Medieval and Renaissance Treatises on the Arts of Painting

Medieval and Renaissance Treatises on the Arts of Painting

Original Texts with English Translations

Two Volumes Bound as One

Mrs. Mary P. Merrifield

Dover Publications, Inc.
Mineola, New York

Copyright

Published in Canada by General Publishing Company, Ltd., 30 Lesmill Road, Don Mills, Toronto, Ontario.
Published in the United Kingdom by Constable and Company, Ltd., 3 The Lanchesters, 162–164 Fulham Palace Road, London W6 9ER.

Bibliographical Note

This Dover edition, first published in 1999, is an unabridged and unaltered republication in one volume of the 1967 two-volume Dover edition of the work originally published by John Murray, London, in 1849. This new one-volume edition also contains the Introduction and Glossary of Technical Terms which was prepared specially for the 1967 edition by S. M. Alexander.

Library of Congress Cataloging-in-Publication Data

Original treatises dating from the XIIth to XVIIIth centuries on the arts of painting, in oil, miniature, mosaic, and on glass
Medieval and Renaissance treatises on the arts of painting : original texts with English translations / Mary P. Merrifield.
p. cm.
Originally published: Original treatises dating from the XIIth to XVIIIth centuries on the arts of painting, in oil, miniature, mosaic, and on glass. London : J. Murray, 1849.
Includes bibliographical references and index.
ISBN 0-486-40440-4 (pbk.)
1. Painting—Early works to 1800. 2. Painting—Technique. 3. Artists' materials. I. Merrifield, Mary P. (Mary Philadelphia), 1804 or 5–1889. II. Title.
ND1130.0747 1999
751—dc21 98-48799
CIP

Manufactured in the United States of America
Dover Publications, Inc., 31 East 2nd Street, Mineola, N.Y. 11501

INTRODUCTION TO THE DOVER EDITION

It is a tribute to Mrs Merrifield's scholarship that her *Original Treatises* merits republication in its original form. Not only are the treatises of interest *per se,* and the translations still adequate, but the author's presentation of her material is a monument of diligent and thoughtful enquiry which continues to take its place with the best of such work today.

Since its appearance in 1849, the *Original Treatises* has been the only publication and English translation of most of the compilations and manuals it contains; it has become one of the standard reference texts in the technology of painting from the Middle Ages to the seventeenth century. Unfortunately, the book has been virtually unobtainable for a considerable time, and current interest in historical materials and methods of production of art objects, manifest among historians in many fields, serves to emphasize the urgent need for a new edition of the volumes.

Mrs Merrifield's work was undertaken during a period of keen interest in the methods of painting of previous centuries, when it was hoped that a close study of ancient texts on the techniques and materials of the Old Masters would contribute to a revival of ancient achievements. A British Royal Commission initiated research in the field and employed Mrs Merrifield as a participant in the work; her books *The Art of Fresco Painting as Practised by the Old Italian and Spanish Masters* (1846) and the *Original Treatises* (1849) were a direct outcome of this

activity. Mrs Merrifield seems to have been well equipped for the task of collecting, translating and explaining early texts on painting techniques. We assume from her later publications—*Practical Directions for Portrait Painting in Watercolours* (1851) and *Handbook of Light and Shade with Especial Reference to Model Drawing* (1855)—that she had some skill as an artist and therefore an understanding of the purpose and character of the treatises she was presenting. Although she states that her two sons prepared the translation of the recipes[1] from Latin, French, Spanish and Italian texts of different periods, Mrs Merrifield herself must have been proficient in these languages in order to supervise the work; her familiarity with Italian is demonstrated by the publication in 1844 of her translation of Cennino Cennini's *Treatise on Painting.*[2] Her capacity for painstaking and thorough research is exemplified in the lengthy introduction to the *Original Treatises*, in which she traces the history of each significant material referred to in the recipes, through literary sources and surviving examples, recording a vast amount of relevant and highly interesting information, interspersed with anecdote and comment. From her introductory pages we get little idea of the author as an individual, the wife of a lawyer and mother of at least three children, with the opportunity in her early forties to spend a period of several years on the preparation of her great book.[3] The personality behind the work is more clearly defined in her *Dress as a Fine Art, with Suggestions on Children's Dress*, published in Boston in 1854, in which she reveals herself as a forceful character with an agreeable sense of humour, and very much the Victorian gentlewoman.

Mrs Merrifield states in the preface to the *Original*

[1] In the prefaces to *The Art of Fresco Painting* and the *Original Treatises*.

[2] *A Treatise on Painting, Written by Cennino Cennini . . .*, London, E. Lumley, 1844.

[3] A short account of Mrs Merrifield's life and work appears in A. C. Sewter's introduction to the 1952 edition of *The Art of Fresco Painting*, London, A. Tiranti (Scopas Handbooks).

Treatises that the research for the work was primarily directed towards establishing the historical techniques of painting, Italian oil painting in particular, as recorded in the early recipes relevant to the subject. However, her selection of texts gives us information of a far wider scope, as the author decided to include treatises outside the area of Italian painting, as well as those predating the appearance of the oil medium in Italy, in order to show the techniques of the period. Thus the treatises of Petrus de S. Audemar and Alcherius, and the greater part of Jean Le Begue's compilation, relate almost entirely to the illumination of manuscripts; Eraclius has a great deal on painting on glass; the Bologna Manuscript has sections on dyeing leather and the fabrication of artificial gems; and the later texts, included for their information on oil painting, also contribute a great deal to our knowledge of ancient practice in other media. The complete title of the book, therefore, *Original Treatises, Dating from the XIIth to XVIIIth Centuries on the Arts of Painting, in Oil, Miniature, Mosaic, and on Glass; of Gilding, Dyeing, and the Preparation of Colours and Artificial Gems*, is fully justified.

The treatises cover a more extensive period of time than was indicated by the information available in 1849. Eraclius, Books I and II, are now thought to be tenth-century[4] and represent one of the few surviving technical manuscripts of that period. Several recipes which Mrs Merrifield traces to the twelfth-century *Mappae Clavicula* may be redated with the bulk of the *Clavicula* text to the eighth or ninth century[5] and probably much earlier, as the

[4] A. Giry, *Notice sur un Traité du Moyen Age, entitulé De Coloribus et Artibus Romanorum*, Bibl. de l'Ecole des Hautes Etudes, Fasc. 35, Paris, 1878; J. C. Richards, "A New Manuscript of Heraclius," *Speculum* XV, 1940, 255–271.

[5] H. Leclercq, *Dictionnaire d'Archéologie Chrétienne et de Liturgie*, vol. X, part ii, 1932, col. 1719–1728.

R. P. Johnson, "Notes on Some Manuscripts of the Mappae Clavicula," *Speculum* X, 1935, 72–81.

———, "Some Continental Manuscripts of the Mappae Clavicula," *Speculum* XII, 1937, 84–91.

Mappae Clavicula itself is a compilation from earlier sources. Similarly, many of the formulae of Jean Le Begue's manuscript are known to be from sources considerably earlier than the fifteenth century. In the history of technical literature generally, however, the manuscripts included in the *Original Treatises* are comparatively late, and fit mainly into a transitional period between the few surviving works predating the thirteenth century, and the more plentiful examples of the sixteenth century and later. It is of considerable assistance to the student of medieval technical literature that Mrs Merrifield published each treatise in full, both in its original language and in English translation, "in order to satisfy the reader that nothing important has been omitted."[6]

The advantage of the manuals dating from the twelfth century and later is the relative ease with which we can understand most of them today. There are very few individual recipes in Mrs Merrifield's collection which we are entitled to view with amused scepticism or to dismiss as unpractical. Several of the ingredients may seem unusual to the modern reader, and the claims made by each author with respect to the efficacy of his recommended procedure may have little consistency with the truth; nevertheless, the validity of the recipes should not be underestimated, at least until practical tests have been made. Apparent confusion on the part of the medieval craftsman, as, for example, in *Experimenta de Coloribus* 30, may be the result of generations of scribes recording each other's misreadings or omissions. The greatest problem facing the modern reader is likely to be the interpretation of technical terms. Over the centuries, most pigments and many other substances have acquired a confusing variety of names, some of which can no longer be identified with accuracy. This edition, therefore, adds a glossary which attempts to collect in one place the data concerning difficult or foreign names and phrases gained from a study of the individual recipes, and the

[6] *Original Treatises*, Preface, vi.

information in Mrs Merrifield's introduction and footnotes to the text.

With this edition of the *Original Treatises,* a classic is restored to the medieval art-technical literature available to the reader of English, and Mrs Merrifield's position is assured in the affections of modern students in the field.

Conservation Center
Institute of Fine Arts
New York University
30 June 1966

S. M. ALEXANDER

GLOSSARY OF TECHNICAL TERMS

This glossary includes terms from Mrs Merrifield's Introduction and footnotes, as well as from the text. The spelling in the text is retained. The interpretation of terms is confined to their use in the treatises included in this book; similar terms in use today frequently have different interpretations.

A word is not included in this glossary if there is only one mention of it with a footnote by Mrs Merrifield on the same page—unless the word happens to be of general interest.

A word is not included if it is mentioned in Mrs Merrifield's Introduction but has no reference to the texts in her *Original Treatises*—unless the word is not explained by her, or unless it is of general interest.

Terms from the "Table of Synonymes" (pp. 18–39) not translated by Mrs Merrifield are included here if they represent actual identifiable materials.

Cross references are indicated by the abbreviation "*q.v.*," since many of the words are synonyms.

Where other researchers may wish to verify the interpretations given here by reference to the recipes, the number of the page in question, or of a typical page, has been supplied along with the definition. Well-known terms, and words extracted from Mrs Merrifield's Introduction which do not refer directly to the treatises she includes, do not have page references.

ABBOZZO. Preliminary sketch of a painting before the colours were applied.

ADAMANT. Fictitious stone of extreme hardness.

AFRONITRE. Perhaps synonymous with saltpetre (*see* Nitre).

AGATINO. Colour made by mixing white lead and red ochre (p. 650).

ALBA CRETA. White earths or chalk, used as a ground (*q.v.*, no. 1) or as a bulk material in pigments made from plant juices and dyes. *Syn.:* Argilla, Creta alba, Gersa, Gypsum, Plastrum (p. 19).

ALBUM HISPANIE. White lead (*q.v.*).

ALBUM PLUMBUM. White lead (*q.v.*).

ALBUS. General term for white pigments. *Cf.* p. 18, note 1; *cf.* Candidus.

ALEMBIC. Early distilling apparatus.

ALOES. Condensed juice from leaves of *Aloe spicata* used as a colouring agent in varnish. The names Hepatic Aloes, Socotrine Aloes and Caballine Aloes indicate juices of different colours from different species.

ALUM. A variety of astringent substances was classed under the name of alum. Sulphates of iron and aluminium, or a mixture of the two, were commonly understood by the term.

ALUME DI PIUMA. Alun de plume (*q.v.*).

ALUMEN. 1. Alum (*q.v.*).

2. White pigment requiring a medium of egg-white (p. 232). Mrs Merrifield suggests that this was the alum scagliuolo used in the preparation of grounds for paintings and for gesso d'oro (*q.v.*), which is not precisely identified.

ALUMEN GLACIAE. Alun de glace (*q.v.*).

ALUMINE ZUCCARINO. Alum ground and heated with rose water, sugar and white of egg, and allowed to harden by cooling. Used as a carrier for lake pigments (p. 62) and as a thickening agent in one of the preparations of verdigris (p. 66).

ALUM OF JAMENI. Alum (*q.v.*).

ALUN DE GLACE. Crystallised alum. *Syn.:* Alumen glaciae.

ALUN DE PLUME. Feather or plume alum, a naturally occurring crystalline ferric potassium sulphate. *Syn.:* Alume di piuma.

AMASSETTE. Early type of palette knife, made of horn, wood or ivory.

AMBER. Translucent fossil resin of the *Pinites succinifer* and other conifers, used as an ingredient in varnish. *Syn.:* Carabé, Glassa.

ANGUILLARIA, ANGULARIA. White pigment prepared from chalk and powdered glass (p. 250).

A PUTRIDO. Technique of painting with decomposed white (p. 282) or yolk (p. 610) of egg as the medium for the pigment.

AQUA DI RAGGIA. *See* Turpentine.

AQUA FORTIS. Nitric acid.

AQUA TARTARI. Water of tartar (*q.v.*).

ARGENTUM. Silver (*q.v.*).

ARGILLA. Alba creta (*q.v.*).

ARMENIAN BOLE. *See* Bole.

ARSICON, ARZICON. Orpiment (*q.v.*).

ARXICA, ARZICA. 1. Yellow lake prepared from the plant weld (*q.v.*) (p. 482).
2. Yellow earth used as a pigment (p. 19). *Syn.:* Terra crocea.

A SECCO. Method of painting on a dry lime-plaster wall with pigments applied in an aqueous medium.

A SFREGAZZO. Method of applying a thin glazing with oil, whereby the finger was dipped into the colour and passed once over the area where a soft shadow was required.

ASPHALTUM. Brownish-black native organic substance; bitumen. Mixed with a drying agent for use as a pigment (p. 748); dissolved in oil or turpentine (*q.v.*) for use as a glaze.

ASSAFOETIDA. Gum resin, mainly from the root of *Ferula fetida*, and probably from other species, used to increase the permanence of a dye (p. 434) and as an insecticide.

ASSISIAM AURI. Gold size (*q.v.*).

ATRAMENTUM. 1. Artificial black pigments including lamp black (*q.v.*) and charcoal black, made from the soot of a variety of carbonised materials (p. 248).
2. Writing ink, incaustum (*q.v.*) (p. 242).
3. Soot of burnt wood, perhaps beech, which when mixed with salt, served as a substitute for gold in the gilding of metal surfaces (p. 220, 222). *See* Bistre.
4. Black dye for leather, made by boiling oil and scales of iron (scoria of iron, *q.v.*) (p. 138, 562). Usually called atramentum sutorium (shoemaker's black).

AURARE. Deaurare (*q.v.*).

AUREOLA. Auripetrum (*q.v.*).

AURIPETRUM. Lacquer, made of gall or saffron or similar materials, applied over base metals such as tin, to represent gilding (p. 158, 240). *Syn.:* Aureola.

AURIPIGMENTUM. Orpiment (*q.v.*). Substitutes such as gall on white earth or chalk base are mentioned (p. 19).

AURUM. Gold, prepared as powder for ink and paint, or laid on as gold leaf.

A VELATURA. Method of glazing large painted surfaces by rubbing on the glaze with the fingers or with the flat of the hand.

AZURE, AZZURRIUM. General term for blue colours. *Syn.:* Lasur, Lazurium.

GERMAN. Azurite (*q.v.*).

INDIAN. Ultramarine (*q.v.*).

LOMBARDY. Azurite (*q.v.*).

PERSIAN. Ultramarine (*q.v.*).

SPANISH. Azurite, or prepared from azurite (*q.v.*).

TEUTONIC. Azurite (*q.v.*).

AZURE D'ACRE. Ultramarine (*q.v.*).

AZURITE. Native blue carbonate of copper, used as a pigment. *Syn.:* German azure, Lombardy azure, Spanish azure, Teutonic azure, Azzurro della Magne, Biadetto, Cendre bleue, Cendrée, Ceneri azzuri, Hungarian blue, Mountain blue, Spanish blue.

AZZURRO DELLA MAGNE, AZZURRUM DE ALEMANNIA. Azurite (*q.v.*).

BAGADEL, BAGADON, BAGUEDEL. Indigo (*q.v.*).

BENZOIN. Balsamic resin from the *Styrax benzoin* tree, dissolved in spirit of turpentine or spirit of wine as an ingredient for varnish.

BERETTINUS. Lombard term for elbidus (*q.v*).

BIACA, BIACCA, BIACHA. White lead (*q.v.*).

BIADETTO. 1. Azurite (*q.v.*).

2. Artificial blue pigment made from copper.

3. Artificial blue pigment made from verdigris (*q.v.*), sal ammoniac (*q.v.*) and tartar.

BIRSUS. Dark red colour made by mixing black and red (p. 21). *Syn.:* Fulvus, Ravus.

BISETUM. Small pieces of rag saturated with plant juices of various shades, which were extracted for use when required, by boiling in an appropriate solution. *Syn.:* Pezzette.

BISTRE. Yellowish-brown soot from charred beech and pine, here used as an ingredient for "gilding" metal. *See* Atramentum 3. *Syn.:* Caligo, Fuligo.

BLACHA. White lead (*q.v.*).

BLANC. French coin of very small value.

BLANCHET. White lead (*q.v.*).

BLAUCCUS. General name for blue colours (p. 20).

BLONDUS. Name applied to different mixtures of blue and white, red and white, green, white and yellow, etc. (p. 21).

BLOODSTONE. *See* Haematite.

BOCALE. Liquid measure, approximately one litre, varying according to locality.

BOLE. Clay material, usually reddish in colour, applied as a ground for gold leaf. The best was thought to come from Armenia. *Syn.:* Armenian bole, Bularminium.

BONE BLACK. Black pigment prepared from the charred bones of various animals.

BRACHA. White lead (*q.v.*).

BRASILEUM, BRASILIUM, BREXILIUM, BREXILLIUM, etc. Brazil wood (*q.v.*).

BRAZIL WOOD. Wood of several kinds of *Caesalpinia* yielding a red dye. Dye extracted by boiling the finely chipped wood, the final colour depending on the acidity or alkalinity of the solution. Used as a pigment or as underpainting for gold leaf (p. 154). *Syn.:* Brasileum, Brexilium, Lignum Braxillii, Verxillium, Verzino.

BRUNO DI SPAGNA. Red ochre (*q.v.*).

BRUNUS. Red ochre (*q.v.*).

BRUSLÉ. Sil atticum (*q v.*).

BULARMINIUM. Bole (*q.v.*).

BUON FRESCO. Painting on newly applied wet plaster with pigments mixed with water; the colours penetrate the plaster and remain fixed on drying.

BURNT ORPIMENT. Realgar (*q.v.*).

BURNT ROCHE ALUM. White powder left after heating alum to remove water of crystallisation, used to prepare lake pigments from plant dyes (p. 658, 678).

BURNT TERRE VERTE. Brown pigment made by heating terre verte (*q.v.*).

BURNT UMBER. Brown pigment made by heating raw umber (*q.v.*).

BURNT VITRIOL, BURNT ROMAN VITRIOL. Artificial red pigment made by heating iron sulphate.

CALCANTHUM, CHALCANTHUM. Copper sulphate, blue vitriol.

CALIGO. Bistre (*q.v.*).

CALX. 1. Product of calcination (*i.e.*, strong heating).
2. Lime (p. 24).

CALX OF GOLD. Powdered gold (p. 532, 334).

CALX OF IRON. Iron oxide (p. 534).

CALX OF TIN. Tin oxide (p. 86, 402).

CALX VIVA. Quicklime, calcium oxide.

CAMILLINA, CAMILLINUS. Colour made by mixing vermilion (*q.v.*), azure and ceruse (*q.v.*); vermilion and ceruse; azure and ceruse, etc. (p. 480, 486).

CAMPEACHY WOOD. Logwood (*q.v.*).

CANDIDUS. Shining white, as opposed to albus, which is matt white (p. 24). *Cf.* Albus.

CANDIDUS CALX. Lime white (p. 20).

CAPRIFOLIUM. Honeysuckle. The ripe berries, after pounding, were boiled in wine; the addition of iron rust gave a bright green ink and dye (p. 158). *Syn.:* Galetrice, Gaterice.

CARABÉ. Amber (*q.v.*).

CARBO. Charcoal black (p. 25).

CARMINE, CARMINIUM. 1. Lake (*q.v.*) from cochineal (*q.v.*) (p. 698).
2. Cinnabar (*q.v.*) (p. 238).
3. White and ochre mixed (p. 252).

CARNATURA, CARNATION. Colour used to represent flesh tint (p. 22, 770).

CEDRA, CEDRE. Excedre (*q.v.*).

CELESTE. Mixture of white lead, smalti and indigo (p. 650).

CENDRE BLEUE. Azurite (*q.v.*) or artificial copper blue.

CENDRÉE. Azurite (*q.v.*) or artificial copper blue.

CENDRE VERTE. Native green ore of copper.

CENERI AZZURI. Azurite (*q.v.*) or artificial copper blue.

CERATE. Unctuous preparation.

CEROSIUS. Green pigment.

CERULÉE. Frit (*q.v.*).

CERUSA, CERUSE. White lead (*q.v.*).

CERVISIA. Beer, used as a medium for pigments (p. 232).

CHIAROSCURO. The disposition of light and shade in a picture.

CHOPINE. Liquid measure, about half a litre.

CHRISARE. *See* Deaurare.

CHRYSOCOLLA. Native green carbonate of copper, malachite (*q.v.*), used as a pigment (p. 248).

CILACETUS. Sillacetus (*q.v.*).

CINERIS PENCHOLINI. Brass burnt and reduced to powder (p. 532).

CINNABAR. Vermilion (*q.v.*).

CINOBRIUM. Vermilion (*q.v.*).

CINOPIS. Red ochre (*q.v.*).

CINOPLE. Red ochre (*q.v.*).

CITRINUS. Colour obtained by mixing yellow with red (p. 22).

CLARE. Solution of gum in water, used as a medium for pigments (p. 294); *cf.* glair, well-beaten egg-white and water, used for the same purpose.

COCCICUS, COCCUS. Kermes (*q.v.*).

COCHINEAL. Natural scarlet or crimson dyestuff obtained from the egg-bearing bodies of the female *Coccus cacti*, introduced into Europe from Mexico in the sixteenth century. *Syn.:* Carmine, Cremisi, Cremisino, Grana.

COLLA. Gum water, size.

COLOPHONY. Rosin (*q.v.*).

COMMON GREEN. Verdigris (*q.v.*).

CONCHILE. Oster (*q.v.*).

COPEROSA. Zinc sulphate.

COPPERAS. Ferrous sulphate, green vitriol, used in dyeing and tanning, and as an ingredient in iron-gall ink. *See also* Shoemaker's black.

CORISCOS. *See* Saffron.

CORROSIVE SUBLIMATE. Mercuric sulphide.

CREMISI, CREMISINO. 1. Cochineal (*q.v.*).
2. Dragon's blood (*q.v.*) with the addition of a substantial amount of alkali.

CRETA ALBA. Alba creta (*q.v.*).

CRETA CIRINA. Terre verte (*q.v.*).

CRETA VIRIDIS. Terre verte (*q.v.*).

CRISICULA. Chrysocolla (*q.v.*)

CROCEA TERRA. Yellow earth (*q.v.*).

CROCEUS. General name for yellow colours.

CROCUS. Saffron (*q.v.*).

CROCUS MARTIS. Saffron of Mars (*q.v.*).

CUBIT. Measurement of length, 45.72 cm.

CUCURBIT. Flask for distillation, forming part of an alembic.

CUM(M)IN. *Cuminum cyminum*, a plant cultivated for its aromatic fruits, used as a spice in the Middle Ages.

CYNOBRE. Vermilion (*q.v.*).

DEAURARE. Latin infinitive, meaning "to gild." *Syn.:* Aurare, Chrisare.

DENARIUS. Coin, mentioned in the recipes as a weight, just over a gram.

DISTEMPER (verb). To add a binding medium to pigments, synonymous with "to temper."

DRAGON'S BLOOD. Dark red resin obtained from the outer surface of the fruit of the *Calamus draco*. Formerly used as a pigment in miniature painting, or as a colouring agent for varnishes. *Syn.:* Sanguis draconis.

DUTCH VERMILION. Artificial vermilion.

EDERA. *See* Gum edere.

ELBIDUS, ELBUS. Latin term for grey colour mixed from black and white (p. 650) with or without the addition of other pigments (p. 654). *Syn.:* Berettinus, Grisus, Neveda, Veneda.

ENDICO BAGATELLO. Indigo (*q.v.*).

ENGLISH RED. Red ochre (*q.v.*).

ESSENTIAL OIL. Volatile oil, such as turpentine.

ESTERLIN. Goldsmith's weight, eighteen and a half grains.

EUPHORBIA. Large genus of plants whose milky juice was used in the preparation of certain substitutes for expensive pigments.

EXCEDRE. Shadow colour for flesh made by mixing red and black (p. 26). *Syn.:* Cedra, Cedre, Exedra.

EXEDRA. Excedre (*q.v.*).

FEL. Gall (*q.v.*).

FENIX. Phenix (*q.v.*).

FENUGREEK. Asiatic herb *Trigonella foenumgraecum*. Oil from the seeds was used in dyeing skins (p. 546).

FERULA. Galbanum (*q.v.*)

FIG TREE MILK. Juice extracted from the young shoots of the tree in spring, or obtained from the young leaves by soaking them in water and alcohol until decomposed. Used as a medium for pigments (p. 96), or as an ingredient in mordant for gold (p. 462).

FLANDERS BLACK. Black pigment made from vine twigs.

FLAVUS. Massicot (*q.v.*).

FLOUR PASTE. Sometimes used instead of size (*q.v.*) for covering canvas before priming (p. 772).

FLOWER OF NITRE. Efflorescence of nitre (*q.v.*) used in the composition of frit (*q.v.*) (p. 804).

FLOWER OF WOAD, FROTH OF WOAD. Scum floating on dyers' vats when woad was boiled after fermentation, used as a colouring agent in the preparation of some blue pigments (p. 390, 414).

FOGLIECTO. Liquid measure, approximately a quarter of a litre.

FOLIUM Vegetable colour used in painting and dyeing, prepared from the juice of *Croton tinctorium*. The hue could be changed from red, through purple, to blue by the addition of alkali (p. 132). *Syn.:* Morella, Turnsole, Worina.

FRANKINCENSE. Yellowish aromatic gum resin from the genus *Boswellia*. Used as an ingredient in varnish and in the purification of ultramarine (*q.v.*). *Syn.:* Incense, Olibanum.

FRIT. Blue pigment made by melting siliceous material with copper and other metallic salts, and grinding the mass to a very fine powder. *Syn.:* Cerulée, Smaltino, Turchino.

FULIGO. Bistre (*q.v.*).

FULVUS. Birsus (*q.v.*).

FUMUS. Lamp black (*q.v.*).

FUSCUS. Lamp black (*q.v.*).

GADUS. Madder (*q.v.*).

GALBANUM. Gum resin from *Ferula galbanifera* used in the preparation of varnish. *Syn.:* Ferula.

GALETRICE. Caprifolium (*q.v.*).

GALL. Secretion of liver from several fish or animals, used as a yellow pigment (p. 193) and as a substitute for gold (p. 160, 308). *Syn.:* Fel.

GALL NUTS, GALLS. Vegetable excrescences, especially on oak trees, produced by an insect. Tannin, extracted from the galls, was used in making ink, as a mordant in dyeing, and for tanning leather.

GAMBOGE. Yellow gum resin from the bark of the *Garcinia hanburii* tree, used as a pigment and as a colouring agent for varnishes. *Syn.:* Gutiambar.

GARANCIA. Gallic name for madder (*q.v.*).

GATERICE. English term for caprifolium (*q.v.*).

GAUDE. French term for woad (*q.v.*).

GENESTRA. Myrrh (*q.v.*).

GERMAN AZURE. *See* Azure.

GERMAN GIALLOLINO. Massicot (*q.v.*).

GERSA. Alba creta (*q.v.*).

GESSO. Aqueous white priming used in the preparation of panels or other supports for painting and gilding. Usually consisted of gypsum (*q.v.*) mixed with glue or size (*q.v.*).

GESSO D'ORO. Very fine and smooth gesso (*q.v.*), called "honey of the plasterers," used as a ground for gilding.

GESSO MARCIO. Type of fine gesso (*q.v.*).

GESSO SOTTILE. Gesso (*q.v.*) prepared from plaster of Paris soaked for several weeks in excess water to prevent setting. Used as a final coat for grounds in panel painting and as a mordant for gold leaf on parchment.

GIALDOLINO, GIALLOLINO. 1. Massicot (*q.v.*).
2. Massicot mixed with giallo di vetro (*q.v.*).
3. Native yellow earth used as a pigment.

GIALDOLINO DI FIANDRE. Massicot (*q.v.*).

GIALDOLINO DI FORNACE. Massicot (*q.v.*).

GIALLO DI VETRO. Pigment made by heating tin and lead together.

GIALLO SANTO. Yellow lake made from a variety of flowers.

GIALORINO. Natural and artificial massicot (*q.v.*).

GIPSUS. Gypsum (*q.v.*).

GLADIUS. 1. Vegetable green from leaves of *Gladiolus communis*.
2. Green colour made by mixing orpiment and indigo (p. 28).

GLASSA. 1. Amber (*q.v.*) (p. 162).
2. Crystallised alum (p. 240).

GLASSE AROMATIQUE. May mean amber (*q.v.*) or sandarac (*q.v.*) (p. 312).

GLAUCUS. Here synonymous with white lead (p. 18, 29), possibly through confusion with *leucos* (*q.v.*).

GLAZING. The last thin coat of transparent colour which softens and gives brilliancy to the pigments.

GOLD SIZE. Ground, usually consisting of bole in a liquid medium, with or without the addition of chalk and pigments, applied under gold which was to be burnished (p. 94, 282). *Syn.:* Assisiam auri.

GOMMA DI GINEPRO. Sandarac (*q.v.*).

GRANA. Kermes (*q.v.*); cochineal (*q.v.*).

GRANETUM, GRANETUS. Colour made by mixing green and white (p. 28).

GRANZA. Madder (*q.v.*).

GREEK GREEN. Verdigris (*q.v.*).

GREEK PITCH. Rosin (*q.v.*).

GREEN CHALK. Terre verte (*q.v.*).

GRENUSPECT. Plant yielding yellow juice which was added to verdigris and wine medium to give green colour (p. 158).

GRISUS. Gallic name for elbidus (*q.v.*).

GROSSINUM. French weight, the *gros*, weighing 3.82 grams at Paris.

GROUND. Used by Mrs Merrifield to mean:

1. The layer of a painting applied to the support to provide a suitable surface for the application of pigment or gold.

2. The background of a picture.

GUADO. Italian term for woad (*q.v.*).

GUM AMMONIAC. Aromatic gum resin from the *Dorema ammoniacum*, used as an ingredient in mordants for gold (p. 156, 622).

GUM ANDRIANUM. Mrs Merrifield suggests this is synonymous with amber (?) or native bitumen (?).

GUM ARABIC. Gum obtained from various species of *Acacia*. The gum is completely soluble in water and was used as a medium for pigments (p. 58), as an adhesive (p. 156), and as an ingredient in gold mordants (p. 156).

GUM EDERE. Gum of certain species of ivy. The dye extracted from the stem turned red on exposure to the air, and was prepared as a pigment by boiling to concentrate the colour. Also used in dyeing and as an ink (p. 190).

GUM LAC. Red pigment prepared from natural red organic dyestuff obtained from the secretion of larvae of *Coccus lacca*. The dye is similar to cochineal in composition, but duller in colour (p. 50, 62). *Syn.:* Indian gum lac, Indian lac lake, Lac.

GUM TRAGACANTH. Gum obtained from several species of *Astragalus*, chiefly used as a binder for pastels and chalks, and as a medium for pigments.

GUTIAMBAR. Gamboge (*q.v.*).

GYPSUM. Native calcium sulphate, used to prepare gesso (*q.v.*) and as a carrier for vegetable pigments (p. 184). Stated to be synonymous with alba creta (*q.v.*).

HAEMATITE. 1. Ferric oxide, highly polished and shaped to form a burnisher (p. 220). *Syn.:* Bloodstone.

2. Red earth used as a pigment (p. 806).

HARTSHORN GLUE. Ammoniacal liquor obtained by the distillation of horn shavings.

HEPATIC ALOES. *See* Aloes.

HERBA MORELLA. The plant *Solanum nigrum* ground with chalk to give a green colour (p. 29).

HERBA ROCCIA. Weld (*q.v.*).

HERBA SANDIX. Madder (*q.v.*).

HERBA VACCINIUM. 1. Plant giving red juice which was mixed with milk to give a violet colour.
2. Plant yielding yellow juice.

HOLCHUS. Membrana (*q.v.*).

HONEY OF ROSES. Mixture of infusion of roses, white sugar and honey, used as an ingredient in mordants for gilding (p. 468).

HUILE DE SAPIN. Pine resin used as an ingredient in varnish (p. 840).

HUNGARIAN BLUE. Azurite (*q.v.*).

INCAUSTUM. Latin term for "ink," including black pigment mixed with gum for writing, and iron-gall ink (p. 30, 150). *Syn.:* Atramentum.

INCENSE. *See* Frankincense.

INDIAN AZURE. *See* Azure.

INDIAN GUM LAC. *See* Gum lac.

INDIAN LAC LAKE. *See* Gum lac.

INDICUS. Indigo (*q.v.*).

INDIGO. 1. Blue vegetable dye from the leaves of plants of the genus *Indigofera*. *Syn.:* Bagadel, Bagadon, Baguedel, Endico Bagatello, Indicus.
2. Blue dye from woad, *Isatis tinctoria* (p. 806).

INTONACO. Final layer of lime plaster on the ground of a fresco painting.

ISINGLASS. Pure form of gelatine prepared from the air bladders of certain fish, especially the sturgeon. Used as an ingredient in some types of media and as an adhesive for gold (p. 192).

IVORY BLACK. Carbon black made by burning ivory chips.

KERMES. Red dyestuff prepared from the egg-bearing bodies of the kermes insect *Coccus ilicis*. Used as a dye and a pigment. *Syn.:* Coccus, Grana, Rubea de grana, Sanguineus, Vermiculus.

LAC. Gum lac (*q.v.*).

LACCA DI CIMATURA, LACHA. Red pigment made by boiling small pieces of cloth dyed with kermes in lye, then precipitating the colour with alum.

LAKE. Transparent dye precipitated on to a translucent base (p. 50, 144).

LAMP BLACK. Pigment made from soot obtained by burning oil or fat and collecting the material on a metallic or other cold surface. *Syn.:* Fumus, Fuscus, Sanctonicus.

LAPIS LAZULI. *See* Ultramarine.

LAPIS NIGER. Terra nigra (*q.v.*).

LASUR, LAZURIUM. Azure (*q.v.*).

LESSIVE FONDISSE. Perhaps a lye solution.

LEUCOS. White lead (*q.v.*).

LEY, LYE. Alkaline solution made from mixing wood ashes in water.

LIGNUM BRAXILLII. Brazil wood (*q.v.*).

LINSEED OIL. Drying oil expressed from the seeds of the flax plant *Linum usitatissimum*, purified for use.

LIQUID VARNISH. Thick varnish composed of oil and resin—usually linseed oil (*q.v.*) and sandarac (*q.v.*)—rubbed while warm on panel paintings.

LITHARGE. Orange-yellow monoxide of lead used as a dryer in paints and varnishes. It is produced as an intermediate step in the preparation of red lead from white lead. Not used as a pigment. *Syn.:* Terraghetta.

LOADSTONE. Magnetite, magnetic iron ore.

LOGWOOD. Heartwood of *Haematoxylon campechianum* from which a purple dye is produced. *Syn.:* Campeachy wood.

LOMBARDY AZURE. *See* Azure.

LOT. Weight, 14.2 grams approximately.

LUMINA, LUMINE. Mixture of pink flesh-tint (membrana, *q.v.*) with lead white, malachite and vermilion, perhaps used as highlight for flesh (p. 314).

LUSTRO DI RASA. Turpentine dissolved with rosin, used as a medium for pigments in painting on glass (p. 696).

LUTUM SAPIENTIAE. Philosopher's lute (*q.v.*).

MADDER. Natural red dyestuff prepared from the roots of the shrub *Rubia tinctorium*. Used as a lake, dye and pigment. *Syn.:* Gadus, Garancia, Granza, Herba sandix, Rubea radix, Sandis, Sandix, Warancia.

MAESTRA. Mordant, used in dyeing.

MALACHITE. Native green carbonate of copper, used as a pigment. *Syn.:* Chrysocolla, Crisicula, Verde azzuro.

MARCHESITE. Iron pyrite, iron disulphide.

MARZACHOTTO. Mixture of sand, soda and potash used as the base material in the production of coloured glass.

MASSICOT. In these recipes it is yellow oxide of lead, an intermediate step in the production of red lead from white lead. *Syn.:* Flavus, German giallolino, Gialdolino, Gialdolino di Fiandre, Gialdolino di Fornace, Gialorino.

MASTIC. Resin from the *Pistachia lentiscus*. Had several uses, mainly as an ingredient in varnish and in media (p. 306).

MEDIUM. Liquid such as water, oil, or a solution of gum, in which a pigment is suspended for painting. *Syn.:* Vehicle.

MELINE EARTH. White earth from Melos used as a pigment (p. 244).

MELLANA. Sinopis de Mellana (*q.v.*).

MEMBRANA, MEMBRAYNE. Pink colour for flesh tints, mixed from red, white and green (p. 144). *Syn.:* Holchus, Olchus.

MENECH, MENESCH. 1. Blue juice used as a colour (p. 31).
2. Medium red tone, perhaps synonymous with madder (p. 31).
3. Dark green colour, the juice of the elder (p. 31). *Cf.* Succus sambuci.

METADELLE. Liquid measure, approximately half a litre.

MILK OF LIME. Solution of calcium hydroxide in water, made by dissolving slaked lime in water. Used for mixing the sand and lime of the plaster coats for fresco painting (p. 788).

MINEVER. White fur from the ermine.

MINIUM. 1. Red lead (*q.v.*).
2. Perhaps sometimes synonymous with vermilion (*q.v.*) (p. 68).

MIRCA. Myrrh (*q.v.*).

MOMMIA. Mummy (*q.v.*).

MORDANT. 1. In dyeing, a mordant is a substance which produces a fast colour on a fibre by combining with the dyestuff and the fibre to form an insoluble compound or lake.
2. In gilding, a mordant is an adhesive for the metal or a ground over which the gold leaf was laid and against which it could be burnished (p. 94, 152).

MORELLA. Folium (*q.v.*).

MORELLO. Violet colour made by mixing blue with various other pigments.

MORELLO DI FERRO. Red pigment from an ore of iron.

MORELLO DI SALE. Unidentified. Perhaps a reddish clay left over from the purification of rock salt.

MOTTÉE DE SIL. Native red or yellow ochre (*q.v.*) used as a pigment (p. 804).

MOUNTAIN BLUE. Azurite (*q.v.*).

MUMMY. Brown bituminous pigment said to be warmer in tone than asphaltum. Used as a pigment, varnish and dryer. *Syn.:* Mommia.

MYRRH. Reddish-brown gum resin from the tree genus *Balsamodendron* boiled with aloes to coat varnished tin in imitation of gold (p. 162). *Syn.:* Genestra, Mirca.

NAPHTHA. Liquid obtained by the distillation of petroleum, used as a solvent for mastic (*q.v.*) in the preparation of varnish (p. 670) and as a thinner for varnish (p. 628).

NATRON. Impure mixture of a variety of saline substances found in the natural state, especially in arid regions. Probably native sodium sesquicarbonate.

NEVEDA. Elbidus (*q.v.*).

NIELLO. Technique in fine metalwork, whereby an engraved design on a gold or silver ground is filled with a black composition of copper, lead, silver and sulphur fused together by heat. *Syn.:* Nigellum.

NIGELLUM. Niello (*q.v.*).

NIGER. General name for black (p. 32).

NIGRI PRUNI CORTEX SECUNDUS. Inner bark of black plum, boiled to give a yellow dye which was mixed with vitriol (*q.v.*) and gum arabic (*q.v.*) to make ink (p. 162).

NITRE. A variety of white substances was classed under the name of nitre, not necessarily corresponding to the modern nitre, which is potassium nitrate. *Syn.:* Afronitre, Sal nitrinum, Saltpetre.

OCHRE. Variety of natural earths coloured in the brown, red, yellow range by iron oxide and iron hydroxide. *Syn.:* Ogra.

OCRA DE RU. Dark-coloured ochre (p. 786).

OGLIO COTTA. Nut or linseed oil boiled with litharge.

OGRA. Ochre (*q.v.*).

OIL OF CHAMOMILE. Oil extracted from the camomile flowers by soaking in olive oil in direct sunlight. Used to dilute pigments.

OIL OF COPAIBA. Resin from the trunk of a species of *Copaifera*, used as an ingredient in varnish.

OIL OF SPIKE. Oil distilled from *Lavandula spica*, used as a diluent for varnish. Its properties are similar to those of turpentine (*q.v.*).

OIL OF TARTAR. Concentrated solution of potassium carbonate, used in one of the preparations of "azure" (p. 398) and of lake (p. 712).

OLCHUS. Membrana (*q.v.*).

OLIBANUM. Frankincense (*q.v.*).

OLIO DI ABEZZO. Resin from the *Pinus picea*. Used as an ingredient in varnish (p. 670), or was mixed with the oil in which brushes had been cleaned, and painted on the back of oil paintings on canvas to re-attach flaking grounds (p. 740).

OR DE COULEUR. Mordant for gold made of oil and yellow ochre (*q.v.*) or bole (*q.v.*) (p. 836).

ORICELLO. Lichen *Roccella* or archil used for dyeing a purple colour (p. 582) or as underpainting for gold (p. 474).

ORPIMENT. 1. Naturally occurring yellow sulphide of arsenic, formerly used as a pigment. *Syn.:* Arsicon, Arzicon, Auripigmentum.

2. Gall adsorbed on to white chalk, used as a substitute for orpiment (p. 19, 198).

OSTER. Purple dye mentioned by Vitruvius, obtained from several types of shellfish. *Syn.:* Conchile.

PAGLIONAZO. Pavonazzo (*q.v.*).

PALLIDUS. Off-white.

PANICELLA. Weld (*q.v.*).

PARAMENTUM. Saline efflorescence found on old walls.

PARATONIUM. White mineral used as a pigment.

PARIS CARMINE. Parisian red (*q.v.*).

PARISIAN RED. Brazil wood (*q.v.*) boiled in lye and mixed with alum (*q.v.*). *Syn.:* Paris carmine.

PASTA DI VESICHA. Sap green (*q.v.*) kept in pigs' bladders (p. 664, 808). *Syn.:* Verde di vesicha.

PASTA VERDE. Sap green (*q.v.*).

PAVONAZZO. Purple colour.

1. Mixture of white lead, azure and red lake (p. 610). *Syn.:* Paglionazo.

2. Purple dye from *Roccella tinctoria* (p. 583). *Cf.* Oricello.

PECE GRECA. Rosin (*q.v.*).

PENCIL. This term, as used by Mrs Merrifield, usually refers to the modern word "paintbrush."

PERSIAN AZURE. *See* Azure.

PERSICUS, PERSUS. Dark blue colour.

PETITTO. Liquid measure.

PEZZETTE. Bisetum (*q.v.*).

PHENIX. Scarlet dye or pigment. *Syn.:* Fenix.

PHILOSOPHER'S LUTE. Cement for sealing vessels; composed of white of egg beaten to a froth, mixed with iron filings and applied in three or four coats. *Syn.:* Lutum Sapientiae.

PIETRA FOCARA, FOCAIA. Flint?

PIGNOLATO. Cloth of linen or hemp.

PINCELIER. Vessel containing oil in which oil-painting brushes were cleaned or placed to prevent hardening.

PLASTRUM. Gypsum (*q.v.*).

PLUMBAGO. Graphite, used for drawing (p. 780).

PLUMBUS ALBUS. White lead (*q.v.*).

PONTELLO. Pontil or punty, working rod for holding glass objects during the process of manufacture.

POSC(E), POSCH, POSECH. Shadow colour for pink flesh, made of ochre, green and membrayne (*q.v.*) (p. 33).

POTTER'S EARTH. Clay used for priming canvas (p. 772).

POUNCE (verb). To perforate for the purpose of using as a stencil in ornamentation.

PRASINUS. 1. Prasin: red pigment, burnt ochre (p. 33, 298). 2. Prasminum, prasis. (a) General term for green. (b) Dark green colour of indeterminate nature (p. 33).

PRUNI NIGRI SECUNDUS CORTEX. Nigri pruni cortex secundus (*q.v.*).

PUMICEUS, PUNICEUS. Reddish colour made by adding red to yellow (p. 34).

PURPLE OF CASSIUS. Richly coloured pigment produced by the action of a solution of tin and iron salts on a solution of gold (p. 388).

PURPUREUS. General name for purple colours.

PURPURINUS. 1. Red colours of various types.
2. Composition of quicksilver, tin or brass, and sulphur heated to produce a yellow metallic powder which, with a medium of gum or egg-white, was used as a substitute for gold (p. 54, 64).

QUICKSILVER. Mercury.

RADIX RUBEA. *See* Rubea radix.

RAVUS. Birsus (*q.v.*).

REALGAR. Artificial or naturally occurring red sulphide of arsenic formerly used as a pigment, and as a preservative for glair (*cf.* clare) (p. 676). *Syn.:* Burnt orpiment, Red orpiment, Red sulphur, Sandaraca, Sandaraque.

RED LEAD. Red oxide of lead made by heating white lead. *Syn.:* Minium, Stupium.

RED OCHRE. Native red clay containing oxide of iron. *Syn.:* Brunus, Bruno di Spagna, Cinopis, Cinople, English red, Rubea terra, Rubigo, Sinople, Spanish red, Synople, Terra rossa, Terra rossa d'Inghilterra, Terra rossa di Spagna, Terra rubea; Vermilion (*q.v.*).

RED ORPIMENT. Realgar (*q.v.*).

RED SULPHUR. Realgar (*q.v.*).

ROCAILLE. White glass or flux to which different minerals were added in the manufacture of coloured glass for painting (p. 792).

ROCHE ALUM. Pure form of alum prepared from alunite.

ROMAN VITRIOL. Copper sulphate, blue vitriol.

ROSA, ROSE. Pink colours of various hues. *Syn.:* Rosette.

ROSACEUM. Pink colour made by adsorbing brazil-wood dye on to white chalk.

ROSETTE. Rosa (*q.v.*).

ROSIN. Resinous constituent of the oleo-resin exuded by various species of pine, i.e., the residue left after the extraction of turpentine from the crude exudation. *Syn.:* Colophony, Greek pitch, Pece greca, Spanish pitch.

ROTHOMAGENSIAN GREEN. Verdigris (*q.v.*).

ROTOLO. Weight of about 907 grams, but varying greatly with locality.

ROUGET. Brazil wood boiled with lime water and alum (p. 808).

RUBEA DE GRANA. Kermes (*q.v.*).

RUBEA RADIX. Madder (*q.v.*).

RUBEA TERRA. Red ochre (*q.v.*).

RUBEUS. General name for red colours.

RUBIGO. Red ochre (*q.v.*).

SAFFRON. Yellow dye obtained by soaking the dried stigmas of *Crocus sativus* in water or white of egg. The best sort, from Sicily, was called coriscos (p. 132). *Syn.:* Crocus.

SAFFRON OF MARS. Native yellow earth used as a pigment. *Syn.:* Crocus Martis.

SAFIREUS. Lapis lazuli. *See* Ultramarine.

SAGIUM. Weight of approximately 1.6 grams.

SAL ALKALI. Potassium carbonate.

SAL AMMONIAC. Ammonium chloride used in the manufacture of purpurinus (*q.v.*) and as a mordant for gold leaf (p. 54).

SAL GEM. Rock salt, sodium chloride.

SAL NITRINUM. Nitre (*q.v.*).

SALT GREEN. Type of verdigris. Green pigment made by sprinkling salt over pieces of copper and subjecting them to the fumes of vinegar or urine in a sealed vessel (p. 116).

SALTPETRE. Nitre (*q.v.*).

SANCTONICUS. Lamp black (*q.v.*).

SANDALICA. Sandalwood (*q.v.*).

SANDALWOOD. Wood of the *Pterocarpus santalinus*, yielding a red dye used for colouring varnishes. *Syn.:* Sandalica.

SANDARAC. Yellowish resinous body obtained from the stems of the conifer *Callitris quadrivalvis*, used in the preparation of varnish. *Syn.:* Gomma di ginepro, Vernix.

SANDARACA. 1. Red lead, minium (p. 140).
2. Massicot (p. 314).
3. Realgar (p. 246, *n*. 3).
Syn.: Sandaracum, Sandaraque.

SANDARACUM, SANDARAQUE. Sandaraca (*q.v.*, nos. 1, 2 and 3).

SANDIS, SANDIX. Madder (*q.v.*).

SANGUINE. General term for red and purple lakes.

SANGUINEUS. Kermes (*q.v.*).

SANGUIS DRACONIS. Dragon's blood (*q.v.*).

SAP GREEN. Colour made from crushed buckthorn berries boiled in alum (p. 662, 808). *Syn.:* Pasta di vesicha, Pasta verde, Succo verde.

SAPPHIRE. Lapis lazuli. *See* Ultramarine.

SBIADATO. Pale yellow colour made by mixing yellow ochre with white (p. 650).

SCAMMONY. Resin obtained from the dried roots of *Convolvulus scammonia* by soaking in alcohol.

SCORIA OF IRON, SCALES OF IRON. Iron oxides from the forging of iron.

SCRINIUM. Container for rolls or books, frequently round, sometimes rectangular.

SCUDELLA. Liquid measure.

SEPIA. Dark brown pigment obtained from ink sacs of various species of cuttlefish. The ink sac is dried immediately after extraction, to prevent putrefaction, is then powdered, dissolved in caustic alkali and precipitated from the solution by neutralising with acid.

SEXTARIUS. Dry and liquid measure, 0.55 litre.

SHOEMAKER'S BLACK. Ferrous sulphate, used as a black dye for leather (p. 138). *See* Atramentum 4. *Syn.:* Atramentum sutorium, Copperas.

SIL ATTICUM. Purple pigment made by quenching heated yellow ochre in vinegar. A substitute was made from plant juices (p. 250). *Syn.:* Bruslé.

SILLACETUS. Yellow lake made from the colour extracted from *Viola lutea* adsorbed on to chalk. *Syn.:* Cilacetus.

SILVER. The metal was used in powdered form as ink or paint, and was a supposed source of blue colour made by subjecting the metal to vinegar fumes (p. 46, 48, 136). *Syn.:* Argentum.

SINDONE. Fine linen.

SINOBRIUM. Vermilion (*q.v.*).

SINOPIA. 1. Red ochre. (*q.v.*).
2. Sinopis de Mellana (*q.v.*).

SINOPIS. Sinopia (*q.v.*).

SINOPIS DE MELLANA. Red lake made from gum of ivy, sometimes boiled with madder (p. 144). *Syn.:* Mellana.

SINOPLE. Red ochre (*q.v.*).

SIZE. 1. Solution of glue or gelatine in water, used for filling pores in supports or to render supports suitable for receiving coatings (p. 772).
2. Gold size (*q.v.*).

SMALT. A frit made by strongly heating a cobalt ore with other ingredients, probably introduced during the later Middle Ages. *Cf.* Frit. *Syn.:* Zaffre.

SMALTI. Coloured glass or enamel used in painting glass.

SMALTINO. Frit (*q.v.*).

SPANISH AZURE. *See* Azure.

SPANISH BLUE. Azurite (*q.v.*).

SPANISH GREEN. Verdigris (*q.v.*).

SPANISH PITCH. Rosin (*q.v.*).

SPANISH RED. Red ochre (*q.v.*).

SPANISH WHITE. White lead (*q.v.*).

STANNUM. Tin, recommended as a substitute for silver or—with the addition of suitable colouring—for gold.

STECCA. Scraper.

STIL DE GRAIN. Transparent yellow lake made by mixing the juice of certain flowers with white earth (p. 808).

STIPATUM. Plant from whose root "gelantina" was extracted for use as a medium for pigments.

STONE YELLOW. Perhaps native yellow ochre.

STUCCO. Fine plaster used for walls or for relief decorations on walls; made of powdered white marble, fine sand, gypsum and water.

STUPIUM. Red lead (*q.v.*).

SUCCO VERDE. Sap green (*q.v.*).

SUCCUS SAMBUCI. Dark green juice from elder (p. 36). *Cf.* Menech 3.

SULPHUR VIVUM. Impure sulphur.
SUMACH. Dried and powdered leaves of various species of sumach, *Rhus coriaria*, used in dyeing and tanning.
SYNOPLE. Red ochre (*q.v.*).

TALC. A hydrous magnesium silicate, called steatite in the compact form. The term was formerly applied to mica and to foliated gypsum. Used to cover paintings to protect them from dust (p. 774, 784).
TAVERTINUS. Travertine (*q.v.*).
TEMPER. Distemper (*q.v.*).
TEMPERA. Medium for pigments.
TEREBINTHINA. Turpentine (*q.v.*).
TERRA CROCEA. 1. Yellow ochre (*q.v.*).
2. Arzica 2 (*q.v.*).
TERRA DA BOCCALI. China clay.
1. When mixed with earth colours and linseed oil, it was used for priming in oil paintings (p. 730).
2. Sometimes mixed with lamp black and used instead of charcoal for drawing.
Syn.: Terra di cava, Terretta.
TERRA DI CAVA. Terra da boccali (*q.v.*).
TERRA DI SIENA. Variety of yellow ochre, more transparent than the usual kind.
TERRA D'OMBRA. Umber (*q.v.*).
TERRAGHETTA. Litharge (*q.v.*).
TERRA GIALLA. Yellow earth (*q.v.*).
TERRA NERA DI CAMPANA. Black colour made from the crust which forms on moulds for casting bells.
TERRA NEREA. Native black unctuous earth used as a pigment.
TERRA NIGRA. Black chalk or graphite. *Syn.:* Lapis niger.
TERRA ROSSA, TERRA RUBEA. Red ochre (*q.v.*).
TERRA ROSSA D'INGHILTERRA. Red ochre (*q.v.*).
TERRA ROSSA DI SPAGNA. Red ochre (*q.v.*).
TERRA VIRIDIS. Terre verte (*q.v.*).
TERRETTA. Terra da boccali (*q.v.*).
TERRE VERTE. Native green earth coloured by iron and manganese. Used as a pigment. *Syn.:* Creta cirina, Creta viridis, Green chalk, Terra viridis, Theodotian, Therdote, Verd de terre, Verde terra, Viride terrenum, Viridis terre.
TEUTONIC AZURE. *See* Azure.
THEODOTIAN, THERDOTE. Terre verte (*q.v.*).
TRAGACANTH. Gum tragacanth (*q.v.*).

TRAVERTINE. Calcium carbonate used as the bulk material in the preparation of lakes. *Syn.:* Tavertinus.

TRIPOLI POWDER. Decomposed siliceous limestone, called rotten stone, used as a polishing powder.

TUCHIA, TUCIA, TUZIA. Impure zinc oxide found adhering to the walls of furnaces for roasting zinc ores.

TURCHINO. 1. Frit (*q.v.*) (p. 804).
2. Mixture of white and blue pigments (p. 651).

TURNSOLE. Folium (*q.v.*).

TURPENTINE. In the recipes, turpentine is the crude resinous liquid from pine trees, used as an ingredient in varnish and in the refining of lapis lazuli. Today, turpentine is the volatile distillate of the above resinous sap. *Syn.:* Terebinthina.

ULTRAMARINE. 1. Blue pigment made from the mineral lapis lazuli by a complicated process of separating it from its associated rock. It was the most expensive pigment of the Middle Ages. *Syn.:* Azure d'acre, Indian azure, Persian azure.
2. Substitute for ultramarine was made from calcined silver, nitric acid and sal ammoniac sealed together in a leaden vessel (p. 808).

ULTRAMARINE SOAP. Mrs Merrifield suggests that this was the Roman soap or alkaline material used in the washing of azure (p. 512).

UMBER. Native brown earth, a hydrate of iron oxide with manganese oxide and clay, varying in colour between yellow- and purple-brown. Used as a pigment (p. 770). *Syn.:* Terra d'ombra.

USTICIUM. Of a colour produced by burning (p. 39).

VACCINIUM. Purple colour prepared from herba vaccinium (*q.v.*, no. 1).

VEHICLE. Medium (*q.v.*).

VENEDA. Elbidus (*q.v.*).

VENETIAN LAKE. Red lake, of which cochineal appears to have been the main ingredient.

VENICE TURPENTINE. Resinous liquid from *Pinus larix*, used in the preparation of varnish.

VERBLEA. Perhaps synonymous with Verde azzuro (*q.v.*, no. 1).

VERCANDE. Vernide (*q.v.*).

VERD DE TERRE, VERDE TERRA. Terre verte (*q.v.*).

VERDE AZZURO. 1. Malachite (*q.v.*).
2. Green colour made from blue and saffron (p. 422).

VERDE DI VESICHA. Pasta di vesicha (*q.v.*).

VERDE ETERNO. Purified verdigris (*q.v.*).

VERDE PORRO. Whitish-green colour; Mrs Merrifield suggests that it might be synonymous with prasinus (*q.v.*).

VERDERAME. Variety of verdigris (*q.v.*).

VERDET. Type of verdigris (*q.v.*).

VERDETTO. 1. Native green pigment from Germany.
2. Yellow-green colour, the juice of certain flowers precipitated on to a white earth.

VERDIGRIS. Hydrated copper acetate, a green substance prepared by suspending pieces of copper over strong vinegar. One of the earliest artificial pigments, no longer in use. Used as a dye (p. 84), as a pigment, as an ink (p. 126, 194), and mixed with varnish for glazing (p. 812). *Syn.:* Common green, Greek green, Rothomagensian green, Spanish green.

VERGAUT. Grey-green colour made by mixing "azure" or indigo with orpiment or yellow ochre.

VERJUICE. Acid liquor from sour apples, grapes and other sour fruit.

VERMICULUS. 1. Kermes (*q.v.*) (p. 38).
2. Vermilion (*q.v.*) (p. 139, 141).

VERMILION. 1. Mercuric sulphide (p. 138). Red pigment artificially produced in the Middle Ages, the natural ore of mercury being used in classical antiquity. *Syn.:* Cinnabar, Cinobrium, Cynobre, Minium, Sinobrium, Vermiculus.
2. Red ochre (*q.v.*). [Perhaps in error.]

VERNICE COMMUNE. Varnish made of turpentine, oil of turpentine and resin melted together. *Syn.:* Vernice grossa.

VERNICE GROSSA. Vernice commune (*q.v.*).

VERNIDE. Undetermined substance used in dyeing (p. 314). *Syn.:* Vercande.

VERNIX. Sandarac (*q.v.*).

VERXILLIUM, VERZILIUM, VERZINO. Brazil wood (*q.v.*).

VERZINO COLUMBINO. Possibly brazil wood (*q.v.*) from Ceylon, thought to be the best quality (p. 554).

VIOLA. Pigment prepared from blue flowers, pounded to press out the juice, which is adsorbed on to chalk.

VIOLACEUS, VIOLETUS. Colour obtained by mixing red and blue (p. 37).

VIRIDE TERRENUM, VIRIDIS TERRE. Terre verte (*q.v.*).

VIRIDIS. General term for green colours.

VITRIOL. Native or artificial sulphates of metals.

WARANCIA. Madder (*q.v.*).

WATER OF TARTAR. Solution of potash. *Syn.:* Aqua tartari.

WELD. The plant *Reseda luteola*, from which a yellow dye is obtained, especially from the seeds and the upper portions of the plant. *Syn.:* Herba roccia, Panicella.

WHITE COPPERAS. Zinc sulphate used as a dryer in oil painting.

WHITE EARTH OF THE FELLMONGERS. Lime.

WHITE LEAD. Basic lead carbonate, a white pigment made by exposing lead metal to the fumes of strong vinegar in a sealed vessel. *Syn.:* Album Hispanie, Album plumbum, Biacca, Biacha, Blacha, Blanchet, Bracha, Ceruse, Leucos, Plumbus albus, Spanish white.

WOAD. The plant *Isatis tinctoria*, whose leaves yield a blue dye, similar in composition to indigo (*q.v.*). *Syn.:* Gaude, Guado.

WORINA. Folium (*q.v.*).

YELLOW EARTH. A native earth, not synonymous with yellow ochre, used as a pigment (p. 810) and as an ingredient in the priming for canvas (p. 772). *Syn.:* Crocea terra, Terra gialla.

YELLOW OCHRE. Natural yellow earth containing iron oxides and clay minerals, used as a pigment. *Syn.:* Mottée de sil, Terra crocea.

ZAFFIRRO, ZAFIRRO. 1. Blue-coloured precious stone. 2. Blue mineral.

ZAFFRE, ZAFFERA. Smalt (*q.v.*).

ORIGINAL TREATISES,

DATING FROM THE XIITH TO XVIIITH CENTURIES

ON THE

ARTS OF PAINTING,

IN

OIL, MINIATURE, MOSAIC, AND ON GLASS; OF GILDING, DYEING, AND THE PREPARATION OF COLOURS AND ARTIFICIAL GEMS;

PRECEDED BY A GENERAL INTRODUCTION; WITH TRANSLATIONS, PREFACES, AND NOTES.

BY

MRS. MERRIFIELD,

HONORARY MEMBER OF THE ACADEMY OF FINE ARTS AT BOLOGNA, TRANSLATOR OF THE TREATISE ON PAINTING OF CENNINO CENNINI, AND AUTHORESS OF 'THE ART OF FRESCO-PAINTING.'

IN TWO VOLUMES.—VOL. I.

LONDON:
JOHN MURRAY, ALBEMARLE STREET.

1849.

TO

THE RIGHT HONOURABLE

SIR ROBERT PEEL, BART.,

THESE TREATISES,

COLLECTED UNDER HIS AUSPICES,

ARE GRATEFULLY AND RESPECTFULLY DEDICATED BY

THE EDITOR.

PREFACE.

In the autumn of 1845 I was honoured by Her Majesty's Government with a commission to proceed to the North of Italy, for the purpose of collecting MSS. relative to the technical part of painting, with a view principally of ascertaining the processes and methods of oil-painting adopted by the Italians. I was also instructed generally to endeavour to procure traditional and practical information on this subject from other sources.

I succeeded in obtaining copies of the MSS. contained in the following volumes. On my return to this country, Sir Robert Peel was pleased to entrust me with the publication of the MSS., and to intimate that a part of the expenses of publication would be defrayed by Government.

I need not say how highly I was gratified by this distinction, for an occupation more congenial to my inclinations could scarcely have been suggested; and I accepted the offer without, perhaps, properly considering the magnitude of the undertaking, and my own incapacity.

The following work, in which I have endeavoured to supply by diligence what I have wanted in ability, is the result of my labours.

In preparing the MSS. for publication, I have adopted, as nearly as possible, a chronological arrangement, considering it was best adapted to show the progress of the art, and the technical methods in use from the twelfth or thirteenth to the eighteenth centuries.

The early MSS., although they do not treat of oil-painting, properly so called, are useful in showing the state of the art of painting at the period when they were written, and the importance attached to the preparation and purification of colours. In an antiquarian and historical point of view these MSS. are also highly interesting. Some of the most valuable facts to be collected from them are mentioned in the preliminary observations prefixed to each treatise. With a view of rendering the MSS. more generally useful, I have prefixed to them a brief sketch of the history and technical processes of the different kinds of painting and other arts, which are alluded to in the MSS.

Among the various recipes, many of which may be traced to a very early period, it will not occasion surprise that some should be found which partake of the barbarism of the times when they were written. Absurd, and perhaps useless, as a few of these may be considered, except as forming part of the History of Art, it has been thought advisable to publish the whole of the MSS. in order to satisfy the reader that nothing important has been omitted. The orthography of the originals has been always scrupulously followed; and no emendations have been permitted, except in one or two instances which are mentioned in the notes.

Much information relative to oil-painting was communicated to me orally by several eminent Italian artists during my tour. This information, which I endeavoured to preserve by committing the substance of their communications immediately to writing, is now published in the original form, with such explanatory notes as appeared necessary to make them intelligible.

It also occurred to me that the statements made in these memoranda would require other confirmation than the oral testimony of living persons, who, although possessing much valuable knowledge acquired by their practice and researches, and much information derived from tradition and the study of works on art, are yet unknown to the reader, and their statements are frequently contradictory. It, therefore, appeared to me, that it would be important to examine and compare the statements of the Italian professors with the treatises contained in these volumes, and with many of the best English and foreign works connected with the fine arts, in order to ascertain how far the statements and practice of these artists were supported in their view of the practice of the old masters; inasmuch as, in these points where they did coincide, it might fairly be concluded that the practice of the old masters was correctly stated by these modern professors. I have accordingly made this examination by comparing these statements with the most esteemed works on this subject. The more important points connected with this examination I communicated to Sir Robert Peel in October, 1846. They are now more fully stated, with additions and corrections, in the following work. I have referred to the authorities from which I have framed my opinions,

and from which the reader will be enabled to judge of the correctness of my conclusions.

In arranging this brief account of the methods and materials adopted in oil-painting in Italy, it is to be observed, that it has not been my intention to give a complete history of all the processes employed in this art, and of the practice of the different schools, but merely to give such a general outline as will render the oral and documentary evidence and information contained in these volumes and now scattered through so many pages, available to the reader. The only variations from the original memoranda which I have permitted myself to make consist in some necessary verbal corrections, and in some omissions of statements and opinions, which, on inquiry, could not be satisfactorily substantiated. I have also considered it unnecessary to mention the names of the professors who favoured me with the communications, although I was careful to ascertain that they were considered by competent judges eminent in their profession.

Although no exertion has been wanting on my part to make the work as useful as possible by a dispassionate and unprejudiced inquiry into the former processes of oil-painting, it may yet be feared that many errors have crept in, or been overlooked, and that many links in the chain of evidence as well as in the technical processes are still wanting. As I have been particular in stating my authorities, the former may be corrected by reference to the works indicated, the latter will be supplied by Mr. Eastlake's promised volume on the Technical Processes of the Italian Painters.

I cannot dismiss the subject of oil-painting without acknowledging the great assistance I have derived from Mr. Eastlake's recent and very valuable work, 'Materials for a History of Oil-Painting;' and I take this opportunity of expressing my sincere thanks to him for the important assistance and encouragement he has so kindly and readily afforded me during the progress of the work.

To the Earl of Ellesmere I beg also to offer my very grateful acknowledgments for the loan of many valuable books, without which it would have been impossible for me to have completed the work.

To Sir Thomas Phillipps I am also indebted for a copy of an interesting work of the middle ages, entitled 'Mappæ Clavicula,' which I have found very useful.

To my highly-esteemed friend, Mr. Seymour, of Dorset Gardens, Brighton, my acknowledgments are also especially due for loans of books, and valuable references to others, which his extensive reading qualified him to give. To Mr. Charles Carpenter, of the Brighton Bench of Magistrates, I am indebted for similar assistance

I beg also to thank Mr. Robert Hendrie, junior, whose recent edition of Theophilus has been of great assistance to me; Mr. Borrer, of Henfield, Sussex; and Mr. Albert Way, Secretary of the Archæological Institute, for their ready attention to my applications.

Mr. Hermann Schweitzer, of Brighton, the eminent analytical chemist, has also afforded me much valuable professional assistance, which I feel great pleasure in acknowledging.

By means of the introductions with which I was favoured by Sir Henry Ellis and Sig. Panizzi, of the British Museum; by M. Champollion-Figeac, of the Bibliothèque Royale, at Paris; and the Cav. Gazzera, of the Library of the University at Turin, I obtained access to the public libraries of many of the principal cities of the North of Italy, and to some private libraries: especially those of the King of Sardinia; the Marquis Trivulzio, and Conte Pompeo Litta, of Milan, author of the 'History of the Noble Families of Italy;' Conte Francesco de' Lazara, of Padua, the nephew and heir of the Cav. Lazara, whose valuable collection of MSS. and works on art is so frequently mentioned by Lanzi; of Sig. Giuseppe Riva, of the Monte Berici, near Vicenza, author of several works of antiquarian interest; of the Canon Ramelli, of Rovigo; of Sig. M. A. Gualandi, of Bologna, editor of an interesting series of original documents and letters of painters; of Professor Longhena and Sig. Vallardi, of Milan: to all of whom I beg to express my obligations for the facilities afforded me.*

---

* My acknowledgments and thanks are also due to many eminent in literature, science, and art on the Continent. I regret to omit the names of any of them, and among others named in these volumes, I feel gratified in expressing my obligations to M. le Comte Charles de l'Escalopier, and M. Delaroche, of Paris; the Cav. Promis, of the Private Library of the King of Sardinia, and Conte Galiteris, of Turin; Conte Giberto Borromeo, and the Cav. Rossi, of the Brera Library, Dr. Zardetti, of the Cabinet of Medals, Drs. Capelli and Vallardi, of Milan; Conte Lochis, President of the Accademia Carrara, Conte Pietro Moroni, Sig. Salvioni of the Public Library, and Sig. Arrigoni, of Bergamo; Conte Luigi Lechi, of Brescia; Conte Orti Manara, and Conte Jacomo Mosconi (known to the literary world as the translator of some of the works of Sir Walter Scott), of Verona; the Ab. Furlanetto, the Ab. Barbaran of the Library of the Seminario, the Ab. Roncetti of the University Library, and Prof. Poli of the University of

In preparing the following treatises for publication, I have been greatly assisted by my sons, Charles and Frederic, who translated the whole of the MSS.

In conclusion I would observe, that the work has been begun and finished under the pressure of great domestic anxiety and ill health, which sometimes rendered it scarcely possible to give that attention which so arduous a task required. Under these circumstances I have to request the indulgence of the reader for any oversights and mis-translations which may be found in the work. These errors will, however, be less important, inasmuch as the translations are accompanied by the original text, and any mistakes in the former may be corrected by reference to the latter. The fatigue of comparing the translations with works in MS. so numerous and so long, can only be appreciated by those who have been engaged in similar undertakings.

The labour, however, has been far from irksome: on the contrary, it has been pursued from beginning to end with intense interest; and from the consolation and stimulus I have derived from the pursuit, in many a

---

Padua; the Baron Galvagna, President of the Academy of Fine Arts at Venice; Sig. Gio. O'Kelly Edwards, son of Sig. Pietro Edwards, who restored the public pictures at Venice; Mr. Rawdon Brown, the Ab. Cadorin, the biographer of Titian; the Ab. Valentinelli, of the Marciana Library; Dr. Vincenzo Lazari, editor of a recent edition of the 'Travels of Marco Polo;' Sig. Cigogna, author of the valuable work entitled 'Iscrizioni Venetiane;' Signori Felice Schiavone, Tagliapietra, and Quarena, of Venice; Dr. Devit, of the Public Library of Rovigo; the Ab. Antonelli, of the Ducal Library, and Sig. N. Cittadella, of Ferrara; Sig. Vegetti, of the Library of the University of Bologna; Sig. Gaetano Giordini, Inspector of the Pinacoteca, and Sig. Masini, Secretary of the Academy of Fine Arts at Bologna; the Cav. Pezzana, of the Ducal Library, and Sig. Scaramuscia, of Parma; Sig. Bombardini, and Sig. Giambatista Baseggio, President of the Athenæum, of Bassano.

weary hour, I take leave of it with the regret which one always feels on parting with an old and agreeable companion.

M. P. M.

Brighton, 6th Nov., 1848.

CONTENTS OF VOL. I.

INTRODUCTION—

CHAPTER V.

CHAPTER VI.

ERRATA.

Page 4,	line 12 from	bottom, *for* Again at Milan, *read* at Genoa.
16,	20	top, *for* Jacobo, *read* Jacobus.
,,	10	bottom, dele "the."
68,	12 & 18	top } *for* in Janua, *read* at Genoa.
82,	5	bottom, } *for* in Janua, *read* at Genoa.
224,	17	bottom, *for* mixed however with oil and a little varnish, *read* a little varnish being mixed with the oil.

INTRODUCTION.

CHAPTER I.

ON THE STATE OF SOCIETY AND OF THE ARTS DURING THE MIDDLE AGES.

History gives but a melancholy view of the state of society in Europe towards the close of the dark ages. The domestic habits and accommodations of the people were rude in the extreme. The nobles were devoted to the pursuit of arms, and when not actually engaged in war their time was occupied in hunting and hawking, of which they were passionately fond. Nor did they disdain, in the intervals of these employments, to become highway-robbers, and to possess themselves by force of the money and baggage of the travellers whom chance threw in their way.[1]

Men so employed could have but little relish for the elegancies and comforts of domestic life. Their castles were merely a retreat from the pursuit of their enemies, and were more suited to secure the defence and safety of their possessions than to display their wealth and magnificence. The walls of these edifices were lofty and substantial, the openings for the admission of light few and narrow, the apertures unclosed with glass; the interior walls, which were bare, had no decorations but arms and the trophies of the chase. The intellectual condition of the nobles was scarcely more advanced

---

1 See Hallam's Middle Ages, vol. iii. p. 368.

than their domestic arrangements; the accomplishment of reading was possessed by few, that of writing was still more rare. Neither Frederic Barbarossa, John, King of Bavaria, nor Philip the Hardy of France, could read; nor could Theodoric or Charlemagne write.[1] Of the barons whose names are affixed to Magna Charta very few could write.

The domestic accommodations were in accordance with the edifices. A passage quoted by Mr. Hallam,[2] from a work written about the year 1300, shows the state of manners in Italy during the age of Frederic Barbarossa.[3] "In those days," the author observes, "the manners of the Italians were rude. A man and his wife eat off the same plate. There were no wooden-handled knives nor more than one or two drinking-cups in a house. Candles of wax or tallow were unknown; a servant held a torch during supper. The clothes of men were of leather unlined; scarcely any gold or silver was seen on their dress."

Such a state of society, it may be readily supposed, afforded small scope for the development of the arts. They were not, however, totally lost. The cloister, while it afforded a shelter and retreat from the more active pursuits of life, afforded also to the monks leisure and opportunity for cherishing the arts, the technical processes of which were preserved in their convents. The magnificent cathedrals which were erected during the eleventh, twelfth, and thirteenth centuries,[4] not only in

1 Hallam, Middle Ages, vol. iii. p. 329. 2 Ibid., p. 409.

3 Frederic Barbarossa was born A.D. 1121, ascended the throne A.D. 1152, and died A.D. 1190.

4 In the eleventh and twelfth centuries the Basilica of St. Mark's at Venice, and the Cathedrals of Pisa and Siena, were erected; and in the thirteenth the Basilica of S. Francesco di Assisi, the Duomo of Florence, that of Orvieto, and the churches of S. Antonio at Padua, Sta. Maria Novella at Florence, S. Croce, SS. Giovanni and Paulo, and the Frari at Venice, and the Campo Santo of Pisa. In other parts of Europe, the Cathedrals of Cologne, of Beauvais, Chartres, Rheims, Amiens, Brussels, York, Salisbury, Westminster, Burgos, Toledo, &c., were built. See, on this subject, Marchese, Memorie dei più insigni Pittori, &c. Domenicani, vol. i. p. 17.

Italy, but in the more northern parts of Europe, gave an additional impulse to the study of painting. It was the delight of the monks to adorn these edifices with painted windows of the most brilliant colours, to cover the interior with pictures representing Scripture stories, which were to serve for the catechism and instruction of the common people,[1] and to embellish the choral books with the most elaborate miniatures.

It is impossible to study the history of the arts of the middle ages without considering the immense influence exercised over society by monastic institutions. It is unnecessary to inquire here whether this influence was the cause or the effect of the darkness which hung over Europe at this period; it is sufficient to state that it extended over all classes of society, for the monks, who were the legislators[2] and physicians[3] of that period, and who possessed almost exclusively all the learning of the age, were almost the only persons skilled in the arts of sculpture, painting, and architecture. Marchese observes, with reference to the services rendered to the arts by the monks in Italy,[4] that "after having taught their ferocious conquerors the duty of forgiveness, struggled against the pride of the powerful, and preached the Gospel in the midst of the barbarous feudal laws, they prepared themselves to build bridges, to embank rivers, to construct magnificent cathedrals and abbeys, many of which remain to record the variety of their genius and the benefits they conferred on mankind. In vain would the patronage of Charlemagne, of Theodo-

---

1 An inscription formerly over the principal door of the Church of S. Nixier de Troyes states that a certain curé had caused three windows to be painted "for the catechism and instruction of the people."—L'Anglois, Essai sur la Peinture sur Verre, p. 16.

2 Mosheim's Eccles. Hist., vol. ii. pp. 26 and 377 n.

3 See Introduction to Mr. Eastlake's 'Materials for a History of Oil Painting.'

4 Memorie de' Pittori, &c., p. 13.

linda,[1] of Theodoric, and of some of the popes have sufficed to save the arts from total ruin, if the monks had not, with so much affection, protected and practised them during so many centuries. They preserved to us the traditions transmitted to them by the Byzantines, and bequeathed them to future ages, stamping them with that expression and melancholy which transpires in them in spite of the inelegance of the forms; and they ennobled by their profession the arts which their barbarous conquerors despised."

The proof that Europe is indebted to the religious communities for the preservation of the arts during the dark ages, rests on the fact that the most ancient examples of Christian art consist of the remains of mural pictures in churches, of illuminations in sacred books, and of vessels for the use of the church and the altar, and on the absence of all similar decorations on buildings and utensils devoted to secular uses during the same period, to which may be added that many of the early treatises on painting were the work of ecclesiastics as well as the paintings themselves. A similar remark may be made with regard to architecture, many of the earliest professors of which were monks.

Painting was essentially a religious occupation. The early professors of the art believed that they had an especial mission to make known the works and miracles of God to the common people, who were unacquainted with letters, "agli uomini grossi che non sanno lettere."[2] Actuated by this sentiment, it is not surprising that so many of the Italian painters should have been members of monastic establishments. It has been observed that the different religious orders selected some particular branch of the art, which they practised with great suc-

---

1 Theodolinda caused to be painted on the walls of the palace of Monza the principal events in the history of the Lombards. See Rio, de la Poésie Chrétienne, p. 20, n.

2 See the Statutes of the Sienese Painters—Carteggio Inedito, &c., vol. ii.

cess in the convents of their respective orders. Thus the Gesuati and Umiliati attached themselves to painting on glass and architecture, the Olivetani to Tarsia work, the Benedictines and Camaldolites to painting generally, and the monks of Monte Casino to miniature painting, while the Dominicans appear to have practised all the various branches of the fine arts (with the exception of mosaics) and to have produced artists who excelled in each.

The various remains of the artistic skill of the monks of the middle ages which have escaped the ravages of time sufficiently attest their mechanical dexterity in these arts, and the excellence of the traditionary practices of which they were for some time the sole depositaries.

Great, however, as the technical skill of the monks undoubtedly was at this period, their paintings were distinguished neither for accuracy of drawing nor for elegance or variety of design. Until the time of Cimabue and Giotto the Byzantine type was adhered to with little variation in Italy, or at least in the northern and southern parts; but in Rome a somewhat different style prevailed, which has been called the Italian. The mural pictures and mosaics throughout Lombardy presented everywhere the same lengthened [1] and attenuated figures, standing on the tips of their toes (for the painters of those days did not possess the art of representing the feet in perspective), with ample and flowing draperies, narrow and ill-shaped extremities, solemn and severe aspects, and large, open, and staring black eyes; the outlines of the figures were hard and black, cutting sharply the gold back-ground, and the expression of the features inspired awe and terror. The same type prevailed in the districts of Southern Italy.

---

[1] The figures of the Byzantine school were sometimes thirteen heads in height.

The good taste of Cimabue introduced in the thirteenth century a better style of art, which was much improved by his gifted pupil Giotto; and such was the influence of their example that the Byzantine style was banished from Tuscany, and wherever the works and influence of these artists extended.

The improvement in the civil condition of the people followed, if it did not keep pace with the advancement of the arts. In the twelfth century there were many influences which had been for some time silently producing a change in the manners of the people. Among these may be enumerated the Crusades, which, by making the turbulent and warlike nobles of Europe acquainted with the arts and luxuries of the more refined and polished Saracens, awakened in them a taste for dress and the elegant enjoyments of life; the commercial enterprise of a few cities,[1] which, in spite of wars and tumults, succeeded in establishing an uninterrupted intercourse with Constantinople and Palestine, and introducing the merchandise of Asia and Africa into the interior of Europe;[2] the settlements in Sicily, in the kingdom of Naples, and in Spain, of the Saracens, who, less distracted with wars than the Europeans, had leisure to attend to the erection of palaces and to the cultivation of the arts; and the establishment of the silk and woollen manufactories,[3] and the consequent increase in the comforts and conveniences of life. To these may be added the occasional cessation of war, which enabled the laity to devote themselves to the study of the arts. During this period the kind

[1] Venice, Amalfi, Pisa, Genoa. See Hallam, Mid. Ages, vol. iii. pp. 367, 388, 389, 390.

[2] Saggio sull' Antico Commercio, sull' Arti, e sulla Marina de' Veneziani, da Jacopo Filiasi, pp. 27 n., 153.

[3] A silk manufactory was established at Palermo in 1148, and in the same century at Genoa. There were woollen manufactories in England in the twelfth century.—Hallam, Midd. Ages, vol. iii. pp. 367, 393.

of painting most practised in Italy was mosaic, but in the western part of Europe painting on glass appears to have been exercised in preference to all others.

In the thirteenth century the manners of the people were still rude and uncultivated, but towards the latter end of this century a sensible refinement took place, especially in Italy. In Venice there were at this period laws in which were mentioned the tariffs regulating the manufactories of gauzes, purple cloth, and cloth of gold;[1] this is sufficient evidence of the establishment of manufactories of these articles and of the increased taste for dress. At this period the commerce of Marseilles with the Levant was in its greatest prosperity. Montpellier and Arles were also engaged in the same pursuit, and at the end of this century or the beginning of the fourteenth the first Venetian vessels arrived at Antwerp laden with spices, drugs, and silk stuffs; to these were added perfumes, cotton, and colours.[2]

The amelioration of the manners and habits of the people was decidedly favourable to the development of the arts in Italy, and the influx of Greek artists, after the taking of Constantinople by the Latins in 1204, gave them an additional impulse, and contributed to their revival in different parts of the country. From the ancient mosaic on the Duomo of Spoleto, dated 1207,[3] works of art, bearing the names of the artists and the date, are of frequent occurrence in the annals of art. Guido da Siena painted the large Madonna in S. Domenico at Siena in 1221; and the works of Giunto da Pisa were executed during the early part of this century.

These artists were succeeded by Cimabue, to whose influence is ascribed the revival of painting in Florence.

---

1 See Filiasi, Saggio, &c., p. 153.

2 Guicciardini, Belgii Descript., Amsterdam, 1613, quoted by Depping.

3 Kugler, Handbook of Painting in Italy, p. 28.

In the middle of this century arose the Florentine school of mosaic painters under Andrea Tafi, who was taught the art by the Greeks; and the family of Cosmati, also painters in mosaic, flourished at Rome about the same period.

In France and England other branches of the art were cultivated with success, especially painting on glass; and a taste for mural paintings appears to have arisen in England.

The arts had also made some progress in Spain during this century, for the corporation of the painters and sculptors of Barcelona dates from the same period.[1] The incorporation of similar societies in Italy appears to have taken place at a later period.[2]

During this century the kings of England found leisure to attend to the decoration of the interior of their palaces. It is ascertained from records preserved at Winchester, that there was a "painted chamber" in this the favourite city of the kings of England, as early as the year 1216;[3] and it appears also from another document that this apartment was decorated with historical pictures.[4] In other documents, paintings, the subjects of which are mentioned, were ordered to be executed in the Hall at Winchester, in the Painted Chamber and Palace at Westminster, in the Castle of Nottingham, and other Royal residences.[5]

---

1 A.D. 1291. Capmany, Memorias, &c., tome iii., cited by Depping, vol. i. p. 264.

2 The statutes of the Sienese painters are dated 1355; those of the goldsmiths, 1361; of the Florentine painters in 1339. Those of Padua were probably some years earlier. The Florentine painters were included in the same company as the physicians and apothecaries. See Gaye, Carteggio Inedito, vols. i. and ii. p. i.

3 Rol. Claus. 4 Hen. III., mem. 16, cited in the Archæological Journal for 1845, p. 69.

4 See Mr. Eastlake's 'Materials,' p. 556.

5 Rol. Liberat. 17 Hen. III. mem. 6, and other documents quoted in the Archæological Journal for 1845, pp. 70–77; and in Mr. Eastlake's 'Materials for a History of Painting in Oil,' vol. i. pp. 552-561.

The analysis of early mural pictures, and the directions of Le Begue, Theophilus, and the author of the Bolognese MS., place it beyond a doubt that the greater part of these paintings were executed in tempera. Many of those which are called fresco paintings, were merely commenced in fresco and finished in distemper.[1] The art of fresco-painting, properly so called, did not arise until some time after the period of which I am now speaking. The paintings on the walls of the Chapel of S. Jacopo di Pistoia were ascertained by Professor Branchi to have been executed upon a ground composed of sulphate of lime (plaster of Paris, the *gesso* of the Italians), carbonate of lime, and a yellowish colouring matter tempered with glue. It has also been ascertained that many of the beautiful mural paintings by Bernardino Luini, in the Chapel of the Monastero Maggiore at Milan, were not painted in buon-fresco, but on white stucco, in the ancient manner.[2]

It appears, from MSS. of this period, that it was sometimes the custom in England to whitewash the exterior of castles, and sometimes to paint them of three colours.[3]

> "This castel is paynted without with thre maner colours:
> Rede brennand colour is above toward the fair tours,
> Meyne colour is y-middes of ynde and of blewe,
> Grene colour be the ground that never changes hewe."

In the thirteenth and fourteenth centuries the houses of the English, of the middle and lower classes, consisted in general of a ground-floor only, divided into two apartments, namely, a hall, into which the principal door opened, and which was the room for cooking, eating, and receiving visitors; and a chamber adjoining the hall, and opening out of it, which was the private apartment of the females of the family and the bed-

---

1 See the First and Second Reports of the Commissioners of Fine Arts.
2 Milano e il suo Territorio, vol. ii. p. 254.
3 See Archæological Journal, Part IV., Jan. 1845, p. 304.

room at night. The greater part of the houses in London were built after this plan.[1] The habitations of the more wealthy classes differed from those of the middle ranks only in having an upper floor, called a *soler*, or *solar*, on which was an apartment called a "saloon." The access to this was by a flight of stairs on the outside of the house.[2] The soler is mentioned in the Le Begue MS., p. 88, probably with reference to an English house, since the term occurs in the recipes given by Theodore of Flanders to Alcherius. A different style of architecture prevailed on the Continent, for it is related that when Henry III. visited S. Louis at Paris, he greatly admired the houses of that city, consisting for the most part of many stories.[3] In houses of this description there was but little room for decoration; and they appear to have been but scantily provided with furniture. Even at a much later period, neither looking-glasses nor chairs are mentioned in the catalogue of the furniture of Contarini, the rich Venetian trader, who resided at St. Botolph's, in London, in 1481;[4] or in that of a nobleman in 1572. The Bolognese MS., however, mentions glass mirrors, in a manner which proves that they were not uncommon in Italy at the time that MS. was written.

In the fifteenth century the taste for decoration extended, as might be supposed, to the castles of the nobility, and the apartments were decorated with historical paintings from the Old and New Testament.

"Ther men myzth se, ho that wolde,
Arcangeles of rede golde,
ffytly mad of o molde,
  Lowynge ful lyzth;

1 See notice of the 'Chronicle of the Mayors and Sheriffs of London from 1188 to 1274,' in the Arch. Journ. for Sept. 1847, p. 282.

2 Illustrations of the Domestic Architecture of the Middle Ages, by Mr. Wright, Arch. Journ., Sept. 1844.

3 Arch. Jour., Sept. 1847, p. 282.

4 Hallam's Middle Ages, vol. iii. p. 428.

With the Pocalyps of Jon,
The Powles Pystoles everychon,
The paraboles of Salamon,
  Paynted ful ryzth.
And the foure gospellores,
Sytting on pyllores,
Hend, herkeneth and heres,
  Gyf hyt be zoure wyll.
Austyn and Gregory,
Jerome and Ambrose,
Thus the foure doctores
  Lystened than tylle.
Ther was purtred in ston,
The fylesoferes everychon,
The story of Absolon,
  That lykyd full ylle."[1]

It will be observed that in all the early MSS. published in this volume clocks are not mentioned, but the hours of the day were reckoned from sun-rise, and shorter periods by the time occupied in repeating Ave Marias, Paternosters, and Misereres. From this we may collect that, although the apartments of castles and palaces might reckon among their articles of domestic convenience—

" An orrelegge (horloge) one hyzth
To rynge the ours at nyzth,"

they were unknown in convents, and among the middle classes, at least until the later half of the fifteenth century.

[1] From a manuscript of the fifteenth century, in the Public Library at Cambridge, quoted in the Arch. Jour., Sept. 1844.

CHAPTER II.

MINIATURE PAINTING.

Having thus taken a cursory view of the state of society and of the arts during the middle ages, it may not be uninteresting to treat more particularly of those arts, the technical processes of which are described in the following MSS., in order to render the various practical directions more available to the student, and more interesting to the general reader.

It has been observed [1] that the rise and progress of painting is better shown by miniatures than by large pictures, because the altar-pieces and frescoes were frequently repetitions of smaller works painted in choral books, and the parchment on which they are executed being better preserved than pictures on walls, and less injured by retouching, represented more exactly the types and traditions of the early schools. Besides the miniatures painted in books, it was also the custom to affix to every picture a predella or gradino,[2] on which the different events of the life of the Saint represented in the picture were portrayed in miniature; the frames were also ornamented with small figures, so that the study of miniature-painting was necessary to all painters. We turn, therefore, with increased interest to the early history of miniature-painting, which, after the revival of the art,[3] must be sought chiefly in the archives of the

---

1 Marchese, Memorie, &c., vol. i. lib. i. cap. xi. p. 175.

2 The step on the top of the altar was so called.

3 The school of miniature painters was very important during the eighth and ninth centuries. Kugler mentions some interesting illuminations executed in manuscripts of this period. (See Handbook of Painting in Italy, p. 20.)

convents of the Benedictine, Camaldolese, and Dominican monks, and in those of the Canons Regular. It is impossible to imagine any employment more congenial to the peaceful and contemplative lives of the monks, in the intervals of their religious duties, than the pleasing and almost luxurious occupation of illustrating the sacred books with stories from Scripture, and of ornamenting with elaborate miniatures the works of Virgil and a few of the other classic authors. It is not surprising, therefore, that this kind of painting should have found so many followers in the cloisters.

The art of miniature painting was divided into two branches: the professors of the first were styled "Miniatori," or miniature painters, or illuminators of books; and those of the second, "Miniatori caligrafi," or "pulchri scriptores." To the first class belonged the task of painting the Scripture stories, the borders, and the arabesques, and of laying on the gold and ornaments of the MSS.

The second wrote the whole of the work, and those initial letters generally drawn with blue or red, full of flourishes and fanciful ornaments, in which the patience of the writer is frequently more to be admired than his genius. The wood-cut[1] in the next page shows a writer of the fifteenth century engaged in this occupation and surrounded with his various implements. With the miniatori may be classed the authors and collectors of many of the MSS. now published, and others of a similar nature. To the second class belongs Alberto Porzello, who is mentioned in the Le Begue MS. to have been "perfect in all kinds of writing, and to have kept a school at Milan, where he taught the art to young men and boys." But the two branches were frequently prac-

[1] Copied from the work of M. Aimé Champollion-Figeac, entitled 'Louis et Charles, Ducs d'Orléans, leur Influence sur les Arts, la Littérature, et l'Esprit de leur Siècle, d'après les Documents Originaux et les Peintres des Manuscrits,' Paris, 1844.

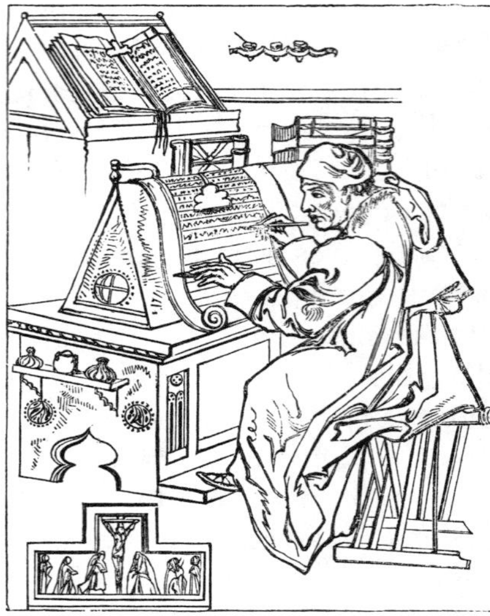

A WRITER OF THE FIFTEENTH CENTURY.
From a Manuscript in the Bibliothèque Royale at Paris.

tised by the same person, whence the term "writing" was also extended to painting, and the word was not confined to miniature painting only, but was applied to painting on glass, which was also called "writing on glass." As to the origin of the word "miniature," it received its name from the practice of writing the rubrics and initial letters with minium or red lead. The French term "illuminer" is supposed to be derived from the custom of illuminating or heightening the lights with gold. The term occurs in the Lucca MS., in the chapter "De Lazuri."

Previous to the invention of printing the art of calligraphy was of great importance. It was the custom and the pride of the large religious establishments to have the books used in the celebration of Divine Service exquisitely written, and adorned with miniatures. The recent researches into the archives of the different Italian cities have brought to light the minutes of expenses of some of these books, which prove the

time occupied in painting them, and the large sums paid to the artists for executing them, or for the purchase of the materials; for the monks did not receive payment for the works intended for their own convents. The choral books of the convent of S. Marco, at Florence, were written and painted by Fra Benedetto del Mugello (the elder brother of Frate Angelico[1]), with the assistance of the monks. The cost of these books was 1500 ducats, and the time occupied in completing them was five years.[2]

The choral books belonging to the cathedral of Ferrara are thirty in number; twenty-two of which are 26 inches long by 18 in breadth, and the remaining eight smaller. They were begun in the year 1477, and completed in 1535.[3] The most interesting of these books, for the beauty of the characters, as well as for the miniatures, were executed by Jacopo Filippo d'Argenta, Frate Evangelista da Reggio, a Franciscan, Andrea delle Veze, Giovanni Vendramin of Padua, and Martino di Giorgio da Modena. The parchment on which these books are written is in excellent preservation. It is worthy of remark that great part of the parchment or vellum for these books was brought from Germany, or, at least, was manufactured by Germans. There is an entry in the records of the cathedral, for the year 1477, of a sum of money paid to M. Alberto da Lamagna for 265 skins of vellum; of another sum, paid in 1501, for 60 skins, to Piero Iberno, also a German; and to Creste, another German, for 50 skins, furnished by them on account of these books.

The magnificent choral books, thirteen in number, which formerly belonged to the Certosa of Pavia, are

1 Called also Beato Angelico.

2 Marchese, Memorie, &c., vol. i. p. 189.

3 Documenti risguardanti i Libri Corali del Duomo di Ferrara, communicated by the Ab. Antonelli, of the Public Library at Ferrara, to Sig. Gualandi, by whom they were published in his Memorie, &c., ser. vi. p. 153.

now in the library of Brera, at Milan. They are of very large size, probably three feet by two, and many of the illuminations are very beautiful.

As a work of art, the choral books of the Monastery degli Angeli in Florence are perhaps more remarkable than those of Ferrara. They are twenty in number, and were all written by one writer, and embellished by one miniature painter. The former, Don Jacopo, was a Camaldolese monk, of the same religious house at Florence; and, according to Vasari,[1] was not only a most excellent person, but the best writer of initial letters that ever lived, not only in Tuscany, but in Europe; and he adds, that these choral books are perhaps, as regards the writing, the finest and largest in Italy; Don Jacopo also wrote other books at Rome and at Venice. The miniatures in the above-mentioned choral books, which are all by the hand of Don Silvestro, are not less excellent than the writing; and so great was the esteem in which these two monks, D. Jacopo and D. Silvestro, were held in their convent, that the right hand of each was preserved in a casket with the utmost veneration. Vasari adds that he, who had seen these books so many times, was astonished at the skill in design and ability with which they were executed, at a period when the art of design was all but lost; for these monks flourished about the year 1350.

The choral books of the Cathedral of Siena have been preserved with the greatest care. They were all attributed by Vasari to Piero di Perugia,[2] but they are known to have been painted by several artists, among whom may be mentioned Liberale di Verona and Ansino di Pietro, whose names are inscribed on their paintings.[3] There were also fourteen magnificent choral books in the convent of S$^{ta.}$ Maria del Sasso,

---

1 Life of Don Lorenzo.

2 Life of Agnolo Gaddi. 3 Marchese, Memorie, &c., vol. i. p. 197.

near Bibbiena, which were executed by Fra Pietro di Tramoggiano, and which were valued at upwards of 1500 scudi. Many of the miniatures were cut out and carried away, others were sent to S$^{ta.}$ Maria Novella, at Florence; but the books are now lost, and the convent does not at the present time possess a single miniature.[1]

The sister arts of calligraphy and miniature painting flourished simultaneously in Italy and in the countries north of the Alps. The celebrated monastery of St. Gall possessed a school of painters, who were distinguished even in the ninth century. In the tenth century, Tutilo, a member of this community, was equally famous as a painter, poet, musician, sculptor, and statuary. But the best miniature painter of the tenth century was Godemann, who was chaplain of the Bishop of Winchester from A.D. 963 to 984, and afterwards Abbot of Thornley. His benedictional, ornamented with thirty beautiful miniatures, is in the possession of the Duke of Devonshire. In the eleventh century schools of painting were formed at Hildesheim and Paderborn; and the art was exercised by ecclesiastics of the highest rank.[2] The reputation of the French miniature painters had reached Italy in the time of Dante, who alludes to the practice of the art

"Ch' alluminare è chiamato in Parigi,"

while recording the merit of Oderigi da Gubbio and Franco Bolognese. Many artists who followed this branch of the profession are enumerated by Alcherius in the work of Le Begue. Some of these were natives of Italy, others of France, and others of Flanders. The Italian miniature painters are numerous. Among the

1 Compendio Storico Critico sopra le due Immagine di Maria S. S. nella Chiesa di Sta. Maria del Sasso, presso Bibbiena, dato in luce dal P. Vincenzo Fineschi, Firenze, 1792, cap. x. p. 72; cited by Marchese, vol. i. p. 209.

2 See Rio, de la Poésie Chrétienne, p. 32–34.

most celebrated miniatori of the fifteenth century was Francesco dai Libri, a native of Verona, called the Old, to distinguish him from his son Girolamo. He obtained the appellation "dai Libri" from his employment, which consisted in illuminating MSS.; and, as he lived before the discovery of the art of printing, he found constant occupation, because those persons who paid the expense of the writing, which was very great, were also desirous of seeing their books ornamented with miniatures. Francesco lived to a great age, and died contented and happy, because, says Vasari, "in addition to the peace of mind which he derived from his own virtues, he left a son who was a better painter than himself." This son was Girolamo dai Libri, whose merits as a miniature painter fully equalled the sanguine expectations of his father. Vasari is warm in his praises. He says, "Girolamo painted flowers with such skill, truth, and beauty, that they appeared like nature itself; and he imitated small cameos and other engraved stones and jewels in such a manner that it was impossible to make them more like, or more minute; and among the figures which he made on cameos and factitious stones, may be seen some which are not larger than a small ant, yet all their limbs and muscles are seen distinctly." Girolamo illuminated many books for religious societies, and especially for the rich monastery of the Canons Regular of S. Salvatore, at Candiani, where he went to work in person, which he would not do at any other place; whilst at this monastery he taught the first principles of the art to Don Giulio Clovio, who was afterwards reputed to be the best miniature painter of his time.[1] Lanzi calls him the prince of miniature painters. Great part of his works were painted for sovereigns and princes, in whose libraries they may be seen, executed with such surprising truth

---

1 Vasari, Vita di Fra Giocondo ed Altri, vol. iii.

and liveliness, that they appear rather to be reflections in a camera obscura than works of art. Some idea of the labour of executing these minute pictures may be formed from the fact, that one work alone, which he illustrated for Cardinal Farnese, with twenty-six subjects, occupied him during nine years. His works are very scarce, but some may be found in the libraries of private individuals. The Sloane Library contains a MS. illuminated by Don Giulio Clovio.

Among the miniature painters of the order of St. Dominic was P. Alessandro della Spina, who flourished during the fourteenth century. Padre Alessandro deserves the gratitude of posterity, and of all miniature painters especially; for to him we are indebted for making known the invention and use of spectacles. Indeed P. Marchese attributes the *invention* [1] of spectacles to Padre Alessandro, but the memorial of him in the Chronicle of St. Katherine, at Pisa, proves that he had seen spectacles made by one who would not communicate the secret, before he made them himself, and that with a cheerful and willing heart he communicated all he knew. The notice in the Chronicle runs thus:—

"Fra Alexander de Spina vir modestus et bonus, quæ vidit oculis facta scivit et facere. Ocularia ab alio primo facta comunicare nolente, ipse fecit, et omnibus comunicavit corde hilari et volente. Cantare, scribere, miniare, et omnia scivit quæ manus mechanicæ valent." [2]

Another monk and miniature painter of the same order, Fra Benedetto, usually called "Bettuccio," deserves remembrance for his brave defence of Giro-

---

[1] "Spectacles had been known at Haarlem since the beginning of the 14th century, and a monument in the church of Sta. Maria Maggiore, at Florence, alludes to Salvino degli Armati, who died in 1317, as their inventor (inventore degli occhiali). Some accurate notices of the use of spectacles by old men appear to have been made in 1299 and 1305." Humboldt's Kosmos, vol. ii. p. 497.—Is it possible that Padre Marchese can have overlooked the monument alluded to by the accurate and scientific Humboldt?

[2] Memorie de' Pittori, &c. Domenicani, vol. i. p. 177.

lamo Savonarola, when the latter was torn from the shelter of his convent of S. Marco, at Florence, to meet a cruel and painful death. Fra Pacifico Burlamacchi, in his Life of Savonarola, relates that "Fra Benedetto armed himself from head to foot, and joined the party of the Piagnoni,[1] to defend a life so dear to him; but Savonarola seeing him, desired him to lay down his arms, adding that the professors of religion should use spiritual weapons only. When Benedetto saw them carrying away his beloved master to prison, he entreated to be allowed to follow him. Then Savonarola, turning round to him, said, 'Brother Benedetto, I command you by your vow of obedience not to follow me, because Brother Domenico and I must die for the love of Christ.' At this instant he was torn from the sight of his sons, who all wept for him. And it was then the ninth hour of the night."[2]

Fra Eustachio, another Dominican monk, was, perhaps, one of the greatest miniature painters that Italy has produced.[3] His merits, passed over by historians, and especially by Vasari, whom gratitude should have prompted to remember him, are recorded by his own order. Padre Timoteo Bottonio,[4] a contemporary of Fra Eustachio, relates that when Vasari was writing the first edition of his Lives of the Painters, he used to come frequently to converse with this old man, who related to him many interesting facts concerning the early and illustrious artists. A Psalter, exquisitely painted by him, still exists in the Convent of S. Marco, at Florence. He has been styled the Porta of miniature painting.

The French miniature painters were undoubtedly numerous, but a Vasari is still wanting to record their merits. The beautiful choral book, painted by Daniel d'Aubonne, in 1621, must not be forgotten. This volume

---

[1] The partisans of Savonarola.

[2] See Marchese, Memorie, &c., vol. i. p. 199. [3] Ibid., p. 202-207.

[4] Annale MSS., vol. ii. p. 303, ann. 1555.

is preserved in the public library at Rouen; it is of very large size, and the writing and illuminations are exquisitely beautiful. Daniel was thirty years in completing it.

Missals and livres d'heures of great beauty are so common in all rich libraries, that it is unnecessary to particularise any in the present work.

As a private collection, perhaps there is no single volume of greater beauty or value than that belonging to Mr. Rogers the poet, whose elegant and correct taste is well known. The volume, formed at great expense, consists of miniatures from different works and different countries; and it is scarcely possible to see more exquisite specimens of the art.

The manner in which these works were executed may be collected from the following Treatises: it is sufficient to observe that the colours were prepared with the greatest care, and that the vehicle was egg, gum, or glue. D'Agincourt, however, mentions some miniatures, the colours of which were insoluble in water; and Dr. Dibdin,[1] in describing the illuminations of a MS. of the Codex Justinianus of the fourteenth century, states that on close examination the colours appear to have been mixed up with a glossy material not unlike oil. These instances appear to have been exceptions to the general character of miniatures, the surface of which usually does not shine. It will be observed that the shades in miniatures were not generally painted with transparent colours, but that white was mixed with them.

The parchment or paper on which these MSS. were written was usually left white; but a purple colour was sometimes communicated to it, by tinging it with a decoction of oricello.[2] When the tint was dry, the letters were written on it with gold or silver. Several MSS. of this kind are preserved in the Bibliothèque Royale at Paris.

---

1 Northern Tour, p. 603. 2 See Bol. MS., p. 474.

CHAPTER III.

MOSAICS AND TARSIA WORK.

In enumerating the arts of the middle ages, we must not omit to mention the beautiful art of working in mosaic, the most durable of all the methods of painting now in existence. Domenico Ghirlandaio used to say that it was the only painting for eternity.[1] Vasari also has a similar remark; he says, with regard to the durability of all works composed of colours, there are none which resist the action of the winds and waters like mosaics.[2]

The art of working in mosaic was known to the ancients. It was practised by the Byzantine Greeks, and appears never to have been entirely lost in Italy. Specimens of this art may still be seen at Rome and at Ravenna, which date from the fourth and fifth centuries.

There were various kinds of mosaics.[3] Those intended for the decoration of vaulted ceilings and other elevated parts of buildings, consisted of cubes of coloured glass, the older specimens being generally inlaid either on a white ground, as in the Romano-Christian school,[4] or on a gold ground, as in the early Christian mosaics of the Byzantine school. The mosaics in the church of SS. Cosmo and Damiano in the Forum at Rome were the work of Roman artists, while the old mosaics

---

1 Vasari, Life of Domenico Ghirlandaio.

2 Life of Gherardo.

3 For an account of the different kinds of mosaic, and of the process employed at Rome, sec Transactions of the Society of Arts, Part I., New Series, 1847.

4 Rio, de la Poésie Chrétienne, p. 41.

in the Apsis[1] of the Basilica of S. Ambrogio, at Milan, which are said to be not later than the ninth century; those in S. Lorenzo, also in Milan; those in the Duomo of Torcello, reputed to be of the tenth century; and some of the ancient mosaics in the church of S. Marco, at Venice, which are of the eleventh century, are represented to be the work of Byzantine artists. Some of the mosaics in the last-mentioned edifice are stated to have been actually brought from the East.

It appears that there were in Italy two principal schools of mosaic painting, established as early as the eleventh century. One of these was formed by the Greek artists employed on the church of S. Mark, at Venice, from which the Florentine school afterwards sprung; the other subsisted in Rome, from an early period until the thirteenth century.[2] Both schools have been praised by different authors as superior to all others; Vasari gives the preference to that of Venice, while Lanzi considers that the Roman artists excelled the Venetians. The Venetian school undoubtedly originated in the decoration of the church of S. Mark, which afforded for several centuries constant occupation to the musaicisti. This church, observes Lanzi, was and is an incomparable museum, in which, commencing from the eleventh century, may be traced, in the mosaics begun by the Greeks and continued by the Italians, the gradual progress of design of every period until the present day.

The earliest artists were undoubtedly Greeks, and the work appears to have been continued by Greek artists and their disciples until about 1250. From that time until 1350, Zanetti states[3] that he was unable to find any records of the progress of the work; but at the

---

1 The *Apsis* was also called the *Tribune*. It was the semicircular recess at the east end of the church.

2 Lanzi, vol. i. p. 6 n.

3 Notizie de' Musaici della Chiesa Ducale di S. Marco—Zanetti, della Pittura Veneziana, p. 561.

last date the doge Andrea Dandolo caused the chapel of the Baptistery to be covered with mosaics. The fourteenth and fifteenth centuries produced many artists, the best of whom was Michele Zamboni, who was the first to abandon the ancient manner, and to improve his design, by studying the works of the best painters of his time. Many of the ancient mosaics having perished, they were replaced by Zamboni, according to the old design. The sixteenth century was the golden age of mosaic painting at Venice. Among the great names of the period may be enumerated Vincente Bianchini, more remarkable for his talents than his integrity, and his brother Domenico, called Il Rosso or Rosetto; Alberto Zio, the priest; Marco Luciano Rizzo; the celebrated Francesco Zuccato, the friend of Titian, who received his first instructions in painting from the father of Zuccato; Valerio Zuccato, the brother of Francesco; and Giovanni Visentin.

The distinctions enjoyed by the brothers Zuccati excited the envy of the other artists, and when the former had completed the pictures from the Apocalypse, the quarrels among the rival painters ran so high, that they reached the ears of the Procuratore Cassiere. A process was instituted to discover the truth. The Zuccati were accused, among other things, of having added to the effect of their mosaics by painting on certain parts, and of having joined the squares badly; Valerio especially was accused of not knowing his business. Among the most violent of the accusers was Bartolommeo Bozzo, a former pupil of the Zuccati, who pointed out some small campanili, and also some clouds in the mosaic of the Apocalypse, which were executed with the pencil, and not with coloured glass and stones, as they ought to have been, according to the rules of the Procuratori. The Bianchini supported the accusation of Bozzo, and an accidental circumstance gave additional weight to the charge against the Zuccati. A mistake

having been discovered by the latter in the word *saxibus*, which formed part of the inscription, they had corrected the error by affixing to it a small piece of painted paper; and when the mosaic was washed to ascertain whether it had been painted or not, the piece of paper was separated, and the Procuratore believed accordingly that some deception had been used. He therefore caused several persons employed in the church to inquire into the affair, and finally he summoned a council of the greatest painters of that time, among whom were Titian, Paolo Veronese, Tintoretto, and Andrea Schiavone, who decided that it could not be denied "that the pencil had been used in some parts, but that when these touches had been removed with a sponge and sand, the mosaics were not injured by it, but were even considered to be improved." Every one praised the design, and the skill of the artists, and Titian, especially, defended his friends the Zuccati with great warmth, saying that the cartoons ought to be examined, to see whether the campanili which had been painted were in them as well as in the mosaics; thinking that the degree of blame attached to these masters depended upon this circumstance. It is doubtful who made the cartoons; Valerio asserted that they were made by "Messer Tiziano," and that they did not contain the campanili, and said that if it were necessary he would produce them with the outlines pricked, as they were. Titian, however, did not acknowledge that these cartoons were his work, although he owned having made others for the Zuccati. The trial concluded by the Zuccati being adjudged to execute again, at their own expense, the parts on which the pencil had been employed; but this decree was never executed, and the painted parts, particularly the small campanili, remain to this day.[1]

The dispute concerning the execution of this mosaic

---

[1] Zanetti, p. 576.

by the Zuccati led to the examination of the other pictures, which had been the work of their rivals; and it was finally concluded unanimously, that the two Bianchini and Bozzo were the best workers in mosaic, but that Francesco Zuccato excelled them all in the knowledge of the art, and next to him in skill was Vincente Bianchini.

The designs for the mosaics executed about this period were by the most celebrated painters, Titian, Tintoretto, Salviati, Sansovino, Domenico Tintoretto, Maffeo Verona, and others; and many of the musaicisti were so little acquainted with the principles of art, that the painters who made the designs were obliged to colour as well as draw them, and they were then servilely copied by the musaicisti. The Procuratori being satisfied by the representations of the professors of the bad consequences likely to ensue from the ignorance of the musaicisti, new regulations were made, the number of masters employed in St. Mark's was reduced, and every one was required, before his election, to give a proof of his skill. In order to determine the respective merits of the rival artists, a design representing S. Jerome was made, and Francesco Zuccato, the two Bianchini, and Bozzo were required to copy it in mosaic. Sansovino, Titian, and Paolo Veronese were the judges, and it was agreed unanimously that Zuccato's picture was the best, Gian Antonio Bianchini's was next, then that of Bozzo, and Domenico Bianchini's was the last, although it was considered the most faithful copy of the design.

Among the later Venetian artists may be enumerated Gio. Antonio Marini, Lorenzo Ceccato, Luigi Gaetano, Jacopo Pasterini, and Francesco Turessio; these worked from the designs of Palma Giovane, of Maffeo Verona, of Leandro Bassano, Aliense, Padovanino, and others. The artists of the seventeenth century were less celebrated, and their works in mosaic executed in the style of that

period were employed as decorations on new walls only; according to Zanetti,[1] it was decreed in the year 1610, that no ancient mosaic should be removed, although the work might be Greek, and the style bad; but that where the danger of ruin was imminent, the design should be copied, and the picture restored exactly as it was at first. By this means a complete series of monuments, unique in their kind, not only in Italy, but in all the world, has been preserved to posterity.

In the middle of the thirteenth century the fame of the Greek artists, who were still employed on the mosaic decorations of St. Mark's, was spread far and wide; it reached to Florence, where Andrea Tafi then practised the art of painting. Andrea, ambitious of transmitting his name to posterity, and having greater confidence in the durability of the materials than in his own talents, prudently determined to adopt the art of mosaic painting; but as the technical part of this art was unknown in the north of Italy, he found it necessary to go to Venice. While residing in this city, he gained the good will of a Greek painter named Apollonio so entirely, that he was persuaded not only to teach him the art, but to accompany him to Florence, where, in the middle of the thirteenth century, he executed, in conjunction with Andrea Tafi, some mosaics in the Tribune of the old church of S. Giovanni.[2] Vasari[3] says that this work was entirely in the Greek manner, that the design was rude and without skill, but that the mechanical part was well executed, the pieces extremely well joined, and the surface even.[4] He adds, that the latter part of the work is much better, or to speak more correctly, not so bad as the portions first completed. After this, Andrea executed in mosaic, without the assistance of Apollonio, a figure of Christ 14 feet high,

---

1 Della Pittura Veneziana, p. 570 n.

2 Now the Basilica of S. Giovanni Battista—the Battistero.

3 Vita di Andrea Tafi. 4 See also Morrona, Pisa Illustrata, vol. i. p. 254.

a work which, Vasari says, spread his fame throughout Italy. "Andrea was really," observes this author, "very happy in living at a time when works of so little merit were so much esteemed." It may be added, that he was fortunate in forming so correct an estimate of his own powers, as to prefer being the head of a new school of painting in the north of Italy, to remaining in the obscurity to which his want of skill in design appeared to consign him. Andrea died in 1294, and his merits were recorded in an epitaph preserved by Vasari—

"Qui giace Andrea, ch' opre leggiadre, e belle
Fece in tutta Toscana, ed ora è ito
A far vago lo Regno delle stelle."

Contemporary with Andrea was Jacopo da Turrita,[1] or, as he was called in Siena, Maestro Mino,[2] a Franciscan friar, to whose merits Lanzi says that Vasari did not do justice. Perhaps the latter judged from the specimens of the works of Jacopo at Florence, which were by no means equal to those conducted by him in Sta. Maria Maggiore at Rome. Some writers have believed that Fra Mino and Tafi both worked in mosaic in the Tribune of the Duomo of Pisa, but Prof. Ciampi has shown that this mosaic was not begun until 1301, at which time Fra Mino and Tafi were no longer living. The mosaic at Pisa, the subject of which was a Maestà, was commenced by one Maestro Francesco,[3] assisted by his son Vittorio, Lapo of Florence, Michele, Duccio, Tura, Turetto, Dato, Tano, and others. Francesco either died or abandoned the work the same year, and was succeeded as Capo Maestro by Cimabue,[4] under whom worked Bardo, Ganaccio, Upechino, and Turetto. The S. Giovanni, on the left hand of the Saviour in the

1 Vasari, Vita di Andrea Tafi. Baldinucci, Vite.
2 Morrona, Pisa Illust., vol. i. p. 247.
3 Ciampi, Notizie, &c., p. 144, and Docum. xxv. 4 Ibid., Doc. xxvi.

same design, is said to be the work of Cimabue, who however left it incomplete; and it was, together with the figure of the Saviour, finished by Vicino, the pupil of Gaddo Gaddi, in 1321. As this is the only work in mosaic ascribed to Cimabue, it has been supposed by some persons that he merely executed the design. The repeated payments, however, to him, on account of this work,[1] in the books of the Duomo, seem to warrant the belief that he actually worked on the mosaic. Giotto also exercised his talents in mosaic painting, and the celebrated mosaic called the "Nave di Giotto," which was executed for the ancient basilica of St. Peter at Rome, attests his eminence in this branch of the art.[2] This work, observes D'Agincourt, "by its ingenious and picturesque composition, as well as by a more correct design, fixes the epoch of the revival of this kind of painting." Kugler says[3] that the mosaic has so frequently changed its place, and thus undergone so many restorations, that the composition only can now be considered as belonging to Giotto.

Gaddo Gaddi was the father of Taddeo Gaddi,[4] and the grandfather of Agnolo, the master of Cennino Cennini.[5] He was the friend of Cimabue and of Andrea Tafi; from the example of the former he learned to improve his style of design, and from the latter he acquired the art of working in mosaic. As he united the mechanical skill of Andrea to a better taste in design, it will readily be supposed that his works were in much request. He executed, in the semicircle over the principal door in Sta. Maria del Fiore in Florence, the mosaic representing the Coronation of the Virgin, which, on the authority of Vasari,

1 Ciampi, Notizie, &c., Doc. xxvi.; Morrona, Pisa Illust., vol. i. p. 249 n.; and see Kugler, Handbook of Painting in Italy, p. 32.

2 Vasari, Int., cap. xxix.

3 Handbook of Painting, Italian School, p. 51.

4 Vasari, Vite di Gaddo, Taddeo, e Agnolo Gaddi.

5 Cennino Cennini, Trattato.

was considered by all masters, foreign as well as native, as the finest work of the kind which had ever been seen in Italy. He afterwards worked at Rome and at Pisa, and died in 1312.

The secret of working in mosaic was inherited by Agnolo, the son of Taddeo,[1] who in 1346 repaired some of the mosaics executed by Andrea Tafi in the roof of S. Giovanni at Florence. He fixed the cubes of glass so firmly into the ground, with a stucco composed of mastic[2] and wax melted together, that neither the roof nor the vaulting had received any injury from water from the period of its completion until the time of Vasari. From Agnolo Gaddi the secrets of the art were transmitted to Cennino Cennini, who, in his Treatise on Painting, left them as an heir-loom to posterity. That Cennini actually treated on mosaics in his work, is related by Vasari;[3] but as this subject is not mentioned in the MS. published by Tambroni, it was considered that Vasari was mistaken, and that he had spoken of the MS. without having read it. Subsequent researches,[4] however, have proved that he was right. Besides the MS. in the Laurenziana, the Riccardiana Library (at Florence) contains a more perfect copy made in the sixteenth century, probably soon after the year 1500, which contains many things omitted in the Vatican MS., among which may be mentioned the arts of working in glass and in mosaic.

It is gratifying to learn that a second edition of this highly interesting work will probably be published at Florence, which will contain the new passages in the MS. of the Riccardiana, and which will be collated with both the Florentine MSS. It has been conjectured from the last words of the MS. of Cennini in

[1] Vasari, Vita di Agnolo Gaddi; Bald., Vita di Agnolo Gaddi.

[2] Bald., Vita di Agnolo Gaddi. Vasari says "mastrice," which signifies cement or glue.

[3] Vita di Agnolo Gaddi.

[4] Antologia—Firenze, 1821.

the Vatican, "Finito libro referamus gratia Christi 1437 a dì 31 di luglio. Ex stincarum f.,"[1] that Cennini was an inmate of the debtors' prison at Florence called "Le Stinche," and our sympathies were excited on behalf of the patient and religious old man, who at an age approaching to eighty could so abstract his mind from the adversity into which he had fallen, as to compose his Treatise on Painting during his confinement in a prison, and to allow no expressions of regret or discontent to escape from his pen. The researches, however, of Signor Benci of Florence prove that the name of Cennini does not occur in the books belonging to the prison of the Stinche in the year 1437, or in some of the later years of the fourteenth century. The addition of the above mentioned words has been accounted for[2] by the fact that it was the custom to employ the prisoners for debt in copying MSS.; and it was conjectured that these words, so expressive of the distaste we may suppose a person indifferent to the art to have felt on the completion of, to him, so irksome a task, were added by the unfortunate prisoner who copied the MS. afterwards placed in the Vatican. If then the date 1437 be that of the copy, the original MS. must be older, and perhaps may be actually a work of the fourteenth century.

Many, if not all, of the early Florentine painters practised this branch of the art.[3] It is said[4] that Alesso Baldovinetto spared no pains to discover the best method of working in mosaic, and that he would never have succeeded in this pursuit, if he had not

---

1 These words are wanting in the Riccardiana MS. See Antologia—Firenze, 1821.

2 Edinburgh Review, 1847, p. 193.

3 Prof. Ciampi (Notizie, &c., p. 92) says the *Musaicisti* called themselves *painters*, and he quotes the inscription on the mosaic by Torriti (or Turrita) in the church of S. Giovanni Laterani at Rome:—" Jacobus Torriti pictor hoc opus mosaycen fecit."

4 Vasari, Vita di Alesso Baldovinetto.

accidentally met with a German who was travelling through Florence on his way to Rome. Alesso gave this man a lodging, and learned from him the whole process, so that he was enabled to set to work with confidence, and to execute some figures in mosaic in the church of S. Giovanni. This work so increased his reputation that he was employed in cleaning the whole roof of the edifice, which had been covered with mosaics by Andrea Tafi, and was then in want of repair. He completed this work also to the satisfaction of his employers. Alesso lived to be eighty years old, and then feeling the infirmities of age stealing over him, he sought a retreat for his declining years in the Hospital of S. Paul. It is related that in order to ensure for himself a better reception, he took with him to his apartments in the hospital a large chest which was thought to contain money, and in this belief the officers of the hospital treated him with the greatest respect and attention. But their disappointment may be imagined when, on opening the chest, after the decease of the aged artist, they found nothing but drawings on paper, and a small book which taught the art of making the mosaics (pietre del musaico), the stucco, and the method of working. At the present time we should have considered this little book a greater treasure than the money which was so much desired. The remarks of Vasari on this occurrence are highly honourable to the venerable old man; he says, "It was no wonder that they did not find money, for Alesso was so bountiful, that everything he possessed was as much at the service of his friends as if it had been their own."

Alesso taught the art of working in mosaic to Domenico Ghirlandaio, who executed, in conjunction with Gherardo, some mosaics in the Duomo of Florence.[1]

The only artists of the early Roman school whose

[1] Vasari, Vite di Alesso Baldovinetto e Domenico Ghirlandaio.

names have descended to posterity are the family of Cosmati.[1] Adeodati di Cosmo Cosmati worked in Sta. Maria Maggiore in 1290, two years after the arrival of Giotto in Rome, and probably about the time that he was employed upon the "Navicella." Jacopo and Giovanni Cosmati also worked in mosaic about 1299 in Rome, and in the Duomo of Orvieto. It is said that these artists were all superior to the Greeks employed in S. Mark's at Venice. It is certain, however, that much encouragement was given at Rome to artists from other parts of Italy, and especially to many Florentines. This city was in fact the general rendezvous of all who were distinguished for more than ordinary skill in the arts, as the place where they might not only improve themselves in their profession by the contemplation and study of works of art, but where their talents might meet with encouragement and reward. The art of working in mosaic was brought to perfection in this city. It became in time the rival of painting, not only by the artful combination of various coloured stones cemented together, but by means of a composition, by which it was possible to produce every colour, to emulate every half tint, to represent every gradation, every touch, as perfectly as with the pencil.[2] As the building of S. Mark's at Venice called forth all the talent of the artists of that period, so the construction and decoration of S. Peter's at Rome occasioned employment to Roman artists. Natural causes concurred in promoting the cultivation of mosaic painting at Rome, for the humidity of S. Peter's was found inimical to paintings in oil, and it was considered advisable, even in the time of Urban VIII.,[3] to substitute mosaics in the place of paintings in oil.

The Roman school in mosaics produced Muziani,

---

1 Lanzi, vol. i. p. 6 n.; Ciampi, Notizie, &c., p. 46.

2 Lanzi, vol. ii. p. 230. 3 Ibid.

Paolo Rossetti, Marcello Provenzale, Gio. Batt. Calandra, a native of Vercelli, by whose discoveries the mechanical part of the art was greatly improved, and the family of Fabio, who copied in mosaic some of the works of Guercino, Domenichino, and Carlo Maratta.

The earliest document known which gives an account of any of the processes of mosaic painting, is the Lucca MS.; but this merely contains some recipes for colouring the glass of which the work was composed. These recipes are repeated in the Mappæ Clavicula. The Bolognese MS. contains directions for making coloured glass, and "Materia Musica;" and the subject is alluded to by Theophilus. The recipes for coloured glass in the MS. of Eraclius may also relate to mosaics. Neither of these authorities, however, describe the stucco in which the mosaic was embedded, nor do they speak of any cement for fastening the pieces of glass together. The omission has, however, been supplied by Vasari,[1] who has mentioned the materials employed for this purpose.

According to this author the stucco, which would remain in a state fit for working for a period of from two to four days according to the weather, was composed of lime, pounded brick, gum tragacanth, and white of egg, and it was kept moist by laying wet cloths upon it. In the Life of Agnolo Gaddi, Vasari mentions that the mosaics of Andrea Tafi in S. Giovanni in Florence, having been injured by the penetration of damp, were repaired by Agnolo, who employed stucco made of mastrice (or mastic according to Baldinucci) and wax, and this composition effectually answered the purpose of excluding the damp. From the same account it also appears that the squares were deeply embedded in the stucco and firmly cemented together. The repairing of these mosaics also gave the artists employed on the work an opportunity of observing that

---

[1] Intr., cap. xxix.

the design had been marked out on the stucco with red outlines, and that it had been entirely worked on the stucco. Prof. Branchi of Pisa thus describes the ground in which the before-mentioned mosaics in the Tribune of the Duomo of that city were embedded :—"The cement or bed of the beautiful mosaic of the Tribune of the Duomo of Pisa consists of two thick strata one upon the other. The lower stratum, which is white, tasteless, of a texture apparently homogeneous, soluble in acids, with liberation of carbonic acid, consisted undoubtedly of a mixture of slaked lime and marble dust. Having tested the weight of 2 denari (grammi 2·358) with acetic acid, there remained only silica and yellow oxide of iron, weighing 1¾ gr. (grammi 0·085). The superior stratum in which the parallelopipeds of coloured glass were embedded, consisted of a yellowish mixture somewhat hard, which acquired on lighted charcoal a colour that was first grey and then blackish. The same acetic acid, to the action of which I exposed an equal quantity of this layer as of the lower, dissolved the lime with slight ebullition, and left 12½ gr. (grammi 0·613) of a substance of a dark-yellow colour, which I found was composed of linseed oil dried, and a small portion of turpentine, and of other resinous matter. The cement of the mosaics of the cloisters of the Basilica of S. Paolo without the walls at Rome was composed of slaked lime and brickdust more or less finely pulverized. It was of a flesh colour, unalterable by fire or by exposure to the sea wind, and of a taste slightly saline. By means of an analysis, sufficiently accurate for the purpose, I found in the same quantity, namely 2 denari, that its constituents were nearly as follows :—

	Denari.	Grains.	Grammi.
Carbonate of lime	1	3½	(1·350
Pulverized bricks deprived by acetic acid of their calcareous parts	0	11⅔	(0·572
Muriate of soda, earthy muriates, and a little calcareous sulphate	0	8⅚	(0·433

By these results I have learned, that the grounds of the mosaics were not always prepared in the same manner. Chambers[1] informs us, that "the composition adapted to retain the different pieces of glass, consisted of lime, and powder of fine bricks, with gum tragacanth and white of egg. From the Encyclopédie we learn, that anciently the cement of the mosaics was composed of white of egg and water, three parts of pulverized bricks, and one part of slaked lime, but that the materials generally employed, and which were preferable to the preceding, were slaked lime, pulverized marble, and linseed oil. As this last composition does not differ essentially from that which formed the superior layer of the Pisan mosaics, it is evident that it was known to the most eminent workers in mosaic of the thirteenth century."

With regard to the oil and turpentine or other resin of which Prof. Branchi found traces in the upper stratum of the ground, I may add that notices have been found by Prof. Ciampi, in the records of the Duomo of Pisa for the year 1303, of payments for oil and turpentine which belong to the mosaics of the Duomo.[2]

---

1 Dict., Art. Mosaics, in which he mentions those of Pisa. [Note by Branchi.] Chambers probably learned this from Vasari (Intr., cap. xxix.), who adds travertine to the other ingredients.

2 "Docum 26 . . . . . Johannes Orlandi coram me Ugolino notario recepit a D. Burgundio operario pro pretio librarum 76 olei linseminis ab eo, et operato. . . . . ad operam Magiestatis* que fit in Majori Ecclesia, lib. iii. Sol. xviiii. . . . . Johannes Orlandi sua sponte dixit se habuisse a d. Operario libras duas den. pis. pro pretio libre viginti novem trementine operate ad operam Magiestatis." Da lib. di am. dell' an. 1301 st. pis. dell' opera del Duomo di Pisa.

"Libras quinquaginta quatuor et solidos decem et octo den. pisanorum minutorum pro pretio centinarum quatuor olei linseminis ad operam Ma-

---

* By a "Majesty" or "Maestà," is meant a representation of the Virgin or Saviour enthroned. See Mr. Eastlake's 'Materials,' &c., p. 170, n. In the present case the maestà consists of the gigantic figure of the Saviour seated on a throne, and holding in his hand a book, on which are inscribed the words "Ego sum Lux Mundi." On one side is the Virgin, and on the other St. John; these figures also are gigantic, and the effect is said to be most grand and sublime. Morrona, Pisa Illust., vol. i. p. 247, 249, n. Murray's Guide to North Italy.

It will be observed that wax does not occur in these documents, neither does it appear that it was found by Prof. Branchi in his analysis of the ground. From this it may be inferred, that it was not used generally, but was employed by Agnolo Gaddi merely as a hydrofuge. Prof. Branchi analysed also some of the glass or enamel of which the coloured cubes were composed, for the purpose of ascertaining the metals with which they were coloured. On this subject he has the following observations:—

"The art of composing the glass and enamels of various colours, by uniting them with glass liquefied by metallic oxides, is at the present time more extensively and perfectly conducted than it was among the ancients. Some chemists assert that the use of the oxide of cobalt in colouring glass blue was known to the ancient Egyptians,[1] but this opinion, as far as I am aware, has never been confirmed by experience. In the observations of the Cav. Rossi, on the vase preserved at Genoa under the name of the 'Sacro Catino,'[2] &c. (Torino, 1807), inserted in the fifth number of the Giornale della Società d'Incoraggiamento delle Scienze e dell' Arte

---

giestatis, et aliarum figurarum que fiunt in Majori Ecclesia, ad rationem denariorum xxviii. pro qualibet libra. . . . . Upechinus pictor pro libris quadraginta tribus vernicis emptis ab eo ad operum Magiestatis." See also Morrona, Pisa Illustr., vol. i. pp. 249, 250, 256.

1 M. de Brongniart (Traité des Arts Céramiques, p. 563) says, that having analysed some of the Egyptian blue glass, he found it to contain silica, alkali, cobalt, and a small quantity of lime. He also says that the Egyptian figurines are coloured blue with copper, and not with cobalt.

2 This was a vessel for a long time supposed to have been formed of a single emerald. There is little doubt, however, that it is composed of glass. As a work of art its value will scarcely be diminished on this account; since it affords evidence of the perfection to which the art of making and colouring glass was brought at a very early period; for this vessel formed part of the spoils won at the taking of Cæsarea in 1101. The author of the Handbook for North Italy observes (p. 106), "The extraordinary perfection of the material, as well as the workmanship, must always cause it to be considered as a very remarkable monument, and of remote antiquity. The colour is beautiful, the transparency perfect, but a few air-bubbles sufficiently disclose the substance of which it is made."

stabilita in Milano,' the following passage occurs:—'Sig. Millin infers from the blue glass, that cobalt was known to the ancients; but this was unnecessary, says the author, because the oxide of copper, which naturally takes a blue colour, was sufficient for this purpose.' I have not been able to analyse the blue glass of the two works in mosaic above mentioned, because too small a quantity was sent me, and because my own private occupations did not permit me to devote as much time to these experiments as was necessary. I observed, however, that in the Roman mosaic and in the fragments of the Pisan [1] seen by refracted light, the characteristics pointed out by Bergman which distinguish glass coloured with cobalt were entirely wanting. I observed also that the last-mentioned glass preserved, as it should do, its own colour after being pulverized and fused by the combined action of fire and of a small quantity of carbonate of soda;[2] whilst that from Rome passed to an amethystine colour, which the Pisan glass also acquired, although in a less degree, having been both pulverized, mixed with carbonate of soda, and exposed to the same degree of heat. Having treated in the same manner the other enamels of various colours and more or less opaque of the mosaic of Pisa, I saw that the red passed to a blue colour; that the purple was changed to an amethystine colour, and that the black became a transparent yellow glass, on the surface of which was an alkaline stratum of a bluish

---

1 The blue glass of the mosaic of S. Paolo is transparent; that of the mosaic of Pisa is opaque, and of much greater thickness. [Note by Branchi.]

2 Sig. Clovet remarks on this subject, "The blue obtained from an oxide of cobalt is the most permanent of all colours; it is equally fine at a low or at a great heat."—Annales du Chimie, Paris, tome xxxiv. p. 222. And in tome ii. p. 434, of the Dictionnaire Portatile des Arts et des Métiers, Paris, 1776, is found the following passage:—"The most permanent colours are, the blue from cobalt, which resists without changing the greatest heat of the fire; then the purple from gold, certain reds prepared from iron, &c."—[Note by Branchi.]

green. Having repeated these last experiments, I obtained from the dark green, light green, and purple enamels, results differing from the preceding in the gradation of colour only. From the red I afterwards obtained a transparent glass of yellowish green colour; from the black, a violet or amethystine glass. These alterations and anomalies, some of which throw light on the nature of the blue glass of the ancients, are to be ascribed to the greater or less degree of oxidation of the metallic colouring matters."

It will be interesting to the practical artist to compare the recipes for the mosaic glass and enamels in the Bolognese MS. with these results of Prof. Branchi's researches. In the Pisan mosaics, the red colour appears to have been produced from copper, while in the MS. it is produced from gold as well as from copper. Another variation also occurs in the blue, which in the old Pisan and Roman mosaics was produced from copper, while in the Bolognese MS. it was coloured with "azzurri ultramarini." The green of the Pisan mosaic was produced by copper, that of the Bolognese MS. by "crocus martis" and salgem.

The gilding of the mosaics of which the backgrounds of the figures were composed was next examined by Professor Branchi. On this subject he observes:— "The gilding of the cubes of common glass and enamel of these mosaics is very beautiful; the leaf of gold is itself defended by a vitreous varnish, which, although not distinguishable on account of its thinness in the Pisan mosaic, except by having a shining surface, different from that of gold, and by the resistance it offers to iron tools, to the action of mercury, and nitro-muriatic acid, is also of such a thickness in the Roman mosaic that even the sight of it alone is sufficient to remove all doubt.

"Chambers,[1] in speaking of the method of gilding

[1] Dict., Art. Mosaics. This also is from Vasari.

glass for mosaics, does not mention this varnish. 'The pieces,' he says, 'to be gilded, are moistened with gum-water, and the leaves of gold are applied; they are then placed at the entrance of the furnace until they are hot. By this means the metal remains fixed to the glass so firmly that it cannot be detached.' In order to varnish the gilded glass and enamels, it is very probable that glass or crystal, easily fusible, was reduced to an impalpable powder; that this powder was distempered with water, or with a solution of gum, or of borate of soda or other liquid; that this mixture was spread over the gilded surface, and that finally the pieces of glass thus prepared were exposed to a degree of heat sufficient to fuse this fine powder, which, when fused, would form the desired varnish.[1]

"The gilding by fire on crystal[2] and porcelain is much superior in beauty to that of our mosaics. The latter, however, besides resisting the above-mentioned reagents, appears, as it were, after the lapse of six centuries, without the slightest alteration, and in the same state in which it left the hand of the artist. This observation, confirmed by so many others, proves that the old masters had the stability of their works much at heart, and that they wished to preserve them, not only for their own sons and grandsons, but also for posterity." The method alluded to by Professor Branchi of mixing

---

1 Leon Battista Alberti recommends fixing the gold to the glass with calcined lead (calcina di piombo), which he says becomes more liquid than any kind of glass. Arch., book 6, cap. x.

2 Kunckel, in the additions to the Arte Vetraria of Neri, treats at length of gilding with greater or less permanence on glass. For gilding which was to be fixed by fire, he recommends that the leaves of gold should be applied with the solution of borate of soda, or the borax of commerce, or with gum and a small quantity of this salt dissolved in a proportionate quantity of water. By bathing that part of the crystal which is to be gilded with a solution of nitro-muriate of gold, mixed with a sufficient quantity of sulphuric acid, and exposing it afterwards to a sufficient degree of heat, a fine and permanent gilding is produced, according to the assertion of Struve and Exsaquet, Giornale di Torino, tom. ii. part i. [Note by Branchi.]

pulverized glass with gum-water, and spreading it over the gold leaf, and afterwards fusing the glass, appears to have been the method followed by Theophilus: while the process described by Count Caylus of placing the design in gold between two plates of glass, and fixing the surfaces together by fire, was the method which Eraclius says was practised by the Romans, and which he describes in Lib. I. cap. v.[1]

TARSIA WORK.

Another art, allied to mosaic painting, was practised in Italy, and was called "Mosaic of wood," "Tarsia" or "Tarsie" work, or "Tarsiatura." This consisted in representing houses and perspective views of buildings by inlaying pieces of wood of various colours and shades into panels of walnut wood.

Vasari[2] says, that at first this kind of work was executed in white and black only; but Fra Giovanni Veronese, who practised it extensively, much improved the art by staining the wood with various colours by means of waters and tints boiled with penetrating oil, in order to produce both light and shadow, with wood of various colours, making the lights with the whitest pieces of the spindle tree. In order to produce the shades, it was the practice of some artists to singe the wood by the fire; while others used oil of sulphur and a solution of corrosive sublimate and arsenic.

St. Audemar (No. 165) mentions that saffron was used to stain box-wood yellow; but he does not say to what use the wood was put when stained.

The subjects most proper for Tarsia work are perspective representations of buildings full of windows and angular lines, to which force and relief are given by means of lights and shades. Vasari speaks rather slightingly of this art, and says that it was practised

---

[1] See pages 187, 188. [2] Int., cap. xxxi.

chiefly by those persons who possessed more patience than skill in design; that although he had seen some good representations of figures, fruits, and animals, yet the work soon became dark, and was always in danger of perishing from the worms and by fire.

Tarsia work was frequently employed in decorating the choirs of churches, as well as the backs of the seats and the wainscotings. It was also used in the panels of doors. The art was cultivated to the greatest extent in the Venetian territories, where three Olivetani monks were particularly distinguished for their skill. The most celebrated of these was Fra Giovanni da Verona, who was called to Rome by Pope Julius II. to decorate the doors and seats of the Vatican with Tarsia work, the designs of which were made by Raffaelle. Fra Damiano da Bergamo, a Dominican monk, attained equal celebrity in this art. So great was his skill that Charles V. refused to believe that the Tarsia work executed by him in the Arca of S. Domenico, at Bologna, really consisted of pieces of wood inlaid, but he thought it must have been the work of the pencil.[1] Nor would he be convinced of the fact until part of the stucco was removed and a piece of the wood taken out; in remembrance of this circumstance the work was left in that state, and has never been repaired.

The inlaid work in wood of various kinds called "Tunbridge ware" is a kind of mosaic, but it cannot be compared with the Italian Tarsia work in the delicate gradations of colour, or the intricacy of the subject represented.

---

[1] Marchese, Vite de' Pittori, &c. Domenicani, vol. ii. p. 257.

CHAPTER IV.

GLASS.

§ 1. Early History of Painting on Glass in Italy.

While the history of painting on glass has been studied in France and Germany, where it has been illustrated by the works of Le Vieil, Langlois, Thibaud, Lasteyrie, and of Fathers Martin and Cahier, its rise and progress in Italy has been but little investigated. A sufficient reason for this may perhaps be found in the superiority of the glass painters of France and Germany [1] over those of Italy in all the mechanical parts of the art, as well as in the fact that all the improvements introduced into this branch of painting may be traced to the northern nations, who in their turn are represented to have received their first instruction from the East.[2] It might be supposed from the celebrity of the glass works at Murano, that the Venetians would have excelled in this art, but this has not been the case; the art of painting on glass was but little practised by them,[3] and the glass manufactured at Murano was found too opaque for this purpose.[4] Still the art was occasionally practised in Italy, sometimes by native artists, who employed their skill either on Venetian glass, or on glass manufactured for the purpose by German or French artists, and some-

1 See Vasari, Int., cap. xxxii.

2 In 687 many Greek workmen went to France, for the purpose of working in glass. Filiasi, Saggio sull' Antico Commercio, &c., p. 148, n.

3 The windows of churches in the Venetian territories are usually filled with small circular panes of colourless glass, about 6 inches in diameter.

4 Vasari, Introduction, cap. xxxii.

times the painted glass was executed entirely by foreign artists invited into Italy for this purpose. The designs, however, were frequently made by the Italians, who excelled the Germans in design and composition. The names of but few painters on glass have descended to posterity, and this is partly explained by the rule which prevailed among the Flemish artists at least, of not affixing their names to their works, or of marking them with their monograms only.[1] The notices of the Italian painters on glass are few and scanty, and have never yet been published collectively. It may, therefore, not be uninteresting to give a short account of some of the most distinguished painters in this branch of the profession.

History has not preserved the name of the artist who executed those glass windows, considered to be the earliest of the kind in Italy, which were painted or stained by order of Pope Leo III. at Rome, A.D. 795;[2] neither is it recorded whether they were by a Greek or an Italian artist. That they were the work of the latter is probable, from the existence of recipes for coloured glass in the Lucca MS., published by Muratori, which was apparently written by an Italian.

From this time until 1303[3] no certain notices of painting on glass in Italy are found. The archives of the House of Savoy show that at this period a sum of money was paid to one Johanneto (Giannetto) for painting certain windows in the Castle at Chambery.[4]

In the fourteenth and fifteenth centuries the art was

---

[1] See Le Vieil, de la Peinture sur Verre, p. 33. Albert Dürer is an exception to this rule; he is said not only to have written his name on his works, but to have added sometimes his portrait also.

[2] Mur., Rer. Ital., tom. iii. part i. p. 196, 197.

[3] At Altare, a village in the midst of the central range of the Ligurian Alps, glass-works are said to have existed from time immemorial. They are reported to have been founded by some fugitive Gauls.—Murray's Handbook for North Italy.

[4] Lettera dal Vernazza al P. Guglielmo della Valle. Giornale di Pisa, 1794.

much cultivated in Tuscany, especially by the Gesuati, who worked in the Cathedrals of Florence, Arezzo, and elsewhere. The names of a few only of these artists have survived. The necrology of the Dominicans, in the convent of Sta. Maria Novella in Florence, has preserved the name of Fra Giacomo di Andrea, a Dominican and painter on glass, who flourished during this century. [1]

Fra Domenico Pollini, a native of Cagliari in Sardinia, lived at Pisa during the first half of the fourteenth century. The Chronicle of the Convent of Sta. Catherine of Pisa thus records his merits: "Frater Dominicus Sardus de Pollinis Kallaritanis fuit valde gratiosus et probus, soavissime conversationis. Cantabat bene, scribebat pulcre, et fenestras vitreas operabatur optime." [2]

The same Chronicle also eulogizes more copiously Fra Michele Pina of Pisa, who is said to have been a perfect master in painting on glass, and who painted the large window in the church of the Dominicans at Pistoia now destroyed, and one in the refectory of the convent of Sta. Katherine. He died in 1340. A lay Dominican named Andrea painted the window of the choir in the same church of Sta. Katherine, as appears by his name being at the foot of it.[3]

The large window in the choir of the church of S. Francesco at Pisa was painted in 1340, but the name of the artist has not been preserved. This window was repaired in 1585 by P. Johanne Antonio Nerucci.[4]

Another window in the same church was painted in 1390 by Jacopo Castelli, of Siena, as is proved by an inscription on the glass.[5] It appears from these notices and from the records of the Duomo that a school of

---

1 Marchese, Vite de' Pittori, &c., Domenicani, vol. i. p. 391.
2 Ib., p. 390.
3 Valtancoli, Annali Pisani, vol. i. p. 428. See Marchese, vol. ii. p. 438.
4 Ciampi, Notizie, &c., p. 116, n. Morrona, Pisa Illust., vol. iii. p. 56.
5 Pisa Illust., vol. iii. p. 60.

painters on glass subsisted in Pisa from the early part of the fourteenth century until 1685, if not later. Lunardo, M. Simone di Domenico of Florence, and Bartolomeo da Scarperia, painted, between 1460 and 1464, the glass for the large windows which sheltered, on the sides exposed to the north and to the marine winds, the walls of the Campo Santo. The remains of the iron employed in fixing the windows may still be seen opposite the pictures of Buffalmacco and Orgagna.[1]

About the same time flourished at Venice one Maestro Marco, who painted certain windows in the church of S. Francesco at Treviso, "which were well executed; for a certain German friar painted [the originals of] all those works formerly in the convent (of the Frate Minori) at Venice, and Maestro Marco copied and sent them to Treviso." This Marco is stated to have been living in 1335.[2]

In the fifteenth century the notices of painters on glass in Italy are more numerous; among those who flourished in the first half of this century may be named Angioletto da Gubbio, who painted some windows in the cathedrals of Orvieto and Siena, and the large window in the chapel of S. Ludovico in the Basilica of Assisi. The original designs for this window, executed in distemper, are preserved in the collection of Conte Francesco Ranghiasi Brancaleone in Gubbio.[3]

In the beginning of this century flourished a Dominican friar named Ambruogio di Bindo, an excellent painter on glass, whose name appears in the archives of the Duomo of Siena from 1404 to 1411.[4]

---

1 Ciampi, Notizie, &c., p. 116, n.

2 Zanetti, Nuova Raccolta delle Monete e Zecche d' Italia, vol. iv. p. 151, cited by Lanzi, vol. i. p. 151, and by Mr. Eastlake, 'Materials,' &c., p. 90, 91.

3 Memorie Storiche di Ottaviano Nelli. Da Luigi Bonfatti. Gubbio, 1843.

4 Marchese, Vite de' Pittori Domenicani, vol. ii. p. 440.

Fra Bartolommeo di Pietro di Vanni Accomandati of Perugia painted a beautiful window in the church of S. Domenico at Perugia,[1] which is said to exceed in the dimensions, in the composition, and in the beauty of the colouring, every other painted window in Italy, with the exception of those by Gulielmo de Marcillat in Arezzo. On the lowest compartments of this window there is an inscription purporting that the window was painted by Fra Bartolommeo in 1411. It has been doubted whether the inscription actually belonged to the window below which it is placed, but the fact appears to be satisfactorily proved by Marchese.[2] A contract for making a glass window in the sacristy of the church of the Dominicans proves that Bartolommeo was living in 1415. The dates of his birth and death are unknown, but he was resident in his convent in 1370, and was elected superior of it in 1413.

It is much to be regretted that the annals of the convent should have been discontinued (excepting a few brief notices) for nearly a century, so that there are no means of ascertaining how Fra Bartolommeo acquired his skill in glass-painting, or where he procured the glass. Even twenty-five years after Bartolommeo completed his celebrated work, the glass made in Italy was not considered good enough for the windows of the Duomo of Florence; for we read that Lorenzo Ghiberti, who delighted greatly in this kind of work, and who had undertaken to paint some of the windows in this cathedral, having considered how large a quantity of glass of the finest workmanship would be required for so great a work, and having heard of a native of Tuscany named Francesco Dominici Livi di Gambasso, who was then living in the city of Lubeck, and who was considered the most eminent master of this art then living, determined to recall him with his whole

---

[1] Marchese, Vite de' Pittori Domenicani, vol. i. p. 393.

[2] Ibid., vol. i. p. 391-402.

family to his own country, for the benefit of which he might exercise his profession.

This design was executed; Livi came to Florence in 1436, and made the glass, which was all painted by Ghiberti, with the exception of one window, which was painted by Donatello. Baldinucci proves the truth of these facts by an entry in the 'Libro di Deliberazione de' Signori Operai,' b. 1436, A.C. 8,[1] which he quotes in his Life of Ghiberti, and thus disproves the assertion of Vasari, that the glass used for this purpose was Venetian.

In reading the history of Italian art there is nothing that strikes the mind more forcibly than that versatility and universality of genius for which so many of the medieval and cinque-cento artists were distinguished, and by which they were enabled to attain so high a degree of eminence in *all* the fine arts. At the present time, in which division of labour is the order of the day, the exercise of one branch of the arts is considered a sufficient employment for the mental powers of an artist during his whole life. When we remember the long period of pupilage through which the Italian artists were accustomed to pass, it is not surprising that there should have been artists who have succeeded in all kinds of painting, as I have mentioned with regard to the painters in mosaic and on glass, who frequently excelled also in oil and fresco painting; but it does appear astonishing that the greatest architect should have been, as was frequently the case, not only the greatest painter of his time, but the greatest sculptor also. Vasari accounts for this fact by saying that "design and invention are the father and mother of all the arts, and not of one only." There is no doubt that he was right, and that the great Italian masters owed

---

1 The same document is published in the Carteggio Inedito, vol. ii. p. 441.

their celebrity to their mental endowments, and not merely to their practical skill. It is said[1] on the authority of Lorenzo Ghiberti that Giotto, painter, architect, and poet, sculptured some of the subjects in marble on his own beautiful campanile at Florence. At a later period the great Raphael changed his manner of painting after having examined the paintings of Michael Angelo, the greatest architect and the greatest sculptor of his age. Francia was a goldsmith before he was a painter. The genius of Benvenuto Cellini was as conspicuous in the jewelled ornaments he made for the pope as in his Perseus. The names of painters who have possessed high mathematical attainments are numerous. But the most remarkable man among the moderns was undoubtedly Lionardo da Vinci, who was at once a painter, poet, musician, mathematician, and natural philosopher, and, as some say, architect and statuary also, whose sagacity anticipated Bacon in declaring that experiment should precede theory—who had described the camera obscura before it was made known by Porta—who wrote on the descent or attraction of heavy bodies to the earth forty years before Copernicus—whose discoveries in hydraulics preceded by a century those of Castelli—and whose observations "on flame and air" were made nearly three centuries before the modern theory of combustion was promulgated.[2] Did Lionardo, when he registered these discoveries in characters that could only be read by reflection in a glass, think, like Bacon, that mankind

---

1 Vasari, Vita di Giotto. Lorenzo Ghiberti left a MS., in which he gives a short account of ancient and modern painters. The most interesting parts of this Essay have been published by Cicognara in his Storia di Scultura.

2 See Amoretti, Memorie Storiche di Lionardo da Vinci, p. 135-142, citing Venturi, Essai sur les Ouvrages Mathématiques de Léonard da Vinci, 1797. See also Humboldt's Kosmos, vol. ii. p. 322, 380, 389, and Hallam's Hist. of Literature, vol. i. p. 303, and note.

were not at that period sufficiently enlightened to profit by his researches into the arcana of nature?

Second to Lionardo only in fame, but his equal in talent, was Leon Batista Alberti. His genius was universal: he was a skilful architect, an accomplished painter, sculptor, poet, and musician, a mathematician and inventor of optical instruments, an author of treatises on painting, sculpture, and architecture, and a moral and dramatic writer.

Lorenzo Ghiberti was another of these distinguished men. He began his career as a goldsmith, but being more partial to the arts of design and sculpture, he sometimes practised painting, and sometimes cast small bronze figures, which he finished with infinite grace. In his maturer years he seems to have occasionally worked at all these arts. He painted an apartment for Pandolfo Malatesta at Rimini soon after the year 1400. In 1439 he made for Pope Eugenius a golden mitre which weighed fifteen pounds; the weight of the pearls with which it was decorated was five pounds and a half, and which, with the other jewels, were estimated at 30,000 golden ducats. It is said that six of these pearls were as large as filberts, and Vasari remarks that, to judge from the design, nothing could be imagined more beautiful than the arrangement of the jewels and the variety of the figures and other ornaments. But the capo d'opera of Ghiberti was the bronze doors of the Baptistery at Florence, one of the finest works of the middle ages, and which alone was sufficient to immortalise the name of Ghiberti. His predilection for painting on glass has been already mentioned. Besides the windows in the Duomo of Florence, he painted others at Arezzo; but in spite of his precautions to secure the best kind of glass, it is related that the buildings were too much obscured by these windows, and this was undoubtedly Vasari's reason for saying they

were made of Venetian glass. Lorenzo taught the art of painting on glass to Parri Spinello, who introduced it into Arezzo.[1]

At Milan during this century the art was practised less successfully. It appears from an entry in the records of the Duomo, dated November 10, 1449,[2] that a dispute having arisen between Stefano da Pandino, the painter, and the authorities on account of some window which he had painted, his work was adjudged to be so badly executed that the artist was obliged to repaint great part of it at his own expense.

In the Venetian territories painting on glass was occasionally practised at this period. In 1473 the window of the choir in the south transept of the church of SS. Giovanni and Paolo at Venice, and another at Murano, were painted by Mocetto from the designs of Vivarini.[3]

But the most distinguished painter on glass of the fifteenth century in Italy was Beato Giacomo da Ulmo, a native of Ulm, in Germany. He was born in 1406, and acquired the art of painting on glass in this city. At the age of twenty-five he travelled to Rome, where he spent his time and money in visiting the sacred edifices of that city; but finding himself at last pennyless, he became a soldier in the service of Alphonso of Arragon, king of Naples, and fought in the great battle in which the Genoese were victorious, and Alphonso lost both his throne and his life. Giacomo having served four years in the army, became disgusted with the profession, and engaged himself as servant to a citizen of Capua. In 1440 or 1441 he determined to return to his native land and embrace

---

1 Vasari, Vita di Lorenzo Ghiberti.

2 Memorie de' Pittori, Scultori, e Architetti Milanesi, Opera MS. dell' Abate Antº Albuzzi, vol. i. This MS. is now in the possession of Co. Gaetano Melzi, to whom I am indebted for the loan of it.

3 See Lanzi, vol. i. p. 152, and Murray's Hand-book for North Italy, p. 354.

once more his aged father. With this view he arrived at Bologna, where, praying before the altar of S. Domenico, he felt himself inspired to renounce his earthly home, and think only of the heavenly. In the thirty-fourth year of his age he entered his noviciate in this monastery, where he lived for fifty years a life so holy that he obtained the honours of canonization. His death took place in 1491.

With the religious habit Fra Giacomo resumed his early occupation of painting on glass. It appears from public archives preserved in Bologna, that he painted windows in the convent of S. Domenico in 1464 and 1465; in the library from 1467 until 1472; and the last time his name was mentioned was in 1480, when he was in his seventy-third year. Some painted glass in a window of the first dormitory in this convent has been attributed to him; but it is considered by Bianconi[1] and by Marchese to be much more ancient—indeed to be the most ancient specimen of painted glass in Bologna.

But the principal works of Fra Giacomo were in the church of S. Petronio in Bologna.[2] It is much to be regretted that it cannot now be ascertained what glass was painted by him, for the windows in this church were the work of several artists, among the best of whom was Frate Ambrogino da Soncino, who had been pupil of Fra Giacomo for thirty years. Besides the glass in S. Petronio, Fra Giacomo is said to have

---

1 Guida di Bologna.

2 The colours in the old glass in S. Petronio are extremely vivid—ruby red, emerald green, ultramarine blue, and opaque black. The two former are transparent, but the blue is semi-opaque, resembling in effect thin plates of ultramarine, rather than blue glass. I could imagine the colour was produced by stirring the ultramarine in powder into glass, as described by Suger when speaking of the blue glass for the abbey of S. Denys. In one of the windows is another kind of blue, more transparent, but the colour is neither so deep nor so pure.—This resembles the blue seen in the old Venetian coloured glass windows.

painted several other windows in Bologna, which still remain.

It appears from an entry in the records of the convent that Fra Giacomo was assisted in the designs by a certain Michele. Bianconi states[1] that the designs for some of the windows in S. Petronio were by the great Michael Angelo Buonarroti. On considering the dates, it will be seen that these designs by Michael Angelo could not have been for the windows painted by Fra Giacomo, because it does not appear that the latter painted after 1480, when Michael Angelo had only attained his sixth year. The reputation of Beato Giacomo was as great in France as in Italy. He was there called "Jacques l'Allemand." Le Vieil (p. 34) says, "The miracles that were wrought at his tomb caused him to be placed among the saints of his order, and the company or guild of the master glass-makers, painters on glass at Paris, celebrate his fête as their second patron on the second Sunday in October."

The discovery of the art of staining glass a transparent yellow with silver has been by some authors ascribed to Van Eyck, but it is attributed with greater reason to Fra Giacomo da Ulmo. The discovery is said to have originated in an accident. Le Vieil (p. 108) gives the following account of it:—Fra Giacomo being one day occupied in placing his glass in the furnace in order to fix the colours, let fall a silver button from one of his sleeves without perceiving it. The button sank into the lime, which is always placed in the furnace under the glass. The furnace being closed, the enamels melted. The button, or at least a part of it, was fused, and it imparted a yellow stain to the glass which lay above it, and this yellow stain was found to have penetrated into the substance of the glass.

---

[1] Guida di Bologna.

Fra Ambrogino da Soncino, the pupil of Giacomo, was also an excellent painter on glass, and his works may be seen in many churches at Bologna. He died in 1517. He wrote the life of his master, Giacomo, from which the biographical facts relative to the latter have been extracted.[1]

Frate Anastasio, also a lay brother of the convent of S. Domenico at Bologna, was another pupil of Fra Giacomo. He died in 1529, having instructed in his art a pupil who left, in a book of Memoranda concerning the Arca of S. Domenico, begun in the year 1521, the following affectionate and pathetic memorial of his master:—"After him (one Fra Petronio, who held the office of Archisti, or guardian of the Arca, until 1521) came my beloved and dear master and predecessor Frate Anastasio, a lay brother, a devout man, a man of God, and of our father S. Domenico. Cheerful, of middling stature, the beauty of his mind was reflected in that of his body; in him I frequently seemed to behold a cherub; one of his hands was worth my whole body; he had great genius, was most skilful in painting on glass, a disciple and imitator of the blessed Giacomo, and during the space of eight years he most faithfully, most fervently, and most devotedly served with the greatest charity and integrity of life, his and our good father S. Domenico, and by him he was richly rewarded."[2]

That affectionate and lasting attachment which so frequently subsisted between the master and the pupils, and which is a beautiful trait in the character of the Italian painters, could only have arisen under their system of working together for a long period of years. The lengthened term of the apprenticeship, frequently extending to twelve years, and the consequent inter-

---

[1] Marchese, vol. i. p. 409, 410.

[2] Ibid., p. 411.

change of benefits given and received by master and pupil, frequently gave rise to a friendship as sincere as it was affectionate, and which terminated only with the death of one of the parties. Thus Taddeo Gaddi, the godson and favourite pupil of Giotto, was the disciple of the latter for twenty-four years; Cennini was for twelve years the pupil of Agnolo, the son of Taddeo. Many other instances are noticed in these pages; many also are recorded by Vasari.

In the 'History of the Duomo of Orvieto'[1] it is stated that in 1444 a certain Fra Mariano di Viterbo, a Dominican, offered himself to paint the windows of the cathedral, and proposed to paint one as a specimen. He did so, but his painting was not approved of, and D. Gasparro di Volterra, a priest, was then invited to paint a specimen. This also was disapproved of, and ultimately the celebrated Benedictine monk D. Francesco di Barone Brunacci was selected, who executed the work to the satisfaction of all parties. Marchese[2] conjectures that he was a pupil of Fra Bartolommeo di Pietro.

In the Necrology of the convent of S. Domenico at Siena, under the year 1515 is mentioned the name of Frater Raphael Peregrini; he is said to have been skilful in painting on glass.[3]

The names of two other professors of this art, Fra Cristophano and Fra Bernardo, have been preserved in the archives of the Duomo of Arezzo. The contract is dated March, 1477, and the colours were to be "*cotti al fuoco, e non messi a olio.*"[4]

A similar stipulation is contained in the contract, dated August, 1513 (preserved in the same archives), relative to the windows to be painted in the cathedral

1 Storia del Duomo di Orvieto, Document lxviii. p. 71.
2 Vol. i. p. 413. 3 Id. ibid.
4 Carteggio Inedito d' Artisti, vol. ii. p. 446.

by Domenicho Pietro Vannis de Pechoris[1] and Stagio Fabiani Stagii;[2] and in another contract, dated April 25, 1515,[3] it was stipulated that Domenicho should execute certain paintings *on good Venetian or German glass.* The price paid for the last windows was at the rate of fourteen "lire piccole" the square braccio.[4] The execution, however, of these works was not such as to satisfy the good people of Arezzo, and one M. Lodovico Bellichini, a physician, and intimate friend of Guglielmo de Marcillat, persuaded the latter, who was then resident at Cortona, to visit Arezzo, where Stagio had the liberality to invite him to reside in his house.[5]

The greatest of all the artists who practised painting on glass in Italy was Guglielmo de Marcillat, whose name is generally translated William of Marseilles. Dr. Gaye, the editor of the 'Carteggio Inedito,' has, however, discovered his real name and designation in a document preserved in the archives belonging to the Bishop of Arezzo. He is there[6] described as "Messer Guillelmo de Piero, Franceze, Priore di S. Tibaldo, di Sto. Michele, diocesi di Verduno" (Verdun, in France), and he subscribes his name thus: "Io Guillelmo de Piero de Marcillat." From this Marchese (vol. ii. p. 212) thinks that *Marcillat* was his family-name, and *Piero* that of his father. He was born in 1475, and acquired the art of painting on glass in France. In order to escape the consequence of being concerned, with some of his friends, in the death of an enemy, he sought refuge in a Dominican convent,

---

1 Carteggio Inedito d' Artisti, vol. ii. p. 446. See also Vasari, Life of Don Bartolommeo, Abate di S. Clementi.

2 Carteggio Inedito, vol. ii. p. 446. Vasari, in the Life of Lazzaro, calls this artist Fabiano Sassoli.

3 Carteggio Inedito, vol. ii. p. 449.

4 A braccio is about 23 inches.

5 Vasari, Vita di Guglielmo de Marcillat, and see Marchese, vol. ii. p. 211, &c.

6 Carteggio Inedito, &c., vol. ii. p. 449.

where he assumed the habit of the order and continued to practise his art.

About this time Pope Julius the Second commissioned Bramante to introduce many windows of glass into the palace. In reply to the inquiries made by the latter for the most excellent among those who practised this art, he was informed that these things were done in a wonderful manner in France, and he was shown a specimen by the French ambassador at the Court of Rome, who had for the window of his study a piece of white glass, on which was painted a figure with an infinite number of colours fixed on the glass by the action of fire. Bramante caused an invitation to be sent to these French artists, offering them good emolument. Claudio, a brother monk, and excellent painter on glass, and intimate friend of Guglielmo, persuaded the latter to accept the offer, and the two artists set out together for Rome, where they were employed by the Pope to paint several windows of the palace, which are now no longer in existence; two only remain of those painted in Sta. Maria del Popolo. About this time his friend Claudio died, leaving him heir to his designs, and the implements used in the art; and Guglielmo henceforward worked by himself. From Rome he went to Cortona, where he painted the front of the house of Cardinal Passerini, and several windows. Leaving Cortona he went to Siena, where he painted a window in Sta. Lucia, in the chapel of the Albergotti, in the bishopric of Arezzo; "which," says Vasari, "may truly be said to be living figures, and not coloured or transparent glass." Some parts of these still remain, and the parts deficient are filled up with white glass. He also painted three windows in the Duomo di Arezzo, as appears by the following contract,[1] dated 31 Oct., 1519:—

---

1 Carteggio Inedito, vol. ii. p. 449.

"I signori operai al Vescovado ano alogato a fare tre finestre di vetro in Vescovado a Maestro Guglielmo di Pietro, franceze, maestro a far finestre di vetro, coiè una finestra sopra la cappella di San Francesco, una finestra sopra la cappella di San Matio, una finestra sopra la cappella di San Niccolò, per prezzo di lire 15 per ciascheduno braccio, *cotti a fuoco, non a olio*, e debale avere finite per tutto Gugno prossimo 1520."

For each of these windows he received 180 ducats, as appears by a record dated 31st Dec., 1520.

He also painted a window in the church of the Dominicans, for which he would receive no recompense, "because," he said, "he was much indebted to that society," alluding to the shelter and protection the Dominicans had formerly afforded him.

Besides other windows, he painted several frescoes which are still in good preservation; the design and composition of these works are good, but the colouring is rather feeble.[1]

He lost his life from his too great application to fresco painting, which he followed summer and winter; the exhalations from the lime occasioned an illness which carried him off in a few days, in the year 1537, at the age of 62.[2]

Many practical details relative to painting on glass are given in the Life of Guglielmo by Vasari, who united to his other attainments a knowledge of this art. Vasari attributes to Guglielmo de Marcillat the honour of having carried the art of painting on glass to perfection in Tuscany. He particularly eulogizes the skill of Guglielmo in the arrangement of the colours, whereby the most forcible colours were employed for the figures in the foreground, while the darker colours were reserved for the more distant objects. He praises also his invention and composition, and the great skill

1 Marchese, vol. ii. p. 223.

2 Vasari, Vita de Guglielmo de Marcillat.

with which he arranged the joinings of the lead and iron, which he disposed in such a manner in the joints of the figures, and the folds of the draperies, that they were scarcely visible, and even imparted to the figures a grace which could not be exceeded by the pencil. Vasari mentions more than once the great dexterity of Guglielmo in applying different colours to the same piece of glass by grinding away the coloured surfaces, so as to leave the white glass, to which another colour was afterwards given; and he informs us that the Gesuati of Florence, by whom this art was much cultivated, having obtained possession of a window painted by Guglielmo, took it to pieces in order to ascertain how it was put together, and removed and experimented on many of the pieces of glass, which they replaced by new ones.

Guglielmo left the materials belonging to the art to Pastorino da Siena, his assistant, who had worked for him many years.[1] Pastorino painted in 1549 the beautiful round or rose window (occhio) in the Duomo of Siena, and others in St. Peter's at Rome. He usually worked from the designs of Pierino del Vaga.

Maso Porro, of Cortona, who was more skilful in joining and in burning the glass than in painting, and Battista Borro, of Arezzo, were also pupils of Guglielmo de Marcillat. The latter taught the art to Benedetto Spadari and Giorgio Vasari, the biographer of the painters.

To these artists may be added Gondrate, who in 1574 painted a window in the Duomo of Parma, from a design by Lattanzio Gambara.

The first glass furnace was introduced into Rimini in 1551 by Geminiano da Modena, whose sons became excellent painters on glass.[2]

---

[1] Vasari, Life of Guglielmo; Bald., Vite, Dec. iv. Part i. del Sec. iv.
[2] Vedriani, Pittori Modenesi, p. 86.

§ 2. On Windows.

We have been so long accustomed to see glass windows in our houses, that few, perhaps, except antiquaries and archæologists, have ever inquired whether they were possessed by our ancestors. It may not, therefore, be deemed uninteresting to relate briefly a few facts relative to this subject, gleaned from history and archæology.

There is reason to believe [1] that glass windows were employed occasionally in ecclesiastical buildings during the early centuries of the Christian era; but the practice was by no means universal, and the most ancient glass windows mentioned to have been constructed in Italy were those ordered by Pope Leo the Third in the eighth century [2] at Rome. The windows of some sacred edifices were closed with valves, or shutters of stone, like those of the Duomo of Torcello[3] erected in 1008. Others were filled with slabs of a transparent kind of talc or alabaster.[4] The only example now known to exist of this kind of window is in the church of St. Miniato at Florence, built in the commencement of the eleventh century, under the Emperor Henry and his wife Cunegonda. The windows, five in number, are in the apsis, and are each filled with a single slab, formed of a kind of transparent alabaster, or marble, called by the Italians "fengite."[5] The effect of these windows is singular. When illuminated by the morning sun, they appear shining with a cloudy roseate light.[6]

---

1 See Theoph., E. Ed., p. 185.

2 Coloured glass is mentioned in the Lucca MS., which is said to be of this century.

3 The windows are now glazed, but this is thought to be a later addition.

4 Vasari, Int., cap. xxxii.

5 Fantozzi, Guida di Firenze, p. 770.

6 Murray's Guide to North Italy, p. 583.

Bede relates that glass was brought to England, A.D. 674, by certain ecclesiastics for the purpose of decorating the churches then erecting in this country; but although makers of glass were brought to England at the same time, the progress of the art in this country must have been inconsiderable, since Matthew Paris relates that, in the reign of Henry the Third, a few churches only had glass windows. In 1135, glazed frames, called "verrinæ," were made for the windows in the chapel and hall of Winchester, and in some of the chambers.[1] The earliest painted glass in York Cathedral was painted about 1200. This slowness of progress must, however, have been the effect of want of encouragement rather than of want of ability, for in 1153 the Queen of England sent a present of a painting on glass to the Comte de Dreux, and his third wife, the Comtesse of Braine, in Normandy.[2] The beauty of the early English painted glass is evident from the windows of Lincoln Cathedral: some of these, which are remarkable for the brilliancy of the colours, were executed in 1220.

In France the art must have been extensively cultivated. A great many churches were erected during the eleventh century, and Le Vieil considers that the art of painting on glass, properly so called, arose in France about this period. In the twelfth century Suger adorned the Abbey of St. Denys with painted windows, and his example was followed in most of the churches newly erected.

The use of glass windows in private houses was

---

1 Archæological Journal for 1845, p. 54.

2 Le Vieil (de la Peinture sur Verre, p. 24), quoting the Chartularium of the Abbey, and the Index Cœnobiorum Ordinis Præmonstratensis. According to Lavoisne, Matilda of Boulogne, wife of Stephen, died in 1152, consequently there was no Queen of England in 1153. The window, however, might have been ordered to be painted some years previously, and perhaps was not completed and fixed in its destined place until 1153.

extremely limited during the middle ages. In France it was not employed until the fourteenth century.[1] At the close of this century, however, and the beginning of the next,[2] several windows were painted for the hotel of the Duke of Orleans in the Rue de la Poterne lez Saints Pol, at Paris. It may be interesting to know that the price paid for this painted glass varied from four to eight Parisian sous the foot. In the document which contains an account of these windows, there is also a charge for "taking down, washing, and replacing several panes of glass, painted and recoloured, in the chamber of Louis Monseigneur de Bourbon." This makes it probable that the glass had been fixed in the windows for some time, since it had become necessary to wash and recolour it. It also suggests the idea that these paintings were not executed with enamel or vitrified colours, which would not have required recolouring, but probably with pigments mixed with egg or oil.

It appears from recent archæological researches that many of the royal residences in England had glazed windows in the thirteenth century. In the twentieth year of the reign of Henry the Third (1235-6), the windows of the chapel and hall of Winchester, and some of the chambers, were glazed.[3] The accounts of Rockingham Castle for the year 1279 also contain an entry of payment "for glazing the windows, 5*s*."[4] It is probable that the dwellings of the nobility were furnished with glass windows in the fourteenth century,

---

1 Hallam's Midd. Ages, vol. iii. p. 425.

2 Between 1399 and 1429. See 'Louis et Charles, Ducs d'Orléans, leur Influence sur les Arts, la Littérature, et l'Esprit de leur Siècle, d'après les Documents Originaux et les Peintures des Manuscrits. Par Aimé Champollion-Figeac (de la Bibliothèque Royale). Paris, 1844.' This extremely interesting publication is very scarce, the work having been suppressed.

3 Archæological Journal for 1845, p. 54, 74.

4 Ibid., Jan. 1845, p. 370.

since they are mentioned in a description of the interior of a castle in a MS. of the fifteenth century[1] (in the public library at Cambridge), containing the metrical romance of Sir Degrevant:—

> "Square windows of glas
> The richest that ever was,
> Tho moynells (mullions) was off bras,
> Made with menne handes."

Glass, however, was not in common use in England until the reign of Henry the Eighth;[2] but it appears to have been employed for windows in Vienna during the fifteenth century. Æneas Sylvius mentions that the houses in that city had glass windows and iron doors.[3]

During the middle ages, glass windows, instead of being affixed to the buildings, were frequently fastened into wooden frames; they were considered as moveable furniture, and were removed with the other effects of families when they travelled. Upon the arrival of the family at the mansion, the glazed frames, or verrinæ, were placed in the windows, where they remained during the residence of the family, and on their departure they were taken out and laid by carefully.[4] A passage in Vasari's Life of Guglielmo de Marcillat proves that this custom of using moveable windows prevailed in France and Italy until the beginning of the sixteenth century. Vasari says that at this period Pope Julius the Second commissioned Bramante of Urbino to make many glazed windows in the palace; and while the latter was making inquiries for persons skilled in this art, he was shown a specimen of one belonging to the French ambassador at the Papal court. This, which he had used for the window of his study, con-

---

1 Arch. Journ., Sept. 1844.

2 Hallam's Midd. Ages, vol. iii. p. 425.

3 Ibid.

4 Northumberland Household Book, Preface, p. 16, quoted in Hallam's Midd. Ages, vol. iii. p. 425.

sisted of a piece of white glass fixed in a frame (telaro), on which was painted a figure with an infinite variety of colours burnt in by the action of fire.

It must not, however, be inferred, because the glasses were moveable, that the windows of houses were destitute of any protection from the weather. The Bolognese MS.[1] describes no less than three contrivances for excluding the air, softening the light, and concealing the inmates of the houses from the gaze of passengers in the streets. The three methods described in this MS. were probably for the windows of the nobility, for it is unlikely that private individuals would incur the expense of painting these substitutes for glass in the manner described. The first substitute was thin parchment stretched on a frame, and afterwards painted and varnished; the second consisted also of parchment, painted as before, but instead of varnish, a coat of linseed oil was applied to make it transparent; the third consisted of linen, stretched on a frame, and then painted. When dry, a coat of white of egg and gum water was applied, and it was then varnished. It is not at all improbable that some of the early transparent paintings executed in Germany, France, and England, may have been intended, and used occasionally, instead of glass for windows.

In France, paper was much employed as a substitute for glass in domestic architecture even at a late period. Le Vieil[2] devotes a chapter of his work to this subject. He says that at the close of the seventeenth century, the persons whose business it was to fix the paper in the windows were called "chassissiers," and the glazier who repaired or cleaned the glazed windows on the inside of the apartments of the palace and its dependences left to the chassissier the care of renewing the double windows of paper. From this it seems

[1] Nos. 214, 215, 216.

[2] De la Peinture sur Verre, p. 235.

probable that glass windows were limited to the habitations of the higher ranks, and that these windows were further defended with other windows, the frames of which were filled with paper. In Le Vieil's time these paper windows were found only in the studios of painters and engravers, who found them useful in diminishing the noise from the street. The light which passed through them was more equal, and less fatiguing to the sight. He adds there was no place of study or religious community, the windows of which were not defended by double casements filled with paper: these had also the additional recommendation of affording an obstacle to the indiscretion and curiosity of those within, as well as without. At Lyons they were used constantly in the time of Le Vieil in the silk manufactories, where they were found to yield a more uniform light than glass. In France, the paper, after being fixed in the windows, was made transparent by the application of poppy oil, or mutton suet, instead of which some persons whose olfactory nerves were more susceptible, employed wax. Paper windows being constantly exposed to the rain, the sun, and the wind, required to be renewed annually, and were consequently found more expensive than glass; this perhaps was a principal cause of their falling into disuse.

These paper windows may still be seen in many villages in the north of Italy.

§ 3. Various Methods of Painting on Glass.

The origin of painting on glass, properly so called, is involved in obscurity. Le Vieil, as has been before observed, attributes it to the French in the eleventh century. It appears certain, however, that it was known and practised at Constantinople in the preceding century. Perhaps the earliest historical notice yet recorded of painting on glass, is the portrait of Con-

stantine VII., which the Arab historian, Ibn Hayyan, states was presented by the ambassadors of that Prince in 949 to Abdurrahman at Cordova. Ibn Hayyan relates that the ambassadors of Constantine, son of Leo, Lord of Constantinah the Great (Constantinople), presented to the Moorish prince a letter, of which he gives the following description:—

"It was written on sky-blue paper, and the characters were of gold. Within the letter was an enclosure, the ground of which was sky-blue like the first, but the characters were of silver: it was likewise written in Greek, and contained a list of the presents which the Lord of Constantinah sent to the Khalif; on the letter was a seal of gold of the weight of four mithkals, on one side of which was a likeness of the Messiah, and on the other those of King Constantine and his son. The letter was enclosed in a bag of silver cloth, over which was a case of gold, with *a portrait of King Constantine admirably executed on stained glass.* All this was enclosed in a case covered with cloth of silk and gold tissue. On the first line of the *Inwan* or introduction was written, 'Constantine and Romanin (Romanus), believers in the Messiah, kings of the Greeks;' and in the next, 'To the great and exalted in dignity and power, as he most deserves, the noble in descent, Abdurrahman the khalif, who rules over the Arabs of Andalus; may God preserve his life!'" [1]

In the absence of all information relative to the manner in which this portrait was painted, conjectures must be useless; it is sufficient for the present purpose to

---

[1] The description of Ibn Hayyan is quoted by the Arab historian, Al Makkari, in his History of the Mohammedan Dynasties in Spain. The work has been translated, with critical Notes, by Pascual de Gayangos, late Professor of Arabic in the Athenæum of Madrid. Printed for the Oriental Translation Fund, 2 vols. 4to. 1840-43. See Blackwood's Mag., vol. 54, p. 442, where the account of the visit of the ambassadors to Abdurrahman is given at length.

establish the fact that a portrait was actually painted on glass at Constantinople and sent to Spain as early as the year 949.

It is generally considered that the earliest glazed windows were filled with stained glass,[1] for it is said to require more skill to make colourless glass than to tinge it with some of the ordinary colours. The pieces of stained glass of which the early windows were composed were small, and they were arranged in a kind of mosaic pattern. The next improvement consisted in forming pieces of stained glass into figures, the outlines and strong shades of which were afterwards formed with black,[2] and fixed by the heat of the furnace. This kind of semi-painting afterwards gave place to painting on glass, properly so called. This was executed in various ways. The colours were sometimes diluted with white of egg,[3] and sometimes mixed with oil, and then varnished.[4] But as it was found that in both kinds of painting the colours were affected by the weather, a new plan was adopted of employing vitrified colours or enamels, which were applied to the glass with gum water, and then fixed by burning them into the glass in the furnace. This method of painting is described by Eraclius and Theophilus. The invention is generally ascribed to the Flemings or Germans. It is quite certain that Italy was supplied with these coloured glasses or "smalti"[5] by some transalpine nation; the Marciana MS. states that they were brought from Germany.[6]

---

1 See Theoph., E. Ed., lib. ii. cap. xxix.

2 The black used for this purpose is described by Eraclius, Lib. ii. No. 20, Lib. iii. Nos. 8 and 49; the MS. of the Marciana, No. 325; Bulengerus de Pictura, &c.

3 See Marciana MS., p. 615.

4 Ibid. See also the Paduan MS., p. 693.

5 The smalti of the modern Italians consist of pieces of glass, about ½ an inch thick, and 6 or 8 inches in diameter.

6 See the Marciana MS., p. 617.

The method of painting on glass practised by Guglielmo de Marcillat and his pupils has been described by Vasari. The following is a condensed account of it.

To produce a good picture on glass, three things were considered necessary, namely, a luminous transparency in the glass selected, good composition, and brilliant colouring without confusion. Transparency was to be secured by selecting the clearest glass, and in this respect the French, English, and Flemish glass was preferable to the Venetian; for the former was very clear, whilst the latter was dark; "and," observes Vasari, "when clear glass is shaded, the light is not totally lost, but appears through the shadows; but Venetian glass, being naturally dark, and being made still darker by the shadows, loses its transparency. Many persons delight in loading the colours artificially applied upon the surface, which being exposed to the sun and air, appear more beautiful than the natural colours; it is better, however, that the glass should be light rather than dark, that it may not be rendered opaque by the thickness of the colour."

To paint on glass it is necessary to be provided with a cartoon, on which are drawn the outlines of the figure, and of the folds of the drapery, which will serve as a guide in joining the glass. The various pieces of red, yellow, blue, and white glass are then arranged in their places as required; and in order to reduce each piece to the form and size indicated by the cartoon, the pieces are laid upon the cartoon and the outline marked with a pencil full of white lead, and a number is affixed to each piece in order to find its place more readily when uniting the various fragments. These numbers are obliterated when the painting is finished. This being done, the pieces of glass must be cut according to the form and size required; for this purpose, the point of an emerald must be drawn along the part to be cut, and the division must be completed by passing a

pointed piece of hot iron over the outline (which is to be first moistened with saliva), being careful not to go too near to it. The superfluous glass is then to be removed with the emerald,[1] and the pieces of glass reduced to the exact size and shape, by filing them with an iron tool called "grisatoio" or "topo," until they fit together accurately. The cartoon being laid on a table, and the pieces of glass thus fitted and laid upon it, the shades of the drapery must be painted with scales of iron ground, and another sort of red rust found in iron mines, or the hard red hæmatite ground, and with this the flesh is shaded, using more or less red or black as required.[2] But in painting flesh, the glass should be previously covered with a coat of this red, and the drapery should be painted with the black, in the same manner tempering the colour with gum, and painting and shading it by degrees until it resembles the cartoon. The painting being completed, in order to produce the high lights, a short and thin pencil of bristles, with which the colour is removed from the lights, is necessary. The high lights in the beards, hair, draperies, casements, and landscapes are to be produced by marking them out with the handle of the brush. There are, however, many difficulties in exercising this art, and he who delights in it may lay various colours on the glass; for if it be required to paint on a red ground a leaf or other small object, which, after being in the furnace, should become of another colour, the surface of the painted glass may be ground away within the outlines of the leaf with the

---

[1] It is evident, from the Bolognese MS., p. 495, that the diamond was used for cutting glass long previous to the time of Vasari. It appears, however, not to have been used for this purpose in France until the time of Francis I. (if the story related by Le Vieil be true), and this will account for the emerald being used by Guglielmo de Marcillat and his pupils.

[2] In addition to the hæmatite, Guglielmo de Marcillat is said to have used for the flesh, scales of copper (scaglia di rame).

iron point, which removes the surface of the glass; for by so doing, the glass remains white, and that red colour (composed of several mixtures), which, when fused by heat becomes yellow, is applied to it.[1] And this may be done with all the colours, but yellow is better when applied over white than over other colours; but when blue is laid on it, it becomes green by the application of heat, because yellow and blue mixed, make green. This yellow colour[2] can be used only on the back of the painting, because by fusing, it would spoil and unite with that colour, which being heated remains red on the surface, but which being rasped away with an iron, leaves the yellow visible. The pieces of glass being painted, they should be placed in a muffle or coffin, on a layer of sifted ashes mixed with burnt lime, then another layer of glass, and another of ashes, until all the glass is disposed of; the whole is then to be placed in the furnace, and heated gradually by a slow fire, until the colours are fused and become fixed to the glass. This burning in of the colours requires the greatest caution, for if the heat be too great it will cause the glass to crack, and if insufficient it will not fix the colours. Neither should the glass be withdrawn, until by repeated trials it is ascertained that the iron coffin and the ashes are red hot, and that the colours are fused.

The windows of the Duomo of Milan were once filled with painted glass of the greatest brilliancy; much still remains, but a great quantity was destroyed by the French, who it is said, on some occasion of rejoicing,

---

[1] From this description it is apparent that the colours were "flashed" on the colourless glass. This is said to have been the case with the red glass which was found among the ruins of old St. Paul's in London. See Boyle's Philosophical Essays, vol. i. p. 458.

[2] In the Life of Guglielmo de Marcillat, this is said to be calcined silver.

placed cannon in the piazza immediately under the windows, which were shattered by the discharge.[1]

The restoration of the painted glass has however been undertaken by the Austrian Government, and several of the windows, including those very large ones in the apsis, have again been filled with glass painted in the vicinity of Milan.

The original windows were painted in the ancient manner, in a kind of mosaic of coloured glass; the result was a picture of the utmost brilliancy. The modern glass is painted with coloured "smalti" mixed with some flux which accelerates the fusion and fixes them firmly to the plate of glass before it melts.[2]

§ 4. Of the various Uses to which Glass was applied.

Another important application of glass was in the composition of factitious gems, which appear to have been made, not for the purpose of personal decoration, but for adorning covers of sacred books, reliquaries,[3] and pictures of the Virgin and saints. It is not, therefore, surprising that so many recipes of this kind should occur in MSS. belonging to convents. Bibles and psalters were frequently bound in ivory covers, beautifully carved, and inlaid with artificial gems, the surfaces of which are always smooth, from their having been formed in moulds, and not cut. Sometimes the covers of books were of silver, or silver-gilt; sometimes they were solid, and carved in relief; sometimes they consisted of a sort of filigree-work in silver, over crimson velvet; and sometimes they were covered with velvet,

---

1 Murray's Guide for North Italy.

2 Dizionario delle Invenzione e Scoperte nelle Arti, nelle Scienze, &c., Milano, 1830. Art. Pittura.

3 A reliquary of brass gilt, set with false stones, was exhibited by Mr. Way at the meeting of the Archæological Institute at Winchester, in 1845. It was of the 11th century, and was of French workmanship.

and strengthened and ornamented with silver or gold studs.

The application of factitious gems to pictures was common. They are expressly mentioned by Cennini, who describes the method of attaching them to the pictures; and they may be frequently seen on paintings executed in Italy during the middle ages. The most remarkable picture decorated with these gems is one by Carlo Crivelli, in the gallery of Brera, at Milan. The picture is highly interesting, not only on this account, but because several portions of it are in relief. It is not less remarkable for the extreme brilliancy of the colours, which are as bright as if just painted. The picture is divided into three compartments. The centre contains the Virgin and Child; on the right hand are St. Peter and St. Dominic; and on the left St. Peter Martyr and St. Geminiano. The surface of each compartment is slightly convex, rising about one inch or one inch and a half in the centre of each compartment; it is quite perfect, without a flaw of any kind. The figures are placed on a gold ground. St. Peter has on his head the papal crown, the gilded ornaments of which are in high relief; and it is set with precious stones, or rather imitations of such. The keys are in his hand, and these are actually modelled, the stem-part of the keys being quite round, and merely attached by a small part of the surface to the picture; the other key lies on this, so that here the relief must be at least one inch and a half. The keys are gilded. The mantle of the Virgin is fastened with a gold or gilt ornament, in which a sapphire is set. The drapery of St. Geminiano is painted to represent crimson velvet, on which is a collar of gold, set with real or factitious pearls, some of which having dropped off, show small holes made in the panel to receive them.

The picture by the same artist, placed next to this in

the same gallery, is, in some respects, a contrast to it. The colours are as brilliant as those in the former picture, and the ground also is of gold; but the glories, instead of being in relief, are indented, and the jewels, with which the mitre is decorated, are painted, instead of being actually affixed to the picture. The artist has given as much transparency and brilliancy to these as if they were actually inlaid, like those in the picture above mentioned. The period of the birth of Crivelli is unknown, but he was living in 1476.

Sacramental cups, both of metal and of glass, were also frequently set with gems, real or factitious; hence the directions given in old MSS. for cements for gems. It is certain that glass was in use in Italy for drinking-vessels in the first half of the fifteenth century. Glass drinking-vessels are frequently mentioned by Cennini, who calls them by the name by which they are still known in Italy—*bicchieri*. Representations of them, of the same shape as those now in use, may be seen in early Italian pictures of the Last Supper, and particularly in the Cenacolo of Lionardo da Vinci. Glass vessels were frequently embossed, or enamelled, with the armorial bearings of their owners, sometimes parcel gilt, sometimes set with jewels, and occasionally they bore designs of high pretension.[1] The museum of antiquities of the middle ages in the Louvre, and in the Hôtel de Cluny, at Paris, afford many interesting specimens of glass of the middle ages, enriched with enamels and jewels. The drinking-vessels and flasks, executed at Murano, were particularly esteemed. Many beautiful specimens of the latter are in the possession of the Marquess Trivulzio, at Milan.

It is generally considered that the art of colouring glass was introduced from the East into Venice. The

---

[1] Arch. Journ., Sept., 1845, p. 264.

time of its introduction is uncertain, but it is known that as early as the commencement of the twelfth century the manufacture of what is called *crystal*, and the art of colouring glass, were carried on at Venice.[1] The mirrors and other works executed in glass in this city were, during the middle ages, the finest works of the kind; and the flasks and other small articles were much sought after, not only in Europe, but also in Asia, and even in the deserts of Africa.[2] Murano was, during four or five centuries, the seat of this manufacture, which the Venetians knew how to vary according to the taste of the times, and for which they found a ready market in the countries of the East. As long ago as 1275 there was a law mentioned in the Chronicle of Dandolo, which prohibited the exportation, not only of sand and the other substances used in the fabrication of glass from Venice, but also of the fragments of broken glass, which other nations might melt and fashion into new forms. It seems that there were formerly large masses of glass, which were employed in the factories.[3] Filiasi supposes that they were brought from Greece, where the composition of glass had attained a certain degree of perfection. By an ancient Venetian law masters of vessels were permitted to import these masses of glass as ballast. Sabellino speaks with admiration of the works executed at the commencement of the fourteenth century in the glass-works at Murano.

It is much to be regretted that no work should be known to exist in which the art of making glass, as practised at Murano, is accurately described. All inquiries for such a work are, however, rendered useless by the fact that the workmen at Murano have always

---

1 Depping, Histoire du Commerce, &c., vol. i. p. 191.

2 Ibid., vol. ii. p. 322, n.

3 Are these the masses of glass mentioned by Eraclius, p. 208, 210?

been sworn to preserve secrecy with respect to all technical processes.[1]

Much information, however, relative to this subject, will be found scattered through the pages of Neri's 'Arte Vetraria,' and the Commentary on this work by Dr. Merret, an Englishman. Cardanus mentions a Venetian MS. on the manufacture of glass, which fell into his hands. This would undoubtedly be a great acquisition if it could be discovered. It was said to have been written by a Venetian named Panteo.

Besides the uses already enumerated, glass was employed in making beads for paternosters, a manufacture which is still carried on to a great extent at Murano. But the favourite material of which the beads or rosaries used in the middle ages were composed, appears to have been amber.[2] The scarcity and high price of genuine amber placing it beyond the reach of the people generally, various attempts were made to imitate it; hence the numerous recipes in old MSS. for "making amber for paternosters;" and hence also the adoption of the term "amber" as a synonyme for beads, in which sense it is frequently used in the Bolognese MS.,[3] where we find directions for colouring the composition red, green, or blue, at pleasure. This fact is a sufficient proof of the estimation in which amber was held during the middle ages. Genuine amber was so highly prized that a statue of the Virgin made of this material, and a set of altar furniture in

---

[1] Gallipado Tallier (author of the 'Nuovo Plico d' ogni sorte di Tinture,' published at Bologna without a date) observes (p. 152), that "The red colour called 'rubino,' which, as every one knows, is made at Murano, is composed of 'oro di zecchino,' but few are acquainted with the process of combining the calcined gold with the liquid crystal." He adds, "The method of calcination is, however, known to me, but it is not lawful for me to discover it."

[2] Secreti di Don Alessio Piemontese, Part ii., p. 35. MS. of the Marciana, p. 609.

[3] Nos. 249—254.

amber, studded with jewels,[1] were considered among the treasures of the Santa Casa at Loreto. At the meeting of the English Archæological Society in 1845, a necklace of rough amber was exhibited, which was found round the neck of a skeleton near Ely, and which was supposed to be of the Romano-British period.[2]

Another art practised during the middle ages was the manufacture of artificial pearls from the bones of the heads of fish, from mother-of-pearl, and other substances; many recipes for these occur in MSS.,[3] as well as for making large pearls out of small ones. Beckmann treats these inventions with contempt, and thinks it impossible to give to any pulverized calcareous matter the hardness and lustre of real pearls. The varnish of caseum, mixed with the milk of the fig-tree, described in the Bolognese MS., No. 245, is certainly curious, and perhaps may hereafter receive a trial.

NOTE ON JEWISH GLASS.

It would appear, on the authority of the third book of Eraclius (p. 245), that lead-glass (see Eraclius, p. 217) was called Jewish glass. I have mentioned in the note to this passage,* that a ruby-coloured glass was formerly sold at Birmingham under the name of Jews' glass; the coincidence was at least curious, but facts were wanting to establish any connection between the Jewish glass of the middle ages and the modern "Jews' glass." It is known that the manufacture of glass was pursued extensively by the Jews during the dark and middle ages. There were Jewish glass-blowers at Constantinople between A.D. 531 and 565. This is proved incidentally by the following narrative, related in the 'History of the Jews:'†—

"It was the custom of the Church to distribute the crumbs of the consecrated host which might remain to children summoned for that purpose

---

1 It contained nearly 7000 pearls, besides diamonds and rubies, and was valued at 200,000 crowns.

2 Archæological Journal for 1845, p. xlii.

3 See Secreti di Don Alessio, Part ii., p. 35. Bol. MS., Nos. 246, 264, 320.

* P. 245. † Hist. of the Jews, vol. iii. p. 230.

from their schools. While Menas was Bishop of Constantinople, the child of a Jewish glass-blower went to the church with the rest, and partook of the sacred elements. The father, inquiring the cause of his delay, discovered what he had done. In his fury he seized him and shut him up in the blazing furnace. The mother went wandering about the city, wailing and seeking her lost offspring. The third day she sat down by the door of the workshop, still weeping, and calling on the name of her child. The child answered from the furnace, the doors were forced open, and the child was discovered sitting unhurt amid the red-hot ashes. His account was, that a lady in a purple robe, of course the Blessed Virgin, had appeared, and poured water on the coals that were immediately around him. The unnatural father was put to death, the mother and child baptized."

Filiasi * relates, that in 687 many Greek workmen went to France for the purpose of working in glass. It is probable that these persons practised the art after the same methods as the Jews, and that they made the processes known in France. It appears that the Jews carried on the art in Syria also. Benjamin of Tudela, whose 'Travels' bear date from 1160 to 1173, states that he found 400 Jews resident in Tyre, who were glass-blowers. This fact certainly shows a great trade in this branch of industry, and may be considered a confirmation of the assertion that the soda found at Tyre was peculiarly fitted for the manufacture of glass.† The glass-works in Syria do not appear to have been confined to Tyre, for Miss Martineau relates,‡ that a glass-house still exists at Hebron. The glass made here, however, appears to be of the most ordinary description, and it seems that the workmen are Arabs, and not Jews.

At the beginning of the ninth century the Venetians traded with the ports of Egypt and Syria; and when, in 1122, the King of Jerusalem requested the Venetian navy to assist him at the siege of Tyre, the Venetians stipulated for the possession of a third part of the city, and the payment of an annual sum of 300 besants. In the fourteenth century the Venetians had still a colony at Tyre.§ The art of glass-making, therefore, with which the Venetians are supposed to have been acquainted as early as the eleventh century, may have been communicated to them by the Tyrian Jews. It appears certain that they acquired it in the East.

It was in the eleventh century that a leaden glaze was, as I have mentioned (p. 177), first found on European pottery. The recipes in the MS. of Eraclius prove that lead-glass was known in some parts of Europe

---

* Saggio sull' antico Commercio, &c., p. 148, n.

† Neri, Arte Vetraria, lib. i. cap. 1, and lib. vii. cap. 117, and Merret's notes on these chapters. The Venetians and Genoese had both settlements at Tyre in the 12th century.

‡ "Next we were conducted to a glass-house, of all odd places to see in Hebron. I would recommend a Newcastle one in preference, as there the glass is not greenish and thin, and the articles made can stand upright. We thought here as before, however, that the Arabs are expert enough at manual arts if they had fair play with tools and materials."—Eastern Life, vol. iii. p. 64.

§ Depping, Histoire du Commerce, &c., vol. i., p. 153, quoting Navigero, Storia della Republ. Veneziana, 819; in vol. xxiii. of Murat., Script. Rer. Ital., and And. Dandolo, Chronic. Venet., ann 828, in vol. xii. of the same work.

at least as early as the thirteenth century; but it appears that it was not generally known even at a later period,* for Neri, who published his 'Arte Vetraria' in 1612, says (lib. iv. cap. lxi.) it was a secret known to but few glass-workers, "Cosa nota a pochi dell' arte vetraria." Merret, the commentator on Neri, in a note to this passage, remarks, that it was not in use in England on account of its want of durability. Both writers speak of the extreme beauty of the colours of the factitious gems made of this kind of glass, and Neri says "that it is the most beautiful and noble kind of glass that is made, for real oriental jewels may be imitated with it; which cannot be done so well with crystal or any other kind of glass; but if great care is not taken, it is so extremely fusible, that it will run through the glass-pots, and be lost among the coals used in heating the furnace." From these facts, therefore, it is considered that there may be some reason for ascribing the invention, or at least the introduction, of glass containing lead, &c., to the Jews, and at the same time of supposing that the correct reading of the above passage in Eraclius has been given.

* A peculiar kind of Venetian glass, containing lead, was used in Italy as a dryer for certain colours. See Mr. Eastlake's 'Materials,' &c., p. 351.

CHAPTER V.

GILDING AND OTHER ARTS.

§ 1. On Gilding.

THE frequent and profuse employment of gilding in every kind of decorative work in the middle ages cannot have escaped the observation of the most superficial observer. The grounds of the most ancient mosaics were of gold, so were those of the pictures of the Byzantine and early Italian schools. The early Italian frescoes, as they are called, were adorned with gold leaf; the same decoration was extended to miniatures, and afterwards to painting in oil, and the use of gilding in pictures was universal, until Domenico Ghirlandaio discovered the method of imitating gold with colours.[1] The directions, therefore, of all old MSS. on painting are diffuse and minute on this head, and although the recipes are alike in principle, there is some variety in the details. The grounds of the ancient gildings were of two kinds; one of which was for miniatures and places not exposed to damp; the other consisted of an oil mordant, which was employed on walls and places exposed to humidity. As the gilding on many old mural paintings is in a remarkable state of preservation, it becomes important to ascertain the manner in which it was executed; and where there is no precise documentary evidence to demonstrate this, it is desirable to have recourse to chemical analysis.

Under this impression, Professor Branchi, of Pisa,

[1] Vasari, Vita di Domenico Ghirlandaio.

analysed some portions of the gold ground of the mural pictures by Benozzo Gozzoli and Buffalmacco in that noble relic of the arts and genius of the middle ages, the Campo Santo at Pisa. Professor Branchi relates in the following words the result of his experiments on this subject.[1]

"With regard to the ancient method of gilding in Pisa, I must observe that my experiments have not enabled me to discover any essential difference between the gilding in Pisa and that of the picture by Taddeo Gaddi, which is still to be seen in the suppressed church of St. Francesco.

"The intonaco is, however, white, fine, and of a thicker consistence. One denaro (grammi 1·779) contained gr. 11¾ (grammi 0·576) of a fine white sand, mixed with a little argillaceous earth.

"The gilding of the fragments of a picture by Buffalmacco in our magnificent Campo Santo, is spread upon a layer of wax of the thickness of about half a line. This yields to the action of the nail, is slightly transparent, inflammable, and lighter than water; it liquefies at a low heat, is soluble in boiling alcohol, from which it separates on cooling in the form of a white and bulky mass; it gives a lustre to wood, and being thrown upon burning charcoal, it diffuses sensibly the odour of wax, which cannot be mistaken for any other substance.[2] It is true that in some parts the gold is seen on both sides; from this I conjecture that this gilding was executed by Buffalmacco, either to repair some part already gilded, and with which he was not satisfied, or it was a reparation made at a subsequent period.

---

1 Lettera del Prof. Branchi al Prof. Ciampi, &c., p. 18.

2 "In making the above experiments I had no indication that a fixed drying oil was mixed with the wax. Among the various mordants which painters were accustomed to use in illuminating with gold, is that which is composed chiefly of the above-mentioned substances." [Note by Prof. Branchi.]

"The gilding of those small fragments which were removed from one of the numerous pictures painted by the celebrated Benozzo Gozzoli in the same Campo Santo is in excellent preservation. The gold being removed with a sharp instrument, discovers a thin layer, not opaque, which may be scraped like wax, and which, like that substance, gives a lustre to wood on which it is rubbed. Below this appears a yellowish tint, which penetrates into the intonaco to a small, but not always uniform depth. When the gold leaf was separated from the fragments by immersion in boiling distilled water, a pellicle of wax appeared on the surface.

"The liquid being filtered, and afterwards slightly evaporated, acquired a yellowish colour, and then formed a pellicle which differed from the preceding, and by complete evaporation left a small quantity of combustible matter—so small that I could not determine its nature.

"From these experiments it appears that our ancient gilding was executed, 1st, by applying on the smooth intonaco a kind of size, that is a liquid and tenacious substance, soluble in water, and coloured yellow; 2ndly, by applying on this a thin coating of wax; 3rdly, and finally, by affixing on this the gold leaf.

"It should here be remarked that the gold leaves being detached without having suffered any alteration in consequence of the liquefaction of the wax, gave me an opportunity of observing how much thicker they were at that period than they are at present. From the time of the Romans until now the art of gold-beating has been continually progressing towards perfection. From one ounce of this metal they were accustomed to obtain 750 square leaves and upwards, four fingers broad on each side,[1] which is certainly

---

[1] Pliny, lib. xxxiii. cap. 3. Modern goldbeaters now make 1200

below the number of those of equal dimension which our best goldbeaters now produce from the same quantity of gold. And as to the wax, which Benozzo applied to the intonaco in order to serve as a mordant, I shall observe that it must have been dissolved either in a volatile or in a fixed drying oil. From its characters I am inclined more towards the volatile than the fixed oil; but in order to form an accurate decision on this point, it would be necessary to have at my disposal a larger quantity of the gilding. I am induced to believe from the experiments which I made on some ancient pictures in 1791 for my particular friend Signor Alessandro Morrona, the author of the celebrated work entitled 'Pisa Illustrata,' that the first of these oils was formerly added to the above-named substance."[1]

Some estimate of the extent to which gold was used on paintings in the fifteenth century may be formed from the document relative to the expenses of painting the chapel of S. Jacopo di Pistoia, which records that 7000 leaves of gold were used for this purpose.

§ 2. Auripetrum and Porporino.

When the parties for whom pictures were painted were unable or unwilling to pay for gold (which was always supplied by the persons who ordered the pictures), it was usual to substitute for it on mural paintings leaves of tin-foil, covered with a yellow varnish.

---

leaves from the same quantity. Cennino (cap. 139) complains that in his time 145 leaves were obtained from the ducat instead of 100; and it appears from Vasari, that in his time 435 leaves of gold were made from three ducats. The size of the leaves is described by Vasari to have been the eighth of a braccio square. Cennino does not mention their size.

1 Vol. ii. p. 162. "Sig. Giov. Fabbroni has proved (Vantaggi e Metodi della Pittura Encausta) that in encaustic paintings the ancients did not unite the wax with mastic as Requeno asserts, nor with an alkali as Lorgna pretends, nor with gums and honey as Astori asserts, but with a volatile oil-like naphtha, or spirit of turpentine." [Note by Prof. Branchi.]

The method of applying and varnishing the tin-foil is fully described in the MS. of S. Audemar, and many other old works on painting. Its actual employment on mural pictures is proved by the above-mentioned document[1] relative to the expenses of the paintings executed in the chapel of S. Jacopo di Pistoia, in which 37 pieces of tin are mentioned. At the time Professor Branchi made his experiments on the gilding and pigments employed on these paintings, ancient treatises on art appear to have been but little studied. Branchi, it is true, mentions the work of Theophilus, which had been published by Lessing and Raspe; but his acquaintance with it must have been superficial, or he would have recollected that Theophilus describes[2] the leaves of tin, and the method of using them on pictures and on books. If he had read this part of the work, he would also have seen that the tin-foil was varnished, and he would then have understood the probable use of the varnish mentioned in the document, for the employment of which he could not satisfactorily account,[3] since he says that the fragments of the gilding, and of the pictures which he had analysed, gave no indication of varnish.[4]

In order to economize gold, the old masters had another invention called "porporino," a composition made of quicksilver, tin, and sulphur, which produced a yellow metallic powder that was employed instead of gold.[5] The Bolognese MS. devotes a whole chapter to this subject. A substance of a similar nature is now in

---

1 Ciampi, Notizie, &c., p. 145.

2 Lib. i. ch. 26 and 32, E. ed. The varnish for the tin leaves is fully described in the MS. of S. Audemar, p. 163, 165.

3 The small quantity of sandarac (one pound) mentioned in the document published by Ciampi was evidently insufficient to varnish the pictures, which, judging from the large quantity of colours supplied, must have been very large or very numerous.

4 Lettera di Branchi, p. 18.

5 See Cennino Cennini, Trattato, cap. 159; Bol. MS., cap. 6.

use in England, and is employed as a substitute for gold on coloured woodcuts and chromolithographs.

§ 3. On the use of Wax in Painting.

The subject of wax-painting during the middle ages has been so fully and ably treated by Mr. Eastlake in his recent work,[1] that but little remains to be added.

It may, however, be remarked that, in addition to the use of wax as a mordant for gilding, in the manner before mentioned, it was employed as a varnish for paintings,[2] for which purpose it is supposed to have been dissolved in an essential oil. That it was also used as a vehicle for painting is established by the two recipes quoted by Mr. Eastlake from the Byzantine MS., and from that of Le Begue. The principle of these two recipes (the solution of wax in caustic potash[3]) is the same in both MSS., but the latter recipe contains mastic in addition to glue and wax. The last-mentioned vehicle must have resembled somewhat the cement, or *cera colla*, which was in use in England about the year 1385, and of which Mr. Hartshorne found the following notice among the documents preserved in Rochester Castle:[4]—"For 3½ lbs. of wax bought for cement (ad cimentum), 21*d*., at 6*d*. a lb. In 2 lbs. of frankincense, 6*d*. In 5 lbs. of lees (coda) and 1 lb. of pitch, 6½*d*."[5] It will be observed that glue is not mentioned in the above entry. Neither does it appear in the varnish used for painting on glass described in the Venetian MS.[6] This varnish

1 Materials, &c., chap. 6.

2 Ibid., p. 163, and n.

3 In the Le Begue MS. (p. 307) the word "flandres" has been erroneously substituted for "cendres"—ashes, which, when boiled with water, made a lixivium, which was rendered caustic by the addition of lime, exactly in the manner now employed by soap-boilers.

4 See Arch. Journ., Jan. 1845, p. 373.

5 The Marciana MS. (p. 626) has a recipe for a cement of this kind, composed of wax, liquid varnish, and black naval pitch.

6 Sloane MSS., No. 416. See Mr. Eastlake's 'Materials,' &c., p. 172, n.

consisted of wax, white turpentine, and mastic, and was of the same nature as the cement employed by Agnolo Gaddi in repairing the mosaics in S. Giovanni at Florence, which varied from the above in being composed of mastic and wax only; its object was to exclude damp.

One of the very few medieval pictures reputed to be painted with wax at present known to connoisseurs, is the Martyrdom of St. Simon the Younger, by Andrea Mantegna, whose name is inscribed on the painting. It is in the possession of Signor Giuseppe Vallardi at Milan, and belonged formerly to the Abbate Boni, of Venice.[1] The picture is very perfect, the colours bright, and the touches sharp. The darks are laid on very thick, but the paint appears to have run into spots or streaks, as if it had been touched with something which had disturbed the surface. It is said, however, that it has never been repaired, and its authenticity is stated to be undoubted. It is evident that the wax has been used liquid, for if the colours had been fused by the application of heat, the sharpness and precision of touch for which this picture, in common with other paintings of this period, is remarkable, would have been lost and melted down. The vehicle, whatever it was, appeared to me to have been as manageable as that of Van Eyck. This picture was painted late in life by Mantegna.

The same collection also contains a modern picture, which may with propriety be said to be in encaustic, since the colours are melted in by the application of a hot iron. This is a small picture of a sleeping Cupid by Appiani, painted by way of experiment on a brick, the surface of which was properly prepared. The colours of this picture were dull, and the effect like that of a fresco; it seemed to be better adapted for

---

[1] See Catalogo dei Quadri di Giuseppe Vallardi. Milano, 1830.

decorative effect than for cabinet pictures. The lights were poor, and did not bear out well.

Wax painting is now practised at Parma. An apartment of the Museo di Antichità, and another in the public library of that city, are now being painted with a wax vehicle, and after a process invented by an artist of that city, which he freely and obligingly communicated to me.

The vehicle used consists of wax and resin dissolved in spirit of turpentine. The mixture is fluid, and of the colour of milk. In this the colours are ground, and are then preserved in small glasses, and spirit of turpentine is poured *upon* them to preserve them. To close these glasses conveniently, the painter employs a cushion of leather larger than the glass, with a button on the top for a handle, and this contrivance effectually defends the colours from the air and dust.

All colours may be used indiscriminately, Prussian blue, orpiment, and others which are not permanent in oil.

For the ground, the wall or ceiling is plastered in the usual way with lime, and is not quite smooth, but is left with a kind of grain or tooth. The painting is executed on this ground when dry, without other preparation.

The method is said to require some practice, as the colours dry fast. When working, the colours are diluted with spirit of turpentine.

This kind of painting has great brilliancy and transparency, and can be seen well from any point of view. If durable, it seems well adapted for decorative purposes. The method has been in use for about six years.

§ 4. On Painting Statues.

The practice of painting statues was common during the middle ages.[1] The proofs of this are numerous.

---

[1] Ciampi, Notizie, &c., p. 118, 142.

The documents recording the wax vehicle, or varnish, called *cera colla*, furnished to Andrea Pisano for painting and varnishing a marble statue over the principal door in the façade of the Cathedral of Orvieto, has been mentioned by Mr. Eastlake.[1] This practice is alluded to more than once in the MS. of Le Begue,[2] and in the Tabula Imperfecta[3] is a reference to some directions contained in Theophilus[4] for painting round images, "ymagines rotundas,"[5] and other sculptured articles which are not covered with leather, cloth, or parchment. The most remarkable example, probably now in existence, of the union of painting with statuary, is in the baptistery near the Cathedral of Novara. The building is circular, and supported by ancient columns: the recesses between the columns contain the events of the Passion. The figures in plastic work are as large as life, coloured; and in some cases the resemblance to life is completed by the addition of real hair. The wall behind the figures, which is painted in fresco, serves as a background to the figures; and the light aërial tone of the painting contributes much to the effect of the figures. The remarks on these groups, in a MS. Journal, quoted by the author of the 'Handbook for North Italy,' are so appropriate and judicious, that I shall make no apology for introducing them here. "They are," he says, "probably by Gaudenzio Ferrari,[6] who excelled in this branch of art; and many of the figures are of exquisite workmanship. The two finest groups are the Garden of Olives, and the Scourging of our Lord, which last, without being in the least disgusting or painful, is most deeply affecting. One of the

---

1 Materials, &c., p. 170.

2 See No. 180 (p. 145), and No. 344 (p. 315). 3 P. 40.

4 Lib. i. cap. 23, E. ed. 5 The word "rotundas" is not in Theophilus.

6 Gaudenzio Ferrari was born in 1484, and died in 1550. He was one of the principal painters of the Milanese school, and his merits, which have been overlooked by Vasari, have been justly appreciated and warmly eulogized by Lomazzo and Lanzi.

executioners is sitting down, tired with his work; the Roman soldier looks on with pity; the other can no longer look, and turns away. These representations are so entirely at variance with our conventional rules, that it requires a considerable degree of mental exertion to appreciate them. The first step in this, and many similar occasions, must be for the observer to forget all that he has read upon the theory of the fine arts; and to form his opinion, as the judge tells the jury, not to mind what they have heard out of court, but to give their verdict upon the evidence before them. In so doing, you must recollect that the only valid plea by which the introduction of images into churches is attempted to be justified by the Romanists, is, that they are books of instruction to the common people; and certainly neither mere painting, nor mere sculpture, can realise the events of Scripture to the mind in a manner so vivid as this union of form and colour. You will rarely enter this baptistery without finding individuals employed in acts of devotion before these scenes; some reading appropriate selections from Scripture, some engaged in prayer, but not praying to the images, for the circumstance of their forming entire groups prevents any one being singled out as the object of worship; and let us repeat, that the independent judgment which we have ventured to advise the traveller to assert in Italy, will be much strengthened by his asserting it in the baptistery of Novara." In the Life of Andrea Verrocchio, Vasari gives a description of some curious effigies of Lorenzo de' Medicis, which were modelled in wax and afterwards painted in oil. His account is as follows:—"On the occasion of the murder of Giuliano de' Medicis, and the narrow escape of Lorenzo his brother, who was wounded at the same time, in the Church of Sta. Maria del Fiore, the friends of Lorenzo ordered several effigies of him to be made in commemoration of this event. Among

others, Orsini, a celebrated modeller in wax, with the assistance and under the direction of Andrea Verrocchio, modelled three images as large as life. Within these was a kind of skeleton of wood, and split canes, which was covered with waxed cloth, disposed in such well-arranged folds, that it was impossible anything could more nearly resemble the reality. The heads, hands, and feet, which were of wax, were hollow within, and modelled from the life, and then painted in oil, real hair being added, and all appropriate ornaments. "These," says Vasari, "represented not waxen effigies, but living men, as may be seen in all three figures, one of which is in the church of the nuns of Chiarito, in the Via di S. Gallo. This figure is habited in the very dress which Lorenzo wore when, wounded in the throat and bandaged, he appeared at a window of his house, that he might be seen by the people, who had collected there to ascertain whether he was alive, as they wished him to be, or dead; and if dead, that they might avenge him." The second figure is in the church of the Servites, at Lucca, in the civil costume worn by the Florentines. The third image was sent to Sta. Maria degli Angeli, at Assisi. There were other wax figures by Orsini in the Church of the Servites. These were distinguished by a large O, within which was an R, with a cross above it. They were all fine works of art, and Vasari remarks that they have been equalled by few. He adds that the art was practised in his time, but whether from want of devotion, or other causes, it was then declining.

The custom of painting figures extended also to the colouring, with a kind of enamel, of figures and bassi rilievi in terra cotta; and the numerous specimens of this kind of decoration which still remain, prove the estimation in which this art was once held.

The most distinguished artist in this line was Luca della Robbia, to whom many improvements in the art are ascribed.

In Spain the art of colouring wooden statues was continued to a comparatively late period. Pacheco[1] gives instructions for painting statues, and it appears that he did not disdain to practise the art himself, and that he even claimed the honour of having introduced a better style of painting sculpture. Alonzo Cano and Montañes are said to have frequently stipulated that none but themselves should paint the images which they had carved.[2]

The practice of painting "ymagines rotundas" was not confined to those carved in wood; it extended also to stone statues, and was frequently employed on the sepulchral effigies of kings and nobles. In this case the dress of the sculptured figure exactly resembled that worn by the person whom it was intended to represent. Among the Germans and English a general custom prevailed of painting monumental effigies. A remarkable instance of this occurs in the effigy of Henry II. of England, at Fontevraud, in Normandy, described by Mr. Stothard in his work entitled 'The Monumental Effigies of Great Britain.' The beard of the figure is painted and stippled like a miniature, to represent its being closely shaven in the Norman fashion. The mantle, Mr. Stothard ascertained by scraping, had been painted several times; it was originally of a deep reddish chocolate.[3] The Dalmatica, or tunic, was of crimson, covered with gold stars. The boots were green, with gold spurs, fastened by red leathers. The gloves have jewels on the centre of the back of the hand, a mark of royalty or high ecclesiastical rank. The crown and the right hand are broken, but the latter still retains the sceptre. The sword lies on the bier by

---

1 Tratado della Pintura, p. 402, &c.

2 For additional information on this subject, see Ford's Hand-book for Spain, p. 110.

3 Probably the deep red colour found on old frescoes, apparently produced by the red hæmatite.

the left side. With the exception of the position of the sword, it will be seen that this description agrees with the account of the burial of Henry II., extracted by Mr. Stothard from the History of Matthew Paris, who says, "the king was arrayed in the royal investments, having a golden crown on his head, and gloves on the hands, boots wrought with gold on the feet, and spurs, and a great ring on the finger, with the sceptre in the hand, and girt with a sword: he lay with his face uncovered." Mr. Stothard continues, "It therefore appears that the tomb was literally a representation of the deceased king, as if he still lay in state. Nor can we, without supposing such was the custom, otherwise account for the singular coincidence between the effigy of King John on the lid of his coffin and his body within it, when discovered a few years since."[1]

§ 5. Implements used in Painting.

The wood-cut, copied originally from a miniature of the fifteenth century, in the Bibliothèque Royale at Paris, appeared in the before-mentioned interesting work of M. Aimé Champollion-Figeac; it exhibits a female artist in the act of painting a statue of the Virgin holding the infant Saviour. The subject is highly interesting in another point of view, because it shows the implements used at that period in painting. The artist holds a pencil or brush in her right hand, and a palette with a handle in her left, thus affording incontestable evidence that the palette was used in France during the fifteenth century. This is, perhaps, the earliest notice of this implement with which we are acquainted. The colours, mixed in shells, as described by Alcherius and other writers, are placed on a small bench by her side, near which are the brushes in a tray, and a second palette, also furnished with a handle.

---

[1] King John was buried in Worcester Cathedral.

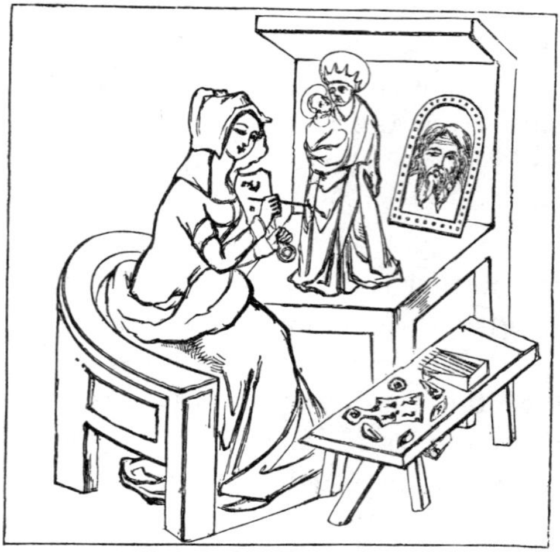

Another illustration of the work of M. Champollion, copied from a miniature of the same period, represents the atelier of a painter of the fifteenth century. He is sitting on a folding stool, holding in his left hand a palette, similar in its form to those represented in the last cut. In his right hand he holds a brush, with which he is painting a picture of the Virgin and Child,

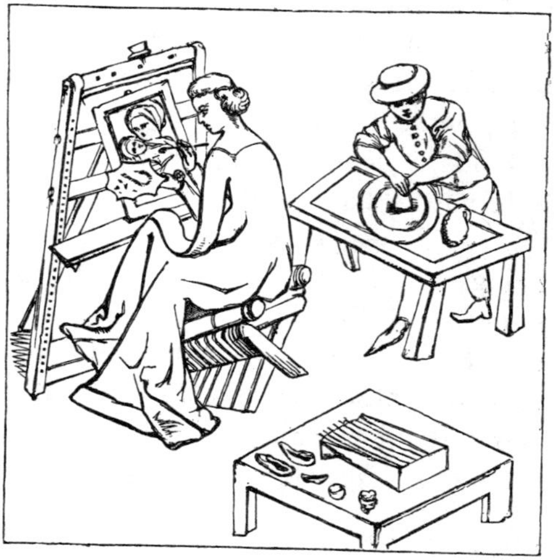

which, from being framed, suggests the idea of being painted on canvass. The picture is placed on an easel, supported by three legs. In the background is a man grinding colours, with a jar by his side. In the foreground is a low table, on which are shells of various kinds holding colours, and a tray full of brushes. The long and flowing sleeves of the painter, and the pointed shoes of the man grinding the colours, will assist in fixing the date of this drawing.

§ 6. Leather.

It has been mentioned that during the age of Frederick Barbarossa, the clothes of men were of leather, unlined. There is reason, however, to believe, from the recipes contained in the Lucca MS., and repeated in the Mappæ Clavicula, that the skins were frequently dyed. During the dark and middle ages, the preparation of leather appears to have been carried on chiefly in the south of Europe, and in the countries inhabited by the Saracens and Moors. The leather of Marseilles was particularly valued at this period; and one quarter of the city, called "La Cuiraterie," was especially set apart for the preparation of this article, with which the markets of Spain and Italy were supplied. In the twelfth, thirteenth, and fourteenth centuries, skins and leather were also imported from Africa into Barcelona, and the merchants of this city occupied, conjointly with those of Marseilles, a certain quarter of the city of Troyes, where they carried on a trade principally in Morocco leather.[1] From the ninth to the middle of the thirteenth century, the city of Cordova, in Spain, was celebrated for the leather called "Cordovan," which was manufactured there by the Moors.

The use of leather was not limited to articles of dress, but as men became more luxurious, the fashion

---

1 Depping, Histoire du Commerce, vol. i. p. 249, 263, 294.

of hanging rooms with leather, painted linen-cloth,[1] or tapestry, was introduced. The walls of apartments were formerly left bare, and on the introduction of leather hangings or tapestry, they were confined to that part of the room which was immediately behind the seats occupied by the owners of the house. These hangings were suspended from hooks fixed in the wall, and, like the glass windows, were removed when the family changed their residence. Frequent examples of these partial hangings of apartments may be seen in miniatures and pictures of the thirteenth and fourteenth centuries. In the fifteenth century, the hangings were continued round the apartment, and the leather was frequently stamped and gilt, or ornamented with tin-foil, and afterwards varnished with a yellow varnish. Descriptions of this varnish are to be found in all technical works relating to art, from the Lucca MS. to the Treatise of Pacheco, inclusive.

Filiasi[2] observes that "the art of gilding skins and leather has been exercised from time immemorial in the [Venetian] lagoon, and to such an extent was the commerce in this merchandise carried on with Spain and the Levant, that, one year with another, the trade in gilt leather brought into Venice a clear profit of about 100,000 ducats and more." Apartments hung with this stamped and gilt leather may still be seen in some of the palaces at Venice. The Barbarigo Palace has more than one room decorated in this manner. Leather hangings were also in use in our own country; the best specimens are at Nonsuch Palace, in Surrey; Hinchinbrook House, near Huntingdon; Ruffor Abbey, in Nottinghamshire; and at Blenheim.[3]

Gilt leather was also applied to other purposes. It

[1] See Mr. Eastlake's 'Materials,' p. 97.

[2] Saggio sull' Antico Commercio, sull' Arti, e sulla Marina de' Veneziani, appended to the 7th volume of his Memorie Storiche de' Veneti, p. 153.

[3] See a paper on this subject in the Art Union for August, 1847.

was used for the covers of books, and for frames of mirrors. Examples of both may be seen in the museum in the Hôtel de Cluny at Paris. Pictures were also frequently painted on plain leather, stretched on a panel. The circumstance is alluded to by Eraclius. Marco Rizzi sometimes painted in tempera on kid-skins;[1] and in the Fondaco de' Tedeschi an apartment is decorated with historical pictures by Paolo Veronese, painted on the gilt leather for which Venice was so famous.[2]

In the commencement of this Introduction full credit has been given to the monks for the preservation of literature and the arts; but it must be allowed that if they have been the cause of the preservation of learning during the dark ages, they have also actually destroyed the writings of many classic authors in order to transcribe on the parchment on which they were written the works of the fathers or the legends of the saints. Some of the lost works of antiquity have been brought to light by the labours of Cardinal Angelo Mai and other learned men; but alas! the ingenious monks had discovered another and more effectual method of destroying the literary treasures of antiquity. This method is revealed in the Bolognese MS.,[3] where we find a recipe "To make chamois leather with sheep or goat-skin *parchment, which has been written on!*" Who shall say how many classic works have been made into leather waistcoats for the warriors of the middle ages or cut into sandals for the sleek and well-fed monks? Who shall even say how many works were obliterated before the destroying process was brought to perfection, and the grand discovery made that parchment which had been written on would make as good leather as that which had never been touched by a pen?

---

1 Zanetti, della Pittura Veneziana, p. 442, n.

2 Ibid., p. 194. 3 Ibid., p. 375.

§ 7. Niello.

Among the arts formerly practised and now fallen into disuse, there is perhaps none which has led to such important results as the ancient nigellum or niello, for to this we are indebted for the invention of engraving. The art was known to the ancients and was practised during the middle ages, as we find from the 'Mappæ Clavicula,' the MSS. of Eraclius, Theophilus, and Le Begue, as well as from specimens of the art still existing in different museums. These examples are extremely rare.

That the art was practised by the Byzantine Greeks is proved by the specimens in the Pala d'Oro, which was made at Constantinople in 976, by order of the Doge Pietro Orseolo, for the church of S. Mark at Venice, where it may now be seen. The material is silver-gilt ornamented with gems and enamels. Some of the inscriptions are in Greek and some in Latin, but the letters are all in niello. The Pala d'Oro was repaired in 1105, in 1209, and in 1345, but it is highly probable that the nielli formed part of the original design. Some fragments of it are now in England. The Marquess Trivulzio of Milan has a collection of about forty nielli, among which I saw a very fine specimen by Maso Finiguerra and another by Peregrino, besides others highly interesting.

This art was much cultivated by the early Milanese goldsmiths, who applied it to the decoration of arms and armour, as well as to religious purposes.[1]

Benvenuto Cellini remarks[2] that the art of executing nielli was nearly forgotten at Florence in the year 1515, when he began to learn the craft of the goldsmith. But, he proceeds, as he was continually

---

[1] Milano e il suo Territorio, vol. ii. p. 244.
[2] Dell' Arte del Niellare, e del Modo di fare il Niello.

hearing from the goldsmiths of the beauty of the nielli, and particularly of the skill of Maso Finiguerra in this art, he applied himself with great diligence to follow the traces of these skilful goldsmiths; but not content with learning to engrave on the silver only, he learned also the mode of executing the nielli, in order to work with more facility and certainty. Cellini has left us the most precise description of the mode of working nielli which is extant. It has been published with his other works.[1]

The art consisted [2] in drawing the design on gold or silver with a style and then engraving it with the burin; a black composition was then made of copper, lead, silver, and sulphur, incorporated together by heat. When cold the composition was pounded and laid on the engraved silver plate, a little borax was sprinkled over it, and the plate was then placed over a charcoal fire until the composition, being dissolved, flowed into all the lines of the design. When cold, the work was scraped and burnished, and the niello presented the effect of a drawing in black on gold or silver.

§ 8. Dyeing.

During the dark ages the Jews appear to have monopolised the trade of dyeing. Benjamin of Tudela relates that when he visited Jerusalem (between 1160 and 1173) he found only two hundred Jews resident in that city, who were all dyers of wool, and who had purchased a monopoly of the trade. Beckmann [3] has shown that the art of dyeing was principally carried on by this people during the same period in Italy. Dye-houses were established in the duchy of Benevento as early as the eleventh century, and in Sicily at the com-

---

1 The Life and Writings of Cellini were published in 3 vols. 8vo., in 1806, at Milan.

2 See Vasari, Int., cap. xxxiii.

3 Inventions, Title *Indigo*.

mencement of the thirteenth. From the Jews resident in Italy the art soon spread to the Italians, who carried it to a greater degree of perfection than the other nations of Europe.

In Venice there appear to have been distinct establishments for dyeing in the thirteenth century,[1] for this city was then celebrated for its purple dyes. The scarlet dyes prepared from the kermes (*grana*) at Florence were particularly prized. About the year 1338 this city contained nearly two hundred of these factories.[2] In the year 1300 the art of dyeing with the purple colour obtained from the lichen Roccella or Oricello was introduced from the Levant; but the secret of preparing the dye was for a long period confined to a single family, who acquired a large fortune by cultivating this branch of industry, and who for this reason received the name of "Ruccellai."

Previous to this period Marseilles, Arles, Montpellier, and other parts of the South of France, were famous for red, blue, and rose-coloured dyes. The statutes of these cities contain regulations relative to the use of madder, kermes, and brasil wood in dyeing.[3]

The date of the introduction of the art of dyeing into England seems uncertain. Hume remarks that "in the reign of Henry III. woollen cloth, which the English had not then the art of dyeing, was worn by them white, and without receiving the last hand of the manufacturer;" and it is certain that as late as the year 1284[4] the English were in the habit of contracting with the Florentine merchants for the sale of their fleeces for a period of one year or more. Mr. Hallam[5] has, however, shown that a woollen-manufactory existed

---

[1] Filiasi, Saggio, &c., p. 153.

[2] Depping, Histoire du Commerce, &c., vol. i. p. 235.

[3] Ibid., vol. ii. p. 293, 300.

[4] Ibid., vol. i. p. 337, quoting Pagnini 'Della Decima e delle altre Gravezze.'

[5] History of the Middle Ages, vol. iii. p. 378.

in England under Henry II., which was noticed in the regulations of Richard I., and which, by the importation of woad under John, may be considered to have been then flourishing. From the importation of woad it may certainly be inferred that the English understood and practised the art of dyeing as early as the time of John. The MS. of S. Audemar alludes to a substance called folium,[1] which was used by the English to dye wool red or purple. The date of this MS. is uncertain, but it is probably not later than the beginning of the thirteenth century.

From the frequent occurrence of treatises on dyeing in old MSS. relative to the arts, it seems probable that this art was formerly practised in monasteries conjointly with painting and medicine. The older MSS., such as that of Lucca and the 'Mappæ Clavicula,' contain recipes for dyeing skins and leather only. The Bolognese MS. contains a long treatise on dyeing, in which various methods of dyeing skins and leather of all kinds, as well as silk, thread, and woollen stuffs, are circumstantially detailed. The Sloane MS., No. 1754, contains also a treatise "de Tincturis," which seems to have been written principally for the use of the monks, the dyeing of the dresses worn by them being described in it. These treatises are generally accompanied by recipes for removing stains from cloth. In the introduction to the MSS. of Le Begue a practice is noticed[2] which prevailed in England, previous to the introduction of printing with blocks, of painting linen cloth intended for wearing-apparel with figures, flowers, and various devices in imitation of embroidery. Recipes of a similar kind are contained in the Sloane MS. above mentioned, and also in the Bolognese MS.[3]

---

1 A vegetable colour employed also in painting, prepared from the juice of the Croton tinctorium.

2 Page 7. 3 Page 491.

CHAPTER VI.

PAINTING IN OIL.

THE fact that in Italy colours were mixed with oil in painting long before the alleged introduction of oil painting by Antonello da Messina, has been established by the clearest evidence; but the method adopted by these early artists was rude and imperfect; and it was only after the middle of the fifteenth century that the process, which had been perfected by the genius and skill of the brothers Van Eyck, was introduced into Italy by their pupils and followers.

In the course of years the Flemish process underwent various modifications, some of the old practices were altered, and new ones introduced, until the example of Titian and Paolo Veronese occasioned a radical change in the technical methods of the Italian painters. After their time the new methods were again modified and changed by succeeding painters, until not only the original Flemish process, but those of the Venetian painters, had fallen into oblivion, and but few traces of the old practices remained. Some of these have been handed down traditionally from master to pupil; others may be collected from works on painting.

It was with a view to collect these scattered reminiscences of art that the present work was principally undertaken.

As traditionary practices might possibly preserve the remembrance of technical processes not recorded in books, or at least serve to confirm those which have been described by writers on art, it appeared to me

most desirable to learn as many of them as I could. With this view, I applied for information to several eminent artists and restorers of pictures in the north of Italy. Nothing can exceed the kindness and frankness with which they answered my inquiries, and communicated all they knew respecting the old methods of painting. On one occasion only was there the slightest degree of reserve.

The information contained in the treatises published in these volumes, and in other works on art, relative to technical details, is frequently concise and incomplete, and sometimes merely incidental. Extensive reading is, therefore, necessary to enable one to form a just idea of the early methods of oil-painting. As many of the processes are described in books which are so rare as to be scarcely accessible to the general reader, I have endeavoured to collect from them, as well as from the communications of Italian artists, such information as will give the reader some slight notions of the Italian practice of oil-painting.

The materials I have collected may be arranged under the following heads:—1st. The communications made by foreign professors of painting. 2ndly. An explanation of the colours used in painting, with some account of the manner in which they are employed. 3rdly. A description of the mode of preparing oils and varnishes, and of the resins of which the latter are composed; and, 4thly, A short account of the process of painting.

§ 1. Opinions of eminent Italian Artists as to the Practice of the Old Masters.

The following particulars relative to old methods of painting were communicated to me by Signor A., an artist who had practised many years at Milan, and is esteemed as a skilful restorer of pictures.

The Society of Painters in the Italian States were

governed by certain rules and regulations among themselves, and when a young man wished to become a painter, he was placed with one of established reputation, with whom he was to continue one year on trial. If at the end of that period the master was dissatisfied with the boy's progress, he returned him to his parents; if he approved of him, the boy was bound to him for twelve years,[1] the first six or seven of which were spent in learning to grind colours, and all the other mechanical parts of the art, as well as in painting "Madonnine," which were sent to the fairs for sale, and the proceeds helped to pay the expenses of the boy's board and lodging. The pupil was sworn never to divulge the secrets[2] of the art until he became a master himself, when he was allowed to teach his own pupils, first binding them to secrecy. Signor A. remarked that a master could not execute large works properly unless he had half a dozen pupils at least, and the object of the long apprenticeship was, that the pupil might by his services repay the master who had maintained and taught him, for in those days pupils did not pay apprentice fees.

He observed that Titian painted on a ground of thin "gesso marcio,"[3] taking especial care not to put too much glue,[4] and this slightly absorbent ground was useful in getting rid of the superfluous oil. He next stated that the two great faults of the moderns were the use of white lead in their grounds, and the little care they took in purifying their colours. He said that any

---

[1] Cennini (cap. civ.) mentions a similar term of apprenticeship. He says the first year was spent in studying drawing; the next six in learning to grind colours, to make glue, to prepare grounds, and to gild; and the remaining six years in learning to paint.

[2] Compare with the Statutes of Sienese Painters, s. xiii. xl. Carteggio Inedito, vol. ii.

[3] See Zanetti, della Pittura Veneziana, p. 101.

[4] Strong glue would have hardened the ground and rendered it non-absorbent. See p. 888.

picture in which white lead was used in the ground would inevitably crack within fifty years after it was painted, and that pictures painted with oil on a white lead ground would moreover turn brown.[1] This practice, he said, was observed by Mengs, who in other respects painted with the true method. He also said that the colours were always *ground* with oil, but that *oil was not used to paint with.* The colours, he said, were of the most common description, as we read in Lanzi and others,[2] but they were carefully purified and washed. Signor A. told me, that when he was at Venice he made a point of going to the Piazza San Salvatore,[3] where Titian used to purchase his colours, to see whether there were any "speziali"[4] there still. He found one, and inquired of him if he had any old colours, such as were used by the old painters, and he was shown an orange-coloured pigment, which resembled a colour frequently found on Venetian pictures. Signor A. gave me an ounce or more of this colour.

He said the blue used by Titian, Correggio, Paul Veronese, and others, was "bleu minerale," (he pronounced this word in the Italian manner;) he showed me his bottle of this blue, and told me I could purchase it for one soldo an ounce, for it was now used for the most common purposes; but that it could not be used with oil, or in any method but his, on oil paintings. He said the Venetians never used ultramarine,[5] which inclined too much to the violet.

As to Titian's method of painting, he said the whole subject was painted in chiaroscuro with this same blue, mixed with white and terra rossa, as if painting with

1 Vasari (Int., cap. xxi.) and Armenini mention that white lead was used in the grounds.

2 Zanetti, della Pittura Veneziana, p. 100.

3 Titian is said to have purchased his colours in Rialto; San Salvatore is on the other side of the Canal Grande.

4 Apothecaries or druggists who sold colours.

5 There is proof that the Venetians did occasionally use ultramarine.

Indian ink; that the lights were laid on with flesh-colour (red and white); the picture was then laid aside for several months (say five or six); afterwards the flesh-colour, consisting of terra rossa, or whatever you please, was glazed over the flesh, and then the picture was again laid by to dry. I think Signor A. said the shades and half tints were then painted, and the picture again dried. The glazing was then repeated until the painter was satisfied with his work, setting the picture aside between every glazing, until quite dry and hard.[1] That the picture was invariably first painted in cold colours, and that the warm colours were afterwards glazed upon them. That the whole surface of the picture, when the painting was completed, was glazed over with asphaltum ("spalto bianco, bitume Hebraico"). "But," I remarked, "if asphaltum is now used, it is almost sure to crack." He answered, "That is because you do not know how to use it." He added, that all Titian's pictures were glazed with it. The effect of daylight discernible in Titian's pictures was, he observed, produced by his studying after the life in the public gardens and the open air, and never in the darkened studio.[2]

I asked whether placing the picture in the sun made any difference: he hesitated. I then related the passage from the letters of Rubens,[3] giving the authority; and he admitted this was necessary to prevent the picture becoming yellow.[4]

He also said it is reported that Correggio was a

---

1 The subject was resumed at another interview, and is more clearly explained in p. cxxiii.

2 See Zanetti, della Pittura Veneziana, p. 99.

3 See Gachet, Lettres inédites de P. P. Rubens, 1840, p. 234.

4 I had been previously informed that it was the custom in Italy to place pictures in the air, and to expose them to the heavy dew, and then to suffer them to dry thoroughly in the sun, that this process was carried on after every coat of paint, and that it was owing to this process that the oil of old pictures did not become yellow. I have myself seen pictures so exposed at Milan.

pupil of Mantegna's, but that he was certain from the manner in which his pictures were painted, that he was a pupil of Giorgione's or Pordenone's. He said it was more difficult to imitate Correggio than any other painter. He spoke of his (Correggio's) St. Jerome, at Parma, which he said was the finest picture ever painted, and stated that Correggio had painted the figure of St. Jerome in two days. The first day he painted the head and half the body, passing from the top of the shoulder to the wrist with one stroke of the brush. The next day, he said, he began at the hips and finished at the toes with one stroke of the brush. "This facility," said he, "he obtained from painting in fresco."

I noticed that some of his own pictures had in places that shrivelled look which is sometimes found on Titian's and Palma Vecchio's pictures, which Merimée mentions[1] as a proof that oil or an oleo-resinous varnish had been used.

With regard to the darks being raised above the surface, he said that in Correggio's St. Jerome beforementioned, the blue drapery was the thickness of a five franc piece above the rest of the picture. He showed me a copy he was painting of Correggio's Marriage of St. Catherine, which was unfinished and without the glazings. The paint seemed to be dry and hard as he rapped it with his fingers, and did not shine, excepting a portion of the drapery. A part of the Virgin's red drapery was glazed; the glazing shone like varnish, and was higher than the lights — that is, it stood up with an edge where it joined the lights. I have reason to think that the vehicle used was amber varnish. I inquired what he thought of Lionardo da Vinci's different processes as related by Lomazzo and others; he said they were "niente, niente." That he (Lionardo) was always experimenting ("soffisticare"),

---

[1] De la Peinture à l'Huile, p. 31.

taking up his oils with little bits of cotton, and so on, *but the oil was of little consequence*; that when Titian was asked about his oil, he said, "If you have good oil, you can make a good picture; if you have *bad* oil, you can still make a good picture."

He observed, "the Englishman Laurent (Sir T. Lawrence) thought the secret consisted in wax; but before his death he discovered his error." He also observed, "some use litharge and the oxides of lead with their oils; but nothing can be worse for the pictures than oxides of lead, for they will always darken the colours." Signor A. also remarked that the difference between the methods of Titian and Rubens consisted in the former glazing the whole picture, while Rubens only glazed parts. The numerous sketches, however, left by Rubens, and the testimony of various writers,[1] show that Rubens painted his pictures in a different manner, Rubens beginning his pictures with rich browns, then the silver gray shades, then the various flesh tints; while, according to Signor A., Titian began with the cold colours and finished with the warm; each attaining transparency by a different road.

He also observed that the old painters never used a mahl-stick on large pictures: that Rubens mentions being obliged to have recourse to one in his old age and in declining health.[2] He allowed that the Dutch used them on small easel pictures;[3] and he said that the great painters used brushes with long handles, and stood at a great distance from their pictures;[4] that the

---

1 Rubens' method of colouring is described at some length by Mr. Eastlake, 'Materials,' &c., 408, 409, 483, 494—508, 516—528.

2 If I am not mistaken, this fact is related by Rubens in one of his letters.

3 Cespides mentions a mahl-stick among the implements necessary for a painter. See Pacheco, p. 395.

4 This is said to have been the case with Velasquez, and in modern times with our own Gainsborough. Vasari recommends that the cartoon should be drawn with a piece of charcoal fixed into a long cane.

practice of keeping a youth drawing for years with a hard point (a pencil) was very injurious to his progress as a painter; that he should be taught to draw with his brush, which was flexible and elastic at the point, and which gives freedom and facility of execution; and that there was no practice so good to form a painter as fresco painting. He added, if a man is not a good painter at the age of 18 or 20, he never will be, because he will be too timid to work with proper boldness.

Signor A. called on me again, and I inquired further respecting the method of Titian. He told me that Titian began by painting in the flesh in chiaroscuro with a mixed tint, formed of biadetto, biacca, and a very little terra rossa. He then painted the lights with flesh colour, and laid by the picture to dry. After 5 or 6 months he glazed the flesh with terra rossa and let it dry. He then painted in the shades transparently (that is, without any white in the shadows), using a great deal of asphaltum with them. Signor A. then stated that Titian always represented his subjects surrounded by daylight, and reflected upon by surrounding objects. He also said that in a blue drapery he painted the shades with lake, and then laid on the lights [with white]. That these colours were laid on with great body, and when dry he took a large brush and spread the biadetto over the whole.[1] Signor A. also told me that the beautiful green used by the Venetian painters was an artificial pigment formed of copper and vitriol (he said he could not describe it

[1] Sig. Palmaroli (note to Marcucci, p. 230 n.) states that he succeeded in imitating certain blue tints in draperies by Titian and Paolo Veronese, by drawing and painting the shadows very transparently with the usual brown tint, broken with lake, next to these the blue tint composed of smaltino and a little verdigris. The lights were painted with white and ultramarine and a little verdigris, and when dry the whole was glazed with ultramarine mixed with varnish.

more accurately because he did not understand chemistry), called verde lavita, or verde vita, which was sold so cheap that it might almost be said to be worth nothing.[1] He added, that all the colours used by the Venetians were cheap and common; but that they were made valuable by their mode of using them. He said, "You may use the biadetto as I have directed you with all the Venetian impasto, but in two years it will become green"[2] (meaning to say it could only be used with his vehicle, which he did not describe). I said that in England painters mixed varnish with the colours, and that the pictures cracked. He replied, "that was because they painted with the colours mixed with varnish before the under colours were dry;" but, he added, painters did not all adopt Titian's manner; some could paint a picture in four hours; Rubens painted his Descent in nine days; and painters could so temper their colours that they could complete a picture as fast as their hands could execute it; that their vehicle gave them complete command over their materials, and that every one added more or less of "certe droghe" (certain drugs), according to their convenience and manner of working.

Sig. A. has an accurate and most extensive knowledge of all the writers on painting, and seems to know every thing in these authors that bears on technical points. He quoted passages from Vasari, Ridolfi, Bellori, Zanetti, Guarienti's 'Abecedario,' &c. I asked him whether he knew anything of Errante's paintings at Rome, and of the work he had written,[3] the object of which was to recommend the addition of ground

---

[1] The Venetians used "verde eterno," which is crystallised or purified verdigris, sometimes called distilled verdigris.

[2] It is well known that biadetto and other blues from copper cannot be used with oil without turning green. See Palomino, vol. ii. p. 52. Paolo Veronese frequently mixed them with size instead of oil. See Boschini, Ricche Minere; and Baldinucci, Vita di Paolo Veronese.

[3] Saggio sui Colori, del Cav. D. Giuseppe Errante, Roma, 1817.

rock-crystal and "smalti" to the colours. Sig. A. replied, that it was "Niente, niente," and added, "see what his pictures become in a few years." But he did not explain in what respect the pictures had suffered.

Sig. A. showed me a picture by Bamboccio (Peter Van Laer), and at the same time informed me he possessed a black mirror which was used by this artist in painting, and in which the subject was reflected, "exactly," he said, "like a Flemish landscape;" "and then," he added, "they had only to paint what they saw in the mirror."[1] This mirror was bequeathed by Bamboccio to Gaspar Poussin; by the latter to some other painter, until it ultimately came into the hands of Sig. A.

In order to prevent insects from eating the panels, Sig. A. stated that roche-alum should be mixed with the grounds. He also told me that to destroy the insects which had already got into the wood or ground of pictures, some assafœtida and sulphur should be burnt in an open vessel, over which the back of the picture should be placed at a proper distance; the whole should be then covered in, so as to enclose the smoke arising from these ingredients, which will effectually destroy the insects. The picture may afterwards be washed, if necessary, but the sulphur will not injure the painting. Assafœtida and garlic were both used by the old masters for these purposes.[2]

Sig A. thinks the old masters used madder-lake, and that they burned it to make it darker.

Verona.—We breakfasted this morning with Count ——, who had invited an artist, principally employed in restoring pictures, to meet us. Among other things this artist said that ultramarine was the only blue pig-

---

1 See Du Fresnoy, de Arte Graphica, l. 286, and the Commentary of De Piles.

2 See Pacheco, Tratado, p. 382, &c. Palomino, vol. ii. p. 49.

ment used by the old masters. That they did not use red-lead, but other colours mixed to imitate it; that the Venetians used cochineal lakes. That if they laid oil upon oil,[1] they waited a year between each painting. That there are few painters who have painted so many times over their pictures as Titian; that he did not apply asphaltum over the surface of the picture, but that he used a yellow varnish; that the old masters did not use oil-varnish in painting; that if new pictures were exposed to the sun they would crack to a certainty, unless they were previously wetted, when the process might be repeated several times. (This reminds me of what I had been previously told about exposing pictures to the dew as well as to the sun.) That the canvass was never primed on both sides. He stated that he had found on a picture of Titian's a coat of thin gesso, then a coat of very strong glue, made from pig's-skin, very hard and shining, upon which the picture was painted.[2] I inquired whether the plan described by Sig. A., of getting in the chiaro-scuro with a blueish tint, was that of Titian? He said it was not. That he painted his pictures first with colours of great body, and then finished with glazings. Sig. A. also said he painted his colours with great body at first. This artist mentioned a kind of strong glue called *crocante*, the nature of which I have not been able to ascertain. He prepared his linseed-oil first by straining it; he then put white-lead into a sieve and filtered the oil through it, when all impurities remained behind in the lead, but he never boiled it. He always found that Guimet's ultramarine, mixed with this oil, turned black.

---

1 To understand this expression, it is necessary to state that I had been previously informed that the Venetians painted the solid colours at once with oil, and finished with varnish, so that one layer of colour mixed with oil was not laid on another.

2 That this coat of hard glue is frequently laid between the ground and the picture is proved by Edwards's Report, p. 888. This glue rendered the ground non-absorbent, of which he did not approve.

Venice.—I was introduced to Sig. B., an artist who had been long employed in restoring the public pictures. He had then just dead-coloured a copy he was making of a picture by Gian Bellino. The dead-colouring of the flesh was not so blue in the shades as Sig. A.'s. There was more red with it; indeed the dead-colouring seemed conducted exactly in the same manner as I have seen it done by artists in England The blue drapery was dead-coloured with bleu de Berlin. The following is a summary of the information I obtained from this artist.

1. The grounds consisted of nothing but gesso and glue, which absorbed the superfluous oil.

2. The dead-colouring was always painted with cold colours, the lights white, and the shades warm;[1] you may then make your picture any thing you please.

3. The warm colours were always glazed, over the more solid tints.

4. The vehicle he used for every part of the picture was linseed-oil, boiled on litharge, which was of a high colour, indeed almost black, and which he purchased in bottles imported from Germany. He also showed me another bottle containing linseed-oil thickened in the sun, and mixed with litharge; more than half the contents of this last bottle was a black sediment. He said he required nothing thinner to dilute the colours; he never used spirit of turpentine or varnish in painting. He used bladder-colours. The lake he mixed with his boiled oil, and it stood up on the palette, and when put on his nail did not flow. He said he exposed his pictures to the sun after every process of painting; that this never occasioned their cracking, and that he did not wet them before exposing them to the sun. He paints on the plan always observed in the Venetian

[1] The first shades in the picture he was copying were painted in cold colours. He must have meant that the shades when finished were to be warm.

school. He does not know the Flemish method, or that of Rubens. He knows that his own method is that pursued by the Venetians, from the frequent opportunities he has had of observation when cleaning their pictures. Sig. B. said that Titian *did* put red shades under his blue draperies.[1] He also said, " If you paint your half tints cold, your shades warm, and your lights white, you may glaze your picture to whatever tone you like."

Sig. B. observed that the Venetians used little besides earths, and never orpiment; but that the modern Romans use it in great quantity.

There was a most beautiful deep lake-coloured drapery in an old picture in the room where he was painting. I asked with what colour was that done? He shook his head, and said he did not know, but that the dead-colouring was done with much white, and when dry it was glazed with lake until it was sufficiently dark.

I asked why in old pictures the darks were always raised higher than the lights? He said it was because the painters went over them a great many times. I remarked that the *blues* are always more in relief than any other colour. In this he agreed, but assigned no further reason. His knowledge seemed entirely practical, and his practice derived from his restorations of old pictures. He said Titian used asphaltum, and that blue draperies were glazed with ultramarine.

Sig. C., another artist, who had been frequently employed during the last thirty years in restoring the public pictures at Venice, informed me that Titian generally painted on a ground of glue and gesso, but great care was necessary, when this ground was used on canvass, to make it soft and pliant; the best means of

---

[1] See p. cxxiii., cxxix.

securing this was to add some *milk* to the glue and gesso. That the use of this gesso ground was to absorb the superfluous oil.

He also observed, that Titian sometimes used a ground composed of terra rossa, with oil. That he laid in the subject in the natural colours, or as nearly as he could to nature, only much fainter, and thin of colour, and when dry painted in the colours more solidly; but that he always painted the shades *cold.* He then put the picture by for a year, and corrected it by glazing. That Titian generally used nothing but oil; that he sometimes went seven, eight, or nine times over the same part,[1] with oil glazings, which is the reason why his paintings become more yellow than others; that he sometimes glazed with varnish. That he did not put red under the shades of his blue draperies; but that when this appearance was perceived it arose from his having used a red ground, and when the blue became thin by being rubbed off, the red ground appeared through. That the blue used formerly was called "Turchino," that it may still be purchased, that some old painters still use it, and that it is very apt to turn green. I mentioned that Baldinucci said that Paul Veronese laid on the blue in distemper. He said it was the fact, and that many restorers did not know it until they found it out by taking off the colour unintentionally in cleaning it. That some of Paul Veronese's blues turned green; but those that best retained their colour were found to have been painted in distemper.

Sig. C. observed that Titian and Paul Veronese both painted "con colori di corpo," that they suffered the colours to dry thoroughly before they painted on them again, and this hard, dry body of colours enabled them to apply the glazings and sfregazzi.[2]

---

[1] See Zanetti, della Pittura Veneziana, p. 102. [2] See note, p. 879.

That the brilliant reds were obtained by glazing lake over terra rossa; that the terra rossa they had formerly is now lost; that the best is now brought from Spain.[1]

That for a green drapery, Titian began with terra verde, with, perhaps, giallolino for the lights. When dry he glazed the whole with verdigris, and the shades with asphaltum; both these colours might be rubbed in with the hand. Sometimes he glazed with asphaltum without the verdigris, when he required a warm rich green.

That asphaltum could be easily dissolved for use in spirit of turpentine.

That litharge mixed with oils was very bad for the picture; and that it corroded the paint, as well as darkened the colours.

I saw Sig. C. on the following day, when I again cross-examined him. The following is the substance of the replies elicited:—

That he had never heard of mixing powdered glass with oil or colours.

That he had heard of encaustic painting, but not of mixing wax with oil.

That he had never heard of dissolving resins in oil, and thus making an oil varnish.[2]

---

[1] I am inclined to believe that the red earth, called sinopia, was a finer colour than any of the iron ores now in use as pigments. I have frequently noticed a red of this description on old mural paintings in Italy, and I have also seen specimens of a fine red colour in a dry state in a volume of drawings by Lionardo da Vinci, in the possession of Sig. G. Vallardi, at Milan. Some of these drawings had been executed on the paper of which the books used for keeping leaf gold were made. Before the gold was laid in these books, the leaves were rubbed over with dry sinopia, as we read in Theophilus (lib. i. cap. 24), and the above instance proves that the custom was continued in Italy at least until the time of Lionardo da Vinci.

[2] As far as I could ascertain, oleo-resinous varnishes are not only obsolete in the north of Italy, but they appear to be almost entirely forgotten. When living artists mentioned the colours being mixed with oil and varnish, they always alluded to the mixture of an essential oil-varnish with linseed or nut-oil. In one instance only had I reason to think an oleo-resinous varnish was habitually employed by a living artist.

That he had never heard of placing pictures in the sun, unless it was for the purpose of cracking a new picture to make it look like an old one.

That the reason why old pictures cannot be repaired with oil colours, is that the oil in the old picture has undergone all its changes, that the new tints are made to match the old with oil that will change; and when this change takes place the colours darken, and cease to match the old paint.

That all restorations are now done with colours mixed with varnish; that Sig. Pietro Edwards was the first who introduced this practice.

Sig. C. then remarked that the reason why spirit of wine dissolved old oil paintings, and not new ones painted entirely in oil, was because the greater part of the oil was dried up, and no more remained in the picture than was sufficient to hold the paint together. In other words, that the oil of the old picture was converted into a resin, and, like other resins, was soluble in spirit of wine.

That the Venetians did not paint on gold grounds after the time of Titian.

That the Venetians sometimes laid a coat of white-lead and oil over the gesso ground.

With regard to the use of ultramarine, he observed that it was occasionally used by the Venetians, chiefly on easel pictures. That as this colour was a stone, and not a metal, it never changed colour; but that if used with oil, in time the oil would dry and leave it, and the colour would come off in powder. That it should be used in distemper, and then it would last; that all those painters whose blues have stood, have applied them in distemper.

He also stated that the lake used by the Venetian painters was called "*Lacca di Cambaneri o di Verzino*;"[1] that it may still be purchased at Venice; that

[1] If this lake was made of verzino, it should probably have been called "Lacca Colombina."

it was always glazed, and used with varnish ; that it will not stand with oil. That the blue tinge of the lake in old pictures was occasioned by adding blue to the lake.

That the Venetians and Titian glazed with varnish.

That red-lead might be used with boiled oil, because as the oil was already oxidised to the highest degree, it would not de-oxidise the red-lead (deut-oxide of lead), which would therefore not change.

He said also that Paolo Veronese had originally glazed his red-leads with giallolino, which had been removed in cleaning ; and that the rich bright yellow colour I had noticed in P. Veronese's picture was gamboge.

That the Venetians of the present day make great use of madder-lake ; and that the old Venetian school also possessed this pigment, because the madder-plant grows in the neighbourhood of Venice.[1]

Sig. C. also informed me that Titian glazed much with asphaltum, and that in glazing he used an essential oil varnish, such as aqua di ragia.[2]

He stated also, that the very fine hair-like cracks in old pictures were the effect of time only.[3]

He mentioned that distemper was frequently employed on early oil-pictures, particularly on parts that it was feared would turn yellow, such as white linen.

With regard to the method of Titian, he observed that Titian always softened the shades of flesh with his fingers ; and that he used sometimes nut-oil, and sometimes linseed-oil, and sometimes both together ; but that linseed-oil was the best, because the nut-oil soon became rancid, and when mixed with the colours underwent a sort of fermentation.

---

[1] This reasoning is not conclusive, and it is probable that the Venetian madder was not the best, since in 1565 madder was imported for dyeing by the Venetians from Flanders, under the name of "robbia o vero roza di Fiandra." See 'Libro intitolato Plicto,' Venezia, 1565.

[2] If this be true, whence arise the wrinkles so frequently observed on Titian's pictures, which can only take place on the tough surface of the oil ?

[3] If so, why do not those of Van Eyck, Lucas Van Leyden, Hammelink, Antonello da Messina, Francesco Francia, and others of that period crack also ?

From what this gentleman said I collect that he deems the rapid drying of the vehicle to be of the first importance to the permanence of the colours, which were not likely to change when once dry, and that it is better to use a dark-coloured oil which will *not* change than any of a lighter colour which will change.

Sig. D., an eminent artist, called on me this evening for the purpose of describing the methods of painting practised by Titian and others of the Venetian school.

He began by stating that the only artists to be considered as examples in the mechanical part of the art are Gian Bellino, Giorgione, Titian, Bonifazio, and the two Bassans. That the decline of the art is to be attributed to Tintoretto, who, to save expense, used bad colours in his immense pictures, and to Palma Giovane.

The following was the plan generally adopted by the first-mentioned artists:—

The grounds were made with gesso and a very thin glue; sometimes a little black was added to this by Gian Bellino and others. Over this one or two coats of glue were applied to prevent the ground being too absorbent.

The glue was made of parings of leather.

An analysis of some pictures by Gian Bellino showed they were painted in the following manner and order:—

The ground as above.

Then the outline with ink.

The chiaroscuro painted very thin with brown.

Then the first flesh colour, very rosy, the colour being spread thin.

Second coat of flesh colour made browner, with more yellow, also very thin.

Third coat thin, and with more white, to match the complexion.

This manner of painting keeps the flesh light and clear, because it permits the white grounds and the rosy tints to be seen through.[1]

These colours are all mixed with oil, but the coats of paint being so thin, the colours dry quickly and hard before the oil has had time to become rancid.

The flesh was finished with glazings of asphaltum.

Draperies.—The lights and shades strongly contrasted, the lights pure white or nearly so.

The darks consisted of the pure colour.

Then the glazings with the local transparent colours.

The whole figure, drapery, &c., finished with glazings of asphaltum and terra di Cologna,[2] not much burnt.

Asphaltum was mixed with olio di sasso (naphtha) or spirit of turpentine.

No part of paintings in oil was executed in distemper.

Titian generally began his pictures like Gian Bellino, but instead of painting the flesh three times only, he painted over it four, five, or six times; consequently the ground would not absorb all the superfluous oil, which rose to the top and darkened the picture.

That he frequently laid on the paint with his fingers.

That he did not paint with a thick coat of colour, but always used his colours thin, for the reason given above.

That he frequently covered the whole picture except the white linen with asphaltum.

He painted no part in distemper.

Bonifazio glazed more than any of the others.

Giorgione began like Gian Bellino and Titian. Did not lay in any part of the picture with distemper.

Paolo Veronese painted generally *alla prima* with

---

[1] As to the lights in early oil paintings being semi-opaque, see Mr. Eastlake's 'Materials,' &c., p. 408.

[2] I am not aware that Cologne earth is mentioned in Italian works, at least previous to the 17th century. The colour might have been terra di Campagna.

more body than Titian (whose patience he appeared to want), so that the finished picture was little more than the abbozzo; that is, that he painted up his picture at once.

That he did not employ distemper on his pictures; but with regard to the appearance of distemper observed on his pictures, it had been remarked that the pictures in the churches in Venice that had hung on south walls for a great many years had the appearance of tempera paintings *because the sun had dried up all the oil*, and that the colours of these pictures would wash off with water.

That the old Venetians always exposed their pictures to the sun, and the dew even, for five or six months, in order to prevent their becoming yellow; that he himself had always done this, and without the least injury to his pictures.

That he had never found glue, &c., between the picture and the varnish in *old* pictures, but that this was the modern practice, because the varnish spread and adhered better on the glue than on the oil.

He said also that *Damara* varnish has been found in old pictures, and not *mastic*, which is modern.[1]

That varnish is found mixed with the paint and oil in old pictures.

That he had never heard of colours having been mixed with vernice liquida, as described by Caneparius,[2] and thinks this practice must have been introduced after the decline of the art.

Sig. D. also mentioned that Chilone, an old painter who died about seven or eight years ago, was acquainted with Canal and Canaletto, and that he had told Sig. D. that these artists used oil boiled on litharge, and re-

---

1 It is almost unnecessary to remark that mastic was used by the old masters, and that Damara resin appears to be only recently introduced.

2 Canepario was a Venetian physician. His work, De Atramentis, was published in London in 1660.

commended him to use it also, and that they frequently spread it over the whole picture.

That mastic varnish was sure to crack if used in painting pictures, but that Damara varnish was not so strong and would not crack.

The reason the darks stood higher than the lights on old pictures was because the painter went over them so often, and generally mixed varnish with them.

He said the oil always rose to the surface of the picture and dried dark; that they (the restorers of pictures) take off this crust of oil with potash.

That the green used by the Venetians was *verd' eterno*, and when used with oil the surface turns black; that when cleaning pictures the crust is scraped off and the green beneath is found as fine a colour as ever.

He told me also that he had made experiments by taking off some of the colours with a knife, and had had them analysed by a very skilful chemist (now dead).

The following are the colours he has found on Venetian pictures of the best period :—

White-lead, yellow, red, and other earths, ultramarine, native cinnabar,[1] cinabro d'Ollanda, verd' eterno, Cologne earth, asphaltum, lakes of kermes and madder; Naples yellow, very seldom used; orpiment, used by Bonifazio only; red-lead, very seldom used, and always with varnish; biadetto and verzino lake, used by Tintoretto only; verd' eterno and lake, always laid on with varnish.

Sig. D. stated that he had found no blue but ultramarine, and the reason this colour was raised so much above the surface of the pictures on draperies was that it was used very thick, because as it was coarsely ground it would otherwise look granular and show the white through.

---

[1] Probably the hard red hæmatite, which was called "cinabro minerale" by the Italians.

With regard to the grinding of the colours, he observed that the Venetians did not grind their colours fine, and that he has often picked out large grains of different colours which he has had analysed.

As to the propriety of early varnishing, he said that the Venetians did not varnish their pictures soon after finishing if they could avoid it, but that early varnishing was safer where the coats of colour had been thin than where they were laid on in great body.

He also remarked that many Venetian pictures which had hung in churches on northern walls had been destroyed by damp,[1] while those on south walls had, by the drying away of the oil, assumed the appearance of paintings in distemper.

In reply to my inquiry how he had ascertained the number of the coats of colour on pictures, he replied, "By taking them off one after another with a knife."

Sig. D. told me he generally used *fresh* linseed-oil unboiled; that he had once filtered the oil through animal charcoal, but that this rendered it too thin. The only preparation he used habitually was to filter the oil through four or five sheets of paper.

In consequence of what Sig. D. told me concerning the painting of Paolo, I inquired of Sig. C. whether colla (glue or size) had ever been found on the pictures of Paolo: he said, "Yes, certainly." But he did not *know* that it had been found on the oil-paintings of any other person.[2]

Having frequently observed in Paolo's pictures at

---

1 Extraordinary precautions were sometimes taken at Venice to defend oil-paintings from damp. See p. 880, n.

2 See Orsini, Elogio e Memorie di Pietro Perugino, 208, n., where it is stated that the blue in a picture by this artist at Montone was tempered with flour-paste, or starch (colla di farina). A part of Van Eyck's celebrated altar-piece at Ghent was painted in distemper. This discovery was made accidentally by some ignorant painters washing off the colour in cleaning it. See also Pacheco, Tratado de la Pintura, p. 373.

Venice that the colour appears laid on at once, the *dark* threads of the canvass being visible on great part of the picture without any appearance of a ground, I inquired the reason of this appearance, and why the white threads of the canvass should appear black. Sig. C. told me it was because Paolo frequently painted without any other ground than a little *colla*, just sufficient to bind the loose downy threads of the canvass and enable the brush to move freely; that this being absorbent the oil soaked into the canvass and turned it black, or nearly so.

It will perhaps be recollected that Pozzo, the Jesuit, generally painted without a ground, for he said the gesso caused the colours to change.[1] Callot, the Venetian, painted on the same kind of ground.

I mentioned having been informed that Titian had begun his pictures in chiaroscuro, and alluded to his early picture in the gallery Manfrin; but Sig. C. would not allow that it was painted in this manner, and he denied that Titian ever began his pictures in this way, but that he always laid in the abbozzo with the local colours, but very thinly and light in colour. In support of his opinion Sig. C. said there was an unfinished picture by Titian at Udine, in which part of the abbozzo may still be seen, having never been covered over. The S. Sebastian in the Barbarigo palace is another example by Titian of an abbozzo in his last manner. From the passage in Paolo Pino's Dialogue it appears that the practice of beginning pictures in chiaroscuro with brown was discontinued some time previous to 1548, the date of Pino's work. The probability is that Titian painted in his youth in the Flemish manner, but that he afterwards changed it to that usually ascribed to him.

In the Manfrini gallery is a picture said to have been painted by Titian when he was only sixteen years of

[1] See Lanzi, vol. ii. p. 228.

age. This picture is evidently painted in the manner described by Sig. D., that is, the chiaroscuro with brown and the flesh colours upon this; the lights of the draperies are white, and the local colours glazed over it when dry: this is seen where the lake has been nearly all rubbed off.

I inquired of Sig. C. whether he had found the description given by Boschini [1] of Tintoretto's method of painting correct. He replied that Tintoretto did not begin his *pictures* in chiaroscuro, but that he made the *sketch* in water-colours in chiaroscuro, and then oiled it; and when it was dry he painted in the local colours with oil. Several of these sketches, he told me, were in the possession of Sig. Bernardino Corniani.

I inquired of Sig. C. whether it was true that pictures which had been hung for a very long period of time (say 100 or 200 years) on a south wall were found in a different state from those which had hung on other walls. He answered "Yes: those which have been hung on north walls are always found destroyed by the damp, or at least much injured; because the damp dissolves the glue of the ground and the picture scales off, while those on the south walls are always found dried up and burnt from the effects of the sun."

I also inquired his authority for saying that colours were frequently mixed with milk; he replied, "It is an old tradition; milk was much used by the ancients, and is mentioned by Pliny."

Another day I observed to the same professor, if the Venetians always required so long a period for their colours to dry before they laid on another coat of paint, how could those pictures be painted that were said to be executed in so short a time? He replied

1 See Ricche Minere. Boschini, speaking of Tintoretto, says, "Abbozzava il quadro tutto di chiaroscuro, havendo sempre oggetto principale di concertare tutta la massa come s' è detto," &c.

that Tintoretto had painted his Crucifixion entirely in twelve days, but that he had painted it up at once, without touching the same part twice, consequently without glazing. I asked whether this picture was in good preservation; his answer was "Benone" (excellent). Sig. C. told me also this picture was painted on a ground of flour-paste.[1]

Signor C. told me it had been found that Paolo Veronese's pictures were painted in the following manner and order:—

A ground of gesso.

The abbozzo.

The solid painting with colours mixed with oil.

A light coat of varnish.

Then the blues, vermilions, red lead, and white linen (biancheria), as well as the vermilion tints in flesh, were laid on in distemper, and over the whole picture was a coat of varnish. He added, the tints in distemper were so firmly united, that they would sometimes bear washing twice without being disturbed, and that the restorers were ignorant of the manner in which they were painted, until, having removed the varnish, they found the colours soluble in water.

I asked, how could the distemper colours be made to adhere upon oil colours? He said the distemper colours mixed with size and milk, adhered firmly to the thin coat of varnish, before mentioned.

Signor C. also said that Paolo used a general tint, composed of Cologne earth, or some other brown pigment, a little white lead, a little blue, and a very little terra rossa, which he spread thinly over the shadows,

---

[1] "La prontezza xè meterse davanti
Una gran tela, e de farina propia
Tamisar, e impastar figure in copia,
E senza natural, far casi tanti."
Boschini, La Carta del Navegar, p. 339.

(which had been previously prepared with a grey tint,) sometimes *a velatura*, sometimes *a sfregazzo*, and that he used this tint on every part of the picture, even on the heads.[1]

Speaking one day of the hardness of the old pictures, that when tried with the file, they scaled off, and presented almost a glassy surface, Signor C. said he had experienced this, but attributed it merely to the viscous nature of the oil, and the varnish with which it was mixed.

He also told me the pictures of Cima da Conegliano were painted with solid colours in a light key, and that the shades were laid on transparently with asphaltum. This also was discovered in the cleaning of his pictures; when the varnish was removed, the shades came away with it.[2]

Signor C. stated that the colour so much used by Titian in shading was not, as is generally supposed, terra rossa, but terra di Siena, burnt to different shades of colour, from yellowish brown to almost black.

I asked whether Titian had painted in tempera on his oil-paintings? Signor C. said No; Paolo Veronese being aware that oil darkened the colours, had employed tempera: but he did not know of any other who had done so. I inquired whether Paolo glazed much? He answered, "Very little, and in the shades only."

Did he use asphaltum? No, not that he was aware of. But Tintoretto used it extensively, and some few used *mommia*, but it was not generally approved of.

With regard to the use of oil, Signor C. said that Titian had used more oil than other artists of the same period; that he frequently glazed with oil, although he sometimes used varnish.

---

1 See Zanetti, della Pittura Veneziana, p. 164.

2 I observed that the blue draperies in the pictures of Tintoretto in the Scuola of S. Rocco were painted with a flat and uniform tint of colour, and that the shades had all disappeared, probably in cleaning.

He again mentioned that the Venetian school used little beside earths, and as few metallic colours as possible; and that the latter were used with varnish, except by Paolo Veronese, who applied them in distemper.

Speaking, again, of the practice of Titian, he observed he lived to a great age, and had time to improve, and he changed his methods several times; but those pictures best retain their colour which he painted in the manner of Gio. Bellino; he added, also, he had seen one picture by Titian the colours of which were very brilliant, and this was painted on a ground of terra rossa; and he added, "I think the terra rossa was laid on in distemper." He mentioned that this picture was on a ceiling.

Signor C. observed it was the same with Giorgione as with Titian; his early pictures were bright and clear, but the later ones were dark. He said that he had seen some pictures by the former as dark as could be. The same remark applied to Tintoretto; but he said Gian Bellino's were always transparent and bright.[1] Signor C. seemed to know nothing of the manner in which these pictures were painted; indeed he told me Gian Bellino did not begin his pictures in chiaroscuro. I then showed him the passage in Paolo Pino's 'Dialogue,'[2] "disegnare le tavole con tanta estrema diligenza, componendo il tutto di chiaro et scuro, come usava Giovan. Bellino, perchè è fatica gettata, havendosi à coprire il tutto con li colori," &c. Signor C. said this method was practised by the Roman school; but the restorers in the Venetian territories seem to know little or nothing of the practice of any but the Venetian school.

I called the attention of Signor C. to some passages in the Marquis Selvatico's work,[3] treating of the practice of oil-painting, where it is observed that the coat

---

1 See Boschini, Ricche Minere. 2 Dialogo di Pittura, fo. 16.

3 'Sull' Educatione del Pittore storico odierno Italiano,' Padova, 1842.

of glue and gesso on the panels was, from the beginning to the end of the sixteenth century, covered with a coat of boiled oil. I asked, had he observed this? He replied he had frequently; but he always added the ground should be very absorbent to get rid of the oil.

He observed Titian never used white lead in the grounds. He also mentioned that Paolo Veronese always laid in the abbozzo with very little colour, so that only a faint impression of the colours should be left; and if the colour was too deep, that it was sometimes the practice to rub it down with pumice stone. On this abbozzo he laid the local colours solidly, but he seldom repeated his colours, or employed glazings; that many coats of paint were never found on any part of his pictures. In this respect his manner was entirely opposed to that of Titian, on whose pictures they frequently found seven, eight, or nine coats of colour.

Returning again to the subject of painting parts of the picture in tempera, Signor C. said that he had found the blue painted with varnish only, and that he had been assured that it was frequently painted in distemper, and that in this case there was no oil paint under it, but that where the skies in Paolo's pictures had turned green, they had been found to be painted in oil.

Speaking again of the old method, and of the different practice of modern artists in restoring pictures, Signor C. observed, "I think we have lost something. Every artist restores in his own way, and the present method of painting is very bad, much worse than it was in the last century." He added, that in restoring he had used oil with a small quantity of thin mastic varnish, in which a little honey was put, and that this had cracked *less* than other vehicles.

Signor C. said it was an error to paint with the colours *too dry*.[1] That this was the case with the

[1] See Requeno, Saggi sul Ristabilimento dell' Antica Arte de' Greci e Romani, vol. i. p. 163.

*

beautiful copy by Baroccio of Raphael's Transfiguration. When this picture was lined, the person entrusted with it neglected to secure the face of the picture by pasting paper over it; the consequence was, that when they attempted to raise the picture after lining it, they found that, by wetting the back in order to fix the new canvass, they had dissolved the ground, and that the picture, which had become very dry, was detached from it, and had dropped to pieces, and that it could never be put together again properly.

He also told me that when he had been painting with oil, and had found the oil penetrate through the gesso ground, he had laid glue and gesso on the back of that part where the oil had soaked through to absorb it,[1] and when that was saturated, he had scraped it off, and had laid on fresh gesso, and had repeated the operation until all the superfluous oil was absorbed; but this was only in cases where he had found it necessary to repeat the coats of oil colour. Everything shows that the Venetians endeavoured to use as little oil as possible.

Signor C. observed that another cause of the darkening of pictures has been the excessive use of asphaltum and mummy; that many used them as solid colours (di corpo), whereas they should be used in glazing only, and very thin, and that they should be mixed with varnish only, and should not be ground with oil or spirit of turpentine. He said, also, that he believed mastic was not much used by the Italians of the time of Titian, and that those who had analysed Venetian pictures had never found wax in them.

He also observed that Paolo never painted the abbozzo with colours tempered with water, and that yolk

---

[1] Merimée (de la Peinture à l'Huile, p. 31) mentions having seen a picture by Sir Joshua Reynolds, in which the latter had employed a similar contrivance to get rid of the superfluous oil, where he had found it necessary to repaint the head.

of egg had not been found on his pictures; that the tempera vehicle used by Paolo consisted of animal glue.

Signor C. showed me a picture painted with boiled oil which had not been varnished. I inquired how the glossy surface was produced? he replied, "by polishing it with a soft cloth."

I saw this morning Signor E., an artist who had restored some pictures by Paolo Veronese. He told me his plan, formed from observation of Titian's pictures, is to lay on the canvass a thin ground of gesso and glue, made of the primings of leather; over this he spreads a coat of colour mixed with oil (the colour is drab, made, I should think, of a little umber, white, and a little black). The gesso ground absorbs the oil, which makes the back of the canvass quite yellow. On this ground the artist paints the whole picture with solid colours, mixed with raw linseed oil, without any glazings. He says that glazings are never permanent, and that nothing can make them so; and as a proof, he told me there were in a certain palace several pictures by Titian, which had always been covered by glasses. That he was present when the glasses were removed for the first time; when, to the surprise of every one present, the glazings were found to have evaporated from the pictures, and to have adhered to the inside of the glass. I considered this incredible, and it certainly appears to require proof, although it must be recollected that Lionardo da Vinci says, "Il verde fatto dal rame, ancorchè tal color sia messo a olio, se ne va in fumo," &c. If the colour evaporated from the picture, it would certainly be retained by the glass; and this artist distinctly said that all the glazings were fixed on the inside of the glass, exactly above the painting, and that the effect of the different colours on the glass was very singular. From that time, he added, that he had left off glazing his pictures.

The same gentleman informed me that he had never found any colours in distemper on Titian's paintings; and that what people took for tempera painting on the pictures of Paolo Veronese was not really so, but was done in the following manner:—

The first painting was executed with colours mixed with oil, and the part to be painted on with metallic colours (or with such as darken with oil) was left to dry until it was *tacky;* the metallic colours were then applied, mixed with *water only.* The water evaporated, and the oil left on the picture in the first painting was sufficient to bind the upper layer of colours firmly to the picture.

Of the Grounds used by some of the principal Painters of Bologna.

[A communication from an eminent liner of pictures in that city.]

Panels were formerly prepared with gesso only, applied with the pencil in the same manner as is done by gilders; after this, the panels received a coat of glue or oil to prevent the colours from sinking in. In this way Francesco Francia prepared his panels, and Samacchini,[1] Sabbatini,[2] and Tibaldi[3] both their panels and canvass. Then came the Carracci. Ludovico[4] used no other priming than a thin coat of white lead and ochre mixed with oil, sufficiently thick to ensure a smooth surface, and he employed this priming as a shadow colour, which we know too well was the cause of the great change observable in his pictures. But Ludovico Carracci was not sufficiently remunerated for his pictures to enable him to incur great expenses in the priming. Annibale, his cousin, sometimes employed successfully on canvass, "creta,"[5] mixed with

[1] He died in 1577, aged 45.

[2] Also called Andrea di Salerno, was born about 1480, and died about 1545.

[3] Called also Pellegrini da Bologna, was born in 1527, died 1591.

[4] Born 1555, died 1619.

[5] Is this "creta" the same as "gesso Bolognese?"

white lead. Instead of "creta," Guercino generally adopted in his early pictures a thin priming of marble dust and size, and his pictures are thought to owe much of their brilliancy to this circumstance. In his second manner, the priming was thicker. When lining Guercino's pictures, it is generally found necessary to remove the ground as well as the canvass. The ground sometimes appears to be composed of hard and gritty terra rossa, and which is thought to have been procured outside the Porta Castiglione at Bologna. Grounds are now prepared extremely well at Bologna and at Rome. The canvass is all the produce of Bologna, which province produces hemp of the finest quality.

The most durable and unchangeable pictures are stated to be those painted on gesso. In the eighteenth century coarse open canvass, the holes of which were filled up with strong glue, was introduced; pictures painted on these canvasses were not durable, for in time the colours scaled off.

The following particulars relative to the method of painting in oil as practised by the Parmasan School were communicated to me by a distinguished painter of Parma:—

1st. That gesso grounds were used.

2nd. That neither size nor varnish was laid over this ground, which was suffered to absorb the oil.

3rd. That the picture was begun in chiaroscuro.

4th. That the first colours were painted with raw nut oil.

5th. That in the glazings and retouchings varnish was used.

I was informed that a professor of that city had devoted much time and attention to the study of the good method of oil-painting, and that he knew more about it than any other person.

The professor had been suffering from illness; but at

the request of the Cav. Pezzana, of the Ducal Library at Parma, he kindly permitted us to pay him a short visit. He perfectly recollected having sent a bottle of varnish to an English artist, and he said that the reason he had not written to him was because he had lost the use of his hand, and could not write legibly; that he had written out the recipe for some person, but that it proved useless, for the varnish could not be made from this recipe on account of the difficulty of the manipulation.

I asked, could he tell me the ingredients? He said it consisted of amber in the natural state, and the higher coloured the better, dissolved in oil of spike, and this was rendered slower in drying by the addition of oil (balsam) of copaiba.

I immediately inquired whether he had found any document showing it was used by Correggio?

He said No; it was the result of his own observation and study.

I asked whether he had ever analysed any of Correggio's pictures?

He replied without hesitation, No, no; and as I saw it was painful to him to talk, I took my leave.

On my return to the library, I was told that the professor *had* analysed parts of pictures by Raphael, and had found amber.

In one respect my informant was probably mistaken, —namely, as to the artist whose pictures had been analysed, since the professor had said the varnish he had made was that of *Correggio*. It appeared, however, quite clear that amber varnish had been found on the pictures of one or other of these great painters.

§ 2. Colours used in Painting.

The Italians appear generally to have exercised the same care in the purification and preparation of their pigments as the Flemish, Dutch, and French artists. This is apparent from the directions preserved in those

manuscripts which treat in an especial manner of the manufacture of colours, but it is seldom alluded to in the treatises on painting. The omission in the last-named works is easily accounted for on the supposition that the different processes of washing, purifying, and grinding colours were taught to the students during the first six years of their long apprenticeship. It is probable also that many studios possessed manuals or handbooks like those published in the following pages. The Byzantine MS. of Mount Athos, the Treatise of Cennini, and several MSS. now in the British Museum, are works of this class. In the MS. of Le Begue several instances are mentioned of the loan of MSS. of this description by different painters to Alcherius; and Cennini wrote his treatise, as he himself informs us, for the benefit of all who studied the arts. It was, therefore, less necessary to introduce such directions in works of higher pretensions.

Next, perhaps, in importance to the purification and preparation of the pigments was their agreement or incompatibility with each other. This subject occupied the attention of artists at a very early period; it is noticed in the third book of Eraclius,[1] and in the Marciana MS.[2] The subject is also alluded to in the Paduan MS. and in the Treatise of Lomazzo;[3] and these passages are useful in showing what pigments were actually mixed together by the old painters, and what mixtures were to be avoided. Among the latter were verdigris and white lead, orpiment and white lead, indigo and cochineal lake, Indian lac lake and white lead. In some cases the mixtures of pigments were not such as would be recommended by modern professors of chemistry; but it is possible that, as the old masters were so select in the choice of vehicles for certain colours, they could regulate the drying of

[1] Cap. lvii. p. 252. [2] P. 609.

[3] Trattato, p. 193—195. See also De Piles' Elémens de Peinture, p. 110.

these pigments in such a manner as to prevent their exercising any chemical agency upon each other. Boschini[1] praises the colours used by Gian Bellino, especially the ultramarine, which, he says, compared with the moderns, put the latter to shame by their greater vivacity and beauty. Boschini attributes this not altogether to the goodness of the colours, but to the skill of Bellino in every part of the art.

The choice of good pigments was another point which engaged the attention of artists: a few hints on this subject may be collected from the work of Volpato.[2] The same work also contains directions[3] for burning earths of different colours.

The different drying properties of the several pigments were also studied by the old painters, and the desiccation of some which were too long in drying was assisted by the addition of pounded glass, white copperas, or verdigris, with or without boiled oil, as the nature of the colour required.

The action of oil on the pigments, and especially on mineral pigments, was also well understood by the old masters; and where oil was known to be injurious, varnish, or, in some instances, size was substituted for it.

White Pigments.

Several white substances used as pigments and in the preparation of colours and grounds, are mentioned in the following treatises. The white pigment universally employed for oil painting is *white lead,* which is mentioned in the MSS. under its various synonymes of albus, blacha, bracha, blanchet, biacca, and ceruse. It was called albayalde by the Spaniards.

White lead is considered a good dryer, and is even used to render oil more drying; it is, therefore, remarkable that it should be classed in the Brussels MS.[4]

---

[1] Ricche Minere. [2] P. 745. [3] P. 745, 747. [4] P. 818.

among the colours which do not dry well. De Piles, however, states[1] that it dries with difficulty, especially in winter, if ground with new oil, or if it has been recently ground. The 'Traité de Mignature' of Christophe Ballard[2] contains "a great secret to make white lead dry without changing." This consists in tempering it with oil of turpentine.

The Italians, and especially the Venetians, were extremely careful in the preparation of their white lead,[3] which was generally purified by washing. Fra Fortunato of Rovigo, in his 'Raccolta di Secreti,' gives the following recipe "for rendering white lead extraordinarily white. Take white lead in scales, select the finest quality, grind it well on marble with vinegar and it will become black, then take an earthen vessel full of water and wash your white well, and let it settle to the bottom, and pour off the water. Grind it again with vinegar and again wash it, and when you have repeated the operation three or four times, you will have white lead which will be as excellent for miniature painting as for painting in oil."[4]

There is scarcely a doubt that the pigment called "*lime*" was the preparation of lime mentioned by Cennini[5] and Imperato,[6] under the name of Bianco San Giovanni. The lime was prepared by macerating it in water until it had lost all causticity. According to Imperato, pulverized white marble was added to the

---

1 Elémens de Peinture, p. 140.

2 Lyon, 1693, 6th Ed., p. 216. The first edition was published in 1682.

3 "Lindo alvayalde de Venecia"—"el meyor alvayalde que se hallare, i lo es sobre todos el de Venecia." Pacheco, Tratado, pp. 354, 387.

4 Per rendere la biacca più bianca straordinariamente. Prendete biacca di piombo in scaglie, elegete la più bella, e macinatela bene sul marmo con aceto, e diventarà nera, allora prendete un vaso di terra piena d'acqua, e lavata il vostro bianco bene, poi lasciatelo bene dar in fondo, e verrate l'acqua per inclinazione. Tornatela a macinare con aceto et a lavare; e fatta questa operatione med^a. 3 o 4 volte, che havera una biacca che sarà perfettam^te bella tanto per miniare, quanto per dipingere a olio.

5 Cap. 58. 6 Istoria Naturale, lib. iv. cap. 13.

lime. This pigment was used in fresco painting. It is known to later authors by the name of *biancho secco*.[1]

White chalk, *marble dust*, *gesso*, the *bone of cuttle fish*, *alumen*, and *travertine*, were occasionally used as white pigments. They were also frequently mixed with transparent vegetable colours to give them body.

Calcined hart's-horn or *bones* were used occasionally as a white pigment.[2]

Egg-shell white was employed in fresco painting. With reference to this pigment, Lomazzo[3] says, that "there is another thing which, in fresco painting, causes the colours to remain unchanged as when first applied on the damp lime; and this, which is one of the rare inventions belonging to the technical part of the art, consists of the shells of eggs finely ground, and mixed in greater or less proportion with all the colours."

Terra di cava, *terra da boccali*, or *terretta*, a white earth used by potters. It is mentioned by Volpato[4] and Baldinucci[5] to have been employed in the priming for oil paintings.

The pigment called *alumen* by Eraclius[6] appears to have been allume scagliuola, a kind of stone resembling talc, of which, when calcined, is made the "gesso da oro," or gesso of the gilders, which is also used for the grounds of pictures. According to Eraclius[7] it was prepared for painting by grinding with gum and water, and was distempered when required with white of egg.

Travertine is a calcareous stone, sometimes light and porous, sometimes dense and heavy. It is of various colours, white, grey, yellowish, reddish yellow, and variegated. It is found at Pisa and Tivoli. The travertine from Tivoli is white. It was used by painters to give a body to lake made from verzino.

---

1 Lomazzo, Trattato, pp. 192, 194.

2 Sloane MS., No. 1754; Strasburg MS., cited by Mr. Eastlake, 'Materials,' p. 133.

3 Trattato, p. 191.

4 P. 730.

5 Voc. Dis.

6 P. 245.

7 P. 232.

White marble is mentioned as a pigment for tempera painting by Palomino.[1]

"A most beautiful white pigment," probably for miniature painting, is described in the Paduan MS.[2] It is composed of powdered Venetian glass (cristallo) and sulphur, and is precisely similar to the opaque white glass used for painting pottery, for which recipes are given in the second and third books of Eraclius.[3]

Yellow Pigments.

Arzica.—Two pigments are known by this name in medieval MSS.

The first kind of *arzica* is mentioned by Cennini (cap. 50), who says that it was much used at Florence for miniature painting. With regard to the nature of the pigment, he observes merely that it is an artificial colour. The Bolognese MS., written about the time of Cennini, or soon after, proves[4] that it was a yellow lake made from the herb "gualda," which is the Spanish and Provençal name for the Reseda luteola. The plant has been used as a yellow dye not only in England but in all Europe, from a very early period. This yellow lake was known to the Spanish painters under the name of ancorca[5] or encorca, and when used for the kind of painting called "estofado," was mixed with lemon juice and weak size.

The second kind of *arzica* is stated to be a yellow earth for painting, of which the moulds for casting brass are formed.[6] A yellow loam is still used for this purpose in the foundries at Brighton. It is brought by sea from Woolwich, and when washed and dried it yields an ochreous pigment of a pale yellow colour.

---

[1] Museo Pictorico, vol. ii. p. 113, 152.

[2] P. 704. [3] P. 201, 205. [4] P. 483.

[5] Indice de los Terminos Primativos de la Pintura, appended to Palomino's Museo Pictorico.

[6] Table of Synonymes, p. 19, 23.

When burnt it changes to an orange colour, which is likely to prove valuable in painting.

Arzicon, or *Arsicon*.—In the Table of Synonymes arzicon is considered synonymous with *arzica*. This is not the case. Le Begue is, however, correct in saying that it is the same as orpiment. It is undoubtedly a contraction or corruption of *arsenicon*, which Vitruvius (lib. vii. cap. vii.) says was the Greek name for orpiment. The term arzicon must not be confounded with *azarcon*, the Spanish name for *red lead*.

Auripigmentum or *Orpiment*.—There was a native as well as an artificial pigment known by this name. The former is found in masses in the neighbourhood of Naples, and in other volcanic countries. It has the great advantage over the artificial pigment of being less poisonous. The artificial pigment only seems to have been known to Cennini.[1] Being difficult to grind, powdered glass was mixed with it, as we are expressly told, for this purpose.[2] And Pacheco directs[3] that orpiment should be mixed with linseed oil, made drying by boiling it with red lead or copperas in powder.[4] For miniature painting it was tempered with gum-water and white of egg. Its brilliant yellow colour renders it a desirable pigment for draperies in oil painting, but it is not durable when mixed with oil, and dries very slowly. The author of the third book of Eraclius says,[5] "If you mix oil with it, it will never dry." Lebrun remarks,[6] that "fat oil should be added to orpiment to make it dry, otherwise it will never dry." Lomazzo also mentions[7] that it was mixed with pulverized glass, but he does not state for what purpose the latter was added. De Mayerne, however, states[8] that Vandyck was accustomed to mix powdered glass with orpiment

[1] Cap. 47. [2] P. 503. [3] Tratado, p. 388.

[4] He was evidently unacquainted with the fact that lead decomposes orpiment. [5] P. 234. [6] P. 813. [7] Trattato, p. 192.

[8] See Mr. Eastlake's 'Materials,' &c., p. 534.

to make it dry. Pacheco[1] recommends it for the same purpose; but there is some doubt as to the propriety of this mixture.

In the third book of Eraclius it is directed[2] that orpiment should be crushed in a leather bag, and then ground upon marble with a little calcined bone; in this respect the directions resemble those given in the Strassburg[3] and also in the Sloane MSS., No. 1754, where calcined hartshorn is said to be the only substance which can be safely mixed with orpiment to lighten it.

Orpiment is mentioned by Biondo[4] among the pigments used by the Venetians; and Boschini states[5] that it was employed by Pordenone and by Paolo Veronese. A professor of painting at Venice informed me that he had found it, by analysis, on the pictures of Bonifazio only. It is generally asserted, and there appears every reason to think justly, that orpiment should not be mixed with any other colour, and especially with white lead, the bad effects of which were well known to the Italians.[6] But there is evidence that the Italians were in the habit of mixing it with ultramarine or with indigo to make a brilliant green.[7] The Marciana MS.[8] recommends that white lead should be laid under orpiment, because it has no body.

This pigment was called jalde, or oropimente, by the Spaniards. Pacheco directs,[9] that for the second or half tints of draperies the orpiment should be burnt in an iron shovel over the fire. Palomino, after describing the method of painting draperies with orpiment, remarks,[10] that he did not approve of the colour, which dried very badly and required many precautions in using it, and that it was, moreover, liable to turn black;

---

1 Tratado, p. 388. 2 P. 239 3 Materials, &c., p. 133, 438.
4 Della Pittura, cap. 24, f. 20. 5 Ricche Minere.
6 See p. 609, and Armenini, lib. ii. cap. 8.
7 Cennini, cap. 53, 55; Borghini, Riposo, p. 170; Marciana MS., p. 611. 8 P. 611. 9 Tratado, p. 388. 10 Vol. ii. p. 252.

this, he adds, may be prevented by varnishing it as soon as it is dry.

Giallolino, *Giallorino*, or *Gialdolino*, strictly signifies a pale yellow. It is a diminutive of *giallo*.

There appears to be so much confusion in the accounts of this colour by different writers, that it will be necessary to treat of it at some length.

According to Borghini[1] and Baldinucci[2] there were two kinds of Giallolino: the first, called "Giallolino fino," which was brought from Flanders, was used in painting in oil, and contained lead; the other, which was brought from Venice, was composed of "Giallo di vetro" and "Giallolino fino" above mentioned. Lomazzo[3] speaks of three kinds of Giallolino, which, he says, are artificial pigments, but the terms in which he mentions them are not sufficiently precise to determine exactly their names or composition.

Sig. Branchi[4] found on analysis that the giallolino of the old pictures at Pistoia, mentioned in the documents published by Ciampi, consisted of the yellow oxide of lead, which, he said, was known by this name in the sixteenth century. In support of this he quotes Cesalpino, who mentions a pigment then prepared from burnt or calcined lead, which was commonly called giallolino—"pigmentum pictoribus . . . quod hodie arte paratur ex plumbo usto, vulgoque giallolinum vocant."[5] And again, Cesalpino[6] says, "the ashes (calx) of burnt lead assume a yellow colour, on account of the black soot mixed with the white; tin, however, gives a white calx.[7] Painters use the former for lights and for representing flame, calling it giallolino. Potters use the

---

1 Riposo, p. 166. 2 Voc. Dis.

3 Trattato, p. 192. 4 Lettera di Branchi, &c., p. 13.

5 De Metallicis, lib. ii. cap. 62. 6 Lib. iii. cap. vii.

7 Thomson (Annals, &c., p. 166) says, that the grey oxide of tin, when brought to a full red heat, takes fire, and acquiring an excess of oxygen, passes to a yellow colour.

latter to give a white colour to their vessels." Professor Branchi adds, that this is confirmed by Ferrante Imperato,[1] a Neapolitan writer of the same century. This author says, "Giallolino, which is made of burnt ceruse (the first degree of alteration by fire), imitates the colour of the yellow broom."

Dr. Fabroni,[2] of Arezzo, analysed the colours of a miniature of the fourteenth or beginning of the fifteenth century, and he ascertained that the yellow pigment consisted of "massicot," which, he says, is the first gradation of the "cerussa usta" of the ancients.

In further confirmation of the above statements it may be observed, that neither Cennini, Borghini, Lionardo da Vinci, Lomazzo, Baldinucci, nor the Paduan MS., mention "massicot," while they all speak of giallolino.[3] It may also be observed, that Lebrun, the author of the Brussels MS., mentions[4] no yellows but ochre and *massicot*; the latter, he says, serves for the fine or bright yellows. Van Mander, Hoogstraten, De Bie, and Beurs,[5] in enumerating the yellow pigments used by the Flemings, mention ochre, massicot, and yellow lake, to which all but De Bie add orpiment. Bulengerus[6] also names massicot, which he calls "fin jaune."

As a further proof of the identity of these pigments, it may be observed, that Haydocke, the translator of Lomazzo's Treatise on Painting, published in 1598, translates *giallolino* by the word *massicot*.[7] The last au-

---

1 Istoria Naturale, lib. iv. cap. 42.

2 Ricerche Chimiche sopra le Miniature di un Manuscritto, Memoria del Dr. A. Fabroni di Arezzo, letta nelle Adunanze Accademiche de' 13 Genn. e 17 Febb. 1811.

3 See Cennini, Trattato, cap. 46. Borghini, Riposo, p. 166. Lionardo da Vinci, Trattato, cap. 352, 353. Lomazzo, Trattato, p. 191, 192, 193, &c. Baldinucci, Voc. Dis.

4 Cap. 1, No. 6; cap. 7, No. 5.

5 See Mr. Eastlake's 'Materials,' &c., p. 438, 440.

6 De Pictura, &c., lib. ii. cap. iii.

7 A Tracte, containing the Artes of curious Painting, Carving, and Build-

thority is particularly valuable on account of the translation having been made so soon after the publication of the original work.

Lomazzo mentions[1] "Giallolino di fornace di Fiandra e di Alamagna." From this it would appear that two kinds of Giallolino were brought from the north into Italy. These were probably the two kinds of massicot mentioned by Félibien, who states[2] they were made of calcined lead, "Le massicot jaune et le massicot blanc," or as they are called in Jombert's edition of the Elémens de Peinture, "le massicot doré et le massicot pâle." Haydocke translates the above-mentioned passage thus, "Yeallowe of the Flaunders fornace, and of Almany, commonly called *masticot* and *generall*."

There is no doubt, therefore, that the "Giallolino Fino" and "Giallolino di Fornace di Fiandra" was massicot, or the yellow oxide of lead, the "Fin jaune" of the French.

The yellow pigment prepared from lead is described by Theophilus (cap. i.), who, however, does not give it a name. The same pigment is mentioned in the MS. of Le Begue.

We now come to the second kind of factitious giallolino which Baldinucci[3] states was brought from Venice, and was composed of the giallolino di Fiandra and giallo di vetro. Borghini says[4] nearly the same. In the Bolognese MS. No. 272, is a recipe for "Vetrio giallo per patrenostro o ambre," the ingredients of which are lead 1 lb. and tin 2 lbs., melted and calcined. The recipe which follows this, No. 273, is entitled "A fare zallolino[5] per dipengiare," and the directions are to

ing, written first in Italian by Jo. Paul Lomatius, painter, of Milan, and Englished by R. H. (Haydocke), student in physick, 1598, p. 99.

[1] Trattato, p. 191. [2] Principes, &c., p. 299.

[3] Voc. Dis. [4] Riposo, p. 166.

[5] It will not escape observation that the *gi* in this word are changed into *z*, as was usual among the Venetians.

take 2 lbs. of the above-mentioned glass, 2½ lbs. of minium, and ½ lb. of sand from the Val d'Arno: the ingredients are to be pulverized finely, and then refined in the furnace. I can scarcely doubt that this is the second kind of giallolino mentioned by Baldinucci and Borghini. It may also be the third variety mentioned by Lomazzo.[1]

It must be observed that Marcucci does not mention giallolino among the modern Italian pigments; he describes[2] three yellow pigments, namely, *giallo di Napoli* (Naples yellow), which he says is composed of the yellow oxide of lead and the oxide of antimony, *massicot*, or the yellow oxide of lead, and *giallo minerale*, which was composed of muriate of lead.

The earliest notice I have met with in Italian writers of a pigment called Naples yellow, is in the work of Pozzo the Jesuit.[3] The name he applies to the pigment is "Luteolum Romæ dicitur Luteolum Napolitanum," and he enumerates it among the pigments to be used in fresco. He also gives a list of colours improper for this kind of painting, among which we find cerussa, minium, and luteolum Belgicum, which can be no other than giallolino di Fiandra. The conclusion then is unavoidable that the luteolum Napolitanum was not the yellow oxide of lead. In the French translation of Pozzo's Treatise on Fresco-painting[4] the term luteolum Napolitanum is very properly translated Jaune de Naples, and luteolum Belgicum by Jaune de Flandres. In other parts of Jombert's edition of the 'Elémens de Peinture,'[5] two kinds of massicot, the yellow or golden and the pale or white, are mentioned; but they are not identified with jaune de Naples, which

---

1 Trattato, p. 192. 2 Saggio, &c., p. 66.

3 The Treatise on Fresco Painting, appended to his work on Perspective, published at Rome, 1693—1702.

4 See Jombert's ed. of the Elémens de Peinture, by De Piles, Paris, 1766.

5 Elémens de Peinture, pp. 252, 286, &c.

is mentioned as a distinct colour. The Italian translator of Pozzo's treatise[1] renders luteolum Napolitanum by giallolino di fornace, which he says is called giallolino di Napoli, and luteolum Belgicum by giallolino di Francia. This writer does not appear to have been aware that giallolino di fornace and giallolino di Fiandra were synonymous. Giallolino di Francia appears to be a mistake for giallolino di Fiandra.

Félibien,[2] Pomet,[3] Pozzo,[4] and the author of the article "Fresque" in the Encyclopédie describe the pigment jaune de Naples as a natural production found near mines of sulphur, which is used in fresco-painting, although it is not so good as the colour formed of ochre and white. M. d'Arclais de Montamy, in his Treatise on the Colours for Enamel Painting, describes it as a stone of a pale or deep yellow colour, which appears to be composed of a species of yellow sand, loosely combined. He believes it to be the production of a volcano. He adds that Naples yellow may be considered as saffron of Mars, first produced by a volcano, and that then the colour was brought to perfection by remaining in the earth, or as a ferruginous substance, the vitrification of which was afterwards decomposed.[5] Cennini's description[6] of this pigment is as follows:— "There is a yellow colour called giallolino, which is artificial and very compact. It is as heavy as a stone, and difficult to break. This colour is used in fresco, and lasts for ever (that is on walls and on tempera pictures). It must be ground like the preceding with water. It is difficult to grind; and before grinding,

---

1 At the end of the Abecedario Pittorico (Naples, 1733).

2 De l'Architecture, &c., 1697, p. 292.

3 Histoire Générale des Drogues.

4 See the French translation of this Treatise in Jombert's edition of the Elémens de Peinture, by De Piles, p. 191.

5 Treatise on Painting and the Composition of Colours, translated from the French of M. Constant de Massoul. London, 1797. P. 137.

6 Trattato, cap. xlvi.

as it is very difficult to pulverize, it should be broken in a bronze mortar, in the same way as the lapis amatito. When employed in painting, it is a very beautiful yellow; and with this colour and other mixtures which I will describe to you, you may paint beautiful foliage and herbage. And I have been informed that this colour is a real stone, produced in volcanoes; and it is for this reason that I said it is formed artificially, but not in the chemical laboratory."

From this account it is evident that Cennini is describing a native mineral which he considers to be produced by volcanic agency—"Però ti dico sia color artificiato, ma non di archimia." The accordance of this description with that of the jaune de Naples just mentioned is apparent. It is therefore certain that there was a native yellow pigment found in the neighbourhood of volcanoes, the nature of which was not well understood, which was known by the name of giallolino or giallolino di Napoli and jaune de Naples. This is the opinion also of Branchi and Watin.[1] In this case therefore giallolino and giallolino di Napoli (Naples yellow) were really synonymous. There is also an artificial pigment called Naples yellow or jaune de Naples, which, by some authors, has been considered to consist of an earth coloured with weld (gaude, Reseda luteola) and by others to be composed of the oxides of lead and antimony with other ingredients. The last is the general opinion, and there appears to be no doubt the modern pigment of this name is composed of these oxides.[2] The vegetable pigment above mentioned is the *arzica* of Cennini, the Le Begue, the Bolognese MS., and Borghini, and the *ancorca* of Palomino.[3]

---

1 Lettera di Branchi, p. 12.

2 See Merimée, de la Peinture à l'Huile, p. 110; Marcucci, Saggio Analitico de' Colori, p. 66; Lettera di Branchi, p. 12; Bachhoffner, Chemistry as applied to the Arts, &c.

3 Indice de los Terminos Primativos de la Pintura—appended to Palomino's Museo Pictorico.

I consider it therefore established that there were three kinds of giallolino employed by the old Italian Masters, namely:—

1. A native mineral yellow pigment known by the names of giallolino, giallolino di Napoli, jaune de Naples, luteolum Napolitanum.

2. An artificial pigment which was composed of the yellow protoxide of lead, and which was called giallolino, giallolino fino, giallolino di fornace di Fiandra, giallolino di fornace, giallolino di Fiandra, luteolum Belgicum, genuli (the last is a Spanish term) and massicot, of which there were two varieties; namely, the golden or yellow and the white or pale massicot.

3. An artificial pigment made at Venice composed of giallolino fino and a certain kind of "giallo di vetro," or vitreous yellow, for which a recipe is given in the Bolognese MS. No. 273, in the Venetian dialect, and which appears to have been the hornaza of the Spaniards.

I consider it also established that there are two kinds of Naples yellow, namely:—

1. A native mineral pigment found in the neighbourhood of volcanoes, the nature of which is not accurately known, and which was called giallolino, giallolino di Napoli, and jaune de Naples, and which is synonymous with the first kind of giallolino above mentioned.

2. An artificial pigment now in use composed of the oxides of lead and antimony, called also giallo di Napoli, jaune de Naples, and Naples yellow, which was not known to the old Italian artists.

From the above statements it will be seen that it is scarcely possible to determine which of the three pigments called "giallolino" is alluded to when the term occurs alone in writers on art. It is certain, however, that one or other of these pigments was much used by the Italian masters. Giallolino was recommended by Lionardo da Vinci[1] to be mixed with white lead and

[1] Trattato, cap. 353.

lake for flesh tints. There is reason to suppose it was also used by Raphael, since it is mentioned in an account of payments for colours found on the back of a drawing by the great painter preserved in the Academy at Venice, and supposed to be in his hand-writing.

It was seldom found among the colours of Venetian pictures which have been analysed. It is stated on the authority of Boschini [1] (who mentions that the pigment was not generally approved by the Venetians) to have been used by Giacomo Bassano and Paolo Veronese, and it is also enumerated among the pigments named by Biondo.[2]

Massicot is however frequently disapproved as a pigment, especially when mixed with white.[3] We have the evidence of Cennini that the native pigment called giallolino was a durable colour. Pacheco remarks that he has employed *genuli*, which has surpassed in brilliancy and beauty the best orpiment, excelling it in durability; he adds that it is preserved in water like white, and is very drying.

Giallo in Vetro, or Giallo di Vetro.—Borghini states[4] that this pigment, which is used in fresco, is made in the glass furnaces, and he recommends that it should be purchased ready made. It is probable, as has been before observed, that this pigment was of the same nature as the vetrio giallo mentioned in the Bolognese MS. No. 272 to have been composed of tin and lead calcined.

The *ochres*, so remarkable for their durability and variety, will always be among the most valuable yellow pigments. Many varieties are enumerated by writers on art, among which may be mentioned arzica, ochre de ru, mottée de sil, &c. The best kinds are sold in Italy in the lump, and Volpato recommends [5] that such

---

1 Ricche Minere. 2 Della Pittura.
3 See Mr. Eastlake's 'Materials,' p. 440. 4 Riposo, p. 166.
5 P. 745.

should be preferred to those which are sold in powder, because the first are in the natural state and no other material is mixed with them; "for," he continues, "the vendors are accustomed to falsify everything."

During the middle ages, an imitation of the Attic ochre of Pliny was in use. This pigment, to which the name of "Sillacetus" was given, was a preparation of white chalk or gesso, saturated with the colour extracted from the wall-flower[1] (Viola lutea).

Vegetable yellow pigments were of two kinds—those which were precipitated on a white earth, such as the different kinds of yellow lake, and those which were used as transparent colours, without any other preparation than that of expressing and inspissating the juice of certain plants. Of the latter kind were *saffron*, the *zafferano* of Cennini, and aloes; the latter was chiefly used for colouring varnishes, or for heightening the colour of verdigris in the manner recommended by Lionardo da Vinci.[2]

Giallo santo was a kind of yellow lake, which was made from various plants. It was sometimes prepared from the berries of the buckthorn[3] (spincervino), sometimes from the flowers of the yellow goat's-beard (barba di becco), sometimes from the flowers of the yellow broom, sometimes from weld or dyer's weed: the latter is the arzica of Cennini and the Bolognese MS. The sillacetus of the Table of Synonymes was a yellow lake.

The French call pigments of this description "*stil de grain*," and include under them not only those pigments which are of a pure yellow colour, but such as incline to green. The English term for this class of pigments is or was "*pink*." Thus we have "*Dutch pink*," "*Italian pink*," "*brown pink*," &c.

Volpato observes[4] that giallo santo should be of a

---

[1] Table of Synonymes, p. 36. [2] Trattato, cap. 120. [3] P. 708. [4] P. 744.

fine colour, that in grinding it should become very liquid, so as to require but very little oil to temper it, and that it should dry very quickly, which is a sign that it is pure; but if it hardens and requires a great deal of oil in grinding, this is a proof that it contains dust and other impurities, and in this case it dries slowly and fades on the pictures.

As another test, he directs[1] that the colour should be exposed to the sun; if it faded, it was bad. He also mentions that it should not be kept in water. Giallo santo appears to have been extensively used by the Italians, and although it is included among the colours which Boschini says the Venetians "detested like the plague," it appears, on his own evidence, that it was employed by Giacomo Bassano in shading yellow drapery. The pigment is also mentioned by Biondo, by Armenini, by Borghini, and in the Paduan MS. Malvasia says that it was used by Tiarini and Cavedone.

Saffron, *zafferano*, the crocus of the middle ages, is produced from the flowers of the crocus. Peter de S. Audemar informs us that saffron was produced in France in his time; but he says the French saffron was not good; he mentions that this drug was imported from Spain and Italy, and that the best kind was brought from Sicily, and was called *coriscos*. The plant is cultivated extensively in England in the neighbourhood of Saffron-Walden, and the name of the place is derived from this circumstance. It was brought into England from the Levant in the reign of Edward III., and the manner in which it was introduced is thus described by Hakluyt:[2]—"It is reported at Saffron-Walden, that a pilgrim, purposing to do good to his country, stole a head of saffron, and hid the same in his palmer's staff, which he had made hollow before on purpose, and so he brought this root into this realm with venture of his

---

[1] P. 744. [2] See Beckmann's Inventions, vol. i. p. 179, n.

life; for if he had been taken, by the law of the country from whence it came, he had died for the fact."

To these vegetable pigments may be added *gamboge*, which is a gum resin that flows from the Hebradendron Cambogioides. It derives its name from Kamboia, a river in Siam, in the vicinity of which the gum is obtained in abundance. It was certainly in use in the Venetian territories at the period when the Paduan MS. was written, and is believed to have been employed by Paolo Veronese. It was sometimes purified by being ground up with lemon juice and roche alum.[1]

Gamboge is prepared for painting in oil by depriving it of its gum. Marcucci recommends[2] the following method:—"Gamboge of the finest colour is to be ground with water; it is then to be put into a china cup, and a sufficient quantity of water is to be poured on it to cover it twice its own height; after being left thus two days, the supernatant water is to be decanted, and the resin which remains at the bottom of the water is to be dried. When quite dry, a quantity of spirit of turpentine sufficient to cover it is to be poured over it, and the cup is to be placed upon warm ashes until the resin is quite dissolved and incorporated with the turpentine. A little nut oil is then to be added, and it is to be preserved for use." Marcucci adds, "this is excellent for glazing yellow and green draperies; for the latter it must be mixed with ultramarine." Other modes of preparation are mentioned by Mr. Eastlake in his recent work.[3]

It appears from the Brussels MS.[4] that gamboge was in use in France in 1635. Palomino remarks[5] that this pigment, which he calls "Gutiambar," was employed to glaze yellow draperies, and that it dried so badly as to require the addition of the common drying oil.

---

1 P. 660. 2 Saggio, &c., p. 135. 3 Materials, &c., p. 442.
4 P. 784. 5 Museo Pictorico, vol. ii. p. 53.

A recipe for an artificial pigment somewhat analogous to the modern pigment called "Gallstone" appears in the second book of Eraclius. It consisted of the gall of a large fish precipitated on a white earth. It was said to have resembled orpiment in colour.

Aloes.—The inspissated juice of the aloë spicata. The plant is a native of Africa. The finest kind of aloes has a brilliant reddish-brown colour, and is translucent at the edges of the fragmented pieces; its fracture is smooth and conchoidal, its odour aromatic and rather agreeable, its powder deep gold colour, its taste intensely bitter and nauseous. But such is rarely found in trade; it is generally opaque, of a dull brown, when it is called *Hepatic aloes*, often passing into black, when it is denominated *Caballine aloes.* It appears to be a mixture of gum, extractive, and a little resin. It is nearly soluble in boiling water, but as the solution cools, some resin and altered extractive are thrown down; the alkalies and their carbonates form with it permanent solutions, and proof spirit dissolves and retains it with only a slight precipitation of resin. Caballine aloes are mentioned by Lionardo da Vinci[1] as an improvement to the colour of verdigris, and he recommends its solution in warm spirit (aqua vitæ).

Orange-coloured Pigments.

The ochreous pigment called *Arzica* in the Table of Synonymes, affords, when burnt, an orange-coloured pigment, which is likely to prove a valuable addition to the palette.

Orange or *red orpiment—realgar.*—This pigment, as well as yellow orpiment, is sometimes found native. It is also prepared artificially by melting it in a crucible over a charcoal fire, and when cool, grinding it.[2]

Burnt or orange orpiment is mentioned by Borghini[3]

---

1 Trattato, cap. 120. 2 Paduan MS., p. 662. 3 Riposo, p. 166.

and by Lomazzo,[1] who observes with regard to this pigment, which was said to be of the colour of gold, "and this is the alchemy of the Venetian painters." Matthioli makes a similar remark; after describing the manner of converting the yellow orpiment into red by burning it, he says, that every one may provide himself with the latter by inquiring for it in the "calle" (lanes or narrow streets) of Venice, where colours are sold. It is probable that red orpiment was used by some of the Venetian artists,[2] since a colour resembling it is frequently seen on pictures of this school, particularly on those of Bonifazio. A few ounces of a pigment of the colour of orange orpiment was given to me at Milan by an artist who told me it was used by Titian, and that he had procured it at an old colour-shop in Venice. He called the colour *rauschel minerale*, and said that he had shown the pigment to a colourman at Bergamo who knew it by that name. From the name, therefore, it may be conjectured, that the pigment was native red orpiment or realgar, and that the name by which it was known to this artist was intended for *rüschegel* or *rauschgelb*. This pigment was called *jalde* or *oropimente quemado* by the Spaniards,[3] and *sandaraca* by the Greeks.[4] It is considered to be less durable than yellow orpiment, and extremely corrosive, for Merimée relates[5] that where it had been employed on flower-pieces, it appears to have corroded the priming. The term *sandaraca* was also applied during the middle ages to *red lead*, or *minium*.[6] With the artists of this period it must have been a favourite colour; if we may judge from the numerous recipes for preparing it which

---

1 Trattato, p. 191.

2 Marcucci is of this opinion: see Saggio, &c., p. 226—228. According to this writer, it was also used by Fra Bartolomeo: see Saggio, &c., p. 215.

3 Palomino, vol. ii. p. 66.

4 Diosc., lib. v. cap. 80, by Matt., p. 1428.

5 De la Peinture à l'Huile, p. 124.

6 See Table of Synonymes, p. 36. S. Audemar, p. 141.

occur in old MSS. on art, and from its being mentioned so much more frequently than vermilion. It was purified by washing it in a horn with wine and water.[1] When to be used on walls it was to be mixed with gum water, when on parchment with egg, but when on wood with oil. For illuminating books it was frequently mixed with vermilion.[2]

It is mentioned by many Italian writers on painting,[3] and has been found on Venetian pictures of the best period. Boschini informs[4] us that it was used by Pordenone, by Paolo Veronese,[5] and by Maffeo Verona. Sig. Pietro Palmaroli states[6] that it was employed by Titian. According to Marcucci, it was also used by Fra Bartolomeo.[7]

Lomazzo states[8] that it was sometimes mixed with lake. Lebrun recommends[9] it in painting flesh, and says, "If some minium be mixed with white lead and a little fine lake, a most beautiful carnation tint will be formed, as I know from experience." Bisagno also observes[10] that in order to make vermilion dry, a little minium may be mixed with it. The general opinion seems to be that minium should be used alone, and according to the observations of the Venetian restorers of pictures always with varnish.

Palomino alludes[11] more than once to its want of durability; he says that, "after a time it throws upon the surface a kind of salt which destroys the juice of the picture." Perhaps this defect may be corrected by purifying the red lead in the manner described by De Mayerne,[12] who observes, "If you extract the salt from

---

1 Le Begue, p. 143, 295. 2 Ibid., p. 141, 297.

3 Biondo, c. 20. Lomazzo, Trattato, pp. 191, 193. Borghini, p. 166. Volpato, p. 745. Paduan MS., p. 655.

4 Ricche Minere. 5 See also Marcucci, Saggio, &c., p. 228.

6 Note to Marcucci, p. 226. 7 Saggio, &c., p. 217.

8 Trattato, p. 195. 9 Brussels MS., p. 820, 822.

10 Trattato della Pittura, p. 206. 11 Vol. i. p. 56; vol. ii. p. 52.

12 See Mr. Eastlake's 'Materials,' &c., p. 452.

minium by washing it with distilled vinegar the remainder does not fade and dries very well." When minium is thus purified, it appears to resemble the pigment formerly known by the name of Saturnine red; which consisted merely of minium washed in large vessels of distilled water, which was changed every forty-four hours, till the surface was quite free from extraneous matter, and the colour ceased to blacken at the edge of the vessel. The colour was afterwards purified with spirits of wine.[1] Pacheco mentions[2] that native red lead (azarcon de la tierra) was used in his time in tempera painting.

Red Pigments.

A great variety of native red pigments have always been used in painting. They all owe their colour to iron.[3] Of this kind were the *sinopia* of Pliny and Cennini, the *terra rossa d'Inghilterra, terra rossa di Spagna, Majolica, ferretta di Spagna, almagre, Pavonazo, Indian red, light red, Venetian red, hæmatite, lapis amatito, sanguine, terra rubea, brunus, brown red, mottée de sil, red ochres.*

The *terra rossa d'Inghilterra*, so frequently mentioned by Italian writers, is still sold in Italy, where it is imported from England.

The colour called *Venetian red* is procured from Verona. Besides its use in painting, this earth was formerly much employed in making the bricks of which many of the old buildings in Venice are constructed. The fine colour of these bricks, heightened perhaps by their contrast with the green waters of the

---

1 Constant de Massoul, p. 205.

2 Tratado, p. 345. Native minium occurs amorphous and pulverulent, but when examined by the lens exhibits a crystalline structure. It is supposed to be an oxide of lead, and to arise from the decomposition of galena, in which it commonly occurs. Phillips, Min., p. 337.

3 The different kinds of red earth used in painting are fully described in the Introduction to my work on Fresco Painting, pp. xiii.—xxxiv.

narrow canals, can scarcely have escaped the observation of travellers.

Hill, the translator of Theophrastus, mentions that what is sold in the shops as *Indian red* is a native red earth [hæmatite] found in England. He states (p. 122, n. 9), "I have a specimen of some from the Forest of Dean in Gloucestershire, very little inferior to the sort brought from Ormuz in the Persian Gulf, which is so much esteemed and used by our painters under the name of Indian red. It is indeed so like, both in colour and quality, that it is used for it, as the people employed in taking it up informed me, and sent to London to be sold under its name. On comparing it with some of the true Persian kind, which I had from the East Indies, I find it of a paler colour, but of a much finer texture." The real Indian red has also a sparkling appearance, which is wanting in the common sort.

The *Sinopia* of Pliny and Cennini was, as has been before mentioned, a red earth originally brought from Sinope, but medieval writers north of the Alps gave the name of *Sinopia*, or *Sinopis de Mellana*, to a kind of lake made either of the gum of the ivy ground with vinegar and mixed with wheat flour, or of the gum of ivy and madder.[1] Sinopis is sometimes written for cinnabar, as in p. 68, where it is said to be made of mercury. The term *Vermiculus* is used by Le Begue[2] to denote the red colour called "coccus," which was undoubtedly the coccus of the ancients. It is synonymous with kermes.[3] In the Bolognese MS. it is put for vermilion.[4] *Cinnabar*, or *vermilion*, is of two kinds, natural and artificial. Both are stated to have been used by the Italians and Spaniards in painting, but the former was preferred for fresco-painting, although the latter was of a much finer colour. If we may judge from the recipes in old treatises, the medieval

[1] Le Begue, p. 145. [2] Table of Synonymes, p. 38.
[3] Matth. 1085. [4] P. 449.

artists employed the latter only. Directions for refining and purifying it are given in the Bolognese MS., the Paduan MS.,[1] and in the recipes at the end of the Abecedario Pittorico.

Lebrun observes,[2] that vermilion is frequently adulterated with lime; to detect this he recommends that some should be put on the blade of a knife and heated; if good, it would, when cold, be of the same colour as before; but if one side of the knife remained black, and then became brown and dark, this would be a proof of its impurity.

Native cinnabar does not appear to be mentioned by writers on art previous to the latter part of the 16th century, when it is spoken of together with the artificial by Lomazzo[3] and Borghini.[4] It is also mentioned and described by the Spanish writers Cespides, Pacheco,[5] and Palomino,[6] and by Félibien.[7] I was informed by a Venetian artist that both native and artificial, or, as he called the latter, Dutch cinnabar, had been found among the colours of Venetian pictures which he had procured to be analysed. It is difficult to imagine how native cinnabar can be distinguished by chemical analysis from artificial, since mercury combines with sulphur in two proportions only, forming the protosulphuret which is black, and the bisulphuret (vermilion or cinnabar) which is red.[8] The difficulty may perhaps be explained by a knowledge of the fact that the name of "mineral cinnabar" was given by the Italians to the hard red hæmatite. Agricola says, that the stone

---

1 See pp. 500, 660, and 664.

2 Brussels MS., p. 814.

3 Trattato, p. 191, 192.

4 Riposo, p. 167.

5 Tratado, p. 342.

6 Museo Pictorico, vol. i. p. 359; vol. ii. pp. 53, 149, 340.

7 De la Peinture, p. 299.

8 The atomic composition is stated to be as follows:

The protosulphuret—1 atom mercury 200+1 atom sulphur 16=216.

The bisulphuret—1 atom mercury 200+2 atoms sulphur 32=232.

According to Phillips (Min., p. 358), the composition of native cinnabar is quicksilver 84·5—sulphur 14·75.

which he calls schist (after Pliny) resembled in appearance *minium*, and that the painters called it *cinnabar*; that when calcined it imitated the colour of cinnabar. This is confirmed by Borghini,[1] who states that lapis amatita (the hæmatite) is called by some persons "mineral cinnabar." Baldinucci[2] and Alberti[3] make the same remark; and Pungelone[4] mentions a design by Correggio, in which may be seen several "pentimenti" drawn with "matita, comunemente detta cinabro minerale." It is not, therefore, unreasonable to conclude, that the mineral cinnabar said to have been found on Venetian pictures may have been the colour procured from the hard red hæmatite burnt; at the same time it must be acknowledged, that if the pigment so called had actually been subjected to analysis, its composition must have been settled beyond a doubt, since no chemist could have mistaken a combination of mercury and sulphur for an ore of iron. Vermilion has been used by all Italian and Spanish painters. Lomazzo[5] and Pacheco[6] direct it to be sometimes employed in flesh tints. Its use by Flemish writers in painting has been mentioned by Mr. Eastlake.[7] Cennini recommends[8] that cinnabar should be purchased in the mass and never bruised or ground, because it was frequently adulterated with minium or pounded bricks.

Lakes.—The red lakes used by the Italian painters were either of animal or of vegetable origin, or a mixture of both kinds.

To the first class belonged the lake produced from kermes or grana, the most common form of which was the lacca di cimatura, lac lake, and cochineal lake. To the second class belonged the lake made from Brazil

---

1 Riposo, p. 168. 2 Voc. Dis.

3 Diz. Enc., tit. *Cinabro minerale*, and *Lapis*.

4 Life of Correggio, vol. i. p. 174.

5 Trattato, p. 312. 6 Tratado, p. 386. 7 'Materials,' &c., p. 448.

8 Trattato, cap. xl.

wood or verzino. The third description was composed of a mixture of the first and second kinds of lake.

Kermes or *Grana.*—The dead bodies of the female insect of the coccus ilicis, which lives upon the leaves of the prickly oak. It appears to have been known from the time of Moses, and has been employed from an early period in India to dye silk. It was called by the Greeks *coccus baphica*, by the Latins *granum infectorium*, by Pliny *coccigranum*, by the Arabs *charmen*, *kermes*, and *chermes*, by the Germans *scharlack ber*, by the Spaniards *grana para teñir* and *grana in grano*, by the French *vermillon*, and by the Italians *grana* or *grana da tentori*.[1]

The kermes grains or berries, whence the name grana, are mentioned (probably as a dye) in the Lucca MS. and the Clavicula[2] under the name of coccarin, and in the latter MS. they are identified with cinnaberin and vermiculum: "Vermiculi tereni qui in foliis ceri nascitur—coccarin nascitur, sicut supra dictum est, in foliis ceri." They are constantly to be traced as a dye during the middle ages in the South of Europe, and are noticed in a commercial agreement between Bologna and Ferrara as early as 1193, and in the Statutes of Marseilles for the year 1287. At Montpellier no other dye was permitted to be used for the finest red stuffs.[3] In the fourteenth century Florence[4] and Venice[5] were celebrated for their red stuffs dyed with kermes, which the latter city exported to other parts of Italy. The

---

1 See Matthioli, p. 1085.

2 See Mappæ Clavicula, p. 41.

3 Depping, vol. i. pp. 241, 293, 300.

4 Ibid., vol. i. pp. 234, 235.

5 Filiasi, Saggio, &c., pp. 153, 154 n. Hellot (L'Art de Teinture, Paris, 1701, pp. 244, 264) said this red colour was called "Ecarlatte de graine," formerly "Ecarlatte de France," and now "Ecarlatte de Venise," because it was much used there, and more was made there than any other place. He adds, "the red draperies of the figures in the old Brussels tapestries were dyed with this ingredient, and their colour, which in some of these tapestries is 200 years old, has lost nothing of its vivacity." In his time kermes was only used to dye wool for tapestry.

red stuffs dyed with kermes or grana found their way into the towns of the North of Europe. Pierce Plowman (whose 'Vision' is supposed to have been written in 1350), in describing the dress of a lady richly clad, says that her robe was of "scarlet in grain;" that is, scarlet dyed with grana, the best and most durable red dye. The import of the words "in grain" was afterwards changed, and the term was applied generally to all colours with which cloths were dyed which were considered to be permanent; in this sense it is still used.

The idea of preparing a pigment directly from the kermes grains appears not to have suggested itself to the early painters, who employed the rather indirect process of boiling the clippings or shearings[1] of cloth dyed with kermes in ley, and then precipitating the colour with alum. The colouring matter, combined with alumina, was well washed to remove the salts, and after being dried on a porous stone or brick was preserved in small cakes. The pigment so produced was the "lacca di cimatura di grana da rosato," commonly called "lacca di cimatura," which appears to have been in common use as a red pigment until the seventeenth century.[2] Neri is probably the first author who gives a recipe for a red pigment prepared directly from the kermes. The method he recommends was, he said, invented by himself at Pisa.[3] Other recipes for lake from the kermes berries are contained in the Paduan MS.[4] Lake from "quermes" was used in France for oil and miniature painting in 1682.[5]

As a dye the kermes was considered among the most durable of all colours. M. Hellot says,[6] "From the

---

1 These consisted of the loose wool, which was removed from the face of the cloth, in order to produce a smooth surface.

2 See Cennini, Trattato, cap. 44; Le Begue, p. 91; Bol. MS., p. 433, &c.; Secreti di D. Alessio, part i. p. 103; Canepario, p. 335.

3 Arte Vetraria, lib. vii. cap. 119.

4 P. 703.

5 See Traité de Mignature de C. Ballard, p. 14.

6 L'Art de Teinture, p. 264.

experiments which have been made with the scarlet dye from kermes, as well by exposure to the sun as by different re-agents, it has been found that there is neither a better nor more durable colour, and yet it is used nowhere but at Venice." This author attributes the solidity of the colour of the kermes to its being nourished on a shrub possessing astringent properties, which have been communicated to the insect; for he remarks "that all barks, roots, woods, fruits, and other substances of an astringent nature, furnish durable colours for dyeing."[1] The Italian painters were aware of this property possessed by astringent substances of rendering colours more durable, and we find accordingly that assafœtida,[2] a handful of the bark of the white beech, or three or four small branches of the Lombardy poplar, were boiled with the lake in order to make the colour more permanent.[3] The bark of the white beech was considered best for rose colours; the practice was not confined to the red from kermes, but extended also to madder lake.

Cremisi, *Cremisino*.—Although there appears to be no doubt that *chermes* and *grana* were really synonymous, yet it also appears that the term cremisino was applied in Italy during the time of Matthioli to the colour procured from certain berries or grains attached to the roots of the pimpinella,[4] as well as to cochineal. Matthioli adds,[5] "There is now brought from the West Indies by way of Spain a new kind of *cremisino*; and as great quantities of it are made in Italy, it has lowered the price of silks of this colour." This cremisino from the West Indies, brought by way of Spain, can be no other than cochineal; it is therefore certain that it was well known and abundant in Italy at least as early as

---

1 L'Art de Teinture, p. 271. 2 Bol. MS., pp. 435, 442.

3 Traité de la Peinture au Pastel. Paris, 1788.

4 Poterium sanguisorba. The Burnet, probably the Bruneta of the Sloane MS. No. 1754. 5 Matt., p. 1085.

1549, the date of Matthioli's work. This may also be considered to be proved by the 'Tariffa Perpetua di Zuane Mariani,'[1] in which *cremese* is mentioned as well as "grana" and "polvere di grana." Both are also spoken of in the 'Plicto.'[2] These notices are certainly evidence that the terms were not synonymous. Matthioli further states that at the time his work was written a lake was made for painters from the cremese or cremisino, and Caneparío [3] carefully distinguishes *grana* from *karbisini* or *cremesi*. Cochineal lake is mentioned in the Paduan MS.[4] In this treatise it is stated to have been prepared for painting by boiling it with lemon-juice, garlic-juice, and burnt alum; this treatment would probably communicate to it a scarlet tint. The anonymous author of the 'Trattato di Miniatura'[5] states that the colour called "lacca fina di Venezia" was made from cochineal after the carmine had been extracted, and that this pigment was made at Paris.

The cochineal insect is produced on different species of cactus. The most perfect variety is that which breeds on the cactus coccinillifer. When the Spaniards first arrived in Mexico they saw the cochineal employed by the native inhabitants in communicating colours to some ornaments and in dyeing cloth. Struck with its beautiful colour, they transmitted accounts of it to the Spanish ministry, who, about the year 1523, ordered Cortes to direct his attention to the propagation of this substance. The pigment prepared from cochineal, though extremely beautiful, is not so durable as those from lac and kermes. It is, however, worthy of trial whether it may not be rendered more durable by

---

1 Published at Venezia, 1567. 2 Venice, 1557.

3 De Atramentis diversi Coloribus, pp. 326, 336.

4 Pp. 661, 699, 703, 709.

5 This work, which was published at Turin in 1758, appears to be a translation of Ballard's Traité de Mignature. In this last work, carmino is stated to be made of cochineal and rocou (Bixa orellana, an American plant).

boiling it with some astringent bark, as recommended with regard to kermes lake.

Lac, Lacca.—The term *lacca* occurs in the Lucca MS., and also in the Clavicula; but it does not appear whether it is used to signify gum lac or the juice of the ivy, which is described by Eraclius in the chapter entitled "De Edera et Lacca." These notices appear rather to refer to a dye than to a colour for painting. In 1220 the Catalans and Provençals imported lac into their ports for the purpose of dyeing.[1] As a pigment lac was known in Italy at least as early as 1409, since recipes for making lake from it are given in the book lent by Fra Dionisio to Alcherius. Other recipes are contained in the Bolognese and Paduan MSS. and in that of Fra Fortunato of Rovigo.

Lac does not appear to have been mentioned in the 'Tariffa Perpetua' of Mariani, but it was used in dyeing at Venice in 1557, when the 'Plicto' was published; and it is among the articles enumerated in the 'Tariffa' of Bartolommeo del Paxi de Venezia.[2] Lac lake was in use at Venice in Matthioli's time, and even as late as that of Caneparius.[3] It was also in use at Naples in 1733.[4]

Madder, Rubea Tinctoria, Robbia overo Roza di Fiandra, Sandis, Granza, Garancia, Warantia, "Rubea Major, id est Waranz."—A red pigment prepared from this root is mentioned in the Sloane MS., No. 1754, and in that of S. Audemar,[5] the same recipe being introduced into both treatises. In the former work it appears also to be alluded to under the term *gorma*:—"Gorma quedam herba est que trahit in purpuram et affertur de quadam regione et hec *rosa* dicitur." Rosa, as has been already mentioned, is sy-

[1] Capmany, Memorias, &c.; and Statuts de Marseille, cited by Depping, vol. i. p. 144.

[2] Venezia, 1503.

[3] De Atramentis, p. 331. This work was published in 1660.

[4] See recipes at the end of the Abecedario, published at Naples.

[5] Le Begue, p. 145.

nonymous with Robbia.[1] It is possible that the *menesch* of Theophilus may have been madder, since *mnitsch* is the Indian name for this plant.[2] In the third book of Eraclius[3] madder is enumerated among colours for painting; it is also mentioned in the Table of Synonymes.[4] From the time the latter work was written until that of Neri all traces of madder as a pigment seem to be lost. This author gives[5] a recipe for madder and verzino lake; he remarks that in making these lakes a larger proportion of madder or verzino must be allowed than of the cimatura, because the colour afforded by the two former is not so deep as the latter. He concludes by observing, "In this manner you will obtain very fine lake for painters at less expense than that made from 'chermisi;' the madder lake especially is very beautiful and pleasing to the eye." From these expressions it may almost be inferred that Neri was recommending what he considered to be a new pigment; had it been known to painters, it would have been unnecessary to advert to the beauty of the colour. With the exception of Neri the pigment does not appear to be mentioned by Italian writers until 1733, when madder lake is noticed among other lakes in the recipes for colours at the end of the 'Abecedario Pittorico.' The French writers are equally silent on this subject until 1788, when the anonymous author of the 'Traité de la Peinture au Pastel' observes, "Madder is, of all the plants known in our climates, that which yields the most durable red, and the addition of the juice of the poplar makes it still more permanent. The juice of the bark of the white beech is still better for rose colours." Constant de Massoul[6] also mentions madder lake, which he says is less likely to change than any other.

---

1 See the 'Plicto.'

2 Nemnich, Polyglotten Lexicon.

3 P. 249, 251.

4 P. 34.

5 Arte Vetraria, Firenze, 1612, lib. vii. cap. 118.

6 Art of Painting, p. 208.

Madder is enumerated among the pigments which it is stated were used by the great Venetian painters.

Madder has been used in dyeing from time immemorial, and by the Orientals as well as the inhabitants of Europe. It was cultivated and used extensively for dyeing in the neighbourhood of Avignon and Marseilles, and it is mentioned in the statutes of the latter city as early as 1287.[1] It grew wild all over Italy, and that produced in the neighbourhood of Rome was at one time much esteemed. In the middle of the sixteenth century Dutch or Flemish madder was preferred to the Italian,[2] since the former only was imported into Venice.

Verzino Lake, or Lake from Brazil Wood.—The identity of these pigments is fully proved from various passages in these MSS.,[3] and the numerous recipes which have been transmitted to us by writers on the arts show the extent to which verzino lake was formerly used. The dyewood from which the pigment was prepared was known to the Hebrews, as appears from the dictionary of the Rabbi David Kimchi, entitled 'Book of Roots,' and was called by the Arabs "albakim" or "bacam."[4]

Verzino Colombino.—Marco Polo states that the best verzino grew in the island of Ceylon, whence Depping supposes that the term "Verzino Colombino" was derived from Colombo, the capital of that island. The colour to which Pierre Pomet[5] and Marcucci[6] give this name was composed not of verzino, but of the clippings of scarlet cloth; the former author remarks that the preparation of this lake is attended with much

---

1 Depping, Histoire, &c., vol. i. p. 293.

2 See 'Plicto.'

3 See Le Begue, p. 53. Bol. MS., p. 441. See also Mr. Eastlake's 'Materials,' &c., p. 114, and Caneparius, p. 297.

4 Dict. Universel, Français et Latin, vulgairement appelé Dictionnaire de Trevoux, Art. Brésil. Paris, 1732.

5 Histoire Générale des Drogues, vol. i. p. 34.

6 Saggio, &c., p. 125; and see also Trattato di Miniatura, p. 29.

difficulty, and that it is seldom conducted successfully out of Venice, because the Venetians add to the alumina a very white earth, which causes the lake to become very light (in weight). A pigment of this description is still sold at Venice in masses of a pink colour and powdery texture, which breaks easily and is remarkably light in weight. It is said this pigment should be well burnt. A recipe for "Laque Colombine," composed of Brazil or other dyewood, will be found in Ballard's 'Traité de Mignature.' Verzino or Brazil wood is not the only wood mentioned in these MSS. which furnished red colouring matter. Red sandal-wood,[1] Campeachy or logwood, are also mentioned; and it appears from Ballard's 'Traité de Mignature' that when that work was published the Brazil wood of America called by the French "le Brésillet de Fernambouc" (*cæsalpinia Brasiliensis*) was used in making lake instead of the Oriental Brazil wood, or verzino (*cæsalpinia Sappan*).

Venetian Lake.—It is difficult to say what this pigment really was. The anonymous author of the 'Trattato di Miniatura' before mentioned states that the "lacca fina di Venezia" was composed of cochineal after the carmine had been extracted. Pierre Pomet[2] says that it was made of cochineal, Brésil of Fernambouc, burnt alum, arsenic, and Egyptian natron, or white soda. According to Palomino[3] Venetian lake was composed of gum lac and grana, or cochineal.

Florentine Lake.—The old pigment was probably the same as lacca di cimatura, since this was the principal kind of lake described by Neri,[4] whose work was published at Florence, although he appears to have resided at Pisa. The modern pigment of this name is made of cochineal and other ingredients.[5]

---

1 P. 517. 2 Histoire Générale des Drogues, vol. i. p. 33.

3 Museo Pictorico, vol. ii. p. 340. 4 Arte Vetraria, lib. vii. c. 116.

5 Dizionario delle Droghe, di Chevalier e Richard, Tradizione da F. du Pré, Venezia, 1830.

Lake from Ivy.—The medieval painters were accustomed to prepare a red colour from the juice or gum which in warm countries flowed from the ivy in the month of March. This colour differed from the lakes before described, inasmuch as the juice or gum was inspissated by boiling, and not precipitated upon a white earth.

The Purple of the Ancients is mentioned in the Table of Synonymes.[1] It is also mentioned in the passages borrowed from Vitruvius in the third book of Eraclius.[2]

It has been observed that the characteristic of the Venetian school was the free and unsparing use of a powerful blue, I would add of a very beautiful and cool lake colour also, which in all pictures of the Venetian school, from the Vivarini to Tintoretto, invariably retains its colour. The Venetian lakes always incline to blue — an effect which was probably produced by the mixture of blue with the lake. Tassi, in his 'Lives of the Bergamasque Painters,' speaking of the beautiful blues and lakes found on the cinque-cento pictures, says: "Where will you find such colours now?"[3] These considerations make it most important to ascertain, if possible, what kind of lakes were used.

The lakes of Florence and Venice were particularly celebrated. We have seen that in both cities the lacca di cimatura was most common. Cennini[4] gives the preference to the pigment prepared from gum lac, and it is generally believed that the latter was the lake most frequently employed by the old masters, especially by those of the Venetian school:[5] the colour of the lake in pictures of this school favours this supposition.

Pacheco, on the contrary, prefers the Florentine to

---

1 P. 25, 33. 2 P. 251.

3 He published in 1793. 4 Trattato, cap. 44.

5 Note by Tambroni to Cennini, Trattato, cap. 44.

the lac lake, as more durable, but he says lake of Honduras is not bad. By the last term he probably meant the lake from cochineal or American Brazil wood. Matthioli states[1] that in his time four kinds of lake were made; namely, 1st, that from *cremesi* or *cremisino*, which was undoubtedly cochineal; 2nd, that made from *grana* or *kermes;* 3rd, that from gum lac; and 4th, that from verzino, which was the worst and least valued of all the others. Lomazzo mentions more than once, in enumerating the colours used, "le lacche tutte," which is a proof that several kinds of lake were used in his time; and in another place he speaks of "grano," whence we may infer that the kermes lake was among the number.

Florentine lake must have had considerable reputation in Venice, since Leandro Bassano contracted to employ it in his picture of the 'Combat of the Angels,' painted for the church of S. Giorgio Maggiore at Venice in 1597.[2]

A Venetian artist told me that the Venetians used kermes (grana) and madder lakes, and that verzino lake was employed by Tintoret only. Another artist, on the contrary, said that the Venetian painters used chiefly verzino lake. A painter and restorer of pictures at Verona believed they used cochineal lake, and, as we have seen, he may be right as far as regards the painters who lived after the middle of the sixteenth century.

From the preceding authorities it will be seen that previous to the middle of the sixteenth century the best lake pigments employed by the Italian painters must have been either the lacca di cimatura or lac lake, or a mixture of one of these with verzino, and that after this period cochineal lake might have been in use. At present there is no evidence which of the two

---

1 Matt. 75. 2 Iscriz. Venet., vol. iv. p. 349.

former was generally preferred: judging from the greater number of the recipes for lacca di cimatura, we should perhaps decide that this was the pigment generally adopted; but if an opinion may be formed from the colour of the lake on Italian, and especially on Venetian pictures, we should say that the lac lake was preferred.

Chemical analysis does not diminish the difficulty; the lake-coloured pigments of a miniature of the end of the fourteenth or beginning of the fifteenth century have been analysed by Dr. Antonio Fabroni of Arezzo, who, after stating[1] that the tint where it was mixed with white was of a bright blood colour, draws the following conclusions from his experiments: "The behaviour of this pigment with re-agents proves that this colour is a combination of a terrene base, and probably of very fine white chalk with a red juice, or perhaps with several juices, either of a vegetable or animal nature. It is, in fact, a composition analogous to our modern lakes, or rather to the 'stils de grain' of the French. . . . From chemical experiments I should be inclined to believe that the dark red colour of the miniature was produced from verzino, if, besides the chronological difficulty,[2] the depth and inalterability of the colour, which are incompatible with the nature of Brazil wood, did not oblige me to abandon this conjecture.

"Carthamus, gum-lac, and madder appear to me excluded by experiment, and by the appearance of the colour to the eye. I think then, that this lake colour can only be attributed to the kermes (the coccus of the ancients) modified by some indigenous vegetable juice."

Perhaps it may be safe to conjecture that where lake-coloured draperies are of the colour of blood they

---

1 Ricerche Chimiche sopra le Miniature di un Manuscritto.

2 Sig. Fabroni probably considered that Brazil gave its name to the wood, whereas it is supposed that the name of the wood was transferred to the country.

have been painted with kermes, and where they incline to the rose-colour, or pink, that lac-lake has been used for them, if painted previous to the middle of the sixteenth century; but if after that period, that either lac, cochineal, or madder may have been employed.

The price of lake does not often appear in old documents, although it is frequently stipulated in contracts that it should be provided by the person who ordered the picture. It is however stated[1] that the lake supplied for the altar-piece, painted in 1521, by Fra Marco Pensaben, at Treviso, was 6 lire the ounce, exactly double the price of the azzurro.

When Guercino was painting the picture called "L'Amore Virtuoso," 25 oz. of lake, besides 21 oz. of lapis-lazuli to make ultramarine, were given to him.[2]

Volpato remarks[3] that lakes should not only be of beautiful colour, but in grinding they should have body, and not become liquid; and De Mayerne observes,[4] "Lake for glazing should be mixed with but a small quantity of oil, and should be ground as thick as butter, so that it may be cut, otherwise it will have no body, and be good for nothing." Lake that is left on the palette cannot be preserved, like other colours, by placing it in water, for that would spoil it.[5] Lakes being slow dryers, the addition of boiled oil or pulverized glass is necessary to promote their desiccation.[6] Palomino[7] observes that the colour which in Spain is called 'Laca de Francia,' and in France 'Carmin,' although very beautiful for illuminations and miniatures, is not durable in oil; for besides losing its beautiful colour, and becoming dark, it dries so badly,

---

1 Memorie Trevigiane.

2 See the Account Book of Guercino, published in the new edition of the Felsina Pittrice.

3 P. 745.

4 MS., quoted by Mr. Eastlake, 'Materials,' &c., p. 451 n.

5 Volpato, p. 741.

6 Bald., Voc. Dis., Tit. *Olio cotto.* Paduan MS., p. 666. Pacheco, p. 390.

7 Museo Pictorico, vol. ii. p. 53.

that after being to all appearance dry, if the picture be washed even six years after it has been painted, the lake will wash off." It was remarked to me at Venice that verzino lake was always applied as a glazing colour, and with varnish.

In painting lake or rose-coloured draperies, the Venetians generally painted the lights with pure white, and glazed with lake until the colour was sufficiently dark. With lac-lake this was a wise precaution; for Mr. Field remarks,[1] that white-lead destroys this colour. We find that it was sometimes the practice to mix the bone of the cuttle-fish, or white chalk, with lake, in order to give it body. The peculiar kind of lake now made at Venice is an example of this.[2]

Dragons'-blood, a resin of a dark red colour, which drops in tears from the tree called Pterocarpus draco. It has been used from a very early period in miniature painting, but is not considered a durable colour. Its tint was varied by adding to it an alkali, or soap, when it was called "carmine," or "ponso." When a large quantity of soap was added, it was called "cremesino."

Pavonazzo, Purple, and Mulberry colours.

Morello di ferro.—Probably some ore of iron, burnt until it assumes a morello or murrey colour; or it might have been the hard red hæmatite, ground without being calcined. It was used for painting in oil.[3]

Vitriuolo Romano abbruciato.—*Burnt Roman Vitriol.*—An artificial pigment, prepared by calcining sulphate of iron, by which process it acquires a red colour.

Morello di Sale.—The nature of this pigment has not been well ascertained. It is distinguished by Lomazzo[4] from morello di ferro, and from burnt Roman

---

1 Chromatography, p. 185.

2 And see Félibien, de la Peinture, &c., p. 299.

3 Lomazzo, Trattato, p. 192.

4 Ibid., p. 191, "Il morello di ferro, e quello di sale, fanno il morello, e oltre di ciò il vetriuolo cotto," &c.

vitriol. The same author also places it among the colours used in fresco painting. Borghini calls[1] it Pagonazzo di sale, and says it was used for painting in fresco and in tempera. Haydocke, the translator of Lomazzo, took much pains to ascertain the nature of this pigment. He says,[2] "But as for morello di sale, it must neede be the rust of salte, called flos salis, whereof Mathiolus, l. 5, c. 88, uppon Dioscorides writing saith, that it is of a saffron colour, in these words: 'There is a reddish colour, like unto rust, digged out of the German salt-mines, much desired of the painters, which, peradventure, is ipse flos salis, the flower itselfe of salt; for it is like it in colour and tast; and is commonly called morello di sale.' Wherefore I rather think that it is the rust of iron, and the rust of salte, making naturally a bay colour; for which cause I have still translated them the rust of iron and salte; though in some places they agree not in colour as they are named in the mixture. So that I imagine there is some errour crept into the booke, which by mine owne paines I cannot yet finde, nor by my conference with many good painters and chemists."

I have been unable to find the passage quoted by Haydocke in Matthioli's translation of Dioscorides, lib. 5, cap. 88, or cap. 87, in which he treats of the various kinds of salts. Matthioli says, in speaking of "fiore di sale," that "it is of a red colour, like rust of salt—that it is very deliquescent, and that by suffering it to repose, the sediment subsides, and the upper portion remains liquid." This description agrees somewhat with the information I received at Venice, namely, that morello di sale is the sediment which subsides from rock-salt when it is purified.

Phillips[3] describes rock-salt as of various colours,

[1] Riposo, p. 174.

[2] Translation of Lomazzo's Treatise on Painting, p. 100.

[3] Mineralogy, p. 193.

namely, white, grey, reddish-brown, brick-red, violet, and green; when coloured it is always more or less impure. He says that red or greyish clay frequently alternates in beds with rock-salt.

It seems probable that morello di sale was the same as the morellen salz of the Germans. From an analysis, made by a friend, the latter pigment is found to consist of peroxide of iron, with a small quantity of silica and alumina. I am informed that there is nothing in these ingredients which militates against the opinion of the Venetians that morello di sale is the sediment formed in the purification of rock-salt. This purification generally takes place in iron vessels, some portions of which may be dissolved and precipitated together with the clay which usually accompanies the salt.

Vasari, it seems, did not approve of this colour in fresco-painting. Speaking of the frescoes of Buffalmacco, he says,[1] "It was the custom of Buffalmacco, in order to paint the flesh with greater facility, to spread a coat of morello di sale over the whole, which in time caused a salt to form, which consumed the white and other colours; whence it is not surprising that these works are spoiled and destroyed, while others which he painted long before are in good preservation. And I, who thought that these pictures had been injured by the damp, have since proved by experience, and by comparing them with other works of this artist, that the injury did not arise from damp, but it was entirely owing to this habit of Buffalmacco that some of them are so ruined, that not even the design is visible; and where the flesh tints were formerly, nothing now remains but the pavonazzo. This method of painting should not be adopted by any one who wishes his pictures to last."

Folium, Turnsol.—Theophilus[2] and S. Audemar[3] describe three kinds of folium, namely, red, purple,

---

[1] Vita di Buffalmacco. [2] Theoph. lib. i. cap. xxxv. [3] P. 132.

and blue, which were prepared from a plant used in England to dye wool. According to these authors, the purple folium was procured artificially by the addition of other ingredients to the red folium.

S. Audemar gives the English name for the plant from which folium was produced; but the word appears to have been so disguised by the French transcriber, Le Begue, that it is quite unintelligible.

Fortunately, however, Mr. Hendrie has ascertained[1] that the name of the plant from which folium was produced, has been preserved in two MSS., one of which is of the fourteenth century, and the other of the fifteenth. In the first of these[2] the plant which is called "morella" is described as growing in the country of St. Giles, and as producing seeds consisting of three grains or berries, with the juice of which were dyed pieces of cloth, which yield a mulberry colour called folium.

The second description of folium, which differs but little from the first, is from a MS. belonging to the Bibliothèque Royale at Montpellier. The directions for the preparation of the colours resemble those in Theophilus and S. Audemar.

From these MSS. it appears that the colour called folium was produced from a plant called "morella," the seeds of which were formed in groups of three berries in a cluster, and that the plant grew "in terra Sancti Egidii." The Venetian MS. in the Sloane Collection (No. 416) describes a plant,[3] from the pulpy

---

1 Theoph., p. 59. 2 Sloane MS., No. 1754.

3 A fare peçolla azurra la quale e molto fina. R. una erba la quale se chiama torna sole che e grande uno braço e la foia sua e fatta chomo lortiga e da il colore a modo de tera v̄de de quela che vende i spiçiali e le semençe soe sono fate al modo che e el mira—solle el so cholore de le dite semençe e verde schuro e la gamba sie bianchaça̦ e se voi a chognossiere la dita ēba tola ī mano e tochate el chollo īcontinente te bruxa e piçara e queste semençe sono quele de le qūle se fa el color arecholgi queste semençe la maitina ꝑ tempo īnāti che lo sole se lieva e volsse arecholgiere a la ussita de Zug°, &c.

seeds of which blue and purple colours were obtained; but this plant is called "tornasole," and not "morella." The description[1] is accompanied by a drawing of a plant which bears three berries, and it is followed by an account of the process of preparing the colour, which corresponds with those given by Theophilus, S. Audemar, and the Montpellier MS.

Now there are two plants mentioned by medieval writers under the name of "morella," one of which is the solanum nigrum, the solatro nero, or ortense, the morella, or herba morella of the Italians, the morelle des jardins, morelle au fruit noir of the French, the black nightshade of the English.[2] Red, green, and blue dyes were prepared from the seeds of this plant, as we find from the MS. of Le Begue, Nos. 94, 338; the Bolognese MS., No. 91; and Paduan MS., Nos. 35 and 100; but on referring to the figure of this plant in Matthioli, we see that the berries grew in bunches of four, and not in three, and that in other respects it differed from the description of the plant in the Venetian MS.

The other plant called "morella" is the croton tinctorium, or crozophora tinctoria, the heliotropium minus tricoccum, which is called in French *tournesole*, but at Montpellier "maurelle."[3] The term *tricoccum* will not escape observation as agreeing with the old descriptions, and the name "tornasole" given to the acrid plant described in the Venetian MS. sufficiently identifies it with the croton tinctorium, the corrosive properties of which are well known.

And now with regard to the place where it grows. The heliotropium tricoccum grows in marshy places, and is a native of the Levant and south of Europe, Provence and Languedoc, especially of Galarques,

---

1 For this recipe from the Venetian MS. I am indebted to Mr. Eastlake.

2 Nemnich, Polyglotten Lexicon. 3 Ibid.

where a colour is still prepared by steeping rags in the juice of this plant,[1] and the neighbourhood of Nismes and Montpellier. The Montpellier and Sloane MSS., it will be recollected, state that it grew in "terra Sancti Egidii," and Egidius is the Latin name for Gilles, or Giles: now about thirteen miles due south of Nismes is *St. Gilles*, a town of great antiquity, the Rhoda Rhodiorum of Pliny, chiefly remarkable at present for its magnificent abbey (which dates from the twelfth century), and other medieval remains. This then is the "terra Sancti Egidii" of the MSS., and the plant morella is the "maurelle" of Montpellier, the modern turnsol. Montpellier and its neighbourhood have always been celebrated for the dyes prepared there, and this city was at one time the centre of the commerce of Languedoc.[2] At the present time it carries on extensive dye and chemical works, and manufactories of colours, some of which are nearly peculiar to itself and neighbourhood.

Having now determined the name and species of the plant from which folium was procured, and the country where it grew, it remains to account for the appellation folium, which, at first sight, appears inapplicable to the juice of a berry. I consider that this is explained by the Montpellier and the Venetian MSS. The directions in the former for preparing the colour are rather indefinite, but the Venetian MS. is more explicit. It directs[3] that pieces of cloth or rag are to be dyed with the juice pressed from the pulp surrounding the seeds; and then dried in the shade, and preserved by laying them between the leaves of a book, like leaves of gold,

1 Marcucci, Saggio, &c., p. 132.

2 Depping, Histoire du Commerce, &c., vol. i. p. 302.

3 —"e quando serano seche le dite peçe mitele ī uno libro de charta bōbaxina e tine lo libro soto lo chavezale aço che nō pia umiditad e quando ne voi adoverar taiane uno puocho e mitelo amoio la sira ī uno chaparaço con uno puocho de aqª la maitina sera fato e lo cholore foro de la peça."

and when required for use, the colour was discharged from the rag by steeping it in water. I imagine the dye derived its name of "folium" from this practice of preserving the pieces of cloth in books.

Some little difficulty has been thrown on this subject, from the statement of Theophilus and S. Audemar, that red, blue, and purple colours were obtained from the same plant. In the Sloane MS. the colour is said to be mulberry. Pierre Pomet says that turnsole en drapeau consists of nothing but rags dyed *red* with the juice of the heliotropium tricoccum, or tornesol, the fruit of which makes a very fine *blue*, but that the least acid turns it red. In the Table of Synonymes it is mentioned among the *red* colours. Nemnich,[1] De Candolle,[2] Léméri,[3] the author of the Paduan MS., and the translators of 'Beckmann's Inventions,' speak of it as producing a *blue* dye. Clusius,[4] De l'Abel,[5] and Merret,[6] who follows Libavius, say it dyes cloth a bright *green*, which changes to *blue* and *purple*. Gerarde[7] mentions a *purple* colour only. Constant de Massoul[8] says, a paste is prepared from the fruit of the heliotropium tricoccum, that grows in gardens in France. This paste being steeped in water, takes a beautiful *blue* tint. It will sometimes appear of a *red* colour, but by adding a little lime-water it will return to its *blue* colour.

All these authors speak of the colour being preserved by dyeing rags in it. It may be considered then that the colour, when fresh, was green, that it became blue on drying, and afterwards purple and red, according to the ingredients used in the preparation.

The rags thus tinged with the juice of the Croton

---

1 Polyglotten Lexicon.
2 Flore Française.
3 Histoire des Drogues.
4 Rariorum Plant. Hist., 1501.
5 Plantarum seu Stirpium Hist., 1576, and Adversaria, 1576.
6 Notes to Neri, cap. 110.
7 The Herball, or Generall Historie of Plantes, 1597.
8 Treatise on the Art of Painting, London, 1797, p. 186.

Tinctorium or Turnsol were called in Italian Pezzette, literally, small pieces, or as we should say, rags; for soft, fine, and worn-out linen cloth was used for this purpose. In Italy the pezzette were of various colours. Cennini speaks[1] of "pezzette di Levante." Don Alessio states, that they were made from "cimatura di grana," or verzino; Pomet and Léméri say that the "tournesole en drapeau" of Constantinople was fine linen or crape, dyed with an acid preparation of cochineal. "Pezzette morelle" were made from the juice of the wild elder; "pezzette pavonaze" from the juice of the myrtle. "Pezzette" of different colours are described in the Bolognese MS.[2]

I have little doubt that the bezette of the Germans was the pezzette of the Italians, and the bisetus of the middle ages.

The folium of Theophilus and S. Audemar must not be confounded with the folium described by St. Isidore, in the passage quoted by M. de l'Escalopier in his 'Theophilus,' p. 293—"Folium dictum, quod sine ulla radice innatans in Indiæ litoribus colligitur. Quod lino perforatum, siccant Indi, atque reponunt. Fertur autem Paradisi esse herba, gustu nardum referens."

The Catholicon gives a nearly similar description of folium, and adds, that the precious ointment called "foliatum" was made from it. The passage evidently relates to the Malabathrum of Dioscorides, which Matthioli[3] says was called "Folio Indiano," and which was valued for its perfume, and not for its colour.

Indigo appears also to have been called "folium Indicum," as may be understood from the following passage from Du Cange, also quoted by M. de l'Escalopier:[4]—"Peto, ut nobis mittas ad decorandos parietes colores diversos, qui ad manum habentur, videlicet auripigmentum, folium Indicum, minium, lazur."

---

1 Cap. x. 2 Pp. 443, 427, 439, 443. 3 Matt., p. 47.
4 Théophile, p. 293, n.

Bisetus, or Biseth Folii.—There is some difficulty in reconciling the few notices I have been able to collect respecting this pigment. It is mentioned in Eraclius,[1] who says "Folium incide de bruno; matiza di *biseto folii*." Again, "misces brunum cum albo, fietque pulcra rosa; incide de bruno, matiza di albo vel de *biseto folii*." "Viride incide de nigro, et matizabis de *biseto*." "Indicum incide de nigro; matiza de azurio, vel de vergaut, aut *biseth*." "Misce auripigmentum cum azurio vel indico, aut ocrum cum indico, vel viride, et erit bonum vergaut; inde de bruno, aut di nigro, undabis; auripigmentum aut de biseth matizabis."

The only information to be collected from these passages is, that it was a colour which served for heightening the others, consequently that it was lighter than they were. In the first case, it was used for the lights of a red, purple, or blue drapery; in the second, of a red drapery; in the third and fifth, of a green drapery; and in the fourth, of a blue drapery.

These passages, therefore, are no guide to the colour; and as Eraclius gives directions for painting changeable draperies in this chapter, it is by no means necessary that the lights should be of the same colour as the shades.

The next notice of bisetus is in the Table of Synonymes,[2] where it is described as being less red than folium, and is said to be taken from that portion which swims on the surface. Le Begue adds, "I believe that this term is applicable in the same sense to the lighter tint of any colour, when tempered in shells (such lighter tint rising to the surface), after the colour has settled a little."[3]

Merret, in his notes to Neri's 'Arte Vetraria' (cap. cx.), mentions bezetta as a synonyme of turnsol, "bezetta seu tornasolis;" this, it will be observed, agrees with the description in the Table of Synonymes. In speaking of this

---

[1] P. 253. [2] P. 21.

[3] I have adopted Mr. Eastlake's translation. See 'Materials,' &c., p. 425.

colour, Merret quotes a passage from the 'Wormianum,' in which Wormius relates that a piece of cloth tinged with a bright and beautiful red colour was given to him by Christopher Herfert (apothecary to Christian V.), who did not know how it was produced; that it appeared to have been coloured with red sandal wood, and was used to give a red colour to food in the same way as the common turnsol; but that it was far superior to it; that it was fit for rouge, and had this peculiarity, that it communicated its colour to water, and with some difficulty to wine, but not to spirit of wine. From this it would appear that Merret considered this piece of red cloth might be included under the general term bezzetta, and that the term was not applicable solely to cloth dyed with turnsole.

My opinion is strengthened by a remark of Nemnich, who says,[1] that cloths dyed with the juice of the turnsol were called in the Levant and at Venice "pezzette," and not "bezzette," as it is usually written. An eminent German chemist informed me that in the laboratory in Berlin, where he studied chemistry, there were several old boxes marked with the word "bezzette," which contained coloured rags. It is probable, therefore, that bisetus or biseth is a Latin term for bezzette, which is a corruption of the Italian pezzette; and that these pezzette might be of different colours; hence the opinion expressed by Le Begue in the Table of Synonymes was probably correct. Whether it is practicable to obtain two tints from folium, that is to say, one from the juice itself and another from the scum which arises on it, and whether this lighter tint was of a pale red only, or sometimes purple or blue, can only be determined by experiment.

With regard to the use of bisetus on the lights in the manner mentioned by Eraclius, it must be observed,

---

1 Polyglotten Lexicon, tit. Croton Tinctorium.

that the colour with which the rags were saturated being transparent, might be made to appear as light as it was necessary, by being much diluted, and that the strength of the colour would depend on the quantity of water with which it was mixed, and the repetition of the colour.

Palomino mentions a colour which he calls "*ur-chilla*;"[1] he states that it is of a morello colour, and known only to a few persons; that it is excellent for illuminating and for shading sketches (or subjects in chiaroscuro); he adds, that although he "could describe the mode of preparation from the juice of morello-coloured lilies and alum, it was not his intention so to do, but merely to mention a beautiful transformation which it undergoes, for by throwing into it lemon-juice instead of water, it changes its colour to that of carmine or dragon's blood; so that, from being one colour only, it becomes two, and both may be used for illuminating, for miniatures, and for sketches." It is unnecessary to observe that if this colour were really made of the juice of blue lilies, it could not have been the oricello of the Italians. Pacheco says[2] that in illuminating, blues were shaded with this colour.

Blue Pigments.

Azzurro.—By this term the early Italian painters appear to have understood Azzurro della Magna.

Azzurro della Magna, Azzurro Todesco, Azzurro Spagnuolo, Azzurro de Anglia, Azzurro de Lombardia,[3] *Lazurstein, Citramarinum.*—I have stated my opinion (supported by what appeared to me satisfactory evidence) in a former work,[4] that this German azure was a native blue ore of copper. I

---

[1] Vol. ii. p. 343. [2] Tratado, p. 354.

[3] Cennini states (cap. lx.) that Azzurro della Magna was found near Siena. It is also stated to be produced at Striscia, in the district of Volterra. See Ricett. Fiorent. [4] Art of Fresco Painting, p. xxxiv.—li.

have since ascertained that the fact has been settled beyond a doubt by Professor Branchi of Pisa.[1] This gentleman analysed a portion of the blue pigment from one of the pictures formerly in the chapel of S. Jacopo di Pistoia. For this purpose he poured a sufficient quantity of concentrated sulphuric acid on the blue pigment, which he afterwards evaporated to dryness; the residue then being dissolved in distilled water, gave a blue colour with ammonia, and a bluish-green precipitate with carbonate of potash. An iron knife-blade being immersed in the liquor, metallic copper was deposited on it. The Professor also obtained the same results from the analyses of the blue pigments of other ancient pictures, especially that from the ground of the very ancient Madonna in the Lunette of the lateral door of the Duomo of Pisa, for which, as appears from the account-roll preserved in the archives, azzurro d'Alemagna was provided. Dr. A. Fabroni, of Arezzo, also analysed a portion of the blue colour of a MS. of the beginning of the fifteenth century. After describing[2] the effects of different chemical re-agents on this pigment, he observes, "At first sight this colour resembles ultramarine, or at least the finest smaltino. Nevertheless it is clearly shown by analysis to be an oxide of copper, and I have satisfied myself by ocular examination, as well as by the comparative effects of re-agents, that it is identical with our *biadetto* (cendre bleue of the French), although it is much deeper in colour. It is to be observed that I have seen the same colour on some ancient fresco paintings which existed in the suppressed monastery of S.S. Flora and Lucilla in our city, which for some centuries have been exposed to the injuries of the air, and yet the colour is very bright." Sig. Fabroni conjectured that the colour was "moun-

[1] Lettera di Branchi, &c., pp. 7, 8, 9.

[2] See Ricerche Chimiche sopra le Miniature di un Manuscritto, published in the Acts of the Soc. of Arts, &c., of Arezzo, 1843, vol. i. p. 3.

tain blue heightened by some acid or saline preparation." But it appears quite possible for the colour to have been produced by the indurated blue carbonate of copper, which is of as deep and fine a colour as ultramarine when first prepared and used, although it differs from the latter in being more easily affected by re-agents, and in fact by being generally less permanent. Professor Petrini has written several articles in the 'Antologia'[1] respecting the pigment azzurro della magna. In one of these, dated August, 1821, after mentioning the experiments of Branchi on the old pictures in S. Jacopo di Pistoia, he says, "the same experiments have been tried with similar success on a great number of pictures of the thirteenth and fourteenth centuries, whence it appears that the painters of that period knew no other mineral azures than ultramarine and azzurro della magna."

De Boot[2] distinguishes two kinds of azure, that which was fixed in the fire, and that which was not fixed. The former was the real ultramarine, which was always brought from the East; the latter was found in Germany, and was commonly called *lazurstein*, and this, he observes, "occupies a mean place between the Armenian stone, which is friable, and the lapis lazuli, which it resembles in hardness. The colour prepared from the lazurstein is called *asurblau*, but many painters do not distinguish between this mineral and the Armenian stone, which they confound together, because the colours extracted from both are alike. Nevertheless, the stones differ in hardness, and the colour prepared from that which is not fixed in the fire is generally more beautiful than that prepared from the Armenian stone. I possess colours prepared by my own hand, which are so fine that they bear comparison with ultramarine."

The above description, as well as those of Cennini[3]

---

1 Published at Florence.

2 Le parfaict Joaillier, p. 351.

3 Trattato, cap. lx.

and the Bolognese MS.,[1] corresponds with the characteristics of the indurated native blue carbonate of copper. The difficulty of distinguishing between these two minerals has always been felt, and there appears to be no test but that of fire, which was known at a very early period.[2]

The mode of preparing this mineral as a pigment is described by Cennini, and in the Bolognese MS.[3] Having shown that the blue pigment in several old paintings, both mural and on miniatures, has been ascertained to be copper, I shall now give a few extracts from documents, proving that it was used on pictures also. The stipulation in the contract to use azzurro della magna must be considered evidence of the esteem in which it was held.

"1453, 10 August . . . . . . Padua.

"Agreement made between the monastery of Sta. Giustina and me, Andrea Mantegna, painter, relative to the painting of an altar-piece to be placed over the altar of S. Luca in the church of Sta. Giustina, by which I, Andrea Mantegna, agree to paint all the figures at my own expense, including the colours, for the price of 50 ducats in Venetian gold, and to inlay with *azzurro Todesco* all the carvings and ornaments of the said altar-piece," &c.[4]

This picture, observes Moschini in 1826, is now fresh and intact at Milan. On my second visit to Milan, Conte Pompeo Litta obligingly procured me an order, which enabled me to obtain a private view of this picture (which, with many others, had been removed

---

1 P. 343. Both kinds of carbonate of copper appear to be described in this chapter. 2 See pp. 247, 341, 385. 3 P. 365.

4 "1453, adi 10 Agosto . . . . . . Padova.

"Pati fati con el Monastero di Sta. Giustina e mi Andrea Mantegna pentor cerca el penger de una so pala da altare da esser mesa a l'altar de San Luca in la dita Gesia di Sta. Giustina soe de depenger tutte le figure a mie spese e colori per prexio de ducati cinquanta doro veniciani con questo che debo campizar dazuro todesco tuti li intagi e adornamenti de la dita pala," &c. Copied from the original contract in the possession of the Conte Francesco de' Lazara, at Padua. The contract has been published by Moschini in his work entitled 'Dell' Origine e delle Vicende della Pittura in Padova,' p. 34 n.

from the gallery of Brera, for the purpose of re-laying the floors). The picture is divided into twelve compartments, separated by columns. In the centre is an evangelist, and in the other compartments are saints; those in the upper row are half-figures, while those in the lower are whole lengths. The figures are painted on gold grounds, and there are several dark-blue draperies, but the blue has turned black. All the colours appear to have darkened, except the lakes, which are as good as ever. The carvings and ornaments inlaid with blue are no longer with the picture. Andrea Mantegna was in his 22nd year when he painted this altar-piece.

By a contract, dated 22nd February, 1474, Giacomo Filipo, a painter of Ferrara, agreed with Fra Ludovico da Forlì, Prior of the old Church of S. Salvatore at Bologna, to paint certain pictures, "de boni coluri a modo stia bene," on a ground of "azuro todesco," of the price of 10 bolognini the ounce.[1]

In the documents respecting the celebrated altar-piece by Fra Marco Pensaben at Treviso, published in the 'Memorie Trevigiane,' a blue colour, which from its price could not have been ultramarine, is mentioned in the following terms:—"1521, 13: Ott. Dati per oncie 10 e mezza d'azzurro, a lire tre l'onza."

Azzurro di Terra, Azzurro di Spagna, Biadetto, Cenere Azzurre, Ceneretta, la Cendrée, Cendres bleues, Cenizas azules, Bleu de Montagne, Bice, Terra biaua, Sanders blue, Ongaro, Bleu minerale, Turchino, Berglblau. —A blue pigment, prepared from carbonate of copper, has been known to artists under the above names from a very early period. It appears to have been of a paler colour than the pigment called azzurro della magna,[2] and in fact not to have exceeded in depth of colour the blue of the sky. It is probable that the azzurro di terra was produced from the earthy blue

---

[1] Gualandi, Memorie di Belle Arti, Ser. iv. p. 91.

[2] See Caneparius, p. 360.

carbonate of copper; but when the latter was of a bluish-green colour it was employed for preparing the pigment called verde azzurro.

It will be seen from the following MSS., that artificial blue pigments prepared from copper were common at an early period. As these azures were easily and cheaply made, and as they were, when freshly prepared, but little inferior in colour to the natural pigments, they found a ready sale, and were not easily distinguishable from the native pigments; indeed it appears from more than one writer of the seventeenth and eighteenth centuries, that it was not generally known whether "cenere azzurre" were natural or artificial productions. The author of the 'Trattato di Miniatura' remarks (p. 52), "It is not known exactly what the 'cenere azzurre' of England really are, or how they are made. They are brought from Dantzic by the English and Dutch, who export them to France and other places, whence they are called 'cenere d'Inghilterra.'" Pierre Pomet says[1] that "cendre bleue" is a composition, or pulverized stone, brought from England or Rouen, whence it is imported into France by the Swedes, Hamburghers, and Danes. Notwithstanding the diligent inquiries I have made, I have found it impossible to ascertain the nature of the "cendre bleue:" some tell me it is a composition made at Rouen; but as those who make it keep it a secret, I could not learn how it is made. The author of the 'Traité de la Peinture au Pastel' appears to have been better informed; he says, "à l'égard de la cendre bleue, c'est une terre chargée d'une certaine quantité de chaux minérale de cuivre; le ton de ce minéral est d'un bleu naissant très agréable."

It is almost unnecessary to observe that sanders blue is a corruption of "cendre bleue."

A blue pigment prepared from the native ore of

---

[1] Hist. Générale des Drogues, vol. ii. p. 385.

copper was in use in Italy at the time of Lomazzo under the name of "Ongaro."[1] This is the pigment which, it is stated on the authority of Pacheco, Michael Coxie obtained from Titian for the purpose of painting the mantle of the Virgin in the copy he was making of the celebrated altar-piece of the Van Eycks at Ghent.[2] Ongaro is mentioned in the Paduan MS.

Biadetto.—This term, which occurs so frequently in technical works on painting, has been applied both to the native and to the artificial pigment prepared from copper. There is no doubt that at an early period of art the natural pigment (which was of a much finer colour than the factitious) was much used.[3] Mr. Eastlake[4] has discovered the true derivation of the term "biadetto" in the 'Bladetus de Inde' of the Venetian MS., which is identified by De Mayerne with "la cendrée," and *beis* or *bice.* "La cendrée" is described to be "made of the blue stone which comes from India, and which is found in silver mines."

The "azzurro di biadetti" of Borghini and Baldinucci was the artificial pigment. The native mineral pigment is mentioned under the term azzurro di vena naturale, and both these are distinguished from azzurro della magna. The biadetto now sold in Italy is the artificial pigment which is imported from England; but I could not ascertain the commercial name. The modern biadetto is described in the 'Secreti' of Fra Fortunato to be composed of verdigris, sal-ammoniac, and tartar.

The name *turchino* is stated to have been applied to this class of pigments in consequence of their being imported at one time into Italy in large quantities by the Turks;[5] others trace the name to the resemblance of the colour of the pigment to the blue stone called turquoise, a mineral which also owes its colour to copper.

---

[1] See Trattato, p. 191. [2] See Pacheco, p. 373. [3] Lettera di Branchi.
[4] Materials, &c., p. 121. [5] See Ciampi, Notizie, &c., p. 57.

A modern blue pigment, known under the name of *copper, mountain, English, Hambro', lime, kassler, mineral,* and *Neuwieder blue,* is prepared from carbonate of copper, with hydrated oxide of copper and lime. "It is obtained by a particular process (which at present is kept in part secret), by decomposing subchloride of copper by a solution of caustic potash, and afterwards mixing the mass with caustic lime, and exposing the mixture for some time to the air. When the greenish-blue colour has become a pure blue, the mass is dried and ground into a rather coarse, crumbling, or dust-like powder. The darker sorts contain only a small percentage of quick lime; but the lighter sorts, on the contrary, from 20 to 70 per cent. Mountain blue is used as a lime colour, but chiefly for colouring rooms, on account of its unchangeability on lime grounds; sometimes as enamel colour instead of oxide of copper." [1]

Although Boschini affirms that biadetto was one of those colours which the Venetians "abhorred like the plague," there is evidence to show that blue pigments from copper were used by Venetian painters. The fact of Titian having in his possession some of the colour called "ongaro" has been already mentioned. Paolo Veronese is stated by Signor Pietro Edwards to have employed "a certain mineral azure which is no longer in use;" and Paolo's well-known practice of mixing his blues with size may be considered a confirmation of this assertion, since the copper blues if used with oil were certain to change. A Venetian artist, whose family have always been painters, and who doubtless possesses much traditionary knowledge, also stated that the Venetians used a "terra azzurra" [2] which is now lost; but he added, that on analysis biadetto had been found on the pictures of Tintoretto only. The 'Tariffa'

---

1 Pharmaceutical Journal, vol. vi. p. 82.

2 Caneparius also mentions (p. 360, 362) a "terra cerulea."

of Zuane Mariana proves that a terra biaua was in 1567 imported into Venice in such quantities as to be sold by the *peso grosso;* and when we consider the immense quantity of blue found on the paintings of the Venetian school, we are obliged to conclude either that ultramarine was much more plentiful than it is at present, or that some other blue pigment has been used. To the above instances must be added the opinion current in Venice that biadetto is the pigment which best matches the blue found in Venetian pictures.

The use of blue pigments from copper appears to have prevailed in other schools of the North of Italy. I was informed at Milan that the blue in the drapery of the Virgin in the St. Jerome of Correggio, at Parma, was painted with biadetto. It appears that either biadetto or azzurro della magna was used by Lionardo da Vinci, since there are the following entries in his MS. book of drawings in the Ambrogiana Library at Milan: "di spesa tra azurro, oro, biaca, giesso, indacho, et cholla; lire 3 . . . . fra smalto, azurro, e altri colori, lire 1½, fra azurro e oro, lire 3½, un' oncia d'azuro, soldi 10." Here we have the exact price of the "azuro," which could not have been ultramarine, and which appears to have been too cheap for azzurro della magna.[1]

With regard to the manner in which these pigments were employed—in the first place it is clear that they cannot be used with oil without turning green.[2] It is true that Borghini, Baldinucci, and Lomazzo state that they may be used with oil; but Bisagno remarks "la ceneretta is but little adapted for painting skies, because it becomes green in time:" and the author of the 'Traité de la Peinture au Pastel' observes that cendres bleues might be employed in tempera painting and in

---

[1] The price of this pigment at Florence, in 1459, was 3 great florins the oz.; see a letter from Benozzo Gozzoli in the Carteggio Inedito, vol. i. p. 193. The author of the Bol. MS. states that azzurro della magna was sold from 10 to 30 bolognini the oz.

[2] See Palomino, vol. ii. p. 52.

unimportant works, that cupreous earths might be used for *peinturage* (by which he probably meant common decorative effects), but never for painting, even in fresco.

Paolo Veronese is stated to have generally painted the blues in his pictures with size; Signor Pietro Edwards mentions [1] that in the picture by Paolo in the ceiling of the Collegio in the Ducal Palace at Venice, the blue sky was painted in tempera, and the clouds with oil.

As the grounds employed by Paolo consisted generally of a thin coating of glue and gesso only, no preparation was necessary before applying the blue of the sky with size. But when the blue was required to be laid upon oil colours, it was necessary to apply a thin coat of varnish, or to rub the surface with juice of garlic.[2] The colour was afterwards varnished. Fra Fortunato of Rovigo states, that to prepare biadetto for miniature painting, so that it should spread well, it should be ground with burnt roche alum, or with a little tartar or sandarac. He adds, biadetto should be ground very fine, and used with varnish made of spirit of turpentine and clear mastic; it will then spread well, glaze brilliantly, and be of a beautiful colour. Blue was sometimes applied in powder. De Boot mentions [3] that "on account of the excessive price of ultramarine, painters were accustomed to dead colour the parts of their pictures intended to be blue with Armenian stone, or a blue glass called smalt, to which white was added for the lights. When this preparation was quite dry, ultramarine, mixed with nut oil and spirit of turpentine, or varnish, was glazed over it. By this means the colours spread beneath, as if under a glass, became brilliant and splendid, borrowing through this veil from the ultramarine, not only beauty but durability; so

---

1 In a document addressed to Sig. Savio Cassier, dated the 25th of Aug., 1780, and now preserved in the Academy at Venice, where I saw it.

2 See Mr. Eastlake's 'Materials,' &c., p. 455.

3 Le parfaict Joaillier, &c., p. 372.

that in two hundred years they lost but little of their brightness and beauty." Volpato directs [1] that azzurro di Spagna should be tempered as firmly as possible with nut oil, and that it should be made to flow with spirit of turpentine.

Bisagno remarks that ceneretta must not be mixed with smaltino, because these colours are inimical to each other,[2] and Constant de Massoul [3] makes the same remark with regard to cendre bleue and orpiment.

There is one peculiarity attending the blue pigments in Italian pictures, which was first pointed out to me by a Milanese artist, and this is that the blues invariably are raised above the surface of the other colours, and that in some cases (and he particularly instanced Correggio's S. Jerome at Parma) they stand up as high as a five franc piece above the canvass. I have myself seen them on some pictures raised to the height of an English shilling. This artist ascribed the effect to the difficulty of using the blue, and to the necessity of repeating the colour several times.

Pacheco's method of using blue pigments has been described briefly by Mr. Eastlake.[4]

Smalto and Smaltini, Email, Azur à poudrer.— There were two kinds of pigment of this name, one of which was a preparation of zaffre, the other was a glass composed of sand, nitre, and copper filings. The latter is the Vestorian azure described by Vitruvius, which was called also azzurro di Pozzuoli. It was chiefly used in fresco painting.[5] The smalto made at Venice in the time of Caneparius seems to have been of the latter kind, since this author describes the first under the term zaphara.

---

1 P. 747.

2 Pacheco, however, recommends that azul de Santo Domingo should be shaded with good smalti. Tratado, p. 391.

3 Art of Painting, p. 176.

4 Materials, &c., p. 431; and see Pacheco, p. 361.

5 See translations of Vitruvius by Orsini, published in 1822; and by Galliani, published at Naples in 1758.

It is not always easy to decide which pigment is intended when these terms are employed, for there is evidence that they were both in use at the same time in Italy. Lomazzo mentions "gli smalti, come quello di Fiandra che è il migliore de gl' altri tutti;" from the last words it might almost be inferred that other vitrified pigments of this kind were known, besides the two above-mentioned. There is little doubt that the "smalto di Fiandra" was *zaffre*, and that it was very similar to the pigment we now call "smalt." The smaltino of the 'Abecedario' was also a preparation of zaffre.

One kind of azzurro di smalto only is mentioned by Borghini;[1] this he states was composed of glass, and was used in fresco, in tempera, and in oil.

Lionardi da Vinci mentions "smalto" among the colours provided for the decoration of the apartments in the castle in which Lodovico il Moro resided;[2] but at the period when these paintings were executed (1492), it is scarcely probable that zaffre was known in Italy. In the absence, therefore, of evidence to the contrary, we must believe that the smalto mentioned by him was of the same nature as the smaltino used by his contemporary Pietro Perugino for the mantle of the Virgin in his picture at Montone. Baldassare Orsini states that the smaltino in this picture was painted in distemper on a ground of black; and to modify the brightness of this blue Pietro had stippled the whole drapery with lake. With regard to the composition of the smaltino, Orsini states that he had analysed this colour, and had found that it was a vitrified pigment like that described by Vitruvius in powder, and that it was tempered with flour paste.[3]

Smaltino appears also to have been occasionally employed in oil-paintings, as we learn from Borghini, and from Bisagno; the latter says it should not be mixed

1 Riposo, p. 173. 2 Amoretti, Memorie Storiche di L. da Vinci, p. 38.
3 Elogio e Memorie di Pietro Perugino, p. 208, and n.

with "ceneretta," and that for painting skies it should be mixed with white lead, and tempered with nut oil. This pigment is called "*cerulée*" in the Brussels MS.[1] Lebrun states[2] that very beautiful blue draperies are made with "azur à poudrer" (smalt):[3] they must be first painted with black and white, the lights being bright (that is to say, very white), and the shades being very dark, and then sprinkled with "azur à poudrer." Mr. Eastlake gives[4] several instances of blue being painted in this manner. Christophe Ballard recommends[5] that email (smalt) should be mixed with oil of turpentine, in order that it may dry and not flow, email, he states, "being very difficult to use; for if it be made too liquid it will flow; and if too thick and firm you will not be able to use it; but by mixing it with spirit of turpentine it may be easily used; for the oil of turpentine evaporates in the air." This author gives the following directions for preventing the colour from flowing (qu'elle ne coule):—"When you have painted your drapery, you will place your picture upon the ground, or upon a table; then you will take some crumpled paper, such as the grey paper used by merchants, tear it into small pieces, and let it fall upon your work. The paper will absorb all the oil; and when the blue is nearly dry, and, as we say, 'embu,' even although it should not be quite dry, the paper will prevent the colour from flowing. To remove the paper, you must strike the picture upon a corner, and all the paper will fall off: and note, that you must not suffer it to dry, or you will not be able to remove the paper; neither must the pieces of paper be too large, or they will mark the drapery."[6]

---

1 P. 804.

2 P. 821.

3 Pierre Pomet, Hist. des Drogues, vol. i. p. 192, 193.

4 Materials, &c., p. 431, 455.

5 Traité de Mignature, p. 216, 217.

6 For other methods of using smalt, see also Mr. Eastlake's 'Materials,' &c., p. 427—432.

In 1676, "the finest ground smalt that ever came into England" was valued at 8*s*. a pound.[1]

The early history of cobalt and zaffre is involved in so much obscurity, and the evidence respecting it appears so conflicting, that it is considered useless to enter into the subject in the present work.[2] The same remark applies to the zaffirro of the middle ages, which, although it decidedly signifies in some cases ultramarine, or lapis lazuli, is yet used so vaguely that it cannot be understood to be limited to this substance only. The difficulty of coming to any decision on this subject may be estimated by the consideration that the term zafirro, saffiro, or saphiro, was used to denote a precious stone of a blue colour as well as a blue mineral, which from its description must be lapis lazuli; that zaffera, saphra, or zaffre was a blue pigment prepared from cobalt, which is now known by the name of smalt, and that safar is the Moorish name for copper.[3] So little variation is there between the terms used to designate the three minerals from which the principal blue pigments are made.

Various kinds of artificial mineral azures were employed in Italy; many of these are described in the Bolognese MS. (cap. ii.). The pigment described at p. 388 is represented to be better than azzurro della magna, and in appearance and colour to be equal to ultramarine. Another of these azures is stated to be worth four ducats the pound;[4] and a third, five gold

---

[1] Walpole's Anecdotes, vol. iii. p. 137.

[2] It may be observed here that the Egyptians were acquainted with cobalt, but they used it only for colouring glass. The small blue figurines are coloured with copper, and neither M. Laurent, M. Malaguti, nor M. Salvetat, have been able to detect any cobalt in them. See De Brongniart, Traité des Arts Céramiques, p. 558, 563. The experiments of Prof. John, of Berlin, prove that the blues in the Egyptian paintings were oxides of copper, with a small intermixture of iron, and that none of them contain cobalt. See 'The Epochs of Painting characterised: a Sketch of the History of Painting, Ancient and Modern,' by Mr. Wornum.

[3] See Mr. Ford's Hand-book for Spain, p. 128.

[4] P. 391.

ducats the pound.[1] Borghini describes [2] several of these artificial azures. But of all the pigments of this class there is none which is mentioned so frequently by all writers on colours as the azure said to be prepared from silver.[3] Yet, in spite of the most diligent inquiry, I have been unable to ascertain that any salt of silver is capable of producing a blue colour. It is probable that the composition of such a pigment may have been suggested by the known fact, that the old bladetus de Inde before mentioned was found in silver mines; and it is very probable that the medieval artists attributed to silver the blue colour which was actually owing to the copper with which the silver was mixed. Whenever a blue colour was really produced from the solution of silver plates in acetic acid, it may be concluded that the colour was produced by the solution of the copper with which the silver was alloyed; and there appears to be no evidence to support the assertion found in some medieval MSS., that a blue colour could be produced from pure silver. The blue pigment composed of sulphur, mercury, and sal ammoniac, has been called Venetian azure.[4]

Bleu Minerale.—There is some doubt as to the nature of the pigment known in Italy by this name. Some persons consider it the same as turchino; and it seems a pigment prepared from copper and lime is still sold under this name. Other persons state that it was a preparation of cobalt, and was brought from Germany. In the Pharmaceutical Journal [5] it is stated to be a cyanide of iron, produced by mixing a solution of sulphate of iron with prussiate of potash, and carefully heating the light precipitate, which is formed with nitric acid, till it assumes a deep blue colour. The white substances used for the finer sorts are alumina, gypsum,

---

1 P. 403. 2 Riposo, p. 173.
3 Le Begue, p. 47, 49. Bol. MS., p. 395, 399. Theoph., E. ed., p. 422.
4 See recipes at the end of the Abecedario Pittorico. 5 Vol. vi. p. 82.

and heavy spar; for the more common sorts, starch or clay. The same author also mentions that Prussian blue mixed with the oxide of zinc, was formerly sold under the name of bleu minerale.[1]

Ultramarine, Azur d'Acre.—The exact period when this fine pigment was introduced is not yet determined. There is no doubt, however, that the real lapis lazuli from Tartary was known in the thirteenth century, since it is mentioned in the work of Yousouf Jeifaschy, who appears to have been a jeweller of Cairo.[2] The term ultramarine must have been common in Italy at the beginning of the fourteenth century, since it occurs in the Italian MS. of Johannes de Modena,[3] and in the recipe given by Michelino de Vesuccio to Alcherius, both of which were copied in 1410. In some MSS. it is called "azurrum transmarinum," in contradistinction to azzurro della magna, which was called azzurrum citramarinum.[4] Ultramarine has always been occasionally used by the Italian painters, and so much was it esteemed that it was frequently the subject of a particular stipulation in contracts. It was generally supplied by the person who ordered the picture, but in some cases the artist himself agreed to employ it. Thus in 1501, Aloese Vivarino di Murano agreed to use ultramarine in his picture painted for the guardians of the Scuola della Carità.[5] It was employed by Paolo Veronese in the "Nozze di Cana;"[6] by Leandro Bassano, in his picture of the Battle of the good Angels with Lucifer, and in that of Sta. Lucia, painted for the church of S. Giorgio Maggiore at Venice;[7] by Pietro

---

1 See Traité de la Peinture au Pastel, where this colour is said not to have been affected by the strongest vapours of liver of sulphur in effervescence with the mineral acids.

2 Depping, Hist. du Commerce, vol. i. p. 147.

3 P. 96, 102.

4 P. 348 and n.

5 For this notice, extracted from the Venetian archives, I am indebted to the Abbate Cadorin, the biographer of Titian.

6 Iscriz. Venet., vol. iv. p. 253.

7 Ibid., p. 349, 352.

Perugino, for his picture in the Duomo of Orvieto;[1] by Palma Giovane, for the pictures he painted in S. Nicolò at Treviso, in 1618;[2] by Gio. Batista Ponchino, for the Pala d'Altare in the choir of the Archipresbiterale at Treviso,[3] in 1551; by Denys Calvart, in 1601, and by Francesco Albano, in 1639,[4] for their pictures in the church of the Servites at Bologna; by Innocenza da Imola, in his pictures in S. Michele in Bosco;[5] by Felice Damiani, in 1593;[6] and by Ludovico Carracci, in 1587,[7] in the picture of the Conversion of S. Paul. It appears, from various entries in the account book kept by Guercino[8] of the receipts for his pictures, that he generally employed ultramarine which was furnished by his employer. Sometimes the pigment, ready prepared, was given to him, and sometimes the lapis lazuli, from which it appears he was to prepare the colour himself. Thus, for the picture called "L'Amore Virtuoso," he received twenty-one ounces of lapis lazuli to make ultramarine.

Contrary to the assertion of some modern artists, Pungeleone states[9] that Correggio always made use of ultramarine, although it appears that he employed "azzurro" (probably azzurro della magna), which cost but three lire the ounce, for the decoration of the "casa del anchona de lo altare grando" at Correggio.[10]

Ultramarine is stated to have been found on Venetian pictures; and although the artists of this school used also the blue pigments from copper, there seems little doubt that the greater part of the ultramarine imported into

---

1 Orsini, Elogio di Pietro Perugino, p. 194 and n.

2 Memorie Trevigiane, vol. ii. p. 59.

3 Ibid., p. 76.

4 Gualandi, Memorie, ser. i. p. 4, 19.

5 Ibid., p. 61.

6 Ibid., ser. ii. p. 4.

7 Ibid., ser. ii. p. 132.

8 The original account book is in the Ercolani Collection at Bologna. It has been published in the new edition of the Felsina Pittrice, by Jacopo Alesandro Calvi, at Bologna.

9 Life of Correggio, vol. i. p. 248.

10 Ibid., vol. ii. p. 68, 69.

Italy was introduced by way of Venice, which was the great emporium of Oriental commerce.

The price of ultramarine at different periods has been preserved by several writers. In 1437 it was sold at Florence for eight ducats the ounce.[1] In 1548 the price at Venice was sixty scudi the ounce.[2] In 1788 the price at Paris was one hundred francs, or even as much as fifty crowns the ounce.[3] The value of ultramarine is not stated in the Bolognese MS., but the price of a pound of lapis lazuli varied, according to the goodness of the specimen, from two to five ducats. De Boot mentions[4] that lapis lazuli was usually sold for eight or ten thalers the pound, and if the stone was good it would produce at least ten ounces of azure. One of the best specimens would yield five and a half ounces of the best colour, worth twenty thalers the ounce. The second quality was worth five or six thalers, the third only one thaler, or one and a half. The price paid by Lely for one ounce of ultramarine was 2*l.* 10*s.*, but for the best kind he paid as much as 4*l.* 10*s.* the ounce.[5]

Pacheco states[6] that ultramarine was not used by the Spanish painters in his time, but it was introduced at a subsequent period, since he himself mentions the colour;[7] and Palomino gives directions[8] for using it. The latter remarks that it was never used in the first painting, because, as it had but little body, it did not cover well; and also because, as it was very dear, it would have been employed uselessly; it was therefore either glazed or worked upon some of the other blues. When employed in glazing it was only necessary to mix it with nut-oil, and to pass it over the drapery with a soft brush, moistened with nut-oil and a few drops of spirit of turpentine, so as to leave it smooth and even.

---

1 Cennini, Trattato, cap. 62.
2 Paolo Pino, Dialogo, p. 18.
3 Traité de la Peinture au Pastel.
4 Le parfaict Joaillier, p. 371.
5 Walpole's Anecdotes, vol. iii. pp. 130, 132.
6 Tratado, p. 391.
7 Ibid., p. 392.
8 Museo Pictorico, vol. ii. p. 68.

If the drapery was to be painted with ultramarine, the light and dark tints were to be mixed with white lead and nut-oil, and the shadows heightened with indigo, and if the drapery were previously glazed with ultramarine it would be more easy to execute. As a dryer, Palomino recommends pulverized smalt; but, he says, it must be used cautiously or it will spoil the colour of the ultramarine.[1]

De Piles also remarks,[2] that ultramarine should not be employed for the first painting, but that the lights and shades should be painted in very distinctly, the high lights consisting of pure white, with common colours; or that the first shade tints, and even the half tints, may be painted with charcoal of the willow, which inclines to blue, or with bone black, and then finished with ultramarine; but he adds, that this last method was not so good as the former, neither were the tints so fresh.

Ultramarine was employed by Simone Cantarini with terra verde in the shadows of flesh, and probably by Guido and some of his pupils,[3] and by Baroccio;[4] and Padre Francesco Lana recommends[5] that it should be mixed with all the flesh tints.

Blue pigments prepared from vegetables are not numerous; the principal are those procured from indigo and woad. Blue colours were also procured from the flowers of the cornflower,[6] from turnsol or folium, and other plants. The use of these pigments was limited to miniature painting. *Guato*, or more correctly *guado*, is the Italian name for the isatis tinctoria, called also glastum sativum—a plant which grows spontaneously in France, Germany, England, and other parts of Europe. It was called glastum by the Romans, and is now

---

1 Museo Pictorico, vol. ii. p. 57. 2 Elémens, pp. 108, 118.
3 Malvasia, Fels. Pitt., vol. ii. pp. 80, 448.
4 Bellori, Vite, &c., p. 118. 5 P. 746.
6 Constant de Massoul, p. 186.

known in France by the names of Pastel, Vouede, and Gaude.

There is sufficient evidence to show that indigo was known as a pigment in the time of the Romans, and that it was used as such during the middle ages in Italy, where it was sold under the name of indigo bagadel, indigo baccadeo or bandas, indacca detto buccaddeo, indaco del golfo.[1] But there is no doubt that the pigment called "indigo," so frequently mentioned by writers on colours in the thirteenth, fourteenth, and fifteenth centuries, was generally prepared from woad, and not from the real indigo. This will appear from various recipes in the Bolognese MS.,[2] in the whole of which woad is the principal ingredient.

It will be observed that the pigment is generally prepared from the blue or purple coloured scum which floats on the dyers' vats, and which is the produce of fermentation. This agrees with the account of Dioscorides, who says there were two kinds of indigo, the first of which was brought from India, but the second, which was made during the process of dyeing, was a purple scum which floated on the surface of the vats. In commenting on this passage, Matthioli observes,[3] "the indigo generally used by the painters was that made in dyehouses, which was procured from woad with which wool is dyed." This passage alone is sufficient to prove that the term "indigo" was applied to woad. Beckmann says,[4] that under the name *indigo* must be understood every kind of blue pigment separated from plants by fermentation, and converted into a friable substance by desiccation; for those who should maintain that the real indigo must be made from those

---

1 Depping, vol. i. p. 141. See Cennini, Trattato, cap. 61. Le Begue, pp. 86, 273.

2 Pp. 412—416. See also Secreti di D. Alessio, parte ii. p. 34; Nuovo Plicto d'ogni sorte di Tinture; and Paduan MS., p. 676.

3 Trans. of Dioscorides, p. 1414.

4 Inventions, tit. Indigo.

plants named in the botanical system *Indigofera tinctoria*, would confine the subject within too narrow limits; as the substance which our merchants and dyers consider as real indigo is prepared in different countries from so great a number of plants, that they are not even varieties of the same species." Although indigo was not considered a durable colour, it appears to have been occasionally used in oil.

The tints were made with white lead. Palomino says,[1] "that it is a fine colour for draperies, and works pleasantly, but that it is necessary to observe the following conditions: 1st, That the lights should not be too light, because the colour fades—therefore the tints should be sufficiently deep; the 2nd and most important, that the tints should not be too oily, but thick, and not tormented with the brush; and 3rdly, that the colour should be well purified." Different modes of purifying indigo are described by Palomino,[2] and in the recipes at the end of the Abecedario Pittorico, and also in the Paduan MS.[3] When carefully employed, Félibien states[4] that it is durable if properly used, but that too much oil must not be mixed with it, and allowance must be made for its tendency to fade.

Green Pigments.

Mineral green pigments, both natural and artificial, are produced from copper. The native green ores of this metal have always been used in painting under the names of *mountain green*, *Hungarian green*, *chrysocolla*, *malachite*, *cenere verde*, *verde de miniera*, *verde di Spagna*, *verdetto*, and *green bice*. To these colours must be added *terra verde*, which is said by some persons to owe its colour to copper;[5] others consider that

1 Vol. ii. p. 67.
2 Museo Pictorico, vol. ii. p. 67.
3 P. 676.
4 Des Principes, &c., p. 299.
5 Marcucci, Saggio, &c., p. 71. Pierre Pomet, Hist. des Drogues, vol. ii. p. 385.

it is a bluish or grey coaly clay, combined with yellow oxide of iron or yellow ochre.[1] It was sometimes called *Prasino* and *Theodote*. Pierre Pomet[2] states that mountain green was a greenish powder in small grains like sand, and that it was distinguished by this sandy appearance from the artificial, which consisted of pulverized verdigris mixed with a little white lead. It was also sometimes adulterated with cendre verte, of which there were many varieties.[3] Mountain green appears to have been but little used in oil painting.

Native carbonate of copper, although sometimes a pure blue and sometimes pure green, was frequently of a mixed colour, when it was called *verde azzurro*.

Prasino or *Prasminum*.—Isidorus gives this name to green earth [4] (terre verte). But in some cases the name has been applied to a white earth saturated with a vegetable juice of a green colour, as in the Bolognese MS., No. 88.

Verde Porro—Perhaps the same as the Prasino of the middle ages. It is mentioned in the Paduan MS., also by Pozzo in his instructions for painting in fresco, and by Baldinucci;[5] the latter states that it was a pigment of a whitish green colour, like that of the leek, whence it takes its name. It appears that during the middle ages the juice of the leek was actually used as a pigment.[6]

Various artificial green pigments were prepared from copper which were known to medieval painters under the names of *viride salsum*, *viride Hispanicum*, *viride Rothomagense*, and *viride Græcum*. In the last may be traced the verdigris (verd de Grèce)[7] of the moderns.

The best kind of verdigris was prepared at Marseilles by a process which has been frequently described.

---

1 Field, Chromatography, p. 233; and see Merimée, p. 191.

2 Hist. des Drogues, vol. ii. p. 286.

3 Ibid., p. 385.

4 See p. 244, n. 4; and Theophilus, E. ed., 101.

5 Voc. Dis.

6 See p. 156.

7 See Mr. Eastlake's 'Materials,' &c., p. 118.

This pigment was known to the Spaniards by the names of verdete and cardenillo. Verdigris was generally purified by redissolving it in vinegar, and then suffering it to crystallize in large crystals, by the evaporation of the vinegar, when it was sold under the name of "distilled" or "crystallized verdigris" and "verde eterno."

Verdetto.—There are several pigments of this name. 1. A mineral green pigment which, according to Borghini and Baldinucci, is found in the mountains of Germany; this probably was mountain green or malachite, the green carbonate of copper. 2. A vegetable pigment mentioned by Lomazzo and in the Paduan MS., which was of a yellowish colour, apparently of the nature of brown pink; Haydocke called this colour holy green. 3. An artificial green pigment prepared from copper, called "Verdet" in the Brussels MS.,[1] and Verdete by the Spanish. These two pigments differ in the mode of preparation.

Verde eterno.—Another name for distilled or crystallized verdigris.[2] It is a neutral acetate of copper, prepared by dissolving verdigris in hot acetic acid, and leaving the filtered solution to cool. It forms beautiful dark green crystals. It is said to have been much used by the Venetian painters. This colour is mentioned by Volpato, who remarks,[3] "Il verde eterno si cristalino chiaro e di color vivace." Baldinucci says[4] it was so called because it never lost its brightness, as all other greens did. He adds that this was nothing else but a glazing of purified verdigris spread thin over silver leaf.[5]

Green pigments prepared from vegetables are numerous. The principal of these are *sap green*, the *verde di vesicha* and *pasta verde* of the Italians, prepared from the berries of the buckthorn (Spincervino—Rhamnus

---

[1] P. 806. [2] Marcucci, Saggio, &c., p. 74. [3] P. 744.
[4] Voc. Dis. [5] See also Mr. Eastlake's 'Materials,' p. 458.

catharticus). The juice being boiled down was inspissated, and when dry was preserved in bladders.

Lily or *Iris* green (verde giglio).—This pigment was sometimes prepared for use by dipping pieces of linen (pezzette) into the juice and then preserving them dry. Green pigments were also prepared from rue, parsley, columbine, and from the black nightshade (the herba morella of the Italians, which must be distinguished from the "maurelle" or Croton tinctorium). The juice of this plant was incorporated with green earth; in this respect it resembled the pigments called by the French stils de grain, prepared from the berries of the Rhamnus infectorius (grain d'Avignon). The colour of these pigments varied from a brownish green (brown pink) to yellow.

It was generally considered that mixed greens, composed of blue and yellow, were more permanent than any of the before-mentioned green pigments. They were frequently compounded of ultramarine and orpiment, of azzurro della magna and giallolino, of indigo and orpiment, and of one of the mineral blues with a yellow lake.[1]

Verdigris, and especially distilled verdigris, or verde eterno, was extensively employed by all the Italian schools for glazing, and especially by the Venetian, and the brilliant green draperies on the pictures of this school were produced by this colour.

Verdigris was sometimes added to black to make it dry,[2] but Le Brun remarks[3] that it must only be used in the shadows, for it is a poison in painting, and kills all the colours with which it is mixed. It appears, from the Paduan MS.[4] to have been sometimes mixed with vegetable greens and yellows, and also with umber

1 See Cennini, cap. 53, 54, 55; Borghini, p. 170. 2 Volpato, p. 747.
3 P. 823, and see De Piles, Elémens, &c., p. 124. Félibien, Principes, &c., 300. 4 P. 652.

and indigo for making dark green. It should, however, be used alone; and De Piles observes[1] that if the smallest particle of it enter into the priming of a picture, it is sufficient to ruin it. It is even necessary, he adds, to avoid using with other colours the brushes which have been employed for verdigris.

Lionardo da Vinci remarks[2] that it was liable not only to fade, but to be removed from the picture by washing it with water, unless a coat of varnish was passed over it.

Volpato also notices the solubility of this colour in water, and remarks that it must be removed from the palette before the latter is put into water to preserve the colours when the day's work is over. In the Venetian school it appears the colour was usually laid on with varnish.

Pacheco directs[3] that purified verdigris should be ground in oil for the first painting, but for the last glazing varnish should be added. Lebrun says[4] that to make a very beautiful green for glazing, verdigris should be used with varnish; it will then be very beautiful, and will not fade. In another place he observes,[5] "Verdigris is very good, if employed with fat oil."

Verdigris is liable to turn black in time, and when in this state the surface has been removed by a penknife, and the colour beneath was found to be perfectly fresh and bright.

Borghini states[6] that terra verde was used in all three (fresco, oil, and tempera) kinds of painting. Lebrun remarks:[7] "Verd de terre is used in the shades of flesh-colour, but it must be employed sparingly, for with age the colour appears crude, which would produce a bad effect." Merimée observes[8] that Rubens had made great use of this colour, not only in landscapes but

---

[1] Elémens, &c., p. 124. [2] Trattato, cap. xcix. [3] Tratado, p. 389. [4] P. 813. [5] P. 815. [6] Riposo, p. 169. [7] P. 813. [8] De la Peinture à l'Huile, p. 192.

in his carnations. He concurs with Le Brun in the fact of the colour deepening in time, and states that for this reason terre verte should be employed cautiously. There are frequent notices in Italian writers of terre verte being employed in painting the shades of flesh, but it is not always clear whether the pigment was used raw or burnt. Thus Malvasia,[1] in speaking of Simone Cantarini's method of painting flesh, remarks, "He was therefore as partial to white lead as he was inimical to lake and umber for his outlines and shades; in which he used to employ plenty of ultramarine and terra verde, learning from Guido the value of these two colours in painting delicate shadows." It is very possible that as the terra verde was used for the shadows, it might have been burnt. Lomazzo directs[2] that the shadow colour for flesh should be made with nero di campana and *burnt* terra verde, or with umber and *burnt* terra verde; and the Paduan MS.[3] states that umber, *burnt* terra verde, and asphaltum were used for the same purpose.

Brown Pigments.

The brown pigments used in the middle ages were very few; those employed by the Italians were not numerous, and they are frequently classed with black pigments. The principal were bistre, which is mentioned by medieval writers under the name of fuligo and by Lomazzo under that of fuligine; umber, raw and burnt; Cologne earth, burnt terra verde, and asphaltum.

Umber is a hydrate of oxide of iron mixed with a variable quantity of oxide of manganese and a small proportion of clay.[4] Merimée says it contains silica and alumina also. The best is reputed to be brought from the Levant, although it is really the produce of

[1] Fels. Pitt., vol. ii. p. 448. [2] Trattato, p. 302. [3] P. 650.
[4] De Brongniart, Essaie des Arts Céramiques, p. 539.

Cyprus.[1] This was probably imported into Venice, and thence to other parts of Europe, particularly to Spain, where the Venetian umber was sold under the name of sombra di Venezia.[2]

Besides its use in painting as a shadow colour both in flesh[3] and yellow draperies[4] and for all colours lighter than itself,[5] it was sometimes boiled with oil as a drier both for painting and mordants.[6] It was also occasionally added to grounds,[7] but for this purpose it was not generally approved.[8] Umber was sometimes called falzalo by the Italians.[9] Mixed with fine lake, it was used as a glazing colour for shadows.

Cologne earth, a bituminous earth, which, although a powerful colour, has the disadvantage of fading and of drying very slowly. The former, according to Merimée, is prevented by mixing it with very durable pigments, the latter can only be remedied by the addition of a drier to the oil. This pigment does not appear to have been known to Lomazzo, Borghini, or the early Italian writers. Neither does the name occur in any of the treatises in this work, nor in the 'Principes de Peinture' of Félibien, nor the 'Elémens de Peinture' of De Piles. It seems to have been used principally by the Flemish and Dutch painters.[10] It is, however, stated to have been employed by the Venetian painters, but this appears to require confirmation.

When *terra verde* is burnt over a slow fire,[11] and the heat gradually increased until the pigment is roasted, it is converted into a fine warm brown, which was used, mixed with other colours, by the Italians for the shadows of flesh.[12] Modern writers do not mention this

---

[1] Merimée, p. 206. [2] Palomino, vol. ii. pp. 52, 149.

[3] Pp. 650, 654. Malvasia, Fels. Pitt., vol. ii. p. 448. Palomino, vol. ii. pp. 62—64. Lomazzo, Trattato, pp. 191, 312.

[4] Palomino, vol. ii. p. 66. [5] Lomazzo, Trattato, p. 197.

[6] Borghini, p. 176. Paduan MS., p. 740. [7] Volpato, pp. 730, 746, n.

[8] P. 813. Merimée, p. 206. [9] Lomazzo, Trattato, p. 191.

[10] Mr. Eastlake's 'Materials,' &c., p. 462. [11] P. 745.

[12] P. 650. Lomazzo, Trattato, p. 191.

colour, but the use of it has been revived by an eminent English artist, under the name of "Verona brown."

Asphaltum, Bitume Giudaico, Nero di Spalto.—Several kinds of asphaltum are used in the arts. The best is considered to be the Egyptian. This will dissolve neither in oil, water, nor turpentine, but it must be fused, and then mixed with linseed oil.[1] There is little doubt from the descriptions of Borghini[2] and Baldinucci,[3] that the old masters used the Egyptian asphaltum, since they mention that it was brought from the Lake of Sodom. Other kinds of asphaltum are brought from China, France, Neufchâtel, and Naples. That brought from Naples is reputed to be next in goodness to the Egyptian. It will dissolve in oil, but never yields that intense black to the same quantity of oil as the real Egyptian. This is probably the kind now employed by the Italians, who dissolve it in oil, spirit of turpentine, and Venice turpentine. It is not always easy to procure genuine asphaltum. Watin remarks[4] that it was frequently adulterated with pitch, and that what is generally sold for asphaltum in Holland is nothing but the residuum left after the distillation of oil of amber. Mr. Wilson Neil states that a similar kind of factitious asphaltum is now made in London, which is not inferior to the best Egyptian. This consists of the residuum left from burning linseed-oil and resin. The mixture of resin with asphaltum may be detected by spirit of wine, which dissolves the resin, but not the asphaltum.[5]

Lomazzo says[6] that it was used to give brightness to light and chesnut hair. Boschini states[7] that it was much employed by Andrea Schiavone, who used it in

---

1 Wilson Neil on the Manufacture of Varnishes, Trans. Soc. Arts, vol. xlix. p. 57.

2 Riposo, p. 164.

3 Voc. Dis.

4 L'Art du Vernisseur, p. 216.

5 Marcucci, Saggio, &c., p. 95.

6 Trattato, p. 198.

7 Ricche Minere.

glazing the shades of the flesh in undraped figures,—that Giacomo Bassano (il Vecchio) employed it mixed with lake in the ultimate retouchings, and that he glazed with this colour all the shadows indifferently, whether of flesh, or drapery, or other things. In the Paduan MS. it is stated to be used for the shadows of flesh mixed with umber and burnt terra verde.[1]

Palomino[2] classes asphaltum among the useless colours, and says its place may be supplied with bone black, mixed with fine carmine and ancorca; that it is a bad drier, and requires the addition of a mordant to make it dry: he adds, that there is no doubt it was used by the great colourists, especially in Seville and Granada, although one may do miracles without it. Volpato directs[3] that it should be mixed with boiled oil and verdigris to make it dry.

The evidence of a modern Italian writer[4] and of several restorers of pictures is decidedly in favour of its having been used as a glazing colour only; according to the latter it was dissolved in oil or spirit of turpentine, and applied, like other glazing colours, with the hand, which insured its being thinly and evenly spread. But even as a glazing colour, it grew darker in time,[5] and the obscurity, so frequently observed and regretted, of many Italian pictures, is attributed to the excessive use of asphaltum. The fact that the Neapolitan asphaltum does not yield so intense a black to the same quantity of oil as the Egyptian, with its known property of darkening with age on paintings, would seem to suggest the propriety of using the Egyptian asphaltum, which being intensely black at first, would probably be less likely to increase in colour. Its extreme blackness would at least cause it to be employed sparingly and very thinly as a shadow colour.

---

[1] P. 650. [2] Museo Pictorico, vol. ii. p. 53. [3] P. 747.
[4] Marcucci, pp. 95, 208. [5] Bald., Voc. Dis.

Marcucci describes a liquid preparation of asphaltum composed in the following manner: one part of Venice turpentine and one and a half part of spirit of turpentine are put into a bottle which is to be placed in a sand-bath to liquefy; two parts of asphaltum are then to be added in powder, and the whole is to be stirred and left over the fire until it boils. When it has boiled for one hour, it is to be removed from the fire, and before it cools a little nut-oil is to be added to give it a proper consistence, and when it is used a small quantity of mastic varnish and some kind of drier are to be added. This, he says, is an excellent colour for glazing, but it must be used sparingly, as it deepens its colour with age.

Mummy is by some[1] considered to be the same as asphaltum, but Marcucci[2] states that the colour of the former is warmer, and the smell more aromatic, and that its external character is different. He remarks that it is a fine colour for glazing oil-paintings, especially in the carnations; it is ground with nut-oil, and is used with varnish and a drier.

Black Pigments.

The principal black pigments were terra nera, coal, terra nera di Campana, nero di schiuma di ferro, and charcoal of various kinds; namely, burnt ivory and bones, oak and vine branches, stones of peaches, shells of almonds, paper, smoke of resin, and of nut-oil.

Terra nera, which may certainly be considered synonymous with *terre noire*, is identified by De Mayerne with "*crayon noir*," or "*black chalke*."[3] The Italians procured terra nera from several places. Cennini[4] mentions a black stone brought from Piedmont, used for drawing and painting, which he describes as soft and unctuous. Later Italian writers mention terra

---

[1] Palomino, vol. ii. p. 53.
[2] Saggio, &c., p. 95.
[3] Mr. Eastlake's 'Materials,' &c., p. 466.
[4] Cap. 34.

nera di Roma and terra nera di Venezia; the latter was procured from Verona. Borghini says[1] that nero di terra is a native unctuous pigment, which may be used in fresco, oil, and tempera painting. The name of this pigment occurs in the Paduan MS.[2] Lomazzo[3] does not appear to distinguish it from nero di scaglia.

A black pigment from common coal (charbon de terre) does not appear to be mentioned by Italian writers, although it is said, on the authority of Lebrun,[4] to have been much used in Italy for external painting, because it was more durable than any other. Mr. Eastlake has shown[5] that it was frequently employed by the Flemish and Dutch painters. The tint furnished by coal mixed with oil is stated to be brownish.

Terra nera di Campana is made from a certain crust which forms on the moulds in which bells and artillery are cast. It is used in all three kinds of painting, but in a short time it fades and spoils the pictures. It is mentioned by Borghini,[6] by Baldinucci,[7] and by Lomazzo.[8]

Nero di Schiuma di Ferro was composed of scales of iron mixed with terra verde and finely ground. Borghini, Lomazzo, and Baldinucci mention this colour.

Ivory Black is distinguished by many writers from bone black. It is described as being intensely black, and very transparent. Lebrun remarks that if it is steeped in vinegar and dried in the sun, it cannot be effaced.

Bone Black was prepared from the bones of various animals, but Palomino states[9] that the best kind was prepared from the bones of pigs, although the bones of stags and oxen were sometimes used. Others employed mutton bones. It is represented to be of a reddish colour, which may even be converted into brown by

---

1 Riposo, p. 164. 2 P. 650. 3 Trattato, p. 192. 4 P. 812 and n.
5 Materials, &c., p. 467. 6 Riposo, p. 164. 7 Voc. Dis.
8 Trattato, p. 193. 9 Museo Pictorico, vol. ii. p. 53.

arresting the carbonization before it is complete, and to dry very slowly. In grinding it with oil it is necessary to use more force than with any other colour, in order to add with more facility the necessary quantity of fat or drying oil.[1]

The blacks made from vegetable charcoal are not of so intense a black as those of ivory and bone;[2] of these some painters preferred the black made from burnt vine-branches, sometimes called *blue black*,[3] which Borghini says[4] is excellent for painting in oil. Other authors mention the charcoal of burnt oak stripped of the bark,[5] of the stones of peaches, and of the shells of almonds.[6] The black of peach stones when mixed with white has a blue tint. Lamp black is used in oil painting, although not approved of by many writers.[7] It is always necessary to calcine it before it is used in oil painting.[8] Ink, and especially printing-ink, was formerly made of the soot collected from burning resin or oil in a paper lantern. This is the ink of which Cennini speaks in the early part of his book. It was also used by Lionardo da Vinci[9] mixed with lake for the darkest shades, and Vasari relates that Fra Bartolomeo wishing to imitate the colouring of Lionardo on a certain picture, also employed this colour and burnt ivory, and that the picture had darkened much in consequence. To the same cause Vasari attributes the darkening of the colours in the 'Transfiguration' of Raphael.[10]

Another charcoal black was procured from the ashes of paper, burnt in a closed iron tube and afterwards ground with water.[11] This black pigment is mentioned

1 Constant de Massoul, p. 215. 2 Merimée, p. 208.
3 Constant de Massoul, p. 215.
4 Riposo, p. 164; and see Cennini, Trattato, cap. xxxvii.
5 Palomino, vol. ii. p. 54. Borghini, p. 164.
6 Cennini, cap. 37. Borghini, p. 164. Baldinucci, Voc. Dis.
7 See p. 823. 8 Marcucci, p. 167. Merimée, p. 209.
9 Trattato, c. 353; and see Vasari, Vita di Fra Bartolomeo.
10 Vasari, Vita di Raffaello da Urbino. 11 Marcucci, p. 167.

by Borghini[1] and by Baldinucci, and appears to be still made in Italy. Marcucci[2] states that he had found it a very good black, and that it did not deepen in colour like some other blacks.

Black pigments are considered slow in drying. Volpato directs[3] that boiled oil and verdigris should be added to lamp-black to make it dry.[4] The Paduan MS.[5] recommends the addition of ground glass, which it is stated will make the colour dry in twenty-four hours. Baldinucci[6] says black earth, bone black, and lamp black require the addition of litharge or ground glass to the boiled oil.

From the preceding account of the principal colours used in painting it will be seen that, notwithstanding the numerous names by which pigments were known in different countries and at different periods, the real number was not in fact so great as might be at first imagined. This is exemplified in the various names by which the blue carbonate of copper and the red ores of iron were formerly known.

It will also be observed that the colours lost or fallen into disuse are the native mineral pigments, for which artificial preparations of a similar nature have been substituted. Thus the native yellow and red orpiment have been superseded by the artificial pigments which bear these names, and which, besides the usual defects of artificial as compared with natural pigments, have the additional disadvantage of being more poisonous. Instead of the native giallorino, or Naples yellow, we have the modern pigment composed of the oxides of lead and antimony, known under the name of Naples yellow. Instead of the native carbonates of copper we have the artificial preparations. Native minium and native cinnabar have also fallen into disuse. The only

---

1 Riposo, p. 164. 2 Saggio, p. 208. 3 P. 747. 4 P. 822.
5 P. 666. 6 Voc. Dis.

exception, perhaps, besides the natural yellow and red ochres, is ultramarine, for which no perfect substitute, possessing properties in every respect equally eligible, has yet been discovered. With the exception of these natural pigments, the colours lost are of little value.

It will be also observed that the more durable lakes prepared from kermes and lac have been superseded by the more brilliant, but less permanent, lake from cochineal.

Another source of confusion, and which has much increased the difficulty of identifying pigments, has arisen from giving the name of a well-known pigment to another which resembled it in colour, but which in other respects differed essentially. Among pigments of this description may be enumerated *sandarace, sandaraca,* which has been used to denote red orpiment, red lead, and massicot; *minium,* the ancient term for vermilion, and the modern term for red lead; *cinnabar,* used to signify a red earth and vermilion; *smalto, smaltino,* sometimes applied to a vitreous blue pigment coloured with smalt, sometimes to one coloured with copper; *indigo,* used to denote both woad and indigo; *arzica,* which signified both a yellow lake and a native ochreous pigment; *verdetto,* which denoted sometimes a native mineral green pigment, sometimes an artificial mineral pigment of the same colour, and sometimes a vegetable green pigment.

Finally, the confusion has been increased by adopting foreign names instead of the original term; thus one of the old pigments called giallorino is now known in Italy under the term massicot, and the original appellation is almost lost.

Of Grinding and Diluting the Colours.

The universal testimony of all writers who have treated on the technical part of painting establishes the fact that the colours (excepting some which were kept in powder) were ground in oil.[1] Vasari, Armenini, Bisagno, Borghini, and Gasparo Colombino[2] give the preference to nut-oil, which, it is stated, is less apt to become yellow. Borghini says,[3] "Let him who would paint in oil on panel . . . . colour it with colours tempered with nut-oil only, and nothing else" (senza più). Volpato directs[4] that white lead should be ground with nut-oil; verde eterno, indigo, and all other blues, charcoal, and other colours with linseed oil. The Marciana MS. also directs[5] that all the colours were to be ground with oil as stiffly as possible, that is, with very little oil, and that they were to be ground so finely that on being felt with the fingers no hard grains could be perceived. This is in accordance with the old Italian practice, as described by Cennini, who repeatedly inculcates the perfect levigation of the colours; and with the example of Michael Angelo, who is said to have ground his own colours,[6] and also with the practice of the Flemish school.[7] But it appears that the later Italians, and especially the Venetians, did not consider this point of importance as far as regards the under colours. If there were any doubt of the colours of the Venetians being coarsely ground, it would be sufficiently proved by the assertion of a professor of painting at Venice that he had with his penknife picked out of Venetian

---

1 Félibien, Principes, &c., p. 295. Bulengerus, De Pictura, &c. Bald., Voc. Dis. Lebrun, p. 771.

2 Discorso del Disegno, &c. Padova, 1623.

3 Riposo, p. 138. 4 P. 739. 5 P. 627.

6 See Lanzi, Storia Pittorica, vol. i. p. 114.

7 "Les peintres Flamands ne prennent que la crême des couleurs, après les avoir délayées et noyées dans une grande quantité d'eau."—Traité de la Peinture au Pastel, &c.

pictures of the best period grains of colour sufficiently large to have them analysed.

The recommendation in the Marciana MS. before mentioned to grind the colours with as little oil as possible is insisted upon by most writers on art.[1] Borghini gives[2] as a reason for this practice that the oil in drying would become dark (nero). Again, he remarks, "If the colours are made liquid with too much oil, it lessens considerably their brilliancy." The use of too much oil is frequently condemned by Malvasia[3] and by Lanzi. The latter attributes[4] to this cause the ruin of so many paintings by the Carracci, by Lo Spagnuolo, and by Pasignano. Armenini also concurs in stating that oil renders the colours dark.

After directing how the colours are to be ground the Marciana MS. continues, "Also, while you are painting, if you find the colours too stiff, dip your pencil into a little oil and stir it well into the colour." The same MS. also directs that the "vernice comune," which might be mixed with colours, was, when too thick, to be diluted with oil. It may be considered certain, then, that during the first half of the sixteenth century it was the practice in Italy to dilute the colours with nut or linseed oil, and not with an essential oil. The anecdote related by Ridolfi, who wrote a century later than this MS., proves that this practice was preserved, traditionally at least, in his time. But although this may have been the general practice, it by no means follows that all colours were thus diluted; and the specification that certain colours were to be made to flow by dipping the brush in an essential oil, is at once an admission that it was the general custom to use linseed or nut oil for this purpose, and also that these oils were not equally adapted

1 Félibien, Principes, &c., p. 298. Requenos, Saggio, &c., vol. i. p. 163. Verri, Saggio Elementare, &c., p. 116. Marcucci, Saggio, &c., p. 201.

2 Riposo, p. 175.

3 Fels. Pitt., vol. ii. p. 450.

4 Storia Pittorica, vol. v. pp. 70, 161; vol. i. p. 196.

for all colours. Thus Volpato observes[1] that painters were accustomed to make Spanish blue flow by dipping their brushes in spirit of turpentine, and ultramarine with naphtha. Pacheco, whose whites and blues were the admiration of Cespedes, and of those Italian painters who had seen them, relates[2] that he dipped his brush in oil of spike when painting to make the colours flow. It appears, however, that the practice of diluting the colours with naphtha was sometimes carried to excess by the Bolognese painters; this was the case with Flaminio Torre, the irrecoverable decay of whose pictures is attributed by Malvasia[3] and Lanzi[4] to the constant use of naphtha. Félibien,[5] who appears to have been well acquainted with the Italian practice, remarks that "those who wish their pictures to remain fresh use as little oil as possible, and keep their colours firmer by mixing a little oil of spike with them; this soon evaporates, but it makes the colours flow and work more easily." From a passage in the Brussels MS.[6] it may be concluded that oil of chamomile was sometimes used for the same purpose.

On the Purification and Bleaching of Oil.

There appears to be no doubt that oil was always purified and bleached before the colours were ground with it. It is, however, somewhat extraordinary that neither Armenini, Vasari, Borghini, nor Bisagno allude to this fact. The precautions taken by Lionardo da Vinci[7] for the preparation of his oils are, however, well known, and incidental allusions to the purification of oil may also be found in Vasari[8] and other authors. The remark of the Gesuato, at the end of his directions

---

1 P. 749. 2 Tratado, p. 392. 3 Fels. Pitt., vol. ii. p. 450.

4 Storia Pittorica, vol. v. p. 105. 5 Principes, &c , p. 297. 6 P. 814.

7 Amoretti, Memorie Storiche, &c., di Lionardo da Vinci, p. 149.

8 See account of Giovan Francesco Caroti, in the Life of Fra Giocondo.

for purifying oil—"Observe that, whenever you find oil mentioned, this purified oil is meant"—may be considered proof of the importance attached to this fact. The recipe of the Gesuato forms part of the directions for preparing ultramarine,[1] and the oil was used in making the resinous pastille into which the powdered ultramarine was kneaded, and the colour worked out into the water. If it was necessary to employ purified oil for this purpose, it was much more important to procure such an oil to mix with colours.

The Marciana MS. directs[2] that purified oil should be used for mordants, and at the end of the recipe gives the following directions for purifying it:—"Boil it over the fire with water for three or four hours, then let it settle, and separate it from the water." In another recipe it is said,[3]—"Take linseed-oil, boiled in the usual way;" from which it appears that the method just described was that which was usually adopted. In the same MS. it is remarked,[4] that if the nut or linseed-oil is inspissated by exposure to the sun, the varnish made with it will be clearer.

Palomino states[5] that all colours were generally ground with linseed-oil, because it was more drying than nut-oil, which was reserved solely for the blues and whites in finishing, and especially for ultramarine; "but," he adds, "if nut-oil cannot be obtained, linseed-oil may be clarified by putting it into a vessel with white-lead in powder, stirring it well until it is quite white, and exposing it to the sun and dew, stirring it up every day, for three days, then let it be used, because if it is kept longer, it will become fat. Pacheco's method of preparing bleached linseed-oil, which might be used with white and blue, was as follows:[6]—"Take a glass vessel, and to one pound of limpid and clear

1 Secreti di Don Alessio, parte ii. f. 62; and see Mr. Eastlake's 'Materials,' p. 327. 2 P. 621. 3 Ibid.
4 P. 635. 5 Museo Pictorico, vol. ii. p. 55. 6 Tratado, p. 393.

linseed-oil, add three ounces of spirit of wine, and two ounces of lavender flowers, place it in the sun for fifteen days, shaking it twice every day, and in this manner it will be purified and clear. Then pouring it into another vessel, it may be used for whites, blues, and flesh tints." Some time since I tried this recipe, and found that in proportion as the oil lost its colour, the spirit of wine acquired it, and the mucilage separating, was carried to the bottom of the bottle with the lavender flowers. The yellow colour of the spirit of wine may, perhaps, be accounted for by the fact, that a small quantity of linseed oil is soluble in spirit of wine; four ounce measures of spirit of wine dissolve one drachm of linseed-oil.[1]

Joannes Zahn recommends[2] the following process for the clarification and bleaching of oil for painting:—"Take the acetous herb, which in German is called 'Sauerampffer' (sorrel), cut it into tolerably sized pieces, and boil it in water over the fire; then strain it through a linen cloth, put it into a tin vessel, or into a vase made of iron, tinned, which must be prepared so as to be long and broad, but not deep. This being done, pour on to this water the oil which is to be clarified and bleached, and then put the vase, with the water and supernatant oil, into a place free from dust, and exposed to the hottest rays of the sun in summer for a few days; in a short time the oil will deposit all its impurities, and be wonderfully clarified and bleached by this process, in the same manner as wax and linen are bleached. The oil thus prepared may be used by painters, not only for making their colours more lively, but also for the preparation of the clearer and more brilliant varnishes." This method of purifying linseed-oil I have also tried, and found it very successful in removing the mucilage, which is thrown down in a few

---

[1] Henry's Chemistry, vol. ii. p. 226. [2] Oculus Artificialis, p. 625.

days, and the oil remains very clear and bright, and of a golden colour: it may afterwards be bleached by exposure to the sun.

The purification and preparation of oil for painting, by exposure to heat and washing with water, has been so fully treated by Mr. Eastlake, that it will be unnecessary to cite the authorities or repeat the processes he has described. It may, however, be interesting to state, that I have bleached and clarified linseed-oil by the following process, suggested by the directions of the Gesuato [1] and those of Dreme.[2] A bottle was filled, about one third with oil, another third with water; it was then corked and shaken, until the water and oil were mixed like an emulsion, when the cork was removed, and a piece of muslin tied over the bottle, which was placed on the boiler of a kitchen-range,[3] and kept in a moderate heat day and night. The oil was shaken every day (the muslin being first removed and the cork inserted in the bottle) for a few days, and then suffered to clear. In about a week the oil was removed from the water into another bottle, and the process was repeated for several weeks until the water below the oil ceased to appear milky, and the oil itself was clear and colourless. During this experiment I observed that the mucilage was thrown down sooner if warm water was added to the oil instead of cold, and that the oil separated more rapidly from the water when the bottle was exposed to a gentle and regular heat, although in a dark situation, than when it was placed in the variable warmth of a sunny window. The addition of salt or sand accelerates the clarification of the oil. Many weeks are necessary to complete the process of bleaching and purification. If the oil is intended to remain fluid, it should be preserved in bottles well stopped.[4]

---

1 See 'Materials,' &c., p. 327.

2 Der Virniss-u Kittmacher, &c.

3 Dreme recommends that the bottle should be suspended in an oven moderately heated.

4 See Mr. Eastlake's 'Materials,' &c., p. 341.

The purification of oil will always be attended with much waste. It may be considered that, with the greatest care, nearly half will be lost in the process. The mucilage alone frequently forms one-third of the oil.

Dryers and Drying Oils.

The necessity of the colours drying quickly, and the circumstance of some drying more rapidly than others, led to the addition of other ingredients to the oil.

The following observations will be limited to the drying ingredients mentioned in the Treatises contained in this work, and to those adopted by the Italian and Spanish painters.

The earliest notice of drying oil which occurs in the following works is to be found in the MS. of Eraclius.[1] In this recipe the oil was boiled with lime,[2] and ceruse being then added, it was placed in the sun for a month or more, and frequently stirred. The use of white-lead as a dryer has been continued to the present day. It was sometimes stirred into the oil, which was then exposed to the sun and dew, and well stirred every day for three days, when it was ready for use.[3] If suffered to remain longer than the time specified, it would become fat. By some modern Italian artists white-lead

---

1 P. 232.

2 The most powerful of all dryers is perhaps chloride of lime in a dry state: a small quantity of this added to clarified oil will convert it into a solid; for this reason it must be employed very cautiously. If too much be used, it may burn the brushes, and injure the colours. It has the advantage of not darkening the oil, and its drying property appears to arise from its absorbing the watery particles of the oil. Chloride of calcium is equally efficacious as a dryer; but the small quantity of iron which it contains dissolves in the oil, and darkens it. It seems probable that if the chloride of lime were judiciously employed, it might prove serviceable as a dryer; but as I am not aware that it has been tried as such by any person but myself, the utmost caution would be required, and some experiments would be necessary in order to ascertain the smallest possible quantity which would answer the purpose intended. As a dryer for house paint it may perhaps be found useful.

3 Palomino, vol. ii. p. 55.

is placed on a strainer, and the oil is suffered to filter through it, when it is ready for use.

The preparation of oil for painting is not mentioned in the Bolognese MS.; but in two of the recipes for making "vernice liquida" directions are given for rendering the oil drying previous to the addition of the resin. In No. 207,[1] the oil is directed to be boiled with burnt roche alum in powder, and minium or vermilion; and after boiling a proper time it is to be set fire to, and allowed to burn for a short time, when it is to be extinguished, and again placed over the fire and burnt as before.

This is, probably, the only recipe for drying oil in which vermilion is mentioned; but as that pigment is not known to possess any peculiarly siccative properties, it may be supposed that it was considered by the writer as synonymous with minium (the cinnabar of the ancients), the term applied to red-lead during the middle ages throughout Europe, and from that time to the present in Italy.

The burning of the oil, recommended in this recipe, was for the purpose of depriving it of its unctuosity, and with this view it is still resorted to by the makers of printing ink.

In the recipe No. 262, in the Bolognese MS.,[2] 2 lbs. of common oil, that is, olive-oil, and 2 lbs. of linseed-oil are boiled with 30 or 40 cloves of garlic, until, on dipping a hen's feather into the oil, it is found to be burnt. This trial with the feather is still the common test of the oil's being sufficiently boiled. The use of the garlic was probably to supply moisture to the oil, and thus prevent its carbonization. Garlic is mentioned as an ingredient in drying oil or fat oil by Pacheco and Palomino; and according to the former the oil was boiled until the garlic was burnt or toasted.[3]

---

1 P. 489. 2 P. 521. 3 Tratado, p. 404.

Garlic yields a gelatinous juice, which does not appear to be miscible with oil. Pacheco also mentions as dryers, minium and white lead, which if added to oil, and placed in a glass vessel in the sun in summer, for fifteen days, stirring it every day, and then straining it, would be very good.

According to Lebrun,[1] drying oil was prepared by suspending a piece of rag containing umber and minium in a vessel with nut-oil, and boiling it. The mordants described in the Paduan MS.,[2] and in the 'Riposo' of Borghini (p. 176), greatly resemble this drying oil. In the first, ochre is added to the other ingredients; in the second, giallorino, calcined bones, and burnt vitriol; which Borghini says is to be "calcined in the fire until it is red; and this vitriol makes all colours which are naturally bad dryers siccative, although it discolours them."[3]

Besides white-lead and minium, litharge, the semi-vitrified oxide of lead, was employed as a dryer for oil. Volpato gives[4] directions for preparing *olio cotto*, by boiling it on litharge, but he does not specify the proportion of litharge. The Jesuit, Father Lana,[5] recommends, for this purpose, two ounces of litharge for each pound of oil. Lebrun calls[6] this preparation "huile grasse," fat oil, which he distinguishes from drying oil.

Lebrun also remarks, that the litharge might be ground on the porphyry with oil, made into a little ball and dried When required for use it was to be boiled until the litharge was dissolved, and, when cold, the oil was said to become as clear as rock-water. This oil was considered very good as a siccative for those colours which did not dry well, such as lakes, black,[7] &c. When used for painting on glass, the proportion of litharge was much increased: thus the Paduan MS.[8]

---

[1] P. 816. [2] P. 692.

[3] Burnt vitriol is sulphate of iron calcined. Iron is to a certain extent soluble in oil, which it renders dark. [4] P. 741. [5] P. 746, n.

[6] P. 816. [7] P. 818. [8] P. 692.

prescribes half a pound of this ingredient to a pound of oil; but for pictures this cannot be recommended. The recipe for "olio cotto," given by Fra Fortunato, differs from these recipes in directing the addition of water, which is to be boiled with the litharge and oil, which he says will cause the oil to become as clear (colourless) as water itself.[1]

In the appendix to the Italian edition of 'L'Idée du Peintre Parfait' of De Piles, drying oil is described as composed of nut-oil boiled with litharge and sandarac. This composition is in fact identical with the old "vernice liquida." It differs but little from the mordant of Cennini,[2] which consisted of linseed oil, vernice (dry sandarac), and white lead. In the former, the dryer was litharge; in the latter, white lead.

In the time of Baldinucci, *olio cotto* was prepared by boiling linseed or nut-oil, either alone, or with litharge or glass, finely ground with water. It is stated by this author to have been used to temper those colours which are slow in drying, such as lake, terra nera, bone, and other blacks, because both litharge and ground glass have the property of making them dry quickly. Oil, boiled without either of these ingredients, was used to accelerate the drying of those colours, which dry well of themselves, such as white lead, minium, terra verde, umber, cinnabar, smalti, and others; but if used with white lead it would become yellow. "Pure boiled oil," continues Baldinucci, "when it is prepared with very clear oil, is also used by painters instead of varnish in the darkest shades, and where the colours have sunk in. And remember, that raw nut and linseed oil are by nature drying, but they do not dry so soon as when

---

[1] "Per far l'olio cotto da Pittore, che sia chiaro, come acqua. Metti il solito piumazzolo col litargirio, et altro come si usa dentro l'oglio di noce, o di lino, a bollire, e con esso mettivi seco dell' acqua a bollire, che questa la fara rimaner chiaro, come l'acqua medesima."

[2] Trattato, cap. 151.

boiled, and especially as when mixed with ground glass and litharge."[1]

Volpato also recommends[2] that "olio cotto" and verdigris should be mixed with asphaltum and black to make them dry.

An eminent professor of painting at Venice stated that Chilone, an old Venetian painter, who died about the year 1834 or 1836, was acquainted with Canal[3] and Canaletto,[4] and that Chilone said these two artists used oil boiled on litharge, which they recommended him to use also, and that they frequently spread it over the whole picture.

It appears certain then from the above evidence, that the preparations of lead were the dryers most approved in Italy, but it may be collected from an expression of Padre Lana's that some doubts had been raised as to their eligibility for this purpose. Speaking of oil boiled on litharge, Lana says, "This application is not so injurious as some persons have imagined; and the advantage is, that it dries quickly, for raw oil is a long time in drying." There can be no doubt, however, that litharge is injurious to those colours which are incompatible with lead, such as Indian lake and orpiment.

The mixture of ground glass with colours as a dryer is not, that I am aware of, mentioned in Italian works written earlier than the seventeenth century: the Paduan MS.[5] and Baldinucci's 'Vocabulary of Design' appear to be the only Italian authorities for it, although it may have been common at the time these works were written. The practice probably originated in the ancient custom of mixing pulverised glass with orpiment, with the object, as some authors say, of making it grind more easily; others say, of making it dry

---

[1] Vocabolario del Disegno. [2] P. 747.

[3] Fabio Canal was born in 1703, and died in 1767.

[4] The real name of Canaletto was Antonio Canal. He died in 1768, aged 71. [5] P. 666.

better. For the latter purpose it was employed by Pacheco, who remarks [1] that when orpiment was ground with linseed oil, it required a dryer, and that some persons added to it glass ground with water; others added linseed oil which has been suffered to fatten by mixing with it red lead in powder. Others, he adds, use a proper quantity of white copperas in powder; but he warns his readers to beware of verdigris, which is its greatest enemy. Pacheco also recommends,[2] as a dryer for carmine, either ground glass or litharge in powder, or a little of the fat oil (with minium) before mentioned, or white copperas tempered with oil, or added in powder.

Ground glass appears to have been a favourite dryer with Palomino, who says [3] that it was excellent for all colours, and that it might be ground with nut or linseed oil like one of the colours, and preserved in a bladder, and a little put on the palette when necessary. This author describes [4] a drying oil for blues and whites, composed of ground glass, litharge, white lead, and red lead, of each one ounce, and half a pound of oil, boiled for a short time together in a water bath. Ground glass also forms one of the ingredients in a recipe given by the same author for drying oil, which, from being boiled longer, appears to have been of a darker colour.

The mixture of pulverized glass with colours is scarcely to be recommended, because a part of the alkali, which is free, is liable to be acted on by the air and other causes.[5] That the alkali is free, may be ascertained by merely boiling some powdered glass in water; on dipping turmeric paper into the water, the paper will be found to have acquired a brown stain. The ill effects

---

1 Tratado, p. 388.

2 Ibid., p. 390.

3 Vol. ii. p. 56.

4 Vol. ii. p. 55.

5 See an article in the Magazine of Science, vol. iv. p. 67, "On the action of water on powdered glass."

liable to ensue from the presence of salts in pictures have been described by Mr. Smith in the First Report of the Commissioners of the Fine Arts: they are also alluded to by De Piles,[1] by Lanzi[2] in a note on Correggio's method of painting, and by Mr. Eastlake.[3] The glass made in Venice contained lead; when this glass was ground and mixed with colours, the lead probably acted on the oil as a dryer, and would affect the colours in the same way as other preparations of lead. In this point of view, therefore, glass can scarcely be an eligible dryer for orpiment, which is decomposed by lead. Manganese was another ingredient in Italian glass; but as the native oxide of manganese is not found pure, but is contaminated with iron, lead, and copper, it may be conjectured that these metals formed part of the glass. The manganese of Piedmont was considered by Neri to be purer than that of Tuscany and Liguria; the latter contained much iron, which gave the glass a dark hue, but it is still probable that the manganese of Piedmont contained the other metals, which cannot be a desirable addition to colours, especially as oils are known to act on copper and iron. If pounded glass has really any drying property (and it must be supposed that it was not classed among dryers without due consideration), this property may be attributed to the metals it contains, which are in the state of oxides.

There is good reason to suppose that white copperas (sulphate of zinc), which is mentioned as a dryer by Flemish and German writers of the fifteenth century, was the dryer of Van Eyck. We owe this discovery to the research of Mr. Eastlake.[4]

With the exception of Padre Vincente Coronelli, white copperas does not appear to be mentioned by any

---

[1] Elémens, p. 141. [2] Vol. iv. p. 71, n. [3] Materials, &c., p. 424, n.
[4] See Materials, &c., p. 130, 136, 284, 299, 311, 365-367.

Italian author as an ingredient in drying oil; but it was employed in Italy in the composition of a mordant for painting on glass by a Venetian friar,[1] about 150 years previous to the date of Coronelli's work. This mordant is described in the Marciana MS.:[2] it consisted of white copperas, mastic, dry sandarac, and roche-alum, ground in purified linseed oil. As a mordant for gold, the effects of this composition could not have been very durable, since it is recommended that vessels on which it was applied should be washed with cold water only, and rubbed or wiped very gently. Copperas is mentioned as an ingredient in a mordant for gilding, and as a dryer, by Pacheco,[3] who recommends it for orpiment and carmine; and by Palomino,[4] who remarks that it may be ground with oil, and placed on the palette like a colour: he says that burnt alum may be added to it, but that he has not tried this dryer. De Piles also states[5] that copperas ground in oil was used as a dryer for lake and ultramarine, but he expresses a doubt whether, on account of its being a salt, it may not, in drying, cover the picture with a white efflorescence, especially in damp situations. There can be little doubt that the objection of De Piles was well founded. It has been already observed that the introduction of any salt into the colours must always be prejudicial, and there seems no reason to make an exception in favour of sulphate of zinc. The same objection does not apply to the addition of this substance to drying-oil: on the contrary, there is reason to believe that calcined sulphate of zinc and the oxide of zinc are the safest of all metallic dryers.[6]

---

1 It is very probable, as was suggested to me by a friend, that this "fratre Veneziano" was Fra Sebastian del Piombo, who was a native of Venice. If this be the fact, it affords additional reason for considering that copperas was the dryer of Van Eyck, inasmuch as Fra Sebastian was the pupil of Gian Bellino, who was contemporary with Antonello da Messina.

2 P. 621. 3 Tratado, p. 388, 390, 418. 4 Vol. ii. p. 56.

5 Elémens, p. 140. 6 See Mr. Eastlake's 'Materials,' &c., p. 349.

Verdigris is one of the most powerful dryers, and its effects have long been known. Cennini mentions[1] it as promoting the drying of mordants. Armenini, and his copyist Bisagno, and De Piles,[2] recommend its being added to black, Volpato[3] to black and asphaltum, and Palomino[4] to black and carmine. But its drying properties appear to be more than counterbalanced by others which are highly injurious to many pigments, and cautions may be found in several writers against the injudicious use of it. De Piles[5] remarks that it is the plague of all the colours, and that if the smallest particle were to be mixed with the priming, it might destroy the whole picture.

There is another dryer mentioned by Italian writers which can only be used in dark primings or mordants: this is the dirty oil pressed from the brushes into a tin vessel kept for this purpose. Volpato says,[6] "this dries like a mordant even in winter." Lebrun remarks[7] that this oil may be used for the dead-colouring or for the priming; Borghini mentions[8] it as an ingredient in a mordant.

Calcined bones, which were so much used by the Flemish painters, do not appear to have been employed to promote the drying of oil by the Italians, although they are mentioned as an ingredient in a mordant by Borghini.[9]

It will be seen, therefore, from the above-mentioned authorities, that the dryers named in works of art as most commonly used in Italy, from the earliest period until the present time, were preparations of lead.

Mastic, which has always been so much used in varnish, has from a very early period been considered a dryer. Mr. Eastlake gives[10] two instances, one of

---

1 Trattato, cap. 151, 152.
2 Elémens, p. 125.
3 P. 747.
4 Vol. ii. p. 56.
5 Elémens, p. 124.
6 P. 732.
7 P. 770.
8 Riposo, p. 176.
9 Ibid., p. 176.
10 Materials, &c., p. 172, n.

which is from the Lucca MS., the other from the Venetian MS. A solution of mastic in nut oil is recommended by Errante[1] as the only eligible dryer. This fact naturally leads to the consideration of the varnishes used with colours in Italy, and of the resins of which they were composed. Before entering on this subject, I shall offer a few observations on some of the essential oils used in painting.

Essential Oils.

The purity of the essential oils is not less requisite than that of the other materials. Mr. Eastlake observes[2] that "their drying property is in proportion to their rectification, and that the lasting purity of their tint may partly depend on the same circumstance."

Essential oils should be kept in close vessels, and excluded from light. By long exposure to air and light, volatile oils become thick, and darker in colour, and assume the appearance of resins.

The essential oils commonly used in painting were naphtha, spirit or oil of turpentine, and oil of spike. The first of these is considered to have been employed in painting by the ancient Egyptians.[3]

Oil of spike should be the foreign oil of lavender; but what is usually sold as such is a mixture of three parts oil of turpentine and one part oil of spike.[4] These ingredients are sometimes rectified together. English oil of lavender is sold for a guinea a pound, while oil of spike may be purchased for twelve or fourteen shillings the pound.

The naphtha, used by the Italian painters for diluting their colours and varnishes, was a natural production of many parts of Italy, particularly of the territories of Modena and Parma. It is also found in

---

[1] Saggio sui Colori, &c. [2] Materials, &c., p. 313.

[3] See D'Agincourt, vol. ii. p. 2.

[4] See Rennie's Supplement to the Pharmacopœias.

Bohemia, Persia, and in Colebrooke Dale in Shropshire; but the finest specimens are furnished by Italy. Naphtha, like turpentine, should be rectified before it is used for painting or varnishes.[1] The naphtha of the shops is distilled from wood; but it probably differs considerably from the native naphtha, which is used by chemists for the purpose of keeping potassium, for which the wood naphtha is entirely unfit. The native naphtha, therefore, should be procured for painting. It is said to be the purest and most unchangeable of the essential oils.[2]

While mentioning essential oils, it will be proper to allude briefly to the volatile oil of linseed or nuts, which was occasionally used in diluting varnishes.

The earliest notice of distilled linseed oil is probably that which occurs in the old part of the Bolognese MS.,[3] (written previously to the introduction of the Flemish process of oil-painting into Italy,) in a recipe for making artificial stones for rings. It will be observed that although the distilled oil in this case was not used for painting, yet it is stated by the author that any pigment put into it will retain its colour for ever.

Vasari's account of the singular experiments, as he calls them, of Lionardo da Vinci on oils and varnish, is not conclusive evidence that he distilled linseed and nut oils, or either of them; he merely states that he distilled oils and herbs to make varnishes;[4] and this may be true with regard to the olio di trementina and olio di spigo, as well as to linseed and nut oil. The passage in Lomazzo's 'Tempio della Pittura'[5] is rather more definite; but even this is not conclusive. In speaking of Lionardo, he says, "della tempera, passò all' olio, il quale usava di assotigliar con i lambicchi, onde è

---

1 Verri, Saggio, &c., p. 138.

2 Mr. Eastlake's 'Materials,' &c., p. 314.

3 P. 507.

4 "Cominciò a stillare oli ed erbe per fare la vernice." See Life of Lionardo da Vinci.

5 P. 49.

causato che quasi tutte le opere sue si sono spiccate dai muri, siccome fra l' altre si vede nel consiglio di Fiorenza la mirabile battaglia, e in Milano la Cena di Christo in Sta. Maria delle Gratie che sono guaste per l' imprematura che egli gli diede sotto."

Besides the passages in Vasari and Lomazzo, which attribute to Lionardo the use of distilled oil, there is the recipe in the 'Secreti' of Alessio,[1] which is conclusive as to the fact that linseed oil was distilled and used to dilute amber varnish. This recipe has been copied by Wecker,[2] by Bonanni, and by Salmon in his 'Polygraphices.' It is stated that this varnish was to be applied on pictures or figures, "sopra alle figure."

Another notice of linseed oil, distilled with other ingredients, occurs in the 'Nuovo Plicto.'[3] In this recipe linseed oil, vernice liquida, roche-alum, nitre, Roman vitriol, and mastic are boiled together, and afterwards distilled. The water which comes over is said to be good for tempering colours in miniature-painting, and for staining or dyeing linen and other things. It must be kept closely corked, otherwise it will evaporate.

The fact, therefore, of linseed and nut oil being used in painting, except for miniatures, appears to rest on the inconclusive testimony of Vasari and Lomazzo that it was used by Lionardo da Vinci; at the same time it will not escape notice that both these authors, who were painters, and undoubtedly acquainted with the method practised at the time they lived, disapproved of the processes of Lionardo, which they evidently considered unusual. As a mere diluent, distilled linseed or nut oil when rectified, and no longer subject to crystallise at a low temperature,[4] may not be more objectionable than spirit of turpentine, oil of spike, or

---

[1] Part ii. p. 74. [2] De Secretis, lib. xvi. p. 643. [3] P. 76, 77.

[4] At the temperature of 40° of Fahrenheit distilled linseed oil is converted into a mass of needle-shaped crystals.

naphtha; but the circumstance of its being so rarely mentioned by writers on painting, when so many must have been acquainted with it, suggests the idea that it was not in general use.

Some caution is necessary in using these essential oils either with varnish or colours upon paint that is not thoroughly dry, lest they should disturb the colours,[1] for they are all powerful solvents. Oil of spike and oil of turpentine are frequently used by picture cleaners to dissolve dirty varnishes, and they often bring away the glazings which have been applied with an essential oil varnish, as well as the varnish itself.

Resins.

Turpentine and Resin.—By turpentine, trementina, and terebinthina is understood the resinous liquid which flows from many kinds of trees; when this liquid is hardened by the sun, or by fire, it is called *resin, ragia,* or *colophony.*

The turpentine of Dioscorides appears to have been what is now called Chio turpentine, the produce of the Pistacia terebinthus of Linnæus; the Terebinthina pistacina, Off. We have no means of ascertaining whether this was the turpentine mentioned in mediæval MSS., for Matthioli relates[2] that in his time the importation of it had ceased for so long a period that the remembrance of it was almost lost, and the resin of the larch had been introduced in its place, and had usurped its name. This author, however, states that the real turpentine tree grew plentifully at Trent, and in several parts of Italy. He also remarks that, although this was the best kind of turpentine, it had only recently (Matthioli's work was published in 1549) been brought to Venice. It was first imported in the dry state, but it was afterwards brought in abundance liquid as it

---

1 See De Piles, Elémens de Peinture, p. 167. De Massoul, Art of Painting, p. 25.

2 Diosc., p. 126.

exuded from the tree. Laguna mentions[1] that Venice was supplied with the best kind of turpentine from Cyprus; but it was so much adulterated that out of one barrel were made twenty. When, therefore, turpentine and larch resin are both mentioned in early medieval MSS., as in the chapter *de Lucide ad Lucidas* in the Lucca MS., the turpentine may be considered to have been of the kind mentioned by Dioscorides; but where turpentine only is spoken of, the point is doubtful. At a later period, and until a few years previous to 1549, trementina may be understood in the works of Italian writers to signify the turpentine of the larch. In this sense, perhaps, the trementina and terebinthina of the Bolognese MS. (in which larch resin is not mentioned) are to be understood.

Venice Turpentine.—Matthioli states that the produce of the Pinus larix (larice of the Italians, mélèze of the French, the larch), called *turpentine of the larch* and Venice turpentine, was formerly called "*laricina.*" His account of this resin is as follows:—

"There is also extracted from the larch that liquid and excellent resin which is called 'terebinthina' in all the druggists' shops in Italy, because it superseded that which is extracted from the terebinthino; for the merchants having ceased to import the terebinthina, the physicians brought into use instead of it that which is produced by the larch, whence it acquired the name of *turpentine* (terebinthina). Nevertheless Fuchsio, in his last book on the Composition of Medicines, was mistaken when he wrote that the apothecaries now use instead of the true terebinthina nothing but the liquid resin of the abeto (Pinus picea of Linnæus), which we call tears (lagrime), for it is known to all the world that the common terebinthina now in use is not extracted from any other tree but the larch. . . . . The

[1] Diosc. ilustrado por el Doct. Laguna. Salamanca, 1570.

peasants inhabiting those mountains call this liquor *largà*, from the larch (larice), whence it exudes.[1] This kind of turpentine is called "largata" by Zuane Mariani,[2] and it appears to have been the only sort of turpentine imported into Venice in 1567.

The liquid resin which was sold in France under the name of térébenthine de Venise, was procured in the neighbourhood of Lyons; and Pomet says[3] that it should rather be called "térébenthine fine du bois de Pilatre ou de Lyon." The Lyonnais called it *bijon*; but at Rouen it was called *berniz*. At the present time much of this resin is brought from the confines of Briançon.[4]

Olio di Abezzo, Strassburg Turpentine, Gomme du Sapin.—The resin which exudes from the Terebinthina abietina, Off., the Pinus picea of Linnæus, the abete of the Italians, the sapin of the French, is the Resina sapini of the Lucca MS. and Clavicula (p. 54). "The abete produces that most excellent liquor commonly called tears (lagrime), or olio di abezzo. . . . . . It is frequently adulterated with the resin of the larch, which is not so dear as the olio di abezzo, and sometimes when the larch resin is very clear and limpid it is sold for the real olio di abezzo; for few apothecaries know one from the other. But the fraud may be detected, first, because the olio di abezzo is much more liquid, and also because it has an agreeable odour, and is much more bitter to the taste than the larch resin; and when it is more than a year old, it acquires a yellowish colour, and becomes somewhat solid."[5] The Marciana MS. mentions[6] that genuine olio di abezzo may be distinguished by its drying rapidly; but when it is mixed with turpentine it dries very slowly.

---

1 Matthioli, p. 118.

2 See Tariffa Perpetua di Zuane Mariani, Venetia, 1567.

3 Histoire des Drogues, vol. ii. p. 62.

4 Diz. delle Droghe di Chevalier e Richard. Venezia, 1831.

5 Matthioli, p. 120.

6 P. 635.

Resin, Resin of the Pine, Gomme de Pin, Bordeaux Turpentine.—This is the produce of the Terebinthina pinea, the Pinus maritima, a variety of the Pinus sylvestris, the Pinus abies of Linnæus.[1] Whenever the word "ragia" occurs in Italian writers, the resin of the pine is always to be understood.[2] This resin is firmer and more solid than that of the larch or the abete. When this resin has been purified by melting it in the sun, and suffering it to run through the small holes perforated in the bottom of the vessel containing it, it is considered equal in quality to Strassburg turpentine. When it is purified by melting it over the fire, and straining it through straw, it is called "yellow pitch or resin," "white pitch," and "Burgundy pitch." If the residuum left after the distillation of spirit of turpentine be stirred briskly with water, it loses its transparency, and acquires a dark yellow colour. In this state it is called "yellow resin or pitch."[3]

Pierre Pomet states that it was called in France "barras," or "galipot," and that there were two kinds, one of which was called "encens blanc," the other "encens marbré." The incense usually burnt in churches is the produce of the Pinus abies.[4]

Pece Greca, or Greek Pitch, Pece Spagnuola, or di Spagna, Pegola di Spagna, Colophony.—The signification of these terms cannot be better explained than in the words of Matthioli:[5]—"What is commonly called pece di Spagna, pece Greca, and colophonia by the apothecaries is nothing but resin boiled in the manner described by Dioscorides. These names were derived from the places whence they were brought. But there was another kind of colophonia described by Dioscorides, which was liquid, and which was called, *par excellence*, colophonia. This was very scarce and

1 Trattato delle Droghe Semplici, da Guibourt, iii. p. 412. 2 Ricett. Fior.
3 Trattato delle Droghe, da Guibourt, p. 415.
4 Humboldt's Kosmos, ii. 441. 5 Trans. of Diosc., p. 126.

dear." Matthioli thinks that the latter was the olio di abezzo, which is not mentioned either by Dioscorides or Pliny.

The hardest of all the resins is colophonia;[1] the terebinthina continues liquid a long time, and the olio di abezzo remains in a moderately liquid state. The best "pece di Spagna" was brought from the island of Pityusa, on the coast of Spain.

In the Greek MS. of Mount Athos, pece Greca is called Pégoula.[2] It appears that it was also known by this name in Italy. Thus Fioravanti states,[3] in his 'Secreti,' "La vernice commune è una compositione, la quale si fa di olio di lino e di pece Greca, con una parte del olio, e tre di *pegola*," &c.

Olibanum, *Thus album*, *Incenso*, *Frankincense*, are synonymous terms in works on art. Under the first name this resin appears to be included among the ingredients in the chapters of the Lucca MS. and Mappæ Clavicula (p. 54, 55), entitled "De Petalo Aureo," and "Lucida quomodo fiant super Colores." This resin is mentioned in the commercial treaty between Bologna and Ferrara in 1193.[4] The best kind was formerly imported by way of Tauris (now Tabreez), whence it was called "Torisino."[5] The tree which produced the Arabian frankincense of Hadhramaut, so famous from the most ancient times, has not yet been discovered and determined by any botanist. There is a similar product in the East Indies, which, according to Colebrooke, has been obtained from the Boswellia thurifera, or serrata. The olibanum of our druggists is the produce of an American plant, the Icica guyanensis, of the same family (Burseraceæ) as the Boswellia.[6] Frankincense was used by the old

[1] Trans. of Diosc., p. 127. [2] Manuel d'Iconographie, p. 40.
[3] Secreti di S. Leonard. Fioravanti, lib. iii. cap. 95. [4] Depping, i. 241.
[5] See the work of Pegoletti and Uzzano, cited by Depping, i. 142.
[6] Humboldt's Kosmos, Sabine's translation, London, 1848, vol. ii. p. 440.

painters in the composition of the pastille with which ultramarine was mixed, as well as in varnishes;[1] and we learn from the Bolognese MS.[2] that when it was dissolved in linseed-oil, the composition was sometimes called "vernice liquida." From the scarcity of oriental olibanum, it was frequently adulterated with gum and resin. The resin held in most esteem in the East for burning as incense was, according to Agricola,[3] amber; but it is probable that for amber we should read oriental copal.[4]

Sandarac.—This resin is brought from the southern provinces of Morocco. In the language of the country it is called "el Grassa;"[5] and by this name it has always been known in Spain. Thus Pacheco says, "Grassa . . . . which is the gum of the juniper, which the Arabs call sandarac."[6] Palomino mentions this resin under the name "grasilla." It was generally believed that sandarac was the gum of the juniper, and as such it is described by Matthioli, Laguna,[7] Bulengerus,[8] and other writers; but it is now known to exude from the Thuya articulata (African arbor vitæ), a dwarf tree somewhat resembling the juniper.[9] In its dry state, sandarac was called vernix, vernice grossa,[10] vernice in grana,[11] vernice da scrivere.[12] The last name was derived from the pulverized sandarac being formerly rubbed over cotton paper to prepare it for writing.

---

1 Pp. 165, 630. 2 P. 489. 3 De Metallicis, p. 243.

4 See Pharmaceutical Journal, vol. v. part iv.

5 Encyc. Brit., tit. Sandarac.

6 "Grassa, que es la goma del enepro que los Arabes llaman Sandaraca." Tratado, 410.

7 Diosc. ilustr. por el Doct. Laguna, p. 62. 8 De Pictura, &c.

9 Mr. Eastlake's 'Materials,' &c., p. 232.

10 Borghini (Riposo, p. 175) says "sandaraca ovvero vernice grossa."

11 "Vernice di sandaraca o vernice in grana," Secreti di S. Leonard. Fioravanti, Torino, 1580, lib. iii. cap. 68. Marciana MS., pp. 609, 621, 631.

12 "Vernice da scrivere, cioè sandracha, cioè gomma di ginepro." Secreti di D. Alessio, part ii. f. 57.

When sandarac was dissolved in linseed-oil, it constituted the "vernice liquida" of the Italians.[1]

Mastic.—This is a resin obtained from the Pistacia lentiscus, a tree which grows in the Levant, and particularly in the island of Chios. Mastic appears to have been always used in the arts as a varnish; and in the Lucca MS.[2] it is recommended to be added to a varnish or mordant composed of linseed-oil, with resins and gums of various kinds, as a dryer. Mastic and mastic-varnish are also mentioned as dryers by Italian writers on art.[3]

Amber, Succinum, Carabe, Glassa, Glas.—The vegetable origin of amber is now universally admitted. On this subject Humboldt remarks:[4]—"Goeppert's excellent researches, which, it is hoped, will soon appear illustrated with plates, inform us 'that all the Baltic amber is derived from a coniferous tree, which, as proclaimed by the extant remains of the wood and bark, were obviously of different ages, came nearest to our white and red pine timber, but still constituted a particular species.' The amber-tree of the former world (Pinites succifer) had a richness in resin with which none of the coniferous tribes of the present world will bear comparison, inasmuch as great masses of amber are contained not only within and upon the bark, but also between the rings of the wood, and in the direction of the medullary rays, which, as well as the cells, are seen under the microscope to be filled with ambreous resin, of a whiter or yellower colour in different places. Amongst the vegetable matters inclosed in amber we find both male and female flowers of indigenous, aci-

1 Bol. MS., pp. 489, 521. Secreti di D. Alessio, part ii. f. 57, 160. Caneparius, de Atramentis, pp. 260, 341, 378, 379. Bulengerus de Pictura, &c., lib. ii. cap. ii. Other authorities are cited by Mr. Eastlake, 'Materials,' &c., p. 238.

2 De Confectio Lucidæ; and see Clavicula, p. 53.

3 See Errante, Saggio sui Colori; Armenini, de' Veri Precetti; and Bisagno, Trattato, &c.

4 Kosmos, vol. i. p. 303, and see vol. ii. p. 412.

cular-leaved, and cupuliferous trees; but distinct fragments of Thuja, Cupressus, Ephedera, and Castania vesca, mingled with others of junipers and firs, indicate a vegetation which is different from that of the present coasts and plains of the Baltic."

Amber, according to Berzelius, "contains *five* substances:—1. An odoriferous oil, in small quantity.—2. A yellow resin, intimately combined with this oil, dissolving freely in alcohol, ether, and alkalis, very fusible, and resembling ordinary vegetable resins.—3. A resin soluble with difficulty in cold alcohol, more freely in hot alcohol, from which it separates on cooling, as a white powder soluble in ether and alkalis. These two resins and the volatile oil, if removed from amber by ether, and then obtained by evaporation of the latter in water, form a natural viscid balsam, very odorous, of a clear yellow colour, and which gradually becomes hard, but retains some odour. There is every reason for supposing this to be precisely the substance from which amber originates, but rather poorer in essential oil than at first; and that the insoluble substances in amber have been gradually formed by a spontaneous alteration of this balsam, but at the same time have enveloped one part of it, and so preserved it from entire decomposition or change.—4. Succinic acid, dissolved with the preceding bodies by ether, alcohol, and alkalis.—5. A body insoluble in alcohol, ether, and alkalis, analogous in some points to the substance found by Dr. John in lac, and called by him the *principle of lac*. This is formed in large quantity when a solution of lac in alkali is precipitated by chlorine."[1]

Amber was formerly found on the coasts of the Baltic, also near the Po and Adriatic: and it is stated by Depping[2] to have been imported from the Maldives.

---

[1] Ure's Dictionary of Chemistry, p. 147.

[2] Histoire du Commerce, vol. i. p. 142.

The amber found on the shores of the Baltic was known to the inhabitants of those countries under the name of glessum, whence *glasse, glassa, glas.* The fact of amber having been found near the Po, and on the shores of the Adriatic, is mentioned by Agricola,[1] and by Matthioli, merely as a report, which they considered to have originated from the circumstance that amber necklaces were commonly worn by the peasant women of these countries;[2] and both authors carefully distinguish amber or succino from the gum or resin which exudes from the black and white poplars growing on the banks of the Po. The latter writer, especially, is very precise in this respect. In quoting the following passage from Serapion, "Et dicitur quod gummi Haur Romi,[3] quod nascitur circa fluvium, qui dicitur Eridanus, quando distillat in flumine illo, coagulatur ibi, et est illud, quod dicitur Alipton, id est electrum; et sunt qui nominant ipsum Arsopodon, et est charabe," and a similar passage from Avicenna, he remarks, they do not affirm that charabe is the gum of the black poplar, but merely that it is said to be. Conder,[4] however, mentions that amber is found in earth impregnated with petroleum, beneath the vineyards and corn-fields in the territory of Modena; and it will also be recollected that in the book lent by Fra Dionisio to Alcherius, a certain gum, Andrianum, which had attractive powers similar to those possessed by amber and resins generally, is stated to have been found on Monte Buono (Bene).[5] Phillips[6] states that amber is actually found in Italy and on the coast of the Adriatic.

---

1 De Metallicis, f. 238. Trans. of Diosc., pp. 155, 156.

2 "The Etrurians carried on considerable trade through the north of Italy and across the Alps, where 'the Sacred Road' led to the distant amber countries." (See Humboldt's Kosmos, vol. ii. p. 164.) These traders probably supplied the Italian women with amber.

3 Haur Romi is the Arab name for the black poplar. See Matt., p. 155.

4 Italy, vol. ii. p. 46. 5 See p. 82. 6 Mineralogy, p. 373.

It may be considered questionable whether the substance reputed to have been imported from the Maldives during the middle ages, under the name of amber, was really amber or oriental copal. Mr. Eastlake has shown[1] that these substances were scarcely distinguished in ancient recipes. Old writers mention two kinds of amber, the white and the yellow; and the only distinctive property they assign to amber is, that of attracting straws, which proves to be common to resins generally, and cannot therefore be considered as decisive. Agricola asserts[2] that amber was certainly found in Africa, but he knew not in what parts: he says it was also found in Syria, in India, and, according to Marco Polo, the Venetian traveller, in the Island of Madagascar. It appears that copal is found in Abyssinia, in Palestine, and in the East Indies; and it is sold in the bazaars of Jerusalem, Mecca, and other places, as a choice specimen of incense.[3] In this respect it agrees with what Agricola says[4] of amber; namely, that the odour of the smoke of amber was more agreeable to the Indians than that of incense. Copal is also brought from Madagascar.[5] There are some grounds then for considering that the amber stated to have been procured from Africa and Asia may have been oriental copal; and that although amber was actually found in some parts of Italy, European nations were principally supplied with it from Germany.

There are two kinds of amber: the best, which is imported from Prussia and Poland, is hard and transparent, and the surface is frequently marked in a peculiar manner, as if, when in a fluid state, it had been enclosed in wood, and had then taken and retained the impression of the fibres of the wood and bark. This kind

---

1 Materials, &c., p. 233, 234.
2 De Metallicis, f. 243.
3 Pharmaceutical Journal, vol. v. No. iv.
4 De Metallicis, f. 243.
5 Guibourt, Histoire des Drogues, vol. ii. p. 526.

of amber makes the best varnish, and dissolves perfectly in oil. The other sort of amber is called sea-amber, and is of the size of coffee-beans, but irregular in shape, darker than the first kind, and much less transparent. Mr. Wilson Neil says,[1] "it is harder to fuse, has less fluidity, and contains more salt, gas, and impurities."

Copal.—A very white transparent resin, used formerly by the aborigines of Spanish America as incense. In the language of these people it signified all kinds of resin exuding from trees.[2] Under the name of copal, therefore, it is useless to look for this resin in works written previous to the period of the introduction of American produce into Europe. At present three varieties are known in commerce, viz., Brazilian, West Indian, and East Indian or Levantine copal. The former, which is called soft copal, exudes from one of the Hymenææ; the latter, or hard copal, is the produce of the Vateria Indica.[3] The last variety was probably the same substance which was called *amber* by the Italians, and which was stated by Agricola and Matthioli to have been imported from Syria and India, and by Marco Polo from the Island of Madagascar; and this supposition is rendered more probable by the fact that the Levantine copal is now brought from Palestine, Abyssinia, and Madagascar. The South African copal is considered the finest in quality, and the best samples which sometimes reach Europe from India were originally procured from Africa.[4] The white resin of Arabia, mentioned in the Paduan MS.,[5] was perhaps African copal, which it appears is sold in the bazaars of Jerusalem, Mecca, and other places, as a species of choice incense, and is at the

---

1 On the Manufacture of Varnishes, Trans. Soc. Arts, vol. xlix. part 2.

2 Ray's History of Plants, p. 1846.

3 Pharm. Times, vol. iii. p. 603.

4 See Mr. Eastlake's 'Materials,' &c., p. 234, citing Tripier-Deveaux, 'Traité Théorique et Pratique sur l'Art de faire les Vernis,' Paris, 1845, p. 40; and Guibourt, Hist. des Drogues, vol. ii. p. 526, on the Copal of Madagascar.

5 P. 695.

present time chiefly employed for this purpose on the altars of Mahomet.[1]

The earliest writer who mentions copal by this name as an ingredient in varnishes is probably Fra Fortunato of Rovigo, the recipes in whose 'Secreti' date from 1659 to 1711. The next author is Palomino, who gives[2] a recipe for varnish composed of copal dissolved in spirit of turpentine. As the solvent in both recipes is the same, it may be concluded that copal was at this period usually dissolved in spirits of turpentine. I have ascertained that copal is perfectly soluble in cold oil of spike, but the solution is not effected in less than five or six years. I possess a specimen of copal varnish prepared in this way, which is very clear and pale.

Black Poplar Resin.—It has been observed that this resin was considered by Serapion, Avicenna, and other writers as synonymous with carabe or amber, and that Agricola and Matthioli had shown that a resin actually exuded from both kinds of poplar, and that the black poplar was the tree known to the Arabs under the name of "haur Romi." Schrœder has, however, the reputation of having been the first who pointed out this resin, which he obtained not from the bark in the manner described by the ancients, but by boiling the buds of the black poplar in water and afterwards pressing them. The buds yield about one-fourth of their weight of resin, which is said to resemble Botany Bay resin.[3] But although new to the moderns, this resin was apparently not unknown to the medieval writers, since we find "flores populi" among the ingredients in two kinds of varnish, for which there are recipes in the Lucca MS., which are copied in the Clavicula.[4]

Lac.—There is some doubt whether the "lacca" of the Lucca MS. and the Clavicula was gum lac or the

---

1 Pharmaceutical Journal, vol. iv. p. 4. 2 Museo Pictorico, vol. ii. p. 328.
3 See London Encyclop., art. Chemistry, p. 494.
4 Mappæ Clavicula, p. 53, 54.

gum of the ivy, but it is certain that Indian gum lac was imported into Spain and Provence as early as 1220.[1] Although the art of preparing a red pigment from this resin was known at an early period, the resin itself appears to have been considered useless, and it was probably only towards the close of the seventeenth century that it came into use as an ingredient in varnishes. The Paduan MS.[2] contains directions for separating the red colouring matter, so that the gum might be used in japanning as a varnish with or without colours. Lac varnish does not appear to have been used for varnishing pictures or in painting until very recently.

Benzoin.—A solid balsam,[3] extracted from incisions made in the Storax benzoe, a tree which grows in Sumatra. According to Depping[4] it was imported at an early period into Europe; but as an ingredient in varnish it does not appear to have been used until the middle of the sixteenth century. It was employed for this purpose by the Italians and Spaniards, and the earliest notices of it probably occur in the Marciana MS.[5] and in the 'Secreti' of D. Alessio.[6] Varnish of benzoin is also mentioned by Armenini,[7] and in the Paduan MS.[8] The benzoin was dissolved in spirit of turpentine or spirit of wine. Benzoin appears never to have been an ingredient in oil varnishes. Palomino and Pacheco mention this balsam under the name of *menjui.*

---

1 Capmany, Memorias, &c.; and the Statutes of Marseilles, quoted by Depping, vol. i. p. 147. 2 P. 686, 688.

3 "Balsams are mixtures of resins and volatile oils. They differ very greatly in consistence, some being quite fluid, others solid and brittle. By keeping, the softer kinds often become hard. Balsams may be conveniently divided into two classes, viz., those which, like common and Venice turpentine, Canada balsam, Copaiba balsam, &c., are merely natural varnishes, or solutions of resins, in volatile oils, and those which contain benzoic or cinnamic acid in addition, as Peru and Tolu balsams, and the solid resinous benzoin, commonly called gum-benzoin."—Fownes, Manual of Elementary Chemistry, p. 501.

4 Hist. du Commerce, vol. i. p. 142. 5 P. 629.

6 Secreti, part i. f. 115. 7 De' Veri Precetti, lib. ii. cap. ix. 8 P. 698.

Copaiva is obtained from incisions made in the trunk of the Copaifera officinalis, a tree which grows in South America and some of the West India islands. It is mentioned as an ingredient in amber varnish, in the Paduan MS., and appears to have been used by the later Venetians both in varnishes and in painting.[1]

Damara Resin.—Terebinta di Dammara is the produce of the Pinus dammara (Lambert), Agathis dammara (Rich., Conifère, tav. 19), a tree which grows in the Indian Archipelago. Its odour is strongly resinous and its taste very bitter.[2] At the present time this resin is much used in the Venetian territories as a varnish, and it is currently reputed to have been employed by the old masters; but this opinion appears to be unsupported by evidence—indeed, its uses are described by Chevalier and Richard as being unknown. It has, however, been recently employed at Munich as a vehicle for painting, for which purpose it was dissolved in spirits of turpentine with a certain proportion of bleached wax.[3] For the following recipe for damara varnish for pictures, I am indebted to a painter of Verona:—Put two and a half ounces of damara resin finely powdered and six ounces of spirit of turpentine into a bottle; shake occasionally until the resin is dissolved, and it will be a strong varnish. No heat is necessary.

Varnishes.

The earliest varnish and that which was most universally adopted in Italy was unquestionably the old vernice liquida, which was composed of linseed oil and pulverised sandarac, commonly called "vernice," "vernice da scrivere," and "gomma di gineparo." The varnishes of Theophilus are referred to under the name

---

1 See Mr. Sheldrake's Essay, Trans. Soc. Arts, vol. xix.; and Marcucci, p. 222. 2 Diz. delle Droghe di Chevalier e Richard, &c.

3 See Appendix to the Third Report of the Commissioners of the Fine Arts, p. 52.

of vernice liquida in the Tabula Imperfecta prefixed to the Le Begue MS. In this table and under the same head is another reference to the recipe of Le Begue: "A faire bonne vernix liquide pour peintres,"[1] which appears to have been compiled by him from the two recipes of Theophilus, with a few additions of his own. From this recipe it may be inferred that Le Begue considered the materials in both the recipes of Theophilus as identical, but a comparison of these chapters of Theophilus with the three recipes in St. Audemar, Nos. 207, 208, and 209, and that in Eraclius (p. 241), make it highly probable that the resin in one case was sandarac and in the other amber.[2] In addition to linseed oil Le Begue mentions hemp-seed and nut oils, which, he says, might be used instead of linseed oil; and it may be remarked that in making varnishes linseed and nut oils were used indifferently.

There is still another reference in the Tabula Imperfecta to a recipe in the Le Begue MS. for "vernice liquida," but as No. 210, the recipe referred to, does not describe a varnish, one of those described in Nos. 207, 208, and 209, and probably the first, must be intended.

The term "vernice liquida" occurs frequently in the early Italian recipes copied in 1409 from the book of Fra Dionisio, and also in the treatise of St. Audemar. It is also frequently mentioned in the Bolognese MS., which contains no less than three recipes for making it. The first of these,[3] the old "vernice liquida," consisted of linseed oil and sandarac, under the name of "gomma di gineparo." The varnish described in the second recipe was composed of linseed oil and incense. This varnish was made clear by the addition of roche alum, and was rendered drying by the addition of minium;

---

1 No. 341, p. 313. 2 See Mr. Eastlake's 'Materials,' &c., p. 241—246.
3 No. 206, p. 489.

the oil, moreover, was set on fire and burnt to deprive it of its unctuosity.[1] From this recipe it is apparent that the term "vernice liquida" was not always limited to the original signification, but was sometimes extended to a varnish composed of oil and incense. When, however, the materials of which the varnish is composed are not specified, the old vernice liquida (linseed oil and sandarac) is generally to be understood. The third varnish was, like the first, composed of linseed oil, sandarac, here called "vernice da scrivere," and thirty or forty cloves of garlic; and when the varnish was nearly cold the whites of several eggs were added to it and well mixed, and the bottle was placed in the sun for one day. Vernice liquida is also frequently mentioned by Cennini not only as a varnish for pictures[2] and for tin,[3] but as an ingredient in cements,[4] and mordants,[5] and other works.

Although vernice liquida is not mentioned in the Paduan MS. or by Volpato, Armenini, Bisagno, or Borghini, the evidence of Matthioli, Caneparius, and others is sufficient to establish the fact that the use of it with colours was not entirely discontinued in the sixteenth and seventeenth centuries. By the Spanish painters this varnish, which is described by Pacheco as that of the "guadamacileros" (leather-gilders), was in his time mixed with colours in a particular kind of oil painting, which this writer calls[6] "las encarnaciones de polimento."

The "drying oil" mentioned in the appendix to the Italian edition of 'L'Idée du Peintre Parfait' of De Piles consisted of vernice liquida made drying by the addition of litharge.

In the course of time the old vernice liquida was modified in various ways. It was sometimes combined

1 P. 521. 2 Cap. 155 3 Caps. 97, 98, 101. 4 Cap. 107.
5 Cap. 151. 6 Tratado, p. 404.

with incense, as in the recipe in the Marciana MS., approved by Sansovino,[1] and sometimes with pece Greca.[2]

Next in importance to the "vernice liquida" was the "vernice comune," or common varnish, of the Italians, which Armenini and Bisagno direct to be mixed with the priming, and with certain colours. There is no doubt that the term was first applied to the varnish of sandarac and oil, which Caneparius calls[3] "common liquid varnish;" but before Armenini's time the appellation "common" appears to have been applied to another varnish also.

Armenini and Bisagno give several recipes for varnish, and after describing one made of mastic and nut-oil, they add that "this varnish may be added to the finer kinds of azure, lakes, and other colours, that they may dry more quickly;" but neither of them states that this is the "vernice comune." A similar varnish is mentioned in the Marciana MS.[4] as a most excellent varnish for lutes, leather, paintings on panel, cloth, &c. In the recipe for making printing-ink the same author says,[5] "Take varnish made for varnishing, and the finer it is the better; but the *common varnish* which the apothecaries sell to varnish wood and other things will do." The composition of "the best vernice comune, which is good for varnishing whatever you please," is described at p. 637, where it is stated to consist of linseed oil and pece Greca. The statement that "vernice comune" was made of linseed oil and pece Greca is confirmed by Leonard Fioravanti,[6] who recommends one part oil and three parts pece Greca. It will be observed that the common Italian varnish corresponds with one of the varnishes in the Strassburg MS.,[7] with

---

1 P. 631. 2 P. 637. See also Venetian MS. in the Sloane Collection, No. 416, f. 139. 3 De Atramentis, p. 260.

4 P. 633. 5 See p. 619. 6 Secreti, lib. iii. caps. 67, 95.

7 Quoted by Mr. Eastlake, 'Materials,' &c., p. 280.

one of those in the Venetian MS.,[1] and also with the varnish of "Péséri" of the Byzantine MS.[2]

Another varnish described in the Marciana MS.[3] "as a most excellent, clear, and drying varnish, proper for colours both in oil-painting and in other kinds of painting," consists of the "vernice comune," with the addition of mastic. This addition was probably made with the view of rendering the varnish more siccative, since mastic was placed among dryers as early as the date of the Lucca MS. The drying properties of mastic varnish are alluded to by Armenini[4] and Bisagno, and the varnish of mastic and nut-oil is recommended by Errante[5] as the safest of all dryers. It is not therefore improbable that this varnish may have borne the name of "vernice comune" as well as the varnish made of nut or linseed oil and pece Greca. It is probable that the varnishes composed of pece Greca, mastic, and incense were much lighter in colour than the "vernice liquida," and therefore were better adapted for mixing with light colours. It must be observed that the common varnish used by the Flemish painters employed by Charles I. in England consisted of Venice turpentine dissolved in oil of turpentine.[6] The "vernix commun" of the French resembled this.

According to Pierre Pomet[7] the latter was nothing more than the turpentine procured from the pine (Pinus abies) liquefied in spirit of turpentine. The same author also calls[8] this varnish "le vernis gros." Pierre Pomet wrote in the eighteenth century, and as a varnish

---

1 Sloane MS., No. 416, p. 139. 2 Manuel d'Iconographie, p. 40.

3 P. 633. According to Bonanni this varnish is used by the Turks for bows, &c.

4 Speaking of the varnish of mastic and nut-oil, Armenini says "e di questa se ne può mettere negli azzurri fini, nelle lacche e in altri colori, acciò si asciughino più presto."

5 Saggio, &c. 6 Mr. Eastlake, 'Materials,' 471–476.

7 Hist. Générale des Drogues, ii. 106. 8 Ib., p. 71.

composed of a balsam dissolved in an essential oil can be traced in Italy as early as the date of the Marciana MS.,[1] and was reputed to be in general use throughout Lombardy about 1580,[2] there is reason to believe that this kind of varnish was of Italian origin.[3] That it was used in Spain is proved by Pacheco, who remarks[4] that the Strassburg turpentine (trementina de veta de Francia) should be used.

But the "gros vernis" of the French was not the "vernice grossa" of the Italians. By the latter, the term was applied sometimes to a dry substance and sometimes to a liquid varnish. When Borghini[5] says, "Prendasi . . . . un' oncia d' olio di spigo e un' oncia di sandarac ovvero vernice grossa," it is probable that he means sandarac in its dry state. Baldinucci defines "vernice grossa" to be a varnish which serves as a preparation for painting in oil on walls (per intonacare a olio), and which is also used in the composition of printing-ink. D. Alessio states[6] that the varnish used for the latter purpose was "vernice liquida." Caneparius[7] is still more precise; he calls it "Common liquid varnish . . . made of Arabian sandarac, which is the gum of the juniper, and linseed-oil." It appears then that the term "vernice grossa" was applied both to dry sandarac and to the old vernice liquida. In the last sense we are probably to understand the words of Vasari in speaking[8] of preparing walls for painting in oil: "Make in a pipkin a mixture of pece Greca, mastic, and vernice grossa, and when this is boiled apply it with a large brush."[9] It can scarcely be supposed that the resins

---

1 P. 635. 2 See Armenini, de' Veri Precetti, &c. Hackert states that this varnish had been in use all over the north of Europe for upwards of 200 years. See Lettera al Cav. Hamilton, sull' Uso della Vernice nella Pittura. Perugia, 1788. 3 See Mr. Eastlake's 'Materials,' &c., p. 470.

4 Tratado, p. 412. 5 Riposo, p. 175. 6 Secreti, parte i. f. 118.

7 De Atramentis, p. 260. 8 Int., cap. xxii.

9 Compare with Vasari's description of Sebastian del Piombo's method of painting in oil on walls, in the 'Life' of that artist.

would spread if they were merely melted without being diluted with oil. In the 'Elémens de Peinture' of De Piles[1] this passage is translated "de poix Grecque, de mastic, et de gros vernis;" but the "gros vernis" of the French was, I have shown, not identical with the "vernice grossa" of the Italians. At a later period, the term "vernice grosse" was also used to denote the common oleo-resinous varnishes. Thus linseed-oil boiled with litharge is said to be of great use in house-painting and in the composition of "vernici grosse."[2]

Amber, the principal ingredient in the German varnish,[3] does not appear to be noticed as a varnish by Italian writers previous to the time of Lionardo da Vinci,[4] who directs that a picture to be painted according to certain directions given by him, should be varnished either with nut-oil and amber, or with nut-oil thickened in the sun.[5] As Lionardo was one of the earliest Italian artists who practised oil-painting upon its first diffusion in Italy, after its introduction by Antonello da Messina, and as the early Flemish painters are known to have used amber varnish, it may be supposed that this varnish of nut-oil and amber was one of the recent improvements introduced from Flanders[6] by Antonello da Messina and the German artists, pupils and followers of Van Eyck,[7] who visited Italy in the latter half of the fifteenth century.

---

1 Jombert's edition, p. 133. Paris, 1766.

2 Diz. delle Droghe di Chevalier e Richard, Traduzione da F. du Pré. Venezia, 1830.

3 See Mr. Eastlake's 'Materials,' p. 288.

4 Lionardo was a pupil of Andrea Verrocchio, who was probably acquainted with the art of oil painting, since Vasari relates that he painted certain wax effigies of Lorenzo de' Medici with oil colours. See Vasari, Life of Andrea Verrocchio.

5 Trattato, cap. 352.

6 It must not be forgotten that the Byzantine MS. of Mount Athos contains a recipe for varnish made of oil and "santalose," which was probably "amber;" amber varnish may therefore have been introduced into Italy by the Greeks; but of this there appears no evidence.

7 Roger of Bruges, Memling, and Justus van Ghent. See Mr. Eastlake's 'Materials,' p. 217.

Notices of amber varnish are not of frequent occurrence in early Italian works on art. It appears, however, to be mentioned in the Marciana MS. under the term "carbone," which has undoubtedly been written instead of "carabe,"[1] the Arabic and Persian term for amber. The varnish made according to the recipe in question would, like all the old varnishes, be very thick, the proportions being one part of amber to three of oil. It was, therefore, diluted with naphtha, oil, or spirit of wine, and was used warm.

The 'Secreti' of Alessio also describes[2] a varnish for pictures consisting of three parts of amber varnish and one of distilled linseed-oil; and another varnish composed of linseed-oil and amber is quoted by Mr. Eastlake from the 'Secreti' of Rossello.[3]

It appears from the MS. of Volpato[4] that amber varnish was in use in his time, and that it was purchased ready-made at the shops, whence it may be inferred that it was in common use. In the absence, however, of any precise recipe for this amber varnish of which Volpato speaks, it cannot be determined whether amber was actually an ingredient, or whether the so-called amber varnish was the old "vernice comune" (linseed-oil and pece Greca) which was known in Bonanni's time under the name of "amber varnish."[5] The ingredients of this varnish were linseed-oil one part, and pece Greca three parts, so that it was, in fact, the vernice comune of the Italians, before described. It is difficult, indeed without additional evidence it is impossible, to assign any reason for the new name given to this varnish. We may, perhaps, be allowed to hazard a conjecture, and

---

1 See p. 628 and note.   2 Part ii. p. 57.

3 Published at Venice in 1575, quoted in 'Materials,' &c., p. 241.

4 P. 743.

5 Trattato sopra la Vernice detta comunemente Cinese, p. 42. The "new" edition was published in 1786.

to suppose that on account of the high price of amber, and the great difficulty of making pale amber varnish, it was customary to purchase it ready made, and that the dealers substituted for it the before-mentioned thick composition of linseed-oil and pece Greca.

In the before-mentioned recipes for amber varnish, the amber was dissolved in oil; but in those which are now to be described, a balsam was substituted for the oil. Such varnishes were perhaps more brilliant, but less solid than the first, which contained oil. In the recipe for amber varnish in the Paduan MS.[1] the amber is dissolved in turpentine liquefied over the fire. The mixture, which when cold is hard, is to be diluted with spirits of turpentine. Another recipe, which is stated by Mr. Sheldrake[2] to have been brought from Venice towards the close of the last century, resembled the amber varnish of the Paduan MS.[3] except that copal was used instead of amber. He tried the recipe and failed, because, as he afterwards found, the Venice turpentine of the shops was not the natural balsam, but common resin dissolved in spirit of turpentine. He tried the experiment a second time with Chio turpentine, and succeeded.

Nearly similar to this is the varnish used by Le Blond on his prints.[4] On this subject Mr. Sheldrake observes, "Le Blond's prints were long neglected, and are now forgotten. Whatever difference of opinion may prevail respecting them, there can be none respecting his varnish, as I have seen some of these prints in

---

1 P. 688. 2 See a paper by Mr. Sheldrake in the Transactions of the Society of Arts, vol. xix. 3 P. 688.

4 The recipe is as follows:—"Take 4 parts of balsam of copavi and one of copal. Powder and sift the copal, and throw it by degrees into the balsam of copavi, stirring it well each time it is put in; I say each time, for the powdered copal must be put in by degrees, day after day, in at least 15 different parts. The vessel must be close stopped and exposed to the heat of the sun or a similar degree of heat during the whole time; and when the whole is reduced uniformly to the consistence of honey, add a quantity of warm turpentine."

perfect condition, notwithstanding they had been thrown carelessly about for nearly sixty years. Le Blond was a pupil of Carlo Maratti. He died at a very advanced age, leaving behind him the character of an ingenious projector." Mr. Sheldrake's conjecture respecting the Italian origin of this recipe appears to be well founded.

It will be observed that these varnishes contained neither linseed nor nut oil; and in this respect they resembled a varnish which a professor of Parma considers to have been that of Correggio. The ingredients of the latter varnish differed slightly from those in the varnish last described; they consisted of amber dissolved in balsam of copaiba (an American production, probably not in use in the time of Correggio), and thinned with oil of spike. Sometimes, as in the receipts of the Paduan MS.,[1] mastic was substituted for amber and copal, and sometimes sandarac and incense. A varnish composed of these last ingredients with Venice turpentine is described by D. Alessio[2] to dry as soon as spread.

The transition is easy from these resinous varnishes containing amber and copal to those composed only of a balsam liquefied in an essential oil like that stated by Armenini to have been adopted by Correggio, which consisted of the olio di abezzo liquefied over the fire, and thinned with naphtha. Count Carlo Verri attempted several times unsuccessfully to make this varnish; at length, having procured genuine olio di abezzo from the Valtellina, and the naphtha having been rectified by a chemist on whom he could depend, he succeeded perfectly.[3]

The above varnish of olio di abezzo and naphtha is

---

1 Pp. 671, 673. 2 Secreti, part ii. p. 57.

3 Verri, Saggio Elementare sul Disegno della Figura Umana, p. 138. The results of Count Carlo Verri's experiments with this varnish are stated by Mr. Eastlake, 'Materials,' &c., p. 481.

mentioned in the Marciana MS.,[1] accompanied by a statement that the olio di abezzo may be diluted with linseed or nut oil inspissated by exposure to the sun, or with naphtha. Count Carlo Verri's failure in making this varnish was probably not the only one; for this MS. requires that the olio di abezzo should be genuine; and in order to test its purity, directs that olio di abezzo and the oil with which it is tempered should be warmed, and then spread over the work: if the olio di abezzo was not genuine, it would be long in drying, which was a proof that it had been mixed with turpentine; but if it dried quickly and perfectly, this was a proof of its purity. From this it appears that pure olio di abezzo was a good drier. The above instances are sufficient to show the importance of procuring the best materials for varnishes.

In addition to the varnishes above mentioned, those composed of a resin or balsam dissolved in an essential oil appear to have been used on pictures. Of these the favourite varnish, if we may judge by the number of the recipes, was benzoin dissolved in spirits of wine: this is mentioned not only in the Marciana MS.[2] but in the Paduan MS.[3] and by D. Alessio, Armenini, Bisagno, Pacheco, and Palomino.

On referring to the recipes for making the varnishes before mentioned, it will be observed that they were so thick as to be sometimes solid on cooling. They were therefore sometimes diluted, while warm, with a proper quantity of purified linseed or nut oil, spirit of turpentine, naphtha, or oil of spike; and, when thick, they were applied on the picture previously warmed in the sun, with the hand or with a sponge. It may be remarked that the varnishes to be mixed with colours were not required to be thin, because a small quantity only was to be mixed with the colours already ground with oil.

With regard to the high colour of oleo-resinous var-

---

1 P. 635. 2 P. 629. 3 P. 699.

nishes, it may be observed that it is the custom in Germany to keep these varnishes in a sunny window; amber varnish, thus exposed to the light, will, it is said, in three years become sufficiently pale for general use.

The use of amber varnish as a vehicle for painting was revived and recommended as long ago as 1801 by Mr. Sheldrake in a paper published in the 19th volume of the Transactions of the Society of Arts. In these papers Mr. Sheldrake endeavours to prove that this varnish was used by the Italian painters; and as his opinion has been in a great measure confirmed by documentary evidence, his papers acquire additional interest from his having recorded the experiments made by himself in painting with this varnish.

The result of Mr. Sheldrake's experiments is thus stated:—

"I dissolved it [amber] in each of the painter's oils, by Dr. Lewis's process, without injuring its colour; and this solution was made in the common way. It was much darker coloured in itself, but produced scarcely any difference in effect when mixed with colour. By experiments with each of these solutions I ascertained the following facts, viz.:—

"Every colour, and all the tints compounded from it, were more brilliant than corresponding tints and colours mixed with the best drying oils to be procured from the shops.

"Colours mixed with amber, after having been shut up in a drawer for several years, lost nothing of their original brilliancy. The same colours tempered with oils, and excluded from the air, were so much altered that they could scarcely be recognised.

"Colours tempered with amber were laid on plates of metal, and exposed (both in the air and close boxes) for a long time to different degrees of heat, from that of the sun in summer to the strong heat of a stove, without being injured. It is needless to observe that

oil-colours cannot undergo the same trials without being destroyed.

"These colours, when perfectly dried in any way, were not acted upon by spirit of wine and spirit of turpentine united. They were washed with spirit of sal ammoniac and solutions of potash for a longer time than would destroy common oil-colours without being injured.

"They dry as well in damp as in dry weather, and without any skin upon the surface. They are not liable to crack, and are of a flinty hardness; whence it appears that this vehicle possesses every desirable property, and it is presumed may be a discovery of some importance to artists.

"Having succeeded thus far with amber, I tried the same experiments upon solutions of gum copal, which is nearly as hard and insoluble as amber itself. The result of these was the same as the former, except that with copal the colours were something brighter than with amber. As it is extremely troublesome to dissolve the copal and amber, I tried those solutions of them in oil which are sold in the shops. When good I found them to answer as well as my own. This is a great convenience, as many might be deterred by the difficulty of preparing this vehicle, who may willingly use it, as it is thus to be procured without that trouble."

Mr. Sheldrake also observes:—

"If my experiments have not misled me, I am entitled to draw the following conclusions from them:—wherever a picture was found possessing evidently superior brilliancy of colour, independent of what is produced by the painter's skill in colouring, that brilliancy is derived from the admixture of some resinous substance in the vehicle. If it does not yield on the application of spirit of turpentine and spirit of wine, separately or together, or to such alkalies as are known to dissolve oils in the same time, it is to be presumed that vehicle

contains amber or copal, because they are the only substances known to resist those menstrua.

"I have been told, and some experiments of my own prove the information to be true, that the Venetian pictures, considered with respect to vehicle, are of two kinds: for some are extremely hard, and not at all affected by any of the above menstrua;[1] others are similar in colour, but so tender that it is scarcely possible to clean them without injury, and in that respect are little superior to turpentine colours. The first, in consequence of the data which I have laid down, incur the suspicion of being painted with amber or copal."

The correctness of Mr. Sheldrake's observations will be acknowledged on comparing them with Mr. Eastlake's remarks[2] on the advantages of amber varnish as a vehicle for painting. The firmest and most durable varnishes were undoubtedly those composed of amber and oil;[3] the next were those composed of other resins, such as sandarac, mastic, and pece Greca, with oil, or of amber or copal dissolved in a balsam; and the last class, which consisted only of resins dissolved in essential oils, was decidedly the least durable.

---

1 "By an attentive examination of pictures which belong to the first epoch of painting in oil, one may be convinced that some of the Italians have employed oil varnishes which are harder than those now used by the Flemings, since they offer greater resistance to solvents."—Merimée, &c., p. 30.

2 Materials, &c., pp. 290, 302, 303, 304 n., 306, 316, 486.

3 See Mr. Wilson Neil on the Manufacture of Varnishes, Trans. Soc. Arts, p. 69. Dreme, Der Virniss-u. Kittmacher, &c. Marcucci, Saggio, &c., p. 163. Merimée, p. 48.

Dr. Lewis, after describing the experiment of Hoffmann mentioned by Mr. Eastlake,* shows that perfect solutions of amber in drying and other oils may be obtained in the following manner:—"In Dr. Stockar's very curious *Specimen Inaugurale de Succino*, printed at Leyden in 1760, there are sundry more important experiments on the subject, made by himself conjointly with my worthy correspondent Mr. Ziegler, of Winterthur. They found that by continuing a simmering heat twelve hours,

* Materials, p. 318.

On the use of Varnish with Colours in Painting.

It has been mentioned that in glazing, varnish was generally mixed with the colours. The practice, however, does not appear to have been universal, and the same artist is reputed to have employed different materials upon different pictures. Sometimes it is said that oil only was used to paint with, and sometimes the

---

and confining the vapour as much as stone-ware vessels would bear without bursting (the danger of which was avoided by making a small notch in the cork stoppers), powdered amber dissolved perfectly in expressed oils, in turpentine, and in balsam of copaiba. A strong copper vessel, with a cover screwed on it, seemed most eligible; and for the greater security a valve may be made in the cover, kept down by a spring that shall give way before the confined vapour is of sufficient force to be in any danger of bursting the vessel. Though such a heat as converts part of the oil into strong elastic vapours, and the forcible compressure of the vapour, are expedient for hastening the dissolution, they do not appear to be essentially necessary; for, by digestion for a week in close stopped glass vessels, in which the compressure could not be very great, solutions equally perfect were obtained.

"The solution in rape-seed oil, and in oil of almonds, was of a fine yellowish colour; in linseed oil, gold coloured; in oil of poppy-seeds, yellowish red; in oil of olive, of a beautiful red; in oil of nuts, deeper coloured; and in oil of bays, of a purplish red. It is observable that this last oil, which of itself, in the greatest common heat of the atmosphere, proves a thick butyraceous consistence, continued fluid when the amber was dissolved in it. The solutions made with turpentine and with balsam of copaiba were of a deep red colour, and on cooling hardened into a brittle mass of the same colour. All the solutions mingle perfectly with spirit of turpentine. Those made with the oils of linseed, bays, poppy-seeds, and nuts, and with the balsam of copaiba and turpentine, being diluted with four times their quantity of spirit of turpentine, formed hard, tenacious, glossy varnishes, which dried sufficiently quick, and appeared greatly preferable to those made in the common manner from melted amber.

"My worthy friend Mr. Ziegler, in an elegant German translation with which he had honoured this work, described a varnish, with the method of using it, which appeared from his experiments to be the best. Fine transparent amber reduced to powder is boiled in a brass vessel having a valve in its cover, with as much drying oil as will just cover it; generally in 5 or 6 hours the amber is perfectly dissolved. Dilute the solution with four or five times its quantity of oil of turpentine, and let it stand some days, that all the impurities may settle to the bottom."—Commercium Philosophico-Technicum, or the Philosophical Commerce of Arts, by W. Lewis, London, 1763, 4to., p. 366, &c.

colours are stated to have been mixed with varnish. The following instances and observations, referring chiefly to the Italian schools, will show that varnish was frequently used, not only in glazing, but in the priming, and with the shadow colours.

Armenini and Bisagno recommend the addition of common varnish to the priming, to those colours which dried with difficulty, and to the glazing colours. Baldinucci states[1] that boiled oil (olio cotto) was sometimes used in the darkest parts *instead* of varnish, and in other parts where the colours had sunk in. From this it appears that it was usual to mix varnish with the dark shades.

As an additional proof of the use of varnish in the dark parts of the picture, may be quoted the following description given by Vasari[2] of the method adopted by Giovan Francesco Caroti:—"He was of opinion, and in this he was not far from the truth, that varnishing was injurious to pictures, and that it caused them to appear old sooner than they would do otherwise; and for this reason, he used varnish and certain purified oils in the shades when painting." This is certainly an admission that varnish was necessary either in the picture or on the surface, and that the former was, by Caroti at least, considered preferable.

De Piles mentions that in painting on walls, varnish was mixed with the colours to prevent the necessity of varnishing afterwards;[3] and in the Italian edition of this work[4] it is stated that painting on wood was executed in the same manner as on walls; whence it may be inferred varnish was mixed with the colours. Canepario, the Venetian physician, says,[5] "others are accustomed to mix colours with liquid varnish and

---

1 Voc. Dis., tit. Olio Cotto.
2 Vita di Fra Giocondo ed altri.
3 These instructions are as old as Vasari. See Int., cap. xix.
4 Published at Turin in 1769.
5 De Atramentis, p. 304.

linseed or nut oil, instead of white of egg and gum-water; for a liquid and oily varnish binds the colours better together, &c." The Marciana MS.[1] describes "an excellent clear and drying varnish proper for colours, both in oil-painting and in other kinds of painting."

These direct proofs of the mixture of colours with varnish are from the works of authors describing the processes of their contemporaries.[2] As an indirect proof, but not the less valuable on that account, is the following anecdote related by Luigi Crespi[3] of his father Giuseppe Maria Crespi, called "Lo Spagnuolo." "One day Cardinal Lambertini was in our house sitting for his portrait, which my father was painting, when one of my brothers entered the room, bringing a letter, just arrived by post, from another brother who was at Modena on business. The Cardinal took the letter, and, on opening it, said to my father, 'Go on painting, and I will read it.' Having opened it, he began to read quickly, inventing an imaginary letter, in which the absent son, with the greatest expressions of shame and humiliation, prostrated himself at the feet of his father, begging his pardon, and saying that he had found it impossible to disengage himself from a stringent promise of marrying a certain Signora Apollonia, whence . . . . . but he had hardly proceeded thus far when my father leaped on to his feet, knocking over palette, pencils, and chair, *and upsetting oil, varnish, and everything else which was on the little bench*, and uttering all kinds of exclamations. The Cardinal jumped up at the same time to quiet and pacify him, telling him as well as he could for laughing, that it was all nonsense, and entirely an invention of his own. Meanwhile my father was running round the room in despair, the Cardinal following him; and thus pleasantly ended the

---

1 P. 633. 2 For additional proof see the work of Gerard Lairesse, cap. v. 3 Lives of the Bolognese Painters, p. 220.

morning's work. After this time, whenever his Eminence came to see my father, before getting out of the carriage, he would whisper, 'that he had no doubt Signora Apollonia was at home with him.'"

It is apparent from this passage, that Lo Spagnuolo was accustomed to use varnish in painting, or the varnish would not have been placed *with* the oil on the low bench by his side while painting a portrait, for which the Cardinal was actually then sitting; it may also be inferred that varnish was still used in painting by Luigi Crespi, his son, who related the anecdote. The period when this scene took place was between 1717 and 1732. Lo Spagnuolo studied first under Angelo Michele Toni, afterwards under Domenico Maria Canuti (who was a pupil of Guido), and lastly under Carlo Cignani; and it is fair to presume that he employed their technical processes. The use made by Sir Peter Lely of varnish mixed with colour, when painting the portrait of Tillotson,[1] may be considered another incidental proof of the use of varnish with colours.

To these proofs from contemporary writers may be added the evidence of those who have cleaned and experimented on old pictures. Among the earliest may be reckoned the declaration of Requeno[2] that some of the pictures of Guercino were painted with oil mixed with pece Greca (the vernice comune of the sixteenth century), others with gums and resins, and some with oil only; and the letter written by Hackert,[3] advocating the use of varnishes in painting. The reply to this letter[4] by a gentleman who at that period possessed the finest collection of Flemish pictures in Rome is equally conclusive. This gentleman

1 Walpole's Anecdotes, vol. iii. p. 129.

2 Saggi sul Ristabilimento, &c., vol. i. p. 169, n.

3 Published at Perugia, 1788.

4 Inserted in the Giornale di Roma, 20th December, 1788.

states that varnish was always used by those Italian schools most distinguished for colouring, and that the works of Domenichino, who used varnish, were in better preservation than those of other pupils of the Carracci. We may also mention the certificate, dated 1754, by Carlo Cesare Giovannini of Bologna,[1] respecting the state of preservation of the celebrated picture by Raphael called the Madonna di S. Sisto, which he says was until that period intact, and had never been touched with varnishes, or otherwise, since the day when it had been placed over the altar of S. Sisto, perhaps by Raphael himself, and on which the varnish used in retouching by Raphael is now visible on close examination in some rancid-looking spots on the body of the infant Jesus, where the varnish had accidentally been left rather thick by the pencil of the master. To these instances may be added the evidence of Marcucci,[2] of Palmaroli,[3] of Requeno,[4] of Merimée,[5] of Sampieri,[6] of the professor mentioned by Lanzi, who restored a picture by Correggio, and of the other professors now living who have been already mentioned in this work. While, however, these authorities appear to leave no doubt as to the adoption by the Italians, during the best period of the art, of varnish with colours on certain parts of the picture, the assertion of Boschini,[7] that in painting flesh the Venetians abhorred like the plague all lustrous or shining surfaces, must not be

---

[1] Gualandi, Memorie, ser. i. p. 29. This picture was purchased, with 62 other celebrated paintings, by Augustus III., King of Poland and Elector of Saxony, for 40,000 Roman scudi, and was taken to Dresden by Giovannini. It was restored by Sig. P. Palmaroli, the author of the Notes to Marcucci's Observations on the Practice of Painting in Oil of the Florentine, Venetian, and Flemish Schools of Painting in their best time.

[2] Saggio, &c., p. 222, &c.

[3] Notes to Marcucci, Saggio, &c.

[4] Saggio sul Ristabilimento dell' Antico Arte de' Greci e Romani Pittori, vol. i. p. 169, n.

[5] De la Peinture à l'Huile, p. xvii. n. xx.

[6] See Lanzi, Storia Pittorica, ed. of Pisa, 1823, note 15 by Boni.

[7] Ricche Minere.

overlooked. This assertion, as far as regards the solid painting, is generally supported by the direction in the Marciana MS.,[1] to grind and temper the colours with oil as stiff as possible, and if they were too stiff to dilute them by dipping the brush in oil, as well as by the evidence of the professors of the art now living at Venice. The latter appear to consider that oil only was used in the solid painting, and that the varnish was reserved for the glazing and finishing colours, and especially for such as would be injured by admixture with oil, such as red lead, cenere azzurre, and others.

The same may also be observed with regard to the later Bolognese school; and this appears to have been the opinion of Lanzi, who, in describing the manner of Lo Spagnuolo, says that "he used gums in painting (per colorire) in the same way as others used them in glazing." The Parmasan school are also stated to have painted in the same manner—namely, the solid colours with oil, and the glazing colours with varnish.

The present state of a picture by Tintoretto in the Casa Barbarigo at Venice is instructive as to the practice of this artist. The surface of the picture alluded to is generally dull, as if the varnish had been removed or worn off, with the exception of certain dark parts, and of the foliage, which are glossy, as if these colours had been mixed with varnish.

Of Varnishing Pictures.

Pictures painted in the Flemish manner, or finished with colours mixed with varnish, did not require the superposition of varnish when complete, and we find that even in the time of Lebrun and Lana the custom of varnishing finished pictures was not universal. The latter remarks (p. 165), " when the painting is finished, some painters are accustomed to varnish it, in

---

[1] P. 627.

order that the work may appear more smooth and brilliant." And Lebrun,[1] after directing white of egg to be spread over the picture to preserve it from dust and fly-marks, adds, "when necessary, the picture may be cleaned by passing a wet cloth over it, which easily removes the white of egg, with the dust attached to it.[2] This," he adds, "could not be done with varnish." These passages, therefore, may be considered evidence of the truth of Vasari's statement that pictures painted according to the process invented by Van Eyck required no varnish. It may also be collected from an expression of Vasari's, in his account of Giovan Francesco Caroti,[3] that the biographer disapproved of varnishing pictures; he says, "Caroti was of opinion, *and in this he was not far from the truth*, that varnishing pictures spoiled them, and made them appear old sooner than they otherwise would do."

The fact that pictures were generally varnished is, however, too well authenticated to require any proof.

On the Preparation of the Grounds.

There is nothing, perhaps, on which the durability of a picture so much depends as on the goodness of the ground; and at the same time there is, perhaps, no part of a picture on which the opinions of artists have been so much divided as on the manner of preparing the grounds; some painters preferring white grounds, others dark grounds; some electing to paint on absorbent grounds, others on non-absorbent grounds; while others reject all preparations but a coat or two of size to fill up the pores of the wood, or the holes of the canvass.

The subject of the preparation of panels and canvass forms an important part of most of the old treatises.

The earliest paintings in oil were generally executed

---

[1] P. 816. [2] See the disadvantages of white of egg as a varnish described in a letter by Hackert, 1788. [3] Vita di Fra Giocondo ed altri.

on panels. The panels were composed of various pieces of wood cemented together with cheese glue, and this glue caused them to adhere so firmly together, that such panels were considered stronger than those which consisted of one piece of wood only. Strips of linen were usually glued over the joinings of the panels, and in some cases the panel was entirely covered with linen. Animal glue was used for this purpose.

Several coats of warm glue, which filled up the pores of the wood, were then to be applied.

The Italian name for the next process is *ingessare*.[1] This consisted in the application of several thin coats of size [2] and *gesso marcio* [3] over the surface of the panel, which when dry was carefully smoothed with a knife or pumice stone.

Upon this preparation the old tempera painters were accustomed to apply a coat of Armenian bole mixed with glue, on which they spread leaf gold; a practice which, though gradually discontinued, was sometimes adopted in oil-painting, and was occasionally practised in Italy.[4] In Flanders the practice was continued to a comparatively late period. The gold ground was considered to give great brilliancy to the colours.[5]

This practice, however, was not universal; the grounds were more frequently left white; but in this state they would absorb the oil from the colours applied

---

1 See Bol. MS., p. 595. Vasari, Int., cap. xx., xxi. Cennini, cap. cxv.

2 The durability of the painting depends much on the glue being employed of the proper strength. It is better that it should be too weak than too strong. See Volpato MS., p. 728, 732; Bol. MS., p. 595; Palomino, vol. ii. p. 47.

3 Plaster of Paris stirred with water until it loses its power of setting.—Third Report of the Commissioners on the Fine Arts, p. 47, n. Cennini, cap. cxvi. Other writers call the plaster "gesso sottile."

4 Zanetti states (Delle Pittura Veneziana, p. 194) that some pictures by Paolo Veronese, in the Fondaco de' Tedeschi at Venice, are executed on gilt leather.

5 See Baldinucci, Vite de' Pittori, vol. vi. p. 262.

on them, unless prevented by the application of several coats of size, varnish, boiled oil,[1] or of colour mixed with oil[2]—practices which prevailed generally in Italy during the fifteenth, sixteenth, and seventeenth centuries, except in Venice, where some artists used absorbent grounds, as will be hereafter noticed; the painters of the other schools, however, adhered to the general practice of employing white and non-absorbent grounds.

The use of linen for grounds is considered to have been an invention of the Germans or Flemings, and by them introduced into Italy.[3] The canvass prepared by the Flemings was in great repute in the time of Borghini, for the facility with which it could be rolled without cracking.[4]

The Venetians are generally considered to have been the first among the Italians who adopted the custom of painting on canvass, on which they were able to execute larger paintings than they could on wood, and which combined the advantages of lightness, cheapness, and portability. The practice, however, necessarily caused an alteration in the nature of the ground, which on canvass was required to be composed of pliant and elastic materials, not liable to crack or be detached when the canvass was rolled up; and this has always been found a great difficulty.

Great diversity of opinion exists among writers on

---

1 Merimée, de la Peinture à l'Huile, p. 15; Lanzi, vol. iv. p. 71 n.

2 Vasari, Int., cap. xxi. Armenini, lib. ii. cap. ix. The colour usually employed for this purpose was a warm tint inclining to yellow or flesh colour; it sometimes consisted of yellow ochre, or minium ground in oil. Fra Bartolomeo is said to have used sometimes one, and sometimes the other of these colours. See Marcucci, Saggio, &c., p. 213.

3 Painted cloth as a substitute for window glass, and waters for painting on linen, silk, or woollen, are mentioned in the Bolognese MS., pp. 491, 493. It is probable that the latter were for articles of dress or the hanging of rooms.

Riposo, p. 136.

painting as to the most eligible mode of preparing canvass; and several processes are recorded as having been employed by good artists. In general the coats of gesso were omitted on cloth,[1] it being considered that they were liable to crack when the picture was rolled.

Vasari recommends that three or four coats of size should be applied, and upon them a mixture composed of flour paste with nut oil, and a little white lead, should be spread with a knife and smoothed with the hand, so as to fill up all the holes; then one or two other coats of weak size should be applied, and lastly the priming. Armenini also recommends several coats of glue, one of which was to be applied on the back of the canvass. The same author states[2] that "painters were in the habit of filling up the holes of the canvass with a mixture composed of flour paste, and a third part of white lead, before the glue was applied. On this preparation the priming, which consisted of white lead, giallolino, and terra di campane, or of verdigris, white lead, and umber, was spread. But the preparation he especially recommended was a light flesh colour inclining to the colour of flame, by means of the varnish, of which rather more than the usual quantity was to be added, because it was observed that "this added to the effect of the colours, especially the blues and reds, without causing them to change; for," continues Armenini, "it is known that oil darkens and sullies all the colours, which appear soiled and dirty in proportion to the darkness of the ground beneath them." He adds that those who were desirous that the colours should not change from the effects of time, made the grounds almost entirely of white lead, adding to them a sixth part of varnish, and a little red, and when this was dry they polished the surface, upon

---

[1] See Vasari, Int., cap. xxiii. Armenini, lib. ii. cap. viii.

[2] Lib. ii. cap. ix.

which they either drew or traced the outlines. In a note to this passage, Signor Palmaroli[1] observes that he has sometimes found in grounds ochre or red lead mixed with the gesso, upon which was laid a coat of oil diluted with spirit of turpentine, applied with a piece of cotton or a sponge.

Borghini states[2] that the Flemish canvass, which could be easily rolled and carried everywhere, was prepared simply with one or two coats of size, and that it was then coloured, taking care to fill the holes of the cloth with the colours. He also recommends[3] one coat of size and two of priming, particularly if the canvass was to be rolled and removed to another country. He mentions that canvass was sometimes prepared by applying a coat of gesso and flour, boiled in linseed oil. Other authors recommend a priming of potter's earth[4] mixed with oil, and applied upon a coat of size or flour paste.[5] Pacheco[6] mentions a mixture of flour paste, salad oil,[7] and a little honey; and when this application was quite dry, and had been smoothed with pumice-stone, then a coat or two of priming was applied. Other painters, he states, first apply size made from the parings of leather, then a coat of sifted ashes instead of gesso, which after being smoothed with pumice-stone was covered with the priming of almagra (a red earth), ground with linseed oil; these grounds, Pacheco says, were used at Madrid. Another kind of priming, according to the same author, was composed of white lead, red lead, charcoal black, and linseed oil upon the gesso ground. Pacheco, however, disapproved of all these methods: he says, "I know by experience that

---

1 Notes to Marcucci, Saggio, &c., p. 207.
2 Riposo, p. 136.
3 Ibid., p. 138.
4 This earth was called by the Italians Terretta, Terra di Cave, Terra da Boccale.
5 Volpato, p. 730.
6 Tratado, p. 383.
7 Palomino (vol. ii. p. 46) says linseed oil should be used, and not salad oil, which is prejudicial to the picture.

flour-paste, gesso, and ashes are, in time, affected by damp, and that they decay, together with the canvass;" and he finally recommends the application of a few coats of size, and then two coats of priming, composed of the potter's clay[1] used at Seville, ground up with linseed oil, each coat being polished with pumice-stone when dry. Upon this was spread a third coat, to which a little white-lead might be added or not, at pleasure. He observes, that although weak size made the cloth more supple, it might be omitted. This, Pacheco states, is the best kind of priming, and that which he always used himself; because he had remarked that the six pictures which he began in 1600, in the cloisters belonging to the monastery of the Order of Mercy, on this kind of ground, were in good preservation when he wrote his work (which was published in 1649), and showed no symptoms of scaling off.

The directions given by Palomino[2] resemble so nearly those of Pacheco that it is useless to repeat them. It may, however, be observed that the former mentions that in Andalusia canvass was frequently primed with a kind of clay, washed up by the rivers when they rose; or, if this could not be had, with chalk, which was ground up with almagra: adding to it, when ground, some old colours (those which are cleaned from the palette and brushes[3]), if they could be obtained, or in default of this a dark colour, called sombre del Viejo, should be added to assist the drying, the clay and chalk being bad dryers.

The custom of using gesso grounds on cloth was, however, never entirely abandoned,[4] and, among other artists, they were used by Bassano. With regard to the

---

1 Called at Madrid "Tierra de Esquivias" (Palomino, vol. ii. p. 48), probably similar to the Terra da Boccale of the Italians.

2 Vol. ii. p. 46—48.

3 See Volpato, p. 733.

4 See Armenini, lib. ii. cap. viii. Borghini, p. 138. Pacheco, p. 383, 384.

pictures of this artist, Volpato mentions having remarked that those painted on grounds prepared with a small quantity of gesso were in good condition, while the colours scaled off those pictures on which much had been used. The directions given by Volpato[1] as to the preparation of grounds need not be alluded to here, as they are contained in the work.

To return to the gesso grounds: it is asserted that they were used also by the Bolognèse painters, Samacchini, Sabbatini, and Tibaldi, both on canvass and panels. Correggio also is said to have prepared his canvass with a very thin coat of size and gesso, over which he laid a coat of boiled oil.[2]

As to the colour of the priming, the weight of authority is in favour of white grounds.[3] Mr. Eastlake observes (Goethe on Colours, p. 378), "the secret of Van Eyck and his contemporaries is always assumed to consist in the vehicle (varnish or oils) he employed; but a far more important condition of the splendour of colour of the works of those masters was the careful preservation of internal light by painting thinly, but ultimately with great force, on white grounds." As an additional argument in favour of white grounds, it may be stated that modern Italian artists are now so convinced of the propriety of employing them, that they have almost all returned to the use of them. When I was in Italy, I was informed that the Academy of Parma had recently decided against the authenticity of a picture attributed to Correggio, because it was painted on a red ground; the Academicians considering that none but white grounds were in use during the life of

---

1 Volpato, p. 729—733.

2 Lanzi, vol. iv. p. 71 and n.

3 See Lionardo da Vinci, Trattato, cap. c.; Du Fresnoy, Art of Painting, with the Commentary of De Piles; Orsini, Vita di Pietro Perugino; Algarotti, Lettere sopra la Pittura, vol. viii. p. 50, 51, Venezia, 1792; Delaval on Colours; and Quatremère de Quincy, Life of Raffaelle.

this artist. There is, however, some diversity of opinion as to the expediency of their being non-absorbent.

Sometimes the grounds were prepared by giving the canvass a few coats of glue only, without other priming.[1] The paintings by Callot, at Venice, are prepared in this way; and a picture by Lionardo da Vinci, or one of his scholars, mentioned by Amoretti, and in the possession of Signor Mussi, is executed on canvass prepared with size only.[2] Pictures so prepared stand well. Pozzo, the Jesuit, also painted on the same grounds, but his pictures are much changed, probably from other causes; for Félibien remarks[3] that if the canvass were not primed at all, but painted on at once, the colours would bear out better and remain more brilliant.

Various grounds were in use in the Venetian school. A Venetian professor communicated, among other particulars, the following information as the result of his experiments on the grounds of the old Venetian pictures:—"The grounds were made of gesso and very weak size; sometimes a little black[4] was added by Gian Bellino and others. Over this were laid one or two coats of glue to prevent the ground being too absorbent; the glue was made of the parings of leather." This information was confirmed by other professors of Venice and Verona.

With respect to the grounds used by Titian, I was informed that this great artist employed a ground of "gesso marcio,"[5] taking especial care not to use too much glue, and that this slightly absorbent ground was useful in getting rid of some of the oil. It is certain,

---

1 Palomino, vol. ii. p. 45.

2 Amoretti, Memorie Storiche di Lionardo da Vinci, p. 165.

3 Principes, &c., p. 297.

4 These grey grounds were also used in the Flemish school. The series of pictures by Rubens of the life of Mary de' Medicis are painted on a grey preparation.

5 Compare Merimée, de la Peinture à l'Huile, p. 241; De Piles, Elémens de Peinture, p. 130.

however, that Titian sometimes employed a non-absorbent ground, since a restorer of pictures at Verona stated that he had found on the gesso-ground a coat of strong glue, made of pig's skin (much used in the Venetian territories), which was very hard and shining, and on which the picture was painted. This was probably the case with Titian's picture of S. Pietro Martire, which, when at Paris, was transferred from panel to canvass. The author of the 'Històire de la Peinture en Italie,'[1] who was present at the operation, remarks, "I observed that the ground and the painting were not consolidated together, but were laid one upon the other."

Titian is said sometimes to have used a red ground made of terra rossa with size, and Merimée mentions that, on analysing the ground of a picture by Titian, he found flour-paste and gesso, but no glue.[2]

Tintoretto is stated to have painted his celebrated Crucifixion in the Scuola of S. Rocco on a simple preparation of flour-paste, and this picture is in excellent preservation. Many painters, and especially Volpato, Pacheco, and Palomino, object to the flour paste. The reason assigned by Volpato is, that if the paste is too stiff, it causes the colour to scale off; and if too weak, the picture is liable to decay from damp. He states, also, that it was frequently used by those who primed bad canvass, which would decay in a few years, because it was useful in filling up the threads of the canvass.

Paul Veronese generally painted on a twilled canvass,

---

1 M. B. A. A., Paris, 1817.

2 Merimée, de la Peinture à l'Huile, p. 241. On this subject Boschini (La Carta del Navegar, &c. p. 339) says—

"La prontezza xe meterse davanti
Una gran tela, e de farina propria
Tamisar, e impastar figure in copia,
E senza natural, far casi tanti."

called in Venice "terlise," which he prepared with a very thin coat of glue and gesso; so thin as to show the texture of the cloth through the paint. This coat, being absorbent,[1] imbibed the superfluous oil which darkened the threads of the canvass.

Sig. Pietro Edwards, whose opportunities of examining pictures of the Venetian school were perhaps greater than ever fell to the lot of any other person, has recorded his opinion that these grounds were best adapted to ensure the durability of paintings; and in support of this opinion he instances the three pictures by Paolo Veronese, representing the legend of Sta. Cristina, which were executed, with very few repaintings, either on a ground of gesso not hardened by strong size, or on canvass, with a thin coating of gesso, the colours of which were, he says, so fresh that they appeared to have been painted but two days instead of two hundred years.[2]

The same favourable opinion of white tempera grounds is expressed by De Piles;[3] but he adds that they have the disadvantage of being liable to crack when rolled up. This was the case with the celebrated Nozze di Cana by Paolo Veronese, which, on its arrival at Paris, was found to be in such a state as to render it necessary to line it with great care in order to prevent its scaling entirely from the canvass. This operation, with some necessary reparations, was performed at the Louvre with all requisite care and attention. But when, in 1815, the picture was about to be restored to Venice, according to the treaty, it was perceived that the colours crumbled off and fell into dust at the slightest movement. To continue the operation, therefore, was to expose one of the finest works of the Venetian school to certain destruction; and the committee decided that the picture

---

[1] See the Dissertation of Sig. Pietro Edwards, p. 887, 888.

[2] See p. 888. [3] Elémens, p. 131.

of Paolo should remain at Paris, and that a painting of Lebrun's should be sent to Venice in its stead.[1]

Absorbent grounds of size and gesso are considered to have been employed by the Parmasan school.

Various contrivances were resorted to in order to prevent the cracking of pictures when the canvass was rolled. Some artists added honey and oil to the preparation of size and gesso;[2] but the Venetian artists are stated traditionally to have used milk for this purpose. All writers speak of the necessity of the grounds on canvass being thin, as a means of preventing their cracking.

With regard to the use of white lead in the priming, the general opinion seems to be that it is injurious. It has been stated that any picture in which white lead was used in the grounds would infallibly crack in less than fifty years; and that pictures painted on a ground of white lead and oil would moreover turn brown. The pictures of Longhi (born in 1702, and living in 1762) are in good preservation, with the exception of the grounds, which are full of large cracks, attributed by the Italian restorers to the use of white lead in the grounds. Neither Palomino, Pacheco, Borghini, Volpato, nor Lebrun recommend white lead in the preparation of the grounds. Vasari and Armenini and some few modern painters, on the contrary, are in favour of it.

---

[1] This account was given by the French painter M. Camille Rogier to Sig. Cigogna, who inserted it in his 'Iscrizioni Veneziane,' vol. iv. p. 328.
It may not be uninteresting to the reader to know that the sum received by Paolo for painting this picture was 324 ducats, and not 90, as asserted by Algarotti. The original contract, with the signature of Paolo, is preserved among the papers belonging to the Monastery of S. Giorgio Maggiore at Venice. It has been copied and published by Sig. E. A. Cigogna in the 4th volume of the 'Iscrizioni Veneziane.' It may also be interesting to know that the date of the contract was the 6th of June, 1562; and the day on which Paolo gave his receipt for the money, on the completion of the picture, was the 6th of October, 1563: so that the picture was begun and finished in 16 months.

[2] Pacheco, p. 383; Palomino, vol. ii. p. 47; and see Ballard's Traité de Mignature, p. 220. Salmon's Polygraphices, p. 80. Marcucci, Saggio, &c., p. 205, n.

The Carracci are said to have used white lead in their grounds. "The only priming used by Ludovico was a slight coat of white lead and ochre, with sufficient oil to ensure a smooth surface, and he made use of this priming as a shadow colour. Annibale, his cousin, sometimes used a mixture of 'creta' and white lead for his grounds. Guercino instead of 'creta' employed marble dust; and with this his pictures in his first manner are thinly primed; in the second manner the priming is thicker."

Some artists, and especially Guido, painted occasionally on silk, which was thought to be more durable than linen cloth. It was frequently prepared for painting by applying a coat of size, to which a little honey was added to prevent its cracking, and on this the priming was laid.[1]

Pictures were frequently painted on copper, and in this case the only preparation necessary was a coat of glue, which prevented the oil from acting on the colours.

The introduction of dark grounds into Bologna is attributed to the Carracci. They were introduced into Venice by Palma Giovane, who has been called the last of the good Venetian painters, and the first of the bad.

On a careful examination of the different authorities, it appears that pictures painted on a ground of gesso are the most durable, but that when this material is used on canvass the greatest care is necessary to prevent its cracking. It also appears that when the surface of the gesso ground has been polished quite smooth with pumice-stone, one or two coats of glue made from pig's skin, and perhaps a coat of varnish or oil, if the picture is to be painted in the Flemish manner, should be applied to prevent absorption. But if the Venetian manner of painting is pursued, the thin distemper ground used by Paolo Veronese is considered best adapted to

---

[1] Ballard's Traité de Mignature, p. 229.

promote the durability of the picture. The great requisites in grounds for canvass are thinness, whiteness, and flexibility, and a perfectly smooth surface.

Methods of Painting.

In examining the technical processes of oil-painting in the North of Italy, it will be seen that they arrange themselves under two great divisions: in the first, which may be called the Flemish process, the picture was begun in chiaroscuro, and finished with the local colours; in the second, or Italian process, which was introduced in the beginning of the sixteenth century, the picture was commenced with the local colours painted solidly with oil, white being introduced into the cool grey or bluish shadows, and was finished with warm glazings. The former system was generally adopted in Lombardy and Bologna; the latter in Venice, where it originated: but this arrangement was not without exceptions, and in later times the Venetian method was preferred to the Flemish, which has almost fallen into disuse and oblivion in Italy. Both methods, however, underwent various modifications according to the genius or the caprice of the different professors of painting, and so great was the diversity in the technical habits of the Italian painters, that the pictures of the same artist are frequently found to have been painted in various manners and with different materials. Thus Titian is said to have changed his method several times, and Requeno relates[1] that he has seen pictures by Guercino in some of which oil only had been used, in others oil and pece Greca, and in others resins and gums. The fundamental principle in all may, however, be traced to one or other of the above-mentioned sources.

In the early period of painting in oil the same pro-

---

[1] Saggi sul Ristabilimento, &c., vol. i. p. 169, n.

cess of painting was observed throughout Italy, as well as in Flanders and Germany. The process may be thus briefly described :—

The ground being properly prepared, the next process was to draw the subject of the picture. This was frequently done with black chalk or black-lead pencil, but in order to insure greater correctness the subject was frequently traced in the usual way from a drawing on paper. Baroccio always adopted the latter method,[1] and the outlines deeply indented, as if with a style, may be seen in a large unfinished picture by him in the library of the Archiginnasio at Bologna. The outline was then secured by marking over it with a brown colour (as in the unfinished picture by Lionardo da Vinci in the gallery of Brera at Milan), or with a tint composed of carmine and dark ochre.[2]

When describing the different kinds of grounds used in painting, I have mentioned that a coat of size, of varnish, or of boiled oil was applied upon the gesso ground to render it non-absorbent;[3] but Mr. Eastlake has proved[4] that the outline was occasionally, at least, drawn before this last application, and the coating of size or the warm transparent oil priming was spread over the outline. It is probable that this plan was adopted in the Venetian school, and it may be observed that sketches by Tintoretto are still in existence which were begun in chiaroscuro with water colours, and then oiled, the local colours being afterwards painted in their places with oil. To this instance may be added the passage quoted by Walpole[5] from the Pocket-book of Mr. Beale, in which it is mentioned that Lely "ap-

---

1 See Bellori, Vite de' Pittori, p. 117. Lanzi, vol. ii. p. 124.

2 Palomino, vol. ii. p. 57, 59.

3 The present state of many of the pictures of Luini and other artists proves beyond a doubt that the ground on which they were painted was non-absorbent. The colours having in some parts scaled off, leave visible the white ground unstained with oil, and of dazzling whiteness.

4 'Materials,' &c., p. 384.

5 Anecdotes, vol. iii. p. 129.

prehending the colour of the cloth on which he painted was too light, before he began to lay on the flesh colour, he glazed the whole place where the face and haire were drawn in a colour over thin, with Cullen's earth, and a little bone black (as he told us) made very thin with varnish." The practice does not, however, appear to have been universal in Italy, especially when the priming was opaque or nearly so, since Vasari, Borghini, Armenini, and his copyist Bisagno direct the design to be traced or drawn *upon* the priming. Perhaps it may not be far from the truth to suppose that when the priming was transparent it was spread over the outline; but when it was opaque the outline was drawn on it.

The subject having been outlined with ink, or black and lake, or brown, the picture was begun in chiaroscuro by washing in the shadows lightly with the same colour, like a drawing in Indian ink, and it was suffered to dry. This practice is alluded to incidentally by writers on painting, and especially by Paolo Pino,[1] where he objects to painters designing their pictures with such extreme diligence, composing the whole in chiaroscuro according to the custom of Gian Bellino, for this, he observes, was labour thrown away, as the whole had afterwards to be covered with colours, &c. Vasari mentions[2] that Fra Bartolomeo di S. Marco was partial to this method of painting, and Malvasia,[3] speaking of Tiarini, relates that he commenced his pictures in chiaroscuro with white lead and bone black, and then covered them with colours and finished with glazings. The custom is also mentioned by Pacheco,[4] who did not approve of it.

When the chiaroscuro had been painted with black, or when the white ground had been covered with a grey

1 Dialogo, f. 16.
2 Vita di Fra Bartolomeo di S. Marco.
3 Felsina Pittrice, vol. ii. p. 206.
4 Tratado, p. 386.

preparation, as in some of the pictures of Gian Bellino and Rubens, the artist proceeded to paint the flesh tints.[1] But where the chiaroscuro was of a rich brown, it was necessary to interpose grey tints between the shades and the flesh tints. The latter, which were made more rosy than nature, were then laid on very thinly, beginning with the lights and proceeding gradually with deeper and redder tints into the shades,[2] laying each tint in its place and not tormenting it with the brush.

The next tints, which were also very thin, had more yellow in them, and the last coat of colours was also thin, and contained more white, and with this the flesh was toned to match the complexion. The number of coats of colour is not to be understood as limited to three.[3] Titian is said to have repeated his colours nine or ten times; the same has been said of Correggio; and it is mentioned on the authority of Mr. Beale,[4] that Lely said he believed Vandyck had painted over a portrait fourteen times. This method of painting keeps the flesh light and clear, because it permits the white grounds to appear through it.[5] Different colours were used for the shadows of flesh: some artists employed a mixed tint of black, lake, and some transparent yellow, or yellow varnish. Armenini says that asphaltum, mummy, and the smoke of pece Greca were commonly used for this purpose. Lomazzo names[6] terra di cam-

---

1 Even where the chiaroscuro has been dark brown, the scumbling of the thin flesh tints over it has produced the effect of grey.—See Mr. Sheldrake's Paper, in the Transactions of the Soc. of Arts, vol. xvi. For the effect of darkness seen through a semi-transparent medium, see Goethe on Colours, by Mr. Eastlake, Nos. 151, 160.

2 See Lomazzo, Trattato, lib. vi. cap. vi.

3 Vasari mentions incidentally that Pietro Perugino had laid three coats of colour on some pictures in the Church of the Servi at Florence. See Life of Pietro Perugino.

4 See Extracts from Mr. Beale's Pocket-books, quoted by Walpole, Anecdotes, vol. iii. p. 125.

5 As to the lights in early oil paintings being semi-opaque, see Mr. Eastlake's 'Materials,' &c., p. 408.

6 Trattato, p. 191.

pana, umber (which he calls also falzalo), burnt terra verde, asphaltum, and mummy. The Paduan MS.[1] mentions umber, burnt terra verde, and asphaltum; and in another place,[2] lake, minium, and umber. Other artists used for the outlines and shadows umber and lake.[3] Pacheco mentions[4] bone-black, umber, charcoal-black, or smoke [of burnt resin], asphaltum, almagra, and carmine. In this method of painting it will be observed that the shadows are transparent, and that the white-lead is reserved for the lights, which are semi-opaque.

It appears to have been the general practice of the Italian painters, from Giotto to Lomazzo, to mix their tints before beginning to paint. The instructions of Cennini[5] and Lomazzo[6] are full and precise on this point. The custom of mixing tints on the palette was not, however, universal, and instances of the opposite practice may be found in works on art.[7]

The method of painting above described appears to have been followed by the Florentine, the Roman, the Lombard, the early Bolognese,[8] and the early Venetian schools. Titian's earliest pictures were painted in this manner, and the process may be seen on some unfinished pictures by Rubens, Vandyck, Fra Bartolomeo, and others.

The beauty of this method of painting consisted in its transparency, every coat of colour being so thin as to show those laid beneath.

The most perfect outline is necessary when pictures are painted in the method just described, because if a part be shaded that ought to be light, the dark colour

---

1 P. 650. 2 P. 654.

3 See Malvasia, Felsina Pittrice, vol. ii. p. 448; Lomazzo, Trattato, p. 198. 4 Tratado, p. 386. 5 Caps. 67, 71—85, 93, 145.

6 Trattato, lib. vi. cap. vi. 7 See Zanetti, della Pittura, &c., p. 401.

8 See Marcucci, Saggio, &c., p. 213. Malvasia, Fels. Pitt., vol. ii. p. 206. Merimée, de la Peinture à l'Huile, p. 15, 16.

will always be visible through the light tints over it, and the colour will look opaque.[1]

The unfinished picture by Lionardo da Vinci in the Gallery of Brera, before mentioned, shows that it was not always customary to complete the chiaroscuro before beginning the painting. In this picture, some parts are finished, or nearly so, while parts of the ground are left white.[2]

---

[1] See Marcucci, Saggio, &c., p. 213 and n.; and see Mr. Eastlake's 'Materials,' &c., p. 397, 398.

[2] This very interesting picture has been mentioned by Mr. Eastlake ('Materials,' p. 392), but as I have alluded to it several times, I shall give a description of it from my own memoranda:—The picture represents the Virgin and Child with the Lamb. It is painted on a white ground, which has a yellowish tint, apparently from being covered with varnish. The ground is full of small hair-like cracks. The subject is drawn with a black pencil. The sky and distance are finished with blue and white, with a slight greenish tint. There is a rock behind the figures, the colour of which, with the earth around, is of a very dark brown, probably formed of black and majorica and a little lake.* A space between the distance and rocky ground is left quite blank, the white ground appearing. The face of the Virgin is more finished than the rest of the picture; it was apparently begun in chiaroscuro with the usual brown—the gray shades incline to black, the lights on the face to lake. The face of the Infant is nearly finished. The hands are just sketched in lightly with the same brown, and the first flesh tints are laid on almost as thin as a first wash of water colours. The same may be observed with respect to the toes: the black pencil-marks are visible on the nails. The drapery, which is scarlet, appears to be formed of earthy reds, with vermilion on the lights. The outer drapery is red also, and is lined with a yellowish green, or perhaps this was to be a changeable drapery, since the shades are red and the lights green. These were Lionardo's favourite colours for drapery. The sleeves of the Virgin, part of the mantle, indeed all that part covering her knees, part of the Infant's drapery, and the whole of the Lamb are left quite blank, excepting that the outline of her knee is marked in pencil. This shows that Lionardo sometimes finished portions of his pictures, leaving the rest untouched, instead of beginning on all parts equally, or even of painting the subject in chiaroscuro. The darks are raised higher than the lights, and the foliage is minutely worked on the dark background. My impression is that this picture was begun upon a non-absorbent white

---

* See Lionardo da Vinci, Trattato della Pittura, cap. 353. Vasari shows that the black used by Lionardo was the lamp black used by the printers, and ivory black. See Vita di Francesco Bartolomeo di S. Marco.

There is little doubt that the method of painting just described was discontinued in Venice in the early part of the sixteenth century. This is proved by the assertion of a professor of painting now residing at Venice, that Cima da Conegliano (of whom nothing is known after 1517[1]) adopted the Venetian method of beginning his pictures with solid colours, and finishing with glazings. In Florence the latter method had been introduced previous to the completion of Vasari's work.[2]

In the earliest oil pictures the touches of the brush are not visible, the whole being softened and blended so as to convey the idea of real shadow, except the sharp touches, which stand up crisply and distinctly in a manner that cannot be imitated with oil alone. This is particularly apparent in the pictures of Van Eyck, Lucas Van Leyden, Lionardo da Vinci, Luini, and others of that time.

At a later period the touches of the brush were often suffered to remain unsoftened; but, in both cases, it is remarkable that, on close observation, the darks will be seen to stand higher above the surface of the picture than the lights: this effect is universally attributed to the use of varnish in the shades.

Four different methods of painting in oil have, at different times, prevailed in Venice. The first was that just described, which was followed by the Bellini[3] and their pupils, and by Titian in the early part of his career; the second was that adopted by Titian in his best time, and by his pupils and followers; the third was that employed by Paolo Veronese; and the last that introduced, it is said, by Palma Giovane, of paint-

ground, and that the yellowish tint is owing to the varnish with which it has been covered.

1 See Ridolfi, vol. i. p. 101.

2 See Vasari, Life of Fra Bartolomeo.

3 See ante, p. cxxxiii.

ing on dark grounds, to which, as it is considered to have led to the decline of the art, it will be unnecessary to advert.

The pictures of Titian are not all painted in the same manner, but the method he frequently adopted was nearly as follows:—When the subject was drawn, the local colours were laid in lightly and thinly with colours mixed with oil,[1] the shades being left very cold. The picture was then exposed to the sun and the dew until perfectly dry and hard; a smooth surface was then given to it by rubbing it down with pumice-stone until quite smooth.

After many months the dead or first colouring or *abbozzo*, as it is called in Italian, was examined and corrected, and fresh colours were laid on;[2] finishing colours were then applied, and the tints were frequently repeated seven, eight, or nine times,[3] until the artist was satisfied with his work, always however suffering a long period to elapse between each layer of colour, and exposing the picture to the sun and dew between each painting. The coats of colour being very thin, the colours dried quickly and hard, and, as the Venetians express it, before the oil had had time to become rancid.[4] Titian, it is said, frequently laid on the paint with his fingers, particularly on the flesh and in glazing.

---

1 Lanzi, vol. v. p. 89, 90; and see Boschini, Ricche Minere, &c.; Verri, Saggio sul Disegno, &c., p. 121, 127. Compare also Marcucci, Saggio, p. 213, n.

2 Boschini, Ricche Minere.

3 Soleva dir el nostro gran Tician"

. . . . . .

"Che per formar el vivo colorito,
No' se possa a la prima (come hò dito),
Fenir le carne con intendimento;
Ma ben con replicar diverse tente."

Boschini, La Carta del Navegar, &c., p. 341.

4 It is related that Bombelli, the Venetian painter, said that he wished his pictures to dry as fast as possible, that the oil in them might not have time to rise to the surface and turn yellow. See Trans. Soc. Arts, vol. xix. p. 329.

When large surfaces were to be glazed, the colour was frequently rubbed on with all the fingers or the flat of the hand, so as to fill the interstices left by the brush, and to cover the surface thinly and evenly. Another way of applying the colour with the finger, frequently used for the soft shadows of flesh, was to dip the finger into the colour and draw it *once* along the surface to be painted with an even movement. These touches were called *sfregazzi*,[1] and were distinguished from the process first described, which was called "velatura." Trial will show that there is no other method by which soft shadows can be so easily produced. The reason given by the Venetians why the fingers are preferable to the brush for this purpose, is because the colour can be laid on thinner in this way, and it has the effect of filling up all the interstices caused by the strokes of the brush. The thinness of the paint also contributed to the durability of the colours, because as the varnish or oil dried more quickly from the thinness of the layer of paint, the colours were preserved from being changed by the action of the air upon them. The shadows were glazed with asphaltum and lake, and Titian is said to have frequently glazed the whole surface of the picture, except the white linen, with asphaltum, or, as others say, with a yellow varnish. The glazings were generally laid on with varnish, although it is said that Titian sometimes used oil for this purpose, which is the reason that his paintings become more yellow than those of other painters.

There is no doubt, however, that Titian used frequently an oleo-resinous varnish in glazing, and to this

---

1 "Quei rossi, e macadure de colori,
Quei sfregazzi co' i' dei, quel spegazzar
Fà le figure vive bulegar;
Quei le fà luser con mile splendori."
Boschini, La Carta del Navegar, &c., p. 340.

is attributed the shrivelled surface so often seen on his pictures.[1]

Paolo Veronese laid in the abbozzo with the local colours thinly on a tempera ground; some say the colours were mixed with oil, others that they were applied in distemper.[2] When these were dry and hard the surface was rasped and smoothed, so as to leave only a thin coat of colour.[3] On this he painted the solid colours, availing himself of a general colour for all the half tints, as well in the flesh as in the draperies and architecture.[4] After this he covered the whole with a very thin coat of varnish to bring out the colours, and then retouched the lights and shades with brilliant and resolute touches, using varnish for vermilion, red-lead,

---

1 Merimée, de la Peinture à l'Huile, p. 31. Mr. Eastlake's 'Materials,' &c., p. 37.

At the public library at Brescia I was shown, among other curiosities, two small miniatures by Titian, painted one on each side of a piece of lapis lazuli, which served for the ground of the painting, a head of Christ on one side, and of the Madonna on the other. Two slight injuries on the painting showed that there was no ground laid under the figures, but the surface round the parts injured looked like glue or resin semitransparent at the edges. I examined the painting with a powerful magnifying glass, and the surface, which was perfect, except in these two places, showed the oil shrivelled as in many of Titian's large pictures, the wrinkles in this picture bearing the same proportionate size to the miniature as those I have observed in his larger pictures.

I observed also in the head of our Saviour another remarkable appearance when examined with the magnifying glass. This was the impression or appearance (for we could not tell which) of threads of silk, so that I almost fancied it had been painted on silk, and cut out and then fixed to the lapis lazuli. The surface of the painting had the usual yellowish brown cast, so frequently observed in Titian's paintings.

2 See Appendix to the Italian edition of the 'Idée du Peintre Parfait,' p. 163; and Félibien, Principes, &c., p. 297. Merimée (de la Peinture à l'Huile, p. 249) says that Paul Veronese, and before him other painters, who lived at the period when artists began to leave tempera for oil painting, were accustomed to begin their pictures with size colours on absorbent grounds. All traditions of oil paintings having been begun in tempera appear to be now lost in Venice.

3 Compare Armenini as to the general practice in Italy, lib. ii. cap. ix.; Bisagno, Trattato, &c.

4 Boschini, Ricche Minere; Zanetti, della Pittura, &c., p. 164.

blues, the tints used in painting white linen, and for the vermilion tints in flesh. He frequently painted the blues in tempera, as in the picture in the Soffitto of the Collegio of the Ducal Palace,[1] in which the blue sky was painted in tempera, and the clouds with oil. These tempera colours are said to adhere so firmly that they will bear being twice washed without being disturbed. The method of Paolo is opposed to that of Titian. The former usually painted "alla prima," seldom repeating his colours; and with few glazings.[2] Titian on the contrary frequently painted over the same part seven, eight, or nine times. His pictures are neither so fresh nor so well preserved as those of Paolo.[3]

After the time of Titian the art rapidly declined in Venice; large pictures and rapidity of execution superseded the more sterling qualities of the art; and the practice of glazing to an almost unlimited extent with asphaltum (for which Tintoretto is greatly blamed), the introduction of dark grounds,[4] and the excessive use of oil, caused the pictures of succeeding painters to become dark.

The honour of having re-discovered and made known some of the early processes of painting in oil, and of the principles which regulated the practice of the old masters, belongs to an Englishman, Mr. Sheldrake, whose Essays,[5] little known in his own country, are

---

1 This is proved by a document in the Accademia at Venice addressed by Sig. P. Edwards to Sig. Savio Cassier, dated the 25th of August, 1780.

2 Bald., Life of Paolo Veronese; Boschini, Ricche Minere.

3 See p. 888.

4 Marcucci (p. 201) attributes the darkening of the later Italian pictures to three causes, namely—first, the badness of the priming, either from being too absorbent or from the use of dark grounds; secondly, the too free employment of "olio cotto;" thirdly, the use of certain black pigments, which deepen in colour in a very short time. See also Zanetti, della Pittura, &c., pp. 374, 401, 438, 528.

5 These essays were entitled 'A Dissertation on Painting in Oil in a manner similar to that practised in the ancient Venetian Schools'—'On the Nature and Properties of Drying Oils'—'On the Use of Amber Var-

appreciated and quoted by foreigners. It is unnecessary to analyse these Essays; it will be sufficient to recommend them strongly to the perusal of the reader, and to state generally, that Mr. Sheldrake considered that the method adopted by the Venetian masters was as follows:—The chiaroscuro was painted with umber on a tempera preparation, composed of umber, broken with red, yellow, or blue, diluted with chalk or whitening to the proper degree of strength. A coat of varnish was then applied, and on this, when dry, the lights were painted solidly with pure white, scumbling it thinner by degrees until it united with the shadows. In this manner the chiaroscuro was finished as much as possible, and the local colour of every object glazed over it. The picture was then varnished.

The general resemblance between this method and that first described as the Flemish or early Italian process is apparent. The principal variation consisted in the absorbent ground, and the solid painting with white on the lights, which was rendered necessary by the coloured priming.

The method of Titian was, with certain modifications, adopted by the other schools of Italy; some artists, however, still continued to adhere to the older method. It is probable that the method of Titian was commonly adopted at Florence in the time of Vasari, for he mentions[1] that Fra Bartolomeo delighted in beginning his pictures in chiaroscuro, as if this custom of his was an exception to the general rule. This supposition is strengthened by the short description of

nish with Colours, and the Method of Dissolving Amber and Copal'—'Conjectures tending to show that these Vehicles were similar in Principle, if not identically the same as that used by several of the older Painters who were eminent for their skill in Colouring'—'An Account of the Process used to separate the Mucilage from Linseed Oil,' &c. These Essays, written between 1797 and 1801, were published in the Transactions of the Society of Arts, vols. xvi., xvii., and xix.

[1] Vita di Fra Bartolomeo di S. Marco.

the process of oil-painting by Borghini, who was a Florentine, and who may be supposed to have been well acquainted with the works of that school. This author directs[1] that when the first colours were laid in with as little oil as possible (for the oil in drying would, he says, cause the colours to darken), the picture should be laid aside for a long time, until the colours were perfectly dry; it was then to be rigorously examined, and the necessary corrections made, and then was to be applied the last coat of the finest colours tempered with very little oil, which would remain bright and lively; for if the (fresh) colours were laid upon the dry dead colouring, the former would retain when dry all their beauty; but if they were applied on the dead colouring before it was dry, the first and last colours would mix together, and the whole would be dusky and darkened, especially when the colours were made liquid with much oil, which detracts much from the brightness of the colours. It will be observed this author does not allude to the use of varnish in glazing.

There is another reason why one layer of colours should be suffered to dry perfectly before another was applied; namely, to prevent their cracking. Some of the early Italian artists, and particularly Pietro Perugino, appear to have bought their experience in this respect. Several of the pictures of Pietro are stated to have suffered from this cause. With reference to some of these pictures, Vasari remarks, "These three pictures[2] are much injured, and the dark parts and shadows are everywhere cracked; and the reason of this is, because when they were painted, the first colour laid on the priming (for three coats of colour were laid one

---

1 Riposo, p. 174.

2 The Christ in the Garden, the Pietà, and the Crucifixion, with Mary Magdalen and Saints, at Florence.

upon the other) was not dry, so that the under colours shrunk in drying, and thus occasioned those cracks on the surface; but Pietro could not have known that this would happen, because in his time artists were only beginning to paint well in oil."[1]

The precaution of waiting long between the dead colouring and the finishing was observed generally by the Italians; Boschini relates that it was the practice of Titian, and its universality may be inferred from the common custom of rubbing down the surface of the picture with pumice-stone, or even scraping it with a knife, as related by Armenini—a process which could not take place until the painting was perfectly dry. This practice seems to have been common to all the later schools, and some unfinished pictures by Guido and Guercino at Bologna present the appearance of having undergone this operation.

But it was necessary that the painting should be quite dry and hard before the surface was thus rendered smooth; and for this reason, as well as to prevent the yellowing of the oil, the painting was exposed to the sun at intervals until it was dry. This last process was repeated after every layer of colour.

During the winter the colours dried more slowly,[2] and when the heat of the sun was insufficient to dry them, or the weather particularly damp, they were exposed to the heat of a stove, which Errante says [3] was the custom of the best colourists. The practice has the sanction of Lionardo da Vinci.[4]

Painters had another reason for exposing their pictures to the sun in the various stages of the painting,

---

1 Life of Pietro Perugino.

2 Gachet, Lettres Inédites de P. P. Rubens; De Piles, Elémens, p. 142.

3 Saggio sui Colori. Rome, 1817.

4 Trattato, cap. 352. The experiments of Mr. Sheldrake prove that paintings executed with amber varnish were not injured by exposure to the strong heat of a stove.

and this was to remove by evaporation the yellow coat of oil which always rose to the surface, and which if not removed by this process darkened the colours. A letter of Rubens,[1] addressed to Peiresc, mentions this defect to which new pictures are subject, and prescribes the only remedy. The letter was written in Italian, and is thus translated by Mr. Eastlake:[2]—"If I knew that my portrait was still at Antwerp, I would cause it to be detained and the case to be opened, in order to see if it is not spoiled after having been so long shut up without air; and whether, as commonly happens to fresh colours [under such circumstances], it has not turned yellow, so as to be no longer in appearance what it was at first. The remedy, however, if it should happen to be in so bad a state, will be to place it several times in the sun, as the sun can dissipate the superfluity of oil which causes this alteration. And, if at any time it should again become brown, it should again be exposed to the sun's rays, which are the only antidote for this disease of the heart."

The perusal of this letter and other evidence which, as it has been given by Mr. Eastlake, it is unnecessary to repeat, induced me about three years since to try and restore by exposure to the sun, the colour of some grounds on canvass which had been made for a particular purpose, of white-lead and marble-dust mixed with oil. They had been turned towards the wall, or otherwise excluded from light and air for some years, and were nearly of the colour of yellow ochre. One of these was placed in a balcony exposed to the afternoon sun. In two days there was a perceptible difference, and in a fortnight the yellow hue had nearly disappeared. A long loop of riband, by which the canvass

---

[1] Dated London, Aug. 9, 1629, published by Gachet.

[2] For much additional information on this subject, see the 'Materials,' &c., pp. 509—519.

(which was old) had formerly hung against the wall, was accidentally suffered to hang over the face of the canvass; on raising the riband it was found that the ground was not bleached where the riband had lain, and this circumstance afforded the means of judging correctly of the effect of the exposure to the sun.[1]

The opinion of Rubens and other evidence of a similar nature suggested the importance of ascertaining whether the custom of exposing pictures to the sun still existed in Italy; and from the inquiries I made, I am induced to believe that the practice of exposing pictures freshly painted in oil to the sun has always existed in Italy, and has descended traditionally from the early ages of oil-painting to the present time;[2] that the custom is now observed by several eminent professors and restorers of pictures at Milan and Venice, and that the picture is by some artists exposed to the dew and then dried thoroughly in the hot sun between every coat of paint; in short, that the great principle in painting is to make the paint dry *rapidly* and *perfectly* between every coat of colour, in order to prevent the pigments being acted on by each other and by the air.[3] The tradition in Venice is that the oil always rises to the surface of the picture and dries dark; and if the colours are long in drying, the oil with which they are mixed becomes rancid and has a deleterious influence on the colours. For this purpose the pigments are to be mixed with as little oil as possible, and the tints laid on extremely thin, where it is intended to repeat the colours fre-

---

[1] In the directions given by Pacheco for cleaning and refreshing old oil paintings, darkened by smoke and varnish, without danger to the picture, he recommends that if they are on cloth, they should be placed in the sun for half a day; but if on panel, they should be exposed to the dew for two nights previous to being washed. Tratado, p. 394.

[2] See Cennini, Trattato, cap. 155; and Ridolfi, Vita di Maffeo Verona.

[3] See the remark of Bombelli (a Venetian painter) quoted by Mr. Sheldrake, Trans. Soc. Arts, vol. xix. p. 329. See also an extract from the letter of an eminent foreign Professor in Mr. Eastlake's 'Materials,' &c., p. 365.

quently, especially in glazing, when the hand is to be used instead of the pencil, for the express reason that the colours can be laid on by it more thinly than with a brush.

With regard to employing colours mixed with size on oil pictures, it was the opinion of Merimée[1] that Paolo Veronese sometimes began his pictures in tempera and finished them in oil. I cannot discover that any Italian author mentions this fact, nor have I met with any traditionary account of such a practice. But the fact that some parts of oil paintings were at times painted with size-colours, is established beyond a doubt, as the practice not only of the Venetians, but of artists belonging to the other schools; and as it is alleged[2] that some part of the celebrated altar-piece of the Van Eycks at Ghent was painted in tempera, it appears probable that the practice has existed from the earliest period of the introduction of oil painting in Italy. Besides this picture of the Van Eycks, it has been ascertained[3] that the blue sky of a picture by Pietro Perugino (the first who practised the Flemish method of oil painting in Perugia) was painted with smaltino tempered with starch or flour paste (colla di farina). There is sufficient evidence to prove that Paolo Veronese frequently painted the blue sky in tempera, and it has been asserted that he applied the more delicate finishing colours in the same manner, but this requires confirmation.

In the Flemish system of painting, which was adopted by the early Italian schools, varnish was added to the oil colours, so that the full effect of the colours was always visible; and as the layers of colour were thin and the colours always finely ground, there was no

---

1 De la Peinture à l'Huile, p. 249—251. 2 Pacheco, Tratado, p. 373.

3 See 'La Vita, Elogio, e Memorie dell' egregio Pittore Pietro Perugino, e degli Scolari di esso.' Da B. Orsini. Perugia, 1804, p. 208, n.

necessity for rasping the surface. But where the local colours were laid on solidly, and not finely ground as in the Venetian school, it was necessary, when the abbozzo was perfectly dry and hard, in order to secure an even surface for the finishing colours, to rub down the surface with pumice-stone.[1]

In the Venetian manner the colours of the abbozzo having been painted with oil only, were dull; and as the difficulty of retouching a picture "in secco," that is with a perfectly dry surface, was felt by all artists,[2] it was considered necessary by some to apply a thin coat of varnish in order to bring out the colours in all their force, as well as to enable the finishing colours to adhere more firmly.[3] This is said to have been the practice of Paolo Veronese, and is still observed by some Venetian artists. Volpato states[4] that white of egg was sometimes used for this purpose, and sometimes varnish or oil. Lana recommends[5] boiled oil to which litharge has been added in preference to raw oil, and De Piles[6] prefers oil to varnish. Armenini and Bisagno direct that a thin coat of oil should be passed over the picture, or at least over the parts to be retouched, and then wiped off immediately, leaving only a slight degree of moisture on the surface.[7] This process is technically called "oiling out."

To conclude, I might have indulged in expressing the feelings of delight with which I contemplated the works of the great Masters of the Italian School; but I feel that this would not have accorded with the technical and practical details of the various subjects treated

---

1 Mengs is said to have adopted this practice.

2 Goethe on Colours, by Eastlake, p. 407. n.

3 Lairesse, le Grand Livre des Peintres, vol. i. cap. v.

4 Pp. 747, 749. 5 P. 746, n. 6 Elémens, pp. 114, 118.

7 See generally Mr. Eastlake's 'Materials,' &c., pp. 476, 304 n.; and see Verri, Saggio Elementare, &c., p. 115.

of in these volumes. It has been my object to support the statements I have made, and the opinions I have expressed, by the authorities quoted, or to which I have referred. From the commencement to the conclusion, the pleasing expectation of discovery has alleviated the labour of research, and smoothed the path of inquiry; and although I have not succeeded to the full extent of my wishes, I indulge the hope that my labours, which have been devoted entirely to this object for upwards of three years, may be found useful, and not altogether uninteresting.

NOTE ON A MANUSCRIPT

Entitled 'Raccolti di Secreti, Specifici, Remedj, &c.; ora adesso di Fra Fortunato da Rovigo, Laico Capucino, Infermiere nel Convento dei Capucini di Verona.'

This MS., which is in two thick volumes in 8vo., is in the possession of the Canon Ramelli, of Rovigo. The MS. consists of several treatises on medicine, and of collections of recipes for colours, with directions for miniature painting. Many of the former are translations from the French, and were probably used by Fra Fortunato in his character of superintendent of the infirmary of the convent. The recipes date from 1659 (soon after the profession of Fra Fortunato) to 1711. A copy from the books of the convent, of the register of his profession, is inscribed in the first page of the MS.

The recipes for painting resemble so closely those in other MSS. of Secreti, that it appeared unnecessary to copy the whole. I have transcribed a few only, which show the colours and methods in use during the time of Fra Fortunato. From these we find that lake was prepared from "grana tinctoria" or "grana di kermes," "cimatura di scarlato," "cremisi" (probably cochineal), "verzino," and "gomma lacca."—"Lacca fina" was made from "cimatura di scarlato overo grana fina, cochiniglia, and gomma lacca."

Among the blue pigments, azzurro di Germania is stated to be composed of mercury, sulphur, and sal ammoniac. "The blue colour made at Pozzuoli" is the old vestorian azure; it was made of sand, "fior di nitro," and copper filings. "Biadetto" was composed of verdigris, sal ammoniac, and tartar. These blue pigments appear to have been difficult to use, since there are especial directions for tempering them. Sometimes a varnish composed of spirit of turpentine and mastic was employed for this purpose. "Biadetto" was to be ground with a little burnt roche alum, or tartar, or sandarac; it was to be ground very fine, and in miniature painting was to be used with a clear varnish of spirit of turpentine and mastic; it would then spread extremely well, glaze brilliantly, and be a most beautiful colour.*

---

* *Biadetto fare, che bene si possi stendere, miniando.*—Si macina bene con un

"Boiled oil for painters, as clear (colourless ?) as water," was prepared in the following manner :—"Put the usual piece of rag containing litharge and other customary things in linseed or nut oil, add water, and boil, and this will cause it [the oil] to be clear (colourless ?) as water itself."*

The recipes for varnish are not numerous. A recipe for one which is ascribed to P. Bonaventura, a monk of Cento, dated 3rd of April, 1707, for paper, wood, and other things, consisted of spirits of wine 6 oz., sandarac 2 oz., olio d'abezzo ¾ oz. Another varnish, which is not injured by hot water, consists of linseed oil and resin; this was the Italian "vernice comune." Another varnish was composed of spirit of turpentine, sandarac, and (concrete) turpentine; and another of "gomma copale" dissolved in spirit of turpentine.

The directions for "painting in fresco on lime with colours that are not mineral (such as lake), and to enable them to resist for a long period the effects of the air," are comprised in a few words, namely, to apply a coat of "gesso da sarto" upon the lime spread on the wall, and then paint on it.

The short instructions for miniature painting contain but little that is new. Fra Fortunato, however, recommends that the gum should be added to the colours, only when required for use, because if the colours were suffered to remain long mixed with gum, they would become dry, and the addition of water to them would cause the more delicate colours, such as lake, giallolino, cinnabar, and azure, to change. From this it appears that it was the common practice to keep the colours for miniature painting ready mixed with gum.

---

poco di alume di rocco, bruciato, o vero con un poco di tartaro, o pure con sandracca. Vedi qui sotto.

Il biadetto macinato ben sottile, e adoprato miniando con vernice fatta con acqua di ragia e mastice, che sia ben chiara, si stende benissimo, vela pulito, e fa colore bellissimo.

* *Per far l' olio cotto da pittore, che sia chiaro come acqua.*—Metti il solito piumazzolo col litargirio, et altro come si usa dentro l' oglio di noce o di lino a bollire, e con esso mettivi seco dell' acqua a bollire, che questa lo fara rimaner chiara, come l' acqua medesima.

MANUSCRIPTS OF JEHAN LE BEGUE.

PRELIMINARY OBSERVATIONS.

In the year 1431, Jehan le Begue, a licentiate in the law and Notary of the Masters of the Mint at Paris, being then in the sixty-third year of his age,[1] composed, or rather compiled, the following manuscript,[2] from a collection of works on painting made by one

[1] See end of manuscript of Le Begue.

[2] The original manuscript of Jehan le Begue is preserved in the Bibliothèque Royale at Paris. It is on paper, and is numbered 6741. For the first information concerning this manuscript we are indebted to Lessing, who mentions it in his Treatise, 'Dom Alter der Oelmalerey aus dem Theophilus Presbyter,' 1774. Lessing, however, did not know the work, but quoted the title only from the Catalogue of Manuscripts in the above-mentioned library, because he believed it contained a copy of the manuscript of Theophilus. It does, in fact, contain great part of the first book of this author. Raspe [a] and Emeric David [b] both mention the manuscript, but with reference to the copy of Theophilus only; the remainder and greater part of the manuscript seems to have been unknown until 1842 or 1843, when M. le Comte Charles de l'Escalopier procured a copy of the whole for the purpose of completing his edition of Theophilus. In the autumn of 1844 I went to Paris to procure a copy of the manuscript, which I obtained after some unavoidable delay. Some extracts from the work have been recently published by Mr. Eastlake, in his 'Materials for Painting in Oil,' and by Mr. Hendrie, in his edition of Theophilus; but the whole work has never yet been published.

[a] Critical Essay on Oil Painting, Lond. 1781, p. 38.

[b] Biographie Universelle—Art. Théophile.

Jehan Alcherius, or Alcerius. The motive that induced Jehan le Begue to undertake the work does not appear. He himself tells us that he was unaccustomed to such writing;[1] and the numerous mistakes throughout the manuscript prove that he told the truth. But, whatever might have been his inducements, the zeal with which he undertook the work, and the manner in which he executed his task, show his attachment to the arts, and his desire to obtain information on all subjects connected with it. The formation and alphabetical arrangement of the Table of Synonymes at the commencement of the work, at a period when the art of printing was unknown,[2] and the sources of information from books must have been very limited, was no small proof of his industry and perseverance. His authorities seem to have been the works collected by Alcherius, and the Catholicon, which was then in manuscript, and which was not printed until twenty-nine years after Jehan le Begue completed his work.[3]

---

1 See [No. 303a]. These numbers refer to the recipes in the text.

2 The first essay of Laurentius, the inventor of printing with separate wooden types, was about the year 1430.

3 The 'Catholicon' was a Latin Dictionary, composed in the year 1286, by Fra. Giovan. Baldi, a Genoese. It was printed at Mentz in 1460, nearly thirty years after it was quoted by Jehan le Begue; and Bettinelli remarks it was the fourth book after the Bible which was printed with moveable types of fused metal, but the author of the article 'Printing' in the 'Encyclopædia Britannica' says it was printed by Guttemberg with types of cut metal, and that Guttemberg used none but wood or cut metal types until the year 1462. Previous to the 'Catholicon,' two other Latin vocabularies had been composed in Italy, the first of which was entitled 'Glossario della Lingua Latina;' this was written by Papia, a Lombard, and, as it is believed, a native of Milan, who was one of the most learned Greek scholars of his age: he flourished about A.D. 1060. This was followed by the Dictionary of Uguccione Pisano, Bishop of Ferrara, in 1190. See Bettinelli's 'Risorgimento d' Italia,' vol. i. p. 110 n.

My reasons for supposing this Table of Synonymes to have been composed by Le Begue are, that the recipes in old French at the end (which the table of contents[1] informs us were added by Le Begue) are referred to in the Table of Synonymes, and also because this Table is full of errors, and contains many statements which Alcherius must have known to be incorrect.

After the Table of Synonymes are two fragments of alphabetical indices, the first of which begins at the letter Q, and concludes with W; the other comprises the letter A only. These fragments, I consider, are both the work of Le Begue, because they contain references to the recipes in old French at the end of the manuscript.

Of the early life and profession of Jehan Alcherius, or Archerius, the manuscript gives no indications. It does not actually appear that he was a painter, but his attachment to the art is unquestionable, or he would not have taken the pains he did to become acquainted with the technical processes, and to write down so many recipes from the dictation of others. In all that related to the art he was superior to Jehan le Begue; he also possessed the additional advantage of understanding Italian, which he acquired in Italy during his occasional visits to that country. The object of these visits does not transpire; it is, however, certain that he frequented the company of painters, and that he neglected no means of obtaining information relative to the art.

The earliest biographical notice of Alcherius is dated

---

1 I am of opinion this table of contents is not in the hand-writing of Le Begue.

March, 1382,[1] at which time he left Milan for Paris, taking with him a recipe for making writing-ink, which had been given to him by Alberto Porzello, "who was most perfect in all kinds of writing and forms of letters, and who, while he lived, kept a school at Milan, and taught boys and young men to write." In 1398 Alcherius was at Paris. On the 28th of July, in that year, he wrote his treatise 'De Coloribus diversis modis tractatur,'[2] from the dictation of Jacob Cona, a Flemish painter, then living at Paris. This treatise relates chiefly to miniature painting, and its usual accompaniment gilding. On the 8th of August following he wrote another short treatise, which also relates to the same subject, entitled 'De diversis Coloribus,'[3] from the dictation of Antonio di Compendio, "an illuminator of books, and an old man," who had tried all the recipes himself. These recipes therefore may be considered to date from the middle of the fourteenth century, at least. In October, 1398, he was still at Paris.[4] Nothing more is known of him from that time until the month of March, 1409, when it appears he was again at Milan, where he copied the recipes at the commencement of the work as far as No. 88, from a book lent to him by Fra Dionisio, a Servite, or, as it is expressed in the manuscript, "of the order of the Servants of St. Mary, which order in Milan is called 'Del Sacho.'"[5] These recipes, from Nos. 1 to 47 inclusive, are for colours of various kinds for painting and writing, and other things belonging to the art of miniature

---

[1] See Preface to No. 302.
[2] See Preface to No. 291.
[3] See Preface to No. 297.
[4] See Preface to No. 303.
[5] See Preface to No. 47.

painting. Nos. 47 to 88 contain various recipes for working in metals; for hardening iron; for a kind of nigellum; for making a sort of pyrophorus—namely, a light which should burn under water, and which could be extinguished with oil only; and also a candle which should burn with water and without fire. In No. 86 a kind of gum is mentioned, which was said to have attractive powers somewhat like the loadstone. It is possible that this gum Andrianum, the name by which it is called in the manuscript, may be another name for amber (of which this attractive power is a known attribute), which is found embedded in stones in various parts of Europe, and in Italy on the coast of the Adriatic.[1] From the description, however, and from a consideration of the locality where it was found, it seems equally probable that it was a sort of native bitumen.

The mountain where the gum is found is called in the text Monte Bono or Buono; it should be Monte Bene. This mountain is on the high road from Bologna to Florence, and is covered with scattered rocks of breccia, and is remarkable for its fine scenery, and for the singular natural phenomena which are found in its vicinity. The height is above 4000 feet. The fires of Pietra Mala, a village near this mountain, are known to all tourists. These extraordinary fires are constantly issuing from a spot of ground three or four yards across. When the air is calm they are seen at a great distance, rising about a foot from the ground, and in

---

1 See Agricola, 'De Metallicis,' f. 238. See also Eastlake, 'Materials,' &c., 234 n.

damp weather are very bright and luminous. They are extinguished by a high wind, but light again spontaneously on the air becoming calm. They resemble the flame of alcohol; and Volta ascertained that the gas emitted is a composition of carbon and hydrogen—probably produced by the decomposition of vegetable remains in the subjacent sand-rock. Between Monte Bene and Montoggioli is a singular spring, which is frequently dry. If a lighted match be brought near the mud of this spring, the gases exhaled from it immediately take fire, burning with a lambent flame.[1]

On the 2nd of February, 1410, Johannes Alcherius wrote a description of the process of preparing ultramarine from the instruction given him by one Master Johannes, a Norman, residing in the house of Pietro da Verona.[2] This Pietro da Verona was probably a painter; and the researches of the Abbate Moschoni have shown that a painter of this name was at Padua in 1398, and that his son Antonia da Verona was also at Padua in 1393.[3] We may therefore suppose that the former was the contemporary of Johannes Alcherius.

On the 11th February, 1410, Johannes Alcherius was at Bologna, where he became acquainted with one Theodore, a native of Flanders and an embroiderer, who had been employed at Pavia by Gian Galeazzo Visconti, and who gave him certain recipes and directions for preparing and using coloured waters, which Theo-

1 See Murray's 'Guide to North Italy.'

2 See Preface to No. 118.

3 See Moschini 'della Origine e delle Vicende della Pittura in Padova.' Padova, 1826, p. 9.

dore stated he had procured at London in England.[1] These recipes, which, it appears from the Note to No. 96, were given in writing, were written in French.

It is certain that these passages relate to the preparation of transparent colours for painting;[2] but I think that they refer also to the art of dyeing, and to the decoration of wearing apparel. No. 92 is evidently a mordant, and was used both to prepare the cloth to receive the colours, and to bleach certain parts of coloured cloths, by which a regular pattern might be given to them. The note of the author attached to this recipe certainly alludes to this operation of the art of dyeing, in which it is expressly stated white letters and figures could be drawn upon a coloured ground; for it is well known if figures, &c., be drawn with the mordant on cloth, and then suffered to dry, and if, when dry, the cloth be dipped into a coloured dye and afterwards dried, it will appear one uniform colour; but if the cloth so coloured be then washed in plain water, the colour will be discharged from those parts on which the mordant was not applied, and the cloth will be marked with a coloured figure on a white ground. This appears to be the process alluded to in the text, No. 92.

An additional reason for supposing that these recipes relate also to the process of dyeing arises from the fact that the stuff to be stained was sometimes made of wool expressed by the French word "drap," and the

---

1 See Preface to No. 89. Gian Galeazzo died in 1402. He had the glory of commencing the 'Duomo' of Milan in 1386, and the 'Certosa' of Pavia in 1396. He was succeeded by Gian Maria Visconti.

2 See Eastlake, 'Materials,' &c., cap. 5. See also Eraclius, lib. iii. No. 26.

Latin "*drapis* coloricis *lane*;" and I am not aware that woollen cloth has ever been used for the purpose of serving as a ground for pictures. The word "tellis," which occurs in the note after No. 99, shows that the staining or painting was not limited to woollen cloths, but extended also to those made of linen. This supposition receives more weight from a passage in the manuscript of St. Audemar (No. 195), where he says, "If you wish to gild leather, or purple cloth, or linen, or silk, stir it (the mordant) up altogether and draw beasts, birds, and flowers upon it; then lay on the gold." This passage can only be understood as applicable to articles of dress, unless indeed the painted or gilded cloths should have been used as altar-cloths or for the hangings of apartments.

The view I have taken of this subject is, I think, confirmed by the fact that the English in the fourteenth century actually wore garments painted with various colours, or in the words of the manuscript chronicle quoted by Mr. Planché, in his 'History of British Costume,' "All that time the Englishmen were clothed all in cootes and hoodes peynted with letters and flowers, and seemly with long beards."

The practice is further illustrated by the epigram which, in 1327, was affixed to the church-door of St. Peter Stangate:—

"Long beirds hertiless,
Peynted hoods witless,
Gay cotes graceless,
Maketh Englonde thriftless."

Nor does it appear to me any objection that the words "lavorare" and "depingere" are used, because it does not appear that at this period blocks for calico-

printing were invented, and consequently the letters and figures were necessarily painted on the cloth by hand. It seems to me very natural that an embroiderer should have learnt the particulars of an invention which must materially have interfered with his own trade.

On the 13th of February, 1410, Johannes caused the recipes numbered 100 to 116, inclusive, to be copied from a book lent to him by "Johannes de Modena, a painter living at Bologna."[1] These are the recipes which, being written in Italian, Jehan le Begue could not read; he, however, procured a Latin translation of them to be made by a friend of his "who was skilled in both languages." They relate chiefly to colours and to mordants for laying on gold. Among the latter is one which will not be affected by the weather, and which consisted of minium, ceruse, verdigris, bole, and ochre ground up with linseed oil and "liquid varnish." There is also a recipe for preparing "gesso sottile" for a ground for the gold.

There is reason to believe that the Giovanni da Modena, the painter mentioned in this manuscript, and Giovanni Rossi da Modena, who was called "Il Negro," the architect, were identical.

Giovanni da Modena is mentioned for the first time as a painter in 1410, when it appears from the manuscript of Le Begue and from some documents preserved in Bologna, that he was then resident in that city.

In 1408, Bartolommeo Bolognini directed by his will

---

1 'Guida di Bologna,' p. 112.

that certain pictures were to be painted in the chapel of S. Giorgio (now S. Abbondio, in the church of S. Petronio in Bologna), which belonged to him, and which he described, as well as the subjects of the pictures to be painted. It appears, from the archives of S. Petronio, that in 1420 Giovanni da Modena was selected to paint some pictures illustrative of stories from the Old Testament in this chapel, and as the subjects of the paintings now there correspond with those ordered by Bartolommeo Bolognini, it is conjectured that some of these paintings are by Giovanni da Modena.[1] His name again occurs as a painter in 1451 in some documents preserved at Bologna, but his works are not mentioned; and from this time until 1455 we hear nothing more of Giovanni da Modena; but about that time Giovanni Rossi executed, for the Duke Borso, the beautiful miniatures in the Bible of the House of Este, now preserved in the Ducal Library at Modena.[2] Lanzi says this Giovanni Rossi exercised his art at Mantua. From the few historical notices of Giovanni Rossi da Modena, the architect, called 'Il Negro,' it appears that he was the son of Martino de Rubeis de Mutina; that he was living at Bologna in 1410,[3] and the archives of S. Petronio

---

1 'Guida di Bologna,' p. 265.

2 Marchese, 'Memorie dei Pittori Domenicani,' vol. i. p. 174. Lanzi, vol. iv. p. 6.

3 While I was preparing these notes, I received the following note (which I translate literally) from Sig. Michaelangelo Gualandi of Bologna, whose archæological researches in the cause of the fine arts are well known and appreciated :—

"We have met with the name of one *Giovanni da Modena*, a painter, between the years 1410 and 1451, but none of his works are named. As to the architect of S. Petronio in Bologna, by name *Giovanni da Modena*,

show that he succeeded Paolo Tibaldi as the architect of that edifice in 1454.[1] His name may now be seen on some architectural designs preserved in S. Petronio. He was living in 1470.

From these facts there appears scarcely a doubt of the identity of the painter and architect; for it has been shown that Giovanni Rossi, or Russi, was an architect in 1454, and that about 1455 a Giovanni Rossi, a painter, executed some miniatures for the Duke of Modena. The identity is further confirmed by the circumstance that both painter and architect resided, at least occasionally, in Bologna from 1410, when Alcherius visited that city, until 1454 or 1455. In addition to these facts it must be remembered that the old masters frequently exercised both professions, to which they sometimes added also that of sculptor. Giotto, the reformer of the Florentine school of painting, was the architect of the beautiful Campanile of Florence. Michael Angelo painted in the Sistine Chapel, and was the architect of St. Peter's. Bramante also was a painter and an architect: there is nothing singular, therefore,

---

I am going to publish some interesting notices respecting him; among others, that dated from Rome, 22nd February, 1454, in which he is described as follows:—'Providum vir *Magistrum Johannem* quondam *Martini de Rubeis de Mutina*, Muratorem Bonon commorantem qui comuniter dicitur M. Johane Negro.' He is styled 'Architecto Magistrum et Ingeniorum.' He lived until 1470, whence it is scarcely probable (supposing him also to have been a painter) that he should have been the same individual who worked in 1410, when he must at least have been twenty-five years of age."

This fact is certainly sufficient to raise a doubt as to the identity of the painter and architect, but instances of longevity are so common among painters, that there is nothing unreasonable in supposing Giovanni da Modena to have attained the age of eighty or eighty-five years.

[1] 'Guida di Bologna,' p. 97.

in Giovanni da Modena being at the same time a painter and an architect.

Giovanni de' Rossi had a son named Antonio, who became a Dominican in the convent of Sta. Maria Novella, at Florence, and who being afflicted with a tedious and incurable malady which rendered him unfit for other studies, occupied himself entirely in writing and illuminating the choral books of the convent. He died of the plague in 1495.[1] The name of Antonio da Modena also occurs among the names of the artists in the book belonging to the Society of Painters in Padua during the year 1441:[2] this was probably Antonio, the son of Giovanni de' Rossi above mentioned.

From Bologna, it appears, Johannes Alcherius went to Venice, where, on the 4th of May, 1410, he procured a recipe for preparing ultramarine from "Michelino di Vesuccio, the most excellent painter among all the painters of the world."[3] The high opinion entertained by Alcherius for the skill of Michelino was general among his contemporaries. Pietro Candido Dicembrio asserts that he was one of the most famous painters of his time—*inter cæteres ætatis suæ illustris.*

The Conte Gaetano Melzi informed me that Michelino was a native of Besuzzo (a village in the province of Milan), which forms part of the estates of the Borromeo family, by whom he was much employed. The present representative of this noble house possessed, until very

---

1 Marchese, 'Memorie,' &c., vol. i. p. 174.

2 See Moschini 'della Pittura in Padova,' p. 23.

3 See Preface to No. 117.

lately, a picture, now entirely decayed, by this artist. Conte Giberto Borromeo was polite enough to search for the picture in order to show it to me, but it was so dilapidated that I could not see it. The following biographical notice respecting this painter is translated from a manuscript volume of Memoirs of the early Milanese Painters, Architects, and Sculptors, kindly lent me by Conte Gaetano Melzi of Milan, a nobleman distinguished for his literary attainments and possessing an excellent library:—

"We may reasonably conclude that this is the Michelino of Milan who is named by Vasari among the disciples of Taddeo Gaddi. He is mentioned by Lomazzo, who says he was a very old Milanese painter who lived a hundred and fifty years before his time;[1] and that he was one of the best of that period, judging from his works, some of which exist to this day. He added that he was 'stupendissimo nel far figure di animali;' and he gives us a description of a picture or drawing in which are represented some peasants in the act of joking and laughing, which was really an extraordinary work of the kind. Pietro Candido Dicembrio, who was a contemporary of this same Michelino, mentions another of his pictures, which was the portrait of Gian Maria Visconti, Duke of Milan. It is also asserted that Michelino was not less skilful in architecture, and that he took a prominent part in the academy instituted by the Duke Gian Galeazzo about the year 1380."

---

1 Lomazzo published his Treatise in 1584; this would bring the date of Michelino at least as far back as 1434.

Michelino, therefore, is another instance of a painter exercising the profession of architect conjointly with his own.

Lanzi (vol. iv. p. 139), after repeating what Lomazzo had said in praise of Michelino, adds, that it appears he was esteemed even by foreigners, for it is mentioned by Morelli (*Notizie, &c.*, p. 81) that the Vendramini family in Venice possessed a small parchment book in quarto, containing animals painted by this artist. The note of Alcherius shows that Michelino was at Venice in 1410. Lanzi says he was living in 1435.

Johannes Alcherius returned to Paris in 1410; and in December, 1411, a year after his return from Italy, he employed himself in recopying and correcting the manuscripts he had collected on painting.[1] This appears to have been his last labour in the service of the arts. From this time nothing more is known of this indefatigable collector of manuscripts on art, whose labours extended over a space of thirty years. Twenty years after we find his manuscripts in the hands of Jehan le Begue, who copied them "with his own hand into one volume," and who probably arranged them in their present form.

I have entered into these particulars because they give authority to the recipes, and authenticity to the manuscripts.

Besides these manuscripts which I have mentioned, the volume of Le Begue contains also a copy of part of the first book of Theophilus; a Treatise on the Com-

---

[1] See Prefaces to Nos. 290, 297, 302.

position of Colours, by Petrus de Sancto Audemaro; and three books by Eraclius, entitled "De Artibus Romanorum."

The whole of the treatise of Theophilus has recently been published, with an excellent English translation and notes, by Mr. Hendrie.

TABLE OF CONTENTS.

Illustra Deus oculum.

CONTINENTUR HOC VOLUMINE.

Illustra Deus oculum.

TABULA de VOCABULIS SINONIMIS et EQUIVOCIS COLORUM, rerumque, et accidencium colorum, ipsisque et arti pictorie conferentium, nec non operum exerciciorumque propiciorum ac contingencium eorum.

[Habitis per presentem tabulam declaracionibus nominum, colorum, rerumque, et accidencium eorum et artis pictorie, et eis conferencium, nec non operum et exerciciorum propiciorum ac contingencium eorum, querantur ipsorum et ipsorum effectus et operaciones in hoc libro, et in capitulis ejus, per primam ex tabulis sequentibus.]

Albus est color, aliter, secundum Grecos, dicitur leucos et secundum Catholiconem dicitur glaucus ; et est cerusa, aliter album Hispanie, et aliter album plumbum dicitur, et aliter bracha seu blacha.[1]

Azurium vel lazurium est color ; aliter celestis vel celestinus, aliter blauccus, aliter persus, et aliter ethereus dicitur.

Aurum est nobilius metallum croceum[2] colorem habens et tenuatur in petulis, quo carentes utuntur stanno attenuato, et colorito colore croceo, et in petulis tenuato.

Argentum est nobile metallum album colorem habens, quo qui caret utitur ejus loco de dicto stanno tenuato, non colorito.

Auripigmentum est color croceus qui aliter arsicon dicitur.

Aureola[3] est color qui aliter pictura translucida vocatur ; et omnis pictura, cujuslibet coloris, in stanno attenuato facta, si

NOTE.—The technical nature of the terms, and the obscurity of many of the explanations, render a translation impracticable.

1 *Albus* appears to signify *white lead.* Blacha was probably written *biacha* (biacca).

2 *Crocus*, *Croceum* is used for yellow. See Croceum.

3 Aureola. This appears to be the auripetrum of Pietro di S. Audemar, No. 202, and the Clavicula.

ipsa liniatur, per eam transparet, et pulcra fit, precipue si in stanno tenuato polito sit.

Attramentum est color niger quo scribitur, aliter incaustum dicitur, et vide in incausto, et de ipso quoque utitur pingendo dum fit de fuligine ardentis candele vel lampadis vel carbone mollis ligni vel vitis.[1]

Auripentrum[2] est color croceus qui stanno lucido suppositus et linitus speciem auri procul intuentibus mentitur.

Auripigmento similis est color qui vocatur (*sic*) et fit de felle piscis magni marini, credo balene, mixto cum creta alba seu gersa et modico aceto.

Arsicon vel *arxica*[3] sicut est auripigmentum, est color croceus, et miscendo succo herbe que scalda bassa dicitur fit viridis et succi gratia quarumdam aliarum herbarum ad hoc boni sunt.

Anguillaria herba facit colorem (*sic*) cum miscetur vitro.

Alba creta est gipsus, aliter gersa dicta, et fit de lapide quodam in fornace usque ad dealbacionem decocto, et de subtiliore ipsius dealbantur tabule altarium. Alii plastrum vocant.

Arxica est quedam terra crocea ad pingendum apta ac etiam ad formas operum cupri fundendorum fiendas utilima.

Alumen glacie[4] quod alibi, precipue in Parisiis glassa dicitur, et si color non sit, tamen pluribus coloribus ad picturam et illuminaturam aptis nimis conveniens est.

Assisiam auri faciendo intrat moniculum[5] quod est quedam (*sic*).

1 Atramentum, then, is charcoal or lamp-black, No. 172.

2 Auripentrum, called auripetrum by Petrus di S. Audemar, No. 202; by Eraclius, No. xliv.; and in the Clavicula. This appears to be the same as Aureola.

3 Arzicon and Arzica are here considered synonymous, but they are not so in fact: the former is declared by Eraclius, No. l., to be the same as orpiment, but the latter is shown by the Bolognese manuscript to have been a yellow lake, made from the Reseda Luteola, Dyers' weed, or, as it is generally called, Weld. Arzicon appears to be a corruption of *Arsenicon*, which Vitruvius (lib. vii. cap. vii.) says was the Greek name for Auripigmentum.

4 Alumen glacie appears to be common alum, see Nos. 42, 299, 313.

5 Gum ammoniac.

Aurare seu deaurare chrisare dicitur, ut dicit Catholicon.

Argilla dicitur creta alba, et aliis modis vocatur ut sequenter in creta dicetur.

Albi colores seu materie et metalla eorum sunt et nominantur, ut et in hac tabula reperies in locis suis, cerusa, blacha, argentum et stannum tenuatum, gipsus, creta alba, candidus calx, gersa, tavertinus.

Bracha seu *Blacha*[1] est color albus, et fit de plumbo vel de ejus corrupcione, sicut rubigo fit de ferro; aliter vocatur cerusa, album plumbum, et aliter glaucus.

Blauccus[2] est color, aliter lazurium vel azurum aliter celestis vel celestinus, aliter persus, aliter ethereus dictus.

Brunus[3] est color quem puto esse bularminium alibi ponitur pro sanguine drachonis qui quasi coloris bularminici est.

Bures[4] est liquor qui in licivio de cinere fabarum coctus facit colorem (*sic*) credo viridem, per ea que continentur in capitulo 247.

---

1 It is probable this word was originally written biacha, the old Italian way of spelling biacca.

2 *Blauccus*, or, as it is written in No. 294, *Blauctus*, and in No. 314 *blauet*, signifies Blue.

3 *Brunus*. Probably Bruno di Spagna, which Haydocke, the translator of Lomazzo's Treatise on Painting (p. 99), identifies with Majolica, and which there is no reason to doubt is the soft red hæmatite, called also Bruno d'Inhilterra. This colour is mentioned by Eraclius, Nos. 282, 286.

4 There is scarcely a doubt that this should be written *Borax*, and not Bures. The word Borax is derived in the first place from the Hebrew Borith, and more immediately from the Arabic Baurach, and was so corrupted by the different nations who practised the arts in which it was used, that it is seldom found in old MSS. written twice alike. By Theophilus it is called "parahas," or "barabas;" in the Montpelier MS. described by Mr. Hendrie (Theoph. p. 429) it is written "Boraxa;" in the Clavicula, Burrago, Borras, Borrax, and Borac. It was also known to the Arabs under another name, derived from Tincal, its denomination in India, whence it was brought to Europe, namely Tincar, whence the Spanish name Atincar. It is a native borate of soda, and is found at the bottom of lakes in Persia, the Mogul territory, in Thibet, China, and Japan.

Bisetus, vel *Biseth* folii,[1] est color minus rubeus quam folium, et de eodem folio cum supernatat acceptus, et credo per hoc etiam potest intelligi quilibet clarescens color supernatans cuilibet ex coloribus cum in conchillis temperati sunt ad pingendum et aliquantulum quieverunt.

Bularminium[2] est color rubeus nigrescens, ut morellus, vel ut sanguis drachonis.

Blacha seu *Bracha*[3] est color albus, aliter cerusa, aliter album Hispanie, aliter album plumbum, et aliter glaucus dicitur.

Braxilium vel *Brexilium*[4] est lignum rubeum a quo cum pistus rixus sit in lixivio forti vel urina cum albumine commiscetur exit color roxeus vel purpureus.

Blaca, dicit Catholicon, est purpura cujusdem animalis colorem mutans; et qui blateus dicitur, purpureus, vel talis coloris, scilicet blauius dicitur ipse.

Blondus est color albo et rubeo mixtus, aliter cerulus vel ceruleus; et ceruleus color alibi ponitur pro colore ex albo et viridi mixto; et facto vel ex viridi, albo, et croceo.

Berettinus[5] color, Lombardice sic vocatus, est color medius inter album et nigrum, qui Latine elbus vel elbidus dicitur, ut in Catholicone scilicet; Gallice grisus appellatur.

Birsus[6] est color rufus vel niger, ut dicit Catholicon.

Blaui[7] colores, seu materie eorum sunt et nominantur ut in

---

1 See Folium. Bisetus, or Biseth folii, a Latin form of "Bezette," which is a corruption of the Italian word "Pezzette." See the note to "Succus."

2 Bularmenium—Armenian Bole.

3 Blacha, or bracha. This should probably be written *biacha* (biacca), Nos. 1, 18.

4 Braxilium, or brexilium, the verzino of the Italians.

5 This colour, which is a true grey, is the veneda of Theophilus.

6 Birsus. This appears to be a dark purple colour. See Cennino Cennini, chap. cxiv., note by Tambroni.

7 *Blaui* colores, that is blue colours. See *ante*, Blauccus. This term occurs in the extracts from the Archivio delle Riformazione di Firenze, published by Gaye, Carteggio inedito, vol. i. p. 449, and in Venetian tariffs. Mr. Hendrie says the word is of Byzantine origin. The resemblance to the German *Blau* is striking.

hac tabula in locis suis reperies, azurium seu lazurium, viola, herbe flos, persicus, persus, indicus, silacetus, safirecus, rubigo argenti finissimi.

Chriso, Chrisas, id est deaurare vel aurare ut in Catholicon dicitur.

Citrinus color aliquantulum differt a duobus coloribus, id est, croceo, et punico vel puniceo, et citrinus est color ex croceo et rubeo mixtus seu factus.[1]

Croceus[2] color aliquantulum differt a coloribus duobus, puniceo videlicet et citrino.

Carnatura,[3] alia membrana, alia cedra, alia holcus vel olcus, alia lumina, alia veneda seu veneda, alia fulvus, menesch, prasis, posech, cerusa, purpureus, folium, sinopis, ruscus, rosa, rubi, succus, menech, exedŕa.

Cedra[4] est color qui fit de rubeo, mixto cum pauco nigri coloris, ad nuda ymaginum humanarum operanda; aliter dicitur exedra.

Coccicus,[5] *ci*, color est rubeus, seu sanguineus; vel etiam genus est tincture coloris medii inter rubeum et croceum: alii coccinum illud vocant, ut, in passione Christi, de colore vestis ejus.

Coccus dicunt Greci, nos vero coccicum, seu cortinum aut coccinum, rubeum colorem qui fit et est ex diversis ut sunt frondes silvestres, flores rose rubee, vel creta, que et terra rubea, et alii colores rubei artificiali; aliter dicitur vernilculus vel vermiletus, et aliter sanguineus.

---

1 Orange colour.

2 Yellow.

3 Under this term the author has included all the tints used in painting flesh, as well the flesh tints as those for shadows.

4 Cedra. The shadow-colour for flesh. See Theophilus, lib. i. chap. xiii., where it is called Excedra or Exedra.

5 Coccicus or Coccicum. By this term was meant the colour called by the Italians "Grana," and which the Arabs called "Alkermes," and we Kermes.

Cortex[1] secundus nigra prunii, si decoquatur facit colorem croceum.

Crocea terra, vel creta crocea, est ad pingendum apta; aliter ocra vel ogra dicitur. Alia terra crocea est que arxica[2] dicitur qua forme operum fusilium cupri fiunt.

Cerulus vel *ceruleus*,[3] dicit Catholicon, id est fulvus ad instar cere viridis, niger, glaucus, et est prope blondus; sed alibi idem Catholicon dicit quod fulvus est aliquantulum rubeus vel cum nigro rubeus mixtus, et, ut idem Catholicon, flavus, albus, rubeus, aut blondus albo et rubeo factus.

Celestinus vel *celestis* est color aliter azurium, aliter blaucus, aliter persus, aliter ethereus dictus.

Cerusa est color albus qui fit de plumbo; aliter vocatur bracha seu blacha, et aliter glaucus et alibi dicitur que cerusa fit de cupro adusto.[4]

Croma Grece, Latine color, secundum Catholiconem, quod est vocabulum universale pro omnibus coloribus.

Color similiter est vocabulum universale pro omnibus coloribus, et Grece croma dicitur, et quot sunt planete, tot sunt colores, videlicet septem, qui sunt, primo duo extremi, albus et niger, et reliqui quinque qui intermedii dicuntur, videlicet, celestis seu Lazurius, rubeus, croceus seu aureus, viridis, et sanguineus seu purpureus aut violetus vel fulvus de quorum singulis reperies in hac tabula in locis suis secundum litteras alphabeti primas nominum eorum et materias quibus fiunt, et de quorum etiam interunpcionibus ad invicem infinite diversitates colorum ad placitum humani ingenii distinguuntur.

Crocus vel *Crocum*[5] est color exiens de saffranno madefacto,

---

1 Cortex. See Nos. 206, 208, 209. This appears to have been used in making yellow varnishes which, being spread over tin, caused it to appear like gold.

2 Is this the "Terra di Matton bianchi" mentioned by Baldinucci? Voc. Dis.

3 Cerulus. This is quite unintelligible.

4 See Eraclius, No. liv.

5 Crocus or Crocum. The zafarano of the Italians. See Cennini, cap. 49.

vel est idem saffrannus; et melior est cicilianus qui coriscos vocatur.

Croceus[1] est color idem exiens de saffranno, et est qui fit ex mixtura fellis et crete albe, et est ocra vel ogra terra quedam, et est color auri, et est auripigmentum, et est etiam quedam terra crocea que arxica dicitur apta ad formas operum cupri fiendas, et alii dicunt ipsam argillam.

Candidus est color albus differens ab albo.

Calx[2] calcis est color albus, videlicet lapis durus in igne usque ad ejus dealbacionem decoctus, de quo lathomi cementum ad muros edificandos faciunt.

Carminium[3] est color rubeus, aliter cinobrium vel sinopis dictus; alibi dicitur quod fit de albo et ocro mixtis.

Cerosius est color viridis, alibi capitur pro quodam succo in 159, et alibi pro (*sic*).

Coriscos est crocus, id est, saffranus perfectissimus, ut ait Ysidorus, nascens in Cicilia insula.

Caligo[4] est color, videlicet, materia illa crocea obscura, quam fumus ignis generat sub caminatis sub quibus continue fit ignis decoquendo fercula.

Caprifolium[5] est herba in Anglico dicta "gaterice," cujus grana in vino trita et bulita si emitatur ferrum eruginatum color viridis fulgentis efficitur, et si addatur atramentum, niger efficitur.

Creta alba, dicitur argilla, est color albus factus de lapide in fornace cocto, qui aliter plastrum dicitur, et aliter gersa, et aliter gipsus, et utuntur ipsa pelliparii; alia est rubea, alia viridis et alia nigra, que terra nigra seu lapis niger vocatur, et alia crocea.

---

1 Croceus may here be considered a general name for yellow pigments.

2 Lime.

3 See Eraclius, No. lvi.

4 This appears to be the colour we call Bistre.

5 Sir Thomas Phillips says, in his Introduction to the Clavicula, that for Gaterice we should read gate-tree, *i. e.* goat-tree.

Creta viridis,[1] cujus melior nascitur in creta cirina insula, et vocatur Grece theodote; alia creta reperitur rubea, et alia alba, et alia nigra, que appellata est lapis niger.

Crisicula[2] est color (*sic*) veniens a Macedonia, et foditur ex metallis ærariis.

Ceruleus color fit ex succo de lutea herba expresso, alibi dicitur quod viridissimum colorem facit, ipsa herba seu succus ejus, precipue si alicui substancioso colori albo admisceatur, ut crete aut cerusie; et alibi ceruseus est color blondus ex albo et rubeo factus.

Carbo[3] est color niger factus de lignis mollibus ustis, ut salix, populus, vitis, et similia.

Cinobrium[4] vel cinopis aliter carminium dicitur.

Conchile[5] vel concile maris circonscise sanguinem purpureum colorem habentem emittunt, quo tinctura purpurea fit pro lanis.

Crocei colores seu materie, et metalla eorum sunt et nominantur ut in hac tabula reperies in locis suis: aurum, auripigmentum, auripigmento similis color, arsica, suffranus, coriscos, caligo, decoctio secundi corticis nigri pruni, ocra vel ogra, fel, grecumspect, stannum tenuatum croce colore in hoc convenienti coloritum.

Celare a celo, celas, id est lanire, sculpere, pingere, figurare, protrahere, designare; et inde celatura, celature, etc.

Drachonis sanguis[6] est color morellus seu rubeus obscurus.

Deaurare, id est, auro aurare, chrisare dicitur, ut in Catholicon.

---

1 This creta viridis seems to be our terra verte.

2 Chrysocolla. This is the native green carbonate of copper.

3 Carbo, that is, charcoal black.

4 Cinnabar or vermilion. The writers of these old MSS. speak of the artificial cinnabar only.

5 This was the purpura of Pliny and the ancients, from which the celebrated Tyrian dye was prepared, and which was procured from a fish of the genus Buccinum found in the Mediterranean.

6 Dragon's blood.

Designare, protrahere, pingere, sculpere, figurare, lanire, celare, quasi idem significant.

Exedra[1] est color ex mixtura rubea et modico nigri ad nuda corporum humanorum fienda aliter dicta cedra.

Edera[2] est herba arboribus herendo, repens, que in Gallico dicitur "yene" vel "lierre," cujus rami ex sobula perforati, vel hinc inde infra eos incisi, ad medium videlicet de mense Marcii emittunt liquorem sanguineum, qui, cum urina coctus, lacca est, qua tinguntur pelles parcium.

Ethereus color aliter dicitur lazurium seu azurium, et aliter persus, aliter blauctus, et aliter celestinus seu celestis.

Elbus,[3]-ba,-bum, vel elbidus,-da,-dum, color est medius inter album et nigrum, ut ait Catholicon, et Gallice dicitur Grisus, set Lombardice Berretinus nominatur.

Flavus[4] color fit de cerusa combusta.

Folium[5] est pro tingendo lanas, et est color rubeus, et quidam alter est purpureus, et alter saphireus, scilicet est quidam alter qui fit miscendo ipsi rubeo cinerem vel lexivium cinerum ligni ulmi, et vocatur folium scampnense.

Fel[6] est liquor croceus, seu color, quo si cuprum cultello rasum et dente politum ungatur quociens conveniat, splendificatur tanquam si deauratum esset, et si ipsum fel misceatur cum creta seu gersa alba, et modico aceto, efficitur color auripigmento similis, videlicet croceus.

Fuscus est color niger, ex carbone, vel ex fumo lampadis

---

1 Exedra. See Theophilus, lib. i. cap. xiii.; and Le Begue, No. 345.

2 Edera, the ivy.

3 In English, *Grey*.

4 Flavus. This appears to be the colour we now call massacot, the protoxide of lead.

5 Folium. See Vocabulary of Colours, *supra*.

6 A similar colour is in use at the present day, called Gallstone. It is a beautiful and very transparent yellow, but it is not permanent. It is used in water-colours.

aut candele ardentis factus, et aliter dicitur fuligo,[1] dicitur aliter fuscus sanctonicus dicitur.

Fuligo est color niger vel quasi niger, ad croceum tendens, et veniens a camino ignis, aliter dicta caligo, et est etiam fumus candele et lampadis nigerrimus recollectus ad scutellam vel aliud vas ferreum, vel cupreum, vel terreum.

Fumus[2] est color niger, si cum ab igne candele sepi vel cere, vel a lampadis lumine exit, colligatur, qui aliter fuscus, et aliter fuligo nominatur.

Fulvus, dicit Catholicon, est rubeus aliquantulum, vel cum nigro rubeus ; et vide sequenter in R. littera super verbo *ravus*, quod ibi aliter dicitur.

Fenix, seu phenix, vel feniceus color rubeus est et feniceon Grece Latine rubeum colori rosarum rubearum similatus.

Ferula,[3] aliter galbanum dicta, est genus, et lac herbe, et est quidem color inde de succo ex palmitibus ejus expresso factus ut dicit Catholicon.

Figurare, pingere, sculpere, protrahere, designare, lanire, celare, quasi idem significant.

Galbanum[4] est genus et lac herbe, que dicitur ferula, et est quidem color inde de succo ex palmitibus ejus factus, et sic dicit Catholicon.

Grisus color, Gallice sic dictus, est color inter album et nigrum, qui Latine elbus vel elbidus dicitur ut in Catholicon, set Lombardice vocatur beretinus.

Grenuspect[5] herba, cujus decoctio vini aut cervisie crocea est, de qua, si temperetur et teretur viride Grecum, fit pulcrum viride, quod credo esse viridegris.

---

1 The colour here described is Bistre.

2 Fumus—Lamp black.

3 Ferula—See Galbanum.

4 Galbanum, a liquor or gum produced by a species of ferula in Africa and Turkey, called Ferula Galbanifera.

5 Grenuspect. Sir Thomas Phillips thinks this should be written "Greningwert."

Gersa[1] est color albus, de quadam terra, vel lapide non duro, cocto in fornace factus, qui aliter gipsus vel creta alba vocatur, et ipsa utuntur pelliparii, et aliter plastra dicitur. Set etiam pelliparii pocius utuntur alia creta alba, que fit de quodam meliori lapide absque coctione albissimo pulverizato, Gallice "croye."

Glades[2] vel *glacies,* cum ex metallis primum exciduntur, gutas argenti vivi exprimunt, pro usu artificum, et sine ipsis es neque argentum inaurari possunt.

Garancia[3] herba est ad faciendum tincturas lanarum et lineorum, et in Ytalico gadus dicitur.

Gadus[4] herba est, in Gallico garancia dicta, ad faciendum tincturas lanarum et lineorum.

Glassa[5] credo quod sit alumen glasse seu glacie.

Gipsus[6] est color albus, aliter gersa, et aliter alba creta dictus, et est terra seu lapis in fornace usque ad dealbacionem decoctus, quo tabule altarium dealbantur ut depingantur.

Granetus est color de albo et viridi factus.

Gladius[7] viridis est color viridis factus de auripigmento et indico mixtus.

---

1 This is plaster of Paris, the gesso of the Italians. The other stone is our English chalk.

2 I believe this passage is from Pliny. See Eraclius, No. 241.

3 Garancia is certainly madder, but its Italian name is Robbia, and not gadus.

4 Gadus. This is a mistake: the French term is Gaude; the Italian, Guado; the English, Woad—*Isatis Tinctoria.*

5 Glassa. In these manuscripts of Le Begue the word Glassa is used in two significations: first, it is used to denote Sandarac or Amber, as in Nos. 208 and 341; and, secondly, it is used in conjunction with Alumen, and appears to mean crystallized alum simply, or Roche alum, as in Nos. 42 and 299.

6 Gipsus. Gesso—plaster of Paris.

7 Gladius viridis. A vegetable green, prepared from the leaves of the Gladiolus communis; in Italian, Gladiolo; in French, Glayeul flambe; in English, the Corn-flag; in Sicilian, Spatulidda. This pigment was much used in Italy. See 'Secreti di Alessio,' part ii. p. 37 b. A blue colour was made from the flowers of the same plant.

Glaucus est color albus, ut cerusa, que aliter dicitur album plumbum, aliter blacha, et aliter album Hispanie.

Gaterice[1] Anglice est herba, cujus grana in vino trita et bullita, si immittatur ferrum eruginatum efficitur color viridis fulgentis et si addatur attramentum niger efficitur.

Gumma[2] edere, lacha est facta ex succo vel liquore exeunte in Marcio de ramis edere herbe arboribus inherentis et repentis, si aculeo ferro perforentur.

Holcus[3] vel olcus est color, qui aliter membrana dicitur, ex rubeo, et albo, et pauco viridis creta compositus ad nuda corpora et membra humana depingenda.

Herba morella,[4] trita cum gersa seu gipso, id est, creta alba, facit colorem viridem.

Herba sandix[5] vocata, est rubea, et de ipsa fit tinctura rubea aut sanguinea.

Herba vaccinium[6] vocata duplex est; una rubea, que temperata cum lacte purpureum colorem facit elegantem, reliqua vero croceum colorem facit.

Herba viola dicta, cujus flos persus seu blavus est, facit colorem blavum si ipse ejus flos misceatur crete albe et teratur.

Herba que *scalda bassa* vocatur in janua facit succum si pistetur et exprimatur, qui mixtus cum arxicon vel arxica, colore croceo, fit color viridis.

Iris est color (*sic*).

Indicus vel indicum est color celestinus obscurus.

---

1 See ante, Caprifolium.

2 Gumma Edera. Gum from the Ivy.

3 See Theophilus, lib. i. cap. i.; and Pietro di S. Audemar, No. 180.

4 Herba Morella (Solanum Nigrum) is here, as in the Bol. manuscript, said to make a green colour.

5 Herba sandix—the madder. The word madder is derived from the Danish, Swedish, and Russian languages.

6 Herba vaccinium, the violet. That from which a yellow colour is made is the Viola lutea, the Wall-flower.

Incaustum est color quo scribitur, aliter attramentum dictum, vide in attramento, id est factum ex decoctione gallarum fractarum, et vitriolo et gummi Arabico, aut ex decoctione mirce que vulgariter genestra dicitur, et dictis vitriolo et gummi Arabico et decoctio etiam corticis hoene ligni aut ceresi ligni posset convenire, nec non cortex secundus nigri pruni arboris ad hoc per decoctionem adaptaretur cum addicione suprascriptorum vitrioli et gummi Arabici.

Jas viride dicitur, ut dicit Catholicon.

Lumina[1] est color ex mixtura membrane et ceruse factus ad illuminandum facies et nuda corpora humana in pictura, seu ad gibbositates in ipsis elevandos.

Lacca est gumma quedam, facta de liquore rubeo, qui exit de liquore edere, arboribus herente et repente, si rami ipsius in mense Marcii aculeo ferreo perforentur.

Lazurium vel azurium fit de lapide lazulli; dicitur aliter persus, aliter celestis vel celestinus, aliter blauctus seu blauus, et aliter ethereus.

Lucee[2] herbe succus coloris cerulei est, et alibi dicitur quod viridissimus est.

Lazuli lapis }
Lapis lazuli } reperitur in montibus vel partibus et est celestis coloris seu persi vel blaui et de ipso fit pulver qui purificatur et postea est azurium.

Lapis niger[3] est, de quo, si satis mollis sit, utuntur pictores et carpentarii, protrahendo ad siccum; et de ipso pingitur terendo ad liquidum; aliter terra nigra dicitur.

Lignum braxillii[4] rubeum seu purpureum colorem reddit si in lixivio vel urina aut in claro ovi cum alumine temperetur.

---

1 Lumina. See Theophilus, lib. i.

2 Herba Luzza, either the Erba lizza, the Tragopogon pratense, yellow goat's beard, or the Erba Lutea of Pliny, the Reseda Luteola, Dyer's weed, or weld.

3 Black chalk, or graphite.

4 The Verzino of the Italians.

Leucos Grece, Latine album, ut ait Catholicon, qui color et glaucus dicitur.

Lanire, celare, sculpere, pingere, figurare, protrahere, designare, quasi idem significant, etc.

Membrana[1] est color quo pinguntur facies et nuda corpora humana ; aliter olcus dicitur, vel holcus, et aliter carnatura.

Minium[2] est color non tam rubeus ut synopis, set magis pallidus, aliter dictus sendracum vel sendaraca.

Menesch ;[3] aliqui dicunt quod est color rubeus, minus clarus quam minicum, et magis clarus quam synopis ; alii ipsum vocant succum, et indici coloris est ; aliter dicitur esse succus sambuci, qui viridis est.

Mellana[4] est color cum quo ex lacha seu gumma edere et flore farine tritici in urina positus fit rubeus color synopis vocatus.

Morella[5] herba trita cum gersa seu creta alba est color viridis.

Mellinus est color metalli speciem habens.

Morellus est color ex rubeo et nigro factus.

Morus Grece, est arbor quam et Latini etiam sic appellant cujus fructus morum dicitur, et ejus succus, mixtus cum creta

---

1 Membrana. See Theophilus, lib. i. cap. 1, and Pietro di S. Audemar, No. 180.

2 The term Sandaraca is sometimes applied to Red orpiment, and sometimes to Minium.

3 Menesch. Mr. Hendrie (Theoph. p. 81) says this is a Romaic word, signifying violet colour ; but I would suggest whether it may not signify "Madder," the Indian name for which is *Mnitsch*. This construction is perfectly compatible with the directions of Theophilus ; and in this case it will also agree with the definition in the Table of Synonymes, on which, however, I acknowledge but little dependence can be placed.

4 Mellana. In the MS. of S. Audemar this colour is called Sinopis de Mellana. It is a kind of lake.

5 Morella. This is one of the Italian names for the Solanum Nigrum, the Black nightshade. It is also called in Italy Solatro Nero, and Cacabo. In French it is called "Morelle," "Morelle des Jardins ;" but it must be distinguished from the "Maurelle," the name which the Croton Tinctorium bears at Montpellier.

alba et aliis rebus convenientibus, simul et separatim, colorem roseum et sanguineum faciunt.

Mirca [1] est arbor vulgariter dicta genestra, que interponitur faciendo incaustum ad scribendum.

Moniculum [2] est (*sic*), quod intrat ad faciendum assisiam auri.

Niger est color terre nigre, que lapis niger dicitur, satis mollis ad protrahendum, et color niger est etiam ex carbone molito, vel ex fumo lampadis aut candele factus; aliter fuscus dicitur, et aliter sanccenicus.

Neveda, [3] seu veneda est color ex mixtura nigri cum modico albo plumbo, et si poni vult in muro, ponatur calx loco dicti albi plumbi.

Nigri pruni cortex secundus, si decoquatur, facit colorem croceum, et si immittantur in ipsa decoctione debite quantitates vitrioli et gummi Arabici, fit attramentum seu incaustum ad scribendum.

Niger color et rufus color vocantur birsus, ut ait Catholicon, et vide in *rufus* et *ravus* quod ibi dicitur, ac etiam in *birsus.*

Nigri colores, seu materie eorum, sunt et nominantur ut et in hac tabula reperies in locis suis, attramentum, incaustum, fuligo, carbo, lapis niger, fuscus, fumus, sanctonicus.

Ocra, }
Ogra, } est color terre crocee.

Olchus [4] color aliter appellatur membrana, ad facies et nuda corpora humana depingenda.

Oster [5] piscis est marinus, cujus sanguis color est rubeus; purpureus vocatus.

---

1 Mirca. See note to MSS. of St. Audemar, No. 206.

2 Probably Gum ammoniac.

3 See Veneda.

4 Olchus. See Pietro di S. Audemaro, No. 180, and Theophilus, lib. i. cap. i.

5 The purpura of the ancients.

Prasis[1] est creta viridis ut dicit Catholicon.

Prasinus[2] est color rubeus; alii dicunt quod habet similitudinem viridis coloris et nigri, set Catholicon dicit quod prasin Grece, latine dicitur viridis.

Posch[3] est color ex mixtura prasini, et rubei combusti, et ocre, et modico cenobrio, factus, ad distinguendas partes membrorum humani corporis in membrana colore, set alibi posch dicitur fieri ex ogra et viridi simul mixtis.

Purpureus, qui est color rubeus, aliter folium vocatur,—vide in *folium;* et Anglici, in quorum terra nascitur, ipsum vocant "unormam;" fit etiam color purpureus ex lapide silicis exusto, et in aceto dum callescit extincto, et oster est certum quid, id est, piscis maris, aut aliud, quo fit color purpureus, vel de sanguine ejus; et concule maris etiam circumcise purpureum colorem faciunt, et similiter creta alba infecta radice rubea, et sic herba que vaccinium dicitur facit purpureum colorem si cum lacte temperetur.

Pruni nigri secundus cortex facit ex decoctione colorem croceum.

Paratonium est color (*Sic*).

Persus est color aliter celestis, aliter lazurium vel azurum, aliter ethereus, et aliter blauus dictus.

Pictura translucida,[4] aliter aureola dicta, est color seu liquor per quem omnes alii colores transparent, si cum in operibus siccaverint ipso linientur, precipue in stanno attenuato et polito.

Pallidus est color non proprie albus, set declinans aliquantulum ad obscuritatem.

Plumbus albus est color ex plumbo factus, aliter albus hispanie, aliter glaucus, aliter cerusa, et aliter blacha dictus.

---

1 Probably Terre Verte.

2 Prasinus, the same as Prasis. See Theophilus, lib. i. cap. ii.

3 Posch. See Theophilus, lib. i. cap. iii. and vii.; and Le Begue, No. 344.

4 See the Chapters 'De Confectio Lucidæ' and 'De Lucide ad Lucidas' of the Lucca manuscript, and Clavicula.

Plastra est terra vel lapis, qui, decoctus fornaci, albissimus est, aliter gersa, aliter creta alba, et aliter gipsus.

Phenix color rubeus est, vel fenix ; et feniceon Grece, latine rubeum.

Pumiceus color seu puniceus, aliquantulum differt a duobus coloribus, id est, a croceo et citrino, que plus continet de croceo, et minus de rubeo, quam citrinno.

Puniceus vel pumiceus, dicit liber de proprietatibus rerum, est color circumdans rubeum colorem, aliter etiam dicitur citrinus, qui est color ab eo parum differens que puniceus plus continet de croceo et minus de rubeo quam citrinus.

Pingere, lanire, celare, sculpere, figurare, protrahere, designare, quasi idem significant.

Rubeus est color qui ex frondibus silvestribus et aliis materialibus diversis fit, et diversis in obscuritate, et claritate, et aliis varietatibus, ut sunt dicti frondes, et etiam flores, ac terra vel creta rubea, et alii colores rubei artificiati ; et Greci ipsum coctum dicunt, nos vero rubeum vel vermiletum.

Rosa est color ex mixtura membrane et modico cenobrii et modico minii factus ad rubricandas facies et membra humanorum corporum in pictura, et fit de vermiculo et albo plumbo, ac de brasilio et alumine cum urina.

Rubi sunt rubei fructus arborum qui apud Grecos morus dicuntur, et fructus ipse eorum morum dicitur, ex quibus succus, mixtus aliis rebus materialibus, ut crete, seu gipso, sanguinei vel rosei colores fiunt.

Rubea radix[1]
Radix rubea } est de qua rubeus color fit, miscendo cum creta alba, id est, gipso.

Rubea terra, seu creta, ex qua trita pingitur.

Rava color niger est fulvo mixtus, dicit Catholicon.

Roseus est color rosarum rubearum colori similatus, et aliter vide in cocticus, coctus, fulvus, fenix seu phenix vel fenicus aut feniceus, per *p* et *h* vel *f* et *e* scribendo, et vide etiam in *purpureus* et in *folium*.

---

[1] Madder.

Rufus color et niger color vocantur birsus ut ait Catholicon.

Ravus, rava, ravum, id est, fulvi color, ut ait Catholicon, et vide ante in fulvus quod ibi aliter dicitur et in eodem Catholicone dicitur ravus talis color, videlicet niger fulvo mixtus, et vide advertenter in birsus quod ibi dicitur.

Rubei colores seu materie eorum sunt et nominantur ut et in hac tabula reperies in locis suis carminium, cinobrium, sinopis, coctinus, cocticus, coctus, vermiculus, herba sandix, herba vaccinium dicta, folium, succus luchet herbe, mellana, sandaraca, minium, sandix, terra seu creta rubea, fenix seu phenix, roseus, et sanguineus; set nota quod colores nominatim in fenix seu phenix in roseus et sanguineus differunt a rubeis, et est de ipsis coloribus sanguineis aliud capitulum generale factum in littera S. in fine.

Sinopis[1] est color magis rubeus quam vermiculus; aliter dicitur cenobrium, aliter mellana, et fit de warancia, et aliter est qui fit ex lacha vel gumma edere, et flore farine bullitis in urina; et aliter sinopis fit ex warancia et lacha suprascripta.

Saffranus, qui reddit colorem croceum, dicitur crocus, et perfectior qui sit Sicilianus, tam in colore quam in sapore, qui vocatur coriscos.

Succus[2] est color trahens ad indicum; alii dicunt esse rubeum minus clarum quam minium et magis clarum quam

---

[1] There was a natural pigment called Sinopia, which is described by Pliny and by Cennini (cap. 38), and which is also mentioned in the Bolognese MS. The sinopis of the text was a red lake.

[2] Succus. In the 'Secreti di Don Alessio Piemontese,' part 2, p. 37, is a recipe for making "Pezzette morelle" from the berries of the Ebuli, or Sambuco Salvatico (Dwarf Elder). The pezzette were pieces of rag which were dipped into the coloured juice of the elder, and other plants, until they absorbed the juice. They were then dried in the shade; when dry, they were then dipped in a solution of alum and again dried. When they were required for use, a piece was put into a shell, and a little gum-water being poured over it, it was stirred about until the colour was discharged, when the rag was thrown away: the colour left, which was transparent, was used for painting.

sinopis, et aliter vocatur menesch, quod aliter dicitur ipse menech esse succus sambuci.

Succus sambuci est color seu liquor viridis obscurus, qui aliter menech dicitur.

Succus herbarum est color viridis seu liquor cui sepe admiscentur alia ad virides colores faciendos.

Stannum attenuatum album utitur scilicet loco argenti, qui caret argento; et loco auri, qui auro caret, depingitur seu coloratur croce colore, et ipso utitur.

Sandaracum[1] seu sandaracha est color minus rubeus quam vermiculus, et est aliter minium dictus.

Scrupulum (*Sic*).

Sandix[2] genus est herbe rubee de qua fit tinctura ut dicit Catholicon.

Sandalica est genus coloris.

Sanguis drachonis[3] est color rubeus obscurus seu est color morellus.

Sillacetus[4] color fit ex violis aridis decoctis, et, expressa aqua, tritis super lapide cum creta alba, id est, gersa.

Safireus color est color quilibet saphiri lapidis assimilans, videlicet proprie inter celestem et rubeum, plus ad celestem trahens colorem quam ad rubeum.

Sanctonicus color aliter fuscus dicitur, qui color niger est.

Sanguineus est color rosarum rubearum colori, ac etiam colorum sanguinis assimilatus, et aliter vide in *roseus* et in aliis locis ibi nominatis.

Scupere, lenire, celare, pingere, figurare, protrahere, designare, quasi idem significant, &c.

Sanguinei colores seu materie eorum sunt et nominantur ut et in hac tabula in locis suis reperies, bullarminium, sanguis

---

[1] Red orpiment is frequently understood by this term. It is used by S. Audemar in the terms mentioned in the text.

[2] Madder.

[3] Dragon's blood.

[4] This is a yellow colour, prepared from the Viola lutea, the Wall-flower, and white chalk or gesso. The name in the text is derived from Pliny.

drachonis, braxillii lignum, lacca, purpura, blacca, sanguis conchillarum maris, coctus, vermiculus, liquor edere herbe, gomma edere, sandix herba, vaccinium herba, mellana, morus, oster maris, rosa, rubi, rubea radix, roseus; et nota quod sanguinei colores a rubeis differunt, ut in capitulo generali de rubeis coloribus dictum est in littera R.

Terreus color fit de cerusa combusta.

Therdote (*sic*) Grece, latine est creta viridis, cujus melior nascitur in creta cirina.

Terra nigra vel lapis niger mollis est, de quo terendo fit color niger; et, non terendo, utuntur carpentarii et pictores protrahendo ad siccum.

Terra seu creta *rubea,* ex qua trita pingitur.

Terra vel creta *viridis* ad pingendum est cujus melior nascitur in creta cirina, et in Greco dicitur Theodote.

Terra vel creta *crocea* est apta ad pingendum et aliter ocra vel ogra dicitur.

Terra seu creta alba, aliter gersa, aliter gipsus, aliter plastra dicitur, qua utuntur pelliparii; et est alia rubea, alia crocea, alia nigra que de terra vel lapide aut creta nigra trita fit, alia viridis cujus melior nascitur in creta cirina, et ipsa in Greco dicitur theodoce.

Tavertinus[1] albus color, seu lapis qui apte rubificatur, si in ligno braxilii, cum urina, vel lexivio, et alumine misceatur.

Viridis vel viride est color ex diversis factus sicut creta vel terra viridis et alii ex herbarum succis et metalli facti virides artificiati.

Violaceus vel violetus color est, qui ex rubeo et nigro, aut ex rubeo et perso vel lazurio, fit miscendo.

---

[1] Travertine. A stone dug in many parts of Italy, particularly in Siena, Pisa, Lucca, and near the river Teverone at Tivoli. It is a peculiar kind of limestone, formed by a deposit from the rivers in these districts. It was much used in Italy for building, and for making lime. See 1st 'Report of Commissioners of Fine Arts,' p. 39, and n

Warancia[1] est color seu materia coloris, quia cocta in aqua cum lacha seu gumma edere fit quidam color rubeus sinopis vocatus et etiam ex ipsa warancia fit color rubeus ad tingendum pelles parcium.

Viridis terra seu creta quedam est, cujus melior est que nascitur in creta cirina, et aliter, videlicet in Greco, theodoce dicitur.

Violetus est color, qui ex rubeo et perso, seu azurio, mixtus, maxime ex rubeo claro, id est, lacha, et azurio fino fit.

Vaccinium[2] est herba rubea que temperata cum lacte facit colorem purpureum elegantem, et est quedam alia herba similiter vaccinium vocata que croceum colorem facit.

Vergaut[3] est color qui est quasi ut azurium respectu coloris, non respectu materie.

Viola est flos cujusdem herbe persus seu blauus, quo cum creta alba fit color blauus, et aliter cilacetus color dictus est.

Vermiculus[4] color rubeus est, qui fit ex frondibus silvestribus, ut dicit Catholicon, et Grece ipsum dicunt coctum ; nos vero rubeum vel vermiletum.

Veneda[5] seu neveda est color factus ex mixtura nigri cum modico albi plumbi, et si poni vult in muro, ponatur calx loco dicti albi plumbi.

Vercanda[6] nominatur in capitulo libri colorum 342.

Verblea[7] nominatur in capitulo 345 libri colorum.

---

[1] Vuarantia. The name by which madder was generally known during the middle ages, especially in the western parts of Europe. It was called "Garance" in French, and "Granza" in Spanish, whence the term warantia is apparently derived.

[2] Vaccinium, the purple violet. The latter is the Viola lutea, or Wallflower.

[3] Vergaut. See Eraclius, No. 282. Perhaps Vertbleu.

[4] By Vermiculus is here meant the kermes, or coccus, the "grana" of the Italians.

[5] Veneda, a true grey. See Theophilus, lib. i. cap. vi.

[6] In the number referred to this word appears to be written "Vernide" and "Vercande," a proof that this part of the table of synonymes was written after Le Begue had added his recipes.

[7] Verblea. Probably Vert-bleu, the Verde Azzurro of the Italians, a native carbonate of copper, of a greenish-blue colour, the Armenian stone of Pliny.

Usticium, usticii, genus est coloris, ut dicit Catholicon.

Virides colores seu materie, et metalla eorum, sunt et nominantur ut et in hac tabula in locis suis reperies, arxica mixta succo viridi herbarum, cerosius, caprifolium, gaterice, ceruleus, succus luree herbe, gladius, herba morella, scalda bassa herba, prassis vel prassinus, succus herbarum diversarum, theodote terra vel creta viridis, jas, succus rute herbe mixtus cum viride eris.

Alia Tabula, licet imperfecta et sine inicio.

[1] Iste liber non est completus usque ad illum numerum.—[Marginal note by author.]

---

[1] Malum premium.—[Marginal note by author.]

Vultum et nudorum corporum colores, scilicet exedram vel posam et alios facere, 133, 317, 344.

Worniam colorem sic in Anglia nominatum qui est aptus ad tingendum lannas est purpureus, aliter folium dictus distemperare, 162, 164.

TABULA ad REPERIENDUM quodlibet capitulum arcium fabulis et aurifabulis et rerum et accidencium illis conferencium nec non operum exerciciorum que et contingencium eorum.

Aqua cavans ferrum, 64.

Arma et alia ferramenta conservare a rubigine, 69, 348.

Attribucio cujuslibet ex metallis alicui ex septem planetis continetur post numerum, 46.

Aurare cuprum fellis pinguedine seu liquore, 226.

Aurare auricalcum, 249.

Aurare metalla fusilia, 252.

Aurare ferrum, 237, 238.

Auraturam facere, 253.

Auraturam metalli perditam recuperare.

Aurei coloris ferrum facere, 67.

Aureo colore metallos colorare, 66.

Auricalcum aurare, 249.

Auricalcum facere, 49.

Auricalcum seu lathonum solidare, 65.

Auricalcum seu lathonum pulcrum facere sicut aurum, 82.

Aurum et argentum fondere, 365.

Argentum et aurum fondere, 365.

Azarium et ferrum temperare, 57, 58, 61, 62, 83, 84, 223, 333, 364.

EXPERIMENTS UPON COLOURS.

1. Know that gold letters are thus written with the following water. Take of sulphur vivum, of the inner bark of the pomegranate, of alum, salt, and gold dust (?), as much as you like, and liquid gum water and a little saffron. Mix, and write.

2. *To erase black letters upon paper.*—Make a water from the following things. Take nitre, and Roman vitriol, of each one pound, and distil them in an alembic, and a clear water will be produced; with this water slightly moisten a sponge, and rub the letters with it.[1]

3. *To make fine azure.*—Take plates of fine silver, and put them into a new jar; cover the jar closely with a tile, and place it in the skins of the grapes for 40 days; then scrape off the efflorescence, which you will find upon the plates, and which is fine azure.

4. *Also azure which is not fine is made in another way.*—Put vinegar into a glass bottle, the mouth of which must be well covered with tenacious earth, and let it be buried in horse dung for a month, and afterwards dry it in the sun.

5. *To make azure.*—Take a vase of pure copper, and put into it a colour [pigment] made of white marble (some recipes say quicklime) so as to half fill it. Afterwards fill it up with very strong vinegar, cover it over, and put in a warm place, or under dung, for a month, and you will find a blue good both for panels and walls.

6. *For the same.*—Take a new glazed jar, or a vase of silver, and put into it plates of very pure silver, as many as you like, rubbed over[2] with good wine, and place the jar under the refuse

[1] The produce of this distillation is nitric acid.

[2] From *sborfato*, a Bolognese word.

EXPERIMENTA DE COLORIBUS.

1. Nota quod auree littere scribuntur sic, cum ista aqua; accipe sulphur vivum, et corticem interiorem mali granati, aluminis, saltis, et de pluvia auri, tantum quantum vis, et aquam gummi liquide, et modicum de croco, et misce, et scribe.

2. *Ad delendum litteras nigras de carta.*—Fac aquam de[1] infrascriptis rebus. Accipe salniterum, et vitriolum Romanum, de quolibet libram unam, et distilla per alembicum, et erit clara aqua, et cum ipsa aqua balnea spongiam modicum, et de ipsa frica litteras.

3. *Ad faciendum azurium finum.*—Recipe laminas argenti fini, et pone in olla nova, et cooperiatur bene cum tegula, et pone ollam in vinariis uvarum per dies xl^{a}, et flos quem repereris super laminas radde, quod est azurium finum.

4. *Item aliter azurum non finum fit.*—Ponatur acetum in ampulla vitrea, cujus orificium bene cooperiatur cum terra tenaci, et sepeliatur in fimo equino per unum mensem, et postea siccetur ad solem.

5. *Ad faciendum azurrum.*—Recipe ampullam de puro cupro et pone intus colorem de albo marmore, ita ut sit dimedia; et in aliis receptis dicitur calx viva. Postea imple de aceto fortissimo, et cooperiri, et pone in loco calido, vel sub fimo, per mensem, et invenies azurrum bonum, in ligno, et in pariete.

6. *Ad idem.*—Habeas ollam novam incretatam, vel vas argenti, et immitte laminas argenti purissimi, quot vis, brofatas bono vino; et mitte vas in profundo viaziarum,[2] per dies

---

[1] Id est infrascriptum et scribitur ut supra causa brevitatis.—[Marginal note by author.]

[2] Vindemiarum ?

of the grapes for 36 or 40 days; and afterwards scrape or shake off into a clean vase the efflorescence which you find round and about the plates, which efflorescence is preserved upon the plates, in the same manner as rust upon iron, and verdigris upon plates or in vases of brass.

7. *To make azure.*—Take very thin plates of fine silver, as many as you like. You must also have a glazed earthen jar, with a cover; and on the middle of the under part of this cover there must be a small hook, to which you must hang the silver plates with a silver thread, so that they may not touch each other; and put very strong vinegar into the said jar, so as not to touch the plates, but to reach near them; and close carefully the said cover with a piece of linen and with glue, and put the jar for 15 days under dung, or over a slow fire or under the refuse of grapes. Afterwards scrape off the azure which you find upon the plates, and if you want more azure, do the same with the plates as you did before.

8. *Green from copper* or brass is made in the same manner with plates of brass, as was directed to be done with silver plates to make blue.

9. *To make perfect azure.*—Take an earthen jar with a cover similar to that in which ceruse is made, and take sheets or plates of fine tin, wetted with strong vinegar, and sprinkled over with powdered white quicklime, place the vase, with the aforesaid plates, in the dung of sheep or horses, for 10 days, and then scrape off the efflorescence which you find on the tin plates, and if you want more of it, put back the jar with the plates as before.

10. *To make perfect ultramarine azure.*—Take of lapis lazuli as much as you like, and grind it very fine upon a porphyry slab. Then make a cake or pastille of the following ingredients, namely, if there is one pound of lapis lazuli, take vi. oz. of Greek pitch, ij. oz. of mastic, ij. oz. of wax, ij. oz. of black pitch, ij. oz. of gum from the pine, 1 oz. of oil of spike or of linseed, and ½ oz. of turpentine. All these things must boil in a pipkin until they are nearly liquefied, afterwards strain them into cold water, and take what drops into the water through the strainer, and knead

xxxvi. vel xl[ta]; postea excucias seu raddas in vas mundum florem quem inveneris in cercuita laminarum, qui flos conservatur super ipsis laminis, sicut fit rubigo super ferro, et viride eris super laminas vel in vasis eris.

7. *Ad faciendum azurrum.*—Recipe laminas argenti fini quot vis subtilissimas, et habeas vas terre vitriatum cum coperculo, et in parte inferiori dicti coperculi sit unus uncinellus in medio, cui suspendas laminas suprascriptas cum filo argenteo, taliter quod lamine non se tangant invicem; et in vase mitte acetum fortissimum, tantum quod non tangat ipsas laminas, set stet prope; et optura bene dictum coperculum cum pecia lini, et cum cola, et pone vas sub fimo per xv[cim] dies, vel ad ignem temperatum, vel sub vinariis; postea radde azurum quod inveneris super laminas, et, si plus velis, fac iterum de ipsis laminis ut fecisti.

8. *Ad viride rami seu eris.*—Fiat eo modo de laminis eris, ut supra dictum est de argenteis pro azurro.

9. *Ad faciendum azurrum perfectum.*—Accipe vas terrenum, cum coperculo tali, ut illud de quo fit cerusia, et habe laminas seu plactas fini stagni, balneatas aceto forti, et sparsas alba calce viva pulverizata, et pone vas, cum laminis suprascriptis in ipso, in fimo pecorum vel equorum, per decem dies; postea radde florem quem invenies super laminis, et, si plus vis, repone vas cum laminis, ut prius.

10. *Ad faciendum azurrum ultramarinum perfectum.*—Recipe de lapide lazulli quantum vis, et teres super lapide porfirico subtilissime, et fac massam seu pastilum ex rebus insertis; videlicet, si dictus lapis est libra una accipe oncias vj. picis Grece, oncias ij. masticis, oncias ij. cere, oncias ij. picis nigre, oncias ij. gummi pini, onciam j. olei spici vel lini, et onciam ½ tremertinæ, que omnia buliant in uno pignatello, usque dum quasi sint strinta [strutta ?], et postea cola in aqua frigida, et tolle quod cadit in aqua, quod est celatum, et deducas, et misces bene

and mix it well with the powder of the lapis lazuli until it is well incorporated; and so let it stand for viij. days; and the longer it stands, the better and finer will be the azure. Afterwards work this paste in your hands, throwing it into water, and keep the first water by itself, and the second by itself, and the third also by itself. And when you see the azure sink to the bottom, pour off the water, and keep the azure.

11. *To make fine lake.*—Take the ashes of oak,[1] and make a ley, and boil in it clippings of fine scarlet of rubea de grana[2] until the colour is extracted from the clippings, and then strain the ley with the colour through a linen cloth. Afterwards take some more ley, similar to what you first took, and heat it, and put into it some finely powdered roche alum, and let it stand until the alum is dissolved. Then strain it through the strainer with the other liquor or ley in which the clippings were put, and immediately the ley will be coagulated, and make a lump or mass, which you must stir well. Remove it afterwards from the vase, and lay it on a new hollow brick, which will absorb the ley, and the lake will be left dry. You must afterwards take it off the brick and keep it for use.

12. *Also to make lake.*—Take 1 oz. of lac, which is a certain gum called lac, or take some of the grana with which scarlet cloths are dyed, and steep it in ley, or in urine, so as to cover over the lac, or the grana, and let it boil for half an hour on a moderate fire without smoke, namely, with smith's charcoal, stirring it continually with a stick whilst it boils. Afterwards take ½ an oz. of roche alum and ½ an oz. of sal gem, and grind them well with ley, and put them into the vase before it ceases to boil. Then remove the vase from the fire, and let it cool. Afterwards take a glazed jar, and a little urine, or strong ley, and empty the before-mentioned jar into it, and stir or shake it every evening and every morning, and after 15 days

---

[1] The Turkey oak, the Cerro of the Italians.

[2] Strictly speaking, "Rubea" means madder, and "Grana" kermes; but as it appears that at this period the kermes was generally used in

illud per dictum pulverem lapidis lazuli, donec bene incorporentur omnia, et sic stent per viii° dies, et, quanto plus steterint, tanta azurrum erit melius, et magis finum; et postea deduc hanc massam per manus, proiciendo cum aqua, et primam aquam serva per se, et secundam per se, et tertiam per se. Et, postquam videris azurrum descensum ad fundum, proice aquam et retine azurrum.

11. *Ad faciendum lacham finam.*—Tolle cineres ligni cerri, vel roboris, et fac lecivium, et in ipso fac bulire cimaturam scarlate fine rubee de grana, tantum quod ex dicta cimatura extractus sit color; postea ipsum lessivium, cum dicta cimatura, colla per pannum lineum; postea accipe de alio lexivio simili suprascripti quod prius accepisti, et calefac, et pone in ipso de alumine roche trito subtiliter, et permitte donec alumen sit fusum, postea cum dicto colatorio cola ipsum in dicta alia collatura vel lexivio, in quo stetit cymatura, et subito dictum lessivium stringetur, et faciet unam bussaturam seu massam, quam mistica bene, et postea trahe ipsam de vase, et pone in madono concavo novo, qui bibet lessivium, et remanebit sicca dicta lacha, quam postea trahe de madone et serva usui.

12. *Item ad faciendum lacham.*—Tolle unciam unam lache, que est quedam gumma dicta lacha, vel accipe de grana de qua tinguntur scarlate, et pone in lissivio vel urina viri, tanta que coperiat lacham seu granam, et fac bullire per mediam horam ad ignem temperatum, absque fumo, videlicet cum carbonibus fabrorum, deducendo cum baculo semper dum bulit. Postea tolle onciam ½ aluminis roche, et onciam ½ salis geme, et mole bene cum lexivio, et postea pone in vase suprascripto antequam cesset bulire. Postea leva vas ab igne, et permitte frigidari. Postea tolle unum vas vitriatum, et unum paucum urini hominis, vel de lessivio fortissimo, et mitte simul de super vase, et deduc vel agita omni sero et omni mane, et post xv^cim^ dies cola

---

dyeing scarlet, and as the recipes for making this "Lacca di Cimatura" generally direct the clippings of cloth dyed with kermes to be used, it is probable that the kermes was meant in the present case, and not madder.

*

strain it by means of a linen bag placed upon a new tile, which will immediately dry the lake, which will remain in the bag, and which you may keep for use, and when you wish to use it, grind it well upon a slab, and work with it. And if you like strain the water again, as before directed; and, if you wish to make more lake, boil the said water, and take more of the before-mentioned ingredients, and do as before, and it will be finer than the first mentioned above.

13. *To make very fine lake.*—Take clippings of very fine scarlet of rubea de grana, and put them into a vase, with sufficient urine to cover the clippings to the depth of one or two fingers' breadths, and let it stand for some days, until the clippings are decomposed, which you may know by touching them with your hand or your fingers. Afterwards take them out of the vase, without squeezing them, and put them on a clean stone, and allow the liquor to flow out by itself. Then grind it well upon a stone, and strain it through a thin piece of linen, and you will have fine lake, to use upon paper, parchment, and upon primed wooden panels, but not on walls.

14. *To make a fine rose colour.*—Take fine brexillium, and scrape it fine, and take strong ley made with the ashes of oak, and make it boil, and pour it over the said verzino into a glazed earthen saucer, so as to cover the brexillium, and let it stand for an hour. Then take egg-shells, pound them well, and grind them very fine on a porphyry slab with clear water, and lay them on a new hollow brick, that the water may be absorbed. Afterwards put them into a glazed earthen jar, and pound up some roche alum, and mix with the powdered egg-shells; afterwards strain the ley in which the verxillium is put, and pour the ley which is dyed red with the verzilium upon the egg-shells, and mix, that the whole may be incorporated together; and afterwards dry the lake, not in the sun, but on a hollow brick, straining it through a linen cloth, and you will have a perfect rose colour.

15. *Also, to make a colour deeper than rose colour.*—Take 1 oz. of scraped verzino and put it in a glazed saucer, with

cum saculo telle lini, posito super tegula nova, que subito siccabit lacham, que remansit in saculo, quam serva ad usum; et cum voles uti, mole bene super lapide, et operare. Et, si vis, recola dictam aquam, prout dictum est; et si plus volueris facere, fac bulire dictam aquam, et accipe de novo de rebus supradictis, et fac ut prius, et erit ista finior quam suprascripta.

13. *Ad faciendum lacham finissimam.*—Accipe cimaturam scarlate fine rubee de grana, et pone in vase cum tanta urina hominis, que coöperiat cimaturam quantum est grossitudo digiti unius vel duorum, et stet per plures dies, donec dicta cimatura sit bene putrefacta, cujus putrefactionem cognosces tangendo cum manu vel digitis. Postea trahe ipsam de vase absque ipsam exprimere, et pone super mondo lapide et dimitte ipsam per se excolare. Postea mole ipsam bene super lapide, postea cola per peciam subtilem lini, et habebis lacham finam pro operendo in cartis et in tabulis gissatis, set non in muro.

14. *Ad faciendum colorem rosete fine.*—Accipe berxillium finum, et rade subtiliter, et accipe de lessivio forti facto de cineribus cerri, quod fac bullire, et ipsum mitte desuper dicto versino, in una scutella terre vitreata tantum quod cooperiat verxillium, et stet per horam; postea accipe corticas ovorum, et trita bene, et molle super lapide porfirico cum aqua clara subtiliter, et pone super madono concavo novo ut aqua decicetur. Postea pone in scutella vitriata, deinde pista de alumine roche, et misce cum dictis corticis tritis, et postea cola lissivium in quo est verxillium, et lessivium illud rubefactum a verzilio mitte desuper dictas corticas, et misce ut incorporentur omnia, et postea desica, non ad solem, set super madono concavo, colando per tellam, et habebis perfectam rosetam.

15. *Ad faciendum etiam colorem plusquam de roxeta.*—Accipe onciam ½ verzini rasi, et pone in scutella vitriata cum tanta

sufficient urine to cover it, and make it boil, on a charcoal fire, for an hour; then, before you take it off the fire, add 1 oz. of honey, and mix it; then remove it from the fire, and leave it so until the next morning, and you will have a fine rose colour.

16. *To make a rose colour for drawing letters.*—Take red brexillium, and roche alum ground upon a stone, and put them both together in whipped white of egg, and let it stand for a day and a night, and you will have what was mentioned.

17. *Item, to make a rose colour.*—Put into a glazed saucer 1 oz. of scraped verzino, and pour in enough urine to cover the verzino and the ingredients which are to be added afterwards. Then add 1 oz. of white marble, ground upon a stone with water, and dried, and ½ oz. of roche alum in powder; and when putting the before-mentioned ingredients into the saucer, let the last thing which is added be the marble dust. Do not mix it until it has stood in the sun long enough for the marble to imbibe the colour; and if it should dry in the sun before the marble has absorbed the colour, add to it some more of the same urine as before, and let it stand in the sun until the marble is sufficiently coloured, and it will become red, or rose coloured. Afterwards strain it through a linen cloth, and dry it upon a baked stone or brick, and keep it for use.

18. *To make flowers and letters of gold.*—Take sal ammoniac, and temper with pure water; then write with that water and draw flowers, and, when they are dry, lay gold leaf upon them.

19. *To make the colour purpurinus.*—Take of sal ammoniac 1 oz., quicksilver 1 oz., sulphur vivum 1 oz., tin 1 oz.; melt the tin over the fire, then pour the quicksilver into it, and allow it to stand for a short time; next grind the sal ammoniac and sulphur together, and add them to the melted tin and quicksilver; put them all together into a glass flask, so that it may be filled only up to the neck, and then cover the flask all over with chalk, of the thickness of one finger's breadth; place it

urina hominis que cooperiatur, et fac bulire ad ignem carbonum per horam; postea, antequam leves ab igne, onciamque j. mellis, et misce, et leva ab igne, et dimitte sic usque de mane sequenti, et habebis colorem rosete fine.

16. *Ad faciendum colorem roxeum pro scribendo litteras.*—Accipe vexilium roxeum, et alumen roxie tritum super lapide, et pone omnia in clara ovi spongiata, et stet per diem et noctem, et habebis quod dictum est.

17. *Item ad faciendum colorem roxaceum.*—Pone in scutella vitriata onciam i. verzini rasi, et pone tantam urinam pueri que cooperiri possit dictum verzinum, et alia que secuntur; postea impone onciam i. marboris albi, triti super lapide cum aqua clara, et siccati, et onciam ½ aluminis roche triti, et ultimum quod ponetur in dicta scutella, ponendo in ipsa ea que dicta sunt, sit dictus marmor tritus; et non misceas, donec steterit ad solem tantum quod marmor ceperit colorem, et si sicaretur ad solem antequam marmor cepisset colorem, pone iterum de simili urina ut prius, et stet ad solem donec marmor ceperit colorem, et devenerit rubeus seu roxaceus. Postea cola per pannum lineum, et fac siccari cum lapide cocto seu madono, et serva ad usum.

18. *Ad faciendum flores et litteras auri.*—Accipe sal armoniacum, et distempera in aqua pura, et de illa aqua scribe, et fac flores, et cum desicate sint, pone desuper folium auri.

19. *Ad faciendum purpurinum colorem.*—Accipe sal armoniacum onciam i., argentum vivium onciam i., sulphur vivium onciam i., Stangnum onciam i., et fonde dictum Stagnum ad ignem, et in ipso mitte argentum vivum, et dimitte stare aliquantulum, et mole dictum sal armoniacum et sulphur simul; et pone in dicto stagno liquefacto, in quo est argentum vivum, et omnia pone in ampula vitri, quod ex ipsis impleatur solum usque ad collum, et sic ipsa ampula, circumlinita de creta

in a small furnace, in a hole at the top of the furnace made for this purpose, so that the flask may only be half way through the hole, and then, by means of a hole made in the side of the furnace, make a strong fire in it, and cover the mouth of the flask with a plate of iron, pierced, in order that the vapour may escape from the flask, and continue the fire strongly until the fumes cease to come from the flask. Then remove it from the fire, let it cool, break the flask, and take your purpurinus; and when you want to use it, temper it with gum-water or with whipped white of egg.

20. *To make a rose-coloured water for shading figures and other things.*—Put scraped verzino into whipped white of egg, and let it stand for a day. Then strain and squeeze through a cloth, and temper what passes through with pure water: shade whatever you like with it, both on parchment and on paper I think that the colour will not be extracted from the said brexillium or verzino, unless a little roche alum be added.

21. *To erase letters on parchment without injury to the paper.*—Take a hare's skin and dress it, and salt it down, afterwards dry it over the smoke of a fire, and reduce it to powder; put some of this powder upon the letters which you wish to erase, and rub them with pumice-stone, and the letters will be erased without injury to the paper.

22. *To make letters which will seem to be of gold.*—Make a small hole in a hen's egg, and take out the white only, and fill the egg with quicksilver; close up the opening carefully, place it under hot dung for 40 days. Then remove the quicksilver, and take 1 oz. of crystal and reduce it to a very fine powder, and incorporate it with the yolk of the egg. Then, with this composition smear the paper, or whatever else you want, and when it is dry rub gold or silver upon it, and it will remain of the colour of gold or silver.

23. *That letters may seem to be of gold.*—Mix sal nitrinum with water and write upon parchment, and illuminate it with juice of celandine and warm the paper, and the letters will appear like gold.

grossa, per grosseciam unius digiti, quam pone in parva fornace per foramen fornacis superius, propter hoc factum, ita quod dicta ampula descendat in dicto foramine solum usque ad medium ampule; et postea, per aliud foramen factum a latere dicte fornacis, immitte, et fac ignem fortem, et cooperi orificium ampule cum lamina ferri forata, ut exeat fumus ampule, et continua fortem ignem usque quo fumus ampule cessaverit exire, et tunc leva ab igne, et dimitte frigidari, et rumpe ampulam, et accipe purpurinum, et ipsum, cum vis operari, distempera cum aqua gummata, vel cum clara ovi spongiata.

20. *Ad faciendum aquam roxeaceam pro umbrando ymagines et alia.*—Pone de verxino raso, in albumine ovi spongiato, et stet per diem. Postea cola per telam, stringendo, et quod exierit distempera cum aqua pura, et umbra quod vis, in carta, et papiro. Credo quod color non exibit a dicto brexillo, seu verzino, nisi ponatur de alumine roze.

21. *Ad delendum litteras de carta absque lesione carte.*—Accipe cossam leporis, et decoria ipsam, et postea in salla, et desicca ad fumum ignis, et pulveriza, et posito de ipso pulvere super litteris quas raddere vis, trahe desuper pumicem, et radetur absque lesione carte.

22. *Ad faciendum litteras, que videantur esse de auro.*—Fac in ovo galine foramen parvum, et extrahe albumen solum, et postea reple ovum argento vivo, et claude bene foramen ovi, et ipsum pone sub fimo calido per dies xl[a]; postea extrahe argentum vivum, et accipe onciam i. cristalli, et pulveris subtilissime, et incorpora cum dicto vitello. Dein cum dicta pasta unge cartam aut quidquid vis, et, cum siccaverit, frica desuper cum auro vel argento, et remanebunt coloris auri vel argenti.

23. *Ut littere videantur de auro.*—Incorpora salnitrinum cum aqua, et scribe in carta, et inlumina cum suco celidonie, et calefac, et videbuntur de auro.

24. *To make gold or silver letters.*—Take sal ammoniac, the juice of pounded vervain mallows, and gum arabic, mix all these together, temper them with urine so as to make them rather liquid; afterwards make the mixture liquid with gum-arabic. Then write whatever you like with this liquid and let it dry. Then breathe upon it well with your mouth, so that the surface of it may be rather damp, and lay gold leaf upon it, and press it on lightly with a piece of cotton.

25. *To make letters of silver.*—Take three parts of quick-silver and a fourth part of tin, melt them together, and let the mixture cool; then grind it on a stone and temper it with a solution of gum-arabic; write with it and let it dry, and polish it with the tooth of a dog or other animal, fit for the purpose, and the letters will be beautiful and brilliant.

26. *To make letters appear like gold.*—Take the horn of a goat, cut it into very small pieces, and distil it in an alembic, and keep the water which comes over, in a glazed jar, in the sun for some days; afterwards write with this water, and the letters will appear like gold.

27. *To erase letters from parchment.*—Take the juice of an orange and dip cotton or sponge in it, and rub it lightly upon the letters, and it will erase them perfectly. But as the parchment will be wetted and made soft, it must be rendered dry and white in the following manner:—Take white lime in powder and mix it with clear water, and afterwards strain through a piece of white linen, dip cotton in the water which has been strained and dab it upon the parchment where it is soft, and it will become white and firm. I think it would be better to dip the cotton in dry lime, and not to wet it.

28. *To make a green ink for writing.*—Take of good vinegar oz. ij., sal ammoniac oz. ij., common salt oz. ij., brass filings oz. ij., put them all together in a glass flask for six days, and it will make a green ink, which you must strain and keep for use.

24. *Ad faciendum litteras aureas vel argenteas.*—Accipe sal armoniacum, et succum alci pisti, et gumirabicum, et hec simul distempera, et postea distempera cum urina, ut sit liquida aliquantulum; postea perfecte liquidam facies cum aqua gumirabici, postea scribe cum hoc que vis, et permitas sicari, et postea flaa desuper cum ore multum bene, ut aliquantulum humectetur superficies, et pone desuper folium auri, super quo deduc leviter bombacem.[1]

25. *Ad faciendum litteras argenti.*—Accipe argentum vivum per tres partes, et per quartam de stagno, et fonde simul, et permitte frigidari, et molle super lapide, et distempera cum aqua gumi arabici, et scribe cum hoc, et permitte siccari, et polias cum dente canis vel alterius animalis ad hoc apto, et erunt pulcre littere et lucentes.

26. *Ut littere videantur de auro.*—Accipe cornu yrci, et ipsum incide minutissime, et distilla per alembicum, et aquam que exibit tene in vase vitriato ad solem per aliquot dies, et postea cum ipsa aqua scribe et littere videbuntur de auro.

27. *Ad delendum litteras de carta.*—Accipe succum pomi ranzii, et in ipso balnea bombacem vel spongiam, et frica leviter super litteras, et optime dellet, et quia carta libri balneatur, et efficitur mollis, remediari debet isto modo, ut sit sicca et alba. Accipe florem calcis, distemperate cum aqua clara, postea cola cum pecia lini alba, et de aqua alba que exibit balnea bombacem, quam ducas super cartam ubi mollis erat, et fiet alba et solida. Credo quod melius esset intingere bombacem in calce sicca et non madida.

28. *Ad faciendum aquam viridem ad scribendum.*—Accipe bonum acetum oncias ii., salis armoniaci ii., salis communis oncias ii., limature eris oncias ii., pone omnia in ampula vitrea per vj. dies, et fiet aqua viridis, quam cola et reserva.

---

[1] Bombacem, id est spongiam ut jam supra vel lanam. [Marginal note by author.]

29. *To make excellent azure.*—Take of sal ammoniac oz. iij., and of verdigris oz. vi., mix them together and make them into a paste with solution of tartar, and put them into a glass jar, which you must stop up, and lute, and place in warm dung, and let it stand there for some days, and when you take it up you will find the green changed to excellent azure.

30. *For the same.*—Take of alum scagliola one part, of vinegar two parts; grind them together upon a slab, and make them boil a little in a glass or other vase, and put them into a glass flask and bury them in dung for five days or more, until you see it is become of a blue colour.[1]

31. *Good ink is thus made.*—Take 1½ lb. of pounded galls, soak them in warm rain water, or warm wine or vinegar, of the quantity of 10 phials, and so let it stand for a day or more; then boil it until the said water, wine, or vinegar is reduced to one-third, and let it be taken off the fire and a phial or two of wine or vinegar be immediately added, and let so much water be added as was boiled away from the said mixture, and let them all be put on the fire again. When the mixture begins to boil let it be removed from the fire; when it is only just warm strain it, and add to it 1½ lb. of gum-arabic in powder and 1 lb. of Roman vitriol, and mix the whole together.

32. *If you wish to make a gold or silver colour for writing.*—Take talc and put it into a glass vase, and pour over it good vinegar made from white wine, and add mercury to it, namely half an oz., and 1 oz. of fish-glue, and put it on the fire, that it may become liquid like water, and write with it, and it will make silver letters. If you wish to make golden letters, add a little saffron.

33. *Cement for joining parchment is thus made.*—Take gum-arabic and whipped white of egg, dissolve the gum in this white of egg and let it dry in the sun, and when you wish to use it wet the edge of the piece with your tongue and lips and

[1] The colouring ingredient seems wanting in this recipe.

29. *Ad faciendum azurrum optimum.*—Accipe salis armoniaci oncias iii., viridis eris oncias vi., et misce simul, et conficiantur cum aqua tartari ad modum unguenti, et ponantur in ampula vitrea, que obturetur, et luctetur, et ponatur in fimo calido, et stet per aliquos dies, et accipe que invenies, viridem conversum in optimum azurrum.

30. *Ad idem.*—Accipe aluminis scarole partem unam, aceti partes duas, tere simul super lapide, et bulire facias parum in vase vitreo vel alio vase, et pone in ampula vitrea, et sepelias in fimo per dies v., vel plures, donec videas devenisse azurri colores.

31. *Attramentum optimum sic fit.*—Recipe galle fracte libram $1\frac{1}{2}$, et pone in aqua pluviali tepida, vel in aceto, aut vino tepido, ad x. fialarum quantitatem, et sic stet per unum diem vel plus, et postea buliantur donec remaneant ad terciam partem dicte aque, seu vini, aut aceti, et deponantur ab igne, et statim super addatur fiala una vel due aceti vel vini; et ponatur tantum de aqua, quantum consummata fuerit ipsa mixtura, et iterum omnia ponantur ad ignem, et cum inceperit bulire deponatur ab igne, et cum ad tepiditatem reductum erit, coletur, et ponatur in ipso libra $1\frac{1}{2}$ gumi arabici pulverizati, et libram 1 vitrioli romani, et simul misceantur omnia.

32. *Si vis facere colorem aureum vel argenteum ad scribendum.*—Accipe talch, et pone in vase vitreo, et superpone acetum de vernazia perfectum, et pone cum ipso mercurium, videlicet onciam $\frac{1}{2}$, et colam piscis onciam i., et pone super ignem ut liquefiat ut aqua, et scribe, et fient littere argentee; et si vis quod faciat litteras aureas, pone cum ipso parum croci.

33. *Colla ad jungendum cartas sic fit.*—Accipe gummi arabici, et clarum ovi spongiati, et dissolvatur gumi in ipsa clara ovi, et siccentur ad solem, et cum operari volueris, balnea caput ipsius masse cum lingua et labiis oris, et trahe desuper cartis

*

apply it to the parchment where the pieces are to be joined, and let it dry in the shade, and the pieces will adhere firmly together. But if you wish to join paper only and not parchment, wheat-flour or powdered bread-crumbs mixed with pure water and slightly boiled is very good for paper. But if you mix a little gum-arabic or whipped white of egg with it, it will do for parchment.

34. *If you wish to erase letters from paper*, take roche alum, and grind it, and make it into a paste with the juice of an orange, and expose it to the wind, and let it dry; afterwards rub it upon the letters, and it will erase them from the paper.

35. *If you wish to make letters of the colour of brass, silver, or gold*, take crystal, and grind it very fine upon a marble or porphyry slab, with white of egg, and write what you like with it; and when the letters are dry, rub them with the metal whose colour you wish them to take, and they will take the colour. Powdered glass will do instead of powdered crystal.

36. *To make lake.*—Take urine, and keep it for a long while, and afterwards make it boil until half of it is evaporated upon a slow and clear fire, skimming it continually, until it is perfectly purified. Then strain it through a linen cloth, and put 4 lbs. of it into a glazed jar of the said urine, and 1 lb. of raw lac well ground, and add to it a sufficient quantity of alumine zuccarino, and put it by and keep it for use.

37. *For the same purpose.*—Take of gum lac, ground very fine, as much as you like, and put it into clear urine for three days, and afterwards make it boil on the fire, and skim it. Add a little Roman vitriol to it, and strain it through a linen cloth of loose texture; then add some urine, and make it boil, always stirring it with the ladle, until one fourth part or more is evaporated; then put it in the sun and let it dry, and keep it for use.

38. *If you wish to remove oil from parchment or letters*, take bones of chicken or capons, and burn them until they are white, and reduce them to powder. Lay some of this powder on the

in locis juncture, et junge, et permitte siccari ad umbram, et tenebunt se simul fortiter. Set si non cartam, set solum papirum, jungere velis, farina frumenti, vel tritura panis subtiliata, et distemperata cum aqua clara, et modicum bulita, optima est pro papiro; set si immisceris parum gumi arabici, vel clare ovi spongiate, valebit pro cartis.

34. *Si vis elevare litteras de carta.*—Accipe aluminis roche, et tere et impasta cum succo pomi aranzii, et pone ad auram, et dimitte siccari; postea frica super litteras, et levabit eas a carta.

35. *Si vis facere litteras coloris erei, argentei, aut aurei.*—Accipe cristallum, et tere subtiliter super lapide marmoris vel porfirici, cum clara ovi, et scribe quod vis de ipso bitumine, et, siccatis litteris, frica desuper metallum illud, cujus colorem vis quod recipiant littere, et accipient; pulver vitri esset bona loco cristalli triti.

36. *Ut facias lacham.*—Accipe urinam hominis bibentis bonum vinum, et diu serva, et postea bullire facias usque ad consumpcionem medietatis, semper despumendo, super lentum et clarum ignem, donec sit optime purgata; postea cola per telam, et pone in vase vitriato libras iiii^or^ dicte urine, et libram unam lache crude, bene trite, et pone de alumine Zucarino quantum sufficit, et repone servando ad opus.

37. *Ad idem.*—Accipe gumam lache quantum vis tritam subtiliter, et pone in urina nitida per tres dies; postea fac bulire ad ignem, et spuma, postea pone in ipsa parum vitrioli romani, postea cola per pannum lineum rarum. Postea adde de urina, et fac bulire agitando semper cum spatula, donec consumatur circa quarta pars vel plus. Postea pone ad solem, et dimittas siccari, et serva ad usum.

38. *Si vis oleum de cartis vel litteris extrahere.*—Accipe ossa pullorum vel castroni, et arde usque ad albedinem, et pulveriza, et de ipso pulvere super pone ubi est oleum, et per-

place where the oil is, and let it stand, in summer in the shade, and in the sun in winter. If necessary, repeat this two or three times. Lime also is good for this purpose.

39. *To make the colour purpurinus as beautiful as gold.*—Take quicksilver and tin, and melt them together; then take sulphur vivum and sal ammoniac, and grind these two together, and mix them with the before-mentioned ingredients, grinding the whole very fine upon a stone, with [1] Then put them into a glass flask well luted, so as not to be quite full of the aforesaid things, and put them on the fire, and let the mouth of the flask be uncovered, and let it stand on the fire until the vapour ceases to issue from the mouth of the flask. Afterwards let it cool, and break the flask, and collect and keep all that is above the dregs, and it will be an excellent colour for using on books and parchment.

40. *If you wish to stain, of a green colour, bones, wood, tablets, or pannels of wood, knife-handles, thread, and linen cloth*, take strong red vinegar, in a glass vase, with brass filings, a little Roman vitriol, and some roche alum, and make all boil together for a short time, and allow it to stand for a few days; and when you wish to stain anything, put it into this mixture, and let it boil a little, and it will become of a good and lasting colour.

41. *To make a water for staining anything of any colour.*—Take of sal ammoniac 1 lb., and of nitre ½ lb., and distil it in an alembic; and if you take 1 oz. of this water, and put into it the weight of two florins of calcined gold, it will make a yellow water; if calcined silver, it will make a blue; if mercury, a black; if calcined copper, a green; if calcined lead, a white water; and if calcined iron, a water of a red colour.[2]

42. *If you wish to dye anything a blood colour*, take a very strong lye, and soak in it shavings of brazillium, and ground

---

[1] So in original.

[2] This water, which dissolves gold, must be Nitro-Muriatic Acid (Aqua Regia).—See Henry's 'Chemistry,' vol. ii. p. 131. The recipe proves that the solvent power of this acid on gold was generally known as early

mitte stare in estate ad umbram, in yeme ad solem, donec oleum exierit a carta. Et, si necesse fuerit, facias hoc bis vel ter ; et calx etiam est bonum ad hoc faciendum.

39. *Ad faciendum purpureum colorem pulcrum et aurum.*—Accipe argenti vivi et stagni, et fonde simul ; postea accipe sulphuris vivi, salis armoniaci, et tere simul hec duo, et pone cum predictis, terendo super lapide subtiliter cum (*sic*), postea pone in ampula vitrea bene luctata, que de predictis non sit plena, et pone ad ignem, et ampula sit discoperta ad orificium, et stet ad ignem tam diu quod fumus cesset exire de orificio ampule ; postea dimitte frigidari, et frange ampullam, et totum quod super feces fuerit collige, et serva, et est color optimus ad ponendum super libris et cartis.

40. *Si vis in colore viridi tingere ossa, ligna, tabulas, seu telas ligni, manubria cutellorum, filum, et pannum lini.*—Accipe de aceto rubeo et forti, in vase vitreo, cum limatura eris, parum vitrioli romani, et de alumine roche, et fac aliquantulum bulire omnia simul, et permitte stare per aliquos dies, et, cum vis aliqua tingere, pone in ipsa mistura, et fac aliquantulum bulire, et fient coloris optimi perdurantis.

41. *Ad faciendum aquam ad tingendum aliquid in quocumque colore.*—Accipe salis armoniaci libram 1, salis nitri libram ½, et distilla per alembicum, et si de ista aqua acceperis onciam unam, et in ipsa posueris pondus duorum florenorum auri calcinati, fiet aqua crocea ; si argenti calcinati, fiet aqua celestis ; si mercurii, fiet aqua nigra ; si cupri calcinati, fiet aqua viridis ; si plumbi calcinati, fiet aqua alba ; et si ferri calcinati, fiet aqua coloris rubei.

42. *Si vis aliqua tingere in colore sanguineo.*—Accipe lessivium fortissimum, et in ipso pone rasuram Brazillii, Alumen

---

as 1409. Mr. Hendrie (*Theoph.*, p. 427) shows that it was known to Geber (*De Alchem.*, Norimb., 1545, cap. xxiii.), who lived during the ninth century.

alumen glaciæ; and let it stand for five days or more, and it will be of a blood colour. Whatever you mean to dye, you must soak in it for three days, and then boil it until what you have put in it is properly dyed.

43. *If you wish to make verdigris*, take a brass vase, and put urine into it to the depth of one finger's breadth. Add a little sal ammoniac to it, and expose it to very strong sunshine until it is dry, when you must scrape off whatever you find in the vase, and it will be very good verdigris.

44. *For the same purpose.*—Take of alum zuccarino oz. vi; of brass filings 1 lb.; of common salt 2 lbs.; of nitre ij oz.; of roche alum, burnt and bleached, iij oz. Reduce all these things to a very fine powder, and smear brass plates with it. Place the brass plates in a well-covered glazed jar; and then, through a hole made in the side of the jar, pour in hot urine or hot vinegar, and close up the hole, and place the vase under warm dung, and let it remain there 40 days. Then take it out, and scrape the brass plates, and you will have a green colour. You can repeat this several times, if you wish to have more colour.

45. *If you wish to make a very deep and beautiful green*, take the herb rue, or parsley, when fresh, and extract the juice from it, and with this juice mix verdigris, and grind it upon a stone; then put it into a shell, adding to it a little strong vinegar coloured with saffron, and it will do even without the saffron. Make it liquid as if for writing, and use it.

46. *If you wish to make a very green colour for dyeing skins*, take of filings of Venus, or copper, 1 part, and of sal ammoniac 2 parts, and temper it with urine. Stretch the skins which you wish to dry upon a hoop, and paint them on the side next the flesh with this colour, and let them dry, and the colour will pass through to the other side.

Whereas in the preceding recipes mention is made of five metals, giving them the names of the planets to which they are appropriated, the following remarks are necessary in order to understand them.

Sol is put for gold, the colour of which is yellow.

Luna for silver, the rust of which is azure.

glacie tritum, et stet per dies quinque vel plus, et erit sanguinea, et quod tingere vis pona in ipsa per tres dies, et postea fac bulire, donec quod in ipsa ad tingendum posueris tinctum sit.

43. *Si vis facere viridem ramum.*—Accipe vas ereum, et pone in ipso urinam, usque ad altitudinem grossesiei unius digiti, et in ipsa pone parum salis armoniaci, et mitte ad fortissimum solem, quousque siccetur, et quod postea inveneris, in vase rade, et erit optimum rami viride.

44. *Ad idem.* — Accipe aluminis zucarini onciam vi., et limature eris libram j., salis communis libras ii., nitri oncias ij., aluminis roche combusti et dealbati oncias iij., pulverisentur hec omnia subtilissime, et unge laminas ereas, quas pone in vase vitriato bene coperto; postea per foramen quoddam, factum a latere vasis, proice urinam calidam vel acetum calidum, postea claude dictum foramen, et pone vas sub fimo calido, et stet ibi per xl dies; postea tolle et radde tabulas, seu laminas, et habebis viridem colorem; et potes hoc pluries reiterare, pro habendo plus de colore.

45. *Si vis coloratissimum et pulcherrimum viridem facere.*—Accipe herbam rute, vel petroxellii, recentem, et ex ipsa trahe siccum, cum quo misce viride eris, et tere super lapide, postea pone in conchilla, et adde de forti aceto aliquantulum, quod sit coloratum cum croco; et etiam absque croco potest fieri; et distempera ut liquidum sicut ad scribendum, et operare de ipso.

46. *Si vis facere viridissimum colorem pro pellibus tingendis.*—Accipe limaturam veneris seu rami, partem unam, et de sale armoniaco, partes duas, et distempera cum urina, et pelles quas vis colorare tende in circulo, et perunge ex ipso colore ex parte carnis, et dimitte siccari ad umbram, et color transibit ad aliam partem.

Quia in precedentibus quinque dicuntur metalla, nominando ea per nomina planetarum quibus appropriantur, ideo ut intelligantur, nota ut sequitur.

Pro sole, aurum, cujus color croceus est.

Pro luna, argentum, cujus rubigo color lazuli est.

Mars for iron, the rust of which is violet, rather inclining to blackness.

Mercury for quicksilver, of which are made sinopis and minium, which are red.

Jupiter for tin.

Venus for copper or brass, the rust of which is green.

Saturn for lead, the rust of which is a white colour.

Also, note, that in the MS. from which I copied the preceding recipes, it was thus written in this place. "The whole that is contained in this unbound book, namely, from the beginning of number 1 to this place, I copied 'in Janua' in the year 1409, in the month of June, having extracted it from an unbound book lent me by Brother Dionysius[1] of the order of the servants of St. Mary, which order is called *del sacho* at Milan."

Also, in the said MS., on the margin of the recipe immediately following, where the number 47 begins, was written, "I had 'in Janua' this receipt on the 1st day of March, 1409."

47. *To make good ink for writing, particularly for books.*—Take 4 bottles of good wine, white or red, and 1 lb. of galls, slightly bruised, which must be put into the wine, and allowed to stand in it for 12 days, and be stirred every day with a stick. The twelfth day it must be strained through a strainer of fine linen, and must be poured into a clean jar, and put on the fire to get hot, until it almost boils. Then remove it from the fire, and when it has cooled so as only to be tepid, put into it 4 oz. of gum-arabic, which must be very bright and clear, and stir it with a stick, then add ½ lb. of Roman vitriol, and stir it continually with the stick, until all things are well incorporated together, and let it cool and keep it for use. And note, that ink made with wine is good for writing books upon the sciences, because, when books are written with it, the letters do not fade, and can hardly be scraped out or discharged from parchment or paper. But if they are written with ink made with water, it is not so, for they can easily be scraped out, and it may happen that the letters written with it will fade.

---

[1] So in original.

Pro marte, ferrum, cujus rubigo violacea est, et pocius nigredini comparata.

Pro Mercurio, argentum vivum, de quo fiunt sinopis, et minium, qui rubei sunt.

Pro jove, stagnum.

Pro venere, ramum, seu es, cujus rubigo viridis est.

Pro saturno, plumbum, cujus rubigo albus color est.

Item, nota, quod in exemplari a quo prescripta sumpsi, in hoc loco, scriptum sic erat, "totum quod continetur in isto quaterno, scilicet a principio numeri 1, usque hic, scripsi in Janua, anno 1409, de mense Junii, extrahendo ab uno quaterno michi prestato per Fratem Dionisium de (*sic*), ordinis Servorum Sancte Marie, qui ordo in Mediolano dicitur 'del sacho.'"

Item, in eodem exemplari, super margine recepte immediate sequentis, qua incipit numerus 47, scribebatur sic, "habui in Janua istam receptam die primo Marcii, 1409."

47. *Ad faciendum optimum attramentum pro scribendo, precipue libros.*—Recipe bocales iiii^or optimi vini vermigii vel albi, et libram i. galle modicum fracte, que ponatur in dicto vino, et stet in ipso per duodecim dies, et agitetur omni die cum baculo, ultima vero die colletur bene subtiliter per colatorium tele linee; postea ponatur in vase mondo ad ignem, et callefiat usque dum quasi bulliat; deinde deponatur ab igne, et cum refrigidatum sit, taliter quod sit tepidum, ponantur in ipso onzie iiii^or gummi arabici bene lucidi et clari, et agitetur cum baculo; deinde ponatur libra ½ vitrioli romani, et semper misceatur cum baculo, donec bene incorporentur omnia simul, et infrigidetur et usui servetur. Et nota quod attramentum factum cum vino est bonum ad scribendum libros scienciarum, que cum de ipso scripti sunt libri, non cadunt littere, neque quasi raddi possunt, nec expelli de carta, nec de papiro. Set si scripti sunt de attramento, seu incausto, facto de aqua, non est sic, que bene radi possunt leviter, et accidere potest quod littere de ipso scripte caduce sint.

*

4 bottles of wine, or water, or half of each.

1 pound of galls of xij. oz. to the pound.

4 oz. of gum arabic.

6 oz. of Roman vitriol.

And if you took equal parts of each, galls, gum, and vitriol, as much of one as of the other, by weight, it would still be good; as, for instance, 6 oz. of each, which would be sufficient for the said 4 lbs. of wine or water, or of wine and water mixed as before.

OTHER EXPERIMENTS NOT UPON COLOURS.

48. *The preparation of Tucia.*—Take as much as you please of Alexandrine tucia, pulverize it well, put it in an iron ladle, and distemper it over the fire until the tucia becomes red. Then take vinegar and urine, and stir it in well with a rod until the tucia becomes of a citrine colour.

49. *To make brass.*—Take thin plates of copper, clean them well with salt, urine, and honey, and when they become red, and are well cleansed, take red honey, and rub it over the plates; then sprinkle powdered tucia on the honey and liquefy it in a shell with [1] (?) of holly, it will then be very good brass.

50. *To write with black on gold or silver.*—Take burnt lead and sulphur, distemper them together, and write on the gold or silver; then heat it with fire, and the desired effect will be produced.

51. *To redden white bones.*—Distemper sal ammoniac with pure water, put any bones into the water and leave them for 2 days. Add some Brazil wood raspings, and a little ley, and leave them for 2 days more. Then take them out, and if they

---

[1] The word is illegible in the original.

Bocales iiii^{or} vini, vel aque, vel per medietatem de utroque.
Lipra i. gallarum, de onziis xii. pro lipra.
Onzie iiii^{or} gummi arabici.
Onzie vi. vitrioli romani.

Et qui caperet gallas, gummam, et vitriolum, quodlibet ad equale, videlicet totidem de uno quotidem de alio, ad pondus, ad huc bonum esset, videlicet ut onzie vi. de quolibet, quod satis esset pro dictis libris iiii^{or} vini, seu aque, vel aque et vini, ut supra.

EXPERIMENTA DIVERSA ALIA QUAM DE COLORIBUS.

48. *Preparacio tuchie.*—Recipe tucie alexandrine quantumvis, bene pulverizate, et pone in ramaiolo ferreo, et distempera ad ignem, tantum quod tucia rubescat. Postea accipe acetum, et urinam pueri, et imbibe, et misce cum baculo, tantum quod tucia deveniat ad modum citrini.

49. *Ad ottonem faciendum.*—Habeas laminas eris subtiles, et purga bene cum sale, et urina pueri, et melle, et quando fuerit rubeum, et bene purgatum, accipe mel rubeum, et unge dictas laminas, et super mel asperge pulverem tucie, et liquefac concham bomb . . . de aggrefolio, et erit optimum ottonum.

50. *Ad scribendum de nigro in auro vel argendo.*—Accipe plumbum ustum, et sulphur, et distempera simul, et scribe super aurum vel argentum, et calefac ad ignem, et feceris quod dictum est.

51. *Ad faciendum ossa alba fieri rubea.*—Distempera sal armoniacum in aqua pura, postea mitte in ipsa aqua osse que vis, et stent per duos dies, et postea adde de verxino raso cum modico lissivii, et stet per duos dies, postea extrahantur ossa, et,

are too red put them in water in which sal ammoniac has been dissolved, and if they are not sufficiently red, do not put them into a fresh solution of sal ammoniac but replace them in the first, containing the Brazil wood raspings, and add more Brazil wood; leave them for some time, and they will become sufficiently red.

52. *To blacken horns or bones of animals.*—Take 2 pints of rain water, 3 oz. of quicksilver, and 2 oz. of quicklime, boil them together for a short time; then take the mixture off the fire, and when it becomes tepid, steep horn or bone in it, and it will become black.

53. *A medicine for silvering divers things in a durable manner.*—Take Lupins, boil them in water until their virtue is imparted to the water. Then strain and boil until the water is reduced to the consistence of honey, and add a quantity of quicksilver equal in weight to the water, stirring it well until the quicksilver is no longer visible. With this you may wash wood, metals, and whatever you please. This will silver them, and this silvering will never separate or fall off.

54. *To make a durable silvering.*—Take clay, pig's blood, vine-wood ashes, and quicksilver, mix them well, then dry and pulverize them; rub anything with this powder and it will be silvered.

55. *To make gold worms, or worms which seem gilt, for gilding anything.*—Take bull's brains, put them in a marble vase, and leave them for 3 weeks, when you will find gold-making worms; preserve them carefully.

56. *To make a powder which shall light a candle without fire but with water.*—Take an ounce of loadstone and 4 ounces of quicklime. Put half of the lime into some strong pipkin, then add to it the loadstone, and fill the pipkin with the remainder of the lime; cover it well, and leave it in a brick-kiln for 9 days, then take it out of the kiln, and when it is cold uncover it entirely: then remove the lime gently, when you will find the loadstone in powder; keep it separately, and when you wish to light a candle take some of this powder, put it on a

si nimis sint rubea, reponantur in alia aqua salis armoniaci. Et si parum, non ponantur in aqua nova salis armoniaci, set in prima in qua prius fuerant, in qua est verxinum, et addatur de verxino, et stent, et fient rubea ad sufficienciam.

52. *Ad nigrandum cornu vel osse animalis.*—Accipe duas pintas aque pluvialis, uncias tres argenti vivi, et uncias duas calcis vive, et fac bulire simul aliquantulum, et depone ab igne, et cum devenerit ad tepiditatem, pone in ipso cornu vel osse animalis, et denigrabitur.

53. *Medicina ad argentacionem perpetuam diversarum rerum materiarium.*—Accipe lupinos, et decoque in aqua, donec virtus eorum transierit in aquam. Postea cola, et fac bulire usque ad spisitudinem mellis, et pone intus de mercurio seu argento vivo, ad pondus aque, et misce bene, ita quod in ea non appareat argentum vivum, et de ipsa lignias ligna, metalla, et alia que vis, et erunt de argentata, et ipsa de argentacio nunquam separabitur seu cadet.

54. *Ad faciendum argentacionem durabilem.*—Accipe terram tenacem, sanguinem porci, cineres de sermento, et argentum vivum, et commisceantur bene, et postea siccentur, et pulverizentur, et ex ipso pulvere frica que vis, et argentabuntur.

55. *Ad faciendum vermes auri, vel qui videantur deaurati, pro deaurando que vis.*—Accipe cerebrum tauri, et pone in vase marmoris, et stet per tres ebdomadas, et invenies intus vermes facientes aurum, et custodi bene.

56. *Ad faciendum pulverem que candelam accendat, absque igne, set cum aqua.*—Accipe calamitem masculum onziam i., et calcem vivam onzias iiii^{or}, et pone medietatem dicte calcis in aliquo pignatello forti, et postea pone in ipso dictam calamittam integram, postea cooperiri pignaculum cum alia parte dicti calcis, et obtura bene dictum pignatellum, et pone per novem dies in fornace in qua cocuntur lateres. Postea leva dictum vas de fornace, et cum frigidum sit apperi plane, et remove moderate dictum calcem, donec inveneris calamittam pulveriza-

piece of paper or on the wick of a candle, and touch it with water or saliva, when the candle will be lighted. But take care you do not keep it in a damp or warm place.[1]

57. *To temper iron well.*—Take powdered glass and burnt goat's horn or stag's bone, well pulverized, heat the iron slightly, and grease it with mutton fat and sprinkle with the powders that part of the iron which is to be made hard. Then heat the iron or the part which you wish to harden and quench it in water which has been distilled from radish-roots and red earthworms which are found in damp places.

58. *To temper iron so that it will be hard enough to cut precious stones.*—Heat the iron in the fire to a convenient heat, and extinguish it in the blood of a goat in the month of March.

59. *To take the impression of seals and other things with engraved or raised surfaces.*—Take 2 parts of gypsum and 1 of flour, mix them together and make them into a paste with glue made of hartshorn and reduce them until they become of the consistence of soft wax. Then make two small tablets of this paste and before they dry press between them the seal or image or other form which must be wrapped in onion skins. Then take out the seal or image, let the tablets dry, then melt lead or wax and pour it into the mould. When cool remove it from the mould or tablets, and you will have what you desire.

60. *To make a perfect glue for fixing hard bodies, such as crystal, glass, and gems, together; or for fixing wood, horn, or other things on to stones.*—Take ceruse made from burnt bricks, that is to say, the powder of them, and finish by grinding it

---

[1] It appears from a passage in Beckmann's Inventions, vol. ii. p. 504, that this recipe was quoted by Cardan, who ascribed it to one Marcus

tam, quam serva per se; et dum vis lumen accendere, accipe de pulvere dicte calamite, et pone in papiro, seu licivo candele, et tange cum aqua dictum licivum, vel cum sputo, et accendetur candela; set cave ne ipsum pulverem teneas in loco humido nec calido.

57. *Ad temperandum ferrum optime.*—Accipe vitrum pulverizatum, et cornua yrci, vel ossa cervi, usta et pulverizata, et calefac parum dictum ferrum, et ipsum unge cepo castrati, *i.e.* muttonis, et asperge de dictis pulveribus simul mixtis, ab illa parte ferri que expedit fieri dura, et calefac ipsum ferrum, seu partem illam ejus quam vis duram facere, et extingue in aqua distillata per alembicum, de radicibus raffanorum, et vermibus terrestribus, seu bombricibus rubescentibus, nascentibus in locis humidis.

58. *Ad temperandum ferrum, quod erit tam durum, quod de ipso poterunt incidi duri lapides preciosi.*—Callefac ferrum ad ignem ut convenit, et extingue in sanguine irci libidine amoris inflammati, id est in marcio mense.

59. *Ad faciendum formam sigilli, et aliarum rerum sculptarum vel levatarum, quas voles extrahere.*—Accipe partes duas gipsi, farine unam, et misce, et fac pastam de ipsis cum cola cervina, et deduc, et confice, donec fit sicut cera mollis; postea fac de ipsa duas tabuletas, et, antequam siccentur, stringe inter ipsas sigillum, vel ymaginem, aut aliud, cujus formam facere vis, et sit involutum in pelliculis ceparum, et postea extrahe sigillum vel ymaginem, et permittas siccari dictas tabuletas, et cola plumbum vel ceram ut vis, et immitte in dicta forma, et dimitte frigidari, et apperi formam, id est dictas tabulas, et habebis quod quesivisti.

60. *Ad faciendum collam perfectam, ad corpora dura firmanda, ut cristallum, vitrum, et gemmas, invicem, vel super petras, ligna, cornua, aut alia.*—Accipe cerussam laterum coctorum, videlicet pulverem ipsorum, et confice subtiliando super

---

Græcus, who, according to some persons, lived in the ninth century, and, according to others, in the thirteenth.

finely on the porphyry slab with painter's liquid varnish. With this preparation you may join anything you like, and then dry it in the sun. And if you have no liquid varnish, take linseed oil with a little lime, and the said ceruse, or powder of bricks burnt in the furnace, and well triturated and pulverized.[1]

61. *To temper iron.*—Take a sufficient quantity of the juice of radish roots, then take earth-worms and put them in salt or sea-water for an hour until they die, and in dying they will be purified from their superfluous humours. Then remove them from the water without squeezing them, but only laying them down and shaking the water from them. Then put them in a glass cucurbit, and pour the radish-juice on them so as just to cover them. Then fix an alembic on the said cucurbit, lute it, place the cup in the ashes, give it a slow fire, and collect the water, which will come off clear as spring water. When your iron is properly heated quench it in this.

62. *For the same purpose.*—Take the herb which is called "famula"[2] and which is like "vidalia," but which has leaves like the "elder," extract its juice, and when your iron is properly heated quench and temper it in this.

63. *To make a water which corrodes iron.*—Take 1 oz. of sal ammoniac, 1 oz. of roche alum, 1 oz. of sublimed silver, and 1 oz. of Roman vitriol, pound them well, take a glazed earthen vase, pour into it equal parts of vinegar and water, then throw in the above-mentioned articles. Boil the whole until reduced to half a cup or a cup, apply it to such parts of the iron as you may wish to hollow or corrode, and the water will corrode them.

64. *A water which corrodes iron, and takes away the spots on all metals, and cleanses wounds.*—Take Roman vitriol and eu-

---

[1] There appears to be some error in this recipe.

[2] Probably "Flammula;" in French, *Clématite flammule;* in Italian, "Flamula;" in English, the sweet-scented Clematis. This is rendered more probable by the comparison of this plant with another species of Cle-

lapide porfirico cum vernice liquida pictorum, et de hac confectione junge quod vis, et dimitte siccari ad solem. Et si non habes, accipe oleum lini, et aliquantulum calcis, cum dicta cerrusa, seu pulvere laterum coctorum in fornace, atritorum, et pulverizatorum subtiliter.

61. *Ad temperandum ferrum.*—Recipe radices rafani, extrahe succum ita quod de eo habeas satis ad quod vis facere, et accipe lombricos, aliter bombricos, terrestres, quos pone in aqua bene salita, vel marina, per horam, donec moriantur, et moriendo purgentur ab eorum humoribus superfluis. Postea extrahe ipsos de aqua absque eos exprimere, set solum jaciendo, et excuciendo aquam, et pone eos in cucurbita vitri, et superpone dictum succum rafani, ita quod succum superet eos aliquantulum, et dicte cucurbite superpone alembicum, et luta, et loca cucurbitam in cineribus, et da ignem lentum et recollige aquam, que exiet clara ut aqua fontis, et in ipsa extingue ferrum debite ignitum.

62. *Ad idem.*—Accipe herbam que vocatur famula, que est ad modum vidalie. Set scias quod habet folia ad modum sambuci; et de ipsa trahe succum, in quo extingue, et tempera, ferrum debite ignitum seu calefactum in igne.

63. *Ad faciendum aquam que cavat ferrum.*—Accipe onciam i. salis armoniaci, et onciam i. aluminis roche, et onciam i. de argento sublimato, et onciam i. vitrioli romani, et pista omnia bene, et accipe unum vas terre vitriatum, et pone in ipso aquam et acetum, de utroque equaliter, et immitte que dicta sunt, et fac bulire, donec devenerit ad quantitatem medii ziatus, vel unius; et, hiis factis, de ipsa linias ferrum, modo quo vis ipsum cavere, seu radere, et radebit ipsum dicta aqua.

64. *Aqua que cavat ferrum et levat maculas ab omnibus metallis et purgat putredinem vulneris.*—Accipe de vitriolo romano

---

matis, the Clematis Vitalba, the wild Clematis, or common Virgin's bower; the Vitalba and Clematite of the Italians; La Clématite des Haies of the French.

phorbia,[1] and distil them in an alembic. Then take the water which is distilled from them and apply it to the wound, and it will purify it and remove the dead flesh without great pain. If you write with this on iron or any other metal, the letters will immediately be made and bitten into it.

65. *To fix one piece of brass to another.*—Take the scrapings of a cask, that is, tartar, burn it until it no longer smokes, and reduce it to powder; then take a fourth part of borax, put it in a small quantity of water, and stir it until it is dissolved; then add the tartar to it, until it makes, as it were, red bubbles, when you must add a little water to make it more liquid: you may then use it to fix anything you please, smearing the article with the said water or mixture. Then put a few copper filings and powdered borax into the said water and smear this mixture as before. Then put what you join into the fire, and when you see the copper filings run or melt, at that instant throw water on the fire, take out whatever you have soldered, and you will find it firmly fixed.

66. *If you wish to give a gold colour to any metal.*—Take powdered red sulphur and red orpiment, heat them in a crucible over the fire, stain your work with this composition, and it will be of a gold colour.

67. *To give iron a golden colour.*—Take alum of Jameni, grind it with urine so as to be of the consistence of ointment, and spread it wherever you like on the plates of iron; then heat it over the lighted coals; what you have spread will become of a golden colour.

68 or 69. *To preserve arms and other iron utensils from rust.*—Anoint them with chicken's grease.

70, 71, 72, 73, or 74. *To make fire which will burn under water, and which cannot be extinguished with anything but oil.*—Take equal parts of quicklime and sulphur, 1 oz. of wax, a

[1] Euphorbia, the spurge, of which there are many species, one of which is mentioned in the Bolognese MS., No. 38, under the name of Turtumagli, a derivation from the Latin Tithymalus, the Euphorbia Esula (Erba Latte,

et euforbiano, et distilla per alembicum, et de aqua que exierit pone in plaga, et expurgabitur, et levabit carnem mortuam absque dolore magno, et si de ipsa scripseris litteras in ferro, vel alio metallo, statim fient et cavabuntur in ipso.

65. *Ad consolidandum unum latonem cum alio.*—Accipe rasuram vegetis, id est, tartarum, et combure donec fumum non faciat, et pulveriza eam; postea accipe quartam partem borratis, quam mitte in modico aque, et misce, et agita eam, donec liquefiat; postea mitte cum ea dictam rasuram, donec faciat bullas quasi rubeas, postea mitte parum aque, ut sit magis liquida, postea de ipsa operare, et consolida que vis, et unge eas de ipsa aqua seu mistura; postea mitte in ipsa mistura aliquantulum limature cupri, et aliquantulum borracis pulverizate, et de ipsa mistura unge ubi supra, et que jonxeris pone ad ignem, donec videbis spargi, seu fondi, linituram dicte mixture positam super jonctura duorum conjonctorum, et subito proice desuper de aqua in igne, et extrahe de igne ea que jonxisti, quia consolidata erunt.

66. *Si vis dare aureum colorem alicui metallo.*—Accipe pulverem sulphuris rubei, auriplumenti rubei, et bulias ad ignem in cruxibulo, et de tali confectione opus tuum intinge, et suscipiet aureum colorem.

67. *Ad faciendum aureum colorem super ferrum.*—Accipe aluminis jameni, et tere cum urina, ut sit quas unguentum, et linias ex ea lamina ferrea ubi volueris, et calefac super carbones ignitos, et fiet linitura color aureus.

68 vel 69. *Ad conservandum arma et alia ferramenta a rubigine.*—Ungantur asungia gallinarum.

70, 71, 72, 73, vel 74. *Ad faciendum ignem qui ardebit sub aqua, nec poterit extingui, nisi cum oleo.*—Accipe calcis vive, sulphuris vivi, ana, onziam i. cera, parum olei, parum petrolei,

Lattaroli; Euphorbe à feuille de pin, La petite Esule, the Gromwell-leaved spurge). All the species are acrid and poisonous.

little oil, and a little petroleum. Mix these things together, smear them over iron or wood, put this under water, and it will burn. If you wish to extinguish it, put it in oil.

75. *If you wish to keep a fire for some time.*—Put lighted coals or charcoal under the ashes of juniper wood, and they will not be extinguished for a long time.

76. *To make maggots and lice fall from your head.*—Anoint your head with the juice of rue.

77. *If you wish to take spots of oil, and so forth, out of woollen cloth.*—Distemper white, or gypsum, or marble dust ground with egg, lay it on the spot, dry it, and then wash it with cold water.

78. *To take stains out of scarlet, velvet, &c.*—Take roche alum, with a little common salt, and grind it, and make it into a paste with yolk of egg and a little vinegar; put this on the spots and dry it. The dried "mixture" may be removed by rubbing, and the cloth will remain free from the spot.

80.[1] *For the same purpose.*—Take burnt tartar of wine, and a little sulphur, grind them and make them into a paste with yolk of egg and water. Put this on the spots, dry it, and remove it by rubbing and beating.

81. *If you wish to stain bones, wood, planks, wooden platters, knife-handles, thread, and linen cloths green,* put some strong red vinegar into a glass vase with brass filings, a little Roman vitriol, and roche alum, and boil all these things together for a short time, and then let them stand for a few days. When you desire to stain anything, put it into this mixture, boil it a little, and it will be of a beautiful and durable green colour.

82. *If you wish to make brass as beautiful as gold,* take 1 lb. of brass plates, ½ lb. of the best tuchia, melt them together in a crucible over the fire, add 2 oz. of tin, stir well, and let the mixture cool. Then melt it a second time, add 3 oz. of tuchia, stir it, and again set it aside to cool. Then melt it a third time, add 3 oz. more of tuchia, stir and cast it in the form of rods, strips, plates, or any other form, and it will be beautiful.

[1] 79 is missing in original.

et hec misce simul, et lignias de hoc ferrum vel lignum, et mittas sub aqua et ardebit; et si vis extinguere, mitte in oleo.

75. *Si vis conservare ignem maximum tempus ne extingatur.*—Pone carbones, seu calcicos accensos, sub cineribus ligni juniperi, et durabunt diu.

76. *Ut lendines et pediculi cadant de capite.*—Unge caput succo rute.

77. *Si vis extrahere de pannis lannarum maculas olei et aliorum.*—Distempera album, vel gessum, vel marmor, tritum cum ovo, et inunge ubi est macula, et dimitte siccari, postea lava cum aqua frigida.

78. *Ad extrahendum maculam de scarlata, et voluto, et talibus.*—Accipe de alumine roche, et parum salis communis, et tere, et impastentur cum vitello ovi, et pauco aceti, et superponatur macule, et siccetur, et confricando expellatur dictum bitumen siccum, et pannus remanebit liberatus a macula.

80. *Ad idem.*—Accipe alumen fecis, et parum sulphuris, et tridentur et impastentur cum vitello ovi et aqua, et superponantur macule et dimittantur siccari, et expellantur confricando et excuciendo.

81. *Si in colore viridi vis tingere ossa, ligna, tabulas, scutellas ligni, manubria cutellorum, filum, et pannum lini.*—Accipe de aceto rubeo et forti in vase vitreo cum limatura eris, parum vitrioli romani, et de alumine roche, et fac aliquantulum bulire omnia simul, et permitte sistare per aliquos dies, et cum vis aliqua tingere, pone in ipsa mistura, et fac aliquantulum bulire, et fient colores pulcri viridis optime perdurantes.

82. *Si vis facere lottonem pulcrum sicut aurum.*—Accipe laminas eris libram i, et optimam tuchiam libras *s*, et simul fonde in igne cum cruxibulo, et pone intus onzias ii stagni, et misce, et dimitte frigidari. Postea fonde secundo, et pone intus de tuchia onzias iii, et misce, et dimite frigidari. Postea tercio fonde, et mitte in ipso onzias iii tuchie, et misce, et jacta in virgis vel laminis platis, vel in qua forma vis, et erit pulcher.

83. *To make a good temper for iron utensils.*—Early in the morning collect a large quantity of celandine when it is wet or full of dew. Extract its juice by pounding, boiling it until one third is consumed, and the two parts remaining will be excellent. Then take the whole of the herb Lattaroli[1] (?), pounded, and extract its juice. Distil this, if possible, and sprinkle some finely powdered antimony on the iron, heat the iron, and quench it in the distilled water.

84. *For the same purpose.*—Take the leafstalks of briony, pound them, and extract the juice. Distil this, and quench the red-hot iron in the water which is distilled from it.

85. *To mend broken vases of earth, stone, and marble.*—Take the white earth of the fellmongers, that is, chalk, which is otherwise called gersa [gesso]; make it into a plaster with white of egg, grind it well on a stone, and use it.[2]

86. *If you wish to attract glass touched with some gum, as iron is attracted by the magnet*, take the gum Andrianum, which is found in the large rocks near Bologna towards Tuscany, in Monte Bono, or Buono, and besmear a stick with this gum. Touch the glass phials on the table with this stick, draw away the stick, and the phials will follow it, as iron follows the magnet.

87. *If you wish to turn black skins white*, take a mole, boil it, then take the water in which it has boiled, and smear a black horse with it, on any part. The black hairs will fall off, and white hairs will grow.

88. *For the same purpose.*—Take cheese, heat it by the fire, press it strongly on the forehead of a black horse, and it will make a star as you know.

After the preceding, it was written in the MS., " All the things contained in this unbound book, namely, from number 47 unto this page, I wrote 'in Janua' in the year 1409, in the month of June, extracting them from a book lent to me by brother Dionysius de (*sic*) of

---

[1] The Euphorbia Esula. See ante, note to p. 78.

[2] This recipe appears to be copied from Pliny, who says quicklime should be used.

83. *Ad faciendum bonam temperam ferramentis.*—Collige summo mane bonam quantitatem celidonie, quando est plena seu madida rore, cujus succum pistendo extrahe, et fac bulire, donec consummata sit tertia pars ejus; due vero remanentes partes optime sunt; et accipe totidem herbam lateranniam, pista, et succum extrahe, et ipsum distilla per alembicum, si fieri poterit, et pulverem antimonii triti pulverizati proice super ferrum, et calefac ferrum, et extingue in dicta aqua distillata.

84. *Ad idem.*—Accipe radicem de foliis brionie, et pista, et extrahe succum, quem distilla per alembicum, et in aqua que exierit extingue ferrum ignitum.

85. *Ad reintegrandum vasa terrea, lapidea, et marmorea, fracta.*—Accipe terram albam pellipariorum, id est cretam, que aliter gersa vocatur, de qua fac emplastrum cum albumine ovi, et subtilia super lapide et utere.

86. *Si vis vitrum tactum de quadam guma attrahere, sicut ferrum attrahitur a calamita.*—Accipe gumam andrianam que invenitur in saxis maximis Bononie versus Tuscam in monte Bono seu Buono, et cum ipsa guma unge baculam, et cum ipso baculo tange fialas vitri positas super mensa, et deduc baculum per mensam, et fiale sequentur baculum, sicut ferrum sequiter calamitam.

87. *Si vis de pellibus nigris facere albas.*—Accipe talpam et fac bulire, et ex ipsa aqua in qua bulierit linias equum nigrum, ubi vis, et cadent pili nigri, et orientur albi.

88. *Ad idem.*—Accipe caseum et calefac ad ignem, et in fronte equi nigri imprime fortiter, et fiet stella sicut scis.

Post predicta scriptum erat in exemplari, " omnia contenta in presenti quaterno, id est, a numero 47, usque hic, scripsi in Janua, anno 1409, de mense Junii, extrahendo ab uno quaterno prestato michi per Fratrem Dyonisium de (*sic*), ordinis Servorum Sancte

the order of the Servants of St. Mary, which order, in Milan, is called Del Sacho; and from that same book I copied also many experiments for making colours for illuminating books, which experiments I wrote in another quire which precedes this."

These are the experiments, Nos. 1 to 47 inclusive.

Also in the same MS., in another unbound book attached to the preceding, it was thus written: "On Tuesday the 11th day of February, 1410, I caused the following to be copied in Bologna from recipes lent to me at that place by Theodore (*sic*) of Flanders, an embroiderer, accustomed to work at Pavia during the life of the late renowned Duke of Milan;[1] which recipes the said Theodore said he had procured in London, in England, from the persons who work with the waters hereinafter mentioned."

The following recipes were brought from England :—

89. *To make black water.*—Take a pint of water from under the grindstone on which knives are ground,[2] and place it over the fire, and throw into it a glass of vinegar and ii. oz. of galls; then take ½ an oz. of alum and an oz. of copperas, and boil it until it is reduced by one-third, and then let it stand for a day.

90. *To make green water.*—Take an ounce of verdigris, half an ounce of alum, a little saffron, and a little parsley; grind the whole well together, and distemper it with one glass of vinegar; then strain it through a cloth into a saucer, and let it rest for a day.

91. *To make red water.*—Take an ounce of rags or clippings of scarlet [cloth], and soak them in a jar in a pint of strong ley; then put the jar over the fire, and throw into it a little alum and gum arabic, and make it boil until it is reduced one-half, and let it rest for a day.

92. *To make the water for staining cloth of all colours, and to make it quite white.*—Take a pint of strong ley, and put it over the fire, and throw into it an ounce of alum and an ounce of saltpetre, and when it is melted take it off the fire and use it.

---

[1] Gian Galeazzo, who died in 1402.

[2] This water probably contained iron-dust. It is also mentioned in the Bolognese MS., Nos. 134, 338.

Marie, qui in Mediolano dicitur 'del Sacho,' et ab ipso quaterno copiavi etiam multa experimenta ad faciendum colores pro illuminando libro, que experimenta scripsi super uno alio quaterno precedenti (*sic*) finis quaterni." [Ista sunt experimenta que scribuntur a pre (*sic*) numeri 1 usque ad numerum 47].

Item in eodem exemplari in quodam alio quaterno precedentibus contiguo scribebatur sic "1410 Die Martis xi Februarii, feci copiari in Bononia, a receptis ibi mihi prestatis per Thedericum (*sic*) de Flandria, rachamatorem solitum operari in castro papie, in vita condam incliti ducis Mediolani, quas receptas idem Thedericus dixit habuisse in Londonia in Anglia, ab operariis infrascriptarum aquarum."

Ab Anglia venerunt recepte sequentes:—

89. *Pour faire l'eau noire.*—Prenez une pinte de l'yaue de dessoulz la meule sur quoy on meult les couteaulx, et la mettez sur le feu, et gettez ung voire de vin aigre, et ii onces de galles, et prenez demie onche d'alon, et une onche de coperose, et le faitez tant boulir, qu'il apetice du tiers, et puis le laissier reposer un jour.

90. *Pour faire l'eaue verte.*—Prenez une once de vert de gris, et demie once d'alon, et un petit de safren, et un petit de persil, et broyez bien tout ensemble, et puis le destrempez en j voire de vin aigre, et puis le coulez parmi un drapel dedens une escuelle, et le laissiez reposer i jour.

91. *Pour faire l'eaue rouge.*—Prenez une once de bourre d'escarlate, ou tondure, et le destrempez dedens une olle, en une pinte de la forte lexive, et puis le mettez sur le feu, et gettez dedens un po d'alun, et de gomme arabique, et le faites tant boulir qu'il apetice de la moitié, et puis le laissiez reposer un jour.

92. *Pour faire l'eaue a destaindre drap de toutes couleurs, et faire devenir tout blanc.*—Prenez une pinte de la forte lessive, et la mettez sur le feu, et gettez dedens une once d'alun, et une once de salepetre, et quant il est fondu mettez le jus du feu et en ouvrez.

NOTE.—It seems also possible to draw, with the said water, on coloured woollen cloths, any letters and other drawings, the parts within the outlines of which only, where the water has touched, will be bleached; and thus there will be white letters and figures; the ground, where it has not been touched by the water, still retaining its own colour.

93. *To make the red water.*—Take an ounce of Brazil in powder and a 6th part of alun de glace, and make it boil well in a vessel of clear water until it is reduced to one half, and then use it.

94. *To make the green water.*—Take an ounce of water of the leaves of the black nightshade,[1] and ½ an ounce of alum and the worth of a blanc[2] of saffron, and ij. oz. of verdigris; grind all together as well as you can, and distemper with a chopine[3] of strong vinegar, and then use it.

95. *To make the violet water.*—Take an ounce of turnsole and soak it in a chopine of strong and tepid ley, and then use it.

What is here called turnsole is to be understood "Bresil."

96. *To make the blue water.*—Take an ounce of indigo of Bandas, that is to say, Baguedel,[4] and reduce it to powder, and then distemper it with ½ a "lot"[5] of strong lessive fondisse, and put it on the fire; and just before it boils, throw into it a 6th part of quicklime, and the same quantity of "meltrac" (?), and then take it off the fire and stir it well, and when it is tepid use it.

Also in the said MS., over the recipe immediately following, was written—"At the beginning of this are wanting several words which had been cut off, as appeared when I caused this to be copied from the MS.; but I think it is for making a water of an azure colour, or a blue or indigo water."

97. Take the worth of a blanc of quicklime, and the same quantity of calcined lees of wine, and of calx of tin, and some "creeres" of indigo, and boil all together in two lots of clear

[1] Morelle. The herba Morella, Solanum Nigrum, Black Nightshade.

[2] A blanc was equivalent to 5 deniers.

[3] Chopine, a half pint. The old French "pinte" was equivalent to 1 quart English.

[4] This was the real Indigo.

[5] Lot, a liquid measure, perhaps what was afterwards called "Litre."

ADDICIO.—Debent etiam posse cum dicta aqua protrahi in drapis coloricis lane quelibet littere, et alie protractiones, in quarum solis continenciis, quantum aqua eadem tetigerit, albificatio fiet, et sic habebuntur ibi protractiones et littere albe, remanente campo in suo colore ubi a qua ipsa non tetigerit.

93. *Pour faire l'eaue rouge.*—Prenez une once de brezil en poudre, et un sisain d'alun de glace, et le faites bien cuire, en desmerlant d'yaue clere, tant qu'il appetice de la moitie, et puiz en ouvrez.

94. *Pour faire l'iaue verte.*—Prenez une once d'eaue de morelle de la feuille, et demi once d'alun, et pour un blanc de saffren, et ij onces de vert de gris, et broyez tout ensemble si bien comme vous porrez, et puis le destrempez d'une chopine de fort vin aigre, et puis en œuvrez.

95. *Pour faire l'eaue violete.*—Prenez une once de tornesel, et le met tremper en une chopine de forte lessive fondisse, et que elle soit tiede, et puis en œuvre.

NOTA.—Quod ubi dicitur tornesel vult dicere Bresil.

96. *Pour faire l'eaue perse.*—Prenez une once de inde de Bandas, c'est à dire, Baguedel, et le met en pouldre, et puis le destrempe en demi lot de forte lessive fondisse, et puis le met sur le feu, et quant il voudra boulir, gette dedens un sisain de chaulx vive, et autant de meltrac, e puis le met jus du feu, et le remue bien, et quant il est tede s'en œuvre.

Item in eodem exemplari et supra receptam immediate sequentem sic erat scriptum. "Hic, in principio, deficiunt plura verba, que ab exemplari erant abscisa, ut apparebat, quando feci hoc copiari ab ipso exemplari; set credo quod sit ad faciendum aquam coloris celestini, aut aquam persam vel indicam."

97. Pren pour un blanc de chaulx vive, et un blanc de cendre de lie de vin, et un blanc de la cendre d'estaing creeres de Inde, et fait tout boulir ensemble en ij lotz d'iaue clere une

water for an instant, and stir it well, and then take it off the fire, and throw into it a glass of cold water; and when it is settled you can use it.

Also in the same MS., over the two paragraphs following, it was thus written—" I think that the following recipes are for making two green waters, as I collect from the contents, and the names and things which are mentioned in them."

98. One oz. of tartar of white wine, 1 oz. of sal gem, 1 oz. of alun de glace, ½ an oz. of alun de plume, 6 esterlins[1] of verdigris, 1 chopine of common salt.

99. 1 oz. of copperas, ½ an oz. of verdigris, 1 oz. of saltpetre, ½ an oz. of rhubarb.

Take a chopine of water and put it into a new earthen jar, and when you see that the water begins to boil put in your powder, and take it off the fire and stir it with a skewer, and let it cool.

I think these words of the above written paragraph relate to both the articles marked 98 and 99.

After the aforesaid, it was thus written in the before-mentioned MS.:—

" The true method of working in England with [coloured] waters.—The aforesaid[2] Theodore, from whom I had the above-written recipes for the aforesaid waters, told me that in England the painters work with these waters upon closely woven cloths, wetted with gum-water made with gum-arabic, and then dried, and afterwards stretched out on the floor of the soler, upon thick woollen and frieze cloths; and the painters, walking with their clean feet over the said cloths, work and paint upon them figures, stories, and other things. And because these cloths lie stretched out on a flat surface, the coloured waters do not flow or spread in painting upon them, but remain where they are placed, and the watery moisture sinks into the woollen cloth, which absorbs it; and even the touches of the paint-brush made with these waters do not spread, because the gum with which, as already men-

[1] Esterlins, 18½ grains, a goldsmith's weight. According to Spelman (*Gloss.* 203) and Dufresne (3, 165), the word was derived from the Esterlings or Easterlings, as those Saxons were anciently called who inhabited the district in Germany now occupied by the Hanse Towns and their appendages, the earliest traders in Europe. See Tomlin's *Law Dict.*, art. *Coin.*

[2] Who is mentioned before in page 84, previous to No. 89.

onde, et le remuer bien, et puis le met jus du feu, et gette dedens un godet d'yaue froide, et quant elle sera rassisse tu en puez ouvrer.

Item in eodem exemplari super ij partes sequentes sic erat. "credo quod hec verba sequencia sint ad faciendum aquas duas virides, ut comprehendo per contentus verborum ac rerum in ipsis verbis nominatarum."

98. Une once de gravelle de vin blanc, une once de sal gemme, une once d'alun de glace, demie once d'alun de plume, vi esterlins de vert de gris, un estrelin de sel commun.

99. Une once de coperose, demie once de vert de gris, une once de salpetre, demie once de rubarbe.

Prenez une chopine d'yaue et la metez en 1 pot de terre neuf, et quant vous verrez que l'iaue commencera a boulir, si metez vostre pouldre, et ne l'ostez hors du feu, et la remuez a une brochete, et laissiez refroider.

Credo quod ipsa verba suprascripti capituli serviant articulis signatis uno 98 alio 99.

Vero modum operandi in Anglia cum aquis.

Post supradicta scriptum sic erat in prefato exemplari, "Antedictus[1] Thedericus, a quo habui ante scriptas receptas prescriptarum aquarum, dixit quod in Anglia operantur operarii pictores cum ipsis aquis, super tellis bene contextis, et belneatis cum aqua gummata de gummi arabico, et siccatis, et postea extensis super solario[2] per terram, super drappis grossis lanne et frixia, incedentes cum pedibus nitidis ipsi qui operantur, iunt, inde per super ipsas telas, operando et depingendo super ipsis imagines, historias, et alia. Et quodque ipse telle sedent et stant in planicie extense, ut dictum est, et super dictis drapis dicte aque colorate pingendo non fluunt, se spargentes, set stant ut ponuntur, et humitidas aquea descendit in drapo lanne, qui eam bibit, ac etiam non sparguntur tractus pincellorum facti ex ipsis aquis, quea gumacio tele facta ut dictum est, prohibet sparsionem

---

[1] De quo supra in 2a. pagina folii precedentis ante numerum 89.

[2] Solario—the *soler*, or upper story of a house. See Illustrations of Domestic Architecture from popular Medieval writers. By Mr. Wright. Published in the Archæological Journal, September, 1844, p. 218.

tioned, the cloth is wetted, prevents their spreading. And when the cloths are thus painted, their texture is not thickened or darkened any more than if they had not been painted, because the aforesaid watery colours have not sufficient body to thicken the cloth."

Also in the beginning of the following quire in the same MS. it was thus written—" On Thursday, the 13th day of February, 1410, I caused the following to be copied at Bologna, by the hand of Dom Johannes de diversis, from a certain book of Magister Johannes de Modena, a painter living at Bologna."

It must also be remarked that the articles which follow, namely, from the article 100 to the article 116 inclusive, were in the book from which I, John Le Begue, copied, as has been already said, the present articles; and that this book was written in the Italian language; and as I did not understand that language, I caused it to be translated into Latin by a certain friend of mine, who was skilled in both languages.

100. *To make lake.*—Take ashes of oak, and boil them in a boiler full of water, namely, in one containing 6 small cups of water, and one parasis, i. e. a large [saucer or] basin full of the ashes, and boil it until it is reduced to three cups. Then let it settle, and when it is clear, pour it into a glazed earthen basin; then take a woollen cloth, and strain the said water, and when it is strained it will be a ley. Put into the said ley a sufficient quantity of the clippings, that is, cuttings of scarlet cloth of rubeum de grana, to be perfectly covered by the ley. Then put it into a glazed earthen jar, and let it rest for twelve hours. Next take that ley, together with the clippings, and put it into a glazed earthen pipkin, and set it by the fire, and let it simmer gently for an hour. After that try it, by putting it on your nail, and if it stands up well on your nail, it is done; then remove it from the fire and strain it through a thick woollen cloth. You must then have a new glazed earthen pot, and pour into it what was strained through the said cloth; add to it vi oz. of roche alum, and stir it together until it is dissolved. Then take a spoon and skim off all the froth that forms over the top of it, and throw away this scum, for it is not good. But the other part is good, and should be put into a glazed earthen vase, and suffered to stand until it

ipsam tractuum pincellorum; et cum telle ipse operate sunt, tamen raritas ipsarum non est inspisata, nec ob fuscata, plus quam si non picte fuissent, quia aquei colores suprascripti non habent tantum corpus, quod possent inspicare raritatem telle."

Item in principio quaterni sequentis in eodem exemplari sicut erat scriptum, "1410, die Jovis xiii[a] Februarii, feci copiari que sequuntur in Bononia, de manu domini Johannis de diversis, a quodam libello magistri Johannis de Modena, pictoris habitantis in Bononia."

Et autem sciendum, quod articuli qui sequuntur, scilicet ab articulo 100 usque ad articulum 116 inclusive, erant in libro a quo ego, Johannes le Begue, presencium articulorum, ut supra dictum est, in ytalico sermone conscripsi, quem sermonem, cum non intelligerem, feci per quemdam amicum meum, utriusque lingue peritum, in latinum vertíi, eo qui sequitur modo.

100. *Ad faciendum lacha.*—Ad faciendum lacha, accipe cinerem de quercu, et fac bulire in una patella plena aque, videlicet quod sint intus sex cassete aque, et una parasis de dicta cinere, videlicet una magna scutella, et fac tantum bullire quod reveniant ad tres cassetas tantum modo. Postea sine clarificare, et, quando est clarificata, ponas in una patella de terra vitreata; postea habeas pannum de lanna, et per ipsum fac colare dictam aquam, et, cum fuerit clarefacta, tum erit lessivium; ponas in dicto lessivio tantum cimature, videlicet burre de panno scarlato rubeo in grana, quod super habundet aliqualiter lessivium dictam cimaturam. Postea ponas totum in uno vase de terra vitriato, et sine morari intus per xij horas. Postea capias illud lessivium una cum cimatura, et ponas in una olla de terra vitreata, quam pones juxta ignem, et fac bulire paulatim per unam horam. Et postea experimentes, et ponas supra unguem, et si teneat se super unguem, tunc est coctum, et hoc facto amovebis ab igne, et fac colorare per pannum grossum de lana. Postea habebis unum potum de terra vitreatum novum, et ponas intus illud quod colaverit per dictum pannum, et accipe vi oncias de alumine de Roch, et ponas intus, et misce ad invicem, usque quo liquefacerit. Postea accipe unum coclearium, et collige tantum illam

has become somewhat dry, when it must be formed into small grains, and be put in the sun.

101. *To make verzino for painting on silver.*—To make verzino for painting on silver or tin-foil, so that the brilliancy of the silver or tin may shine and appear through it, put a piece of white lime about the size of an egg into water to dissolve, and let it stand in the water for three days and three nights. Then rasp or scrape verzino, and add it to the lime-water, and let it stand for an hour; then put it on the fire in a small jar, and let it boil until, when you put it upon your nail, it remains upon it. Then take isinglass, or, as some say, turpentine, a piece about the size of a bean, and put into it, and remove it from the fire. Take a little roche alum, which you must stick in the end of a small stick and tie it there, and dip it into the said mixture, and let it remain there until you see that it is dissolved. Then take a strainer, and strain or filter the water through it.

102. *To make [a liquid] for dyeing.*—Take the whites of six eggs, and put them in a glazed basin, and break or beat them well with a sponge. Then take an ounce of verzino and scrape it, and add it to this white of egg, and let it remain in it for three days. Then take a little roche alum and scrape into it, and set it to strain or filter through a strainer. Then place it in the sun, and let it stand until it dries. Temper it with a little weak gum, that is, gum-water, made with gum arabic, having but little gum in it, on account of the viscosity of the white of egg, which is sufficient for it.

103. *To make gesso sottile.*—Take fine gesso sifted, that is passed through a sieve, and put it into water to dissolve, and change the water every day, and stir it together every day, and

spumam que veniet desuper, et illud quod remanet desuper separes, quod non est bonum. Alterum vero est bonum, et ipsum ponas in uno vaso de terra vitreato, et sinas stare intus usque quo aliqualiter desiccetur, et, quando desiccatum fuerit, fac de ipso parva grana, et ponas ad solem.

101. *Ad faciendum verzin super argento ponendo.*—Ad faciendum verzin super argento vel stagno verberato, ponendo taliter quod splendor argenti et stagni splendeat et lucescat, accipe calcem albam tantum, quantum est unum ovum, et ponas in aqua ad liquefaciendum, et sine stare in dicta aqua per tres dies et tres noctes. Postea habeas feltrum, et per ipsum cola dictam aquam. Postea ratices sive radas verzin, et ponas in dicta aqua de calce, et sine stare intus per unam horam, postea ponas super ignem in una parva olla, et sinas tantum bulire, quod si posueris super unguem, ibi remaneat. Postea habeas de cola piscium, et aliqui volunt dicere de Trementina, tantum quantum unum granum fabe, et pone intus et removeas ab igne, et habeas parumper de alumine de roch, quod ponas in summitate unius parvi baculi, et liges ipsum, et emerge in dicta aqua commixtionata, et sine stare usquequo videris esse liquefactum. Postea habeas unam stamineam, et per ipsam fac penetrare sive colare dictam aquam.

102. *Ad faciendum pro tingendo.*—Accipe clarum sex ovorum, et ponas in una scutella vitreata et deducas, sive percussias, bene cum una spungia. Postea habeas unam onciam de verzin, et ratices, et ponas in isto claro ovorum, et sinas stare intus per tres dies. Postea habeas aliquantum de alumine de roch, et ratices desuper, et pone ad colandum, sive penetrandum, in una staminea. Postea ponas ad solem, et sine stare tantum quod sit siccum. Postea tempera ipsum cum aliquantum de gumma debili, id est de aqua gommata de gummi arabico, que parum gumme in se habet, causa viscositatis clari ovi jam impositi, que sufficit.

103. *Ad faciendum gessum subtile.*—Accipe de gesso subtili sedassato, id est, penetrato per aliquam stamineam, et pone in aqua ad liquefaciendum, et cotidie renoves aquam, et cothidie

do this for a month. Then strain or filter off the water, and take the part that remains behind and put it into a fresh vase, in which you must let it remain till it has settled properly; then make it into a cake, and let it dry.

104. *To lay burnished gold upon paper.*—Take gesso sottile and grind it on a stone with water. Then let it dry, and when it is dry take some glue, not very strong, and mix with it, and add a little minium and ceruse—*i. e.* blanchet—and lay the gesso on the paper, and let it dry. Then scrape it, and lay over it Armenian bole well ground with white of egg, and when it is dry, lay gold upon it with white of egg, and burnish it in proper time.

105. *To lay fine gold upon gilt tin.*—Take white of egg, and whip or beat it well with a sponge, with which wet also the tin, but the sponge must not be too wet. Then take fine gold, and lay it on the tin, and let it stand until it is fit to burnish.

106. *To make a mordant with garlic.*—Take garlic, and pound or grind it very fine, and strain or sift it through a very fine sieve. Then take what passed through, and put it on a stone with a little minium and ceruse, viz., blanchet and a little bole, and grind and mix all these together, and let the mixture stand till it becomes tacky.

107. *To make a mordant which will not be affected by the weather.*—Take a little minium and ceruse, viz., blanchet, also verdigris, bole, and ochre, and grind all together with water, and let them dry until the water is completely evaporated. Then take what remains and grind it with oil and linseed, and add a little liquid varnish to it, and a little gold size, and grind all these things well together, and apply the mordant, and when you have applied it lay on the gold.

108. *To make lake.*—Take verzino and rasp it with glass, and take travertine rasped to powder, and a little roche alum, and grind it, and soak all these things in a ley, and let them

commisceas ad invicem, et in tali statu sine morari usque ad unum mensem; postea cola sive penetra aquam, et abstrahe illud quod remanserit, et ponas in uno vase novo, ubi sinas morari usque quo fuerit bene repausatum, postea fac panem, et sine siccari.

104. *Ad ponendum aurum bornitum in carta.*—Accipe gessum subtile, et tere super petra cum aqua. Postea sine siccari, et quando erit siccum, habeto de cola non valde forti, et extempera cum ipso et pone aliquantulum de minio, et de ceruza, videlicet blanchet, et pone istud gessum super carta, et sine siccari. Postea radas et ponas super bolarminum, bene tritum cum claro ovi, et quando est siccum, pone super aurum cum claro ovi. Postea bornisce quando tempus est.

105. *Ad ponendum aurum finum super stagno aurato.*—Accipe clarum ovi, et deducas sive percutias bene cum spungià, et balne stagnum de dicta aqua cum spungia, et non valde; postea accipias aurum finum, et vade ponendo super stanno, et sinas tantum quod sit ydoneum ad borniendum.

106. *Ad faciendum mordentem de aleo.*—Accipe de aleo, et pista, sive tere, bene nitide, et cola, sive penetra, bene nitide per unam pessiam. Postea collige illud quod penetraverit, et ponas supra petra cum aliquantum de minio, et de cerusa, videlicet Blanchet, et aliquantum de bolo, et omnia ista tere et commisce ad invicem, et sine tantum quod efficiatur conglutinosus.

107. *Ad faciendum mordentem qui stet ad aerem.*—Accipe parumper de minio, et cerusa, videlicet blanchet, et de verderamo, et de bolo, et de ocrea, et tere omnia ista ad invicem cum aqua. Postea sine siccari usquequo aqua exiverit. Postea accipe illud quod remanserit, et tere cum oleo et semine lini, et pone intus cum aliquanto vernicis liquide, et aliquantum de auratura; et omnia ista tere bene invicem, et ponas in opere, et quando pungit pone super aurum.

108. *Ad faciendum lacha.*—Accipe verzin, et ratices cum aliquantum de vitreo, et accipe tevertini raticatum in pulvere, et accipe alume de roch, et tere. Et omnia ista pone ad lique-

stand for a day. Then mix the whole well together, and put the mixture in a new earthen jar, and make it boil for a quarter of an hour. Then take a small bag, and pour the whole into it, and let it remain until the moisture has passed or run through, and let it fall into a saucer or stone basin.

109. *To make a yellow colour.*—Take an ounce of orpiment, and an ounce of sulphur vivum, and temper this colour with the milk of a fig-tree, and it is done.

110. *To make a green water.*—Take buckthorn berries, and mix them in the same way as is done with wine or raisins when they are boiled in a cauldron to make wine, and cover them up, and let them remain for six days. Then squeeze them into a parasis, viz., a basin of glazed earthenware, and add to it a little [1] alum, lest it should be spoiled. Proportion the alum to the quantity of the liquid, and place it in the sun to dry. And when you wish to use it add a little ley to it; and if you wish to have a beautiful green take some fine azure and mix with this water; and note, that for this purpose azurrum de Alemannia, provided it is good and perfect, is better than ultramarine.

111. *To make ultramarine azure.*—Take 3 lbs. of lapis lazuli, and pound finely in a copper mortar, and afterwards sift it with a sieve such as perfumers use when they sift their perfumes after having pounded them. Then take 3 lbs. of turpentine, and put into a glazed earthen saucer, and place it on the hot ashes. Then put into it a little olive oil, and when you see that it begins to boil take it from the fire, and immediately put in the powdered lapis lazuli, little by little, stirring it well with a stick, so that the turpentine may be well incorporated with the said powder. Then keep the saucer, with the pastille thus made, for three days, and the longer it stands the better. Afterwards take another larger saucer, and put the pastille into it, and take some clean tepid water, and pour

---

[1] So in original.

faciendum cum lexivio, et sine morari per unum diem. Postea misce omnia ista bene, et pone in una olla de terra nova, et fac bulire per quartam partem unius hore. Postea habeas unum parvum succum, et pone intus omnia ista, et sine morari usquequo succus penetraverit, sive colaverit, et fac cadere in una paraside, sive catino, de petra.

109. *Ad faciendum colorem croceum.*—Accipe unam unciam de orpimento, et unam unciam de sulfure vivo, et distempera istum colorem cum lacte de figu, et est factum.

110. *Ad faciendum aquam viridem.*—Accipe grana de spino cervino, et ammusces sicut fit de vino sive raisinis, quando fit bullire in cuva pro vino faciendo, et tege et sine morari usque ad vj dies. Postea premas in una paraside, videlicet, in uno catino de terra vitriato, et pone intus aliquantulum de alume de (*sic*), ne corrumpatur, et ponas de dicto alume secundum quantitatem dicti liquoris, et pone ad solem, et sine siccari. Et quando vis de ipso operari, accipe aliquantum liscivii, et mitte intus; et si vis facere pulcrum colorem viridem, fac quod habeas pulcrum azurrum, et misce cum ista aqua; et scias quod ad istud negotium melius est azurrum de Alemannia, quam ultramarinum, dum modo sit bonum in perfectione.

111. *Ad faciendum azurium ultramarinum.*—Accipe libras tres lapides lazuli, et pistes valde bene in uno mortario de cupro, et fac postea penetrare per unam stamignam, qua utuntur aromatarii, quando faciunt penetrare aromata postquam pestaverint. Postea habeas libras tres de trementina, et ponas in una scutella vitreata, quam pones super cinerem caldum. Postea pone intus aliquantum de oleo olivarum, et si tu vides quod inceperit bulire, removeas ab igne, et statim pone intus dictum pulverem lapidis lazulli, paulatim, miscendo, et bene incorporando cum uno baculo, per modum quod illa trementina sit bene incorporata cum dicto pulvere. Postea conserva dictam scutellam cum dicto pastillo taliter confecto per tres dies, et si plus staret, melius valeret. Postea habeto

over the pastille as much as would fill a small saucer of the size of the saucer in which the pastille was kept, and wash the pastille well with your hands in the water, and then strain the water through the cloth; and having strained the water from the pastille in that manner three times, keep it in another larger saucer, for in it you will have the flower of the azure. Also pour water again over the pastille in quantity about three saucers' full, pouring it over three times, one saucer full at a time, and do as you did before, and you will have good azure, but not so perfect as the first. Also pour water on the pastille a third time, and do as you did before, and you will then have another azure, yet not so perfect as the first or the second.

112. *To make the pastille with which the azure is prepared.*—Take 3 oz. of olive oil, also 2 oz. of turpentine, also ½ oz. of liquid varnish, also 2 sagii[1] of good incense; and, in my opinion, each sagium makes 1 sterling and a half. Afterwards prepare the oil in the following way:—Take a glazed jar, and first put some of the oil into it, and next the two ounces of turpentine, and place it on a clear fire, and let them boil together for so long as it would take to say a Paternoster and Ave Maria. Then put in the said 2 sagii of incense, and let them boil together for as long as it would take to say the *miserere mei Deus* twice. Then add the half ounce of liquid varnish, and let them boil together for as long as it would take to say the *miserere mei Deus* twice. Lastly, pour in the remainder of the oil, and afterwards strain it through a clean closely-woven linen cloth, and preserve it in a clean jar.

113. *To extract the azure from the pastille.*—Put the pastille into an earthen vase, and rub it very well with linseed oil, and afterwards make the said pastille into a round cake. Then

---

[1] A Sagium, or scruple, according to the Ricettario, weighed 24 grains. The saggio mercantile weighed 24 grains.—*Ricett. Fior.*, p. 126.

unam aliam scutellam majorem, et in dicta pone dictum pastillum, et habeas de aqua nitida et clara tepide, et in dicto pastillo pone quantitatem unius parve scutelle, que scutella sit quantitatis que erat prima scutella, in qua prius conservasti dictum pastillum, et cum manibus lava bene dictum pastillum in dicta aqua, et tunc cola dictam aquam in dicto panno, et illam aquam, taliter colatam de pastillo, tribus vicibus reserva in una alia majori scutella, quia in ista tu habebis florem azurii. Item altera vice ponas aquam in metipso pastillo, in quantitate trium scutellarum, ponendo per tres vices, et qualibet vice unam scutellam, et fac sicut fecisti prius, et habebis azurum bonum, set non tam perfectum sicut primum. Iterum, tercia vice, ponas aquam in metipso pastillo, et fac sicut fecisti alteris duabus vicibus, et tunc habebis alium azurum, set non erit in perfectione sicut primum nec secundum.

112. *Ad faciendum pastillum de quo fit azurrum.*—Accipe tres oncias de oleo olivarum, item duas oncias de trementina, item dimidiam onciam vernicis liquide, item duos sagios boni incensi; et, secundum opinionem meam, quodlibet sagium facit unum sterlingum cum dimidio. Postea confice dictum oleum isto modo: in primis accipe unam ollam vitriatam, in qua pones prius de dicto oleo, postea duas oncias de dicta trementina, postea pones juxta ignem clarum, et sine bulire ad invicem, tantum quod diceretur semel pater noster et ave Maria. Postea pones dictos duos sagios incensi, et dimitte bullire invicem tantum, quod bis diceretur "*miserere mei Deus.*" Postea pone dictam dimidiam unciam de vernice liquida, et sine bulire tantum, quod diceretur bis *miserere mei Deus.* Postea finaliter pone residuum de dicto oleo, et postea cola per unum pannum lineum nitidum bene intextum, et ponas in uno vaso nitido.

113. *Ad trahendum azurrum de pastillo.*—Pone dictum pastillum in uno vaso de terra, et frica valde bene cum oleo de semine lini, et postea fac de dicto pastillo unum panem ro-

take warm ley, well strained and clear, and pour it on the pastille, and do the same thing a second and a third time, and thus you will have three sorts of azure. Then remove the ley as well as you can, and put it afresh into another ley, and make it boil slowly and gently, and skim it. Then let it boil for an hour, and remove it from the fire, and pour off the ley, and wash and strain it well. Make every three portions boil in this way, and also each by itself; and also, if you wish to strain it together with the ley you can do it.

114. *To make the pastille from which the ultramarine is made.*—Take 1 lb. of lapis lazuli and grind it well, and take three sagii of new wax. In my opinion these sagii are equal to 1 sterling and a half each. Also three sagii of mastic, also one sagius of coarse incense, also one ounce of the before-mentioned prepared oil, and then make a pastille in the following manner. First take the wax, and chew it well with your teeth, and put it into a glazed jar. Then place it on the fire, and let it melt. Next add the incense, and let it melt; and then add the mastic, and let it boil slowly and gently for so long as it would take you to say the *miserere mei Deus* once. Then add half an ounce of the oil, and let it stand by the fire until it boils. Then remove it from the fire, and keep stirring it till it is cold, or nearly so, when you must add the powder of lapis lazuli, and stir it until it becomes hard. Then take water that is slightly warmed, and put the pastille into it, and mix it until the water is well coloured. Then put it into a parasis or basin of glazed stoneware, and the perfect azure will immediately sink to the bottom of the basin, and you must then pour off the water carefully; or, you may keep it, if you wish to do so, and then pour off the water: add cold water, and wash the said azure well, mixing it with a stick. Then strain it through a closely-textured linen cloth, and pour off the water and dry it, and you will thus have perfect azure.

115. *To extract perfect azure.*—First take a phial of cold ley, and put into it one drachm of the stone tuzia, well ground with the said ley, then wash the azure in it, and afterwards wash it

tundum; postea habeas lessivium tepidum bene colatum et clarum, et pone in dicto pastillo, et simili modo iterum facies bina et trina vice, et sic habebis de tribus maneriebus azurri. Postea atrahes lixivium quam melius poteris, et de uno pone in alio lexivio, et fac bulire paulatim et plane, et schiumabis [from schiumare] desuper; postea sine bulire per unam horam, et retrahe ab igne, et abstrahe lexivium, et lava bene, et similiter bene colabis, et fac omnibus tribus vicibus sic bullire, et qualibet vice pro se; et etiam, si velis colare una cum lessivio, facere poteris.

114. *Ad faciendum pastillum de quo fit azurum ultramarinum.*—Accipe unam libram de petra vel lapide lazuli, et tere bene, et accipe tres sagios de cera nova, qui sagii faciunt, videre meo, quilibet unum sterlingum cum dimidio. Item tres sagios de mastich, item unum sagium large incensi, item unam onciam de oleo supradicto confecto, et postea fit pastillum tali modo. In primis accipe ceram, et mastica bene cum dentibus, et pone in una olla vitriata. Postea pone juxta ignem et sine liquefieri. Postea ponas dictum incensum, et sine liquefieri; postea ponas dictum mastich, et sine bullire paulatim et plane, tantum quod diceretur semel "*miserere mei Deus.*" Postea ponas dimidiam onciam de dicto oleo, et sine tantum stare juxta ignem quod buliat. Postea remove ab igne, et commisce tantum quod sit refrigeratum, vel quasi; postea pone dictum pulverem de lapide lazulli, et misce tantum quod veniat dura; postea accipe de aqua parumper calida, et pone supradictum pastillum, et tantum misceas, quod aqua sit bene colorata. Postea ponas in una paraside, sive catino, de lapide vitreato, et statim azurrum perfectum submergetur in profundo cathini; postea diligenter abstrahe aquam, et, si vis ipsam reservare, potes, et abstrahe dictam aquam, et ponas de aqua frigida, et laves bene dictum azurrum, miscendo bene cum uno ligno. Postea cola per panum lineum bene intextum, et abstrahe illam aquam, et siccabis, et sic habebis azurrum perfectum.

115. *Ad abstrahendum azurrum perfectum.*—In primis accipe unam fiolam de lissivio frigido, in qua pones intus unam dragmam de lapide tuzia bene trita cum dicto lixivio, postea lavabis

with cold water, until it remains pure and brilliant, and thus you will have a perfect blue.

116. *To obtain a blue, not quite so perfect.*—If you like you may also make up the pastille again, as before directed, except that you must not add to it any of the before-mentioned lapis lazuli, and you must keep and knead this second pastille as before directed with regard to the first, and thus you will have a second and a third kind of azure not so perfect.

Whoever wishes to try all these experiments must observe and note that the pounds mentioned here must be understood as of twelve ounces each, according to the Italian mode of reckoning.

Also in the said MS. it was thus written—" I received the following receipt at Venice, on Tuesday the 4th day of May, 1410, from Michelino di Vesuccio, the most excellent painter among all the painters of the world."

117. *Azure is thus made.*—Take 1 lb. of lapis lazuli and grind it well upon a porphyry slab; then wash it with water and dry it, and reduce it to powder. The pastille is thus made:—To each pound of powdered lapis lazuli take 1 lb. of Greek pitch, ij. oz. of liquid varnish, j. oz. of mastic; put into a rough jar iij. oz. of good common oil, *i. e.* linseed or olive oil, and make it boil; then put the mastic and varnish in powder into the oil, and stir it well with a stick, and when you see that they are dissolved add the Greek pitch in powder, and let it boil a little, until the whole is incorporated. Then strain it through a cloth into cold water and knead it with your hands greased with common oil, and then incorporate the powdered lapis lazuli very carefully upon a slab with the pastille, and let it stand for three days with the pastille. Afterwards extract the azure from the pastille in this way:—Stir it about with a stick in water that is a little more than tepid, and keep it in as long as any colour flows out; but if you cannot extract the colour put hotter water to it, and so keep adding water hotter and hotter by degrees until it brings out the colour. Lastly, pour off the water when it is at the hottest, and having extracted all the azure and separated it from the water, make a very strong ley, and put the azure into smooth vases, and pour

azurrum, postea etiam lavabis cum aqua frigida, tantum quod remaneat purum et nitidum, et sic habebis perfectum azurrum.

116. *Ad habendum azurrum non adeo perfectum.*—Si vis, fac pastillum etiam de novo, sicut dictum est de super, excepto quod tu non debes ponere aliquid de dicto lapide lazullino, et istud secundum pastillum debes custodire et incorporare, sicut dictum est de super in primo, et sic habebis azurrum in secundo et tercio modo non adeo perfectum.

Sit autem monitus, vel advertat, quicumque habet omnia ista experiri, quod libre, de quibus in eis fit mencio, intelligantur de duodecim unciis quelibet libra, secundum morem italicum.

Item in eodem exemplari sic erat scriptum, "hoc sequens experimentum hujusmodi, in Veneciis, die martis, IIII maii, anni 1410, a Michelino de Vesucio, pictore excellentissimo inter omnes pictores mundi."

117. *Azurrum sic fit.*—Recipe libram unam lapidis lazuli, et tere bene in lapide porfirico. Postea ablue ipsum cum aqua clara, deinde desica et reduce ipsum in pulverem. Pastillum sic fit; ad libram unam pulveris lapidis, pone libram unam picis grece, oncias ij. vernicis liquide, onc. i. masticis; ponantur in olla rudi onc. iij. olei communis, id est lini, vel olive, et boni, et fac bullire, et tunc mastice et vernicem pulverizatam pone in oleo, et bene moveas cum ligno. Et cum videas resoluta, pone piscem pulverizatam, et permitte parum bullire, donec omnia fuerunt bene incorporata. Postea cola per pannum in aqua frigida, et manicetur manibus oleo communi, et postea pulver lazulli incorporetur super lapidem cum dicto pastillo, et optime, et dimittatur per tres dies in dicto pastillo. Postea extrahatur azurrum de pastillo hoc modo; misceatur cum baculo in aqua calida, parum plusquam tepida, et taliter teneatur, quousque aliquid exiverit. Si vero non exiret, ponatur aqua magis calida, et sic gradatim, mittendo aquam calidiorem, et miscendo, donec aliquid exiverit; ultimo ponatur aqua quando magis fervet, et extracto toto azurro, et separato ab aqua, et sicato, fiat lexivium fortissimum, et ponatur azurrum in planis vasis, et superius ponatur lexivium, sicut nosti, ut exeant immondicii pastilli, quo purgato, dulcifica cum aqua clara, etc.

the ley upon it, in order, as you know, to get rid of the impurities of the pastille. Having thus purified it, wash it with clean water, &c.

In the year of the Circumcision of Christ, 1410, on the 2nd day of February, after that Master Johannes de (1) (a Norman, who was residing in the house of Master Petrus de Verona, who knows how to refine or make ultramarine azure, and does refine or make the said azure when he wants it) had told me, Johannes Alcherius, at Paris, the process which is used in making the said ultramarine azure, I noted down and made the present writing, according to my opinion, and according to the things which I heard from him, and also according to the things which I saw in divers treatises concerning this, and as I heard from divers other persons.

118. *To clean, refine, or make ultramarine azure with a pastille; or to make it with lapis lazuli ground to powder, and to purify the powder with a pastille.*—Pound and grind very fine and dry in a copper mortar fine ultramarine lapis lazuli, which is the better in proportion as it is of a deeper and more brilliant sky blue, namely when the colour is not too pale or whitish, and the stone itself is not mixed with parts that are not of a blue colour, but of a yellow or earthy and whitish colour. And if, as it sometimes happens, the stone cannot be obtained in pieces, but the powder of it, which the salesmen call azure, can be obtained, although not refined or purified, take it and try whether it is fine, by heating it in the fire upon an iron plate. If it does not change its colour or get dull it is good. Then grind this powder excessively fine, upon a hard and smooth stone, with clean water, in the same way that colours are ground. Then dry it, and reduce it to powder, and make the pastille for purifying the said powder or azure, of the following things, in this manner:—

Put into a glazed earthen vase, 8 oz. of turpentine. This must be softened by warming, so that it may be stirred and washed; and it must be washed several times with pure warm water, stirring the water and the turpentine with a stick, and

---

1 So in original.

Anno circoncisionis 1411, die ij Februarii, post quam magister Johannes de (*sic*), Normanus, commorans in domo magistri Petri de Verona, qui sit afinare vel facere azurrum ultramarinum, et afinat diatim, seu facit, cum expedit, dixit mihi Johanni Alcherio, in Parisiis, modum quo utitur afiniando, seu faciendo ipsum azurrum, notavi, et feci presentem scripturam, secundum avisum meum, et juxta eaque ab ipso audivi, et juxta eaque per diversas scripturas vidi de hoc, et a diversis aliis personis audivi.

118. *Ad purgandum, vel afinandum, seu faciendum, azurrum ultramarinum cum pastillo, seu ad faciendum illud de lapide lazulli, trito in pulvere, et purgando pulverem cum pastillo.*—Pulverizatur et teritur subtilissime ad siccum, in mortario cupri, lapis lazulli ultramarinus finus, cujus bonitatis est major, quanto est magis celestis coloris, et vivi, videlicet quod non sit nimis clarus color et albescens, seu quod lapis ipse non sit immixtus de partibus non celestini coloris, set crocei, vel terrestis, et albescentis; et si, ut quandoque accidit, non invenitur lapis, et inveniatur pulver de ipso factus, quem vendentes appellant azurium, dato quod non sit afinatus seu purgatus, accipiatur et probetur si fit finum, ponendo ipsum ad ignem super lamina ferri, et si non mutat colorem, vel pejorat, est bonum; deinde pulver illud teratur super lapide duro, plano, bene subtiliter cum aqua clara, ut teruntur colores, postea siccetur, et redigatur in pulverem, et fiat postea pastillus, pro purgando dictum pulverem seu azurium, de rebus sequentibus, hoc modo. Accipiantur in vase terreo vitreato uncie octo tormentine, que si vel sic intepidetur, ut sit aliquantulum mollis, ut possit agitari lavando eam, et lavetur pluries cum aqua clara tepida, agitando aquam et tormentinam simul cum baculo, et jactando aquam, ita quod termentina fiat bene alba, clara, et purgata,

then throwing away the water, so that the turpentine may be bleached, cleaned, and purified. This is my own advice, although Master Johannes did not say that it would be better. Then add to it 2 oz. of pine resin, or Greek pitch, and 2 oz. of new wax, and melt or liquefy all these things together over the fire, and mix them well, and it will make the pastille, which must afterwards be allowed to cool a little, so that it may be just tepid and soft, and not liquid, but rather solid.

Then add viij., x., or xij. oz. of the said powdered lapis lazuli, putting it in by degrees, and mixing the pastille and the powder with a stick, so that the powder may be well incorporated with the pastille, and let it rest for about a day and a night or longer.

Then pour over it a quantity of warm water sufficient to cover the pastille, and let it stand for a short time, so that it may not be melted, but only warmed and softened sufficiently to allow it to be kneaded and stirred with the stick. Afterwards, if the water has become too cold, add more hot water, which thus being added to the former becomes and also causes the pastille to become of a convenient heat. It would therefore be more convenient in summer than in winter on account of the heat. Stir the pastille gently with a stick or a wooden spoon, and pour off the water, and the azure that is extracted with it, into another glazed earthen jar. And because the azure on account of its weight sinks presently to the bottom of the water, the water must be immediately poured off into another glazed earthen jar, lest any yellowish or white and earthy impurities, which are not so heavy as the azure, and which therefore do not sink to the bottom so soon, should, perhaps, render the water turbid; and if the water should be turbid, these impurities will sink to the bottom along with the azure, which it will contaminate by being mixed with it. Afterwards wash the said pastille again several times in the same manner with warm water, not allowing it to cool or harden, but keeping it at a proper degree of heat and softness; always pouring off the water of each washing, together with the azure which

quod advisavi ego, dato quod ipse magister Johannes non dixerit erit melius. Postea ponantur in ipsa oncie due picis rase, seu grece, et oncie due cere nove, et fundantur seu liquefiant hec omnia simul ad ignem, et misceantur bene, et iste erit pastillus, qui postea dimittatur aliquantulum infrigidari, ita quod sit solum tepidus et mollis, et non liquidus, set aliquantulum obduratus. Deinde ponantur in ipso oncie viii°, vel x^cem^, vel xii^cim^, dicti pulveris lazulli lapidis, paulatim imponendo, et cum baculo pastillum cum pulvere miscendo, ita quod bene incorporetur pulver cum pastillo; postea dimitatur per circa diem et noctem, vel plus, deinde ponatur de aqua calida, ita quod pastillus cooperiatur, et stet paucum, ut efficiatur non liquefactus, sed tepidus et mollis, ut possit cum baculo agitari et misceri. Postea, si aqua erit nimis infrigidata, et suponatur de alia calida, que sic fit alteri adita remaneat, et pastillus cum ea ad tepiditatem convenientem reducatur. Igitur melius fit hoc in estate, pro calido, quam in hieme; et misceatur pastillus cum baculo, vel spatula ligni, moderato modo, et azurrium, quod exibit cum aqua, immittatur, cum ipsa aqua lavature sue, in alio vase terreo vitriato. Et quia azurium subito, pro ejus ponderositate, descendit ad fondum aque, est cito post ejus descensum proficienda est aliquo alio vase terreo vitreato, ne aliqualis turpitudo albescens, vel crocea, et terrestris, que non est tam ponderosa, ut azurrium, et igitur nec tam cito descendit ad fundum, et qua turpedine forte ipsa aqua es aliqualiter turbida, si aliqualiter ex ea turbida erit, descendat ad fondum cum azurrio, et ipsum deturpet se sibi immiscendo; et postea iterum relavetur simili modo dictus pastillus pluribus vicibus cum aqua tepida, non dimittendo ipsum pastillum infrigidari nec indurari, set tenendo ipsum in tepiditate et mollicie debita, et semper aquam, ad quamlibet lavaturam cum azurro exeuntem quem secum traxerit et dixerit, mittendo in dicto vase, in qua prima missa erit, donec videatur quod azurrium incipiat exire a pastillo tanto minus bonum, seu minus pulcrum in colore ejus, quam primum, quod ex nimia differencia conveniat non plus ipsum ulterius ex aliis lavaturis exeuntem

comes off with it and is mixed with it, into the vase in which the first was put, until you see the azure come out of the pastille so much inferior in colour that on account of the too great difference of colour it is not proper to mix this last with the azure proceeding from the former washings, but it should be kept separate. You must then put what comes off with the subsequent waters into another vase, separate from the first, and pour off in a similar manner the water of the washings into the same vase in which you put the water of the former washings. And afterwards wash the azure again secondly as many times as you were directed to wash the first sort aforesaid, namely until the colour changes so materially for the worse, and then, on account of the too great change in the colour, let the subsequent waters be poured off into another third vase, until the whole pastille is washed in such manner that all the colour which can be extracted from the pastille is obtained. There will thus be three sorts of azure.

Next, pour off the water of all these different washings into the other vase, which contains the rest of the water of the said washings, and let the azure, which was thus made and refined, dry, and keep it for use in painting pictures. Then stir the aforesaid water, consisting of a mixture of all the washings of the three sorts of azure, well from the bottom with a stick, so as to mix up the grounds of the azure and the earthy parts, and so that the water may be as turbid as possible; let it stand for a very, very short time, and then immediately pour the water quickly off, with all the earthy impurities mixed with it, leaving in the bottom of the vase any azure which may sink to the bottom, if there should have been any portion of it with the water, as there usually is in this manner of refining the azure, namely with the water which is poured off from the three sorts of azure.

And note that when it is wished to use the ultramarine azure, which is made from the three sorts of waters above mentioned, it must not be ground upon a stone, as is done with sinobrium and other colours, because the grinding which it had

miscere cum primo, set teneri separate; et tunc quod exibit ad alias sequentes lavaturas pastilli suprascripti ponatur in alio vase, separatim a primo, et similiter mittendo aquam dictarum lavaturarum in dicto vase, in quo alia aliarum lavaturarum missa erit. Et postea iterum secundo per tot vices lavetur, quod similiter ut de suprascripto primo dictum est, videatur quod nimis mutet colorem in minori pulcritudine; et tunc, ab ipsa nimia mutatione coloris antedicta, ponantur tertio sequentes lavature in alio vase, donec pastillus totus sit taliter lavatus, quod extractum sit de ipso totum azurium quod extrahi poterit; et sic erunt tres sortes azurii, de quibus dictis lavaturis similiter iniciatur aqua in predicto alio vase, cum alia aqua omnium aliarum lavaturarum predictarum, et postea desiccari permittatur azurium, quod sic erit afinatum et factum, et servetur ad usum operum fiendorum, et qua predicta, acumulata de omnibus dictis lavaturis dictarum trium sortarum azurii, agitetur fortiter cum baculo usque ad fondum, ut fecies azurii et pars terrestris commoveatur, et turbidetur aqua quantum poterit; deinde valde parum stet, et postea proiciatur cito ipsa aqua, cum tota turpedine suprascripta terrestri in ipsa immixta, et retineatur in fundo vasis illa aliqua pars azurii que in ipso fondo erit descensa, si aliqua pars adherit, ut esse solet, in talibus affinaturiis azurrii de dependenciis, scilicet dictarum trium sortarum azurii; et nota, quod cum dicto azurrio ultramarino dictarum lavaturarum ipsarum trium sortarum in opere ponere volueris, non debet teri super lapide, nec aliter, prout fit de sinobrio et aliis coloribus, quia suffisit de prima suprascripta tritione facta, et etiam quia azurii color fortiter pejaretur et vastaretur, sed debet sic ut est destempari cum aqua gomata, seu cum clara ovi, vel cum cola liquefacta, aut cum oleo seminum lini, prout volet operari, et pertinebit operi fiendo; postea si voluerit lavari de alio azurrio, accipiatur totidem de tormentina, et pice, et cera, ut antea est dictum, et fiat alter pastillus, et fiat ut prius, et tociens quociens fieri voluerit, semper refaciendo novos pastillos, secundum quantitatem que expedit volenti facere et purgare azurrium. Set credo quod, pro

at first is sufficient for it, and also because the colour of the azure would very likely be spoilt or deteriorated, but it should be tempered just as it is with gum-water, or with white of egg, or melted glue, or with linseed oil, according to the choice of the artist and the nature of the work which is to be done. Afterwards if any more azure is to be washed, the same quantities of turpentine, pitch, and wax as were mentioned before must be taken and another pastille must be made as before, and the same method adopted; and this may be done as often as is wished, always making up new pastilles, according to the quantity convenient to the person who wishes to wash or refine the azure.

But I think, that in order to diminish the expense, the former pastille might be cleansed from all the impurities which it has contracted in the operation for which it was used, if it is put over the fire to boil and liquefy in clear water, because the pastille, being melted by the heat of the boiling water, would liquefy and float upon it. It should then be stirred with a stick or a wooden spoon, beating it up violently and quickly in the water with the stick, so that the pastille may be well mixed with the water and that the impurities of it may be dissolved by the water, and leave the pastille and enter into the water, and that when the stirring has ceased the melted pastille may separate and float upon the top of the boiling water, entirely cleansed from all earthy and other impurities, which by their weight will sink to the bottom. If it is afterwards taken off the fire and allowed to cool, the pastille being allowed to remain as it is in the said water, when the water is cold and the pastille has become hard, it can be taken out of the water, and the water with the impurities can be thrown away; and having been thus renewed, it may be used again for the same purpose as before, and thus it would be useless to incur any expense in making fresh pastilles; but the labour of washing the azure might be repeated as often as convenient, until the whole of the washing necessary for the quantity of the azure has been completed.

faciendo minorem expensam, posset primus pastillus purgari ab omni sorde in ipso inserta, pro operatione de ipso facta, si poneretur ad ignem, ad bulliendum in aqua clara, et liquide faciendum; quia cum ex caliditate bullientis aque esset fusus et liquidus, supernataret ipse pastillus in ipsa aqua bullienti; et, si agitaretur cum baculo vel spatula ligni, cum veloci strepitu agitando cum ipso baculo usque ad aquam, ita quod im-misceretur pastillus cum aqua, turpedo ipsius dilueretur, et exiret ab ipso, et intraret in aquam; et, cum cessaretur a dicta agitacione, adunaretur ipse pastillus liquefactus, supernatatando in superficie dicte aque bullientis, totus purgatus ab omni sorde terrestri, et a quacumque alia que, ut ponderosa, ad fondum descendasset; et postea, si levaretur ab igne, et permitteretur infrigidari sic, ipso pastillo stante in dicta aqua, cum frigidatus esset et durus, posset levari ab aqua, et abici aqua cum sorde, et de ipso iterato refici opus primo de ipso factum, et sic non expediret fieri expensa, pro aliis pastillis novis fiendis, set, quociens expediret, posset opus predictum lavacionis azurii eodem dicto modo reiterari et refici, usque ad totalem expedicionem lavende necessarie quantitatis azurrii.

OF THE MS. OF PETRUS DE S. AUDEMAR.

PRELIMINARY OBSERVATIONS.

THIS MS. affords internal proof that Petrus de S. Audemar (Pierre de St. Omer ?) was a native of or a resident in the northern part of France. Many passages in the MS. prove that it is of French origin; among these I may mention that in which is described the Rothomagensian green, which derived its name from Rothomagus, the Latin name for Rouen on the Seine. Madder also, which is called in French Garance, is mentioned under the term Warancia, and in No. 201 a recipe is given for making a green colour after the Norman manner. There are indications also of some of the recipes being derived from English or Anglo-Saxon sources, and thence communicated to their fellow-subjects in Normandy. In No. 162 the English name for Folium is mentioned, and in Nos. 199 and 201 two other English plants are named. These last recipes are to be found in the Mappæ Clavicula, but without the addition, in No. 201, of the words "according to the Normans." Several other recipes belonging to this MS. are also in the Clavicula; some are found in the 1st book of Theophilus, and some in the Sloane MS., No. 1754.

The date of the MS. is doubtful. Mr. Eastlake (Materials for a History of Painting in Oil, p. 45) says

it cannot be placed later than the end of the thirteenth or beginning of the fourteenth century. The fact of some of the recipes being in the Clavicula, which is supposed to be of the twelfth century, affords no evidence of the age of the MS., because some of them are comprised in the body of the work, but the greater part are to be found in the very beginning, even before the table of contents, and these seem to have been an addition to the original work. It is by no means improbable that these recipes were selected in both cases from some well-known originals as yet undiscovered.

The MS. contains the usual recipes for colours, for ink, and for gilding. Among the colours we find *greens* prepared in different ways from copper and vegetables; *white* from lead, *black* from charcoal, *blue* from silver, from copper, and from flowers. Ultramarine does not appear to have been known to our author. It seems from the description of the mode of purifying the blue pigment in No. 168, that it was a natural blue ore of copper, the Azzurro della Magna of Cennini (chap. lx.), which was extensively used both before and after the introduction of ultramarine, and which was produced in great abundance in the mines of Chessy, near Lyons. This mine was worked for a long period, and continued to produce great quantities of the blue ores of copper. It is now, however, closed. In the year 1845 I saw many specimens of these ores exposed for sale at Lyons.

The *red* pigments consisted of artificial vermilion, red lead, which the author calls "minium" and "sandaraca," and lake made from the gum of the ivy. It

will be observed that the latter is also called "Sinopis de Mellana."

The only yellow pigment is saffron, but the principal use of this colour appears to have been in colouring varnishes, the yellow in old pictures being more frequently represented by gold.

Like Cennini, Peter de S. Audemar teaches what vehicles should be used with each colour, and from these instructions we learn that the colours were applied on walls in secco, tempered with egg or gum; in books, that is, miniatures with gum or egg; and on wood with oil—thus affording certain proof of the use of oil in painting at this period in France.

That varnish was used, is incidentally mentioned in the recipe for making auripetrum, which was a varnish to which a golden colour was imparted by saffron, and which, when spread over tinfoil, was employed to imitate gold. A similar recipe is given in Eraclius, and another will be found in the Lucca MS., which has been copied into the Clavicula, a proof of the extent to which it was used. A gold colour was also given to tin by applying over it several coats of gall (see No. 203), and also by applying a solution of aloes, No. 206. Other varnishes are described in Nos. 207, 208, and 209; and it seems these also must have been highly coloured, because they were to be used like the auripetrum, for colouring tin to imitate gold, the price of which placed it beyond the reach of all but the rich. As to the materials of the varnishes, one was composed of linseed oil, resin, and *vernix*, that is, sandarac; another of linseed oil boiled with the inner bark of

the black plum, *glassa*, alum, and dragon's blood; and the third of the same linseed oil previously boiled with the inner bark of the black plum, resin, and *frankincense*. We must therefore suppose that three different ingredients were used for varnishes, for it is as reasonable to conclude from the text that they were *all* synonymous, as that *vernix* and *glassa* were the same in this instance, for it can scarcely be supposed that Peter de S. Audemar, who must have been in the habit of making these varnishes, should have used a different term, if any two had been synonymous.

It will also be observed, that there is no allusion in this MS. to the application of varnish upon colours or pictures, or to any other preparation of oil, except boiling it with the inner bark of the black plum (the object of which, if we may believe the Table of Synonymes, was to give the oil a yellow colour) before it was mixed with the resins; at the same time there is nothing to show that this boiled oil was not used in painting. The fact of "liquid varnish" being mentioned in the recipe for Auripetrum, No. 202, is sufficient proof that it was in use at this period, and that the drying effect produced on oils by boiling was known, because sandarac is not soluble in raw oils, and distilled oils were not used at this period. The recipes Nos. 208 and 209 much resemble those in the Paris MS. of Eraclius, No. 274.

HERE BEGINNETH THE

BOOK OF MASTER PETER OF ST. AUDEMAR ON MAKING COLOURS,

AND FIRST THE

INTRODUCTION.

By the assistance of God, of whom are all things that are good, I will explain to you (at whose request, as you know, I undertook this work) how to make colours for painters and illuminators of books, and the vehicles for them, and other things appertaining thereto, as faithfully as I can in the following chapters.

150. *The way to make a green colour with salt.*—First hear how to make a green colour with salt:—Stir some salt together in a jar or in a ladle, and heat it, stirring it frequently until it loses its former colour and becomes dusky—*i.e.* darkish. Then pound it, and, if necessary, pass it through a sieve, shaking it with your hand, in the same way that boys are accustomed to shake dust in a bottle ; sift it into a jar, or any other vase which will hold it, in order that, if by chance any hairs or other impurities be mixed with it, they may be separated ; as otherwise, if it continue white, or if any impurities remain in it, the colour will be dirty. Afterwards crush it well, dry as it is, upon a flat slab, either of marble or wood, with a smooth wooden block made for this purpose, or with a stone. Then temper some soap with wine or vinegar. Vinegar is made as follows.

151. *How to make vinegar.*—Take good wine, or wine as sour as you can get it, and put it into a jar or any other vase,

INCIPIT LIBER

MAGISTRI PETRI DE SANCTO AUDEMARO DE COLORIBUS FACIENDIS,

ET PRIMO

PROHEMIUM.

DEO opitulante, cujus sunt omnia que bona sunt, tibi, sicut novisti, cujus rogatu hoc opus sum aggressus, de coloribus pictorum et illuminatorum librorum faciendis, de temperamentis que eorum, et de aliis hiis convenientibus, quam fidelius potere in sequentibus explicabo.

---

150. *De modo faciendi viridem colorem de sale.*—Primo quo modo ex sale fiat intellige; salem igitur commiscens in olla seu patella torribis, sæpius movendo, usque quo primum colorem amittat, et fuscus fit, id est subniger. Deinde pulvemorizabis, et, si opus fuerit, induces cum stamino, et manu movendo, sicut pueri pulverem in catrasia positum agitare solent, et transire facies in ollam, vel in aliud quodcumque vas, illud recipiens ut si forte pili, vel aliæ sordes, ei commixtæ fuerint, seque ferentur alioquin, si albus remanserit, aut aliquod turpe in ipso remanserit, turpis color erit. Postea super tabulam æqualis superficiei, vel marmoream, vel ligneam, bene subtiliter ita siccum conteres cum ligno ad hoc parato equali, vel cum lapide. Deinde savonem cum vino vel aceto distemperabis. Acetum vero sic fit.

151. *Quomodo fit acetum.*—Sume vinum optimum, vel quantum acrius habere potes, et in ollam positum, seu vase alio,

and let it stand for 5 or 8 days, or for as many days as you like, in a vase covered with a plank or a stone, and not entirely closed, in order that it may feel the changes of the air, which cause it to turn sour; and let it acidify by exposing it to the sun, or suspending it over the fire. You can then put it by, and preserve it as long as you like.

If you have no soap, never mind; yet, nevertheless, wet plates of copper or basins,[1] cut into pieces or strips, all over with pure wine, without water, or else with the vinegar. Afterwards spread salt well and evenly over the metal, so that the copper may be entirely covered, but very thinly and evenly, because, if it be covered too thick, the colour will not be good. You must have a vase prepared for the purpose, either of earth or of wood, in the bottom of which you must pour a little wine or beer, or stale urine, which is better than fresh, and place the copper, salted as before directed, inside the vase. But, in order that it may not slip into the wine or urine, let it be supported by putting a piece of wood over the jar, to which the said slips or curved pieces (if formed by cutting up basins or cups) must be suspended side by side, so as not to touch one another. Then stop up the mouth of the jar, lest any dung should fall into it, and put plenty of horse-dung all round it, and under it and over it, and leave it in that manner to heat in the dung for 8 or 9 days, and you will then find your salt turned green, and of an excellent colour. The hotter the dung is, the sooner it will be done. You may, if you like, wait for 17 or 18 days before you uncover it and remove the colour. And in winter and summer, according as you find the heat of the dung greater or less, you will so time your work; and also according to whether the plates are made of copper or brass, as aforesaid, knowing that if they are of copper the work will be done—*i.e.* the colour will be made sooner; but if they are made of brass it will be longer before it is made. Heat accelerates the formation of the colour, cool weather retards it, and

[1] When the word "basin" is used alone, a vessel of copper or brass should be understood.

quinque, vel octo, vel quot volueris diebus, vase cooperto asce vel lapide, et non obturato, ut aeris mutaciones sentiat, quæ acuere facit, et ad solem, vel super ignem, suspensum, acui permitte, et sic quantum diu volueris repositum servare poteris.

Si autem savonem non habueris, non sit tibi cure, nihilominus tamen ex vino puro absque aqua, si vel ex dicto aceto, laminas cupreas ex omni parte humectabis, vel bacinos decisos per pecias seu laminas. Et postea ex ipso sale asperge bene et equaliter per totum, ita ut cuprum totum coopertum sit, tamen tenuissime et equaliter, quia si spissum fuerit non habebit optimum colorem. Unum vero vas habebis ad hoc paratum, vel ligneum, vel fictile, in cujus fundo pones parum vini, vel cervisiæ, aut aceti, vel urinam, nihilominus vetustam, quæ melior ad hoc probatur, et desuper in ipso vase pones cuprum, sicut jam dixi, salitum. Sed ne labatur in vino vel urina, sustineatur ligno superposito, cui suspendantur dictæ laminæ in aere, sive autem recte sint laminæ, seu curvæ, ut de de bacinis, vel patellis incisis, sint juxta se alia post aliam, non se tangente. Postea os ipsius olle obtures, ne fimus introcadat, et fimum equinum habundanter, et sub vase, et in circuita, et superpones, et sic isto modo, in dicto fimo califactum, octava vel nona die salem viridem recipies, et optimum. Et quanto fervencius callescet fimus, tanto fiat citius. Et tum nihilominus, si volueris, usque ad xvii. vel xviii. dies expectabis, antequam discoperias vas, et recipias colorem. Et in estate, et in hyeme, sicut senseris calorem stercoris vel fimi majorem vel minorem, ita tuum laborem moderabis; et tam de æneis, quam cupreis tabulis, sicut dixi, sciens que si cupreæ fuerint, citius fiet opus—i. e. colorabitur—si vere æneæ, tardius. Calor ejus accelerat colorem, sed tepiditas tardat; frigiditas vero nil agit; et notandum est, quod si dictum vas cooperieris in fimo existenti in stabulo equi, in alio secreto et calido loco, melius valet, et opus acceleratur, quia interius calefit. Hoc idem agere potes in cumulo vinciarum, ad pressorium vini. Hunc autem colo-

cold stops it altogether: it must also be remarked, that if the vase is covered with dung in a horse-stable, or in some other warm and close space, it is better, and the work will progress more rapidly, because it is better warmed. The same thing can be done in the heaps of grape-skins by the wine-presses. You must then scrape and shave off the colour with a knife, or any other instrument, from the aforesaid plates, and if you find that any white salt has remained mixed with the green colour, you need not be vexed at it, but just pick it out with a knife or with your hand; and you must afterwards wash these tablets with water, preserving the water, if necessary. Then wash, scour, and clean them a second time, with wood-ashes, rubbing them down with a linen cloth before you put fresh salt upon them, lest, if any of the old remained upon it, it should be a hindrance. You must allow the water of the first washing, which was done without the ashes, to remain quiet, so that you may collect the colour which sinks to the bottom, throwing away the supernatant water. This colour may be distempered and mixed with water, or still better, with vinegar, and also with linseed-oil, or even with white of egg.

152. *How to make and temper white and green.*—White and green colours, without salt, are made and tempered as follows: Pour very strong vinegar into a vase, and place twigs of trees across it inside the vase, and then place strips of lead, and other strips of copper or brass, suspended in the air by means of the twigs, so as not to touch the vinegar or each other. Then close the vase very carefully, and lute it with clay or cement, or wax, so that there may not be the least hole through which the vinegar may exhale. Then cover it with horse-dung, and, after 30 days, on account of the acidity of the vinegar or the wine—for the wine, on account of the heat of the dung, will become vinegar—on account, I say, of the acidity of the wine or vinegar, the copper or brass will be found to be turned green, and the lead white. Take the white, dry it, and grind it, and temper it with wine, and use it for painting on parchment, and mix it with oil for painting on wood and on walls. In the same manner

rem postea cum cultello, vel alio instrumento, a laminis predictis extirpere et radere debes, et si aliquantulum de albo sale cum viridi remansisse invenies, non sit tibi curæ, sed caute cum cultello vel manu separa, et projice. Viridem autem reservandum excipe, et postea ipsas tabulas debes primo cum aqua lavare, si opus fuerit, servando aquam. Deinde secundo etiam cum cinere, et panno lineo fricando, lavabis, detergas, et nitidas, antequam super ipsas alterum salem ponas, ne si quid ex veteri remansit, impedimento fiat. Cujus lavationis primæ aquam, quæ absque cinere erit, quiescere dimitte, ut colorem, qui in fundo remanet, colligas, projiciendo aquam. Hic color cum aqua, vel melius cum aceto, et etiam cum oleo lini, distemperatur, et mollitur, nec non et cum vitello ovi.

152. *De albo et viridi colore quomodo fiunt et distemperantur.* —Albus autem et viridis color, absque sale, hoc modo fit et distemperatur. In vase aceto acerrimo imposito, et desuper virgulas ligneas, intra vas, et sic tabulas plumbeas, et alias æneas, vel cupreas, pones virgulis suspensas in aere, ne tangant acetum, nec se invicem. Deinde vas diligentissime claudes, liniesque de argilla, vel cemento, vel cera, ne aliquod spiraculum remaneat, per quod exalatio fiat. Deinde co-operiatur in fimo equino calido; post dies autem xxx. vas aperiatur, et ex fortitudine aceti vel vini, quod vinum excalore fimi devenerit acetum, et ex fortitudine ipsius vini vel aceti, cuprum vel æs virideum, plumbum vero album invenientur. Sumptum autem et arefactum album, teratur, et temperetur cum vino, et pingetur in pergamenis, et cum oleo in lignis et in materiis. Similiter virideum cum oleo teres, et distemperabis, et operaberis in lignis, sed in materia cum vino, vel, si mavis, cum oleo. In

grind and temper the green with oil, and use it for painting on wood; but on walls with wine, or, if you prefer it, with oil. On parchment, however, you must not grind it with oil, but you must temper it with very clear and good wine, or with vinegar.

153. *Of a green water, or colour, for writing.*—But if you wish to write letters, put the green powder of brass in wine or vinegar as aforesaid, and then stir it round a little with your finger only, and immediately the whole of the wine or vinegar will be green. If the wine, before it has cleared itself from the dregs of the said green powder, is very green, you may know that it has enough of the powder of brass. If it seems of a dirty colour, appearing contaminated by the admixture of yellow impurities, you must know that this is because a sufficient quantity of the green powder has not been added to it: you must therefore add a little more, and stir it again with your finger, and again let it rest; and if it is not yet of a beautiful colour, add more of the powder, and stir it again with your finger, and, if necessary, do this a third time. But if you wish it to be very beautiful, add a little saffron; and when it has settled so that the impurities have sunk to the bottom, pour off the clear green liquid which stands uppermost in the vase, and you will thus separate it from the impurities and gross substance of the saffron that was put into it. If you wish to write with it immediately, you cannot do so unless you first let it boil over the fire to make it thicker; or you may let it stand in the shade, or in the mild breeze of the evening or morning; but it must be done when the wind blows gently, and must not be put in the sun.

154. *To make minium out of the before-mentioned white colour.*—The white colour which we mentioned before, is called, I believe, by the armourers ceruse, and you may convert it into minium by putting it into a jar and torrefying it over the fire for two days and two nights, stirring it frequently in the vase or jar with any instrument; and this is the way to make minium. Take care not to let any flame get inside the jar, but make the fire of charcoal only without flame; you must heap the charcoal

perchamenis vero non teres cum oleo, sed in vino clarissimo et bono, seu aceto, temperare debes.

153. *De aqua vel viridi colore ad scribendum.*—Si vero litteras scribere volueris, pone viridem pulverem æris in vino vel aceto, ut dictum est, et sic digito tantum fricabis, et statim totum vinum vel acetum virideum erit; quod si valde virideum fuerit illud vinum, cum necdum a fece sua dicte pulveris viridea sit purgatum, scias quod sufficienter habet depulvere eris superscripto. Si vero turpem colorem videatur habere, et quasi crocei, turpidis commixtione corruptum, scias esse hoc habere parum pulveris ipsius viridis. Et ideo aliquantulum adde, et digito iterum commisce, et postea paululum quiescere sines, et si non ad huc pulchrum colorem habet, iterum adde de pulvere, et iterum digito fricabis, et postea adhuc sines quiescere, et, si necesse fuerit, fac similiter tercio. Et si vis quod miræ pulcritudinis fiat, adde aliquantulum de croco et cum quieverit, ita quod feces ad fundum decensa sint, mitte clarissimum virideum desuper stantem in vasculo, et sic ipsum separabis a fecibus, et a substancia grossa crossi imposite; et si ex ipso statim scribere volueris, non poteris, nisi prius ad ignem ipsum fervere permiseris, ut spissior fiat, vel in umbra solis, vel mane, vel vespere, ad auram dulcem; quando sed ventus suaviter flat ponendus est, non autem in sole.

154. *Di minio faciendo de albo colore ante dicto.*—Album autem colorem de quo supra diximus, scutarii, sicut puto, cerusam vocant, quem in minium vertes, si in olla posueris duobus diebus noctibus que, eandem sæpe movendo, in vase, seu olla, ipsa cum aliquo instrumento ad ignem torrueris, et sic minium facies. Cave autem ne in olla flamma nullo modo tangat, sed tantum carbones, verum absque flamma; de quibus fac congeriem albam, usque ad medietatem ollæ, et eam ore aperto in

round the jar, so as to reach half-way up the jar, which must be put in the middle. The charcoal should be large, so that the air may pass through the spaces of it, and keep up the heat; it should not be small, for it would then be useless. When it begins to get hot, stir the colour which is inside it with a spoon, or with a strip of iron or brass, or a stick: so that the hot colour, which is next the side of the vase, may be mixed with the tepid part in the middle; for this stirring is the principal cause of the perfect preparation of all which is thus torrefied; and this stirring must be repeated four or five times in the space of every two or three hours. This process must be continued, as I said before, for two days and two nights following: not sleeping all the time, unless you have another person to supply your place and to continue stirring it, as well as to take care of the fire, and to manage the operation, otherwise your labour will be in vain. When the large charcoal is all consumed, take the jar off the fire with a blacksmith's pincers, or a twisted stick, or any other instrument, and throw away the small coal and ashes, and put fresh charcoal. We shall mention this colour frequently hereafter.

155. *How to make the green from brass which is called Greek or common green.*[1]—If you wish to make the copper-green which is called Greek, take a new jar, or any other concave vase, and put into it the strongest or most acid vinegar, so as not to fill it, and put strips of very clean copper or brass over the vinegar, so that they may not touch the vinegar or each other, being suspended to a stick placed across the vase. Then cover the vase and seal it, and put it into a warm place, or in dung, or under ground, and leave it so for six months, and then open the vase and scrape and shake out what you find in it, and on the strips of metal, into a clean vase, and put it in the sun to dry.

156. *To make Rothomagensian green.*[2]—If you wish to make Rothomagensian green, take strips of very pure copper or brass,

---

[1] This recipe and the next are in the Clavicula.

[2] Rothomagus, Rouen on the Seine. This recipe is in the Clavicula, and the Sloane MS., No. 1754.

medio compone, carbones autem sint magni, et per rimas eorum, ventus entret, et calorem exerceat; non minuti vero, quod non perficerent. Cum autem torreri cœperit, colorem, qui intus est, cum cocleari, vel lamula ferrea, vel ærea, vel lignea, commove, ut qui circa testam seu ollam calet, illi qui in medio loco tepet, misceatur. Nam commotio hæc est principalis causa omnibus que coquuntur, ad perfectionem decoctionis ipsorum; hoc autem per duarum vel trium horarum spatium, quater vel quinquies. Duobus enim diebus ac noctibus continuis est agendum, sicut dixi, non dormiendo nisi alter accedat, qui hoc ipsum procuret, et commociones ipsas, et ignis curam, et manutenaciones agat; alioquin frustra laborabis. Cum autem carbones grossi consumpti fuerint, vel forcisibus ferieris, vel virga conterata, vel alio quodum instrumento, ollam a foco extrahe, et minutos carbones et cineres abjicies, et alios adhibe. De hoc eodem colore aliquanti spei in sequentibus loquimur.

155. *Quomodo fit viride eris quod Grecum dicitur seu commune.*—Si vis facere viride eris quod Grecum dicitur, accipe ollam novam, aut aliquod aliud vas concavum, et mitte in eo acetum fortissimum seu acerrimum, ita quod vas non sit plenum, et laminas cupri mundissime, vel æris, pones supra acetum, ita ut non tangant acetum, aut se invicem, suspendendo eas ad aliquod lignum, in vase extranverso positum, et ita cooperi vas, et sigilla. Et sic pone illud in calido loco, aut in fimo, aut in terra, et ita dimitte usque ad sex menses, et tunc aperies illud vas, et quod in eo et circa dictas laminas inveneris, rade, et excute in vase mundo, et mitte ad solem siccare.

156. *De viride Rothomagense faciendo.*—Si vis viridem Rothomagensem facere, accipe laminas purissimi cupri, vel

smear them over with good soap, and put them into a clean vase made for this purpose, and pour into it some pure vinegar; then suspend the strips of copper or brass in the vase to a stick stretched across it, which should be placed as high up as possible, so that the strips may not touch each other or the vinegar. Then cover up the vase and seal it, and put it into a warm place, such as horse-dung, or the refuse of the wine-press; or, in winter, cover up and bury the vase in a deep hole under ground, and thus leave it for one month; then open it, and shake and scrape off what you find upon the strips, putting it in a bason or an earthen vase; place it in the sun to dry, and preserve it for use.

157. *Also, how to make verdigris for writing.*—Whoever wishes to make a green colour for writing, let him pour into a copper or brass vessel equal quantities by weight of honey well mixed with vinegar, and then bury the vessel in horse-dung, in the hottest part of the heap. After 12 days are passed, he may take the colour out of the vase, scraping it out; then dry it in the sun, and keep it for use.

158. *Also, how to make green without brass.*—If you wish to make earth-green, take, in the middle of May, a bunch of the flowers of the herb columbine; pound them well in a mortar, and strain the juice through a linen cloth. Then put this juice into a vase, and place it in the sun until it is hard. This must be tempered, first with water, and then with egg, on wood or on walls; but on parchment it must be used like ceruse.

159. *Also to make green.*—If you wish to make a green colour, take urine, or vinegar, and put it into a vase, and make a plate of brass, and place it over the liquid in the said vase so as not to touch the urine, and afterwards set the vase in a warm place and cover it up for 9 days, then take it out and collect the colour which is produced. This is tempered first with water, and afterwards with egg on wood or on walls. When you put verdigris upon paper, put cherry juice [or cervisia?] in it. If it is not of a fine green, mix *viride terrenum.* If it is too green, so as to be too dark, mix pure orpiment with it.

160. *Also verdigris is thus made.*—Take vinegar and put it

æris, et liniis ipsas in circuitu de optimo savone, et mitte ipsas in vase mundo ac hoc facto, et pone in ipso de puro aceto, et superpone in ipso vase dictas laminas cupreas vel æreas, suspensas ad virgulam in vase ex transverso, altius quam poteris, sitam ita ut lamine non se invicem, nec acetum tangant. Postea cooperies vas, et sigilla, et in calido loco, ut in fimo equino, aut in vinaciis pressorii vinarii, aut in hyeme sub terra, in profundo loco cooperias, et sepelias, dictum vas. Et sic dimittas uno mense, et postea aperies, et quod inveneris in circuitu laminarum excuties et rades, et mittendo in bacino vel vase terreo, et pones ad solem siccare, et usui reserva.

157. *Item de viridi eris, quo modo fit pro scribendo.*—Colorem viridem qui vult ad suum usum scribendi facere mel cum aceto valde mixtum equo pondere infundat ac deinde in sterquilinio equorum ubi plus calet in vase cuprea vel æreo cooperto positum sepeliat. Postea bis senis diebus transactis illud recipiet de vase ipsum colorem radendo et ad solum siccet et reservet pro usu.

158. *Item de fiendo viridi aliter quam eris.*—Si vis facere terreum viride in medio maio accipe massam florum herbæ quæ vocatur aquileia et pila in mortario optime et cola succum per pannum lineum. Deinde pone ipsum succum in vase et pone ad solem siccare usque quo durum sit. Hoc distemperatur primum cum aqua, deinde cum ovo ad lignum vel murum, in carta pone sicut cerosium.

159. *Item de viridi faciendo.*—Si vis facere colorem viridem, accipe mictum hominis, *i. e.* urinam, vel acetum et mitte in vas, et fac laminam eream, et pone desuper in dicto vase ita ut mictum non tangat et pone postea vas in calido loco et cooperi per novem dies postea trahe foris et colorem exortum execute. Hoc distemperatur primum cum aqua post cum ovo ad lignum vel murum. In cartam dum ponit viride eris pone succum cerosium in ipso si non bene est viridis misce terrenum viridem. Si nimium est viride ita ut nigrescat misce auripigmentum purum.

160. *Item eris viride sic fit.*—Accipe acetum et pone in vaso

into a brass or copper vase, and place it on the coals so as to boil strongly, skim it well, and grind it with a little alum upon a marble slab. Afterwards put it in a brass vase, and then leave it to settle for a day or two. Then pour off the supernatant liquor which floats over the dregs at the bottom into another vase, separating it from the before-mentioned impurities, and put it away and keep it for use. Then pour more vinegar into the aforesaid sediment, and mix it well. Leave it so for four days, so that everything may settle, and it will then be good green. But if it is too clear or liquid, put it upon lighted charcoal without flame, so that it may boil a little and thicken, and then put it into the vase, and keep it for use.

161. *How to make a beautiful green.*—Mix Spanish green with saffron, and distemper them both together, and the colour will be of wonderful beauty.

162. *Of folium, how it is distempered.*—The purple colour called *folium* by the laity, by whom (or rather by the English, in whose country it is prepared, and who call it *worina*) it is used in dyeing wool, is not always tempered in the same manner; for some persons distemper it with urine, or with ley made from the ashes of ash-trees, and particularly on walls; while others, on parchment, distemper it with cheese-glue, made as follows.

163. *How glue is made from cheese.*—Fresh cheese is first to be washed in hot water, until the milk is washed out, and then ground with lime and water, in a little mortar or on a marble slab; and a little before this is done—namely, while the cheese is being ground—the colour is soaked in water again. Then, when the cement is prepared, so as to be as white, clear, and shining as milk, it is put into a small vase, and the colour is scraped into it with a knife, and care must be taken not to let the air have access to the mixture; and when the colour is seen to be good, it may be used for writing at pleasure.

164. *Of folium stamipiensi, a purple colour, how it is tempered or made.*—Take the wood of the tree which is called elm and burn it in the fire, and collect such a quantity of that flowery ash which appears upon the coals as you think will be

æreo vel cupreo et super carbones pone ut fortiter bulliat et spuma illud optime et ex eo cum alumine modico super marmorem tere viridem. Postea in vase æreo mitte et sic uno die vel duobus dimitte ut resideat. Illud autem quod super feces in fundo descensas nataverit in aliud vas a dictis fecibus separando, mitte et reserva deinde acetum iterum mitte in fecibus superscriptis, et misce bene. Postea dimitte sic per quatuor dies ut quicquid quiescat et tunc forte bonum viride erit. Si vero nimium clarum seu liquidem fuerit pone super carbones ignitos absque flammis ut modicum bulliat et spissum fiet tunc mitte in prædicto vase ad servandum usui.

161. *Quomodo pulchrum fiat viride.*—Viridi Hispanico admisce crocum et distempera simul et miræ pulchritudinis erit.

162. *De folio quomodo distemperatur.*—Purpureus color quem folium vocant laici qui lanam inde tingunt vel potius Anglici in quorum terra conficitur worina vocant non uno semper modo distemperatur. Nam aliqui cum urina vel lexivia de cinere fraxini facta ut in parietibus precipue alii in pergamenis cum visco de caseo ita facto.

163. *Quomodo viscum de caseo fiat.*—Primum recentum caseum in aqua calida lavant, donec lac eliciatur et sic illum in mortariolo vel super marmorem terunt cum calce et aqua et paulo antequam hoc agant dum scilicet teritur caseus, iterum ipsum colorem in aqua temperare permittunt. Deinde cum viscum preparatum habent, sic album et nitidum et clarum velut lac. Inducunt in vasculo et super incidunt cultello ipsum colorem jam temperatum in aqua et tunc cavent ne ventus tangat ipsam confectionem et si cum viderit colorem esse bonum scribunt inde prout ipsis placuerit.

164. *De folio Stamipiensi* (sic) *purpureo colore quomodo distemperatur seu fit.*—Sume tibi ligna arboris quæ ulmus vocatur et arde in ignem, illum vero florem cineris qui super carbones apparet tolles et in unum pones quantum tibi sufficere putas et in

sufficient for you, grind it in a mortar, and distemper it with urine so that it may be as thick as dough; make it into cakes as thick as you like, and put these cakes upon two trays or plates of iron, or baked bricks, in order that they may burn for a day and a half. Then take them out of the fire and put them into a mortar and pound them until they are reduced to powder. Then sift this powder through a sieve, or make it pass through a sifter. Again, while you are doing this, you must have a jar prepared full of urine, and let it boil over the fire three or four times; then remove it from the fire, and add to it of fresh urine one half or less, until it is tepid, and then stir them together. Afterwards take the colour, which is called folium, and put it into a vase, and wash it with this prepared urine, rubbing it between your hands, and hold it against one side of the jar and throw away the urine; then take the above-mentioned ashes and fill one ladle with them, and take another ladleful of folium, and lay one couch of ashes in that vase by sprinkling them, and then one of folium, and do so until the folium and the ashes are all mixed. Then again rub them between your hands, and so leave them for three days, well covered up by the fire, that they may keep warm. But the best colour will of itself, when it begins to get warm, be covered all over with a purple bloom. If you wish to dye anything, put the water into a vessel; but if you have nothing to dye, let the water and the folium cool, so that you may make it into small cakes, and you may keep it as long as you like, and put it into an oven.

165. *Of the different sorts of saffron.*—You must not take all kinds of saffron for painting or writing with, for you must know that that which grows in our country of Gaul, as well as throughout the whole of France, is not good; and although it has some resemblance to the good sort, yet it has not the exact colour, smell, or taste of the perfect sort; for there is a certain herb with whitish leaves and roots, the flowers of which we call *crocus*, but which the laity call *saffron*. When you see these flowers have a certain whiteness at the top of one side, you

mortariolo fortiter teres, cum urina distemperabis ita ut panis crudus spissum sit, facies que de ea tortellos quantum grossos volueris quos super duas dolatiles seu laminas ferreas vel lateres coctos pones ut ibi super carbones usque ad dimidium diem ardeant. Dein trahe ab igne item que in mortariolo pones et multum fortiter usquedum pulvis fiat. Pestabis; postea attenuabis per satacium vel per staminiam, transire facias. Iterum dum hoc facies, habebis ollam paratam plenam urina et cum tribus vel quatuor vicibus bullire permittes. Postea ab igne retrahes et cum ea de urina cruda, medietatem vel minus, usque dum tepida fuerit vel fiat similiter misces. Posthæc accipies illum colorem qui folium vocatur et in uno vase pones abluesque de illa mixta urina inter manus tuas fricando, attrahes que in unam partem et feces urinæ projicies foris. Tunc accipies illum suprascriptum cinerem et unam scutellam de eo implebis et de folio aliam facies que in illo vase de cinere pulverando unum lettum et unum desuper de folio sic que facies usque dum folium et cinis mixta sint. Iterumque inter manus tuas fricabis et sic dimittes usque tribus diebus bene coopertum juxta ignem ut calefiat. Ipse vero optimus color de se ipso emittet colorem purpureum super se cum cepit calescere. Si vero aliquid tingere volueris pones aquam in sartagine. Si vero tingere non habes dimittes aquam et folium sic refrigerari ita ut possis ex eo parvos tortellos facere et servare poteris quantum volueris et in forulo pone.

165. *De croco et de diversitatibus ejus.*—Omnem crocum ad pingendum assumere non oportet vel ad scribendum. Illum enim qui in hac nostra patria galliæ ut in toto Francia crescit bonum non esse non nescias. Et quamvis aliquam similitudinem boni habeat tamen vere colorem nec odorem nec saporem illius perfecte habet et enim quedam herba albo silis foliis et radicibus cujus flores nos crocum laici vero safran vocant. Quos flores cum videris gestare quandam candorem ex una parte in summittate scias quod non est bonus cum duos digitos saliva

may know that they are good. When you wet two of your fingers with saliva, and rub the saffron a little between your fingers, if your fingers immediately become yellow, you may know that the saffron comes from Italy or Spain, and is good; but in Sicily, as a certain Ysidius [Isidorus] says, the best is that which is called *coriscos;* and a great deal of excellent saffron comes from thence, very fragrant to the smell, and of a colour superior to gold. Some temper this with egg; others both grind and temper it with egg, or mix it with water, and strain it through a linen cloth, and then they paint with it. However, I do none of these things, but only put clear water into a very clean vase; I then sprinkle the saffron over it, and, after a little while, when I see the water well impregnated with it, I put it on the coals for a short time, leaving the saffron in it, and then, with a pencil or pen prepared for this purpose, I paint upon skins and other things, and upon box-wood, in order to colour it yellow, or to redden it, by mixing the saffron with wine, and then laying it on the box-wood. If you wish to make the wood shine, let the saffron dry, and then lay on some more with oil.

166. *That there are three kinds of folium, and of the way to temper the purple folium.*[1]—There are three kinds of folium; one purple, another red, and a third sapphire blue, which you must temper as follows. Take ashes, and sift them through a cloth, pour cold water over them, make them into cakes like loaves of bread, and put them into the fire until they are quite white hot. When they have been burnt for a long time, and have afterwards cooled, put part of them into an earthen vase, and pour urine over, stir them with a stick, and, when they have settled clear, pour the liquor on the red folium, and grind it a little on a stone, adding to it one-fourth part of quicklime, and when it is ground and sufficiently moistened, strain it through a cloth, and lay it with a pencil wherever you like, first thinly, and afterwards more thickly. And if you wish to

[1] This is a transcript of chap. xxxv. of the first book of Theophilus.

humectabis et florem inter eos paululum fricabis et statim crocos habueris inde digitos scias quod ex Italia vel Expania venit et bonus est. In Sicilia autem, ut Ysidius ait quidam, melior est qui coriscos dicitur, unde crocum plurimum et optimum venit. Spiramine flagrantius et colore pulchrius auro. Hunc cum ovo distemperant, alii etiam cum ovo terunt et distemperant vel cum aqua per lineum pannum transire faciunt et sic isti pingunt. Ego vero nichil horum facio sed tantum in mundissimo vasculo claram aquam mitto, Dein crocum desuper spargo et post modicum cum videro aquam totam inde confectam super carbones paululum simulque crocum permitto et deinde cum pincello vel pennula ad id parata in pellibus pingo et alibi et super buxum ut croceus fiat vel rubicundior ubi crocus cum vino distemperandus est et sic buxo superponendus est quod si volueris ut ipsum lignum luceat permitte prius crocum siccari. Postea cum oleo eum super illum pone.

166. *Quod folii tria sunt genera, et de modo distemperandi purpureum.*—Tria sunt folii genera; unum purpureum, aliud rubeum, turcium saphirum que sic temperabis. Tolle cineres et crebra eos per pannum; Perfondes eos aqua frigida fac inde tortulas ad similitudinem panis mittes que ea in igne donec omnino candescant. Postquam diutissime canduerint et postea friguerint mitte partem in vas fictile perfunde urina, move ligno, cum que residerent lucide perfunde rubeum folium et teres illud modice super lapidem addens ei quartam partem vivæ calcis, et cum tritum fuerit, et sufficienter perfusum cola per pannum et trahe cum pincello ubi volueris tenue deinde spissius et si placet in similitudinem palii in pagina facere purpureo folio eodem temperamento absque calce profuso pinge penna vel pincello.

represent a robe on the page [of a book], paint it with purple folium, moistened with the same vehicle, but without lime, with a pen or a hair pencil.

167. *Of azure; how and with what vehicles it is tempered.*—Of the etherial colour, or, to speak in common language, the azure or blue colour, I have nothing very certain to say, as some grind and temper it with goat's milk, others with woman's milk, and others with white of egg; and either of these is sufficiently good.

168. *How azure is prepared and purified.*—But I shall not conceal how I purify it when it comes to my hands. I first pour it into a bason, and put a little water along with it, and rub it with my finger until it is thoroughly moistened, and then I pour in more water and stir it well, and let it rest. When it has settled, I pour off the water, turbid from the impurities, into another vase, keeping the precious colour which remains at the bottom of the vase, for its nature is such that the finer and purer the colour is the heavier it is, and therefore the sooner it reaches the bottom; and the impurities, or the whitish or yellowish parts, which are lighter, float or remain above it in the water. And, if necessary, I repeat this process several times, pouring water out and in until it is purified; and when it is well purified and ground with water, after I have put it into a horn, I pour in very clear whipped white of egg, and paint upon the places in which I wish to paint anything; and I afterwards throw away the same white of egg within the space of one hour, for if it remains in it any longer it spoils the colour by depriving it of its fine appearance and beauty. And after I have thrown away the white of egg, I immediately fill the horn with cold water and stir up the colour, and wash it with water, throwing away the same water after an hour, while the colour settles and sinks to the bottom; for, as I said, if the egg, or the said water impregnated with the said egg by the washing of the colour were to remain any longer, the colour would be deteriorated. This colour is used on walls with egg and with water; but on wood it is ground with oil, like other colours.

167. *De azurio quomodo distemperatur et cum quibus liquoribus.*—De etherio colore, vel ut juxta vulgare loquar lazurio vel perso quid certius dicam non habeo quia alii cum lacte caprino alii cum lacte mulieris alii cum glarea ovi molunt ac distemperant et satis utrumque bonum est.

168. *Quo modo preparetur et purgetur azurium.*—Sed quo modo cum admanus meas venerit illum preparare non tacebo. In primis fundo id opus in bacino simulque cum eo, paululum aquæ mitto, et cum digito, tamdiu frico quousque totus madefactus sit, ac deinde habundancius aquam infundo et bene misceo et quiescere permitto. Postquam quieverit eamdem aquam sic turbatam ex emundicia in alio vase recipio reservaturque colorem preciosumqui in fundo remanet vasis, nam hujus modi naturæ est ut quanto pulchrior et purior est tanto ponderosior et ideo tanto ad fundum labatur ; et immundicea seu pars albescentis vel croceantis coloris qui nimis gravis est superius natet vel maneat et si necesse fuerit id ipsum sæpius repeto aquam sæpe infundendo et effundendo donec pergatus sit. Et jambene purgatum et cum aqua tritum postquam in cornu reposuero postea loca in quibus inde aliquid facere voluero glaream ovi multum clarum immitto et operor. Postea glaream eamdem prius unius hore spacium jecturus nam si diutius intus remanserit corrumpet colorem illi precipuam speciem et pulchritudinem auferendo. Et postquam glaream ejecero statim illud cornu aqua frigida repleo et misceo colorem et lavo cum aqua, eandem aquam post horam dum color ad fundum quescendo descendit rejecturus. Nam ut dixi si diutius remaneret ovum vel dicta aqua, de dicto ovo ex ipsa lavatione coloris infecta color corrumperetur. Hunc colorem cum aqua et cum ovo in materia ponet in ligno vero cum oleo ut tritos colores.

169. *How azure is made.*[1]—If you wish to make azure, take a new jar that has never been used, and put into it strips of very pure silver, as many as you like, and so cover it up, and seal it, and put the jar among the grape-skins, and keep it well for 14 days and then open the jar, and scrape into a very clean vase the efflorescence which you find on the silver, which will be a perfect azure, and of a blue colour, provided that the silver contains no alloy or mixture of any other metal, but only consists of the purest and finest silver. If it contains any brass, you will obtain a colour which is rather green, than blue or azure. If you afterwards want any more of it, do again as before directed.

170. *To make azure not so good* [*as the last*].[2]—If you wish to make another azure, take a jar of very pure copper, and put lime into it until it is half full, and then fill the jar with very strong vinegar, and so cover it up and seal it. Then place the jar under ground, if it is in winter, that it may be warm there, or among the grape-skins, or in hot horse-dung, or in any other hot place, and so leave it for one month. Afterwards, open the jar, and scrape off what you find upon it, and put it in the sun to dry. This azure is not so good as the last, but it is useful for wood or walls.

171. *Also of another way of making blue with the juice of blue flowers.*—If you wish to make a third kind of azure, take blue flowers, that is, of an azure colour, and grind them, and press out the juice, straining it through a cloth into a very clean vase. And you must first make the ground of your work, whether on wood or on parchment, with white lead, which is called ceruse, and put over it three or four, or five coats of this expressed blue juice or colour, and repeat this until you find the colour appears like azure, letting it dry each time you lay it on, before you apply a fresh coat.

---

[1] This recipe is in the Appendix to the MS. of Theophilus in the British Museum, and in the Mappæ Clavicula, p. 7.

[2] This recipe and the next are also in the Mappæ Clavicula, p. 7.

169.—*De azurio quo modo efficitur.*—Si vis facere azurrium optimum accipe ollam novam que nunquam in opus fuerit et mitte in eas laminas purissimi argenti quantas vis et sic cooperi eam et sigilla et mitte ipsam ollam in vindemia et serva bene usque ad quindecim dies et sic aperies illam ollam et illum florem qui erit in circuitu laminarum argentearum excucies in mundissimo vase. Quod perfectum azurium erit et celestini coloris dum tamen argentum laminarum mullum alligamentum vel mixturam alterius cujus que metalli in se continuerit preterquam purissimum ac finissimum argentum. Quid si in se aliquid eris continuerit viridatis potius quam celestis vel azurii colorem obtinebis et si postea amplius volueris habere, iterum fac ut superscriptum est.

170. *De azurio alio non tam bono faciendo.*—De alio azurio si vis facere, accipe ampullam purissimi cupri, et mitte in eam calcem usque ad medium, et sic imple ampulam fortissimo aceto et ita cooperi et sigilla. Et tunc mitte ipsam ampulam in profundo terræ si erit in hyeme ut ibi calidum sit aut in vindemia aut in fimo equimo calido, aut in alio calido loco, et ita dimitte usque ad unum mensem et postea aperies ampulam et ex ea rade quod in ipsa inveneris et mittes ad solem siccare. Illud azureum non est ita bonum sicut aliud, tamen valet ad lignum vel materiam.

171. *Item aliter modo fiendo azurio cum succo florum persarum.*—Tertium azurium si vis facere, accipe flores blauos id est celestini coloris et teres et exprime colando per telam in mundissimo vase et fac prius campum tui operis sit in ligno vel sit in pergameno, De albo plumbo quod cerusa dicitur et mitte desuper tries aut quatuor aut quinque lectos de ipso succo seu colore blauo expresso, et tantum ita fac usque quo videas ipsum colorem similem esse azurio permittendo qualibet vice quam posueris siccare antequam reponas.

172. *How to make a black colour in various manners.*—Every black colour which is used in painting on skins, we know to be atramentum, distempered in various manners, except that with which we stain the skin, which is commonly called *corduanum* (cordovan). But that black colour is made of oil and scales of iron, boiled together for a very long time, and it is laid on the skin, not with a pen or a brush, but with a very sharp piece of wood, namely boxwood. But on walls, or on wood, we take charcoal, made of leather, or of hay, or of wood of any kind, except oak, which, on account of its hardness, can scarcely ever be sufficiently ground. If you wish to lay black over other colours on parchment, you must not put incaustum, but know that you must take charcoal distempered with egg, and the same on walls either with water or with egg, and on wood with oil; and whoever takes the soot of rushes and oil, where they are burnt together over a lamp, and calcines it in a jar upon coals, and grinds it with water or with egg, or with oil, will find it a very excellent colour wherever he wants it.

173. *Also of another mode of making black.*—Take the bark of the wood which is called elm, and cut it into small pieces, and put it into a vessel to boil with water; and take the rust which is at the bottom of the water under a workman's grindstone, and mix it with the said bark, in order that they may boil over the fire together; and add to them atramentum distempered with the aforesaid water of the bark. Afterwards, if you wish to dye anything, put it in while the water boils, and so leave it from morning until the third hour of the day (*i.e.* from 6 to 9 A.M.), until it is diminished to a third of the quantity. And if what was put into it is not well dyed, put it in again, and add a little atramentum, in order that that which is put into the composition may be better dyed.

174. *To make vermilion.*[1]—If you wish to make very good vermilion, take a glass flask, and lute it outside. Then take one part by weight of quicksilver, and two parts of sulphur of a

---

[1] This recipe is also in the Clavicula.

172. *De nigro colore quomodo fit diversi mode.*—Omne atrum colorem unde pingitur in pellibus scimus attramentum esse variis modis distemperatum præter illum de quo tingimus illam pellem, quam vulgus corduanum vocat. Illud autem nigrum ex olio paleaque ferri diutissime simul coctis fit et in eadem pelle non cum penna nec cum pincello sed cum ligno acutissimo scilicet buxeo pingitur. In parietibus vero vel in lignis assumimus carbones scilicet de lignis cujus libet generis, vel de corio vel de feno factos præter querqueos que vix unquam pro eorum duritie suffienter teri possunt. Sed si in pergamenis supra ceteros colores ponere volueris nigrum non pones incaustum sed scias quod carbones cum ovo distemperatos assumes, in materiis similiter, vel cum aqua, vel cum ovo, et in lignis cum oleo. Fuligine quoque junci et olei ubi simul in lampade ardent qui ceperit si in testa super carbones torruerit et cum aqua vel cum ovo vel oleo triverit valde optimum colorem ubique voluerit comprobabit.

173. *Item, alio modo de nigro faciendo.*—Accipe corticem ligni quod elna vocatur et per particulas incides mittes que in sartaginem *i.e.* patellam cum aqua bullire. Accipies que ferruginem que est in fundo cum aqua subtus in ollam fabri. Et mitte cum dicto cortice ut simul ad ignem bulliat ponesque cum eis attramentum de illa supradicta aqua dicti corticis ligni distemperatum. Postea in volueris aliquid tingere mittes intus dum aqua bullierit et sic id dimittes a mane usque ad terciam. Et si bene tinctum non fuerit, quod intus positum fuerit, iterum intus reponatur adjiciatur que parumper de attramento ut melius tingatur id quod in compositione mittetur.

174. *De vermiculo faciendo.*—Si vis facere vermiculum optimum accipe ampulam vitream et lini de foris luto. Et sic accipe unum pondus argenti vivi et duo pondera sulphuris albi

white or yellow colour, and put them into the aforesaid flask, which you must afterwards place upon four stones, and make a very slow fire of charcoal piled round the flask, and cover up the mouth of the flask with a tile; and when you see a blue vapour come out of the mouth of the flask, cover it up; and if a yellow vapour comes out, cover it up also. But when there comes out a vapour nearly as red as vermilion, then take it away from the fire, and you will have excellent vermilion in the flask.

175. *Another way of making vermilion.*—Take a glass jar, and quicksilver and sulphur, and weigh them, so that two parts may be of sulphur, and the third of quicksilver, and fill the flask with them up to the neck. But first cover the flask with three coats of very good clay, then put in the aforesaid articles, so that the sulphur may be underneath, and the quicksilver above, and put red tile, well pounded, from the neck to the top of it, and place it upon three stones over a charcoal fire, and let it burn until a blue vapour comes off, and then it will suffice.

176. *How to make minium, otherwise called sandaraca.*—If I am not mistaken, minium, that is sandaraca, and white lead, that is ceruse, are of one nature. If you put ceruse into the fire it takes a new name, and colour, and strength; because, the more it is burnt the redder it is, and the less it is burnt the more it retains its former colour, that is, its whiteness or its paleness; and in laying it upon walls, it is ground with gum-water, but never with egg. It can, however, be laid upon parchment, distempered with egg; but on wood, with oil.

177. *How minium is mixed with vermilion.*—If any one wishes to illuminate a manuscript he must not do that with minium only, because, although the letters may be well formed yet they would not be beautiful, for they would be too pale; he must therefore mix minium with vermilion, that the colour may be brighter. But as I have certainly known some persons who are ignorant about this mixture, not knowing how much to put of one sort, or how much of the other, if they will give their

aut crocei coloris, et mitte in ampulam suprascriptam quam postea pones super quatuor petras et ignem lentissimum de carbonibus in circuitu ampullæ positis facias cooperto ore ampullæ tegula et quando videris fumum ex ore ampulæ exire blauum, cooperi; si vero fumus crocei coloris, iterum cooperi; quando autem exierit fumus rubeus quasi ut est vermiculum, sic tolle ab igne et habebis vermiculum optimum in ipsa ampula.

175. *Alio modo ad faciendum vermiculum.*—Accipe ampullam vitream et vivum argentum et sulphur, et libra ita ut duæ partes sint de sulphure et tertia de argento vivo, et intus pone ut veniat usque collum ampullæ et primitus lini ampulam de argilla optima tribus vicibus et intus pone supradictas partes, ita ut sulfuris pars subtus sit bene diminuta et argenti vivi pars supersit et rubeam tegulam bene diminutam a collo usque ad summum mitte et super tres lapides ampulam in igne de carbonibus et dimitte combuere donec ignis inde exeat glaucus et tunc satis est.

176. *De minio faciendo aliter sandaraco dicto.*—Nisi fallor minium id est sandaracum et album plumbum id est cerusa unius naturæ sunt, si in ignem mittas cerusam, nomen et colorem et fortitudinem accipit quia quanto plus ustum fuerit plus rubet, et quo minus ustum plus pristinum colorem retinet, id est alborem vel pallorem et ponendo ipsum in materiis teritur cum aqua gummata numquam vero cum ovo. In pergamenis vero poni potest cum ovo distemperatum, sed in lignis cum oleo.

177. *Quomodo misceatur minium cum vermiculo.*—Si quis codicem illuminare satagit non id de sole minio debet facere quia quamvis litteræ forent bene formate pulchre tamen non essent quia nimio pallore essent obfuscate, ideo minium cum vermiculo misceat ut pulchriores sint. Verum tamen quia aliquos de hac commixtione novi certe, nescientes quantum ex uno nec quantum ex altero mittere deberent si mihi assint animo de hoc intimabo, quod mihi notum est, ut teneant. Si ipsum

attention to me I will teach them all that is known to me, that they may remember it. If the vermilion is very good and new, I put two parts of it, and scarcely the third part of minium. But if the minium is dusky and very old, put a half or a third part of the vermilion, and make the remainder of minium; and you must know, that the older the vermilion is by nature, the darker and the less useful it is; and the darker it is, the less of it must be added to the minium. When you have ground this minium thus cautiously mixed with vermilion well in clear water, if you wish to write with it immediately, allow it to dry completely, and then distemper the same with stale white of egg, namely, three or four days old. And if you wish to write or paint with this minium, which will shine with a sort of varnishy brilliancy, you must mix but a little clear water, or nothing at all, with the above-mentioned white of egg, with which you distemper the minium; and then lay it sufficiently thickly on the parchment while you are writing, that is to say, you must paint the letter thick; and if, after this, it should happen that the work does not shine, you may know that this is to be imputed to the quality of the air, or the weather, if it be damp. And you must know this also, that if it is dried at the fire, it will undoubtedly shine; but it will turn black in the sun. The minium may be either fresh or have been prepared for some time.

178. *How minium is to be washed.*—But if, when you are illuminating any book, the minium is old, and of a dirty colour, you must wash it thus. Take water and wine, so that the third or the fourth part may be of wine, and put it into a horn with the minium, and mix it well, stirring it. Afterwards let it rest. When it has settled and is fallen to the bottom, throw out the water and the wine, and pour in a sufficient quantity of white of egg, and use it.

179. *Of sinopis.*—Sinopis, as I have heard, is a certain colour redder than vermilion, so that when the vermilion itself is very precious on account of its beauty, the heralds praising it call it sinopis, although the vermilion only resembles it on account of its redness.

vermiculum valde optimum et novum fuerit duas partes ex illo et vix tertiam partem ex minio. Si vero minium fuscum et vetussimum fuerit dimediam seu tertiam partem ex illo vermiculo mitte et reliquas de minio facito. Et sciendum est quod vermiculum natura quanto vetustior tanto nigrior et minus utilis et quanto nigrior est tanto minus de illo mittendum est in minio. Quod minium sic ex vermiculo caute mixtium postquam bene triveris cum aqua clara. Si statim ex inde scribere volueris permitte penitus prius exsiccare deinde cum vetusta glarea ovi trium scilicet aut quatuor dierum ipsum idem distempera. Et si tibi accidat scripturam vel picturam ex eodem minio facere velle quasi que verniciata nitore subluceat glarea suprascriptæ qua ipsum minium distemperas parum aquæ claræ vel nil omnino commisceas et exinde inter scribendum sufficienter pergameno suppone crassam scilicet litteram debes facere. Sane si post hoc opus ipsum non lucere contingerit noveris hoc imputandum qualitati vel auræ vel tempori si humidum sit. Hoc autem scire debes quod si ad ignem exsiccetur procul dubio venitescet. Sole vero fuscabitur minium potest esse vel noviter vel ex multo tempore paratum sit.

178. *Quomodo lavatur minium.*—Si autem cum aliquem librum illuminas minium vetus sit et turpis coloris. Debes ita lavari. Sume aquam et vinum, et ita ut tertia vel quarta pars sit vinum et mitte in cornu cum minio et commove bene miscendo. Postea permitte quiescere. Cum autem sedatum et ad fundum deductum erit eice aquam et vinum et mitte glaream quantum opus sit et operetur.

179. *De sinopide.*—Sinopis est quidam color magis rubeus ut didici quam vermiculum. Unde et ipsum vermiculum sit valde preciosum in pulchritudine fuerit quasi laudando scutarii sinopidem vocant cum tantum modo vermiculum in rubeo teneat ejus similitudinem.

180. *How the colour olchus, otherwise membrana, is made.*—The colour olchus, otherwise membrana, is so called from its appearing like the human flesh on the face, the hands, and the other parts of the body. It is made of red or vermilion, and white or ceruse, and he who has no vermilion, must make it of minium and white mixed together in proper proportions of each, according to the greater or less ruddiness, or paleness, or whiteness, which he wishes to give to the naked figure, in painting it. And because a greenish colour is proper for it, mix a little green with it, in proper proportion as you may think proper. And if you have no green, mix orpiment with lazur, and you will have a green which you may use. Others also collect the flowers of a certain herb, the name of which has escaped me, which they grind or mix with the olchus, and thus make the colour.

181. *How lake is made.*—Take filings or scrapings of Brazil wood, and let them boil over the fire in a clean vase with red wine. Then add lake distempered with urine, and let them boil together, and having done this, strain and squeeze them. Then take alum and mix with the other ingredients in the vase over the fire, and stir it a little. Then remove it from the fire, and pour the contents into a basin. Then grind it well upon a stone, and collect the lake together and let it dry in the sun. Afterwards preserve it in a box.

182. *Item.—How to make sinopis de mellana.*—If you wish to make sinopis de mellana, take lac, that is, the gum of ivy, with which parcium is dyed, and grind it very fine, and temper it with vinegar or urine. Then, adding wheat flour well cleansed from the bran, make it into little cakes, and bake it in an unglazed jar; and, while it is being baked, put a little of it upon a stick with a twig, until you see that it is of a very good colour. If you wish to have it very red, bake it but little; if less red, bake it more.

183. *As before.—To make the same sinopis in a different manner.*—If you wish to make excellent sinopis, take lac, that is, the gum of ivy, and madder, and boil it for a short time in a

180. *Quomodo componitur olchus color seu membrana.*—Olchus color aliter membrana vocatur qui sicuti humana caro in facie in manibus et aliis partibus et membris corporis demonstratur. Componitur ex rubeo seu vermiculo et albo seu cerusa. Et qui non haberet vermiculum componeret ex minio et albo simul ad proportionatas quantitates utriusque ipsorum juxta majorem vel minorem rubedinem vel palliditatem, vel albedinem quam dare voluerit nudo ymagini pingens ipsam. Et quia virideus color in ipso convenit aliquantulum viridis per debitam portionem sicut placuerit. Et si viride non habetur auripigmentum cum lazurio misceat et viride habebit quo uti poterit alii colligunt colligunt (*sic*) etiam cujusdem herbe flores cujus nomen excidit quos cum olcho terunt seu miscent et colorem inde facit.

181. *Quomodo efficitur lacha.*—Accipe Brasilis ligni limaturam vel rasuram, et in uno vase mundo cum vino rubeo permitte ad ignem bullire. Deinde lacham cum urina distemperatam cum ea pone et simul bulliant et hoc facto colantur et exprimantur. Postea alumen accipe et misce cum eis in vase ad ignem existente et move parumper. Tunc ab igne tolle et in scutella mitte. Deinde super petram fortiter tere et collige et ad solem siccare permitte. Postea ad servandum in ferulo vel pixide pone.

182. *Item de faciendo sinopide de mellana.*—Si vis facere sinopidem de mellana. Accipe de lacca id est gumma ederæ de qua parcium tingitur et optime tere et distempera cum aceto vel urina. Deinde farinam triticeam bene a furfure mundatam adjungens, fac quasi pastulas et coque in olla rudi et frequenter cum coquetur ex eo cum festuca super virgulam tuam pone, donec videas optimi chloris esse et si multum rubeum volueris minus coque si minus rubeum magis coque.

183. *Sicut supra de eodem synopide aliter faciendo.*—Si vis facere optimum sinopidem, accipe laccam id est gummam ederæ et Waranciam et coque in ollam aliquantulum cum aqua postea

jar with water, and afterwards take it out of the jar, and let it cool a little. Then grind it well in a mortar, and strain it through a cloth, squeezing it well out, and afterwards heat it carefully in a basin or saucer, taking care not to let it boil, but only simmer. And while it is on the fire put it frequently with a twig upon your rod to try it; if it is thick enough, remove it from the fire, and let it cool and harden, so that you may be able to make it into cakes. Having made it into cakes, cut it up, and put it into a small hole, and keep it for use.

184. *Of lake.*—In the month of March, cut branches of ivy crosswise in various places, or pierce them with a bodkin, and there will exude a liquid, which you must collect every third day. This is boiled with urine, and turns to a blood colour, which is also called lacha, with which the skins, commonly called parcie, are dyed with alum. The above-mentioned liquid is useful for many purposes.

185. *Of writing, or painting, with tin.*—When you are going to make gold or silver writing or painting, if you have neither of them, that is to say, neither gold nor silver, you must make use of the following process. Cast very pure tin into strips of half a foot or little more in length, namely, like those of which glass windows are made. Then scrape with a knife one or more of them, as many as you like, into very small pieces, until they, or it, are, or is, entirely scraped away; and then put the shavings into a mortar made of very hard metal, namely, of that of which bells are made, which must be prepared for this purpose, and fixed in a plank. You must also have a muller or pestle of the same metal, which must revolve in the mortar. Afterwards put these clippings into the mortar, and pour water upon them, and grind them by pulling a thong backwards and forwards; but when the muller begins to stick a little, so that it will not turn, take it out, and pour or tip out the water and tin into a very clean vase; and then, letting the tin remain in the vase, pour the water cautiously off, without pouring away the tin. Afterwards let the tin dry by the fire or in the sun. Then put it on a very thick linen cloth, and make the fine parts

extrahes ab olla et aliquantulum refrigerari permitte. Deinde in mortariolo fortiter tere et per pannum extorquendo cola, et postea in bacina vel in testa coque cum diligentia cavens ne bulliat sed tantum fremat. Et dum coquitur frequenter cum festuca super virgulam tuam pone temptando; si satis spissum ab igne tolle et permitte frigescere et durescere. Itaque inde possis pastillos facere. Et factis pastillis excisea et pone in forulo et serva usui.

184. *De lacca.*—Mense Marcio ramas in diversis locis incide de edera extransverso vel cum aculeo perfora et egredietur liquor quem de tertio in tercium diem collige qui cum urina coquitur et in sanguineum colorem vertetur, qui et lacha dicitur ex qua pelles alutine tingentur que vulgo parcie dicuntur. Liquor superdictum ad multa valet.

185. *De stannea scriptura vel pictura.*—Auream seu argenteam scripturam vel picturam facturus, si neutrum habeas, scilicet nec aurum nec argentum hac utere compositura. Stannum purissimum funde in laminas quas dimidii pedis vel paulo plus longitudinis fac ad instar scilicet earum ex quibus fenestre vitree componuntur. Deinde unam earum vel plures quot vis cum cultello vel quo instrumento necesse fuerit minutatum erade vel errade quo ad usque tota consumpta vel consumptæ sint. Et deinceps ipsas encisuras in mortariolo pone quod de metallo durissimo sit, quo scilicet campanæ fiunt ad hoc opus parato et in ligno infixo. Habeas simulque molam seu pistillam qui in mortariolo vertitur, de eodem metallo. Postea in ipso mortario pone ipsas incisuras. Et super ipsas infunde aquam et sic eas mole trahendo corrigiam et retrahendo seu relaxendo. Ubi autem mola stare ceperit paululum nec jam posse verti extrahe illam et aquam et stannum in mundissimo vase rejecta vel reversa. Et ipsum stannum retinendo in ipso vase eice caute aquam absque ejiciendo stannum. Et postea permitte ipsum stannum siccari ad ignem vel ad solem. Deinde panno lineo valde spisso indue ac fac transire subtiles minucias;

pass through; but the coarser parts, which will not pass through the cloth, put back into the mortar, and grind as you did before: and you must always make the finer parts pass through a cloth as before, and then put them with the other similar parts; and so, when you have reduced the tin to a very clean powder, draw upon the parchment and upon the cloth flowers and images, and whatever else you like. And in painting you must put glue upon the places which you wish to gild or silver, with a brush of ass's hair, which glue you must thus make from ox-skins:—

186. *How to make glue from the skin of an ox or a cow.*— Take the skin of an ox or a cow, as thick as you can find it, which has already been tanned for shoes, and put it in a jar and pour water upon it, and make it boil over the fire from daybreak on a summer's day until nearly the third hour of the day, pouring water into it when necessary, or, when it is much diminished, pour off the water, which has boiled so long, and pour in clean water, and make it boil again until the sixth hour. Then pour off this water, which will be nearly all evaporated, and again pour clean water into the jar over the same leather, and do not renew it more than once or twice more. And take great care not to let it boil over, and then, having boiled it down to one-third, pour it into a vase, and leave it to cool all that day and night. In the morning of the next day, if it is coagulated in the vase, put your finger upon it. If any part of it remains sticking to your finger, you may know that it is not good, and may throw it away as refuse. Afterwards fill up the jar with water as before, in order to boil it with the leather; and you must not fill it up any more, but take all possible care not to let it boil over. You will know when it is good by (after you have boiled it sufficiently and let it cool) putting your finger upon it as before, to see whether it is hard; and the harder you find it, the better you may know it to be. Afterwards putting a small portion of it into an earthen vase, set it on the coals and make it rather warm. Then, removing the vase from the fire, keep it at a moderate heat over a slow fire made of a few pieces of charcoal, lest it should be con-

grossiores vero quæ per pannum transire non poterunt iterum in ipso mortario mitte et molle sicut antea feceras. Et semper minutiorem partem per pannum transire facias sicut dictum est et repone cum similibus minutiis et sic postquam in mundissimum pulverem redegeris stannum protrahe super pergamenum et super pannum flores et imagines et quodcumque opus volueris. Et in ipso opere per loca que de aurare vel argenteare voles, pones viscum cum pincello asinino quod viscum sic facies de corio bovis.

186. *Quomodo viscum vel gluten fit de corio bovis vel vaccæ.*—Corium bovis vel vaccæ quod spissius invenire poteris jam ad calcimaenta instinctum mitte in ollam simul que aquam et a primo deluculo usque ad horam pene tertiam temporis æstatis fervere fac ad ignem, aquam infundendo cum opus erit vel cum comminuta fuerit. Postea projicies ipsarum aquam que tandiu fervuerit et infundas claram aquam et iterum fervere facies usque ad horam sextam. Postea ipsam aquam pene consumptum projice atque iterum in olla cum corio eodem aquam claram mitte nec augeas plusquam semel aut bis sed diligenter observa ne ex inundando exiliat tunc usque ad tertiam partem coctam ipsam in vase recipe et refrigerari permitte tota die illa et nocte. Mane die altera si coagulatur invanis digitum suppone. Si digito aliqua pars adhærens remanserit, scias non esse bonam et projice illud velut stercora. Post hoc iterum aqua ollam implebis similiter ut cum eodem corio excoquatur, nec augebis amplius sed cum qua possis diligencia custodi ne exiliat sciens quod bona erit si digitum, postquam sufficienter bullierit et frigidari permiseris, supposueris ut supra et durum inveneris, et quanto duriorem senseris tanto meliorem esse scias. Postea sic aliquam partem de ea sumptam in testeo vasculo pone eo super carbones aliquantulum fac fervere. Ex igne autem in vasculum quem ad levem ignem paucorum carbonum ad moderatam caliditatem tunc ne congelitur pincellum minimum ad hoc paratum ea intinge et super pergamenum et super pannum quidquid protrahendo vel de protractis volueris fac et linias atque statim ut

gealed, and dip into it a very small paint-brush made for this purpose, and draw on the parchment or canvas whatever you like, or fill in any former drawings; and as soon as you have drawn your paint-brush over a few places, before the glue is congealed, quickly, and without delay, in order that the tin may adhere before the glue dries, sprinkle plenty of the powdered tin over it, so that none whatever of those parts, which you spread over with the paint-brush full of glue or cement, may remain bare, or not covered with the powdered tin. And so go on by degrees with the remaining parts of the work, until you have completely filled in all that you intended to colour with it. Lastly, collect and put by the superfluous powder of the tin which is lying scattered about here and there on the paper, not adhering to the work, and leave your work until the next day to dry.

188. *How to know good tin.*[1]—Good tin is known as follows. Put a plate of tin to your ear, and bend it to and fro several times with both hands, as if you wished to know whether it was broken, and if it rings, that is, creaks or crackles, it is good. Also, if you cut a strip from the plate with a knife, and do not entirely separate it, but bend it to and fro six or seven times, as if you were going to break it off, and if it does not break, you will by that means prove the said tin to be very good.

189. *How to make ink.*[2]—If you wish to make ink, you must take, they say, the bark of blackthorn, and when you have torn it off clean from the wood, you must fill a vase with it, mixed also with plenty of water, which must not be renewed, and put it on the fire, and let the bark boil down over the fire like beef, and then take it out, and squeeze out of it the water which it has soaked up, and let the water boil quickly over the fire till it is reduced to one-half. Afterwards, pour it into the first vase, and let it boil still, and when it is reduced, pour it back into the other vase, and make it boil away.

---

[1] No. 187 is missing in the original.

[2] The word atramentum is written in the margin of this chapter in the original.

aliquantulum in aliquibus locis pincellum traxeris priusque congeletur glutem cito non tardando ut stannum tenere possit et antequam siccetur, habundanter stannum pulverisatum super spargas et ita ut nil omnino de his quæ cum pincello de ipso visco vel glutine linieris vacuum remaneat quin stanno pulverizato cooperiatur. Deinde sic fac paulatim procedendo ad reliquas partes operis usquequo intoto compleveris quod perficere ex eo decreverit. Demum stanni pulverem quod super habundaverit et hac illuc dispersum erit non adherens operi, colligas et recipe et opus tuum usque in crastinum siccari permitte.

188. *De cognitione boni stanni.*—Sic autem bonum stannum cognoscitur. Accipe lamina stanni juxta aurem tuam et cum utraque manu plices sepius illam quasi qui velis scire an facta sit et osculta diligenter et si tinuit id est stridet vel crisnat bonum est, et si de lamina cum cultello crispam sceveris nec tamen omnino abrumperis sed quasi qui velis eam frangere, sexcies vel septies plicueris et sine fractura remanserit optimum fore dictum stannum isto modo comprobaverit.

189. *De incausto quo modo efficitur.*—Quisquis igitur incaustum conficere voluerit sumens ut aiunt corticem nigræ spinæ quam cum de ligno ad purum evulserit impleat inde vas mixta pariter habundantissime et semel tantum cum aqua qua imposita igni sinat corticem dequoqui more carnis vaccinæ eo que extracto extorqueat ab eoquam ebiberat aquam et ipsam aquam igni prestolatur excoqui ad medietatem. Postea ipsam transfundat in vas primus et adhuc bullire permittat et cum comminuta fuerit refundat in aliud vas et ebullire faciat. Et cum ad ultimum iterum comminuta erit evacuet in minimo

And when lastly it is again reduced, empty it into a very small vase, and make it boil away. And when the ink has become thick like porridge, take it off the fire, because it is sufficiently boiled. But when you wish to prepare it for writing, take some part of it, and put it into an earthen vessel with double the quantity of wine, and take great care, when it begins to get hot, to throw away the impurities which sink to the bottom, separating them from the ink by straining through a cloth. But what cannot be omitted is, that care must be taken not to let it run over the edge of the vase, for otherwise you will lose a great part of your labour. But when, as I had begun to say, it is still hot, mix up with it two pieces of burnt atramentum, and after four days or a week you will be able to write with it. And if the ink should remain pale, or soak the parchment like water, put it on the fire again, mixing with it a little incaustum and atramentum. But do not throw it away while it is still hot, for it is atramentum.

190. *How to lay gold on a wall, or on parchments.*—If you wish to lay gold on a wall, or on paper, or on wood, or upon a block of marble, grind gypsum by itself separately. Then grind brown separately in the same manner, and take three parts of gypsum and one of brown, and take glue made from parchment or leather, and distemper them together, mixing the said parts, and lay upon it [the object to be gilded] one coat of this mixture with a paint-brush, and then another; and so lay three or four coats. And when the last is dry, scrape it with a knife or other iron instrument fitted for the purpose, so that it may be very smooth; and then burnish it with a tooth or a stone, and lay over it, with the paint-brush, only one very thin coat of the gypsum, and let it dry. When it is dry, lay the gold upon that mordant, as you have been taught. Afterwards lay upon the gold a very fine cloth that has been two or three times warmed; or apply it as I do, not so warm, in order that the gold may be the better polished.

191. *Also how to lay on gold.*—Take gypsum and grind it

vase et ebullire faciat. Cum que ipsum incaustum in modum pultium densatum fuerit extrahat illud ab igne, quia ad plenum est decoctum, cum vero ad scribendum volueris aptare tolles ab eo aliquam portionem pones in vas fictile, duplum que vini, solicitate que procaveat ut cum ceperit fervere sordes in fundo immergentes rejiciat separando eas ab incausto colando ipsum per telam. Hoc vero quod pone preteriri poterit observet ne vel tunc vel quando confectatur in caloris ora vasis transeat. Alioquin magna parte quassabitur suo labore. Cum vero ut dicere ceperam ad huc calet attramenti duo frustra cremata commisceat quatuor que diebus vel ebdomada exacta inde scribere poterit. Et si in pallore perduraverit vel pergamenum transierit more aque appone iterum igni miscendo aliquantulum incausti et attramenti sed tunc cum ad huc efferfuerit non abiciat quod attramentum est.

190. *Quomodo in muro vel in pergameno ponitur aurum.*—Si vis aurum ponere in muro vel in carta vel in ligno vel super petra marmorea, tere fortiter gypsum per se separatim. Deinde brunum similiter teris separatim facies que de gypso tres partes et quatuor de bruno. Accipies que colam de pergamenis vel de corio factum et distemperes simul, miscendo illas supradictas partes, facies que de ipsa mixtura unum lectum de super cum pincello et ad huc de super alium. Et sic facies tres vel quatuor linitiones : cum vero siccum fuerit rades cultello vel alio ferro ad hoc parato ita quod sit bene adequatum deinde burnias dente vel petra et cum pincello de super tantum una vice trahe de ipso gypso postea siccabitur. Postquam siccatum fuerit pones de super ea distemperatura tua aurum sicut doctus es. Postea pannum delicatissimum super aurum duabus vel tribus vicibus calefactam pones, vel sicut ego facio minus calefactum, ad modum vel melius polia-tur, super eum pone.

191. *Item de ponendo auro.*—Accipe gypsum et mola eum

well with water. Then take your glue which is made of bull-skin and mix with it a little white of egg, and distemper the gypsum. But when you wish to lay on the gold, cover the place with gypsum with a paint-brush, and let it dry. Do this three times. Then scrape it, that it may be smooth, and burnish it, and again lay another coat of the glue or mordant upon it, and then your gold upon that, and remove the dirt gently with cotton, and then let it dry. But if you wish to polish it, do so with hæmatite, or with a dog's-tooth.

192. *Also how to lay on gold.*—Take *brasilium*, newly distempered with white of egg, well whipped with a sponge or otherwise, and draw and paint with it whatever you like on vellum or on any other thing you wish to gild, and immediately lay the gold upon it, and remove the dirt with cotton, scarcely touching it, and leave it to dry for half a day or a whole day if you like. Then take a dog's-tooth, and begin to burnish at first gently, lest you should spoil it all, and then harder, and afterwards so hard that your forehead is wet with perspiration. And if you wish to lay gold on parchment made of sheep's-skin, add a little plum-tree gum, otherwise gum arabic, which is excellent for working on any kind of parchment, namely, from calf-skin, sheep-skin, and goat-skin, as we shall declare in the following [recipe]. And either kind of gum must be distempered as follows :—

193. *The mode of tempering the gums for laying on gold.*—Take whichever of these gums you like, and tie it up in a very clean linen cloth, and put it in a glass vase, and let it lie in water for a whole day and night, although indeed, if you want to make haste, you may stir up the water with your finger. Then draw whatever you like on the parchment, and lay the gold on it as before mentioned.

194. *Of the precautions required in gilding.*—But take notice that you ought to work in gold and colours in a damp place on account of the hot weather, which, as it is often injurious in burnishing gold, both to the colours on which the gold is laid and in [the operation] of gilding, if the work is done on parch-

fortiter cum aqua. Deinde accipe gluten tuum quod fit de taurino pinguedine et misce cum eo parumper de glarea ovi, et distempera gypsum. Ubi vero aurum ponere volueris ibi cum pincello de gypso trahes, dimittes que siccare. Hæc facies tribus vicibus; postea raddes eum ut sit planum et burnies; iterum de dicto glutine seu cola de super trahes et illico aurum tuum pones et de cotho suaviter turpedines ipsum et ita dimitte siccare si vero polire eum vis de emate vel dente canino polies ipsum.

192. *Item ad ponendum aurum.*—Accipe brasilium noviter distemperatum cum glarea ovi optime fracta cum spungia vel aliter et de ipso protrahe et pinge quæ vis in pergameno vitulino vel alio ubi ponere aurum volueris et statim aurum de super pone et de cotho quasi non tangens turpedine, dimittesque dimidium diem siccare vel per totum diem si vis. Postea accipe dentem caninum et brunire incipias primum quidem suaviter ne totum dissipes, deinde fortius postea tam fortiter ut frons tua sudore madescat. Et si aurum in pergameno de ariete ponere volueris addes parumper de gumma cinea aliter gumma arabica quæ mirabilis est ad operandum in utroque pergameno scilicet vitulino, arietino et capretino sicut in sequenti declarabimus utrumque etenim gummam distemperabis sic.

193. *Modus distemperandi gummas ad ponendum aurum.*—Accipies gummam qualem vis unam de duabus hiis et ligabis in pannum lineum nitissimum ponesque in vitreo vase tota die et nocte in aqua jacere vel certe si festinare vis, distemperabis eam digito tuo cum ipsa aqua. Sic que in pergamenum penna protrahe omne quod vis et illico pone aurum ut suprascriptum est.

194. *De advertentiis habendis in ponendo aurum.*—Sed inde adverte quomodo operari te oportet de auro, et coloribus in humido loco propter calidum tempus quod sicut sepe nocet ad brunien dum aurum et ad colores de quibus aurum ponitur et de auro operari si opus fiat in minus humido et nimis sicco

ment that is too dry and not sufficiently moist; so also it is injurious when the weather is too dry and arid, or too damp, while applying colours or gilding.

195. *Also how to lay on gold.*—Take gum arabic and distemper it as aforesaid. Then take gum ammoniac distempered with hot water over the fire, and mix it with the gum arabic, and stir it with your finger, and put it in the sun, that it may be well mixed and liquefied. Next, take gypsum, and distemper it with white of egg, and mix it with gum ammoniac and gum arabic. And when you wish to gild leather or purple cloth, or linen or silk cloths, stir it up altogether, and draw beasts and birds and flowers upon them with a very sharp stick, and let them dry. Then take the gold, and blow gently on the flowers, and lay on the gold directly, and press it down with a burnishing tooth or stone, and burnish it as before.

196. *Of certain kinds of gum or glue.*[1]—If you have not the air-bladder of a sea-fish, cut up thick vellum in the same manner, and wash it. Also wash carefully three times in warm water the dried bones of the head of a pike, and boil them. Whichever of these you boil, add to them one-third part of very clear gum, that is, gum arabic, and boil a little; and you may keep this as long as you will.

197. *How and with what vehicles to temper colours for painting in books.*—When mixing colours for painting in books, make a vehicle of the clearest gum arabic and water, as before, and mix with it all colours except green and ceruse, minium, and carmine. Salt green is of no use in a book. Spanish green you must temper with wine, and if you wish to shade it, add a little of the juice of sword grass, or cabbage, or leek. You must mix minium and ceruse, and carminium, with white of egg. Grind azure with soap, and wash it, and mix it with white of egg.

198. *How that various tints are made by the mixture of the*

[1] This chapter is a paraphrase of chap. xxxiii. of the first book of Theophilus, English ed.

[2] See Theophilus, lib. i. cap. xxxiv. (Eng. ed.), of which this is a para-

pergameno. Sic de coloribus vero operari et ponendo aurum in tempus nimis rigidum vel siccum ac etiam minus humidum.

195. *Item ad ipsum aurum ponendum.*—Accipe gummam arabicam et distempera ut dictum est. Accipiesque moniaculum distemperatum cum aqua calida ad ignem et misces cum arabica, distemperabis que digito tuo et pones ad solem ut bene distemperetur et liquefiat. Postea accipe gypsum et distempera cum glarea ovi et clarum misce cum moniculo et arabica. Et quando aurum in corio vel in purpura vel in pellis lineis vel siricis ponere volueris movebis omnia simul et facies bestias et volucres et flores cum baculo acutissime de super dimittesque siccum. Postea accipe illud et super flores modice suffla et statim aurum impones et imprima dente vel lapide ad bruniendum, et brunias ut supra.

196. *De quibusdam generibus gummi vel glutinis.*— Si vesicam non habueris piscis marrini pergamenum vituli spissum eodem modo incide, lava quoque ossa etiam capitis lupi piscis sicca, diligenter lota in calida aqua ter illa coque; qualemcumque horum coxeris. Adde eis terciam partem gummi lucidissimi, *i. e.* arabici et modice coque et poteris servare quam diu volueris.

197. *Quomodo temperantur colores in libris ponendis et de quibus liquoribus.*—Temperando colores in libris ponendos fac temperamentum ex gummi arabico lucidissimo et aqua ut supra et tempera omnes colores excepto viridi et cerusa et minio et carminio; viride salsum non valet in libro, viride hispanicum temperabis vino et si volueris umbras facere adde modicum succi gladioli vel caulis vel porri; minium et cerusam et carminium temperabis claro ovi. Azur mole cum sapone et lava et distempera claro ovi.

198. *Qui ex mixturis colorum ad invicem plurimæ ipsorum*

---

phrase; the last sentence excepted, which is not in Theophilus, but part of it will be found in the Clavicula, p. 61.

colours with one another.—All colours whatever are diversified and varied in various ways and manners, by mixtures being made with them or laid over them, of other colours, that agree with them in proper manners and quantities. If you require these mixtures for painting figures and other things, mix and temper them as before for books. And all colours are to be laid on twice, in books, and on parchment, first very thin, and then thicker; but in letters only once.[1]

199. *Of black, and ink, and of a black and green colour.*[2]—Take ripe berries of honeysuckle, that is, in English, galetrice, and pound them well in a mortar. Afterwards boil them carefully in wine, adding also some rust of iron to the decoction. This is a green and brilliant ink. If you wish to colour a cloth or a skin green, paint it over with a paintbrush. But if you wish it to be black, add ink to the composition, as usual.

200. *Gum prevents the ink from running.*—If you wish to prevent the above written, or any other ink from running when you are using it, add the gum of a plum-tree or of an apple, in the boiling, and boil it together.

201. *Also how to make green, according to the Normans.*[3]—Take the herb which is called grenuspett [or gremispett], and boil it with beer or wine, so that the beer may be coloured yellow by the herb. Then strain it. Then grind sufficiently some Greek green with the beer, and afterwards let it stand in a basin or a copper vase in the sun to ripen.

202. *How to make auripetrum.*—Spanish saffron, distempered with very clear glue or liquid varnish, and laid over very clear, that is, very bright and well polished tin, assumes the appearance of gold to those that look on it, for it receives its colour from the sun, and its brilliancy from the tin, and thus may be made excellent auripetrum.

---

[1] The latter part of this chapter is from Theophilus, lib. i. cap. xxxiv.

[2] This recipe and the next are in the Mappæ Clavicula, p. 43.

[3] This recipe is also in the Clavicula (p. 43), without, however, the remarkable addition "according to the Normans."

varietates fiunt.—Omnes et quicumque colores ex mixturis aliorum eis convenientium debitis modis et quantitatibus eis adhibitis et impositis diversificantur et variantur plurimis modis et differenciis. Quas mixturas si indigueris ad pingendum imagines et alia, compone et distempera in libris ut supra. Et omnes colores bis ponendi sunt in libris et pergamenis in primus tenuissime, Deinde spissius in literis vero semel.

199. *De attramento et incausto et de negro et viridi colore.*—Accipe grana matura caprifolii hoc est anglice galetrice et in mortario bene contere. Post vino diligenter fac bullire ferrum aruginatum decoctione similiter addiciens. Hoc est viride et fulgens incaustum et si vis pannum vel corium habere viride, pincello desuper linias. Si vero vis ut niger sit huic compositioni adde solito attramentum.

200. *Quod gumma cum prohibet fluxum incausti.*—Si vis facere quod superscriptum incaustum vel aliud non decurrat cum de ipso operatur, pone gummam cini vel pomi in coctione et simul coque.

201. *Item de viridi faciendo secundum normannos.*—Accipe herbam que dicitur gremispect et bulli cum cervesia aut vino adeo ut cervisia crocea sit de herba. Postea cola Deinde pulverem de viridi Greco mola cum ipsa cervisia ut satis sit, postea stet in baccino vel cupreo vase contra solem ad maturandum.

202. *Quomodo efficitur auripetrum.*—Crocus hispanicus cum lucidissimo glutine seu vernicio liquido distemperatur et stanno limpidissimo, *i.e.* pene polito et claro, superpositas speciem auri intuentibus mentitur quod a sole colorem et stanno accipit fulgorem et inde optimum fit auripetrum.

203. *Also, in the same manner, a coat of gall gives the appearance of gold to copper vases.*[1]—By scraping copper with a knife, and burnishing it with a bear's tooth, it is polished. Then lay gall evenly over every part of it with a paintbrush; and, when it is dry, lay on more and more coats of gall, and it imitates the colour of gold.

204. *How to colour copper.*—Take copper that has been well filed and polished and afterwards varnished over, and warm it frequently before the fire, and it will turn of a red colour. Afterwards scrape it with a sharp knife in several places and cover it again with some colour, and then the fire will turn it of a different colour; and so in proportion to the warmth.

205. *Also, the manner of beating out tin-plates, so as to appear gilt, to use in painting, on account of the price of gold.*—If you wish to make [imitate] gold leaf, take pure tin or silver and make it into very thin plates; and take dry saffron flowers, and wrap them up in a linen cloth and lay them in gum water, and leave them there until they are soft. Then take them out, being careful not to squeeze them. But if the saffron which you intend to soak in water is fresh, you must first put the flowers in the sun in a linen cloth by themselves, to dry, and when they are dry soak them in water as before directed. Afterwards take the beforementioned water and lay it thinly once over the plates and let them dry. Then take the flowers, dried as before directed, and soak them in white of egg, which has been whipped a little, and stir it with your finger, and let the plates lie in it a short time, until each piece has been dipped three times, letting the pieces dry separately between each of these three times, and afterwards polish them with an onyx stone; and if you have no onyx, grease the tin with the oil which is made from linseed, and let it dry, and put it on paper or on wood in this manner. Take the above mentioned gum and put it in tepid water, and allow it to remain for so long as it takes to sing a mass.[2] Afterwards lay pure white colour in

[1] See Eraclius, lib. ii. No. XVI.

[2] About a quarter of an hour.

203. *Itemque sic vasa cuprea linicio fellis deauraturam mentitur.*—Cuprum raddendo cum cultello et bruniendo dente ursino splendificatur. Deinde cum felle linies pincello per omnes ejus partes tracto equaliter; quo siccato iterum atque iterum fel superpone et auri mentitur colorem.

204. *Ad colorandum cuprum.*—Cuprum bene limatum et planatum postea vernicio tinctum ad ignem sepe calefaciat et contrahet colorem rubeum. Postea cum acuto cultello radde in diversis locis et iterum illini aliquo colore et ibi alium colorem habebit ad ignem et quanto plus calefiet.

205. *Item de modo attenuandi laminas stanni ut auratæ videantur ex carentia auri utendas in operibus.*—Si vis facere petonas de auro accipe stannum purum vel argentum et fac laminas multum tenuas et accipe crocum florem siccum et involve in panno lineo et pone in aqua ubi gumma est et dimitte ibi usquequo mollescat. Postea tolles eum et cave ne constringas eum; si autem crocus recens est quum ipsam accipis pro ponendo in aqua debes prius ponere ad solem in panno lineo florem separatim siccare et dum siccus fuerit mitte in aquam temperare ut dictum est superius. Post hec accipe aquam supradictam et tinge laminas subtiliter semel et admitte siccari. Dehinc accipe florem siccatam sicut dixi et pone in glaream ovi aliquantulum vapulum et cum digito fricabis. Et laminas dimitte jacere aliquantulum in ea donec omnes laminæ infusæ sint ter. Ita tamen ut unaquaque vice exipsis tribus permittas eas sigillatim siccari, postea liccabis eas cum onchino, si non habes onchinum unge laminas de oleo quod fit de lini semine et permitte siccari, et eas pones in carta vel in ligno hoc modo. Accipies gummam supradictam et pones aquam tepidam et iterum tantum permittes jacere, quantum spatii est cantare missam. Postea pone purum album colorem sicut ponere debes in locis in quibus ponere vis laminas et dum

a proper manner on those places on which you wish to apply the tin, and, when they are dry, polish them with an onyx stone; then lay the gum water upon the white colour, and let it dry. Then polish it as before; after this cut the tin according to the form required, lay it on with the said gum-water, and let it dry; and clean it with a sponge dipped in cold water; then rub it down with a linen cloth well wrung out, and rub the tin, and afterwards polish it, as before mentioned.

206. *Also as before, how to gild leaves or beaten plates of tin.*—Take the herb which is called myrrh,[1] and aloes, of each equal weights, and having mixed them together, put them in a proper quantity of water. Then boil them well, and after they have been boiled, pour the water into a vessel, and take the leaves of tin well covered on one side with varnish, immerse it in the liquor as long as necessary. Then boil the middle bark of the black plum well in a vessel, and afterwards dip the same tin in this water. Then lay it on a table to dry.

207. *Also as before.*—Mix linseed oil and resin, an equal weight of each, and add the same measure of vernix, put these ingredients into a jar and boil them well. Then dip leaves of tin well varnished into it [the jar], and afterwards dry them in the sun.

208. *Also as above.*—Put linseed-oil and the inner bark of the black plum into a new jar, and boil it well for a short time upon charcoal or upon a clear fire. Then clean your glassa, by weight as much as you like, and put it into another jar, and take about half the quantity of alum, and of dragon's blood, and put it all into the jar, and lastly add a little resin, and melt the whole well together, and as soon as all the ingredients

---

[1] It seems probable that the gum-resin myrrh is meant, particularly as myrrh is named among other gums and resins in the recipe entitled "Lucida quo modo fiant super colores," in the Clavicula, p. 53, and in the Lucca MS., published by Muratori. At the same time it must be observed, that the author writes "the herb which is called myrrh;" and in the Table of Synonymes myrrh is said to be the "tree vulgarly called genestra." The plant called "myrrha," myrrhis, &c., is the Scandix odorato,

siccum fuerit licca eum onichino et sic pones aquam in qua gumma est super album colorem et dimitte siccare. Item licca ut supra; post hoc incide laminas secundum modum loci ubi ponere volueris, et pone eas cum dicta aqua gummata, et permitte siccari et cum spongia intincta in aqua frigida purga postea ipsas laminas ubi posuisti eas, postea cum panno lineo extersa optime et frica ipsas laminas et postea licca ut supra scriptum est.

206. *Item ut supra de modo deaurandi folia seu laminas stanni attenuatas.*—Accipe herbam que dicitur myrra et aloem uno pondere ambas et commixtas simul pone in illam aquam secundum modum appositam. Deinde fac bullire bene, et post coctionem herbarum mitte aquam in sartaginem et folia stanni bene illinita una parte de vernix appone et bene merge quantum opus fuerit. Deinde medianam corticis pruni nigri fac bullire, in sartaginem bene et postea mitte eadem folia in hac aqua. Deinde appone folia super tabulam ad siccandum.

207. *Item ut supra.*—Oleum de lini semine et picem uno pondere mixtum et eamdem mensuram de vernix pone in ollam et fac bullire bene. Deinde mitte folia stanni bene verniciata intus et post modum siccata ad solem.

208. *Item ut supra.*—Oleum lineum et medianam corticem nigri pruni mitte in ollam novam ac fac bene bullire super carbones vel claro igne paulatim, deinde munda glassam tuam quantum volueris cum pondere et pone in alteram ollam et aluminis quasi mediam partem et sanguinem drachonis et omnia hæc mitte in ollam et ad ultimum mixtum picem adjunge et bene funde et quam citius hec omnia fondentur appone

---

Myrrhis magno semine longo sulcato, Myrrhis major cicutaria odorato. Myrrhenkerbel, Aniskerbel. In English, the sweet-scented Cicely, or myrrh. Cerfeuil odorant ou musqué, Cerfeuil d'Espagne, Fr. Cerfoglio odoroso, Miroide, Ital. Matthioli and Laguna say that the Cerfeuil of the French was synonymous with the Gingidio of the Greeks (the Scandix cerefolium): therefore, instead of "Genestra," we ought perhaps to read "Gingidio."

are melted, add the abovementioned oil, and, as if you were making a compound ointment, let them boil well together, and stir them frequently, and afterwards dip your nail into the composition and try whether it is good or not.

209. *Also as before.*—Collect twigs of black plum, and put them in the sun for a week or a fortnight, and then throw away the outer bark, and take the inner bark, and put it into a rough jar, so as to fill it. Then take linseed or hempseed-oil, and pour into the jar as much of it as it will hold, and heat it slowly over the fire, until the bark is reduced to charcoal. Then throw away the bark, and strain the remainder of the oil through linen, and take resin and white frankincense, and clean the jar well, and then put all the ingredients into it again, and heat it as long as you please.

supradictum oleum et secundum unctionem confectionis et sine bene bullire simul et sæpe move et post modum intinges ungulam tuam et temptabis utrum bonum sit an non.

209. *Item ut antea.*—Collige virgulas de nigro pruno et pone ad solem per octo dies aut quindecim et postea primum projicies corticem accipies que secundum et pones in olla rudi ita ut plena sit. Deinde accipies oleum de lino vel de canapo, et in olla quantum intrare poteris impones et lente igne tam diu coques donec ipse cortex in carbonem redigatur et tunc projicies et per lintheum quod remanserit oleum colabis et postea accipies picem et thus album et ipsam que ollulam fortiter mundabis, totum que simul repones iterum intus et quantum tibi placuerit coques.

MANUSCRIPTS OF ERACLIUS.

PRELIMINARY OBSERVATIONS.

Two ancient copies only of the MS. of Eraclius have been hitherto discovered, and it is somewhat singular that both are bound up with MSS. of Theophilus.

The most ancient of these is that discovered by Raspe in the library of Trinity College, Cambridge, and which he afterwards published in his work on Painting in Oil (London, 1801). This MS. is written on vellum, and is of the latter half of the thirteenth century.[1] It is now in the British Museum.[2] The first two books are in verse; the last, which consists of twenty-four or twenty-five chapters, is in prose.

The MS. next in point of antiquity is that which forms part of the MS. of Le Begue. It is written on paper, and was transcribed in the year 1431, probably from an older MS., the property of John Alcherius, which passed with his other MSS. into the hands of Le Begue. The third book of this copy contains a great many additional chapters, and the whole of those published by Raspe, with the exception of one chapter, "De probatione auri et argenti."[3]

---

1 Raspe, 'On Painting in Oil,' p. 42; Eastlake, 'Materials for a History of Painting in Oil,' p. 33.

2 Egerton MSS., 840, A.

3 Raspe, p. 117.

There is reason, however, to suppose that many copies of this MS. existed formerly, and that they were as widely scattered as the copies of the MS. of Theophilus. That this was the case is, I think, proved by the fact that fragments of the Treatise of Eraclius are found in other works, although they are ascribed not unfrequently to other authors. I shall mention, in the first place, those works in which the metrical chapters are to be found.

The most ancient work in which this occurs is the Treatise of Theophilus, the copy of which in the British Museum contains fifteen chapters of the first and second books of Eraclius, some of which, like the original, are metrical, while the others are paraphrases in prose; and this is certainly a proof that this part of the Treatise of Eraclius was written before that copy of Theophilus.[1]

---

1 The mere fact of one MS. containing parts of another, is not of itself sufficient to prove the age of a MS.: as these old writers borrowed from each other without acknowledging their obligations, it is impossible to say which is the oldest, unless other circumstances assist in determining the age. In the case of Theophilus it is apparent that the poetical parts are borrowed, because they form part of another work written entirely in verse, while no part of Theophilus is in verse except the commencement, and the measure of the latter verses differs from those of Eraclius, for the former are Leonines, which is not the case with the latter. If this proof be insufficient, the passage in Theophilus, lib. iii. cap. cvi., will be quite conclusive. He says, "Ex vitro si quis depingere vascula quærit, et te verte ad hanc artem quæ in primo libro scripta est. Hæc enim ita se habet." The chapter referred to is not in Theophilus, but in the first book of Eraclius. In the case of the Clavicula, it is not so easy to determine whether it is older than Eraclius, because both contain copies of certain chapters which perhaps belonged to a third work, for some of them are repeated two or three times in the Clavicula. The age of the MS. must be settled by the consideration of other circumstances, and these favour the presumption that the Clavicula preceded the third book of Eraclius.

The earliest writer, after Theophilus, whose name I have yet found attached to the verses of Eraclius is Arnold de Villeneuve.[1] The verses ascribed to him occur in the Secreti of Wecker,[2] published at Basle in 1598, pp. 428 and 449. They relate to precious stones and crystal.

Other metrical chapters of Eraclius, eight in number, will be found in the same edition of Wecker (p. 643-645); but these chapters, instead of being ascribed to Arnold de Villeneuve, have the name of Marcellus Palingenius attached to them.[3]

---

1 Arnold de Villeneuve, a physician and alchemist. He travelled in Italy and Germany. He was born A.D. 1245, and died previous to 1311.

2 The work of J. J. Wecker, 'De Secretis,' was originally a translation of the secrets of Don Alessio Piemontese; the first edition was, according to Haller, printed at Basle in 1559. "Every edition," says Beckmann, "seems to differ from the preceding; many things are omitted, and the new editions are, for the most part, of little importance. I have the edition of Basle, 1592, 8vo., in which there is a great deal not to be found in that of 1662, and which wants some things contained in the edition of 1582. The latest editions are printed from that improved by Theod. Zuringer, Basle, 1701, 8vo. The last edition by Zuringer was published at Basle in 1753." The edition of 1598, the preface of which is dated 1582, is the only one to which I have had access; I cannot say, therefore, whether the extracts from Eraclius are contained in other editions.

3 The real name of this Marcellus Palingenius was Manzelli, or Manzoli; he was a native of the neighbourhood of Ferrara, and being a reformer, he narrowly escaped being put to death by the Inquisition. He published a Latin poem, called the Zodiac; the first edition of which was published not prior to 1534. The measure of these verses is different from that of Eraclius, and I could not discover that the work of the latter formed a part of it. Another work has also been ascribed to Marcellus, entitled 'De Corallorum Tincturâ.' (See Potts' 'Chemical Dissertations,' translated by Demachy.) The fragment from Eraclius may have formed part of this work, for which I have inquired in vain in many public libraries. When I was at Ferrara I inquired for this and other works of Marcellus Palingenius of the Abb. Antonelli, the learned librarian of the public library of that city, and I showed him the verses in Wecker, but he could give me no information, except that the King of Prussia, when he was at Ferrara, had

With regard to the chapters of the third book contained in other MSS., I shall at present mention only that some of them are to be found in the Clavicula. These have been collated with the MS. of Eraclius, and the variations are inserted in the present work. It is probable that many more chapters may be incorporated into some of the works entitled "Secrets;" but there appears to be no inducement to undertake the labour of searching these works, since they would neither add to the practical knowledge of the arts they describe, nor make us acquainted with the history of Eraclius or of his works, since they do not bear his name.

Of the biography of Eraclius nothing is known: his country and the date of his work are equally uncertain. The same uncertainty attends the work; for there is some doubt whether the whole of the MS. ascribed to him in the Le Begue collection was actually written by him or not. I shall first offer some remarks on the work itself, and shall then state the conclusions I have drawn from a careful consideration of it.

With regard to the composition of the work itself, it appears to consist *primâ facie* of three books, the first two of which are metrical; the third is in prose.

The metrical part consists of twenty-one stanzas or

---

appeared to take a personal interest in Palingenius, and had procured such of his works as he could collect. On my return to England, Sir Henry Ellis was so obliging as to give me a letter of introduction to Dr. Pertz, the librarian of the King of Prussia, to whom I wrote, requesting to know whether he could inform me if these verses, of which I inclosed a copy, formed part of any work of Palingenius which might be preserved in the Royal Library at Berlin. Dr. Pertz very kindly searched both the Royal Library and the King's private library, but without success.

chapters. It commences with a prologue, which is preceded in the Cambridge MS. by these words, "Incipit Liber Eraclii sapientissimi viri de coloribus et artibus Romanorum." The commencement of the second book in the same MS. is "Incipit Lib. II. de colore auripigmento simili;" while in the Paris MS. the word "metricus" is inserted in the title of both books after "primus" and "secundus." The third book in the Cambridge MS. has no heading; but in the Paris MS. it is headed "Incipit tertius liber et prosaicus Eraclii antedicti de coloribus et artibus prædictis." These various readings certainly suggest the idea that the headings of the chapters were not written by Eraclius himself, and that the work consisted originally of the metrical parts only; and this supposition gains ground from a consideration of the difference of style observable between the first and second books and the third part, and from the fact that the metrical parts contain frequent allusions to the arts of the Romans, which is not the case in the third book, with the exception, perhaps, of the extracts from Vitruvius and Isidore. The chapter "De edere et lacca" is singular, and seems to indicate that the author was a native of Italy. Eraclius says,

> "Hujus enim frondem nimium coluere *priores*,
> Ad titulum laudis; erat ipsa corona poetis."

while the parallel chapter in Theophilus (E. Ed. p. 394) runs thus: "Poetarum enim carmina cum recitarentur in theatro ante conventum *romanorum* coronabantur hederâ." From this it may be inferred, not only that Eraclius was a native of Italy, and that Theophilus (supposing the *whole* of the MS. in the

British Museum ascribed to Theophilus to have been included in his work)[1] was aware of the fact, but also that the latter was not an Italian, otherwise he would not have changed the phraseology of Eraclius.

The first chapter of the second book describes a yellow colour, composed of the gall of a large fish, called "Huso," mixed with chalk, which produced a colour like orpiment. A similar recipe, which is entitled "colore aureo Lombardico," is contained in a small MS. in the Bibliothèque Royale at Paris.[2] This is another intimation of an Italian origin.

Although the name of Eraclius appears to be Greek,[3] and not Latin, I am induced to suppose that Eraclius, the author of the first two books, was an Italian, a native perhaps of some part of the Lombard dukedom of Benevento, which, says Sismondi, "had preserved, under independent princes and surrounded by the Greeks and Saracens, a degree of civilization which in the earlier part of the middle ages was unexampled throughout the rest of Italy. Many of the fine arts and some branches of science were cultivated there with success. The schools of Salerno communicated to the West the medical skill of the Arabs, and the commerce of Amalfi introduced into those fertile provinces not only wealth, but knowledge. From the eighth to the tenth century

1 I have before observed, that the copy of the MS. of Theophilus in the British Museum contains no less than fifteen chapters taken from the first and second books of Eraclius. Some of these are transcripts, others are paraphrases. It is impossible to say whether these additions to the work of Theophilus were actually made by himself, or by one of his transcribers. The former appears to me probable, because I think it is evident that Theophilus was well acquainted with the MS. ascribed to Eraclius.

2 No. vi. MDCCXLIX., B. No. 9.

3 Raspe, p. 44.

various historical works, written, it is true, in Latin, but distinguished for their fidelity, their spirit, and their fire, proceeded from the pen of several men of talent, natives of that district, some of whom clothed their compositions in hexameter verses, which, compared with others of the same period, display superior facility and fancy."

The custom alluded to of composing works in hexameter verses, will not fail to recal to the mind of the reader the metrical work of Eraclius, the literary merit of which, however, certainly does not entitle it to rank among the works alluded to by Sismondi.

It appears to have been also the custom in Italy during the twelfth and thirteenth centuries, to place inscriptions in Latin verse on works of art, as well of architecture, as of sculpture and painting, and even in mosaics. Many of these inscriptions have been published by Ciampi.[1] The verses were sometimes hexameters, and sometimes leonines. It is not improbable, therefore, that the first two books of Eraclius were written during the prevalence of this custom.

The last book of the Cambridge MS. which follows the metrical chapters without any title, contains about twenty-five chapters which are arranged with some regard to order. Nos. I.—IV. relate to pottery; two of these I have before observed are versified in the second book. Nos. V.—XII. treat of glass and precious stones. In these chapters is given a narration, taken from Isidore, who had copied Pliny, of the discovery of the art of making glass, with the marvellous legend of the

---

1 Notizie inedite della Sagrestia Pistoiese, &c., pp. 27, 37, 38, 43, 46, 48.

cup of flexible glass which, it is said, cost the inventor his life; to which are added from other sources the method of making glass of various colours and of cutting and polishing precious stones. Nos. XIII.—XXIII. relate to gilding on metals, and the last two chapters relate to painting. There is reason to suppose that this third book of the Cambridge MS. is incomplete, because there is a reference in one of the chapters to auripetrum, the composition of which is not described in this MS., but in that of Le Begue.

The third book in the Le Begue MS. contains all the chapters enumerated above, with the exception of one "De probatione auri et argenti," to which are added above thirty other chapters which treat chiefly of painting. The arrangement, however, observable in the Cambridge MS. is not the same in the MS. of Le Begue, in which the different recipes appear to be thrown together at random without any regard to the subject. As it was therefore necessary to select between the arrangement of the Cambridge MS. and that of Le Begue, I have adopted the former as the most methodical, and have arranged the remaining chapters of the third book as systematically as it was possible. I have however retained the numbers of the Le Begue MS. for the convenience of reference, and have attached to them other numbers which commence with the third book. As the last chapters of the Cambridge MS. treat of preparing wood and colours for painting, the chapters which relate to the preparation of grounds and vehicles are placed next. After this is a recipe for dyeing Cordovan leather, followed by recipes for colours, for gilding on pictures, and then

for executing Nielli. Next follow several chapters relative to colours which are extracted principally from Vitruvius, and lastly three chapters on painting which have evidently formed part of some Byzantine MS.

While preparing this MS. for publication, I have had occasion to remark, that several chapters in the third book, contain words and expressions and allusions to arts, which appear to belong to the twelfth or thirteenth centuries. From these expressions it also appears to me quite clear, that the author of certain portions of the third book was neither a Greek nor an Italian; on the contrary it seems to me extremely probable, from the fact of some of the foreign words introduced being of French origin, while others occur in French MSS., that this part of the work was written by a Frenchman, under which term I include also the Normans, who were at that period English subjects.

I shall first notice the word "cerasin," which appears to me to be derived from the French, and if this could be proved it would at once fix the country of the author, for he says "quod *nos* Cerasin vocamus." If this be the fact, "Galienum" may also be considered a French term, for although it is mentioned in the Index of the second book of Theophilus (who calls it "Gallien"[1] and not "Galienum"), yet it will be recollected that this author professes to teach "quicquid in Fenestrarum preciosa varietate diligit *Francia*," and in lib. ii. cap. xii., he again mentions the skill of the French in this art. Besides, the term "Gali colour, red,"

---

1 "De vitro quod vocatur Gallien." See the Wolfenbüttel MS. of Theophilus, published by Lessing. There is a reprint of this work in the 8vo. edition of Lessing's works, published in 1839.

occurs in the MS. of Mayerne in an extract from the book of "Mr. Colladon" entitled "Couleurs des Esmaulx ou Vernix de la Poterie de Faience; Copie de l'original d'un Maistre potier Anglais."[1]

The term "Grossinum," which occurs in No. VIII. and No. XLIX., appears to denote a gros, which was a French weight equal to 1 drachm or the 8th of an ounce; it may also denote a small German coin, but in the present case the former may be fairly considered to express its real signification.

Among the terms which are peculiar to the north and west of Europe may be enumerated "Cervisia," also "Warancia," which is mentioned in the recipe for Cordovan leather No. XXXII., and which in the extracts from Isidore No. LIII., is written "Garancia,"[2] and is identified with Sandis (madder); "Glassam" called in German "Glas," and in French MSS. "Glasse," amber, and several others.

It is to be observed that several recipes occur in the

---

[1] It is observed by all writers on glass-painting, that the colours used for one art are always applicable to the other. See Le Vieil, de la Peinture sur Verre, p. 113.

Le Vieil (p. 25) observes, "A great many of our French churches, which date from the twelfth century, contain coloured glass windows, which consist only of different compartments of glass, the ground of which is generally red, and this red glass was so common then, and is now so rare, that it is only with regard to this fine red colour that we can truly consider the art of painting on glass as a secret now lost."

[2] Granza is the Spanish for madder; and Isidore, from whose work the passage in question was copied, was Bishop of Seville in the seventh century. Madder is called in French, Garance. In medieval MSS. the term Warantia is generally used.

The fact of the madder plant being mentioned under four different terms, two only of which are mentioned to be synonymous, is certainly a proof that the recipes were written by different persons. In No. XXXII. the term "Warancia" occurs; in No. LIII. we find "Sandis, id est Garancia;" and in No. LV. the plant is called "Rubea."

third book, which are merely variations of some in the first book. This occurs so frequently in old MSS., that no conclusions can be drawn from this fact alone, as to the antiquity or originality of those of the first book. No. XVIII. in the first book is a metrical version of No. I. in the third book; No. XIX. of the first book, of No. II. in the third book; No. XXI. of the first book, of No. IV. in the third book. There is no evidence to show which of these are the most ancient.

The same thing may be observed of the recipes for sculpturing or engraving gems and hardening iron, three of which occur in the first book; a similar number are contained in the third book. The recipes are all somewhat different, but they are alike in principle, and Eraclius informs us (Lib. i. No. VI.) that they were derived in the first instance from Pliny. Several of these are found to be in the Clavicula.

As to the date of the third book of Eraclius, it appears to me that it must not be considered earlier than the twelfth, or later than the thirteenth century.

The allusions to the arts of the Saracens or Arabians, in Nos. IX., XXXII., XLVI., and XLVII., prove that the work could not have been earlier than the ninth century, and the recipe for dyeing cordovan leather[1] (No. XXXII.), in which the word "Warancia"

[1] Cordova was taken by the Moors A.D. 711, and in the year 759 Abdurrahman established his royal residence there. From that time Cordova became the centre of the arts, of industry, and of genius. It was distinguished for the excellence of its manufactures, and was especially celebrated for its leather, hence called "Cordovan." The remains of the tan-pits employed in the process, which are still to be seen on the north side of the Guadalquivir, prove that the art was of Moorish origin, for they were formed of baked earth, a material, says Mr. Murphy, much used by the

occurs, affords a strong presumption that it was much later, in order to give time for the Moorish art to become known in those countries where madder was called by the above name.

The lead glaze mentioned in No. III. will, however, probably enable us to fix the earliest date at which this third book could have been written, for De Brongniart, the director of the manufactory at Sèvres, who certainly may be considered good authority on this subject, remarks in his Traité des Arts Céramiques, p. 304, "J'ai déjà dit que jusqu'à présent on n'avait reconnu aucune potterie Européenne qui avant le xiie siècle eut reçu une glaçure plombifère."[1] He also says that lead glazing was applied to pottery at Pesaro about 1100; that it had been found on pottery in a tomb at Jumièges, the date of which was 1120. He also remarks, that pottery with a lead glaze was found at Alsace in the thirteenth century.

The directions given by Eraclius for the preparation of oils and varnishes, and for painting generally, correspond with the practice of the thirteenth century, especially in England, as Mr. Eastlake[2] has shown from various documents preserved in the public records. I should also observe, that the real Lapis Lazuli is mentioned in No. LI., with the test by which it was distinguished from the Azzurro della Magna, which certainly does not occur in Theophilus, the Lucca MS., the Clavicula, or

---

Moors in Spain. The prospects of Cordova continued to increase until the dissensions which distracted the Moorish power in Spain, towards the close of the tenth century. After that period it continued to decline until the expulsion of the Moors in 1236. The trade in Cordovan leather was then nearly destroyed, and the Moors carried it with them to Morocco.

1 See also pp. 96, 97, 98.

2 'Materials for a History of Painting in Oil,' pp. 49–57, and 552–561.

S. Audemar, and I think not in the first or second books[1] of Eraclius. Brazil wood also is mentioned in the third book of Eraclius, and in S. Audemar, but not in Theophilus, the Lucca MS., or the Clavicula.

The probability is, that the third part was written after the Clavicula,[2] and shortly before the MS. of Theophilus, who appears not only to have introduced some of the metrical parts of the work into his own; but it seems probable that he had the third book before him when he composed his own second book, although he has enlarged, and I must say, very much improved upon his original, which I think I can trace in several chapters of the second book of Theophilus, and I also think that three of the missing chapters mentioned in the table of contents of the second book of Theophilus will be found in the MS. of Eraclius. Red glass, called "Gallienum," and green glass, are described in No. VII., and blue glass in No. VIII. and No. XLIX. of Eraclius.[3]

The extracts from Isidore relative to glass are contained in both MSS., those relating to pigments are in the Le Begue MS. only. Some of these are abstracted in so imperfect a manner, as to be scarcely

---

[1] The lazur mentioned in the second book seems to have been native carbonate of copper, and not lapis lazuli, because it turned *black in the fire.*

[2] The date of Sir T. Phillips's copy of the Clavicula (the only one known) is of the twelfth century, but the earliest copies of Eraclius and Theophilus are of the thirteenth century. There is, however, internal evidence of the Clavicula being older than the third book of Eraclius, especially those parts which relate to painting in oil, and which are found in the Paris MS. only.

[3] The fourth of the missing chapters (De Coloribus qui fiunt ex cupro et plumbo et sale) seems to be contained in cap. xxxi. of the second book of Theophilus, entitled 'De Anulis,' where we find the following words:— "Deinde acquire tibi cineres, sal, pulverem cupri, et plumbum."

intelligible. It is easy, however, to perceive that Nos. L. to LV. inclusive, are an abridgment of Chapters VII.—XIV. of the 7th book of Vitruvius, interspersed occasionally with a few original observations relative to colours generally, and to a few pigments which were employed during the middle ages.

Chapters LVI. and LVIII. appear to be translations from some MS. of Byzantine Art, which was current wherever painting was practised at this time, and parts of which also appear, with the variations likely to be met with in translations by different persons, and perhaps by persons of different nations, from the same original, in the Clavicula, in the MS. of S. Audemar, in the appendix to the Theophilus of the British Museum, and at the greatest length in the Sloane MS., No. 1754.

From the fact of all these translations appearing in MSS. of northern origin (always supposing Theophilus to have been a German), and of the white pigment so frequently mentioned being called Album de Pullia, or Apuleya, I have formed the opinion that the original MS. of Byzantine art was written by a Greco-Italian of the Duchy of Benevento (which included Apulia), and that the MS. was perhaps communicated by some descendant of the Norman followers of Robert Guiscard[1] to the Normans settled in the west of Europe.

---

[1] In 1002 or 1003 the Normans first landed in the Neapolitan territory: in 1015 they made their first settlement there. In 1019 the Normans under Raynulf, uniting with the Lombards and Greeks, drove the Saracens out of Sicily; and the Greeks, who, on the arrival of the Normans, were in possession of about two-thirds of the kingdom of Naples, re-established themselves, and made a distinct province in the western part of Apulia, under the name of Capitanata. In 1056 Robert Guiscard, the Norman, was made Duke of Apulia, and his successors continued to enjoy the dignity until 1195, when the Normans submitted to the Emperor.

After a careful perusal of the MS. attributed to Eraclius, I have formed the following conclusions :—

That it is a collection of works on art, somewhat of the same nature as the MS. of Le Begue.

That the metrical parts only constituted the Treatise de Coloribus et Artibus Romanorum of Eraclius, and that this part is more ancient than great part of the third book.

That the third book consists of a miscellaneous collection of works on art, which may be arranged under three heads: first of an abridgment or paraphrase from Vitruvius and Isidore on making glass and on colours; secondly, of some translations of a Greek or Byzantine MS.; and thirdly, of original matter, or of recipes collected from contemporary artists, many of which appear to be of French origin.

That these MSS. fell into the hands of some person who did for them what Le Begue did for the collection of Alcherius, namely, united them into one work, and who also extended to the whole work the title which was probably intended for the first and second books only. I think there is some proof of this in the epithet added in both MSS. to the name of Eraclius, "Vir sapientissimus," which, whatever might have been the opinion of Eraclius relative to his own abilities—and he certainly did not underrate them—he would scarcely have ventured to place there himself.

I think it of some importance to the arts that the time of Eraclius should be fixed. If my reasons are not satisfactory, I shall probably be corrected by those more skilled than myself on this subject.

EXPLANATION OF SYMBOLS

REFERRED TO IN THE NOTES TO THE TREATISE OF ERACLIUS.

P. denotes the MS. in the Royal Library at Paris.

R. the MS. published by Raspe.

W. the chapters printed by Wecker, and by him ascribed to Arnaldus de Villanova and Marcellus Palingenius.

T. the chapters of Eraclius found in the MS. of Theophilus in the Harleian Collection at the British Museum.

(T.) those chapters of which a prose version is given in the last-mentioned MS.

S. the chapters of the third book of Eraclius contained in the MS. No. 1754, of the Sloane Collection at the British Museum.

C. the chapters of the third book of Eraclius contained in the treatise called 'Mappæ Clavicula.'

Cant. The MS. formerly at Cambridge, but now in the British Museum.

HERE BEGINS THE

FIRST AND METRICAL BOOK OF ERACLIUS,

A VERY WISE MAN,

ON THE COLOURS AND ARTS OF THE ROMANS.

AND FIRST THE

INTRODUCTION.

I have described, brother, various flowers for your use, as I best could. I have added to the flowers the arts which relate to, and are proper for writing; to which, if you pay attention, you will find them true in practice. I indeed write nothing to you, which I have not first tried myself. The greatness of intellect, for which the Roman people was once so eminent, has faded, and the care of the wise senate has perished. Who can now investigate these arts? Who is now able to show us what these artificers, powerful by their immense intellect, discovered for themselves? He who, by his powerful virtue, holds the keys of the mind, divides the pious hearts of men among various arts.

INCIPIT

PRIMUS ET METRICUS[1] LIBER ERACLII,

SAPIENTISSIMI VIRI,

DE COLORIBUS ET ARTIBUS ROMANORUM.

ET PRIMO

PROHEMIUM.[2]

Ut potui levius varios tibi frater ad usus
Descripsi flores, adjeci floribus artes,
Congrua scripturis quæ sunt, et idonea[3] scriptis,
Que si perpendis, utendo vera probabis.
Nil tibi scribo quidem, quod[4] non prius ipse probassem.
Jam decus ingenii quod[4] plebs Romana probatur
Decidit, ut periit sapientum cura senatum.
Quis nunc has artes investigare valebit,
Quas isti artifices, immensa mente[5] potentes,
Invenere sibi, potens est ostendere nobis ?
Qui tenet ingenii claves virtute potenti
In varias artes resecat pia corda virorum.

---

[1] *Primus et metricus* omittit R. [2] *Et primo prohemium* omittit R.
[3] *Idone* R. [4] *Quæ* R. [5] *Meree* R.

II. *How various colours fit for writing are made from wild flowers.*[1]

He who wishes to convert flowers into the various colours which, for the purpose of writing, the page of the book demands, must wander over the corn-fields early in the morning, and then he will find various flowers fresh sprung up. Let him make haste to pluck them for himself; and when he gets home, let him take care not to mix them together, but let him do what this art demands [namely], grind these flowers upon a smooth stone, and grind raw gypsum along with them. So you can preserve these colours dry. And if you wish to change the colour to green, mix lime with the flowers. You will then see what I have bid you [do], which is as I have already tried it myself.

[1] See Theoph., E. Ed., p. 392. Wecker, p. 643.
The early painters were accustomed to prepare many vegetable pigments for painting in miniature. Indeed there are scarcely any plants which yield colouring juices, which have not, at some period, been used for this purpose. The process employed in the text was simple enough: it consisted in grinding the flowers first by themselves and then with sulphate of lime, which, while it gave body to the vegetable pigments, did not affect the colours. The text shows that the effects of lime in changing vegetable blues to greens, even at that early period, were well understood.

III. *To paint earthen vases.*[1]

If any one wishes to paint vases with glass, [let him grind Roman glass well on marble, and when it is like dust, let him paint earthen vases with it, with the clear fatness of gum, mixed with spring water; and when dry, send them to the furnace. Let the earth [clay] be good, so as to stand the fire; and at length he will take out of the furnace shining vases good enough for kings.] Let him choose for himself two stones of red marble, between which let him grind the Roman glass, and when it is

[1] See Theoph., E. Ed., p. 398; and Wecker, p. 644.

II. *Quomodo fiant diversi colores de floribus campestribus ad scribendum apti.*[1]

Flores in varios qui vult mutare colores,
Causa scribendi quos[2] libri pagina poscit,
Est opus ut segetes in summo mane pererret,
Et tunc[3] diversos flores ortuque recentes
Inveniet properetque sibi[4] decerpere eosdem.
Cumque domum[5] fuerit,[6] caveat ne ponat in unum
Illos, sed faciat quod[7] talis res[8] sibi poscit[9]
Desuper[10] equalem petram contriveris istos
Flores ; incoctum pariter tum[11] contere[12] gypsum[13]
Sic tibi siccatos poteris servare colores.
Ex quibus in viridem si vis mutare colorem,[14]
Calcem commisce cum floribus ; inde videbis[15]
Quod tibi mandavi, veluti prius ipse[16] probavi.

[1] Sic P. ; R. et T. habent *de floribus ad scribendum;* W. *Carmen de floribus seu coloribus, ad scribendum, pingendum,* &c. [2] *Quis* P. [3] *Et inter* R. [4] *Sibi* omittunt P. R. [5] *Domi* W. T. [6] *Fuerint* T. [7] *Quæ* P. R. [8] *Quis* W. [9] *Poscit vel quærit* T. [10] *Dum super* W. T. [11] *Tu* P. R. [12] *Congere* T. [13] Sic W. T. ; *Gipsum* P. R. [14] *Recentem* W. [15] Hanc lineam omittit W., errore forsan typographico. [16] *Veluti prius ipse* W. ; *verum velut ipse* P. R. ; *veluti ipse* T.

III. *Ad vasa fictilia depingenda.*[1]

E vitro[2] si quis depingere vascula[3] quærit,
[Vitrum[4] Romanum bene marmore conterat, et cum
Ut pulvis fuerit, claro pinguedine gummi,
Fontis aqua mista, figulorum vascula pingat,
Siccaque fornaci mandes : sit terra probata
Quæ valeat flammis obstare, nitentia tandem
Regibus apta satis ex furno vascula tollet.]
Eligat ipse duas rufo de[5] marmore petras

[1] Sic W. ; *De preciosa pictura vitri* R. ; *De pictura ex vitro* T. ; *Quomodo fialæ terreæ ex preciosa pictura de vitri bitumine facta ornantur* P. [2] *Ex vitro* T. ; *De vitro* W. ; *De vitro fialas* P. [3] *Vascula* omittit P. [4] In [ ] inclusa in W. solum continentur. [5] *De rufo* T.

pulverized as fine as the dust of the earth, let him make it liquid with the clear fatness of gum. After this let him paint the vessels, which the workman has finely moulded in clay, and when they are dry, let him put them into the furnace. And let him take care to put them into [vessels of[1]] good clay, that they may thus be able to check the heat, and make them shining with perfect beauty.

[1] Compare with the last sentence in No. III. lib. iii.

IV. *Of sculpturing glass.*[1]

O all you artists, who wish to engrave in a beautiful manner on glass, I will now show you what I myself have tried. I sought fat worms, which the plough turns up from the earth; and the art useful in these things bid me at the same time seek vinegar, and the warm blood of a large he-goat, which I had cunningly fed for a short time on strong ivy, tied up under cover. After this, I threw the worms and vinegar into the warm blood, and anointed all the bright shining vessel, after which I tried to carve the glass with the hard stone called pyrites.

[1] See Theoph., E. Ed., p. 396; and Wecker, p. 644.

V. *Of phials decorated with gold.*

The Romans made themselves phials of glass, artfully varied with gold, very precious, to which I gave great pains and atten-

Inter quas vitrum Romanum conterat,[1] et cum
Ut pulvis terræ fuerit pariter resolutum,
Hoc faciat [2] liquidum clara pinguedine gummi
Post hæc[3] depingat petulas[4] quas finxit honeste
Figulus. Hoc facto succensæ imponat[5] easdem
Fornaci, caveatque simul quod[6] terra probata
Has teneat, quo[7] sic valeat[8] obstare calori[9]
Illas que faciat[10] plena virtute nitentes.

[1] *Conteret* P. R. W. [2] *Faciet* P. R. [3] *Post hoc* P. W. [4] Sic P. R. *Paginas* T.; *Peculas* W. [5] *Figulus e terra; siccatas ponat* W. [6] *Quæ* P. R.; *quo* T. [7] *Qua* W. [8] *Valeant* W. T. [9] *Colori* P. R. [10] Sic T.; *Illasque faciet* W. P.; *Illas qui facies* R.

IV. *De sculptura vitri.*[1]

O vos artifices qui sculpere vultis honeste[2]
Vitrum, nunc vobis pandam,[3] velut ipse probavi,
Vermes quæsivi pingues quos vertit aratrum
Ex terra,[4] atque simul me quærere jussit[5] acetum
Utilis ars istis rebus, calidum que[6] cruorem
Ex hirco[7] ingenti, quem sollers[8] tempore parvo
Ex hedera[9] forti pavi tecto religatum.
Sanguine cum calido; post hæc[10] vermes et acetum
Infudi,[11] ac totam fialam clare renitentem
Unxi; quo facto, temptavi [12] sculpere vitrum
Cum duro lapide piritis[13] nomine dicto.

[1] Sic R. and T.; *De Sculptura vitri, quomodo fit* P.; *Modus pingendi vasa, et vitra* W. [2] *Honesti* W. [3] *Pandam vobis* W. [4] *E terra* P. R.; Per terram T. [5] Sic W.; *Jussit me quærere* alii. [6] *Atque* W. [7] *Hyrco* T. [8] *Solito quem* W. [9] *Ex Hedera* W.; *ex herba* P. R.; *herba ex hedera* T. [10] *Posthoc* P. [11] *Infondi* P. [12] *Quo pacto tentavi* W. [13] *Piritis*, sic R. P. T.; *Smerilli* W.

V. *De fialis auro decoratis.*[1]

Romani fialas, auro caute variatas,
Ex vitro fecere sibi, nimium preciosas;

[1] *De fialis vitri auro decorandis* P.

tion, and had my mind's eye fixed upon them day and night, that I might thus attain the art by which the phials shone so bright; I at length discovered what I will explain to you, my dearest friend. I found gold-leaf carefully inclosed between the double glass.[1] When I had often knowingly looked at it, being more and more troubled about it, I obtained some phials shining with clear glass, which I anointed with the fatness of gum with a paint-brush. Having done this, I began to lay leaf-gold upon them, and when they were dry I engraved birds and men and lions upon them, as I thought proper. Having done this, I placed over them glass made thin with fire by skilful blowing. After they had felt the heat thoroughly, the thinned glass adhered properly to the phials.

[1] A small design in gold and silver is mentioned by Count Caylus in his work entitled 'Recueil d'Antiquités,' tom. iii. p. 193, which is thought to be enclosed between two strata of glass, probably in the manner described in the text. One stratum of the glass mentioned by Caylus was blue, the other was colourless. From the recipe in the text, it may be conjectured that this method of gilding on glass was followed by the Romans, and early Italian school, which existed contemporaneously, although independently of the Byzantine school, at the time when the MS. of Eraclius was written. The process taught by Theophilus (lib. ii. cap. xiii.), and usually adopted in the Florentine school of Mosaic painters, who were taught by the Byzantine Greeks, appears to have been different. See Lettera di Branchi al Prof. Ciampi, Notizie Inedite, &c., p. 25, n.

VI. *Of engraving precious stones.*[1]

Whoever wishes to cut with iron the precious stones in which the kings of the Roman city (who anciently held the arts in high estimation) much delighted, upon gold, let him learn the discovery which I made with profound thought, for it is very precious. I procured urine, with the fresh blood of a huge he-goat, fed for a short time upon ivy, which being done, I cut the gems in the warm blood, as directed by Pliny, the author who wrote upon the arts which the Roman people put to proof, and who also well described the virtues of stones; of which he

[1] See Theoph., E. Ed., p. 402; and Wecker, p. 428.

Erga quas gessi cum summa mente laborem,
Atque oculos cordis super has noctuque dieque [1]
Intentos habui, quo sic attingere possem
Hanc artem, per quam fialæ valde renitebant;[2]
Tandem perfexi tibi quod Carissime pandam.
Inveni petulas[3] inter vitrum duplicatum
Inclusas caute. Cum sollers sepius illud
Visu lustrassem, super hoc magis et magis ipse
Commotus, quasdam claro vitro renitentes
Quæsivi fialas mihi,[4] quas pinguedine gummi
Unxi pincello. Quo facto[5] imponere cepi
Ex auro petulas super illas; utque[6] fuere
Siccatæ volucres homines pariterque leones
Inscripsi ut sensi; quo facto desuper ipsas
Armavi[7] vitrum docto flatu tenuatum
Ignis; sed postquam pariter sensere calorem
Se vitrum fialis[8] tenuatum junxit honeste.

[1] *Diebus* P. [2] *Nitebant* P. [3] *Paculas* P. [4] *Michi* P. [5] *Ex auro* male supplet R. [6] *Atque* P. [7] *Ornavi* P. [8] *Fialæ* R.

VI. *De preciosorum lapidum incisione.*[1]

Qui cupit egregios [2] lapides irrumpere ferro
Quos dilexerunt nimium reges [3] super aurum
Urbis Romanæ, qui celsas jam tenuere
Artes,[4] ingenium quod ego sub mente profunda
Inveni, accipiat [5] quoniam valde est [6] preciosum.
Urinam [7] mihi quæsivi, pariterque cruorem
Ex hirco ingenti, modico sub tempore pasto
Herba, quo facto, calefacto sanguine gemmas
Incidi, veluti monstravit [8] Plinius [9] auctor.
Artes qui scripsit quas plebs Romana probavit,

[1] Sic P. R. *De sculpendis gemmis* T. *Gemmarum sectio* W. [2] *Egregio* W. [3] *Reges nimium* W. T. [4] *Arces* W. [5] *Capiant* W. [6] Sic P.; *est* omittet R.; T. habet *quem valde est;* et W., *quoniam nimis est.* [7] *Uriciam* R. [8] *Monstrante* R. [9] *Plenius* P.

who knows the powers, esteems them most. For the first kings, who anciently held the city, adorned with gems their garments, gleaming with gold; of these the most remarkable was Aurelian, who interwove his own robes with gems and gold.

VII. *Of golden writing.*[1]

Whoever wishes to execute beautiful writing with gold, let him read what I say in lowly verse. Let him grind gold with pure wine, until it is well dissolved. Then let him wash it frequently, for the white page of the book demands this, and then make it [liquid] with the fatness of ox [gall, if he pleases, or with the clear fatness of gum]; and I also request him to stir it with a reed when he uses the gold, if he wishes to write beautifully. When the writing is dry, let him make it very brilliant with the tooth of a savage bear.

[1] See Theoph., E. Ed., p. 392.

VIII. *Of ivy and lake.*[1]

The strong ivy is very useful for these purposes. Our ancestors were very fond of its leaves as a mark of honour: it was used as a crown for poets. In the spring all things rejoice,

[1] See Theoph., E. Ed., p. 394.

It appears that the resinous juice exudes from the ivy in warm countries only. See *Nemnich*, *Polyglotten-Lexicon*, *Tit.* Hedera. It will be observed, that the juice, when it first flowed from the ivy, was not red, but that it gradually acquired that colour.

Atque simul lapidum virtutes scripsit honeste,
Quorum qui noscit[1] vires, plus[2] diligit illos.
Nam primi reges, urbem qui jam tenuerunt[3]
Gemmis ornarunt vestes auro renitentes.
Ex quibus insignis primus fuit Aurelianus
Qui proprias vestes gemmis contexit et auro.[4]

[1] Sic T. W.; *nescit* R. P. [2] *Minus* R. P. [3] *Tenuere* R. P. [4] Hos quatuor versus ultimos omittit W., et eorum loco ponit "*Primus ait versus quot habet sententia sensus.*"

VII. *De aurea scriptura.*

Scripturam pulcram quisquis bene scribere quærit,[1]
Ex auro, legat hoc quod[2] vili carmine dico.
Aurum cum puro mero[3] molat, usque solutum
Hoc[4] nimium fuerit. Tunc sepius abluat illud;[5]
Nam quia[6] deposcit hoc candens pagina libri.
Exin taurini faciat[7] pinguedine [fellis[8]
Hoc liquidum, si vult, seu cum pinguedine] gummi.
Atque rogo pariter calamo cum ceperit aurum
Illud[9] commoveat, pulchre si scribere quærit.
Hinc siccata sicut[10] fuerit scriptura, nitentem
Hanc[11] nimium faciat ursi cum dente feroci.

[1] *Si quis scripturam quærit sibi scribere pulcram* T. [2] *Hic quæ* R. [3] *Mero* T., *Menio* P.; omittit R. [4] *Hoc* T.; omittunt R. P. [5] Sic R. P. *Moneo quod sæpe lavet illud* T. [6] *Namque* R. P. [7] *Faciet* R. P. [8] Ex T. In R. P. male omissum. [9] *Illum* T. [10] *Sed ut* T. [11] *Hunc* T.

VIII. *De edera et lacca.*[1]

Propositis rebus edere satis utile robur.
Hujus enim[2] frondem nimium coluere priores
Ad titulum laudis; erat ipsa corona poetis.
Vere novo, reduci cum gaudent[3] omnia succo,

[1] Sic R.; in P. vero *De edera herba et lacca succo ejus rubeo ab ipsa exeunti.* [2] *Ut* R. [3] *Cum gaudent* P. *Congaudent* R.

being refreshed with new sap; and the spring brings back the moisture to the trees, while the winter refuses them the power of growing. The ivy is similarly affected; for the offshoots of the branches, pushed into barren places, give out a juice, which, whoever collects, should put into a red vase of baked earth, and it will gradually assume a blood colour. This the painter loves, and the scribe equally delights in. Hence also is made the parcia dyed with a rose colour. It also serves to dye the skins of goats and sheep.

IX. *Of gold-leaf, how it is laid on ivory.*[1]

You will decorate carvings in ivory with gold-leaf. Now hear in what manner this thing is done. . Seek to obtain the fish which is called "huso,"[2] and keep its air-bladder liquefied by being boiled in water, and with this mark over the place where you wish to lay the gold; and you will thus easily be able to fasten it to the ivory.

[1] See Theoph., E. Ed., p. 404; and Wecker, p. 645.

[2] The Huso or Huson (Acipenser Huso) was the large sturgeon from which isinglass is procured. It was the Ichthyocolla of Pliny; the Ittiocolla, Usone, Colpesce, of the Italians; the Copese of the Venetians; the Isinglass fish of the English; the Huizenblasfisk of the Dutch; Der Hausen of the Germans; and the Bjeluga of the Russians. See Nemnich, Polyg. Lexicon.

X. *How gems are polished.*[1]

If you wish to give a shining splendour to gems, obtain for yourself a piece of smooth marble, and lest it may be injured by this, lay it on the gem and rub it gently, and a polish will be given to the stone. The harder it is, the brighter polish will it take.

[1] See Theoph., E. Ed., p. 402; and see Wecker, p. 645.

Arboribusque refert humor, quas bruma negabat
Crescendi vires, ederam talis probat ordo.
Nam subula rami, loca per deserta forati,
Emittunt viscum, quem qui sibi sumpserit illum,
Transferet in rubeam coctum prurigine [1] formam ;
Sanguineumque sibi leviter capit ille colorem.
Hunc sibi pictor amat et scriptor diligit eque.
Hinc etiam roseo fit parcia tincta [2] colore.
Quæ [3] quoque caprinas, quæ [3] pelles tingit ovinas.

[1] *Prurigine* P. ; in R. lacuna relicta sic—. . . .*rigine*. [2] *Parva tinctura* P. [3] *Quam* R.

IX. *De petula auri, quomodo in ebore mittatur.*[1]

Sculpturas eboris auri petulis [2] decorabis
Quo tamen ipsa tibi [3] res ordine congruat audi.
Quære tibi piscem qui dicitur usa [4] liquentem
Vesicam tamen [5] serva cum flumine coctam
Inde locum petulam cui [6] vis componere signa
Sic ebori facile poteris ipsam consolidare.

[1] Sic R. ; *Quomodo petula auri in ebore mittatur, et cum quo visco* P. ; *De pictura eboris* W., qui hunc versum cæteris premittit—"*Pingere si quis ebur vult sic procedere debet.*" [2] *Pecula* W. [3] *Tibi* omittunt R. P. [4] Sic P. ; *Husa* W. ; R. lacunam habet. [5] *Tantum* P. ; W. vero habet *Vesicam serva decoctam fluminis unda.* [6] *Petulam quem* P. ; *Pecula quem* W., qui sequentem versum omittit.

X. *De gemmis quomodo lucidæ fiunt.*[1]

Si vis splendentem gemmis inferre nitorem [2]
Partem quære tibi tantummodo marmoris æqui
Gemma superposita petræ, sed flumine pauco
Hinc ne lædatur, tractu leviore limetur.[3]
Quanto durescit, tanto magis ipsa nitescit.[4]

[1] Sic P. ; *De gemmis quomodo luceant* R. ; *Gemmæ ut nitescant* W. [2] *Colorem* P. R. [3] Sic emendavi. W. habet "*Gemma supposita petræ, sed flumine pauco : sed ne lædatur, tractu leniore limetur.*" P. et R. vero "*Hinc ne lædatur, tactu leviore limetur Gemma superposito, sed petre lumine tracto.*" [4] *Nitescit* P. ; *Accescit* R. ; *Nitebit* W.

XI. *Of a green colour for writing.*[1]

If you wish to embellish your writing with a green colour, mix vinegar together with strong honey, and then cover up the vase itself in very hot dung; and so take it out after twelve days shall have elapsed.

[1] See Theoph., E. Ed., p. 396.

The vase mentioned in this chapter must have been of copper or brass. The colour produced in that case would have been verdigris, which is an acetate of copper.

XII. *How to cut crystal.*[1]

Crystal can easily be cut by the following artifice:—Seek for yourself a convenient plate of lead, and join two boards to it, one on each side, with a centre piece of iron, so as to keep the lead steady; for to the lead alone belongs the business of cutting, and the outer plates are as guides to make it run round evenly. But you would not be able to overcome such great hardness by the unassisted softness of the lead, unless you join to it some powder, such as the pulverized fragment of a furnace, which you will be able to fasten to the tender plate, for this addition will make the lead sharp, and the fragments of brick also have equal force; you must cut it, adding to it a little river water. But let the blood of a goat first temper it, for this blood makes the iron so hard that even adamant is soft compared with it.

[1] See Wecker, p. 449.

Compare with Theophilus, lib. iii. cap. xciv. (E. Ed., p. 387). Crystal is defined by Theophilus to be "water hardened into ice." In this, Mr. Hendrie observes, he has repeated the opinion of Pliny. The term "crystal" was also applied to glass made from pulverized quartz or sand fused with an alkali. In an extract from the book of Mr. Colladon, quoted in the Mayerne MS. and by Mr. Hendrie (Theoph., p. 180), crystal is defined to be "very clear glass of Venice."

XI. *De viridi colore ad scribendum.*[1]

Si quæris viridi scriptura[2] colore notari,
Aeri commissum melli miscebis acetum;
Hinc valde calido vas ipsum contege fimo.
Sic et bissenis hoc extrahe solibus[3] actis.

[1] Sic R.; *ad scribendum quomodo fit* P. [2] *Scripta* R. [3] *Talibus* R.

XII. *Quomodo cristallum possit secari.*[1]

Cristallum tali facile[2] valet arte secari.[3]
Opportuna[4] tibi quæratur[5] lamina plumbi;[6]
Huic[7] etiam binæ claves[8] jungantur utrinque,[9]
Ex ferro medium, quæ firmant[10] undique plumbum;[11]
Nam plumbo soli[12] tribuetur cura secandi.
Ipsi custodes laminæ sint exteriores,
Ut sibi dent rectum recto consumere[13] cursum.
Sed nec duritiem[14] poteris prærumpere[15] tantam
Mollitie plumbi, nisi quædam junxeris[16] illi
Tanquam pulverulas fornacis fragmine micas[17]
Quæ teneræ poteris laminæ connectere plumbi[18]
Hæc etenim plumbum conjunctio reddet[19] acutum.
At quum rursus[20] habent lateris fragmenta vigorem
Concidis adjuncta paulatim fluminis unda[21]
Sed[22] vim cristalli cruor antea temperet hirci
Sanguis enim facilem ferro facit hic adamantem.[23]

[1] Sic R. *Quomodo cristallum possis secare* P. *Cristalli sectio* W. [2] *Cristallus tali durus* W. [3] *Parari* P. [4] *Oportuna* P. R. [5] *Quæretur* W. [6] *Ferri* P. R. [7] Hinc? P. R. [8] Sic R. *Bene clavos* P.; *Bini clavi* W. [9] *Utrumque* P. [10] *Qui solito medium consument* W. [11] *Plumbi* P. [12] *Solo* P. R. [13] *Conamine* P. R. [14] *Duriciam* R. P. [15] *Prorumpere* R. P. [16] Ita emendavi. *Nec quiddam junxeris* R.; *Nisi quoddam junxeris* P.; *Nisi quædam junxerit*, W. [17] Sic P. R.; *Tanquam pulvereas fornacis fragmine mittas* W. [18] Sic W.; *Contere, quas teneræ poteris* [*possis* P.] *connectere laminæ* P. R. [19] Hunc versum omittit W. *Reddit* P. [20] *Et quum rursum* P. R. [21] Hunc versum omittunt P. R. [22] *Si* W. [23] Sic P. W.; Hunc versum omittit R.

XIII. *Of tempering iron [hard for cutting stones.]*[1]

[You must thus make iron hard for sculpturing gems.] Whoever wishes to cut stones with the solid iron, must observe the following rules to temper its edge. At the time when the goat is in heat his fat alone is fit for this purpose. For if any one quenches the hot iron in its fat, it immediately becomes hard with a firm edge.

[1] See Theoph. p. 404. Wecker, 428.

XIV. *Of the gems which you wish to make from Roman Glass.*

You will thus be able to make beautiful shining gems of every sort with Roman glass. Hollow out some clay for yourself as a mould for the stone; and put into it some glass broken into small pieces. You may easily prepare this [the mould] by this artifice. Let a certain reed be skilfully turned round and round, and when it [the clay] begins to harden, and the rod sticks tight, then fix it on the rod on both sides, and let the rod be held by the glass placed round it; and then put the clay, guarded by a hollow iron, into the fire, and when the glass is thoroughly liquefied, press it into the hollow with a bright iron, so that you may have no bubble or flaw in it.

XIII. *De temperamento duro ferri ad incidendum lapides.*[1]

Qui quærit solido[2] lapides irrumpere ferro,
Hos habeat ritus, ut acumen temperet ejus.
Tempore quo solito magis uritur[3] hircus amore,
Solus adeps hujus fit ad istos aptior usus.
Hujus enim calidum[4] si quis pinguedine ferrum
Extinguit,[5] subito durescit acumine firmo.

[1] Sic P. ; *De temperamento ferri* R. ; *Gemmarum sculptura* W., qui hunc versum alteris præmittit—*Sic gemmis durum sculpendis effice ferrum.* [2] *Qui quæret solido* R., *quisquis vult solito* W. [3] *Uritur magis* P. [4] *Candens* W. [5] *Restinguet* R. ; *refrigeret* P.

XIV. *De Gemmis quas de Romano vitro facere quæris.*

Sic ex Romano poteris conficere vitro
Splendentes pulcros generis cujusque lapillos
Ad modulum lapidis cretam tibi quippe cavabis ;
Hic pones vitrum per quædam frusta minutum.
Hunc ergo facile poteris hac arte parare.
Subtiliter[1] quædam circumvolvatur arundo,
Qui dum durescit, dum virga firmius[2] hæret,
Tunc ipsi virgæ superimponetur utrinque,[3]
Et circumposito teneatur virgula vitro ;
Atque cavo tectam ferro post[4] insere cretam
Igni ; fit[5] vitrum ; cum fit[6] penitus liquefactum,
In fossam lato fulgenti[7] comprime ferro ;
Quo vesica sibi, quo lesio nulla supersit.

[1] *Subtilis* P. [2] *Durius* P. [3] *Utrumque* P. [4] *Ferro post* P. *Penitus* R [5] *Fit.* Sic emendavi ; codices *sit* habent. [6] *Fit.* Sic R. *Sit* P. [7] *Fulgenti* P.

HERE BEGINS

THE SECOND AND METRICAL BOOK,

AND FIRST

XV. *Of a colour resembling orpiment.*[1]

You will easily be able to make a colour resembling orpiment thus; preserve it carefully in your memory. The gall of a large fish is very useful for this art. The liquor of the gall must be received in a marble stone, and you must mix a little vinegar with it, and then add some white clay to the fatness of the gall, and this mixture will make the colour brilliant.

[1] A recipe similar to this is contained in the small Paris MS., No. vi. MDCCXLIX. B., where it is called "Colore aureo Lombardico."

XVI. *Of copper gilt with the fatness of gall.*[1]

If you wish to prepare copper with the fatness of gall, so as to appear gilt, you may do it in this way. Having scraped it with a knife, burnish it by rubbing it with a bear's tooth, and then sprinkle it with a pencil [dipped in] the liquor of the gall, and lay it evenly all over; afterwards give it another smooth coat, and upon this a third; and each time pass the quill evenly all over it, lest any scratch, or lump, or bubble should make the copper rough.

[1] See Theoph., E. Ed., p. 406. S. Audemar, No. 204.

INCIPIT

LIBER SECUNDUS [METRICUS,

ET PRIMO][1]

XV. *De colore auripigmento simili.*

Sic facile similem poteris servare colorem
Auripigmento; memori tu mente teneto.
Hinc piscis magni fel multum congruit arti,
Marmorea cujus petra liquor excipiatur,
Cui vetus et paucum tamen[2] admiscebis acetum,
Fellis et hinc albam tum[3] cum pinguedine cretam.
Reddet splendentem commixtio tanta colorem.[4]

[1] In [ ] omittit R. [2] *Tum* R. [3] *Ter* P. [4] *Liquorem* R.

XVI. *De cupro fellis pinguedine deaurato.*

Si velut auratum fellis pinguedine cuprum
Condere curabis, sic hoc implere valebis.
Cultello rasum splendens hoc effice tactum.
Ursi dente; quidem calamo post[1] sperge liquorem
Fellis; et hoc eque tamen[2] apponatur ubique.
Appones alium post[3] equo tramite. Rursum
Huic alium junges; vice tamen undique duces
Equali calamum, ne qua divisio cuprum
Ne quis monticulus vel ne tumor efferat[4] ullus.

[1] *Post* P.; *penitus* R. [2] *Tegmen* P. [3] *Penitus* R. [4] *Offerat* P.

XVII. *How to make a green colour for painting what you please.*[1]

Thus, O painter! you may obtain for yourself a green colour! Grind white earth with the leaves of the black nightshade.[2] Grind them both evenly together on a marble slab until they become liquid for the use of the pen, and afterwards take this juice and try it with your paintbrush. Then adorn any writings you please with the colour; but take care previously not to add too much earth.

[1] See Theoph., E. Ed., p. 394.

[2] This chapter must have been written by a person who habitually spoke Italian or French, because the Solanum Nigrum is not known by the name of "Morella," or "Morelle," except in the countries where the Italian and French languages are spoken. The expression in the MS. of Theophilus runs thus: "herba quae vulgò morella nuncupatur." The term "morelle" occurs more than once in the MS. of Le Begue, and also in the Bolognese MS. It must not be confounded with "Maurelle," the name by which the Croton Tinctorium is known at Montpelier.

XVIII. *How green glass is to be made for painting earthen vases.*[1]

By these things the effect of precious glass is shown. Take sulphur burnt in the fire, and [burnt] copper, and grind shining glass with the powder of these, and take care to make it liquid for yourself with gum only, and then place the jar, painted over with this, into the fire, for the painting will assume a green colour, when the outside of the jar begins to turn red.

[1] See Theoph., E. Ed., p. 398. Wecker, p. 644.

XIX. *Of white glass for painting earthen vessels.*[1]

You must thus make white glass fine enough for painting. Grind white glass mixed with sulphur. With these, ground

[1] See Theoph., E. Ed., p. 400. Wecker, p. 644. This probably describes an opaque white glass, resembling those threads of white glass which Theo-

XVII. *De viridi colore quomodo fieri possit ad quæ volueris depingere.*

Sic poteris viridem tibi pictor habere colorem.
Cum foliis albam morellæ[1] contere cretam;
Hæc in marmorea pariter quoque contere petra,
Usus ad pennæ liquidum dum fiat utrumque.[2]
Et post[3] hunc succum pincello sume probandum.
Hinc quascunque cupis scripturas conde colori,[4]
Ne cretæ nimium ponas tamen ante caveto.

[1] *Morellam* male habet R. [2] *Utrinque* R. [3] *Penitus* R. [4] Sic emendavi. *Coloribus* P. R.

XVIII. *De vitro viridi quomodo fieri debeat, ad vasa fictilia*[1] *depingenda.*

His rebus vitri patet effectus preciosi:
Igni combustum sulphur, quærasque cupellum,[2]
Atque teras horum splendens cum pulvere vitrum;
Hoc cures solo liquidum tibi[3] reddere gummo.
Attamen inde litam post[4] ignibus injice testam,[5]
Assumet viridem quoniam[6] pictura colorem,
Exterior testæ cum cœperit ipsa rubere.[7]

[1] *Figuli* P. [2] *Quærasque cupressum* P., *assum quare cuprum* W. [3] *Ter* W. [4] *Penitus* R. [5] *Coctam* P. R. [6] *Qualem* R. [7] *Rubore* P.

XIX. *De vitro albo, ad vasa fictilia*[1] *depingenda.*

Album picturis vitrum sic[2] attenuabis[3]
Candens permixtum cum sulphure contere vitrum

[1] *Vasa figuli* P., *Fictilia vasa* W. [2] *Sic vitrum* R. [3] *Attenuabit* R.

---

philus (lib. ii. cap. 14) says were sometimes made to surround long-necked bottles. Le Vieil (p. 27) says that white opaque glass was used for the windows in the churches belonging to the monasteries of the Bernardines and Cistercians.

together until they are like dust, you must paint a thick jar all over the outside. Then put it in to be baked by the flame of the furnace; and when it is red-hot, and the painting adheres to it, take it out; so also you may paint vases in the manner described in the first book.

XX. *Of black glass for painting earthen vases.*[1]

In the same manner also you may make black glass useful for painting. Grind the azure that is found in the earth with gum; and then breaking clear glass upon a marble slab, mix it up with it, and grind them again. This mixture will assume a blue colour, which, however, the force of the fire will turn to a beautiful black.

[1] See Wecker, p. 645.

XXI. *Of glass which is very green.*[1]

So also you may make glass of a very deep green. Take very small fragments of burnt copper, which you must afterwards mix with the rust of the same. Then grind it again, with an admixture of shining glass. Afterwards, put the jar, painted with this, into the furnace; and when the flame makes it white hot, take it out. It will not be of a beautiful appearance until it is cold; for while the glass is made intensely hot, the violence of the flame takes away the real beauty of the colour.

[1] See Wecker, p. 645. Theoph., E. Ed., p. 400.

His simul attritis, postquam[1] fuerint quasi pulvis
Exterius spissam depinges[2] undique testam.
Injice post ipsam fornacis ab igne coquendam.
Cum[3] simul ipsa rubet, sibi cum pictura coheret,
Extrahe. Sic etiam[4] pinges hinc vascula quædam,
Ars velut in primo notat insinuata libello.

[1] *Penitusque* R. [2] *Depurges* P. [3] *Quam* P. R. [4] *Ea* W.

XX. *De vitro nigro ad vasa fictilia*[1] *depingenda.*

Sic etiam nigrum pingendi transfer in usum.
Qui terra capitur cum gummo[2] contere lazur;
Et sic[3] perspicuum frangens in marmore vitrum,
Ipsi miscebis, rursumque terendo parabis.
Hæc quoque cæruleam sumet[4] commixtio formam
Quam[5] tamen in nigrum vertet vis ignia[6] vitrum.

[1] *Vasa figuli* P., *ea vasa* W. [2] *Gummi* R. [3] *Ut sit* W. [4] *Sumat* W. [5] *Quæ* W. [6] Sic emendavi; *vertetur insignia* P. R., *convertet singula* W.

XXI. *De vitro quod nimium viret.*[1]

Sic etiam nimium tu virens effice vitrum.
Accipies assi subtilia fragmina cupri,
Quæ tamen ejusdem post[2] cum rubigine mittes;
Rursus et admixto splendenti contere vitro,
Protinus hinc[3] pictam fornacibus injice testam.[4]
Postquam lucentem dabit ipsi flamma colorem,
Accipe. Non[5] pulcram capiet nisi[6] frigida formam,
Nam dum fit vitrum nimis fervere, coloris[7]
Huic auffert propriam[8] flammæ violentia formam.

[1] Sic P. R. *De vitro valde virente* W. [2] *Penitus* R. [3] *Hic* R. [4] *Flammam* R. [5] *Nam* R. W. [6] *Hinc* W. [7] *Nimio fervore vaporis* W. [8] *Propria* R.

HERE BEGINS

THE THIRD AND PROSAIC BOOK OF THE AFORESAID ERACLIUS,

ON THE AFORESAID COLOURS AND ARTS,

AND FIRST

I. [232][1] *On painting earthen vases with green glass.*[2]—Take green glass and burnt thunderbolts,[3] and also burnt copper, in powder, and mix them with clear glass, previously ground on a smooth stone. And if you wish to paint a vase with it, temper it with the aforesaid gum water, and lay it on the vase with a paint-brush, and put it into the furnace until it appears thoroughly red hot. When cool it will be of the colour of green glass.

II. [233] *To whiten earthen vases with white glass.*[4]—If you wish to make white glass for the purpose of painting, grind hot sulphur carefully with white glass, and lay it on a thick piece of earthenware, and put it into the furnace. And when it has run together, take it out of the fire; and if you wish to paint saucers and phials, made of earthenware, with it, grind it up as if for writing, and do as before directed for the green glass.

III. [259] *How earthenware vessels are glazed.*—Take the strongest potter's clay you can procure, and put it into the furnace with the other vases, or in any other fire, and bake it until it is quite red hot. When it is cool, put it into any vase, and

---

1 The figures in [ ] refer to the numbers in the Le Begue MS. at Paris.

2 See lib. ii. No. xviii.

3 The nodules of iron pyrites found about the chalk-rocks at Brighton and other parts of the coast of Sussex, are still called by the lower orders "thunderbolts." The same term is also applied to the fossils called "Belemnitæ;" but I consider that, in the present case, it can apply only to one of the minerals called "pyrites."

4 See lib. ii. No. xix.

INCIPIT

TERCIUS LIBER ET PROSAICUS ERACLII, ANTEDICTI,

DE COLORIBUS ET ARTIBUS PREDICTIS,

ET PRIMO[1]

I. [232] *De vasis testeis depingendis ex viridi vitro.*[2]—Viridis vitri et usti fulminis pulverem, item usti cupri, accipe, et misce cum claro vitro[3] prius bene[4] super marmoream petram planam[5] trito. Si ex eo testam ornare volueris,[6] cum gummi liquore supradicto temperes, et cum[7] pincello testam ex his[8] intinges, et in fornacem pones ut bene rubeat.[9] Refrigerata vitri viridis representabit[10] colorem.

II. [233] *Ad vasa testea albo vitro dealbanda.*[11]—Album vitrum si facere vis ad usum pingendi,[12] calidum sulphur cum vitro albo diligenter tere, et super spissam testam pone, et in fornacem mitte. Cum autem glutinatum fuerit, extrahe ab igne, et si ex eo scutellas[13] arte figuli factas vis dipingere, illud contere[14] ad usum scripturæ, et fac quemadmodum[15] ante dictum est de viridi vitro.

III. [259] *Quomodo vasa figuli*[16] *plumbeantur.* — Accipe terram figulorum quantum[17] fortem poteris invenire, et in furno cum aliis vasis mitte,[18] ubi tantum lento igne coques, vel in alio igne, quousque tota sit rubea. Quando[19] frigida fuerit, mitte eam

---

[1] Ex P. [2] Ex P. *De vasis testeis pingendis* R. [3] *Cum claro misce* R. [4] *Bene* omittit P. [5] *Planam* omittit R. [6] *Temperes* hic inserit P., et post omittit. [7] *Cum* omittit R. [8] *Hic* R. [9] *Ut tantum rubea appareat* R. [10] *Resplendabit*. Cant. [11] Ex P. *Item ut supra* R. [12] *Tere* hic inserit P., et post omittit. [13] *Et fialas* inserit P. [14] *Contere illum* P. [15] *Scripturæ qualiter* R. [16] *Fignul* R. [17] *Quantumvis* R. [18] *Mitte* omittit R. [19] *Et quando* P.

grind it until it is reduced to powder. Then take water and mix with it, and pour off the water into another vase, and let it remain so until the next day, and then throw away that water. Then take [some of] the clay that is left behind, and mix it with other clay without sand, and with two parts of the aforesaid very strong clay. Then pound it with a mallet, and make whatever kind of vase you like with it. Afterwards, take [some more of] that clay which you allowed to settle, and mix oil with it, and spread it all over the vase which you have made, before it is baked. Then put it away in a secret place until it is quite dry, and do not let the draught get to it. If you wish to glaze the vessel, take wheat flour, and boil it in a jar, and let it cool, and wash over the vessel with this water. Then take lead well dissolved. But if you wish to make the vase green, take copper or brass, which is better, and melt it with lead in the following manner. Take lead and melt it well in a vase. When it is quite liquid, shake it round the vase with your hands until it is reduced to powder, and then mix six parts of brass filings with it, and while the vase is wet with the flour paste, you must immediately dust the lead over it [that is, dust it over with the aforesaid filings]. But if you wish it to be yellow, dust it over with the powder of lead alone, without the filings. Then place this vase in another larger vase, and put it into the furnace, that it may be more brilliant and beautiful, but with a slow fire, so as to be neither too strong nor too weak.

IV. [234] *Also to finish earthenware vessels with green glass.*[1] —Grind rust of copper and copper filings with clear glass, and afterwards paint a jar with them as before, and put it into a very hot furnace. Then take it out of the furnace, and you will have a precious colour.

---

[1] See lib. ii. No. xxi.

in quodam vase, et tamdiu tere, quousque tota sit quasi pulvis. Deinde accipe aquam, et misce cum ea, et in alio vase cola, et usque ad alium diem sic eam dimittes. Postea illam aquam projicies foras. Deinde accipe illas feces, et cum alia terra quæ sine sabulo est misces, cum duabus partibus illius fortissimæ terræ supradictæ. Postea tere eam cum malleo. Deinde qualecunque vas volueris facies. Postea accipe illam fecem quam sivisti quiescere, et cum oleo misces, et illud vas quod fecisti, antequam coquatur, per totum linies. Deinde pones eum in secreto loco quoadusque totum siccetur, et ne ventus ei contrarius sit. Si vero eum plumbeum facere volueris, accipias[1] farinam de frumento, et in ollam bullire eam facies, et refrigerari permittes, et de ipsa aqua eam per totum in circuitu linies. Postea accipe plumbum bene solutum. Si tamen viride eum volueris[2] facere, accipe cuprum, vel auricalcum, quod melius est, et cum plumbo misce sic. Accipe plumbum, et in vase eum optime funde. Quando totum liquefactum fuerit, circumvolve manibus tuis illud in vas usque dum pulvis fiat et ita[3] VI partes limaturæ auricalci[4] cum eo misces. Cum vas illud de aqua farinæ humefactum fuerit, statim pulverabis de plumbo [id[5] est, suprascripta limatura pulverabis]. Si vero vis ut croceus sit, de puro plumbo,[6] et sine[7] limatura, pulverabis. Deinde in majori vase intus vas illud repone, et in furno mitte ut sit plus splendidum et pulcrum, lento tamen igni, ut non nimis fortiter nec nimis flebiliter.[8]

IV. [234] *Item, [ad[9] testea vasa, id est, figuli, viridi vitro perficienda.]*—Rubiginem cupri et pulverem ejusdem,[10] cum vitro claro tere, et postea ex hoc[11] testam ut supra pinge, et in fornacem valde succensam mitte. Deinde a fornace extrahe,[12] et preciosum habebis colorem.[13]

---

[1] *Accipies* P. [2] *Virideum volueris eum* P. [3] *Ita,* sic P.; R. lacunam habet. [4] *Auricalci limature* P. [5] Ex P. [6] *Deinde pones plumbo.* Cant. [7] *Suprascripta.* Cant. [8] *Nimus fortiter nec minus flebis* R. [9] Ex P. [10] *Rubiginem vitri* R. [11] *Ex hoc* omittit R. [12] *Abstrahe* R. [13] *Preciosum colorem habeas viridem* P.

V. [255] *How and when glass was invented.*—Glass is so called, as Isidorus says, because it has the property of being transparent to the sight; for with regard to other metals, whatever is inclosed in them is concealed. But with regard to glass, whatever liquid or substance is contained in it, appears inside just as it appears outside, and is visible, however it may be inclosed. Its origin was as follows: In the part of Syria which is called Phœnicia, and which borders on Judea, at the foot of Mount Carmel, there is a swamp, in which the river Belus rises, which after a course of 5 miles flows into the sea just by Tholomaïs [Ptolemaïs], the sands of which are washed by the water flowing over them. At this place, as it is reported, a vessel of nitre-merchants was wrecked, and when they were preparing their food here and there upon the sands, having no stones to support their [cooking] vessels, they placed lumps of nitre [natron] under them; which being ignited, and mixed with the sand of the shore, streams of a new and transparent liquor began to flow, and this is asserted to have been the origin of glass.

Then as the ingenious skill of men was not contented with the glass alone, endeavours were made to extend and improve this art, with other mixtures; for it is heated with light and dry wood, together with copper and nitre, and is melted in constant furnaces like brass, and is made into lumps. Afterwards these lumps are again melted in the workshops, and some is formed into shape by blowing, some is ground on a lathe, and some is sculptured like silver. It is also tinged in many ways so as to imitate hyacinths and green sapphires and onyx stones, and other colours of gems. And there is no material fitter for mirrors, or for pictures especially, than the white glass, and particularly that which is made like crystal; so that for drinking cups it has driven gold and silver quite out of use. Glass was formerly made in Italy, and throughout Gaul, and in Spain. Very soft white sand was triturated with a pestle and mill. It was then mixed with three parts of nitre, by weight or measure, and when melted was transferred to other

V. [255] *Quomodo et quando inventum fuerit vitrum.*—Vitrum dictum,[1] ut ait Ysidorus,[2] quod visui perspecuitate transluceat. In aliis enim metallis quicquid intrinsecus continetur absconditur. In vitro vero,[3] quilibet liquor vel species[4] interius, talis[5] exterius declaratur, et quodam modo clausus[6] patet.[7] Cujus origo hæc fuit. In parte Syriæ quæ Fenicis vocatur, finitima Judeæ, circa radicem montis Carmeli, palus est, ex qua nascitur Belus amnis,[8] V millium passuum spatio in mare fluens, juxta Tholomaida, cujus arenæ, decurrente[9] fluctu, sordibus eluuntur. Hic[10] fama est, quod, expulsa[11] nave mercatorum nitri,[12] cum sparsim[13] per litus epulas pararent nec essent lapides[14] pro attollendis vasis, lapides, glebas nitri vasi subdiderunt.[15] Quibus accensis, permixta arena littoris, translucentis novi liquoris, vitri scilicet,[16] fluxisse rivos,[17] et hanc fuisse originem vitri.

Mox, ut[18] ingeniosa hominum[19] solertia non fuit contenta solo vitro, sed et aliis mixturis hanc artem studuit[20] in melius ampliare, levibus enim et] aridis lignis concoquitur, adjecto cipro ac nitro,[21] continuisque fornacibus, ut æs, liquatur, massæque fiunt. Postea ex massis rursus funditur in officinis, et aliud flatu figuratur, aliud torno teritur, aliud argenti modo celatur. Tingitur etiam multis modis ita ut jacinctos saphirosque virides imitetur,[22] et onichinos, et aliarum gemmarum colores. Neque est alia speculis aptior materia, vel picturæ accommodatior. Maximus tamen in candido vitro, proximaque in cristalli similitudine, unde et ad potandum argenti et auri metalla[23] repulit. Vitrum olim[24] fiebat[25] in Italia, et per

---

[1] *Deinde* P. [2] *Proprietatem habet* supplet P. [3] *Vero* omittit R. [4] *Quælibet* supplet R. [5] *Taliter* R. [6] *Clarius* R. [7] Inter hæc duo verba lacunam habet R. [8] *Belus rivus* R. [9] *Decrescente* R. [10] *Hæc* P. [11] *Quod expulsa* P.; *pulsa* R. [12] *Mercatorum nitri* omittit P., et loco ejus *ibidem* supplet [13] *Sparsius* R. [14] *Lapides* omittit R. [15] Ex R.; *cum ad ignem in navi apponi deberent pro ferculis decoquendis, glebas igitur nitri, loco lapidum utendas, navi subdiderunt;* P. [16] *Vitri scilicet* omittit R. [17] *Asseritur* supplet P. [18] *Est* supplet R. [19] *Hominum* omittit R. [20] Ex P.; *nam* R. [21] *Et vitro* supplet P. [22] *Immittetur* P. [23] *Argenti metalla et auri* R. [24] *Enim* P. [25] *Et* supplet R.

furnaces. This mass was called "Admovitrius," and from this, when re-melted, pure and white glass was made. Among the kinds of glass, the stone obsidian[1] is also enumerated. This is black and occasionally greenish, and sometimes translucent, and of a coarser appearance, and when used for mirrors, shows a shadow instead of an image. Many persons make gems of it. It is said that this stone is produced both in India and Italy, and in Spain near the ocean.

VI. [256] *How that a person was beheaded by order of the Emperor because he had discovered the art of making flexible glass.*[2] —It is related that in the reign of Tiberius Cæsar a certain artist had discovered a way of making glass flexible and ductile. When he was admitted into Cæsar's presence, he handed a phial to him, which Cæsar indignantly threw on the ground, and it bent like a brazen vessel. The artist took up the phial from the pavement, and then taking a hammer out of his bosom he repaired the phial. Upon this Cæsar asked the artist whether any other person was acquainted with that method of making glass. When he affirmed with an oath that no other person knew the secret, Cæsar ordered him to be beheaded, lest, when this was known, gold and silver should be held dirt cheap, and the prices of all the metals be reduced. And, indeed, if glass vessels did not break, they would be better than gold or silver.

---

[1] Mr. Phillips observes that obsidian occasionally bears a great resemblance to common glass. The origin of this substance has been warmly contested: it is common in the neighbourhood of volcanoes, and has been considered as vitrified lava, whence it has obtained the familiar name of *volcanic glass*. It is found on Hecla, and in almost every part of Iceland, in the Lipari Islands, in one of which it constitutes the greater part of the mountain "della Castagna"; near the Peak of Teneriffe; in Peru, Mexico, and New Spain. In Europe, obsidian is made into reflectors for telescopes; in Mexico and Peru, it was made into looking-glasses and knives. Phill. Min. p. 135, 136.

[2] It is merely necessary to observe with respect to this tale, which is repeated by every writer on the subject, that it is universally disbelieved.

The

Gallias, et in Hispania. Arena alba mollissima pila molaque terebatur. Dehinc miscebatur tribus partibus nitri pondere vel mensura, ac, liquata, in alias fornaces transfundebatur quæ Massa vocabatur Admovitrius,[1] atque hæc recocta fiebat vitrum purum et candidum. In genere vitri et obsianus lapis adnumeratur. Est autem virens interdum, et niger, aliquando et translucidus crassiore visu, et, in speculis parietum, pro imagine umbras reddente.[2] Gemmas multi ex eo faciunt. Hunc lapidem et in India, et in Italia, et ad Oceanum in Hispania nasci tradunt.

VI. [256] *Quod quidam decapitatus fuit jussu Imperatoris, quia modum faciendi vitrum flexibile invenerat.*[3]—Fertur autem sub Tiberio Cesare quendam artificem excogitasse vitri temperamentum ut flexibile esset et ductile. Qui, dum admissus esset ad Cesarem, porrexit[4] fialam Cesari, quam ille indignatus in pavimento projecit, quæ complicaverat se tanquam vas æneum. Artifex autem sustulit fialam de pavimento, deinde martulum de sinu protulit, et fialam correxit. Hoc facto, Cesar dixit artifici, numquid alius scit hanc condituram vitrorum? Postquam ille jurans negavit alium[5] hoc scire, jussit illum Cesar decollari, ne, dum hoc cognitum fieret, aurum et argentum[6] pro luto haberentur, et omnium metallorum precia abstraherentur. Et revera quod si vasa vitrea non frangerentur, meliora essent quam aurum et argentum.

---

[1] *Admonitem* P. [2] *Reddere* P. [3] Sic P. *De artifice* R. [4] *Prorrexit* P. [5] *Alterum* R. [6] *Et argentum* omittit R.

The problem, however, of making malleable glass was always a favourite subject with the alchemists, and Raymond Lully expressly declares, that "one of the principal effects of the philosopher's stone was to render glass malleable." The Hon. Robert Boyle mentions (Philosophical Works, vol. i. p. 58), on the authority of an expert chemist, a piece of transparent red glass which, after receiving several strokes with a hammer, was found to have stretched under it (although it had begun to crack on the edges), growing more thin on the beaten part, and leaving visible impressions made on it by the edge of the hammer. Mr. Boyle, very prudently, declines expressing his own opinion on this subject.

VII. [257] *How to make white glass, and glass of various colours.*—Glass is made with the ashes both of fern and of "faina"[1]—that is, of the small trees which grow in the woods. The fern is cut before the Feast of St. John the Baptist, and well dried, and is then put into the fire and reduced to ashes. So also the "faina" is reduced to ashes in the fire. Then take two parts of fern, and one-third part of "faina," and mix them together. Then make a furnace of stones, faced with clay mixed with horse-dung. You must make the foundation quite smooth to the height of half a cubit, and leave a hollow in the furnace without any materials—that is, you must put nothing in the middle of the furnace, because the fire must be in the middle of the furnace while it is at work. Upon the foundation of the furnace you must begin to make three small compartments, which are called "archæ," in which there must be small windows. You must make the middle arch large, with two windows in it, one on one side, and one on the other. In the middle arch, just opposite the door of the arch, must be placed two jars, very well baked, which they call "mortariola," in which the ashes, or sand, as it may be called, is melted, and the glass is made. And you must make the other arches, one on the right hand and one on the left of the middle arch, and the one on the right hand smaller than the one on the left. In the arch on the left hand side you must heat the ashes for a day and a night; and you must heat them until they cohere into a mass. In this arch also you must bake your melting pots perfectly, in order that they may be firm and hard, so as to hold and melt the glass without breaking. When the whole of the ashes have been well baked, and for a very long time, put them into your melting pots with an iron spoon, and melt them until they become white. If you wish it [the glass] to become red,

[1] Theophilus employs the ashes of beech-wood, "ligna faginea." It seems to me, therefore, not improbable that "faina" may have been an old French term for the seedling beeches which grew wild in the woods, the beechnut being still called in French "faîne." The ashes of the beech-tree are mentioned afterwards, in treating of the purple and flesh-coloured glass.

VII. [257] *Quomodo efficitur vitrum* [*album*[1] *et etiam de diversis coloribus*].—Vitrum efficitur de cineribus, id est,[2] de filicis cinere,[3] et de faina, id est,[4] de parvulis arboribus quæ sunt vel crescunt in sylvis. Accipitur autem filix ante Festum S. Johannis Baptiste, et optime siccatur, deinde ad ignem mittitur et fit cinis. Similiter et faina efficietur cinis per ignem. Accipies itaque duas partes de filice, et terciam partem de faina, et simul misces. Deinde facies furnum de petris argilla linitis mixta de stercore jumentorum. Fundamentum ejus altitudine dimidii cubiti totum planum facies; profundum furni dimittes sine materia, id est,[5] in medio furni nihil facies, quod in medio ejus ignis quando operatur semper faciendus est. Super fundamentum furni incipies facere tres mansiunculas, quæ arche nominantur, in quibus erunt fenestrellæ. Mediam archam magnam facies, in qua duæ fenestræ erunt, una ex parte una, et alia ex parte altera. In istam archam intus ante os archæ duas ollas optime coctas ponunt,[6] quas mortariola vocant, in quibus cinis sive[7] arena, ut dicetur, funditur, et vitrum efficitur. Alias autem archas facies unam a dextris mediæ archæ, et alteram a sinistris. Illam autem quæ est a dextris minorem facies illa quæ a sinistris est.[8] In archa sinistræ partis una die et una nocte cinerem coques. In tantum vero coqui facies, ut simul[9] sit agglutinatus.[10] In hac quoque archa mortariola tua penitus[11] coqui facies, et, ut firma sint et duriora ad vitrum sustinendum et coquendum, ne frangantur. Quando autem cinis totus et diutissime et optime coctus fuerit, tunc mittes eum in mortariolis tuis cum coclea ferrea, et funde eum tamdiu, donec efficiatur album. Si vero vis ut efficiatur rubeum, de cinere non[12] bene cocto, sic facies. Accipe limaturam cupri, et arde eam quousque pulvis sit, et mitte illum in mortariolis, et erit vitrum rubeum, quem Galienum vocamus. Viride vero vitrum ita facies. De eodem

---

[1] Ex P. [2] *Id est* P.; *Et* R. [3] *Cinere* omittit R. [4] *Id est* P.; *Aut* R. [5] *Id est* P. *Et* R. [6] *Ponunt* omittit R. [7] *Seu* P. [8] *Quæ est a sinistris* R. [9] *Similiter* R. [10] *Conglutinatus* P. [11] *Primitus* P. [12] *Tamen*. Cant.

you will do as follows, with ashes not well baked. Take copper filings, burn them until they are reduced to powder, and throw them into your melting pots; and this will make red glass, which we call "galienum." Green glass you will make thus. Throw, of the same powder of burnt copper into your melting pots, as much as you think proper, and stir it, and it will be green. Yellow glass is thus made. Take raw ashes, and put them into the melting pot and melt them, and throw a little sand in with them, and a little, if I am not mistaken, of the powder of copper, and stir the whole together; and it will make a yellow glass, which we call "cerasin." Purple and "membranaceum" are made differently, with the ashes of the beech-tree, which are baked like white ashes, and put into a melting pot, and melted and boiled until they burn to a purple colour. While the glass is boiling, stir it about frequently, like the other glass, as we have said before. When you see it turn to a purple colour, take what quantity you like of it, and do whatever you like with it, until you see it turn pale. From this pale colour it changes to another colour, which is called "membrun."

But when you wish to make tablets or plates, take iron tubes of the length of one cubit, more or less, as you may think fit, and at the end of each tube a little wooden tube, having a very small hole, through which you must blow when you wish to make a vase. When you begin to work the glass, take one tube, and look into the melting pot to see whether the glass is well cleared and melted. Then dip the tube into the melting pot and take up a little glass upon it, like dough, and whirl it round in your hand, and form whatever you please upon the iron slab which is placed at the mouth of the furnace. And you must make a screen of brickwork, to avoid being scorched by the fire; and inside this you must put the iron slab, which is called "marmor," upon which you must shape the glass which you are working, and you may form whatever kind of vase you like. When your vase, or cup, or saucer, or phial, is made, you must put it into the arch which is on the left hand

pulvere cupri combusti [1] in mortariolo pones quantum tibi visum fuerit, et movebis, et erit[2] viride. Croceum quoque vitrum sic efficitur. Cinerem crudum accipies, et mittes in mortariolo, et fundes eum, projicies que modicum sabuli intus cum eo, et parum, ni fallor, de pulvere cupri, et movebis simul, et efficietur croceum vitrum, quod nos Cerasin vocamus. Purpureum et Membranaceum[3] aliter efficiuntur[4] de cinere arboris fagi, et, sicut cinis albus, ita coquitur, et mittitur in olla, et tamdiu funditur bulliendo, quousque vertatur in colorem purpureum. Dum bullit sepe movebis, sicut et aliud vitrum, ut[5] supra docuimus. Quando videbis[6] eum verti in purpureum colorem, illico tolle quantum vis, et fac opus quod volueris usque dum videris eum mutari [in pallorem.[7] De colore pallido mutatur] in aliud quod membrun[8] vocatur.

Quando vero vasa vel tabulas facere volueris, habebis virgas ferreas intus cavatas longitudine unius cubiti, aut plus, vel minus [ut videbis opportunum[9]] et in summitate virgæ parvulum lignum intus cavum, habens[10] unum foramen parvissimum per quod sufflabis quando operari volueris aliquod vas; et quando de vitro operari incipies, accipies virgam unam, et in mortariolo, si sit[11] bene purgatus vel fusus[12] fuerit cinis, aspicies. Tunc mittes virgam in mortariolo, attrahesque modicum vitri quasi parumper pastæ, et circumduces manu tua in girum, et formabis quod tibi placuerit super marmorem ferri qui positus est juxta os furni. Nam ibi[13] facies obstaculum quoddam[14] macerie, ne ab igne consumeris, in quo pones tabulam ferri quæ marmor vocatur, super quem formabis vitrum quando operaberis, et facies qualecunque vas placuerit tibi.[15] Facto autem vase vel[16] cipho vel scutella vel fiala, mittes in archa quæ est in sinistra parte furni ut ibi temperetur donec refrigescat.

---

[1] *Cupri combusti* omittit R. [2] *Et erit* R.; *eritque* P. [3] *Membranum.* Cant. [4] *Efficitur vel efficiuntur* P. [5] *Sicut* R. [6] *Videris* R. [7] Ex R. [8] *Membranum.* Cant. [9] Ex P. [10] *Concavum habentem* P. [11] *Sit* Inserit P. [12] *Fondatus vel fonditus* P. [13] *Tibi* P. [14] *Quadam* R. [15] *Qualecunque vas sicut placuerit in oculis tuis* P. [16] *Id est* P.

side of the furnace, that it may be annealed there until it is cool.

But when you wish to spread out plates of glass—that is, to make them smooth—heat them again in the furnace, and spread them out in the small window, which is called "explanaria," which is near the left hand side of the arch. When they are spread out, put them into a small furnace made on purpose, and let them remain there until quite cold. And there must be put live coals in the furnace, and as they go out, so the glass cools.

VIII. [271] *How glass is made of lead, and how it is coloured.*[1]—Take good and shining lead, and put it into a new jar, and burn it in the fire until it is reduced to powder. Then take it away from the fire to cool. Afterwards take sand and mix with that powder, but so that two parts may be of lead and the third of sand, and put it into an earthen vase. Then do as before directed for making glass, and put that earthen vase into the furnace, and keep stirring it until it is converted into glass. But if you wish to make it appear green, take brass filings, and put as much as you think proper into the lead glass; and then, if you wish to make any vase, do so with the iron tube. Afterwards take out this vase with the glass, and let it cool. You may, if you like, mix some of this leaden glass with a grossinum of sapphire for painting on glass, adding to it one-third part of scoria of iron. And this pigment is to be ground on an iron slab.

IX. [235] *How to cut glass and other stones.*[2]—The Saracens whip the udder of a goat well with sting-nettles, and then rub it with their hands to get the milk down into it. It is then

---

[1] The latter part of this chapter should be compared with No. xlix., "Quomodo pingitur in vitro."

[2] See Mappæ Clavicula, p. 63.

Tabulas autem vitri quando volueris extendere, id est, planas facere, recalefacies in furnum, et extendes[1] in fenestra parva quæ explanaria vocatur, quæ est juxta sinistram partem archæ. Explanata vero repones eam in parvum furnum ad hoc opus factum, et ibi dimittes donec omnino sit frigida. Carbones autem vivi erunt in furno preparati, qui quanto magis extinguitur[2] tanto plus refrigescit[3] vitrum.

VIII. [271] *Quomodo efficitur vitrum de plumbo, et quomodo coloratur.*[4]—Accipe plumbum optimum[5] et nitidum, et pone in ollam novam, et arde in ignem usque quod[6] pulvis sit. Deinde tolle eam ab igne ut refrigeretur. Postea sabulum sume, et misce cum pulvere illo, ita tamen ut duæ partes sint de plumbo, et tercia de sabulo, ponesque in testeo vase. Facies vero sicut supra[7] scriptum est ad vitrum faciendum, et illud vas testeum pones in furnum, et semper movebis, usque dum vitrum efficiatur. Si vero ut videatur[8] virideum facere cupis, accipe limaturam auricalci, et intus cum plumbeo vitro quantum tibi visum fuerit pone. Deindeque[9] si aliquod vas facere[10] volueris cum fistula ferrea facies. Postea[11] vas illud cum vitro tolle et refrigerari sine. [De isto[12] vitro plumbeo poteris, si vis, cum gallino[13] saphireo miscere ad pingendum in vitro, apposita tercia parte de scoria ferri. Et hæc pictura in marmore ferreo est terenda.][14]

IX. [235] *Quomodo inciditur vitrum*[15] [*et alii lapides*].—Cum acri urtica ubera capræ Saraceni acriter urticant,[16] et palmis tundunt,[17] ut in eis lac[18] descendat. Postea[19] lac in vas emulgitur,[20]

---

[1] R. lacunam habet sic— ;. . . . .*tendes*. [2] Sic emendavi. *Quanto extinguitur* R. *Tanto magis extingueritur* P. [3] *Refrigescet* P. [4] Sic P. *Quomodo efficitur de plumbo* R. [5] *Di Vitro*, Cant. [6] *Quod* omittit R. [7] *Superius*, Cant. [8] *Efficitur* P. [9] *Denique* R. [10] *Facere vas* R. [11] *Posthæc* R. [12] *Pisto*, Cant. [13] *Grossino*, Cant. [14] Sic R.; in P. vero, *de isto vitro plumbeo, illo scilicet qui cæruleus est, quæ de duobus coloribus potest fieri, poteris, si vis, cum pulvere saphireo miscere ad pingendum in vitro.* [15] Sic P. In [ ] omittit R. *Ad vitrum incidendum* C. [16] *Saraceni acriter urticant* sic C.; *urticantur* R.; *acriter urticantur* P. [17] *Tenduntur* P. R. [18] *In ea* C. [19] *Ex eis* supplet P. [20] Sic C.; *mulgetur in vas* R.; *mulgatur in vas* P.

milked into a vase, into which the glass, with the iron with which it is to be cut, is to be put for one night until it becomes soft. The iron must be tempered in the milk itself. When necessary the milk should be warmed to the same degree of heat which it had when first milked. The glass must be always kept warm in it, and so it must be cut. Other stones are cut in the same way. The goat must be fed on ivy.

X. [236] *How precious stones are cut and polished and made brilliant.*[1]—Sume hircum qui nunquam coierit, et pone in cuppa per tres dies [quousque totum digerat quod in ventre habet. Postea hederam da ei edere per iiij. dies]. Posthæc purgabis dolium, ut urinam ejus accipias. Posthoc occides hircum et sanguinem ejus urinæ commiscebis; et sic lapidem impone per unam noctem, et posthæc vel comprime in figuram, vel sculpes si vis. To make it beautiful, procure a leaden plate, and sprinkle upon it white flint, ground fine like pepper, and rub the stone upon it until you have ground down the roughness of it. Then tie up some of the said powdered flint in a linen cloth, with which rub down the angles which you could not do on the plate. And then, in order to restore it to its former lustre, make some nut oil, and rub over it. You must also rub it down with a waxed cloth to make it shine and remove the greasy appearance.

XI. [254] *How to cut crystal.*[1]—Take the crystal, and wrap it up in a linen cloth wet with sudore capræ, and bury it, together with the cloth, in cow-dung; and afterwards cut it with a knife just as you like, but with care. After you have done this, put the crystal into cold water, and then polish it with a leaden plate, and with flour or bran.

---

[1] See Mappæ Clavicula, p. 64.

et in eo per unam noctem, vitrum cum ferro ponitur[1] cum quo debet incidi [temperabitur in ipso lacte ferrum, aut in lotio parvæ puellæ rufæ, quod excipitur ante ortum solis[2]]. At vero lac,[3] cum necesse fuerit, recalefiat cum[4] eadem calitudine, qua fuit prius[5] mulsum, et in eo semper vitrum calefiat [donec[6] molle fiat] et sic incidatur. Sic et alii lapides.[7] [Capra vero hedera pascatur.][8]

X. [236] *Quomodo sculpuntur preciosi lapides, poliunturque, et splendificantur.*[9]—Sume hircum qui nunquam coierit, et pone in cuppa[10] per tres dies [quousque totum digerat quod in ventre habet. Postea hederam da ei edere per iiij. dies].[11] Posthæc purgabis dolium, ut urinam ejus accipias. Posthoc occides[12] hircum et sanguinem ejus urinæ commiscebis;[13] et sic lapidem impone per unam noctem, et posthæc[14] vel comprime in figuram, vel sculpes si vis. Ut pulcrum facias, fac tibi tabulam plumbeam, et super hanc asperges album silicem contritum, ut piper, et lapidem desuper fricabis, quoadusque asperitatem lenies.[15] Postea liga de eodem silice contrito in laneo panno, et inde fricabis angulos quos prius[16] aptare nequisti[17] in lamina. Deinde, ut pristinam lucem recipiat, fac tibi oleum de nucibus, et inde fricabis. Adhuc debes eum linire panno cerato, ut splendeat et sudore deficiat.[18]

XI. [254] *Quomodo incidatur*[19] *cristallum.*—Accipe cristallum, et involve in panno lineo intincto in sudore capræ, et cum ipso panno in fimo bovis involve, et sic cum cultro incide, ut volueris, et tamen caute. Postquam[20] feceris, mitte in aquam frigidam. Dehinc lica cum lamina plumbea, et farina vel furfure.[21]

---

[1] *Ponatur* P. R. [2] Ex C.; alii omittunt. [3] *At vero lac* C.; omittit P.; *at vero* R. [4] *Cum* omittunt P. C. [5] *Primitus* C. [6] Ex C. [7] *Aliæ petræ* C. [8] Ex C. [9] Ex P.; *quomodo sculpuntur lapides* R.; *ad cristallum comprimendum in figuram* C. [10] *Cupam* P. R. [11] Ex C. [12] *Vel incides* supplent P. R. [13] *Miscebis* P. R. [14] *Posthoc* P. [15] *Lenieris* R.; *Linieris* P. [16] *Prius* omittunt P. R. [17] *Nequivisti* C. [18] *Et sudare desinat* C. [19] *Incidetur* P. [20] *Posteaquam* R. [21] *Cum farina vel sulfure* P.

XII. [266] *How stones are polished.*—Take the stone which is called hæmatite, which must not be too hard, or veined, but very smooth and bright; and go to a grindstone, and make it as smooth as you can. When it appears sufficiently even, make it still smoother upon a tile, and afterwards, that it may be still smoother, rub it upon a whetstone. Then polish it upon a leaden plate, and again polish it still better upon the hairy side of a cow's skin, which must be very smooth and clean. Afterwards polish it again on a very smooth and polished piece of the wood which is called aspen or poplar. You may also polish the teeth of beasts in this way, and not only teeth, but also whatever gold you have used either on walls, or wood, or even on parchment.

XIII. [276] *Of gilding* [*tin foil*].—Gilding is composed of quicksilver and tin, in the proportion of three parts of quicksilver to four of tin. Take a plate of tin, and varnish it very thinly two or three times, and let it dry. Then take soot[1] and cervisia, and mix them together. Then strain them and place them upon charcoal. When they have boiled a little, dip the tin into the dish containing the soot and cervisia, and when you see that it is sufficiently done, take it out of that colour, and put it into a saucerfull of cold water, and it will then appear to you to be good. Afterwards, when you take it out, it will look like gold.

XIV. [253] *How to gild.*—Take seven parts of quicksilver and one of gold, and mix them together, and then put them into a saucer, or cup, or basin, and wash them with water, and gild whatsoever you like with them. But if you wish to keep the gold very long, squeeze out the quicksilver through a clean cloth, and the gold will remain, which you may put into a vase, and so you may preserve it. And when you wish to gild with it, mix it afresh with quicksilver, and wash it.

---

[1] Probably the soot from burnt wood, of which the pigment called "Bistre" was made.

XII. [266] *Quomodo politur lapis [et dens animalis.]*[1]—Sume lapidem qui dicitur emantes, qui non sit nimis durus, neque venatus,[2] sed admodum planus, et clarissimus, et vade ad molam fabri, et ut volueris planum facies. Cum tibi visum fuerit satisfactum, inde super tegulam levius planabis; postea iterum, ut dulcius fiat, cum cote; deinde super tabulam plumbeam, ut poliatur. Hinc iterum super corium vaccæ illa parte quæ[3] pilosum fuit, quod planissimum et mundissimum[4] sit volo, super quod[5] iterum melius polies. Posthoc super lignum quod tremulum vel populus[6] vocatur, optime et multum planatum, polies iterum.[7] Dentem vero bestiarum poteris hoc modo polire; non tantum dentem, sed et aurum, quocunque posueris, sive in muro, seu in ligno,[8] vel etiam in perchameno.[9]

XIII. [276] *De deauratura [petulæ stagni.]*[10]—Deauratura efficitur de vivo argento et stanno[11] ita ut tres partes sint de vivo argento, et quatuor,[12] de stagno. Sume laminam stagni, et vernicia illam duabus vel tribus vicibus multum tenuiter, et dimitte siccare. Postea accipe fuliginem et cervisiam, et misce simul.[13] Postea[14] cola. Deinde pones super carbones. Cumque aliquantulum bullierit, tunc in patella cum fuligine et cervisia mitte, et cum videris satisfactum, abstrahe de hoc colore,[15] et mitte in scutella plena aqua frigida,[16] et tunc tibi non videbitur bonum. Postea, cum eum tuleris, velut aurum eum[17] videbis.

XIV. [253] *Deauratura quomodo fit.*—De argento vivo vii. partes,[18] et unam de auro accipies, et misces simul. Deinde in scutella vel in[19] cipho vel in bacino mitte, et de aqua ablue, et deaura quod volueris, [si[20] vero diu multumque servare volueris] per pannum nitidum[21] argentum vivum projicies foras, et remanebit aurum, et in vase pones. Sicque servare poteris. Quando vero deaurare volueris, iterum cum argento vivo misces, et ablues.

---

[1] Ex P. [2] *Veratus* P. [3] *Quæ* P.; *vel qua* R. *Quod.* Cant. [4] *Mundum* R. [5] *Qua* R. [6] *Vel populus* omittit R. [7] Novum capitulum hic incipit R. [8] *Sive in ligno sive in muro* R. [9] *Pergameno* P. [10] Ex P. [11] *Stagno* R. [12] *Quarta* R. [13] *Similiter* R. [14] *Post* P. [15] *Calore* R. [16] *Et plena aqua frigida in scutella mitte* R. [17] *Eum* omittit R. [18] *Partes* omittit R. [19] *In* omittit R. [20] Ex P. [21] *Accidum* R.

XV. [252] *How brass, or silver, is gilt.*—Take soot and pure salt, and grind them well, and take white of egg, and distemper them with it. Then spread it over the silver, or gold, or copper, or whatever else you wish to gild, laying this mixture on those parts between which you wish to gild it, and put it upon charcoal, and when it is dry, gild those parts upon which the mixture was not laid, and when it is gilt, wash off the mixture, and burnish.

XVI. [249] *How to gild brass.*—Take three parts of atramentum and one part of salt, and grind them with vinegar; then mix quicksilver with them, and grind them all together again. Next take a clean cloth and dip it in atramentum, and rub the brass strongly with it. Then put it into the fire until it is thoroughly red-hot, when it must be removed from the fire and suffered to cool. You may then gild it like gold or copper.

XVII. [237] *How to gild iron.*[1]— Grind brass filings with vinegar in a brass mortar, with salt and alum, to the consistence of honey: some persons use water instead of vinegar. Then the iron, well cleaned, and slightly warmed, must be anointed and rubbed with this, until it is of the colour of brass. It is then washed with water and wiped, and gilt like silver, and the quicksilver driven off in the usual manner by heat; and in order to make it shine it is rubbed with an iron.

XVIII. [238] *Otherwise.*— Globular alum (?)[2] and salt, which is called sal gem and calcanthum, are ground with vinegar

---

[1] See Clavicula, p. 37.

[2] The different readings of these words have cast much obscurity over the passage. The word "glumen," however, does not appear to be susceptible of any other explanation than the reading in the Mappæ Clavicula (p. 39), which has been followed in the text. Additional weight is given to this construction by the word "alumine" being used in a manner somewhat similar in the recipe immediately preceding. The correspondence of the other parts of the recipes will also be observed. Salt, which is mentioned in the first, is substituted for the sal gem (the purest kind of rock salt) of the second, and the brass filings of the first recipe for the calcanthum (sulphate of copper) of the second.

XV. [252] *Quomodo deauratur æs, vel auricalcum, vel argentum.*[1]—Accipe fuliginem et purum sal; teres fortiter, accipiesque gleream ovi et distemperabis. Deinde linies aurum, vel argentum, vel cuprum, vel aliud quod volueris deaurare, et ibi ubi volueris interim deaurare illam distemperaturam superpones,[2] et super carbones mittes. Cum fuerit siccatum, deaurabis ubi non fuerit positum, et quando deauratum fuerit, ablues distemperaturam, et burnies.

XVI. [249] *Quomodo deauratur auricalcum.*[3]—De atramento tres partes, et salis unam partem accipies, et cum [aceto [4] fortiter teres, deinde argentum vivum cum eis misces, et in simul iterum teres]. Postea accipe pannum nitidum, et intinges in atramentum, et auricalcum fortiter fricabis. Deinde mitte in ignem quousque totum rubeum fiat. Postea retrahe [5] ab igne, et sine refrigerari. Tunc poteris deaurare sicut aurum vel cuprum.

XVII. [237] *Quomodo ferrum deauratur.*[6]—Eris [pulvis [7] vel] limatura teritur[8] cum aceto in mortario æreo,[9] et [10] cum sale et alumine, usque ad mellis spissitudinem. Aliqui pro aceto aqua utuntur. Deinde ferrum bene purgatum,[11] et leviter calefactum, hac mixtura inungitur,[12] et fricatur, donec colorem æris[13] accipiat. Posthæc[14] abluitur aqua,[15] et tergitur,[16] et sicut es vel[17] argentum deauratur[18] et calefactum, recedente[19] vivo argento, sicut mos est,[20] ut splendorem accipiat, ferro defricatur.

XVIII. [238] *Aliter.*[21]—Alumen rotundum, et sal, quod gemma vocatur,[22] et calcanthum,[23] ex aceto acerrimo teruntur in æreo

---

[1] *Quomodo deauratur vel aurum vel argentum* R. [2] *Suppones* R. [3] *Oricalcum* R. [4] Ex P., R. habet *eis misces et insimiliter tercium teres.* [5] *Trahe* P. [6] Sic P. R.; *inauratio ferri* C. (p. 64). In C. (p. 37) partem alterius capituli facit. [7] C. (p. 37). [8] *Teratur* P. R. [9] *In eneo mortario* C. (p. 37), *in hereo mortario* C. (p. 64). [10] *Et* omittit C. [11] Sic C. (p. 64); *Deinde ferrum multum purgatum* P. R. *Denique bene purgatum ferrum* C. (p. 37). [12] *Inungatur* P. [13] *Eis* P., *Heris* C. (p. 64); *eris* C. (p. 37). [14] *Posthoc* P.; *posthac* R.; *tunc* C. (p. 37). [15] *Abluta aqua* R., *aqua abluitur* C. [16] *Teritur* C. (p. 37). [17] *Aurum et* R.; *es vel* C.; omittit P. [18] *Deauratum* P. [19] *Recedendo* R. [20] *Et* supplet P. [21] Sic P. R. C. (p. 64). In C. (p. 37) partem facit capituli cxlvj. [22] Ex C. (p. 37). *Glumen rotundum et salvandum, quod sal Gemma vocatur* P. R.; *alumen rotundum et salvandum, quod salis gemma vocatur* C. (p. 64). [23] *Calcantum* C.

in a brass mortar. This is rubbed over the clean iron with a cane or any other light stick, and, when it has the colour of brass, it is washed and gilt. The quicksilver is then driven off, and it is cooled with water, and then rubbed down with a very smooth and bright iron until it is well polished.

XIX. [239] *How ivory is bent and ornamented.*—If you wish to bend and adorn ivory, put it into the aforesaid mixture for three days and three nights.[1] Having done this, hollow out a piece of wood in whatever manner you like, and then put the ivory into the cavity, and turn and bend it just as you like. A plate of copper, 10 inches in breadth, and the same in length, can be gilt with [the weight of] one denarius[2] of gold.

XX. [250] *How to restore gold.*—If you have gilt any vase which, through negligence, has lost the gilding, take atramentum and salt, well ground together, and spread some of it over the vase. Then place it before the fire to dry; and give it another coat, then place it again before the fire. Do this three or four times, and it will recover its former colour, which it had lost.

XXI. [267] *How to varnish gold so that it will not lose its colour.*—If you wish to varnish gold that has been laid upon gypsum, varnish over the gold, not with pure varnish, but with that colour which is made for preparing auripetrum,[3] mixed, however, with oil, and a little varnish, lest it should be too thick. And so, if in any part the colour of the gypsum should appear through [the gold], it may be covered with this colour. But you may varnish figures and other colours with pure varnish or with thick oil.

XXII. [248] *How to solder gold, or silver, or copper, or brass.*—Take three parts of brass, and three parts of tin, and melt

---

[1] See Clavicula, p. 64.

[2] It is obvious that the author is here speaking of the weight of the coin, for the denarius was not a gold coin. Celsus informs us that, from the time of Tiberius to that of Vespasian, seven of them were made from one ounce Troy weight. At a later period eight were made from the ounce Troy. In the lower empire they scarcely weighed half so much in pure silver.

[3] The composition of this colour is described in No. xliv., which is not in the Cambridge MS. From this it would appear that the MS. published by Raspe was really defective.

mortario. Ex [1] his ferrum purgatum, cum ferula,[2] vel alia qualibet levi hastula,[3] defricatur, et, cum æris habuerit colorem,[4] detergitur,[5] et deauratur; deinde,[6] exfumigato vivo argento[7], aqua refrigeratur,[8] et [9] usque ad splendorem, ferro valde plano et limpido, defricatur.

XIX. [239] *Quomodo dirigitur et ornatur ebur.*[10]—Quod si volueris ebur dirigere et ornare,[11] in hac supradicta confectione mittatur tribus diebus et tribus [12] noctibus. Hoc facto, cavabis lignum quali modo volueris; deinde, posito ebore in cavatura,[13] diriges illud, et plicabis ad placitum.[14] Tabula cupri quæ decem pollices habet in latitudine, et totidem in longitudine, denario auri deaurari [15] potest.

XX. [250] *Quomodo recuperatur deauratura.*—Si aliquod vas habueris deauratum, et per negligentiam deauraturam perdiderit, accipe atramentum, et sal cum eo bene tritum, et lini illud vas. Postea pone ad ignem seccare, et iterum linies, et ad ignem pones. Hoc facies tribus vel [16] quatuor vicibus, et recuperabit colorem pristinum.[17]

XXI. [267] *Quomodo vernicietur aurum ne perdat colorem.*—Si aurum super gypsum positum verniciare volueris, non de [18] puro vernicio, sed de illo colore qui efficitur ad auripetram [19] faciendum, mixto tamen [20] cum oleo modico vernicio, ne nimis sit spissum,[21] vernicietur [22] super aurum. Ideo si aliquid [23] gipsei coloris apparuerit,[24] hoc colore operiri poterit. Imagines vero et alios colores de puro vernicio, vel de crasso oleo, poteris verniciare.

XXII. [248] *Quomodo poteris solidare aurum vel argentum vel cuprum*[25] *vel auricalcum.*—Accipe tres partes de auricalco, et

---

[1] *Ex* omittit C. (p. 37). [2] *Ferura* C. (p. 64). [3] *Hattula* R.; *astula* P. [4] *Cum eraminis colorem habuerit* C. (p. 37); *cum heris colorem habuerit* C. (p. 64). [5] *Extergitur* C. (p. 37); *retergitur* C. (p. 64). [6] *Ac deinde* C. [7] *Argento vivo* C. (p. 37). [8] *Refrigeratum* C. (p. 37). [9] *Et* omittit C. [10] Sic P.; omittit R., qui septem prima verba capituli rubricavit. *De ebore* C. (p. 64). [11] *Vel carvare* C. [12] *Tribus* omittit C. [13] *Cavitura* R. P. [14] Quod sequitur omittit C. [15] *Decorari* R. [16] *Et* R. [17] *Pristinum colorem quem perdiderat* R. [18] *Circumde (conde)* R. [19] *Aurum petrum* R. [20] *Unde* R. [21] *Ne sit spissum nimis* P. [22] *Verniceter* R. [23] *Aliqui* R. [24] *Apparuerunt* R. [25] *Vel cuprum* omittit R.

them together in a ladle over the fire, and reduce the mass to powder, and put it away in a box. Then take three parts of paramentum, and burn it in an earthen vase in the fire like atramentum. Then take salt, and dry it well upon coals. Then grind the salt and paramentum together with wine. When you wish to solder brass or copper, put some of this preparation, made with the salt, upon the brass or copper, wherever you wish to solder it. Then immediately put some of the aforesaid powder on it, and heat it in the fire and it will be firmly soldered.

XXIII. *On trying gold and silver.*[1]—All pure gold, of whatever weight, is denser, by one-twentieth part of itself, than any silver, similarly pure. This may be proved as follows: If one pound of pure gold be weighed in the balance, under water, with an equal weight of pure silver, the gold will be found heavier than the silver, or the silver lighter than the gold, by xii denarii, or one-twentieth part of its weight. Wherefore if you have any article made of gold, with which silver appears to have been mixed, and you wish to know how much gold, and how much silver, is contained in it, take silver or gold, and having found the weight of the said article, make a mass of either of the metals, of exactly equal weight, and, putting them into the scales, immerse them in the water. If the mass which you made is of silver, the said article will preponderate. If the mass is of gold, the gold will preponderate, throwing up [the scale containing] the said article. And it will happen, that by as many parts as the gold is heavier, by so many parts the silver is lighter; for whatever there may be in the said article, under water, besides the usual weight, belongs to the gold on

[1] This chapter does not form part of the MS. of Le Begue; but it will be found, with some variations, in Mappæ Clavicula, p. 45. From the chapter in the text, it will be seen that the value of the denarius was much diminished, since, at the time the above was written, 20 denarii were equal to an ounce, and 240 to a pound.

tres partes de stagno, et funde [1] simul in conca ad ignem, pulveremque facias, et in buttam [2] recondes. Postea accipe paramentum tres partes [3] et quasi atramentum in testeo vase arde in igne. Accipiesque sal, et super carbones optime siccabis. Deinde paramentum et sal [4] macerabis simul cum vino. Cum vero auricalcum vel cuprum solidare volueris, pones super auricalcum vel cuprum de ista confectione, et de sale, et temperamento facta ubi volueris solidare. Statimque de pulvere supradicta [5] pones, et ad ignem calefacies, et firmiter solidabitur.

XXIII. *De probatione auri et argenti.*[6]—Omne [7] aurum purum, cujus libet ponderis, omni argento similiter puro, ejusdem [8] tamen ponderis, densius est parte sui vicesima ;[9] quod ita probari potest. Si purissimi auri libra cum equo [10] puri [11] argenti simili pondere [12] sub aqua conferatur in statera, xii denariis,[13] id est [14] vicesima [15] sui parte, aurum gravius argento, vel argentum levius auro invenietur. Quapropter si inveneris opus aliquod [16] auro formatum, cui argentum permixtum esse [17] videatur, scireque [18] volueris quantum auri, quantumque [19] in eo argenti contineatur, sume argentum sive aurum, et examinato supradicti operis [20] pondere, nec [21] minus pensantem massam de utrovis [22] metallo fabricato, atque utraque et opus et [23] massam stateræ [24] lancibus imponito,[25] aquisque immergito. Si argentea fuerit [massa quam fecisti, opus preponderabit ; si aurea fuerit [26]] alleviato [27] opere, aurum inclinabitur. Hoc tamen ita fiet, ut quot partibus inclinatur aurum, totidem partibus sublevatur [28] argentum ; quia [29] quicquid in ipso opere fuerit sub aquis præter solitum pondus,[30] ad aurum, propter densitatem,

---

[1] *Fonde* P. [2] *Buscam* P. [3] *Tres partes paramentum* P. [4] *Sal et paramentum* P. [5] *Suprascripta* P. [6] Sic R. ; *de auri pondere* C. (p. 45). [7] *Omnem.* Cant. [8] *Eidem.* Cant. [9] *Parte sui xxiiij. et insuper ccxl.* C. [10] *Eque* C. [11] *Puri.* Omittit Cant. [12] Ex. Cant. [13] *xj. denariis* C. [14] *Et* R. [15] *xxiiij. et ccxl.* C. [16] *Opus aliquod inveneris* C. [17] *Per commixtionem inesse* C. [18] *Que* omittit R. [19] *Quantumve* C. [20] *Examinato inspectione* C. [21] *Non* C. [22] *Utrius* R. [23] *Utrumque opus scilicet, et* C. [24] *Stantem* C. [25] *Imposito* R. [26] Ex R. [27] *Allevato* C. [28] *Sullevetur* C. [29] *Quod* R. [30] *Ponderis* C.

account of its greater density; and whatever deficiency there may be is to be attributed to the silver, on account of its greater rarity. And in order that you may perceive it more easily, you must bear in mind that, in weight for gold, and in lightness for silver, x denarii signify a pound, as I have already stated in the former part of this chapter.

XXIV. [268] *How wood is to be prepared before painting on it.*[1]—Whoever wishes to adorn any wood with divers colours, let him hear what I say. First make the wood very flat and smooth by scraping it, and lastly by rubbing it with that herb which is called shave-grass. But if the piece of wood is such that you cannot smooth down its inequalities, or you have reasons for not wishing to do so, and at the same time are not willing to cover it with leather or with cloth, grind dry white-lead upon a stone, but not so finely as if you were going to paint with it. Then melt wax over the fire in a vase, add tiles ground fine. Then mix it with the white-lead which you had ground, stirring it frequently with a small stick, and so let it cool. Then heat an iron, and with it melt the wax into the little fissures, until they are level, and then scrape off the rough parts with a knife. And if you hesitate about mixing white-lead with the wax, know that the more you mix with it, the harder it will be. And when you have made it smooth, as I was saying, mix plenty of white-lead very finely ground, with linseed-oil, and lay an excessively thin coat of it wherever you intend to paint with a brush of ass's hair adapted for that purpose. When this is dry, lay on, as you did before, another and a thicker coat of it, not thicker by having a greater quantity of colour, but by having less oil in it. For you must take very great

---

[1] The mode of preparation described in this chapter differs essentially from those usually followed; inasmuch as several coats of white lead and oil are laid immediately on the wood, without a previous preparation of glue and gesso.

pertinet; quicquid autem levitatis, ad argentum, propter raritatem, conferendum est.[1] Et, ut hoc[2] facilius possit adverti, considerare debes, tam in gravitate auri, quam in levitate argenti, x denarios[3] significare libram, sicut in[4] prima lectionis hujus fronte prefixum est.

XXIV. [268] *Quomodo aptetur lignum antequam pingatur.*—Quicunque aliquod lignum ornare diversis coloribus satagis, audi quæ dico. Imprimis ipsum lignum multum rade equalem, et planissimum radendo, et ad ultimum fricando cum illa herba quæ dicitur asperella. Quod si ligni materies talis fuerit, ut non possis equare ejus asperitates,[5] vel non velis, propter aliquas occasiones, nec tamen[6] cum corio illud[7] velis cooperire,[8] vel panno;[9] album plumbum teres super petram siccum, sed non tantum[10] quantum si inde pingere[11] velis. Deinde ceram in vase supra ignem[12] liquefacies, tegulamque tritam subtiliter; albumque plumbum, quod ante trivisti,[13] simul commisces, sepius movendo cum parvo ligno, et sic sine refrigerari. Postea aliquod ferrum fac calidum, et, cum ipso, ceram[14] funde in ipsas cavernulas donec equales sint, et sic cum cultello desuper abrade ea quæ sunt scabrosa. Si autem album[15] plumbum miscere cum cera dubitas, scito quod quantum plus miscueris, tanto durius erit. Et, sicut dixi, jam equali facto, habundancius plumbum, valde subtilissime tritum cum oleo lini,[16] desuper, per totum ubicunque pingere vis, tenuissime extendendo[17] cum pincello asinino,[18] sic aptato; deinde ad solem exiccari bene permitte. At post,[19] cum siccatus fuerit color, iterum superpone, sicut prius fecisti, de eodem, et spissiorem pones; sed non ita spissiorem, ut abundancius[20] colorem super-

---

[1] *Est referendum* R. [2] *Hoc* omittit R. [3] *Denarios* xj. C. [4] *In* omittit C. [5] *Asperitatem* P. [6] *Id* supplet P. [7] *Illud* omittit P. [8] *Operire* R. [9] Quod sequitur novum capitulum facit P., cum titulo "*Quomodo ligni cavernaculas seu fossulas implebis.*" [10] *Tantum* omittit P. [11] *Inpinge* P. [12] *Super igne* R. [13] *Trivisses* P. [14] *Ipsam* supplet P. [15] *Album* omittit R. [16] *Lini* omittit R. [17] *Extendo* P. *Exterende* Cant. [18] *Afornio* vel *Aforino* P. [19] *Post* omittit R. [20] *Abundanciorem* R.

care never to lay on the colour too fat, for if you do this, and lay on a great deal of it, when it begins to dry, wrinkles will form on the surface of it.[1] But now, in order that I may omit nothing that relates to the subject, I beg you will let me return to where I was speaking of the bare wood [if you were willing to cover it with a leather or with a cloth]. If the wood, which you wish to paint upon, is [not] smooth, cover it with leather made of horse-skin or with parchment.

XXV. [262] *How a column is prepared for painting.*—If you wish to paint on a column or slab of stone, first let it dry very perfectly in the sun or before a fire. Then take white, and grind it very finely with oil upon a marble slab. Afterwards, the column being well smoothed and polished, without any crevices, lay on it two or three coats of that white, with a broad paint-brush. Then rub very stiff white over it with your hand or with a brush, and let it remain a short time. When tolerably dry, press your hand strongly over the white surface, drawing your hand towards you. Continue to do this until it is as smooth as glass. You will then be able to paint upon it with all colours mixed with oil. But if you wish to imitate the veins of marble on a general tint (brown, black, or any other colour), you can give the appearance, when the ground so prepared is dry.[2] Afterwards varnish it in the sun.

XXVI. [280] *If you wish to paint a linen cloth, and to lay gold upon it, prepare it thus.*—Take parchment, or clippings of parchment, and put them into a jar with water, which must be placed over the fire and made to boil as before directed; then dip a cloth into it,. take it out immediately, and stretch it out on a wet panel, and let it dry. Then burnish or polish it all over with a glass muller, and stretch it out, fastening it on to a

---

[1] See Mr. Eastlake's remarks on this subject, in his recent work, Materials for a History, &c., p. 37.

[2] I have adopted Mr. Eastlake's translation of this sentence. Ibid. p. 34.

ponas, sed ut oleum minus habeat. Nam et in hoc multum cavendum est ut nunquam crassiorem colorem superponas; quod si feceris et abunde posueris, cum exiccari cœperit, rugæ desuper erunt. Nunc autem ut ea quæ supersunt[1] simul omnia dicam, superius queso me redire permitte, ubi de ligni nuditate locutus sum, [si[2] illud corio vel panno operire volueris]. Quod si lignum, quod pingere volueris, non[3] fuerit equale, corio equino vel perchameno operi illud.

XXV. [262] *Quomodo preparatur columpna ad pingendum.*—Si vis aliquam columnam vel laminam de petra pingere, inprimis optime ad solem vel ad[4] ignem siccare permittes.[5] Deinde[6] album accipies,[7] et cum oleo super marmorem clarissime teres.[8] Postea illam columpnam jam bene sine aliqua fossula planam et politam, de illo albo cum lato pincello superlinies duabus vel[9] tribus vicibus. Postea imprimes cum manu vel brussa de albo spisso, et ita dimittes paululum. Cum vero modicum siccatum fuerit,[10] cum manu tua album[11] planando fortiter retrahes. Hoc tamdiu facies donec planum sit quasi vitrum. Tunc vero poteris desuper[12] de omnibus coloribus[13] cum oleo distemperatis pingere. Si vero marbrire volueris, super unum[14] colorem, vel brunum, vel nigrum, vel alium colorem, cum siccata fuerit[15] marbrire poteris. Postea vernicia[16] ad solem.

XXVI. [280] *Si vis pingere lini pannum, et aurum in ipso ponere, sic præpara.*—Accipe pergamenum vel minutias pergamenorum, et mitte in ollam cum aqua, et pone ad ignem, et fac bullire sicut suprascriptum est, et mitte in ea pannum, statimque extrahe, et desuper tabulam in aquam extende, et ita dimittes siccare, et tunc cum petra vitrea burnies, seu lissabis, per totum; postea extendes ipsum, ligando in lignis cum filo,

---

[1] *Superius* R. [2] Ex P.; omittit R. [3] *Volueris, non* P.; *vis* R. [4] *Ad* omittit P. [5] *Permittas* P. [6] *Dein* R. [7] *Accipe* P. [8] *Tere* P. [9] *Vel* omittit R. [10] *Fuerit album siccatum* P. [11] *Album* omittit P. [12] *Desuper poteris* P. [13] *Et* supplet P. [14] *Unum* omittit R. [15] *Fuerunt* R. [16] *Verniza* P.

wooden frame with the thread. You may then paint upon it with colours distempered with size, or egg, or gum.[1]

XXVII. [281] *How to lay gold on the cloth.*—And if you wish to lay gold on the cloth, apply it with the before-mentioned size, and polish it.

XXVIII. [285] *Of the general practice in grinding all colours.*—You must know, however, that all colours may be ground with clear water, if they are afterwards allowed to dry; and then with white of egg, or oil, or gum-water, or wine, or cervisia, when they are mixed or tempered.

XXIX. [260] *How oil is prepared for tempering colours.*—Put a moderate quantity of lime into oil and heat it, continually scumming it; add ceruse to it according to the quantity of oil, and put it in the sun for a month or more, stirring it frequently. And know that the longer it remains in the sun, the better it will be. Then strain and keep it, and distemper the colours with it.

XXX. [263] *How alumen*[2] *is distempered.*—Grind the alumen with gum and water upon marble, and let it dry; and when you wish to do anything with it, distemper it with white of egg.

XXXI. [284] *Of the manner of preparing white of egg for tempering colours.*—When you are going to prepare white of egg, take a filter, and dip it in water, and wet it well, and afterwards receive the white of egg mixed with water in this filter, which must be folded up so as to be pointed at the bottom and open at the top; and so, squeezing it, make it pass through seven or eight times, or oftener or less frequently, if necessary, for you must do this until the white of egg becomes like water, and runs through without drawing into threads. Then take it and put it by; or, if you wish, write with it. Two vases are necessary for preparing it.

---

[1] The sized cloth mentioned in this recipe was probably used for the transparent painting practised by the English and Germans. See Eastlake, Materials for a History, &c., p. 100.

[2] See No. L., where alumen is said to be a white colour.

deinde cum coloribus, cola, vel ovo, vel gummi distemperatis, desuper pingere poteris.

XXVII. [281] *Quomodo aurum ponitur in panno.*—Et si aurum desuper ipso panno ponere cupis, cum distemperatura suprascripta pones et polies.

XXVIII. [285] *De pratica generali in movendo omnes colores.*—Sciendum autem est quod omnes colores cum aqua clara moli possunt, si postea exsiccari permittantur, ut postea glarea, vel oleum, vel aqua gummata, aut acetum, seu vinum, necnon cervesia, quomodo misceantur aut temperentur.

XXIX. [260] *De oleo, quomodo aptatur ad distemperandum colores.*—Calcem in oleo mensurate pone, et illud despumando coque; cerosium in eo secundum quod de oleo fuerit pone, et ad solem, per mensem, vel eo amplius, frequenter removendo, pone. Scito quod quanto diutius ad solem fuerit, tanto melius erit. Postea cola, et serva, et colores inde distempera.

XXX. [263] *Alumen quomodo debet distemperari.*—Alumen cum gumma et aqua super marmorem tere, et dimitte siccári, et cum aliquod ex eo facere volueris, cum glarea ovi distempera.

XXXI. [284] *De modo parandi glaream ovorum, ad colores ex ea temperandos.*—Glaream paraturus sume staminium, et in aqua intinge illud; et madidum sit, ut postea glaream aque mixtam, in eodem staminio duplicato, subter summato (*acuminato?*), desuper autem expanso, excipe, et sic exprimendo, fac transire vel septies vel octies, vel sæpius, vel minus, si necesse fuerit, tamdiu scilicet debes hoc facere, donec glarea quasi aqua fit, et tenuis, sine filo, distillet. Hinc susceptam reconde, vel, si vis, scribe. Ad hanc autem parandam, duo vascula sunt necessaria.

XXXII. [270] *How yolk of egg is prepared.*—Orpiment is ground and prepared with the yolk of egg in the following manner, and the yolk of egg is thus prepared:—Take the yolk in the middle of your hand, and prick it with a thorn or a needle, and, putting your finger upon it, press it out, and receive it in a vase; and, adding a drop of water to it, mix it with the orpiment. If you mix oil with it, it will never dry. Mix it therefore with yolk of egg.

XXXIII. [258] *How Cordovan leather is dyed.*—Take the leather which is called "Cordovan," not dyed with colour, but pure and white, and wash over the side on which the hairs grew with alum. Then take madder, and heat it over the fire in a brass vessel with wine or with water, so that you can just bear your finger in it. Then dip the aforesaid leather into the vessel, and take it out; see if the colour is sufficiently deep; if it is, well and good; if not, dip it in again. Then spread it out on a smooth table, burnish it with a piece of box-wood; and then take fat, and grease the skin all over, and suffer it to dry.

XXXIV. [277] *How to make use of brasilium.*—Take a brass dish, and scrape as much brasilium into it as you may think necessary; then fill it up with urine; add powdered alum to it, and so let it remain for a night. The next day set it upon the coals, make it boil up once or twice; remove the dish from the fire, and put a little quick-lime with the brasilium and alum and stir it up, and so let it stand till it settles thick, and the water floats on the top; then throw away the water, and let the remainder dry in the sun, and keep it as long as you like. You may use this colour both on wood and on walls; but with greater brilliancy on parchment.

XXXV. [289] *To make a rose-colour with braxilium.*—To make rose-colour, add urine to the braxilium before you put the alum; and this is the way it is to be done.

XXXVI. [288] *How ceruse is made, and how red minium is made from that.*—If you wish to make red minium, or the white which is called ceruse, take lead plates, and put them into a

XXXII. [270] *Quomodo vitellum ovi paratur.*—Auripigmentum cum vitello ovi molitur et distemperatur sic, et vitellus hoc modo paratur. Sume vitellum in media manu, et spunge vel spina vel stila, et digito superposito, exprime, et in vase recipe, mittens guttam aque ex auripigmento misce. Si autem oleum miscueris, nunquam siccabitur. Ideo misce cum vitello.

XXXIII. [258] *Quomodo corduanum tingitur.*—Accipe corium, quem corduanum vocant, nondum coloribus tinctum, sed purum et album, illamque partem, quæ prius pilis tegebatur, de alumine ablues. Accipiesque Waranciam, et ad ignem in vase æreo calefacies cum vino, vel cum aqua, et tantum ut digitum tuum in ea mittere possis, et tunc corium antedictum in vase merges et trahes, videbisque ; si fuerit rubeum, bene quidem ; si non, iterum merge, dimittesque siccare ; postea super tabulam planam extendes, et cum baculo buxeo burnies ; deinde adipem accipies, et pellem per totum inunges, sicque siccare permittes.

XXXIV. [277] *Quomodo poteris de bresilio operari.*—Accipe patellam æream, et brasilium intus rade, quantum tibi visum fuerit. Postea imple eam urina, pulveriza desuper alumen, et sic una nocte dimittes. In crastino super carbones mitte, unam aut duas undias bullire facies, et retrahe ab igne patellam, et pone parumper de viva calce cum brisillio et alumen, et insimul move, et ita dimittas ; dum spissum fuerit, et aqua desuper nataverit, projice foras, et reliquum ad solem permitte siccum fieri, et serva quantum volueris. De hoc colore in ligno et in muro operari poteris, mirabilius tamen in pergamenis.

XXXV. [289] *Quomodo rosa color fit de ligno braxillii.*—Rosam faciendo, urinam pones cum brixillio priusquam pones alumen, et sic faciendum.

XXXVI. [288] *Quomodo fit cerusa, et de ipsa rubeum minium.*—Si vis facere rubeum minium, vel etiam album, qui cerusa dicitur, accipe laminas plumbeas, et mitte in ollam novam, et

new jar, and so fill the jar with very strong vinegar, and cover it up and set it in some warm place, and leave it so for a month. Then open the jar, and put what you find adhering to the slips of lead into another jar, and place it upon the fire, and keep stirring up the colour until it becomes as white as snow. Then remove it from the fire, and take as much as you like of that colour, which is called ceruse. Put the rest back over the fire, and keep stirring it until it becomes red minium. I recommend you to continue stirring it, because, if it is not stirred, it turns back again to white lead. Then take it from the fire and let the jar cool.

XXXVII. [265] *How terre verte is distempered.*—Take mallow, and distemper it with vinegar or with very good wine, and with this juice distemper the terre-verte, and it will be a good colour for walls.

XXXVIII. [273] *How to make a green colour from salt.*—I have often mentioned a green colour, and now I will tell you how I make it. I take a piece of oak, of whatever length and breadth I please, and scoop it out into the shape of a scrinium. I then take copper, and cause it to be hammered out into plates as long as I choose; that is, so that their length may cover the breadth of the hollow wood. Afterwards I take a ladleful of salt, and pressing it strongly down, I put it into the fire for a night, and cover it up with coals; and the next day grind it very carefully upon a dry stone. I then take small twigs, and place them in the aforesaid wood, so that two parts of the hollow wood may be underneath and the third above. Then smearing the copper-plates on both sides with honey, I sprinkle the salt all over the honey, then shake the plates over the ladle to avoid waste, and then place the plates upon the twigs. I next cover up the hollow wood with another piece made for this purpose, and lute it all round with clay well mixed with asses'-dung. But before I cover up the hollow wood, I pour into it hot vinegar or hot urine, so as to fill one-third part of it, and then cover it up, and afterwards do as before directed with this colour.

sic imple illam ollam fortissimo aceto, et cooperi, et mitte in aliquo calido loco, et sic uno mense dimitte; et tunc aperies ollam, et quod inveneris in circuitu laminarum plumbearum mitte in aliam ollam, et pone super ignem, et semper movebis ipsum colorem, donec efficiatur albus sicut nix, et tunc tolles ab igne, et sumes de ipso colore quantum vis, et iste color vocatur cerusa; reliquam partem pone super ignem, et semper movebis donec efficiatur rubeum minium. Propterea moneo ut moveas, quod si non moveris, semper iterum vertetur in album plumbum, et sic tolle ab igne, et ipsam ollam dimitte refrigerari.

XXXVII. [265] *Quomodo distemperatur viride terrenum.*—Accipe malvam, et distempera cum aceto, vel optimo vino, et de isto jussu terrenum viridem distempera, et erit boni coloris in muro.

XXXVIII. [273] *Quomodo efficitur viridis color cum sale.*—Sæpe tractavi de viridi colore, quali modo efficiatur. Nunc vero quomodo id ipsum facio narrabo. Lignum quercinum sumo quantæ latitudinis et longitudinis voluero, et illud in modum scrinii cavo; deinde cuprum accipio, et facio illud attenuari in laminas tam longas quantum mihi placet, scilicet ut longitudo ejus operiat latitudinem concavi ligni. Posthoc accipio scutellam plenam salis, et, comprimens eum fortiter, mitto in ignem per noctem, et cooperio carbonibus, et in crastinum super lapidem molo diligentissime siccum. Postea accipio surculas graciles, colloco eas in predictum lignum, tamen ita ut duæ partes ligni cavi sint inferius, et tertia superius, sicque liniens laminas cupreas utraque parte melle, et desuper mel sal aspergens per totum, moxque excutio laminas in scutellam, ne pereat, sicque super surculas illas laminas pono. Tunc lignum concavum altero ligno adhuc aptato cooperio, et in circuitu totum argilla bene fimo asini mixto linio. Antequam autem lignum illud concavum cooperuerim, ponam intus vel acetum calidum, vel urinam calidam, ita ut tertia pars impleatur, et mox cooperio; tunc deinceps facio quod de hoc colore suprascriptum est.

XXXIX. [287] *A manner of making green with copper or brass.*—Fill a basin with white wine vinegar, and put into it strips of copper, and throw into it any other copper that you can procure; let it remain there for the space of one, two, or three months, and you will then find an excellent green colour.

XL. [261] *How orpiment is prepared for use.*—Crush the orpiment in leather, and afterwards grind it with water upon marble, adding to it a little calcined bone, and so let it dry there. Distemper it afterwards with egg for painting on wood, or on walls; but on paper, distemper it like ceruse. If it is not good, mix ochre with it, and then it will do.

XLI. [264] *How to lay on gold.*[1]—Take ochre and distemper it with water, and let it dry. In the mean while make glue with vellum, and afterwards whip some white of egg. Then mix the glue and the white of egg, and grind the ochre (which will by this time be well dried) strongly upon a marble slab, and, as soon as the ochre is dry, lay it on the parchment with a paint-brush, wherever you wish to lay the gold on the parchment, and then apply the gold, and let it remain so without pressing it with the stone. When it is dry burnish it well with a tooth. This is what I learned by experiment, and have frequently proved, and you may safely believe that I have told you the truth.

XLII. [278] *How to gild on parchment.*[2]—Take gypsum and white of Apulia, and carminium,[3] that is to say, cinnabar, namely, one third part of gypsum, and two equal parts of white and of carminium. Mix them well, and grind them on a marble slab, and add to them only a little thin glue; and with this mordant you may lay on gold wherever you like, and you may keep it a long time.

---

[1] See Sloane MS. No. 1754. [2] Ibid.

[3] Carminium is here represented to be synonymous with Cinnabar; but at p. 252 it is said to be composed of white and ochre.

XXXIX. [287] *Modus faciendi viridem cupri vel æris.*—Imple pelvim de aceto albo vini, et quicquid cupri poteris habere, projice intus, et sic stare permittes per spatium unius mensis vel duorum vel trium, et postea optimum viridem procreatum invenies.

XL. [261] *Quomodo auripigmentum præparatur ad operandum.*—Auripigmentum confringe in corio, postea tere cum aqua super marmorem, addens ei parum ossis combusti, et ibidem siccare permitte. Postea distempera cum ovo ad ponendum in ligno vel in muro, sed in carta pone sicut cerosium. Si non est bonum, misce ocrum; postea valet.

XLI. [264] *Quomodo ponitur aurum.*[1]—Accipe ocrum, et distempera cum aqua, sicque dimittes siccare. Interim de pergameno[2] vitulino colam facies. Postea glaream de ovo facies. Tunc colam et glaream insimul misces, et ocrum jam[3] bene siccatum[4] fortiter super marmorem teres, et ubi volueris ponere aurum in pergameno, statim ut molitum fuerit ocrum, super pergamenum cum[5] pincello trahes, sicque aurum desuper illico pones, dimittesque siccare[6] ita sine impressione coti.[7] Postea, cum siccatum fuerit,[8] cum dente fortiter burnies.[9] Ecce ut sæpe experimento didici, multociens probavi, et tua certa fide verum dixi.

XLII. [278] *Quomodo aurum in pergamenis ponitur.*[10]—Accipe gipsum, et album de Pullia[11] et carminium, i. e. cinobrium,[12] tertiam partem de gipso, et de albo, et[13] de carminio[14] duas partes equales, et misce simul, et tere super marmorem, adjungesque eis[15] modicum colle, tenue tamen,[16] et de hac distemperatura poteris aurum ubicunque volueris ponere, et multum[17] diu servare.

---

[1] Sic P.; *De temperamento auri* S. No. 63. [2] *Percameno* passim S. [3] *Jam* omittit S. [4] *Teres* hic inserit et post omittit P. [5] *Percameno illo* S. [6] *Siccare* omittit P. [7] *Et* supplet S. [8] *Cum siccatum fuerit* omittit S. [9] Quæ sequuntur omittit S. [10] Sic P. *Item de distemperatura auri* S. [11] *Apuleya* S. No. 64. [12] *Carominium id est sinobium* S. [13] *Quod* P. [14] *Carominio* S. [15] *Cum iis* S. [16] *Tantum* P. [17] *Multum* omittit S.

XLIII. [279] *How to write with gold.*[1]—Take a glass vase and fill it with urine, and let it rest until it appears clear. Then take the white of an egg well whipped, and divide it into two parts, and mix it with the urine, and stir them both together, and put them into a horn with gold dissolved, that is, ground, and then washed. You may write with this gold as with any other colour.

XLIV. [274] *Of auripetrum.*—Secundum Magistrum R. Take oil made from linseed, and put it into a new jar, and take the bark of "vesprum" very well dried and well ground in a mortar, and let it lie for a night in the oil. The next day boil it as long as you may think proper, but not much, and then pass it through a cloth into another jar, and boil it again a little over the fire with myrrh and aloes. Strain it again, and immediately put *vernix* with it, and heat it upon the coals. But if you have no *vernix*, take *glassa*, and put it with the aloes and myrrh instead of *vernix*, and, as I said before, strain it again. If you have not the bark of *vesprum* take dry *incaustum*, or else the bark of black-thorn dried and ground, and, as I said before, boil it with the myrrh and aloes, and afterwards remove it from the fire, and when it is cold, put it away in a vase to preserve as long as you like. You must collect the bark in March or April, and dry it in May, and keep it as long as you like.

XLV. [275] *How to gild upon tin.*—Take tin and place it on a tablet well whitened for this purpose, and well dried. Hammer the tin out well, and polish it with water and flint, rubbing it both along and across. Then take a polished iron made for this purpose, and polish it again with water. When it is very bright, let it dry, and then take it again and lay it on a table and burnish it with flint. And you may work with this gold on wood or on walls, and wherever you wish to gild.

---

[1] See Sloane MS. No. 1754.

XLIII. [279] *Quomodo scribitur de auro.*[1]—Sume tibi vas vitreum, et urina tua illud imple; sicque, donec appareat clara, requiescat; postea accipe glaream ovi optime fractam,[2] et fac duas partes, miscesque cum urina, et movebis utrumque [3] insimul, et pone in cornu cum auro soluto [*i.e.* molito et postea lavato [4]], itaque [5] poteris de tali [6] auro scribere sicut de alio colore.

XLIV. [274] *De auro petro.*—Secundum magistrum R. Accipe oleum de lini semine factum, et pone in ollam novam. Accipies que corticem de vespro optime siccatam, et in mortario bene tritam, et in oleo eam unam noctem jacere permittes. In crastino ad ignem bullies; quando satis tibi visum fuerit, tamen non multum, protinus per medium pannum in aliam ollam transire facies, deinde iterum ad ignem cum mirra et aloe parumper bullies. Iterum colabis, statimque vernix cum eis pones, et super carbones calefacies. Si autem vernix non habueris, accipies glassam, et pones cum aloe et mirra pro vernix, et, ut dixi, iterum colabis. Si autem corticem de vespro non habueris, accipe incaustum siccum, vel etiam corticem de nigra spina siccatam et tritam, et, sicut supra scripsi, cum mirra et aloe bullies, post hoc retrahes ab igne, et, cum frigidum fuerit, ad servandum in vase, quanto tempore volueris, repone. Cortices autem in Martio vel in Aprili accipies, et in Majo siccabis, et servabis quamdiu volueris.

XLV. [275] *Quomodo ponitur aurum super stagnum.*—Accipe stagnum, et pone super tabulam ad hoc opus optime dealbatam, et bene siccatam, extende, et cum silica et aqua in longitudinem et latitudinem poli; deinde sume ferrum totum aceratum, ad hoc opus factum, et iterum cum aqua poli. Cum multum et stans fuerit, sic siccare dimittes; postea accipies iterum, et super tabulam pones, et cum silice burnies eum. Poterisque de hoc auro in ligno vel in muro operari, et ubi volueris ponere.

---

[1] *De* omittit S. No. 65. [2] *Factum* S. [3] *Utrumque* omittit S. [4] Ex P. Omittit S. [5] *Et* S. [6] *Tali* omittit S.

XLVI. [246] *How borax*[1] *is distempered and kept.*—Take bean-ashes, and strain them through a cloth into a jar three or four times, and afterwards boil them [with water] over the fire until the ley is thick like ink, and then take the liquor which is called borax, and grind it in a vase or cup like cummin or pepper, and then mix it with the aforesaid ley. Then make it boil again, and keep stirring it, and then remove it from the fire, and put it into a leaden vase, and you may keep it as long as you like.

XLVII. [247] *Also on the same subject in another manner.*—Also, take the same ley, fresh made, and mix it with a little borax previously well ground in a shell, and then take copper reduced to powder of the weight of 12 denarii, (⊢÷⊣), and grind it well in a shell, like pepper, and mix it with the ley and borax, and boil it over the fire, and afterwards let it cool, and put it into a copper vase, and preserve it as long as any remains.

XLVIII. [248] *How to make nigellum.*—When you wish to make nigellum, take quicksilver, and copper, and lead, in equal quantities by measure, and put them into a shell to fuse together. Then take 6 denarii by weight of sulphur, and mix with the other ingredients, and stir them well. Then remove the mixture from the fire, and let it cool, and put it into a vase; then take atramentum distempered with wine, and draw what you like upon the silver with the atramentum, and immediately lay the powder made of the quicksilver, copper, and lead upon it [and heat it] until it melts, and it will make a beautiful nigellum.

XLIX. [272] *How to paint upon glass.*—I must tell you how to paint upon glass. Take a grossinum of sapphire, and the scales which are beaten off red-hot iron upon the blacksmith's anvil; and you must put one-third part of this with the grossi-

---

[1] I have no doubt that "Bures" should be read "Borax," and I refer to the note on this subject in the Table of Synonymes. It will be observed that the Bures of the text is said to be a liquor; it is unnecessary to remark that this is scarcely consistent with the direction to "grind it like cummin or

XLVI. [246] *Quomodo distemperatur bures et servatur.*—Accipe cinerem fabarum, et cola per pannum in ollam tribus vicibus aut quatuor, postea ad ignem bullire facies donec spissum sit quasi incaustum; deinde accipias illum liquorem qui vocatur bures, et teres in vase vel cipho quasi caminum vel piper; tunc misces cum laxiva suprascripta, iterumque bullire facies, semperque movebis. Postea tolle ab igne, et in plumbeo vase pone, et poteris servare quamdiu volueris.

XLVII. [247] *Item de eodem aliter.*—Item accipe eandem laxivam cum nuper fuerit facta, et misces cum ea parum de bures bene in conca prius maceratum; deinde accipies pulverem de cupro factam pensantem xii^{cim} denarios, et macerabis fortiter in conca velut piper, et cum lexiva bures misces, et ad ignem bullire facies. Postea sine refrigerari et in vase cupreo mitte, et serva quantum duraverit.

XLVIII. [248] *Quali modo nigellum facies.*—Quando volueris nigellum facere, accipe de argento vivo, et de cupro, et plumbo, equali mensura, et mitte in conca, ut simul coquantur. Tunc accipe sulphuris pondus vj denariorum, et cum eis misces, et movebis. Postea retrahe ab igne, et sine refrigerari, in vase pone; deinde accipe attramentum cum vino distemperatum, et facies quod volueris super argentum de attramento, statimque pulverem de argento vivo et cupro et plumbo superpones, donec fundatur, fietque pulcrum nigellum.

XLIX. [272] *Quomodo pingitur in vitro.*—Dicendum quomodo pingere debes in vitro. Accipe grossinum de saphiro, et palleam, quæ excutitur de calido ferro super incudem fabri, cum grossino tertiam partem pones, et plumbeum vitrum, Judeum

---

pepper." A similar direction is repeated in the following recipe. I consider that in both cases the Borax was prepared as a flux for the nigellum in No. xlviii.

num, and mix it with lead glass, that is, Jewish glass,[1] and grind it well on an iron slab, and so you will be able to paint.

L. [240] *On the various kinds and names of the principal and intermediate colours. And on the advantage of mixing them together; and on the places in which they are found, and are produced, or exist, and on the means of knowing the goodness of them.*—Of colours, some are white, and some are black, and some are intermediate. And the species of white are ceruse, lime, and alumen. The blacks are fuscus and those which are made from twigs. The intermediate colours are red, green, yellow, purple, prasinus, azure, and Incicus [Indigo ?], which are each of them, in themselves, beautiful; but are more so when mixed, because, by their variety, they give beauty to one another. And then, in composition they have a different hue, for as in medicinal preparations the various drugs mixed together modify each other; so colours of different kinds are mixed together, in order that they may partake of the nature of the others as well as of their own, and make as many, and beautiful, and pleasing, varieties as possible.

In this mixture, and in the order in which one is laid over another in painting, great skill is exercised. For after white, black or red should be put as an intermediate, because yellow, in composition, is in the second degree of mediocrity, for a colour too thick or too thin, soon alters.

Reds are produced in many places, but the best are found in Pontus and Spain.[2] "Paratonium"[3] is named from the place where it is dug. In the same manner, also, "Meline earth," a kind of metal, is found in some of the Cyclades, and receives its name from it. Green earth[4] is found in many

[1] In an extract published by Mr. Hendrie from a copy of the MS. of Le Begue, "judicatim scilicet" is inserted instead of "Judeum scilicet." So little is known of the history of glass-making, that it is impossible to say whether the glass mentioned in the text resembled in *any* respect the "Jews' glass," which used to be sold at Birmingham.—(See a paper in the 'Philosophical Magazine' for Dec. 1836.) The latter was a ruby-coloured glass, coloured with gold; but as Bulengerus says ('De Pictura,' &c. lib. ii. cap. v.), "Sine plumbo nullum metallum in vitrum transire

scilicet, misces, et super marmorem fortiter teres, sicque pingere potes.

L. [240] *De diversis colorum principalium et intermediorum speciebus et nominibus et de utilitate mixtionis eorum ad invicem, et de locis in quibus inveniuntur, et nascuntur, vel sunt, et de cognicione perfectionis eorum.*—Colorum alii sunt albi, alii nigri, alii sunt medii. Et albi quidem species, cerusa, calx, alumen. Nigri vero, fuscus, et qui ex sarmentis componitur. Medii, rubeus, viridis, croceus, purpureus, prasinus, azur, et incicus; quorum expressio per se cujuslibet pulcra est, sed interdum sic invicem permixti pulcriores fiunt, quia sua varietate graciam alter alteri præstant: Dein compositi aliud monstrant, nam ut in medicinæ confectionibus species sibi permixtæ invicem conferunt, sic colores non ejusdem qualitatis, ut partem ex alterius natura, partem ex sua trahant, et quam plurimas eorum varietates pulcras et delectabiles reddant, simul commiscentur. In qua commixtione, et in eo modo quo in pictura alter alteri post se ponuntur, summa est subtilitas; siquidem post album, niger, aut rubeus medius, convenit; quoniam crocus, in temperacione, mediocritas secunda est, quia color nimium spissus, et nimium tenuis, cito deficit.

Rubi itaque multis locis generantur, sed optimi Ponto, et in Hispania, nascuntur. Paratonium ex ipso loco unde foditur habet nomen. Eadem racione et melinus quidem, metalli species, per insulas Cycladis, inde dicitur. Creta viridis pluribus locis nascitur, sed optima in Creta Cirina, quæ Græce dicitur Theodote quædam, in cujus solo primum est inventa. Arzicon, id est, auripigmentum, in Ponto nascitur. Sandaraca

potest," it is not improbable that glass coloured with gold was composed partly of lead; and if, as appears from the text, lead glass was called "Jewish glass," this may sufficiently account for the appellation given to the glass made at Birmingham.

[2] See Vitruvius, lib. vii. cap. vii.

[3] Paratonium and Meline earth, or Melino, are both white minerals.

[4] The author of the French Commentary on Pliny, published at London in 1725, observes that Isidore mentions green earth, which he calls "Prasinus."

places, but the best in "creta cirina," which in Greek is called Theodote,[1] in which territory it was first found. "Arzicon,"[2] that is, orpiment, is found in Pontus. "Sandaraca"[3] is found in many places, but the best is found in Pontus, and by the river Ysparis.[4] Azure is mentioned as having been first found in the Ephesian territory and afterwards in Spain, and with it are connected the following inventions.[5]

LI. [241] *On trying azure.*—Now azure must be tried in the following manner: Put it on an iron plate, and hold it over the fire until it is red-hot. Then take it out and let it cool. If it does not change colour, it will be good; but if it does change colour, it is adulterated.

When ice,[6] therefore, is first cut off metals, drops of quicksilver are pressed out, which artificers collect for various purposes, for neither silver nor brass can be gilt without it. When the drops of quicksilver are run together, so as to fill a measure of 4 sextarii, they will weigh one hundred pounds. If upon this liquor you place a stone weighing a hundred pounds, it will float on it. If you put a scruple into this liquor, it will sink, whence you may see that the difference does not consist in the weight of the substance but in the nature of it. Also, if the goldsmith wish to obtain the gold from the tinder of burnt frieze, let him wash it, and mix it with quicksilver, and then press it in a linen or cotton cloth, so that the quicksilver may be expressed, and the gold remain.

---

[1] Vitruvius says it was called "Theodotion," because the name of the owner of the estate where it was found was Theodotus.

[2] The word Arzicon appears to be a corruption of "Arsenicon," the Greek name for Orpiment.

[3] The term "Sandaraca" is applied to red orpiment and also to red lead; both are occasionally found native.

[4] Hypanis, according to Vitruvius.

[5] A native mineral azure is here described, which appears, from the test mentioned in the next chapter, to be Lapis Lazuli. The author of this work appears to have been unacquainted with the azure described by Vitruvius, which consisted of a blue glass formed of nitre, sand, and copper filings.

[6] This obscure passage appears to be an abridgment of cap. viii. of the 7th book of Vitruvius. The original MS. may have been imperfect, or

pluribus locis generatur, sed optima in Ponto et juxta flumen Ysparim. Azurii autem natura, primum Ephesiorum solo reperta, memoratur deinceps in Hispania, cujus natura has invenciones habet.

LI. [241] *De probatione azurii.*—Verum probacio azurii sic erit observanda. In lamina ferrea mittatur, et super ignem ponatur, tamdiu donec lamina rubescat. Tunc retrahatur ut refrigescat. Si colorem non mutaverit, optimum erit; si autem mutaverit, viciatum erit.

Glaces itaque, vel glaciens, cum ex metallis primum exciduntur, argenti vivi guttas exprimunt, quas artifices ad plures usus colligunt. Neque enim argentum, neque æs, sine hiis inaurari possunt. Nam confuse in unum guttæ argenti vivi, ita ut quatuor sextariorum mensuram habeant, centum libræ pondus efficiunt. Supra cujus liquorem centenarium saxi pondus si posueris, sustinebit; scrupulum si posueris, descendit. Unde intelliges non ponderis esse, sed naturæ distinctionem. Itaque si aurifex pannis tostilibus adustis ex friso in rudi vase fictili solidari pulverem voluerit, lava, postea mixtum argento vivo, vel in panno, vel in linthiolo, cumprimis, ut liquor argenti vivi expressus emanet, et aurum extrinsecus remaneat.

---

something may have been omitted by Le Begue, for this paragraph is evidently unconnected with the first part of the chapter. The following extract from Vitruvius (lib. vii., cap. viii.) may render the passage more intelligible:—"Ingrediar nunc Minii rationes explicare.....Foditur enim gleba, quæ Anthrax dicitur antequam tractionibus ad minium perveniat, vena uti ferreo magis subrufo colore, habens circa se rubrum pulverem; cum id foditur, ex plagis ferramentorum crebras emittit lacrymas argenti vivi, quæ a fossoribus statim colliguntur."

LII. [242] *On the mixture of colours, and what the colours are, particularly lakes, which are used for want of other colours.*—It is evident that all colours are corrupted by mixing them; although, indeed, in tempering "folium," lime made from hard stone is used, lest the colour should fade for want of body. For when "folium" is distempered with a pernicious quantity of albumen, that is white of egg, it can [not?] be employed with great beauty and advantage. The juice of dragon's blood, and "sandis," that is, madder—is used either pure or with red chalk; other juices of a similar kind are also mixed with green or yellow earth. "Crisicula[1]" [chrysocolla] comes from Macedon, and is dug in copper mines. *Indicus* by its name shows whence it is brought.

LIII. [243] *How atramentum of various kinds is made.*[2]—The method of making ink is as follows, for it is necessary, not only for use in painting, but even for every day writing. A vase is put into a hollow chamber; and a furnace is made so as to have nostrils, that is, apertures, through which the smoke can penetrate into the vase. Some tiles must then be laid in the furnace, and upon these hot tiles resin must be put, so as to drive all the smoke and soot into the vase. Afterwards grind the soot very fine, and you will make a very bright atramentum, with which you must mix painter's size. To accelerate the process, soft charcoal of wood, or of peach-stones, ground up with glue, is useful. Charred twigs also will imitate the appearance of atramentum; but the blackest twigs must be used. If good wine is poured over them, and glue be added, they will form a colour which will appear to imitate the softness of daylight.

LIV. [245] *How to make a "purpurino"*[3] *colour out of various things in various ways.*—Stones or flints, that is, stones emitting fire, seem very necessary for painting, when they are heated in the fire, and quenched with very strong vinegar, and they will give

---

[1] See Vitruv., lib. vii. c. ix. [2] Ibid. c. x.

[3] Ibid. cap. xi. This chapter treats of red or crimson colours, and not of the "Purpurino" of the Italians.

LII. [242] *De colorum commixtione, et quales ipsi colores sunt, præcipue infectivi, quibus utitur propter aliorum colorum inopiam.*—Colores autem omnes commixtione corrumpi manifestum est. Siquidem in temperamento folii utilitur calx ex duro saxa facta, ne minus pressus pereat. Quippe aqua distemperato folicio, cum perniciosa quantita albuginis, id est, glarea ovi, pulcherrime et utiliter miscetur. Sanguis drachonis aut sandis, id est, garancia; ejus autem purus succus, aut creta rubea, viridi quoque, et croceo, alii suæ qualitatis permiscentur. Crisicula a Macedonia venit, foditur autem ex metallis ærariis. Indicum ab ipsis ostenditur ubi nascitur.

LIII. [243] *Quomodo fit attramentum diversarum specierum.*—Attramenti vero compositio sic erit observanda, quæ non solum ad usum picture necessaria videtur, sed etiam at cothidianas scripturas. Vasculus curva camera servatur: fornacula sic componatur, ut nares, id est, suspiracula, habeantur in vasculo, quibus fumus possit intrare. Tegulæ in eadem fornace intendantur. Super tegulas ardentes resina mittatur, ut omnem fumum et fuliginem per nares in vasculum exprimat. Postea fuliginem diligenter conteres, et attramentum facies nitidum, pictorum autem gluten misceas ipsi. Ad accelerationem etiam operis, carbones molles ligni, et ossium persicorum, cum glutino contriti, valent. Nec minus sarmenta exusta attramenti qualitatem imitabunt, sed sarmenta quæ nigrioris coloris sunt, si in optimo vino perfundantur, postea exusta fuerint, addito glutino, imitari etiam diei suavitatem monstrabunt.

LIV. [245] *Quomodo fit purpurinus color ex diversis diversimode.*—Utique plurimum necessaria in operibus picturæ videntur glebæ vel silices, id est, lapides ignem emittentes, cum in igne cocuntur, tunc, aceto acerrimo perfuso, extinguuntur, et

a purple colour. Copper burnt becomes ceruse.[1] The oster[2] also, the blood of which is used for a purple colour, is found in many places, but the best are found in the island of Cyprus, when they grow with the sun [i. e. in the spring]. Having, therefore, cut them round, pound them, and they will give out drops of a purple colour, which, being run together, are tempered as a purple pigment. This pigment is called "oster," because it is obtained from the above liquor, which soon solidifies on account of its saltness.

LV. [245] *Of lakes; and how they are made of various substances in various manners.*[3]—Purple colours are also made by straining [a decoction of] boiled madder roots. So also other colours are dyed with flowers. Thus, when painters wish to imitate sil atticum they put dried violets[4] into a vase of water over the fire to boil, and, when boiled down, they are strained through a linen cloth, and rubbed down in a mortar with chalk, and so a colour like sil atticum is made. In the same manner, tempering "vaccinium" with milk, a very elegant purple colour is made; so the herb which is called "litea"[5] gives out an azure juice; and a very deep green colour is also made. These are called "infectivi;" and are used for want of simple colours. In the same manner, also, mixing formosa or angularia[6] with glass, they make colours with it.

LVI. [282] *On mixing colours together in painting, and in illuminating; and of the ways in which pictures are filled in with them, and how the lights and shades are laid on.*[7]—Mix azure with ceruse; shade it with indigo; lay on the lights with white-lead. Shade pure vermilion with brunum or with dragon's

---

[1] There is probably some mistake here. See Vitruv., lib. vii. cap. xii.

[2] Ibid. cap. xiii.

[3] Ibid. cap. xiv.

[4] The Viola lutea, or Wall-flower.

[5] Lutea—The Reseda Luteola—Dyer's weed, Weld. See Vitruv., ibid.

[6] The annularia of Vitruvius and Pliny.

[7] This chapter and the next are certainly translations from some Byzantine MS. The term Bisetum, Biseth, occurs frequently. It is a corruption

reddent purpureum colorem. Cuprum adustum fit cerusa. Oster autem, cujus sanguinem qui pro colore purpuræ temperatur, pluribus locis nascitur, sed optimum in insula Cipri, cum solis cursum habentur. Concute itaque, cum circumcisæ fuerint, lacrimas in purpureum colorem emittunt, quibus collectis, purpureus color temperatur. Hoc autem oster est appellatum, quod ex humore licetur, qui cito ex salsugine inhærescit.

LV. [245] *De coloribus infectivis, et quomodo fiunt ex diversis diversimode.*—Fiunt etiam purpurei colores, infecta cocta rubea radice. Similiter ex floribus alii colores inficiuntur. Itaque pictores, cum voluerint silvaticum imitari, viola arida in aqua cum vase ad ignem ponatur, ut ferveat, et decoctam in linteolo exprimunt, et in mortario cum creta terunt, et faciunt silasacetum colorem. Eadem ratione, vaccinium cum lacte temperantes, purpureum faciunt eleganter, uti herba quæ litea appellatur, succum efficit cæruleum, et utuntur viridissimo colore. Hæc infectiva appellantur, quibus utitur propter inopiam colorum simplicium. Simili modo cum in formosam seu angulariam vitro miscentes, inficiunt ex ea colores.

LVI [282] *De miscendis inter se coloribus pingendo et illuminando, et de modis cum de ipsis implentur opera et matizantur et inciduntur alter ex altero.*—Azurium misces cum cerosio; incides de indico; matizabis de albo plumbo. Vermiculum purum incides de bruno, aut de sanguine draconis; matizabis

---

of Pezzette, the Italian name for those pieces of rag dipped in the juice of certain plants, which were used in painting, and for other purposes. The Turks and inhabitants of the Levant still call them "Bezerere Rubré" (see Pierre Pomet, Histoire Générale des Drogues, Tit. Tornesole). In the west of Europe they were called Bezette or Bezeth. From the term "Vergaut," which occurs in this recipe, and which appears to signify "Vert bleu," "blue green," or "Verde azzurro," I should think the translation was by a Frenchman.

blood; lay on the lights with orpiment or minium. Also mix vermilion with white-lead, and make the colour which is called rosa; shade with vermilion; lay on the lights with white [and] rosa, or with white-lead. Also make a colour with dragon's blood and orpiment; shade it with brunum; lay on the lights with orpiment. Shade carminium with brunum; vary with minium. Shade folium with brunum; lay on the lights with bisetum folii. Also mix folium with white; shade it with folium; lay on the lights with white-lead. Shade ochre with vermilion; lay on the lights with white [and?] ochre. Also shade ochre with green; lay on the lights with white. Shade white with pure minium; and vary with azure. Shade brunum with black; lay on the lights with azure or minium. Also mix brunum with white, and it will make a beautiful rose colour; shade with brunum; lay on the lights with white or with bisetum folii. Also mix brunum with minium; shade with black; and lay on the lights with red minium. Mix orpiment with azure or indigo, or ochre with indigo, or green, and it will be good "vergaut;" then vary with brunum or black; lay on the lights with orpiment or with bisetum. Shade green with black; lay on the lights with bisetum. Mix green with white; shade with green; lay on the lights with white. Shade brunum with black; lay on the lights with vergaut or with minium mixed with brunum. Shade indigo with black; lay on the lights with azure, or vergaut, or bisetum. Shade orpiment with vermilion; lay on the lights with white [and?] orpiment. Carminium is made with white and ochre.

LVII. [283] *On colours incompatible with each other.*—Now, if you wish to know which are the colours that are incompatible with each other, they are these:—Orpiment does not agree with folium, or with green, or with minium. Nor does green agree with folium, namely, in the mixture of the materials of the said pigments, and in the works in which they are employed together.

de auripigmento aut de minio. Item, vermiculum misce cum albo plumbo, et facies colorem qui vocatur rosa; incide de vermiculo; matizabis de [alba[1] rosa, aut de] albo plumbo. Item, facies colorem de sanguine draconis et de auripigmento; incide de bruno; matizabis de auripigmento. Carminium incide de bruno; de rubeo minio undabis.[2] Folium incide de bruno; matiza de biseto folii.[3] Item, misce folium cum albo; incide de folio; matiza de albo plumbo.[4] Ocrum incide de vermiculo; matiza de albo ocro. Item, ocrum incide de viride; matiza de albo. Album minii purum incide, et undabis simul de azuro. Brunum incide de nigro; matiza de azurio vel minio. Item, misces brunum cum albo, fietque pulcra rosa; incide de bruno; matiza de albo, vel de biseto folii. Item, brunum misces cum minio; incides de nigro; matiza de rubeo minio. Misce auripigmentum cum azurio vel indico, aut ocrum cum indico, vel viride, et erit bonum vergaut; inde de bruno, aut de nigro, undabis; auripigmento aut de biseth matizabis. Viride incide de nigro, et matizabis de biseto. Misce viride cum albo; incide de viride; matiza de albo. Brunum incide de nigro; matiza de vergaut, aut de minio mixto cum bruno. Indicum incide de nigro; matiza de azurio, vel de vergaut, aut biseth. Auripigmentum incide de vermiculo; matiza de albo auripigmento. Carminium fit de albo et ocro.

LVII. [283] *De coloribus sibi contrariis.*—Modo si vis scire qui sunt colores qui sibi invicem alter alteri sunt contrarii, hi sunt. Auripigmentum non concordat cum folio, nec cum viride, nec cum minio. Nec viride concordat cum folio, scilicet in mixturis materiarum ipsorum colorum, et operationibus mixtis eorum, quæ discordantiæ non sunt in qualitatibus colorum, nec

---

[1] Ex P.; in alteris omittitur. [2] *Matizabis de rubeo minio.* C. [3] *De albo plumbo* C. [4] *Albo folio* P.

And these discordances are not in the mere [optical qualities of the pigments, nor in their accidents of colour; for there are no colours, or qualities of colours, either simple or mixed, which, as regards the colour only, do not agree with any other sorts of colours in mixtures, namely, for composing other different mixtures; and you may thus have at pleasure almost innumerable varieties of colours. But the said discordances are, and are to be understood as being, in the other natural conditions, incident to the substance of the said pigments, they being contrary to each other in such manner that, if they are mixed together, one substance, by a certain natural incompatibility, either changes the other or is changed by it; and so the quality and beauty of the pigments themselves, as well separate as mixed, and their own substance, and the work done with them, are spoiled and destroyed. They therefore do not bear to be mixed together; and so, in the art of painting, besides the consideration that is to be had for the varieties of colour, and these and other things relating to the said art, we must not forget the proper and necessary considerations, drawn from a true theoretical and practical knowledge of and acquaintance with the natural conditions and contrarieties existing in the materials and liquors of the said colours, and of the contrarieties of the other things incident to that art.

LVIII. [286] *Of the care which must be taken with regard to the nature of the colours and of the way of mixing them together, and of the method to be observed in shading and laying on the lights, on which another chapter has been inserted.*—If you wish to know well the natures of the colours, and the mixtures of them, as whether they are transparent or opaque, give attention to what follows. And note, that you must shade azure with black; and lay on the lights with white lead. Also mix azure with white lead; and shade [with azure, and lay on the lights] with white lead. Shade vermilion with brunum; and lay on the lights with orpiment. Also mix vermilion with white lead, and make the colour which is called rosa; shade it with vermilion; lay on the lights with white lead. Shade orpiment with vermilion, and orpi-

ex accidentibus colorativis eorum; quia nulli colores, nec colorum qualitates, sunt, simplices aut mixtæ, quæ et qui, quantum ad colores, non conveniant quibuslibet aliis in mixturis, ad componendas, scilicet, alias diversas et quasi innumerabiles qualitatum varietates ad placitum habebis: sed dictæ discordantiæ intelliguntur et sunt, quantum ad ceteras naturales conditiones insistentes in materiis ipsorum colorum invicem taliter contrarias, quod, si simul miscentur, una materia, ex contrarietate quadam naturali alterius, vel alterat alteram, et altera alteram, et colorum ipsorum qualitas et pulcritudo, tam distincta quam mixta, necnon eorum materia, et opus ex ea factum, vastatur et deletur. Igitur mixtiones ad insimul invicem non tolerant; et sic non prætermittendum est, quin in arte pictoriæ, ultra debitas considerationes quantum ad colorum varietates, ac eorum et aliarum rerum in ipsa arte concurrentium differentias, habeantur etiam debite et necessarie considerationes, ex vera theorecali vel practicali scientia et cognitione conditionum et contrarietatum naturalium, insistentium materiis et liquoribus ipsorum colorum, et rerum contrarialibus in ipsa arte intervenientium.

LVIII. [286] *De diligentia quæ haberi debet circa naturas colorum, et de modis miscendi, eos inter se, et incidendi, et matizandi, cum in operibus distinguuntur, ut etiam aliud capitum de hoc antepositum est.*—Si vis bene scire naturas colorum et mixtiones eorum, ut hi sunt clari et spissi, diligenter autem intentum appone. Et nota quod lazurium incides de nigro; matizabis autem de albo plumbo. Item, misces lazurium cum albo plumbo [incides[1] de azur, matizabis] de albo plumbo. Vermiculum incides de bruno; matizabis auripigmento. Item, miscebis vermiculum cum albo plumbo, et facies colorem qui vocatur rosa; incides de vermiculo; matizabis de albo plumbo. Auripigmentum incides de vermiculo; et illi matizatura non est, quia stercorat omnes alios colores. Tum si vis facere gladium viridem,

[1] Ex. T.; *et incides* P.

ment has no light tint, because it mars all colours. Then, if you wish to make lily-green, mix orpiment with indigo; shade it with black; lay on the lights with orpiment. Shade dragon's blood with black; lay the lights on with white lead. Also mix dragon's blood with orpiment; shade with dragon's blood; lay on the lights with orpiment. You must shade green with black, and lay on the lights with white lead. Also mix green with white lead; shade with green; lay on the lights with white lead. Shade granetum with green; lay on the lights with white lead. Shade indigo with azure; lay on the lights with white lead. Also mix indigo with white lead; shade with indigo; lay on the lights with white lead. Shade flesh colour with black; lay on the lights with white lead. Also mix saffron with white lead; shade with saffron; lay on the lights with white lead. Shade folium with black; lay on the lights with white lead. Mix folium with white lead; shade with folium; lay on the lights with white lead. If you wish to make a colour like lily green, mix azure with white lead; shade it with azure; lay on the lights with white lead; and when it is dry, cover it over with clear saffron. Orpiment does not agree with green, or with folium, or with red minium, or with white minium, as we have already said.

auripigmentum misce cum indico; incides cum nigro; matizabis auripigmento. Sanguinem draconis incides de nigro; matizabis de albo plumbo. Item, misces sanguinem draconis cum auripigmento; incides de sanguine draconis; matizabis de albo plumbo. Item, misces sanguinem draconis cum auripigmento; incides de sanguine draconis; de auripigmento matizabis. Viride incides de nigro; matizabis de albo plumbo. Item, miscebis viride cum albo plumbo; incides de viridi; matizabis de albo plumbo. Granetum incides de viridi; matizabis de albo plumbo. Indicum incides de lazurio; matizabis de albo plumbo. Item, misce indicum cum albo plumbo; incides de indico, matizabis de albo plumbo. Carminum incides de nigro; matizabis de albo plumbo. Item, misces crocum cum albo plumbo; incides de croco; matizabis de albo plumbo. Folium incides de nigro; matizabis de albo plumbo. Misces folium cum albo plumbo; incides de folio; matizabis de albo plumbo. Si vis facere colorem similem gladio viridi, misce lazurium cum albo plumbo; incides de lazurio; matizabis de albo plumbo; et quando fuerit siccus operi de claro croco. Auripigmentum non concordat cum viridi, nec cum folio, nec cum rubeo minio, nec cum albo minio, ut antea jam dictum est.

THE FOLLOWING IS

A TREATISE UPON COLOURS OF VARIOUS KINDS.

AND FIRST

THE INTRODUCTION.

290. In the year of the Circumcision of Christ 1398, on Sunday, the 28th day of July, JOHN ARCHERIUS wrote and noted down, at Paris, the following chapters concerning colours for painting, according to the words and instructions given him by Jacob Cona, a Flemish painter then residing at Paris, who, as he said, had himself tried, and used, during the whole period of his life, the recipes contained in the following pages.

And afterwards in the month of December, in the year of Christ 1411, the said John, more than a year after his return from Lombardy, corrected them in several places, according to various information which he had since received, both from other authentic books relating to such things, and otherwise; and which he copied fairly as follows:—

291. *For laying gold in different ways upon various articles so that it may be burnished, and the cautions to be observed concerning this in painting.*—For laying gold on parchment,[1]

[1] *Carta et papiro.* It is difficult to translate these words accurately: there is no doubt that in this sentence *carta* means *parchment*, which would otherwise be omitted in enumerating the substances on which gold was laid. *Papirus* also may be understood to mean *paper*, since cotton and linen paper were both in use at this time. The next time the author mentions the word "carta" he explicitly speaks of that kind called

DE COLORIBUS DIVERSIS MODIS TRACTATUR
IN SEQUENTIBUS.

ET PRIMO

MODUS PROHEMII.

290. Anno circumcisionis Christi 1398 die dominicæ 28 Julii, JOHANNES ARCHERIUS scripsit et notavit in Parisiis sequentia capitula de coloribus ad pingendum, per verba et signamenta quæ sibi dixit Jacobus Cona flamingus pictor commorans tunc Parisiis, qui toto tempore suo ut dixerat temptaverat et usus fuerat ipsemet de contentis in sequentibus. Et post ea anno Christi 1411 de mense decembris, idem Johannes reversus de partibus Lombardiæ jam per plusquam unum annum, correxit ea in pluribus locis secundum plures informationes, quas inde postea per ceteros libros autentiquos de talibus narrantes et aliter habuerat, et ad nettum rescripsit ut sequitur.

291. *Ad ponendum aurum burniendum super diversis diverse mode et de cautelis habendis circa hoc pingendo.*—Ad ponendum aurum in carta, papiro, tela linea; sindone, et in ligneis tabulis

---

" parchment" (pergamenum), of the clippings of which, he adds, the size might be made. In the earlier part of this MS. I have translated the word " carta" always by " parchment," but it appears that it was also applied to paper at this period, 1382—1411.

The exact date when the Egyptian paper, made of the papirus, fell into disuse in Europe is not known, but it appears from the testimony of Eusta-

paper, linen cloth, sindone,[1] and on primed wooden panels, which gold may be burnished, that is polished. Take the white gersa, which is otherwise called white chalk, which is found in abundance at Bologna and at Paris; and a little Armenian bole, in quantity about one-fourth of the chalk, or a little *crocus*, which is commonly called saffron. This Armenian bole and this saffron are not added because they cannot be omitted without great inconvenience by any one who wishes to do so, but merely that the colour may not be white, but yellowish or reddish; and not for any other reason than this, namely, that when it is laid upon the paper, it may differ from the whiteness of the paper, and thus the things which are made of it are better seen than they would be if the colour of it was white like that paper which is called parchment. Grind all these things very fine upon a hard stone, well polished, and broad, with another stone to be held in the hand, polished in the same manner with clear water from a well or a spring, and let the

---

chius, the learned commentator on Homer, that it was no longer in use in his time, 1170.

The invention of paper made from cotton is believed to have occurred in Greece in the tenth century. The most ancient MS. that Montfaucon saw on this paper, with the date, was written A.D. 1050.

Theophilus, lib. i. c. xxiii., mentions "*pergamenum græcam quæ fit ex lana ligni.*" This is the reading of Raspe, from a MS. of the thirteenth century, and may certainly be understood to apply to the cotton paper made in Greece, which was called by the Italians "Carta Bambagina;" but the copy of the MS. of Theophilus, which formed part of the MS. of Le Begue, which is of the fifteenth century, and which is in his hand-writing, instead of "ligni," has the words "*lini id est papirum.*" Le Begue then may be considered to have understood this passage, if indeed he did not interpolate the words "*id est papirum,*" as applying to paper made of rags or linen. We may therefore, I think, consider that, where *papirus* is used in the MS. of Jehan Le Begue, paper made of rags is meant.

I am the more strongly inclined to this opinion, because the author of the article 'Paper' in the 'Encyclopædia Britannica,' quoting the work of the Abbé Andrez, published at Parma in 1782, entitled 'Dell' Origine, Progressi, e Stato attuale d'Ogni Letteratura,' says that paper made from silk was anciently fabricated in China, and that the art of making this paper was

---

[1] *Sindone,* a kind of very fine linen, such as cambric or lawn.

dealbatis, quod aurum burniatur, id est, poliri possit. Accipe gersam albam quæ aliter dicitur creta alba de qua habundanter *reperitur bononiæ et Parisiis,*[1] et accipe parum bularmenii circa quantitatem quartæ partis cretæ, vel parum croci, qui vulgariter dicitur safran et qui bularmenius et saffranus non ponuntur quia non possunt absque magno inconvenienti dimitti cui vult, sed ponuntur solum ut ipse color non sit albus sed sit croceus vel rubescens et non per alia causa, ad hoc quod dum ponitur in opere super cartam quæ differenciet ab albedine cartæ et quod per hoc melius videantur quæ fiunt de ipso quod videri possent si ipse color esset albus ut est carta quæ dicitur pergamenum. Et ea omnia tere valde subtiliter super lapidem durum bene politum et latum et cum alio lapide manuali similiter polito, viz. cum aqua clara putei vel fontis et fiat tempera seu color qui in gallico dicitur *assiete,* quæ postea si vis tamen antequam penitus siccet, dum tamen induratus jam sit, quia postquam siccus sit potes distemperare cum aqua colata, ex cola facta de

---

carried from China to Persia about the year 652, and to Mecca in 706. The Arabs substituted cotton, the production of their own country, for silk, and introduced the paper into Spain. The Spaniards, from the quantity of linen to be found in the kingdom of Valencia, seem first to have adopted the idea of using linen rags, and the most ancient paper of this kind is that of Valencia and Catalonia. From Spain it passed into France, as may be learned from a letter of Joinville to St. Louis about 1260. It is discovered to have been in Germany in 1312, and in England in 1320. In consequence of the paper made from cotton in the Levant, the paper from linen was introduced much later in Italy. "Carta Bambagina" is frequently mentioned in the MS. of Cennino Cennini, written at Florence in 1437, and it is still made in the Levant.

The precise period of the introduction of paper made from rags into France and Italy is not known, but Montfaucon could find no book on this paper antecedent to the death of St. Louis.

We may then conclude, that during the time of Jehan Le Begue, paper made from linen rags was used in France and Germany, and that in Italy paper was made from cotton, while parchment, which had become scarce, was employed occasionally throughout Europe.

It will be observed that in the following chapters Alcherius writes "pergamena *seu* carta."

---

[1] Sic sublin. in MS., sed in atramento recentori.

mixture or colour be made, which in French is called *assiete*,[1] which you may afterwards, if you like, before it is quite dry, but after it has set, distemper with glue water, made with glue from cuttings of the white leather of which gloves are made. Clippings of parchment also are good for this purpose, but the cuttings of the white leather make the glue stronger. Lastly, let the size, or sized water, be warm; I say warm, lest it may be conglutinated, because if the size is as it ought to be, when it is cold it will be congealed like jelly for *galantina* [brawn] not very hard, and this on account of the glue which is made to enter into the water by the decoction of the cuttings of leather or of parchment in that water, which is congealed by cold. And therefore summer weather is very convenient for this, both because it does not allow the colour to congeal or chill, and because it makes the colour dry quickly when it is laid on. And with this warm size, you must, as has been said before, distemper the said powdered colour or tempering for laying on gold, so that it may be soft and liquid like good ink for writing, or as it may seem convenient. Having done this, write, draw, and fill in or paint whatever you wish with it, and rather with a paintbrush than a pen, because if it were done with a pen, and were to become chilled in the pen, it would not flow so well as with a paintbrush; moreover, when using a paintbrush, the colour may be held in the hand, which, by its warmth or heat, will not allow it to congeal; this, however, can also be done well with a pen, but a paintbrush is much more convenient. And, in painting with a pen, as well as with a paintbrush, it is a good thing to keep the colour over a slow fire of charcoal, at such a warmth, that it may not congeal, but may remain liquid. Afterwards let those things dry which you have drawn and painted, and when they are dry burnish them, that is, polish or smooth them gently with a tooth of a horse or a boar, or with a polished hard stone fitted for this purpose, in order that all the roughness may be softened down,

[1] Hence our terms "size" and "gold size."

inciseriis corii albi de quo fiunt chirothecæ, et minutiæ pergamenorum etiam sunt bonæ ad hoc, sed meliores sunt dictæ incisæ corii albi quia faciunt colam firmiorem; denue cola seu aqua colata sit tepida, dico tepida ne sit conglutinata quod si ipsa aqua sit qualis debet esse cum ipsa erit frigida erit congelata in modum gelii galantinæ non multum duri, et hoc causa colæ in ipsa aqua insertæ ex decoctione dictarum minutiarum corii vel pergameni facta in ipsa aqua, quæ per frigidum congelatur. Ideo tempus æstatis in hoc multum prodest, tam quod non permittit colorem congelari neque frigidari quam quia facit colorem cito siccari cum positus est in opere. Et de ipsa aqua colata tepida debes ut dictum est distemperare dictum colorem tritum seu temperamentum ad ponendum aurum taliter quod sit mollis et liquidus quantum est bonum incaustum ad scribendum, vel ut conveniens videbitur. Et hoc facto scribe pertrahe et imple seu pinge quæ vis ex eo, et potius cum pincello quam cum calamo, quod si fieret cum calamo et infrigidaretur in calamo, non tam bene curreret sicut facit cum pincello; ac etiam operando cum pincello potest ipse color extendi super manum, quæ pro tepiditate sua seu caliditate non permittit ipsum colorem congelari, quod tamen potest etiam bene fieri cum calamo sed multo melius pincello convenit. Et operando tam cum calamo quam cum pincello, bonum est quod color ipse teneatur cum lento igne carbonum in tali tepiditate, quod non possit conglutinari, sed stet liquidus; et postea dimitte siccari ex quæ scripseris pinxeris et protaxeris [protraxeris] et quando siccati fuerint, burnias, id est polias seu lisses leniter cum dente equi vel apri, vel cum lapide duro polito ad hoc apto, ut adæquentur omnes scabrositates in ipsis præcipue locis in quibus ipsam assisam seu colorem posuisti, deinde rettera et adhuc in ipsis locis repone pinge et pertrahe tanquam prius cum ipso colore et postea permitte siccari et adhuc polies et burnias ut prius. Postea vero tertia reponas et repinge ea ipsa quæ prius de eadem assisia seu colore, sed fac quod ista

particularly in those places in which you have put this size or colour. Then grind some more, and again paint over and draw upon those same places, with this colour, as before, and afterwards let it dry, and then polish and burnish it as before. Afterwards go over and repaint those places which you did before, with the same mordant or colour, but let this third and last coat of colour be tempered with white of egg whipped or beaten, so as to be liquid and without any particles conglutinated or adhering together; because this white of egg makes a size or vehicle sufficiently strong to hold the gold for burnishing and to resist the shaking and violence of the friction and rubbing the burnisher over the gold. Then, before the colour on the places in which you put it, is dry apply the gold quickly, and allow it to dry, and afterwards burnish all these things with the same tooth, stone, or other instrument, you used before as above mentioned, but first pressing lightly and drawing the burnisher over the gold; then rather harder, and afterwards harder still, particularly on parchment, paper, and panels; but on cloth and sindone not pressing so hard, and taking great care lest what has been done should crumple up and be broken, and so those things which you drew and painted, and upon which you laid the gold, will remain clean and polished; and the forms and lines made with this colour will remain brightly gilt.

But it must be observed, that on parchment, paper, and panels it is sufficient for the said colour to be put on once only, tempered with size, and afterwards, for the last coat, with white of egg, provided that it is laid on well the first time when tempered with size. But on cloth or sindone it is more necessary that this colour should be laid on twice, while tempered with size, before it is put on for the last coat tempered with white of egg. And this is because sindone and cloth, owing to their porosity, are too absorbent, flowing, flexible, and unstable, and therefore soak up the colour, so that there does not remain a good and firm substance of colour upon the cloth or sindone, unless, as useful experience tells us, it is laid on several times.

tertia et ultima vice temperatus sit ipse color de clara ovi spongiata aut verberata, ita quod sit liquida absque aliquibus partibus conglutinatis et sibi adhærentibus quia ipsa clara ovi facit ipsam assisiam seu temperam fortem satis ad tenendum aurum ad burnissionem et ad strepitum et violentiam fricationis et deductionis ipsius super ipso auro. Et tunc velociter antequam siccetur color in locis in quibus posueris, pone sursum aurum et sic permitte siccari, et postea ea omnia burnias cum eodem dente lapide vel alio instrumento quo prius ut supra, sed primo leniter premendo et trahendo burnissorem desuper aurum, postea aliquantulum fortius, et postea adhuc fortius, præcipue in carta papiro et tabulis, sed in telis et sindone non tam fortiter et cum majori studio ne plicetur et diripietur quod factum est, et sic remanebunt quæ pertraxeris de ipso colore pinxeris et auro ut dictum est posueris purgata polita et ex ipsa deauratura lucida juxta formas et pertractiones ex dicto colore factas.

Sed notandum est, quod in carta, papiro, et tabulis, sufficere quod ponatur dictus color solum una vice, temperatus cum cola et postea ultima vice cum clara ovi, dum bene ponatur ad primam vicem cum cola temperatus. Sed in tela et sindone magis est necesse poni bis, primo cum cola temperatus ipse color, antequam ultima vice ponatur temperatus cum claro ovi etc., et hoc quod sindon et tela, pro raritatibus eorum sunt nimis labiles, decurrentes, flexibiles, et instabiles; et ideo bibunt colorem ipsum nisi pluries, prout expediens experientia doceat, reponatur ita quod in superficie telæ vel sindonis non remanet bene valida substantia coloris; neque etiam dicta flexibilitas et ductibilitas ipsorum, sindonis et telæ, per aliquem alium modum corrigi potest, et ad stabilitatem quandam, quam illis ex hoc causa viscositatis et tenacitatis colæ infertur reduci potest. Ideo haberi debet etiam advertentia, quod si tempus sit ventosum, impedit, nisi ponens aurum sit in loco recluso; et si aer sit nimis siccum, color non bene capit aurum; et si nimis humidum, color non tenere potest aurum ad burnissorem. Et provideatur etiam quod tela et sindon cum ca-

And this flexibility and instability of the cloth or sindone can be corrected and reduced to firmness in no other way than by the tenacity and viscosity of the glue laid over them for this purpose. And therefore care must be taken as regards the situation, because windy weather is a hindrance, unless the gilder is in a closed place; and if the air is too dry, the colour does not take the gold well; and, if too wet, the colour cannot hold the gold under the burnisher. Care must also be taken that the linen or sindone which is chosen for this purpose be well woven and strong, and as close in the texture as possible. The colour itself ought not to be applied too thick or too cold, lest by the curve made in folding them the colour should scale off and fall away along with the gold; particularly under the stroke of the burnisher, while the gold upon it, as has been already mentioned, is being burnished; and so your labour should be thrown away. And even supposing that the cloth, sindone, paper, or parchment, on which gold has been laid in the manner hereinbefore described, should be folded into slight creases, as frequently happens spontaneously and by chance, and unless they are folded and rubbed together, cracking the priming by violent and voluntary force, the gold will not fall off or start from the places in which it was laid.

292. *For laying on gold in various ways, and upon various articles, when it is not to be burnished.*—For laying gold on parchment, paper, cloth, and sindone, with size alone, or with a mordant tempered with size, and this by a short and quick method, but so that it ought not, nor can be burnished, particularly on cloth and sindone, which, on account of their flexibility, instability, softness, and porosity, can ill bear the stroke and pressure of the burnisher, nor can they stand it so that the gold will not be spoiled in burnishing; and also because the size which is to be used for laying on the gold, or for tempering the colour on which the gold is to be laid, is not strong enough to hold the gold against the stroke of the burnisher, as white of egg would be, if it were tempered with white of egg. Take the glue with which bows and spears are glued, and put it to soak in cold

piuntur pro operando sint bene texti et fortes, et minus rari in eorum textura quam possunt. Sed neque etiam debet ipse color esse nimis grossus seu spissus et frigidus, ne ex ductu plicationum contingentium eis, ut necessario convenit, cadat et resiliat color cum auro, et specialiter ad strepitus burnissoris, quando aurum desuper, ut dictum est, burnitur, et quod sic opus perdatur. Et dato quod tela, sindon, papirus, et carta in quibus positum erit aurum modo quo dictum est complicentur aliquantum in rugas sicut a casu per se accidit, dum modo non violento et voluntario rigore confringendo plicentur et fricentur, aurum tamen non cadit nec resilit a locis in quibus positum est.

292. *Ad ponendum aurum diversi mode super diversis, quod non burniatur.*—Ad ponendum aurum in carta, papiro, tela et in sindone cum cola tantum vel cum colore de cola temperato et hoc brevi modo et veloci, quod burniri non debeat, nec possit, præcipue in tela et sindone qui pro eorum flexibilitate ductibilitate mollitie et raritate strepitum et impressionem burnissoris male sustinent nec possint pati quin burniendo aurum deleretur, et etiam quia cola imponenda ad ponendum aurum vel ad temperandum colorem, de quo poni debet, non est fortis ad tenendum aurum ad strepitum burnissoris ut esset clara ovi si de clara ovi distemperetur. Accipe colam de qua colantur arcus et hastæ et pone ad distemperandum in aqua frigida, et quum est bene mollis pone ipsam in vase cum circa totidem de dicta aqua, quotidem debito respecta est colla et non plus, et pone ad ignem

water, and when it is well softened put it into a vase with about an equal quantity of the said water, that is, as much as the glue requires, and no more, and put it on the fire so as not to boil, but only keep hot, until the glue is dissolved in the water, or is melted, and incorporated with the water. And having done this, not allowing the glue to cool, but keeping it at a moderate heat with a slow fire, for fear it should be congealed, so that it could not be used, write and draw whatever you wish with this glue, upon a linen or other cloth, or upon sindone, or even on parchment, or paper, with a soft pen, or a small paintbrush of hogs' bristles, which brush must be obtuse, that is, must have short bristles which are stiff or hard, that is to say, like those which are used to mark the canvass upon bales of goods with ink; and write, fill in, or paint, and draw any letters or other broad designs, whatever they may be, with the said stiff and blunt paintbrush. But if you are working on fine cloths or sindone, and on parchment and paper, it is better for the paintbrush to be made of the hairs of the tails of minever, blunt or pointed as you see best, according to the nature of the work you have to do. When you have done this, leave it to dry, and afterwards with the same glue go again over those things which were drawn before, particularly on cloth and sindone, which usually absorb the first coat of size so strongly, that scarcely any of it remains upon the surface to hold the gold which is to be laid on them. It is therefore proper to lay it on twice, if it should seem necessary; afterwards at the last coat, before the letters and drawings are dry, apply the gold and allow them to dry. And know, that if the cloth, sindone, paper, and parchment, on which the gold is laid in the above mentioned manner, are folded into a crease, and rubbed, as sometimes happens accidentally, and not by violent and voluntary force, yet the gold laid on in this manner will not fall off, or be spoiled. This is because the size, with which the gold is laid on, or with which the mordant is tempered, if a mordant is used, makes the mordant itself less rigid and more flexible and yielding, by reason of its soft condition and nature, than the white of egg, which is firmer and stiffer.

ita quod non bulliat sed solum calefiat, usque ad hoc quod colla fundatur in aqua seu sit liquefacta et incorporata cum aqua. Et hoc facto, non permittendo infrigidari colam, sed tenendo ipsam ad temperatam caliditatem cum lento igne, ne conglutinetur, ita quod de ipsa possit operari, scribe et pertrahe quod vis de ipsa cola super telam lineam vel aliam, vel super sindonem, aut etiam super papirum, aut pergamenum, seu cartam cum calamo non duro vel cum pincello parvo setarum porci, qui pincellus sit obtusus, id est, habeat setas curtas ut sint rigidæ seu duræ, viz., sicut sunt pincelli ad signandum balas mercium super earum cavenatiis [canevatiis ?] cum incausto ; et scribe, imple, seu pinge et pertrahe, quascumque literas et alias pertractiones grossas, quæque sint, fac cum dicto pincello sic rigido et obtuso. Sed si operaris in telis subtilibus ; vel in sindone, et in carta, aut in papiro, melius est quod pincellus sit de pilis caudarum vayrorum, obtusus vel acutus secundum quod videbis magis convenire juxta qualitatem operum faciendorum. Et hoc facto dimittas siccari, postea de eadem cola rescribe et reimple iterum semel, et repertrahe quæ pertracta jam fuerant ; specialiter super telam et sindonem quæ solent lambere tam fortiter primam colam, quod de ipsa quasi nil remanet in superficie eorum quo possit aurum desuper ponendum teneri. Ideo advertatur de ponendo vis si necesse videatur, et postea, ad ultimam vicem, antequam siccentur literæ et pertractiones pone aurum desuper et dimitte siccari. Et scias, quod dato quod tela, sindon, papirus, et carta, ubi positum erat aurum modo supradicto, complicentur in rigam et fricentur sicut accidit a casu, et non cum rigore violento et voluntario, tamen aurum illo modo positum, non cadit, seu non vastatur, etiam quia cola qua positum est aurum, vel qua temperatus est color de quo positum est aurum si de colore ponatur, reddit colorem ipsum magis flexibilem, non rigidum, et consentientem contingentibus flexionibus ex sua molli conditione et natura, quam facit clara ovi quæ fortior et rigidior est.

293. *A good rose colour for linen cloth, sindone, parchment, or paper, and primed panels, is made in this way.*—Take *brasilium* rasped or scraped with a knife, or with glass, pounded in a mortar; but it is much better to have it scraped; then let it be put with a little raw alum in powder into a ley, or into urine. Then make it boil for a long time over a charcoal fire, not a wood fire, lest by chance the smoke, which the wood makes, should spoil the colour. Afterwards let it be strained through a linen cloth, retaining in the cloth the substance of the wood brasilium, lest it should be mixed with the colour that is to be made, and then let it be put into a glazed jar with white chalk or gersa [gesso], in powder, or with powdered bracha [biacha—biacca], which is otherwise called white lead, otherwise ceruse, otherwise Spanish white; and let it be allowed to incorporate with the said chalk or ceruse. Next let it be ground altogether upon a hard stone without adding water or urine, on the contrary, keeping it as little liquid, *i.e.*, as thick as it can be ground; and although it should be less liquid than it was at the beginning before it was ground, and yet not sufficiently thickened in the grinding, because the water of the ley or the urine had not been sufficiently poured off or dried; let the colour be put to dry upon a hollow stone of chalk or gersa, or upon a concave brick made of clay, and baked in the furnace, which will immediately absorb the moisture of the ley, so that the colour remains suddenly almost dry, *i.e.*, inspissated. Afterwards let the colour be put away; and when it is necessary to use it, take whatever is wanted of it and temper it with white of egg, or with gum water made of gum arabic, in the way cinnabar is used. But if it is used with white of egg, it shines where it is used, and is more beautiful. And write and draw and paint with this colour whatever is wanted on parchment, and primed panels, as well with the pen as with the paintbrush. And the less ceruse or chalk there is in it the darker will be the colour; and so, on the other hand, the more there is of it the lighter the colour will be.

293. *Color rosæ bonus in tela linea, sindone, papiro, pergameno, seu carta et in tabulis dealbatis fit hoc modo.*—Accipe brisilium raspatum seu rasum cum cultello vel cum vitro aut pistum in mortario, sed multo melius tamen est habere rasum; deinde cum pauco aluminis crudi pulverizati ponatur in lexivio vel in urina hominis ebriatoris quæ optima est, et melior est vetera et diu facta quam nova. Et fac bullire diu ad ignem carbonum; non lignorum, ne fumus quem ligna faciunt vastet colorem. Et postea coletur dictus color ita callidus per telam lineam, dimittendo in tela substanciam ligni brisilii ne immisceatur colori faciendæ, postea ponatur in vase vitreato cum creta seu gersa alba pulverizata vel cum bracha pulverizata quæ aliter dicitur album plumbum aliter cerusa, atque aliter album Hispaniæ, et dimittatur incorporari cum ipsa creta vel cerosio. Et postea teratur totum simul super lapidem durum absque addendo aquam nec urinam ymo minus liquidum, *i. e.*, magis spissum quam teri poterit vel possit; deinde si minus liquidus erit quam sic esset a principio antequam tereretur, et quod terendo non satis inspissatus fuerit, quod aquositas lexivii vel urinæ non erat satis comminuta et desiccata ponatur ad siccandum super concava lapide cretæ vel gersæ aut super latere concavo facto de terra et cocto in fornace, qui subito bibunt humiditatem lexivii taliter quod remanet color subito quasi siccus, viz., inspissatus. Postea reponatur et quando oportet operari accipiant de illo quantum necesse sit, et distemperetur cum clara ovi vel cum aqua gummata de gummi arabico ut distemperatur cinobrium. Sed si distemperatur cum claro ovi, relucet cum in opere est, et pulcrior est. Et scribantur ex eo et pertrahantur ac pingantur in carta in papiro et in tabulis dealbatis de ipso colore, quæ velint tam cum calamo quam cum pincello. Et quanto erit in ipso minus de cerusa aut de creta, tanto erit color plus obscurus; et quanto plus, sic converso magis clarus.

294. *A blue colour, that is, azure, which is not ultramarine, nor is it so beautiful, but which is good on linen, sindone, parchment, or paper, and primed panels, that is panels covered with gersa.*—Take fine indigo, which is called by the name of Bagadel, and Spanish white, otherwise called ceruse or blacha, and mix both together, and grind them on a hard stone, with white of egg beaten and mixed with pure water, or with gum water, made with gum Arabic, and in the manner in which sinobrium, that is, sinopis is ground when alone. When it is ground, temper it in a shell or a horn with the clear part of beaten white of egg, not mixed with water, as has been already directed for the rose colour, and write or draw whatever you want with this colour. This is the way in which it must be made if you wish to use it immediately. But if you do not want this colour for immediate use, but wish to keep it, you must not add any egg or gum water to it when you grind it on the stone, but only mix it with pure and clean water; and when it is ground up with water, let it dry up or inspissate upon a brick of baked clay, or a hollow stone of white chalk, which immediately absorbs the moisture in such a manner, that the colour remains thickened and like juice, and afterwards allow it to dry completely in the shade, or in the sun, and put it away and preserve it. And when you wish to use it, take some of it and temper it in a shell or a horn, with white of egg not mixed with water, or even with the said gum water, and make it of a reasonable and moderate softness or liquidity, according to what is required for the work you intend to do with it, and just as you would do with sinopis. And the lighter or less dark you require it, the more blacha or ceruse you must mix with it; and, on the other hand, the darker you wish it, the less you must put of the said ceruse, that is, white-lead, that is to say, while you are grinding the colour upon the stone.

295. *To make letters of a green colour, and to draw and paint all other things on linen, parchment, or paper, primed panels, and sindone.*—Take fine indigo, called Bagadel, and

294. *Color blauetus id est celestis, qui non est de lazurio, nec tam pulcher, et est bonus in tela linea, sindone, papiro, pergameno seu carta et in tabulis dealbatis, id est gersatis.*—Accipe Indicum finum qui cognomine bagadellus vocatur, et de albo hispaniæ aliter cerusium vel blacham, et misce ambo simul et tere super lapidem durum cum claro ovi spongiato et mixto aqua clara, aut cum aqua gummata de gummi arabico, et ad modum quo teritur sinobrium solum, id est sinopis; et postquam erit tritum, distempera in conchilla vel in cornato cum claro ovi spongia liquidato, non mixtum aqua ut dictum est antea de colore rosæ, et scribe et pertrahe quæ vis cum ipso colore. Et hic est modus quo fieri debet, volendo ipsum de præsenti ponere in opere. Sed si non vis ipsum colorem de præsenti ponere in opere et quod velis ipsum servare, debes isto modo nullum ovum nec aquam gummatum ponere quum ipsum teris super lapidem, ymo solum ponas de aqua munda pura et simplici, et cum tritum sit cum aqua, fac ipsum siccari vel inspissari super laterem terræ coctum aut super laterem coctæ albæ concavum qui subito bibit humiditatem aquæ taliter, quod remanet color subito inspissatus et quasi succus; et postea desiccari penitus permittas ad umbram aut ad solem et repone et serva. Et cum vis operari accipe de ipso et distempera in conchilla vel in corneto cum claro ovi non mixto aqua, vel etiam mixto vel cum dicta aqua gummata, et fac ipsum de rationabili et moderata mollitie, seu liquidate secundum quod requiritur in faciendo ea quæ vis de ipso facere et sicut de sinopide faceres. Et quanto vis clariorem seu minus obscurum, tanto pone plus de blacha seu cerosio; et e converso, quanto vis magis obscurum, pone minus de dicto cerosio, id est de albo plumbo, scilicet quando teres ipsum colorem super lapidem.

295. *Ad faciendum literas viridis coloris et ad protrahendum et pingendum omnia alia in tela in papiro in carta seu pergameno in tabulis ligneis dealbatis et in sindone.*—Accipe Indicum

orpiment, and mix and grind them together upon a hard stone with clear water from a well or a spring, and it will be a green colour, and the lighter you require it, the more orpiment you must add; and the darker you require it, the less orpiment you must put, and the more indigo. When you have ground it very fine, let it dry; and if it is put upon a stone of white chalk, that is gersa, or upon a clay brick baked in the furnace, and concave so that it may hold the colour, the moisture will directly dry up or be absorbed into the stone, and the colour itself will remain hard and thick, and you may then allow it to dry by itself, and when it is dry, put it away and keep it. And when you wish to use it, take as much as you want of it, and put it into a horn, or into a shell which is found in fresh water, or even a sea-shell that is fit for this purpose, and temper it with white of egg, or with gum water, as is done with sinopis, and with it write and draw whatever you like, in the same manner as is done with vermilion or sinopis. But if, omitting and not putting the indigo, you mix fine ultramarine with the said orpiment instead of indigo, you will have a much finer green.

296. *To prepare parchment, or paper, primed panels, and linen, so that you may be able to draw upon them in black, with a pencil or stile of gold, silver, bronze, or brass, as is done upon panels of boxwood whitened or covered with bone or stag's-horn burnt and whitened in the fire.*—Take bones of any animal or bird, or stag's-horn, which is better, and burn it, and make it white and friable and soft by long and violent boiling, and afterwards grind it upon a hard stone with pure water. Then put it on a brick of baked clay or of white chalk, that the moisture may enter into it, and that the bone may remain thickened and almost dry. Remove it from the stone, and burn it a second time in a charcoal fire, and make it perfectly white and fine in a crucible in which silver or gold is usually melted, and afterwards, that it may be made still more fine and white, grind it a second time upon a stone with water, in the same way as you did before; and then if you wish to use

finum quod bagadellum nominatur, et auripigmentum, et misce et tere simul super lapidem durum, cum aqua putei vel fontis clara et erit color viridis. Et quanto volueris ipsum magis clarum, pone magis de auripigmento. Et quanto magis obscurum pone minus de dicto auripigmento et plus de Indico. Et cum tritus sit valde subtiliter, pone ad siccandum, et si ponatur super lapidem album cretæ i. e. gersæ aut super laterem de terra coctum in fornace et concavum ita quod capax sit coloris, subito aquositas siccabitur seu intrabit in ipso lapide et color remanebit durus et spissus, et postea permittas per se siccari et cum siccus sit repone et serva. Et quando vis de ipso operari, accipe quantum vis de ipso et pone in cornu vel in conchilla quæ reperitur in aquis dulcibus vel etiam in mari apta ad hoc et distempera cum claro ovi, aut cum aqua gummata ut fit sinopis, et de illo scribe pinge et pertrahe quæ vis ut fit de vermiculo seu sinopide. Sed si cum dicto auropigmento, loco Indici, præmisso Indico et non posito, misceris finum azurium multo pulcriorem viridem habebis.

296. *Ad aptandum papirum, et pergamenum, seu cartam, tabulas ligneas et telam, modo quo possis super ipsas protrahere nigro, cum grossio seu stilo auri, argenti, latonis, vel æris, sicut super tabulas busuli dealbatas seu intinctas cum osse vel cornu cervi combusto et dealbato in igne.*—Accipe de osse cujusvis animalis vel avis, aut de cornu cervi, quod melius est, et arde illud et albifica et tritibilem et dulcem facies longa et forti decoctione, postea tere super duro lapide cum aqua clara; postea pones super latere terræ coctæ, aut cretæ albæ, ut in ipso entret humiditas et inspissetur et remaneat ut quasi siccum: postea eleva a lapide, et iterum in ignem carbonem secundo decoque et perfectissime albifica et subtilem facies illud in crusibulo in quo solet fondi argentum vel aurum; postea ut iterum magis subtilietur et dealbetur, tere illud secundo super lapidem cum aqua ut prius feceras; deinde si prompte vis operare, de ipso distempera quantum velis in conchilla vel in scutella figuli

it immediately, wet up as much of it as you require in a shell or a glazed earthen jar, with size made from glue or from clippings of white leather or parchment, and which must be of a moderate consistence and warmth. Having done this as directed, paint or draw with it, with a broad paint-brush, upon paper which has been polished with a boar's tooth. Also lay it over parchment, cloth, sindone, and wooden panels, and permit it to dry. And then, if the first coat is not sufficient for it (which may be known by drawing on it with a stile of brass, or bronze, or copper, or still better of silver, and seeing whether it makes black marks or not), you must give it another coat of the said bone-dust, keeping it warm in the vase in which it stands over a slow fire, particularly in winter, lest it should be congealed by the cold, on account of the glue with which it is mixed, which hardens with cold; afterwards let it dry, and try it again by drawing upon it with a stile as before. And so you must apply this bone or horn as many times as you see necessary, though it is true that the second coat usually suffices, and frequently the first. And note, that if you wish the paper, after it is thus painted, to be very smooth and polished and without any inequalities or roughnesses, that it may be better to draw upon, you must polish and burnish it, holding it under another paper not painted on, upon which you must rub a boar's tooth, or a hard and polished stone, or any other instrument fit for burnishing. And know, that if you wish to make this preparation of various colours, it is necessary, while grinding the horn or bone upon the said stone, and wetting it in a shell or a glazed earthen vessel, when you wish to paint the paper, that you should mix with the horn or bone whatever colours you wish, separately, which must however be ground very fine upon the said stone with pure water. Afterwards, if any of the said horn remain, whether white or coloured, it can be preserved, because, although what remains becomes dry by keeping, it may still be of use to lay upon other paper, like any other colours, by being wetted up with pure water, not sized; because, although the water of the first wetting dries up, yet the glue of

vitriata, cum aqua colata de cola seu de incisuris corii albi vel pergameni, et quod sit colata moderato modo et tepida. His itaque talimodo factis pinge vel pertrahe de ipso cum pincello grosso super papyrum quod primo sit lissatum cum dente apri. Item pinge de eo pergamenum telam sindonem et tabulas ligneas, et permitte siccari; postea, si prima depinctio facta non sufficit, quod scitur protrahendo desuper cum stilo æris vel latonis aut cupri; et melior esset de argento; si non bene pertrahit nigros tractus. Quod si sic sit debes iterum repingere de eodem osse, tenendo ipsum tepidum in vase in quo est lento igni, præcipue si sit in hyeme ne conglutinetur ex frigore pro cola qua temperatus est, et quæ pro frigore induratur; postea dimitte siccari et iterum tempta protrahendo desuper cum stilo ut prius. Ita sic ipsum ossem vel cornu totiens ponas quotiens videbis esse necessarium, dato quod verum est quod si secunda vice pingatur, solet sufficere et multotiens pro prima. Et nota quod si velis ipsum papirum postquam taliter pictus sit esse valde politum et equale absque fossulis et scabrositatibus ut melior sit ad protrahendum super, ipsum lisses et burnias tenendo ipsum sub uno alio papiro non picto super quem trahes imprimendo dentem apri, aut lapidem durum politum, aut aliud instrumentum ad burniendum aptum. Et scias quod si de diversis coloribus ipsas depictiones facere velis, oportet quod terendo cornu vel osse super dictum lapidem distemperando illud in conchilla vel scutella figuli vitriata, quando papirum vel cartam vis pingere, quod in ipso cornu vel osse misceas separatim quales colores velis, tritos tamen ut subtiliores super lapidem cum aqua clara. Postea si de dicto cornu tam albo quam de coloribus remanent partes illæ residuæ possunt servari, quia dato quod resedentiæ postea stando siccentur, possunt tamen sicut est de omnibus aliis coloribus adhuc alias valere ad ponendum in opere, scilicet distemperata cum aqua clara non colata; quia dato quod aqua primæ distemperaturæ sit desiccata, tamen iterum remanet ibidem cola ipsius primæ distemperationis, quæ sufficit; quia in exhalatione et desiccatione aquositatis primæ distemperaturæ, non frustrata nec exalata

the first wetting still remains there, and in sufficient quantity; for in the exhalation and evaporation of the moisture of the first wetting, the strength or substance of the glue is not exhaled or evaporated, but only the water. And if any of the first quantity of bone or horn, not mixed with any colour or glue remains in the vase, shell, or saucer, you may put it on a lump of chalk, or on a brick of baked clay, that the water which is contained in it may be dried up, and may be exposed to the air or the sun, that it may dry completely; and afterwards, when you wish to use it, you must temper it with size as originally directed, as there is not any size or glue mixed with it. You can also colour it with various colours, mixing them with it, as before, according to your taste, as above mentioned. And note, that if you have no stag's-horn, the bones of the stag are good, as also those of any other animal or bird, as has been already mentioned.

est virtus nec substantia colæ, sed solum aqua. Et si de primo osse vel cornu non mixto de colore ullo et in quo non est cola remanebit ulla pars in vase seu scutella vel in conchilla, potes ipsum ponere super lapidem cretæ, aut super laterem terræ coctæ, ut siccetur aqua quæ in ipso est et reponere ad aërem vel ad solem, ut ex toto desiccetur, et postea quum de ipso eges ad operandum, debes illud distemperare cum aqua colata ut prius dictum est. Ex hoc quia in ipso non fuerat umquam cola seu aqua ulla colata. Et potes etiam colare illud de diversis coloribus, ut prius commiscendo eos in ipso ad libitum tuum, ut dictum est supra. Et nota, quod si non habes cornu cervi, pro faciendo quod dictum est, bona sunt ossa sua et etiam ut supra est declaratum ossa aliorum animalium et avium.

A TREATISE UPON VARIOUS COLOURS,

AND FIRST THE

INTRODUCTION.

297. In the year of the Circumcision of our Lord Jesus Christ, 1398, on Thursday, the 8th day of August, Johannes Alcherius wrote, and noted down, at Paris, in the house of Anthonio de Compendio, an illuminator of books, and an old man, according to the words told him by the said Anthonius, who, as he said, had tried, during the whole time of his life, all the following recipes, namely, the following chapters concerning colours for illuminating books. And afterwards, in the year 1411, in the month of December, the same Johannes, who had then returned more than one year from Lombardy, namely, from Bologna, where there was a *curia apostolica* newly united, corrected them in many places, according to further information, which he subsequently received by means of several authentic books treating of such subjects, and otherwise; and copied them fairly as follows:—

298. *For laying gold upon various articles, so that it may be burnished, and various cautions concerning it, for illuminating.*—To lay gold on parchment, or paper, and on wooden panels primed with white chalk, which gold may be burnished or polished. Take gersa, or white chalk, and a little ocra de ru, equal to one-third part of the chalk, and pound them both together, and grind as thick as you can, i. e. with little water,

DE DIVERSIS COLORIBUS

IN SEQUENTI TRACTATU,

ET PRIMO MODUS PROHEMII.

297. Anno circumcisionis domini Jesu Christi 1398 die Jovis octavo Augusti, *Johannes Alcerius* scripsit et notavit in Parisiis in domo *Anthonii de Compendio* illuminatoris librorum, antiqui hominis, a verbis quæ ipse Anthonius sibi dixit. Et qui omnia quæ sequuntur tentaverat toto tempore vitæ suæ, ut dixit, de coloribus scilicet ad illuminandum libros, sequentia capitula. Et postea anno 1411 de mense decembris, idem Johannes qui jam per plusquam annum reversus fuerat a partibus Lombardiæ, viz., a Bononia, ubi erat curia apostolica noviter unita, correxit in pluribus partibus ea, secundum plures informationes quas inde postea per plures libros autentiquos de talibus narrantes, et aliter habuerat, et rescripsit ea ad nettum ut sequitur.

298. *Ad ponendum aurum super diversis quod burniatur, et de diversis cautelis utendis super hoc, illuminando.*—Ad ponendum aurum in papiro, in pergameno, seu carta, et in tabulis ligneis, creta alba dealbatis, quod aurum burniatur seu poliatur. Accipe gersam seu cretam albam et modicum ocræ de ru, per tertiam partem quantitatis cretæ et totum simul subtilia, et tere cum aqua clara magis spissum quam poteris,

upon a smooth hard stone, with a muller also made of stone. Afterwards put the colour, which is otherwise called the tempera or size of the gold, in a shell or a glazed earthen saucer, or a glass vase. And when you wish to use it, take as much as you like of it in another smaller shell, and temper it to a reasonable softness or consistence, with whipped white of egg, in order to paint or write with it; and if you have time, allow the mordant to get stale, for several days or weeks, for it will be better putrid than fresh. Afterwards write, paint, and draw whatever you like, and where you like, and let it dry. Then, when you wish to lay on the gold, go into a closed place and choose a proper time, as has been before mentioned. And having chosen a fit time and place, and used the proper precautions, lay the gold on those parts of the parchment or paper on which you put the colour or mordant, and draw over it, first pressing lightly, and afterwards more forcibly, the burnisher, namely, the tooth of a boar or a horse, and polish the said gold until it adheres to the colour, and becomes shining, as was said before. Therefore, when the gold is to be laid on, the mordant which was left from a previous gilding is better than any other, provided that in the interval, by looking at it, stirring it and mixing egg or water with it, it has been kept sufficiently liquid, so that it may not be completely dried up, or have been too much putrified or altered.

299. *To make a rose colour.*—To make a rose colour for painting on parchment, paper, and wooden panels primed with chalk. Take brixillium scraped very fine with a knife or with glass, and tie it in a fine piece of linen, not tight, but loose and easy. And put it, tied up in that manner, into a new glazed earthen jar, to soak in ley, or in urine; and if the urine is stale, so much the better. If you cannot have any such, take very strong ley and put with the said piece of linen containing the brixillium, some of the white chalk of three or four times the weight of the brixillium, more or less, as by looking at it you may think fit, according to the goodness of the brixillium. Afterwards add some

i. e. cum pauca aqua, super lapidem equalem durum cum molleta lapidis similiter. Postea pone ipsum colorem qui aliter tempera vel assisia auri dicitur, in conchilla aut in scutella figuli vitriata, aut in vase vitri. Et cum operari vis, accipe de ipso in conchilla alia parviori quantum vis et modera ipsum cum claro ovi spongiato ad rationabilem mollitiem seu liquidatem pro pingendo aut scribendo de ipso, et si habes tempus cum temperaveris, dimittas inveterari per plures dies vel septimanas ipsam temperam, quia melior erit putrida quam recens. Postea de ipso scribe pinge et pertrahe quæ vis et ubi vis et dimittas siccari. Postea sis in loco recluso cum aurum vis ponere et elige tempus idoneum ut supradictum est. Et habitis idoneis loco et tempore et remediis; ponas aurum in locis cartæ aut papyri quibus ipsum colorem vel assisiam posuisti, et super trahe, et premendo primo leviter, postea fortius burnissorem, scilicet dentem apri vel equi et polias tantum dictum aurum quam adhæreat colori et lucidum fiat ut supra jam dictum est. Ideo cum aurum poni vult, color talis remansus de alia positione auri alias facta melior est dum ex interpolata visitatione deductione et ovi aut aquæ interpositione conservatus sit in debita liquiditate, ita quod ad totalem siccitatem vel nimiam putrefactionem et alterationem deductus non sit.

299. *Ad faciendum Rosam.*—Ad faciendum rosam pro operando in carta, et in papiro, et in ligneis tabulis creta dealbatis. Accipe brixillium rasum subtiliter cum cultello vel cum vitro, et liga in subtili pecia lini non stricte sed late et fluctuanter. Et sic ligatum pone in vase figuli vitriato novo ad temperandum in lixivio aut in urina hominis ebriatoris potantis forte vinum, et si urina sit vetera tanto melius, et si non possis habere talem, accipe lessivium fortissimum et pone de creta alba in ipso lessivio, cum dicta petia in qua est brixillium et per quantitatem de tribus vel quatuor vicibus quantitatis brixillii ad pondus et etiam sicut inspiciendo melius videbis convenire plus et minus secundum bonitatem brixillii. Postea pone

pulverized raw alum, in quantity about one-fourth part of the chalk or thereabouts, more or less, and mix all these things together, always leaving the said brixillium tied up in the said piece of linen, and leave it so for about one hour. Next, place the jar upon a fire, not of wood, but of charcoal, and let it boil, but not too fast, for the space of a quarter of an hour or less, so as just to melt the alum. Then take the said bag of brixillium out of the vase, and press it and screw it out well, in order that the whole of the colour may run out of it into the said vase; and then remove the colour, hot as it is, from the fire, and put it on a hollow lump of chalk or upon a brick of baked clay, in order that the urine or ley may be immediately absorbed into the stone, and the colour itself remain thickened and half dry. Afterwards let it dry completely in the sun, and then remove the colour, which is of a rose colour, from the stone or brick with a knife, and put it by for use. When you wish to use it, take as much as you require and powder it, that is, grind it upon a hard and smooth stone with gum water, which must be made of two-third parts of gum arabic dissolved in so small a quantity of water as barely to cover the colour when the water is added and strained through a linen cloth, and one-third part of clear water mixed with the said gum so dissolved and strained. And with the gum water, thus made, temper your rose colour to a proper consistence, and use it for whatever you please, as well for writing, as for painting and drawing.

300. *To make corrosive green, without substance or body.*— To make a green transparent in its nature, and without body, that is, having no substance, such, for example, as is the colour of saffron, *i. e.* of crocus, which does not cover up other colours so as to conceal them, on account of its thinness, transparency, and rarity, owing to which other colours appear through it, wherefore this colour as well as the said green colour is overpowered, and shows little or not at all, nor can it be much seen over other colours. But this green colour is not mild like saffron, on the contrary it is, by nature, acrid and corrosive, so

de alumine glaro crudo pisto in pulverem, quod sit tantum quantum est quartum dictæ cretæ vel circa, et autem plus quam minus, et misceas hæc omnia insimul dimittendo semper ligatum in dicta pecia dictum brixillium et dimittens sic per horam unam vel circa. Postea ponas vas ad ignem non lignorum sed carbonum et bulliant non nimis fortiter et per spatium quartæ partis horæ vel minus, ita quod solum alumen fondatur. Postea de ipso vase tollatur dicta pecia brixillii et exprimatur et extorqueatur fortiter ut color de ipsa totaliter exeat in eodem vase; postea tollatur ipse color ita callidus ab igne et ponatur super lapidem cretæ concavæ vel super lapidem de terra &c., ad hoc quod urina seu lessivia intret in lapidem subito et color ipse remaneat ibi inspissatus et semisiccus. Postea facias ex toto siccari ad solem, deinde eleva ipsum colorem, quæ rosa est cum cultello a lapide vel latere, et repone servando pro usu. Et cum de ipsa operari vis, accipe de ipsa quantum vis et subtilia, id est tere super lapidem durum et planum cum aqua gummata quæ fit per duas partes gummi arabici fusi in tam pauca aqua, quod pene cooperiatur ipsa aqua cum in ipsam ponitur aqua, et colati postea per telam lineam, et per tertiam partem fit aqua clara insimul cum dicto gummi fuso et colato; et de ipsa aqua gommata ipso modo factam distempera dictam rosam ad debitam mollitiem et operaberis de ipsa quæ volueris, tam scribendo quam pingendo ac protrahendo.

300. *Ad faciendum viride corrosivum absque substantia seu corpori.*—Ad faciendum viride in substantia clarum et non corpulentum id est substantiam non habentem, ut verbi gratia clarus atque sine substantia est color safran, i. e. croci qui non cooperit alios colores pro ejus subtilitate claritate et raritate, qua alii colores apparent per medium ipsum, et ex hoc ipse pro raritate sua ut et dictus color viridis remanet obfuscatus, et nil vel minimum apparet, neque multum apparere potest super alios colores. Sed ipse color viridis non est dulcis sicut est dictus color croci, ymo ex sua natura est acer et corrosivus,

that it destroys and corrodes other colours if it is put over them, or they over it, and this on account of the verdigris which is in it; and such is its nature, and it is used upon parchment and paper. Take verdigris and a little of the dried lees of wine, which in Latin is called *tartarus,* and in French *gravelle,*[1] and pulverize it and grind both the ingredients together upon a hard and smooth stone with vinegar. Afterwards draw all those things which you wish, both in parchment and paper, and the empty spaces which are between the lines of black; afterwards fill in with the green colour made in the above manner, and colour according to your taste, the things which you have so drawn as aforesaid. And note, that no other colour can be laid over this green colour, as has been already observed, nor can it be laid over others; nor can it be used otherwise than by itself and upon white paper and parchment, because this green colour, made as above, is corrosive and acrid, and, by reason of its acrid nature, it destroys other colours, as has been already mentioned above.

301. *To make a green colour, which has body and is not corrosive.*—To make a mild green body colour, for painting on parchment, on paper, on linen, and on primed wooden panels. Take verdigris and the juice of the herb which is called in French *flamma,*[2] and strain the juice of the herb through a linen cloth, and grind up the aforesaid green with it upon a stone, adding a little gum water to it. Then put it into a shell or a glazed earthen saucer, and temper it with the gum water, and the juice of that herb. The gum water must be made of clear gum arabic, and must be strained, lest, when the gum is poured into the colour, it should contain any straws, earth, or other impurities. Afterwards write, draw, and paint whatever you like with this green colour, and note, that the juice of rue would be better than that of the above written herb for putting into the above-mentioned composition of the said green

---

[1] Anglicè "Tartar."

[2] Flambe, Glayeul. It. Gladiola; E. Cornflag; L. Gladiolus Communis.

taliter quod destruit et rodit alios colores si ponatur super ipsos, vel ipsi super ipsum, et hoc pro viride æris qui in ipso ponitur et est talis conditionis et ponitur in carta et in papiro. Accipe viride æris et modicum de fæce vini sicca, quæ dicitur in latino tartarus et in gallico *gravella*, et subtilia et tere super lapidem durum et planum insimul quæ dicta sunt cum aceto. Postea omnia quæ in carta et in papiro protrahere vis, protrahe, ac vacuum, viz. per lineas de colore scilicet nigro, postea de ipso colore viridi sic facto ut dictum est colora ad libitum ea quæ ut dictum est protraxeris. Et nota quod super ipsum colorem viridem ut dictum est, nullus alter color debet poni neque ipse super alios nisi solum super cartam albam vel papirum, et non super colorem aliquem album artificiatum seu pictum, quia ipse color viridis illo modo factus est fortis seu acer et pro sua acritudine destruit alios colores ut supra jam dictum est.

301. *Ad faciendum colorem viridem cum corpore et non corrosivum.*—Ad faciendum colorem viridem dulcem et corpulentum, pro operando in pergameno, in papiro, in telis, et in tabulis ligneis dealbatis. Accipe viridem æris seu arani et succum herbæ quæ dicitur in gallico flamma et ipsum succum herbæ cola per telam lineam et cum ipso tere super lapidem viridem suprascriptum addendo aliquantulum de aqua gommata, postea ipsum pone in conchella, vel in scutella figuli vitriata, et distempera cum dicta aqua gummata et cum dicto succo ipsius herbæ, et dicta aqua gummata debet fieri de gummi arabico lucido, et collata, ne cum infusum sit gummi in ipsa, adsint in ipsa ullæ palleæ, terra vel aliæ turpitudines. Et postea de ipso colore viridi scribe protrahe et pinge quæ vis. Et nota quod succus rutæ esset melior quam suprascriptæ herbæ ad ponendum in dicta compositioni dicti viridis coloris. Et alii sunt

colour. There are some persons who put the juice of certain other herbs.

The aforesaid colour is such that you may paint upon it with other colours, and lay gold upon it, &c., in the same manner as upon sinopis or ultramarine, or upon rosa, and other similar things, because there is no vinegar in it, and the acrid nature of the verdigris is corrected by the juice of the said herb.

302. *Introduction to the following chapter, concerning the manner of making writing ink.*

Also in the aforesaid year, 1398, on Saturday the xijth day of October, the aforesaid Johannes Alcherius wrote at Paris, and in this place, after the preceding, added this chapter concerning the way to make good atramentum, or incaustum, which chapter had been long previously, even before the year 1382, given to him in writing at Milan, by the since deceased Master Alberto Porzello, who was most perfect in all kinds of writing and forms of letters, and who, while he lived, kept a school at Milan, and taught boys and young men to write; and who, as he said, had frequently tried and made ink in the manner described in this chapter, and had found it very good, as he told the said Johannes. And the said Johannes, himself, afterwards tried this method at Milan, and also found it very good. And afterwards in the said year, 1382, in the month of March, when the said Johannes Alcherius went from Milan to Paris, he carried with him a copy of the said recipe, which is as follows. But afterwards, in the year of Our Lord Jesus Christ, 1411, in the month of December, having then been returned to Paris more than one year from Lombardy—viz., from Bologna, from the newly-formed Apostolical *curia*, he corrected in some places the following recipes, and copied them fairly as follows:—

303. *To make ink for writing.*—Observe that choice and tried writing ink must be made in this way. Take iij ounces of galls, the goodness of which may be known by their being wrinkled. Take an equal quantity of gum arabic, the goodness of which may be known by its being bright and easily broken, and the smallest is the best. *Item.* Take 3½ oz. of Roman vitriol [sulphate of copper ?], the goodness of which may be known by its being of a blue colour, and solid, and coarse after the manner of coarse salt. Afterwards take four pounds,

qui ponunt succos quarundam aliarum herbarum. Et color suprascriptus est talis quod potest super ipso pinge cum aliis coloribus, et super ipso poni aurum etc. sicuti posset fieri super sinopide vel super lazurio, vel super rosa et aliis similibus, quia ibi non est acetum, et acritudo viridis æris mitigata est ex dicto succo herbæ.

302. *Prohemium super capitulo sequenti de modo ad faciendum incaustum pro scribendo.*

Item anno prædicto 1398, die sabati xii. Octobris, antedictus Johannes Alcherius scripsit in Parisiis, et hic post precedentem addidit hoc capitulum de modo faciendi bonum atramentum seu incaustum ad scribendum, quod capitulum jam diu usque ante annum 1382 sibi dederat in scriptis in Mediolano nunc quondam magister *Albertus Porzellus* perfectissimus in omnibus modis scribendi et formis literarum, qui tunc dum vixit tenuit scolas in Mediolano et docebat pueros et juvenes ad scribendum. Et qui temptaverat ipsemet multotiens et fecerat attramentum in modum in ipso capitulo contentum, et invenerat valde bonum ut dixit dicto Johanni. Et postea dictus Johannes ipsum modum temptavit Mediolano et invenit similiter valde bonum. Et postea dicto anno 1382 de mense Martii, quum dictus Johannes Alcherius ivit a Mediolano Parisiis, portavit secum copiam dicti capituli quæ talis est ut sequitur. Sed postea anno ejusdem domini nostri Jesu Christi 1411 de mense decembris dum jam per plusquam annum de partibus Lombardiæ viz., a Bononia veniens, ab apostolica Curia noviter unita, rediisset Parisiis, in aliquibus partibus ea quæ dicta sunt sequentia, et rescripsit ad nettum ut sequitur.

303. *Ad faciendum incaustum seu atramentum pro scribendo.*—Nota quod atramentum electum et probatum hoc modo debet fieri. Accipe unciæ tres gallæ, cujus bonitas apparet si minuta in crispa est. Totidem accipe de gummi arabico, cujus bonitas apparet si lucidum et de facili frangatur, et minutum magis valet. Item accipe oncias tres et dimidiam vitrioli Romani, cujus bonitas apparet si est cœlesti coloris et solidum et grossum, quasi in modum salis grossi. Postea accipe quatuor libras de onciis duodecim per libram aquæ claræ, quæ si

of twelve ounces to the pound, of clear water, which if it is rain water, or water from a cistern in which rain water is kept, is better than well, spring, or river water; and put into a new metal or glazed earthen jar, which has never been used for any thing else, in order that it may be pure and clean from all filth; and into this water, put the galls roughly pounded so that each grain of gall may be broken into four or five pieces, and then let the galls boil in the water without gum or vitriol, until the water is reduced to one-half. Then let it be strained through a cloth or piece of linen, and be put back without the substance of the galls in the vase over the fire, and let it remain there until it begins to boil, and then put into it the gum ground and pulverized, and let it boil gently for a short time, namely, until the gum is dissolved. Having done this, pour into it directly two pounds of the best pure and white wine, and stir it a little, and immediately add the vitriol well pulverized, stir it again a little, and then immediately remove the vase from the fire, and mix the whole together in order that the vitriol may be well incorporated with the galls, and the gum, and the water. Having done all these things in order, put the vase with the ink in the open air, and let it stand for one night, in order that the air may make it brilliant and more black. And therefore if it be done in fine weather, it will be better and finer. Afterwards strain it through a cloth, and put it by, and keep it for use.

303*a*.[1] *Another Recipe to make Ink.*

Another recipe for making one quart of good atramentum, or incaustum, which, however, does not belong to the present treatise; but was added in this place on account of its connexion with the matter of the preceding chapter, by me, Jehan Le Begue, licentiate in law, who wrote with my own hand, although not accustomed to it, the present work, or the chapters in this volume contained, in the Year of Our Lord MCCCCXXXJ, and in the year of my age lxiij, as I found the same recipe elsewhere, written as follows:—

Take a quarter of a pound of gall-nuts of the weight of iiij.

[1] The succeeding chapters, to the end of the volume, were added by Le Begue.

est pluvialis vel de cisterna reservante aquas pluviales melior est quam putei nec fontis nec fluvii et pone eam in vase metallino vel figuli vitriato novo, quod non sit alteri usui deputatum, ut sit purum et mundum ab omni sorde, et in ipsa aqua mitte gallam grosso modo tritam, ita quod de quolibet grano gallæ fiant quatuor vel quinque particulæ, et sic bulliat galla in aqua absque gummi et vitriolo, donec aqua reddatur ad medium comminuta. Postea coletur per pannum seu telam et absque substantia gallæ reponatur in vase ad ignem et sic tantum stet quod incipiat bullire, et tunc gummi tritum et pulverizatum mittatur in ipsa et bulliat aliquantulum, scilicet leniter usque: quo gummi liquefactum sit. His factis, immediate apponas duas libras optimi vini puri et albi et aliquantulum misce, et immediate mitte vitriolum bene pulverizatum et misceas parum, et statim eleva vas ab igne, et misceas simul totum, ita quod bene incorporetur vitriolum cum galla, et gummi, et aqua. Omnibus his peractis ex ordine pone vas cum ipso attramento ad aerem serenum, et stet per unam noctem, ut serenum reddat ipsum lucidum et magis nigrum. Et ideo si fiat sereno tempore, magis valet et pulcrius est. Et postea coletur per telam, et reponetur, et usui servetur.

303*a*. *Autre Recepte pour faire encre.*

Alia recepta pro faciendo unam quartam attramenti seu incausti boni, quæ tamen non est de præsenti compilatione, sed hic, propter connexitatem materiæ capituli precedentis, fuit addita per me *Johannem Le Bégue licentiatum in legibus* qui præsens opus seu capitula in hac volumine aggregata, propria manu, licet non assuetus, scripsi Anno Domini MCCCCXXXI ætatis vero meæ lxiij, prout eandem receptam alibi scriptam reperi sub hac forma.

Prenes ung quarteron de noiz de galle de iiij deniers parisis

Parisian deniers, and let them be beaten to powder. Put it [the powder] into a quart and a half of water, and let it boil for an hour and a half or more on a good charcoal fire until the water is reduced to a quart; and when it has thus boiled put into it a quarter of a pound of gum of the weight of iiij. Parisian deniers and a cup full of vinegar; and then make it boil another hour, and when it has boiled, take it off and put into it a quarter of a pound of copperas in powder of the weight of iij. Parisian deniers, and let it cool, and then put it into an inkstand. And if it is too pale add to it a little more copperas, and you will have good ink.

304. *To make a rose colour from Brazil wood.*—Take a mixture of equal quantities of water from a cistern, and wine, and boil in it shavings of the said brexillium; and, having extracted and pressed out the colour, and strained the red liquid through a linen cloth, and removed the substance of the wood, add to the water a little roche alum in powder; and when it is dissolved, put in some white gypsum, which has been ground upon a stone with pure water and dried, or some bracha prepared and ground in the same way as the gypsum is directed to be done, in sufficient quantity, and mix and incorporate them all well together, and keep for use. This water can also be used without putting in gypsum or bracha, but only for shading, and not as a body colour, for it has no body or substance; and when the bracha or gypsum is added, then it can be used as a body colour as well as for shading, because the gypsum or bracha, which have body, give their body to the colour.

305. *Tracing paper*, through which all things are visible that are drawn and figured on other parchment or on paper or on panels when laid under it, and therefore all drawings which are put under it, or all drawings or pictures over which it is put, can be drawn correctly and perfectly on this tracing paper. It is made in this way. Grease thinly with mutton suet a smooth and polished stone of the breadth and length you wish your tracing paper to be. Then, with a broad brush, spread clear and transparent melted glue over the stone, and let it dry.

et faites batre en pouldre, puis la metez en quatre et demie diaue et la faites boulir une heure et demie ou plus a beau feu de charbon et jusques atant que leaue soit revenue a la quarte; et puis quant elle aura ainsi bouli, y mettez un quarteron de gomme de iiij deniers et plain gobelet de vin aigre; et puis le faites boulir une autre heure et puis quant elle aura boulu, la descendez et y metez un quarteron coperose en pouldre de iij deniers parisis, et le laissiez refroidier puis metez en un cellier. Et se elle est trop clere blanche si y metez encore un pou de coperose et vous aurez bon encre.

304. *Ad faciendum colorem ligni Brexillii rosaceum.*—Accipiantur aqua cisternæ et vinum album per medietatem, et in ipsis coquatur rasura dicti brexilii et extracto colore postea expressa et colata dicta aqua rosacia per telam et ablata substantia ligni suprascripti ponatur in ipsa aqua parum aluminis rosiæ triti quo fuso ponatur in ipsa aqua de gipso albo bene trito super lapidem cum aqua clara et desiccato aut de bracha eodem modo ordinata et trita quo dictum est de gipso ad quantitatem quæ sufficiat et incorporentur et misceantur et operetur de hoc, et etiam potest operari de ipsa aqua antequam ponatur gipsum nec bracha, sed solum umbrando, et non ad corpus, quia corpus seu substantiam non habet, et quando apposita est bracha vel gipsus, tunc potest operari ad corpus et etiam umbrando quia gipsus seu bracha qui corpus habent incorporant colorem ipsum.

305. *Carta lustra,* per quam transparent quæ sub ipsam sunt posita protracta et figurata in aliis cartis vel in papiris aut in tabulis et possunt igitur in ipsa carta lustra penitus et recte abstrahi qualia sunt quæ sub ipsam ponuntur protracta vel protractiones et picturæ super quas ipsa extenditur. Fit hoc modo. Perungas subtiliter sepo arietino lapidem æqualem et politam latitudinis et longitudinis tantæ quantæ vis facere cartam. Postea cum pincello lato lineas ex colla liquefacta clara et lucida lapidem ipsum et dimitte siccari. Postea eleva ab uno angulo

Afterwards lift up from one of the corners of the stone a little of this skin of dried glue, which will be as thin as paper, but transparent; and see whether it is thick enough, that is, whether it is not too thin; if so, do not pull it off, but leave it there and give it another coat of the same glue, and let it dry; and then again, as before, try whether it is thick enough. And repeat this until it is sufficiently thick. Afterwards take it quite off the stone, because the above-mentioned greasing with mutton fat will enable you to take off the said coat of glue easily, for it will not allow it to fasten or stick to the stone; and so you will have tracing paper for the purposes aforesaid.[1]

306. *How the colours are tempered.*—All colours are distempered with the gum of the pine or of the sapin,[2] except minium and ceruse, which are tempered with white of egg. All kinds of green must be tempered with glue except Spanish green, which must be tempered with vinegar.

307. *To clean and renovate minium that is too old and dirty.*—Put it into water mixed with one-fourth part of wine in a horn, and stir it up well; then let it settle well and pour off and remove the water, and pulverize the colour and distemper it with whipped white of egg, and do as you please with it.

308. *To make a colour which makes all other colours, except orpiment, sinople, and saffron, bright, brilliant, and lustrous, and which is called "Clare."*—Put gum arabic to soak in clean water in a clean vessel, until it is dissolved, and with this distemper your colours, or stir them with it and leave them moist for a day or two; and if you wish the clare to be made quickly, place it over hot ashes.

309. *To make a very good lake.*—Take an ounce of lake,[3] and

[1] Compare this with Cennino Cennini, chap. xxv.

[2] The article being repeated, it would seem that the author intended two kinds of pine resin. The latter was the Pinus Picea of Linnæus, the Silver Fir of the English, the Abete of the Italians—whence they procured the Olio di Abezzo, which was used in making varnishes. See Nemnich, art. 'Pinus;' and see Matthioli, pp. 118, 120.

[3] The lac lake.

lapidis aliquantulum linituram illam collæ siccatæ quæ erit subtilis ut carta sed erit lustra, et vide si non sit satis grossa seu spissa, viz., quod sit nimis subtilis, et non eleves sed permittes, et adhuc linias desuper de eadem cola et permitte siccari, et ut prius tempta si satis grossa sit. Et totiens hoc reiteres quod fiat sufficienter grossa. Postea ex toto eleva a lapide quia suprascripta perunctio lapidis ex adipe arietino facta dabit facilitatem elevandi ipsam cartam quam non permisêrit lapidi glutinari nec adhærere et sic habebis cartam lustram ad ea quæ dicta sunt facienda.

306. Toutes couleurs sont destrempées de gomme de pin ou de sapin, fors mine et ceruse qui se destrampent de glaire dœufs. Tout vert droit estre destrempe de glux, se ce nest vert despagne qui doit estre destrempez de vin aigre.

307. *Se mine est trop vielle et trop orde pour la renouveler et abellir.*—Mettez le en yaue avecques la quarte partie de vin, en un cornet et la mouvez tres bien, puiz la laissiez bien rasseoir, puis purez et ostez leaue et le brisiez et destrempez de glaire dœf et en faites vostre volente.

308. *Pour faire une couleur qui fait toutes autres couleurs reluisans clers et replendissans qui est nommee clare; hormis orpiment sinople et safran.*—Mettez tremper gomme arabice en eaue nette en un vaisseau net tant que elle soit fondue et soit expresse par raison, et de ce destrempez vos couleurs ou vous les mouvez avecques, et les laissiez moitier par ung jour ou deux. Et se vous voulez qu'il soit tost fait si le mettez dessus les cendres chaudes.

309. *Pour faire trés bonne laque.*—Prenez une once de laque

rasp finely a little Brazil wood, put it into a clean vessel, then add to the Brazil wood some clean and clear beaten white of egg, and a little alum water. Grind the lake with that water and dry it in the sun, and when you wish to use it, distemper it with this water, especially on parchment; and the more you grind it up with this Brazil wood water, the better it will be.

310. *To write or paint with gold.*—Put quicksilver with powdered gold into stag's leather, and press it; the quicksilver will pass through the leather, and the gold will remain; then put the gold with the quicksilver over the fire, but take care that the crucible does not burn. And you must add to it a little well-pulverized salt, until the mercury evaporates, which you may catch in a vessel anointed with grease, and suspended above it. Then wash the powdered gold with water in a basin as you would wash minium; and when it is dry, stir into it a glue made with parchment or vellum, which you must put into a vessel over hot water, and it will presently be dissolved. When this is the case, grind it well, and fill with it your pen or pencil, and write or paint with this distempered gold.

311. *To illuminate a book or other thing with minium.*[1]—Do not use minium alone, for the letters would be too light coloured, and would not look well, but put minium with vermilion; and if the vermilion is very red and new, put two parts of that to one of minium. And if it is old and brown, put equal quantities of each, or two-thirds of minium, for the older the vermilion the darker and browner it is. When it is ground up with clear water and dried in heaps, if you wish to use it and to have it appear brilliant, distemper it with varnish and white of egg beaten to a froth, and add a little clean water; with this you may write large letters [initial] and small on parchment. If the colour is

[1] This is nearly a repetition of No. 177.

et rayez un pou de bresil soubtillement et mettez le en un vaissel nett, puiz mettez dedens le bresil glaire dœf batu clers et net et puiz un pou deaue en quoi il ait un pou dalun mis avecques, et puis de celle eaue moules le laque, puiz le laissiez secher au soleil et quant vous en voulez ouvrer vous le destremprerez de ceste yeaue especialment en parchemin. Et quant plus de foys le ferez broyer et mouldre a cette yaue de bresil, et resuer, tant mieulx vauldra.

310. *Pour escrire ou paindre dor.*—Mettez argent vif avecques or molu en pouldre en cuir de cerfs, et le espraignez si passera largent vif par le cuir et lor demourra ou cuir, puis mettez lor avecques largent vif sur le feu maiz gardez bien que le crosel narde. Et mettez avecques un pou de sel bien moulu et crible tant que le vif argent se parte par fumee, lequel vous pouez recevoir en une escuelle ointe de graisse pendue au hault au dessus puis lavez la pouldre dor en un bacin en yaue, comme vous feriez mine. Puis mettez la pouldre dor quant elle est seche en glus faite de parchemin orculin [ou velin] lequel mis en vaissel sur eaue chaude est tantost resolu et quant tout sera resolu moelez bien et mettez en vostre plume ou pincel et escrisiez ou paindez dicellui or trempe.

311. *Pour enluminer de mine, soit livre ou autre chose.*—Ne mettez pas mine par soi, car la lettre en seroit trop clere et mal parant, mais mettez mine avecques vermillon, et se le vermillon est bien rouge et novel si en mettez deux parties et le tiers de mine. Et sil est viel et obscur ou brun mettez de mine la moitié ou les deux pars, car plus est vermillon viel et plus est noir et obscur, et quant il sera mouluz ensamble a leaue clere et sec par monseaux se vous voulez eu ouvrer et quil soit luisant trempez le de vernix et de glaire dœufs rompue a lespurge, et y mettez pou deaue clere et de ce escrisiez en parchemin grosse lettre et menue et quant il est sech, sil nest bien luisant, et que

not brilliant when dry, and the weather is moist, dry it by the fire, and thus it will shine; but if the weather is dry and hot, it will be better to dry it in the sun.

312. *To write with brass, gold, and silver.*—File some brass of a good colour very finely, then grind it on the porphyry, which is a very hard stone; put it into a clean vessel and let it settle; then pour off the water and prepare your tempera of gum arabic. Distemper it with this, and use it on your pencil, and when it is dry you must rub and burnish it well with the stone which is called *ametiste* [hæmatite]. You will act in the same manner for writing with gold and silver.

313. *Orpiment [atramentum] is thus made.*[1]—Take oil and ink, and juice of the blackthorn, and its middle bark well ground in a mortar; put the whole together in a pot, and let it stand for a night. Then boil it gently and strain it; boil it gently again with myrrh and aloes, and again strain it. Then add to it a little verjuice or glace,[2] and put the whole to boil gently over the coals without flame; then take it off and keep it.

314. *To make a blue colour like azure.*—Take the juice of the corn-flower,[3] and make on wood or parchment a ground of white-lead; lay the juice on the said ground, three, four, or five, or more times, if necessary, and thus you will have an azure colour.

315. *To paint walls.*—Put a little lime with ochre, that it may be lighter coloured, or mix it with simple red or prasin,[4] or with a colour which is called posce,[5] which is made with ochre, green, and membrayne;[6] or you may take of a colour

---

[1] See *ante*, No. 189.

[2] Glace, probably Alumen Glacie, or glarum, as in No. 41.

[3] The blue-bottle, the Corn Centaury, the corn-flower. Ciano delle biade, Ciano ceruleo, Blaveolo, Fiore di Zaccaria, Centaurea cyanus.

[4] *Prasinus.* See Theophilus, lib. i. c. ii., and see *ante*, pp. 236 and 244. This colour was sometimes called "Prasminem;" and by the Italians "Verde Porro."

[5] *Posce.* See Theophilus, lib. i. c. iii.

[6] See Theoph., lib. i. c. i. See also *ante*, pp. 144 and 180, where this

le temps soit moite, sechez le au feu, si resplendira ; et se le temps et sech et chaut elle seroit mieulx sechee au soleil.

312. *Pour escrire de laton et pareillement dor et dargent.*—Limez tres subtilement laton de tres pure couleur et puis le molez soutiliment sur le porphire qui est pierre tres seure, puis le mettez et un net vaisel et le laissiez asseoir, puis ostez leaue et ayez vostre detrempe de gomme arabiche, et len destrempez puis en ouvrez de vostre pincel, et quant ce sera fait et sech, si le frotez et burnissez tres bien, d'une pierre qui est nommee ametiste et ainsi povez vous escrire dor et dargent.

313. *Orpiment se fait ainsi.*—Prenez oille et encre et jus despine noire et son escorce moienne bien broyee en un mortier et mettez tout ensemble, en un pot, et li laissiez une nuit reposer, puis le metez un poi boulir, puis le colez, puis le metez boulir un pou avec mirre et aloes et derechief le coulez. Puis metez avee un po de verjus ou de glace, et remetez tout ensemble sur les charbons sans flamme un petit bolir, puis le ostez et le gardez.

314. *A faire couleur blauet comme d'azur.*—Prenez jus de bleues net et faites en bois ou en parchemin un camp de blanc de plomb, puis mettez le jus dessus le dit champ, trois ou quatre ou cinq lis ou plus si mestier est ; si avez couleur dazur.

315. *Pour peindre murs.*—Mettez un po de chaux avec ocre pour avoir plus grant clarte, ou vous la mellez avec rouge simple ou avec prasin ou avec une couleur qui est nommee posce qui est faite de ocre vert et de membrayne ou vous pouvez

---

colour is described by S. Audemar under the name of "Olchus seu Membrana."

The method of mural painting described in the text was probably that which was generally practised by the painters of the middle ages ; and there is reason to suppose that the old paintings recently discovered on the walls of churches in so many parts of England were painted in this manner.

which is made of sinople, ochre, lime, and posc, &c. And walls should be painted rather moist than otherwise, because the colours unite together better, and are firmer. And all the colours for walls should be mixed with quicklime.

316. *Black* is made with charcoal ground with water or wine, and distempered with oil or garlic; but the best is made with atramentum, unless it is charcoal which is made of scales of iron boiled and heated with oil. Or take the bark of alder and grind it with iron filings in water, and put it with atramentum, and distemper it.

317. *The flesh colour of images is thus made.*—Take terre verte, white, and lake, mix them together, and fill what you please with them. Then make a shade [tint] of green and ochre so that it may be like green, and mix with it a little lake, and mark out the shadows with it; then make the rose colour with white and synople, and lay it wherever you may think proper. Then make the flesh colour of ochre and white, with a little synople, and fill up the solid parts, but that which is laid on the rose colour should be very thin. Then take some of that colour and lay it on the eyebrows, and under the feet, on the mouth, chin, neck, and ears. Then draw as it were veins, and then with pure lake mark the eye-lashes, nostrils, eyes, and limbs. Then shade again lightly with lake mixed with a little oil; then whiten the lights with pure white, and then draw the eyelids, eyes, and other members.

318. *To gild with gold leaf.*—Grind well some gypsum with pure clean water, dry it; then grind it with synople like rose, and with fish-glue dissolved in very good white wine, and with the pencil spread it where you please, covering well with it the part to be gilded. Then dry it, and make it smooth with the knife, apply the gold, fix it with the hæmatite and polish it,

prandre dune couleur qui soit faite de synople et docre et de chaux et de posc etc. ; et doivent estre murs paint plus moiste que aultre chose pour ce que les couleurs se tiennent mieulx ensembles et soient plus fermes. Et doivent toutes couleurs pour murs estre melles avecques chaux vive.

316. *Noir* est fait de charbon broye avec eaue ou vin et destrempez doile ou deil, mais le bon est fait darrement,[1] etc. Se ce nest carbon qui est fait de paille de fer boulu et cuie avec oille. Ou vous prenez escorce dalne et le broiez en eue avec molure de ferre en yaue, et mettez avec arcement et destrempez.

317. *Charnure dymages se fait ainsi.*—Prenez vert terrin blanc et laque, et mellez ensemble et emplissiez la ou vous vouldrez, puis faictes ombre de vert et ocre en telle maniere que ce soit comme vert et mellez avecques un po de laque, et signez vos lits, et puis ombre et puis rose de blanc et de synople, et roses la ou vous plaira, puis faites charnure docre et de blanc et dun po de cinople et mettez dedans les signemens espes et cil qui sera sur la rose sera tres sutil, puis prenez de celle couleurs et mettez sur les surcils et dessoubs les piez et sur la bouche et au menton et a la goile et aux oreilles. Et en faut si comme se fust vains, puis designez de pur lac les cilles et narines et les yeulx et tous les membres. Et metez de rechief dedens umbre legierement et de lac loignez un petit, puis le blanchissez de blanc pur, puis designez les cilles et les yeulz et les autres membres.

318. *Pour mettre or de feuilles battues.*—Molez gipse tres bien avec yaue pure et nette, puis le sechiez, puis le molez avec cinope si comme rose, et avec cole de poisson qui soit fondue avec tres bon vin blanc et le mettez au pincel la ou vous vouldrez et soit bien couvert et le sechiez puis le raez dun coustel plainement et mettez lor dessus et le fermez de ame-

---

[1] That this word is really "atramentum," is proved by a similar passage in S. Audemar—see *ante*, No. 172. See also 'Materials for a History of Painting in Oil,' by Mr. Eastlake, p. 132, n.; and Halliwell's 'Dictionary of Archaic and Provincial Words.'

and if it does not succeed well, take the above-mentioned glue, spread it over the drawing, and over that the gold leaf.

319. *If you wish to prepare oil for distempering all kinds of colours.*—Take quicklime, and equal quantities of ceruse and oil; expose these to the sun without moving it for a month or more, as the longer it remains the better it will be. Then strain it and preserve the oil well. With the oil, thus kept and prepared, you may distemper all colours either separately or mixed.

320. *To write with gold and silver.*—Take leaf gold, grind it with salt on the marble, leave it for a long time in water, stir it and let it settle. Then pour off the water to remove the salt, and the gold will remain at the bottom. Distemper it with gum for writing, and the letters you make will be dark; but when they are dry, polish them with a tooth and they will be of a beautiful yellow shining gold colour. If you choose you may write with silver in the same manner.

321. *To make silver letters without silver.*—Grind alum with salt; then wash it in order to remove the salt; then distemper it with gum and write with it. When it is dry, if you polish it with the tooth, it will lose its darkness, and will take the colour of silver.

322. *A recipe for grinding gold.*—Take some very fine and pure gold filings, grind them in a mortar such as is used by the apothecaries, which is made of three parts copper and one part of tin or lead; such are their mortars. But previous to this, your gold filings should be well washed in a basin or in a shell with a pencil. Then grind all your gold in the above-mentioned mortar, so that when finished it shall be left clear. And in like manner you may grind copper, silver, brass, pewter, and all other metals; but take care that the gold does not burn, as it would then be necessary to regrind it. When the operation is finished, remove the water and impurities, let the gold settle, then place it over the coals with water, and warm, and stir it.

tiste, et le lissez. Et se il ne vient bien prenez de la cole dessus dicte et metez au dessein, et tantost la feuille de lor dessus.

319. *Si vous voulez appareiller oile pour destremper toutes manieres de couleurs.*—Prenes chaux vive avec autant de ceruse comme est de loile, puiz metez au soleil et ne le movez jusques a ung moyt ou plus tar quant plus y sera, et mieulx vaudra, puis le colez et gardez tres bien loile, et de celle oille gardee et ainsi preparee, povez destremper toutes couleurs ensemble et chacun par soy.

320. *Pour escrire dor et dargent.*—Pren feuille dor et la broye sur le marbre avec sel, puis le fay estre longuement en eaue, et le leve et laisse rasseoir puis prenez leaue pour oster le sel, si demourra lor au fons. Si le destrempe a gomme et en escri, si auras lettre noire et quant elle sera seche, si la poli dun dent, si sera belle et gaune et luisant en bonne couleur dor, et ainsi puez tu escrire de argent se tu veulz.

321. *Pour faire lettre dargent sans argent.*—Broyez alun avec sel, puis le leve pour oster le sel puis le destrempe a gomme et escri et quant il est sec, si le poli du dent, si perdra sa novete et ara couleur d'argent.

322. *Pour or mouler recipe.*—R. tres fin or lime bien menu et le broyez en un mortier suzille tel que les appoticaires ont, cilz de cuivre les trois pars et la quarte partie de staing ou de plomb, tels sont leurs mortiers; mais avant ce doit estre votre limeure d'or bien lavee en un bachin ou en une conche de limeterie a un pincel et en ce mortier dessus dit, molez tant or que have qui y sera mise soit au departir clere. Et en telle maniere pourrez molez cuivre argent loton estaing et tout autre metail, mais gardez que lor ne se haerde car il le fauldroit remouldre de rechief. Et quant ce sera fait, ostez liaue et les ordures et laissiez lautre rasseoir, puis le metez sur les charbons avec eaue et le chauffez et mouvez.

323. *To grind gold, and how it should be softened.*—Take well-filed gold, grind it well on a porphyry slab with two parts of sal gem [rock salt], a little yellow sulphur in a glass vessel, changing it frequently from one vessel to another until it is well washed and purified. Then put it into a horn, and when you wish to use it, distemper it with gum arabic, which must be put into a glass vessel with water and exposed to the rays of the sun, until it is dissolved. When it is dissolved put it into a saucer with as much silver as water, and let it be tepid when you write with it, which you must do the same day before the fire. When dry, let it be burnished with a tooth.

324. *To make what appear to be gold and silver letters, without the use of either gold or silver.*—Make very thin plates of fine brass for gold letters, of fine tin for silver letters, and each separately; and let the plates be as thin as gold leaf, and let them be well ground and bruised with water and dried in the sun, and then strained through a cloth; afterwards regrind the coarser portion which remains in the cloth in a mill or mortar of iron or copper, such as is used by the apothecaries. Then fill the letters or portraits with minium, if you mean to gild, but if you intend to lay on silver put no minium; and when the minium is dry, fill those letters or portraits, by means of an ass'-hair pencil, with a glue made in the following manner.

Boil some clean and white pieces of the leather of cows, oxen, calves, or sheep, early in the morning, until two-thirds have evaporated. Then pour off that water, add some fresh water, and boil again for an hour. Then pour off one-third of the water and let the rest boil for two hours more, when you must take out the leather and keep it in a clean vessel; and if it is then thick and sticks to the fingers, it is good; if it does not do so, you must boil it again. Then take some of this glue and put it into a vessel over the coals, and while hot or tepid, lay it on those portraits or letters with the pencil. Afterwards dust on to it the said brass powder or tin powder, and leave it for a day to dry, then polish it with a tooth. Again, an-

323. *Pour escrire dor et comment il se doit mollir.*—Recevez or bien lime, et le moulez tres bien sur une porfire avec ij pars de salgemme et un poy de souffre jaune et moulez tout ce tres bien ensamble avec lor puis en vaissel de voire, et le mettez souvent de vaissel en autre tant qu'il soit fort bien lavez et bien purifiez, puis le mettez en un cornet. Et quant vous en vouldrez ouvrer si le destrempez de gomme arabic et lequel mettez avec yaue en ung vaissel de voire au soleil afin quil fonde. Et quant il sera fondu, mettez avec argent autant comme et de leaue en une paelle et faites que elle soit tiede quant vous vouldrez escrire et escresiez ce jour devant le feu. Et quant elle sera seche si le burnissez dun dent.

324. *Pour faire lettre qui semble dor et dargent, qui na ne or ne argent.*—Face plattes moult tenues de fin loton pour lettre dor, et de fin estaing pour lettre dargent, et chacun a part, et soient les plates tenues comme feuille dor a dorer, et soit molu tres bien et crible avec yaue et laissie seichr au soleil et coule par ung drapel et remoler le plus gros qui demorra en le drapel et moule tous dits en ung moulin ou mortier de cuivre ou de fer tel quil sont chieux les appothicaires, puis emplissiez les lettres ou pourtraictures de mine, en cas que veuillez faire dor ; et se dargent, ne y mettez point de mine, puis quant le mine est mis et est sech, mettez a un pincel de poil dasne en icelles lettres ou pourtraictures cole ou glus facte en tele maniere.

Faites boulir pieces de cuir de vaiche ou de bœuf ou de veau ou de mouton purs et blans, du matin jusques a tierce, pus ostez leaue et metez de lautre et faittes boulir une heure puis ostez le tiers de leaue et laissiez boulir lautre encore ii heures puis ostez les cuirs et gardez leaue en un vaissel pur et net, et se lautre tour elle est expresse et que elle se tienne aux doiz elle est bonne. Et se non faictes boulir de rechief puis prenez une partie de ceste cole et la mettez en un vaissel sur les charbons et la mettez chaude ou tiede a tout le pincel sur icelles lettres ou pourtraictures. Et tantost mettez dessus de la dicte pouldre de loton ou de celle de estaing et laissiez

other way, without using brass powder: boil parchment with the said glue, then take out the parchment, and put much saffron with the glue, and let them cool together. In the morning give your parchment a coat of glue on a very smooth table, lay your tin powder on it, and then leave it exposed to the sun for four or five hours, that it may dry; after this you must polish it with a boar's-tooth, when it will be of the colour of gold. Or thus, scrape your parchment with a knife where you wish to draw, and make the glue with the saffron boil a little. Then put a little of this into an iron spoon, warm it over the coals, and while tepid, lay it where you please, by means of the pencil, having your powdered tin in the other hand, which you must then apply all over it, and burnish it with a tooth. Also, if you wish to make gold letters, put saffron with your tin and glue; but if you wish them to be of the colour of silver, use no saffron; after this you may put on other colours. And you must know that sometimes the letters become pale; this arises either from its not being sufficiently polished, or from the too small quantity of saffron.

325. *If you wish to make a water proper for distempering all colours.*—Take a pound of lime and 12 pounds of ashes;[1] then take boiling water and put the whole together, making them boil well; after which let the mixture settle and strain it through a cloth; then take four pounds of that water, heat it well, take about two ounces of white wax, and put this to boil with the water; then take about $1\frac{1}{2}$ oz. of fish-glue, put it in water, and leave until it is well softened, and as it were melted, when you must manipulate it until it becomes like paste, and throw it into the water with wax, and make all boil together; then add to it about an ounce and a half of mastic, and boil it with the other ingredients. Take some of this water on a knife-blade, or piece of iron, to ascertain whether it is done: if it is like glue, it is all right. Strain this water while hot or

[1] I have no doubt that the word originally written was *cendres*, and not *Flandres*.

secher par un jour, puis polissiez dun dent. Item autrement sans pouldre de laton boulez parchemin avec la dicte cole et ostez le parchemin et metez foison safran avecques la cole et laissiez refroidier ensamble, et au matin faictes ou liniez le parchemin de vostre cole sur une table bien pleine, et mettez vostre pouldre destaing dessus, et puis le laissiez au soleil secher par quatre ou cinq heures, puis le polissiez dun dent de porc et sera couleur dor. Ou ainsi ; raez vostre parchemin dun coustel la ou vous vouldrez pourtraire et faictes la cole avec le safran un tant et boulir et en mettez un poy en une cuiller de fer et faictes a tiedir sur les charbons, et en prenez tout tiede et en mettez au pinceau la ou vous voulez et tenez la pouldre de vostre estaing en lautre main et le appliquez tantost dessus et laissiez secher et burnissez a un dent. Item se vous voulez faire lettre dor mettez safran avecques vostre estaing et vostre cole. Et se vous voulez dargent, si ny mettez point de safran. Et apres pourrez vous mettre les autres couleurs, et est a savoir que la lettre aucune fois palist, et cest quant elle nest mie bien polie ou quant on ni met pas le safran a point.

325. *Se vous voulez faire yaue conosite a destremper toutes couleurs.*—Prenez une livre de chaux et douze de Flandres puis prenez eaue boulant et metez tout ensamble et les faictes assez boulir puis le laissiez bien reposer, puis le coulez bien parmy un drapel et de celle yaue prenez livres quatre et la faictes bien ardoir, puis prenez cire blanche environ ii. onces et la mettez boulir avec lyaue puis prenez cole de poisson environ j once et ½, et la mettez en eaue et li laissiez tant quelle soit bien emollie et si comme fondue puis la maniez tant que elle soit comme paste puis la mettez en lyaue avec la cire et la faites ensamble boulir, et mettez mastic dedens environ once et demie et faictes boulir ensamble, puiz prenez de ceste eaue et mettez sur un coustel ou sur fer pour savoir sil est bien cuit et sil est comme glue il est bien. Puis adonc coulez celle

tepid through a linen cloth, let it settle, and cover it well. With this water you may distemper all kinds of colours.

326. *To make skins and all other things of a red colour, or any other colour.*—First put the skins in alum-water which has been boiled with some bran, and then skim it well and let it settle, and when the heat of the water is so reduced that it is just tepid, so as not to burn the skins, throw them in. After this you must dry them; then boil some brazil wood in the above-mentioned water, and when it is well boiled sew your skins into the form of bags, and fill them with the said water while tepid and not boiling, as in that case the skins would burn: they will thus be well coloured. And in this manner you may stain anything with any colour.

327. *To gild copper or brass without gold.*—Take clean and pure brass or copper, and scrape it well with a knife, and burnish it with a boar's tooth; then grind some ox-gall or other suitable thing; then take your pen or pencil, soak it in the gall, rub it on the above-mentioned brass or copper, and let it dry. Do this three times and you will have a colour similar to gold.

328. *To make fine letters of gold.*—Grind gold and mercury together, put them into a crucible over the fire until the mercury is evaporated; then stir the gold well until it is reduced to powder, when you must grind it up with saffron boiled in water, and expose it to the sun in a phial with gum-water. When you use it, take it from the sun and write with it.

329. *If you wish to make three kinds of vestures on parchment, one purple or red, another violet, and another white.*—Mix together a green made from the juice of any herb with a little ochre, and with this fill the vesture of the pourtrayed image. As to the second mix a little cinople with orpiment, and with this fill the dress of the other image. For the third mix orpiment with the juice of a tree called in Latin sambucus, and in

yaue chaude ou tiede parmi ung drap linge, et laissiez reposer et la covrez bien et de celle eaue povez destremper toutes manieres de couleurs.

326. *Pour taindre peaux et toutes autres choses en couleur rouge, et en toutes autres couleurs.*—Mettez les peaulx premierement en eaue alumee, qui soit boulie et du son dedens et puis laissiez bien escumer et reposer, et quant leaue ne sera que tiede tellement que en mettant les peaulx dedens elles nardent, mettez lors dedens celle eaue les dictes peaulx puis les mettez sechier, puis faictes boulir bresil dedens leaue dessus dicte et quant elle sera tres bien cuite cousez vos peaulx en maniere de sacz et mettez leaue dessus dicte dedens, tiede comme dit est et non boillant afin que les peaulx nardent, et ainsi seront elles tres bien coulorees. Et par ceste maniere povez taindre toutes choses et de toutes couleurs.

327. *A dorer cuivre ou arain sans or.*—Prenez arain ou cuivre pur et net, et le reez bien dun coustel, puiz le burnissiez dun dent de porc puis moulez fiel de torel ou autre chose convenable, puiz prenez vostre penne ou vostre pincel et le moilliez au dit fiel et en frotez sur le cuivre ou arain dessus dit, et laissiez secher, et se faictes pour trois fois, si aurez couleur semblable dor.

328. *A faire lettre dor fin.*—Molez or et vif argent ensamble et metez en un crosel sur le feu tant que le vif argent soit evapore, puis le movez tres bien tant que ce soit pourre, puis molez safran avecques et les cuisez en yaue, puis le metez en yaue de gomme au soleil en un fiale, et quant vous vouldrez escrire prenez la fiale au soleil et du dit or escrisiez.

329. *Se vous voulez faire trois manieres de vestemens en parchemin, lun pourpre ou rouge, lautre violet, et lautre blau.*—Mellez ensemble vert avec jus daucune herbe et y adjoustez un po docre et emplissiez le vestement de limage pourtraicte. Et en aprez pour le second, mellez un po de cinople avec orpiment et emplissiez le vestement de lautre ymage. Tiercement mellez orpiment avec jus des feuilles dun arbres qui es

French seur,[1] and fill the third dress with this. But these are not good on walls.

330. *To make a colour which is called venede or veneda.*[2]—Take black, and mix white lead with it, if it is to be used on parchment, but if it is to be used on walls employ lime instead of the said white lead.

331. *To make a green colour for writing.*—Mix good vinegar with sour honey, and put it in a [copper] vessel under very hot dung. In 12 days it will be of a beautiful green.

332. *To make a blood-like colour which is called lake.*—In the month of March cut some ivy, which in Latin is called edera, and which climbs on the trees and forests, and put the juice which exudes into a glass vessel every three days; then boil it in urine and use it in drawing with the pencil.

333. *The following is for tempering iron and steel.*—When the he-goat is in heat take his blood and temper your iron or steel in this; it then becomes very hard. The he-goat is an animal whose Latin name is hyrcus.

334. *To make the colour of red roses.*—Put some Brazil wood raspings into an earthen vessel glazed with lead, adding urine and powdered alum; let it stand for a night, and in the morning place it over the coals without flame and boil it well for a little; then take it off the fire, add a little powdered quick lime, and mix it well with the other ingredients; then pour off the clear part, and dry that which is thick so that you may use it when necessary.

335. *If you wish to redden tables or other things.*—Take linseed, or hemp-seed, or nut-oil and mix it with minium or cinople on a stone without water; then with a pencil illuminate what you wish to redden with this.

336. *To write with gold.*—Grind gold with clear and pure wine, then pour off the wine and distemper it with gum or ox-gall. When you desire to paint or write with it, you must stir

---

[1] The elder. [2] See Theophilus, lib. i. c. vi.

nomme en Latin *sambucus*, et en Francais *seur*, et emplissiez le tiers vestement, mais en murs ils ne sont pas bons.

330. *A faire une couleur qui se nomme venede ou veneda.*—Prenez couleur noir et y mellez un pou de blanc de plomb avec pour mettre en parchemin, mais se vous voulez le mettre en mur, mettez en lieu du dit blanc plomb de la chaux.

331. *A faire couleur verde pour escrire.*—Mellez bon vin aigre avec miel aigre, et le mettez en un vaissel en fiens bien chaut et li laissiez douze jours et sera bon vert.

332. *Pour faire couleur sanguine qui est appelee laque.*—Trenchiez du mois de mars yerre, qui est une herbe en Latin appelee *edera*, et rampe sur les arbres et forets, et recevez en un vaissel de voirre le jus qui en ystra de iij jours en trois jours, et le cuisiez en orine et puis en ouvrez au pinceau vos portraictures.

333. *Trempeure de fer et dacier forte se fait ainsi.*—Quant le bouc est en amour, se on prent son sang, et on y trempe dedens fer ou acier. Il est moult dur, et le bouc est beste que on nomme en Latin *yrchus*.

334. *A faire couleur de roses vermeilles.*—Raez bresil en un vaissel de terre plomme et y metez de lorine et aussi pouldre dalun, et le laissiez une nuit reposer, et a landemain le mettez sur les charbons sans flambe, et le faites tres bien boulir une onde ou deux, puis lostez du feu et mettez avec un pou de chaux vive en pouldre, et mellez tres bien ensamble, et ostez le cler, et mettez lespez secher pour garder et pour en ouvrez quant est besoing.

335. *Si vous voulez rougir tables ou autres choses.*—Prenez oile de lin ou de chanvre ou de noiz, et mellez avec mine ou cinope sur une pierre sans yaue. Puis en luminez a un pincel ce que vous voulez rougir.

336. *Pour escrire dor.*—Molez or avec vin cler et pur, puis lostez du vin et le destrempez de gomme ou de fiel de torel, et quant vous vouldrez paindre ou escrire, si le mouvez et en

it and use it with a pen or pencil, and when dry polish with a boar's tooth.

337. *Several modes of distempering saffron.* — Saffron is sometimes distempered with water, sometimes with egg, sometimes with wine; but the best way is to put the saffron into a clean vessel with a great quantity of water until it is soaked, and then to boil it over the coals. You may then write or paint with it whatever you please, and you must know that saffron is redder when distempered with wine.

338. *To make green.*—Boil the leaves of the Morelle [so-anum nigrum] with ochre and grind them on a stone. If you were to put saffron instead of ochre, or saffron and ochre, the colour would be very good.

339. *To paint and write with gold on cloth, parchment, tables, and everything else.*—Fill a glass vessel with urine and let it settle until it is clear, then take two parts of white of egg and mix it with your fresh urine and put it with some dissolved or ground gold into the horn; and with this gold you may write as with any other colour, and paint on cloths and all other things.

340. *To make the colours of flowers.*—At the rising of the sun go into the fields and collect divers corn flowers and other herbs; bruise and grind each kind of flower separately with well-baked gypsum, then dry them and keep each colour separately so as to be ready when wanted for use; and if you wish for a green colour mix quick lime with the flowers and you will have a good colour.

341. *To make a good liquid varnish for painters.*—Take glasse aromatique, which is dark or dull outside, and inside when broken is clear and shining like glass; put some of it in a new jar, which must stand on the mouth of another jar, which must be well luted to it. The upper jar must be well covered so as to be smoke-proof, and its bottom must be pierced. Then light a fire beneath it, and leave it until the glasse is melted, when you must take two parts of linseed, or

ouvrez a la penne ou au pincel et quand il est sec polissiez le dun dent de sangler.

337. *A destremper safran en plusieurs manieres.*—Safran est aucunefoiz destrempez dyaue aucunefois dœuf aucunefois de vin, mais la meilleur maniere et de mettre le safran en yaue en un vaissel bien net jusques a tant quil soit confis et fault quil ny ait une grant quantite deaue, puis le mettez sur les charbons boulir un po ensamble et puis en ecrisiez ou paindez ce que vous vouldrez ; et est a savoir quant le safran est destrempe de vin, il est plus rouge.

338. *Pour faire vert.*—Cuisez feuille de morelle avec ocre puis le broyez sur la pierre. Et cui y mettroit safran en lieu de locre, et autour avec locre, bon seroit.

339. *A paindre et escrire dor sur telles, parchemins, ou tables, et toutes autres choses.*—Emplissiez de votre orine un vaissel de voirre et si le laissiez reposer tant que elle soit bien claire, puis prenez glaire doefs tres bonne deux parties et les meslez avec vostre orine novelle ensemble, et le mettez avec or solut ou broye, dedens le cornet et de cest or povez escrire comme dautre couleur, et paindre sur draps et toute autres choses.

340. *A faire couleurs de fleurs.*—Alez au matin soleil levant aux champs et assemblez diverses fleurs de bles et dautres herbes, et criblez bien et molez chacun par soy avec gips bien cuit, et mettez le sechier et gardez chascun par lui et en ouvrez quant est besoing. Et quant vous vouldrez avoir couleur verde, meslez chaux vive avecques les dictes fleurs, et avez bonne couleur.

341. *A faire bonne verniz liquide pour paintres.*—Prenez glasse aromatique qui est obscur par dehors et par dedens quant on le brise il est clair et luisant a maniere de voirre et en mettez une partie en un pot neuf qui soit assis sur la bouche dun autre pot et soient bien lute ensamble, et le pot denhault bien couvert que fumee nen ysse et soit percie au fons et faites feu dessoubz, tant que vous santez que la glasse sera fondue. Puis prenez oile de lin, ou de chanvre, ou de noix deux parties,

hemp-seed, or nut-oil, and heat this oil slowly over a fire, not making it too hot. You must then pour it on to the said glasse, make the fire hotter, and let it boil for an hour, taking care that the flame does not touch it. Then take it off the fire and put it into a clean vessel, and when you wish to varnish any dry painting take some of this liquid and spread it over the painting with your fingers, for if you were to do it with a pencil it would be too thick and would not dry. You will thus have good varnish.

342. *To make a yellow colour.*—Cook some vernide well in a clear ley, add to it a little verdigris, and distemper it with black, and the more verdigris you add the redder it will be; for instance, 2 oz. of verdigris and 5 of vercande, put the thread in while it is hot or boiling and it will give you satisfaction.

343. *The nature and condition of minium, sandaraca,*[1] *and ceruse, and the way to distemper them.*—They are all of the same kind and nature, but when exposed to heat they change their name, strength, and colour; for that which is the most heated is the reddest, and that which is the least heated is the whitest or palest, and they should be distempered with water for mason's work, with egg for parchment, and with oil for wood.

344. *To make a colour which is called posc for the undraped parts of images.*—Mix a little cynobre with simple flesh colour and a little minium and you will have the said posc[2] colour, with which you will redden teeth (gums), nostrils, mouths, hands, the under part of necks, the wrinkles of foreheads, the temples, and the articulations and other members in all the undraped parts of painted and round figures.

345. *To make two colours, one called lumine*[3] *and the other cedre or excedre, for the undraped parts of figures.*—Mix flesh

---

[1] The colour here called sandarace appears from the description to have been massicot.

[2] See *ante*, p. 300, No. 315.

[3] See Theophilus, lib. i. c. v. ix. and xiii.

et le chauffez au feu petit a petit et ne li laissiez pas trop chauffer, puis le getez par dessus avec la dicte glasse, et faites bon feu et le faites bien boulir par lespace dune heure, et gardez tres-bien que la flamme ne la touche. Puis lostez du feu et mettez en vaissel cler et net, et quant aucune euvre de painture sera faite et seche et la voulez vernicier si prenez de ceste liqueur et la tandez dessus la painture a voz doiz ; car se vous le fasiez du pincel il seroit trop espez et ne pourroit secher, et ainsi avez bonne vernix.

342. *A faire couleur jaune.*—Cuisiez bien vernide en lexive clere et nette et y mettez un po de vert de gris et le destrempez de seurs et quant plus y mettez du vert de gris et plus sera rouge s. ij oz. de vert de gris et v de vercande, puis mettez dedans le fil tiede ou boulant, et sera a vostre plaisir.

343. *La nature et condition de mine, sandarace, et ceruse, et la maniere de la destremper, et que ils sont dune maniere et dune nature, mais par feu ilz muent, noms, force, et couleurs.*—Car celui qui est plus cuit et plus rouge et le moin cuit est le plus blanc ou plus pale, et doivent estre destrempez deaue en maconnage et de œufs en parchemin, et de oille en sustages.

344. *A faire une couleur qui est appelee posc pour faire le nus de ymages.*—Mettez avec simple membrane un poi de cynobre et un poi de mine, et vous avez la dicte couleur posc, de laquelle vous rougirez dens, naselles, bouche, mains, col par dessoubs, et les fronces du front, et les tremples, et les articles et les autres membres en tous nus dimages pourtraictes et rondes.

345. *Pour faire deux couleurs, lune appelee lumine et lautre cedre ou excedre, pour le nud des ymages.*—Mellez avec cynobre

colour, well-ground ceruse, and verblee [vertbleu] with cynobre, and you will have a colour which is called *lumine*, with which you will illuminate the eyebrows, the upper part of the nose, and the nostrils with very fine lines. The other colour is made by mixing red with a little black, which produces a colour called cedre or excedre, with which you will make the touches round the pupils of the eyes.

346. *To make a glue for flesh.*—Take the root of the plant which is called "stipatum," put it into a cauldron or kettle with pieces of flesh boiled in water; when cold, the water will coagulate, and is called "gelantina." And pure water in which the said roots are boiled is useful for distempering colours on account of the glutinous properties which it takes from the root; and even if that root alone was left in water for a day and night without being boiled it will be of equal value.

347. *Water for tempering colours.*—Water in which linseed-oil has been steeped for a day and night receives a glutinous quality from that seed, which makes it proper for distempering colours.

348. *To prevent anything made of burnished iron or steel from rusting.*—Take saltpetre, otherwise called afronitre,[1] or sal nitre, of the size of a nut, and half a goblet of olive oil, distemper and boil the whole together, then strain through a linen cloth and keep it clean, and anoint with it the said things, or armour, or other works by means of a linen or woollen cloth, which must be moistened with the oil without laying it on too thickly; for it is better to lay it on thinly and then at any time after two or three months the articles may be again rubbed down with the oiled rag.

349. *To make fine azure.*—You must take the Indian or Persian azure stone which comes from beyond the sea, and which is kept by the apothecaries, who use it in some of their medicines. That which has white veins is better than that which has gold veins, and if you heat it over the fire on a hot

[1] Froth of nitre. The saline excrescence which forms on walls.

membrane ceruse bien molue et verblee si avez couleur qui est appellee lumine, de laquelle vous enluminerez les sourcils, le nez au long, et sur les pertuis des narines, faisant les trais soubtilz ; et lautre est se vous mellez avec rouge un po de noir vous avez couleur qui est nommee cedre ou excedre, de quoi vous ferez les trais environ les pupilles.

346. *Ad gellantinam carnium faciendam.*—Herba quædam stipatum vocata est, ejus radix in cacabo vel lebete posita cum carnium frustris in aqua coquentibus ea coagulat cum ad frigidatem reducuntur quæ sic gelantana vocantur, et aqua pura in qua bulirentur ipsæ radices dictæ herbæ utilis esset ad temperandum colores, pro ejus glutiniositate ab ibsa radice sumpta. Ac etiam si solum radix ipsa in aqua staret per diem et noctem saltim, absque quam bulita æque valeret.

347. Aqua in qua semen lini diu per diem et noctem saltim steterit, recipit ab ipso semine glutinositatem quæ ipsam facit aptam ad distemperandum colores.

348. *Pour garder denreullir aucune chose de fer ou dacier burnies.*—Prenez salpetre, autrement appellee assafetide [afronitre ?] ou salnitre, le gros dune noiz et la moitie dun gobelet duille dolive, et deffaites tout ensemble, et le faites boulir, et puis le coulez par un drapel de lin et le gardez nettement et en oindez les dictes choses armoures ou autres besoignes a un drapel de lin ou de laine qui seroit meilleur moillie en icellui ille sans le mettre trop gros, car il est mieulz a le mettre delie, et puis aucune fois de deux ou troiz moiz les torcher et remettre.

349. *Pour faire fin azur.*—Vous devez prendre la pierre de lazur qui est Inde ou Pers, et vient des parties doultremer, et se treuve sur les appothicaires qui en font aucunes medicines ; et celle qui a vaines blanches vault mieulx que celle que les a dor, et se vous le mettez ou feu recuire, ou sur une platine de

plate of iron and when cool find it of the same colour as before, it is good. If you buy the said stone in powder, you must prove it in this manner, and then pound and grind it well on a flat piece of porphyry or other hard stone; then make a cement of turpentine and to a quarter of a pound of the said powder by weight add 4½ ounces of turpentine, and mix and incorporate together the powder and turpentine in a well-glazed earthen vessel, the turpentine being tepid before the powder is put into it. You must leave them in this state for the space of sixteen hours or thereabouts; then heat some water until it is tepid, throw it into the pot until the said mixture is covered with it, and stir the whole well together quickly and for a long time with a stick; then take the water, which will be rendered opaque by the blue colour, let it clear, and throw it into another new well-glazed earthen vessel, and let it settle, when the blue will fall to the bottom; then pour some more water on the mixture and stir it harder than before, and throw the water, which will thus be full of the blue colour, into another clean glazed vessel, and let it settle, when the blue will fall to the bottom. Then pour in tepid water for the third time, and stir the said mixture of turpentine and blue; pour off the water into another pot and let it settle, then pour the water off all three vessels, dry the blue and keep it. The first will be worth its weight in gold, the second its weight in silver, and the third is good for making grounds. For this reason each sort should be kept apart.

350. *When a horse has bad and troubled eyes.*—Take three or four leaves of *waide* [woad?] and the white of an egg, with salt of the size of a bean; put all these things in an egg-shell; sweep the hearthstone clean; put it on it, and let it dry until it can be easily powdered, then apply to the eye of the horse.

351. *To cure quartan fevers.*—Take an herb which is called "tettes de souris," of the size of a gall-nut, distemper it with white wine, and make the sick person drink it on the day he expects to be seized with this fever: he will be immediately cured.

fer chaude chaufer et puis le laissiez refroidier et il revient ou est de telle couleur que devant il est bon. Et pareillement eprouverez au feu la poudre de la dicte pierre se vous lachetez broye puis le devez bien broyer et mouldre bien sutil sur une pierre platte de porfire ou autre bien dure. Puis faites siment de termentina et pour un quarteron de la dicte pouldre a pois fault iiij onces et demie de termentine, et doit on en une paelle de terre bien plommee encorporer et mesler la dicte pouldre et pierre ou azur, avec la termantine qui soit un pou tiede, avant que la pouldre y soit mise et laissier ainsi par lespace de seize heures ou environ; et puis chauffez de leaue que elle soit tiede et en boutez en la paelle grant foison tant que celle mixtion soit couverte et remues ce bien et fort et hastivement et longuement a un bastonnet. Et liaue qui lors sera bien trouble de lazur, purez et boutez en une autre paiellete de terre neufve bien plommee et la mettez rasseoir et vostre azur se traira au fons. Puis mettez encor sur la dicte mixtion de leaue tiede et remuez plus fort que devant, et puis leaue qui ainsi sera trouble de lazur et la boutez en une autre paelle nette plommee et le laissiez aussi rasseoir et lazur descendre au fons. Puis remettez la tierce fois de leaue tiede, et remuez la dicte mixtion de trementine et dazur, et purez leaue en une autre paelle et laissiez rasseoir, et de toutes trois getez leaue et sechez et gardez lazur. Le premier vault son poiz dor, le second son poiz dargent, et le tiers est bon pour faire assiete. Et pour ce chacune sorte soit tenue apart.

350. *Quant un cheval a mauvais yeux et troubles.*—Prenez troiz ou quatre feuilles de waide et le blanc dun œufs et du sel le gros dune feve et mettez toutes ces choses en lescaille de lœf et netoiez lastre du feu et le metez dessus, et le laissiez tant secher que on en puisse faire pouldre et en mettez en leul du cheval.

351. *Pour garir de fievres quartainnes.*—Prenez dune herbe que lon appelle tettes de souris, le gros dune noiz galle, et le destrempez de vin blanc, et en faites boire le malade le jour que les fievres le doivent pranre, et tantot garira.

352. *To make cleret, which in Lombardy is called stellerie.*—Take an ounce of chanelle [canelle ?], half an ounce of ginger, 6 cloves, 8 grains of paradise grains, a little nutmeg, all these things well pulverized, half a pint of virgin honey, and a little wine. Distemper all these things together and strain them through a bag, the bottom of which is pointed into the vessel which contained the wine; and if it is not clear the first time of straining, replace it in the bag over the other, which meanwhile has been dripping, and on straining it will become clear.

THANK GOD.

This Book is composed by Master Jehan Le Begue, a Licentiate in the Law, Notary-General of the Masters of the King's Mint, at Paris, Anno Domini 1431, when he was 63 years of age.

352. *Pour faire cleret qui en Lombardie est appelle stellerie.* —Prenez une once de chanelle et demie de gingembre et six clox de girofle et viij grains de grainnes de paradis, et un po de noiz muscade, tout broye en pouldre, et demie pinte de larme de miel et un pot de vin, et les trempez tous ensamble, et puiz les coulez par le sachet agu dessoubs en le pot ou estoit le vin; et se le premier qui descend nest bien cler, remetez le au dit sachet sus lautre qui tondis coule et il revenra cler.

DEO GRATIAS.

Compositus est liber iste a magistro Johanne le Begue, Licentiato in Legibus, Greffario Generalium Magistrorum Monetæ Regis Parisiis, anno Domini 1431, ætatis vero suæ 63.

END OF VOL. I.

Medieval and Renaissance Treatises on the Arts of Painting

Volume II

CONTENTS OF VOL. II.

CAP. V.

CAP. VI.

CAP. VII.

CAP. VIII.

ERRATA.

Page 339, line 15 from top, *for* couch *read* coat.

377, dele *note* (1).

610, line	3 from	bottom, *for* "a putrido" is, *read* "a putrido," *i.e.* with.
668,	6	bottom, *for* sandals, *read* taffeta.
674,	6	top, *for* a stone impervious to water, *read* an absorbent stone.
712,	14	bottom, *for* with goatskin, and rub the work well, *read* and rub the work well with goatskin.
730,	14	bottom, *for* Riformati, *read* Riformate.
748,	8	top, *for* abazzo, *read* abbozzo.
796,	10	bottom, *for* Villalpandur, *read* Villalpandus.

BOLOGNESE MANUSCRIPT,

ENTITLED

"SEGRETI PER COLORI."

BOLOGNESE MANUSCRIPT.

PRELIMINARY OBSERVATIONS.

THIS MS. is of the fifteenth century. It is a small volume in duodecimo, on cotton paper, and is preserved in the Library of the R. R. Canonici Regolari in the convent of S. Salvatore in Bologna. It is numbered 165. On the outside of the fly-leaf is written "D'acquisto di D. Gio. Giuseppe Trombelli," and on the other side of the same "Libro di P. Gio. Batta Nozzi, di carte 240."

The first intimation we had of the existence of this MS. was from the 3rd series of the "Memorie di Belle Arti," p. 111, of Sig. Gualandi (Bologna, 1842), who mentions that it was with other MSS., in number about 500, carried to Paris, where the words "Bibliothèque Nationale" were stamped on it, and whence it has been since restored to its original depository.

On my arrival at Bologna Sig. Gualandi very kindly introduced my son to the Generale of the Canonici Regolari at the convent of S. Salvatore, and obtained permission for him to copy it.

It is a book of recipes rather than a treatise, and affords interesting notices of all the decorative arts practised at that period in Bologna. The arrangement

is systematic, and I consider it an arranged collection,[1] the author having copied different recipes as he became acquainted with them, and arranged them in their proper places, leaving blank sheets between each chapter or subject, for additional recipes. The name of the author does not appear; but as we find that the last sections in many of the chapters are written in a different character, it may safely be inferred that these additions were made at a period somewhat later than the rest of the MS., and probably after the death of the original collector. The additions, which appear by the handwriting to have been made at least half a century after the other part of the work, are written with fewer contractions, in a more running character, and with finer strokes to the letters; the black ink is not so pale, and the rubrics have nearly disappeared, while those of the earlier writing are as bright as at first. The later sections are distinguished in the present work by the letter B in the margin.

The language in which the MS. is written, is sometimes Italianised Latin, and sometimes Italian, with a mixture of Latin words, as was usual at that period, and the different recipes contain words from most of the dialects of Northern Italy, in which, however, the Lombard seems to prevail, and the same word is frequently spelled in three or four different ways.

The precise date of the MS. is not mentioned, but there are allusions to circumstances which seem to fix the date to the first quarter, or at latest, to the middle of the fifteenth century.

---

[1] That some of the recipes were copied is proved by the occasional blanks that are left in the MS.

In No. 136 is a recipe for making a "colore cardinalesco," in the later handwriting. Now the "colore cardinalesco" at this period was *crimson*, as appears from this chapter, and not scarlet. As the Cardinals did not assume the red dress until 1464,[1] it follows that this additional chapter must have been written previous to this date, and therefore that the original MS. was some years older. The author also desires that alabaster of Constantinople should be used for a certain purpose, a proof that the communication with that city still subsisted. This city was taken by Mahomet in 1452, and it is well known that the importation of pigments was impeded, if not altogether stopped, when the Turks became masters of Constantinople. (See Agricola, de Metallicis.) The different articles mentioned in the MS. show that Bologna at this period had considerable intercourse with other states. We find Giallolino and Azzurro della Magna, Spanish pitch, Roman tin, Venetian tin, Alexandrine borax, lapis lazuli from Damascus and Cyprus, sand from the Val d'Arno, besides the usual gums and resins, Indian lac, indigo, &c.

The first five books treat of the preparation and manufacture of blue, green, and lake-coloured pigments. The first book treats of natural blue pigments, by which we learn the old masters possessed two, namely, Ultramarine and the Azzurro della Magna of Cennini, also called in this MS. Azzurro Todesco or Azzurrum Teothonicum, Azzurro Spagnolo, and Azzurro di Lombardia. The author teaches how to distinguish one pigment from the other, and to prepare both for painting. The

---

1 See note by Sig. Tambroni to Cap. 42 of the Treatise of Cennini.

second book treats of factitious mineral blue pigments. The third book of blue pigments made from flowers. The fourth treats of green pigments. The fifth book shows that at this period lakes were made from lac, from kermes, and from Brazil wood, which last is identified with verzino — "verzino o vero Brasilio." The sixth book is devoted to the composition of "porporino," which was an imitation of gold. It also contains directions for gilding.

The seventh book is a practical course of painting after the manner of Magister Jacobus de Tholeto, who was probably a Spaniard.[1]

This book also commences with recipes in Italian for making certain colours, among which is the "arzica" of Cennini, and then follow directions in Latin, which appear to be from an older work, "ad fatiendum incarnatum pro incarnare figuras," "ad incarnandum crucifixum," "ad fatiendum incarnatum," &c. The author also gives instructions for preparing panels, and "gesso sottile" for painting.

The style of painting, as appears from the seventh book, resembled that which, according to Malvasia, prevailed in Bologna in the early part of the fifteenth century.

If we may be allowed to form an opinion of the skill of Magister Jacobus from his writings instead of his paintings, I fear we cannot assign him a high rank as a painter. The flesh colour was first to be laid on, then the eyes and outlines of the limbs were to be marked with black, the eyebrows with sinopia and black, the pupils of the eyes black, and a shade of sinopia under

---

[1] See No. 245. There was a Spanish college at Bologna; and S. Maria Maddalena, formerly an hospital under the title of S. Onofrio, was built in 1343 for the Spaniards.

the chin. These directions are sufficient to identify Jacobus with one of those painters who were contemporary with, or immediate successors of Lippo Dalmasio, described by Malvasia,[1] who, uninfluenced by the good example of Lippo, persisted in following the barbarous Greek style introduced from Constantinople. These artists lived in Bologna during the latter end of the fourteenth and beginning of the fifteenth century. Pietro di Lianori, who retained the Greek manner, and who surrounded his figures with black outlines, painted in the year 1415 a picture in the ancient church of S. Fidriano di Lucca in Bologna, then belonging to the R. R. Canonici Regolari, in whose library the original MS. from which the present is copied is still preserved, and there is nothing unreasonable in supposing that the MS. may describe his method of painting.

The vehicle used by Jacobus appears to have been egg and gum-water, but when it was required to make a drapery of a fine and beautiful rose colour, lac and ceruse were ground with linseed oil and white of egg.

After this we have an "aquam que est bona ad ponendum super figuris et altris miniis." This consists of oil of aloes, linseed oil, and "vernice liquida." And in order that no information should be wanting to his readers, Jacobus de Tholeto tells us how to make linseed oil, and then how to make "vernice liquida," for which he gives two recipes, the first made of linseed oil and "gomma de gineparo," the second of linseed oil, roche alum, and incense.[2]

---

1 Felsina Pittrice, vol. i. pp. 30, 31.

2 A third recipe, probably written by a later hand, for vernice liquida made of linseed oil and "vernice da scrivere," is given in No. 262.

It was the belief of Malvasia and Tiarini,[1] that Lippo Dalmasio and Pietro Lianori, both of whom must have been contemporaries, or nearly so, with the author of this MS., painted in oil; but chemists have asserted that it is impossible to decide whether paintings have been executed with colours mixed with oil, or whether they have been painted in distemper and then varnished.

There is nothing in the present MS. to show that the art of painting in oil was known at this period in Bologna (otherwise than in the imperfect manner before mentioned), although there is proof that the effects of boiling the oil, and not only of boiling, but of setting fire to it, were well understood. It is therefore probable, that the old pictures in Bologna which Malvasia says were painted in oil, were, in fact, painted in distemper, and then covered with the varnish described in the MS.; for if painting in oil had been practised at Bologna at the time the MS. was written, the author could scarcely have failed to become acquainted with it, and to record it in his work, as St. Audemar, Le Begue, and Cennini have done.

The art of distilling oils was also known and practised at this time in Italy, for the distilled or volatile oil of linseed is mentioned in No. 238, accompanied with a remark, that colours mixed with it will last for ever; and spirit of turpentine, the "acqua di ragia" of the Italians, is also spoken of in No. 246.

In No. 236 directions are given for preparing earths for use "in muro o in calcina." As these were tem-

---

[1] Felsina Pittrice, vol. i. p. 27.

pered with strong gum water, or with the white and yolk of an egg well mixed, and beaten with the branch of a fig-tree cut into small pieces, it is clear that the author does not speak of painting in "buon fresco;" at the same time it is doubtful whether he is speaking of painting, or merely of the letters or legends which were at that time frequently written on pictures.

The next subject treated of is the making of artificial gems, in which the author appears to have again had the assistance of his Spanish friend. The base of these factitious gems consists principally of a glass composed of crystal, calcined stag's bones, and sal alkali, without lead.

The early recipe in No. 268 for colouring glass red with copper, will be read with interest. The art of composing this colour was lost, although recipes for it have always existed. The note in the text alludes to a difficulty which exists in preparing this colour, from the tendency of the copper to pass into the state of peroxide, in which state it tinges glass green.[1]

The application of the diamond to cutting glass was, it is said, suggested by the well-known anecdote of Francis I., who, in order to let the Duchess d'Estampes know that he was jealous, wrote the following lines on a pane of glass, which, says Le Vieil (De la Peinture sur Verre, p. 206), may still be seen in his castle of Chambord:—

"Souvent femme varie
Mal habil qui s'y fie."

"The effect," he continues, "of the impression of one of the points of this diamond on the glass, caused

[1] See Beckmann's Inventions, tit. Coloured Glass, which contains some interesting notices respecting this colour.

it to be remarked that the characters were not only engraved on it, but that the glass was actually cut; thus an accident proved that the diamond was adapted for cutting glass, and doubtless gave rise to the practice which soon became general."

It is a pity to spoil so good a story by proving the invention to be older, but the truth must be told, and it will be seen by No. 217, that the art of cutting glass with a diamond was known and practised in Italy at the period when this MS. was written, that is, more than a century previous to the time of Francis I. The circumstance, trifling as it may appear, is useful in ascertaining the period when coloured glass was executed.

The same chapter (No. 217) also proves that the art of corroding glass by means of an acid was known and practised contemporaneously with the last-mentioned invention. The directions for preparing the acid liquor are so clear as to place this beyond a doubt. "When," says the author, "you wish to use this liquor, take equal quantities of each of these three waters; mix them together, draw with the mixed liquor upon the glass, and it will be cut exactly as you wish wherever it is wetted by this water." The fact of the three liquids being kept in separate bottles is a proof of their effects when mixed. They would probably have corroded the glass, which perhaps contained lead or other metals, easily acted upon by acids.

The invention of this art has been attributed by Beckmann to Henry Schwanhard, glass-cutter to the Emperor Rudolph in 1670; and the invention is said to have originated in the following occurrence:—Some aqua-fortis having one day fallen accidentally on the spectacles of Schwanhard, the glass was corroded by it,

and from this he learned to make a liquid by which he could etch writing and figures upon plates of glass.[1] Beckmann remarks, that it is not known how Schwanhard prepared this liquid, and that "at present we are acquainted with no acid, but that of fluor-spar, which will corrode every kind of glass."[2]

The conclusion of the same chapter in the MS., No. 217, also shows that glass mirrors were in general use.[3]

It will also be observed, that the art of painting on glass with enamels of various colours is distinctly described in No. 270; and the "smalti," or enamels, are also mentioned in No. 1. It is usually considered that these were not in use until after the middle of the sixteenth century: the chapter in the text will, I think, disprove this fact. The same "smalti" are also mentioned in the MS. of the Marciana (No. 325, which is of the sixteenth century), with the additional information that they were brought from Germany. It is probable, therefore, that they were in general use for painting on glass in Italy during the fifteenth and sixteenth centuries. Gaye has shown[4] that the windows in the Duomo d'Arezzo, painted in 1477 by Frati Cristophano and Bernardo, were to be executed with colours "cotte al fuoco e non messi a olio." The colours "cotte al fuoco" were, probably, these smalti, or enamel colours.

---

1 See Sandrart, Teutsche Akademie, vol. i. p. 346; Doppelmayer, p. 250.

2 Inventions, tit. Glass-cutting.

3 Glass mirrors are known with certainty to have been used in the thirteenth century.

4 Carteggio Inedito d'Artisti, vol. ii. p. 446.

This MS. also gives the composition of the old pigment Giallolino, which was made of lead, tin, red lead, and sand; and a method of applying leaf gold on glass, in which a solution of borax is the flux.

The author next treats of Mosaics, and first of the white material which serves as a base for the colours. The blue colour is produced by adding ultramarine to the white material. The red colour for the Mosaics is formed of tin and calx of gold, with other ingredients, thus affording a certain proof of the antiquity of red colours produced from gold.[1] While on the subject of the production of colours from gold, it may be mentioned that in No. 32 there is a description of the process of procuring a purple from gold, by dissolving it in aqua regia (nitro-muriatic acid), and then precipitating it with the oxide of tin, a process which seems analogous to the preparation of the purple of Cassius, and the date of this must be at least 150 years previous to the first notice of the purple of Cassius in the history of art. It will also be observed that No. 318 describes a yellow colour for painting made from silver, the discovery of which has been ascribed, although without sufficient foundation, to Van Eyck. The production of a yellow colour, for painting on glass, from silver, has always been attributed to the Flemings; but this recipe bears strong evidence of a French origin, for *French* ochre is directed to be used, and the ingredients are weighed by the usual French weights "denari." At the same time, however, it will be observed that the

---

[1] Mr. Hendrie (Theoph. E. E. p. 174) quotes some recipes for factitious gems from an old MS. in the British Museum (Sloane MSS., No. 3661), in which gold is used.

word "giallo" is written according to the Venetian dialect. The term "anconitani" proves that it was in use in Italy, and probably for painting on pottery as well as on glass. No. 322 also describes a gold colour made from silver, for painting vases previously glazed. This is one of the additional chapters, and may therefore have been written at a later period.

The next subject, glazes for pottery, is interesting because it shows what glazes were in use at this period. The base of the glaze employed was tin, to which was generally added Marzachotta, which was not the yellow oxide of lead, but probably a kind of frit like the composition called Mastichot, or Massicot, by the Dutch.

The colour with which the vases of Majolica and Damascus were painted is also described. These vases were known in Italy in the beginning of the fifteenth century. They are mentioned by Cennini as well as by the author of this MS., and in neither case as novelties.

Vasari attributes the invention of glazing pottery with a vitreous glaze, composed of tin, litharge, antimony, and other materials, to Luca della Robbia; now many of the glazes mentioned in this MS. contain tin and litharge [terraghetta], but none contain antimony. It is also worthy of remark, that one of the recipes teaches how to make blue in relief in the *Florentine* method. Some of these recipes may, therefore, have been similar to those used, or invented, by Luca della Robbia.[1] They certainly existed in Italy during the

1 Vasari (vol. ii. p. 47) says Luca was born at Florence in 1388. Passeri also (Storia delle Pitture in Majolica fatte in Pesaro e ne' luoghi circonvicini) attributes the invention of this art to Luca; others, observes Lanzi,

period when Luca was living, and are not mentioned as new inventions.

"Les pièces d'art," says M. de Brongniart, in his Traité des Arts Céramiques,[1] "dues à cette famille d'artistes Faienciers[2] [the family of Luca], ont pour gla-

vol. ii. p. 118, say the art was brought from China, whence it passed into the island of Majorca, and from thence into Italy, where it was principally cultivated in the state of Urbino. It was employed not only for vases and table-services, but also for statues and groups in relievo, some of which were coloured. The art reached the highest point of perfection in the period between 1540 and 1560. During this short interval were executed the most beautiful vases and table-services that were ever made of this material. (See De Brongniart, Traité des Arts Céramiques, p. 58.) In the early part of the fifteenth century Giorgio Andreoli, commonly called Maestro Giorgio, invented the beautiful ruby red colour which is seen on pottery of this period. He worked at Gubbio between 1511 and 1537. The Duke Guidobaldo of Urbino took great interest in this art, and maintained a factory of it at his own expense. In order to secure good designs he prohibited the artificers from designing the works themselves, and compelled them to use prints after great artists, and especially after Raffaello; and this gave rise, observes Lanzi, to certain reports concerning this artist and his father, and the nickname of the "Boccalajo di Urbino," which was given to the great painter.[a] Many designs of Michael Angelo, of Raffaello del Colle, and other great artists, were executed in this material, and many painters were employed in making designs purposely for it; and Taddeo Zuccaro relates, that the designs for the service made for Philip II. of Spain were by Batista Franco. Services were made also for Charles the Fifth and other princes; and they were held in such esteem that Christina of Sweden offered to replace with silver vessels those which are now in the S. Casa at Loreto, which she desired to possess. See Lanzi, vol. ii. p. 117—120. De Brongniart, Traité des Arts Céramiques, pp. 55—59.

[1] See Traité des Arts Céramiques ou des Poteries considérées dans leur histoire, leur pratique, et leur théorie. Par Alex. Brongniart. 2 vols. 8vo. Paris, pp. 55—57.

[2] The French term "fayence," earthenware, was derived from Faenza, in Italy, where it was formerly made.

[a] Another reason for this appellation was, that one of the most skilful painters of this porcelain was also called Raffaello—his surname was Ciarla. His works then were truly said to have been painted by Raffaello, and the vulgar supposed they were by Raffaello Sanzio. See Lanzi, vol. ii. p. 119, n.

çure un véritable émail stannifère, bien glacé, dur, sans gerçure." The principal colours employed are, according to the same writer:—

A tolerably pure yellow, produced by lead and antimony.

An opaque, pure, and dark blue; sometimes like enamel, sometimes as if applied on the surface.

Copper green.

The dirty violet from Manganese.

He adds, "These baked earths, with ornaments in relief of white and coloured enamels, were, for some time, the only coloured stanniferous pottery made in Italy. The manufacture of this varnished pottery, which Passeri calls 'semi-porcelain,' is still continued at Pesaro. This glazing was very beautiful."

It is evident that the pottery described by M. de Brongniart resembles that for which the recipes are given in the MS. They have the same ornaments in relief of white and colours, and the colours used appear to be nearly the same.

The principal variation is in the yellow, which De Brongniart states consisted of lead and antimony; but he does not add that this statement is the result of analysis; and he may have named antimony on the authority of Vasari, who wrote above 100 years after the death of Luca, and who might therefore have been deceived as to the time when antimony was first used. It will be seen by referring to the MS., that the yellows were produced by lead (see Nos. 298, 299), and by silver (see No. 318).

The pure, dark, opaque blue appears to have been ultramarine. In No. 303, the blue colouring matter is called Zafirro, and in other recipes "azurro" only; but

to judge from the colour and appearance of the blue on old Italian pottery, there is every probability that it was produced by ultramarine.

The copper greens are mentioned in Nos. 300, 301; the violet azure in No. 311. The latter was produced by adding Manganese to the azure.

This is the only colour approaching to red which is mentioned in these recipes, excepting that which may be produced by exposing "crocus martis" to the action of fire, for the colouring of the Damascus or Majolica vases. See No. 316.

The recipe in No. 284, for making a baked vase white without painting it, is worthy of notice as a historical fact; because Passeri, the great authority on this subject, says, "It was only towards the year 1500, that the idea occurred at Pesaro, of employing this stanniferous glaze, as the glazing of earthenware, and as the white ground, on which were executed those beautiful paintings, which have given so much celebrity to this pottery, under the name of Majolica, and even under that of porcelain, a name which it owes to the beauty of its enamel."

It is singular that although the author treats of making artificial gems of glass, of Mosaics, and of glazes for pottery, he should have omitted to treat of painting on glass[1] for windows; which was certainly known long previous to the date of this MS.,[2] and which was practised at this period in England, France, Flanders, Germany, and in some parts of Italy.

---

[1] Unless windows may be included under the head of "any other works in glass," in No. 270.

[2] See the MSS. of Theophilus, Book ii., and of Eraclius.

On looking, however, into the early history of Bologna, it will be found that the most ancient painted glass in that city (which is in the Church of S. Petronio) was not executed until the middle, or end, of the fifteenth century (consequently after the date of this MS.) by a lay Dominican, Beato Giacomo da Ulmo,[1] who was much addicted to painting, or, as it was then called, "writing" on glass; and who "was the only person at that period who practised this art in Bologna."

But although our author does not mention painted glass windows, he mentions three substitutes, or imitations, which, he says, "will appear like real glass." The first[2] consists of parchment, which is to be painted, and then varnished on the painted side; the second of parchment painted, and then covered with a couch of linseed oil; the third of linen also painted, and varnished with Vernice Liquida.

It is not mentioned whether these windows were intended for churches or private houses.

The MS. concludes with a treatise on dyeing silks, thread, linen, and leather; on the last subject it is very voluminous. To these are added a few miscellaneous recipes, among which are some for glues and cements of various kinds.

The unfinished Table of Contents is by another hand, probably of the seventeenth century.

---

1 B. Giacomo was born at Ulm in Germany in 1407. In his youth his devotion led him to Rome, then he became a soldier. Afterwards he went to Bologna, where he assumed the habit of a lay Dominican, and gave himself up to painting on glass and working miracles. He died in the odour of sanctity in 1491. See the Guida di Bologna. Marchese, Vite de' Pittori, &c., Domenicani.

2 See No. 165.

SECRETS FOR COLOURS.

HERE BEGINS A TREATISE

ON PREPARING VARIOUS KINDS OF NATURAL AZURES. AND FIRST WE MUST TREAT OF THE KNOWLEDGE OF THE SPECIES AND NATURE OF THE UNDER-MENTIONED LAPIS LAZULI, FROM WHICH NATURAL AZURE, THAT IS, ULTRAMARINE AZURE IS MADE. AND I WILL DESCRIBE THE MODE OF TRYING THE STONE.

1. *To know the quality and nature of good stones without amalis.*[1]—Know that lapis lazuli is a mineral stone which comes from beyond the sea. Many persons sell it in powder, and some sell it in entire pieces; it is of various sorts, and one stone may be of much greater value than another. Some stones are of a purple colour, and some of a dark violet, with red veins, and in some of the crevices is red earth; and this stone is not so brilliant as smalt.[2] And if its vein is white, or if there should be no spots of white here and there upon it, and if it should break easily, such stones are not very fine, because you cannot extract from them more than half their weight of fine azure; and in exchanging these stones you lose a great deal, therefore none will trouble themselves about them but those that are unpractised. Many say that the best lapis lazuli is a stone of a blue colour, which appears to have something of a violet tinge, with vein-like spots of gold in it; and it is mixed with a whitish stone, and is very hard to break. And observe that the following is the test by which to distinguish the good from the bad:—First take a piece of the stone and

[1] Amalis. Query, Amulets or Charms?

[2] It is almost unnecessary to observe that the colour we call Smalt was not known until long after the date of this MS.; I have, however, retained

SEGRETI PER COLORI.

INCIPIT TRATATUS

DE MULTIS ET DIVERSIS AZURRIS NATURALIBUS FIENDIS. ET PRIMO DICENDUM EST DE COGNITIONE SPETIE ET NATURA SUBSCRIPTI LAPIDIS LAZULII EX QUO FIT AZURRUM NATURALE SCILICET AZURRUM OLTRAMARINUM. ET DICAM DE PROBATIONE IPSIUS LAPIDIS.

1. *Ad cognoscendum qualitatem et naturam bonorum lapidum ab aliis sine amalis.*—Sappi che lo lapis lazuli e una petra de minera che vieni ultra mare. Molti la vendino impolvere e alcuni la vendino impezi integri e sonno de piu ragioni e de molto piu fia una pretra che un altra. Alcune petre sonno de colore pavonazo, alcune de colore violato scuro e tiene la sua vena de rosso e in alcuni de li suoi canthoni hala terra rossa e non e la dicta petra troppo splendente quemadmodum de smalto. E se la sua vena fusse bianca o non fusse in qua e in la alcuna gocia de bianco e sia tenera a rompere : queste cotale petre non sonno troppo fini perche non se ne po cavare oltra a la meza de bono azurro e a mercatare queste cotale petre se ne scapita in grosso impero non se ne vole impaciare che qualunque non ha bona pratica. Molti dicano che lo lapis lazuli optimo e una petra che celistrineggia e pare che tenga in se uono colore violato cum sentille di vene doro e ha misture de petre bianchette e de asa ben dura a romperla. E nota che questa e la sperientia de sapere quale sonno bone e quale sonno rei. Prima tolli uno pezo de le dicte petre e metila in nel

the name for want of a better term. I consider it to mean those coloured glasses, or enamels, mentioned in the MS. of the Marciana, No. 325, which were brought from Germany, and which were used in painting on glass.

put it into the fire, and let it become quite red hot, then take it out and let it cool by itself; and when it is cold, if the stone retains its colour and does not become pale, it is good. But if it both improves and retains its colour, it is both good and perfect. As for those stones which change the beauty of their primitive colour, we must consider how many degrees they have changed, because there are some stones which the more they lose the finer they are. And let us suppose that the loss of colour does not proceed from the quantity of earthy matter contained in the stone, that is to say, that what azure it does contain is of good quality. But if it should proceed from the mixtures which are contained in the stone, we must nevertheless consider the difference made by this loss of colour, because it will yield less; and this is known by its not being of an uniform colour after it has been in the fire, but retaining its colour better in one part than in another. If it happens that the stone loses all its colour, then from whatever part it may have been dug, it is not ultramarine and is not fine, and consequently you cannot procure ultramarine azure from it, because the base of the azure, that is the stone, is not ultramarine. And even if it were ultramarine, it may contain so little substance as not to make it worth while to work it, because you would spend money without any advantage whatsoever; and the price of these stones in Italy commonly varies from 2 to 5 ducats a pound, according as they are more or less fine.

2. *To distinguish German or Teutonic azure from the other; and some notice of the stone from which this German azure is made.*—Know that the German azure is of several sorts, as is well known to those who have any knowledge and experience of it, because it usually contains in itself the stone from which this colour is made; it is partly of a pale and opaque blue, and partly earthy, of a yellow colour and frangible, so as to be broken by the nail; and these are the noblest azures of Germany that are found, and they usually appear somewhat translucent or transparent if you keep your eyes steadily fixed on them; but in this experience is the best guide. The value of

fuoco e farla ben infocare de vantagio poi il tra fuora e lassala fredare da se stessa e quando sera refredata se la dicta petra sta in suo colore che non smortisca e bona. Ma se migliorasse collore che lo mantenga e perfecta e bona. Ma quelle che mutano la bellezza dal primo collore e da considerar in quanti gradi se mutano per che ce sonno de quelle che quanto piu smontano tanto sonno piu fini. E poniamo che lo smontare non procedesse da la quantita de la terra de la petra cio e che quello cotanto che tene de azurro e de bona natura. Ma se procedesse dale misture che sonno cum la petra nondimeno e da fare la defirentia per lo callo imperho che renderia meno e questo se cognosce quando e stato in el fuoco non torna tuta duno collore, in alcun luoco se mantieni melglio che in uno altro. Ma se devinisse che la petra perdesse tutto el colore suo questa tale petra de qualunque parte fussero cavate non sonno de ultramare e non sonno fini e per consequentia non ne poresti cavare azurro ultramarino perche lo suo fondamento cio e la petra non e de de oltramare. E ben che fussero de ultramare possino tenere tanto poco de substantia che non seria da impaciarsine imperho che faresti la spesa senza utili alcuno e li pregi de le dicte petre in nele parte de ytalia communamente combatino da li doi ducati infino in cinque la libra e secondo che sonno più e meno belle.

2. *Ad cognoscendum azurrum almaneum sive Teothonicum ab alio et aliquam notitiam ipsius lapidis ex quo fit predictum azurrum almaneum.*—Sappi che lo azurro de la magna e de piu maineri secondo che ello e manifesto a chi de esso ha alcuna notitia e sperientia imperho che sole havere in se la petra che che se ne fa el dicto azurro parte de vena camillina e parte terra e de de collore croceo e sono frangibili a romperle cum l' ognia e quelli sono piu nobili azurri de lamagna che se trovino e soglino esse piu penetrabili e trasparenti a chi tiene ben gliochi fissi in questo la experientia da molto piu dotrina che altra cosa. E li pregi loro in partibus ytale combatano dali

these stones in Italy varies from 12 bolognini[1] a pound to 20 or even 30 bolognini, when they are of very good colour and appearance. And know that the price of the azures, when extracted and refined, commonly varies from 1 to 3 ducats the pound, more or less, according as they are more or less fine.

3. *Here begins the practice of extracting the azure from the lapis lazuli, and of refining it.*[2]—Azure is of two kinds, namely natural and artificial; it is refined in the following manner:—Take the stone, which is a mineral, and after washing it with ley, heat it on burning charcoal, and afterwards extinguish it in good and very strong white vinegar; then break it with a mallet on an iron anvil. Choose the good pieces, and grind them fine in a brass mortar well covered, lest the finer particles should escape; when very finely ground put the powder into an earthen dish and pour over it hot water or hot ley with a little honey and clay, rubbing the azure with your hands or with a stick, in order to extract the refined azure, and note that the water comes off of a green colour. Afterwards strain it through a linen cloth into a well-glazed earthenware basin,[3] and pour off the water, or, still better, the ley, leaving the powder of the lapis lazuli settled in the basin; wash the azure with tepid but not hot water in a porphyry vessel, until the saline particles of the ley are washed away, and let the azure dry in the shade in the porphyry vessel; keep it in a bladder or in a purse of chamois leather: and note that if it is not of a good colour, or if it inclines to paleness, boil "Brasil-wood"[4] reduced to powder, in good ley or pure water, and then strain it through a cloth and put into it a little "alumen jameni," or glasso,[5] and mix with your azure already re-

---

1 Bolognini, coins of the value of six quattrini, or a bajoccho, equal to an English halfpenny.

2 There is another version of this chapter in a small MS. in the Bibliothèque Royale, at Paris, No. vi. MDCCXLIX. No. 9, entitled "Anonymous Tractatus de Coloribus." The volume of which it forms part was dated 1481. The principal variations have been noticed.

12 bol la libra o ali vinti bol e per infino trenta bol la libra quando fussero avantagiati in colore et in apparentia. E sapi che li pregi de li azurri tracti e affinati comunamente combatino da uno ducato in fino a 3 ducati la libra e piu e meno secondo che sonno belli.

3. *Incipit pratica ad extrahendum azurrum de lapide lazuli et ipsum affinando.*—Duplex est azurrum, scilicet naturale et artificiale et ipsorum vero affinatio in modo asignatur isto. Accipiatur lapidem istum qui est mineralis et igniatur post lavationem lexivii inter prunas ignitas postea extinguatur in perfecto et acerrimo aceto albo postea frange ipsum cum malleo in ferrea incudenea et elige bonas partes et subtiliter terrantur in mortario hereo optime coperto ne vapor ejus evalescat et cum fuerit per optime tritum ponatur in patella terrea et de super pone aquam calidam sive lexivium calidum cum modico melle obluto et ipsum azurrum manibus fricando vel cum baculo ut exeat azurrum afinatum et nota quod prædicta aqua efficitur viridis colloris postea cola per pannum lineum in lavella terrea ben vitriata post aquam sive lexivium quod melius est effundatur et pulvis lazuli in lavella residens postea ablue dictum lazurinum cum aqua tepida et non nimis calida in porfido donec salsedo lexivii exeat et permitte ipsum azurrum ad umbram siccari in prædicto porfido et servetur in visica in bursia camussi. Et nota quod si non est boni colloris vel tendens ad pallorem dequoque [Brasilium] in pulverem deductum in bono lixivio vel aqua pura postea per pannum cola et impone aliquantulum aluminis Jameni vel glasso, et

[3] The Paris MS. has "patella ferrea bene plumbata."

[4] Brasilium. The word has been supplied from the Paris MS.

[5] The parallel passage in the Paris MS. has "Alumine glaro," which appears to be synonymous with roche alum. See Cennino, chap. lxii., and the MS. of Le Begue, Nos. 42 and 299, where it is called "Alumen glacie" and "Alumen glarum;" and in No. 313 it is called simply "glace." I have little doubt that in all these passages roche alum is to be understood.

The term Alumen Jameni occurs in Geber's work on Alchemy. It also occurs in the Le Begue MS.

fined, and this gives it a good colour and will increase its weight.

4. *The mode of working the powder of the before-mentioned stone into the pastille.*—Take of mastic 1 lb., strained fine resin ½ lb., soap from goat or mutton suet ½ lb., new wax 2 lb., liquid varnish 2 lb., linseed oil 1 oz. First melt the wax and soap in a glazed jar, then the resin and the mastic in powder, and afterwards the varnish and oil, and mix them with a spatula so as to incorporate them, and afterwards try if the composition is well made and sufficiently thick by putting one drop into water; the mixture hardens if it is well done, if not, boil it until it becomes hard, which done, strain it through a linen cloth into a basin full of clear cold water and put it by. When you want to use it, take equal quantities of the pastille and of lapis lazuli, and incorporate your mineral, reduced into very fine powder, with the pastille; then put the pastille mixed with the powder into some glazed jar, and let the jar be half full of cold water, so that the water may cover the pastille by three fingers' width at the most, and let it remain in the water for 15 days, and the longer the better; afterwards remove the pastille from the water, and take good strong ley, which should be rather warm, and with it extract the azure from the pastille, rubbing it with your hands in a glazed jar, and pouring by degrees the warm ley over it; when you see the ley become blue pour it off by itself and put it into another glazed jar, and continue to do this until you have two other azures, not so fine as the first, and this you will know by experience. Then boil each sort separately with the ley and take off the scum neatly and carefully with a spoon; when you have done this let it stand for a day and a night until all the azure settles at the bottom; then separate the ley from the azure with a sponge, and wash the azure with clean water until all the saltness of the ley is extracted from it, then let it rest and the azure will sink to the bottom; when settled pour off the water, let the azure dry in the shade, and afterwards keep it in lambskin or sheepskin, and take care not to expose it too much to the air.

misce cum tuo azurro jam affinato et per hoc dat bonum collorem et augmentabitur in pondere.

4. *Modus autem ponendi dictum pulverem ipsius lapidis in pastillum.*—Accipe de mastice lb. unam, ragia pini collata lb. mediam, et de sapone caprino vel aretino lb. mediam, cera nova lb. duas, vernicis liquidæ lb. duas, olei seminis lini oz. 1; primo funde ceram et saponem in olla vitriata postea pone ragiam et pulverem masticis postea vernicis et olei et cum spatula misce ut incorporantur postea tenta si fuerit cottum et spissum dico ponendo guttam unam in aquam si firmatur bene est si non coque ut dum firmatur quo viso cola per pannum lini in quodam vase pleno aqua clara et frigida et serva quum volueris eo uti accipe tantum de dicto pastillo quantum de pulvere lapidis et incorpora mineram tuam in subtilissimam pulverem reductam cum prædicto pastillo postea mite dictum pastillum cum dicto pulvere mistum in quodam vase vitriato et in dicto vase sit aquam claram usque ad medium vel tribus digitis ad plus supra pastillum et dimite stare in dita aqua per 15^im^ dies et quanto plus tanto melius postea extrahe dictum pastillum de dicta aqua et habeas lescivium bonum et forte et cum dicto lescivio aliquantulum calido extrahe azurrum de dicto pastillo et ipsum manibus fricando in alico vase vitriato et paulatim de dicto liscivio calido desuper mitendo et quando videbis azurrum extrahe de per se et mite in alio vase vitriato et sic continua donec habeas alios duos azurros variatos non ita bonos quam primum et demostrabitur per experientiam et cum dicto liscivio facias aliquantulum bulire quemlibet sortem de per se et cum uno coclario acipias spumam suavis et ingeniose et quando erit sic operatum permicte sic stare per diem et noctem donec totum azurrum petat fundum postea sepera liscivium ab azurro cum spongia et ablue dictum azurrum cum clara acqua donec omnis salsedo liscivii exseat et permicte possare donec azurrum petat fundum postea eice aquam soprastantem et dictum azurrum permicte sicari ad humbram postea conserva eum in corio agnilino vel aretino et cave ne ayer nimis tanget eum. Et intellige quod azurrum ultramarinum

And know that citramarine[1] azure must be refined by a ley and not by a pastille, because it is coarse and not heavy, and cannot be extracted in any manner by means of a pastille, or otherwise than by a good ley impregnated with Roman soap, and this ultramarine, or German or Spanish azure, or that which is brought from Lombardy, is refined in the following manner by means of a ley. Take very clear ley made from the sifted ashes of brushwood[2] and dissolve a considerable quantity of Roman soap so as to make it very viscid, put your mineral reduced to a very fine powder into the ley and afterwards make it boil a little over the fire; stir it gently with a spoon, then, pouring off the ley by degrees, you will find a very beautiful refined azure at the bottom of the jar; afterwards wash it with pure water, to remove the viscosity, and strain it through a linen cloth, and you will have natural azure.

5. *Another sort of pastille is made thus.*—Take of the best dried pine resin 6 oz., mastic 6 oz., of new wax 2 oz., of linseed oil 4 oz.; put all these things upon the fire, and do with everything as you were directed to do for the other pastille. When you wish to incorporate the pastille with the powder directly, take the pastille out of the water and rub it well in your hands, which you must grease with linseed oil. If the pastille spreads well, it is right; if not, repeat the boiling until you can spread it out well, and knead it like wax; then take a porphyry slab, oil it with linseed oil, spread out the pastille flat upon it, and immediately sprinkle over it some of the powder of lapis lazuli, kneading it up with your hands until one pound of the powder is kneaded up with 16 oz. of the pastille, then put the pastille, together with the powder, into cold water in any glazed jar, and let it remain as before in

---

1 This part of the chapter is nearly a transcript of part of the Paris MS. before mentioned.

I have supplied the word "Citramarine" from the Paris MS., which appears the most correct. In the first part of the Bolognese MS., the author has described the method of preparing the true Ultramarine, or Azurrum Transmarinum, with the pastille; but he is now speaking of another kind of azure, for which a ley was to be used instead of a pastille. This last

debet debet affinari per capitellum et non per pastillum: quia grossum est et non ponderosum nullo modo extrahitur pastillo nisi bono capitello sapone romano infecto et dictum azurrum ultramarinum vel almaneum vel ispaneum vel de lombardia aportatum affinatur hoc modo per viam capitelli. Acipe lescivium de cineribus crebellatis et sit bene clarum in quo dissolve saponem romanum in bona quantitate ut sit bene vischosum in quo pone mineram tuam in subtilissimam pulverem reductam postea ad ignem fatias aliquantulum bolire fatias et eum move plane et moderate cum spatula postea paulatim effuso capitello invenies azurrum[2] pulcherrimum in fundo vasis affinatum postea eum lava cum pura aqua ut auferatur ab eo viscositas et postea colabis per pannum lineum et habebis azurrum valde naturalem.

5. *Alium pastillum sic fit.*—Summe ragia pini optime sicce oz. 6, masticis oz. 6, ceræ nove oz. 2, olei seminis lini oz. 4, hæc omnia pone super ignem et fac per omnia ut supra habuisti in alio pastillo. Et quando vis dictum pastillum cum pulvere incorporare subito acipe dictum pastillum de aqua et ipsum ducas per manus multum bene perunta manus de oleo lini et si dictum pastillum bene extenderetur bene est si non reitera decotionem donec se possi bene extendere et ducere per manus sicut cera tunc habeas porfidum et undem unge cum oleo lini et de super pone dictum ditum pastillum extensum super dictum porfidum sic splanata et aspergas subito de dito pulvere lazuli desuper et ipsum manibus incorporando donec una libra dicti pulveris incorporetur cum sexdecim unciis dicti pastilli et hoc facto pone dictum pastillum cum pulvere incorporato in aqua frigida in quodam vase vitri-

---

azure, he says, was brought from "Almania ut de Anglia ut Ispanea seu Lombardia;" a proof that this pigment was not produced in Germany only. Cennini also speaks of its being found at Siena.

[2] Subcarbonas Potassæ impurus, Impure potash, or pearl-ash. It is generally prepared by burning land plants, or wood; in Italy vine branches were generally used for this purpose.

another pastille not so good, and do as before; and note that if you wish to colour the azure, take a little spirit of wine and put it into the water with some good verzino; but this does not belong to the art of preparing azure.

6. *To extract the gold from the lapis lazuli.*[1]—Take the before-mentioned mineral lapis lazuli, and break it on an anvil or in a covered brass mortar, and put it in a basin of cold water, and you will see that it has veins of gold, and that sort is good. If you want the gold, pick it out piece by piece.

7. *To make good azure and refine it by means of a pastille.*—Take as much lapis lazuli as you like and pound it very finely and carefully in a brass mortar, afterwards grind it on porphyry with clear water so as to become almost impalpable, because in this state it will work better, and let it dry.

8. *The manner of working the before-mentioned azure into a pastille.*—Take for every pound of lard, one pound of pine resin and one ounce of Spanish pitch; then take a jar, free from fat, and melt the lard in it, and when it is melted and strained add clean pine resin, and mix it well, so that the ingredients may be incorporated together, afterwards add the Spanish pitch; mix all thoroughly together, and let the mixture be as liquid as water. Then pour upon it a little common oil, or linseed oil, and remove the jar from the fire, continually stirring it with the stick while it is cooling. When you wish to put the powder of the lapis lazuli into this pastille, take equal quantities of the pastille and of the stone reduced to powder, and melt the pastille over the fire in a glazed vessel, and when it is liquid like water put your stone into it, and mix it well with a stick; afterwards take it away from the fire, and let it remain from evening to morning, or even longer; then heat it at the fire until nearly liquefied. You must place by the fire a pot full of water, tepid, but not hot, in which you must put the pastille for a short time, then take a glazed jar

---

[1] Gold is not actually found in the Lapis Lazuli; but the spots and veins which resemble this mineral consist of sulphuret of iron, which is always more or less present in the mineral. The Romans called the Lapis Lazuli

ato et permitte stare ut supra in alio pastillo non tam bono et sequere ut supra. Et nota quod si vis ipsum collorare acipere modicum aquæ ardentis et intus in ipsa aqua pone aliquantulum de virzino bono tamen non est de arte azurorum.

6. *A cavar loro de lo lapis lazuli.*—Accipe dictum lapidem mineralem lazurrinum et eum frange in ancudenea sive in mortare hereo coperto et pone ipso in quodam vase ut sit de aqua frigida et videbis venas aureas habentes et illud est bonum. Et si vis aurum acipe ipsum paulatim paulatim.

7. *Affare azurro bono et afinarlo per via de pastillo, viz.*—Recipe de lapide lazuli quantum vis et eum pista in mortareo hereo valde bene et caute postea macina ipsum in porfido cum clara aqua quantum potest ut veniat subtile quasi sine tacta quia melius operabit deinde demicte eum sicari.

8. *Modus ponendi sopradictum azurrum in pastillum.*—Summe per omni libra lardi lb. unam ragia pini et et untiam unam pegule spagnole postea habeas ollam unam multum nitidam a pinguedine deinde mitte lardum dictum in ditta olla ad colandum et quando colatum fuerit tunc mite ragia pini munda et mistica bene ut incorporantur postea impone desuper dictam pegulam spagnolam et insimul incorpora valde bene ut deveniat sicut aqua deinde impone desuper aliquantulum olei communis vel seminis lini postea remove dictam ollam ab igne semper mistando cum baculo dum refrigiatur. Et quando vis mittere dictum pulverem lapidis lazuli in hunc pastillum accipe tanto de dicto pastillo quanto de dicto lapide in pulverem redutto deinde recipe dictum pastillum et mitte eum ad ignem ad liquefaciendum in quodam vase vitriato e cum liquefactum fuerit ad modum aquæ tunc impone lapidem tuum et mistica bene cum uno baculo postea sepera eum ab igne et dimitte sic stare a sero usque ad mane vel plus deinde calefac eum ad ignem ut deveniat quasi liquidum et habeas ad ignem ollam unam aquæ plenam dico quod aqua sit tepida et non

---

of this description, Saphirus Regius, under the supposition that it contained gold. See Bachhoffner, Chemistry applied to the Arts.

with hot water and pour it on to the pastille, mixing it continually; and as the pastille loses its azure, keep continually adding hot water; and note, that if the pastille should break, you must not knead it, but let it stand a little, and pour off the water from the pastille, then pour some other hotter water on the pastille, in the manner you did before, and mix it: and observe, that when the azure changes colour, you must immediately pour off the coloured water into another vase; and it will be of less value than the first. If you choose to return this into the first pastille another time, then it will come out like the first azure; and know, that when you take the second azure extracted from the pastille, you can put it back a second time, and it will come out a better azure. And note also, that all the powders of lapis lazuli, when they are put into the pastille, diminish and lose one half. If you wish to extract completely the whole of your azure from the pastille, make it boil in ley until the pastille becomes white, and then prepare it in this way:—Take the first jar (and do the same with the others) and strain the contents into another jar through a thick piece of white linen cloth; then take another clean jar and rub the piece of linen to and fro upon the bottom of it, and all the good azure will be extracted: if it were squeezed, the azure would get into the pores of the linen. Then pour it into that which has been strained through the linen, and let it settle until it all sinks to the bottom; throw away the water, and heat the powder with clear ley so that it may boil a little; then throw it into another jar, and let it rest until it sinks to the bottom; next take out the ley dexterously and cautiously with a sponge, and pour clean water into it and mix it well. Then let it stand, and take out the water in the same way that you did the ley, and let it dry in the shade, and keep it in a purse.

9. *To make ultramarine azure another way.*—Take the mineral stone of the lapis lazuli, which has veins of gold, and which is of a blue colour, and this is the finest sort. Divide the stones into three classes; and first select the cleanest and

calida et in ipsa olla cum aqua tepida mite aliquantulum dictum pastillum postea habeas catinum unum vitriatum cum aqua calida et mite intus dictum pastillum semper misticando et quando pastillum deficit de azurro renova semper aquam magis calidam. Et nota quod si pastillum frangeretur cave ne tu misticas sed dimete ipsum stare aliquantulum et separa aquam a pastillo et desuper pastillum impone de alia aqua magis calida per supradictum modum et mistica. Et nota quod quando azurrum mutat colorem statim sepera aquam azurrinam in alio vase et erit minoris pretii quam primum. Et si vis retornare aliam vicem in pastillo primo dum supradictum veniet ut primum azurrum. Et intelige quando tu acipias azurum secundum extractum de pastillo tu potest eum remictere alia vice in pastillo veniet tibi meliorem azurrum. Et nota quod omnes pulveres lapidum lazulorum ut mictantur in pastillum defitiunt et callant per medium et si vis extrahere penitus azurrum de pastillo fac eum bullire in lexivio dummodo pastillus deveniat albus postea acipe azurrum illum et eum quoque per hunc modum acipe primum catinum et sic reitera cum aliis et cola in uno alio catino per unam petiam spissam panni lini albam et acipe alterum catinum netidum e poi mena la dita peza suso per li fondi e tuto lo azurro buono uscira fuora perchè se se stringesse intraria in la peza e poi metilo in quello che sia colato con la peza e poi lo lassa posare infino che e tutto al fondo poi gietta via laqua et fallo bulire cum liscia chiara tanto che bolla uno poco poi giettalo in uno catino e lassalo possare tanto che vada al fondo poi cava la liscia fuora dextramente et ingeniose cum una spongna poi mecti dentro de laqua chiara e misticalo bene poi lassa posare e cava fora laqua per lo modo che cavasti la liscia poi lassalo secare a lombra et servalo in bursia.

9. *Affare azurro ultramarinum per alium modum.*—Tolli de la petra minerale de lo lapis lazuli la quale tene de vene doro e de di collore cillistrino e quella e la più fina della quale preta ne farai tre sorte prima elleggio le piu nectc e le piu

finest, which contain no stone or earth; second, choose those that are of the middling sort; and, thirdly, those that remain, which belong to the third sort; and put each sort by itself. Then put those which you wish to use into a crucible, cover it with a tile, and put it on a charcoal fire or in a hot oven for a whole day; then quench the stone in hot vinegar, and afterwards pound it in a bronze mortar, well covered, and sift it very fine. Then put the azure into a glazed jar with pure water, and stir it with your hand or with a stick, and let it rest. Remove the water carefully with a sponge, then grind the azure well on a porphyry slab, and afterwards put it into pure water in a jar, and stir it well with a stick. Then let it rest for the space of a *pater noster*, after which pour that water into a clean glass, because the finest azure is that which will remain at the bottom. You must grind the inferior azure which remains a second time, as before. Then take out the coloured water and lay it aside, and do as before; then grind it again, and do this until there remains no more azure, and when you have put away all the waters by themselves, let them settle well, so that all the azure may sink to the bottom and the water remain clear above. Then take off the water with a sponge as before, and when you have completely removed it, wash the azure with tepid caustic ley[1], stir it well with a stick, let it settle, and then take out the ley as you did the water, and let it dry in the shade. This is the true preparation of ultramarine.

10. *Mode of making a pastille to extract the azure from the lapis lazuli.*—Take of pine resin oz. viij, Greek pitch oz. iiij, mastic half an ounce, linseed oil oz. ij; then take a glazed pipkin, and put it upon a tripod over a slow and clear fire, and when it begins to get hot, put into it first the linseed oil, and let it warm a little; then add the Greek pitch in powder, and incorporate it thoroughly with the oil, mixing it with a stick until it is done; and you will know when it is done by trying it

[1] Ranno da Capo is probably the same as *Capitello*. The term *ranno* is Tuscan.

belle le quale non tengano de spetie de alcuna altra petra o vero de terra. Secundo eleggie la mezana sorte. Tertio eleggie quelle che avanzano che e la terza sorte e metti omni una da per se e poi meti quelle che tu voi lavorare in uno crugiolo e coprilo cum una tegola e mectilo al fuoco de carboni o vero in lo forno caldo tuto uno di e poi immortalo cum aceto forte poi lo pista in uno mortaro de bronzo ben coperto poi lo stamegna ben sotili e poi pone lo azuro in uno catino vitriato cum aqua pura e rimenalo cum mano o cum uno bastoni e lassalo ripossare poi cava lacqua con una spogna moderatamente poi torai lo azurro e macinalo sopra uno porfido molto bene poi lo porai in aqua pura in uno catino poilo rimena bene cum uno bastone poi lo lassa repossare per spatio duno pater nostro poi mecti quella aqua in uno vaso de vetrio netto imperhoche lo azurro subtilissimo e quello che remara al fondo e quello azurro più grosso che te romara atritalo bene una altra volta commo prima e poi cava laqua azurra e mectila da parte e fa commo prima poi la trita de novo e cusi farai tante volte in fino a tanto che ce niente de azurro e quando tu haverai poste tutte laque da per se lassale ben possare si che tutto lo azurro vada al fondo e laqua remanga chiara de sopra poi cava laqua cum la spogna commo e di sopra ditto e quando laverai tucta cavata multo bene lava lo dito azurro cum lo ranno [1] da capo tepido e remenalo molto bene cum lo bastone e lassa possare poi cava la liscia commo laqua e lassa secare a lombra e questa e verissima preparatione.

10. *Pratica a fare pastillo per cavare lo azurro de lo dicto lapis lazuli.*—Piglia ragia de pino oz. viij. pece greca oz. iiij mastice once meza olio de semi de lino oz. ij poi tolli uno pignatto vitriato e pollo sopra a uno tre piei cum lo fuoco sotto lento e chiaro e commo comincia ad esser caldo mectice prima lolio de semi de lino e lasselo uno poco scaldare poi ce pone la pece greca spolverizata e incorpora multo bene cum lolio misticando cum uno bastoni per infino che sera cotto che lo

---

[1] Liscivio.

in the same manner as you tried the first-mentioned pastille. Then strain it like the other, and when it is cooled in the water, put the pipkin on the fire as you did at first; and when it begins to get hot take oz. ij of linseed oil, and add to the said pastille, and when it is well melted, add an ounce of turpentine, always mixing it well; then take the pipkin, and while it is still boiling put oz. viij of the powder of the mineral, pounded very fine, by degrees into the pipkin, keeping it still boiling gently; then throw the pastille into cold and clear water in a basin, and when it is cold, grease your hands with linseed oil, and work the pastille about this way and that in your hands like dough; and when you have worked it sufficiently, put it back into the water, and let it stand several days, changing the water two or three times every day; and at the end of six days take the pastille, and some warm honey-water (that is, take ten measures of clear water and one of honey, and let them boil for the tenth part of an hour, scum well, and then strain the liquid through a linen cloth, and it is done); wash the pastille with the honey-water previously warmed, and extract the azure the first time; the second time let the honey-water be a little warmer, and the third time a little warmer still, as in the other recipe. And know that the first time it is very troublesome to extract, the second time it is easier, and the third time it is easier still; and the reason is, that each time the water is a little warmer; but take care not to have it quite so hot as to melt the pastille: if this should happen, cool it by throwing cold water over it. Take care that the water is tepid the first time, warmer the second time, and warmer still the third time, otherwise you will never be able to extract the azure.

11. *To make azure and to refine it well.*—Take lapis lazuli, and pound it in a bronze mortar as carefully as you can, in order that the powder may not escape, and when it is well pounded, if the powder is of a greenish colour, it must be ground upon a marble or porphyry slab with clear fine white honey; but if it is not of a greenish colour, grind it with strong

conoscerai in quando sera cotto al segno de laltro pastillo poi locola commo laltro e quando sera freddo in laqua mecti la pignata al fuoco commo fecisti prima e quando comincia a scaldarse tolli oz. ij. de semi de lino e poi meti el dicto pastillo e quando sara ben disfatto mettivi una oncia di trementina sempre menando bene poi tolli la pignatta e cusi bolendo mectivi oz. viij. de polvere de la dicta preta ben sotili a poco a poco ne la pignatta sempre bolendo competentimente poi gietta lo pastillo nella aqua fredda e necta in uno catino e quando sera freddo ogniti le mano cum olio de lino e tolli lo pastillo e tiralo in qua e in la in mano commo pasta e quando laverai ben menato remetilo in la sua aqua e lassalo stare alcuni di e ongni di li muti laqua doi o tre volte e in capo de vj di tolli lo pastillo e cum laqua de mele calda cio e tolli x. mesure de aqua chiara e una de mele e bolla la decima parte de hora una e schiumala bene poi la cola cum panno de lino e de fatta e lava lo dicto pastillo cum la dicta aqua de meli calda e cava lo azurro la prima volta la seconda volta sia uno poco piu calda e la terza uno poco piu commo ne l' altra pratica. E sapi che la prima volta e grande fatica a cavarlo in la seconda meglio e in la terza melglio la ragione e che omni volta laqua e uno poco piu calda ma guarda che non fusse in tuto tanto calda che lo pastillo se disolvesse e se purre ocurisse aiutalo getando supra de laqua fredda. E habbi cura che la prima aqua sia tepida la seconda piu la terza piu imperhoche altramenti non lo caveresti mai.

11. *Affare azurro e afinarlo bene.*—Torrai la petra lazuli e pistala in uno mortaro di bronzo piu cautamente che tu poi acio non sfuita e quando sera ben pisto se questa polvere havera colore verde sci e da macinare sopra lo marmo o porfido cum lo mele chiaro e bello e bianco. Ma se non tene de colore verde macinalo cum aqua gommata ben forte sopra porfido

gum water upon porphyry until it becomes almost impalpable like ointment, and then put it into a glazed jar, and pour over it a sufficient quantity of strong white wine vinegar to cover it; mix it well and let it stand 4 or 5 hours, then pour off the vinegar carefully from it, and wash the azure with fresh water 3 or 4 times, or until it comes off clear, and then incline the basin to the rays of the sun so that the water may dry up completely. The azure must then be treated as follows: take a new pipkin with a little pine resin, a little new wax, a little common oil, and a little white wine at discretion. Mix up these things with the azure, so that it may become liquid like honey, first straining the pastille through a linen cloth, and then pouring it by degrees on to the azure, mixing it up well with a stick; take care to have plenty of the pastille, so that there may be no want of it; for if there should not be enough, the azure would be lost; then put the paste with the azure incorporated with it, upon a linen cloth, coarse but loosely woven, which must also be damped, and put it into a basin of clear water, and take up all the corners of the cloth in your hand, leaving the azure in the middle of it, and move the cloth about backwards and forwards as if you wished to sift it under the water. It must then be strained again through a coarse cloth, from which it will press out like pills, and the earth and the impurities will all go to the bottom, and that will show when the azure is well cleaned. You must put the mass of azure into a coarse linen cloth spread out, and then take up the corners of it all together, and keep continually moving the azure about with your hand, and there will remain good and excellent azure in the cloth; then put it little by little carefully into a clean vase, and you must mix up with the azure enough common oil to make it liquid, so that it may appear to be all oil, and putting it upon the fire, add to it a little white soap, well thinned and beaten up, for the space of two paternosters; then pour in the soap ley and beat the whole well together. When the composition is well boiled put it into a small bag made of horsehair like a sieve, rub it well with

tanto che venga quasi impalpabili ad modo de onguento di poi lo metti in uno catino vitriato e metice di sopra tanta quantita daceto forte di vino bianco che la materia venga coperta e mistica bene e lassa cusci stare per 4 o 5 hore da poi ne cava lo aceto cautamente e lava la materia cum aqua frescha 3 o 4 volte o per infino che se schiare da poi inchina lo catino al ragio del sole che nescha totalmente laqua de poi se vole acconciar el dicto azurro in questo modo tolli una pignatta nova cum un poco di ragia di pino e uno poco de cera nova e uno poco dolio comuno e uno poco de vino bianco a tua descritione e tucte queste cose incorpora cum lo dicto azurro per modo che vegna liquido commo mele e cola prima la dicta matheria cum panno de lino poi la pone sopra a lo azurro a poco a poco incorporando bene cum uno bastone e fa che magiormente habunda la dicta matheria che non mancha per che se manchasse alcuna parte lo azurro se perderia e alhora pone la dicta matteria cum lo azurro incorporato sopra a uno panno de lino grosso e raro de trama e sia humido e ponilo al catino de laqua chiara pieno alhora tene el dicto panno de ongni capo cum mano e lo azurro in mezo del dicto panno e va menando el panno in la e in qua commo volesti crevellate infra doi aque e alhora la dicta matheria se vole arecolare per uno panno frugato che vegna commo pilole e la terra e la feccia vada tucta in fundo del catino e alhora sera signo che lo azurro sera ben purgato e la dicta adunatione de lo azurro se vole porre in uno panno de lino frustro seperato in qua e in la e adunnalo tucto insiemi e mai se vole cessare de menare le mano per lo dicto azurro e rimara optimo e buono azurro in el panno e subito remitilo in uno vaso necto a poco a poco e vol se incorporare cum lo dicto azurro de lolio communo tanto che sia bene liquido e quasi tutto olio e stando sopra al foco mettice uno poco de sapone bianco molto ben asotigliato e bactuto per doi patri nostri alhora fortemente pone el capitello insiemi li rompe e poi quando sera ben cotta la dicta matheria in uno sachetto facto de pelo de cavallo ad modo stacia e sempre sfregando cum mano, overo cum doi bastone da poi pone in el sachetto el

your hand or with two sticks, and put the ley into the bag; rub it so that all the azure may be pressed out, and then wash the azure with a ley made of the ashes of vine branches, and having done this two or three times, put it to dry in the shade, in whatever way you like, and when it is quite dry, if it should not be of a good colour, you must proceed in the following manner.

12. *To give a good and fine colour to the azure, when it is not well coloured.*—Take several eggs, and make them boil till they become hard, then open the eggs in the middle with a knife, take away the yolk, and fill up the hard white of the eggs with sal ammoniac in very fine powder; then cover it with the other parts of the eggs, and tie them so that they will not come open, and put them in a new glazed jar for one night in a place which is very damp; in the morning you will have a water made from the sal ammoniac, which you must pour upon the azure so that it is entirely covered with the water, and it will make the azure of a most beautiful colour, and of twice the value that it was before. Dry it in the shade, and keep it in a leather purse, or in a box, and expose it as little as possible to the air.

13. *How to prepare the azure and to work it into the pastille to refine it.*—Take the lapis lazuli which has golden veins; the deeper it is in colour, and the purer from other mixtures, the better, and of the more perfect kind it is. You must put it into a shell, and let it stand over a charcoal fire until it becomes red hot; then throw it into strong vinegar, and repeat this 3 or 4 times, each time making it red hot, and quenching it in fresh vinegar, because by calcination it is more easily pounded and reduced to powder. And if the lapis lazuli is not of a perfect sort, it must not be heated, because it will lose its colour, and know that it is much better to take the lapis lazuli pounded and reduced to powder, because you can see its colour better. But if it is in pieces, the pieces must be pounded in a bronze mortar, well covered, lest the powder should escape into the air; then you must grind the

capitello e sfregalo si che tucto lo azurro escha fuora de poi lava el dicto azurro cum lo capitello facto de sementi e facto questo doi o tre volte metilo a secare a lombra commo a te piace e quando sera ben secco se non havesse in tutto bello collore farai in questo modo commo seguitara di socto.

12. *A dare bono e bello collore a lo azurro quando non fusse bene collorato.*—Recipe parechi ova e falli tanto bollire che diventano duri de po apri li dicti ova per mezo cum uno cortello e leva via el torno giallo e impelo albumi duro de li dicti ova de polvere ben subtili de sale armoniaco e de poi copri con l'altra parte de li dicti ova e ligali bene che non se aprino e polli in una pignata vitriata nova per una nocti in loco che sia ben humido e la matina haverai laqua facta del sale armoniaco la quale porai sopra alo azurro in tanto che sia tutto coperto de la dicta aqua e renderalli beletissimo collore e dopio pregio che prima e seccalo a lombra e serbalo in saculo de curami in una scatola e fa che senta meno haiere che poi.

13. *Pratica a sapere fare la preparazione de lo azurro e porlo in lo pastillo per affinarlo.*—Accipe la preta de lo lapis lazuli che habia vene doro e quanto e de piu pino collore e necto da laltre misture tanto e migliore e de piu perfecta sorta lo poi ponere in uno coccio e lassa la tanto stare sopra al fuoco de carboni che diventi bene infocata e rosscia e cosi infocata gietala in lo aceto forte e cosi farai 3 o 4 volte omne volta reinfocandola e spingendola in nuovo aceto bianco perche lo calcina meglio per poterla pastare e redurla in polvere. E se lo lapis lazuli non fusse de perfecta sorte non se vole infocare perche perderia lo collore E sappi che e molto meglio torre lo lapis lazuli pisto e reduto in polvere perche se vede meglio de che collore le. Ma se sonno in pezi se voglino pistare nel mortare de bronzo coperto multo bene perche la polvere non valesca al vento poi lo macina sopra al porfido e quando sara

powder upon porphyry, and when it is very fine, let it dry. When dry, you may grind it with ley or with tragacanth, because this makes it more easy to grind, and let it dry; and so much for the preparation of the lapis lazuli.

14. *The way to make the pastille, and to refine the before-mentioned lapis lazuli.*—Take 3 oz. of pine resin, oz. j of Spanish pitch, oz. j of mastic, oz. j of linseed, and put it all over the fire in a glazed pipkin to boil slowly together, and let the composition boil until a drop of it thrown into cold water, and taken up in your wet fingers, ceases to stick to your fingers, when it is done. Then take it from the fire and immediately strain it through a cloth, receiving it in a basin of cold water; when the pastille is hardened, grease your hands with linseed oil, and take the composition, and pull it to and fro like bird-lime; then make it into a cake, and you can then keep it a long time, either in or out of water, and so much for the preparation of the pastille.

15. *The way to incorporate the pounded lapis lazuli with the pastille to refine it well.*—Take of the powder of the lapis lazuli one pound for every 10 oz. of the pastille, and put the pastille into a glazed pipkin and make it almost boil; then take the powder and put a little at a time into the pipkin, and mix it well together with a stick, and throw the mixture while hot into a basin of cold water; then oil your hands with linseed oil, as you did before, and knead the paste very well in order to incorporate the ingredients thoroughly together; then make them into a cake and put this back into a basin of clear cold water. You may keep it as long as you like, and you must keep it at least a fortnight; and so much for incorporating the powder with the pastille.

16. *The way to wash the powder out of the pastille to refine it.*—When you wish to extract the azure, put the pastille into a glazed pipkin, with tepid water; and there must be enough water to stand four fingers' breadths over the pastille; let it remain so for the space of ten paternosters, and then throw away that water, and add some more water to it, and do this three or

bene subtilissimo lassalo seccare e quando e secco lo poi macinare cum lisciva o vero cum draganti perche lo fa piu palpabili e lassalo seccare e questo e quanto ala preparatione de lo dicto lapis lazuli.

14. *El modo affare el pastillo e affinare la dicta preparatione de lo lapis lazuli supradicto.*—Recipe oz. 3 de ragia de pino oz. j de pece spagnola, oz. j de mastice, oz. j de semi de lino e mecti omni cosa al foco in una pignatta vitriata a bulire pianamente e tanto bolla che gietandoni una goccia in aqua fredda e poi pigliandola cum li deta bagnati non se apicha ale deta alhora e cocta e cosci calda tolla dal fuoco e subito colala in uno panno e ricogliendolo in uno catino daqua fredda e quando el pastillo e ben indurato ongniti le mani cum lolio de semi di lino e piglia la dita compositione e tirala in la e in qua come se fa el vischio poi lo reduce ad modo duno pano e conservare el poi longho tempo o voli in aqua o senza aqua e questo basta a la compositione del pastillo.

15. *El modo da incorporare la sopradicta preta pista in lo pastillo per affinarla optimamente.*—Summe de la polve de lo dicto lapis lazuli per omne libra oz. x de lo dicto pastillo e mectilo in una pignatta vitriata e fallo tanto scaldare che sia per bollire alhora tolli lo dicto lapis in polvere e metilo a poco a poco in la pignatta e misticalo bene insieme cum uno bastone e gietalo cosi caldo in uno catino daqua fredda poi ongiti le mano cum lolio de semi de lino commo facesti la prima volta e tiralo molto bene acio se incorpora bene poi lo reduce commo uno pane e rimetilo in uno catino daqua fredda e chiara e poilo tenere quanto voli ma vole almanco stare per xv di naturali e questo basta in quanto alla incorporatione de la polvere.

16. *El modo da cavare la dicta polve de lo pastillo per afinaria.*—Quando voli cavare el sopradicto azurro del pastillo poni el dicto pastillo in uno catino vitriato e metivi de l aqua tepida e e vole esser tanta aqua che stia 4 deta sopra al pastillo e lassalo cusci stare per dire X patri nostri poi sparge via quella aqua e metice de laltra aqua calda e fa cusi iij o iiij volte

four times until the pastille is warmed through. Then take two clean sticks a foot long, and of the thickness of one finger, round at the ends; and with these sticks you must knead the pastille in the warm water, turning it inside out with the sticks and continue doing so, and changing the warm water, until the azure begins to come out of the pastille, and when the water is full of the azure, empty it into another basin, holding back the pastille in the basin with the sticks. Then pour some hotter water over it, and continue to do so until all the azure is extracted. When you see the ashes, which are of a dull colour, work out, put them away into another vase, because they are not good, compared with the first sort. Pour the 3 or 4 first washings into the first basin, and as many more into the second, and all the rest in the third basin. The first will be of a fuller colour, but not so finely pulverized; and the second will be of a very good colour, but not like the first, and the third will be of a whitish colour and very finely pulverized. Then put each sort by itself, and take out the water, then clean the azure with eggs, beaten up with the branch of a fig-tree, and make the azure into a paste with these beaten eggs; then wash the azure with clear and weak ley until the ley comes off clear, frequently renewing the ley, and then dry the azure in the shade, out of the way of dust, and keep it in a little bag of chamois leather.

17. *The way to make "azurro di lamagna," or German azure, or Spanish azure, and to refine it well.*—Take the mineral stone of the colour of smalt, or of a yellow colour, break it in pieces, and free it from other mixtures and impurities, and then pound it very fine in a bronze mortar, covered over, in order that the powder may not escape and be blown into the air, and sift it with a very fine sieve. Then take very strong and clear ley, made from baked ashes, with which you must wash the powder of the lapis lazuli four or five times, and receive all the waters in a basin, and pour the ley carefully off the azure, which will settle at the bottom of the basin. Then take very clean and white honey, and grind up the azure with the honey, a little at

tanto che el pastillo se scalde de dentro poi tolli doi bastoni longhi mezobracio e grossi uno deto polliti e necti per tutto e tondi in capo e cum questi bastone se vole cemenare el dicto pastillo nela dicta aqua calda e revoltando quello dentro de fora cum li dicti bastoni e tanto farai cusci scambiando laqua calda per infino che lo azurro cominciara ad huscire fora del pastillo e quando laqua e ben piena de azurro voita quella aqua azzurra in uno altro catino retinendo el pastillo nel fondo del catino cum li dicti bastoni poi li rimecte suso del aqua piu calda e tanto fa cusci che nescha fora tucto lo azurro e quando tu vedrai uscire fora el cinaraccio che e di colore smorto metilo da parte in uno altro vaso perche non e buono apresso quello de prima. Mecti la prima lavatura 3 o 4 volte nel catino e altratanto nel secondo e tucte l'altre nella terza sorte el primo sera piu pino de collore ma non sera cusi subtili e el secondo havera assai buono collore ma non commo el primo e el terzo sera de collore bianchetto e sera sutilissimo poi mecti cescuno da per se e cavarai laqua e poi purga lo azurro cum gli ova sbactuti cum una rama de fico e impasta lo dicto azurro cum questi ova sbattuti poi tolli liscia chiara e dolce e lava lo dicto azurro cum essa liscia tanto che la liscia nescha chiara renovando spesso la dicta liscia e poi lo pone a secare a lombra dove non vi vada polve e serba lo in saculo camusi.

17. *Pratica affare azurro de lamagna o vero azurro thodesco o vero azurro spagnolo e afinarlo optimamente.*—Tolli de lo lapis minerali de collore de smalto, o vero de collore crocio e rompilo bene e acapalo de l' altre misture e immonditii poi lo pista molto bene in uno mortaro de bronzo coperto primo che non sfuita et non vada la polvere alaiere poi lo staccia cum una stacia subtili de poi tolli liscia fortissima e chiara facta de cenere recotta cum la quale lava la polvere de lo ditto lapis in fino a quattro o cinque volte e coglie tutta la lavatura in uno catino e lassa bene scolare la liscia de lo azurro che stara in lo fondo del catino poi tolli del mele molto bene netto e bianco e vieni macinando lo dicto azurro allo dicto mele a pocho a poco

a time, on the porphyry slab, until it is ground fine; then take four or five glazed basins, and put the azure into one basin, in which you must distemper it with strong ley, mixing it well with your hands; when it is well mixed, pour it off very quickly into another vase, and continue washing it until the ley becomes clear, and let the coarse azure remain at the bottom; then grind up again the coarse azure which you have left at the bottom, as you did before, and when it is ground put it with the first, and wash it all together as you did before. When you have washed it well, let it rest for the space of one *pater noster;* then pour it off slowly into another basin, and wash it until you have washed away the fine parts. Then grind up the coarse parts as before mentioned, if you like, and mix all together, coarse and fine—that is to say, the first, second, and third washings; and when you have washed the powder well, so that the ley separates entirely from it, let all the ley run off, and put the azure into a glazed pipkin, and pour over it strong white vinegar, so as to cover the azure, and as much common salt as is sufficient. Let it stand so for two natural days; then pour off the vinegar into a basin, and when it is run off, wash the azure in three or four clear waters, and throw all those waters on to the vinegar which first ran off the azure, as there may perhaps be something useful in it, which you must put with the good. You must then separate the fine azure from the coarse in this manner:—Take a new glazed jar, into which put the azure; then take ley so warm that you can just bear your hand in it, and some soap scraped very fine with a knife, add to each pound of azure half an ounce of soap, mix all these things together, and then have ready a small bag in which you may shake up the mixture together until it froths; then empty the pipkin carefully, taking off the scum with a spoon, so that only the coarse part may remain behind; next take the scum, and put it back into another pipkin with a little more fresh ley, and do the same as you did before; then pour off into the first basin the coarse parts which remain, and grind it again, and do as before; afterwards grind that which is with the soap with

in su lo porfido prima che vegna subtili e commo sera tutto macinato bene habbi 4 o 5 catini vitriati poi metti el dito azurro in uno catino nel quale stempera el dicto azurro cum liscia forte remenandolo bene cum mano e quando sera bene stemperato e tu presto presto scola in uno altro vaso e cusci seguita lo lavare per infino ne vieni la liscia chiara e lassa romanere lazurro grosso al fondo e de novo remacina quello grosso che te remasto al fondo commo prima e commo e macinato metilo insiemi cum lo primo e lavalo tucto insiemi commo da prima e commo tu laverai ben lavato lasselo reposare per uno pater nostro poi scolalo pianamente in uno altro catino poi lo lava tante volte che se ne cava lo sotile e poi de novo macina el grosso se te piace commo di sopra e dicto e tucto lo ricoglie insiemi grosso e suctili cio e el primo e el secondo e el terzo e da poi che lai molto bene lavato tanto che nescha la liscia chiara e lassalo bene scolare da la lixia poi lo metti in una pignatta vitriata e e mectivi sopra de lo aceto forte e bianco tanto che lo azurro stia coperto e tanta quantita de sale communo che sia sufficienti e lassa cusci stare per doi di naturali e poi scola el dicto aceto in uno catino e commo e scolato lavalo a tre o a quatro aque chiare e tucte quelle aque bucta in su lo aceto che cavasti prima de lo azurro acio se vi fusse niuna cosa bona la quale mecti insiemi cum lo buono da poi sepera lo azurro buono dal grosso in questo modo tolli uno pignatto novo vitriato nel quale mecti el dicto azurro poi tolli liscia ben calda quanto se li possa soffririre la mano e habi del sapone raso ben sottili con lo cortello e vole esser tanto che sia per omne libra de azurro meza oncia de sapone e mistica tutte queste cose insiemi poi habbi uno sachetto cum lo quale tu volte e travolte molto bene le dicte cose per infino a tanto che faccia una buona schiuma de poi scola la dicta pignatta in uno catino caute tirando suso la schiuma cum uno cochiaro infini romane solamente lo grosso e da poi tolli la dicta schiuma e de novo lo rimecti in una altra pignatta cum uno altro poco di liscia nova e fa el simili commo da prima poi scola nel primo catino el grosso che te remane remacinalo una altra volta e fa commo prima poi vieni lavando

clear and clean ley, and then take a glazed jar with urine in it, and boil the urine, and for every pound of azure add half an ounce of gum arabic, and scum it well, and put some scent into it. When it has boiled, take it off the fire, and when cool put the azure into it, and let it stand so for a night; then pour off the urine, and let the azure dry in the shade, and turn the azure frequently with a stick; then put it into a little leather bag before it is quite dry, and squeeze it well in your hands, or put it into an ox bladder, which must be prepared by soaking the bladder for one night in vinegar and salt; and keep it well, and you will have an azure like ultramarine.

18. *To make azure by means of the pastille.*—Take pine resin oz. iij, Greek pitch oz. j; pound the pitch and mix the whole with oil, and put it to boil slowly in a glazed jar until it is done, and this may be known in the following manner:—Take a drop of the composition and throw it into cold water, and if it does not stick to your wet fingers it is boiled sufficiently. When it is done, take a glazed basin of cold water, and strain the said composition into the water through a cloth, screwing and squeezing it with a split stick so that it may all come out of the cloth, and let it harden a little in the water; and when you wish to use the pastille, warm it a little, and take for every half pound of the pastille, half a pound of azure—that is, of the stone pounded into a fine powder—and mix and incorporate well the powder and the pastille, and let them lie for a week. Then take a glazed jar, and put into it some tepid water; put the pastille into this water, and wash it very well in the same way that birdlime is washed, pulling and kneading it to and fro in the hand, and taking care not to break it, and continue doing this until the water becomes blue, renewing the water frequently. Then set aside that azure water, and take another basin of water a little warmer than the first; put the pastille into it, and do as you did before until it becomes blue, and put it apart as you did the first, and do this until the water no

quello che e in nel sapone cum liscia ben chiara e netta poi tolli uno pignatto vitriato cum orina e fa bullire la dicta orina ne la quale mecti per omni libra dazurro meza oncia de gomarabico e schiumalo molto bene e metili dentro alcuna cosa odorifera e quando ha bulito levalo dal fuoco e commo e refredato e tu vi mecti dentro lo azurro e lassalo cusi stare per una nocte e poi scola via la ditta orina e poi pone asciugare lo dicto azurro a lombra e apre el dicto azurro spesso cum uno bastone poi lo ripone in uno sachecto de corami in nanti che sia in tutto fornito de sciugare e menalo bene per mano o vero tu lo pone in una visicha de bove la quale sia attuata in questo modo farai stare la visicha in lo aceto e sale per una notte e servalo bene e haverai azurro simili al oltramarino.

18. *A fare azurro per via de pastillo.*—Tolli ragia de pino oz. iij, pece greca oz. j, e pista la pece e mistica omne cosa cum olio et mettilo a bullire a poco a poco e mectilo in una pignatta vitriata infino a tanto che sera cotto e questo se cognosce in questo modo tolli una gocia de la dita compositione e gietala in aqua fredda e se non se apicha ale deta che sieno bagnati e cocta poi quando e cotta tolli uno catino vitriato cum aqua fredda e cola la dita composition in questa aqua cum uno panno spregnendo e ritorcendo cum uno ligno fesso siche tutto vegna fora del panno e lassalo indurare uno pocho nel aqua poi quando voli operare el dito pastillo rescaldalo uno poco e tolli per omne meza libra de pastillo una libra dazurro cioe la preta pista in polvere sotili e mista insiemi la polve el pastillo molto bene incorporando poi lo lassa stare per 8 di naturali poi tolli uno catino vitriato e metice dentro del aqua tepida e metti lo pastillo in questa aqua e lavalo molto bene commo se lava lo vischio tirando e remenando in qua e in la cum mano e guarda che tu non lo rompi e cusi farai in fino a tanto che laqua diventa azurra renovando spesso laqua alhora pone quella aqua azurra da parte poi tolle uno altro catino cum laqua che sia uno pocho piu calda che laltra prima e mecti dentro lo pastillo e fa commo prima intanto che diventa azurra e serbala da parte commo prima e farai cusci infino a tanto che laqua non

longer comes off blue, and put each water away by itself; cover it up, and let it settle until the azure sinks to the bottom; then take up the water with a sponge cautiously, so as not to move the azure, and when all the water is removed, let the azure at the bottom of the basin dry, and keep it; and know that the first is perfect azure, and is worth five ducats the ounce, the second less, and so the third.

19. *To make azure another way.*—Take lapis lazuli of a violet tinge, very clean from earth and impurities and particularly from pyrites, and break it in a bronze mortar, afterwards grind it very fine upon porphyry or marble, and then dry it. Then make a pastille from the following ingredients, viz.: take for one pound of the stone, 4 oz. of new wax, the same quantity of colophony, 4 oz. of naval pitch, and one ounce of powdered incense, and you must first liquefy the wax in a glazed jar; you must then put 5 ounces of linseed oil, only half of which is to be used at first, the other part is to be reserved. Then add all the other things, pulverizing all that should be in powder, and when they are melted or dissolved, strain them through a linen cloth into a glazed vase, such as a washing basin, filled with clear cold water; then take the pastille with the powder of the lapis lazuli, and put it on a marble slab, and incorporate one with the other. The proof of their being perfectly incorporated is, that the pastille breaks while kneading it in your hands, but it must be done a little at a time, a piece, for instance, of the size of a chestnut, and the whole must be made into a cake, and must be suffered to stand 3 or 4 days. When you wish to extract the azure, do it with hot water, having an assistant to throw the water over your hands while you are kneading and washing the pastille, letting the water run into a glazed vessel, and setting apart three waters, and changing the water until it is no longer coloured. Then let it settle and pour off the water, strain the azure through a cloth, and let it dry, and it will be done.

20. *To make azure another way.*—Take of lapis lazuli one pound, and grind it well and sift it through a linen cloth; after-

diventa piu azurra e metti omne aqua da per se coperta e lassala tanto possare che lo azurro sia andato al fondo poi cava tutta laqua cum una spogna cautamente che lo azurro non se mova poi che sera cavata tucta laqua lassa seccare lo azurro nel fondo del catino e conservalo e sappi che lo primo e perfecto azurro e vale cinque ducate loncia lo secondo vale mancho e cosi lo terzo.

19. *Ad faciendum azurrum per aliam viam.*—Accipe lapis lazuli bene multumque mundum a terra et superfluitate et maxime a marchesita et sit coloratus colore violatii et ipsum tere in mortario bronzi postea macina super porfidum sive marmorem suctiliter postea desicha ipsum deinde fac pastillum ex istis rebus, viz., sume pro una libra dicti lapidis uncias quatuor cere nove et tantumdem colofonie et untias 4 pice navalis et untiam unam incensi pulverizati et unam ollam habeas vitriatam in qua liquefac ceram super quam pone untias 5 olei seminis lini sed primo non ponas nisi medietatem dicti olei lini et aliam partem serva deinde pona et omnes alias res pulverizatas quæ pulverizanda sunt et quando erunt destrute sive disolute tunc cola per pannum lineum in uno vase vitriato sicut est lavella in quo sit aqua clara et frigida tunc sume pastillum cum pulvere lazuli et pone in marmore et simul bene incorpora unum cum reliquo. Signum vero perfecte incorporationis est quando trando pastillum cum manibus frange tamen debet incorporari ad modicum ad modicum proice qualibet ad quantitatem unius castanee et tunc ex omnibus fiat panis unus et permicte stare diebus tres vel quatuor. Et quando vis exthraere azurrum extrahe ipsum cum callida aqua ita tamen quod unus proiciat aquam super manus tuas et tu move pastillum lavando ipsum et aqua cadat in vase vitriato seperando aquam ter et mutando tantum quod plus non colloretur et permitte posare et sepera aquam et cola azurrum per pannum subtile et permitte sicari et erit factum.

20. *Ad faciendum azurrum per alium modum.*—Summe lapidem lazurinum libram unam et eum tere bene et cribra per

wards grind it fine upon porphyry, and let it dry; then take Greek pitch, naval pitch, olibanum, mastic, vernicem annarii (?), clean new wax 2, 4̦, 2,[1] and common oil 2̦, 1; melt all these things together in a saucer and mix them well. Then take a basin full of clear water, and strain into it through a cloth all those things which you melted in the saucer, and anoint your hands with oil, and take the composition which you put into the basin, and knead it well before the fire like wax; then by degrees incorporate the powdered lapis lazuli with it, and let the mass remain in a ball for 3 or 4 days, and the longer the better. Next take a large glazed vase, and put the ball into it, and pour hot water upon it, stirring it with a wooden stick, and working it well until the water is coloured with the azure; separate it, and add fresh hot water, and do as you did before, and put it into another basin. Do this as long as the water comes off coloured, and if there seems to you to be any colour left in the ball, take some common ley almost boiling, and pour it upon the ball and stir it strongly, then put it back with coloured water from the third washing; afterwards, when the water has cleared, pour it off so that none of it may remain, and then cover over those vases with a sieve in the sun, and let them dry. This must only be done in clear weather.

21. *The way to make coarse azure.*—Take the stone called "viterola de lamanea,"[2] which is like pumice stone, and grind it fine without any liquid. Then take a little turpentine, new wax, and naval pitch, and put it to melt, and when the whole is melted put into it some of the powder of the stone, and stir it with a stick to mix it well; then take warm water and a ladle or a stick, and work it till the azure is extracted, frequently changing the water and setting it aside. Let it dry, and keep it in a leather purse.

---

[1] These numbers probably refer to pounds, ounces, and drachms; the figure with the comma under it stands for ounces.

[2] The Viterola de Lamanea is probably native blue Vitriol, or sulphate of copper; because in the Nuovo Plico (p. 126), it is said, that "when Viterolo de Lamanea is boiled with the Verdigris and Sal Ammoniac in strong vinegar, and a piece of iron put into it while boiling hot, when cold

pannum lineum postea tere eum subtiliter in porfido et permicte siccari deinde accipe pecem grecam et picem navalem, olibanum, masticem et vernicem annarii et ceram novam mundam 2, ℥, 2 (*sic*), oleum comune ℈, 1, omnia ista fundantur impatella et fortiter incorporentur postea habeas parasidem unam aque clare plenam et cola per pannum omnia que intus infusisti scilicet in patella et tunc acipe de oleo et unge tibi manus et acipe ea que in paraside posuisti et duc bene ad ignem ac si esset cera postea paulatim incorpora dictum pulverem lazurrinum et permitte dita massa stare admodum palle per 3 vel 4 dies et tanto plus tanto melius erit deinde accipe unum vas cupum et et magnum ut sit vitriatum et intus pone dittam pallam et infunde de aqua calida deinde remove eum cum baculo de ligno et duc fortiter quousque aqua fuerit bene collorata colloris azurri et sepera illam et pone de nova aqua calida et fac sicut prius et mite in alia paraside et sic reitera dummodo aqua venit collorata. Et si tibi videtur quod remanserit de azurro in ditta palla accipe de comuni liscivio quasi bullito et micte desuper palla et duc fortiter et repone in tertia lavatura cum alia aqua azurra postea quando aqua erit clara proice illa ut nil remaneat et tunc coperias parasides illas cum stamenia ad solem et dimicte sicari et hoc non debes facere nisi per tempus clarum.

21. *Modus faciendi grossum azurrum.*—Summe lapidem qui dicitur viterola de lamanea et est ad instar pumicis, tere ipsum sine aliquo licore subtiliter tunc recipe modicum terebentine et cere nove e pice navalis et pone ad liquefaciendum quando erunt liquefacta tunc micte intus pulverem dicti lapidis et move baculo ut sint bene admisia et inde habeas aquam calidam et accipe misculam sive baculum et move tantum quod azurrum exeat mutando semper aquam et secuando ad partem et permicte sicari et serva in bursia corii.

---

the iron is found to be of the colour of copper;" being in fact actually coated with copper.

Native Sulphate of Copper occurs massive, stalactitic, and pulverulent; it is rarely found crystallized. When a portion of it is dissolved in water, and spread on the surface of iron, the latter is immediately covered by a film of copper. See Phil. Min., p. 313.

22. *To make German azure.*—To make azure like German azure, take of rasscia[1] as much as you like, that is to say, that rasscia which comes from Germany, and which is like stone; crush it upon a marble slab and grind it well, then take gum arabic, and dissolve it in twice the quantity of water, and distemper the gum, and then with this gum water distemper the rasscia, and when they are well incorporated, take strong ley made from the ashes of vine branches, and wash the azure two or three times with this ley; then let it settle to the bottom, separate the ley, and let it dry, and the work is done.

23. *To extract sol,* i. e. *gold, from the lapis lazuli.*—Take lapis lazuli, and pound it very fine on an anvil or in a bronze mortar, or, if you like, grind it on porphyry, first heating it in the fire, and when it is well ground take for every pound of powder an ounce of mercury, and mix it well together with the powder; then take a linen cloth, not of too close a texture, or a sieve, and put these things—that is to say, the powder and the mercury—into whichever of these you choose, and press the piece of linen in order that the quicksilver may pass out with the gold; then pour the quicksilver into a crucible, and put it in the fire, when the mercury will go off in vapour, and the gold will remain behind.

24. *To make azure, and to know the place where it is produced.*—Take lapis lazuli, which is a stone that comes from Organia, in the country of Tartary,[2] and which is dug from the

---

[1] I have not been able to find the word "rasscia" in any Vocabulary. From the imperfect description of the text, I should consider it to signify the indurated Blue Carbonate of Copper.

[2] Beckmann says, that the real Lapis Lazuli is found in the mountains of that part of Tartary, called Bucharia, which extends eastward from the Caspian Sea; and particularly at Kalal and Budukschu. This is confirmed by Tavernier in his 'Travels.' I believe it is not found in Hungary, which country we are to understand by the word "Organia," or in Cyprus; but in both these countries are copper mines, which produce the blue ore. From the former, the blue pigment called "Ongaro" by Lomazzo (Trattato della Pittura, p. 191), which Pacheco says was used by Titian (Tratado de la Pintura, p. 373), was prepared. The blue copper ores of

22. *Ad faciendum azurrum almaneum.*—A fare azurro commo de lamagna tolle la rasscia quella parte che tu vole cio e quella rasscia che vene delamagna la quale e commo petra rompilo in sulo marmo e macinala molto bene poi tolli gomma rabico e doi parte piu che la goma de aqua e stempera la dicta gomma e cum quella aqua gomata stempera la dicta rasscia e quando sonno bene incorporate e tu tolli ranno forte facto de cenere de sciermento e lava lo dicto azurro cum esso ranno doi o tre volte poi lo lassa andare al fondo e sepera lo ranno e lassalo seccare et de facto.

23. *Ad extraendum sol,* i. e. *aurum, de lapide lazuli.*—Ahvve lo lapis lazuli et tritalo bene subtili in su lancudini o vero in mortaro de bronzo o voi spolverizarlo in porfido metendolo ad infocare nel foco poi commo e bene trito tolli per omne libra dela dicta polve una oncia de mercurio vivo e miscola insiemi cum la dicta polvere ben de vantagio poi tolli panno de lino che non sia troppo ficto o vero una stamegna et in qualunqua tu voli metivi dentro le dicte cose cio e la dicta polvere cum lo ariento vivo e spremi la dicta peza acio nescha lo argento insiemi cum loro poi poni lo dicto ariento in uno crugiolo e pollo al foco lo argento andara via in fumi e el sole remarra in lo fondo.

24. *Ad faciendum azurrum et cognoscendum locum ubi nascitur.*—Tolli lo lapis lazuli lo quale e petra che vene de Organia de paese de tartaria et la se cava la dicta preta de le montagne

---

Cyprus have always been celebrated, and are still produced there. It is almost unnecessary to observe, that this blue pigment from Hungary and Cyprus is the Azzurro della Magna formerly mentioned. Large quantities of blue copper ore have also been found in Persia; and have frequently been mistaken for Lapis Lazuli. Tavernier gives the following account of it:—

"In the copper mines of Persia, veins of lazur, which is much used in that country, and with which the flowers on the ceiling and roofs of apartments are painted, have also been found. Before these were discovered the Persians had no other lazur than the real kind, which comes from Tartary, and is exceedingly dear. The Persian lazur is a sort of copper ore; and when the stone is pounded and sifted, which is the process employed with

mountains of that country, and where also are found sapphires and other precious stones. The stone is also dug in the country of Damascus, and in Cyprus; and the people of those parts, who are Tartars and infidels, call it in their tongue "agiara,"[1] that is to say, azure stone. When you want to use this stone, take it, and if the said stone is in large lumps, put them in the fire so as to be heated throughout; suffer them to remain in the fire for ten hours, and let the fire be burning all round them, and if you allow them to stay longer in the fire they will be finer; and if you put them into a pipkin they will be still better refined in the following manner:—Take an unglazed pipkin pierced with many holes at the bottom, and with a few at the sides, and put charcoal around it; then put the large lumps of lapis lazuli into this perforated pipkin, which must be placed on a tripod, and when the stone has been burnt for the above-mentioned space of time, take strong ley made of ashes of oak, or glass ashes—that is soda—and the ley will be so much the better if you take equal quantities of both of these, with a little quicklime, and make a ley as clear and clean as you can, and then put the stone red hot into the cold ley, and let it remain for three days; next pour off the ley, and let the stone dry, and then pound it in a metal mortar, and reduce it to as fine a powder as you can; and if the stone should contain any gold, you will extract it with quicksilver as was before directed. When it is well sifted, so as to be very fine, put it into a shell of cold water, and mix it with a clean spoon, and then let it settle in that water till the powder is all gone to the bottom, and all the impurities remain above; then separate the water from the dust with a sponge, softly, so as not to disturb the powder or the

---

the real kind, it forms a fine paint, which appears very bright and pleasant. After this discovery, the Persians durst no more purchase the Tartarian lazur; and Mahomet Beg issued an order that painters should not use foreign but Persian lazur. This prohibition, however, did not long continue; for the Persian lazur could not stand the effects of the atmosphere like the real kind, but in the course of time became of a dark and dismal colour. Sometimes it was full of scales, and would not hang to the end of a soft

che sonno in quelli paesi e la se trovano zaffirri et altre prete pretiose. Et ancora se cava de la dicta preta in le parte damasco et in le parte de cipre et la gente de quelli parte che sonno tartari et infideli la chiamano in loro lingua agiara cioe petra de azurro. Et quando voi lavorare la dicta preta prendila e se la dicta preta fusse in zuppi grossi mecti i peze nel fuoco che arda da omne parte e lassali stare nel foco per x hore e fa che habia bene il foco da omne parte e se piu la lassi stare nel foco piu se affinara. E se tu la mecte in una pignatta ancora se affina melglio in questo modo: tolli una pignatta non vitriata e mecti de intorno carboni e la pignatta vole esser forata nel fondo cum spessi bugi e cum alcuni bugi de intorno poi poni in la dicta pignatta bugiata li pezi de lo dicto lapis grossi e la dicta pignatta vole esser sospesa in uno tre pei poi che sera la dicta preta bene cocta et bene infocata per lo dicto spatio habi liscia forte facta de cenere de cerro o de cenere de vetrio cioe soda tanto megliore serà la liscia se tu vi poni de luna e del altra cenere anna et cum uno pochettino de calcina viva et fa liscia chiara et necta quanto piu poi poi cusci calda mecti la petra in lo dicto ranno freddo e lassa stare per 3 di poi sepera la dicta liscia e lassa resciugare la dicta preta poi la pista in uno mortaro de metallo e fa polvere piu subtile che poi et se la dicta petra tenesse doro farai cum lo argento vivo commo e di sopra dicto et commo e ben staciata che sia ben subtili mectila in una concha daqua fredda e mista bene cum una mescola necta bene e poi la lassa ben reposare in quella aqua che la polvere sia bene andata al fondo et omne cativita rimara de sopra et sepera laqua de la polve cum una spogna pianamente che non movi la dicta polvere o dicto azurro e se vedesci che

---

hair brush. On this account it was soon neglected as a coloured earth, and the lazur of Tartary again introduced."

[1] Agiara. The usual term for Azurro in those parts of Italy situated between the Apennines and the Po. It occurs in contracts for pictures by Denys Calvart, and Marc Antonio Seccadenari in 1601, and by Ludovico Carracci in 1587.

azure; and if you see that it is not well cleansed, wash it another time in the before-mentioned manner; and when it is quite clean let it dry, and grind it dry on the porphyry as fine as you can, a little at a time; and if you should have any trouble in grinding it dry, add a little water to it, and when you have ground it fine put it into a large and flat glazed earthenware pan, spread it along, and let it dry, and then grind it again on the porphyry, and sift it very fine. It must then be refined with the pastille, made according to this recipe:—Take 1 oz. of white resin, 1 oz. of incense, 8 oz. of Greek pitch, 1½ oz. of turpentine, 1 oz. of linseed oil, and if you wish to make a greater quantity make it according to this proportion; then take a glazed pipkin, and put it on the fire on a tripod, and make a fire of charcoal without flame; first put the oil into the saucepan, and let it get warm, and then the Greek pitch, mix them together with a clean spoon, and when the pitch is well melted add the resin, and keep continually stirring it; then add the incense, and then the turpentine, and mix all together, and take care to keep a moderate fire, in order that the mixture may not catch fire inside; then remove the vessel from the fire, and strain the contents through canvass like a strainer. Next take a basin of glazed earthenware, and fill it half full of clear cold water, and put that canvass over the basin, and then strain the mixture which is in the pipkin into this water, and when you have strained it all, take it out of the water, and put it where it will not get dirty. If you wish to refine one pound of lapis lazuli, take two pounds of this pastille, and it will even bear another ounce of azure. Then take a clean glazed saucepan, and put it over a moderate fire, and add another ounce of Greek pitch, and it will be sufficient for making a larger quantity; put the oil into it, and do as before, and let it melt slowly; then remove the saucepan from the fire, and pour it while hot over the lapis lazuli, and mix it well. When it is well incorporated, before it gets cold, take a shell of fresh water and pour it on the hot pastille which you have in the pipkin, and the whole will sink to the bottom and adhere together; and when

non fusse bene depurgato lavalo una altra volta alo dicto modo e commo sara bene depurgato lassa lo sciugare poi lo macina in su lo porfido cusci dasciuto quanto piu poi a poco per volta et se te fosse fatiga a macinare dasciuto metice uno poco daqua poi che lai macinato subtili metilo in uno vaso de terra vitriato largo e piano e stendivilo suso et lassalo sciugare bene poi lo aremacina in lo dicto porfido e statiarlo che sia ben subtili poi se vole darli la concia cum lo pastillo cioe cum questa maestra. Tolli oz. j de ragia bianca, oz. j. de incenso, oz. 8 de pece greca, oz. 1½ de trementina, oz. j de olio de seme de lino se ne voi far maggior quantita fallo secondo questa proportione poi habbi uno tegami vitriato e pollo al foco in su li tre pej et fa fuoco de bragia e non de fiamma prima mecti in lo dicto tegami lolio et lassalo uno poco scaldare et poi la pece greca e mescola insiemi cum una mescola necta et quando la pece e ben disfatta mettivi la rasina et vene sempre mescolando poi lo incenso poi la trementina et mista et fa che lo foco sia molto temperato accio non se acenda dentro poi levalo dal foco e colalo cum uno canavaccio ad modo duno colatoro poi tolli uno catino de terra vitriato et fallo mezo daqua chiara et fredda et mecti quello canavaccio sopra alo catino poi cola et metivi suso quella decotione che e in lo dicto tegami et fa bene colare dentro in questa aqua poi che lai colata tucta cavala de laqua et ponila in loco che non se imbrutta. E se voi afinare una libra de azurro tolli doi libre de questo pastillo et anco comportara una oncia de azurro piu poi tolli uno tegami necto vitriato e ponilo al foco temperato et mectivi oz. j. piu de pece greca et basteralti per farne maggiore quantita et metivi dentro lolio et fa commo de sopra et lassalo strengiare adagio poi leva lo tegami dal foco et cosi caldo mectivi su la polvere de lo lapis lazuli e mista bene et quando sara bene incorporata prima che se freddi habbi una concha daqua fresca e metivi in su questa materia cosci calda che hai nel tegami et tucta la materia andara al fondo et arapicarasse insiemi et commo e bene arapicato cavela de laqua et rimenala per mano commo pasta tirando et distendendola bene poi lo pone nel aqua del catino et se apicha ale

it coheres firmly, take it out of the water and knead it in your hands like dough, pulling and spreading it well. Then put it into the water in the basin, and if it sticks to your fingers anoint them with linseed oil; let the pastille remain in the said water for six days, changing the water in summer twice each day, and in winter once; and when you wish to extract the azure, take a glazed basin and put the pastille into it, with tepid water; let the pastille get warm, and cover it with a ladle and press it. When it is well melted, put a little hotter water to it, or else warm that same water in a vase, and so wash it eight times with that same water, and then let it cool, and the pastille will float upon the top, and the azure will go to the bottom; and you must keep the water covered, in order that no dirt may get into it. Then remove the water with the pastille softly, in order that the azure which is at the bottom may not be disturbed; warm the water that was removed, and return it upon the azure, and then let it cool, and the pastille will float upon the top. Then separate the water and make it boil, and when boiled return it upon the azure as before, and take out the pastille, which will be good for making other azures, and put it away in a clean place; and know that the first azure is the finest, the second less fine, and the third still less; and you must keep the azure in a chamois leather purse, or in a glazed earthenware jar.

25. *The way to refine the pastille; and if it should happen to get burnt so that the azure does not work out, the way to cure it.*—Put cold water into a pipkin and place it over the fire. When the water is hot, put the burnt pastille into it, and when the pastille also begins to get hot, take it out of the water, and put it into a glazed jar, and again place it over a slow fire; then add to the pastille the following things. If the azure and the pastille together weigh two pounds, add 1 oz. of new wax, 1 oz. of olive-oil, 1 oz. of turpentine, and mix all well together with the pastille, and take the pipkin from the fire and pour cold water into it and let it cool; then knead and work it as before, and if it should stick to your hands, anoint them with

mano ongite le mano cum lolio de semi di lino et lassa stare in la dicta aqua per 6 di mutando laqua destate doi volte el di et de inverno una volta et quando voi cavare el dicto azurro tolli una catino vitrio et mectivi dentro el dicto pastillo et habi aqua tepida e lassa rescaldare el dicto pastillo et coprilo cum una miscola et vienlo spremendo et quando lo pastillo e bene disfacto metivi uno poco daqua piu calda o vero rescalda quella aqua medesima in qualche vaso et cosi cum quella medesima aqua calda lo lava 8 volte poi lassa refredare et el pastillo rimara de sopra et lazurro andara al fondo et tene coperta la dicta aqua acio non vi vada alcuna bruttura poi cava laqua de sopra insiemi cum lo pastillo pianamente che lazuro che e in nel fondo non se mova poi pone quella aqua a scaldare et ritornala sopra a lo azurro et lassa poi reposare et el pastillo arivra a sommo poi sepera la dicta aqua et falla bullire et ritornala bulita sopra a lo azurro al dicto modo et cava fora el pastillo che e buono per chavare deli altre azurre e riponilo in loco netto et sappi che el primo azurro e piu fino lo secondo meno lo terzo mancho et serbali in saculo camusci o vero in albio de terra vitriato.

25. *Modo affinare el pastillo se caso fusse che te venisse arso che non ne uscisse lazurro pratica a raconciarlo.*—Tolli uno pagnolo et metivi dentro aqua fredda et ponilo al foco et quando e calda metivi dentro lo pastillo arso et commo se cominza a rescaldarse cavalo fora et habbi uno tegami vitriato et pollo al foco et metivi dentro el pastillo et dalli il foco lento et giongivi sopra del pastillo queste cose se fusse infra lo azurro et lo pastillo libre doi oz. j de cera nova, oz. j de olio de olivo, oz. j de trementina et miscola omne cosa bene insiemi cum lo pastillo et leva el tegami dal foco et metivi dentro aqua fredda et lassa lo refredare poi lor mena et extiralo commo prima et se se apicasse ale mano ongiti le mano cum olio et per questo

oil, and in this way you will make it right, and you may wash the azure out of it as before, and it will be good azure.

26. *The way to make the pastille to prepare one of these stones when it is much finer than the rest.*—Take 4 oz. of white resin, 8 oz. of Greek pitch, 1 oz. of turpentine, 1 oz. of mastic, 1 oz. of linseed-oil, and use this for a pound of the lapis lazuli, and do as you did before.

modo lo riconciarai et cavane poi lo azurro commo de sopra et sera fino azurro.

26. *Modo da fare el pastillo per lavorare una di queste prete quando fusse piu fina de vantagio piu che laltre.*—Pilglia oz. 4 de ragia biancha et oz. 8 de pece greca, oz. j de trementina, oz j de mastice, oz. j de olio de semi de lino et questo adopera per una libra de la dicta preta dazurro et fa la pratica commo di sopra.

HERE BEGINS THE SECOND TREATISE

CONCERNING MANY AZURES THAT ARE MADE ARTIFICIALLY: AND FIRST WE MUST TREAT OF THE TRIAL OF AZURES, WHETHER THEY ARE NATURAL MINERAL AZURES, OR WHETHER THEY ARE ARTIFICIALLY MADE.

27. *How to know ultramarine azure from the artificial, by trial and examination.*[1]—Take the dust of the mineral, or a little of the azure extracted from the mineral, and put it on a red-hot plate of iron shining and without rust. If it does not change colour, it is excellent. If it turns black, it is of little value. If it is adulterated, the ash will be pale. If it turns whitish, it is made artificially.

28. *It is known in another way by experience.*[2]—Put a little azure in your hand, or into a shovel, pour clean water upon it, and rub it with your fingers, and if it immediately settles into the cracks of your hands or of the shovel, that azure is very fine and good; otherwise it is not so.

29. *To make azure artificially.*—Take one pound of brass filings, and the same quantity of sal ammoniac[3] or a little less, and dissolve the sal ammoniac in aqua tartari; then, with that water, make a paste with verdigris, and put it into a glass cucurbit covered and sealed up like a blind alembic,[4] and let it stand under hot dung for 15 days; then take out what is inside and put it into a crucible in a place where it will melt, but uncovered; when melted take it out, and when it is cool, grind it on a stone with aqua tartari, and let it dry, and you

---

[1] This recipe is also in the Paris MS. vi. MDCCXLIX. No. 9. If the mineral turn black, this is a proof that it is copper ore, and not Lapis Lazuli. Eraclius mentions the same test for distinguishing the true Lapis Lazuli.

[2] This recipe is also in the Paris MS.

INCIPIT SECUNDUS TRACTATUS

DE MULTIS AZURRIS PER ARTIFICIUM FIENDIS ET ARTIFICIALITER FACTIS: ET PRIMO DICENDUM ET VIDENDUM EST DE PROBATIONE AZURRORUM SI SUNT NATURALIA DE MINERA AN ARTIFICIALITER FACTA.

27. *Modus cognoscendi azurrum ultramarinum ab artificiale per experientiam et examen.*—Accipe pulverem minere ejus aut parum de azurro extracto de minera et eum pone super laminam ferri ignitam et nitidam absque erugine. Si non mutaverit collorem optimum est. Si vero revertit ad nigredinem parum valet. Si vero affalsatum est cinis smortua efficietur. Si vero revertitur ad albedinem artificialiter factum est.

28. *Alio modo cognoscitur per experientiam.*—Pone aliquantulum de azurro in manu tua aut pone in scutella et desuper infunde aquam claram et frica cum digitis postea subito si aderat per manus rimmulas aut per scutellam azurrum illud valde pulcrum et bonum est aliter non.

29. *Ad faciendum azurrum per artificium.*—Abbeas libram unam limature heris et tantundem salis armoniaci vel parum minus et solutum sit sal in aqua tartari sive oleo deinde cum aqua ista fac lutum de viride heris et micte in cucurbita vitri coperta et sigillata ad modum factum elembicum cecum et dimitte sub fimo calido quindecim diebus—postea extrahe quod est intus et micte in crugibulo et micte in loco fusionis discoperto tamen ut fundatur deinde extrahe et cum refrigidatum fuerit ducas super lapidem cum oleo sive aqua tartari et per-

---

3 Sal Ammoniac is now called Hydrochlorate of Ammonia, and "aqua tartari sive oleo" is a solution of Potash.

4 A blind Alembic appears to be an alembic without a pipe for conveying the vapour to a receiver.

will have azure; and if you wish to make it brilliant, colour it with a solution of scraped verzino in white wine, in the same manner as you were directed in the other recipe concerning natural azure.

30. *To make azure artificially.*—Take four parts of a stone brought from beyond sea, which is called mercury, and it must be sublimed according to the usual method, that is to say, it must be held on a red hot and burning plate, for a considerable space of time, in order that it may be reduced to powder, then take two parts of sal ammoniac, and one part of sulphur, grind each well by itself; then mix them well, and put them into a glass vase, lute the vase with the philosopher's lute,[1] and let it dry. Then put the vessel into the furnace, and give it a moderate fire, and when you see the white smoke come out of the mouth of the vase, make no more fire; and when it is cold break the vase cautiously and you will find good azure.

31. *To make artificial azure.*—Take fine marble, and about an equal quantity, by guess, of the flower of metal[2] which the dyers use, and grind them well together, boil them in good red wine, put the mixture in the sun to dry; afterwards grind it again, adding more of the said flower, then grind it and dry it again. Afterwards take verdigris and indico, and grind them well together, and then you must have "lac calvisei," otherwise called starch, and mix the ingredients until the colour pleases you. Put it in the sun to dry and it is done.

32. *To make azure.*—Take of Roman vitriol 1 lb., saltpetre ½ lb., of cinnabar 2 oz., of roche alum 3 oz., of sal ammoniac 1 oz., of orpiment 1 oz., of verdigris 1 oz.; and let each be ground separately very fine, and then let them be mixed together, and afterwards put them to distil in an alembic; first with a very slow fire,

---

[1] Lutum Sapientæ consisted of white of egg beaten to a froth, and mixed with iron filings. A coat of this was to be applied on the vessel to be luted, and when this was dry, another coat was to be given; and so on until three or four had been applied. (See Breve Compendio di Maravigliosi Segreti dal Sig. F. Domenica Auda Venezia e Bassano. And see I Secreti di Don Alessio Piemontese, Part I., p. 137. Ed. Venezia, 1557.)

micte siccari et habebis azurrum et si vis illuminare ipsum mitte verzinum abrasum in vino albo et collora ut habuisti in alia recepta de azurro naturale.

30. *Ad faciendum azurrum per artifitium.* — Tolli parte quattro duna preta ultramarina che se chiama mercurio e volse solimare secondo el loro modo cioe che se vole tenere in su la piastra infocata e acesa per spatio duno pezo acio che se possa spolverizare poi tolli doi parte de sale armoniacho et una parte de solfano e macina bene omne una da per se e poi le mistica bene et mectile in uno vaso de vetrio et lutalo cum luto de sapientia o vero philosophico et lassa seccare poi lo mecti in lo fornello et dalli el fuoco moderato et quando tu vederai uscire el fumo bianco per la bocca del vaso non fare piu foco et quando e freddo rompe lo vaso cautamente et trovarai buono azurro.

31. *Ad faciendum azurrum artificiale.*—Summe de lapide pulcro marmoreo et tantundem ad extimationem de flore mectalli quo tintores utuntur et tere simul bene et fac deinde bullire in vino rubeo bono et pone ad solem ut siccetur postea iterum tere adendo de dicto flore et sicca deinde iterum tere et sicca postea accipe de viride ere et de indica, et bene simul tere deinde habeas lac calvisej aliter vocatur amido et simul misce donec color tibi placet et pone ad solem ut siccetur et erit factum.

32. *Ad azurrum faciendum.*—Recipe vitrioli romani libram unam, salis nitrii libram mediam cinabrii oz. 2, aluminis rocze oz. 3, salis armoniaci oz. j, auripiumenti oz. j, viridis æris oz. unam et quodlibet per se teratur subtiliter deinde insimul corporentur et postea pone ad distillandum per elembicum primo

---

[2] I think this is a mistake, and that for "mectalli" we should read "guati," as in Nos. 36, 40, 75, 76, and 77. The explanation of the term is given in No. 75, where it is said to be the froth which floats on the dyers' vats when they are dyeing with woad. This froth is the produce of fermentation.

and take off the first water by itself, until the alembic reddens, then put away that water by itself, and collect the next water, that is the second water.[1] You must know, as I said before, that the fire must be gentle at first, for the first 6 hours; and you must then increase the fire until the alembic gets white hot, and no longer emits a red smoke, which shows itself in the recipient vase; then let it cool, and this water will be stronger than any water in the world. For this water dissolves and corrodes, and reduces to water all things under the sky, namely, stones and metals, and is white and clear like spring water; and, if heated, gives out a very red smoke; it is strong and acrid, and must therefore be kept securely closed. And when you wish to make azure, take that second water, which you set apart, and dissolve verdigris in it, keep it in a glass vase, and warm it a little at the fire, as the jewellers do, because it will dissolve sooner, and when it is dissolved, put some oxide of tin into it and evaporate the water, and in the bottom of the vase you will find very beautiful azure. And if you wish it to be more beautiful and like ultramarine azure in appearance, take very fine brass filings, and put them into the before-mentioned water, and do as above directed; when they are dissolved, put oxide of tin into the mixture, and do as before, and you will have an azure better than German azure, and in appearance and colour it will be equal to ultramarine. If in that water you dissolve the golden marcasite, as before, you will find a beautiful purple, and if you dissolve iron filings in it, and put calcined brass into that water, you will have a red colour, which is called "minius."

33. *To make azure.*—Take of lime made from marble or travertine, obtained from the living rock, one pound, of verdigris one pound, of sal ammoniac two pounds, and grind the whole together to a fine powder; make the whole into a paste with spirit of wine like rather stiff dough, and then put the com-

---

[1] The water described here is evidently nitro-muriatic acid, the aqua regia of the Alchemists. This recipe is a proof that the colour called the "Purple of Cassius," was known at least 150 years before the period of its

cum igne lentissimo et accipe aquam primam per se donec erubescat elembicus tunc remove aquam illam per se et collige aquam per se aliam scilicet secundam aquam et scias ut supra dixi ignis primus esse debet lentus per 6 horas deinde auge fortem ignem donec alembicus albescat et non amplius mictet fumum rubeum qui in vase apparebit tunc dimitte frigidari et supra dicta aqua est fortior quam aquam mundi. Nam hæc aqua solvit et corrodit et in aquam rediget omnia quæ sub celi sunt viz. lapides et mectalla et est alba et clara sicut aqua fontis et si calefit emitet fumum rubicundissimum durum et fortem et ideo serva eam bene obturata. Et cum vis azurrum facere, acipe secundam aquam quam servasti et in ea disolve viridem eris et tene eam in vase vitri et aliquantulum calefac ad ignem in modum orifici quia citius disolveretur et disolutum desuper pone de calce Jovis et evapora aquam et infundo vasis invenies azurrum valde pulcrum et si vis eum pulcriorem quasi azurrum ultramarinum in aparentia. Accipe limaturam eris vel octoni subtilissimam et pone in prædicta aqua et fac ut supra ut disolvatur et disolutum desuper pone calcem Jovis et fac ut supra et habebis azurrum meliorem quam almaneum et in apparentia et in collore est sicut azurrum ultramarinum. Et si in ista aqua disolveris marchesitam auream ut supra pulcrum pavonatium invenies. Et si disolveris in ea ferrum limatum et in tali aqua posueris es ustum invenies colorem rubicundum qui vocatur minius.

33. *Ad faciendum azurrum.*—Accipe calcina marmorina o vero travertina in petra viva libri unum verderamo libre j sale armoniaco libre 2 et macina omne cosa subtili et in pasta cum aqua vite in modo duna pasta de pane durecto poi pone la dicta compositione in uno panno de lino grosso et forte et poninolo

---

reputed discovery. The golden marcasite (auriferous iron pyrites) being dissolved in the aqua regia, was precipitated by the oxide of tin, and the result was a beautiful purple colour.

position into a thick and strong linen cloth, and place it in dung for the space of a month. Then take it out, when it will have become hard like a stone ; and if it does not become hard, let it remain beneath the hot dung until it hardens, and then pound it fine and grind it on marble, and take for every pound of this composition two ounces of the flower of woad, and grind them together, and rub them up with a little spirit of wine, and incorporate all well together ; then let the composition dry, and keep it in a bag of chamois leather excluded from the air.

34. *To make azure.*—Take of sal ammoniac two pounds, and brass filings two pounds, and sublime the mixture 6 or 7 times. Put the azure which is at the bottom upon a marble slab in a damp place, and it will dissolve into a blue water, and do the same with the sal ammoniac, mixing it with the azure, which it will soon soak up, and put it to dry. And know that this can be done with every metal, but brass and copper are the best, and the least expensive; and this azure is worth 4 ducats the pound.

35. *To make azure.*—Take 1 oz. of sal-ammoniac, and 6 oz. of verdigris, and grind these powders very fine with oil of tartar upon marble ; then put them into a glazed vase, and let them stand some days, and you will find the verdigris converted into a very beautiful azure.

36. *The way to make azure.*—Take the shells of hens' eggs well washed, and put them into a new jar, and lute the jar with lutum sapientiæ. Calcine the shells and then grind them fine upon a stone ; afterwards take clean indigo[1] liquefied with common water, and mix the lime with that colour by grinding it upon the stone, a little at a time, until it assumes a good colour. But if you have no indigo, use the froth of dyer's woad instead of it, and do as before ; and know that while the woad is boiling in the dyer's cauldron, you must take away the froth and mix it with the egg-shells, and afterwards dry and keep it.

37. *To make azure.*—Take of refined saltpetre, brass filings, sal-ammoniac, sulphur vivum, and quicklime, each one ounce,

---

[1] This is the true Indigo.

socto lc litami per spatio duno mese de po el tra fora essendo tornato duro in forma de petra et non tornando duro lassalo tanto stare sotto lo litami caldo che diventi duro et de poi lo pista subtili et macinalo in marmo subtili poi tolli per omne libra de la dicta compositione oz. 2 de fiore de guato et macina de compagnia et sborfandoli cum uno poco daqua vite et incorpora bene insiemj poi lassa sciutare et serbalo in saculo de camosscio che non stia alayere.

34. *Affare azurro.*—Tolli sale armoniaco lb. 2 limatura de octone lb. 2, e fa solimare sei o 7 volte et pone lo azurro che e in fondo sopra uno marmo steso in loco humido e disolverasse in aqua cilistrina et el simili fa del sale armoniaco et agiungi insieme et imbevera lo azurro de sopra ditto sopra el marmo et imbeverasse presto e pollo a secare et sappi che se po fare de omne metallo ma loctone et lo ramo e piu digno et cum mancho spesa et el dicto azurro vale ducate 4 la libbra.

35. *Ad faciendum azurrum.*—Accipe sale armoniaco oz. j verderame oz. 6 et macina queste polve bene subtili cum olio de tartaro sopra marmo poi lo pone in uno vaso vitriato et lassalo stare alcuni di et troverai lo verderamo convertito tucto in azurro asa bello.

36. *Modus faciendi azurrum.*—Recipe testas ovorum gallinarum ben lotis et mitte in olla nova et luta luto sapientiæ et calcina et deinde tere subtili super lapidem tunc accipe indicum bene mundum et liquefactum cum aqua comuni et cum isto colore misce super lapidem terendo dictam calcem paulatim paulatim quoutque habeat collorem bonum. Si autem non habes dictum collorem indici loco ipsius pone spumam guati tintorum. Eodem modo fac ut supra et scias quando guatum bulit in caldarea tintorum debes spumam auferre et miscere cum dictis testis ovorum et postea sicca et serba.

37. *Ad azurrum faciendum.*—Summe salnitrij affinati limature octonis salis armoniaci sulphuris vivi calcis vive an. oz. j

grind what is necessary to be ground, and put the ingredients into a glass jar, and pour very strong white vinegar upon them, so as to cover the powders. Lute the jar with lutum sapientiæ, and put it in dung for 15 days; then grind the powder, and preserve it in a purse of chamois-leather.

38. *To make azure in another way.*—Take one drachm of indigo, and grind it well, and take a great quantity of the juice of the euphorbia,[1] and mix and incorporate them well. Put them in the sun, let them dry, and preserve them.

39. *To make azure.*—Procure some very white marble or travertine, and bake it in a furnace in a linen cloth, lute it with lutum sapientiæ; then take the lime, and put it into water, and wash it three or four times. Afterwards take indigo, wash it in water, and let the lime absorb that water; then dry it in the shade. Repeat the operation until the colour suits you.

40. *To make azure.*—Take very white marble, and roast it in the fire for a day and a night, and when it is calcined grind it fine upon another marble slab; then take the froth of indigo or woad which is in the dyer's vat, and soak the powder in it, and do this until the colour of the azure pleases you, then dry it; and when you require it, take and use it.

41. *To make artificial azure.*—Take of sal-ammoniac 1 part, of verdigris 2 parts, of ceruse ½ a part, grind them well together, and make them into a paste with oil of tartar, and put the whole into a glass vase luted in the manner of the philosophers; and when the lute is dry put it into the oven while the bread is baking, and when the bread shall have been baked 7 times, the process will be completed.

42. *To make good azure.*—Take the third part of a pound of lime made from marble or travertine, 4 oz. of verdigris, and two oz. of sal-ammoniac, grind the whole together with strong white vinegar, in the manner of a sauce, and then put it into a jar well closed, and expose it to the air for three days and

[1] Lac Turtumagli—the juice of a species of Euphorbia. Matthioli (p. 1318) names seven species; but it is probable that the species from

pro quolibet teranturque que terenda sunt et pone in olla vitriata et super-pone acetum album fortissimum ut supernactet pulveribus et luta ollam luto sapientiæ et pone sub fimo diebus 15^{im} deinde macina ipsum et repone in bursia camuscij.

38. *Ad faciendum azurrum per alium modum.*—Tolle unam dragmam indici et bene molle et habeas multum lac turtumagli et simul misce et bene incorpora et pone ad solem et dimitte siccari et repone.

39. *Ad azurrum faciendum.*—Invenies marmorem sive travertinum colloris albissimi et quoquatur in furno in panni lini lutato luto sapientiæ deinde accipiatur cals et ponatur in aqua et lavetur ter vel quatuor postea accipe indicum et lavetur in aqua et cals illius aque potetur deinde siccetur in umbram et iteretur operatio donec color tibi placeat.

40. *Ad azurrum faciendum.*—Recipe marmorem albissimum et alla ipsum in igne per diemque noctem et cum calcinatum fuerit super alium marmorem subtile tere deinde Recipe spumam indici sive guati quam in caldaria tintorum est et imbibe per dictum pulverem fortiter et cum siccum fuerit iterum imbibe et hoc tamdiu facies donec collor azurri tibi placeat et sica et cum opus fuerit tolle et utere ipso.

41. *Affare azurro artificiale.*—Accipe sale armoniaco parte j. verderame parte 2 biacha parte meza spolverizati bene insiemj et impasta cum olio de tartaro et pone omne cosa in uno vaso de vetrio alutato al modo filosofico poi che e secco lo loto ponilo in lo forno del pane quando el pane se coce poi che sera cocto el pane 7. volte sera facto.

42. *Affare azurro bono.*—Summe lo terzo duna lb. de calcina marmorina o travertina et oz. 4 de verderamo et oz. doi de sale armoniaco poi macina omne cosa insiemj cum aceto forte e biancho ad modo duno sapore poi lo mecti in una ampolla bene turata et mectila alayere per tre di et tre nocti poi la soc-

---

whence this milky juice was extracted was the Euphorbia Esula, the Tithymalus Pinea, called in Italian Erba latte and Lataroli.

nights; then bury it, and let it have rain, wind, sun and air, and suffer it to remain for the space of six months, and let it be exposed both to the winter and summer. At the end of 6 months or thereabouts take it out, and break it, and you will find the azure, at which you will rejoice; grind it well with strong ley, put it into a glazed vase, and let it rest until it sinks to the bottom; then pour off the ley and wash it again with very weak and clear ley, and do as before. Then wash it with clear cold water, and let it settle, the good azure will sink to the bottom, and the bad will remain in the water like indigo. Then remove that blue water with a sponge so as not to disturb the azure that is at the bottom, and let it dry in the shade, and you will have good and fine azure. Keep it in leather so that the air may not have access to it.

43. *To make azure.*—Take of verdigris 6 oz., sal-ammoniac 1 oz., unburnt gesso 1 oz., grind each dry by itself, then mix them together and soak the powders with water of tartar, so that the water may cover the powders, and put all into a flask, and stop well the mouth of the flask. Tie a string round its neck, and hang it to the chain in the smoke for some days, and you will find the azure, which you must grind well, and then preserve it.

44. *To make splendid azure.*—To make splendid azure for walls. Take a glass [copper?] flask, and put into it enough powdered travertine, well and finely ground, to fill it half way, and pour upon it very strong vinegar distilled through an alembic, so as to fill the flask. Then seal up the mouth of the flask, and put it in dung or in the refuse of grapes for a month. Afterwards take it out, and you will have azure, which you may grind and keep.

45. *To make azure.*—Take very thin plates of silver, and fasten them skilfully over the vapour of very strong vinegar in a jar, so that there may be a space of one finger's breadth between the vinegar and the plates; cover the jar well to exclude the air, and put it in a warm place, such as dung or the refuse of grapes, for a month, then uncover it, and you will see the azure upon the silver plates. This you must rub and scrape

terra et fache habia aqua et vento et sole et ayere et lassala stare per spatio de 6 mesi et fache ella participa delo inverno et dela state in capo de 6 mesi o circha cavarala fora et rompila et troverai lo azurro del quale tene alegrarai et macinalo sotili in marmo cum liscia forte et pollo in uno vaso vitriato et lassa posare tanto che vada al fondo poi sepera la liscia et lavalo una altra volta cum liscia dolce dolce et chiara et fa commo prima poi lo lava cum aqua chiara et fredda poi lo lassa possare et lo azurro bono andara al fondo et el grosso stara per laqua ad modo duno endico et cava fora quella aqua cilistrina cum una spongna per modo che non conturbi lo azurro che e al fondo et lassa secare alombra et haverai azurro bello et bono et serbalo in corami che non senta ayere.

43. *Ad azurrum faciendum.*—Recipe verderame oz. 6. sale armoniaco oz. j guersa cruda oz. j et macina cescunj subtili dasciuto poi le mista insiemi et imbevera le dicte polvere cum aqua de tartaro che laqua sopravanza ale dicte polvere et mecti omne cosa in una ampolla et obtura bene la bocca de lampolla et legala in lo collo et appiccala al fumo sopra ala catena per alcuni di et troverai lo azurro el quale macinalo bene et serbalo.

44. *Ad faciendum azurrum feriale.*—Ut habeas azurrum feriale per murum. Recipe ampulla vitrii et intus pone tantum de pulvere travertini bene triturati et subtili ut dimidiam sit et desuper pone acetum fortissimum distillatum per alembicum ut vas sit plenum et os ejus optime sigillatum et pone sub fimo aut venacia per unum mensem postea extrahe et habebis azurrum quod tere et serba.

45. *A* (sic) *faciendum azurrum.*—Summe laminas argenteas subtilissimas et liga ingeniose supra vaporem aceti fortissimi in olla ita quod remaneat unius digitis de vacuitate inter acetum et laminas et coperi bene ollam ut non respiret et pone eam in loco callido ut est fimus aut venatia per unam mensem et descoperias et videbis azurrum super laminas quem frica et rade et repone dictas laminas ut supra et sic reitera donec consumentur

off, and then put back the plates as before, and repeat this until they are consumed. And if you have no silver plates put brass plates instead, and do as before; but it will not be so beautiful.

46. *To make azure.*—Take one part of sulphur vivum, two parts of Roman vitriol,[1] both in fine powder, and two parts of quicksilver. Put these articles well mixed into a flask, and heat them as you did the vermilion; when it is done it will give out a blue smoke. Then take it from the fire, and when it is cool grind and keep it.

47. *To make azure.*[2]—Take 2 ounces of quicksilver, 3 ounces of sulphur, and 4 ounces of sal-ammoniac; grind the sulphur and sal-ammoniac very fine, and then take a flask with a long neck, and lute it with lutum sapientiæ on the outside the thickness of one finger from the neck downwards, and let it dry. Then put the before-mentioned ingredients into the flask, and stop up the mouth of the flask with a cork, make a very small hole in the middle of it, and put this flask into a new unglazed jar nearly full of sifted ashes, so that it may be covered half way up the neck by the ashes. Then put the jar over a charcoal fire, let the fire be very slow for the first four hours, and increase the heat until you see white or blue smoke issue out of the flask. Then immediately remove the fire, let the flask cool and then break it; grind the azure fine on porphyry, and keep it in a place free from air, and you will have good azure.

48. *To make azure.*—Take of roche alum, Roman vitriol, and saltpetre, each one ounce; distil them through an alembic, and then keep the water in a vessel securely closed. Then take calcined egg-shells, and grind them with the distilled water, and let them dry: do this three or four times. Then take very strong vinegar, and for every pound of vinegar take 5 oz. of verdigris; grind it up with the vinegar, and distil it through an alembic, and with that distilled vinegar soak and grind the egg-shells three or four times. Then dry the mass, and keep

---

1 I think that in this case, Roman Vitriol signifies Sulphate of Copper.

et si non habes laminas argenti loco ipsius pone laminas octoni et fiet ut supra sed non ita pulcrum.

46. *Affare azurro.*—Accipe parte j. de solpho vivo et parte doi de vitriolo romano spolverizati subtili et parte doi de argento vivo et mecti le sopradicte polve in una ampolla bene incorporate et cocilo commo lo cinabrio et quando sera cocto fara fumi azurro alhora tolli via el foco et quando sera freddo macinalo et serbalo.

47. *Ad azurrum faciendum.*—Summe once doi dargento vivo once tre de solphino et once quatro de sale armoniaco et macina bene subtili lo solfo et lo sale predicto poi tolli una ampolla che habia el collo longo et inlutala cum luto de sapientia de fora grosso uno deto dal collo ingiù et lassalo sciuctare poi mecti queste cose sopradicte in nel ampolla et obtura la bocca de lampolla cum suvera et lassali in el mezo uno foro picolino poi mecti questa ampolla in uno pignatto novo non vitriato quasi pieno de cenere crebellata poi pone lampolla in la dicta cenera che sia coperta fino al mezo del collo de la dicta cenera et poi ponila dicta pignatta al foco de carbone et dalli el foco lento lento da prima per 4 hore poi lo vieni crescendo per infino attanto che vedrai uscire de la dicta ampolla fumi bianco o vero fumi azurro alhora subito levali el foco et lassa refredare poi rompe lampolla et macina lo azurro in porfido subtili poi serbalo in loco senza ayere et haraj bono azurro.

48. *Ad faciendum azurrum.*—Accipe alumi de rocho vitriolo romano sal netrio ana oz. j, e stilla per lambicco poi serba laqua bene opturata poi torrai calcina de cociole dova et macinala cum la dicta aqua stillata et lassa secare et cosi farai 3 o 4 volte poi toraj aceto fortissimo et per omne libra daceto torai oz. 5 de verde ramo et macinalo cum lo dicto aceto poi lo pone a stillare per lambicco et cum quello aceto stillato imbevera et macina lo sopradicta calcina 3 o 4 volte et poi lo secca et serbalo in bursia corj et haverae bello azurro et cosi

---

2 This recipe is of the same nature as that in No. 30, but the proportions vary.

it in a leather purse, and you will have fine azure. You may do the same with lime made from travertine or marble, but lime made from egg-shells is better.

49. *To make azure.*—Take a flask of pure copper, and put lime made from white marble into it, so as to fill it half way; then fill it with strong white vinegar, and put it, well covered over, into a warm place for a month; then take it out, and grind the mass, adding to it some indigo, and put it away, and it is done.

50. *To make azure.*—Fill a glazed earthenware vase half full of urine; then take strips of copper, as thick as for a copper cauldron, and suspend them in the air at about two fingers' breadth above the urine; stop up the vase, and let it stand for two months, and you will see the azure upon the strips of copper; and if you wish to scrape them you may do so; and if you wish them to remain until they become quite brittle, they will become so in seven months.

51. *To make azure.*[1]—Take of verdigris 2 oz., sal ammoniac 1 oz., white lead ½ oz., pounded together; make them into a paste with oil of tartar, and put all these things into a glass vase luted with philosophers' lute, and put the vase into the oven for baking bread, and when the bread has been baked six or seven times the process will be completed.

52. *To make azure.*—Take indigo and verdigris well ground, and a great quantity of the juice of the euphorbia, and grind them well together. Place the mass in the sun, and dry it well; then wash it, and it will be good azure.

53. *To make azure from silver.*—Take 3 oz. of silver, and 1 oz. of copper; melt them together, and make them into very thin plates, and suspend them over the vapour of vinegar in a vase, well covered to prevent evaporation; then put the vessel into hot dung for thirty days; the azure will remain attached to the plates; then take it away, and renew the operation as long as the plates last.

---

[1] A repetition of No. 41. This recipe is given in "Secrets des Arts et des Métiers."

porai fare cum la calcina del travertino o marmo ma la calcina de le cocciole e meglio.

49. *Ad azurrum faciendum.*—Ahbeas ampulla de puro cupro et pone intus calcem de albo marmore ita ut dimidia sit et adibe acetum album fortissimum ut plena sit et eam pone in calido loco copertam optime per unum mensem postea extrahe et macina dictam massam adendo sibi de colore indici et repone et est factum.

50. *Ad azurrum faciendum.*—Tolli orina et mectila in uno vaso de terra vitriato et el vaso vole essere per mita poi tolli piastre de ramo a modo de caldare grosso et mectili in ayere che stia discosto dalla orina doi deta et obtura el vaso et lassa stare a termine de doi mese et vederai sopra le lamini lo azurro e se tu le vorai radare se ponno radare et se tu le volesscie lassare stare tanto che tucti vengano frangibili et farasse in secte mesi.

51. *Affare azurro.*—Recipe verderamo oz. 2 sale armoniaco oz. j biacha oz. ½ spulve[ri]zati insiemi et impasta cum olio de tartaro et pone tute queste cose in uno vaso de vetrio lutato de luto philosophico et metilo in lo forno del pane quando sera cocto el pane 6 o 7 volte el sera facto.

52. *Affare azurro.*—Tolli indico verderamo bene macinato habbi multo lacte de tortomaglio et macina bene insiemi poi lo pone al sole a seccare bene poi lo lava e de facto bono azurro.

53. *Affare azurro de argento.*—Ahvve oz 3. dargento e oz. j. de ramo, et fondi insiemj et fanni piastre sutilissime et polle sopra alo vapore de laceto sospese in uno vaso bene coperto che non possa evaporare poi lo poni socto lo litamj bene caldo per 30 di et lo azurro remara atacato ale lamine et levalo via poi reitera la pratica per infino le lamini saranno bonne.

54. *To make azure.*—Take of sal ammoniac 1 oz., verdigris 3 oz., and mix them together with water of tartar until they are as soft as dough, or rather softer. Put the mixture into a hot oven in a well-closed glass vase, and let it remain there for several days, and you will find good azure, which you must keep in a sealed jar, or in a bag of chamois leather.

55. *For the same, in another way.*—Take 2 oz. of burnt copper, 1 oz. of sulphur, and 1 oz. of tartar of wine;[1] grind the whole together, and make it into a paste with urine passed three times through a filter, or with strong white vinegar; then put it into a glazed vase, and boil it over the fire, stirring it well. Take it off, and put it into a glass vessel; stop up the mouth of it, and let it remain in the sun for fifteen days, and you will find azure; and if it is not crystallized with the urine or vinegar, leave it in the oven after the bread is taken out.

56. *For the same, another way.*—Take 1 lb. of very fine brass filings, 3 oz. of quicklime, 5 oz. of tartar pounded fine and calcined, for it will be better than raw, 4 oz. of terra verde, 1 oz. of sal ammoniac; mix all these things together with strong white vinegar, so as to be like dough, or rather thick, and put the mixture into a glass or glazed earthenware vase, well closed, so as to exclude the air, and place it in horsedung or the refuse of grapes, and let it remain there, well covered up at the depth of about two or three feet, for fifteen days; then take it out, and grind it well on porphyry, and put it into a leather purse; and know that this azure is better for walls, upon mortar, than for any other purpose.

57. *To make azure for walls, upon mortar.*—Take finely-powdered and very fine white lime from marble, and put it into a new glazed jar, so as to fill it about half, or rather less; and know that the lime must be very fresh and fine. Then fill the jar with very strong red or white vinegar, and lute the jar so as to exclude the air; put it under horsedung, or under the refuse of wine, for one month or forty natural days; then open

---

[1] An impure supertartrate of potash.

54. *Ad faciendum azurrum.*—Recipe salis armoniaci oz. j, viridis eris oz. 3, confitiantur simul cum tartari aqua donec molle fiat sicut pasta vel modicum plus et ponatur in furno calido in vase vitrio per otime obturato et stet ibi per aliquos dies et invenies azurrum bonum et reserva in vase plumbato sive saculo camusii.

55. *Ad idem per alium modum.*—Accipe oz. 2 rami combusti et oz. j sulphuris et oz j feccis vini et terantur omnia et impastentur cum hurina distillata per filtrum tribus vicibus vel impasta cum aceto albo forti postea pone in aliquo vase vitriato et bulliat ad ignem et commisciatur bene postea elleva et pone in vitreo vase et bene os ejus obtura et dimicte stare ad solem per 15 dies et invenies azurrum et si non fuerit zellata hurina sive aceto dimicte in furno post extractionem panis.

56. *Ad idem per aliam formam.*—Summe limaturam rami subtilissimam lb. j. calcis vive oz. 3 tartari pulverizati subtili et calcinati quia melius erit quam crudi oz. 5 terre viridis oz. 4 salis armoniaci oz. j omnia confice insimul cum acerrimo aceto albo ut sit in modum paste et potius magis spisse et pone in vase vitrio vel terreo vitriato per optime obturato ut non respiret et pone sub equino fimo vel venatias et ibi maneas bene coperto per tres vel duos pedes circum circha per 15 dies demum extrahe et trita bene eum in porfido et repone in bursia camusi. Et scias quod hoc azurum magis bonum est per muros in calcina quam in aliis rebus.

57. *A fare azurro per muro in calcina.*—Havve calcina de marmo bene sotili et canida et metila in una pignatta vitriata nova tanto che sia mezo o mancho piu tosto che piu et sappi che la calcina vole esser freschissima et bene subtili poi empi la pignata de fortissimo aceto rosso o biancho poi copri la dicta pignatta cum luto che non respire poi la poni sucto lo litami de cavallo o vero socto la venaccia per uno mese o 40 di naturali

the vase, and you will find at the top bright azure good for walls, and underneath it impurities—that is, the lime—which you may throw away.

58. *To make azure by means of aqua fortis.*—Take of Roman vitriol 1 lb., of refined saltpetre ½ lb., and 4 oz. of vermilion, grind all these things together very finely, mix them well together, then put them in a bottle and distil them through an alembic with a gentle fire at first, and receive the first water until the alembic begins to get yellow, or to redden; then remove the recipient, and put on another, and lute the edges well, so as to be air-tight, and receive the next water, and throw away the first water, for it is useless for this operation, and then increase the fire, and let the recipient have all the vapours from the large bottle as long as you see any come off, and keep this water in a vessel well closed so as not to evaporate; and this water is useful for making good azure almost like ultramarine. It is also useful for gilding all kinds of things.[1]

First, if you wish to make azure, take calcined tin, and put it into a glass or glazed jar, and pour some of the before-mentioned aqua fortis over it, so as to stand half a finger's breadth over the oxide of tin; let it stand so until the calcined tin is well sunk to the bottom, and is highly coloured; then pour off the water, and you will find good and fine azure, which you may sell for 5 gold ducats the pound.

If you wish to make calcined tin, take tin and put it into an earthenware vase, place it on the fire, and let it melt, and when it is melted, continue to mix it until it cools, and do not let it clog together, and you will have a calx (oxide) with which you may make the azure. You can also make the calx of tin in another way. Take tin filings and put them into a glazed jar and pour over them distilled vinegar, and cover the jar closely. Place it in dung, and let it remain until the tin and vinegar

---

[1] The description in the text appears to be imperfect. It is probably an inaccurate version of the recipe in No. 32, for making "an azure better

poi descopre el vaso e troverai de sopra azurro bono per muro et bello et de socto fecia cio e calcina la quale gieta via.

58. *A fare azurro per via daqua forte.*—Tolli vitriolo romano lb. j salnitrio affinato lb. ½ et cinabrio oz. 4 et tucte queste cose macina bene subtilissimi et poi le mista insiemi multo bene et polle in una boccia et destillale per lambicco prima cum lento foco et colglie la prima aqua per infinj che lo lambico se comincia affare croceo o vero rosigiare alhora remove l'ampolla et mectinie una altra et tura bene le junture che non spirano et coglie l'altra aqua et la prima gietta via che non vale niente in questa opera et alhora cominza a fare un poco magiore foco che prima et fa che lampolla receva bene i fumi da la boccia grandj per infino che tu vedi che ne vieni et serva questa aqua ben turata che non respire et questa aqua e bona da fare azurro bono quasi simili a lo azurro oltramarino. Et e bona ancora da dorare omne lavoro.

Prima se tu voli fare azurro tolli calcina de stagno et metila in uno vaso de vetrio overo vetriato et desopra ce pone de la dicta aqua forte dicta desopra tanto che sopravanze mezo deto de sopra ala calcina et lassa stare cosi tanto che la calcina sia bene andata al fondo et bene colorita poi sepera laqua et trovarai azurro bono et bello del quale azurro venderai ducati 5 doro la libra.

Et se tu volesci fare la calcina de stagno tolli delo stagno et pollo in uno vaso de terra et metilo al foco et lassalo desfare et commo e disfatto non finare mai de mistarlo per infino a tanto che se fredda et non lo lassare apicare insiemj et sera facta calcina cum la quale poi fare el dicto azurro. Ancora poi fare la dicta calcina de stagno in uno altro modo: tolli limatura de stagno et polla in una olla vitriata et disopra ce pone aceto distillato per lambiccho et copri bene la dicta olla et polla sub fimo et lassa tanto stare che lo stagno et aceto siano

---

than German azure, which, in appearance and colour, equals ultramarine."

are dissolved, because it will then be converted into a very fine and almost impalpable powder; and with this you can make the azure.

If you wish to gild iron or any other thing, take the thing you wish to gild, and varnish it, and let it dry; then draw what you like on the varnish, and put some of this water upon it. Warm it at the fire, and when it is hot, rub it with a linen cloth, and it will be well gilded.

B 59.[1] Take strong ley, and as much as you like of indigo, grind it with the ley, according to the depth of colour you wish for. For example, if you wish the colour to be very deep, grind more indigo with the cold ley, and then make the ley boil with the indigo for the space of one *miserere*, and afterwards remove it from the fire, and immediately put a little roche alum in powder into it, and mix it and let it cool until it is tepid or almost cold. Then put it into a piece of linen and rub it upon a chamois leather skin, and the skin will become blue. Dry it in the meridian sun or at the fire, and when it is dry, rub it with your hands and make it soft, and it will have become a beautiful blue skin, &c.

---

1 The title is wanting. It appears to be a recipe for dyeing skins rather than for painting. The hand-writing is more recent than that in the preceding chapters.

disoluti perche se convertira in polvere subtilissimo quasi senza tatto et cum questo poi fare el sopra dicto azurro.

Et se tu volesse dorare ferro o altro tolli la cosa che tu voli dorare et invernicala et lassa sciucare poi designa quello che te piace in la dicta vernice poi vi meti desopra de la dicta aqua et scald(a) al foco poi commo e bene calda sfrega cum panno de lino et vira dorato bello.

B 59. Recipe liscivium forte et indicum quantum vis et macina eum cum dicto liscivio et pone tantum emdicum secundum vis ut sit coloratum viz. si vis ut sit magis coloratum pone magis indicum ad macinandum cum dicto liscivio frigido demum fatias dictum liscivium bollire cum dicto indico per spatium unius miserere et postea extrahe ab ingne et immediate pone in eo unum modicum aluminis rocci pulverizati et misce et dimicte frigidari dummodo tepidum fiat et quasi frigidum demum pone eum in petia linea et frica super pellem camusciam et fiet azurram et sicca ad meridiem aut ad ingnem et quando erit sica frica manibus et reduc eam ad morbitatem et erit facta pulcram pellem turchinam et cetera.

HERE BEGINS THE THIRD CHAPTER

ON MAKING AZURES FROM THE JUICES OF HERBS, WHICH ARE USED ON PAPER, ON MINIATURES, ON CANVAS, AND ON GESSO; AND FIRSTLY, THAT IS TO SAY—

60. *To make azure from the juice of herbs.*—First collect in the beginning of the month of July those violet flowers which grow in the fields, and with the juice of them fill a glass flask, and pour strong vinegar or urine into it until it is full; let it be well covered over, and put it in dung or in a heap of quick-lime, or in the refuse of grapes for a fortnight, then take it out, and you will find your azure made.

61. *Also, to make azure from herbs.*—Take the blue flowers which are called "oculos pulcini," and boil them with vinegar and powdered resin and roche alum, and let the vase be air-tight; afterwards strain the liquor through a cloth, and you will have a good blue colour. You may keep the dried flowers for a whole year.

62. *On the same subject, to make blue from herbs.*—Take the flowers of wild peas, and select only those petals which are inside and above the others, and which are of a dark purple, and pound them; extract the juice from them, and incorporate the juice with white lead, and you will have a durable and tried blue colour.

63. *To dye linen cloth blue with juice of herbs.*[1]—Take the berries of the "chacabassia," and bruise them well on a thick and white, but not new, linen cloth, on both sides of the cloth. Then take a vessel full of urine, and put the cloth over it so as

---

[1] This appears to be a version of one of the recipes for "Pezzette." I cannot find the explanation of the term "Chacabassia"; perhaps, as was suggested to me by a gentleman well acquainted with the subject,

INCIPIT TERTIUS CAPITULUS

DE AZURRIS FIENDIS DE HERBARUM SUCCIS QUIBUS UTUNTUR IN CARTA SUPER MINII ET IN TELA ET IN GISSO ET PRIMO VIDELICET—

60. *Ad faciendum azurrum ex succo herbarum.*—Primo collige in principio mensis Julij illos flores violatos qui nascuntur in campis et ex succo eorum impleas unam ampullam vitream et desuper infunde fortem acetum vel orinam usque ad summum et sit optime copertam et pone sub fimo aut sub acerva calcis vive vel sub venatias per 15^{im} dies postea extrahe et invenies azurrum factum.

61. *Ad idem de azurro herbarum.*—Collige flores azurrinos qui vocantur oculos pulcini et fac eos bullire cum aceto et cum ragina pulverizata et aluminis rozi ita quod vasculum non possit aspirari postea collabis per pannum et habebis bonum colorem azurrinum et poteris servare per totum annum flores siccos.

62. *Super eodem de herbarum azurro.*—Recipe fiore de peselli salvatice et tolli solamente quello fiore che e de dentro in suso l'altro fiore el quale e pavonazo scuro et quelli pista et cavani lo sugo et incorpora lo dicto sugo cum biacca et haverai colore cilestro durabili et provato.

63. *A fare la peza azurra de sugo derbe.*—Tolli delle pomellj de la chacabascia e sfregali bene in uno panno de lino grosso et bianco non novo da omne lato de la pezza poi tolli uno catino pino de orina poi pone questa pezza sopra a questo

---

it may be the same as "scaldabassa," which is mentioned in the Le Begue MS., and which was certainly a blue colour, because it was used with yellow to produce a green colour.

*

not to touch the urine, and let it stand for three or four days. Then take it up and it will have become blue; and when you want to use it take a small piece of that cloth, put it into a shell; add a little gum water, and let it stand to soak for the space of one *miserere;* then press it, and with what you press out, paint what you like on paper, on miniatures, or elsewhere, and it will be a fine colour.

64. *To make blue in another manner with juice* [of plants].—Summe stercho canino bianco, et spolverizalo bene subtili et stemperalo cum orina ad modo de collore et cum questo stercho stemperato cum orina, scrive, depinge quello che tu voli et lassalo sechare, poi tolli lo sugo delli granelli dellebe, et pollo cum lo pennello sopra le lettere o fogliami della mistura de lo stercho et subito diventara collore azurro bello, et se misti el dicto sugo cum lo stercho, et cum lorina, et mistica bene insiemj, vira azurro, ut supra.

65. *How to grind azure to use with the pen and in body colour.*—Take the azure, and put it into a glazed pan; then add some very clean honey and incorporate them well together, then grind the honey with the blue upon marble or porphyry until it becomes an almost impalpable powder. When it is ground fine put it back into the pan and wash it several times with warm water, and when it is well washed with warm water, wash it with cold water, and after each time let the azure sink to the bottom. Continue this until it is well washed, cleaned, and purified; then take the azure and put it to soften in clear and clean ley in a glass vase, such as a tumbler, and let it stand for the space of seven days; change the ley every two or three days, and then wash it well with fresh and clear water, and let it dry in the shade in a place where no dust will get to it. And if you wish to use it as a body colour, distemper it with size made from clippings of white chamois leather and it will be good. And if you wish to use it with the pen or for miniatures, take the azure and distemper it with glue made from parchment clippings, or with gum water and prepared white of egg, and it will do well.

catino per modo che non tochi lorina et lassala stare 3 o 4 di et poi la leva et sera diventata azurra et quando la voi operare tolli uno poco de quella peza et metila in una cocia et metice uno poco daqua gommata et lassa stare a mollo per uno miserere et poi lo spremi et cum quella spremitura dipenge quello che te piace in carta sopra aliminii o altrove et sera bello colore.

64. *Affare azurro per altro modo cum sugo.*—Summe stercho canino bianco et spolverizalo bene subtili et stemperalo cum orina ad modo de collore et cum questo stercho stemperato cum orina scrive depinge quello che tu voli et lassalo sechare poi tolli lo sugo delli granelli dellebe [ellera?] et pollo cum lo pennello sopra le lettere o fogliami della mistura de lo stercho et subito diventara collore azurro bello et se misti el dicto sugo cum lo stercho et cum lorina et mistica bene insiemj vira azurro ut supra.

65. *Commo se macina lo azurro per adoperare a penna et fare corpe.*—Accipe lo azurro et mectilo in una scudella vitriata et poi mectivi del mele ben necto et incorpora bene insiemj poi macina el mele insiemj cum lo azurro supra marmo o porfido et macinalo tanto che venga quasi senza tacto et quando sera bene macinato aremetilo in quella scudella et lavalo piu volte cum aqua tepida et poi che sera bene lavato cum laqua tepida lavalo cum aqua chiara et da luna volta et laltra lassa andare lo azurro al fondo et tanto continua che sia bene lavato purificato et necto poi tolli lo dicto azurro et metilo amollo in ranno da capo necto et chiaro in uno vaso de vetrio commo e uno bichiere et lassalo stare per spatio de 7 di et omne doi o 3 di mutali lo ranno novo poi lo lava molto bene cum aqua frescha et chiara et lassalo sciugare a lombra in loco che non vi vada polvere. Et se tu el voli adoperare per fare corpe distemperalo cum colla de retalglie de camoscio bianco et stara bene. Et se tu el voli per operare appenna o per minij tolli de lo azurro et distemperalo cum colla de rasura de carta o vero cum aqua gommata et cum chiara dovo preparata et stara bene.

66. *To mix azure for writing.*—Take whatever kind of azure you like and grind it gently with prepared white of egg and ley upon porphyry, and then put it into a horn. When it is quite settled, throw away that ley and white of egg, and do this three or four times, and the last time throw away the ley, drain it and then let the azure dry. When you wish to use the colour add a little gum water to it and mix it well; and when it is settled, throw away that gum water and put some fresh, and use the colour. Some mix it with white of egg, but if you use white of egg, you must renew it every day, because if it remains too long, it turns the azure black. And if you put in it some wax from your ears, it makes the colour flow much better. Some persons say that if you put gum water into the azure, it turns black; and it is said that the azure should be ground with ley made from the ashes of the oak or with calcined ashes. Distemper it, when it is dry, with white and yolk of egg, and this makes it more beautiful, more shining, and more pure.

67. *The way to refine the azures when they are impure.*—If you have azure which is not clean, take the azure and put it in urine to soak for the space of one month, and then wash it with clear water, and distemper it as above, and it will become clean and beautiful.

68. *For the same purpose.*—Take the azure and distemper it with white of egg and tragacanth, well beaten and incorporated together, and distemper your azure with this.

69. *To purify azure.*—If the azure is too earthy, it may be purified as follows:—Take white and clean ashes, and an equal quantity of quicklime, and let it be very white; then take equal quantities of vinegar and water, and put them into a new and clean jar, and boil them with the ashes and lime, and afterwards let them cool and settle, and with that ley wash the azure, and know that after such washing the azure will appear black. Then wash the blackened azure with white wine, and let it dry, and put it into a shell with about a fourth part of gum water.

70. *To colour the azure.*—Take verzino, scrape it fine with

66. *A distemperare azurro per scrivare.*—Reccipe de qualunque sorta de azurro te piace et macinalo legiermente cum chiara dovo preparata et lisciva da capo sopra porfido poi mectilo in lo cornecto et commo ello e bene reposato et tu giecta via quella liscia et chiara et cosci fa 3 o 4 volte et l'ultima volta gieta via la liscia et lasselo bene scolare et lasselo seccare. Et quando tu lo vorai operare mectice uno poco daqua gommata et misticalo bene et commo e bene possato gietta via quella aqua gommata et mectice della nova e doperalo. Alcuno lo tempera cum chiara et aqua gommata. Ma se tu lo conciaraj cum chiara se vole renovarla quasi omne di perche standoce troppo fa lo azurro negro. Et se tu ce misti de la bruttura de le orecchie lo fa piu corrente assai. Et alcuni dicano che mettendo de laqua gomata in lo azurro diventa nero et dicano che se de macerare in liscia facta de cenere de cerro o cenere recotta et distemperarlo poi quando sera sciuto cum chiara et torno dovo et questo lo fa piu bello et piu lucente et piu puro.

67. *El modo dafinare li azurri quando fussero grossi.*—Se tu havessi azurri che non fossero necti tolli lo dicto azurro in lorina amolli per lo spatio de uno mese et piu poi lo lava cum aqua chiara et distemperalo commo e dicto disopra e vira necto et bello.

68. *Ad idem.*—Accipe lo azurro et temperalo cum chiara dovo et draganti sbatuti bene insiemj et bene incorporati luno cum laltro et con quello tempera el tuo azurro.

69. *Ad purgandum azurrum.*—Si azurrum est nimis terrestre sic purgatur. Recipe cininerem candidum et mundum et totidem de viva calce et sit bene alba et acetum et aquam equaliter et mitte in vase novo et mundo et fac simul cum cineribus et calce bulire postea permite infrigidari et clarificari et cum tali liscivia lava azurrum et sias quod post talem lavationem azurrum apparebit nigrum et deinde lava cum vino albo dictum azurrum nigrum et permicte siccari deinde pone eum in coculeam cum aliquantulo aque gumate per quartam partem.

70. *Ad colorandum azurrum.*—Reccipe verzinum et subtiliter

glass, and put the scrapings into prepared white of egg for a day and a night, so that the raspings may be covered with the white of egg; add a little pounded roche alum, then strain all these ingredients through a piece of white linen, and temper the azure with this coloured white of egg.

71. *To "multiply" your azure.*[1]—Take azure with a little ceruse, mix them together, and distemper them with white of egg; and if you wish the colour to be paler, add more ceruse, and it will be "multiplied."

72. *To colour your azure very well.*—Take 3 oz. of oil of bitter almonds, and an equal quantity of olive oil, put them into a stone vase with azure, and boil them, without smoke, for 7 hours; do this three or four times, and afterwards wash the azure with tepid ley, then with cold and clear water, so as to clean it well. Then dry it, and it will be well coloured, and you may temper it as you like.

73. *To make indigo.*—Take the herb woad and pound it very fine, and make it into little balls like apples; then take for every pound of woad two ounces of common salt, three ounces of sulphur vivum, and one ounce of roche alum; grind all these things with the herb, and afterwards put them into a copper vessel of clear water, and mix them to the consistence of sauce not too thin, then put the vessel over a clear fire, and let it remain until it becomes like dough; next put it on a table, and spread it out rather thin, and afterwards cut it with a knife in any manner you please and let it dry, and you will have good indigo.

74. *To make indigo.*—Take two ounces of "gesso sottile," and grind it with 10 oz. of dried woad, that is to say, the flower (or froth), and grind it well; then mix a little albumen of eggs, that is to say, prepared white of eggs, with it, and incorporate the whole well together, and dry it in the sun, and when it is dry cut it into pieces just as you like. And note, when you

---

1 To "multiply azure," *i. e.*, to increase the quantity. In the present instance this is done by adding white to it, which also diminishes the inten-

rade cum vitro et pone rasuram illam in clara ovi preparata per diem et noctem ita quod rasura illa sit coperta a dicta clara cum modico aluminis rocci pulverizati deinde colabis hec omnia cum petia panni lini alba et cum predicta clara colorata temperabis azurrum.

71. *Ad multiplicandum azurrum.*—Tolle azurrum cum modico ceruse et misce simul et distempera cum clara ovj et si vis magis clarum micte plus de cerusa et multiplicatur.

72. *Ad colorandum azurrum optime.*—Invenies oleum amamgdolarum amarum oz. 3 et totidem olej olive et pone in lapideum vasem et fac bullire cum azurro sine fumo per 7 horas et sic ter vel quatuor faties postea ablue cum liscivio tepido deinde cum frigida aqua et clara ut sit bene mundum postea sicca et coloratum erit congrue et tempera eum quomodo vis.

73. *Ad fatiendum endicum.*—Reccipe guatum in herba et eum pista valde bene subtiliter et fac pallottas sicut poma postea accipe pro omni libra dicti guati ontias duas salis comunis et ontias tres sulphuris vivi et untiam unam aluminis rocci deinde bene trita omnia simul cum dicta herba postea pone omnia in uno vase rameo cum aqua clarissima et stempera ad modum salse non nimis clare postea pone super ignem clarum et fac tantum stare ut veniat ad modum paste postea pone super unam tabulam et stende aliquantulum subtile hinc ad modicum incide cum gladio ut tibj placet et mite sicari et erit factum indicum finum.

74. *Ad faciendum indicum.*—Tolli once doi de gesso subtili et macinalo cum x once de guato secco cioe el fiore et macina bene subtili et poi ce mistica uno poco de albume dova cioe chiara dova preparata et incorpora omne cosa bene insiemj poi el pone asciugare al sole et quando e seccho fannj pezi commo te pare. Et nota che quando tu el macini mectice

---

sity of the colour. The term "multiply" was much used by the old Alchemists in the above sense.

grind it, mix with it a little roche alum dissolved in water, and it will be good and fine indigo.

75. *To make fine indigo.*—Take one part of flower of woad, which flower is collected in the dyers' vat when they are boiling woad; bake it well in an earthenware shovel, until it is well burnt; then grind it fine, and take 5 parts of the white earth which the fellmongers use,[1] pound it and mix it well with the powder of the woad; afterwards grind the whole with clear water upon a stone, like paint, then spread it on a smooth table, and let it dry a little in the sun; afterwards break it into small pieces, and let it dry again in the sun. Then take some of the first composition, and make it of the consistence of a rather thin soup, and put the pieces into it to soak; then take them out and dry them in the sun or at the fire, and if the colour is not sufficiently deep, renew the process as often as you think proper; afterwards dry it, and keep what you have made.

76. *To make indigo.*—Take gesso, ground very fine, three parts, and flower of woad six parts; mix and grind them well together until they become like paste of a good colour. Then take alum water made with roche alum, and again wet up this gesso and flower, add more fresh flower of woad until it is as thick as porridge; and before you put in the alum water you must spread the mixture of gesso and woad on marble or hard stone until it is very dry. It must then be wetted up again with the alum water; afterwards spread it out, and let it become very dry, and preserve it.

77. *To make indigo another way.*—Take flower of woad, and make it up into a paste with urine and strong vinegar; make a cake of it, and dry it in the sun, and if it is pale add more flower of woad to it, until it becomes of a fine colour; then cut it into pieces, and finish drying it, and it will be done.

78. *To make indigo.*—First you must know that the various sorts of this colour are made of a certain herb which is called

---

[1] There is no doubt that this was lime.

uno poco dalumj de rocho disoluto in aqua e sera bono et bello indico.

75. *Affare bello indico.*—Reccipe partem unam floris guati qui flos colligitur in caldarea tintorum quando guatum dequoquatur et ipsum bene coque in pella terrea donec peroptime comburetur postea tere eum subtile deinde accipe terram albam qua utuntur pelliparij et pulveriza et tolle de ea partes 5 et bene missia cum pulvere predicto guati postea cum aqua clara omnia simul conjunge supra lapidem ad modum colloris deinde extende supra tabulam politam et dimitte aliquantulum sicari ad solem postea fac parva frustra et iterum dimite sicari ad solem hoc facto acipe de primo composito et fac unum brodum aliquantulum currens et impone ipsa frustra ut imbibantur deinde extrhae et sicca ad solem vel ad ingnem deinde si non est satis coloratum reitera donec videtur tibi postea sicca et serva quod factum erit.

76. *Affare indico.*—Tolli gesso macinato subtilmente per terza parte e fiore de guato per sesta parte et mistica et macina bene insiemj tanto che venga ad modo de pasta che habbia bono collore poi tolli aqua alumata cum alumj de rocho et reintridi questo gesso et fiore de novo cum la dicta aqua alumata cum piu fiore de guato novo tanto che sia commo una farinata. Et nanti che tu ce mecti laqua alumata se vole stemdare lo gesso et lo fiore in uno marmo o vero sasso vivo in fino che e ben secho poi se vole reintridare de novo cum la dicta aqua alumata poi lo stende et lassalo seccare si che sia ben secho et ripollo.

77. *Affare indico per altram viam.*—Reccipe fiore de guato et impasta insiemi cum orina et aceto forte et fanne uno migliacio et secalo al sole e se ello bianchegiasse metice piu fiore de guato et cusi fa tanto che habbia bello colore poi ne fa peze e fornissce lo de seccare et sera facto.

78. *Ad faciendum indicum et confitionem ejus.*—Primo sciendum est quod genera istius coloris fit de quadam herba que

woad, and this herb is boiled down in a jar until no part of it remains; it is then dried, and is called by different names; it is made in various places, and is nearly perfect azure.

79. *To make indigo.*—Take prepared gesso, ground fine, and mix it with flower of woad, and grind it until it becomes like soft and watery paste, and has a good colour. Then take roche alum, and distemper it with hot water; then wet up afresh the gesso and flower with the said alum water, so as to be like a thin porridge; let it remain so until it begins to shrink, then spread it out, and let it dry; afterwards wet it up again with the alum water and flower of woad, and spread it out again on a plank or table of polished walnut wood, or well-polished marble or stone. When nearly dry, cut it into pieces just as you like, and let it finish drying, and it will be good indigo.

80. *To make indigo in another way.*—Take flower of woad and very white starch, knead them together with urine prepared and strained through a filter, and strong white vinegar, equal parts of each. Make the whole into a cake, and dry it in the sun; and if it is not sufficiently coloured, add to it more flower of woad, and put so much of it that it may be of a lively colour, and it will be done.

81. *To make indigo by another method.*—Take woad in the herb, and pound it well, and put it in the sun in a vase, and let the sun always shine upon it, and let it stand so for several days, and every day wet it with urine until it breeds worms, and it will produce large worms of a blue colour. Then take these worms and pound them, and extract the juice of them by means of a linen cloth, not too tight; then let the mass remain by itself, and when it begins to shrink make it into a cake like dough, not too thick, and put it to dry; and when it is nearly dry, so that the juice can be pressed out well, cut it in pieces just as you like, and let it finish drying, and it is done.

vocatur guatum et illa herba coquetur in vase donec nil de substantia remaneat deinde desicatur et diversis nominibus nominetur et in diversis partibus conficitur et quasi azurrum est.

79. *Affare indico.*—Tolli gesso curato macinato subtili et mistalo cum fiore de guato et tanto lo vieni macinando che sia commo pasta intrisa brodosa per modo che habia bono collore poi tolli alumj de rocho et distemperalo in laqua calda poi reintridi de novo lo dicto gesso et fiore cum la dicta aqua alumata per modo che sia commo una farinata liquida e lassalo cusci stare per infino che se cominzia a stregnare poi lo stende e lassalo sciugare poi de novo lo intridi cum la dicta aqua alumata e fiore de guato e de novo lo stende in una tavola de noce o asse bene polita o marmo o petra bene polita e lassala quasi secare poi ne fa li pezi a tuo piacere e lassalo fornire de secare et sera bono indico.

80. *Affare indicho alio modo.*—Ahvve fiore de guato et amido bene canido e impasta insiemj cum orina preparata e stillata per filtro et cum aceto bianco e forte tanto de luno quanto de laltro e fanne uno migliacio e secalo al sole e se venisse che non fosse bene colorito metivj piu fiore e tanto vi ni mecti che habia bono e vivo collore e de facto.

81. *Affare indicho per altra forma.*—Tolli guato in herba e pistalo bene e mectilo al sole in uno vaso e fache lo sole li dia di continuo e lassalo stare piu di e omne di lo bagna cum orina per infino a tanto che inverminisce e fara verminj grossci de collore azurro poi tolli quei verminj e pistali e tranne el sugo per uno panno de lino non troppo stretto poi lassalo reposare per se medesimo e commo se comincia a stregnare e tu ne fa una focacia come se fusse pasta non troppo grossa e mectila a seccare e quando sera a presso che secca che lo sugo se tirera bene e tu ne fa in pezze commo te pare et lassali compire de secare e de facto.

HERE BEGINS THE FOURTH CHAPTER

ON MAKING GREENS FROM COPPER AND FROM THE JUICES OF HERBS IN VARIOUS MANNERS. AND FIRST—

82. *To make verdigris.*—Take very thin slips of copper, and put them into a vase, and then place the vase three palms deep in horsedung, underground, in a damp place, and let it remain thirty or forty days; then take it out, and rub the slips well with very strong vinegar; then put them back under the dung in the vase, and let them remain well covered for the space of one month, when the verdigris will be formed.

83. *To make verdigris.*—Take a copper pot, with a cover that can be luted on to it, and fill it with very strong vinegar, then put on the cover, and let it remain sixty or seventy days underground in a warm and damp place; then take out the vase, and scrape away the verdigris that adheres to the bottom; then put back the vinegar, and return it as before, and continue this as long as any of the basin remains.

84. *To make verdigris.*—Take plates of copper, and suspend them over the vapour of strong vinegar in a jar covered with clay and well closed, so as to be air-tight; then put the jar into dung or the refuse of grapes, in the time of the vintage, for the space of fifteen days, when you must open the jar, and you will find the verdigris adhering to those plates. Scrape it away, and return it as before.

85. *To make verdigris.*—Take very thin copper and cut it into pieces of half an ounce or one ounce each; arrange them in a glazed vase with common salt—that is to say, one stratum of copper and another of salt; then fill the vase with strong vinegar, and cover it with lutum sapientiæ; put it underground in a damp and warm place for a month, and you will have good verdigris.

INCIPIT QUARTUS CAPITULUS

DE FIENDIS VIRIDIBUS RAMIS ET DE VIRIDIBUS FACTIS CUM ERBARUM SUCCIS IN DIVERSIS MODIS. PRIMO

82. *Ad faciendum viridem ramum.*—Accipe fecte de ramo subtilissimi et mectile in uno vaso e poi lo pone socto lo litami de cavallo socto terra in loco humido socto tre palmi et lassalo stare 30 o 40 di poi el tera fora et sborfa molto bene cum aceto fortissimo le dicte lamine poi le ritorna socto quello litami in quello vaso et stiano bene coperte per spatio duno mese et sera facto verderamo.

83. *Ad viridem herem faciendum.*—Tolli uno catino de ramo cum uno coperchio che li stia sogillato et inpe lo catino de fortissimo aceto poi lo copri cum lo suo coperchio et lassalo stare per 60 di socto terra che habia caldo et humido poi tolli fora el vaso et rade via el verderamo che se teni al fondo poi remectili suso quello aceto et tornalo al modo disopra et fa similmente per infino a tanto che lo catino ne mena.

84. *Ad faciendum viridem ramum.*—Summe le piastre de ramo et sospendi le sopra alo vapore de lo aceto forte in una pignatta coperta cum creta bene obturata che non spire poi lo poni in lo litami o vero venacia al tempo de vendemia per spatio de 15 di poi apre la dicta pignatta et troverai el verde ramo che sera apicato a quelle piastre et rade via quello et poi lo torna al modo sopradicto.

85. *Ad viridem ramum faciendum.*—Habbi ramo subtilissimo et fannj peze de meza oncia o duna oncia luno et acconciale in uno vaso vitriato cum sale communo cioe uno strato de lamine et uno de sale poi impe lo vaso daceto forte et coprilo vaso cum luto de sapientia et mectilo socto terra per uno mese in loco humido et callido et sera facto bono verderamo.

86. *To make green for painting on gesso.*—Take 5 ounces of strong white vinegar, of copper-foil and Roman vitriol equal quantities, and a little alum; grind them all together, and let them dry, and when you want to use the colour distemper it with gum water, and it will make a good green.

87. *To make green.*—Take orpiment and indigo "de bagadon,"[1] and grind them well with water. When the colour settles, grind it again with gum-water, and it will make a green; and, if you please, take orpiment and grind it, and mix with it white lead and indigo, and do as before, and it will be green.

88. *For the same.*—Take viridem presimum and grind it with water; let it dry, then temper it with gum-water, and if you wish it lighter, put in a little more orpiment, and it will be of a good colour.

89. *To make a good green with buckthorn.*—Take small berries of buckthorn[2] when quite ripe, put them into a glass vase, and crush them well with your hands; then place them in the sun, and let them remain until the juice rises above the berries; then strain the refuse, and throw it away, and if the juice weighs one pound put into it the weight of two quattrini[3] of roche alum in powder. Place the mixture in the sun in a well-closed glass vase, and let it stand three or four days, stirring it well three or four times every day; and if it should happen to dry after a time, distemper it with clear ley, with a little gum.

90. *To make green.*—Take indigo and grind it with plenty of saffron, and with a little white lead and gum-water, and it will become green.

91. *To make green.*—Take the juice of the plant "morella,"[4] and incorporate it with white earth, such as the fellmongers use, and mix a little gum-water with it, and it will become green.

---

[1] The true Indigo.

[2] Spincervino. The Rhamnus catharticus, Sap green.

[3] Quattrini. Small copper coin, worth about the fifth part of a crazia, or the 60th part of a Florentine lira; perhaps so called because a quattrino was of the value of four denari or piccioli, now no longer in use. Alb. Diz.

86. *Affare verde da dipengiare in gesso.*—Tolli once 5 de forte aceto bianco poi tolli battitura de ramo vitriolo romano ana et un pocho dalumi de rocho et macina omne cosa insiemj et lassalo secare et quando tu voraj operare stemperalo cum aqua gomata et sera bono verde.

87. *Ad viridem faciendum.*—Invenies aurum piumentum et indicum de bagadon et tere bene cum aqua et cum se residerit tere cum aqua gumata et fiet viridem et si tibi placet acipe de auropiumento et tere et simul misce de biacha et de indico et fac ut supra et erit viridis.

88. *Ad idem.*—Tolle viridum presimum et tere cum aqua et dimite sicari et deince tempera cum aqua gumata et si vis magis clarum impone aliquantulum auripiumenti et congrue colorabitur.

89. *Affare verde bono cum spingerbino.*—Recipe granelli de spinogerbino quando sonno bene mature et metili in uno vaso de vetrio et amalpali bene cum le mano et metili al sole et lassali stare tanto che leve suso li grappi e quelle venacie poi li cola et premili bene et gieta via quella venacia et grappi et se lo dicto sugo fusse una libra metice doi quattrini dalumi de rocho spolverizato poi lo pone al sole in vaso de vetrio ben serato et lassalo stare 3 o 4 di et omni di lo mistica 3 o 4 volte molto bene atorno et per spatio de tempo se secasse distemperalo cum ranno da capo chiaro cum uno poco di gomma.

90. *A fare verde.*—Havve indico et macinalo cum zaffarami asso et cum uno pocho de biacha et uno poco de aqua gomata et cum quella aqua gomata macina li sopradicte cose et vira verde.

91. *Affare verde.*—Tolli sugo de herba morella et incorpora cum terra bianca la quale usa li piliciarj et mistace uno poco daqua gomata et sera verde.

---

4 Solatro Nero, Cacabo, It. Black Nightshade, Eng. Solatrum hortense, vulgare, officinarum, uva vulpus, lupina-strychnos, Lat. Morelle, Morelle des Jardins, Fr. Hierba mora, Sp.

92. *To make a light green, excellent for miniatures.*—Take dark blue lilies, pound them well, and extract the juice from them; then take roche alum dissolved in water, and in this alum-water wet some pieces of white linen three or four times, and each time dry them in the shade; then wet the pieces of linen in the juice six or seven times, and each time let them dry well in the shade; then keep them closely shut up in a box, in order that the air may not have access to them. When you wish to use the colour, take a small piece of that linen and put it into a shell, and soak it in gum-water just sufficient to cover it. Let it stand so for a night; then press it well, and stir it about in the shell in order to extract the colour; and if you choose to make it more brilliant, put it to soak in prepared white of egg, and use it for miniature and for drawing leaves upon paper.

93. *To make dark green.*—Take berries of buckthorn, not too ripe; pound them, and extract the juice from them, and then do the same as was directed in the other recipe for making light green.

94. *To make green.*—Take myrrh and put it into a glazed vase, and fill it with strong white vinegar for the space of several days. A scum will rise on the top of the vinegar, and that scum is good and fine verdigris.

95. *To make good green.*—Take honey and strong vinegar of each as much as you like, and incorporate them very well together; then put the mixture into a well-luted copper vase, place the jar a foot deep in every direction in warm dung, in a place where the sun shines strongly, and let it remain so for a fortnight; then take it out, and you will find all the matter converted into fine verdigris of a perfect kind.

96. *To make blue green.*—Take some of our own azure,[1] and saffron well soaked in clear water, grind it on a marble slab with the azure, and incorporate them well together until the colour becomes a fine green; let it dry in the shade, and dis-

---

[1] Probably azzurro de Lombardia, mentioned in No. 4.

92. *Affare verde chiaro per miniare optimo.*—Recipe li gilglj azurrini scuri e pistali bene et tranni lo sugo poi tolli alumi de rocho disoluto in aqua et in questa aqua alumata ce bangna le peze bianche de tovalglia doi o 3 volte et omne volta le sciuga alombra poi bagna la dita peza in lo dicto sugo 6 o 7 volte et omne volta la pone a sciugare alombra molto bene et poi la conserva in bossola bene serata acio non vengha laiere. Et quando la vorai operare tolli uno poco de quella peza et metila a molle in aqua gommata in una coccia tanto che stia coperta da la dicta aqua et lassa stare per spatio duna nocte et poi la preme molto bene et rimenala in la coccia acio lo colore escha fora et se te piace per farlo piu lustro la poi porre a molle in chiara dovo preparata et usalo per miniare a fare fogliame in carta.

93. *Affare verde scuro.*—Ahve grani de spingerbino che non siano troppo maturi et pistali et cavane lo sugo et poi fa similmente commo e disopra dicto in laltra ricetta dalo verde chiaro.

94. *Affare verde.*—Tolli mirra e metila in uno vaso vitriato et impelo vaso de aceto forte bianco per spatio de alcuni di questo aceto fara fiore de sopra et quello fiore e bono verde ramo e fino.

95. *Affare verde bono.*—Ahvve mele e aceto forte ana el tuo volere et incorpora multo bene insiemj poi lo pone in uno vaso de ramo bene coperto poi lo pone socto lo litamj bene caldo et stia in loco dove el sole ferisci forte et fa che lo vaso stia socto lo litamj uno pei per omne verso et lassalo cosi stare per 15 di poi lo cava fora et trovarai tucta la matheria convertita in verde ramo bello in grado perffecto.

96. *Affare verde azurro.*—Summe azurro nostramo e zaffaramj bene mollo in aqua chiara et atritalo sopra lo marmo cum lo azurro et incorpora bene insiemj tanto che vegna bello verde et lassa secare alombra et distemperalo cum aqua gommata.

temper it with gum-water. If you like, you may put instead of the saffron, yellow earth dyed with the juice of buckthorn,[1] and it will become green; or the juice of buckthorn only.

97. *To make a green water for painting on canvas.*—Take ripe French beans, and put them into a small bag of strong canvas, place the bag in a press, extract the juice, and set it to boil, and let it be reduced one-half. Then add some powdered roche-alum, and remove it from the fire, and it will be a good and fine colour.

98. *To make a natural blue green.*—Take azure of whatever kind you like in fine powder, and put it to soak in soft water; then take fine verdigris, grind it very fine with soft water, and add to it so much saffron as will make it a dark green. Then put it into a glass cornet and mix it well, let it rest so as to sink perfectly to the bottom, and the water will remain above the verdigris clear and of a green colour, and this green water must be separated cautiously from the verdigris. Next take some of that soaked azure, and pour off as much of the water as you can from it. Then take the green water, and throw it upon the azure, and mix them well together, stirring them with your finger, and you will have a perfect blue-green, and it will maintain its colour; and when it is dry, if you wish to use it, pour some of the green water upon it, and soften the blue-green with your finger, and if it is weak, distemper it with fine gum, and it will be a most perfect blue-green.

99. *To make good green.*—Take the pips of the "pero citrino" which are ripe at the time of   , and extract the juice from them; then take an equal quantity of white wine, and boil them down till reduced by one-half; then take roche alum in powder at discretion, and add it to the liquid when it boils; then take it off the fire and set it to cool, and when it has settled and cooled strain it, and keep it in a glass vase, and use it for painting.

100. *To make "verde alommo."*—Take the scum of woad, and

[1] See No. 105.

Et se te piace tu poi torre in loco del zafferamj quella terra gialla tenta cum lo sugo de spino gerbino et vira verde o vero cum lo sugo de spino gerbino.

97. *A fare aqua verde da dipengiare in panno.*—Havve fagioli maturi e metili in uno sachetto de canavaccio bene forte et mitilo a strigere et tranj lo licore mitilo a bulire et lassalo disimare per mita poi li pone uno poco di polve de alumi de rocho e toto dal foco et sera bona et bella tenta.

98. *Affare verde azurro naturali.*—Tolli azurro de qualunque sorte voi bene subtili et metilo amollare in aqua dolce poi tolli de lo verde ramo fino et macinalo cum aqua dolce ben subtili poi lo metti tanto zaffarami che diventa verde scuro poi lo pone in uno cornetto de vetrio et mistalo bene poi lo lassa reposare siche vada bene al fondo la quale aqua te remara disopra alo verderamo chiara collorita in verde la quale aqua verde se vole separare da lo dicto verderamo cautamente poi tolli el tuo azurro mollificato et sepera via quella aqua quanto piu poi et de po tolli la dita aqua verde e gietala sopra a lo azurro et incorpora bene luno cum laltro remenandolo bene cum lo deto et haverai verde azurro perfecto et mantira lo colore et quando fosse secco e tu lo volesci operare gietali de la sopraditta aqua verde et molifica lo verde azurro cum lo deto e se fusse debili distemperalo cum gentili gomma et sera perfetissimo verde azurro.

99. *A fare verde bono.*—Tolli li acini del pero citrino maturi al tempo de (*sic*) e trannj lo sugo poi tolli altretanto vino bianco et mistica insiemj et fa bulire per mita po tolli alumj de rocho in polvere el tuo parer e gietalo suso quando bolle e misticalo uno poco poi lo leva dal foco et pollo afredare et commo e reposato e fredato et tu lo cola et serbalo in uno vaso de vetrio et usalo a dipengiare.

100. *Affare verde allommo.*—Tolli la fiorata del guato e seccala

dry it until it becomes a powder, and temper it with gum water and a little roche alum, and it will make a good green.

101. *To make green.*—Take verdigris, and grind it very fine with strong vinegar, and put it on a new brick which has a hollow in the middle; let it stand until the moisture and the vinegar are removed, that is, until the brick has soaked up the moisture. Do this four or five times, and each time soak the verdigris with fresh and very strong vinegar; and this is called purifying the verdigris. This purification is also done with ley made from ashes in the manner before-mentioned. Then take the purified verdigris and mix it with a little white lead or a little orpiment, and distemper it with gum-water, and it will become a fine and good green.[1]

102. *To make green.*—Put the ripe seeds of the buckthorn into a boiler with an equal quantity by weight of strong white vinegar, and boil it down to one-half; afterwards strain it through a piece of linen cloth into a glazed vase, and when you wish to use it, take some of it, and use it as you please.

103. *To make green.*—Take as much as you like of strong white vinegar, and add to it some verdigris reduced to a fine powder, a little powdered roche alum, a little saffron, a small quantity of the juice of rue, and a little powdered gum arabic. Let it all stand in the vinegar for 5 days, then mix a little ceruse with it, and it will become of a fine green colour.

104. *To make a light green for miniature—proved.*—Take violets in the month of March, pound them well, and squeeze the juice into a glazed saucer; put in a little well ground roche alum, and mix it up; afterwards take some pieces of very white linen cloth, not too thick, and dip them into the saucer three or four times, and the oftener the better, and each time dry them in the shade, and when you wish to use the colour distemper it with gum water.

---

[1] This appears to be purified, or, as it is sometimes called, Distilled Verdigris, the Verd' Eterno of the Venetians.

in polve poi la stempera cum aqua gomata e cum uno pocho dalumj de rocho et sera bono verde.

101. *Affare verde.*—Ahavve verderamo et macinalo cum forte aceto multo subtili tolli el ditto verderamo cum lo aceto macinato et mectilo in uno matone novo el quale habia una concava in mezo et lassalo stare tanto che la humidita et lo aceto sia andata via cioe che lo matone habia bevuto quella humidita et cosi continua 4 o 5 volte et omne volta reintride el dito verderamo cum novo aceto fortissimo et questa se chiama la purgatione de lo verderamo et anco se fa la dita depurgatione cum lo ranno facto de cenere recotta il modo desopra poi tolli de lo dicto verderamo depurgato mistalo cum uno poco de biaccha o vero uno poco de oropiumento et distemperalo cum aqua gummata et vira bello verde e bono.

102. *A fare verde.*—Recipe semina spini cervini matura et micte eas in caldario et tantumdem aceti forti et albi scilicet quantum est pondus semina predictorum et fac devenire usque ad medium postea cola cum pezia pannj lini et eum pone in vitriato vase et cum vis operare tolle de ipso et utere ad beneplacitum tuum.

103. *Ad viridem faciendum.*—Summe aceti albi forti quantum vis et in eo pone viridem ramum in pulverem subtilis reductam et aliquantulum pulvis aluminis rochi et modicum zafferami et modicum succi ruuite et aliquantulum pulvis gumme arabici et in aceto permite stare per 5 dies et deinde misce cum eo aliquantulum ceruse et efficitur color magis viridis.

104. *Affare verde chiaro per minio provato.*—Recipe de mense Martij violarum et pista bene et exthrae succum in una scutella vitriata et impone aliquantulum aluminis rocci optime triti et misce simul postea recipe pezias panni lini albissimi et non nimis subtiles et infunde eas in dicta scutella ter vel quatuor et tanto plus tanto melius et pro qualibet vice sicca eas ad humbram et cum vis eas operare stempera aqua gumata.

105. *To make a splendid yellow, finer than orpiment or German giallolino.*—Take berries of buckthorn, when they are quite ripe, extract the juice from them, and keep it in a glass jar well closed for a fortnight. When you wish to use it, take strong ley, clear and fine, and for each mezzetta[1] of ley take an ounce of roche alum in powder, and make it boil with the ley for the space of one paternoster in a glazed vase; then remove it from the fire and let it cool. Next take for every tumbler of ley with alum one-third of a tumbler of the juice, and incorporate it well with the ley and alum, which will become a sort of dark green water, and let it stand thus incorporated for a night or more. Then take very fine white earth such as the fellmongers use, and incorporate it gradually with the green ley, in a vase, such as a saucer, with your finger, and add to it so much earth that it may be of the consistence of dough; keep mixing it with your finger as long as you can, and set it to dry in the sun; and if you please you can soak it two or three times in the green ley, in order that it may become more beautiful and of a brighter colour. Distemper it with clear ley, and an equal quantity of prepared white of egg, and with powder of gum arabic, and let it remain together for two nights. And if you wish to use the yellow before it dries, that is, when you have just made it, take some of the green ley and mix it with a very little white earth, and paint with it whatever you like, and it will remain a most beautiful yellow. And know that the juice is good all the year, but is nevertheless better stale than fresh. If it becomes hard, mix a little ley with it.

106. *To make a good and natural green—proved.*—Take verdigris and grind it very fine with water; then dry it. Next take some of the before mentioned yellow and mix with the verdigris, that is to say, three parts verdigris, and one of yellow, and it will become a noble and durable green, and you may mix more or less yellow, as you please, because the more yellow you put, the lighter it becomes.

---

[1] A glazed earthen vessel used to measure wine; it holds the fourth part of a Florentine Fiasco. Alb. Diz.

105. *A fare giallo belitissimo piu che oropiumento o giallolino delamagna.*—Tolli granelli de spingerbino quando sonno ben mature et trannj lo sugo et serbalo in una ampolla de vetrio ben turata et lassa cusi stare per 15 di et quando tu lo vorai operare tolli ranno da capo forte chiaro et bello et per omne mezo de ranno tolli una oncia dalumi de rocho in polvere et fallo bollire insiemj cum lo ranno per uno paternostro in uno vaso vitriato poi tolo dal foco et lassa refredare poi tolli per omne bichiero de ranno alumato il terzo duno bichiero de lo dicto sugo et incorpora bene insiemi cum lo dicto ranno alumato che diventara ad modo duna aqua verde scura et lassa stare cosi incorporato una nocte o piu poi tolli terra biancha ben subtili la quale opera li piliciarj et incorpora cum lo dicto ranno verde a poco a poco in uno vaso commo e una scutella cum lo deto et tanta terra vi meti che vemgna duretta ad modo de pasta et sempre mistica cum lo deto quanto poi et pollo a secare al sole et se te paresse tu poi darli doi o tre bangni cum lo dicto ranno verde acio che vengha piu bello et cum piu vivo collore et distemperalo cum ranno chiaro et altratanta chiara preparata et cum polvere de gomarabica et lassa stare insiemj doi note et cum quello lo distempera. Et se tu lo vorai operare el dicto giallo nante che se secche cioe quando tu lo fai che e fresco tolli de lo ditto ranno verde et mistavi poco poco terra biancha et dallo dove te piace et rimara giallo belitissimo. Et sappi che lo dito sugo e bono tutto lanno e de migliore stantio che frescho e se se indurasse mistali uno poco de ranno acio diventi morbido.

106. *A fare uno bello et naturali verde provato.*—Tolli verderamo et macinalo ben subtili cum aqua poi lo secca poi tolli de lo sopradito giallo et mistica cum lo dito verderamo cioe le tre parte de verderamo et una de giallo et vira nobili verde durabili et poi mistare piu e meno giallo commo te pare perche commo piu giallo vi meti piu chiaro vene.

107. *To make a very dark green—proved.*—Take indigo and grind it very fine; then incorporate it with a little of the before mentioned yellow, and it is done. Distemper it with white of egg or gum water.

108. *To prepare blue-greens, or blues when they are impure.*—Take the blue-green or blue, and put it into a piece of linen cloth and squeeze it, and wash it in a saucer of fresh and clear water, and when you have washed it well, the colour will sink to the bottom. When it is well settled throw away the water at the top, and then add a little clean white honey and mix it until it froths; then grind it well on porphyry, put it into a glazed vase, and wash it with tepid water until the water comes off clear. Then wash it with clear ley, and afterwards with clear water two or three times, and let it settle well; pour off the water cautiously, and then distemper it with prepared white of egg, or with size made from clippings of leather, and it will do well.

B 109. *To make a green tincture for writing.*—Take 2 lbs. of calcined verdigris, reduce it to fine powder, and distil it in an alembic, and keep the water that comes over and it is good for writing and dyeing thread, &c.

107. *Affare uno verde scurissimo probata.*—Ahvvi indico et macinalo bene sotili poi incorporalo cum uno poco de lo supraditto giallo ed e facto et distemperalo cum chiaro o aqua gommata.

108. *Aconciare verde azurri o azurri quando fussaro grosci.*—Havve lo verde azurro o azurro et metilo in una peza de panno de lino stretto e lavalo in una scutella daqua frescha et chiara et commo lai bene lavato lo colore andara al fondo et quando sera bene reposato gieta via laqua de sopra poi li mecte uno poco de mele bianco et netto et mistica bene per infino atanto che fara una schiuma poi lo macina in porfido molto bene poi lo pone in uno vaso vitriato et lavalo cum aqua tepida tanto che laqua nescha chiara poi lo lava cum liscia tepida poi cum laqua frescha doi o 3 volte poi lassalo bene repossare separa via quella aqua cautamente poi lo distempera cum chiara dova preparata o cum colla de branche de ritalglie de corami et stara bene.

B 109. *A fare tentura verde da scrivare.*—Recipe lb. doi de verderamo abrusciato et fanne polvere subtili et polla a distillare a lambico et serva laqua e de bona da scrivare et da tegnare filo etc.

HERE BEGINS THE HEADING OF THE FIFTH CHAPTER

ON THE MAKING OF LAKES, PURPLES, AND VERZINO IN VARIOUS MANNERS, AND FIRSTLY,

110. *To make good and fine lake.*—Take 1 lb. of clippings of Rosato,[1] and put them into very strong ley made of ashes, such as the dyers use, in a new glazed jar, and set it on the fire to boil, and boil it slowly for the space of two *paternosters*, then pass the ley and the shavings through a clean linen strainer, and press it strongly with the hand so that all the ley may pass out ; then put back the ley to boil again without the clippings, and when it is boiled, throw it on the shavings which are in the strainer, and press the strainer hard with the hand so that all the ley may run out, and put it by. Throw away the shavings and wash the strainer well, so that there may not remain in it any hairs of the shavings. Next take 5 oz. of roche alum in fine powder, and put it a little at a time into the ley, until the ley begins to settle, which you may know by its turning almost entirely to a thick scum, from top to bottom, and you must keep on mixing the ley with a clean spoon until it becomes cool and settles ; then put the ley into the clean strainer and strain it all off, and the lake will remain on the strainer. Let it remain on the strainer until quite dry, and then put it into a small basin of glazed earth full of clear and cold water, and stir it and rub it up well with the hand until it diffuses itself; all the scum which rises to the top at first must be thrown away with a feather; then wash the strainer well and pour into it the water in which you have put the lake, and the clear water will pass out along with the alum, and this is called purifying it

[1] Rosato is a kind of woollen stuff dyed with "grana," that is Kermes.

INCIPIT DISTINTIO QUINTI CAPITULI

DE LACCIS ET PAVONATIIS FIENDIS IN DIVERSIS MODIS ET VERZINIS. ET PRIMO, VIZ.

110. *Affare laccha bona et bella.*—Tolli lb j de cimatura de grana de rosato e mectila in ranno fortissimo facto de cenere la quale usa li tentori in una pignatta vitriata nova et polla al foco a bullire et bolla pianamente per spatio de doi pater nostri poi mecti el ranno et la cimatura per uno collatoro netto de panno de lino et premilo forte cum mano siche tutto el ranno escha fora et poi repone el dicto ranno a bullire de novo senza ala cimatura et bolito el gieta sopra ala cimatura che e in lo collatoro et preme forte el colatoro cum mano siche tutto el ranno escha fora bene et ripollo da parte et la cimatura gietta via et lava molto bene il colatoro siche non vi rimanga veruno pelo de la ditta cimatura poi tolli once cinque dalumi de rocho spolverizato subtili et metilo a poco a poco per volta in el dito ranno per infino che el ranno se strenge che lo conoscirai quando el dito ranno tutto quasi se converti in una schiuma grassa in fino al fondo et mai se vole finare de mistare el dicto ranno cum uno cochiaro netto per infino che se fredda bene e che se strenga poi meti el ditto ranno stretto in lo dito collatoro lavato et cola tucto lo ranno et la lacha remara de dentro et lassala tanto stare in lo ditto collatoro che ella se seche bene poi la pone in una catinella de terra vitriata piena daqua fredda et chiara et rimenala et sfregala bene cum le mano tanto che se diffaccia et tutta quella schiuma che vene a summo da principio se vole giettare via cum una penna et lava bene lo colatoro et ripone suso questa aqua ove hai stemperato

from the alum. And when the lake is nearly dry, remove it from the strainer, and spread it out with a broad knife on a new tile, let it dry in the shade, and before it has done drying, cut it into pieces according to your fancy, and let it dry, and it is done. And know that the more it is purified from the alum, the more beautiful and lively, and the better it is. And observe this secret, that if you wish the lake to have a brighter colour and one which will never change, when the shavings are boiling, add a lump of assafetida[1] as large as a chesnut.

111. *To make lake in another manner.*—Take baked ashes, such as the dyers use, and make a caustic ley, and keep it clean and clear; then put the ley to boil in a glazed jar, and when it boils, put a lump of quicklime, not slaked, into it, and strain it through a close cloth. Then take 2 "petitti" of this ley clean and fine, and put it into a new glazed pipkin and add to it half a pound of shavings of cloth, mixing it well; then put the ley over a clear fire, and make it boil until reduced to one-third. When it is so reduced, add to it 3 oz. of roche alum, and make it boil until it is reduced one-third; then strain it through a straining cloth into a glazed vase, and put the lake on a new brick that has a hollow in the middle, a little at a time if the brick will not hold it all at once, and let it remain for the space of 5 hours; then take it out and do this as long as any lake remains. Then put it into a basin to finish drying in the heat of the sun, and when it is nearly dry, spread it on a very smooth table, and when quite dry, cut it into pieces according to your pleasure.

---

[1] The virtue of this gum resin probably lay in the bitter or extractive principle, for it is known that lakes are more durable if the water used in making them be previously boiled with some astringent bark, such as the bark of the beech, or the small branches of the poplar. (See Traité de la Peinture au Pastel, du secret d'en composer les couleurs, avec indications d'un grand nombre de nouvelles substances propres à la Peinture à l'huile, et le moyen de prévenir l'altération des couleurs. Par M. P. R. de C. C. à P. de L. Paris, 1788.) The permanence of the colour of the Kermes is thought to be owing to the astringent matter it contains.

la lacha et laqua chiara uscira fuori insiemi cum lo alumi et questa se chiama la purgatione de lo alumj et quando la dicta lacha sera quasi sciuta et tu latra del dicto colatoro et cum uno colltello largo la spiana in una tegola nova et lassalo seccare alombra et nante che se fornischa de secare fanni li pezi a tuo modo et lassa secare e de facta. Et sappi che quando se fa quella purgationi de lo allumj tanto e piu bella piu viva et melglio. Et nota questo secreto che se tu voli che la lacha habbia piu vivo collore et mai non perda quando la dicta cimatura bolle metice tanta assa fetida quanto una castagna et stara bene.

111. *Affare lacha per altro modo.*—Recipe cenere ricolta et fa capitello et fanne ranno la quale cenere usa li tentore et serbalo necto et chiaro et poi pone a bullire el dicto ranno in una pignatta vitriata et quando el ditto ranno bolle metice una zuppa de calcina viva che non sia disolta poi la cola cum uno panno stretto et colgli lo ranno netto et bello poi tolli doi petitti de de questo ranno et metilo in una pignatta nova vitriata et metice meza libra de cimatura de grana mistando molto bene poi la pone al fuoco chiaro et falla bollire tanto che le tre parte revengna luna et quando e rentrata per terzo et tu ce pone tre once dalumi de rocho poi lo fa bullire tanto che a rentre per terzo poi la cola per uno telo de staccia in uno vaso vitriato poi la pone in uno matone novo el quale habia uno concavo in lo mezo et metice la dicta lacca a poco a poco se non ce po capire tucta e lassala stare per spatio de 5 hore et poi la cava et cosi farai per infino che tu nai poi la pone in una lavella a fornire de secare al sole bene caldo et quando e per secarse stendila in suso una tavola bene polita et quando e bene secca fannj li pezi al tuo piacere.

That Assafœtida was used occasionally by painters, is proved by a Document, dated 1347, which was discovered by Professor Ciampi, in the Archives of S. Jacopo di Pistoia. Professor Branchi, of Pisa, to whom the document was submitted, together with fragments of paintings from S. Jacopo, which he analyzed, could form no opinion as to its probable use, which appears to be explained by the text. See " Lettera dal Prof. Branchi al Sig. Seb^no^ Ciampi sopra gl' ingredienti di varj musaici e di varie antiche pitture."

112. *To make lake in another way.*—Take quicklime, and put it into a vase to boil, with sufficient water to cover the lime two fingers deep, and mix it well with a stick. Let it boil for the space of 3 Ave Marias; then suffer it to cool for a night, and afterwards filter the liquor which stood on the lime. Put the verzino scraped fine into this water, by which it should be covered; then take fine flour, or starch in powder, and put it into the water with the verzino, and mix it well together. Let it remain so for a night, then separate the water carefully, and make the starch or flour into a ball as if it was dough, and put it to dry in the oven after the bread is taken out, or even later, in order that it may not burn, and let it dry well. Then knead it again with the water of the verzino, and let it rest. Throw away the water, and make the paste into little balls like hazel-nuts, and put them to dry in the shade where no dust or other dirt can get to them, and the lake will be made. And if you wish the lake to have a bright and perfect colour, take shavings of rosato and put them to boil in the lime-water, and let them boil until reduced one-half; then strain the liquor and put the verzino to soak in the water, and follow the recipe as before.

113. *To make verzino good for painting flowers on miniatures.*—Take a piece of lime, reduce it to powder, and put it into white of egg, and stir it well with a stick, in the same manner as the white of egg is prepared for vermilion; let it settle, and then separate the scum and filter off the white of egg. Then take verzino scraped fine with glass or with a rasp, and put it into the filtered white of egg, and let it soak for two days, and there must be enough white of egg to cover the verzino and it is done.

114. *For the same, another way.*—Take quicklime and put it to soak in a vase with sufficient water to cover the lime three fingers deep, stir it well with a stick until you see that it is well slaked; then let it settle for two days, and take the clear water and some scrapings of verzino, and put the verzino to soak in the water for the space of three days. Then put the

112. *Affare laccha per altra via.*—Tolli calcina viva et metila in uno vaso a bullire cum tanta aqua che sopra avantia a la calcina doi deta et mistila bene cum uno bastone et bolla per spatio de 3 ave marie poi lassa fredare per una notta poi destilla per filtro la ditta aqua che e sopra a la calcina et in questa aqua pone el verzino raso subtilmente et fa che lo verzino stia coperto da la dicta aqua poi tolli fiore de farina o vero amido in polvere et metilo in la ditta aqua dove e el verzino e mistica molto bene insiemj e lassa cusi stare per una nocte poi sepera la dicta aqua cautamente ed e quello amido o vero fiore de farina ne fa una pallotta commo se fusse pasta et polla a secare in lo forno quando e tratto el pane o piu tardo che non se abruscia et lassala bene secare poi la reintride cum la sopradicta aqua del verzino poi la lassa reposare e gietta via quella aqua e de la pasta ne fa pallottecti ad modo de avellane et polla a sciugare alombra dove non vi vada polvere ne altra brutura e de facta. Et se tu volesci fare che la dicta laccha habbia vivo et perfecto collore tolli cimatura de rosato et polla a bollire in la sopra dicta aqua de calcina et tanto bolla che arentre per mita poi la cola et in la dicta aqua pone a molle el verzino et seguita la recieta al modo de sopra.

113. *Affare verzino da fiorire minij bono.*—Recipe calcina impetra et fanne polve et metila in chiara dova et rimenela bene cum uno bastone commo se concia lachiara per lo cinabrio et lassa possare poi sepera via la sciuma et distilla quella chiara per filtro poi tolli del verzino raso subtili cum vetrio overo cum la raspa et metilo de dentro in la dicta chiara stillata et lassalo stare a molli doi di e vole esser tanto chiara che lo verzino stia coperto e de fatto.

114. *Ad idem alio modo.*—Ahvve calcina viva et metila a molle in uno vaso cum tanta aqua che sopra avanza ala calcina 3 dete et rimenela cum uno bastone molto bene per infino a tanto che tu veghi che la calcina sia bene disciolta poi la lassa posare per doi di e colglie laqua chiara e bella poi tolli de lo verzino raso et pollo a molle in la dicta aqua per spatio de 3 di,

whole on the fire and boil it down to one-half or less; then add some pounded alum and a little gum arabic, take it off the fire, and let it settle; when cool strain it through a piece of linen cloth and it will be fine verzino.

115. *To make verzino, another way.*—Take verzino, scrape it fine, and put it into a glazed vase to soak with a sufficient quantity of cold and purified urine to cover the verzino; then add 2 parts of alum zucharino, one of white-lead, and a little pounded gum. Let the whole stand to soak for two days, then strain it through a linen cloth, and put it to dry; afterwards distemper it with gum water, and it will be good verzino.

116. *To make verzino and to preserve it in powder.*—Take verzino, scrape it fine, put it into a cup, and pour upon it a quantity of prepared white of egg sufficient to cover the verzino, add a little roche alum so as not to make it froth; then add a drop or two of honey, and let it stand for one natural day. On the second day, add a little whipped white of egg, and scrape into it some of the before mentioned alum, as you did before, so that it may not froth, and do this for three or four days; afterwards strain it through a clean piece of linen, put it into a shell and let it dry in the sun; then scrape it out of the shell and preserve the powder. When you wish to use it, put the powder into a shell with some ley in it, to soften, and do as you please with it.

117. *To make pavonazzo with the juice of herbs.*—Take thick pieces of linen cloth, not new and white, but such as pieces of old towelling and sheeting; then take roche alum and dissolve it in boiling water and then let it cool. Soak the rags in this water, wet them well, and dry them in the shade; then take the juice of a plant which is called "gilosia,"[1] and wet the linen rags many times in this juice, and between each time let them dry well in the shade. Keep them in a place open to the air, such as a saucer; and when you wish to use the colour take a little of that linen, and put it to soak in a shell with gum water,

---

[1] Erba Gilosia. The Amaranthus Tricolor.

poi lo pone al foco a bollire per la mita o mancho poi li pone uno poco di alumi pisto et uno poco de commarabico et tolo dal foco e lassa possare poi lo cola quando sera freddo cum una peza de panno de lino et sera bello verzino.

115. *Affare verzino per altra via.*—Havve verzino et radilo subtilmente et metilo in uno vaso vitriato a mollo cum tanta orina fredda et porificata da le fecce che copra el verzino poi ce poni alumj zucharino parte 2 et per terza parte biacha et uno poco de gomma pista et lassa stare a mollo doi di poscia lo cola cum una pezza et pollo a secare poi lo distempera cum aqua gommata et sera fatto bello verzino.

116. *A fare et conservare lo verzino in polvere.*—Summe verzinum et subtile rade et pone in parascide et desuper infundi claram ovi preparatam ita quod coperiatur verzinum et impone desuper aliquantulum de lumine rochi ita quod non facia spumam et deinde mite unam aut binam guctam mellis et permite stare per unum diem naturalem. In secunda vero die addas aliquantulum de clara ovi rupta et abrade super de predicto alumine ut prius fecisti ita quod non fatia spumam et sic faties per tres vel quatuor dies—postea cola cum pettia munda panni lini et micte in coculea et dimitte siccari ad solem postea abrade de coculea et serva pulverem et cum vis operari mitte de dicta pulvere in coculea cum lexivio ad mollificandum et fac velle tuum.

117. *A fare pavonazzo cum sugo dehrbe* (sic).—Accipe peze de panno de lino grosse et non siano nove bianche commo e peze de tovalglie et peze de coltrice use poi tolli alumj de rocho et disfallo in laqua bolita poi lassa fredare et in quella aqua aluma le peze et bagnale molto bene poi le sciuga alombra poi tolli lo sugo duna herba che se chiama gilosia et in quello sugo bagna le peze piu e piu volte et da una volta et laltra lassale sciugare alombra bene et conservale in loco che le dia hayere commo e una una scatella et quando la vorai operare tolli uno poco de quella peza et metila a mollo in una coccia cum aqua

and let it stand for the space of an hour; then press it out and paint with it.

118. *To make the colour brasilium.*—Take verzino or brasilium, scrape it and put it into sufficient gum water to cover the verzino, in a glazed vase for a day and a night, and then boil it until the third part is consumed; then add some roche alum to it and boil it a little, and then pour into it one-third part of strong white vinegar, and let it boil a short time, afterwards strain it and keep it excluded from the air.

119. *To make verzino another way.*—Take scraped verzino, steep it in prepared white of egg for two days; afterwards strain it through a piece of white linen drop by drop on a new brick, and let the verzino remain until dry; then take it off carefully with a knife, and put it away, and when you wish to use it, soften it with water, and write whatever you like.

120. *To make a colour like grana with verzino.*—Take verzino scraped fine, and soak it in ley as strong as you think proper for the space of 3 days; then let it boil over a slow fire in a glazed vessel until the fourth part of it is consumed; then add to it immediately a little alum zucarino, and a little roche alum in powder, and mix it well with a stick; then let it cool, pass it through a filter, wrap it up closely, and put it away, and you will have a good colour like grana.

121. *To make verzino over the fire.*—Take half an ounce of verzino scraped fine, and a sufficient quantity of white wine to cover the verzino; then put these ingredients into a new glazed pipkin, and let them soak for the space of one natural day. Then add to them one-eighth part of roche alum, and the same quantity of gum arabic in powder, and let the whole stand another day. Boil until the liquor is reduced one-half, let it cool, then strain it through a piece of linen, and keep it in a well closed glass bottle, and it will be good.

122. *To make good verzino, proved excellent.*—Take verzino collombino[1] scraped fine, and put it to soak in very strong and

[1] Verzino Collombino. Marco Polo, the Venetian traveller, says, the best Brazil wood, or, as he calls it, Verzino, grew in the Isle of Ceylon.

gomata et lassa stare per spatio de una hora poi la spremj et con quella depengie.

118. *Ad faciendum collorem brasilium.*—Recipe verzinum sive brasilium et rade et pone in aqua gummata ita quod coperiat verzinum in vase vitreato per diem et noctem postea pone ad bulliendum donec terzia pars consumetur postea pone intus de alumine roccj et bulliat parum postea pone de forti aceto albo quantum fuerit tertia pars aque et bulliat parum postea cola et serva bene turatam.

119. *Ad faciendum verzinum per aliam formam.*—Abeas verzinum rasum et mitte in clara ovj preparata per duos dies postea cola eam cum pezia parni lini gutatim super matonem novum et fac manere donec siccatur postea cum curtello elleva diligenter et repone et cum vis eum operare mollifica cum aqua et scribe quicquid vis.

120. *Affare collore de grana cum verzino.*—Tolli verzino raso subtilj et metilo a mollo in ranno da capo forte bene quanto te paia che stia bastevole per spazio de 3 di poi lo fa bullire al fuoco lento in uno pignatto vitriato per infino a tanto che sia consumpta la quarta parte poi poni subito uno poco dalumj zucarino et uno pocho dalumj de rocho spolverizato poi lo mistica cum uno bastone bene et poi lo lassa fredare et poi lo stilla per filtro et ripollo bene turato et haverai bono collore de grana.

121. *Affare el verzino al fuoco.*—Tolli meza oncia de verzino raso subtile poi tolli tanto vino bianco quanto copra el dicto verzino poi lo pone in uno pignatello vitriato novo et lassalo mollare per spatio de uno di naturali poi tolli una otava dalumj de rocho et altratanto gommarabico spolverizato poi lo pone in lo dicto pignatello dal verzino et lassalo stare uno altro di poi lo pone a bullire al foco et quando sera arentrato permita poi lo lassa fredare poi lo cola cum una peccia de panno di lino et serbalo in ampolla de vetrio bene turata et sera bono.

122. *Affare verzino bono provato optimo.*—Recipe verzino collombino subtilmente raso et metilo a mollj in ranno da capo

Depping supposes the term "Verzino Collombino" was derived from Colombo, a city of Ceylon. See Depping, Histoire du Commerce entre

clear ley, and let the ley be 3 fingers deep over the verzino. Let it soak in a glazed pipkin two natural days, and then put in a good pinch of the clippings of cloth dyed with grana, and let them soak well. Then put the liquor over the fire to boil until reduced one-half, add a little roche alum, a little gum arabic in powder, and a little assafœtida, and let it boil slowly for the space of two misereres, so that it may not boil over, as it makes much froth; let it cool, and strain it through a piece of linen, and keep it in a well closed flask.

123. *To make verzino in the sun.*—Take the verzino, scrape it fine, and then put it into a large fish shell, or in a glass vase, with sufficient red wine to cover the verzino; let it soak for a day and a night in the shade, not exposed to the night air; put it in the heat of the sun, and let it stand for 3 or 4 hours; and take roche alum and a little gum, pound them both fine, and add them to the verzino; and let the verzino stand in the sun for 3 or 4 days, but do not expose it to the night air. Then strain it, and keep it in a well closed jar, in order that it may not change its colour, and it will be good.

124. *To make verzino in another way.*—Take verzino, and scrape it with glass, and then put the rasped wood into a shell half full of water, and let it stand for a day and a night; and having done this, strain it through a cloth, and press it into another saucer, and put into it a piece of alumen scabis,[1] the size of a bean, and afterwards set the lake in the sun, and let it dry, and preserve it. When you wish to use it take a little drain water, and distemper it with that water, and use it.

125. *To make a pavonazzo colour.*—Take blue flowers which grow in the corn when it blooms, and extract the juice, and then do as before directed for the other purple made with the pieces of linen, and it is done.

126. *To make a pavonazzo colour, perfect for painting on walls.*—

---

le Levant et l'Europe depuis les Croisades jusqu'à la fondation des Colonies d'Amériques, 2 vols. Paris, 1830, p. 146 n. Verzino Colombino is mentioned in the Tariffe of Pisa quoted by Pagnini in the work entitled

fortissimo et chiaro tanto che lo dicto ranno avantia sopra al verzino 3 o 4 deta e lassalo stare a molle in uno pignattino vitriato doi dj naturali poi li mete una bona piccichata de cimatura de grana et fa che se mollifica bene poi lo pone al fuocho a bullire per mita poi tolli uno poco dalumj de rocche et uno poco de gommarabico in polvere et uno poco de assa fetida et lassa bollire per doi miserere pianamente acio non si sparga per la schiuma che fara poi lassalo refredare et colalo cum una pezza et serbalo in ampolla bene turata.

123. *Affare el virzino al sole.*—Tolli el verzino et radilo subtili poi lo pone in una coccia de pessci grande overo vaso de vetrio cum tanto vino vermilglio quanto che copra el dicto verzino et lassalo mollificare per uno di et una nocte alombra in loco che non li dia lo sereno poi lo meterai al sole bene caldo et lassalo stare 3 o 4 hore poi tolli alumj de rocho et uno poco de gomma et pista subtile luno et lalltro poi lo meti in lo dito verzino poi lassa stare al sole el dicto verzino 3 o 4 di ma la nocte fa che non stia alo sereno poi lo cola et serbalo in una ampolla bene turata acio non se smortisca et sera bono.

124. *A fare verzino alio modo.*—Recipe verzinum et rade cum vitrio et postea tolle cocleam et pone in ipsa cum lingno rupta cujus medietas sit aqua clara et permite per unum diem et unam noctem hoc facto tolle ipsum et cum panno cola et exprime in aliam cocleam et immise tantum alumen scabis quantum est unum ciceris postea pone ad solem et permicte scicari deinde serva et cum volueris operari tolle aliquantulum aque chloche et distemperabis cum ea aqua et opera.

125. *Ad faciendum colorem pavonatium.*—Tolli fiori torchi i quali nascano in lo grano quando spiga et tranni lo sugo poi fa a modo di sopra in laltro pavonazzo cum le peze et de fatto.

126. *Affare collore pavonazzo perfetto per operare in muro.*—

"Della decima e delle altre gravezze del commune di Firenze," &c. Lisbon e Lucca, 1765-66.

[1] Query Alumen Scagliuolo?

Take yellow ochre, clean from all other mixtures, and put it into a vessel which will stand the fire, and set the vase with the ochre to bake in a brick or glass furnace; and know, that if you put it at the top of the furnace it will become of a red colour like vermilion. And if you put the vase at the bottom of the furnace in a place where it will have more heat, it will become of a fine pavonazzo colour, and you must let the vase remain in the furnace from the time that the fire is first lighted, until the furnace is emptied, when it will be done.

127. *To make a very durable and beautiful verzino.*—Take calcined tartar and make as clear a ley with it as you can; and if you make the ley with white wine, it is better than making it with plain water, but either will do. Then take verzino scraped very fine, as much as you like, and put it to soak in the ley so that the verzino may be just covered by the ley, and no more, and let it remain so for a day and a night. Then put it into a glazed jar, and let it boil down one-third, that is to say, let it be reduced by one-third; then add gum arabic in fine powder, as much as you think will suffice, and let it boil a very little. Add a little roche alum, in fine powder, and immediately take it off the fire and let it cool and settle; then strain it through a linen cloth, and keep it in a well-closed phial, and throw away the lees.

128. *To make a light and brilliant pavonazzo for using on paper, that is to say, for boxes, and on parchments.*—First give the parchment or boxes, or other similar things, a coat of vermilion distempered with gum water, and let it dry; then take scraped verzino and put it to soak in white of egg well broken and beaten up, clear and without froth, that the verzino may be covered with the white of egg, and let it stand for two natural days. Then separate the verzino from the white of egg, and with that coloured white of egg, give 3 or 4 coats over the vermilion, each time letting it dry in the shade, and you will have a bright and beautiful pavonazzo; and know that you must not put any gesso whatever upon the parchment, but only give a coat of vermilion on the bare paper, just as it is, because if

Havve terra gialla et ben necta da altre misture et ponila in uno vaso bistugio o altro vaso che arestia a foco et mectilo dicto vaso cum la dicta terra a cociare in fornace de matone o vetrio e sappi che se tu lo mecti desopra a la fornace vira uno collore commo cinabrio rosso e se tu mecti lo dicto vaso in fundo de la fornace in loco che habia piu caldo vira uno collore pavonazo e bello. E volse lassare stare el dicto vaso in la fornace da principio quando se accende foco per infino che se sforna la dicta cocta.

127. *Affare verzino bellitissimo et durabili.*—Tolli cenere de feccia et fanne liscia bene chiara quanto tu poi e se tu farai la dicta liscia cum vino bianco e meglio che a farla cum laqua cummuna ma omne una e buona poi tolli verzino bene raso subtili la quantita che voli e pollo a mollo in la dicta liscia per modo che lo verzino stia coperto da la liscia et non piu et lassa cusci stare per di uno et una nocte poi lo pone al foco in uno pignatino vitriato et lassalo bollire per terzo cioe che arentre la terza parte poi li pone tanto gommarabico bene pisto quanto te paia che sia bastevili et lassalo bollire uno poco poco poi ce pone uno poco de alumj de rocho bene subtili et subito lo leva dal foco et lassalo refredare et reposare poi lo cola cum panno de lino et serballo in una ampolla bene turata et le fecce gietta via.

128. *Affare pavonazzo chiaro et lucido per operare in carta cioe fare scatole et pargamene.*—Prima campeggia le pergamene o scatole o altre cose simili de cinabrio cum aqua gommata distemperato et lassa sciugare poi tolli verzino raso et pollo a mollo in chiara dova bene fratta o dibatuta et chiara senza schiuma tanto che lo verzino sia coperto da la dicta chiara et lassa stare per doi di naturali poi sepera lo verzino da la chiara et de quella chiara collorita darai 3 o 4 mane sopra a lo lecto de lo cinabrio et omne volta lassa sciutare alombria et haveraj pavonazo chiaro et laudabili et sappi che ale dicte parchamene non se li vole dare giesso de niente de fora ma solo dare lo cinabrio in carta schietta commo sta perche se tu li daessi lo gesso lo verzino lo faria crepare per

you were to put gesso on it, the verzino would make it crack on account of the white of egg. And upon the pavonazzo colour, you can make flowers with other colours and paint just as you like; and this is a tried recipe.

129. *To make good lake.*—Take of urine as much as you like, and put it into a vase for the space of a week; then pour it into a pipkin and make it boil until no more scum arises. Then make it into a ley with strong ashes. Next take raw gum lac and pound it as small as panic, put it into a new glazed pipkin, and add to it some of the ley of urine, which must be quite clear, and mix it well with a stick; let the urine or ley be warm when it is poured upon the gum, and when it is well mixed, pour off gently the ley so coloured, and put it into a glazed jar. Then take roche alum in fine powder and mix it with water; then put some of this alum water into the shell containing the ley coloured with the lac, and when you see that it begins to froth, do not put any more. Then put that which has coagulated into a piece of linen like a strainer, hang it up high, and let the water run off; then take the drainings and put them back into the pipkin where the gum was still left, and mix it up well. Then pour it out, and repeat this another time, thus making 3 sorts of lake; the first best; the second not so good; and the third worst. And know that the ley must be very strong, made with urine, and baked ashes, and it must be poured very hot upon the powdered gum, putting the gum on a strainer or filter of linen; then pour the hot ley several times upon it; afterwards add the alum, and dry it; and also dry by itself what remains in the strainer, and it is done.

130. *To make lake as before in another manner.*—Take of gum lac 5 lbs., reduce it to powder and sift it through a close sieve; then take filtered urine, which has stood for 20 days, and place a small kettle on the fire, into which put the urine, and when you see the scum which floats upon the urine, remove it with a perforated ladle, and when the urine is well skimmed and warm, add 3 oz. of roche alum in powder, and

amore de la chiara et sopra el dicto pavonazo poi fiorire cum li altre collore e dipengiare commo a te pare e piace e de probata.

129. *Affare lacha bona.*—Accipe orina d'homo quella quantita che voj et mectila in uno vaso per spatio de 8 dì poi la pone in una pignatta e falla tanto bollire che non faccia piu schiuma poi ne fa lixia cum cenere forte poi tolli gomma de lacca cruda et pistala minuto commo panico poi la pone in uno pignatto novo vitriato poi vi pone de la dicta liscia de hurina che sia bene chiara et necta et miscola bene cum uno bastone et fa che la hurina o vero la dicta liscia sia calda quando la pone sopra ala gomma et commo e bene mista poi ne cava fora quella liscia pianamente cosi collorato et metila in una concha vitriata poi tolli allumj de rocho bene subtili et stemperalo cum aqua poi de questa aqua alumata ne pone in questa concha dove e la liscia gomata e collorita et quando tu vede che se comincia a pigliare non vene mectare piu poi tolli quella che e arapresa et mectila in una pezza a modo de uno colatoro et apicala ad alto et lassala scolare poi tolli quella scolatura et rimectila in su la pintola dove arimase la gomma et mista bene poi nella cava et fa commo facesti prima poi reitera una altra volta et cosi ne fa de tre sorte la prima e migliore la seconda meno la terza mancho. Et sappi che la liscia vole esser fortissima facta de hurina et de cenere recocta et mecterla sopra ala gomma pista bene calda et mecti la gomma in una torcefecio o colatoro de panno de lino poi ve mecti suso lo ranno bene caldo piu volte poi la luma et secala et quello che te rimane nel colatoro ancho secalo daparte et e facto.

130. *Affare laccha ut supra per altro modo.*—Summe gummam lacce libras 5 et eam pista et cribella cum spisso cribello et demum habeas orinam humanam pausatam per xx dies et stillatam per filtrum et habeas unum caldareum parvum et pone ad ignem cum supra dicta hurina et quando videbis spumam habeas capitem foratam i. e. miscolam perforatam et cum ea proice spumam que supernatat urinam et quando urina erit

make it boil again, and then again while it is still boiling take off the scum with the ladle, and when it is well skimmed and clear, take gum lac, sifted, and put it into the urine and alum, continually mixing it over a slow fire for the space of 3 misereres. Then take it off the fire and put it into a clean wooden vase, and afterwards take 6 ounces of verzino in very fine powder, either rasped or pounded in a bronze mortar, and put it over the fire in a small glazed jar with a little water, and make the said verzino boil; afterwards strain it into a vase through a thin and close woollen cloth, and let it cool for one natural day; then take the urine with the alum which is in the before mentioned wooden bowl, and put into it this water which has been boiled with the verzino and then strain and mix it well together. Afterwards take 2 lbs. of roche alum, and put it into two metadelle[1] of clear water, boil it, and afterwards put the alum water into the urine, and mix it well and let it settle for a day; strain it through a strainer and let it settle for another day. Then let it dry, and when nearly dry, cut it into pieces as you please, and let it dry hard. And observe, that you may make lake in this way from various stones and of various kinds, namely, from that from which the crimson colour is made, from dragon's blood, from grana, from vermiculis, from minio, from verzino, and from the flowers of herbs.

131. *To make lake by another process.*—Take urine, pour it into a new glazed jar, and put it over the fire, make it boil well, and while it is boiling take off the scum which arises with a stick, and let it boil until one half is consumed. Afterwards put the gum lac into the urine, and let it boil with a small quantity of gum arabic, and a little alum zucharino, or roche alum. When it has boiled for the space of one hour, strain the liquor through a thin linen cloth, and let it settle in a glazed jar, and the lake will sink, that is, will go to the bottom. Then

---

[1] Metadella, or Mezzetta, a liquid measure still used in Italy.

bene dispumata et calida habeas oncias tres aluminis rochi spulverizati et pone in hurina et iterum fac bullire et denovo buliendo acipe spumam cum predicto capite et quando erit bene spumata et optime clara acipe gummam lacce setaciatam et pone intus cum hurina alumata semper miscendo ad lentum ignem per spatium trium miserere demum eleva ab igne et pone in uno vase ligneo nitido postea tolle oncias 6 verzini subtilissime spolverizati cum raspa aut pisto in brunzi mortario et pone ad ignem in parva olla vitriata cum modica aqua et fac bulire dictum verzinum postea cola eum in vase per petiam laneam subtilem et spissam et dimicte infrigidari per unum diem naturalem demum acipe urinam alumatam que est in vase ligneo predicto et pone intus hec aqua cocta cum verzino et colata et insimul bene misce postea habeas libras duas aluminis rochi et pone in aqua clara ut sit aqua in quantitate duarum metatellarum et fac bullire insimul postea pone hanc aquam alumatam intus in orina et misce bene et permicte pausare per unum diem demum cola per colatorium et dicmitte pausare per alium diem et dimicte sicari et quando erit apud sicitatem fac de ipsa frusta ad libitum et permitte ad sicitatem duredinem. Et nota quod poteris componere laccha isto modo de pluribus lapidibus et diversis speciebus silicet de quo fit color crimusinus, de sanguine draconis, de grana, de vermiculis, de minio, de verzino, et de floribus herbarum.

131. *A fare laccha per altra forma.*—Recipe urinam humanam et ponas in olla nova vitriata et pone ad ignem et fac bene coqui et dum bullit acipe spumam que facit cum aliquo baculo et tantum bulliat quod medietas consumitur post modum pone intus gumma lacce et bulliatur aliquantulum gummi arabici parva quantitate et modico et aluminis zucharinj vel aluminis rocci quo bulito per spatium hunius hore fatias hanc materiam colare per pannum lineum radum et permite pausare in vase vitriato et laccha petit, *i. e.*, ibit ad fundum quo facto proice

pour off the urine which remains upon the lake, taking care not to pour off the lake also, and let the lake dry by itself, and not by the fire, nor in the sun, and it will be good and perfect lake.

B. 132.[1]—Take of verzino, scraped with glass or with a rasp, whatever quantity you like. And if you have a drinking-glass full of scrapings, reserve half of the verzino, and put the other half to soak in so much ley as just to cover the verzino ; let it soak for the space of one night. Then put it to boil slowly over the fire, and when it has boiled while you can say one ave maria, take some of the verzino which you reserved, and put a small quantity, little by little, upon that which is boiling, and continue to do this as long as you have any left, always waiting a little after each time ; and when you have no more left, and the verzino is reduced to one-half, stir in as much roche alum (and it must be well powdered) as you think sufficient, and immediately take it away from the fire and let it rest and cool. Then strain through a thin piece of linen that part only which comes away of itself, without pressing out the dregs. Put it into a well-closed glass phial, and place it in the heat of the sun for a day or two, and it will be fine and perfect verzino for writing. And if you wish the colour to be darker, add to it, when it boils, a piece of quicklime as large as a bean, and it will be done.

B. 133.—Take one ounce of verzino, scraped with a rasp or with glass. Put a third part of the verzino to soak in sufficient spirit of wine to cover it, for the space of one natural day, and add to it the weight of one quattrino of roche alum in powder. Put it over the fire, and let it boil for the space of one paternoster, strain it, and keep it in a phial, and also put by the verzino. Then take the rest of the verzino, that is, the other two-thirds, and put it to soak in very clear vinegar, and add to it a quattrino or more of alum and a quattrino of gum arabic, and a good half drinking-glass full of vinegar. Let it soak for 8 or 10 days, and then soak in this liquid the verzino which

---

[1] The rubrics are wanting in this chapter and the next.

urinam que supra lacha erit taliter quod non pritias lacha postea permite laca sicare non ad ignem neque ad solem per se ipsa et erit bona et perfecta lacha.

B. 132.—Tolli verzino raso cum vetrio o cum la raspa la quantita che tu voli. Et se la raditura fosse pieno uno bichiero tolli la mita de lo dicto verzino et pollo da canto et l'altra mita micti a molle in tanto ranno da capo che lo verzino stia bene coperto dalo dicto ranno et lassa stare a molle per spatio duna nocte poi lo pone a bullire al foco temperatamente et commo ha bulito per una ave maria et tu tolli de quello verzino che reservasti et mettivini supra a quello che bolli a poco a poco et cusi continua per infinj che nai sempre staendo uno poco da una volta alaltra et commo non nai piu et che dicto verzino sia arentrato per mita et tu tolli tanto alumj de rocho quanto te pare bastevilj et metivilo dentro et mistalo uno pocho et sia bene spolverizato et subito poi lo leva dal foco et lassalo reposare bene et fredare bene poi lo cola per panno de lino raro solamente quello che nesce da se senza aspremare le fece de niente. Et poi lo pone in una ampolla de vetrio bene obturata et polli al solle bene caldo per uno di o doi et sera bello et perfecto verzino da scrivare. Et se tu lo volesti piu scuro metice quando bollj quanto uno cece de calcina viva et sera facto.

B. 133.—Recipe una oncia de verzino raspato cum la raspa o cum vetrio e tolli el terzo del deto verzino et mectilo a mollo in tanta aqua viti quanto stia bene coperto per spatio de uno di naturali et mectici uno quattrino de alumj de roccho pista et poi lo pone al foco et bolla per uno patrenostro et colalo et serbalo in una ampolla et lo verzino ancora reserba poi tolli el resto de quello verzino quelli altri doi terzi et pollo a mollo in aceto ben chiaro et ponce un quattrino o piu de alumj et uno quatrino de gomma rabico et lo aceto vole essere uno bono mezo bichiero et lassalo stare a molle per octo o dece di et poi ce repone a mollo el verzino che resto dalaqua vite sopra ali altri

was taken out of the spirit, adding it to the other two-thirds, in the sun; then add to it another quattrino of pounded alum, and let it stand in the sun in a glass vase for 4 or 6 days; then put it away in a phial, after straining it. When you wish to use the colour, take some of the verzino that was in the spirit, which will be almost yellow, and mix it with one-tenth part of the verzino which was in the vinegar, and write with it, and it will be fine; and if you wish to have it darker, put more of the verzino made with the spirit into it, and if lighter, less. And the verzino will be better if made in this manner, viz.:—Take the verzino, scraped as before; then take a tumbler of vinegar, and let it boil for the space of one paternoster, and put into it 2 or 3 quattrini of pounded alum, because when the vinegar is boiling the alum dissolves and liquefies sooner; and if it does not all dissolve it is of no consequence. Then put the verzino and the gum to soak in it, and place it in the sun for 8 or 10 days, and it will be good, and mix it with the other verzino, steeped in the spirit, and it will be light or dark as was before mentioned.

B. 134. *To make a perfect black.*—Take a small jar of the juice of sumach,[1] and put it to boil until reduced by one-fourth, and add to it a good ladleful of dirt from a grindstone, and reduce it two fingers more, and then add of Roman vitriol in powder 3 oz. and 3 oz. of pounded galls, and when you have added these things make it boil till it is reduced by two fingers' breadth.

B. 135.—Take 1 lb. of "panicella," and let it boil in a vessel of strong ley until it is reduced four fingers' breadth, and put into it whatever you wish to be yellow; and if you wish this yellow to be green add a ladleful of the seed of "ghebbi" and a little verdigris pulverized, and strained through a cloth, and put the yellow into it, and it will become green.

B. 136. *To make a perfect colore de grana, such as is worn*

[1] Rhus Cotinus, Cotinus Coriaria, Venus's Sumach, the Venice Sumach.

doi terzi al sole et poi ce agiungi uno altro quatrino dalumi spolverizato et lassalo stare al sole in uno vaso de vetrio per 4. o sei di et poi lo repone in vostra ampolla collato che de et quando lo vorai adoperare tolli una parte de quello verzino de aqua vite che sera giallo quasi et amistalo et amistalo (*sic*) cum la decima parte de laltro verzino de lo aceto et scrivi cum esso et sera bello et se lo voi piu scuro piu verzino daquaviti ce pone et lo [se ?] lo voi piu chiaro ce ne pone meno. Et se tu farai in questa forma sera mellglio affare dicto verzino, viz. :—Tolli el verzino raso commo di sopra poi tolli uno bechiero de aceto et bolla per spatio di uno patrenostro et mectice dentro 2 o 3 quattrini de alumj pesta perche bollendo lo aceto lalume se consuma et liquefasse meglio et se non se liquefasse tucta non fa nientj poi ce poni a mollo lo verzino et la gomma et polla al sole per 8 o 10 di et colalo et sera bello et mistalo cum laltro verzino de aquevite che vera chiaro o scuro commo tu hai hauto di sopra.

B. 134. *Affare colore nero perfecto.*—Tolli uno orciolo daqua de scotano et metilo a bollire tanto che calli la quarta parte et mectice una bona scutella de loto de rota et falla calare doi deta et poi ce pone de lo vitriolo romano pisto 3 oncie et 3 oncie de galla pista et quando ce mecti queste cose fa bullire tanto che calli doi deta.

B. 135. Tolli libra una de panicella et mectila a bollire cum uno broco de lisciva forte tanto che calli quattro deta et mecti dentro cio che voi che sia giallo et se tu voli che questo giallo sia verde tolli una scutella de seme de ghebbi et uno poco de verderamo spolverizato et colalo per panno et mecti dentro quello che fu giallo et sera verde.

B. 136. *A fare perfecto collore de grana cardinalesco cum*

The plant is used in dyeing yellow. From its astringent properties, it is used as a substitute for galls.

by cardinals,[1] *with verzino.*—Take a pound of verzino, and rasp it, or cut it across as fine as possible, and put it to boil in half a kettleful of clear rain or river water; reduce the water one half, and before you take the kettle off the fire, add a pound of roche alum, and make the water boil for the space of one pater-noster, and it will become red, then remove it from the fire and let it cool until you can keep your hand in it, and pour white vinegar into it. And if you require a colour such as cardinals wear, do not put vinegar to it, but strong ley. And you will have 3 colours if you like to boil what remains at the bottom of the kettle in the strongest ley that you can get; let it be reduced by two-thirds, and it will be a perfect violet.

B. 137. *To make lake.*—Take one ounce of crude lake or grana, put it into a small pipkin, and pour on it sufficient urine or ley to cover the lake, and make it boil on a moderate fire for half an hour without smoke. When it boils keep mixing it, and when it has boiled take ½ oz. of roche alum, and ½ oz. of sal gem,[2] and grind them well with ley, and put them into the jar before it has done boiling; then take the vessel from the fire immediately and let it cool. Next take a wash-hand basin and a petito of stale urine, or of strong ley, and throw the whole into the basin, and mix it together, and stir it very well with a stick, and put it for 15 days in a place free from dust, stirring it every evening and morning; at the end of a fortnight take a small linen bag and strain it, and put what you have remaining on a new and clean tile, and dry it directly in the shade, and you will have fine lake. Put it back into a box and cut it into pieces, &c.

B. 138. *To make fine lake another way, for miniatures.*—Take clippings of fine "scarlato de grana," and put them into a glazed jar, and pour upon them sufficient urine to cover the clippings by two fingers' breadths, and put it, well covered over with a cloth, in a place not exposed to the air, and let it

---

[1] That this colour was crimson, and not scarlet, is proved by the fact of the verzino assuming a "colore Cardinalesco" when mixed with an alkali, because alkalis have the property of changing vegetable reds to blues;

verzino, etc.—Tolli una libra de virzino et raspalo overo taglialo atraverso minuto quanto se po et mectilo a bollire in aqua pioviana chiara overo aqua de fiume cioe che sia mezo broco et fallo bollire tanto che se sceme per mita et innante che leve la caldara dal fuoco habbi una libra dalumj de roco et fallo bollire per uno patri-nostro et sera virmiglio et levalo dal fuoco et lassalo fredare tanto che tu ce possi tenere la mano et mectice dentro aceto bianco et se tu el voli cardinalesco non ce mectare aceto ma mectice lisia forte et haraj tre colore. Et se voli che quello che romane al fondo de la caldara a bolire ne la piu forte liscia che poi havere et fa che calle le doi parte et sera perfecto violato etc.

B. 137. *Affare laccha.*—Recipe una oncia de laccha cruda overo grana et mectila in uno pignatello et mectivi suso urina dhomo overo ranno tanto che sia coperta la ditta laccha et falla bollire al foco temperato meza hora senza fumi et commo bolle sempre mestala poiche ha cosci bollito tolli meza oncia de alume de marocho et meza oncia de salgemmo et macinali bene cum ranno et mectilo nelo pignatello nanze che romangna de bollire poi lo leva subito dal fuoco et lassalo fredare poi tolli una lavella et uno petito dorina dhomo reposata overo de ranno forte et cacialo suso in la lavella et mistica omne cosa insiemj et remenala molto bene cum uno bastone et polla per 15 dj in loco che non ce vada polvere et remistalo omne sera et omne matina et in capo di xv di have uno sachetino de panno de lino et colalo et quello che romane in lo colatoro pollo suso una tegola nova et bene necta et li la secha de bocto alombra et haverai lacha fina et reponla in una scatola et fanne pezze etc.

B. 138. *Affare laccha per altro modo per minij fina.*—Recipe cimatura de scarlacto de grana fina et mectila in uno vaso vitriato et de sopra ce pone tanta orina domo che la cimatura sia coperta per doi deta de sopra de la orina dhomo et polla bene coperta cum uno panno in loco che non venga aiere et

whereas, if the vinegar had been added instead of a strong ley, the colour would have been scarlet, and not "Cardinalesco."

The purest kind of rock salt.

remain there until the clippings rot, and when they are rotten pour the urine off; then grind the clippings, and when they are perfectly ground cover them up on a piece of very thin linen cloth, and you will have fine lake, &c.

B. 139. *To make lake.*—Take cloth or clippings of [cloth dyed with] grana, but the rosato or scarlet cloth is best, because it has more substance. Put them into ley made from the ashes of bean-stalks, and let the ley be strong. Put the ashes into it and strain it 8 or 10 times, and it will be very strong; then put the cloth into the ley, and the colour will soon be dissolved. Strain it and let it settle; and if you wish to give body to the lake, take roche alum, and mix with the lake, and put it to dry, and it is done. And know that the ashes may be of oak or burnt tartar of wine, &c.

B. 140. *To make lake in another manner.*—Take 1 lb. of gum [lac], and put it into very strong boiling ley, and let it dissolve; then take three glasses of tepid water in which 2 oz. of roche alum have been dissolved, but first put the water into a large shell, throw on it the boiled ley, and let it remain so for 2 days; then take a glass and take also that gum and water and ley, and strain it in a small woollen bag; let it run through and the lake will remain at the bottom.

lassala costi stare tanto che dicta cimatura se immarcisca et sia fragida et quando sera ben fragida scola via quella orina bene et poi macina la cimatura molto bene et quando sera bene macina coprili sopra una pezza de panno de lino bene subtili et averai laca fina etc.

B. 139. *Affare lacha.*—Recipe panno o veramente cimatura de grana ma el rosato o panno de grana e migilore perche ha piu substantia et mecti in lesciva de cenere de fava et questa liscia vole esser forte et fa cosci octo o dece volte mectendo dentro la cenere et colala che sera fortissima et in la dicta liscia poni el dicto panno el quale se consumera presto et poi el cola et lassa possare la colatura et se tu voli dare a lo dicto collore corpo tollj alume di rocho et mistica cum la dicta lacca et polla a secare et e facta et sappi che la cenere se po fare de cenere de cerro overo de fecia de vino etc.

B. 140. *Affare lacha per altro modo.*—Recipe lb. una de gomma laquale porai in liscia fortissima quando che bolle et lassala disfare bene poi habi tre zayne dacqua tepida in la quale sia doi once dalume de rocho ma prima mecti laqua in una concola grande et desopra butaraj la liscia bulita et lassa stare cosci doi di poi tolli una zaina et piglia questa gomma et aqua et liscia et polla a collare in una sachecta de tela et lassa uscire fora et la lacha romara al fondo.

HERE BEGINS THE HEADING OF THE SIXTH CHAPTER—

HOW TO MAKE PURPURINI AND GOLDEN COLOURS; AND HOW TO LAY ON GROUNDS AND MORDANTS FOR GOLD. AND FIRST TO MAKE A GOLDEN PURPURINO.

141. *To make purpurino, that is to say a golden colour.*—Take quicksilver and Venetian tin, of each as much as you like; melt them together over the fire, and then let them cool; grind the mass, and then take a glass flask, and lute it with philosopher's lute, and let it dry. Put the powder into it, place the glass in a furnace over a slow fire, and leave open the mouth of the flask; when it ceases to smoke, remove the fire, and when it is cold break the flask, and you will find a splendid purpurino, which you must grind fine upon porphyry. Distemper it with gum water and use it.

142. *To make purpurino another way.*—Take equal quantities of quicksilver and Roman tin, and melt them together, and when cool grind the mass fine; then take sulphur vivum and sal ammoniac, of each equal quantities, that is to say, the same quantity as the quicksilver or tin, and grind all together to a very fine powder; then take a small bottle, and put these ingredients into it, lute the bottle with lutum sapientiæ, and put it into the furnace with a slow charcoal fire; do not close up the mouth of the bottle. When it leaves off smoking, remove it from the fire; and when it is cold, break the bottle and you will find the purpurino.

143. *To make a fine gold colour another way.*—Take beaten tin, sulphur vivum, quicksilver, and sal ammoniac, of each equal quantities; put all into a flask, lute the flask with lutum sapientiæ, and close the mouth of the jar with a cork; then pierce the cork in the middle with an awl, put the jar in

INCIPIT DISTINTIO SEXTI CAPITULI

AD PURPURINOS ET COLORES AUREATOS FATIENDUM. ET AD SCISAS ATQUE MORDENTES AD AURUM PONENDUM. ET PRIMO AT FACIENDUM PURPURINUM AUREUM.

141 *Affare purpurino scilicet colore doro.*—Recipe argento vivo et stagnao vinetiano ana el tuo volere et liquefac ad ingnem insimul et dimite infrigidarj postea macina omnia insimul postea tolle ampullam vitream et luta eam cum luto philosofico et dimite siccarj deinde pone intus dictas res et pone in furnello cum lento ingne et ne os ampulle claudatur et cum desinerit futere fumum subtrhae ignem et cum fuerit fridda frange ampulla et invenies purpurinum nobilem quem macina super porfidum subtiliter et stempera cum aqua gummata et utere.

142. *A fare purpurino alio modo.*—Tolli egualmente ariento vivo stamgno romano et fallo strugiare insiemj quando e freddo macinalo bene subtili poi tolli solfo vivo sale armoniaco ana cio e quanto fu l'argento vivo e lo stagno et macina omne cosa bene subtili insiemj poi tolli una bocciecta et mectice dentro le dicte cose poi la inlota cum loto de sapientia et mettila in lo fornello et falli al foco de carbone lento et non obturare la bocca della boccia et quando non fumara piu levali el foco et quando e freddo rompi la boccia et troveraj el purpurino.

143. *A fare collore doro bello per altra via.*—Avve stagno batuto solpho vivo argento vivo et sale armoniaco tanto deluno quanto delaltro poi mecti omne cosa in una ampolla et inlutala cum luto de sapientia et serra la bocca della ampulla cum una suvera poi fora la suvera cum una lesina in lo mezo et polla al

the fire and let it remain there moderately heated, till the smoke comes off yellow. Then let it cool, and break the jar, and you will find good purpurino. Distemper it with gum water, and use it for painting miniatures and other things.

144. *To make purpura, in whatever quantity you like.*—Take 1 oz. of sal ammoniac, 1½ oz. of sulphur, 1 oz. of quicksilver, and 1 oz. of tin. Then take a bottle with a very low neck, and lute it with lutum sapientiæ up to the neck; then mix the tin and quicksilver together over the fire, grind them with the other things, and put the whole into the bottle, and make a clear charcoal fire under it. When you see the smoke issue from it, continue the fire, and let it remain until you see a silvery line round the bottle; then let it cool, and preserve it, and when you wish to use it, take this porporino, and grind it, and then put it into a vessel with gum water, and it will do; and know that it will bear a great deal of gum water. Lay it upon colours or other miniatures.

145. *To make a gold colour in another manner.*—Take 2 oz. of tin, and mix it with one pound of quicksilver, and when they are well mixed[1] add 2 oz. of sal ammoniac well ground; mix all well together in a glass vase, such as a urinal; put it in the furnace, and give it a moderate fire for a day and a half. Then remove it from the fire, and let it cool, and you will find a fine golden colour, with which you can write. Distemper it with white of egg well beaten.

146. *To make a good and fine gold colour.*—Take a hen's egg, make a small hole in it, take out the white, and leave the yolk in the shell; then fill it with quicksilver, and stop up the hole securely and put it under a sitting hen for the space of 30 natural days, and you will have a golden colour,[2] which you must distemper with gum water.

147. *To make golden fringes with the paintbrush.*—Take

---

[1] For the method of mixing the tin with the quicksilver, see No. 168.

foco et falla tanto stare et cociare temperatamente che per lo bugio escha lo fumo giallo allora tolli via lo foco et lassa fredare et rompi lampolla et troverai lo purpurino bello et bono et distemperalo cum aqua gommata et adoperalo a fare minj et altre cose.

144. *A fare purpura secondo la quantita che voi.*—Havvi once j de sale armoniaco, once una et mezo de solpho once j dargento vivo et once j de stagno poi tolli una boccia cum lo collo basso basso et inlutala cum luto de sapientia per infino al collo poi tolli lo stagno et lo argento vivo et incorporalo insiemj al fuoco poi lo matina cum le altre cose sopradicte et metili in nella boccia et polla in lo fornello et falli lo foco de carbone et sia chiaro et quando tu vedi uscire el fumo continua lo foco et lassalo stare per infino che tu vederai uno signo atorno ala boccia ad modo dargento et lassa fredare poi lo conserva et quando lo vorai operare tolli questo porporino et macinalo poi lo pone in la ghiavella cum aqua gomata et lavalo doi o 3 volte cum dicta aqua gomata et stara bene et sappi che porta asa aqua gomata e dalla sopra li collori o altri minii.

145. *A fare collore doro per altra forma.*—Tolli once doi de stangno et metice dentro una libra dargento vivo et commo sono bene incorporati insiemj mectice doi once de sale armoniaco ben trito et mistica bene insiemj in uno vaso de vetrio commo seria uno orinalj et mectilo al fornello et falli lo foco temperato per uno di et mezo poi lo leva dal foco et lassalo fredare et trovarai collore doro bello et cum lo quale poterai scrivare et distemperalo cum chiara dova rupta bene.

146. *A fare collore doro bello et bono.*—Tolli uno ovo de gallina et falli uno bugio picolo et cava fora la chiara et lo ventello lassa in la cocia poi lo impe de argento vivo et serra bene quello bugio cum colla poi lo pone socto la gallina covante per spazio de 30 di naturali et haveraj collore doro et distemperalo cum aqua gommata.

147. *Ad fatiendum fregios aureos cum pennello.*—Recipe ar-

---

2 See a recipe somewhat similar in the collection of Le Begue, No. 22.

gum ammoniac,[1] and cut it small with a penknife, and soak it for a night or a day in strong white vinegar or in urine, and afterwards grind it with a little white of egg, and make flowers with your pen, or write upon gold with the paintbrush, and make a fringe or whatever else you like; and when it is dry, breathe on it slightly, lay on the gold and press your hand upon it. When the gold has set, take some cotton, or a hare's foot, and rub it on the gold, and remove the loose gold. And if you wish to make a fringe or flowers with your paintbrush upon figures, add also a little ochre.

148. *To lay dead gold upon colours.*—Take incense, white gum, and sugar candy, of each equal quantities, grind them together, and distemper the mass with strong vinegar or wine, and make it sufficiently liquid not to clog the brush; and it must be thoroughly mixed so as to dry well when applied with the pencil. Lay it on where you wish to put the gold, and when dry, lay the gold upon it, and press it with the cotton; when you have pressed it down well, rub it with the cotton, and the gold will remain clear and fine.

149. *To lay gold upon books, that is, upon paper.*—Take white of egg, well whipped with the milk of the fig-tree, and gum arabic in fine powder, about as much as a nut. Soak it in the white of egg, add to it a little pure saffron, and let it also soak in the white of egg for the space of one natural day. Then take a small sponge or a paintbrush and dip it in the composition, and spread it thin where you wish to lay the gold, and immediately apply the gold; then press it with cotton, let it dry well, and burnish it with a tooth, and it will become bright.

150. *To gild cloth or canvas.*—Take gum ammoniac and put it into a little urine, and let it stand for a night; then make it into a paste with ceruse and a little honey; then lay on the mordant, and the next day lay on the gold. This is good also for laying gold upon paper.

---

[1] This is the gum resin Ammoniac, and not Armenian Bole, which is mentioned in No. 160 under the term "Bolarminium;" and again in No.

moniacum et incide minutatim cum curtello et pone in forti aceto albo vel in orina ad mollificandum per noctem vel diem postea macina eum cum aliquantulo clare ovi et fatias flores cum penna vel scribe supra aurum cum pennello et fac fregium et quicquid vis et cum siccum fuerit aliquantulum satage et pone aurum et preme manum super aurum et cum captum fuerit aurum habeas de bombage vel pedem leporis et duc super aurum et tolle aurum non captum. Et si volueris facere fregium vel flores cum penello super figuras adde aliquantulum et de ocrea.

148. *A mectere oro senza lustro in suso li collore.*—Havve incenso gomma biancha et zuccaro candio ana, et macina le predicte cose insiemj et stemperale cum aceto forte o cum vino et fallo tanto liquido che non se abombola et vole essere bene remenata tanto che sciuga bene dalo penello et dallo dove voi porre loro et quando e sciuto ponci suso loro, et fermalo cum lo bambagio et quando haverai premuto bene sfregalo cum lo bambagio et loro remara necto et bello.

149. *A mettere oro in suli libri cioe in su le carte.*—Avve chiara dova rupta cum fici lacte multo bene poi torai tanto gomarabico quanto una avellana subtilmente spolverizato et metilo a mollo in la dicta chiara poi torrai uno poco de zaferamj Integro et metilo a molli in la predita chiara per spatio duno dj naturali poi tollj uno poco di spogna et bagnala in la dita compositione o vero cum uno pennello et gratalo dove tu voli metere loro subtilmentj et subito mecti loro et poi lo ferma cum bambagio poi lo lassa bene sciucare et brunisce cum dente et sera lustro.

150. *De aurando panno vel tela.*—Summe armoniacum et pone in modica orina et ibi stet per noctem postea conficitur cum cerusa et modico melle et tunc ponitur dicta ascisa uno die et alio die pone aurum et etiam valet ad ponendum aurum in carta.

161, both "armoniaco" and "Bolarminium" are mentioned. See similar recipes in D. Alessio, Part I. p. 114.

151. *A golden colour for gilding.*—Take gum of almonds and saffron, and grind them on a mortar, and put them into a glass vase; place the mixture by the fire to warm, and afterwards mix some whipped white of egg with it, and paint wherever you like, and it will be of a golden colour.

152. *To make a mordant for gilding on walls.*—Take calcined bone, ground fine with weak glue, such as parchment glue, and let it dry; and when quite dry grind it up afresh with linseed oil, and make it rather stiff; then take a little liquid varnish, and incorporate it with the bone-dust. Add to it a little saffron, sufficient to give it colour, and make it rather stiff. When you wish to put the gold on the wall, the mortar must be dry, and the mordant must not be applied too thick. Let it remain 5 or 6 days, and then put on the gold.

153. *To write with silver.*—Take the silver marchesite,[1] and grind it very fine on porphyry with strong vinegar; then wash it and purify it well with other vinegar. Distemper it with gum-water, and write whatever you think proper.

154. *To make a good and fine silver colour.*—Take tin filings and quicksilver, of each two parts, well pounded with gum arabic wetted with water, and write whatever you please with it; let it dry, and then you may burnish it.

155. *To gild all bodies.*—Take tartar, atramentum,[2] quicksilver, and salt, and distemper the whole with strong vinegar, and warm the mass a little at the fire, and when you wish to gild, put a little water in the glass, that is to say, some of the above-mentioned water, so as to cover what you cast.

156. *To make a golden colour for writing.*—Take juice of celandine,[3] and put it into a well-closed glass flask, place it under horse dung, or the refuse of grapes, and let it remain there for a month; afterwards take it out and grind a little orpiment with the liquor, and put it back into the dung for a fortnight, and then it will be purified. And when you wish to write with

---

1 See Beckmann, Inventions, Tit. *Zinc*, and Agricola De Metallicis p. 435, 436, Venezia 1550.

151. *De auro collore ad aurandum.*—Habeas gummam amangdolarum et crocum et molle in mortario et recollige in vase vitrio et pone justa ignem ut calefatiat postea misce de clara ovj fracta et pinge ubicumque volueris et erit color aureus.

152. *A fare mordente da mectere oro in muro.*—Tolli osso calcinato et subtili macinato cum colla dolce commo colla de carta poi lo lassa seccare poi che e bene secho remacinalo de novo cum olio de semj de lino et fallo uno poco duretto poi tolli uno poco de vernicj liquida et incorporala cum lo sopradicto osso poi li pone uno poco de croco quanto li dia collore et vole essere uno poco duretto e quando voli mectere loro in muro la calcina conviene essere secha poi pone lo mordente non troppo grosso et lassalo stare 5. o 6. di poi mecto suso loro.

153. *A scrivare dargento.*—Pilglia marchasita che tengha de argento et macina la in porfido bene subtili cum aceto forte poi lavala et purificala bene cum laltro aceto poi la distempera cum aqua gummata et scrivi quello te pare.

154. *A fare collore de argento bello et bono.*—Tolli stamgno limato argento vivo ana parte doj pisto bene cum gummorabico humecttalo in aqua et scrivi quello te piace cum esso et lassa secare poi le porai brunire.

155. *A mectere a oro omne corpo.*—Avve tartaro atramento ariento vivo et sale et distempera omne cosa cum forti aceto et scaldalo uno poco al foco et quando tu voli dorare pone uno poco daqua in uno vaso cio e de la sopradicta aqua tanta che copra cio che tu giette.

156. *Ad fatiendum aureum collorem pro scribendo.*—Recipe succum celidonie et pone in ampulla vitrea et bene clausa ponatur sub fimo equino aut venatia et ibi maneat per mensem postea extrahe et molletur aliquantulum de auropiumento cum ipso licore et remitatur in fimo per quindecim dies tunc erit purificatus quum autem vis scribere mitcte aliquas guctas dicti

---

2 It is by no means clear what the Italians understood by this term. The MS. of Le Begue shows that it had different significations.

3 Celidonia, Chelidonium. A yellow lake is made from this plant.

it, pour a few drops of this liquid into a shell or cornet; then put in a leaf of fine gold, and liquefy them together, and afterwards write with a pen whatever you like, and burnish the writing when dry.

157. *To make gold letters.*—Take gesso, with which panels are primed, and with which the tailors mark their thread, and ochre, and also a little white of egg, well beaten with a sponge, or otherwise; grind all these things together for a considerable space of time, and add a little wax from your ear, in order that it may flow freely from the pen. Write where you like, and let it dry, afterwards put the gold on and fix it with cotton; when dry, burnish it with the tooth of a wolf, or of a sucking calf, or of a mule, or of an ox, or with a stone, or knife.

158. *To write in gold with a pen.*—Take water of cinnabar, and saltpetre, of each equal quantities, one grain of common salt, and one leaf of fine gold, which you must put into a shell along with the before mentioned ingredients in the evening, and let it remain all night; in the morning write, and the letters will be most beautiful.

159. *To make water for gilding.*—Take 3 jars of water, $\frac{1}{2}$ lb. of roche alum, and 1 oz. of white, that is, calcined tartar, of verdigris about as much as a bean, and one handful of common salt; pound all well together, and boil them down to one-half or more, and with that water paint what you like.

160. *To make size for gilding.*—Take of gesso sottile about as much as a nut, grind it with clear water, and make it tolerably stiff; afterwards take some Armenian bole, about as much as a bean, and grind it by itself with clear water. Then mix it with the gesso, and add a sufficient quantity of fine glue already dissolved, a little white sugar, and a little ear wax, and grind all these ingredients together. And know that the glue must be made so as not to stick to the porphyry in the grinding, and when you wish to use it, place it upon hot ashes in order to liquefy it. And note, that if the glue has remained melted in the vase for several days, it is better and lighter;

licoris in coclea aut cornetto deinde pone unum folium auri fini et liquefac insimul postea scribe cum penna quid vis et quando erit sicce burnias.

157. *Ad faciendum literas auratas.*—Summe gissum cum quo ingessatur tabulas et ocrea i. e. cum aqua saccatoris tingunt filum et modicum et clare ovi bene rupta cum spungia aut aliter et omnia ista insimul macina per magnum spatium deinde tolle modicum de sorde aurium et macina insimul ita quod currat scribendo deinde scribe ubi vis et dimicte siccarj postea pone aurum desuper et firma eum cum bombige et quando fuerit siccum burnias cum dente lupino vel victule lactentis vel mule aut bovi vel cum lapide aut telbella [coltello ?].

158. *Ad scribendum aurum cum callamo.*—Tolle aqua cinabrij sal nitrij et unum granum salis comunis ana et unum folium auri fini quem pone in una coclea simul cum predittis rebus in sero per noctem et in mane scribe et erunt pulcherime.

159. *Ad fatiendam aquam ad aurandum.*—Habeas tres orciolos aque et libram mediam aluminis roccj et untiam unam tasi albi i. e. calcinati et viride ramum quantum est faba et manipulum unum salis comunis et bene ad invicem pistentur et tantum bulliat quod deveniat ad medietatem vel plus et cum aqua illa pinge quid vis.

160. *Affare scisa da mectere oro.*—Habeas gissum subtilem quantum est nux et macina cum aqua clara et fatias eum aliqualiter sodum postea Recipe bolum arminium quantum est faba et macina eum de per se cum aqua clara postea missce cum preditto gisso deinde habeas collam nobilem distemperatam et mite intus quantum necessarium est postmodum pone intus aliquantulum zucheri albi et aliquantulum fectie auricularum et predicta insimul macina. Et scias quod colla debet esse taliter quod in macinando se adhereat porfido aliquantulum et quando vis operare pone eam super calidum cenigem ut bene liquescat et nota quod si colla staret aliquibus

and if the mordant is laid too thickly upon the paper, scrape it smooth and thin. When you wish to lay the gold on it, bathe it with clear water, put on the gold, and fix it with the cotton, and when it is dry burnish it well with a tooth. If the mordant is too soft, put a little white of egg into the water, when you are applying the gold, or add some to the mordant, and it will be good.

161. *To make size for gilding.*—Take gum ammoniac, and grind it first without water, and then with the juice of garlic, to which add a little Armenian bole, and when the mass is dry, it must be ground up again with the garlic juice; then apply it where you please, and afterwards lay on the gold.

162. *To draw outlines of gold with size.*—Take gesso sottile,[1] and grind it with white of egg, neither beaten nor whipped, add to it a little honey of roses,[2] and a drop or two of weak size at discretion, with a little ear wax. Then make the outlines or other things, and, when dry, breathe upon them a little, and immediately apply the gold, and press it gently with the cotton; then burnish it, and it will be lustrous and beautiful.

163. *To make letters of gold—proved, and true.*—Take fine gold, and grind it on porphyry with roche alum; then take up very carefully the gold and alum, and put the mixture into a glass saucer; wash it several times with tepid water, then with cold water, and each time let it settle, in order that the gold may sink to the bottom; when the gold is well purified and cleansed, let it dry. When you wish to use it, distemper it with gum water, and write whatever you please; let it dry, and then burnish it if you think proper.

164. *To write gold letters with a pen as before.*—Take fine gold leaf and mix it with white honey in a saucer, then grind it upon porphyry very fine with common salt, wash it with hot water like "smalto," and do as before.

---

[1] See No. 213.

diebus in vasculo distemperata esset melius et levius et quando ascisa esset nimis grossa super cartam rade eam ut sit bene equales et subtilis et quando vis super eam aurum ponere balnea eam cum aqua clara et pone aurum et firma cum bombice et cum siccum fuerit bene cum dente burnias, et si esset nimis dulcis pone in aqua quando mictis aurum pone desuper ascisa vel cum aqua aliquantulum clare ovi et bonum erit.

161. *A fare scisa per mectare oro.*—Recipe armoniaco et macinalo senza aqua poi tollj sugo dalglio et macina lo armoniaco cum lo ditto sugo et mectice un poco de bolarminio et quando fusse secco se vole remacinare cum lo dicto sugo e dallo doi voi poi mete loro.

162. *A fare il profilo doro cum scisa.*—Tolli gesso subtili et macinalo cum chiara dovo che non sia rupta ne dibatuta et metice uno poco de mele rosato et alcuna goccia de colla dolce a tua discretione cum uno poco de scarcatura de orechie et poi fa li profili, o altro et quando e secco ansciare suso uno poco e subito mette loro et calcalo uno poco cum lo bambagio poi lo brunisse et sera lustro et bello.

163. *A fare lettere doro provata et vera.*—Havve oro fino et macinalo in porfido cum alumj de rocho molto bene subtili poi recolgli el dicto oro et alumj macinato molto bene et metilo in una scudella de vetrio poi lo lava piu volte cum aqua tepida et poi cum la fresca et omni volta lassa possare acio loro se ne vada in fundo et quando loro sera bene purificato et netto lassalo secare et quando lo vorai operare distemperalo cum aqua gomata et scrivi quello te piace et lassa seccare e poi lo brunissci parendoti.

164. *A scrivare oro cum penna ut supra.*—Havve oro fino in folglio et mistalo cum mele bianco in una scudella poi lo macina in porfido overo macinalo in porfido cum sale comuno molto bene subtili poi lo lava cum aqua tepida ad modo de smalto et seguita commo de sopra.

---

[2] The Ricettario Fiorentino gives a recipe for this compound. It consists of Infusion of Roses, 6 lbs.; white sugar, 2½ lbs.; best honey, 1¼ lb.

165. *The same—another way.*—Take a little gum, white, fine, and clear, and soak it in a shell with a little rose-water for the space of one natural day or night; then take a clean glazed saucer, and moisten the saucer with the liquefied gum. Next take fine gold leaf, and mix it with the gum, and having ground it fine, wash it as you did before, until it be well washed, purified and cleaned. Distemper it with gum water, in the manner I mentioned in the other recipes.

166. *To make a mordant for burnishing and laying on gold.*—Take of gesso sottile as much as a nut, a little vermilion, sufficient to give it colour, and a piece about twice as large as a bean of hepatic aloes,[1] and grind all together with clean water on porphyry or marble, until reduced to a very fine powder. Then let it dry, and grind it again with water; let it dry again, then grind it afresh with gum-water mixed with half as much again of white of egg, and with a little honey of roses, and a piece about the size of a bean of sugar candy; grind all these things well together, and while grinding add a little wax from the ear. When ground, put the powder into a small horn and let it settle for the space of two or three days; then throw away all the scum which will rise to the top, use it, scraping away the thicker parts, and immediately apply the gold and burnish it.

167. *To make a good mordant for gilding, which is easily prepared.*—Take good weak glue, with a little gesso sottile and a little saffron, grind it all together; then lay the mixture wherever you like and let it dry. Then, breathing on it, lay on the gold and burnish it.

168. *To make a golden colour for writing with a pen on paper and canvas.*—Take tin and quicksilver in equal quantities at pleasure, first put the tin to melt in a crucible, and when it is melted pour into it the quicksilver, and mix the ingredients well with a stick, and incorporate them together, and they will

[1] This substance was formerly much used in varnishes to give them a yellow colour. See No. 204.

165. *Ad idem per aliam viam.*—Tolli uno poco de gomma bianca et bella et chiara et metila a mollo in una coccia cum uno pocho daqua rosata per spatio duno di naturali o nocte poi tolli una scudella vitriata bene necta et unge la dicta scutella cum la dicta gomma liquefatta poi tolli oro fino in folglio et mistalo cum la dicta gomma poi lo pone a macinare bene subtili et lavalo commo facesti disopra tanto che sia bene lavato purificato et necto et lo distempera cum aqua gomata ut te certiorem feci in aliis receptis ut supra.

166. *A fare scisa per brunire et porre oro.*—Avve gesso subtili quanto una noce et uno poco de cinabrio quanto li dia collore et quanto seria doi fave de aloe pattico et macina omne cosa insiemj cum aqua chiara in porfido o in marmo tanto che sia sutilissima poi la lassa secare poi la macina una altra volta cum aqua et lassa secare poi la remacina de novo cum aqua gomata et chiara dovo la mita piu che laqua gomata et un poco de mele rosato et quanto una fava de zucaro candio et macina multo bene insiemj omne cosa et macinado metice uno poco de bructura de orechie et macinata che sera metila in lo corneto et lassala possare per spatio di doi o tre di po gietta via tutta quella schiuma che ella mandara di sopra poi ladopera radendo le parti grosse poi ansciando et subito mete loro et brunissce.

167. *A fare scisa bona et breve per mettere oro.*—Piglia colla gentili che sia dolce cum uno poco de gesso subtili et uno poco de zaferamj et macina omne cosa insiemj poi lo pone dove voglj et lassa secare poi ansciandoce mecti loro et brunissce.

168. *A fare collore doro da scrivare cum penna in carta et in tela.*—Tolli stangno argento vivo ana el tu volere prima pone lo stagno in uno crugiolo a fundare et quando sera bene fuso buttace dentro lo argento vivo et mistalo molto bene cum uno bastone et incorporali bene insiemj et vira ad modo de polvere

become like dust; then throw this dust into a saucer, and take sulphur and sal-ammoniac of each the same quantity as of the quicksilver; pound the whole very fine, and mix it all together, put it into a bottle luted from the neck downwards. Close the bottle well with an iron cover and lute the top of it with lutum sapientiæ; then set it to boil over the fire until the moisture is evaporated and consumed by a slow fire. Let it cool, and break the vase, and you will find a fine and good golden colour; and when you wish to write, take some of this mixture, and grind it very fine with white of egg; then put it into a horn and write, and the letters will appear fine and shining.

169. *To lay gold on paper for letters.*—Take gesso sottile, and grind it with glue not too strong; then add small quantities of Armenian bole, sugar candy, red sugar, and honey of roses, grind the whole together, and apply it wherever you like, and when dry, scrape the rough parts, and breathe on the paper, and immediately put on the gold, and then burnish it.

170. *To make a mordant for burnishing and gilding.*—Take a little gesso well ground, and then take one-third part of parchment glue, and soak it in water; grind it all together with a little minium, and it will be good.

171. *To make mordants for gilding on figures, on canvas, on stone, on wood, on gesso, and on mortar or walls.*—Take litharge, verdigris, and a little ochre, and grind them with a little linseed oil and liquid varnish; incorporate them well together, and then gild in the usual manner.

172. *To make a water for gilding all things.*—Take the marcasite of gold,[1] and grind it well upon porphyry with very strong vinegar; then boil, and treat the mixture like salts; afterwards distil it through an alembic, and three waters will

[1] Auriferous Iron Pyrites. Phillips (Mineralogy, pp. 219, 324) says this mineral contains gold. Beckmann (Inventions, Tit. Zinc) remarks, that that was the true Marchasita aurea which contained Zinc. He adds this is properly a stone, the metallic particles of which were so entirely sublimated by fire, that nothing but useless ashes remained behind.

poi butta questa polvere in una scudella poi tollj solfo et altretanto sale armoniaco egualmente quanto fu lo soprascripto argento vivo et pista menuto bene subtilj et miscola insiemj omni cosa et metila in una boccia alutata dal collo ingiuso et obtura molto bene la bocca cum uno coperchio de ferro et disopra obtura cum luto de sapientia poi lo pone a bullire al fuoco per in fino che le humedita de le dicte cose siano giallate via et consumate cum fuoco temperato poi lassa fredare et rompe lo vaso et troverai collore doro bello e bono et quando tu voraj scrivare tolli de la dita mistura et macinala cum chiara dovo bene subtili poi lo pone in uno cornecto et scrivi poi apareranno lustre et belle.

169. *A mectare oro in carta cum litera.*—Tolli gesso subtili et macinalo cum colla non troppo forte poi ce pone uno poco de bolo arminio et uno poco de candio et uno poco de zucaro rosso et uno poco de mele rosato et macina insiemi et dallo dove voi et quando e secco rade le parti grosse et ansciace suso et subito mete loro poi brunissce.

170. *A fare scisa da brunire e porre oro.*—Avve uno poco de gesso ben trito poi tolli la quarta parte de colla de carte et polla a mollo cum laqua poi macina omne cosa insiemj cum uno poco de minio et sera bona.

171. *A fare mordenti da metere oro in figure in panno in petra in ligno in gesso e in calcina o muro.*—Recipe litargirio verderamo et uno poco de ocria e macinale cum uno pocho de olio de seme de lino et cum uno poco de vernice liquida et incorpora multo bene insiemj poi fa commo se fa per mectere oro.

172. *Ad afare una aqua da dorare omnia.*—Summe marchesitam auri quam optime tere super porfidum cum aceto acerrimo et inde bullant ut fiant sicut sala postea distilla per alembicum et exibunt tres aque cum prima scribitur in carta cum

---

It contained fixed quicksilver, communicated a colour to metals, burned in the fire, and was at length entirely consumed. Agricola had said the same thing 200 years before. Compare Agricola de Metallicis, pp. 181, 343, 376, 433, 438, Ed. Venezia, 1550; and see Matthioli, 1443.

come over. With the first you may write on paper; with the second, which is red, you may write on canvas, on iron, or on gesso, and when it is dry rub it with a rough cloth, and it will become fine and shining gold; and with the third, which is black, you may write upon glass, and when it is dry you may rub it with a very harsh and rough cloth, and it will be splendid gold.

173. *To make a mordant for gilding on paper, and for burnishing according to the German manner.*—Take gesso sottile and white clay in equal quantities, and temper them, as if for writing, with white of egg beaten up with the milk of a fig-tree; write whatever you like upon paper previously polished with a tooth. Then let it dry and scrape off the rough parts. Then take white of egg coloured with saffron, lay on the white of egg by degrees with the paint-brush, and directly afterwards apply the gold or silver leaf, press it lightly with the cotton, and let it dry. When dry, clean it with bread-crumbs, first polishing it with a tooth, and it will stand well.

174. *To make purple oricello.*—Oricello has a purple colour; boil some water, when it is hot liquefy the oricello in it, and rub it hard, and press it through a strainer into a glass goblet, boil the water as you did before, and strain it two or three times. Then put a strip of saffron and a piece of gum into an egg-shell, and warm it on the coals, and do this 2 or 3 times, and the next day, when that water has settled, strain it well through a strainer and distemper it, and lay it upon paper, and write, and then let it dry. Then take gum ammoniac and grind it well with ley, and mix a little vermilion with it, and write whatever you like upon the oricello with a paint-brush or a pen, and let it dry. Having done this, take a leaf of gold between your little finger and thumb, blow upon the leaf, and place it upon the gum ammoniac, and fix it well first with your finger and afterwards with a stone, but do not rub it. Clean it with bread crumbs; do this once or twice; if you mix the oricello with lake or vermilion it will be brighter.

175. *For the same, another way.*—Take the milk of the fig-

secunda que est rubea scribitur in tela aut ferro vel in gisso et ea sicca fricatur cum panno aspero et fiet aurum pulcrum et lustrum: cum tertia vero aqua que est nigra scribitur super vitrium et ea sicca fricatur cum acerrimo et aspero panno et fiet aurum nobilissimum.

173. *A fare scisa per metere oro in carta e per brunire secondo luso thodesco.*—Invenies gissum subtilem et cretam albam equaliter et bene tempera cum clara ovj que sit rupta cum fici lacte et eam tempera ad usum scribendi et scribe quid vis in carta prius cum dente polita et permicte siccarj et inde rade rudes partes deinde tolle claram cum crocho coloratam et cum penello paulatim supermite claram et postea statim supermicte folium auri aut argenti et firma eum modicum cum bomboce et permitte sicari et sicco purifica eum panis mulica prius cum dente polita et peroptime manebit.

174. *Ad auricellam purpuream fatiendum.*—Auricellam purpureum habet collorem sed bulli aquam bene et captefacta auricellam liquefac intus et frica fortiter et frica per stamineum in parascide vitreo et iterum bulli aqua similiter ut prius fecisti et pro bis vel ter cola aquam illam et sic filo croci et gummj in testa ovi et calefac super prunam et feceris bis vel ter in sequenti die aquam preditam cum resedit bene iterum cola per stamen et colata tempera et in carta pone et scribe inde permitte sicari postea tolle armoniacum et ipsum fortiter tere cum urina et immisce aliquantulum de cinaprio postea super auricellam cum penello vel pennam quod vis scribe et permitte sicari. Hoc facto tolle folium auri et digito parum vidat et ad maximam druge folium et super armoniacum pone et cum digito ferma bene postea cum lapide et noli fricare et cum panis mulica purifica hoc fac semel vel bis demum sublimj capum auricelle cum laccha vel cinabrij et clarius erit.

175. *Ad idem alio modo.*—Summe lac ficus et misce cum

tree, mix it with white of egg reddened with vermilion, and write what you please upon paper, and let it dry; then lay the juice upon it and do not rub it, but press it with a stone, and polish it with a fine cloth.

176. *To make water of quicksilver*[1] *for gilding ostrich feathers and other things very beautifully.*—First lay a stratum of common salt in a retort, and on that lay quicksilver, cover the vessel with an alembic with a very large head, and let the retort be a very long one. Distil it with a slow fire, and afterwards preserve it, and when you wish to use it, take some of the water and dip in it an ostrich feather, wetting it on each side, and let it dry well; do this twice, and the third time dip it and do not dry it, and while it is still wet spread gold leaf on both sides of it, and hold it to the fire and shake it, for the whole feather will then become gilt.

B. 177. *To make a mordant for gilding on paper, on walls, and on everything else, &c.*—Take parchment glue, pour on it a little cold water, and let it stand 3 days in the shade; then put it in the sun until it becomes decomposed, and if there is not enough water, add more to it; and when quite decomposed, reduce to powder some tiles or red earthen vessel not over-baked, or gesso sottile, and mix them well together, and then spread the mixture thinly wherever you like, lay the gold on it, and let it dry, and then burnish it with a boar's or a horse's tooth.

B. 178. *To write in gold on any cloth you like.*—Take ox-gall dried in the smoke, distemper it with gum arabic, and write wherever you like; when it is nearly dry, apply gold upon it, and it will be good, &c.

---

1 In this recipe, the term "Azoch" is used to denote the metal mercury or quicksilver. It is derived from the Arabic. From the Arabic it passed into the vocabulary of the Alchemists, where it was used to denote the mercury of metals, the first principle of metals, and an universal medicine. Paracelsus used to boast that he had a spirit at his command, called "Azoth,"

clara rubificata cum cinabrio et quodvis scribe in carta et permitte sicarj deinde superpone succum et noli fricare sed cum lapide firma et cum pano levis purifica.

176. *Ad fatiendum aquam azoch ad deaurandum pennas strutii et alia valde pulcherrime.*—Primo fac stratum salis comunis in urinali et superpone azoch vivum et superpone alembicum cum capite valde magnum et sit orinale bene longum et distilla cum lento igne postea serva et cum vis operari tolle de dicta aqua cum qua madefatias pennam strutii ab utroque latere et dimicte bene sicari et sic fatias bis terzia vice balnea et non sicces et super eam sic balneatam extende folia solis ab utraque parte et monde ad ignem, et scurla quia tota ibi penna efficitur aurea.

B. 177. *Affare scisa da pore oro in carta muro et in omni altro luoco.*—Recipe colla de carta et mectili uno poco daqua chiara et lassala stare tre di alombra poi la pone al sole tanto che diventa tucta putrefacta et marcia et puzzolento et se mancasse laqua agiongnicine et quando e bene diffatta fa polvere de tegoli o de coppi rossi non tracotti overo gesso subtili et misticale insiemj et poi dalla ove tu [vuoi ?] subtili et desopra pone loro et lassa secare de poi lo inbrunisce cum uno dente porcino o cavallino etc.

B. 178. *A scrivare doro in omne drappo che voi.*—Recipe fele de bo secco al fumo et distemperalo cum gomarabico et scrivi ove tu voli et commo e quasi secco pone sopra loro et sera bello etc.

---

whom he kept imprisoned in a jewel; and in many of the old portraits he is represented with a jewel inscribed with the word "Azoth" in his hand. The Spanish name for mercury, Azogue, is derived from Azoth.

HERE BEGINS THE HEADING OF THE SEVENTH CHAPTER

ON MAKING VERMILIONS, AND MANY OTHER COLOURS OF DIFFERENT KINDS. AND ON THE MIXING OF COLOURS; AND OF THE TEMPERING OF COLOURS, ACCORDING TO MAGISTER JACOBUS DE THOLETO. AND FIRST TO MAKE VERMILION.

179. *To make vermilion.*—Take of quicksilver two parts, of sulphur one part; first melt the sulphur, then add the quicksilver, mix them well, and reduce them to powder, and then put the powder into a flask luted with lutum sapientiæ as high as the neck. Place the flask on the ashes until all the humidity is driven off; then close the mouth of the flask with cotton, and give it a tolerably strong fire until the matter rises to the neck of the flask and is very red; then take it from the fire, let it cool, and it is done.

180. *To make vermilion.*—Take 1 lb. of sulphur vivum, with one pound of quicksilver, and 4 oz. of tin; put them into a crucible well covered with lutum sapientiæ, apply heat until a knife held to the opening of the crucible is no longer discoloured or turned blue, and you will have good vermilion.

181. *For the same, another way.*—Take of sulphur vivum 3 lbs., put it into a basin, and cover it with another basin, and make a fire under it, and, when it is melted, add a pound of mercury, and incorporate them well by mixing them until they harden; when cold, grind the mass well upon marble, put the powder into a bottle, and close up the mouth of the bottle with earth; make a moderate fire under it, and when you see the contents rise so as to fill the whole of the bottle, remove it from the fire, and let it cool. Then break the bottle, and it will be perfect vermilion.

INCIPIT DISTINTIO SEPCTIMI CAPITULI

DE CINABRIIS FIENDIS. ET MULTIS ALIIS DIVERSIS COLLORIBUS. ET DE MISTURIS COLLORUM. ET AD COLLORES DISTEMPERANDUM SECUNDUM MAGISTRUM JACOBUM DE THOLETO. ET PRIMO AD FATIENDUM CINABRIUM.

179. *Ad cinabrium faciendum.*—Reccipe argento vivo parte doi soplfaro parte una et prima disfa lo solpho de po ce pone lo argento vivo et misticali bene et redulli in polvere depoi lo pone in una ampolla lutata da luto de sapientia in fino al collo poi la pone sopra le cinige per infino a tanto che le humidita sieno andate via poi serra la bocca de lampolla cum lo bambagio e dalli lo foco uno poco grande per infino che la materia monta a presso el collo de lampolla e sia bene rosso de po li tolli lo foco e lassa fredare e fatto.

180. *Ad faciendum cinabrium.*—Summe libram j sulphuris vivi cum una libra argenti vivi et quatuor untias stangni et pone in crisole bene obturato cum luto sapientie et quoque tam diu quod cultellus non blueatur a foraminibus crugibuli et habebis cinabrium bonum.

181. *Ad idem alio modo.*—Recipe sulphur vivi libras tres et pone in una paraside et coperi eam bene cum alia paraside et fac subtus ingnem et quando est liquefactum pone intus unam libram mercurii et incorpora bene mistando dummodo induratur et quando frigidum fuerit macina eum bene super marmorem et pone eam pulverem in una bocia et claude os botie terra e- fac subtus unum modicum ingnis et quando vides quod ellevat tur intantum quod impleat totam bociam tunc remove ab igne et dimite frigidari deinde frange bociam et erit cinabrium perfectum.

182. *To make vermilion.*[1]—Take 1 part of quicksilver and two parts of sulphur, clean, yellow, and well ground; put all into a bottle and cover it lightly with lutum sapientiæ; then put it into the furnace, and give it at first a gentle fire; cover the mouth of the bottle with a tile, and when you see a yellow smoke, keep up the fire until you see the smoke come off red or scarlet; then remove the fire, and when it is cold you will find fine vermilion.

183. *For the same, another way.*—Take a glass jar luted with lutum sapientiæ up to the neck, then take 2 parts of white sulphur well ground and one part of quicksilver; afterwards put them into the flask; then make a small charcoal fire, and place four stones round it; set the flask upon them, and cover it with a tile. Uncover it frequently; and when you see a blue smoke come out of it, cover it up until you see a red smoke; then take it away from the fire, for it is done.

184. *To make a yellow for drawing gold flowers on paper.*—Take a little saffron and a little white lead, and distemper them together with gum-water; let them stand so as to be well incorporated for half an hour, and it is done.

185. *To make a very beautiful white.*—Take egg-shells and well-pounded glass and mix them together; then put the mass into an earthen jar, and place the jar in a furnace for one natural day. Then take it out and keep it. And when you wish to use it, grind it very well upon marble, and distemper it with gum-water.

186. *To make vermilion quickly.*—Take 1 lb. of lead, ½ lb. of quicksilver, and 4 parts of yellow sulphur; grind all these things well together, and put them into an earthen jar over the fire for 14 hours, and it will be done.

187. *To make camillina.*—Take vermilion, azure, and ceruse, and grind them together; and if the colour is to be dark, put more vermilion and azure, and it will be good.

---

[1] Recipes nearly similar to this and the next are contained in the MS. of Le Begue, Nos. 174, 175.

182. *Ad faciendum cinabrium.*—Tolli una parte de argento vivo et doi parte de solfo giallo e necto e ben macinato poi pone omne cosa in una bocia et incoprila legiermente cum luto de sapientia poi la pone in lo fornello et dalli da prima lo foco ligiero et copre la bocca della bocia cum una tegola, e quando tu vederai lo fumi giallo continua lo foco per infino che vederai uscire el fumo rosso o vermeglio alora tolj via lo fuoco et quando sera freddo troverai bello cinapro.

183. *Ad idem alio modo.*—Habeas unam ampollam vitream lutata de luto sapientie usque ad summum collj deinde recipe partes duas sulforis albi et bene triti et partem unam argenti vivi postea pone in ampulla sopradicta et fac de carbonibus ignem lepidissimum et circa eam cum quatuor lapidibus et pone ampullam desuper et coperi eum cum tegula et sepe discoperias et quando videbis fumum lividum coperi dummodo videbis exire fumum rubeum tunc tolle ab igne quod factum erit.

184. *Affare collore giallo per fiorire in oro in carta.*—Reccipe un poco de zaffaramj e uno poco de biaccha et stempera insiemj cum aqua gomata et lassa cusi stare acio se incorpora per una mez' hora et sera facto.

185. *A fare biancho bellitissimo.*—Tolli cociole dova et vetrio bene pisto et misticali insiemj et poi la pone in uno in uno vaso de terra et mectilo in una fornace per uno di naturali poi lo cava fora et serbalo. Et quando lo vorai operare macinalo molto bene in marmo e distemperalo cum aqua gomata.

186. *A fare cinabrio brevemente.*—Abeas libram j plumbi et mediam libram mercurii et quatuor partes sulphuris gialli et omnia insimul acriter tere et pone in vase terreo ad ignem per horas 14^{im} et erit factum.

187. *A fare camillina.*—Tolle cinabrium azurum et cerusam et macina insimul et si esset obscurum micte plus de cinabrio et de azurro et bonum erit.

188. *To make a violet colour.*—Take a little indigo, a little vermilion, and a little ceruse, grind them very fine and distemper them, and you will have a fine violet colour.

189. *To make the red colour for shading gold letters on paper.*—Take scraped verzino and put it in a horn-shaped vessel, with sufficient white of egg to cover it; let it remain in the sun for a day; afterwards press it out, and keep it in a well-closed glass flask; and, when necessary, use it for the red outlines of gold letters.

190. *To make a flesh colour for painting the flesh of figures.*[1]—Take sinopia and ceruse, and apply it wherever you wish to paint flesh; when it is dry, take black and mark the eyes and limbs, and lay on the lights with pure ceruse; and for the eyebrows use sinopia and black together, and it will be brown; the pupil is made with black and no white, and the shade of the jaws with sinopia, and the effect will be good.

191. *To colour the flesh in painting a crucifixion.*—Take ochre, ceruse, and a little terra verde, mix them together and lay them on the figure, and when dry, mark out the limbs with black made with charcoal, with which mix a little sinopia, lay on the lights with ceruse, and do as you like. Paint the hair with sinopia and charcoal mixed and pounded together.

192. *To make flesh colour.*—Take indigo mixed with orpiment, and it will make green, which, mixed with ochre[2] and white, makes flesh colour.

193. *To make another camillina colour.*—Know that by mixing ceruse with verzino it will become a camillina colour; and if you wish to make violet add a little azure. And if you wish to make green take a little indigo and orpiment.

194. *To make good and fine arzica.*—Take one pound of weld, which the dyers use, cut it very fine, then put it into a glazed or tinned vase, and add to it enough water to cover the herb. Make it boil until the water is half wasted, and if there

---

1 It is probable that this and some of the following recipes were derived from the Greek (if not immediately translated from it). Sinopia is mentioned for the first time in this recipe; it is also probable that this colour

188. *A fare colore violato.*—Prima tolli uno poco de indico et uno poco de cinabrio et uno poco de cirusa et macina bene subtili et distempera et vira fino violato.

189. *A fare collore per porre sopra la rosecta de loro in carta.*—Summe verzinum abrasum et pone in corneto cum tanta ovorum clara preparata ut coperiatur et dimite manere ad solem per unum diem postea exprime eum et serva in ampulla vitria bene obturata et quando necesse est utere in li profili de la lectra de la rossecta de loro.

190. *Ad fatiendum incarnatum pro incarnare figuras.*—Tolle sinopiam et cerusam et micte ubi vis incarnare et cum siccum fuerit tolle nigrum et reinvenias oculos et alia membra et illumina cum cerusa viva et super cilia sinopia et nigrum insimul et erit brunum luciula fiet de nigro et puntum album et in mascillis umbra de sinopia rubea et bene stabit.

191. *Ad incarnandum crucifixum.*—Abeas ocream et cerusam et aliquantulum de terra viride et misce simul et pone in crucifixo et cum siccum fuerit reinvenias membra cum nigro facto de carbone et misce cum eo aliquantulum de sinopia ét expleas opus cum cerusa et fac sicut tibi videtur pilos fac de sinopia et carbone misto et insimul pisto.

192. *Ad faciendum incarnatum.*—Capias indicum mistum cum auripiumento et fiet colorem viridem ocrea et album insimul incorporata veniet incarnatio.

193. *Idem alius color camillinus.*—Scias quod ponendo cerusam cum verzino erit color camillinus et si vis facere violatum pone aliquantulum de azurro. Et si volueris facere viridem pone modicum indici et auripiumenti et fiet viridem.

194. *A fare larzica bona et bella.*—Piglia libra una de herba gualda la quale opera li tentore et tagliala ben minuta poi la pone in uno vaso vitriato o vero stagnato et metice tanta aqua che copra la dicta herba et falla tanto bulire che torni per

---

was the Sinopia of Cennini (the Red Hæmatite), and not the colour of this name, described by S. Audemar, p. 145.

[2] This must be burnt ochre.

is not enough water add a sufficient quantity and no more; then take 2 oz. of travertine finely ground, or 2 oz. of white lead, and $\frac{1}{2}$ oz. of roche alum ground very fine, then put all these things together a little at a time to boil in the vase directly, before the water cools, and stir the water continually, remove the vessel from the fire, and when nearly dry, pour off the water. Then take a new brick hollow in the middle, lay the arzica on it, and let it settle perfectly; then put it on a small and well polished board to dry, and it is done.

195. *To make white lead.*—Take leaden plates, and suspend them over the vapour of very strong vinegar in a vase, which after being luted must be placed in dung for two months; then scrape away the matter that you will find upon the plates, which is the white lead. Do this until the plates are consumed.

196. *To make minium quickly.*—Take calcined litharge, and lead, prepared together over the fire, and you will have minium.

197. *To make paste for sculpturing all kinds of things, that is to say, figures and medallions, and to make moulds.*—Take white lead and mastic, and put the mastic to soak in sufficient clear water to cover it for the space of one night; then make this water with the white lead into a hard paste like dough, and knead it well with your hands. When you wish to model anything, knead the paste with your hands, having previously greased them well with lard. Then impress whatever you like on the paste and let it dry, and the impression will be sharp and fine. And you may make the paste of any colour you like, by mixing up some colour with the paste.

B. 198.[1]—Take 1 oz. of tragacanth, and put it to soak in sufficient water to cover it for the space of one day and one night; then take a pound of white lead and grind it with the moist tragacanth. Then let it harden till it is as stiff as dough, and knead it well with your hands, adding to it a little white

[1] The Rubric is wanting. It appears to be a recipe for making artificial Cameos.

mita et se mancasse laqua arigiognicine quanto bolla et non piu poi poi tolli once doi de travertino molto bene macinato overo doi once di biacca et meza oncia de alumj de roccho bene subtili poi mete tutte queste cose a bulire in lo dicto vaso subitamente nante che laqua se fredda e mete queste cose a poco a pocho tuttavia remenando laqua et leva dal foco et quando sera a presso che fredda et tu ne cava via laqua poi tolli uno mattone novo cavato in mezo et metice dentro lo colore de larzica et lassala reposare multo bene poi la pone in su una asicella bene polita a secare e de fatta.

195. *A fare biacha.*—Tolli lamine de piombo et metile disopra alo vapore de lo aceto fortissimo in uno vaso et coprilo bene cum luto et metilo socto lo litamj per doi mesi poi rade la matheria che e la biacha che trovarai sopra ale lamini et fa per lo sopradito modo per infino che sonno consunte.

196. *A fare minio brevemente.*—Avve calcina de litargirio cum piombo confectato insiemj al foco et sera minio.

197. *A fare pasta da scolpire omne lavoro cioe figure medaglie e fare forme.*—Piglia biacha et mastice et pone la mastice a mollo in tanta aqua chiara che stia coperta per spatio duna nocte poi impasta la dicta aqua cum la dicta biacca dura ad modo de pasta et menala bene per le mano. Et quando vorai scolpire ungite le mano cum lardo bene et menala bene per mano poi imprompta quello che tu voj et lassa secare e vira necto et polito et poi la fare venire de quello colore che tu voli mistando insiemj cum la pasta.

B. 198. Recipe once una de draganti et mectili a mollo in tanta aqua che se coprino per spatio de uno di et una nocte et poi tolli una libra de biacca et macinala cum lo dicto draganti mollo et poi lo indura ad modo duna pasta et menalo molto bene per mano et mistace uno poco de mele bianco acio non

honey in order that it may not crack. Anoint your hands with the honey, and let the paste be well kneaded; then impress whatever you like upon it, and the impression will be sharp and fine. You may make it of whatever colour you please by mixing some colour with it, and when you have taken the impression, you must glue it on with glue made from parchment clippings, and let it dry, and when it is well dried polish it with a tuft of cotton, and it will become shining like a bone, &c.

199. *Also another colour.*—Take green and ceruse, and make a drapery or a leaf, shade it with pure green, and then make the outlines with black or with verzino; lay on the lights with ceruse, and do this with all the colours, and when you wish to make flowers with azure, add a little yolk of egg; and for roses add a grain of salt.

200. *To make another camillinus colour.*—Azure mixed with white is a camillinus colour; with orpiment a splendid green; with saffron, it is also green; and with dragon's blood, or with lake, it will be a purple colour.

201. *To make a rose colour, very good and beautiful.*—Take 1½ oz. of lac, and the same quantity of ceruse; grind them with linseed oil [1] and prepared white of egg, and apply upon paper. If you wish the colour to be very good, take an equal quantity of grana, and grind with the other ingredients, and you will have a finer colour.

202. *To make a blue colour.*—Take orpiment and lac, of each equal quantities, and grind them together with prepared white of egg; and you will have a blue colour.

203. *To make a light rose colour for miniature.*—Take travertine pounded fine, as much roche alum as travertine, and an equal quantity of scraped verzino; boil the verzino with strong ley, and, when it boils, add the other ingredients and reduce it one half; then strain the liquor through a loosely woven cloth, and you will have a fine rose colour.

---

[1] It appears from the treatise of Cennini, chap. cxliii., that it was a common practice to mix lake with linseed oil for draperies.

crepe et ungite le mano cum dicto mele et fa che sia bene remenata et poi impronta quello te piace et vira necto et bello et poila fare venire de che collore tu voli mistando cum essa el dicto colore et commo tu hai improntato se vole incolarla cum colla de carnicia et lassa sciugare et quando sera bene sciucta et tu la polisce cum uno matoffo de bambagio et vira lustra como uno osso etc.

199. *Idem alius color.*—Tolle viridem et cerusam et fac vestimentum vel folium postea umbra cum viride puro postea profila cum nigro vel verzino deinde illumina cum cerusa et sic poteris facere de omnibus colloribus et quando vis facere flores cum azurro pone aliquantulum de vitulo ovj et quando rosas pone unum acinum salis.

200. *Ad faciendum alium colorem camillinum.*—Azurrum cum albo misto est color camillinus cum auripiumento est viridis pulcer cum zafaramino est etiam viridis et cum sanguine draconis aut lacca erit color purpureus.

201. *Ad faciendum colorem rosatum optimum et pulcrum.*—Recipe lac untiam unam cum dimidia et tantundem ceruse et macina cum oleo seminis lini et cum clara ovj preparata et pone in carta et si vis magis coloratum et optimum acipe tamtumdem grane et macina insimul et habebis.

202. *Ad fatiendum colorem perseum.*—Habeas auripiumenti et lac de utroque tantum et insimul macina cum clara preparata et habebis.[2]

203. *A fare la rosecta per miniare.*—Tolli travertino subtilmente pisto et tanto alumj de rocho quanto fu lo travertino et altratanto verzino raso et mecti lo verzino a bulire cum ranno forte et quando bolle mectice le sopradite cose et fa bolire che arentre per mita et poi lo cola per una peza rareta et haveraj bella rosetta.

---

[2] There is apparently a mistake here, for "perso" signifies dark blue, and orpiment and lake would produce an orange colour.

204. *To make a certain water which is good for applying upon figures and other miniatures.*—Take oil of aloes, linseed oil, and liquid varnish, of each equal quantities; boil these ingredients together, and put them into a flask. When you wish to use the liquor, anoint with it the figures or miniatures when they are dry, and not before, and they will be shining and very beautiful.

205. *To make linseed oil.*—Take one quart of clean and pure linseed, damp it a little and then put it into a vase over the fire and stir it up with a spoon, and then push the spoon several times to the bottom so as to moisten all the seeds. You must add a little water in order to soften them; then put the seeds into a strong woollen cloth, place it in the press, and the oil will flow out.

206. *To make liquid varnish.*—Take of the gum of the juniper [sandarac], two parts, and one part of linseed oil, boil them together over a slow fire, and if the varnish appears to you to be too stiff, add more of the oil and take care not to let it catch fire, because you would not be able to extinguish it, and even if you could extinguish it, the varnish would be dark and unsightly. Let it boil for half an hour, and it will be done.

207. *To make liquid varnish in another manner.*—Take 1 lb. of linseed oil, and put it into a new glazed jar, and then take ½ a quarter [of an ounce?] of roche alum in powder, and an equal quantity of minium or vermilion ground fine, and ½ oz. of incense also ground fine. Mix all these ingredients together and put them into the oil to boil, stirring it with a stick; and when the oil is boiling, as it is likely to run over, have another glazed jar ready, and put it by that which contains the oil, so as to catch the oil that runs over, in order that it may not run on the ground, and in this manner make it boil up 3 or 4 times, and each time pour back what has run over, on that which is boiling in the jar. Having done this, set fire to the oil on the right hand side with a lighted straw, and let the oil burn on the upper part, but so that the jar may not burn on

204. *Ad fatiendam quemdam aquam que est bona ad ponendum super figuris et altris miniis.*—Abeas oleum aloe oleum seminis lini et vernice liquida de unoquoque tantum et hoc fatias simul bulire et repone in ampulla et quando opus est unge figuras aut minios dico ipsis desicatis et non ante et erunt lustre et pulcherrime.

205. *A fare olio de semj de lino.*—Pilglia uno quarto de semj de lino necta et pura et amachala uno poco poi la pone in uno vaso al foco et cum uno cochiaro la vienj mistando poi va piu volte in lo fondo del dito vaso cum lo ditto cochiaro et falli spatio che se li possa infondare la granatella et volse imborsarla cum uno poco daqua acio diventi morbida poi la mecte in panno de lana forte et polla ali frescoli et uscira fuora lolio.

206. *A fare vernice liquida.*—Tolli gomma de gineparo le doi parte et olio de semj de lino et fa bulire insiemj cum fuoco temperato et chiaro et se te pare esse troppo sodo et tu ce pone piu olio predicto et guarda che la fiamba non se li aprenda perche non lo poriste spingiare et se purre lo spingesse viria negra et brutta et bolla per meza hora et sera facta.

207. *A fare vernici liquida per altro modo.*—Recipe libre j de olio de semj de lino et metilo in una pignatta nova vitriata poi tolli mezo quarto de alumj de rocho spolverizato et altratanto minio o cinabrio subtili macinato et meza oncia de incenso bene trito poi mista omne cosa insiemj et ponile in lo dito olio a bulire insiemj mistando cum uno bachetto et quando lolio ha lo bollo per volere prosperare de fora habi aparichiata una altra pignata vitriata et metila apresso quella de lolio per modo che quello che se spande vada in laltra pignatta acio che lolio non se spanda in terra et in quello modo fa levare el bolore 3 o 4 volte disopra et ongnj volta retorna quello che va disopra in su quella disocto che bolle facto questo acende lolio de lo lato dextro cum una paglia apresso de essa ma lassa ardare lolio uno poco dal canto disopra per modo che la pig-

the inside, on account of the too great heat, for otherwise the oil would smell unpleasantly. When you light the oil with the straw, remove the jar from the fire, and let it burn while you can say three paternosters, then extinguish the oil with a wooden cover, putting it upon the jar, and when it is extinguished, remove the cover in order to let the vapour escape. Then put it back over the fire; do this 3 times, and it is done.

208. *To purify ceruse.*—Take ceruse, put it into a clean jar, which should be placed over the fire, stir the ceruse continually with a stick, and it will become white.

209. *To make a pigment from the shavings of cloth, of the same colour as the cloth.*—Take quicklime and baked ashes, of each equal quantities, and make a caustic ley; take the ley, clean and clear, put it into a clean vase, and make it boil, and when it boils add to it the clippings of cloth of what colour soever you like, and, after it has boiled down to one-third, add to it a little roche alum at discretion; then strain it and put it to dry on a clean tile or upon a table, and spread it out, and when nearly dry, cut it in pieces as you like, and it is done.

210. *To make a water for painting on linen cloth or silk.*—Take 2 oz. of sal-ammoniac, 2 oz. of salgem, 1 oz. of saltpetre, pound the whole together, and then distil it, and keep the water until you need it; you may paint on whatever cloth you like.

211. *To make a yellow water for drawing and painting on linen or woollen.*—Take of roche alum 1 oz., of saffron 2 oz., and a little ley, and boil all these things together till reduced by one-third, and it is done.

212. *Glue for making any mould you like for casting figures.*—Take Armenian bole, flour, and clear water, and knead them together until they form a rather stiff paste; model what you like with it. Sulphur will do equally well, it only requires melting.

213. *To make gesso sottile.*—Take gesso and soak it in a vase so that the water may cover the gesso; mix and stir it up

nata non arda de dentro per troppo caldo altramente lolio puzaria. Et quando tu acendj lolio cum la paglia remove la pignata dal fuoco et lassa ardare tanto che tu diche 3 patri nostri poi aramorta lolio cum uno coverchio de ligno et mitilo sopra ala pignata et aramorto che le remove lo coperchio per che el fumj escha fora poi ritornalo al foco poi cosi farai 3 volte et sera fatta.

208. *Ad purgandam cerusam.*—Ahbeas cerusam et eam pone in ollam mundam et micte super ignem semper movendo cum baculo dictam cerusam et efficitur alba.

209. *Ad fatiendum colorem de cimatura panorum cujus coloris erit talem colorem habebis.*—Pilglia calcina viva et cenera recocta tanto de luna quanto de laltra et fa lisia per capitello et tolli la liscia necta et bella poi la pone in uno vaso necto et fa bullire et commo bullj mectice la cimatura de que colore che tu volj e quando havera bulito tanto che sia rentrata per terzo et tu ce pone uno poco de alumj de rocho a tua discretione poi la cola et polla a sciugare in una tegola pollita o vero in una tavola et distendila et quando sera quasi sciuta fannj li pezj a tuo piacere e de facto.

210. *A fare aqua da dipengiare in panno de lino o de seta.*—Ahvvj once 2 de sale armoniaco once 2 de sale gemmo once j. de sal nitrio et pista omne cosa insiemj poi le metti alambichare et serba laqua al bisogno et porai dipengiare suso omne panno che tu volj.

211. *A fare aqua gialla da disignare et dipengiare in panno de lino o de lana.*—Tolli alumj de rocho once j zafaramj 2 et uno poco de liscia et fa bolire queste cose insiemj quanto che callj per terzo e de facto.

212. *Colla da fare omne forma che tu voli per gietare figure.* —Havvj bolarminio fiore de farina cum aqua chiara et incorpora tanto che sia duretta et fa che forma tu volj. Et ancora el solphano fa quello medesimo et sia solo disfatto.

213. *A fare gesso suctili.*—Piglia la chiavarda del gesso lucido et metila a mollo in uno vaso siche laqua stia disopra al

3 or 4 times every day, and at the end of 5 days take a strainer and strain off the water; and if you grind it, it will be finer. Then make it into cakes, and put them upon new tiles or bricks to dry; then put them away, and take care to preserve them from dust and dirt, and it will be fine gesso sottile.

214. *To make a window of goat-skin parchment which will appear to be real glass.*—Take the skin of a kid or a sheep or a goat, macerate it, remove the hair without lime, and scrape it very fine; then take a drachm of clean and clarified honey, mix it with 8 or 10 whites of eggs well beaten together with the honey in the same way as white of egg is beaten up for vermilion. Put the skin to soak in the white of egg and honey, squeeze it with your hand while in the composition, and let it remain in soak for 2 or 3 hours at the most; then take it out and stretch it well on a frame, and let it dry. Then paint upon it what you please, and let the colours dry well. Afterwards varnish it on one side, that is, on the side on which the colours are, and dry it in moderate sunshine, and it will appear like glass.

215. *For the same in another way.*—Take kid or sheep-skin parchment, scraped very fine, wet it with warm water; then stretch it on a frame, and let it dry; afterwards paint upon it, and again let it dry. Then take rather warm linseed-oil, and rub it over the parchment, and let that dry also, and it will resemble glass in appearance.

216. *To do the same with linen cloth.*—Take a linen cloth, very clean and close, and stretch it out well upon a frame; then take white of egg well whipped, separate it from the scum, and add to it one-third part of gum-water. Then lay it over the cloth with a sponge, so as to soak the cloth with it all over, and let it dry, and then paint upon it in any manner you like, and let that dry also; then give it another coat of the white of egg and gum-water, and let it dry again. Afterwards apply a coat of liquid varnish, and it will appear like crystal.

gesso et miscola molto bene omne di 3 o 4 volte et in capo de 5 di tolli una stacia et cola fora laqua et se tu la triti sera piu subtili de poi fanne pagnetti et mectile sopra coppi novi o vero matone acio che se sciugano poi la ripone et fino che se sciugano guarda non vi vada polvere ne altra bructura et sera bello gesso subtili.

214. *A fare una finestra de carta caprina che parera vetrio naturali.*—Tolli una pelle de capretto o montone o duna capra et macirala et de pela la sezna [senza?] calcina et radila subtilissimamente poi tolli una dragma de mele spumato et necto et mista lo cum octo o x chiara dova bene dibatuti insiemj cum lo mele ad modo se dibacte la chiara per lo cinabrio, poi mecti la dita pelle a mollo in la dicta chiara et mele et spremila cum mano in la dicta compositione et poi la lassa stare a molle in la ditta chiara per doi o tre hore al piu poi la tira fora et apicala bene stesta ad uno telaro et lassala sciugare et fa che la sia bene tirata poi la dipenge commo te piace et lassa sciugare bene li colori poi la invernica da uno lato cioe da lo lato de li colore et polla a sciugare al sole temperato et aparera de vetrio.

215. *Ad idem per aliam formam.*—Ahvvi carta de capretto o montone rasa subtilmente et bagnala in aqua tepida poi la stende insuso lo telaro et lassa sciugare poi la dipenge et lassa sciugare poi tolli olio de semj de lino uno poco caldo et dallo disopra ad ala dita carta et lassa sciugare et sera commo vetrio in aparentia.

216. *Ad idem in panno lini.*—Havvi panno de lino bene polito et fitto et pollo in su lo telaro bene tirato et steso poi tolli chiara dova ben dibatuta poi seperala dala schiuma et mistace per lo terzo de aqua de gomma poi la da sopra alo dito panno cum una spongia tanto che lo panno sia ben trapassato per tucto et lassa sciugare poi la dipenge cum gliochi o commo voj et lassa sciugare poi li da una altra mano de la dita chiara et aqua gommata et lassa sciugare poi li da la virnice liquida et sera commo christo vetrio.

217. *To make a water for cutting glass.*—Take vitriol, which comes upon the walls, and make a distilled water from it, and keep it in a vessel well closed. Then take Roman vitriol and pound it well, distil it, and keep the water also in a close vessel; then take sal-ammoniac and distil it, and keep this also. When you want to use the liquor, take equal quantities of each of these waters, mix them together, and draw with the mixed liquor upon the glass, and it will be cut exactly as you like wherever it is wetted with this water. And also, if you wish to cut glass, or to make small mirrors out of large ones, take a fine diamond, and draw upon the mirror with the point of the diamond, and immediately put the glass into water, and it will break directly by tapping the glass dexterously wherever you have touched it with the diamond.

218. *To make an earth for casting any fine thing.*—Take of potter's clay sifted fine 20 parts, and of common salt 1 part, then take ½ a bocale of water, boil it, and dissolve the salt in it, let it cool, and make the clay into a paste with the salt and water, and work the mass into a cake; set it to bake until it becomes red like fire, then pound and work it again with the salt water. Next take the thing which you wish to cast or mould, and lay it on something smooth and polished, and take a hoop, and put into it the thing which you wish to mould, and then lay the earth upon it, and press it down well, let it dry over a slow fire, and cast it according to your fancy, and it will be fine and clear.

219. *To make a paste for modelling that will withstand the fire.*—Take scales of iron and pumice-stone and pound well together, then make them into a paste with white of egg well beaten up, and model whatever you like with it. Let it dry slowly, and it will become very hard and will stand fire.

220. *To make a paste with which you can do both good and evil, and can seal and unseal any letter, and can model whatever you like, and which will become very hard after you have moulded it, if you suffer it to dry, and to which you may give whatever colour you please.*—Take gum-tragacanth and gum-

217. *A fare aqua da tagliare el vetrio.*—Tolli vitriolo che nasce per le mura et fanne aqua a lambico et serbala bene turata poi tolli vitriolo romano et pistalo bene et fanne aqua a lambico et serbala bene turata poi tolli sale armoniaco et fanne aqua alo lambico et serbala bene et quando la voraj operare tolli de le ditte aque de omne una tanto et mistale insiemj et disegna lo vetrio cum dita aqua et tagliarasse dove sera bagnato cum dita aqua a tuo piacere. Et ancora se tu volesse taligliare vetrij o spechj grandi farli picolj tolli uno diamante fino et disegna cum la punta de lo dito diamante in su lo specchio et subito lo mecte in aqua et erompirasse subito percotendo lo vetrio dextramente dovj tu haverai tochco cum lo diamante.

218. *A fare una terra da gietare omne suttili cosa.*—Recipe terra da fare pignatti staciata subtili parte 20 sale comuno parte una poi tolli mezo bocale daqua et falla bulire poi ce pone quello sale a disfare poi lassa fredare poi impasta la terra cum la ditta aqua salata et fannj pane et metila a cociare tanto che tornano rossi ad modo foco poi la strita et staciala de novo et impastala de novo cum la dita aqua salata poi tolli la cosa che tu voli gettare o formare et metila in loco pollito et piano et tollj uno cerchiello et mecti dentro la cosa che tu voli formare poi mecti suso la dicta terra et calcala bene poi la lassa seccare a lento foco poi gieta la tua fantasia et virà necta et bella.

219. *A fare pasta da impromptare che aresta a foco.*—Tolli schaglie de ferro et pumice et pista bene omne cosa insiemj poi impasta cum chiara dova bene dibattuta poi imprompta quello che tu voli et lassa secare adagio e diventara durissima et arestara a foco.

220. *A fare pasta cum la quale poi fare el bene et el male et poi disigillare et sigillare omne lettera et poi impromptare quello te piace diventera durissima poi che averai impromptato et poi farla vinire de quello colore che tu voli ponendola a sechare.*—Piglia gomma draganti et gommarabico ana et mecti tuctj

arabic, of each equal quantities, and steep them in sufficient water to cover them for 20 hours; then pound them very fine in a mortar. Next take 1 lb. of white lead to each ounce of the gums, and mix the whole together like dough; and, if you wish to have the paste white, do not add anything more to it. If you wish to have it of any other colour, mix with it whatever colour you like in fine powder, and work the ingredients well together, in order that they may be thoroughly incorporated one with another. Then anoint your hands with castor-oil, or linseed-oil, or oil of bitter almonds, and take this paste, and knead it very well in your hands; and when you have kneaded it well, you can impress whatever you choose upon it. If you wish the paste to remain soft, put it into a cabbage-leaf, and it will remain soft for as long a period as you like.

221. *To make musk soap.*—Take a vase of whatever size you like, made of good earth, and let it be rather thick in order that the weight of the lime may not break it, and near the bottom of it there must be a hole, closed with a peg, and on the inside, in front of the hole, you must put a wooden platter, and upon the platter you must put a lump of tow, enough to cover the bottom of the jar, and upon the tow, in front of the hole, put a small piece of thin linen. Then mix two parts of ashes from the baths with one part of quicklime, and place the mass upon the piece of linen that is upon the tow in the vase, and spread it well all over it. Then take rain-water, according to the quantity of the ashes, and pour it into the vase at two or three times, because it boils up and absorbs the water, and there must be enough water to cover the ashes to the depth of two fingers'-breadth or less, and when it ceases to boil, let it stand for a whole night, and in the morning take out the peg and let out the ley; and when you have drawn off a bocale full of it, pour it back into the vase, and it will become rather thick; do this two or three times, and the last time let it rest a little, and then strain it; and if it comes away too fast, press the ashes down a little in the vase, because it must issue from the whole like a thread in order that the ley may

queste cose in tanta aqua che stiano a molli per 20 hore poi pistale bene in uno mortaro che siano bene piste poi tolli lb. j. de biacha per omne oncia de le dicte gomme et incorpora omne cosa insiemj commo pasta. Et se tu la voj canida et bianca non ce metare piu niente. Et se tu la volesci daltro colore collorita mistace quello colore che te piace bene subtili et mista bene acio se incorporano luno cum laltro et poi te unge le mano cum olio de riciuta [ricino?] o olio de semj de lino o olio de amandole amare poi piglia questa pasta et menala molto bene intra le mano et commo e bene menata porai impromptare quello te piace. Et quando la volesse mantinere liquida dicta pasta mectila in una foglia de colo et sempre stara morbida per omne tempo.

221. *A fare sapone moschato.*—Habbi uno vaso de la capacita che tu voj facto di bona terra et sia ben grosso a cio la possanza de la calcina non lo rompa et apresso del fondo vole esser uno bugio el quale se convene serrare cum uno spinello e dal canto dentro nante el bugio se vole metarce uno tagliere et sopra al tagliere se vole metarce una faldella de capecio che copra el fondo del vaso et sopra el capecio nante al bugio mectice uno poco de peza rada poi tolli doi parte de cenera de bagno et una parte de calcina viva poi la incorpora cum la cenere poi la pone sopra a la peza che e sopra al capeccio in lo vaso et distendila bene per tutto poi tolli aqua pioviana secondo secondo che e la cenera et mectila in el vaso in doi o 3 fiate per che ella bolle et resciugase et vole esser tanta aqua che stia sopra ala cenera doi deta o manco et quando non bolle piu lassa stare cusi tucta una nocte et la matina cavala spinella et lassa colare el capitello et quando naj cavato uno bocale remitilo disopra al vaso et vira uno poco brutto et questo fa doi o tre volte et lultima volta lassa uno poco reposare poi lassa colare et se venisse troppo forte calca uno poco la cenera del vaso perche la spinella vole gietare a filo acio che lo capitello vengna netto e bello poi che lo capitello e tutto vinuto che la cenera sia senza aqua tollj

run off clear. And when the ley has entirely run off so that the ashes remain dry, take half a jug of water, and pour it over the ashes in the vase, and when it is strained pour it back 3 or 4 times into the vase, and the last time draw off the ley clear. And if you wish to know whether the ley is properly made, put a fresh egg in it; if the egg goes to the bottom it is not good, and if the egg floats it is good. Then take 9 bocali of this ley, and one roll of deer's or cow's tallow, which makes lb. 2 oz. 9, and melt it well over the fire; and when it is well boiled pour it into this ley, and keep stirring it for the space of half an hour; then let it rest for a night or more, and if you wish to add musk or any other scent to it, reduce it to a fine powder, and add it to the tallow which is in the ley, mix it up well and let it settle. Then put the soap in the sun in order that it may refine itself better, and it will harden so that you may make it up into balls, and it is done.

222. *To make good camphor.*[1]—Take 1 lb. of mastic, and steep it in two pounds of distilled vinegar, and put it in a round flask, and place it in dung for 3 days; afterwards place it in the sun, and close up the mouth of it, to exclude the rain, for thirty days in summer, and you will find a congealed mass, and will have very fine camphor.

223. *To make Alexandrine borax.*[2]—Take roche alum, and make it into pieces of about ½ an oz. each, and then put them into a glazed jar, and pour some milk over them so that the milk may cover the alum by two fingers' breadths, and each day change the milk for 8 days, or until you find it mild to the taste. Then take beef-marrow and an equal quantity of oil of

---

[1] D. Alessio also gives a recipe for making factitious Camphor (Part II. p. 43), which he says was almost as good as that which was brought from Constantinople.

[2] It appears that two kinds of Borax were in use, the natural and the factitious; the former was brought from Alexandria, whence its name. D. Alessio (Part I. p. 129, 130) describes different modes of imitating it, among which is that mentioned in the text. According to this writer, borax was used in medicine, and in cementing gold.

meza trocha daqua et metila sopra ala cenera che e in lo vaso et colata che sera remectila 3 o 4 volte suso in lo vaso et lultima volta recoglie el capitello chiaro. Et se voj sapere quando lo capitello e facto fino se conosce in questo modo tiene uno ovo frescho desopra se lovo va al fondo non e fino et se sta a galla e fino. De poi tolli 9 bocali de questo capitello et uno rotulo de sego de cervo o de vacha che sonno libre 2, 2 [oz. ?] nove e fallo bene strugiare al foco et bene bolito metarlo in questo capitello et sempre remenalo per spatio de meza hora poi lo lassa possare una notte o piu et se tu ce volj metere musco o altre cose odirifare pulverizale bene subtili et metili sopra al sego che e in lo capitello et misticalo bene de vantaggio poi lo pone a reposare poi lo pone al sole acio che se afina meglio et restringerasse per modo che lo porai a palotare e de facto.

222. *A fare la camphora bona.*—Tollj libram unam masticis et pone in duabus libris aceti stillati et pone in palla rotunda clausa sub fimo per tres dies postea pone ad solem et obtura bene ejus os propter pluvias in estate per triginta dies et invenies massam congelatam et habebis camphoram nobilissimam.

223. *A fare borace alixandrina.*—Recipe alumj de rocho et fannj pezuoli de meza oncia luno o circha poi li pone in una pignatta vitriata poi li pone desopra de lo lacte tanto che lo lacte avanza desopra alalumj doi deta et omne di li rimuta el lacte per infino a octo di tanto che tu veghi a la lingua che te paia dolce poi tolli merolli de ossa de bovi et altratanto

---

It was also used in reducing or fluxing metals and nielli, and by ladies as a cosmetic to whiten, soften, and cleanse the skin. Alexis does not allude in the most distant manner to the use of Borax in painting; and he appears so well informed on the subject, that it is scarcely probable that he should have been unacquainted with the fact, if it had been so used. The real Alexandrine Borax is mentioned in No. 269, where it is used as a flux in gilding on glass.

almonds, melt them in a pipkin, and then strain them and pour them into the jar with the alum and milk, and let the oil and marrow cover it by three fingers' breadths. Then put it into the sun for three months, that is to say, June, July, and August, and take care that neither rain nor dust falls into it, and it is done.

224. *To prepare vermilion for using with the paint-brush, and as a body colour.*—Take of vermilion whatever quantity you like, and grind it dry to a fine powder on marble or porphyry, and afterwards grind it with clear water, or with ley, until the powder is very fine and almost impalpable; let it dry upon the marble and put it into a horn, and wash it very well with clear and strong ley until it is very clean, and afterwards wash it again with fresh water until you think that the ley is well washed out of it; then suffer it to become nearly dry and wash it again with hot water and let it settle, and when nearly dry add to it some white of egg prepared with saffron and with twigs of fig-trees ground up, and make it liquid enough to flow well in the pen while writing. And if you wish it to use in body, put a little yolk of egg along with the white. And if you wish it for writing or making flowers, do not add the yolk of egg to it, and that it may be without froth or gloss add a little ear-wax to it; if too glossy, throw away that white of egg, and put some fresh to it without saffron or ear-wax; if it hardens so as not to flow in the pen add to it two drops of rose-water. And if you wish the white of egg not to smell, add to it (that is, to the white of egg) a little realgar (red orpiment) or camphor.

225. *To prepare azure to use as a body colour, and to use with the pen.*—Take the azure and put it into a glazed saucer, and then add some clean honey to it, and incorporate them well together; grind the honey with the azure upon marble, and the more it is ground the finer and better it will be. Then put it back into that saucer and wash it with warm water, until the water runs off clear; then wash it with cold water, and between each washing let the azure sink to the bottom, and continue to

olio damangdole et metile in una pignatta a disfare et poi le cola et mectile disopra a la ditta pignatta de lo alumj et lacte et fa che lo dito olio et merolle sopra avanzano 3 deta poi la pone al sole per 3 mesci cioe giugno, luglio et agosto et guarda non li piuova ne vada polvere e fatta.

224. *A preparare il cinabrio per adoperare a penna et fare corpi.*—Piglia del cinabrio la quantita che voj et macinalo molto bene asciutto in marmo o in porfido et poi lo macina cum aqua chiara o vero cum ranno da capo quanto sia bene subtile quasi senza tatto et lassalo seccare in su lo marmo poi lo mecti in lo cornetto et lavalo molto bene cum ranno chiaro et forte tanto che sia bene netto poi de novo el lava cum aqua chiara tanto che tu crede che ne sia bene uscito quello ranno poi el lassa quasi seccare poi lo lava de novo cum aqua calda et lassalo posare et quasi secare poi metice sopra chiara dova preparata con zaferamj et cum rami de fico triti et fallo tanto liquido che scorgha bene per la penna scrivendo. Et se tu el voli per fare corpi metice uno poco de rosso de ovo insiemj cum la chiara. Et se tu el voli per scrivare o fiorirj non ce metare lo rosso del ovo. Et per farlo che non facia schiuma et lustro metice uno poco de scarcatura de orechie et se fusse troppo lustro gietta via quella chiara et metice de la nova dove non sia zafaramj ne brutura de orechie et se se indurasse che non scorisse per la penna metice doi gocie daqua rosa. Et se volesi che la chiara non puza mectice dentro uno poco de risa gallo o de canfora et cioe in la chiara.

225. *A preperare azurro per fare corpi et per adoperare a penna.*—Accipe lo azurro et metila in una scudella vitriata poi ce metti del mele bene netto et incorpora bene insiemj poi macina lo mele cum lo azurro sopra marmo e tanto piu sera macinato tanto vira piu fino et migliore poi lo remetti in quella scudella et lavalo cum aqua tepida tanto che laqua nescha chiara poi lo lava cum aqua frescha et da luna volta alaltra lassa andare lo azurro al fondo et tanto continua che sia bene

do so until it is well washed and purified. Then let the azure dry, and soak it in clean and strong ley in a glass vase, such as a drinking-glass, and let it stand for the space of 7 days; each day change the ley, and then add some fresh to it, and let it dry in the shade in a place free from dust. And if you wish to use it as a body colour, distemper it with parchment-size, or with size made from clippings of white chamois leather, and it will do well. And if you wish to use it with a pen or for miniatures, distemper it with gum-water and with prepared white of egg, and it will do well.

226. *To prepare white lead for painting.*—Take the white lead, and wash it several times in hot water, and then take two grains of clear gum-arabic and 3 grains of white incense, grind them very well with a little clear water, and then add the washed white lead, and grind the whole together, and collect it and add to it as much gum-water as you think it will bear, and if it is too hard put a little fresh water to it, and it will do well.

227. *To prepare verdigris for painting.*—Take verdigris and grind it well with very strong vinegar, and then make a hollow in a new brick, and put the verdigris into the hollow, until the brick has soaked up the vinegar, and do this 3 or 4 times, each time grinding up the verdigris with the vinegar afresh. Then take a little gum arabic, and grind it up together, and if you wish it lighter, add a little giallolino to it, and it will be well coloured.

228. *To prepare orpiment for using as a body colour.*—Take orpiment, and grind it dry, and know that it is hard to grind. In order to grind it quickly, grind some glass with it, and it will grind quickly, and, when it is well ground, distemper it with gum water and yolk of egg.

229. *To make gum water.*—Take clear water in a glass cup with gum arabic in powder and make it rather warm over the fire until it is well liquefied, and then keep it in a phial and use it.

230 *To temper prasminum.*—Take prasminum, grind it

lavato et purificato poi lassa sciugare lo azurro poi lo mecti a mollo in ranno da capo netto et forte in uno vaso de vetrio commo e uno bichiere et lassalo stare per spatio de 7 di et omne di li muta el ranno poi ce meti del novo poi lo lava cum aqua frescha et lassalo sciugare alombra in loco che non vi vada polvere. Et se tu el voli adoperare per fare corpi distemperalo cum colla de carta caprina o vero colla de ritalglie de camoscio bianco scamosciato et stara bene. Et se tu el voli per operare a penna o per minii distemperalo cum aqua gommata et cum chiara dovo preparata et stara bene.

226. *A preperare la biacha per dipengiare.*—Tolli la biacha et lavala piu volte cum aqua calda poi tolli doi granelli de gomarabico chiaro et 3 granelli de incenso biancho et macinali molto bene cum uno poco daqua chiara poi ce metti la biacha lavata et macina omne cosa insiemj poi la racogli et metice tanta aqua gommata quanto te pare che comporta et se fusse troppo dura metice uno poco daqua chiara et stara bene.

227. *A preparare il verderamo per dipengiare.*—Havvi verderamo et macinalo cum fortissimo aceto multo bene poi lo pone poi fa uno cavo in uno matone novo et pone el dito verderamo in dito concavo per infino a tanto che lo matone havera surbito quello aceto et cusi continua 3. o 4 volte omne volta remacinando lo verderamo cum lo aceto poi tollj uno poco de gommarabico et macina insiemj et se tu lo volesci piu chiaro macinace uno poco de zalulino et congrue colorabitur.

228. *A preperare loropiumento per fare corpi.*—Tolli oropiumento et macinalo dasuto et sappi che e duro a macinarlo per macinarlo presto macinace insiemj cum esso del vetrio et macinarasse presto et commo e bene macinato distempera cum aqua gomata et trolo dovo rosso.

229. *A faciendum aquam gummatam.*—Summe aquam claram in ciato vitrj cum gummarabico triturato et fac aliquantulum calefacere ad ignem donec sit bene liquefactum deinde serva in ampulla et utere.

230. *Ad distemperandum prasminum.*—Accipe prasminum

with pure water, and let it dry, and when you wish to use it, temper it with gum water, and if you wish to have it lighter, add some orpiment to it, and it will be well coloured.

231. *To temper minium.*—Take minium and grind it with pure water, and put it into a vase, and when it is settled, separate the water well, and temper it with gum water.

232. *To temper giallolino.*—Take of giallolino whatever quantity you like and grind it on porphyry very fine with fresh ⊡, and then let it dry. Then grind it again with clear water, and let it dry, and then temper it with gum water and a little yolk of egg.

233. *To temper the rossetta.*—Take the rossetta and grind it well with gum water, and it will become hard like the other colours. When it is hard, temper it with fresh water.

234. *To prepare saffron.*—Take saffron, and soak it in a shell with prepared white of egg for 3 hours, and it will be a fine yellow.

235. *To temper lake to use in body.*—Take the lake and grind it in gum water with 2 or 3 grains of white and clear incense, and when it is hard, temper it with fresh water.

236. *To prepare the earths for painting on walls or on mortar.*—Know that you must first grind red earth, and green earth, and every other earth for painting on walls, dry, afterwards very finely with clear water, then let the colour dry, and temper it with very strong gum water, or with egg, that is to say, with the yolk and white mixed and well beaten up together, and with fig wood cut small into the white of egg, and with this vehicle temper any letters, and they will look well.

237. *To lay flat tints and make [ornamental] foliage.*—If you wish to make foliage, lay on a flat tint of what colour you like, and let it dry very well. If you lay a flat tint of green, use the pezzette made from the blue lily[1] for the shade, and giallolino for the light. If you lay a flat tint of azure, use the

[1] See ante, Nos. 92 and 125.

et eum tere cum pura aqua et permitte sicarj et cum vis operare tempera cum aqua gummata et si vis eum magis clarum pone cum eo de auropiumento et congrue colorabitur.

231. *Ad distemperandum minium.*—Habeas minium et tere cum aqua pura et mitte in vase et cum resederit sepera aquam optime deinde tempera cum aqua gummata.

232. *A distemperare el zallulino.*—Tolli del zallulino la quantita che voi et macinalo in porfido cum urina frescha subtilissimamente et poi lo lassa secare poi lo rimacina de nuovo cum aqua chiara et lassa secare et poi lo distempera cum aqua gummata et uno poco de rosso dovo.

233. *A distemperare la rossecta.*—Piglia de la rossecta et macinala bene cum aqua gummata et indopiasse commo li altri collore et quando e dura stemperala cum aqua chiara.

234. *A preparare el zafaramj.*—Abbi zafaramj et metilo in la tua cocia a mollo cum chiara preparata et lassala stare a molle per 3 hore et sera bello zallo.

235. *A distemperare lacha per fare corpi.*—Tolli la lacha et macinala cum aqua gommata et cum doi o tre granelli de incenso bianco et chiaro et quando se indurasse stemperala cum aqua chiara.

236. *A preperare le terre per adoperare in muro o in calcina.*—Sappi che la terra pagonaza et terra verde et omne terra da dipengiare in muro se macina prima da secco et poi cum aqua chiara molto subtilmente poi se lassa sechare poi se distempera cum aqua gommata ben tenace o vero cum lovo cioe chiara et rosso misto et dibatuto bene insiemj et cum lingno de fico sminuzato in lovo et cum esso distempera tucte lettere et stara bene.

237. *A campeggiare et fare fogliami.*—Se tu volj fare fogliami campeggia prima de quellj collore che tu volj et lassali sciucare bene de vantagio. Se tu campeggie de verde la pezola de lo giglio e lombra sua et el zallulino e lo suo relevo. Se tu campeggie de azurro lombra sua e la pezola pavonaza et la

purple pezzette for the shade, and white lead for the light. If you lay a flat tint of red, use verzino for the light.

238. *To make stones for rings, that is to say, precious gems clear and of a fine colour. And you may, in this way, quickly and easily, make pearls, rubies, and balas rubies which are artificial, and not natural.*—Take of the good stone which is called alabaster of Constantinople[1] as much as you like; first make it hot like iron and quench it in very strong white vinegar; afterwards grind it fine in a bronze mortar, and put the whole of it into linseed or olive oil, and let it remain for 3 days or more. Afterwards put it into a cucurbit, and distil it through an alembic, and collect and keep what comes over. And when you wish to colour it, put into that water whatever colour you like, and it will keep its colour for ever. So if you want to have a sapphire, put ultramarine azure into it. If you wish to have an emerald, put in some verdigris. If you wish to have a topaz, put in some oil from the yolks of hen's eggs and tin, and a certain water must be made by soaking the colour in it for 3 days with some alum zucarino or scagliola, and then strain this coloured water through a fine and close linen cloth, and in the same manner do what you please. Then thicken it by the fire to the consistence of dough, and take some of that paste and cut it into whatever shape you like, a stone or a cup, or a vase, boiling it well with olive or linseed oil, or with oil of bitter almonds; dry it in a hot sun upon a polished board, and it will be like true and natural stone, and preserve this recipe as of great use and advantage.

239. *You may make in the following manner with crystal, painted and factitious stones, such as topazes, sapphires, &c.*[2]—Take 1 lb. of the best crystal, and grind it in a mortar and sift it, so that it may be in a very fine powder. Then add 5 lbs. of stag's bones, calcined to perfect whiteness, and if you cannot

---

1 The Alabaster appears to supply the place of the pounded bricks used in the common process of distilling oil. The object of employing it was to equalize the heat and to economise time and fuel. It probably also prevented the danger of the oil boiling over.

biccha e el suo relevo. Se tu campeggie de rosso el suo relevo e el verzino.

238. *Ad lapides anullorum componendos scilicet gemmas pretiosas claras et laudabilis colloris. Et margaritas rubinos et balascios que sunt artificiales et non naturales poteris ita componere cito et facile.*—Recipe de bono lapide qui vocatur alabastrum constantinopolitanum quantum vis et illum primo ignias ut ignitum ferrum et extingue in acetum album acerrimum postea tere in brumzi mortario subtiliter et totum pone in oleo lini vel olive ubi stet 3^{bns} diebus vel plus postea pone in cucurbita et stilla per elembicum cujus distillationem collige et serva. Et cum autem vis collorare pone in ipsa aqua quem colorem vis et perpetue tenebit colorem. Nam si vis habere zafirrum intus pone azurrum ultramarinum. Si vis habere smiralgdum intus ponem viridem herem. Si vis habere topatium intus pone oleum vittollorum ovorum gallinarum et ♃ [stannum] quequidem aqua fiet cum interposito collore 3 diebus rasine aluminis zucarini vel scaioli deinde aquam coloratam cola per pannum lineum spissum et subtilem et idem fac quid vis. Nam congela juxta ignem ut veniat ad duritiem paste et de tali pasta tolle portionem et incide ad quam formam vis lapidem vel coppam sive vasem bene buliendo cum olive oleo vel oleo seminis lini aut oleo amangdolarum amarium in freventi sole ad desiccandum super asidem politam et erunt tamquam vere et naturales et hoc habeas pro magno dono ac utilitate.

239. *Sic fiunt de christallo lapides picti contrafacti ut topatii zafirri etc.*—Abeas libram j cristalli optimi et tere in mortario et cribra ut sit subtiliter pulverizati postea pone 5 libras ossum cervinum combustum usque ad albedinem perfectam si vero non poteris habere zervinum ossum habeas bovinum ossum sive

---

[2] This recipe somewhat resembles one in the Sloane MS., No. 3661, but in this last MS. it is said that the sapphire is to be imitated with "Azzurro Ultramarino," while in the text "good azure" only is mentioned. See Theophilus, E. ed., p. 176.

have stag's bones, take beef bones or buffalo bones. Then take of sal alkali 5 lbs., grind it fine, and mix it all together, and put this powder in a strong covered jar, luted with lutum sapientiæ, and place it into a glass furnace where it may remain 5 or 7 days at the most, and melt it into glass there. Afterwards put some good azure upon it, and knead both up together, and a blue colour will be produced and you may make up small or large sapphires, which you may set with the stone called emerald. If you wish to have a topaz, add saffron. If you wish light rubies put vermilion, if dark, verzino. If pomegranate coloured put verzino or oricella or rose colour. If you wish jasper, put burnt orpiment; for what is made of glass, is made of crystal, as before.

240. *To make pearls.*—Take very clear crystal glass, and reduce it to as fine a powder as you can, and incorporate it with white of egg, and slime of snails, and with that paste make pearls in moulds, so that they may be round, perforate them with a hog's bristle, and then put them in a hollow vase over the fire, so that they may become white hot; then quench them in cold water, and they will be very beautiful.

241. *To make beautiful saucers of crystal.*—Calcine bright crystal or white marble stones, and then take 6 rotoli[1] of this very white calx, 2 rotoli of burnt tartar, and 1 rotolo of sal alkali; put them all into the glass furnace, and let them melt there, and you may make saucers and whatever you like, and they will be as beautiful as crystal; and if you paint them with saffron of Mars, and heat what you have painted at the fire, it will be like fine gold.

242. *To make rubies.*—Take of roche alum 2, 1, of saltpetre 3, 1, and reduce them to fine powder together; then take verzino boiled with wine till reduced one half, and with this wine mix and knead up the said powders to the consistence of sauce; put them into a glass vase with a gentle fire, that the liquid

---

[1] Rotolo, a Venetian weight of about 32 oz.; also a Sicilian weight of 2½ lbs. But see No. 221, p. 499.

buffalinum deinde tolle salis alcali lb. 5 et subtiliter tere et commisce bene insimul et hunc pulverem pone in forti olla coperta et luto sapientie lutata et pone in formace vitrialorum ubi stet quinque diebus vel seeptem ad plus et illic fundatur vitrium postea superpone de bono azurro et insimul stempera et fiet color cilistrinus et conficias zafiros grossos vel parvos quos actabis cum petra que vocatur smiraglius. Si vis habere topatium pone desuper crocum. Si rubinos claros pone cinabrium. Si obscuros pone verzinum. Si granatas pone verzinum sive oricelle aut rose. Si iaspides pone exustum de auripiumento nam quod fit de vitro fit de cristallo ut predictum.

240. *Ad fatiendum margaritas.*—Accipe vitrum cristallinum lucidissimum et subtiliter pulveriza quantum potes et incorpora cum albumine ovj et spuma lumace et de illa massa forma perlas cum formis ut sit bene rotunda et perfora cum una seta porci deinde pone eas in uno vase cupo ad ignem tantum quod fiant albe postea extingue eas cum clara aqua et erunt pulcherrime.

241. *Ad fatiendum pulcras scutes de cristallo.*—Habeas lapides vivos cristallinos sive marmorinos albos et de ipsis fac calcina de quo vis deinde accipe de ista calcina albissima rodulos 6. tartari usti rodulos 2. et sal alcali rodulos unum et pone in fornace vitri et ibi fac fundere et poteris facere scutellas et quodquumque volueris et erunt pulcre ut cristallus et si pingis de croco ferri et calefatias ad ignem picturas erunt sicut aurum finum.

242. *Ad rubinos componendum.*—Tolle aluminis rocci 3. j. salis nitri 3. j. et pulveriza subtiliter insimul deinde accipe verzinum bulitum in vinum ad medium et cum dicto vino impasta et incorpora dictos pulveres ad modum saporis et pone in vase vitrio cum parvo igne ut siccetur et in unam massam reducetur

may evaporate, and that the whole may form one mass. Take it off the fire, and let it stand 7 days, and you will find a well-coloured substance like dough, mould it into any shape you please.

243. *To make balas rubies.*—Put a stone of pure crystal into a hollow iron ladle, and make a good fire under it. When the whole of the ladle, with the stone in it, is red hot, take clear and cold spring water, and throw a drop of it upon the stone, and afterwards put it back gently to the fire; then take dragon's blood in fine powder, make it into a lump, and anoint the stone, and put it back to the fire so that the ladle may get red hot with a little fire, and then remove it from the fire and let it cool near the fire, and when it is almost cool, rub it with a piece of very rough woollen cloth, and it will be well done.

244. *To make fine pearls, and of a good colour to all appearance.*—Take stones from the heads of fishes in fine powder, and incorporate the powder with white of egg to the consistence of dough, and then shape the pearls that they may be perfectly round; perforate them with a hog's bristle, and pass a horse-hair through the hole; then place them in the sun to dry. Then boil them in new milk, and let them cool in a place free from wind and dust until they become hard.

245. *To make pearls, which are just like natural pearls, and undoubtedly real and good.*—Take mother of pearl, or very fine pearls, or that shining matter which is in pearls' shells, pound it fine, and take two parts of this powder, and one part of very white powdered gum arabic, mix the whole with dew, and then make up the pearls into a good shape and dry them before the fire, and before they are quite hard perforate them with a hog's bristle, and then let them get very hard, and polish them gently with the tool with which the goldsmiths polish stones. Then take very white cheese and some milk of a fig-tree, and put the powdered cheese into that milk, and expose it to the open air in a clean vessel, and it will be dissolved. Then string your pearls on a horsehair or thread, warm them well before the fire,

et leva ab igne et dimicte stare per 7^{m} dies. et invenies matheriam in modum paste bene coloratam et fac aut forma quid vis ad libitum.

243. *Ad fatiendum balascios.*—Accipe lapidem cristalli puri et habeas unam palectam ferri concavam et ea micte lapidem et fac subtus ignem bonum et cum fuerit ignita tola palecta cum lapide intus habeas claram et frigidam aquam surgentem et proice unam guctam super dictum lapidem postea suaviter repone ad ignem et habeas sanguinem draconis finum pulverizatum subtiliter et fatias ex eo unam maxam et unge lapidem et remite ad ignem ut palecta veniat rubea cum parvo igne deinde elleva ad igne et permitte frigidarj justa ignem et cum fuerit quasi frigida frica eam cum pettia panni lini acerrimj et bene erit factum.

244. *Ad fatiendum pulcras perlas tamquam et laudabilis coloris in aparentia.*—Habeas lapides pisscium de capitibus pulverrizatos suctiliter et incorpora cum albumine ovj ut pasta forma postea et fac ut sit bene rotunda post perfora cum seta porci per quod foramen pone setam equi et dimite ut ad solem siccentur demum quoque eas in lacte recenti et dimicte fridare in loco sine vento et pulvere donec in duritiem convertantur.

245. *Ad fatiendum margaritas sive perlas tanquam naturales et optimas et veras sine dubio.*—Summe matrem perle sive perlas minutissimas aut lucidum illud quod est in conchiliis perlarum et pulveriza subtilissime et de eo pulvere acipe partes duas et partem unam albissimam gummam arabicam pulverizatam et misce cum aqua roris demum informa optime et desicca ad humbram et antequam multum induresca nt perfora cum seta porcina et dimitte fortiter durescere postea poli plane cum quo poliunt aurifices lapides postea acipe casum albissimum et lac fici et pone in eo lacte ditum casum pulverizatum et dimicte ad serenum in vasculo mundo et disolvetur postea micte perlas tuas in seta caballi aut in filo et calefac bene eas ad ignem postea merge eas in tali disolutione et eleva et dimitte sicari demum

dip them into this solution, and take them out and let them dry, and then warm the solution. Dip the pearls in it and dry them, and repeat the process until you have very bright pearls; then bury them in barley meal for 2 hours, and rub them well with a cloth. And a certain Spaniard[1] told me that I might dissolve them in lemon juice, and dry the powder, and make up the pearls with snails' slime, so as to be like dough. Then shape them, and take a piece of stale and tender beef, cut it open, and, making holes in the meat, put each pearl into a separate hole, and join the pieces together, and tie them well lest the vapour of the pearls should escape, and bake them in the oven until the meat is well dressed for eating, and they will be good and perfect; but if by chance the meat should be too much burnt for eating, give the pearls to a pigeon to swallow for a day or more, and they will then be very bright.

246. *To make large pearls out of small ones.*—Grind small pearls fine in a bronze mortar, and then take the juice of citrons, and filter it; next take urine and spirit of turpentine, of each one-third part of the quantity of the citron juice, and knead up the powder with this water so that it may become like dough; let it stand for 3 days in the sun, and afterwards knead it well together and put it upon glass, and make pearls just as you please with "oleo muscellino,"[2] and then perforate them with a hog's bristle, and pass a horsehair through the hole and leave them in the sun until they are dry. Then put them into the belly of a fish, having thrown away the inside, and bake it as if it were a pie; then take out the pearls, and you will find them converted into hard stones. Rub them well in a linen cloth with barley meal, and they will be very bright.

247. *To clean pearls.*—Take pearls, and wash them well in clear water in a very clean cloth, and then take ultramarine soap,[3] and dissolve it in water, and wash them as before.

---

1 Probably Jacopo de Tholeto before mentioned.

2 A composition of oil, water, spices, and odoriferous drugs. See Ricettario Fiorentino.

iterum calefac dictam disolutionem et sumerge et desica et sic tandiu reitera donec habeas perlas luccidissimas deinde sepelias eas in furfure ordeacio per duas horas et frica optime cum panno. Et quidam Ispanus dixit mihi ut eas in succo limonum solverem novem recottam et siccetur et cumglutinetur cum glutine limatii et sint sicut pasta et formentur postea accipe frustrum carnis veteri et macer tauri et divide frustrum et facta fovea incarne colloca singulas perlas in singulis foveis et reiunge carnes et liga perfecte ne vaporet fumus perlarum et infurno bene assa et sint bone ad comedendum et erunt bone et perfecte sed si forte erunt nimis aduste da comedere columbo per diem vel plus et erunt lucidissime.

246. *Ad fatiendum perlas grossas de minutis.*—Tere parvas margaritas in mortario brunzi subtiliter demum accipe citositatem citrorum et distilla per filtrum et de urina et de aqua rasi quantum est tertia pars aque citri et impasta dictum pulverem cum hac aqua ita quod deveniat sicut pasta et dimicte per tres dies ad solem postea cum glutina diligenter et depone super vitrum et forma margaritas ad libitum cum oleo muscellino postea perfora cum porcina seta per quod foramen pone setam equinam et dimite ad solem donec sicentur demum pone in ventre piscis bucefallj egeritis interioribus et sue sive cuscias ventrem et fac inde pastillum et quoque et extrage et invenies lapides duros. Et frica eas cum furfure ordei in panno fortiter demum da collumbo vel gallo comedere per diem j vel amplius sicut videtur et iterum frica cum furfure ut prius et erunt lucidissime.

247. *Ad margaritas sive perlas clarificandas.*—Accipe perlas et lava fortiter in aqua limpidissima in panno mundissimo et tunc acipe saponem ultramarinum et disolve in aqua et lava ut supra.

---

[3] Probably the Roman Soap, with which it was said in No. 4, that the Azurum Citramarinum was to be washed.

248. *To make an emerald of crystal.*—Take crystal, and soak it in alum for 12 days, and then cook it in verdigris, and it will be in appearance a fine emerald, like a real one. And so you may make a sapphire and all other precious stones according to the colour you add to the crystal, proceeding in the same manner as before, and you will have imitations of all the precious stones.

249. *To make a chrysolite with crystal.*—Take a crystal, and steep it in alum for 15 days; then cook it in orpiment, and it will appear a chrysolite.

250. *To make amber.*[1]—Take burnt tartar, and make a ley with very strong vinegar, reduce it by boiling to one half, strain it again through the burnt tartar, and let it settle and clear itself. Then take yolk of eggs for the red, and white of egg for the white, and beat them well, and let them stand for 3 days in the sun until they are decomposed; then put the vinegar with the eggs into a glass vase, place them near the fire, and make them boil, and for each egg put 2 [oz.], 5 [dr.] of spirit of wine and of honey; of tempered saffron, 3, 1; of myrrh, 3, 5; and of cherry gum, 3, 5. Strain all these things so prepared, boil them for an hour, and let them cool, and make amber [beads] just as you please; then pierce them with a hog's bristle, and afterwards anoint them with linseed oil, and at length, when they are dry, anoint them with liquid varnish, and they will be very beautiful.

251. *To make amber (beads).*—Take the whites of hen's eggs, and whip them with a sponge till they cease to froth; add a little roche alum, colophony well powdered, and some cherry gum. Strain the mixture through a cloth, and put it into a flask well closed and luted, and set the flask in a jar full of water; boil it for an hour, and then put it to cool in the open air, and dry it, and afterwards wrap it up in a linen cloth and bury it in dung for 3 days, and it will then be liquid, so that you may work it in your hands, and make beads and whatever you please. While you are modelling them, anoint your hands

---

[1] The value of amber at this time may be estimated by the numerous

248. *Ad fatiendum smiralgdum de christallo.*—Habeas cristallum et micte in allumine per dies duodecim postea quoque in viride ere et erit smiraldus nobilis in aparentia ut esset finum. Et sic poteris habere zafirrum et omnes lapides pretiosos secundum colorem quem vis mictere cristallum et fac in supradicto modo et habebis omnes lapides pretiosos contrafactos.

249. *Ad fatiendum crisolitum de cristallo.*—Tolle cristallum et micte in alumine per 15 dies demum quoque in auripiumento et apparebit crisolitum.

250. *Ad fatiendum ambra*.—Accipe cinerem fetie et fac liscivium cum aceto albo fortissimo et deinde fac eum bullire per medium ut revertatur et iterum cola per dictum cinerem et fac eum quiescere ut sit bene clarum demum acipe ovorum vitella pro rubeis et albumina pro albis et percute bene et permitte per tres dies ad solem quiescere donec fiant putride deinde tolle dictum acetum cum dictis ovis in uno vaso vitrio et pone ad ignem et fac bullire et pro omni ovo mitte 2. 5. aque vite et mellis ana, et croci stemperati 3. j. mirre 3. 5. gumme ceresarum 3. 5. stringentur ea et omnia sic preparata fac bullire per unam horam et micte frigidari et forma ambra ad libitum tuum et fora ea cum porcina seta et postea unge ea cum oleo seminj linj demum quando sunt sicce unge ea cum liquida vernice et permitte sicare et erunt pulcherrime.

251. *Ad ambra fatiendum.*—Tolle albumina ovorum gallinarum et cum spungia tantum perchute ne aliqua spuma appareat et mite aliquantulum aluminis rocci et colofonie optime pulverizate gume cerese et per pannum cola et pone in ampulla bene clausa et lutata et pone in olla aque plena et fac bulire per unam horam demum pone ad refrigidare ad serenum ut siccetur postea involve in panno lineo et pone sub fimo per 3 dies postea erit liquida qua poteris ducere in manus et forma ambra et quicquid vis aliud et cum formabis ea unge tuas manus comuni oleo et fora ea et pone ad siccandum et erunt facta.

---

recipes for imitating it. The use of this factitious amber appears to have been for making "beads for Paternosters," as it is expressed in No. 272.

with common oil, pierce the beads, and let them dry, and they will be done.

252. *For the same.*—Take white of eggs, beaten as if for distempering vermilion, and put it into a flask and boil it in very strong vinegar until it coagulates; then break the flask, and make beads of it.

253. *For the same purpose.*—Take arsenic in crystals [1] and roche alum finely pounded, of each equal quantities; distemper these ingredients with white of egg well whipped, and then put them into a very clean budello di castrone, which must be boiled until it becomes hard. When you wish to use it and soften it, boil the budello with white vinegar, and make the beads as you please. If you wish to make them yellow, add some saffron, and mix the ingredients well together in powder; then strain the powder through a linen cloth, and boil it as before directed. And if you wish the colour to be red, mix the white of egg used for vermilion with sandal-wood [2] in powder, and do as before directed. And if you wish the colour to be green, take verdigris, and mix it with white of egg, and do as before. And if you wish it to be blue, take azure, and do as before directed.

254. *For the same, as before.*—Take purified white of egg, coagulate it over a slow fire, and make beads of it; then let it dry in the sun, and you may make it of whatever colour you like by putting into it the colour which you wish to give it, but it must be coagulated in a round shape.

255. *To calcine crystal.*—Take small pieces of crystal of the size of chesnuts, wash them well, and dry them; put them in a reverberatory furnace, until they are red hot, then throw them into clear water. Do this 4 or 5 times, and then pound what was calcined; and in the same manner the emerald must be calcined.

---

1 The method of preparing arsenic in crystals is thus described by Matthioli :—" Crystalled Arsenic, so called because it is transparent, like crystal, is not found native with orpiment, as my countryman Vannoccio writes in his Pyrotechnia; but is prepared artificially from pounded orpiment and salt, by heating and subliming them together in certain covered earthen

252. *Ad idem.*—Habeas albumen ovorum ruptum in modum ad temperandum cenabrium et micte in ampulla ut impleatur et in aceto acerrimo fac bullire donec congeletur demum frange ampulla et forma ambra.

253. *Super eodem.*—Piglia arsenico cristallino alumi de roccho bene pisto ana et distempera queste cose cum chiara dova rucpta bene poi mecte queste cose in uno budello de castrone bene necto et fa bullire tanto che divente sodo et quando el vorai adoperare et indolcirlo fa bulire lo dicto budello cum aceto bianco poi forma limbra [lambra ?] a tuo piacere. Se tu le voi fare gialli mistace del zafaramj et remista bene insiemj in polvere poi lo cola cum panno de lino et cocilo commo e dicto disopra et se lo voi rosce mista cum la chiara del cinabrio cum li sandoli in polvere et fa commo e disopra dicto. Et se lo voi verde tolli verderamo et mista cum chiara et fa commo disopra. Et se volesce azurre tolli azurro et fa per lo modo sopra dicto.

254. *Ad idem ut supra.*—Habeas ovorum clara purificata et coagula lento igne et fac ambra postea dimite ipsum sicare ad solem et potes facere de quolibet colore vis colorare pone intus colorem sed formam rutundam debet coagulari.

255. *Ad calcinandum cristallum.*—Capias pecios christalli parvos ut castanea et ipsos bene lava et desica demum pone in igne reverberationis donec rubiscentur postea proice in aqua frigida et ita fac 4. vel 5 vicibus deinde pista quod calcinatum est. Et idem modo calcinabitur smiriglium.

---

vessels, made for the purpose; the arsenic sublimes and attaches itself to the covers, and becomes clear and transparent, especially in the centre." Matt. p. 1428.

[2] Sandali Rossi. The wood of the Pterocarpus Santalinus. It is used in dyeing, and for colouring varnishes.

256. *To prepare crystal.*—Take crystal, make it very hot, and quench it in cold water; break it and reduce it to powder; and when it is powdered, take 5 parts of the powder, 1 part of calcined tartar, and 1 part of sal-alkali; melt them together until the tartar and sal-alkali are consumed, and then colour the glass with any colour you choose, if you think proper, and do what you choose with it.

257. *To make factitious crystal.*—Take the whites of 30 eggs, beaten to a froth, and ℥. 2 of common salt, put them into a jar to boil till reduced to one-third; then fill the jar again, and add of oil of chamomile[1] ℥.ij; boil it again till it dries, and then set it by to cool. Make it into any form you please. With oil it will make amber, and without oil it will appear like crystal.

258. *To soften crystal.*—Take roche alum, and grind it well upon marble with very strong vinegar, then put it into a glazed vase, and make it boil until it is dry. Having done this, take it out and grind it again, and do this 5 times, and afterwards put it in a glass flask beneath dung until it is dissolved. Then throw away the supernatant water, and you may then give a colour to the crystal, and mould whatever you like.

259. *To imitate precious stones with crystal.*—Take roche alum, alum zucarino, Roman vitriol, and "salis copertum," of each equal quantities, and put these ingredients into clear and strained ley, and dissolve them, and you may colour the crystal. For a sapphire, add azure; for an emerald, add verdigris; for a ruby, add vermilion; for a balas ruby, add verzino or "stupio;" for hyacinth, sky-blue and a little azure; for amethyst, some oricella; and so you may imitate all stones by adding different colours. Remember, however, that the crystal and the colours must be dissolved like colours and coagulated. Then boil them till they become like stones.

260. *To soften crystal previous to stamping or carving it like wax.*—Take fine crystal and put it to soak in the blood of a

---

[1] The old method of preparing this oil was by steeping chamomile flowers in olive oil, and exposing the bottle to the sun for 40 days. See Ricet-

256. *Ad fixandum cristallum.*—Tolle cristallum et calefatias eum valde fortiter et proice in aqua frigida et ipse frange et reduc in pulverem et eo pulverizato recipe de ipso partes 5 et partem j de tartaro calcinato et partem j de sale alcali et funde insimul donec tartarum et sal alcali consumentur et ibi colora ipsum de quo colore vis colorare si placet et fac de ipso opus tuum.

257. *Ad fatiendum christallum contrafactum.*—Habeas album triginta ovorum et ℥ : 2. (*sic*) salis comunis et bene spumatum pone in ampulla ut bulliant donec reducatur ad tertium et iterum repleatur ampulla et in ea ponatur olei camomille ℥. ij (*sic*) et iterum buliatur ut desicetur et pone ad refrigidandum et forma quic vis cum oleo erunt ambra et sine oleo aparebit cristallum.

258. *Ad molificandum cristallum.*—Accipe aluminis rocj et tere bene super marmorem cum fortissimo aceto deinde pone in vase vitriato et fac bulire donec desicetur hoc facto extrahe et iterum tere et sic fac vicibus 5. postea pone in ampulla vitria sub fimo donec solveatur deinde aqua que supernatet proiciatur et tunc poteris dare collorem christallo et formare quicquid vis.

259. *Ad faciendum lapides pretiosos contrafactos de cristallo.*—Abeas aluminis rocce, aluminis zucarini, vitrioli romani, salis copertum ana et tere bene simul et pone in urina colata et clara et dimite ut disolvitur et poteris colorare cristallum pro zafirro pone azurrum pro smiralgdo pone viridi es et pro rubino cinaprium pro balascio brasilem sive stupio pro iacinto celeste parum azurri pro amastito ex oricella et sic poteris habere omnes lapides ponendo colorem. Memento tamen quod cristallus et collores debent resolvi ad modum coloris et congellare deinde bulliant in modum lapidum.

260. *A mollificare el cristallo primo che porai impromptare et tagliare commo cera.*—Recipe el cristallo fino et metilo a

tario Fiorentino, p. 248. At the present time a distilled oil is made from Chamomiles.

lamb, or of a calf fresh killed, and it will soon become soft, and when it is cold it will again become hard and shining as before.

261. *This is a hidden philosophical operation, that is to say, to make large corals out of small ones in this way.*—Take whatever quantity you like of the small seed corals, and pound them and pulverize them so as to be almost impalpable, and then take lemon-juice, well purified, as follows:—Take the juice and first strain it through a thick woollen cloth, and do this 3 or 4 times, and then filter it until it is perfectly clear, and knead up the powder with this juice in a glass vase; and, when well incorporated and soaked, let the juice cover the powder by two or three fingers' breadths, and then you will see that it will produce a certain creamy or thick liquor on the top of it. Take this and put it aside in a clean jar; then take the powders, and let them dry until they become as hard as stiff paste, and with this paste make large corals, or images, or horses, or figures, or branches of coral, or whatever you like, and put them into a place secure from dust, smoke, wind, and sun, and let them dry a little; and before they are quite dry, anoint them with that creamy liquor which you reserved; let them dry well and completely, and you will have a fine and polished and genuine work, which is of considerable profit.

262. *To make good liquid varnish.*—Take 2 lbs. of common oil, and 2 lbs. of fresh linseed, and boil them together in a glazed pipkin until it is reduced one-half, and then pour it into another glazed vase, such as a pipkin, and take a tripod and place the pipkin on it, and make a clear fire under it, and when the liquid begins to boil add to it 30 or 40 cloves of garlic, cleaned and scraped fine, and a little roche alum at discretion, and let it boil; and if you wish to know when it is well done, take a hen's feather and dip it in the mixture. If the feather is burnt it is done well; take it from the fire, and before it is cold add to it one pound of sandarac well pounded, a little at a time, and keep continually stirring it round with a

molle in sangue dagnello o de vitello quando se amaza, e poco stara che sera morbido, et commo sera freddo retornara duro et lustro comme prima.

261. *Questa e un opera oculta filosoficale: cioe fare coralli grossi de li piccoli in questo modo.*—Accipe quella quantita che tu voi de li coralli picoli finissimi et pistali tanto et polverizali tanto subtilmente che paiano essere senza tatto de poi tolli el sugo de limone che sia bene depurgato in questa forma tolli lo sugo et prima lo distilla per uno panno de lana grosso et questo fa 3 o 4 volte poi lo distilla per filtro tanto che sia bene chiaro poi impasta cum lo dicto sugo la predita polvere in uno vaso de vetrio et commo sonno bene incorporate et imbeverate de vantagio fa che ce sia tanto sugo che avanze sopra alla dicta polvere doi o tre deta de poi tu vederai che produra de sopra una certa graseza o licore grasso piglialo et pollo da parte in uno vaso neto poi tolli le polvere et lassale seccare tanto che fornano dure ad modo duna pasta uno poco duretta de la quale pasta forma li coralli grossi o forma vase o immagine o cavalli o figure o branchi de coralli o quello che te piace et polle in loco dove non sia polvere ne fumj ne vento ne sole et lassale alquanto secare ma prima che siano fornite de secare ungile con quella graseza o licore che reservasti de poi lassale seccare bene in tucto et haverai opera polita et bella e vera et de bono guadagno.

262. *A fare vernice liqquida bona.*—Ahvvi lb doi dolio comune et doi libre de semj de lino fresca et fa bullire insiemj in una pignatta vitriata tanto che calla per mita poi la mecti in uno altro vaso vitriato commo uno pignato poi havvj uno tre pei et disopra vi mecte la dicta pignatta et falli di socto el foco chiaro et commo comenza a bullire e tu ce pone 30 o quaranta spighi de alglio mondato et bene alanato sutili poi ce pone uno poco de alumj de rocho a discretione et lassa bulire et cociare et se voi sapere quando e bene cocta tolli una penna de gallina et bagnala in la dicta cocictura se la penna vieni pellata e cocta et facta et levala dal foco e nante che se fredda mectice una libra de vernice da scrivare bene pesta a poco per

stick, and when it is nearly cold add six or eight whites of egg, well beaten and cleared, as they are used for vermilion, and mix the whole well, and then place the varnish for one day in the sun, stir it every hour, and keep it in a cool place, and it will be good.

263 *To make vermilion.*—Take quicksilver, and two parts of yellow or white sulphur, incorporate the sulphur well ground with the quicksilver, and put it into a bottle well luted with lutum sapientiæ, and let it dry. Then put it into the oven and give it a gentle fire, and cover the top of the vase with a tile, uncover and cover it frequently, and when you see a yellow smoke come over it is nearly done; let it remain, and give it more fire until a red smoke, almost purple, arises. Then extinguish the fire, and let the bottle cool, and you will have fine vermilion.

264. *To make, with* [1] *pearls, one fine and very good pearl.*—Take the juice of moderately ripe lemons, and put it into a glazed saucer, and distil [or strain it?] [2] and take care not to let dust or smoke or any other dirt have access to it. Then pour the juice into a glazed vessel, such as a cup, and put into the juice as many pearls as you like, let the pearls be perfectly free from all dirt, and let them remain closely covered up until they are well softened. Then take them out of the lemon juice and wash them well with clear water, so that no greenness may remain on the pearls. Then make them up into a paste with water of slugs, which is made in this way. Take the slugs and clean them well, and put them into a glazed saucer, and sprinkle a little salt well pounded upon them, in order to clean them from all slime, and then a little sal-ammoniac, and let them remain so for a day and a night, after which distil them in an alembic, and use the water that comes over for your purpose. Then take a piece of very clean glass in the palm of each hand, and with the pieces of glass make your pearls dexterously round, whether you wish

[1] and [2] These words are illegible in the original.

volta e sempre vienj mistando intorno cum uno bastone poi quando sera quasi fredda et tu la cola cum una stamegna poi quando sera fredda mectice sei o 8 albuma dova bene dibatuti et chiara commo se fa per lo cinabrio et mista bene poi la mecti uno di al sole et mistala ad omne ora et serbala al fresco et stara bene.

263. *Affare cinabrio.*—Abbi argento vivo et doi parte de zolpho bianco o giallo et incorporalo lo solpho bene trito cum largento et pollo in una boccia alutata bene de luto de sapientia et lassa sciutare poi la pone nel fornello et falli foco ligiero et copri la boca del vaso cum una tegola et spesso lo scopri et ricopre et quando tu vedi vuscire el fumo giallo sera apresso che facto et lassalo tanto stare et dalli lo foco che facia lo fumo rosso quasi pavonazo ahlora toli via lo foco et lassa fredare e de facto fino cinabrio.

264. *Affare de perle una bella perla et bona de vantagio.*—Tolli sugo de limone i quali siano mezanamente maturi et mectilo in una scutella vitriata et distillalo per lingua et fa che non vi possa andare polve ne fumj ne altra bructura poi pone lo dicto sugo in uno vaso de vetrio commo e una taza poi mecti in lo dicto sugo quanti perlj che tu voj esiando le dicte perle ben necte da omne loto et sallavezza et lassale stare ben coverte per spatio che siano ben mollificate dapoi le remove dal sugo e lavale bene cum aqua chiara bene scrillente per modo che non rimanga nisciuna verdeza ale perle poi le impasta cum aqua de lumache la quale se fa in questo modo. Tolli le lumache et mondale bene et mectili in una scutella vitriata poi li pone suso uno poco de sale bene trito acio depurga omne baviglia poi li pone suso uno altro poco de sale armoniaco et lassale stare cusi per uno di et una nocte et poi le pone a stillare per lambicco e de questa aqua usarai ala tua opera poi habbi doi peze de vetrio bene polite in cescheduna palma de le mano et cum li dicti peze de vetrio le ritonda dextramente o vo fare una o doi o 3 perle o

one, two, or three pearls, or as many more as you like; and when the pearls are perfectly round string them upon a clean hog's bristle, first boring them with a silver thread or horsehair, and hang these pearls between two saucers of glass, suspended between the two saucers so as not to touch them in any part. Fasten the two saucers closely together, and then put them in the sun to dry; and when they are hard rub them well with the dust of emeralds and with a cloth. Then take barley-meal, and mix it with the pearls and powder, and rub them well again with the cloth, and they will be bright and fine.

265. *To make sapphire, and to refine and colour it.*—Take a crystal, or a transparent stone, and whichever you take heat it strongly and then quench it several times in cold water; then pound it, and take an equal quantity of sal alkali, and melt them together. Afterwards put them into a furnace, and add a little zaffirro. And if you wish to have the colour green, add a little minium, and note, that some say that "callamita femina" [1] makes a transparent red. Note also, that these stones are found upon Mount St. Bernard, and are good and perfect crystals, as if they were really mineral.

266. *To make a gold colour.*—Take ley and ochre, of each equal quantities, and grind them with linseed oil; then mix a little verdigris and black, and grind them together, and then put them in a small jar over the fire, and when the oil begins to boil take it off the fire, and spread it wherever you like, and it will be of a gold colour.

267. *To purify zafirro.*—Take the zafirro and wash it with salt and vinegar, and then keep it in strong vinegar for the space of 6 days, change the vinegar every day, and keep doing this until the impurities are removed and the colour is refined.

268. *To make red glass.*—Take 1 lb. of copper, and melt it,

---

[1] Agricola (De Metallicis, Lib. v. p. 249) says there were several kinds of minerals called Calamites; that they differed in appearance and in properties; that some attract iron powerfully, and these are called the "male calamites;" others attract it less powerfully, these are called the "female

quanto voli et quando le dicte perle seranno bene retonde mectile in una seta de porcho bene necta et forale prima cum uno filo de argento o cum una seta de cavallo lungha et mecte queste perle in mezo de doi scudelle de vetrio suspese suso in la dicta setula de cavallo per tal modo che le dicte perle stiano in mezo de le dicte doi scudelle in aiere suso in le dicte sete che le dicte perle non tochano in nisciuna parte et le dicte scudelle siano bene serate insiemj poi le pone al sole a seccare et quando seranno duri tu le pone suso de la polve de lo smeriglio et sfregale bene cum quella polvere de lo smeriglio cum uno canavaccio poi tollj semola dorzo et mista cum le dicte perle et polvere et sfrega de novo molto bene cum lo dicto canavaccio et saranno lustre et belle.

265. *Ad fatiendum zaffirrum et ipsum affinando et colorando.*—Accipe christallum vel lapidem trasparentem et quod vis accipe et eos calefac fortiter demum extingue in aqua frigida pluribus vicibus postea pistetur deinde tolle totidem de sale alcheli et insimul funde et postea pone in furnum et adde secum parum de zaffirro. Et si vis quod fiet viridis adde parum de mineo. Et nota de callamita femina aliquis dicit quod facit rubeum trasparentem. Et scias quod dicti lapides inveniuntur in montagna sancti Berardi et sunt perfecti et boni cristallini tamquam de propria minera.

266. *A fare collore doro.*—Tolli ranno et ocria ana et macina cum oleo de semj de lino poi ce mista uno poco de verderamo et de nero et macina insiemj poi lo pone in uno pignatino al foco et quando cominza a bolire levalo dal foco et lavoralo dove voi et sera in collore doro.

267. *A porificare el zafirro.*—Ahavve el zaffiro et lavalo cum lo sale et aceto poi lo tienj a molli nello aceto forte per 6 di et omne di li muta laceto et tanto fa chusci che lo loto o stista vada via ed e facto fino.

268. *Affare vetrio rosso.*—Tolli libra j de ramo et fundilo et

calamites." In the former it is not difficult to recognise the loadstone or magnet; the latter from the properties ascribed to it, such as making copper white when added to it, was probably Electric Calamine, or siliceous oxide of zinc. See Phillips' Min., p. 354.

and when it is melted add 4 oz. of lead, and incorporate them well with each other and throw the mass into cold water, and it will be broken small like grains of corn. Then grind it as fine as you can, and stir it into the glass, and it will become red glass, for making *paternosters* and other articles.

Also note that copper filings thrown into the glass make a red, but they require a very gentle fire. Calcined lead has the same effect, and so also has minium and white lead.

269. *To lay gold upon glass.*—Take very thin bladders of crystal glass, as clean and pure, and liquid as possible, and break them just as you please, and lay real gold upon them. And Frate Giovanni told me that in order to fix the gold on to the glass, it was necessary to employ a solution of borax, the Alexandrian borax,[1] which the goldsmiths use, for this water makes the gold adhere well. And when you have laid the gold on to the white glass, put it in the mouth of the furnace, that is, where you stand to work, so that it may become hot, and take care as it dries to have ready in the furnace the glass upon which you wish to lay the gold, and with this glass some very fine saffron of Mars of the alchemists must be mixed, in order to serve as a mordant for the gold, which will appear of a deeper colour. Then take out of the furnace the quantity of glass which you require, and heat it upon the marble slab upon which you make drinking glasses, and be quick, and take it with the iron for making drinking glasses, and lay upon it the piece covered with gold, and put the gold on the under side of it, that is, let it be between the two glasses. Then put it in the furnace to spread, and spread the glass with the gold in it with another iron, and when you see that it is well spread out and that it adheres well together, take it out and set it to cool on the top, where you set the rest of the glass to cool, and then use it for your own purpose just as you please.

270. *To paint glass, that is to say, cups or any other works in glass with smalti of any colour you please.*—Take the smalti[2]

---

[1] This is the true Borax.

[2] The composition of these smalti is not described. They were probably, as I have mentioned in a former note, like those coloured glasses, or

quandc e fuso metice oz. 4 de piombo et lassalo bene incorporare et butalo in laqua fredda et vira minuto commo granelli de grano poi lo trita piu se poi poscia lo mecte nel vetrio et vira vetrio rosso da fare patrenostri et altre lavore.

Idem nota la limatura del ramo messa nel vetrio fa rosso ma vole poco foco et lo simile fa lo piombo arso et simili fa lo minio et la biacha.

269. *A mectere oro in el vetrio.*—Tolli vesiche de vetrio subtilissimi che siano de vetrio christallino polite et necte et cocto quanto piu poi et rompilo commo a te piace et metivj suso loro vero et che frate gioahnne me disse per apiccare bene loro al vetrio se voleva torre aqua de borace quella borace Alisandrina che adoperano li orefici et cum quella apicare loro in su lo vetrio la quale aqua lo fa apichare bene et quando hai apicato el dicto oro in su lo vetrio bianco pone lo in su la bocha de la fornace cioe dove stai a lavorare in si facta forma che se scalde poi habbi cura commo e secchо poi debbia el tuo vetrio aparichiato nella fornace in su lo quale voi mectere loro nel quale vetro vole essere miscolato crocum ferri subtilissimo de Archimista et questo vi vole essere dentro acio che facia lo lecto a loro che parera piu collorito poi cava de la forma cio e quella quantita de vetrio che voi et scaldala in su lo marmo dove lavore i bichiere et fa presto poi la piglia cum lo ferro che piglie li bichierj et pone suso la peza dove e loro et pone loro ala parte de socto cioe fa che sia atramendoi queste vetrie poi lo pone nella fornace a stendare cum uno altro ferro et stende quella peza de loro si che sia bene stesa et quando vede che e bene stesa et bene apiccata cavela fora et metila de sopra a fredare dove mectj li altre vetrj poi ladopera al tuo lavoro commo te piace.

270. *A dopengiare li vetrij cum li smalti de omne collore che tu volj commo sonno tazze o altre lavore de vetrio.*—Tolli ismalte

enamels, spoken of in the MS. of the Marciana, No. 325, which were brought from Germany, and which were used for painting on glass.

you wish to use, and let them be soft and fusible, and pound them upon marble or porphyry in the same way that the goldsmiths do. Then wash the powder and apply it upon your glass as you please and let the colour dry thoroughly; then put the glass upon the rim of the chamber in which glasses are cooled, on the side from which the glasses are taken out cold, and gradually introduce it into the chamber towards the fire which comes out of the furnace, and take care you do not push too fast lest the heat should split it, and when you see that it is thoroughly heated, take it up with the "pontello" and fix it to the "pontello" and put it in the mouth of the furnace, heating it and introducing it gradually. When you see that the smalti shine and that they have flowed well, take the glass out and put it in the chamber to cool, and it is done.

271. *To make blood red glass.*—Take 100 lbs. of white glass and melt it in the furnace, and then take 8 lbs. of calcined manganese pounded, and 8 lbs. of sal alkali, which is to be mixed with the manganese, put these ingredients into a jar in the furnace to remain white hot for one day, and mix them well with an iron rod, and then take the mass out and reduce it to powder. Next take 3 lbs. of this powder and put it with the glass, that is to say, with 10 lbs. of glass; stir it well with the iron and let it fine itself. If it is too dark, add white glass to it; and if too light, add more of the material to it, and it will be good and perfect.

272. *To make yellow glass for paternosters or beads.*—Take of lead 1 lb., of tin 2 lbs., melt and calcine them, and make glass for paternosters.

273. *To make giallolino for painting.*—Take 2 lbs. of this calcined lead and tin, that is 2 lbs. of this glass for paternosters, 2½ lbs. of minium, and ½ lb. of sand from the Val d'Arno pounded very fine; put it into a furnace and let it fine itself, and the colour will be perfect.

che tu volj adoperare et fa che sieno ben tenere et corrente et pistali in su lo marmo o porfido nel modo che fanno li orifice poi lo lava et pollo ne lo tuo vetrio nello modo che lo voi porre poi lo lassa bene seccare poi lo pone in su lorlo de la camera dove se freddano li bichierj dallato dove se cavano i vase frede e a poco a poco lo spigni nela camera verso lo foco che escie da la fornace et habbi cura che non lo metesci troppo presto acio per troppo caldo non scopiassce poi che vedi che e ben caldo tolo con lo pontello et apiccalo al pontello et pollo a la bocha de la fornace a poco a poco li da el caldo metendolo dentro et quando tu vedi che i smalte lucano et che sonno bene stesi et apicati cavali fora et pone a fredare nella camera e de facta.

271. *A fare vetrio incarnato.*—Accipe lb cento de vetrio bianco et mectilo a cociare nella fornace poi tolli lb octo de maganese pisto de quello arso poi tolli lb 8 de sale alchali et mistica cum lo dicto maganese et mecti le dicte cose in uno testo nella caldara ad imbiancare per uno di et mistalo bene cum uno ferro poi cavalo fora et pistalo et fanne polvere poi toi 3 lb de questa matheria et mecti sul vetrio cio e in X. lb de vetrio et mista bene cum lo ferro et lassalo afinare et se fusse troppo scuro metivj dento vetrio bianco et se fusse troppo chiaro agiongivi de la dicta matheria et sera bono et perfecto.

272. *A fare vetrio giallo per patre nostro o ambre.*—Tolli piombo lb j. stagno lb doj. et fundi et calcina et fa vetrio per patrenostro.

273. *A fare zallolino per dipengiare.*—Havve lb doi de questo stagno et piombo calcinato et doi lb de questo vetrio da patrenostrj et doi lb et $\frac{1}{2}$ de minio et meza lb. de rena de valdarno sotilmente pista et mecti in fornace et fa affinare et sera perfecto.

HERE BEGINS A TREATISE ON MOSAIC COLOURS.

AND FIRST HOW TO MAKE THE MATERIAL FOR THE MOSAICS.

274. Take lead and tin, of each 1 lb., melt them together, and calcine them with common salt, until the whole is reduced to powder, in a reverberatory furnace, and then melt the mass and add to it its own weight of raw tartar, and reduce it to powder, and mix it again with common salt and put it in the reverberatory furnace for one natural day. Then wash the salt out with common warm water, and add more salt and calcine it again and continue this until it becomes a white calx. Take 7 lbs. of this calx and 1 oz. of calcined bones, and mix all together and put the mass into a glass pot, melt it and let it remain in fusion for 3 days, and try with an iron rod whether it is well digested and mixed, and it will be mosaic or white glass, of which you may make all other colours in glass as follows. To 8 lbs. of the said material, put one ounce of zaffirri in powder, and mix it well with an iron rod, and when it is quite melted, try with a little of it whether it is a good blue; if not, add a little zaffirro, and let it continue liquid until it is of a good colour. Then cast it, and it will take whatever shape you like, but take care of the wind while you are casting it.

275. *Another kind of mosaic.*—Take 1 lb. of crystal glass, and put it in the fire, and when it is red hot, throw it into spirit of wine in which roche alum is dissolved and so quench it 16 times, and then pulverize it on porphyry and mix with it three times its own quantity of ceruse in powder. Fill a jar half full with it and cover it and lute it down, and put it in a soda furnace and let it remain there as long as if it were soda, and when it is cold you will find your material fit to receive whatever colours you like.

INCIPIUNT COLLORES MUSAICI.

ET PRIMO AD FATIENDUM MATERIAM MUSICAM.

274. Accipe plumbum et stagnum ana lb j et funde insimul et calcina cum sale comuni quousque fuerit totum pulverizatum ad furnum reverberationis post funde cui adjunge pondus sui tartari crudi et pulveriza et iterum mise de sale comuni et pone in furno reverberationis per diem naturalem postea lava inde sal cum aqua comuni calida post redde aliud sal et iterum calcina ut prius et sic fac tamdiu quod fit calx alba de quo acipe lb 7. ed oz. j. ossum calcinatum et omnia insimul misce et pone in patella vitri et fac fundere et stet ita fusum in fusione per tres dies et cum virga ferrea vide si sit bene degestum et comistum et erit musaicum seu vitrum album intus et extra quo poteris componere omnes alios colores vitreos in tali forma in octo libris supradicte matherie pone oz. j zaffirri pulverizati et misce bene simul cum vergha ferrea et cum fuerit bene fusum proba cum modico si fuerit in collore azurri quod si non esset adde modicum de zaffirro et stet in fusione quousque habeat bonum colorem postea proice et erit in forma quo volueris custodi tamen a vento quando proicis.

275. *Alius modus musaici.*—Tolle christallinum lb j et pone ad ignem et cum fuerit ignitum proice in aquam ardentem in qua sit desolutum polvere aluminis roccj et ita extingue 16 vicibus post pulveriza super porfidum et misce cum eo ter tantum de cerusa pulverizata et pone in olla ut sit semiplena et coperi et luta et pone ubi dequoquitur soda et ibi stet tantum sicut soda et cum infrigidatum fuerit invenies materiam tuam preparatam ad recipiendum omnes collores quos volueris.

276. *To make a saffron coloured, that is golden coloured, mosaic.*—Take some of the prepared material, and add to it 1 oz. of saffron of Mars, and mix with it 8 lbs. of the prepared white material, and let it stand until it is of a gold colour. If it does not become so, add a little more saffron of Mars, and it will certainly be like gold.

But if you wish to make a red mosaic, put into the white material 1 oz. of alcucu, (?) and 1 oz. of calcined brass to 8 lbs. of the said material, and it will be red. But if you wish to make black mosaic, melt 1 oz. of iron, and 1 oz. of tin, and throw powdered sulphur upon it and it will make a very good black.

277. *To make red mosaic.*[1]—Take three parts of the white material, 1 part of calx letitiæ, that is, calx of gold, 1 part of ashes of verzino and three parts of sal gem in powder; mix the whole well together upon porphyry, and set it to melt in a glass pot in a glass furnace and let it remain there for 4 or 6 hours. Then take it out, and you will have a red mosaic.

278. *To make a rose coloured mosaic.*—Take 3 parts of the white material and 3 parts of calx letitiæ, that is calx of gold, and 2 parts of cineris pencholini, *i. e.* brass burnt and reduced to powder, and 3 parts of sal gem, pulverize the whole together, and do as you did before.

279. *To make a pomegranate-coloured mosaic.*—Take 3 parts of the said material, and 1 part of calx solis, *i. e.*, calx of gold, half a part of manganese [?], and 1 part of salgem, and do as before.

280. *To make a blue mosaic.*—Take 3 parts of the said material, $2\frac{1}{2}$ parts of ultramarine azure, and 3 parts of salgem, and it is done.

281. *To make a green mosaic.*—Take 3 parts of the said

[1] This and the succeeding chapter are proofs that the art of producing a red colour from gold was known and practised at this early period. It is not likely that the verzino mentioned in the first recipe could have produced the red colour, for it must have been converted into charcoal long

276. *Ad faciendum musaicum croceum* i. e. *colorem aurj.*—Capias de dicta matheria preparata et pone cum ipsa oz j. croci ferri et misce cum ea 8 libris de dicta materia preparata et alba et stet quousque sit in collore aurj si non fuerit adde adhuc de dicto crocho ferri et certe fiet ut aurum.

Si autem volueris facere musaicum rubeum pone in dicta matheria alba oz. j alcucu, j. es ustum in octo libris dicte materie et fiet rubeum. Si autem volueris facere musaicum nigrum funde oz. j ♀ martis et onciam ♄ Jovis et proice desuper sulphur pulverizatum et fiet nigrum valde bonum.

277. *Ad fatiendum musaicum rubeum.*—Accipe partes 3 de dicta materia alba et partes j calcis letitie *i. e.* solis et partem j. cineris brasilij et partes tres salis gemme pulverizatj et misce omnia simul multum bene super porfidum et pone fusionj in una patella vitrj in furno vitri et stet per 4 vel 6 horas demum extrahe et habebis rubeum musaicum.

278. *Ad fatiendum musaicum rosatum.*—Tolle partes 3 de dicta matheria et partes 5 calcis letitie *i. e.* solis et partes 2 cineris pencholimj *i. e.* es ustum et pulverizatum et partes 3 salis gemme et pulveriza omnia simul et fac ut supra fecisti.

279. *Ad fatiendum musaicum granatum.*—Habeas 3 partes dicte materie et partem j. calcis solis *i. e.* auri et partem mediam de maneriaci et partem j. salis gemme et fiet ut supra.

280. *Ad fatiendum musaicum azurrum.*—Tolle partes 3 dicte materie et partes 2 cum dimidia azurri ultramarini et partes 3 salis gemme et fiet.

281. *Ad fatiendum musaicum viridem.*—Capias partes 3.

---

before the glass melted. I requested the opinion of an eminent chemist on the probable effects of these three recipes, and he told me, that there was nothing in them which could have produced the red colour but the gold.

material, and 2 parts and 2 oz. more of calx of iron, and 3 parts of sal gem, and it is done.

282. *To make a crysolite, i. e., glass of the colour of gold, viz.* —Take 5 parts of the said material, 10 parts of calcined lead, 10 parts of sal-gem ; put the whole together into the furnace for 5 hours, and it is done.

materie dicte et partes duas cum duabus oz. magis calcis martis et partes 3 salis gemme et fiet.

282. *Ad fatiendum crisolitum, i. e., vitrum colloratum collore auri viz.*—Tolle de dicta materia partes 5 saturni arsi partes x. salis gemme partes x et pone omnia insimul in furno per 5. horas et fiet.

HERE BEGINS A TREATISE ON THE VARIOUS COLOURS WHICH POTTERS USE TO INCREASE THE BEAUTY OF THEIR VASES.

AND WE MUST SPEAK OF THEM IN ORDER; AND FIRST,

283. *To make fine white with marzachotto.*[1]—Take 4 lbs. of calcined tin, 2 lbs. of marzachotto, 2 lbs. of stone,[2] and 3 oz. of litharge. This is a tried recipe for painting vases.

284. *To make a baked vase white without painting it, if you wish the vase to be white and clean.*—Take 100 lbs. of litharge ground fine with water and with 20 lbs. of powdered tin, and grind the whole together, and then lay it on the jar liquid with water, and it will make it white.

285. *To make a white with glass.*—Take 5 lbs. of tin, 3 lbs. of "pietra fucara de la viersa," 2 lbs. of good glass; and if you wish to improve it, so as to have it still finer, take 1 lb. less of the said stone.

286. *To make a white on which to lay azure.*—Take 8 lbs. of marzachotto, 5 lbs. of stone, and 4 lbs. of tin.

287. *To make white for azure.*—Take 5 lbs. of white glass, 3 lbs. of stone, and 4 lbs. of tin.

288. *To make white for azure.*—Take 2 lbs. of marzachotto, 1 lb. of stone, and 1½ lb. of tin.

289. *To make white.*—Take 6 lbs. of tin, 3 lbs. of stone, and 4 lbs. of marzachotto.

---

[1] The composition of this substance, which served as a base for the white covering of pottery, is not described. It probably resembled Mastichot or Massicot, which Kunckel (Art de la Verrerie de Neri, Merret, et Kunckel, 2e partie, Livre 2, § première, traduit de l'Allemand par M. D. . . [Baron d'Holback], Paris, 1759, p. 407) says was used for this purpose by the Dutch. It consisted of 100 parts of sand carefully washed and calcined, with 40 parts of soda and 30 parts of potash. For the second preparation

INCIPIUNT DIVERSI COLLORES QUIBUS VASARII UTUNTUR PRO VASORUM PULCRITUDINE

PER ORDINEM DICENDUM. ET PRIMO,

283. *Affare bianco fino de marzachotto.*—Accipe lb. iiij de stagno cocto *i. e.* stagno calcinato et lb. ij de marzachotto et lb. ij de petra et oz. iij de terra gietta et deprovata per dipengiare vase.

284. *Affare biancho el vaso cocto senza dipentura se tu voi che lo dicto vaso sia biancho et necto.*—Habeas lb cento de terra gietta macinata subtilmente cum aqua et cum lb vinti de Jove spolverizato et macina tucto insiemj poi mecte cum aqua liquido et fara biancho.

285. *Affare biancho de vetrio.*—Tolli lb 5 de stagno et lb 3 de petra fucara de la viersa et lb ij de bono vetrio et se lo voi corregiare che sia piu bello tolli una lb meno de la dicta petra.

286. *Affare bianco per mectare azurro.*—Ahvve lb 8 de marzachotto et lb 5 de petra et lb 4 de stagno.

287. *Affare bianco per azurro.*—Piglia lb 5 de vetrio biancho et 3 lib. de petra et 4 lb. de stagno.

288. *Affare bianco per azurro.*—Tolli lb 2 de marzachotto una lb de petra una lb et mezo de stagno.

289. *Affare biancho.*—Havvi lb 6. de stagno lb 3. de petra lb. 4 de marzachotto.

---

of this massicot, 100 parts of massicot were mixed with 10 parts of salt, and the mixture was calcined several times. The Venetian MS. in the Sloane Collection, No. 416, mentions "Mazachoto provenzale" as an ingredient in the preparation for working "with azure upon vessels of yerth."

2 See No. 285, where it is called "pietra fucara (focaja), (*i. e.*, stone which reddens in the fire, silica flint), de la Viersa."

290. *To make white for a thin and flat coat of azure.*—Put in the mortar 4 lbs. of marzachotto, 2 lbs. of stone, and 3 lbs. of tin.

291. *To make white for painting certain colours devised just as you think proper.*—Take 6 lbs. of marzachotto, 9 lbs. of tin, and 3 lbs. of stone.

292. *To make a white for laying a flat tint of azure.*—Take 6 lbs. of calcined tin, 3 lbs. of stone, and 4 lbs. of marzachotto.

293. *To make white.*—Take 6 lbs. of marzachotto, 8 lbs. of stone, 9 lbs. of tin, and it is done.

294. *To make white for azure.*—Take 12 lbs. of marzachotto, and 12 lbs. of stone, and 13 lbs. of tin, and it is done.

295. *To make white for azure in relief.*—Take 20 lbs. of tin, 10 lbs. of marzachotto, and 12 lbs. of stone.

296. *To make white for azure in relief.*—Take 5 lbs. of fine marzachotto, 6 lbs. of tin with lead, and 4 lbs. of stone.

297. *To refine whites that are hard in the fire.*—Take 10 lbs. of calcined tartar and 1 oz. of manganese.

298. *To make the vase yellow.*—Take litharge only, and it will be yellow, and take care that the earth contains no copper, for it would make it greenish.

299. *To make yellow for glazing on the inside.*—Take 6 lbs. of litharge, 2 lbs. of stone of La Viersa, and 2 lbs. of tufo from Civitella.

300. *To make the vase green.*—Take strips of copper, and grind them fine, and you will make a fine green.

301. *To make a green for glazing.*—Take 12 lbs. of litharge, 6 lbs. of stone, and 4 oz. of copper-parings.

302. *To make a deeper green.*—Take 4 lbs. of tin, 2 lbs. of marzachotto, 2 lbs. of stone, and 4 oz. of copper-parings.

303. *To lay on azure with the paintbrush.*—Take 1 lb. of marzachotto, 1 oz. of zaffirro, 3 oz. of stone, and, if it does not melt, add to it one quarter [of an ounce] of Venetian tin.

304. *For the same purpose, to make azure to lay on with the paintbrush.*—Take 10 lbs. of marzachotto, 2 lbs. of stone, 1 lb. of azure, 1 oz. of smalto; and, if it does not melt, add an ounce more of smalto.

290. *Affare bianco per azurro subtili spianato.*—Recipe nella pila lb 4 de marzachotto lb 2 de petra lb 3 de stagno.

291. *Affare biancho per dipengiare certe collore divisati commo te pare.*—Ahvve lb 6 de marzachotto lb 9 de stagno, e lb 3 de petra.

292. *Affare biancho per metare azurro spianato.*—Tolli lb sei de stagno calcinato, lb 3 de petra et lb 4 de marzachotto.

293. *Affare biancho.*—Piglia lb 6 de marzachotto lb 8 de petra et lb nove de stagno fornito.

294. *Affare biancho per azurro.*—Tolli lb xij de marzachotto et lb xij de petra et lb xiij de stagno facto.

295. *Affare biancho per azurro relevato.*—Ahvve lb xx de stagno lb x de marzachotto et lb xij de petra.

296. *Affare biancho per azurro relevato.*—Havve lb 5 de marzachotto fino lb 6 de stagno cum piombo et lb 4 de petra.

297. *Ad affinare i bianchi duri a foco.*—Recipe lb x de taso cocto et oz. j de manghanese.

298. *Affare giallo el vaso.*—Tolli solo la terra gietta liquida et sera zallo et guarda che la terra non tenga de rame che lo farebbe verdegiare.

299. *Affare giallo da vitriare dentro.*—Ahvve lb. 6 de terra gietta et doi lb. de petra de la viersa et doi lb. de tufo de quello de civitella.

300. *Affare verde el vaso.*—Piglia loppe de le rame et macinale subtili et farai verde bello.

301. *Affare verde per invetriare.*—Tolli lb. xij de terra gietta et lb. 6 de petra et lb. j. et j. oz. de ramina.

302. *Affare verde de vantaggio.*—Tolli lb. 4 de stagno lb. 2 de marzachotto lb, 2 de petra e oz. 4 de ramina.

303. *A mectere azurro a penello.*—Ahvve lb. j. de marzachotto oz. j de zaffirro oz. 3 de petra et se non fundesse vi mete uno quarto de stagno venitiano.

304. *Ad idem affare azurro per mectare a penello.*—Havve lb. x de marzachotto lb. doi de petra lb. j de azurro oz. j de smalto et se non fundesse mectivi oz. j piu de smalto.

305. *Azure to use with the paintbrush.*—Take 4 oz. of marzachotto, 1 oz. of stone, and 3 quarters [of an ounce] of azure.

306. *Azure to use with the paintbrush.*—Take 12 oz. of marzachotto, 4 lbs. of stone, 1 lb. of azure, and 1 oz. of smalto, and it is finished.

307. *To make azure in relief after the Florentine fashion.*—Take 12 lbs. of marzachotto, 4 lbs. of stone, 1 oz. of enamel, and 1 lb. of azure.

308. *To make azure.*—Put into the mortar for the white 5 lbs. of calcined tin, 4 lbs. of marzachotto, 3 lbs. of stone.

309. *To lay it on with the paintbrush.*—Take 1 lb. of marzachotto, 1 oz. of azure, 2 or 3 oz. of stone, half an ounce of sal gem.

310. *To make azure in relief to lay on with the paintbrush.*—Take 7 lbs. of marzachotto, 18 oz. of stone, 6 oz. of azure, 3 oz. of blue smalto.

311. *To make violet azure.*—Take 14 lbs. of marzachotto, 2 lbs. of stone, 1 lb. of azure, 1 oz. of manganese; and, if it is not sufficiently purple, add half an ounce more of manganese.

312. *To make a good light blue colour.*—Take 18 oz. of terraghetta, 12 oz. of stone, 1 oz. of fine azure.

313. *To make a fine coat of azure.*—Take 18 oz. of tin, 6 oz. of azure, and 6 oz. of marzachotto.

314. *To calcine tin and lead.*—Take 100 lbs. of lead and 25 lbs. of tin, and put them into a reverberatory furnace.

315. *An earth for mending broken vases.*—Take 2 lbs. of dry [potter's] earth kneaded, and 3 lbs. of ground stone—a tried recipe.

316. *To make a colour for painting vases, such as Damascus vases or Majollica.*—Take 2 oz. of pietra focara, 1 oz. of lead, 2 oz. of "crocus Martis," that is, yellow [hydrate] of iron, and it requires a moderate fire, and 3 oz. of marzachotto well purified.

317. *To make azure to use with a paintbrush.*—Take 12 lbs. of marzachotto, 1 lb. of azure, 2 lbs. of stone, and one quarter [of an ounce] of scarlet enamel.

305. *Azurro per operare a penello.*—Tolli oz. 4 de marzachotto, oz. j. de petra et 3 quarti de azurro.

306. *Azurro da penello.*—Capias lb xij de marzachotto lb 4 de petra lb j. dazurro et una oz. de smalto fornito.

307. *Affare azurro relevato a modo Fiorentino.*—Piglia lb xij de marzachotto lb. 4 de petra oz. j de smalto et una lb de azurro.

308. *Affare azurro.*—Mecti nella pila per lo bianco lb 5 de stagno scharso lb. 4 de marzachotto lb 3 de petra.

309. *Per mectare a penello.*—Avve lb j de marzachotto oz j. dazurro doi o 3 oncia de petra meza oncia de salgemmo.

310. *Affare azurro relevato per mectare a penello.*—Tolli lb 7. de marzachotto oz. 18 de petra oz. 6 de azurro oz. 3 de smalto azurrino.

311. *Affare azurro violato.*—Avve lb 14 de marzachotto lb 2 de petra lb j de de azurro oz. j de Manghanese et se non fusse tanto violato metivi meza oncia piu de manghanese.

312. *Affare colore de azurrino bono.*—Havve 18 once de ghetta once xij de petra oncia j d azurro fino.

313. *Affare azurro subtili spianato.*—Tolli once 18 de stagno oz. 6 de azurro et 6 once de marzachotto.

314. *A cociare i. e. calcinare stagno et piombo.*—Piglia lb C de piombo et lb 25 de stagno et metilo in fornello de reverberatione.

315. *Terra per araconciare vasi rocti.*—Tolli lb 2 de terra seccha lavorata et lb 3 de petra macinata provata.

316. *Affare collore per dipengiare vase commo vase damasco e de mayollica.*—Ahvve once 2 de petra focara once j. de piombo once 2 de crocho de marte i. e. crocho de ferro et vole foco temperato et once 3. de marzachotto bene purgato.

317. *Affare azurro da penello.*—Tolli lb xij de marzachotto lb j de azurro lb doi de petra et uno quarto de smalto vermiglio.

318. *To make a fine yellow for miniatures and other things.*—Put two "Anconitani" of fine silver into a crucible to melt, and heat them in a blast furnace, and, when they are melted, add some well pounded yellow sulphur, and mix all well together. When the sulphur is consumed, add more to it, and continue this until the silver is quite dissolved; then take it out of the crucible, and throw it into an iron trough. When cold, pound it, and grind it upon porphyry; and if it does not grind well, that is, if it is not sufficiently burnt, return it again to the fire in the same manner, and continue this until you can grind it very fine. When the matter has been well ground with clear water, take French ochre, pound it and put it on an iron shovel, and let there be 3 oz. of it, and 6 denarj of common salt calcined; mix, and heat the ochre upon the iron with the salt until it becomes red, and then grind it with the silver upon a brass plate, or upon a smooth brass basin with clear water as fine as possible, and let it dry. When you wish to use it, distemper it with gum water, and use it wherever you like, and you will have a fine yellow for painting and making flowers on black, white, azure, and green, and wherever else you like.

B 319. *To make a water to dissolve pearls.*—Take 2 lbs. of sal-ammoniac, distil it through an alembic, and reduce it to water, and keep it in a well-closed bottle. Put the pearls into this water, and they will be converted into water, &c. This is a water that dissolves pearls, &c.

B 320. *To make pearls just like natural pearls.*—Take pearls and pound them fine, and then put them into the before-mentioned water; then place the vessel containing the water with the pearls dissolved in it on the hot ashes to dry; and when the water is nearly evaporated, and the pearls remain at the bottom of the vase, take it out, and add to it white of egg well beaten as if for vermilion, and knead up the pearls with white of egg like smooth paste. Then take moulds and make the paste into pearls, and let them dry; pierce them, and let them boil in linseed oil. Then take them out and rub them in bran, and

318. *A fare zallo bello per minii o altro.*—Recipe doi anconitani de fino ariento et mectili in uno crugiolo et mettili a fondare et fa fuoco a vento poi commo sonno fusi metice solfaro giallo ben pisto et mista bene insiemj et quando e brusciato el dicto solfaro aragiongivinj piu et cusi fa tanto che el dicto ariento sia bene corupto poi cava la matheria del crugiolo et gietala in canale de ferro et quando e fredda et tu la pista poi la macina in su lo porfido se non se macinasse bene cioe che non fusse tanto brusciato. Iterum lo ritorna al foco in lo dicto modo et tanto fa cosi che tu la possi macinare subtilissimamente poi che è bene macinato la dicta materia cum laqua chiara tollj ocria francese et pistala et polla in su una palecta de ferro e fa che sia tanta che arivj a tre once et sei denaj o vero denaratj o deratj de sale comuno arso et mista insiemj et scalda la dicta terra in suso lo ferro cum lo sale arso per infino a tanto che torne rossa poi la macina cum lo dicto ariento in una piastra de octone o voi in uno bacili piano de octone cum laqua chiara quanto piu subtili poi lassa siucare et quando la voj adoperare distemperalo cum aqua gomata et adoperala dovj te piace et haveraj bello giallo per dipengiare et fiorire in nero bianco azurro et in verde et doi voi altrove.

B 319. *A fare aqua da disolvere perle.*—Recipe sale armoniaco lb doj et distillalo per lambiccum et reduc in aquam et eam serva in ampullam turatam et pone in dicta aqua perlas et convertuntur in aquam etc. hec est aqua disolvens margaritas etc.

B 320. *A fare perle naturale quasi.*—Recipe perle et pistali subtilmente poi le pone in la supradicta aqua a disolverle et pone a zelare la dicta aqua cum le perle solute in le cenere calde et quando laqua e quasi andata via et le perle remangano nel fondo del vaso et tu le cava fora et ponli in albumj dovo ben dibatuta commo per cinabrio et intridi le dicte perle cum la dicta chiara al modo de pasta bene incorporata et habi le forme et fanne perle et lassale scuhare [sciugare?] et falli forare et poi le pone a bollire in olio de seme de lino et poi le toglie et caciale in lo gozo ad uno piaonj per 5 hore et

afterwards in a linen cloth. And if, instead of pearls, you put mother-of-pearl, it is good, and will make good pearls, &c.

Also, the mould for making the pearls must be of fine silver, and gilt, like that for a "Ciara botana,"[1] but small. And many persons have them perforated in order that they may pass a horse-hair through the hole, and that they may be easier to pierce, &c.

B 321. *To make a stucco for making imitation corals.*—Take the white horn of a cow, break it, and soak it in strong ley for the space of a fortnight; then make it boil over the fire until it becomes soft like glue, and so that you can strain it through a cloth or a strainer; and when it is strained, take vermilion in the finest powder, and mix it up with the strained liquid, so as to be like dough, and make paternosters of it in moulds like pearls as before; then boil them in linseed-oil, and let them dry. And if you scrape the horn with a glass, and then soak it in the manner above mentioned, it will soften so that you may strain it more easily, and do with it as before, and you will have fine and beautiful imitation corals.

B. 322. *To make a gold colour for painting earthen vessels previously glazed.*—Take pure silver calcined and burnt with alum, and arsenic and sulphur, three parts of lime, and one part of eggshells; mix the whole together with white of egg and with juice of celandine and distemper it with gum arabic, and with this paint the vases before they are baked.

---

1 The word is frequently used by Benvenuto Cellini, who writes it "ciorbatana." Florio (Dict., Ital. and Eng., London, 1598) defines it to

renchiude lo pianoj in loco che lo possce havere et poi cavali et stropiciali in lo remolo et poi in lo panno de lino. Et in loco de perle anco se ce pone la matre perle e bona et faraj perle belle etc.

Item le forme da fare dicte perle voglino esser dargento fino et dorato ad modo de quello de ciarabotana ma piccolini et anco ce sono multi che le fanno forate acio possino poi mectare una seta de porco per mezo el bucio a cio siano piu facili a forare etc.

B 321. *A fare stucho per fare coralli contrafatti.*—Recipe corno bianco de bo et rompilo et mectj lo a mollo in ranno forte per spatio de xv dj poi lo fa bollire al foco tanto che tornj molle ad modo de colla et per modo che se colara cum panno de lino o stamegna et collato che sera tolli cinabrio subtilissimo et bene macinato de vantagio et incorpora cum detta colatura ad modo de pasta et fannj patrenostrj cum le forme commo le perle de sopra et poi li fa bollire in olio de semj de lino et lassale seccare. Et se tu radesti el corno sopra dicto cum uno vetrio et poi lo mectesti a mollo in lo modo sopradicto et molificarasse in modo che lo colarai piu facilmente et fa commo de sopra et haverai coralli contrafacti et belli etc.

B 322. *A fare collore doro per pegnare vase de terra primo vitriate.*—Recipe argento puro calcinato et abrusciato cum alume de arsenico solphoro parte tre de calcina gusce de ova parte una tucta cum chiara dova mestica cum sugo de celidonia e distempera cum gomarabico et pigne luase innante che se cocano.

---

be "a trunke to shoot pellets with one's mouth. Also a kind of mortar-chamber or short bumbard."

HERE BEGINS THE TITLE OF THE EIGHTH CHAPTER.

ON DYES FOR DYEING CLOTH, SILK, SKINS, AND CHAMOIS LEATHER, AND DIVERS OTHER THINGS. ALSO HOW TO MAKE CHAMOIS LEATHER IN MANY AND VARIOUS WAYS. AND FIRST HOW TO DYE CHAMOIS LEATHER.

323. *To dye kidskins with verzino.*—Take kidskins and wash them and press them well with the hand as much as necessary, and then take 9 oz. of verzino well pounded, and add to it 24 bocali full of plain water, and 1 bottle of water of quick-lime, which lime must be slaked with a little, that is to say, half a glass, of ley made from the ashes of the vine, and when you see the lime begin to smoke, add to it three bocali of lime water, and pour it into the verzino and let it boil until it is reduced one-third; then strain it and spread the skins one upon another. Then take 4 oz. of roche alum, with 4 bocali of water, and dissolve the alum in the water over the fire, and when the water is tepid, apply it lightly on both sides of the skins with a paintbrush gently, giving them one coat only; then set them to dry in the shade, until they are half dry. Next take the said verzino and make it boil for a quarter of an hour, and then remove it from the fire, and take 1 oz. of fenugreek, and 1 oz. of linseed, well pounded together, and put them into the water with the verzino, let the mixture cool so as to become tepid, then give two or three coats on each of the skins, and each time let them dry until they are soft to the hand, but not quite dry, and stretch them on the pummel. And if you wish to have them of a fuller colour, the more coats of dye you give them the darker they will be. Put them to dry in the wind or in the air in a place where they will not be exposed to the sun, and fold and pull them to

INCIPIT DISTINTIO OPCTAVI CAPITULI

DE TINTIS AD TINGENDUM PANNUM SETAM ET PELLEM IN CAMUSSIUM ET MULTA ALIA. ET DE CAMUSIIS FIENDIS PER MULTOS ET DIVERSOS MODOS. ET PRIMO AD TINGEN-GENDUM CAMUSSIUM.

323. *A tegnere caprete in verzino.*—Reccipe li caprete et lavali et premili bene cum le mano tanto che sia bastevile poi tolli once nove de verzino bene pisto et metilo in vintiquattro bocali daqua comuna et j. bocali daqua de calcina viva la quale calcina se vole spengiare cum uno poco de liscia de cenere de vite cioe mezo bichiere de quella liscia et quando lo vede che comenza affumare et tu ce mectj tre bocali daqua de calcina et mecti nel dicto verzino et lassa bulire tanto che manche el terzo poi lo cola et tolli li caprete et stendilj tuctj uno sopra alaltro poi tolli once quattro de alumj de rocho cum quatro bocali daqua et metti lo alumj a disfare in dicta aqua al foco et commo laqua e divinuto tanto che sia tepida et tu ne da de questa aqua ale pelle cum uno penello da tucti doi li late de le pelle una volta ligiermente poi le pone asciugare alombra tanto che se sciugano per mita poi tolli el dicto verzino et fallo bullire per uno quarto de hora poi lo leva dal foco et tolli once j. de fingreco et once j. de semj de lino pisto bene insiemj et metilo in nel aqua del verzino et lassa refredare che vegna tepida pioi ne da ale pelle doi o tre volte per pelle et omne volta le lassa sciugare che siano pastose ala mano et non siano secche in tucto poi le mecte ala storta o ala stroppa. Et se piu le voi pine de collore quanto piu li darai la tinta tanto viranno piu cupi et mectili asciugare al vento o alaiere dove non habiano sole et mectile alla stroppa et falle morbide. Et ancho chi volesse piu pino collore tolli uno torlo dovo et

make them soft. And if you wish the skins to be of a still deeper colour, add for the maestra the yolk of an egg to this solution of verzino and stir them together and the colour will be very fine.

324. *To dye kidskins in scarlet.*—Take kidskins soaked with alum, and wash them well until the alum is washed out of them, and for every dozen of skins take 8 oz. of verzino pounded or rasped with a rasp, and put it over the fire with as much water as you may think sufficient for the skins, but the usual quantity is 3 bocali of water for every ounce of verzino, and let it boil until the verzino becomes nearly black. Then remove it from the fire, and let it settle for a night, and in the morning there will appear a certain scum on the top of it, which you must remove gently, because it would soil the skins. Pour one half of this dye into a basin, and put the skins into the other half to soak one by one, and manipulate them well, that is, stir them about and squeeze them and then put them on a string to dry without wind or sun, and when they are nearly dry, put them back into this dye or water one by one, take them out gently, and do not squeeze them. Then put them to dry as before, and when they are nearly dry, work them about well in your hands, and for the maestra take two ounces of tartar, and put it into a glazed jar, and make it boil until reduced one half, or more, and this is the maestra. Then take that first quantity of dye which you set apart, and add to it a little of the maestra and mix them well together, and try it upon your hand; if you see that it has not enough colour add a little more to it, and take care not to add too much, because it would make the dye too dark. And when the dye is tepid, apply it with a sponge on both sides of the skins and put them dripping as they are, upon a string to dry without wind or sun, because that would make them too hard, and when they are nearly dry, stretch them well with the hand or with a wooden hammer until they are quite soft, and this is the best and most masterly practice for dyeing.

mectilo in questa aqua de verzino et stempera insiemj et mectilo per maestra in nella tinta et viranno beletissime.

324. *A tegnare caprecte in vermiglio.*—Tolli pelle de caprette alumate et lavale bene tanto che nescha lo alumj et per omne dosina de pelle tolli 8 once de verzino pisto o raspato cum raspa et pollo al foco cum quella aqua che te pare che sia bastevile per le pelle ma il consueto e questo che per omne oncia de verzino vole tre bocali daqua et lassalo tanto bolire che el verzino diventi quasi negro ahlora levalo dal fuoco et lascialo posare per una nocte et la matina aparera uno certo panno et quello levalo via legiermente per che faria machiare le pelle poi tollj una catinella et metivj una parte de questa tinta et metila da parte poi tolli laltra mita et metivi dentro a bagnare le pelle a una a una poi le concia bene cum mano cio e remenale et spremile bene cum le mano poi le cava fora et mectile in una corda asciutare alombria senza vento e sole et quando seranno apresso che sciute et tu le rimecte in questa medesima aqua o intinta a una a una commo prima et cavale legiermente et non le torcere et polle a sciugare al modo disopra et quando sonno a presso che sciute et tu le rimena per mano molto bene et per sua maestra tolli doi once de alumj de feecia et metila in una pignata vitriata et fallo tanto bulire che calli per mita o piu poi tolli de questa aqua per sua maestra et poi tolli quella prima in tenta che reserbasti et mistace uno poco de quella aqua de maestra et miscola bene insiemj et fanni el saggio in su le mano se tu vede che non agia asa collore et tu ve ne gionge un poco piu et guarda non ve ne mectissce troppo perche te daria la tinta troppo cupa et quando la tinta sera tepida vienj bagnando le pelle cum una spogna da tucti doi li cante poi le pone cosi sgociolante in su una corda a sciugare senza vento e senza sole perche le faria incrudire troppo et quando sonno a presso che sciutte et tu le stendi bene cum le mano et cum la stroppa tanto che siano bene

325. *To dye sheepskins scarlet, on the side of the flesh, for shoes.*—Take the skins, and wash and wring them, and work them well with three or four waters, and then beat them well with a wooden hammer in order to press out the water, and then take a dyer's horse and spread the skins upon it and scrape them with a knife so as not to cut them, and squeeze them well, and then stretch them out upon a cord, and let them dry a little, and then beat them with the hammer until quite dry, in order that the dye may not penetrate through the skin. And for every dozen of sheepskins take 9 oz. of verzino well ground, and put it on the fire with two metadelle of water for each ounce of verzino, and boil until the water is reduced one half. Then pour it into a glazed earthen vessel, and cover it up so as to confine the vapour, and put back the lees that remain behind, with ten metadelle of water, and make it boil until reduced to less than one half, and then begin to dye the skins with this last water, of which you must give them two coats, and mix up the lees, and after each time let the skins dry, and the third time give them the stroppa and open them well, and when they are well opened, give them a third coat of the first colour, and then give them a second coat of this colour, and when nearly dry, rub them lightly with your hand; and then, for the fourth time, put for each dozen of skins one metadella, and one-third of ley into the dye, for its maestra. Some persons, in order to make the colour deeper and more brilliant, add two yolks of eggs. When they are dry, dye them with the dye into which you put the maestra, and, when again dry, rub them gently, and they will be done.

326. *To dye sheep-skins scarlet on the side of the hair, to make shoes.*—Take the skins well washed and cleansed from lime, and 4 oz. of galls well pounded, and boil them [in water ?] until reduced one-third, and let them become tepid. Put the skins into this water and gall, and wring them well, and then let them remain in the water for a night; then take them out and let

morbide et questa e la migliore pratica et maestra che se facia per tegnare.

325. *A tegnare montone in vermiglio da lo lato de la carne per fare scarpe.*—Avve le pelle et lavale et storcile et rimenale multo bene a tre o a quattro aque poi torcele multo bene ala stroppa acio nesca quella aqua bene poi habbi uno cavalecto et distendile multo bene cum una costa non che taglie et spremile bene poi le stende in una corda et lassale sciugare uno poco poi li da la stroppa o la steccha tante volte che sia bene sciucta acio la tenta non passa la pelle. Et per omne dozina de pelle de montone tolli nove once de virzino bene trito et mectilo al foco cum doi metadelle daqua per oncia de verzino et fallo tanto bolire che advenga per mita poi lo pone in uno vaso de terra vitriato et coprilo bene che non sfiate poi lo cola et rimecte la feccia che rimane al foco cum dece metadelle daqua et fa bullire tanto che mancha piu che la mitta poi comenza a tringiare queste pelle cum questa ultima aqua de fecie et dalinj due mano di questa ultima aqua et rimista le fecie et da una volta et laltra lassale sciutare et la terza volta tu li da la stroppa et aprele bene poi che sonno ben aperte et tu li da el primo collore questa terza volta et daglini doi mane et quando sono apresso che sciutte stropale ligiermente cum mano poi la quarta volta tu vi ni mecte per dozina una metadella et uno terzarulo de ranno in lo collore per sua maestra et alcuno ce mettj per fare piu lustrenti et piu pino el collore doi torlj dova et quando sono scucte et tu le tengne cum questa tanta che hai dato li dentro la maestra et quando sonno sciute et tu le stroppa ligiermente et sonno facte.

326. *A tegnare montonj in vermilglio dal canto del pelo per fare scarpe.*—Abbi le pelle bene lavate et divolte dala calcina poi tollj once quattro de galla bene pista et falla tanto bollire che aventre per terzo poi la lassa devenire tepida et in questa aqua gallata mectj le pelle et storci le bene poi ce le lassa stare per una nocte et poi le tira fora et polle asciutare et quando sonno

them dry, and when they are nearly dry, give them the stroppa, and then take ½ oz. of roche alum to each skin, and make it boil in a vessel with a small quantity of water, and soak the skins in this alum water, and squeeze and wring them so that all the water may run well out. Then take a piece of lime which has not been slaked, put it into a basin, and add to it enough water to cover it by one finger's breadth, and stir it well, so that it may be perfectly dissolved; then let it settle, and when it has settled for one night take off the scum or crust which the lime forms on the top of the water, and then take two bocali of fresh water, and pour them into a pan, and when the water boils put into it 2 oz. of verzino well pounded, and boil it until it is reduced one-half, add to it a little pounded gum arabic, and remove it from the fire, and when it is tepid take away the skins, and sew them up all round so that the side of the flesh may be outside, and leave the neck open, and pour in the dye through the neck, and stir and shake it well 4 or 5 times in the dye, so that the dye may cover the whole of the skin. And if you wish to have a fuller colour, add to it for its maestra as in the last recipe a yolk of egg, well beaten up, adding it a little at a time to the dye until the colour appears full enough. Then pour it into the skin, and shake it all over it, so as to touch every part. When the skins are dry, polish them on a smooth bench with glass, and they are done.

327. *To dye dog-collars and couples a good and fine scarlet.*— Take the skins, wash them well with fresh water, and let them dry; then take 3 oz. of roche alum to each skin, boil the alum [in water], and when it is dissolved and tepid give each skin two or three coats of it. Then take for each skin 3 or 4 lbs. of galls well pounded, boil them a little, and let them cool so that you can bear your hand in the liquor, and then put this water and galls into a bucket, and shake the skin well about in this water, and let it remain in it a day and a night that it may become soft. Then put it to dry, and while it is drying, work it about in your hands that it may become soft. When it is well dried, take 3 oz. of verzino well pounded for each skin, and to

apresso che sciute et tu le stroppa et stecchale poi tollj una oncia dalumj de rocho per pelle et fallo bulire in uno padelecto cum una bocalecta daqua poi mectj le pelle a mollo in questa aqua alumata et spremile et storcile bene siche nesca via quella aqua multo bene. Et poi tollj de la calcina in petra che non sia disciolta et metila in una catinella et metive tanta acqua che sopra avance uno deto et mista bene che se disolva tucta de vantagio poi lassala riposare et commo e bene riposata per una nocte et tu li leva via uno certo solo o panno che la calcina perdura disopra alaqua poi tollj doi bocalj daqua frescha et mectila in uno padelecto et quando bollj et tu ve pone dentro doi onci de verzino ben pisto et fallo bollire tanto che manche la mita de et mectivj uno poco de gommarabico pisto et levalo dal foco et commo e tepido et tu tollj le pelle et coscile de intorno intorno per modo che lo lato de la carne vegna di fora et lassa el collo scoscito et per quello collo scuscito vi mettj la intenta et manegiala et rimenala multo bene de vantagio in qua et in la cum la intenta 4 o 6 volte tanto che la intenta agiungha per tutto la pelle. Et se tu volesci lo collore piu pino metivj per sua maestra la derieta volta uno torlo dovo bene sbatuto et metilo in la dicta intinta a poco a poco tanto che te paia che sia pino poi lo mecte in la pelle et dallj bene de intorno dela et di qua remenando la dicta pelle poi che sonno tente et tu le liscia in uno banco polito cum lo vetrio et sonno facte.

327. *A tengere pelle de sovatto in vermiglio bone et belle.*—Havvj le schinj et lavale bene cum laqua chiara et lassale succare poi tollj once tre de alumj de rocho per cescuna schina et fallo bollire et quando e tepido che sia bene disfacta damnj doi o tre mane per schina poi tolle per omne schina lb j. de galla bene pista et mectila a bollire uno poco et lassala refredare tanto che tu ce posse patere la mano poi mectj questa aqua gallata in una bigoncia et menerai la schina multo bene per quella aqua et lassala stare cusci undi et una nocte che se molla bene poi la pone a sciucare et infinentre che se sciucca et tu le palmegia acio diventano morbide et quando e bene sciuta tolli once tre de verzino per cescuna schina bene pisto et per omne oncia de

each ounce of verzino put two bocali of water, and then add two glasses of solution of tartar, and put it into the verzino when it is boiled, and then add ½ oz. of gum arabic, and put this dye into a glass vessel, as clean as possible. Then take the grounds of the verzino, and add to it 3 glasses of water, and make it boil until reduced one-half, and with this water, boiled on the grounds, begin to dye the skin with a paintbrush or a sponge, and let the dye be tepid, and so put it on as often as necessary, but do not put too much tartar (which is its maestra), that it may not be too highly coloured; and when you dye it, let it dry each time, and when it is dry rub it with your hands, and then with the stick on the side of the flesh to make it soft, and it is done.

328. *To dye scarlet.*—Take ½ lb. of sandal wood and ½ lb. of madder, boil them together with plain water until reduced to one-half, and then add half a fogliecto[1] of ley for its maestra to make the colour deeper, and a piece of quicklime, and boil it until reduced to one-third; then prepare the skins for dyeing as in the other recipes.

329. *To dye very fine scarlet.*—Take 1 lb. of verzino columbino well ground, and soak it in clear water for the space of two days, and then put it into a boiler containing 3 or 4 bocali, to boil until reduced by one-third, add to it 2 oz. of quicklime and 3 oz. of roche alum; and if the colour is pale add 2 oz. of fenugreek; and if you wish to have it of a fuller colour add a fogliecto of boiled ley and it will be of a fine colour.

330. *To dye skins of a very beautiful and good purple colour.*—First take the skin prepared like chamois leather, and dip it two or three times in clear water, and shake it and wring it, and then take 2 oz. of roche alum, and put it into two bocali of plain water, and make it boil, and let it cool. Then take the skin, and dip it in the alum water, and wash and wring it well, and let it dry in the shade. Then take 2 oz. of

[1] A liquid measure used at Florence.

verzino metivj doi bocali daqua et poi ce mectj doi bichiere de aqua de alumj de fecia et polla in lo verzino quando e cocto poi ce mectj meza oncia de gommarabico poi mecti questa tinta in uno vaso de vetrio neto quanto poi poi tolli quello fondaccio de verzino et mectice dentro 3 bichiere daqua et fallo bollire tanto che manche la mitade et cum questa aqua del fondaccio comenza a tegnare in su la schina cum uno penello o vero una spogna et fa che la tenta sia tepida et cusi vi ni da tante volte che sia asai et non cemectare troppo alumj de fecia che e sua maestra acio non havesse troppo collore et quando tu li daraj la tinta lassa sciugare per omne volta et quando e facto et tu la mena cum mano et poi cum la stecca dal canto de la carne che divente borbida (*sic*) e de facto.

328. *A tegnare in vermiglio.*—Tolli meza libra de sandoli et meza lb de robbia et fa bullire insiemj cum aqua comuna per in fino divengha piu che la mita poi ce mectj meza foglieta de ranno da capo per sua maestra et piu pino lo colore mectice una zupa de calcina viva et fa bullire tanto che arentre per tertio poi nutrica le pelle per tegnare commo in le altre recepte.

329. *A tegnare in verzino bellitissimo.*—Abbi libre j de verzino columbino bene trito et metilo a molle in aqua chiara per spatio di doi di poi lo mecte in uno caldaro de 3 o 4 bocali a bullire tanto che calli per terzo poi ce mecti doi once de calcina viva et 3 once de alumj de rocho et se el collore fusse chiaro mectice doi de fino greco et se lo volesti piu pino mectice una foglicto de ranno bollo et sera bono collore.

330. *A tegnare le pelle in colore de pavonazzo bellitissimi et bone.*—Prima tolli la pelle concia in camoscio et bagnala doi o 3 volte in laqua chiara et remenala et storciala poi tollj doi once de alumj de rocho et mectilo in doj bocali daqua comuna et fallj levare el bolore poi la lassa fredare poi tollj la dicta pelle et bagnala in la dicta aqua alumata et lavala et storcila bene poi la pone asciucare alombra poi tollj doi once de verzino bene

verzino, well pounded, and put it into a boiler with three bocali of water, and make it boil until it is reduced by one-third, and take the skin, very dry, and stretch it well, and then take the verzino, which must be tepid, and spread it over the skin with a paintbrush, or with a sponge, and let it dry in the shade, and out of the wind. When it is dry give it two other coats of the verzino, letting it dry between each coat. Then take a lump of quicklime, and put it into a piece of linen, and tie it closely and dip it into what remains of the verzino, and while you are thus wetting it, press out all that you can into the verzino, and then take the skin, and give it another coat, and it will become purple and beautiful. And if you wish to dye more than one skin, take for each skin 2 oz. of alum and 2 oz. of verzino, and as much water as was mentioned above, and make it boil as before.

331. *To dye skins red.*—Take the root of knot grass, otherwise called blood wort,[1] which children put to their nose or tongue to make it bleed; then take one metadella of strong white wine vinegar, and put into it some of this root very well pounded, and make it boil until reduced one half, and then put this dye into a pan, and when it is tepid dye the skins, and give them so many coats that they may have a good colour. And you may reduce this root to powder, because it is then good for dyeing all the year round. When the skins are dry rub them in your hands to make them soft.

332. *To dye kidskins green.*—Take of the grains or berries of the plant or shrub called privet, by some called also "fioria," and by others "oriola," which has a leaf like the laurel, and its leaf grows crosswise upon the bough, and at the end of the bough there grow several berries, black like pepper, which resemble ivy berries, and which are ripe in the month of September. Take 1 oz. of these berries for each skin, and then take several tender twigs of a fig tree, and cut them into little bits, and then distemper the said privet berries with two cups

---

[1] Poligonum Aviculare.

pisto et metilo in uno caldaro cum 3 bocali daqua et fallo tanto bollire che arentre per terzo poi tollj la dita pelle bene sciuta et stendila bene poi tollj el verzino che sia tepido et dallo sopra ala dicta pelle cum uno penello o spogna et metila a sciugare alombra et senza vento poi che e sciuta dallj doi altre mane de lo dicto verzino et sempre da una mano alaltra lassa sciutare. E de poi tollj una zuppa de calcina viva et metila in una peza de panno de lino et lega la bene poi tollj la dicta peza et bagnala in quello verzino che te rimase et commo tu la bagni cusi la vieni spremendo in lo dicto verzino quello che cenuscira poi tolli la pelle et darai li una altra mano et lassa sciugare et sera pavonaza et bella. E se tu volesci tegnare piu che una pelle tolli per omne pelle doi once de alumj et doi once de verzino et tanta aqua quanta fu dicto sopra et fallo tanto bulire.

331. *A tegnare in rosscio la pelle.*—Ahvvi radice de herba spagnola alias dicta Saguinarella che li fanziulli se la mectano al naso o vero alla lingua per fare uscire el sangue poi tollj una mectadella de aceto forte de vino bianco et metivj dentro de questa radice pista bene et fa tanto bullire che manche la mita poi mecti questa tinta in una catinella et quando e tepida vienj tingendo le pelle et dalinj tante mane che habia bona tinta et de questa radice fanne polvere perche e bona tucto lanno per tegnare poi che le pelle sonno sciute menale per le mano acio diventano morbide.

332. *A tengnare caprecte in verde.*—Tolli de quelli grani o acinj che fa questa herba o arbore che se chiama olivella et alcuno la domanda fioria et chi la chiama oriola che fa la folglia commo lorbacho et fa la folglia in cruce in su la rama et in capo ce fa parecchj granj commo pepere nigri et sonno commo acinj o pipere de hellola et sonno mature del mese de setempre colglie de li dicti granelli once j per pelle poi tollj parecchi ramictinj de fico tenere et talglialj in frustri menuti poi distempera cum doi scudelle daqua la dicta olivella et bene sbactuti

of water, and beat it all up well together and let the water boil for a quarter of an hour, and then set it to cool until it becomes tepid, and before you boil it, put into it a glassful of strong vinegar; and when it has become tepid, lay two or three coats of this dye upon the skin, until it is well dyed. And if you wish to have the dye of a deeper colour, add more of the privet berries, and it will be a fine bright green.

333. *To dye skins green.*—Take ripe buckthorn berries and put them into a boiler, and add an equal quantity of vinegar, that is, an equal weight to that of the berries, and let it boil a little, and then strain it through a piece of linen cloth, and pour it into a glazed vase, and when you wish to use it, take the skins, and spread the colour upon them with the paint-brush, and they will become green, and you can keep this colour or dye for a whole year, if kept well closed.

334. *To dye the skins green.*—Take some "pero citrino" when ripe, and extract the juice, and then add some good and strong white wine to that juice, that is to say, for every petitto of juice, two of wine, and boil them together until reduced one half; then take a hare's foot or a paintbrush, or a small sponge, and dip it in the juice and dye the skins once or twice with it, until you consider the colour to be sufficiently deep. It must be dried without sun or wind.

335. *To make a green dye for dyeing cloth, thread, or silk.*—Take roche alum, and dissolve it in a boiler, and let it boil till it is well dissolved; then take it off the fire, and let it cool so that you can bear your hand in it, and then put the cloth, or silk, or thread, into it, and let it remain for a day and a night, and then take it out and let it dry well. Next take a little verdigris and make it boil in the water, and then remove it, and when the water is become tepid, put the cloth into it, and work it well in your hand, and let it dry, and if you give it another wetting with a little roche alum, it will become of a brighter colour. If you wish it to be darker, add more verdigris.

336. *To dye skins blue.*—Take for each skin 1 oz. of indigo,

insiemj et poi pone a bullire dicta aqua per uno quarto dhora poi la pone a fredare tanto che diventj tepida et nante che tu faci bulire metice dentro uno bichiero daceto forte et commo sera divenuta tepida et tu da de questa intinta a le pelle doi o 3 mane tanto che sia ben tento. Et se le voj piu cupi mectivj piu de quelli granellj et vira verde chiaro et bello.

333. *A tegnare pelle in verde.*—Accipe semina spinj cervinj matura et micte in caldario et tamtumdem fortis aceti scil. quantum est pondus semina predictorum et fac ut buliat parum demum cola cum peza alba linj pannj et eum pone in vitriato vase et cum vis operare acipe pellas et da super eas collorem illum cum penello et veniet virides et potes servare dictum collorem sive intintam per totum annum bene clausa.

334. *A tegnare la pelle in verde.*—Tolli del perc citrino quando sonno mature et trannj el sugo poi tollj vino bianco bono et grande et mectilo in quello sugo cioe per omne pectito de sugo doi de vino et fa bullire insiemj tanto che callj per mita de poi tolli uno pe de lepore o uno penello o uno poco de spogna et bagna in quello sugo et tegne le pelle una volta o doi secondo che te pare che habia vivo collore per omne volta vole essere sciuta senza sole e senza vento.

335. *Affare tenta verde da tegnare panno, o refe o seta.*—Recipe alumi de rocho et metilo a strugiare in una caldara et fallo bullire tanto che se distrugia bene poi lo leva dal foco et lassalo refredare tanto che tu vi possci patere la mano poi ce mecti dentro lo panno o sete o refe et lassalo per uno di et una nocte poi lo tira fora et lassalo bene sciucare poi tolli uno poco de verderamo et fallo bullire in la dicta aqua et poi la leva via et quando laqua sera diventata tepida et tu vi mecti lo panno et manegialo bene cum mano et pollo a sciutare et se tu li darai uno altro bagno cum uno poco dalumj de rocho vira cum piu vivo collore et se piu cupo lo volesci mectivi piu verderamo.

336. *A tegnare pelle azurre.*—Summe pro qualibet pelle

and grind it well with strong vinegar, and to each ounce of indigo take one foglietta of vinegar, and dip a paintbrush or a hare's foot into it, and lay it upon the skins, and dry them in the shade. Then give them a second coat, and let them dry, and they will be very beautiful. And if you boil the vinegar a little with the indigo, the skin will be of a much brighter and fuller colour.

337. *To dye the skins black.*—Take the skin prepared with sumach and scrape it on the side of the flesh and rub it well with pumice stone; then take whites of egg, and lay them on the side which you have pumiced, and let it dry. Next take fine black, and lay it with a paintbrush upon the white of egg which you laid upon the skin, and let it dry, and then take the maestra mixed up with oil, and lay it upon the black with a paintbrush, and let it dry in the shade, and then break it with the stecca, and it will be like silk, and its maestra is lime water mixed with common oil.

338. *To make a black dye for dyeing skins, that is to say, fine shoemaker's black, without iron.*—Take a boiler full of the juice of sumach, and add to it some dust from a wheel [or grindstone] and let it boil until reduced by two fingers' breadths in depth; and when it is cool you may dye the skin with this dye, and every hour it will be a finer dye.

339. *To dye kidskins a fine and beautiful black.*—Take the skins, and wash them very well in three or four waters; then squeeze them and wring them well in the stroppa until the water is run well out of them. Then stretch them upon a string to dry, and for every dozen of kidskins take 2 oz. of verzino ground, and boil it until it is reduced to one half, and then take it off the fire, and when it is tepid begin to lay the colour on, and squeeze it well with your hands, and each time let the skin dry a little, and do this 3 or 4 times, and the 4th time put a little very clear lime water into the dye with which you dyed the skins, and this is its maestra, and dye them the fourth time, and when they are nearly dry, give them the stroppa until they are dry. Then take a little oil with a sponge, and

oncia j de indico et eum bene macina cum forti aceto et pro qualibet oncia indici unam foglietam acetj et infunde penellum aut leporis pedem et da super pellas demum sicca eas sine sole deinde desuper alteram vicem dictam tintam et permite sicari et erunt pulcherrime. Et si facies bulire aliquantulum dictum acetum cum dicto indico venient tibi multum magis clare et colloris plene.

337. *A tegnare le pelle in nero.*—Tolli la pelle concia in scotano et radda ben dal canto de la carne poi tolli una pumice et pumiciala bene poi tolli chiare dova et dalli dal canto che tu hai pumiciato et lassa sciugare poi habbi lo nero fino et dallo cum lo penello sopra a la dicta chiara dova che desti sopra ala pelle et polla a sciugare poi habbi la maestra incorporata cum lolio et dalla sopra a lo nero cum lo penello et polla a sciugare alombria poi la rompe ala torta poi la rompe ala stecca et sera morbida commo seta et la sua maestra sci e aqua de calcina viva mista cum oleo comuno.

338. *A fare tenta nera per tegnare pelle cioe tenta da calzolare fina senza ferro.*—Ahvve uno caldaro daqua de scotano frugato e falla tanto bullire che calli quatro deta poi ce mectj de lo lozo de rota et bolla tanto che calli doi deta et quando sera fredda cum questa aqua tu porai tegnare la pelle et omne hora sera piu fina tenta.

339. *A tegnare caprecti in nero fini e belli.*—Tolli le pelle et lavale molto bene a 3 o a 4 aque poi torcele et spremile bene alla stecca o ala stroppa tanto che nesca bene quella acqua poi le stende insuso una corda asciugare et per una dozina de pelle de capretti tollj once doi de verzino trito et fallo bollire tanto che manche per mita poi lo leva dal foco et quando sera tepido et tu li comencia a dare el collore et premili bene cum le mano et da luna volta et laltra lassale uno poco sciugare et cosci fa 3 o 4 volte poi la quarta volta pone in nella tinta che hai tinti li caprette uno poco daqua de calcina viva che sia ben chiara et questa e la sua maestra et tinge la quarta volta et polli a sciugare et quando sonno a presso che sciutte et tu li da la stropa tanto che siano sciucte poi tolli uno poco dolio cum

lay on the kidskins as much of it as they will take, and then give them the stroppa in order that the oil may penetrate well into the skins. When you have done this, roll up each skin into a lump by itself, and let it stand so for a night, and then give them the stroppa again, and spread them out in the shade, and they are done. And know, that the more you soften them with your hand or with the hammer, the softer they will be.

340. *To dye sheep or kidskins a fine and good black.*—Take the kidskin or sheepskin, and wash it and wring it till the water comes off it clear; then take galls well pounded, which you have proved to be strong by trying them in your mouth, and put them into a pipkin, let them boil, and then let them cool so as to become tepid. Then take the skin and gall it well; afterwards wash it with fresh water, and squeeze the water well out. Then take shoemaker's dye, that is, atramentum; steep the skin in it and let it soak for the space of 4 hours; then wash it well, until the water comes off clear and clean. Then take ley and a little oil, and wet the skin with this mixture, and it will become as soft as silk.

341. *A way of preparing skins with the hair on, or without the hair, that is to say, deerskin or wolfskin, or badgerskin, or other skin, or kidskin, or goatskin, or the skin of other animals. And it is a well tried preparation.*—Take skins which have been taken off the animal in proper time, and not from unhealthy beasts, and let them be dried without sun, or let them be a little salted, and put them into a tub of water, and let them remain there for the space of 5 natural days, in order that the flesh may be well macerated, and in the course of these 5 days renew the water 2 or 3 times on account of the unpleasant smell which arises from them. Then take them out, and let them drain, and when they are drained, put one upon the other on the bench for cleaning the skins from flesh, those that are fleshy, I mean, and then strip the flesh from the skins just as you think proper, and so lay one upon another in order that you may not cut them with your knife, and when you have

una spogna et dallo a li caprette quanto ne ponno portare poi li da la stroppa acio lolio penetra bene le pelle facto questo et tu reingoluppa omne pelle da per se commo uno pane et lassa stare cusi per una nocte poi la da la stroppa de novo et distendile alombra et sonno facte et sappi che quanto piu le remorbidiraj cum le mano tanto piu seranno morbidi et cusi cum la stroppa.

340. *A tegnare montone o capretto in nero belli et bonj.*—Piglia la pelle de capretto o de montone et lavala et storcila tanto che nesca laqua chiara poi tolli galla ben pista che tu senti ala bocha che sia forte et metila in uno pignato et lassa bullire poi lassa fredare che divente tepida poi tollj la pelle et gallala bene che ella sia ben gallata poi lavala bene cum laqua frescha et torcila bene che nesca quella aqua poi tolli tenta da calzolare cioe lagrimento et mecti la pelle in la sopradita tenta et lassala mollare per spatio de 4 hore poi la lava multo bene tanto che nesca laqua necta et chiara poi tollj liscia et uno poco dolio et bagna la sopradita pelle et vira morbida ad modo duna seta.

341. *Modo da conciare pelle cum lo pelo et senza pelo cioe pelle de cervo o de lupo o de tasso o de lotrie o de capretti o de capre o daltri animali e de concia probata.*—Recipe pelle scorticate a stagione e non sieno de bestie che habiano insanita et sieno secche senza sole o vero alquanto insalate et metile in una tina daqua et lassale stare li dentro per spatio di 5 di naturali acio lo carnacio sia ben macero et infra questi 5 di renova laqua doi o 3 volte ale dicte pelle pelle per la puza che fanno poi le cava fora et lassale scolare et scolate che sonno pune luna sopra alaltra in el banco da scarnare pele cum carne in tende bene poi excarna le dicte pelle commo te pare et pone cusci luna sopra a laltra acio non te vengano guaste cum lo cortello et scarnate che sonno levale dal banco et lassale scolare bene poi tollj uno barile daqua et falla bulire et in questa aqua pone libre 4 de sale et commo el sale e disfacto bene et tu la lassa refredare tanto che divente tepida et in

stripped the flesh off, remove them from the bench and let them drain well; then take a barrel of water, and make it boil, and put into it 4 lbs. of salt, and when the salt is quite dissolved, let it cool until it becomes tepid, and into this tepid water put half a wheaten loaf, and move it about with your hands until it is well dissolved. Then add to it some flour made from corn (barley flour is best), and put as much as you think sufficient, so that the water may be tolerably thick, and know that the flour must not be bolted or sifted, but must be mixed with the bran just as it comes from the mill. Having done this, and having mixed the tepid water with the meal, put in the skins one by one, stirring them well with your hands without stretching them, and let the flesh be underneath, stretching out one skin nicely over another. Let them remain in this way for the space of 2 days, then take them out and let them drain well for the space of half a day, and in the evening put them back into the water, and let them remain in it 3 days, and stir them well, and at the end of three other days repeat the process, and put the skins back again into the water, and let them remain for the space of 6 days in all, besides the other two days before mentioned; and this is done in order that the hair may adhere more firmly. Then take them out of the preparation and put them to dry in the shade for the space of one night; then arrange them in order, one upon another, upon planks or boards to remove the flesh from them, which you must remove just as you think proper. And when you have done so, scrape them well, and take roche alum in crystals, and not in powder, for it is better, and put for 12 wolfskins, or deerskins, or similar skins 12 lbs. of roche alum, so that each skin may have a pound of alum, and 24 petitti of water, which will make two petitti for each skin, and let the alum dissolve well in the water over the fire, and do not let the alum and water boil. Then put into the water 4 lbs. of salt, and when it is perfectly dissolved, let the water cool until it is tepid; then soak the skins in it, allowing for each hide one petitto of the solution of alum and salt, stirring the skin well with your hands

questa aqua tepida metice mezo pane de formento et menalo bene per le mano tanto che sia ben disfacto poi mecte in la dicta aqua farina de grano ma e meglio dorzo cioe quella farina che te pare bastevile et che laqua dala farina sia uno poco spessa la prima volta sappi che la farina non vole essere staciata ne stamignata ma vole essere con la remola commo ella viene dal molino facto questo essendo laqua tepida cum la dicta farina mectj dentro le dictj pelle ad una ad una et menandole bene cum mano senza extirarle et fa che lo carnaccio sia desocto bene steso luna pelle sopra alaltra et lassale stare in questo modo dentro per spatio de doi dj da poi le tira fora et lassa le bene scolare per spatio de mezo giorno et la sera le remecte in nela dicta aqua et lassacele stare dentro 3 dj et mistale bene et in capo de tre altre di fate purre a questo modo et remetile purre de dentro et lassale stare per spatio de sei di in tucto et questi altre doi di desopra et questo se fa perche el pelo se ferma meglio de poi le tra fora de la dicta concia et polle asciugare alombra per spatio duna nocte poi le pone ordinatamente luna sopra alaltra in tabole o assci da scarnare et poi scarna commo te pare et scarnate che sonno scrullatile bene poi tolli alumj de rocho che sia in peze et non in polvere che e melglio et mecti per xij pelle de lupo o de cervo o similj a queste xij libre dalume de rocho che omne pelle ne venga ad havere una libra e 24 petitti daqua che vengano doi petitti per pelle et lassa ben disfare lo alumj al foco in questa aqua et fa che laqua non bolle cum lo alumj poi ce mecte dentro quatro libre de sale et commo e bene disfacto lassa tanto refredare laqua che advenga tepida poi mecte in comfetione le dicte pelle et per omne pelle li da uno petitto de la dicta aqua cum lo dicto alumj et sale et menandole bene per mano in nella dicta aqua tepida per spatio de uno miserere extirandole et manegiandole ad una ad una bene sucte sopra ne la dicta aqua poi la goluppa et pon le cum la dicta confetione et ponile da parte et cosi fa actuctj lavanzo de le pelle et lavanzo de laqua che te remane o vero confetione gietala sopra ale dicte pelle et fa che le pelle sieno stese in la tina luna sopra alaltra et

in the tepid water for the space of one miserere, stretching and turning them about well one by one in the water. Then roll the skin up, and put it in the composition, and lay it aside; do the same to all the rest of the skins, and pour the remainder of the water or composition upon the skins, and let the skins be stretched out in the tub one upon another and so let them remain for the space of a day and a night, and know that if the skins are small, such as kidskins, two skins require but 1 lb. of alum. Then take them out, and let them drain for the space of half a day, and collect what runs off them, together with the other water that was left from the skins, and set it aside. And then, in order perfectly to clean the skins, take corn flour, (but barley flour is the best,) that has been bolted, that is to say, as much flour as you may think sufficient, and wet it with the alum water which you reserved, and let the flour be mixed up well with the water like paste for making fritters. Then put into this paste 16 eggs, as well the shell as the white and yolk, with a glass of oil, rather less than more, and mix them up well together. Let the water be rather warm before you add these ingredients, and mix the whole well together. Then take the skins one by one, and fold them in the middle, that is, so that the hair may come on the inner side, and not be soiled by the preparation. Then put the skins one by one into the preparation or mixture, which must be tolerably liquid, and let them be thoroughly wetted by the mixture; then pile them one upon another, and if you have any of the mixture remaining, throw it upon the skins. Let them remain for a day and a night, and then take them out, and put them to dry in the sun, or, which is still better, in the shade, and take good care not to stretch them in the least until they are dry; and when they are dry rub them down well upon a sharp piece of wood made expressly for this purpose, in order that the flour may fall off. Then cut off the flesh with a very sharp knife, and scrape them with an osier wand, and afterwards rub them well with the hand, that they may become soft. And know that this preparation is better in April and May, and also in September and October,

lassale stare dentro per spatio duno di et duna nocte et sappi che se sonno pelle picollinj commo e pelle de capretto le doi pelle vogliano una libra de alumj et de poi tirale fora et lassale scolare per spatio de ½ di poi recoglie la dicta scolatura cum questa altra aqua che ce advanzata dele pelle et ripolla da parte. Et poi per affinare perfectamente le dicte pelle tollj farina de grano ma e meglio de orzo che sia afiorata cioe quella farina che te pare che sia bastevile et stemperala cum laqua de lo alumj che reservasti da parte et sia bene misticata la dicta farina cum la dicta aqua ad modo duna pasta da fritelle et poi in questa pasta ce mecte 16 ova cum le coze et cum tucti chiare et vintellj et rompili bene insiemj et metice uno bichiere dolio o manco che piu et mistica bene insiemj poi fa che la dicta aqua sia uno poco calda prima che tu ce mecte le dicte cose et mistica omne cosa bene insiemj poi tolli le dicte pelle aduna aduna et indopiale per mezo cioe che lo pelo venga per de dentro et el carnazo sia de fora et acio che el pelo non se habia troppo ad imbrutarse per la dicta concia et metile in la dicta concia o vero pinta et sia competentemente liquida et mecti dentro le pelle ad una ad una et fa che sieno bene impastate da la dicta pinta et pone luna sopra alaltra et se te avanza de la dicta pinta gietala sopra ale dicte pelle et lassale stare per spatio de uno di et una nocte poi tirale fore et polle asciugare al sole o a lombra che e melglio et guarda bene che non le stirassce per veruno modo per infino che non sonno sciuche et quando seranno sciuche sfregale bene sopra ad una stecha de merollo bene tagliente facto a quello mistiero acio che la farina se ne cagia tucta poi le scarna cum lo cortello bene tagliente et scruttale bene cum una vengastra poi le remena bene cum mano acio che diventano morbide. Et sappi che questa concia e meglio daprile et de magia che in tutto lanno et anco de setembre et de octobre. Et sappi che per le pelle picole commo sonno dagnelli o de volpe se vogliano conciare cum la mestra dele grande cum tucti li modi sopradicti. Et sappi che la concia de pelle senza pelo se vole tenere tucti li modi sopradicti salvo che vogliano essere pellate le dicte pelle in calcina et poi

than all the rest of the year. Know also that the small skins, such as foxskins and lambskins, must be prepared with the maestra for the large skins, with all the before-mentioned operations. And in the preparation of skins without the hair, the above directions must all be observed, except that the hairs must be taken off with lime, and then the preparation must be applied in the same manner as for those with the hair, except that they must be rubbed much more with the hand, to give them a finer surface.

342. *The preparation of a skin.*—Take of roche alum in powder 2 oz., and 2 eggs well beaten, a good handful of flour, as much salt as is sufficient to salt down a pound of flesh, as much oil as would warm a dish of soup, and a large foglietta of warm water. Put into the water, first the alum in fine powder, then the flour, and then the salt, and mix these ingredients; then add the eggs and the oil, and stir the whole together while the water is hot, put in the skin from which the hairs have been removed, and stir and manipulate it well, taking it out, and putting it back into the water; then let it stand for a night or for 4 hours at the least. Take it out without stretching it, and you may then dry it, and beat it well with the hammer; afterwards rub it down on both sides with pumice stone and it is done.

343. *To make chamois-leather.*—Take skins that have had the hair taken off by lime, and wash them well in water; then take warm water, and put into it 5 oz. of roche alum to each skin, and an equal quantity of dough made with wheaten flour, and make a sort of gruel, into which put the skins, and then stir them about for a considerable time with your hands. Let them stand for a night, then take them out and dry them in the shade, and press them.

344. *To make chamois-leather, dressed on both sides.*—Take a round piece of wood, as thick as the thigh, and as long as a man is high, and place it up against the wall as the fellmongers do. And if you wish to prepare a kidskin quickly in one day, take the skin, which must be fresh, and lay it upon this piece of wood, and with the blade of a knife take off the hair and the

li da la concia ordinatamente commo quelle dal pelo ma vogliano essere piu remenate assa cum mano perche levano piu bella grana.

342. *Concia per una pelle.*—Havve alume de rocho in polvere once 2, doi ova bene dibatutj poi tollj uno bono pugno de farina cio e el fiore et tanto sale quanto bastasse per insalare una libra de carne et tanto olio quanto condisse una menestra et una bona fogliecta daqua calda et mecti in la dicta aqua prima lo alumj bene subtili poi la farina et poi el sale et miscola bene poi mectice li ova et lolio et mista bene et quando laqua e calda mecti dentro la pelle depilata et manegiala bene et strocila bene traendola et remitendola in la dicta aqua calda poi premila et remenela in la dicta aqua calda poi lassala stare per una nocte o 4 hore almancho poi la tra fora senza astirarla et polla asciugare et remenala bene a la stroppa poi la pumicia da luno lato et laltro e de facto.

343. *Ad camussium faciendum.*—Summe pellas depilatas in calce et sint bene lotas in aqua demum habeas calidam aquam et in ea pone pro qualibet pelle oncias 5 aluminis rochi et tantumdem de pasta levata cum farina de frumento et fac ut farinatam et intromicte pellas et dehinc inde diu manibus misce et permicte per unam noctem deinde exthrae et sicha ad humbriam et remena ad torquam.

344. *A fare camoscio cum nervo o senza nervo cioe scamosciato da omne parte.*—Tolli uno lingno retondo et grosso quanto la cossa et longo quanto lhomo et al muro appoggialo commo fanno li conciatore de corrame. Et se volesci fare una pelle de capretto subtitamente in uno dj tollj la pelle che sia fresccha et polla insuso questo ligno et cum una costa de cortello per

scarf-skin. And if it is a large skin, let it remain in lime as the fellmongers do when they wish to make leather of it, and then rest it upon the before-mentioned beam, and with the knife-blade take off the sinews, and wash the lime well off. Then take 3 fogliette of water, into which put ½ oz. of roche alum and half a handful of common salt, set the water over the fire in order to dissolve these ingredients. Then add a little oil, and remove it away from the fire; and while the water is tepid, add to it an egg well beaten up, and mix it well in the water; then dip the skin into it 3 or 4 times, and each time let it dry a little, and the last time let it dry well, and then beat it with the wooden hammer.

345. *To make chamois-leather without fat.*—Take milk, fine flour, and oil washed with ley, that the skins may not be soiled, mix the whole together with hot water, and put the skins into this water for three days; then turn them over on to the other side for 3 days more; afterwards let them dry, and do not stretch them. When they are dry beat them with the hammer.

346. *To make good chamois-leather.*—Take for each skin 3 oz. of flour, one tumbler of milk, 1 oz. of butter, and a little wheaten bread, and wet the whole well together with a little ley, in order that the ingredients may be well incorporated; and if it is not sufficiently wet, add to it nothing but clear ley, and let it remain for 5 natural days, and then put it to dry, and beat it with the hammer.

347. *To make chamois-leather quickly.*—Take 1 oz. of white soap and distemper it with ley, and then put the skins into the ley for the space of 4 days; then dry them, and stretch them on a stick, and they will be white and soft.

348. *To make chamois-leather as white and soft as silk.*—Melt pork-fat in a pipkin, and then take warm water, and wet up flour with it, and add to it the pork-fat, and mix all well together; then take another pan, and spread out the skins in it, and take a bocale of milk, and pour it upon the skins, and then put in the above-mentioned preparation, and let the skins

forza de braccio li leva via el pelo et lo nervo. Et se fusse una pelle grande falla stare in calcina commo fanno li conciatore quando le voglano conciare per corame et poi lapoggia al dicto ligno et per forza de la costa li leva lo nervo poi la lava bene da la calcina poi tollj 3 fogliecte daqua et in la dicta aqua ce pone una oncia e meza dalume de rocho et mezo pugno de sale comuno et mecti laqua al foco che se disfaccia le dicte cose et poi ce pone uno poco dolio et levalo dal foco et quando e tepida laqua et tu ce pone uno ovo bene dibatuto bene et mistalo bene in la dicta aqua poi ce mectj la pelle 4 o 5 volte et da una volta a laltra lassala uno poco sciugare et lultima volta lassala bene sciugare poi la mecte alo lavello o ala stroppa e de facto.

345. *A fare camosscio senza grasso.*—Ahvve lacte fior de farina et olio lavato cum ranno da capo acio le pelle non vengano machiate et mista omne cosa insiemj cum aqua calda et mecte le pelle in la dicta aqua per 3 dj poi le revolge da laltro lato per 3 altre dj poi le pone asciugare et non le stirare et quando sonno sciuche et tu li da la stecha et stroppa.

346. *A fare camoscio bono.*—Piglia per cescuna pelle once 3 de fiore de farina et uno bichiero de lacte et una oncia de butiro et uno poco de pane de formento et distempera omne cosa insiemj cum uno poco de ranno da capo molto bene acio che le dicte cose se incorporano insiemj et se fusse poca concia non ce agiongiare se non de lo ranno chiaro et lassa stare per 5 di naturali poi lo pone a sciutare et dallj la stroppa.

347. *A fare camoscio brevimente.*—Recipe oncia j. de sapone bianco et stemperalo cum lo ranno poi mecte le pelle in lo dicto ranno per spatio di quattro dj et poi le pone a sciutare poi le stira ala stecca et seranno bianche et morbide.

348. *A fare camoscio che sia bianco et morbido commo una seta.*—Tolli grasscia de porco et strugila in uno pignatto poi tolli aqua calda et distemperala cum farina poi ce mectj la dicta grasscia et mista bene insiemj poi tolli uno altro vaso et stendice le pelle poi tollj uno bocale de lacte et mectj sopra ale dicte pelle poi mecti la dicta concia et fa che le pelle sieno

be well covered by it, and let them remain there for 5 days, and they will be white and soft.

349. *To make chamois-leather which will always remain soft.* —Take milk, barley meal, and oil, washed with ley to soften the skins, and mix it all together with warm water; then dip the skins in the mixture several times, and let them nearly dry each time. Afterwards leave them to dry in the shade, and beat them with the hammer.

350. *To make chamois-leather water-proof.*—Take for each skin 4 eggs, and a good quantity, that is, a good glassful of milk for each skin, and a little oil; beat it all up well together, then let the skins soak in the mixture for 7 days, and turn them over once a day. Let them dry, and beat them with the hammer.

351. *To make chamois-leather.*—Take the skins and soak them in water for 5 or 6 days, and then in warm water for one night; then remove them from the water, and take off the hair with a horse's rib, and sprinkle them well with clear water and let them drain a little. Next take roche alum in fine powder, and 2 eggs to each skin, and flour well bolted, with a little wheat, and mix all these ingredients well with hot water, like paste for fritters, and then put the skins into the mixture for 3 days. Then take them out, and let them nearly dry; then mix some brass well with warm water, into which put the skins for 3 days more. Then dry them well without stretching them, and beat them with the hammer, and they are done.

352. *To make chamois-leather from parchment.*—Take parchment and anoint it with olive oil, and rub it well with your hands, and afterwards mix soap with warm caustic ley, and dip the parchment in it, and rub it well in your hands until it is finished, and then press it.

353. *To make chamois-leather from parchment.*—Take the parchment and soak it in water for 3 natural days, then take it out and let it half dry, and do not stretch it at all. Then soak it in a pan of warm water, with a handful of bran in it, mix all well together, and let the mixture stand so for 2 days;

bene coperte da la concia et lassa stare per 5 di et seranno bianche et morbide.

349. *A fare camoscio che arestia morbido sempre maij.*—Ahvve lacte farina dorzo olio lavato cum lo ranno acio le pelle pigliano la morbideza et mista omne cosa insiemj cum aqua tepida poi ce pone le pelle piu volte et lassandole apresso che sciucare da una volta a laltra poi le pone asciutare alombra et dallj la stroppa.

350. *A fare camoscio che arestia alaqua.*—Tolli 4 ova per pelle et lacte assa cioe uno bono bichier per pelle et uno poco dolio molto bene menato insiemj et poi ce mectj le pelle a molle per spatio de 7 di et omne di le remena subtusopra una volta et polle a seccare et dalli la steccha.

351. *A scamosciare le pelle.*—Havve le pelle et mettile a mollo in laqua per 5 o 6 dj poi le pone a molle in laqua tepida per una nocte poi le leva via dala dicta aqua et levalj via el pelo per forza duna costa de cavallo poi le sciaqua cum aqua chiara multo bene et poi le pone a scollare uno poco poi tollj alumj de rocho et sia bene subtile et doi ova per pelle et farina bene stacciata cum uno poco de formento et mista bene insiemj cum aqua calda ad modo de pasta da fritellj et poi ce mecte le dicte pelle per spatio de 3 di poi le tira fora et lassale quasi sciutare poi tolli remola et mistala cum aqua calda bene poi ce pone le dicte pelle per 3 altri di poi le sciuta bene senza astirarli et dalli la steccha e de facta.

352. *Ad camussium de carta caprina faciendum.*—Accipe cartam pecudis et eam unge oleo comuni et duc cartam inter manus fortiter postea distempera saponem cum liscivo capitis tepido et intromicte dictam cartam et multum duc manibus quousque perficitur et etiam duc ad torquam sive steccam.

353. *Affare camoscio de carta pecorina.*—Havve la carta et mettila a molle nellaqua per 3 di naturali poi tirala fora et lassala quasi sciugare per mita et non la stirare de niente poi la pone a molle nellaqua tepida in uno vaso et mistace cum quella aqua tepida una pugnata de remola et mista bene omne

then take it out and wash it in 2 or 6 waters, or until it is washed enough, and squeeze it well. Then take a vase, and fill it more than half full with water, and add to it as much alum as you think necessary, according to the quantity you wish to make, and one or two eggs beaten up; and do it all in order: first putting the water into a pipkin, and heating it over the fire; then adding the alum, and when the alum is dissolved let it cool until it is tepid, and then put it into a clean shell, adding to it a little wheat flour and an egg or two, and mix the alum-water well with the other ingredients; then put the said parchment into it, and stir it well in the liquor. Then let it remain for 3 days, and let the said parchment be well covered with the preparation, and keep it free from dust or other dirt. Then take out the parchment and squeeze it well, and repeat the process; then put it to dry in the shade, but do not stretch it at all, and then beat it with the hammer, and it is done.

354. *To make chamois leather with sheep or kidskin parchment that has been written on.*—Take the parchment that has been written on, and soak it in a pan of water, so as to be well covered. Next take a piece or two of quicklime, according to the quantity of the parchment, and put it into the water and let it dissolve and remain in it one natural day, and then rub it well with the water, using your hand for this purpose, or rub down the written side with a piece of hard quicklime, and when the letters have disappeared put them into the liquor previously directed for preparing parchment that has not been written on.

355. *To make excellent chamois leather.*—Take the skin from which the flesh has been stripped inside and outside, and then daub it all over with flour and water mixed like paste for wafers, and let it remain some days, that is, for three days or more; then wash it well, and put it into a pan; then take a new glazed pipkin, fill it with water, and put it over the fire, that is, put for each skin one metadella of water, and one ounce and a-half of roche alum. Let the alum dissolve in the pipkin, then put an equal quantity of common salt, and when they are well dis-

cosa insiemj et lassa cusci stare per doi dj poi la tira fora et lavala a doi o 6 aque o tanto che sia ben lavata et spremuta poi tollj uno vaso et fallo piu che mezo daqua poi ce pone tanto alumj quanto tu credi che sia bastevile secondo la quantita che tu voli fare et uno ovo o doi dibatuto e falla ordinatamente in prima mecte laqua in una pignatta et falla scaldare al foco poi mete dentro lo alumj et quando lo alumj sera disfatto bene et tu la lassa tanto fredare che sia tepida poi la mecte in una concha necta poi li mecte uno poco de formento di smolglio et uno ovo o doi et mista bene la dicta aqua alumata cum le dicte cose poi ce mecte dentro la carta sopradicta et remenala bene in la dicta decotione et poi lassa stare per 3 dj et fache la dicta carta stia ben coperta da la dicta concia et stia in loco che non vi vada polvere ne altra brutura poi cava fora la dicta carta et spremila bene poi factj da capo et remenala bene intra le mano et poi la pone a sciutare alombra et non la stirare per viruno canto et poi li da la stecca e fatta.

354. *Affare camosscio de carte pecorine scripte o de carte de capretti scripte.*—Tolli le carte scripte et metile a molle in acqua in uno vaso tanto che siano bene coperte poi tollj una petra de calcina viva o doi secondo la quantita dele carte et metila in la dicta aqua et lassala bene sciogliare et stare uno di naturali poi le sfrega cum la dicta aqua et cum mano o vero tu le sfrega cum calcina soda disopra ala scriptura et poi che sonno andate via le letere meteraile nella concia commo e dicto disopra de la carta caprina non scripta.

355. *A fare camoscio bonissimo.*—Pilglia la pelle bene scarnata dentro et de fora et poi la creta tucta de farina cum aqua ad modo de pasta da fare cialde et lassala stare alcunj dj cioe per di 3 o piu poi la lava bene et mectila in una concha poi habbj una pignata nova vitriata et impila daqua et polla al foco cioe mecti uno mezo daqua per pelle et mectj una oncia et meza dalumj de rocho per pelle poi mectj lo dicto alumj a disfare in la dicta pignatta et poi ce pone altratanto sale comuno et commo sonno bene disfacti et tu leva dal foco la dicta pignata et mecti

solved remove the pipkin from the fire, and pour the water in which the alum and salt were dissolved into a pan, and when it is just tepid add for each skin 3 or 4 eggs well beaten. Mix them well with the water, to which add a little flour well beaten with the other ingredients, and a little oil, less than the fourth part of a foglietta to each skin, and mix all well together; then put the skin into the liquor and stir them well in the preparation; let them remain in it covered closely for 3 days. Then take out the skins, and squeeze them well one by one, and then rub them in your hands one at a time in order, and put them to dry sheltered from sun, wind, or smoke; then beat them with the hammer.

356. *To make a preparation for chamois leather, good, and true, and tried.*[1]—Take dry skins well seasoned and from healthy beasts, and put them into a tank of water to soak for 3 days, and then wash them well in the tank from all dirt that may hang about them, and when they are well washed throw away the water. Then take fresh quicklime, and put it into the tank, and mix it well with water, and when the quicklime is well slaked and dissolved so that it is very thin and liquid, put the skins into it one by one, continually stirring the lime water, and let them remain in soak for three or four days, more or less, according to the state of the skins, and until the hair comes well off. Once every other day, or every day at the most, take them out of the lime water, and hang them over the tank for an hour to drain; then put them back into the tank, and when the hair comes well off, lay them to drain well in a trough for two hours. Then take a beam supported on two feet, and lay the skins upon it in order, one upon another, and then take a crooked stick of the shape of a horse's rib, and scrape the hair with the stick from each skin, and when the hair is all stripped off, put them back to soak in the tank containing the lime and water for 16 or 20 days, and every other day stir them about well in the lime water; after 16 or 20 days take them out, and carry them to a running

[1] This recipe is distinguished in the original by a hand drawn in the margin.

laqua alumata et salata in una concha et commo la dicta aqua e divinuta tepida et tu ce mectj 3. o 4 ova per pelle bene dibatutj et mistalj bene cum la dicta aqua et poi li mecte uno poco di formento disfacto bene cum la dicta aqua et mective uno poco dolio cioe manco che el quarto duna foglietta per pelle et mistica bene omne cosa insiemj poi ce pone le pelle et menale bene per la dicta concia et lassa stare per 3 dj le dicte pelle bene coperte dala dicta concia et passati i tre dj cava fora le dicte pelle et spremilj bene ad una ad una poi le remena per mano ad una ad una ordinatamente poi le pone a sciutare in loco che non habia ne sole ne vento ne fume et ponele ala stroppa o stecca.

☞ 356. *A fare concia in camoscio bona et vera et probata.*—Tolli le pelle stagionate et non sieno de bestie insane et sieno le pelle seche et metilj in uno mastello daqua a molle per tre dj poi le lava molto bene in lo dicto mastello da omne immunditia che le pelle havessaro et commo sonno bene lavate gietta via quella lavatura poi tollj calcina nova et viva pollo in lo dicto mastello et distempera la dicta calcina cum aqua molto bene et commo la calcina e ben disfatta et disolta et che ella sia ben brodosa et liquida et tu ce pone dentro le dicte pelle ad una ad una sempre remenando la dicta aqua et calcina et lassale stare a molle li dentro per 3 di o 4 o piu o meno secundo le pelle et per infino a tanto che se pelano bene. Et omne di o vero omne doi di al piu le cava fora una volta da la dicta aqua et calcina et polle sopra alo dicto mastello per una hora a scolare poi le ritorna dentro in lo mastello commo prima et commo se pelano bene et tu le pone a scolare in una caviglia molto bene per doi hore poi habbi uno cavallecto da doi pei et mettice suso le dicte pelle ordinatamente luna sopra laltra poi tollj una bastone retratto in forma duna costa de cavallo et mandato giuso el pelo cum lo dicto bastone molto bene a pelle per pelle poi che sonno ben pellate remectile a molle in lo dicto mastello dove te rimase la dicta aqua et calcina per spatio de 16 o 20 di et omne capo

stream, and wash them and squeeze them well, to remove the lime from them. And when they are well washed and clean, throw away the lime and water from the tank, wash it very clean, and pour into it as much lime water as you think will just soak the skins, and then put into it sufficient bran to make the warm water pretty thick. Put the skins, when well washed, one by one into the bran and water, and let them remain so for 3 days; then take them out and wash them in a running stream to remove the bran, and afterwards carry the skins well washed to a ladder or a trough, and then take the skins one by one and wring and squeeze them well so that there may not remain any water in them, and the better they are squeezed and pressed the whiter they will become. And if in pressing the skins any bladders should form, prick them with a needle in order that the water may drain out; and when the skins have well drained, and have been all squeezed separately, smooth the skins one at a time by pressing the hand all over them, and lay them one upon another well stretched at the neck, at the shoulders, and all over the skin, and then make the tank very clean, and put into it as much tepid water as you think the skins will well bear, and rather more than less. Then take an ounce of roche alum well pounded, and an equal quantity by weight and not by measure of pounded salt, and ½ oz. of gum arabic well pounded; put the powders into the tank with the tepid water, and mix them well in order to dissolve them; then take the skins one by one well stretched out, and dip them into the water in which the powders are dissolved, pressing them and dipping them, and stirring them well, that they may soak up more of the alum water, and do this to each skin separately, and when the skins are well stirred and soaked put them to drain for an hour, and let the drippings fall into the water in which the skins were dipped. Then take as much flour as you think sufficient for the skins, and wet the flour with the drippings of the skins which you reserved, and distemper it so that it may be like paste for making fritters. Add to the paste an ounce of oil, or one egg for each skin, and know that when you mix

de doi di le remena molto bene in la dicta aqua calcinata de poi 16 o 20 dj et tu le cava fora et portale alaqua corrente et lavale et spremile molto bene acio la calcina escha fora. Et commo sonno bene lavate et nectj tolli lo dicto mastello et gietta via quella aqua et calcina et lavalo per modo che sia bene necto et mectice tanta aqua tepida chiara quanto tu crede che le pelle possano ben stare a molle poi ce pone dentro tanto de remola grossa che la dicta aqua tepida vengna uno poco spessa poi tollj le dicte pelle ben lavate et metile dentro in la dicta aqua remolata ad una ad una et cosi le lassa stare per 3 di poi le cava fora et lavale molto bene alaqua corrente acio tucta la remola vada via poi porta le pelle bene lavate ad una scala o vero ad una caviglia poi tollj le dicte pelle ad una ad una et dallj lo torcholo et premile bene che non ce rimagna niente daqua et quanto seranno meglio spremute et atorcholate tanto piu bianche viranno. Et se in lo torcolare le pelle facessaro alcune vesiche apuntale et forale cum uno acho acio la pelle se possa bene scolare dalaqua et commo le pelle sonno bene scolate ad una ad una et bene spremute de vantagio stendile cum le mano per tuta la pelle ad una ad una et pone luna pelle sopra laltra ben distesa al collo a le branche et per tucta la pelle poi tollj lo dicto mastello bene necto cum tanta aqua tepida quanto tu poi comprehndare che le dicte pelle possano bene ricevare et innanze piu aqua che meno poi tollj una oncia dalumj de rocho bene pisto cum altretanto de sale pisto a misura et non a peso et meza oncia de gomarabica bene pista poi pone le dicte polvere in lo dicto mastello dove e la dicta aqua tepida et remistale bene acio se disolvano poi tollj le dicte pelle ad una ad una bene stese et metile in la dicta aqua tepida dove sonno disolute le dicte polvere spremendole et reimbeverandole et remenandole bene acio pigliano meglio quella aqua alumata et cusci fa a pelle per pelle et commo le pelle sonno ben remenate et et imbeverate et tu le pone a scolare per una hora et ricoglie la scolatura sopra alaltra aqua che te remase de le pelle poi tollj farina afiorata tanta quanta te pare bastevilj ale pelle et distempera la dicta farina cum la dicta scolatura dele pelle che reservasti et dis-

the flour, the drainings must be tepid and not hot. Mix them well together, then take the skins one by one and put them into the paste or composition, and let them remain for three natural days at the most; then take the skins just as they come, without stretching them at all, and put them to dry upon a string in the shade, and as they dry you must stretch them, and then beat them with the hammer, and rub them well with your hand that they may have a finer surface, and the work is done. And know that each kidskin, and skin of the same size, requires the alum and the other things of the weight above given. And if the skins are those of sheep, or goats, or such like, they require 3 oz. of alum and 3 oz. of oil, or 3 eggs and 1½ oz. of gum arabic for each skin. Follow the recipe as above directed.

357. *To dye silk or cloth red.*—Take 1 lb. of silk, and 4 oz. of soap, and put them into a cauldron with water, and let it boil until you see the silk appear starred. Then take it out, and wash it well in clear water until the silk becomes white; drain it well, and wring it with your hands, and then spread it out, and this is done when the silk is not boiled. Then take 4 oz. of alum in another small vase and boil it, and dissolve it in clear water, and when it is dissolved take another larger vase, and fill it with fresh water, and put the alum into it, and then put in the silk, and let it remain 3 days and 3 nights, and then wash it and stir it about well in fresh water, wringing it well with your hand until the alum is washed out. Then take a kettle of fresh water, and 3 oz. of powdered verzino, and let it boil until reduced one third; then fill it up with fresh water, and boil it again till reduced one finger's breadth. Then take it off the fire and divide the water into two portions, and into one of these put the silk and let it stand till it is cold. Then wring it with your hand, and put it back into the other water which you reserved, and let it be as hot as you can bear

temperala per modo che sia commo pasta da fare fritelli poi pone in la dicta pasta una oncia dolio per pelle o vero uno ovo per pelle et sappi che quando tu distempere la dicta farina la scolatura vole essere tepida et non calda et mistica bene insiemj poi tolli le dicte pelle ad una ad una et metile in la dicta pasta o compositione et lassale stare per 3 di naturalj al piu poi tolli le pelle commo le venghano senze extirarle de niente et polle in su una corda a secare alombra et commo se venghano secando cusci le vienj stirando poi le pone ala steccha et remenale bene per mano acio levano piu bella grana et diventano piu morbide e de facto.

Et sappi che omne pelle de capretto o similj a quelle vogliano lo alumj et laltre cose al peso dicto de sopra. Et se fussaro pelle de castrone o capre o altre simili vogliano 3 once de alumj per pelle et cusci 3 once dolio o vero 3 ove per pelle et una oncia et ½ de gomarabica et seguita la recepta alo sopradicto modo.

357. *A tengnare sirico o drappo rosscio.*—Tolli una libra de sirico et 4 once de sapone et mectilo in uno caldaro cum aqua et bolla per infino che vede aparere lo sirico ad modo de stelluccie da poi trallo fora et lavalo ben in aqua chiara per infino che lo sirico sera facto bianco et scolalo bene et torcilo cum mano dapoi lo stende. Et questo se fa quando lo sirico non e cocto. Ma poi tolli oz. 4 dalumj in uno altro vaso picolo cum la bolitione et strugilo in aqua chiara commo e structo tollj uno altro vaso magiore et impilo de aqua chiara et mectj dentro lo dicto alumj et poi ce pone lo dicto sirico et stia li dentro tre di et tre notte poi lo lava et rimenalo bene in aqua chiara torcendolo bene cum mano tanto che quello alumj escha fora poi tollj uno caldaro cum aqua chiara et tolli 3 once de verzino trito et fallo bollire tanto che arentra per terzo poi reimpe lo dicto vaso daqua chiara et bolla de novo tanto che calli uno deto poi levalo dal foco et parte per mezo la dicta aqua de verzino et in una de queste parte ce pone lo dicto sirico et lassa stare per infino che se refreddj de poi lo torce cum mano poi lo repone in laltra aqua che reservasti et sia tanto calda che tu ce possce

your hand in it. Then drain it and wring it well, and spread it out in the sun and it will be fine.

358. *To dye silk or thread saffron coloured or yellow.*—Take 1 lb. of silk and 4 oz. of soap, and boil it until it gives the before mentioned sign of little stars, and then distemper it with 4 oz. of alum as before and put the silk into it, and let it remain in soak for 1 natural day. Then draw it out, and do not let it be stirred or washed in the water, but take it out and dry it in the sun so as not to crease it. Then take 2 lbs. of "herba roccia," called also "panicella," and put it to boil in a cauldron until it is well boiled and prepared, and then take a vase, and put fresh water into it, and an equal quantity of the decoction of this herb, and let both these waters be so hot that you can but just bear your hand in them. Then put in the silk and let it soak for 3 or 4 hours; then wring and put it back two or three times into the decoction, which must be tolerably hot, and without any other mixture, and then spread it out to dry.

359. *To dye silk or thread purple.*—Take 4 oz. of soap and boil [the silk] as before directed, until it appears starred, and let it be washed in clear water, and then be spread out; then take a vase with clear water, and put into it 2 lbs. of oricello to every pound of silk, if the oricello is good; if the oricello is not very good, put 3 lbs of it into a cauldron for 2 hours, and let the fire be moderate; then let it cool, and wring it well, and put it into a very clean woollen cloth and squeeze it well, and let it remain so for 3 days, and then wash it well in clear water, wring it, and then stretch it out in the shade, and when it is dry roll it up in a white linen cloth tolerably tight.

360. *To dye silk or thread violet.*—Take 2 or 3 lbs. of oricello, and divide it into two portions, and put one part of it into water to boil with the silk, and let it boil for an hour; then draw out the silk and stretch it out, and fold it up; afterwards put the other half of the oricello to boil together with the former portion until there remains but a very little water.

patere la mano poi lo scola et torcilo bene et stendilo al sole et sera bello.

358. *A tegnare sirico croceo o vero giallo o refe.*—Havve una libra de sirico cum 4 once de sapone et bolla tanto che facia lo sopradicto signale de stellucie dapoi distemperalo cum 4 once dalumj commo e dicto desopra et mectj dentro lo sirico et stia a molle per uno dj naturali poi tiralo fora et non sia remenato nella dicta aqua ne lavato ma sia tracto fora et steso al sole per modo che non se intriche poi tolli doi libre de herba roccia cio e panicella et metila a bullire in caldaro per infino che sia ben cotta et confectata poi tollj uno vaso et metice aqua chiara et altretanta aqua de la cocitura de la dicta herba cotta et tucti doi quelle aque siano ben calde che tu ce possce patere la mano poi mectj dentro lo sirico et stia a molle per 3 o 4 hore poi lo torce poi doi o 3 altre vole mectj lo sirico a molle in la dicta aqua cotta et sia ben calda senza altra mistura poi lo stende a sciutare.

359. *A tegnare sirico pavonazzo o refe.*—Ahvve once 4. de sapone et cocilo commo e di sopra dicto che apare certe stelluccie et sia lavato in aqua chiara et poi sia steso poi tollj uno vaso cum aqua chiara et mectice doi libre de rogello per una libra de sirico se lo rogello e buono se non fusse troppo bono meticene 3 libre et fa bene bollire cum lo sirico in uno caldaro per doi hore et sia lo foco temperato et poi lo pone a fredare et poi torcilo bene et metilo in uno panno de lana bene necto et stringilo bene et cusci lo lassa stare per 3 dj poi lo lava bene in aqua chiara et torcilo bene et poi lo stende alombra et commo e sciutto metilo in uno panno de lino bianco ordinatamente strecto.

360. *A tegnare sirico violato o refe.*—Tolli doi o 3 libre de rogello et partilo per mita et una parte sia messo in aqua a bullire cum lo sirico et bolla per una hora poi tira fora lo sirico et sia steso et revoltato dapoi sia messo laltra mita de rogello a bollire insiemj cum lo sopradicto per infino che aremanga uno poco daqua poi levalo dal foco et stia lo sirico in quella

Then take it away from the fire, and let the silk remain in that water to cool for one natural day. Then wring it and wash it with clear water and let it dry in the shade, and then put it into a linen cloth rolled up tolerably tight as before.

361. *To dye silk and thread black.*—Take ½ lb. of galls well crushed, and boil them in a cauldron with water, until they are well boiled, and then put in the silk to boil in the decoction of galls for half an hour. Then take it out and let it dry in the sun or in the wind, and then take 3 pitchers of shoemaker's blacking, and 1 pitcher of the decoction of galls, and two petitti of dust from a grindstone, and mix the whole together and make it boil for an hour. Then let it cool and clear very well, and then separate that clear water from the lees in another vase, and add an ounce and a half of well pounded vitriol and set it to boil, and when it has boiled for the fifth part of an hour, add to it half a glass of common oil, and then put in the silk to boil for half an hour. Then remove it from the fire and let it remain so for a day and a half, and then take it out and wash it in clear water and wring it well, and spread it out in the sun, and this dye as long as it lasts is good for dyeing. And know that the silk must be always boiled, and if it has not been boiled it cannot be dyed; and it must be boiled in the before-mentioned manner with soap. And the silk that has not been boiled is distinguished in the following manner from the silk that has been boiled. Put the silk into your mouth and chew it a little, and let it be wet with the saliva, then rub it with your fingers; if it rustles while it is wet it is not boiled.

362. *To dye silk or thread green.*—First make the silk yellow with "panicella" as was before directed for yellow silk, and then take 1 lb. of silk and 4 oz. of indigo, and put it into a saucepan with a little water to boil for half an hour or less, and then take it away from the fire, and cover it for half a day with a cloth, and if the indigo is not dissolved, rub it up with your fingers in the water, and let it clear itself; then separate the water from the lees, and put the water into a vase that is

poca daqua a refredarse per uno dj naturalj poi sia torto et lavato in aqua chiara et pollo a sciucare alombra poi metilo in uno panno de lino agullupato competentemente strecto commo e dicto desopra.

361. *A tegnare sirico negro o refe.*—Piglia lb ½ de galla bene amachata et cocila in uno caldaro cum aqua che sia cocta bene poi mecte dentro lo sirico a bollire in nella dicta aqua gallata per meza hora poi lo tira fora et pollo a sciutare al sole o al vento poi tolli tre brocche de tenta da calzolare et una broccha de quella aqua gallata et tolli doi petti de loto de rotta et mista omne cosa insiemj et fa bullire per una hora poi lassala refredare et multo bene reschiarare et poi sepera questa aqua chiara dale fecce in uno altro vaso et in questa aqua chiara mecte una oncia e ½ de vitriolo ben pisto et pollo a bullire et commo ha bollito per uno quinto dhora et tu ce mectj mezo bichiero dolio comuno poi ce mectj lo sirico a bullire per meza hora poi tollj via dal foco et lassalo cusi stare per uno di et mezo poi tiralo fora et lavalo in aqua chiara et torcilo bene poi lo stende al sole et questa tenta dummentre che ella dura e bona per tegnare. Et sappi che lo sirico deve essere sempre cocto et se non fusse cocto non se poria tegnare et cocilo in lo modo sopradicto cum lo sapone et quando lo sirico non fusse cocto se cognosse in questa forma da lo sirico che e cocto se vole mectare lo sirico alla bocha et masticarlo uno poco et fa che sia bagnato cum la saliva et da poi lo sfrega cum li deta et se quella bagnata stride non e cocto.

362. *A tegnare sirico verde o refe.*—Prima fa lo sirico giallo cum panicella commo e disopra dicto de lo sirico giallo poi tollj una libra de sirico once 4 de indico et metilo in uno caldareto cum poca aqua a bullire per meza hora o manco poi tola dal foco et coprila per mezo di cum uno panno et se lindico non fusse desfato atritalo cum li deta in la dicta aqua et lassa reschiarare poi sepera laqua chiara dale fece poi mete la dicta aqua in uno vaso che sia bono da tengiare et quando tu

fit for dyeing. And when you wish to dye it, take the solution of indigo and put it to warm, and when it is hot, take a lump of quicklime as big as an egg, and half a pound of honey, to every pound of indigo. Then put one-third part of the lime into the water, and when it is hotter, put in another third part, and when it is nearly boiling, add what remains, and then remove the water from the fire, because if it were to boil, it would boil over the saucepan. Then pour the decoction into a vase, and let it be well covered over like a stew, and when it is cool enough to bear your hand in, put in gently the yellow silk, which must have first been dipped in fresh water and well wrung. Then put it into the solution of indigo, and warm it gently, and if it is but slightly coloured put it back again into the dye, and you may repeat this several times with the dye as long as any of it remains, if you preserve it; and when you wish to dye anything, put in fresh indigo and honey, but not in such quantity as before.

363. *To dye silk a dark green.*—Take the silk dyed with a purple or violet colour; and when you have taken it out, dip it in alum, and then dye it with "panicella," as was before directed for a yellow dye; and when it is so dyed, you will do as before directed for a green colour, and you will have a dark green.

364. *To dye silk or thread blue.*—Take the silk boiled and washed as before directed for boiling silk white and without alum, put it into the indigo-dye, and you will have a fine light blue.

365. *To dye red.*—Take for every pound of thread 3 oz. of roche alum well ground, and put the alum into a vase with water over the fire; and when it has boiled a little, put the thread into it, take it off the fire, and let the thread remain soaking in it until it is cool. Then take it out and wash it well until the water comes off clear; and take 1 oz. of verzino in powder, either scraped or rasped, and pour water upon it, and boil it for an hour and a half. Then remove it away from the fire, and strain it through a linen cloth; then first set the strained liquor to boil, and when it is nearly boiling put the

vole tegnare tollj la dicta aqua indicata et metila a scaldare havj poi che e calda una zuppa commo uno ovo de calcina viva et meza libra de mele per libra de indico et poi mectj in la dicta aqua la terza parte de quella calcina et quando sera piu calda mectj laltra terza parte et quando sera per bollire metice laltra vanza et alora remove la dicta aqua dal foco perche se bollisse usciria fora del caldaro et mectj la dicta bullitione in uno vaso et stia bene coperta ad modo duno stufo et quando sera tanto fredda che tu ce possce patere la mano pianamentj mectice lo dicto sirico giallo e bagnato in nelaqua chiara prima et bene spremato poi lo mete in la dicta aqua indicata et calda pianamente et se havesse poco collore de novo lo remectj in la dicta tinta et cusi poterai fare piu fiate cum la dicta aqua per infino che durara se tu la conserve et quando tu volesti tegnare renova la calcina et lo mele et non in tanta quantita quanto prima.

363. *A tegnare lo sirico verde scuro.*—Ahvve lo sirico tento in collore pavonazo o vero violato et tracto che laj fora tingilo in lo alume poi lo tegne cum la panicella commo e dicto de sopra in lo colore giallo et cosci tinto farai commo e dicto disopra in lo colore verde et haverai verde scuro.

364. *A tegnare lo sirico in turchino o refe.*—Tolli lo sirico cocto et lavato commo e dicto desopra dela cocitura de lo sirico cosci bianco et cocto senza alume commo e dicto desopra mectilo in la dicta aqua indicata et haveraj bello turchino.

365. *A tegnare in roscio.*—Havve per omne libra de refe once 3 de alumj de rocho bene trito et mectj lo dicto alume in uno vaso cum laqua al foco et commo ha bullito uno poco et tu vi mectj dentro lo refe et levalo dal foco et lassa cusci stare lo refe nel bagno fino che se fredda poi lo tira fora et lavalo bene per infino che nesci laqua chiara poi tollj once j. de verzino in polvere o raso o raspato cum la raspa et metice suso de laqua et fallo bollire per una hora et ½ poi lo leva dal foco et colalo cum uno panno de lino poi pone la dicta collatura a bullire et quando sera per bollire et tu ce pone lo dicto refe et lassalo

thread into it, and let it boil for an hour, and then take out the thread and put it upon a stick to dry. Next add to the liquor which remains one glassful of very strong ley for each pound of thread, and stir the liquor well, in order for it to unite with the ley, and then return the thread into it and boil it for a quarter of an hour; afterwards stretch it out to dry in the shade, and it will be fine.

366. *To dye thread with verzino.*—Take verzino, and boil it in water as long as you think sufficient, and then take the thread and gall it well; afterwards wash it in fresh water, and then alum it, and let it nearly dry; warm the verzino, and dip the thread several times into the dye to colour it, and dry it well in the shade.

367. *To dye thread red.*—Take some madder well pounded, and put it into a little ley made from vine ashes, and let it boil, and put the thread to boil in the ley for some time; then remove it from the fire, and let it dry; when it is dry alum it, and then boil it in a little verzino well boiled with water and ley mixed together; then dry it in the wind without sun, and it will be fine.

368. *To dye silk black.*—Take soot, and scrapings of boilers, and well rusted iron, and boil these ingredients in red wine till reduced more than one-half, and when it has become tepid, put in the thread well dipped and dried several times in the dye, and it will become fine black thread.

369. *To dye cotton or silk black.*—Take 1 lb. of iron filings, 2 oz. of galls well pounded, 1½ oz. of Roman vitriol, rinds of pomegranates, bark of the roots of walnut-trees, 2 oz. of verzino well ground, and strong vinegar; boil all together until reduced to one-fourth, and let the decoction cool, and put it in the sun for 3 or 4 days, stirring it 8 or 10 times every day. Then strain it, and when you wish to dye silk or cotton set the decoction to boil, and boil the silk or cloth in it for a quarter of an hour; then dry it in the shade, and the more you dip it, the finer and more beautiful it will be.

370. *To dye cotton cloth.*—Take 5 lbs. of galls well pounded,

bullire per una hora poi cava fora lo dicto refe et pollo sopra uno bastone che se sciuta poi mectj in lo dicto bagno che te aromasto uno bichiero de ranno fortissimo per cescuna libra de refe et mista bene lo dicto bagno acio se incorpora cum lo ranno poi tornalj lo dicto refe et ponalo abullire per uno quarto dhora et poi lo pone asciugare alombra steso et sera bello.

366. *A tegnare refe in verzino.*—Tolli verzino et cocilo in aqua tanto che te paia che sia bastevile poi tolli lo refe et gallalo bene et poi lo lava alaqua chiara poi lo aluma et lassalo quasi sciutare poi scalda lo verzino et mecte a tegnare lo refe piu volte in la dicta tenta et sciugalo bene alombra.

367. *A tegnare refe in roscio.*—Ahvve uno poco de robbia bene pista et metila in uno poco de ranno facto de cenere de vite et fallo bullire et mecti lo refe a bullire in lo dicto ranno per una peza poi lo leva dal foco et pollo a sciutare commo e sciuto et tu lo aluma poi lo pone a bullire in uno poco de verzino bene cocto cum aqua et ranno misto insiemj poi lo sciuca al vento senza sole et sera bello.

368. *A tegnare in nero lo refe.*—Tolli fuligini raditura de caldaro et ferrj bene aruginatj et fa bullire queste cose in vino vermiglio piu che per mita et quando sera divinuto tepido et tu ce pone lo refe bene callato et sciucho piu volte in essa tinta et vira bello refe nigro.

369. *A tegnare guarnello o seta in nero.*—Ahvve una libra de limatura de ferro once 2 de galla bene pista once 1 et ½ de vitriolo romano scorze de mele granare scorze de radice de noce poi tollj once 2 de verzino ben trito poi tollj aceto bianco forte et fa bullire omne cosa insiemj tanto che torna per quarto et poi lassa fredare pone la dicta decotione al sole per 3 o 4 dj et omne dj lo mista 8 o x volte poi la cola et quando tu vole tegnare mecti a bulire la dicta decotione et metice la seta o panno a bullire dentro per uno quarto dhora et poi lasciuta alombra et commo piu ce la metera piu se fara bella et piu fina.

370. *A tegnare guarnello.*—Tolli galla bene pista lb 5 et

and put them into hot water with 10 lbs. of "pignolato,"[1] and then add 5 lbs. of Roman vitriol well pounded, and mix the whole well together, and let it stand a night, and it will be good.

371. *To dye bones green.*—Mix finely powdered verdigris with the very strong vinegar, and put white bones into a vase closely covered, warm them a little, and they will become green.

372. *To dye bones red.*—Take verzino scraped, and put it into a glazed jar, and pour urine and ley upon it; then dip bones into it, and they will be red.

373. *To dye skins a light grey.*—Take 12 bocali of water and 3 oz. of galls well pounded, boil until reduced one-third, and then strain the liquor, and add 6 oz. of Roman vitriol to the decoction of galls, and dye the skins. And if you wish to have a dark grey add to it a bocale of ley, one glass of oil, and boil it, but the vitriol must not be boiled.

374. *To make good writing ink.*—Take a bocale of good and strong white wine, 4 oz. of galls well crushed, one handful of dried rinds of pomegranates, one handful of the fresh bark of mountain ash scraped with a knife, and one handful of fresh bark of roots of walnut trees, and 2½ oz. of gum arabic; mix the whole together with the wine, and let the mixture remain for 6 or 8 days in the sun, stirring it well 4 or 6 times every day. Then add 2½ oz. of Roman vitriol, and mix it frequently, and let it remain so for several days; then put it over the fire to boil for the space of one *miserere*, let it cool, and then strain it and leave it for 2 days in the sun. If you then put in it a little roche alum it will make it much brighter, and it will be a good and perfect writing ink.

375. *To dye bones of oxen, buffaloes, and goats, of all colours inside and out.*—Put the bones into strong vinegar, and let them remain for 7 days; then boil them with that vinegar until reduced to one-half. Add to them the colour with which you wish to dye them, and boil it with them; then put in a little sal-

---

[1] Guarnello is a kind of cloth made of cotton, but the term is also used

polla in aqua calda poi ce pone lb x de pignolato poi ce pone lb 5 de vitriolo romano bene pisto et mista bene insiemj multo bene et lassa stare una nocte et sera bono.

371. *A tegnare losso in verde.*—Capias acetum acerrimum viridem erem subtilissimum et pone in dicto aceto et intus pone ossa alba in aliquo vaso bene coperto et aliquantulum calefac et efficitur viridis.

372. *A tegnare losso in rosscio.*—Tolle verzinum rasum et pone in olla vitriata et intus pone de hurina et de liscivio et intus pone de ossis et fient rubeis.

373. *A tegnare pelle in bretino chiaro.*—Tolli 12 bocalj daqua et once 3 de galla bene pista et fa tanto bullire che arentre per terzo et poi la cola et tolli once 6 de vitriolo romano et metilo in la dicta aqua gallata et poi tegne le pelle. Et se volesci bertino scuro metice uno bocale de liscia uno bichiere dolio et mecti a bulire ma non vole bulire el vitriolo.

374. *A fare inchostro bono et da scrivare.*—Tolli uno bocale de vino bianco grande et bono et once 4 de galla amachata bene et una manciata de scorze de mele granate seche et una manciata de scorze de ornello fresco rase con lo cortello et una manciata de scorze de raiche de noce fresche poi tollj once 2 et ½ de gomarabico et mistica omne cosa insiemj cum lo sopradicto vino et fa stare per 6 o 8 di al sole et omne di lo mista 4 o 6 volte molto bene poi ce pone doi once et ½ de vitriolo romano et mistalo spesso et stia cosci per alcunj di et poi el pone al foco a bullire per spatio duno miserere et lassalo fredare et poi lo cola et metilo doi dj al sole et se ce mectj poi uno poco dalumj de rocho farallo piu lustro assa et vira perfecta et bona intinta da scrivare.

375. *A tegnare ossi bovini bufalini et caprini dentro et di fora in omne colore.*—Aabeas de forti aceto et ossa micte intus et ibi dimicte stare per secptem dies demum fac bullire cum illo aceto usque ad medium et quem collorem vis colorare pone intus cum ipsis ad bulliendum deinde pone intus cum ossis aliquan-

to denote a woman's dress made of this material. Pignolato is a sort of cloth made of linen or hemp.

ammoniac with the bones, and let them boil until they are coloured inside and out.

376. *To dye box wood black.*—Take box wood, and leave it for a night in oil and sulphur, then boil it for an hour, and it will be as black as coal.

377. *To dye bones green.*—Put bones well cleaned into a vase full of ley, with goat's milk and verdigris very finely powdered; cover the vase closely, and bury it in dung for the space of 10 days, and the bones will become green inside and outside.

378. *To make a cement which will resist water and oil.*—Take liquid varnish ½ oz., raw ceruse, very white quicklime, and white of egg, each ½ oz., and incorporate them together, and cement what you please.

379. *A wonderful cement for crystal and gems, and for stone and wood.*—Take ceruse and grind it up well with varnish, cement what you please, and dry it in the sun.

380. *To make a cement to fasten on gems.*—Take two parts of powdered vitriol, 1 part of mastic, 4 parts of pitch, and melt them together, and they will form a very strong cement.

381. *To make a cement for vases.*—Take the yellow earth of the apothecaries, a little orpiment in powder, a little quicklime, and a little liquid varnish, and put all into a pipkin, mixing the ingredients together over the fire, and, while hot, cement what you please.

382. *To make a cement for vases in another way.*—Take liquid varnish, ceruse, and a little Armenian bole, to make the cement more tenacious, grind the whole together, and cement what you please.

383. *To make a cement for wood work.*—Take of Greek pitch 2 parts, pounded bricks, and a little mastic, and grind the whole up well, and then with a hot iron cement whatever you like.

384. *To soften bones.*—Take common salt and Roman vitriol in equal quantities, and grind them very well together; then distil them through an alembic, and keep the distilled water in

tulum de sale armoniaco et dimite tantum bulire quod habeat illum colorem intus et extra.

376. *A tegnare bosso in nero.*—Recipe bussum et eum permicte in oleo cum sulfure per unam noctem et postea permicte bullire per horam unam et fiet nigrum ut carbonem.

377. *A tegnare ossa in verde.*—Ttolli losso ben pollito et metilo in uno vaso pieno de ranno et de lacte de capra et de verderamo bene subtili et copri bene lo dicto vaso et mectilo socto lo litamj per spatio de x dj et sera facto verde dentro et de fora.

378. *A fare colla che tene aqua e olio.*—Ahvve vernice liquida oz. ½ biacca cruda clacina viva et bene bianca et chiara dova ana oncia ½ et incorpora insiemj et incolla quello che tu volj.

379. *Mirabilis colla ad christallum gemmas et super petram vel lignum.*—Accipe ceruse et confice cum vernice bene et incolla quicquid vis et dimite secare ad solem.

380. *Ad fatiendum collam ad gemmas retinendas.*—Summe vitrioli pulverizati partes 2, masticem partem j. picis partem 4 et insimul distempera et erit colla fortissima.

381. *Affare colla per vasa.*—Tolle terra gialla da li spitiali et uno poco doropiumento in polvere et uno poco de calcina viva et uno poco de vernice liquida et mecti omne cosa in uno pignatino et mista molto bene sopra al foco et incolla cusi calda quello che te pare.

382. *A fare colla per li vase per altro modo.*—Ttollj vernice liquida cerusa et uno poco de bollarminio perche sia piu tenace et macina omne cosa insiemj et incolla quello che te piace.

383. *A fare colla per lignamj.*—Ahvve pece greca parte 2 polve de matone et uno poco de mastice et macina bene insiem poi incolla cum uno ferro infocato quello che tu volj.

384. *A mollificare losso.*—Tolle sale comuno vitriolo romano ana et macinalj insiemj molto bene poi distilla per lambico et serva laqua distillata ben turata. Et quando vorai mollificare

a vessel well closed. When you wish to soften bones or horn or ivory, put them into the said water for the space of 5 hours, and it will soften so that you may impress on them what you like, and they will afterwards become hard as before.

385. *To make fish-glue.*—Take the bones of a pike or of any other large fish, dry them, and reduce them to powder in a bronze mortar; then put the powder into a new pipkin, with as much water as you think sufficient for the bones or dust, and make the water boil until the bones are liquefied; then touch the water with your fingers, and if they stick together it is good and perfect. Then take it from the fire, and strain it through a linen cloth, let it cool, then cut it into pieces, and dry it in the wind without dust.

386. *To prime panels for painting on.*—Take the panels and give them 3 or 4 coats of very hot glue; after each coat let them dry tolerably, but let the last coat dry perfectly. Then take gesso in fine powder and well ground, so as to be very fine; distemper it with warm water, and lay it upon the panel with a stick, and let it dry; then scrape it, that is, scrape off the rough parts with a knife blade. Then take gesso sottile, with very clear size, not too strong, and lay it ten times, if necessary, with a paintbrush upon the first coat of gesso; and, when it is dry, rasp it very thin, and draw upon it if you like with soft charcoal of willow or vine; and if you do not like that, take a goosequill and put the charcoal into it so as not to soil your hands. And if you wish to gild it, take Armenian bole ground very fine with white of egg, which is to be diluted with one cupful of pure water, and beaten for one hour; grind the Armenian bole very fine, and lay it on wherever you wish to gild, not twice only, but even so many as eight times, continually adding Armenian bole, until the priming is very thick; and so you will have what you want. Wet the part you wish to gild twice with clean water, lay on the gold, and remember to let it remain for one hour, and then burnish it.

387. *To soften bones.*—Put the bones into ley made with quicklime and baked ashes in equal quantities, and let them

losso o corno o avorio et metilo in la dicta aqua per spatio de 5 hore et molificarasse che porai impromptare quello che tu voli et indurarasse commo prima.

385. *A fare colla de pescio.*—Tolli ossa de Luccio et de omne altro pesscio grandicello et sechali poi li spolveriza in lo mortaro de bronzo et poi mecti la dicta polve in una pignata nova cum tanta aqua che te paia che sia bastevile ali dicti ossa o polve et falla bollire tanto che sia ben liquefacta poi tocca quella aqua se tene insiemj e bona e de facta poi la leva dal foco et colala cum uno panno de lino et lassa fredare poi ne fa li peze et polla asciugare al vento senza polve.

386. *Ad ingessandum tabulas causa pingendi.*—Accipe tabulas et super eas da ter vel quatuor vicibus cum colla bene calida ab una vice ab altera permite sicari aliquantulum et ultima vice permitte sicari valde bene postea habeas gissum pulverizatum et bene macinatum ut sit subtile et distempera cum aqua tepida et da super asidem cum sticca et permite sicari quo facto rade eum gladio scilicet partes grossas deinde habeas gissum subtile cum colla clara bene et non nimis forte et da super gissum positum deties si expediens fuerit cum penello et desicato eum subtilissime rade si vis demum designa cum carbone dulci aut de salce aut de vite et si non consentiret tibi habeas pennam anseris et sepera nigredinem carboni. Et si vis ponere aurum habeas bolarminium subtilissimum et macinatum cum clara ovi fratta et distempera cum aqua pura viz. cum uno ciato aque per unam horam et tempera ipsum bolarminium subtilissimum et da ubi vis ponere aurum nedum bina vice sed multotiens usque octo vice adendo semper bolarminium ut grossus multipliciter et sic habebis intentum balneando cum aqua clara ubi vis ponere aurum bina vice sed posito auro memento stare per unam horam et demum burnias ipsum aurum.

387. *Ad mollificandum ossa.*—Pone ossa in liscivo facto de calce viva et cinera recotta ana et maneant per diem novem

remain for 9 days, and the bones will become as pliant as you wish. And if you wish to colour them, put in any colour you like, and having formed them into shape, anoint them with linseed-oil, and let them dry in horse-dung for 7 days.

388. *To dye skins green.*—Take the sloes which grow upon the blackthorn in the month of September, put them into a kettle, and pound them well; let them boil, and ferment like wine in the sun for 3 days. Then separate the clear liquor from the lees; then take roche alum and a little urine, and twice as much strong white wine vinegar as urine, and dissolve the alum in the vinegar and urine; and when it is cold, alum the skins with the solution; and when they are nearly dry, wash them with that wine made from the sloes, and dry them in the shade. And the more coats you give them, the finer colour will be; and you will thus have a fine colour for dyeing chamois-leather.

389. *To know good galls.*—Good galls are known by their being small and wrinkled, and being hard within and appearing powdery without.

390. *To know good vitriol.*—Good vitriol is known by its being blue within and very granular without.

391.[1] [*To make cheese glue.*]—Take cheese of any sort, tolerably old, and scrape it as thin as paper, or slice it very fine; and then take the scrapings and put them to soak in fresh water for a day. Strain off the water carefully, and then take warm water, as much or rather less than what you threw away, and put the scrapings into the warm water. Knead the whole well with your hands, just as dough is kneaded for bread, in the warm water until all the fat is extracted from the cheese. Continue changing the water, then make the cheese into a cake, and put it into a vase of fresh water, so that it may always be covered with water. And when you wish to use it, take whatever quantity you want of the cake, and mix it with a little quicklime upon a very smooth board, kneading it well with a

---

[1] The Rubric is wanting.

tunc habebis passadutilem ad libitum et si vis colorare impone quem colorem vis et retucta in forma lineas cum oleo linj et dimicte sicari per 7 dies in equi fimo.

388. *A tegnare la pelle in verde.*—Tolli granelli de brugno che hanno le spinj del mese de setembre et metile in uno catino et pistalo bene et lassalo bolire et levare suso quelli venaciuoli commo se fa colo vino al sole per 3 dj poi sepera lo licore necto da la venacia et poi tollj alumj de rocho et uno poco de hurina et el dopio de lorina de aceto forte de vino bianco et disfa lo alumj in lo dicto aceto et urina et quando e freddo et tu aluma le pelle cum lo dicto aceto et hurina alumata et quando sonno quasi sciute et tu li da el bagno cum quello vino de le brugne et sciutale alombra et commo piu li daraj piu bello collore haveramno et haverai bona tenta verde per tegnare pelle de camosscio.

389. *A cognosciare la bona galla.*—La bonta de la galla se cognossce se e minuto et se e crespa et se e soda dentro et apara polverosa.

390. *A cognosciare lo bono vitriolo.*—La bonta delo vitriolo se cognosse se e cillistrino de dentro et de fora bene granoso.

B 391. (*sic*) ecipe cascio de qualunque ragione che sia vechio mediocramente et radilo subtilimente commo se rade la carta o vero tu lo pialla bene subtilj poi tollj quella radetura et metila a mollo in aqua chiara per uno di poi cola via quella aqua de la radetura cautamente poi tollj altratanta aqua calda o mancho quanto quella che hai getato via et de dentra ala dicta aqua calda ce pone la dicta raditura et remenala cum mano molto bene commo se mena la pasta da pane et tanto la remena in la dicta aqua calda che nesca tucta la graseza che ha el cascio et vienj mutando spesso spesso laqua poi la redu et fanne uno pane et metilo in uno vaso cum aqua chiara che lo dicto pane stia sempre a molle. Et quando lo voi adoperare tollj de quello pane la quantita che voj et incor-

wooden stick; then add to it a little sifted gesso, and mix the whole up again for a considerable time, and it will become cheese-glue for cementing wood-work and vases, and it must be used as fresh as possible, because then it takes a better hold.

B 392. *To make a green and red and purple dye for dyeing bones, cloth, thread, and whatever you like, &c.*—Take as much as you like of strong white vinegar, and put it in a glazed vase, and add to it scales of copper and copper-filings of a good red colour, Roman vitriol, roche alum, and a little verdigris; let everything be well ground and mixed with the vinegar, and let it remain so for 7 or 8 days and nights, and this vinegar becomes a good green tint for dyeing silk, bones, linen cloth, and other things as well as for painting. And if in this liquor you put bones raw or boiled, and boil them and let them remain in the liquor for the space of a month, they will become green for ever. And note that scales of copper make the best tint when fresh beaten. In the same manner things may be dyed red and crimson, using vermilion or minium or verzino, and put whatever you wish to dye into the liquor, and it will dye it well. The same can be done in yellow, using orpiment and proceeding as before directed; and, if you like, you may put urine instead of vinegar.

poralo bene cum uno pochetino de calcina viva in suso uno asse bene polito et cum uno pastello de ligno li compiglia insiemj poi ce agiongi uno poco de gesso statiato et rimena da capo omne cosa insiemj per gran spatio e de diventata colla de cascio per incolare lignamj e vasa et operala piu frescha che poi perche fa migliore presa.

B. 392. *Affare tenta verde et rossa et pavonaza a tengnare ossi panni refi et cio che volj etc.*—Recipe aceto bianco fortissimo quanto voi et pollo in uno vaso vitriato et mectice suso bactitura de ramo et limatura de ramo bene colorito rosso vitriolo romano alume de rocho et uno poco de verderamo omne cosa sia bene macinato et mista cum lo aceto et stia cusi per 7. o 8 dj et nocte et questo aceto diventa bona tenta verde per tegnare seta osso panno lineo et altre cose et per depegnare et se in questa cocitura mecterai osso crudo o cotto et faraicilo bolire et de poi stare per uno spatio de mese diventara verde imperpetuo nota che la bactitura de lo ramo fresca fa migliore tenta.

Et cosi se po fare de lo colore rosso come e dicto de lo verde et pavonazo cum lo cinabrio o minio et verzino et mecte a tengnere omne cosa che voi et tignirallo bene et simili se po fare de loropiumento in giallo et fa come de sopra et se voj in loco de lo aceto ce pone orina humana.

EXTRACTS FROM A MANUSCRIPT

OF THE

LIBRERIA MARCIANA AT VENICE,

ENTITLED

"SECRETI DIVERSI."

MARCIANA MANUSCRIPT.

PRELIMINARY OBSERVATIONS.

THE following extracts relative to painting, and the composition of varnishes, were selected from a Manuscript of the sixteenth century, now in the Library of S. Marco at Venice, but which formerly belonged to the Patrician Nani. The Abbate Morelli thus describes[1] the Manuscript:—

"It is a collection of recipes which make us acquainted with many compositions of the old professors, used in medicine, surgery, farriery, chemistry, painting, illuminating, gilding, working in stucco, varnishing, and similar works. Some of the recipes are common, others but little known. They are written in the Tuscan dialect, and sometimes the names of those by whom they were practised are prefixed. Among these are Andrea di Salerno, Frate Venetiano, Sansovino, Giovanni da Udine, Fundano, &c."

These various recipes appear to indicate that the MS., like many others, was compiled for the use of a convent by some monk or lay brother, who presided over the infirmary of the convent, compounded the

[1] Catalogo de' Codici Volgari della Libreria Naniana, Venezia, 1776, p. 31.

medicaments, and prepared varnishes and pigments—occupations which, during the middle ages, were frequently carried on by the same person.

The recipes for farriery appear to me sufficient proof that the MS. was not written by an inhabitant of Venice, where they would have been useless, since there were no horses in that city in the sixteenth century.[1]

The names of the artists alluded to in the MS. show that the author lived during the beginning and middle of the sixteenth century. It is probable that some at least of the recipes were collected at Rome; for the author remarks, in No. 238, "This I had from Master Andrea di Salerno:" and it does not appear that Andrea ever resided at Florence. Dominici[2] says that he was for a short period the pupil of Raffaello, whom he left at Rome, in 1513, to return to his own country.

---

1 In the fourteenth century, while Venice consisted almost entirely of the Island of Rialto, and that on which stand the Piazza and Church of S. Marco, horses were used there, and it was the custom for the senators to ride on horseback to the Council Chamber; it was even considered beneath their dignity to approach it in any other way. This fact, perhaps, accounts for the number of monuments in the different churches in Venice of men on horseback, which placed, as they generally are, high on the side wall, or over a lofty doorway, present a singular appearance. Shortly after this time the bounds of the city were enlarged by banking up the islands and deepening the canals; and gondolas, which soon became the favourite mode of conveyance, were introduced. The different parts of the city were united by bridges: but as the level of the streets was scarcely above high-water mark, the bridges were necessarily elevated in order to allow the gondolas to pass under them; and as the ascent and descent would have been too steep for foot passengers, the surface was cut into steps, which still remain. These bridges, of course, led to the disuse of horses, which in a short time were no more seen at Venice.

2 See Lanzi, vol. ii., pp. 82, 251. Andrea di Salerno was also called Sabbatini. He was born in 1480, and died in 1545.

Unless, therefore, it can be shown that this recipe was written in the kingdom of Naples, we must suppose that it was written a short time previously to 1513. In this recipe it was recommended to mix the blue pigments employed in fresco painting with milk; and as Andrea di Salerno worked with Raffaello, it may be inferred that this was the practice of the best masters of that period.

A recipe invented by Giovanni da Udine, for making Stucco, is given in this MS. Giovanni also worked at Rome under Raffaello, who had been invited by his kinsman, Bramante, to decorate the Stanze of the Vatican for Pope Julius II.[1] This invitation must have been given previous to 1513, for Julius died in that year. In 1527 Rome was sacked, and many artists left the city after this melancholy event, to seek in other parts of Italy a home more congenial to the arts; among these was Giovanni da Udine, who for some time resided at Florence, where he decorated the Palace and the Chapel of S. Lorenzo. Giovanni died in 1561, or 1564.[2] This recipe was communicated by another artist named in this MS., who, although a sculptor and architect by profession, exercised considerable influence on the sister art of painting. This was Jacopo Tatti, usually called Sansavino or Sansovino,[3] a native of Florence, who studied painting under Andrea del Sarto. Sansovino, whose fame extended beyond the bounds of his native city, went also to Rome, on the invitation of Giuliano di S. Gallo, the

---

[1] Julius II. was made Cardinal in 1471, and Pope in 1503.

[2] Lanzi, Indice de' Professori.

[3] Lanzi, vol. iii., p. 152; and Indice de' Professori.

architect of Julius II. He continued to reside in this city, returning occasionally to Florence, until the sack of Rome, when he was obliged to take shelter at Venice, where he died in 1570, at the age of 91.

From the above statements it appears that these three artists were at Rome between the years 1503 (the period when Julius II. ascended the Papal throne) and 1527 (when Rome was sacked); and it is highly probable that the recipes were collected during this period. The notices, therefore, of the preparation of the colours and oil, and the various recipes for varnish, will be read with much interest; and may fairly be considered to have been employed at Rome and Florence during the best era of Italian art.

The following facts appear to be established by this MS.:—

1st. That colours for painting in oil were ground with oil only; and, when too stiff for use, they were to be diluted with oil incorporated into the colour by working it in with the pencil.

2nd. That linseed oil was purified by boiling it over the fire with water for three or four hours. It was then suffered to settle and purify.

3rd. That olio-resinous varnishes were considered proper for colours and paintings in oil; but whether they were mixed with the colours, or otherwise, does not clearly appear.

4th. That powdered glass was used as a dryer for lakes and other colours which dried slowly in oil.

5th. That all varnishes were extremely viscous, and were thinned for use as required.

6th. That oil varnishes were common at this period.

7th. That the "vernice comune" sold by the apothecaries or druggists at this period was composed of linseed oil, pece greca, and calcined alum.

The MS. contains some information relative to painting on glass, and we find that there were several methods then in use:—

1st. With certain metallic colours applied on the glass with gum-water, which, by the application of heat in the furnace, penetrated into the glass.

2nd. With transparent colours mixed with oil, which were to be afterwards varnished.

3rd. With coloured glasses or enamels brought from Germany.

4th. With colours tempered with glue, or white of egg.

The first and third methods were probably united, and there is documentary evidence that painting on glass with vitrifiable pigments was known and practised in Italy during the fifteenth century; since in the latter half of this century it was usual to stipulate in contracts for painting windows, that the colours should be burnt in the fire, and not laid on with oil—"cotti al fuoco, e non messi a olio."[1]

The method of gilding on glass, described in No. 339, and attributed to a Venetian friar, may have been practised in the glass-works which have been carried on during so long a period at Murano.

---

[1] See Carteggio Inedito d'Artisti, vol. ii., p. 446—449; and see also the Introduction to this work.

EXTRACTS

FROM

A MANUSCRIPT IN THE MARCIANA LIBRARY AT VENICE,

ENTITLED

"DIVERS SECRETS."

214.[1] *Yellow paste like amber.*—Take of gum arabic oz. 3, of varnish in grains[2] oz. 2, pulverize and mix them well together, place them in a glazed pipkin, and mix them with a drachm of saffron tempered with common water, and let them remain in that state until they become like a paste; then take the yolk of an egg, strain it through an old but good linen cloth, incorporate it with the before-mentioned ingredients, and model with it what you please. Then dry it in the sun until it is hard, and anoint it with white of egg which has been well beaten; dry this also in the sun, and then varnish and gild it according to your pleasure.

301. *Divers colours for painting works in oil, or "a putrido," &c.*[3]—And mark that the colours are of two kinds, one of which consists of those which have no body, and which do not conceal the colours laid under them, but only tinge them, as saffron for instance; the other consists of those which have body and which cover every other colour over which they are laid, and many of these colours are inimical to each other, so that by mixing together they spoil each other, as white lead and verdigris and white lead and orpiment.

---

[1] The numbers in the margin refer to those in the original.

[2] That is, in grains or tears.

COPIA ESTRATTA

DAL CODICE INTITOLATO

"SECRETI DIVERSI,"

ESISTENTE NELLA BIBLIOTECA MARCIANA.

214. *Pasta gialla come ambra.*—Togli gomma arabica oz : 3. vernice in gran oz : 2. polveriza bene ogni cosa et mescola et poni in una scodella invetriata et mescolavi una dramma di zafferano stemprato con acqua comune, et stieno tanto cosi che diventino come pasta, poi togli uno tuorlo duovo, et colalo per peza lina vecchia ma buona, poi lo incorpora con le predette cose, et improntane quello che vuoi ; poi seccha al sole che sia duro, poi ugni con chiara d' uuovo che sia sbattuta ben et seccha al sole, poi vernica et indora a tuo proposito.

301. *Colori diversi per dipingere e lavori a olio o putrido etc.* —Et nota che e colori sono di due sorte una che non hanno corpo e non proprono quello che trovono sotto, ma solamente tinghono, come è verbigratia el zafferano etc. un altra sorte è che hanno corpo e quali quoprono ogni altro colore che essi trouovono sotto, et molti sono inimici l'uno del altro in modo che mescolandogli insieme si guastono, come è biacca e verderame et biacca et orpimento.

[3] A putrido—that is, with white of egg which has been suffered to stand until it has become decomposed. See MS. of Jehan Le Begue, No. 298, p. 282.

If, then, you wish to make *white*, take good white lead, and if you wish red, take lake or minium or cinnabar. The lake has no body, therefore take cinnabar, and according as you wish the colour to be more or less dark, take more or less lake. If you wish to make it still lighter add a little white lead, so that it may become lighter coloured, &c.

302. If you wish to make *flesh colour* take white lead and lake, and make it lighter or darker as you please.

If you wish *green*, take verde azurro, and mix it with giallolino and white lead, making it darker or lighter as you please. If you have no verde azurro, take giallolino, or orpiment and azure; mix them together, and you will have a green, adding more or less of one or the other according to the degree of obscurity which you may desire.

303. "*Paglionazo*" [*pavonazzo.*] — Take white lead and azure and red lake, mix well together, and if you wish the colour to be darker, add more azure; if lighter, add more white lead, and if you wish it redder, put more lake.

304. *Yellow.*—Take pure giallolino, item pure orpiment, item ochre; and because these colours have no body, lay white lead underneath.

305. *Black.*—Take peach stones and char them, or burn ivory, which will make perfect black, &c.

306. *Grey.*—Take white lead, verde terra, ochre, and black; mix together, and put more or less of one or the other until the colour is to your mind.

The colours which have no body are these:—

309. Verdigris, lake, ochre and verde terra, and they are very proper for mixing with those colours which have body.

The tempera of these colours, prepared " a putrido," is water and the yolk of an egg, and the quantity to be used is rather less than half the quantity of colour.

Se adunque vuoi fare bianco pigli biaccha stietta, se rosso togli laccha, o minio, o cinabro. La laccha non ha corpo, pigla adunque el cinabro, et secondo che tu lo vuoi, più o mancho scuro, pigla piu o mancho laccha. Se lo vuoi fare anchora più chiaro mettivi un poco di biaccha secondo che tu vedi che rischiara, etc.

302. Se vuoi fare incharnato piglia biaccha e laccha tanto che lo faccia piu oscuro o piu chiaro come vuoi.

Verde, piglia verde azurro et puossi mescolare con giallolino, et con biaccha, et sarà piu o mancho oscuro secondo che vorrai, et se non hai verde azurro piglia del giallolino, o vero orpimento, et azurro et mescola insieme et farà verde, et mettivi più et mancho dell' uno et del altro secondo che lo vuoi piu o manco oscuro.

303. Paghonazo o piglia biaccha et azuro et rosso-laccha, et mescola insieme et se vuoi che sia più oscuro, mettivi più azurro, se piu chiaro più biaccha. Se più rosso più laccha.

304. Giallo piglia Giallolino stietto, item orpimento stietto. Item ocria, et perchè non ha corpo campeggia sotto di biaccha.

305. Nero, piglia noccioli di pesche et fane carboni o vero avorio arso, et fa perfetto nero, etc.

306. Bigio, piglia biaccha, verde terra, ocria, et nero, et mescola insieme et mettivi piu o manco dell' uno o dell' altro secondo che tu vedi, e viene a tuo modo.

Colori che non hanno corpo sono questi :—

309. El verderame, la laccha, l'ocria, el verde terra; et son buoni a mescolare con quelli che hanno corpo.

La tempera di questi colori fatti a putrido .I. a acqua e el tuorlo del vuovo un pocho manco che la meta del colore etc.

314. *To make "indaco."*—Take flowers of woad and alum water, boil them together, strain through a linen cloth into a vase; then take what remains on the cloth, spread it out on a tile, dry it well, and it will then be fine "indaco."

315. *To make fine azure.*—Take 6 ounces of copper filings, 3 ounces of calcined eggshells, 4 ounces of sal alkali, and 2 ounces of quicklime. Pulverize them well and mix together; then place them in a vase of tinned copper, adding as much of the strongest white vinegar as will cover them, then make the vase air tight, and put it under dung (horse-dung is best) for 20 or 25 days, after which you may take it out, and it will be done.

323. *A most beautiful red from verzino for painting or writing.*—Take lime and make ley, and when you have made it and strained it through a cloth, take any quantity you please, and scrape into it some good verzino, using the quantity which seems best to you, and leave it in that state for 2 or 3 days, until you see that the ley has well extracted the colouring matter of the verzino; then strain it through a cloth, and put on it as much pulverized roche alum as will make the whole of the material feel its virtue,[1] and let it dissolve. Then add to it as much pulverized gum arabic as will give the colour sufficient body, and expose it to the sun for 3 or 4 days, stirring it occasionally that the gum may be dissolved and well incorporated; and when you think it is well purified and of the proper colour, take it from the sun, strain through linen, and keep it for use.

The longer it is exposed to the sun the thicker it will be, &c.; and if you leave it so long as to become hard enough to require distempering when used, you may distemper it with a little of the same ley, and your writing and painting with it will then be very beautiful, &c.

You may add that portion of the verzino which remains on the cloth after the first straining to other verzino, and repeat

---

1 That is, a quantity sufficient to coagulate it.

314. *A fare lo Indaco.*—Togli fiore di guado, et acqua alluminata, et fa bollire insieme, et con un panno lino cola sopra un vaso questa cocitura et quello che rimane in sul panno distendilo in su una tegola et fallo asciughare bene, et e indaco fino etc.

315. *A fare azurro fino.*—Togli limatura di rame oz. 6 scorze di vuova calcinate oz. 3. sale archoli oz. 4. calce viva oz. 2 polveriza ogni cosa et mescola bene insieme et ponile in uno vaso di rame stagnato, et mettivi tanto aceto bianco fortissimo che quopra questa materia, et turalo che non respiri, et mettilo sotto el litame et maxime di cavallo per 20 o 25 giorni, di poi lo cava et sarà fatto.

323. *Colore bellissimo rosso di verzino per dipingere et scrivere.*—Togli calcina et fa liscia et quando l'hai fatta et colata per peza pigliane quella quantità che tu vuoi, et rastiavi su del verzino buono tanto quanto pare a te et lascialo stare cosi due o 3 di tanto che tu veggha che la liscia habbia cavato la sustantia bene del colore del verzino, poi lo cola per peza, et mettivi su tanto allume di roccha polverizato che tutta quella materia ne possa sentire destramente della sua virtù, et mestalo che si solva, et mettivi tanta goma arabica polverizzata che gli dia corpo discretamente, et tienlo tre o quattro di al sole, et rimestalo qualche volta accioche la goma si solva et incorporisi per tutto, et quando ti pare che sia bene purgato et fatto di colore a tuo muodo, lievalo dal sole et colalo per peza lina, et serbalo et adoperalo.

Quanto più sta al sole tanto più si fa corpulento etc. Et se tu lo lasciassi stare tanto al sole che riventassi si sodo che poi allo adoperare havessi bisogno di stemperare, stemperalo con un poco di quella liscia, et scrivi, et dipingi con esso, et farai una cosa bella etc.

Quella materia del verzino che rimane della prima colatura, vi puoi aggiugnere verzino eodem modo et rifarne e o simile al

the process in the same manner, either adding the same kind of wood as at first, or using a more common sort, according to the quantity which you may add, &c.

325. *Divers colours for colouring window-glasses and other works.*—If you wish to make a beautiful black which will penetrate into the glass, take fine iron filings, especially those of needles, if you can procure them good, or otherwise those scales which fall from the iron when it is beaten while red hot on the anvil; then take an equal quantity of burnt lead or tin, or perhaps rather more of the lead than of the iron, which you will learn by experience, and grind them well together, with water on the porphyry like any other colour. Then distemper the mixture with gum water made with soft water, and draw your subject on the glass with this, letting it dry in the shade; place it in the furnace of a potter (who will generally know how to regulate the heat), and heat it according to the best of your knowledge in an iron vase, otherwise cover it with ashes only, and it will be beautiful.

Burnt lead or tin is prepared in the following manner:—Put as much as you wish of it into a vase over the fire and liquefy it; and from time to time, while it is still over the fire, take off the scum, and continue to do this until no more arises. In order to refine it, put the whole into an empty vase; and while it is over the fire, stir it so that the whole of the contents may be well calcined, and then keep it for use.

If you wish to make a beautiful yellow colour[1] which may penetrate into the glass, grind some silver leaf with a little honey and water, that it may hold together; then wash it in

---

[1] Silver, "either in the metallic or any other form, possesses the singular property of imparting a transparent stain, when exposed to a low, red heat, in contact with glass. Modern glass painters are accustomed to obtain three colours from silver, yellow, orange, and red. For this purpose no flux is used, the prepared silver is merely ground up with ochre or clay, and applied in a thick layer upon the glass. When removed from the furnace the silver is found not at all adhering to the glass; it is easily scraped off, leaving a transparent stain, which penetrates to a certain depth. If a large proportion of ochre has been employed, the stain is yellow; if a small

primo, o del più dozinale secondo la quantità che ve ne aggiungi etc.

325. *Colori diversi per colorire vetri da finestre et da altri lavori.*—Se lo vuoi fare nero bello et penetra nel vetro togli limatura fine di ferro, et maxime limatura d' agoro quanto se ne potessi havere, è buona, o di quella scaglia del ferro che cascha quando si batte caldo in su l' anchudine, et togli piombo o stagno arso, d' ognuno parte eguale et più presto un poco piu piombo che scaglia come per experientia vedraj, et macina bene con l' acqua in sul porfido, et fanne a uso di colore, poi lo tempera con acqua di ghoma che sia dolce, et dipingi quello che vuoi in sul vetro et lascia secchare a l' ombra, poi gli metti in fornace di questi che fanno stoviglie, e quali gli sanno communemente quocere et quocigli ut scis in vaso ferreo assuoli con la cenere et verrà bello.

El piombo o lo stagno arso si fa cosi. Metti quella quantità che tu vuoi in uno vaso al fuoco e squaglialo, et stia cosi al fuoco, et quella stiuma che egli fa di mano in mano cavala, et tanto fa cosi che si consumi in questa, poi per raffinarla mettila tutta insieme in quel vaso dove non sia altro, et stando sopra el fuoco, rimescolala in modo che si arda tutta bene, poi serbala al bisogno.

Se vuoi fare colore giallo et bello el quale etiam penetra nel vetro. Macina ariento in foglio con un poco di mele acciocchè si tenga insieme et con l'acqua, poi lavalo con le ditta nella

---

proportion, it is orange-coloured; and by repeated exposure to the fire, without any additional colouring matter, the orange may be converted into red. This conversion of orange into red is, I believe, a matter of much nicety, in which experience only can ensure success. Till within a few years this was the only bright red in use among modern glass painters; and though the best specimens certainly produce a fine effect, yet it will seldom bear comparison with the red employed in such profusion by the old artists." Extract from an Essay on the Art of Glass-painting in the Philosophical Magazine for December, 1836.

water with the fingers until it is well purified, in the same manner as powdered gold is treated. Distemper this silver with gum water made with soft water, dry it, then heat it in a furnace as before, and it will become very beautiful, &c.

If you wish to paint with other colours which, although beautiful, do not penetrate into the glass, but remain on the surface, especially with verdigris, fine lake, peach-stone black, or charcoal black, and generally all the colours which have no body, and also with fine azure, that is, ceneri azzurri, give a coat of nut oil or linseed oil, which last is to be preferred for painting on glass, according to the painting which you wish to execute, and let it dry in the shade; then grind up the colour with the same oil, and paint upon the coat of oil and let it dry, and it will be beautiful; and although the colour does not penetrate, it will for a long time remain beautiful, and you may even varnish it afterwards, according to the best of your skill.

And with these colours, and with coloured glasses brought from Germany, and with ornamental works done with gold "ut scis," on glass, you will make beautiful windows and other works.

And when you paint with the verdigris, if you grind some saffron in the same manner with the before-mentioned oil, and with this distemper the verdigris, it will be a green so much the more beautiful, &c.

You may also paint with these colours on window glasses and on drinking glasses, and on other utensils made of glass; and you may also fasten on the glass leaf gold and silver; and on this you may paint with colours or smalti, whichever you please; and in the same manner you may lay divers colours over each other, and you will thus execute most beautiful works on glass or crystal, on vases, windows, and bell-glasses, and on plates of glass which are to be afterwards joined together, and a thousand different kinds of painting according to your taste, &c.

328 *If you wish to paint on glass "a putrido."*—First lay

acqua tante volte che sia bene purghato come si fa al' oro macinato: poi tempera questo ariento con acqua di ghoma che sia dolce et lascia secchare; poi quoci in fornace ut supra et verra molto bello etc.

Se vuoi colorire d' altri colori e quali saranno begli ma non penetrano nel vetro, ma stanno in superficie: et maxime verderame, lacha fine, nero di noccioli di pesca arsi, o di carbone et universalmente tutti e colori che non hanno corpo et azurro fine . I . di cenere, etc. Da col pennello una mano di olio di noce, o di lino è meglio in sul vetro secondo la dipintura che vuoi fare, poi lascialo bene secare a l' ombra, poi macina el colore con detto olio, et dipingi sopra quello, et lascia secchare; et sarà bello, et benchè non penetri durera assai tempo bello, puoi etiam poi invernicarlo ut scis.

Et con questi colori et con vetri coloriti, che vengono della magna, et con lavori fatti d' oro ut scis in sul vetro farai bellissime finestre et lavori.

Et quando tu dipingi col verderame, macina del zafferano al medesimo modo con detto olio et con questo tempera el colore del verderame et sara tanto piu bello verde etc.

Puoi etiam in su vetri da finestre et bicchieri, et altri lavori di vetro fare lavori di questi colori et puoi etiam appicchare in sul vetro l' oro et l' argento di pezi, et in su quello lavorare di colori et di smalti quello che vuoi etiam di diversi colori l' uno sopra l' altro, et in questo modo farai lavori bellissimi sopra vetro o cristallo, sopra vasi, finestre, et campane, et piastre di vetro da congiungerle poi insieme, et fare mille lavori secondo la tua fantasia.

328. *Se vuoi dipigniere in sul vetro a putrido.* – Da prima

on a coat of soft and hot glue, and when this is dry paint on it.

You may temper the colours with yolk of egg, and also with weak and slightly warm glue, the blue and white especially, for these two colours are much more beautiful and bright when distempered with glue than with yolk of egg.

When you paint with blue in fresco, that is, on walls, and you desire that it may retain its colour and not turn black, as generally happens to the blues, distemper the colour with the milk of goats or of any other animal. This I had from Master Andrea de Salerno.

329. *The mode of making the best black printing ink.*—Make a large lantern, two feet and a half broad on each side, and ten or twelve feet in height, and cover it with cotton paper or parchment, for one is as good as the other, and let there be a door at the foot of it, and put into it a tripod, and on the tripod a pan, and on the pan two pounds of Greek pitch. Set the pitch on fire, then shut the door; take care that the lantern is air-tight, and let the pitch burn until it is entirely consumed, when the smoke from it will affix itself to the interior of the lantern like soot; then take out the earthen pan and the tripod, shut the door, and with a rod beat the outside of the lantern, when the black will fall to the bottom, leave it to settle there; then take it out and preserve it for use. But if you wish to clean the lantern more perfectly, tie some hen's feathers to a rod, and sweep the inside of the lantern with these, and add the black which you thus sweep off to the other black. When you desire to make printing ink, take the varnish which is used for varnishing, and the more perfect its quality the better. But in default of other, you may use that common sort which is sold by the apothecaries[1] for varnishing wood and similar things, and procure a wooden rod, such as is used in making carpenters' glue, with which the varnish is to be stirred; and put some of the black into it, and liquefy it as you require it; and with this you know books are printed, &c.

[1] See the recipe for "Vernice comune," No. 405.

una mano di colla dolce et calda et quando è secchа dipingivi sù.

Et puoi temperare i colori col tuorlo dello vuovo, et etiam con la colla dolce et un poco calda, et maxime lo azurro et el bianco per questi due colori vengono più begli et piu chiari a temperargli con la colla che con l' uovo.

Et quando tu dipingi con l' azurro, in fresco cioè in sul muro et tu voglia che mantenga il colore et non riventi nero come comunemente fanno gli azurri, temperalo col latte o sia di capra o d' altro non importa. Hoc habui a Magistro Andrea de Salerno.

329. *Modo di fare el nero da stampare e libri optimo.*—Fa un lanternone largo per ogni verso un braccio et quarto et alto cinque o sei braccia, et incartalo di carta bombagina o pecora non importa; et da pie fa che habbia uno sportello et mettivi un tre pie et in sul tre pie un tegame; et nel tegame due libre di pece greca et metti fuoco nella pece, et serro lo sportello, et fa che el lanternone non sfiati da alcuna parte, et lascia ardere, tutto el fumo che riesce s' appicha per il lanternone, a uso di filiggine; alhora cava el tegame et el tre pie, et sera lo sportello, poi batti di fuora el lanternone con una bacchetta, et quella materia chascherà in fondo, lasciala riposare, poi la cava et serbala et se tu vuoi meglio nettare il lanternone, in sur una bacchetta legate penne di gallina et spazalo dentro per tutto, et questo serba col primo, et quando voi fare la compositione per istampare, togli vernice fatta da invernicare, quanto migliore è tanto è meglio: ma basta di quella comune che vendono gli speziali per invernicar legname et ogni cosa: et habbia un menatoio di legno di quegli da fare colla da legnaiuoli, et rimena di questa vernice et mettivi di questa materia, et falla liquida a tuo proposito, et con questa si stampa i libri come tu sai, etc.

339. *Mordant for gilding glass, which has been tried by a Venetian friar.*—Take one ounce of mastic which has been roasted, not burnt, but dried carefully, one ounce of coperosa[1] which must be fine and white and not grey, one ounce of varnish in grains, and half an ounce of burnt roche alum. Pulverize the ingredients finely, and grind them up with well purified linseed oil. When you use this mordant, grind it with linseed oil well purified, and when you use it distemper it with the same oil, so that it may be of the consistence of ink, lay it on the glass, and expose it to the sun when it does not shine very strongly, and if the sun is very hot, place it in the shade, but in such a place that the sun may be reflected on it, and let it dry so far that when touched with the finger a slight impression may be left on it. When this is the case, lay on the gold and let it dry well; then clean it with the cotton, varnish the gold, and let it become perfectly dry.

But do not wash vases gilded in this manner except with fresh water, and be very careful in rubbing them.

Linseed oil is thus purified:—Boil it over the fire with water for 3 or 4 hours, then let it settle and separate it from the water.

[2] *Tried by the painter Fundano.*[3]—A most excellent mordant for laying gold on oil paintings, on walls, on wood, on leather, on silk, and on cloth, and on everything you please, first laying on glue (and fish glue is best) wherever you may wish to lay on gold; and the glue must be applied thinly on cloth and similar things in order that the cloth and silk may not absorb it. The glue being laid on and dried, the mordant is applied, and then immediately the gold, leaving it to dry, and not burnishing it. So where there is no glue lay on the mordant, and immediately after apply the gold.

346. *On marble and stones.*—Take linseed oil boiled in the usual way, and take giallolino and verdigris and tow (?) in equal parts; grind these things dry, then mix them with

---

[1] Sulphate of Zinc. [2] From p. 167 of MS.

339. *Mordente per porre oro in vetro ex fratre vinitiano provato.*—Togli mastice abbruciato, ma non sia arso, ma diseccato discretamente once una, et coperosa che sia bella et bianca et non bigia oncie una. Vernice in grani oncie una. Allume di rocha arso oncie mezza. Polverizza ogni cosa sottilmente, et macina con olio di lino bene purificato: et quando lo adoperi stemperalo etiam cum questo olio che vengo come inchiostro cioe corrente; et pollo in sul vetro, et poi pollo a sole che non sia molto caldo; et se el sole fussi caldo assai pollo a sechare a l'ombra dove el caldo del sole reverbera, et secchisi tanto che resti in modo che toccandolo col dito pizichi un poco et all'hora poni loro et lascia seccare poi spaza e campi con la bombagnia quando è secco bene. Et poi davi su la vernice in su loro et falla bene seccare.

Ma non lavare questi vasi dorati in questa maniera, se non con acqua fresca et stropicciali discretamente.

L'olio di lino si purifica cosi: fallo bolire al fuoco tre o quattro hore con l'acqua, poi lascialo riposare poi separalo dall' acqua.

Ex pinctore fundano provato.—Mordente ottimo a porre oro in muro sopra dipinture a olio in su legno in cuojo et seta in tela, ma dando prima la colla et in su ogni altra cosa che vuoi, dando la colla dove bisognassi darla: et di pescie è meglio, et in su tela o simili cose da la un poco tenaretta accioche la tela o seta non la bea, et data la colla et seccha si pone el mordente et subito l'oro et lascia secchare et non brunire, similmente dove non si pone la colla, poni el mordente et subito l'oro.

346. *In sul marmo et pietre.*—Togli olio di seme di lino seconda la quantita che ne vuoi fare, cotto ut scis et togli giallolino, verderame, et stoppino in parte eguale, macina queste

[3] Lanzi mentions seven painters of the name of Fontana, most of whom flourished in the sixteenth century.

oil, and lay the first coat on the marble or stone, and let it dry. This is done on account of the fragility of the marble, in order that it may not spoil the other things which are laid on it, &c.

Then lay on a coat of liquid and hot glue, and proceed as above directed.

Although these coats must be very dry they should not remain long exposed to the sun, but for a short time only, especially in winter, and then rather to prevent their being cold than for the purpose of drying them in the sun.

[1] And observe, as an universal rule, that all oil mordants resist the water, and that those in which no oil is used do not withstand the water, &c.

Also when you wish to lay the mordant on polished iron or marble, or any other polished surface, you must first lay on a coat of glue neither too thin nor too thick, and let this dry; then lay on the mordant, and then the gold, because without the glue, the mordant would not adhere firmly.

351. *Item. A most excellent mordant of garlic juice for gilding all things, pasteboard, panels, walls, iron, marble, tin, gesso, and leather, even if they are rough.*—Take gum ammoniac, reduce it to powder by pounding it on a stone with garlic juice, and while grinding it, add a little gum arabic in such quantity that all the substances which you are grinding may have a slight proportion of it, because if you were to put too much it would dry too quick. Then grind up so much bole as will colour the whole substance, and grind up all these things together one after the other with garlic juice strained through linen, and if during the grinding these ingredients should become too viscous on account of the garlic juice and consequently difficult to grind, add some vinegar, but not more than is necessary. It is then finished, and you may use it immediately, distempering it with vinegar so that it may be sufficiently liquid and may flow well on the pencil. If you wish to preserve it ready made, it will keep for some

---

[1] From p. 171 of MS.

cose asciutte et mescola con l'olio, et da il primo letto in sul marmo o pietra, et lascia secchare, et questo si fa per la fragilità del marmo acciò che la non guasti l'altre cose che vi si pongano su etc.

Poi da una mano di colla liquida et calda poi fa tutto come è detto di sopra.

Queste cose anchora che bisogni sieno bene secche non vogliono molto stare al sole se non un poco, et maxime di verno, più per conforto del freddo che per secchare col sole.

Et nota che universalmente, tutti e mordenti a olio reggono a l'acqua il che non fanno gli altri che non sono fatti con l'olio etc.

Item quando vuoi dare il mordente in sul ferro pulito, o marmo o altra simile cosa liscia: da prima una mano di colla, non troppo liquida ne troppo tenace, et lasciala seccare, poi da el mordente, poi poni l'oro: perchè senza quella colla non si appicherebbe bene el mordente.

351. *Item. Mordente di sugho d'aglo ottimo per porre oro in su ogni cosa, cartoni, tavola, muro, ferro, marmo, stagno, gesso, sopra corame etiam che fusse crespo* —Togli armoniaco et pestalo in polvere prima, poi lo macina in su la pietra con sugho d'aglo poi vi metti macinando un poco di gomma arabica, tanta che tutta quella materia macinata ne senta per tutto modestamente, perchè la troppa sarebbe troppo di secchativa, poi simul etiam macina tanto bolio che dia colore a tutta questa materia, tutte queste cose macina insieme l'una dopo l'altra con sugo d'aglo colato per peza, et se nel macinare queste cose le fossino troppo viscose per amore del sugo, et non le potessi cosi bene macinare, mettivi dello aceto quanto puoi forse tanto che basti a fare bene macinare et è fatto: Et lo puoi adoperare al' hora se tu vuoi, et stemperalo con l'aceto tanto che sia liquido che corra bene col pennello a tuo proposito. Et se tu lo vuoi serbare fatto dura assai tempo et quando ne vuoi adoperare sendo sodo stempera con aceto ut dictum est.

time, and when you wish to use it, distemper with vinegar as previously directed.

353. *Item. A mordant of garlic juice.*—Pound the garlic, and pass the juice through a linen cloth, then grind up this juice with a little white lead to give it proper body, adding Armenian bole in quantity sufficient to colour it entirely, and as much urine as is sufficient to enable you to grind and incorporate it well, to make it sufficiently liquid to be applied well with the pencil. Then lay it on your work, let it dry, moisten it by breathing on it, lay on the gold and fix it with cotton; then let it dry. You may preserve this mordant for some time after it is made, and when you wish to use it, if you find it hard distemper it with urine, then gild and burnish the work. And I think, according to the experience that I have had of the simple garlic juice, that it is good for laying gold on almost everything, even on marble, and it is not affected by the dampness of the marble, or by the dampness of its situation unless it is exposed to the rain, and in this case every mordant of garlic is affected.

And if you wish to gild on silver with amalgam in some places only, and not all over, lay garlic juice with the pencil over those parts to which you intend the gold shall not adhere, and let it dry. Then lay on the gold with the amalgam all over, just as any other thing is gilded with amalgam, and the gold will not adhere to those parts on which garlic has been applied, and you will thus have the gold alone on clean grounds. You may then remove the garlic juice from the work and clean it well, and in this manner you may execute beautiful works.

Take also any work executed in tin after your own design, and clean it well, then cut, or pound, or bruise a clove of clean garlic, and anoint well with it the tin over the design on which you wish to lay the leaf gold; then gild and fix the gold with the cotton, and let it dry; afterwards burnish it dexterously, and, lastly, uncover the ground of tin which you did not intend to gild. On these you may paint or enamel, or varnish, and execute most beautiful works.

353. *Item. Mordente di sugo d'aglo.*—Pesta l'aglo et passalo per peza, poi macina di questo sugo con un poco di biacca tanto che gli dia corpo a discritione, et poi tanto bolio armenio che tinga quella qualità che tu macini, et tanta orina che basti a farla bene macinata, et incorporata, et liquida a tuo proposito per darlo col pennello, et pollo in sullavoro et lascialo secchare, poi lo rinvieni con l' alito caldo, et poni l' oro, et fermalo con la sua bambagia, et lascialo seccare ; poi spaza e campi ut scis. Questo mordente, dura assai tempo fatto, et quando ne vuoi adoperare et fussi duro, stemperalo con l' orina, pruova a brunire. Et credo secondo la esperientia che ho del sugo d' aglio semplice che sia buono a porre olio quasi in su ogni materia ; et etiam in sul marmo, et non rinviene propter humiditatem marmoris nec loci humidi, nisi desuper pluat, il che fa etiam ogni mordente d' aglo.

Et se vuoi dorare sopra argento com malgama et vuoi che resti dorato in alcun luogo et non per tutto, dove tu vuoi che l' oro non si appichi ; da col pennello sugo d' aglo, et lascialo secchare ; poi da l' oro con la malgama per tutto come si dora ognaltra cosa con malgama, et dove sarà il sugo dello aglio, non si attacherà, et cosi harai l' oro solo in su campi netti, poi puoi levare el sugo del aglio et nettare bene, et farai lavori begli et netti.

Togli etiam el lavoro di stagno fatto a tuo modo et nettalo bene, poi habbia uno spicchio d' aglo mondo, et taglialo o soppestalo, o masticalo et poi ugni con esso sottile lo stagno sopra el disegno dove tu vuoi porre l' oro di pezzi et ponvi loro et fermalo bene con la bambagia poi lo lascia secchare, poi lo brunisci destramente, et poi scoprire poi e campi dello stagno dove tu non vuoi che sia loro, puoi etiam sopra loro dipignere smaltare invernicare, et farai lavori bellissimi.

You may also draw what you please on the tin, and gild the remainder of the ground; thus the works will be tin, and the ground gold.

You may also try the experiment on parchment or cotton paper, first polishing it, and then anointing it with the cut clove of garlic, having previously bruised or pounded the garlic, if necessary, gilding it as above and burnish it if you please.

370. *Colours tempered with oil are prepared in the following manner.*—Grind up the colour with linseed or nut oil as stiff as you can, that is, with as little oil as possible, and so that it may be very fine, and that on being felt between the fingers, no hard grains can be perceived; and when you paint with it, if you find the colour too stiff, dip the pencil in a little oil and incorporate it well with the colour.

377. *A most excellent glue for damp and moist places which always becomes harder, but only fears the heat, and fixes everything to wood and stone, which must be as smooth as porphyry.*—Take one pound of good yellow wax, nine ounces of liquid varnish, and one pound of black naval pitch. Put the varnish into a pipkin over a slow fire, that is hot enough to liquefy without burning it;[1] then throw in the wax, liquefy it in the same manner and incorporate it well with the varnish; then do the same with the pitch, having previously pounded it, etc. Then take Armenian bole ground to a fine powder, and stir some of it into the other ingredients until the whole material becomes liquid, and yet so tenacious that it fixes and holds together firmly the things which you wish to glue together; and you must stir the ingredients well together and use them warm, because in a short time the cement hardens so that you cannot glue with it. And when you have applied it where you please, and wish to make the surface smooth and polished, take a firebrand from the fire and bring it near to the glue until the heat causes it to liquefy and spread; you should also move about the firebrand

[1] A proof that varnish was extremely viscous, if not absolutely solid.

Et puoi etiam disegnare lo stagno secondo che tu vuoi et poi el resto de campi mettere a oro et cosi e lavori saranno bianchi, et el campo doro.

Puoi prouare anchora ad ugnere la carta pecora et bambagina, prima lisciata et poi ugnerla sottilmente con lo spicchio del aglio tagliato, et se bisogna masticato o sottoposto et porre l' oro ut supra et vedere se esibrunisse.

370. *E colori temperati a olio si fanno in questo modo.*—Macina el colore con olio di lino, o di noce et macinalo duro quanto puoi, .|. con poco olio, quanto puoi, et macinalo tanto che sia bene sottile che tu lo senta col ditto senza nocciolino o rendina alcuna: similmente quando tu dipigni e ti fussi troppo sodo toca un poco d' olio col pennello et incorpora bene col colore.

377. *Colla ottima per luoghi humidi et molli che sempre più indurisce, ma solo teme el caldo et appicha ogni cosa insino a legno con pietra et che la pietra sia liscia come porfido.*—Togli cera gialla buona libbra una. Vernice liquida oz. nove. Pece nera navale lib. una. Metti la vernice in uno pignattino, et poni al fuoco lento che si scaldi bene, et si squagli et non arda, poi mettivi lacera et squagliala similmente et incorpora colla vernice ben, poi fa similmente della pece la quale prima sia pesta bene etc. poi habbia bolio armenio pesto bene in polvere et mettivene su tanto che tutta questa materia resti tanto liquida che possa essere tenace in modo che si possa bene appicchare, et tamen pigli et tenga forte a cose le quali vuoi incollare insieme, et incorpora bene ogni cosa insieme, et subito cosi calda incolla quello che vuoi, perchè aspetta poco et indurisce poi in modo, che non potresti incollare. Et quando tu l' hai posto dove tu vuoi, et tu lo voglia fare liscia et pulita di sopra, togli un tizone di fuoco et accostalo alla colla tanto che senta el fuoco et si distenda per se medesima, et va menando il tizone per tutto et falla distendere, et assottigliare a tuo modo, et verra

over the surface of the glue, and melt it so that it at length becomes smooth and beautiful, &c. And on putting the work which you have cemented into water, it will immediately become very hard.

394. *Modes of making divers varnishes ; and first, of "bengivi" (Benzoin), which will dry in the shade.*—Take 2 oz. of spirit of wine which has been distilled 4 times (that which has been distilled 3 times will do, but not so well), and one ounce of benzoin. Put the ingredients into a bottle, and shake them until the benzoin is dissolved; the varnish is then finished. It must be kept in a vessel closely stopped. This is a very fine varnish upon miniatures and all other delicate works, on paste, or glue, or wood, and also on paper and glass.

395. *Item, a varnish.*—Take one pound of linseed oil, boiled "ut scis,"[1] etc., and anoint the vessel with it while hot, and 4 ounces of pounded carabe;[2] place it to dissolve with the bottle closed on the coals, and when it is nearly dissolved pour in the hot oil and stop it up; afterwards, at the proper time, when the whole is dissolved, stir in 3 oz. of alum.

Dilute the varnish with the necessary quantity of naphtha, or linseed oil, or spirit of wine, and use it warm.

396. *Item, a varnish of benzoin, which dries very quickly and may be used on everything, because it is pale and admirable for all delicate works.*—Put into a large glass vessel 5 ounces of good spirit of wine, with an ounce of fine benzoin pounded into very small pieces; stop the vessel closely, and agitate it until the benzoin is well dissolved. Then let it stand for a day and a night; pour off the clear part, throw away the sediment at the bottom, and keep the liquid in a well-closed glass vessel: this liquid is the varnish.

397. *Item, an excellent varnish which is made without the aid*

---

[1] Ut scis, &c. See ante, No. 339, p. 620.

[2] The word is written "Carbone" in the MS. in the Marciana, and "carabone" in recipes somewhat similar in the Nuovo Plico and Abecedario. I have ventured to translate it "carabe" (amber), because it is quite

liscia et bella etc. Et mettendo il lavoro incollato nell' acqua fresca si farà subito durissima.

394. *Modi di fare vernice di Verse et prima di bengivi che secha etiam al' ombra.*—Togli acqua vite stillata quattro volte, tre volte fa, ma non si perfettamente oz due bengivi oz una diguaza in ampolla usque ad solutione belzui ut scis, et è fatta: serbala turata: questa è cosa finissima, quasi sopra miniature, et ogni altro lavoro fine di pasta, o colle o legname et cartoni, et vetro.

395. *Item vernice.*—Togli olio di lino libre una cotto ut scis etc. ugni la boccia cum illo calido: carbone oz quattro, pesta et poni a solvere con la boccia turata in su carboni, et quando è quasi soluta inmitte olium calidum et tura; de inde tempore suo quantum est solutum, inmitte tres uncias alluminis.

Stempera con olio di sasso .l. petronio o di lino o acqua vite q̃n op̃z caldar. ut scis etc.

396. *Item Vernice di bengivi che seccha prestissimo et puossi dare in ogni luogo perchè è chiara et mirabile in su ogni lavoro finissimo.*—Metti in una ampolla grossa di vetro oz cinque d' acqua vite buona, et una oz di belzui buono pesto in pezzuoli minuti, et metti tutta detta acqua et tutto il bengivi et tura l' ampolla bene et diguazala tanto che el bengivi si solva bene: poi lascialo posare un giorno, et una notte poi cavala per declinatione et buta via el fondaccio che resta, et serva questa acqua bene turata nella ampolla et questa è la vernice.

397. *Item vernice ottima la quale si fa senza fuoco, et seccha*

---

clear that carbone does not liquefy over the fire, and because, after a diligent search, I can attach no other meaning to it. I consider this to be the common recipe for amber varnish: the amber being dissolved in a vessel previously greased to prevent it from burning, before the hot oil is added.

of fire, which dries very quickly without being exposed to the sun, and remains very clear, and with which may be varnished anything painted on panel, pasteboard, or iron.—Take spirit of wine which has been rectified at least three times, because otherwise it would not dissolve the benzoin properly, and put it in a glass vessel; then take some benzoin and add either at once, or a little at a time, that quantity which you know to be sufficient. Then stop up the bottle and agitate it until the benzoin is entirely dissolved; and if, after it is dissolved, it is of the consistence of good "vernice liquida," and, as it were, tenacious, and varnishes well, it is finished; but if it is too thick, add more spirit of wine until you bring it to the correct standard; and if it is too thin, add more benzoin. You may then preserve it for use.

398. *Item, a varnish tried by Master Jacopo de Monte San Savino, the Sculptor, which is proper for every kind of work and on all materials.*—Take one ounce of sandarac, ground to a very fine powder, and 3 ounces of clear nut oil. Heat the oil in a glazed pipkin over a slow fire in the same manner as linseed oil is boiled; then add the powdered sandarac a little at a time until it is dissolved; add to it also at the same time so much clear incense finely powdered as will impart a pleasant savour to the whole mixture, stirring it well that it may dissolve, and, if you please, you may also add a sufficient quantity of burnt and pounded roche alum to have a sensible effect on the whole composition; and the addition of the alum will improve the varnish if you stir it until it is dissolved. It should then be strained through a linen cloth, and afterwards exposed to the sun and dew until a sediment is formed, which should be separated by pouring off the clear varnish, after which it will be ready for use.

399. *Item, a varnish which spreads like oil, dries quickly, and is very lustrous and beautiful, appearing like a glass mirror, and which is admirable for adhering firmly and for varnishing lutes and similar things.*—Take one pound of linseed oil, boil it in the proper manner in a clean glazed pipkin, add to it half

senza sole prestissimo, et resta molto chiara, et si può vernicare ogni lavoro dipinto in tavola o in cartoni o sul ferro.—Togli acqua vite che sia passata tre volte almanco perchè non solverebbe bene altrimenti et mettila in una ampolla di vetro, et togli del bengivi et mettivene dentro quella quantita, tutta a un tratto, o a poco a poco che sia abastanza ut intelliges: et tura l' ampolla, et diguaza tanto che el bengivi si solva tutto bene, et se quando è soluto ti resta come vernice liquida buona, e che sia in modo tenace che invernichi bene, a l' hora è fatta. Sin autem, se fussi troppo dura aggiungivi tanta acqua vite che torni ala misura, et se fussi troppa liquida aggiugnivi tanto bengivi che torni al proposito, et serbala et adoperala.

398. *Item vernice ex Mag^{ro}. Jacobo de Monte S. Savino scultore provata. Et serve a ogni lavoro et in ogni materia.*—Togli una oz di vernice in grani macinata sottilissima et tre oncie di olio di noce chiaro; quoci l'olio lento igne in pignattino invetriato, come si cuoce l' olio di lino: poi mettivi su la vernice a poco a poco, mestando anche quousque solvatur: poi mettivi su al medesimo modo tanto incenso chiaro polverizato sottile, che condischa discretamente tutta la materia et mescola tanto che si solva bene, et se vuoi poi mettivi tanto allume di roccha arso et pesto che condischa questa materia virtute sua: tanto sarà miglore, et mesta quousque solvatur. Poi colala per peza lina poi tienla al sole, et al sereno poi colala per declinatione, et serbala et adoperala etc.

399. *Item Vernice che si distende come olio et secchа presto et è molto lustrante et bella et pare uno specchio di vetro et per stare a la cosa et sopra liuti et simile cose è mirabile.*—Togli per una misura: una libra d' olio di linseme, et quocilo come si fa in una pignatta invetriata netta, poi vi metti su meza

a pound of well pulverized clear and fine Greek pitch, and stir and incorporate the whole over a slow fire; then add half a pound of powdered mastic, and the moment you have done so, withdraw the pipkin gradually from the fire, because it swells up, and incorporate the ingredients thoroughly; then replace the pipkin on the fire, and keep it there until everything is well dissolved and mixed, when some burnt and pounded roche alum of the size of a nut should be added and mixed, until that also is entirely dissolved and incorporated. Then take the varnish off the fire and strain it through an old linen cloth. Your varnish is then made, and it will be found to be beautiful varnish for wood, iron, paper, leather, and all kinds of painting and works, and for withstanding water. When you find it too viscous, dilute it with linseed oil in the proper manner.

400. *Item, a most excellent varnish of mastic for lutes, leather, panels, cloths, woód, and pasteboard.*—Take 3 ounces of strained and clear linseed oil, and boil it. Then take half an ounce of mastic pounded and ground, and add it gradually to the oil, mixing it in such a manner that it may be entirely dissolved and incorporated with the oil, and that it be properly evaporated and made into a varnish "ut scis;" then put in a little pulverized roche alum at discretion, but sufficient to affect all the varnish; keep it over the fire until it is entirely dissolved and incorporated with the varnish and evaporated, after which you may take it off the fire, and strain it through an old and good linen cloth, when it will be finished. But observe that everything should be done over a charcoal fire and with great care.

401. *Item. A most excellent mastic varnish.*—Take one pound of mastic, half a pound of naphtha, and half an ounce of clear nut oil; melt them together in a bottle or glass over a charcoal fire, and strain through an old linen cloth.

402. *Item. A most excellent clear and drying varnish proper for colours, both in oil-painting and other kinds of painting.*—Take 2 ounces of clear and good nut oil, one ounce of clear and good Greek pitch, and half an ounce of clear and good mastic;

libbra di pece grecha chiara et bella et polverizzata et mesta quando la metti, tanto che si incorpori bene a fuoco dolce, poi vi metti su mezza libra di mastice macinato, et quando lo metti perchè si rigonfia leverai però la pignata da fuoco et mettilo su a poco a poco mestando et incorporandolo bene, poi torna la pignata al fuoco et mesta tanto che si solva ogni cosa bene, poi mettivi quanto una noce di allume di roccha arso pesto et mesta che si solva et incorpori bene poi lievala dal fuoco et colala per peza lina vecchia et serbala, et per legname, et per ferro et per carta et corame et per ogni dipintura et lavoro farà un opera bellissima et per stare alla aqua, et quando ti pare soda stempera con olio di lino come si fa etc.

400. *Item Vernice di Mastice optima per Liuti, quoio, dipinture di Tavola et di tela, per lavori di legname et cartoni.*—Togli tre oz d' olio di lino colato et chiaro, et quocilo, poi abbia un oz ½ di mastice pesto et macinato, et mettilo in sul' olio a poco a poco mestando in modo che si solva et incorpori bene con l' olio et che sia sfumato ben et fatta vernice, ut scis; poi mettivi un poco di allume di roccha arso et pesto, et sia a discretione secondo che tutta la quantità della vernice ne participi: et sta al fuoco tanto che si risolva et incorpori la virtu sua colla vernice et svapori, ritíralo poi dal fuoco, et colala con peza lina vecchia et buona, et è fatta. fa ogni cosa con fuoco di carboni et discreto.

401. *Item. Vernice di mastice optima.*—Togli mastice libre una, olio petronio libre meza, olio di noce chiaro oz meza fondi insieme in boccia o in bicchiere sopra carboni. cola con peza lina vecchia et è fatta.

402. *Item. Vernice ottima chiara et diseccativa ben per colori et a olio et per ogni dipintura.*—Togli per una misura: due oz. d' olio di noce chiaro et bello, et una oz. di pece greca chiara et bella, et meza oncia di mastice chiaro et bello, macina la pece

grind the pitch and the mastic [separately] to a very fine powder, and place the oil in a clean glazed pipkin over a charcoal fire, and let it boil gently until it is done sufficiently, that is, until one-third has evaporated; then put in the powdered pitch a little at a time, mixing and incorporating it well; afterwards throw in the mastic in the same manner, and when it is dissolved, take the varnish off the fire and strain it through a fine and old linen cloth.

And if you wish it to be still clearer, prepare the mastic with tepid water in the following manner:—Take the largest and clearest tears of mastic that you can find, and soak them in tepid water, so that they may become tender; then select the best pieces, dry them, and pound them.

You may also try the effect of adding a little burnt and pulverized roche alum when the other ingredients are dissolved, so that the whole may virtually be seasoned with it, straining it afterwards. This is done in order to purify it better.

403. *Item. A varnish of "olio di abezzo," which dries both in the sun and in the shade.*—Take "olio di abezzo," which must be genuine and not adulterated, and if you wish to know whether it is falsified, distemper it with nut or linseed oil, or naphtha, heating both the oils, &c., and spread it on a work, when, if it is not genuine, it will not dry for a long time, and then badly, because it is adulterated with turpentine, but if it is genuine it will dry quickly and perfectly.

If you desire to varnish delicate works which will not be exposed to water, but merely to bring out the colours and show their beauty, distemper the olio di abezzo as above. But if you wish to varnish more permanently on works which are intended to resist water, do not distemper the olio di abezzo with other ingredients, but heat it in a vase, melt it, and varnish with it.

When you distemper it with linseed or nut oil, let it be with oil which has been exposed to the sun to evaporate, and the varnish will be much clearer.

et il mastico sottile, et poni a fuoco di carboni in uno pignattino netto et invetriato l' olio et fallo bollire dolcemente tanto che sia bene cotto .I. tanto che scemi el terzo: poi vi metti su la pece macinata a poco a poco mestando ed incorporando, poi vi metti el mastice simili modo, et quando è bene soluto, ritirala et colala con peza lina sottile et vecchia.

Et se tu vuoi che la sia ancora più chiara; acconcia el mastice con l' acqua tiepida in questo modo. Togli i grani del mastice piu grossi et chiari che puoi et metti in acqua tiepida tanto che intenerisca. Cavane el midollo et secchalo, poi lo macina.

Puoi etiam provare quando ogni cosa e soluta a mettervi un poco di allume di roccha arso polverizzato tanto che condisca virtualiter tutta quella materia poi la cola. Questo si fa per farla più purgata.

403. *Item. Vernice d' olio di beza che seccha al sole, et senza sole.*—Togli olio di bezza che sia schietto et non falsato et se vuoi conoscere se è falsato stemprane un poco con olio di noce, o di lino, o di sasso caldi tutti due etc., et distendine in sur un lavoro, e non seccherà se non con gran tempo et male, perchè lo falsano anche con la trementina, ma se e schietto seccha presto et bene.

Se tu vuoi invernichare lavori gentili che non habbino a stare a l' acqua, ma per colori et bellezza stemperalo ut supra. Ma se tu vuoi invernicare più fermamente in lavori che reghino alla acqua non lo stemperare con altro, ma scaldalo in un vaso et struggilo et invernica.

Quando tu lo stemperi con l' olio di lino o di noce, togli che siano stati al sole a svaporare et sera più chiara assai.

404. *A most excellent varnish for varnishing arquebuses, cross-bows, and iron armour.*—Take of linseed oil, lbs. 2 ; varnish in grains (sandarac), lb. 1 ; clear Greek pitch, oz. 2.

Boil the oil, then dissolve in it the other ingredients, and strain through a much worn linen cloth, and when you wish to use the varnish, scrape and polish the work, and heat it in a hot oven, because that is the best place to heat it ; and when it is of a proper heat, that is, when the varnish adheres to it firmly and does not fry [bubble or blister from too great heat], then lay it on thinly with an instrument of wood, so that you may not burn your fingers, and it will make a beautiful changing colour.

And if you supplied the place of Greek pitch with naval pitch, I think it would make the work black when you varnished it.

When making the varnish you must boil it well, even to such a degree as to make it foam and bubble, if necessary, in order that it may be clear and thick.

405. *Item. An excellent common varnish, good for varnishing whatever you please.*—Take 2 ounces of clear and good linseed oil, and one ounce of good and clear Greek pitch, but 2 ounces of the latter also will make the varnish thicker and give it more body ; boil the oil over a slow fire, and then put in the pounded pitch a little at a time, that it may incorporate well, and add a little roche alum previously burnt and pounded, and when it is incorporated and boiled sufficiently, that is, when you try a little of it in your fingers and find that it is done, strain it and keep it. When it is used it will be beautiful and good ; if it is too tenacious you will dilute it with a little oil.

And if you wish it commoner so as to sell it at a larger profit, take 10 ounces of oil to one of pitch ; and if you use black pitch it will be good for pommels of swords, spurs, and similar things.

406. *Item. Varnish [pounce] for writing paper.*—Take the shells of unboiled eggs, soften them in water for a fortnight, then take off the pellicles and wash them ; dry them well by exposing them to the heat of the sun or the fire, then pound and grind

404. *Vernice ottima per invernichare archibusi et balestre et armadure di ferro.*—Togli olio di seme di lino libre 2. vernice in grani libre 1. pece grecha chiara oz 2.

Quoci l' olio, poi struggivi dentro l' altre cose, poi cola con peza lina usata, et quando vuoi invernicare el lavoro, limala o nettala prima bene, poi lo scalda in un forno caldo perche fa meglo che scaldarlo altrove, et quando è debitamente caldo, cioè caldo in modo che la vernice vi si appiccha su bene et non frigge alhora invernicha et dalla sottile, con uno istromento di legno, acciò non ti quocha le dita, et farà un bello colore cangiante.

E se tu vi mettessi in luogo di pece grecha pece navale, credo farebbe il lavoro nero quando tu lo invernicassi.

Quando la fai falla bollire assai, et stiumala si oportet acciocchè la sia bene chiara et spessa.

405. *Item. Vernice ottima comune et buona da invernichare quello che vuoi.*—Togli olio di lino chiaro et buono, oz. 2. Pece Grecha chiara et bella, oz. una ma se ne toi due verrà più tenace et corpulenta : quoci l' olio lento igne, poi vi metti la pece pesta a poco a poco tanto che incorpori bene, poi mettivi un poco di allume di roccha arso et pesto, et quando è incorporato et cotta a sufficientia : e quando ne pruovi un poco fra le dita et sentila fatta : colala et serbala, et usala, et sera bella et buona, et quanhai adoperarla fassi un poco tenace temperala con olio.

Et se la vuoi più dozinale per vendere con più guadagno togli x oncie d' olio et una di pece. Et se la togli nera sara buona per pomi di spade et sproni, et similia.

406. *Item. Vernice da porre in su le carte da scrivere.*—Togli guscia d' uova non cotte, tienle in molle nella acqua per 15 di, poi lieva bene le pillicule et lavale bene, poi le asciuga bene al sole, o al caldo del fuoco, poi pestale et macinale, et

them and sift them through very fine rags. Then add to a pound of these ½ an ounce of clear incense, also strained through rag and grind them up together; then pass them again through rag. This is found to succeed well.

393. *Tried by Master Jacopo di Monte S. Savino, the sculptor. Admirable stucco for making and modelling figures, and for colouring them, and it resists water.*[1]—Take of finely powdered travertine lb. v., and if you would have it finer and more delicate, take fine marble instead of travertine, and 2 lbs. of slaked lime; mix them together with water, and stir and beat them well together like a fine paste, and execute what works you please with it, either by forming it with your hands or in moulds, and dry it in the shade. And if you wish to colour it white, when the work is dry enough to be tolerably firm, but not quite dry, grind white lead with water in the same way as colours are ground, and flower [or finest particles] of sifted lime, and apply it with the pencil, and it will be very white, and will effectually resist water. And if you wish to colour it with other colours, let the work dry perfectly, and then colour it; but these colours will not resist water, like the white, because they do not incorporate or unite so well as that does with the materials of which the work is composed. If, then, you wish the colours to resist water, apply on the work the abovementioned composition (which is to be used in the manner described), and paint on it with oil-colours.

You may also colour the stucco with colours ground up dry, but these will not be so bright as if they were applied afterwards.

---

[1] The invention of this stucco is ascribed to Giovanni da Udine, on the following authorities:—Morelli,[2] in his description of the Marciana MS., observes, . . . " M. Jacopo da Monte, whose method of making varnish and stucco is there shown; the stucco is the same as that which, on the authority of Rafaello Borghini (Riposo, p. 402) and of others, was invented by Giovanni da Udine, and by him employed in the celebrated Loggie of the Vatican." Borghini's

[2] Catalogo de' Codici della Libreria Nani, p. 32.

passale per istraccie che sieno finissime, poi mescola una libra di questa con ½ oz d' incenso chiaro, passato come questa et macinale insieme, et passa iterum per straccio et è buona, et provata, et riesce bene.

393. *Ex Magistro Jacopo de Monte S. Sauino Scultore—prouato. Stuccho mirabile per fare figure &c. et etiam improntare et colorirlo, et regge allacqua.*—Togli treuertino macinato sottile v libra, et se uuoi che sia più gentile et delicato, Togli marmo fino in luogo di treuertino, et togli dua lib. di calcina spenta et mescolale insieme con acqua et rimenale et battile bene insieme come pasta fine et fanne che lauoro tu uuoi, o con mano o impromptato con le forme, et secchalo alombra et se lo uolessi colorire di bianco, quando il lauoro è tanto seccho che sia fermo, ma non secco interamente, macina la biaccha con l' acqua auso di colore, et fiore di calcina colata, et dalla col pennello, et sara bianchissimo, et stara forte allacqua, et se lo uuoi colorire d' altro colore, lascia secchare il lauoro perfettamente; poi lo colorisci, ma questi colori non reggeranno à lacqua come quello bianco, perche non si incorporanno, ne si vniscono con la materia del lauoro come fa quello. Se a dunque tu uuoi che questi colori reghino à lacqua da insul lauoro la inzuppatura disopra detta la quale si da come qui dice, et poi dipigni à olio.

Puoi etiam colorire lo stuccho co' colori macinati asciuttj: ma non uenghono tanto vivi, quanto a colorirgli poi.

Borghini's account of the invention of this stucco is as follows: "While Giovanni was working with Raffaello at Rome, excavations were made in search of antiquities among the ruins of the palace of Titus, and some apartments were discovered decorated with grotesque paintings and small historical figures and ornaments in relief, composed of stucco. Giovanni and Raffaello went together to see them, and were lost in admiration. Pictures of this kind being found in grottoes, were called 'Grotesques.' They were carefully copied by Giovanni, who made many imitations of them in various places, and nothing was wanting but to discover the mode of making the ancient stucco; he, therefore, tried so many things, that at last he discovered that he could make the ancient stucco with lime made from white

travertine, mixed with white marble in the finest powder; and so, these stucchi, with beautiful grotesque ornaments, and many new and rare designs, were employed by the order of Pope Leo (X.) in the Loggie of the Vatican."

Vasari, in his Life of Giovanni da Udine, mentions these experiments at greater length, and informs us what materials he tried before he succeeded in imitating the ancient stucco.

MANUSCRIPT

PRESERVED IN THE

LIBRARY OF THE UNIVERSITY OF PADUA,

ENTITLED

"RICETTE PER FAR OGNI SORTE DI COLORE,"

ETC.

PADUAN MANUSCRIPT.

PRELIMINARY OBSERVATIONS.

THIS Manuscript, without the date or name of the author, is certainly Venetian. It is in quarto, is written on paper, and is numbered 992.

The handwriting is of the seventeenth century; and although, from the following circumstance, the MS. may have been written during the latter part of the sixteenth century, I think it more probable that it was composed during the middle, or latter part, of the seventeenth century.

In the fly-leaf preceding the commencement, and in the same hand-writing, and in similar coloured ink, is a sonnet (dedicated to Prince Emanuel Philibert, of Savoy), which appears to have been composed by the Canonico Michael Angelo Blanchiardi di Torino, as his name is affixed to it.[1]

Now, Emanuel Philibert died in 1580; if, therefore, Dr. Blanchiardi composed the MS., he must have done so previous to this period, and the MS. might have been written soon after the sonnet.

---

1 The work on colours is followed by a copy, in a more recent handwriting, and with blacker ink, of a letter from "Il principe D. Anton. Ottoboni al Sig. P. Pietro suo Figlio hora Cardinale eletto dal Ste Papa Alessandro Ottavo suo Zio. 1698."

Some parts of the early sections of the work, from No. 1 to No. 13 inclusive, bear such strong resemblance to parts of the 3rd book of Lomazzo's Treatise on Painting, that it can scarcely be supposed that one was not copied from the other. Lomazzo's work was published in 1584; if, therefore, parts of the MS. were taken from this, the date must be later than that period.

But independently of these considerations, the work bears intrinsic evidence of having been composed at a later period. A change seems to have taken place during the interval that elapsed between the composition of the MS. of the Marciana and the Paduan MS., not only in the pigments used, but in the varnishes. Essential oil varnishes are introduced in great abundance; Spirit of Turpentine, Oil of Spike, and Naphtha, are the diluents; while the hard varnishes, made with amber and sandarac, have nearly given place to mastic and olio di abezzo.

Among the varnishes for pictures is one (No. 94) described as "Alla Fiaminga," which is composed of spirit of wine, sandarac, and olio di abezzo. "Oglio cotto," prepared by boiling nut or linseed oil with litharge, is twice mentioned, namely in No. 70 and No. 96.

One recipe only is given for making Lac Lake, but Gum Lac is frequently mentioned, being applied to the novel purpose of composing varnishes, by which the Indian Japan work was to be imitated. The MS. contains recipes for varnishes of this description composed of different ingredients; and for the preparation of the colours used in Japanning.

Gamboge was used at this period as a pigment, and

was prepared for painting by grinding it with lemon-juice and roche alum. I do not know when this substance was first used as a pigment, but it was first employed for medical purposes about 1603.

Articles of American produce are mentioned as in use; among these are Campeachy wood (or Logwood) and Cochineal lake, which seems almost to have superseded the lac lake as a pigment. Cochineal is said to have been introduced in the beginning of the sixteenth century.[1] It seems at this time to have been usually prepared with lemon-juice, or crystallized arsenic.

In order that the Lakes, and some other colours, should dry when mixed with oil, glass, very finely pulverized, was mixed with them; and it is added, that they would then dry in twenty-four hours.

We also find that paintings in oil had begun to suffer from the effects of age; and that they required, or it was believed that they required, to be washed with some corrosive liquid, and to be re-varnished. Directions, or rather recipes, for both these processes are given.

No. 83 contains some recipes in Latin (the only part of the MS. written in that language), which seem to have been considered secrets.

A method of transferring prints on to a plate of glass is described (in No. 95), in which it appears that the design was fixed by means of heat. It was probably painted afterwards, for in No. 96 a recipe for painting and gilding on glass is given, in which the colours are to be ground with boiled oil. The fact of this method being described in two Italian MSS., and the stipulation

---

[1] It was introduced into Spain soon after 1523.

respecting it in contracts, proves the extent to which it was used in Italy.

Two different recipes for etching grounds, and aquafortis, are mentioned in this MS.

In conclusion I shall observe, that in addition to the subjects I have mentioned, the MS. contains the usual recipes for colours used in miniature painting.

PADUAN MANUSCRIPT;

ENTITLED

RICETTE PER FAR OGNI SORTE DI COLORI," ETC.

RECIPES FOR ALL KINDS OF COLOURS.

1. *Of Colours in general, and of what materials they are composed, &c.*[1]

White is made with gesso, lime, white lead, powdered marble, egg-shells well pulverized and sifted, and with the bone of the cuttle fish ground to a very fine powder.

Yellow is made with "gialdolino di fornace" of Flanders and Germany,[2] orpiment, and ochre, with saffron and gamboge for water-colour painting.

Blue is prepared with ultramarine and Hungarian[3] blues. Others are made with "smalti" and "smaltini"[4] of every kind, especially with those of Flanders, which are the best, with "biadetti"[5] and similar pigments.

Green is made with the "verde azzurri,"[6] verdigris, "verdetto,"[7] which is called "gialdo santo," and approaches to yellow,

[1] The whole of this chapter so closely resembles the fourth chapter of the third book of Lomazzo's Treatise on Painting (although additional colours are named in each class of painting), that it is scarcely possible to suppose that the author of the MS. had not seen that work; unless, indeed, it could be proved that both writers had made use of some common original work, which had been used as a text book by the Lombard painters, in the same manner as the old Byzantine MSS., so variously rendered into Latin, in the Paris copy of Eraclius, the Clavicula, the Sloane MS., and the Theophilus of the British Museum.

[2] In Haydocke's translation of Lomazzo, written in 1590, the names of these two colours are translated "Masticot" and "generall."

RICETTE PER FAR OGNI SORTE DI COLORI.

De' Colori in generale, e di qualli materie si componghino.

Il Bianco si fa col gesso, calcina, biacca, marmo pesto, gusci d' ouo bene polverizati, et settazzati, e con osso di sepia benissimo macinato.

Gialdo si fà col gialdolino di fornace di Fiandra, et Alemagna, orpimento et ocrea, col zaffarano et Gomma gute, quali sono per l' acquarello.

Turchino si prepara con gl' azuri oltramarini et ongari et altri si fa ancora con gli smalti, e smaltini d' ogni sorte, massime con quelli di Fiandra, che sono li migliori, con li Biadetti et simili.

Verde si fà con li verde azurri, verderami, verdetto, che si chiama gialdo santo, e tira al gialdo, terra verde, verde porro,

---

3 Hungarian Blue. Native blue carbonate of copper.

4 Smalti and Smaltini. The smalti of Flanders were probably preparations of Zaffre; the smaltino was most likely the blue glass, "Azzurro di Pozzuoli," described by Orsini and Galliani in the notes to Vitruvius.

5 Biadetti. The artificial carbonate of copper.

6 Verde azzurri. Armenian stone, also a native carbonate of copper, in which the blue colour is mixed with the green. Haydocke translates this "Green bize."

7 Verdetto is defined by Borghini (Riposo, p. 169) to be a native green pigment brought from the mines of Germany. Giallo Santo is usually considered to be a yellow lake made from the flowers of the plant called "Barba di Becco," the yellow goat's beard; also from the Reseda Luteola (weld

"terra verde," "verde porro,"[8] and for water-colours, "verde di vesicha" or "pasta verde" [sap-green], the juice of rue, and of blue lilies.

Mulberry colour is made with "morello di ferro" and "morello di sale," burnt Roman vitriol, "celeste," and dark indico; and for water-colours, Turnsol.

Red is made with cinnabar, terra rossa, and fine lake.

Orange is made with minium and burnt orpiment.

Black is made with the smoke of burnt nut oil, burnt almond shells, smoke of burnt rosin, and black earth.

The shadows of the flesh are made with terra d' ombra, terra verde burnt, and asphaltum.

2. *The composition and mixtures of the colours, and first of white lead.*[9]

Sbiadato is made with white lead mixed with ochre, and is a colour similar to straw, or white lead with terra gialla.

Biondo is made with white, ochre, and gialdolino.

Celeste is made with white lead, and blue or smalti, and indico.

Pale green is made with a mixture of white lead and verdigris.

Bright green is made with white lead, verderame, or gialdo santo, or the juice of rue.

Yellow is made with white lead and gialdo santo.

Agatino is made of white lead and morel di ferro.

Blue is made with white lead and blues, or indico together.

The colour of unripe strawberries is made with white lead and cinnabar, but with more cinnabar than white lead.

Berettino and smoke colour are made with white lead and black well mixed together.

---

or dyer's weed) and other yellow flowers. From a comparison of this chapter with Haydocke's translation of Lomazzo, it appears that the colour here called Verdetto was one of those lakes to which the name of "Pink" has been given. The colour in question, perhaps, resembled "Brown Pink."

e poi l' acquarella, verde di vesicha, o sia pasta verde, succo di ruta, di gigli azurri.

Morello si fà con morello di ferro, e di sale, vitriolo romano cotto, celestro, et indico oscuro, e per acquarella il tornasole.

Rosso si fà col cinaprio, terra rossa, lacca fina.
Ranzetto si fà col minio et oropimento arso.
Negro si fa col fumo d' oglio di noce arso, guscio di Mandola arso, fumo di ragia, et terra negra.
Umbra delle carni si fà con terra d' ombra terra verde arsa, e spalato.

Compositione e mischia di colore e po. della biaca.

Sbiadato si fà con biaca mischiata con l' ocrea, et è color simile alla paglia, o biaca con terra gialla.
Biondo si fà con biaca, ocrea, e gialdolino.
Celeste si fa con biaca, e azuro, o smalti, et indico.

Verde smorto si fa con biaca e verderame mischiati.

Verde vivo si fa con biaca, verderame, o gialdo santo, overo suco di ruta.
Gialdo si fà con biaca e gialdo santo.
Agatino si fa con biaca e morel di ferro.
Turchino si fa con biaca e azurri, overo indico insieme.
Color di fragole mal mature si fa con biaca e cinaprio ma più cinaprio che biaca.
Berettino e color di fumo si fa con biaca e negro ben mischiati insieme.

---

8 Verde Porro. Perhaps the same as the Prasminum or Prasino of the old writers. Baldinucci (Voc. Dis.) says that it is a pigment of a whitish green colour, like that of the leek, whence it takes its name.

9 Compare this passage as far as No. 13 with Lomazzo's Treatise, lib. iii., cap. vii.

Rose colour is made with white lead and cinnabar, but more cinnabar than white lead.

The colour of stone, wood, bark of trees, and hair, is made with white lead and umber.

Straw colour is made with white lead and gialdolino.

3. *Mixtures of Gialdolino.*

Green colour for the distance in landscapes is made with gialdolino, blue, smalti, smaltino, and white lead.

Green is made with gialdolino and indico together.

A brighter green is made with gialdolino, indico, and orpiment.

The colour of flames and glories is made with gialdolino and cinnabar.

Orange colour is made with gialdolino and cinnabar, but with more cinnabar than gialdolino.

4. *The mixtures of blues, smalto, and "biadetti."*

Dark green is made with blue and giallo santo.

For purple and dark morello, blue and lake are mixed together.

A morello a little lowered in tone is made with blue, lake, and umber.

A morello of a very low tone is made with azzurro, lake, and black.

5. *The mixtures of verdigris.*

For bright green, verdigris is mixed with gialdo santo.

Bright green for water-colour painting is made with verdigris, rue-juice, and saffron.

Dark green is made with verdigris, indico, and umber, and it is lowered by adding black.

6. *The mixtures of Indico.*

Dark purple is made with indico and lake.

Color di rose si fa con biaca e cinaprio, ma più cinaprio che biaca.

Color di sassi, legni, scorze d' alberi e capelli si fa con biaca e terra d' ombra.

Color di paglia si fa con biaca e gialdolino.

Mischio del Gialdolino.

Color verde per lontani paesi si fa col gialdolino, e azurro, smalto o smaltino, e biaca.

Verde si fa col gialdolino et indico insieme.

Verde più vivo si fà col gialdolino, indico, et orpimento.

Color di fiame e splendori si fa col gialdolino e cinaprio.

Color di Naranzo si fa con gialdolino e cinaprio, ma più cinaprio che gialdolino.

Mischie degli azurri smalti e biadetti.

Verde oscuro si fa con azurro e gialo santo.

Pavonazzo e Morello scuro, si mischia azurro con biaca.

Morello che perde un poco si fa con azzurro, lacca, e terra d' ombra.

Morello che perde assai si fa con azzurro, lacca, e negro.

Mischie del verderame.

Verde vivo si mischia il verderame col gialdo santo.

Verde vivo per l' acquarella si fà col verderame, succo di ruta e zafferano.

Verde perso si fà con verderame, indico, e terra d' ombra, e si perde assai più aggiungendovi il negro.

Mischie dell' Indico.

Pavonazzo oscuro si fa col indico e lacca.

The colour of iron, silver, tin, &c., is imitated with indico, lake, and black.

7. *The mixtures of cinnabar.*

The colour of ripe strawberries is imitated with cinnabar and lake.

Scarlet is made with cinnabar, lake, and white lead.

Blood colour is made with cinnabar and lake.

The red colour on the cheeks of beautiful flesh is represented with cinnabar, lake, and white lead.

The colour of burnt ochre is imitated with cinnabar and black.

8. *The mixtures of lake.*

The colour of cinnabar is imitated with lake and minium.

The shades of the flesh are made with lake, minium, and umber.

The colour of black velvet is made with lake, blue, or indico and black.

The colour of velvet of a berettino colour [grey] is imitated with lake, cinnabar, ochre, and white.

Flesh colour is made with lake, cinnabar, ochre, and white.

Violet colour is made with lake and blue.

Dark morello colour is made with lake and blue or indico.

9. *The mixtures of minium.*

Orange colour is made with minium alone.

A light orange colour is made with minium and gialdolino.

10. *The mixtures of Gialdo santo.*

The colour of green grass or verdure is represented with gialdo santo and verdigris.

Emerald colour is imitated with gialdo santo, rue-juice, and verdigris, for miniature painting.

11. *The mixtures of black.*

Light berettino is made with black, white, terra d' ombra, lake, and indico.

Color di ferro, Argento, stagno, et simili, si fa con indico lacca e negro.

Mischie del cinapro.

Color di fragole mature si fa con cinaprio e lacca.

Color di scarlato si fa con cinaprio lacca e biacca.

Color di sangue si fa col cinaprio e lacca.

Color di guancie colorite di bella carne si fa con cinaprio, lacca, e biacca.

Color d' ocrea arsa si compone col cinaprio e negro.

Mischie della lacca.

Color di cinaprio si fa con lacca e minio.

Ombra di carne si fa con lacca, minio, e terra d' ombra.

Color di veluto negro si fa con lacca, azurro overo indico, e negro.

Color di veluto berettino si fa con lacca, azurro o indico, negro, e bianco.

Color di carne si fa con lacca, cinaprio, ocrea e bianco.

Color di viole si fa con lacca e azurro.

Morello oscuro si fa con lacca, e azurro overo indico.

Mischie del minio.

Color di naranzo si fa col solo minio.

Color ranzato chiaro si fa col minio e gialdolino.

Mischie del gialdo santo.

Color di verde pianure si fa col gialdo santo e verderame.

Color di smeraldo si fa col gialdo santo, succo di ruta, e verderame per miniare.

Mischie del negro.

Berettino chiaro si fa col negro, bianco, terra d' ombra lacca et Indico.

Smoke colour is made with black and white.

12. *The mixtures of white.*

The colour of the tops of mountains is made with white, ochre, and maiolica,[1] and they will appear as if touched by the sun.

Flame colour is made with white, gialdolino, and cinnabar.

13. *Of the shades in general, and how each of the above-mentioned colours should be shaded.*[2]

We must first warn you that the shades must not be laid on lighter or darker than the colour which is to be shaded can bear. All the mixtures of compound colours must be shaded with the darkest of the colours of which they are composed, used pure, and in the following manner :—

Celeste made with blue and white, must be shaded with pure blue.

Green made with white and gialdo santo, is shaded with gialdo santo.

Light morello mixed with umber, must be shaded with dark morello.

Blue made with indico and white lead, is shaded with pure indico.

Cinnabar mixed with white, is shaded with cinnabar alone.

Umber mixed with white, is shaded with umber alone.

Blue, black, smaltino, and biadetto, are shaded with indico, lake, and black.

Verdigris is shaded with indico or black.

Pure gialdo santo is shaded with umber.

Dark morello is shaded with black.

White is shaded with black or berettino.

Gialdolino is shaded with ochre, or terra gialla, and umber.

---

[1] Majolica, a red earth. (Terra Rossa.)

Color di fumo si compone col negro e bianco.

Mischie del bianco.

Color delle cime de' Monti si fa con bianco, ocrea, maiolica, e pareranno toche dal sole.

Color di fiamma si fa col bianco, gialdolino, e cinaprio.

Dell' ombre in generale, e come si debba ombreggiare ciascheduno de suddetti colori.

Avertasi prima a non dar ombra più oscura, ne più chiara di quello che può comportare quel colore che si deve ombreggiare. Tutte le mischie fate di più colori si devono ombrare in quel colore pure, che nella mischia resta più oscuro, e nel modo che segue.

Celeste, fatto con azurro e bianco, l' ombra con puro azurro.

Verde fatto di bianco e gialdo santo, l' ombra col gialdo santo solo.

Morello chiaro cioè mischiato d' ombra con morello scuro.

Turchino fatto d' indico e biaca, o bianco, s' ombra con indico puro.

Cinaprio mischiato con bianco, s' ombra con cinaprio solo.

Terra d' ombra mischia con bianco, s' ombreggia con terra d' ombra sola.

Azurro, negro, e smaltino, e biadetto, s' ombrano con indico, lacca, e negro.

Verderame, s' ombra con indico e negro.

Gialdo santo puro, s' ombra con terra d' ombra.

Morello oscuro, s' ombra col negro.

Bianco, s' ombra col negro o berettino.

Gialdolino, s' ombra con ocrea o terra gialla, e terra d' ombra.

---

[2] See Lomazzo, lib. iii. cap. viii.

Saffron for water colours is shaded with the same saffron, mixed with a little lake and umber.

Orpiment is shaded with terra gialda and a little umber.

Cinnabar is shaded with lake, or a mixture of cinnabar and black.

Dark yellow is shaded with a mixture of lake and black.

Umber is shaded with black.

A red made with lake, and white, and other mixtures, is shaded with lake alone.

Cinnabar is shaded with lake.

All light colours, except white, are shaded with umber.

14. *How gum water for dissolving and distempering the colours for miniature painting is made.*—Take what you consider to be a proper quantity of very clear and clean gum arabic, leave it infused in rose water for a night with a little candied sugar, in a clean glass vase, which you will then place in a pipkin or other vessel, with common water in it; let the water in the pipkin boil for a short time, and the gum water will then be perfectly prepared, so that the colours will not crack or scale off.

15. *To make a good green from blue lilies.*—The flowers must be pounded with lemon juice, a little burnt roche alum, and glassmaker's soda, and then strained through a fine linen cloth, put in shells, and dried in the shade.

16. *To make a good green of verderame.*—Take 10 parts of verdigris, 2 of corrosive sublimate, ½ a part of saffron, ¼ of galls of Istria, and ½ of sal ammoniac, grind them up with very strong vinegar (distilled vinegar is the best), put them into a glass vase, and when the vinegar is clear and coloured, let it be decanted and evaporated in a glazed vase. Then pour fresh vinegar on the remainder, mix again and do as before, until the part which settles ceases to colour the vinegar, and if you pour the coloured vinegar into shallow open vases, it will dry much quicker either in the sun or in the shade. When dry remove

Zaffrano per l' acquarella, s' ombra con l' istesso zaffrano meschiato con poco di lacca, e terra d' ombra.

Orpimento s' ombra con terra gialda, e puoca terra d' ombra.

Cinaprio s' ombra con lacca, ovvero cinaprio e negro meschi.

Gialdo scuro s' ombra con negro e lacca meschi.

Terra d' ombra s' ombreggia col negro.

Rosso fatto di lacca, e bianco, et altri mischie, s' ombra con lacca sola.

Rosso di cinapro, s' ombra con lacca.

I colori chiari, eccetto che il bianco, si ombreggiano con terra d' ombra.

Come si facci l' acqua di gom̃a per disciogliere e temperar i colori per miniare.—Piglierai quella quantità di gomma arrabica ben chiara e netta che ti pare, la porai in infusione per una notte in acqua rosa con un poco di zucchero candito in un vaso di vetro ben netto, quale indi metterai in una scudella, o altro vaso in acqua com̃une dentro, che poi facendo bollire per poco tempo l' acqua della scudella che havera dentro il uasetto con l' acqua gom̃ata, che cosi restarà cotta a perfettione, e non creparanno li colori, meno si spicaranno.

Per cavar un bel verde da gilij azurri.—Si pestano li fiori con succo di limone, puoco alume di rocca bruggiato, e soda di vetriari, e colato per pezza sottile, si mettono in conchilie, e si lasciano asciugare all' ombra.

Per fare un bel verde di verderame.—Verderame^{10}, solimato^{2}, zafrano$^{\frac{1}{2}}$, galla d' Istria$^{\frac{1}{4}}$, e sal amoniaco$^{\frac{1}{2}}$. Si macina il tutto con acetto fortiss^{mo}, e se fosse distilato sarà meglio, poi si meta in vaso di vetro, e quando il d^{to} acetto sarà chiaro e colorito si decanti, e si m̃eta in vaso vitriato ad asciugare; e sopra le residenza si metta novo acetto, si mescoli sempre, e si facci come sopra sin à tanto che le residenze non rendino più colorito l' acetto, et quelli acetti coloriti mettendoli in vasi spanti si sciugaranno più presto all' ombra, et anco al sole, et seccati gen-

the colour gently by dipping the pencil in vinegar, and afterwards grind up the colour with a little roche alum and a little gum arabic, so as to make it into a cake.

17. *To make another brilliant green.*—Take oz. vi of the best verdigris, oz. ij of tartar of Bologna, and dr. j ss. of roche alum; pulverize the whole, and grind each article separately, then grind them together rather stiffly with distilled vinegar, put the powder into a glass vase with a little saffron, and expose it to the sun. Then pour on it a bocale of distilled vinegar, and the longer it is exposed to the sun the more beautiful will be the colour.

18. *How to make yellow.*—Take flowers of wall-flowers, grind them up with roche alum, strain through rag, and preserve the juice.

19. *How gamboge is refined.*—It is ground up with lemon juice and burnt roche alum.

20. *How cinnabar is refined.*—It is boiled with vinegar and roche alum.

21. *How to prepare lake for miniature painting.*—Steep the pounded lake in rose water for 12 hours to soften, then grind it up with gum water made in the before-mentioned manner, adding lemon juice, vinegar, burnt alum, and candied sugar at discretion. Observe, that burnt lake makes a beautiful shadow colour.

22. *How to prepare cochineal.*—Boil it with lemon juice, garlic juice, and burnt alum.

23. *How paper of "rosseto di Spagna" is used.*—Apply first a coat of lemon juice, then one of alum water, and lastly another of lemon juice, letting each coat dry before the next is laid on. Afterwards, dipping the pencil in lemon juice, take the rosseto off the paper as you require it.

24. *How ultramarine blue is distempered.*—It is softened in boiled water for a night, and is then taken out and tempered with clear glue.

25. *How to purify the turnsole.*—Boil it with urine, then strain and squeeze it through a cloth.

26. *How to grind gold and silver for writing and miniature*

tilmente col pennello bagnato d' acetto li anderai leccando, e raccogliendo il colore, qual poi con poco d' alume di rocca lo remacinerai, et puoco di gomma arrabica acciò si faccia in pietra.

Per fare un altro verde lustro.—Piglia verderame ℥ vi del più bello, tartaro di Bologna ℥ ij, alume di rocca ʒ j ss, si polverizi il tutto e si macini separatamente, poi messi insieme con acetto stilato, macinato alquanto duretto, mettasi in vaso di vetro al sole con poco di zafrano, e vi si aggiunga sopra un bocale d' acetto stilato, e più che starà al sole sarà più bello.

Gialo come si facci.—Si pigliano fiori di uiolette gialle, si macinano con alume di rocca, e colato per pezza il succo si conserva.

La gomma gute come si raffini.—Si macinerà con succo di limone et alume di rocca bruciato.

Il cinaprio come si raffini.—Facciasi bollire con accetto et alume di rocca.

La lacca come si prepari per miniare.—Mettasi in mole la lacca pesta, in acqua rosa per 12 hore, poi si macini con l' acqua di gomma d^{ta} di sopra, giongendoui succo di limone, accetto, alume bruciato, e zuccaro candito il tutto a discretione. Nota che la lacca bruciata serve per far ombre belliss^{me}.

La coccioniglia come si prepari.—Facciasi bollire con succo di limone, succo d' aglio, et alume bruciato.

La carta di rosseto di Spagna, come s' adopri.—Prima se le darà sopra una mano di succo di limone, poi un' altra d' acqua alluminata, poi un altra di succo di limone, lasciando però s' asciughi ciascheduna volta prima. Poi bagnando il penello in succo di limone, lo cavarai dalla carta a suo bisogno.

L' azurro oltramarino come si tempri.—Si mette a molle l' azurro per una notte in acqua bolita, poi si cava e si tempera con acqua chiara di colla di carnuzza.

Il torna sole come si purghi.—Si purga facendolo bollire con orina, poi si cola e si preme con pensia [pezza?].

Per macinar oro et argento per scrivere e miniare.—Prendasi

painting.—Take of the finest and yellowest gialdolino di Fiandra oz. i ss. and of gold leaf oz. ss., little more or less; grind them up together with fresh water a little at a time on a piece of porphyry; then put the mixture in a glass, let it settle and pour off the water. In grinding silver, supply the place of gialdolino with nitre.

27. *A glue which holds as tight as a nail.*—Take Greek pitch, resin of the pine, and powder of baked bricks; mix them all together, and when it is to be used make it very hot.

28. *How to make ink that will remain black when water is added.*— After the inkstand has once been filled with ink of a good colour, a piece of red orpiment should be put into it, and if a piece of the same [*i. e.* the red orpiment] be put into white of egg, it will keep for a long time without putrefying.

By boiling roche alum in water until one-third of the water has evaporated, and while still hot, washing it over paper with a pencil or sponge, when it is dry you may paint on it even if it were common blotting paper, which is not then liable to blot.

29. *To make a good yellow for writing and miniature painting.*—Take what quantity you please of the berries of buckthorn while they are still green and unripe, bruise them coarsely in a mortar, put them into a vase with enough ley to cover them, and place them to boil over a slow fire until half the ley is consumed; then strain through a cloth, and put the strained liquor again over the fire, with a little roche alum, not heating it to the boiling point, and when you have done this, put it into shells to dry, and preserve it well-covered from the air.

30. *To make a most beautiful orange-yellow colour.*—Take orpiment, put it in a jeweller's crucible, and melt it over a charcoal fire, then take it from the fire, let it cool, and preserve it, and when you wish to use it, grind it finely, and temper it with gum water.

31. *How pasta verde* [sap green] *is made.*—Take the grains or berries of the buckthorn when they are quite ripe, and this will be about the end of September; let them soften for 7 or 8 days in a vase with water in which roche alum has been dissolved in

di gialdolino di fiandra del più fino e gialo ℥ i ss., di fogli d'oro ℥ ss. poco più ò meno, il tutto si macina con acqua fresca poco à poco, sopra pietra di porfido, poi si mette in un bichiero, si lascia posare, e si cola l' acqua ; per macinar l' argento si mete in loco del gialdolino, salnitro raffinato.

Colla che tien forte come un chiodo.—Piglia pecce greca, resina picea, e polvere di quadrelli cotti, mescola ogni cosa insieme, e dovendola adoperare falla scaldar bene.

L' inchiostro come si mantenghi negro con aggiungervi acqua.—Dopo ch' una volta sarà aggiustato il calamaro con buona tinta, vi si metta dentro un pezzo di risigallo, e mettendo l' istesso nella chiara d' ovo si conserverà longo tempo senza putrefarsi.

Facendo bollire allume di rocca in acqua che cali duoi terzi, e con quella cosi calda bagnando la carta con penello o spongia, asciuto che sarà vi si potrà dipingere sopra ancor che fosse carta strazza e leva le macchie.

Per fare un bel gialdo da scrivere e miniare.—Piglia quella quantità ti piace di grani o sia pomelli di spincervino ma verdi et immaturi, fracassali nel mortaro grossamente, ponili in uaso con dentro liscia, che basti per coprirli, indi li metterai a lento foco a bollire sino sia consumata quasi la mettà della liscia, ciò fatto li collerai per una tella, et la collitura di nuovo metterai al fuoco con un poco di lume di rocca facendola solamente scaldare, finalmente la metterai in conchiglie ad asciugare, e lo difenderai ben coperto dall' aria.

Color giallo ranzo bellissimo.—Piglia orpimento, mettilo in grisolo da orefici e fallo liquefar à fuoco di carboni, indi levalo dal fuoco, lascialo rafredare, e serbalo, e quando vorrai servirtene, macinalo sottil^{te} e tempralo con acqua di gomma.

Pasta verde come si faccia.—Piglia bacchi o sia granelli di spincervino beniss^{mo} matturi, il che sarà la fine di 7bre ; lasciali a mogio in un vaso per sette o otto giorni mettendogli dentro acqua nella quale sia disciolto alume di rocca, e sarà per ogni

the proportion of 1 ounce of alum to 6 of the berries, and boil it well until nearly half the water is consumed; then cool it, strain through a linen cloth, put the part that is strained into pigs' bladders, and dry them in the sun or smoke; and this is called "pasta di vesicha."

32. *How to refine verdigris.*—Take the verdigris, grind it well, steep it in the best vinegar for 3 or 4 days, strain it, then pour the strained liquor on other well-ground verdigris; let it settle for 2 days more, strain it again gently, leaving the lees of the verdigris at the bottom of the vase; put the liquid which has been strained in a glass vessel with a little saffron, and keep it well covered.

32. *A most beautiful green colour.*—Take the powdered verdigris, dissolve it with lemon-juice, and let it settle for 24 hours; then strain the most fluid portion very carefully, leaving the lees at the bottom of the vase. Put the strained liquid into a glass vase, and add to it a little of the above-mentioned pasta verde, let it dry, and when you use it, add to it some more lemon juice, and the more you add the more beautiful the colour will be, so that it will be like an emerald; take care, however, that you do not permit the pencil to touch water.

34. *How to prepare cinnabar for miniature painting.*—Grind the cinnabar on the porphyry with clear water, and let it dry; then put it in a glass vase with urine, mixing the two substances well together; then let it settle, so that the cinnabar will fall to the bottom, and pour off the liquid gently. Then add more urine, mix as before, and continue to do thus for 4 or 5 days, morning and evening, so that the cinnabar will be well purified. Then take some white of egg well beaten with a small piece of dry wood, pour it over the cinnabar to the depth of a finger, mix them well together; let the cinnabar fall to the bottom, and wash it as before for 2 or 3 days, so that the smell will be removed from the cinnabar; and then, when it is well purified, pour in some more white of egg, and mix well together. Leave it thus, and it will be most perfect. When it is used, stir it well.

sei oncie di grani uno d' alume, e cocendo molto bene sino alla consumatione quasi della metà dell' acqua, lasciala raffredare, si colli per tella di lino, e la collatura si ponghi in vesiche di porco, di poi si mettono a seccare al sole overo al fumo, si chiama pasta di vesicha.

Verde rame come si raffini.—Si piglia il verderame, si tritta bene, poi s' infonde in boniss^{mo} aceto per due o tre giorni, indi si cola, e la colatura, lasciando le fecci, si metti sopra altro verderame ben tritto, si lascia posare per due altri giorni, collasi di novo gentil^{te} lasciando la feccia del verderame nel fondo del vaso, e la collatura liquida si mette in ampola di vetro con poco di zafferano, serbasi ben coperto.

Color verde belliss^{mo}.—Si piglia il verderame polverisato, si disolve con succo di limoni, e si lascia posare per hore 24, indi si cola pian piano il più liquido tralasciando le fecci nel fondo del vaso, e la collatura si mette in vaso di vetro, e se gl' aggionge un poco della sod^{ta} pasta verde, e si lascia sciugare, e quando vorrai servirtene, li aggiongerai altro succo di limone, e quanto più ciò farai, tanto sarà più bello in modo che parerà un smeraldo, avertendo però che il pennello non tocchi acqua.

Come si prepari il cinaprio per miniare.—Macina il cinaprio sopra il porfido con acqua chiara, e quando sarà macinato, lasciallo seccare, poi mettilo in vaso di vetro con orina sopra, mescolando ben insieme, poi lascialo posare tanto che vadi in fondo, poi getta via l' orina piano, poi metti dell' altra sempre mescolando come prima, e cosi farai per quattro o cinque giorni, sera e mattina, che sarà beniss^{mo} purgato. Poi habbi chiara d' ouo ben batutta con un legnetto secco, e mettila sopra il cinaprio che sopravanzi un dito, e stempralo bene insieme, lascia andar in fondo il cinaprio, e fa come del orina per doi o tre di, che levarà tutto il tuffo al cinaprio, poi essendo ben purgato mettevi altra chiara, e mescola bene e lascia così che sarà perfettiss^{mo}, e volendo adoperare, mescolano bene.

35. *Green for writing.*—Take the black nightshade, extract the juice, strain it, and write with it, and it will answer well. You may also do the same with the juice of rue.

35*a*. *To make lake, indico, and lamp-black, dry quickly.*—Grind them with oil, then take glass ground to a very fine powder, and incorporate with the colours by grinding them together again; and thus, in the space of 24 hours, they will dry.

36. *To gild the leaves of books.*—Having first put the book in the press, and cut it very evenly, give it a coat of well-beaten white of egg, and let it dry. Then take Armenian bole of the size of a nut, and candied sugar of the size of a small pea, grind them well together dry; then grind them again with well-beaten white of egg, and give the book another coat, neither too thick nor too thin; let it dry; then bathe it with the pencil dipped in clear water; and before it dries, lay on the gold-leaf dexterously with the cotton, and when dry polish with the tooth.

37. *To make a very strong glue.*—It is made with ceruse, minium, umber, and litharge of gold, all well ground up with boiled nut oil, and made into a paste which serves for cementing stones to wooden handles or other parts of small machines, but it ought to be dried in the sun.

38. *Mode of etching on copper or iron with "aqua fortis," and how the said "aqua fortis" is made.*—The plate of copper must be made very even and then burnished, and it must be varnished with a varnish made of wax, mastic, and the smoke of rosin made into a cake by the heat of the fire, then heating the plate of copper in such a manner that when this cake is rubbed over it, it may be liquefied and united smoothly. It is then allowed to cool, and the design is drawn on it with a sharp style, and the plate is then placed so that it may hang over a varnished vessel which contains the aqua fortis made in the following manner:—

39. *"Aqua fortis."*—Pulverize verdigris, sal ammoniac, and galls of Istria, and put the powder into strong vinegar, and

Verde per scrivere.—Piglia solatro ortense, cavane il succo, colalo, e scrivi che riuscirà beniss^mo^. Il mede potrai ancor fare col succo di ruta.

Per far asciugare prestamente la lacca, indico, e negro di fumo. Macinati a olio, si piglia polvere di vetro ben pesta, e macinati sottilm^te^, poi s' incorpora con li sud^ti^ colori, rimacinandoli di nuovo, e cosi in spazio di ventiquattro hore s' asciugheranno.

Per indorare le carte de libri.—Primieramente messo il libro nel torcolo tagliato ben uguale le darai una mano di chiara d' ouo ben battuta, e lascia seccare, poi piglia bollo armeno quanto una noce, zuccaro candito quanto un cece, macina bene insieme a secco, indi torna macinare con chiara d' ouo battuta, poi ne darai una mano, che non sia troppo liquido ne troppo spesso sopra il libro, e lascialo seccare, e poi bagnalo con acqua chiara col pennello, et auanti s' asciughi mettili li pezzi d' oro in foglio sopra destramente col bombace, e seccato, liscia con il dente.

Per far colla gagliardiss^ma^.—Si fa con cerusa, minio, terra d' ombra, e litargirio d' oro, si macina il tutto beniss^mo^ con oglio di noce coto, e se ne fa pasta, qual serve per incolare pietre con manichi di legno o d' altra materia per far macinini, ma devesi lasciar seccare al sole.

Modo d' intagliare in rame e ferro con l' acqua forte, e come si faccia d^t^ acqua.—Si prepara la piastra di Rame ben spianata e lustra, e s' invernicarà con vernice fatta con cera, mastice, e fumo di raggia, formandone al calor del fooco una pallotta, poi si fa scaldare la piastra a segno tale che passandovi, e fregandovi sopra detta mistura si liquefaci con unirla legerm^te^ sopra detta piastra, poi si lasciarà rafredare, e con un stecco aguzzo farassi il disegno che si vuole, poi si collocherà deta piastra in modo che sia pendente sopra d' un vaso vernicato, nel quale sia l' acqua forte seguente.

Acqua forte.—Pigliasi verderame salarmoniaco, accetto forte, e galla d' Istria, il tutto polverizzato, e messo nel detto accetto,

after beating it continually with a spoon or "spatula" for four hours, pour it over the suspended plate (but if you have to engrave on iron, instead of the sal ammoniac, put to it some corrosive sublimate), and let that water remain on the plate for the space of 6 or 8 hours.

40. *To make the colours stand in fresco.*—They should be distempered with milk; this is found to succeed wonderfully, especially with the smalti and smaltini.

41. *Verdigris for painting in water-colours.*—Take of verdigris oz. vj, and of refined tartar of wine about oz. j, pound them both separately. The verdigris is to be put with half a bocale of very strong vinegar, weighing about oz. xij, into a new pipkin, and to be allowed to boil until, on a pencil being dipped in the vinegar, it will be seen to stain a piece of paper.

During the boiling the above-mentioned tartar must be added, and when it is done it must be placed, cold, in a glass flask, together with what remains at the bottom, and the water must be allowed to clear; and if, when it is used, the colour is too deep, more strong vinegar may be added, and while it is used the pencil must not be allowed to touch clear water.

Remember that the pipkin must not be uncovered during the boiling, lest the vinegar should evaporate; a small hole in the cover, large enough to admit a small piece of wood, will be quite sufficient for stirring the mixture while it boils.

42. *To lay the colours on silver for flowers* [for ornamenting].—After you have laid on the silver, take lake and whatever colour you please, grind it up well with pure water, and give the silver 3 coats, one thin and the other two thicker; and when it is dry, draw the ornamental foliage or other works with the style, and then apply the varnish warm.

43. *To lay gold on sandals, paper, or other things.*—First apply a coat of strong Lyons' glue (?), in which you will boil some white lead and yellow earth ground up together with a little honey; then gild, and it will succeed wonderfully.

44. *Oil gilding on stone.*—Take nut oil which has been boiled with litharge of gold, yellow earth, and minium, well

qual poi per quattro hore continue si fa passare sbattendolo con cucchiaro, o palletta sopra d^{ta} piastra pendente, ma dovendosi intagliare in ferro, in loco del sal armoniaco, si mette in d^{ta} acqua del solimato, qual acqua si lascia passarvi sopra la piastra per lo spacio di sei o otto hore.

Per far restare i colori a fresco.—Si deuono stemperare con latte, e ciò riesse beniss^{mo}, massime ne smalti e smaltini.

Acquarella di verderame.—Si piglia di verderame ℥ vj, si pesta beniss^{mo}, poi si pesta di tartaro di Bote raffinato ℥ j circa.

Si mette d^{to} verderame in un pignatino novo con mezo bocalo d' aceto fortiss^{mo} come sarebbe ℥ xij e si lascia bollire poi fintantoche pigliando un pennello, e bagnandolo in d^{o} accetto si vedrà tinger bene la carta.

A mezo il boglio se li metterà il tartaro sud^{to}, e doppo che sarà fatto si metterà freddo in una caraffa di vetro, insieme con la residenza che sarà in fondo, e si lasciarà chiarir l' acqua, la quale quando nell' adoperarla restasse col color troppo carico, se le potrà aggiongere nel ampola altro aceto forte, ne bisogna nel adoperarla che il pennello tocchi acqua chiara.

Avertasi nel bollir à non lasciar il pignatino scoperto acciò non svapori, bastando un piccolo pertuggio nel coperto per mettervi dentro nel bucco un legnetto, e mescolar il tutto mentre bolle.

Per metter colori sopra argento per fiorire.—Dopo ch' hauerai dato l' argento, piglia lacca, e qual si voglia colore, e macinalo bene con acqua semplice, e ne darai tre mani sopra l' argento, una chiara, e l' altre due più spesse, e sciugato farai i fiorami o lavori con stecco indi li darai la vernice calda.

Per metter oro sopra zendalo carta o altro.—Prima darai una mano di colla forte di lione, nella quale bollirai un poco di mele con biacca, o terra gialda macinati insieme, indi metterai l' oro e riuscira benissimo.

Per metter oro sopra pietra a oglio.—Prendi oglio di noce bollito con litargirio d' oro, e terra gialda, e minio ben macinati,

ground; give three coats of this, and let it remain thus for 2 or 3 days, when you will lay on the gold.

45. *A clear and fine varnish.*—Take of clear Venice turpentine oz. iij, and of odoriferous oil of spike oz. j, melt them well together over a slow fire, and use the varnish hot, recollecting that if you are using it on wood you must first give it a good coat of glue, or distemper the colours with gum water, in order that the varnish may not penetrate.

46. *A varnish which has been tried.*—Take equal parts of white mastic and linseed oil, put them into a new pipkin over a slow fire, and when the oil is hot, add to it a little "olio d' abezzo," and continue to mix.

47. *Another good varnish.*—Take equal quantities of red mastic well powdered and linseed oil with a little resin; put them over the fire in a new pipkin, stirring the ingredients continually for a quarter of an hour, when it will be finished.

48. *Another varnish.*—Take of oglio d' abezzo, naphtha, and white mastic, all at discretion; put the whole into a new pipkin over a slow fire, and boil until all the mastic is dissolved; if there is plenty of the olio di abezzo the varnish will be better.

49. *A varnish which dries directly.*—Take equal parts of boiled linseed oil and white mastic, place them over the fire in a new pipkin with a little oglio di abezzo; let them boil while you can say a credo; then add to them spirit of turpentine, equal in quantity to half the linseed oil, mixing it well with the other ingredients.

50. *Another varnish which dries directly.*—Put into a pipkin a proper quantity of mastic, cover it with a somewhat greater quantity of naphtha, and leave the pipkin over the hot coals until the mastic is dissolved.

51. *A varnish which does not dry immediately.*—Take of white mastic oz. j, of nut or linseed oil oz. ij, and of oglio di abezzo oz. ss; put the whole into a pipkin, and boil over a slow

e ne darai tre mani, e lascierai stare cosi per due o tre giorni, indi darai l' oro.

Vernice sottilla e chiara.—Piglia trementina di Venetia chiara ℥ iij, oglio di spico odorifero ℥ j, fa fondere bene insieme a lento foco, poi la darai caldo a tuo modo, auertendo di dar prima una buona mano di colla sopra se sarà lavoro di legno, ovvero stemprerai li collori con acqua gommata acciò la vernice non trapassi.

Vernice provata.—Piglia mastice bianco et olio di lino, di ciascuno parti uguali, metti ogni cosa in un pignatino nouo al foco lento, e come sarà caldo l' olio, metterai dentro un poco d' oglio d' abezzo e mescola sempre.

Altra vernice bona.—Mastice rosso ben pesto, et oglio di lino, tanto dell' uno quanto dell' altro, con poco di Raggia, metti ogni cosa in pignatino novo al fuoco, mescolando sempre per lo spatio d' un quarto d' hora, et è fatta.

Altra vernice.—Si piglia oglio d' abezzo, e oglio di sasso e mastice bianco, il tutto a discretione, si pone il tutto in pignatino a foco lento, e si fa bollir sin tanto che il mastice sia disfato, e sarà più gagliarda con assai abezzo.

Vernice che subito s' asciuga.—Oglio di lino cotto con mastice bianco, parti uguali, pongasi in pigna^{no} nouo con poco d' oglio d' abezzo al fuoco, lascia bollir per spacio d'un credo, poi mettivi dentro un poco d' acqua di raggia, tantoche sia per mettà del oglio di lino mescolando sempre.

Altra vernice che subito asciuga.—Metti in pignatino tanto mastice quanto ti piace, coprilo con olio di sasso che sopravanzi un poco, lascia il pignatino sopra le ceneri calde sintanto che sia disfatto il mastice.

Vernice ch' aspetta.—Di mastice bianco ℥ j, olio di noce over di lino ℥ ij, d' oglio d' abezzo ℥ ss., metti ogni cosa in un pignatino, e fa bollire a foco lento sin tanto sia disfatto il mastice, poi mettegli dentro poco oglio di sasso a discretione.

fire until all the mastic is dissolved; then add a little naphtha at discretion.

52. *A varnish which has been proved to dry instantly.*—Take of coarsely pounded white mastic oz. j, of spirit of turpentine oz. j, of naphtha oz j, and of oglio di abezzo oz. ij; put all the ingredients into a glass vessel closely covered with paper; then put a tin pot over the fire, to the handle of which the glass must be suspended, being secured to it by a string; and put into the tin pot sufficient water to cover the glass. Boil the water for half an hour, and until the mastic is dissolved, taking care not to take out the glass while the water is boiling, as it would crack.

53. *Another varnish.*—Let any quantity of oglio di abezzo, naphtha, and mastic, be placed in a pipkin in the summer and exposed to the sun, and in this way excellent varnish will be made.

54. *How to wash old pictures previous to varnishing them.*—Take tartar and black soap, and boil them with water. With this old paintings are washed, and afterwards varnished with the following varnish.

55. *A varnish for old pictures.*—Take linseed or nut oil, oil of spike, and powdered mastic, all at discretion; put them into a pipkin over a slow fire. This is found to succeed.

56. *Another mode of washing old paintings.*—Take some weak ley and soap with a little of that amalgam[1] which is used for the backs of mirrors, and rub the amalgam all over the picture; leave it in that state for a short time, then wash it off with a new ley, and lastly wash off the whole with common water. This has been tried.

57. *A varnish which does not dry immediately.*—Take a

---

[1] Amalgam for the backs of looking glasses. The process of silvering mirrors at Murano was described by Porta to be as follows:—" The tin, hammered to thin leaves, was spread out very smoothly, and quicksilver was poured over it; and when the tin was saturated it was covered with paper. The glass, wiped exceedingly clean, was then laid above it, and while the workman pressed it down with his left hand, he drew out very

Vernice che subito sciuga—provata.—Di mastice bianco mezo pesto ℥ j, d' acqua di raggia ℥ j, d' oglio di sasso ℥ j, oglio d' abezzo ℥ ij, metta ogni cosa in un ampolla ben otturata con carta poi metti una stagnata al foco, et in essa metti l' ampola che con spago sia legata sospesa al manico, e metti nella stagnata tant' acqua che copra l' ampola, fa bollir l' acqua per spacio di mez' hora, e sin tanto che il mastice sia disfato, avertendo di non tirar fuori l' ampola dal acqua nel tempo che bolle, perche l' ampola creperebbe.

Altra vernice.—Oglio d' abezzo, oglio di sasso, e mastice, ogni cosa a discretione, pongansi in pignatino l' estate al sole, che in questo modo si fa perfett^{ma}.

Come si lavino li quadri vecchi nanti di dargli la vernice.—Si piglia alume di feccia, e sapon negro, si fa bollir con l' acqua, e con quella si lauono bene i quadri vechi: poi se li da la seguente vernice.

Vernice da darsi à quadri vechi.—Si piglia oglio di lino, ouero oglio di noce, oglio di spico, et mastice pesto, ogni cosa a discretione si mette in pignatino a foco lento, e riesce.

Altro modo di lauar quadri vechi.—Si piglia della liscia dolce, e sapone con un poco di quel stagnolo che sta dietro i specchi, e si va con deto stagniolo sfregaciando sopra il quadro, e vi si lascia stare poco, poi si lava giù detto stagnolo con noua liscia, poi con acqua comune si lava giù ogni cosa—provato.

Vernice che aspetta assai.—Piglia un pignatino e poni mastice

---

carefully with his right the paper that lay between the tin and the glass, over which weights were afterwards placed." In Germany, however, according to Garzoni, an amalgam was used, composed of a mixture of lead, tin, the silver marchesite, and tartar; while Porta says the mixture consisted of antimony, lead, and colophonium. (See Beckmann's 'Inventions,' vol. ii. p. 78, 79.)

pipkin, and put into it white mastic, linseed, or nut oil, at discretion; then boil it over a slow fire until all the mastic is dissolved.

58. *Mode of preparing lime for fresco painting.*—Take quicklime, quench it in water; then grind it well with water, and after it is ground place it on a stone impervious to water; let it dry, and it will then be ready for use.

59. *A varnish for picture-frames coloured like walnut wood.*—Take a pipkin and pour into it a proper quantity of the strongest spirit of wine, add to it some dry pine resin in the following proportions, namely: of resin, a piece equal in bulk to 5 nuts to a drinking glass of spirit; then put the pipkin over the fire, and when the resin is dissolved, the varnish will be finished; but take care that the flame does not approach the pipkin. You may then use it on any work you please, but remember that dust before it is dry will injure it much.

60. *Secret for writing with leaf gold.*—If you wish to write with gold on parchment or paper, take of candied sugar oz ij, and fine ochre oz. j; grind them well on a colour-grinder's slab, then distemper with urine or barber's ley, and make the mixture so liquid that you can write with it. Then prepare your pen, and write on the paper as if you were writing with ink. When you have finished writing, let it dry well; then take up the gold on some small pieces of cotton, breathe on the letters so that they will become rather moist, and then apply the gold dexterously, pressing it slightly with the cotton. In this manner the gold will remain fastened to the letters, and you must then rub gently with paper or something else on that part which is not written on to remove the loose gold; and if the letters should be capitals, like the Roman letters, you may with a penknife proceed to take off the gold where it is not wanted. If in any place the gold does not adhere to the letters, you may put on some more; and lest that also should not adhere, you may retouch the letters with the above-mentioned mixture, and again apply the gold when the composition is dry; and this is

bianco et oglio di lino o di noce a discretione fa bollir a lento foco sin che il mastice sia disfatto.

Modo d' accomodar la calcina per servirsene a fresco.—Piglia calcina viva, e strugila in acqua, poi macinala bene con acqua, e dopo macinata ponila sopra pietra viva, lasciala seccare, e adoprela.

Vernice da dare a Cornici colorite di color di noce.—Si piglia un pignati^{no}, e dentro vi si mette dell' acqua vita galiardiss^{ma} quella quantità si uol fare, e poi vi si mette dentro della raggia di pino secca, cioè in un bichiero d' acqua vita, si ponerà tanta raggia quanto sarà cinque noci in circa, poi si mete al foco, et a forza di foco si fa disfare, e come sarà disfata la raggia all' hora sarà fatta. Ma averti di non lasciar accostar la vampa del foco al pignatino, quella poi si da al lavoro che ti piace, avertendo che la polvere le fa danno non asciuta.

Secretto per scrivere con oro in foglio.—Volendo scrivere con oro in carta pecorina o altra carta, piglia Zuccaro candito ℥ ij, ocrea fina ℥ j, macina sottilm^{te} sopra una pietra da macinar colori, poi distempera con orina, overo liscia di barbiero, e lafarai tanto liquida, che si possi con essa scrivere, poi accomoda la tua penna, e scrivi sopra la carta come se scrivessi con l' inchiostro, e quando haverai fornito di scrivere, lascia asciugare bene, poi piglia l' oro sopra un poco di bombace a pezzetti, e con il fiato li soffierai sopra le lettere tanto che doventi un poco humida poi va applicando destramente l' oro premendolo alquanto col bombace, che in questa maniera resterà l' oro attaccato alla lettera, e dove non è scritto se ne anderà via fregando legier^{te} con una carta o altra cosa, e se le lettere fossero Miuscole (sic) come le Romane con un temperino li puoi andar rappezzando, e levar l' oro dove non fà bisogno, e se in alcun loco l' oro non fosse attacato ne porai dell' altro, e caso che non s' attacasse, si ritocca con la mistura sud^{ta}, poi ponivi l' oro dopo asciugata e cosi si fa. E se vuoi fare in altro modo più facile, piglia succo d' aglio e con quello scrivi, e lascia asciugare indi metti sopra

the manner in which letters are gilded. And if you would gild in an easier manner, take garlic juice, write with it, let it dry, and lay on the gold in the above-mentioned manner. But this mode does not please me on account of the smell.

61. *How very fine ink is made.*—Take of strong white wine lb. 8, and of well broken galls of Istria oz. viij, put them together in a glazed vase, and expose them to the heat of the sun or in a covered furnace for 8 days, stirring them frequently; then separate the wine from the galls, strain it, and add to it of Roman vitriol oz. vj, and leave it in the shade for a week longer, stirring it frequently. Then take of gum arabic oz. ij, dissolve it in a pint of rose-water, and for 8 days more continue to mix this with the wine, at the end of which time use the ink with a little boiled wine, and you will find it good.

62. *To write with cinnabar.*—Among all the methods tried, the following is esteemed the best:—Take the whites of two fresh eggs, and put them into a new pipkin; then break the bough of a fig-tree, containing the milk, into minute pieces, which you will add to the eggs; and with another fig-tree bough beat the mixture up until the white of egg is well broken. Then strain it through a fine linen rag, and place it in a well closed glass vessel, with an equal quantity of roche alum. Distemper your cinnabar with this white of egg, which must be first well ground with clear water, and dried so that you can write with it, and you must mix it well in using it.

In order to preserve the white of egg for a year, take red orpiment of the bulk of a chestnut, and put it in the white of egg, which consequently will never spoil; and this serves for grinding the gold for writing.

63. *How to prepare indico so that when used it shall be beautiful.*—Grind it well with simple water, dry it on paper in the shade, grind it again with urine, and again dry it. When you wish to use it thus in powder, mix it with white lead with as little oil as possible, and it will thus be beautiful when used, if you first grind up the white lead very finely, and then distemper the indico.

l' oro al modo che di sopra s' è detto, ma per l' odore non mi piace.

Inchiostro finiss^{mo} come si faccia.—Vin bianco galiardo lb. 8, Galla d' Istria ben franta ℥ viij, quale per otto giorni stia nel vino in vaso vitriato al sole, o nel fornello coperto mescolandoli spesso, poi separato il vino dalla galla, e collandolo, mettivi vitriolo Romano ℥ vj, e stiavi dentro altri otto giorni all' ombra mescolandolo spesso, poi piglia di gomma arabica ℥ ij e posta in ○ j acqua rosa, et per altri otto giorni mescola col vino, nel qual tempo con poco di vin coto, et incorporate insieme, te ne servirai, e sarà bono.

Per scrivere con cinaprio.—Fra tutte le maniere provate questa si stima boniss^{ma}. Pigliarai donque la chiara di due oua fresche e messa in scudella nova, romperai una bachetta di fico verde che habi il late in minuti pezzi, e la porai nella chiara, e con una bachetta pure di fico la sbatterai sino che la chiara sia ben dirota, il che fatto colerai per pezza di lino sottile, e la porai in vaso di vetro ben turato, e vi porai altrettanto alume di rocca. Distempra il cinaprio con questa chiara che sii prima ben macinato con acqua chiara, et asciugato in modo che possi scrivere, e l' anderai mescolando nel adoprarlo.

Per conservare un anno la chiara d' ovo, piglia tanto risigalo, come una castagna, e ponili nella chiara, che mai si guasterà, e questa serve per macinar l' oro per scrivere.

Come s' accomodi l' indico che in opra resti bello.—Macinalo bene con acqua semplice, poi mettilo a seccare sopra carta all' ombra, e poi tornalo a macinare con orina, e tornalo a seccare, e quando si vol adoprare cosi in polvere mischiato con la biacca con manc' olio si potrà, e cosi resterà bello in opera macinando prima la biacca un poco tenera poi stemprerai l' indico.

64. *How to purify cinnabar and minium for miniature painting.*—If you wish cinnabar and minium to be beautiful, grind them with fresh urine, and it will succeed well.

65. *A secret for making an unequalled green.*—Take the purple lilies, that is, the flowers, and of these the petals only are to be used, and pound them until they are well bruised, and leave them until they begin to ferment; then take burnt roche alum at discretion, grind and incorporate it well with the lilies, leave them on the grindstone for 5 or 6 hours; then prepare the shells, and take a worn linen rag, put the lilies into it, and press the juice dexterously into the shells or vases; then dry the colour in the shade, and you will have a beautiful green; and if you wish to make the colour lighter, add to it a little quicklime at discretion.

66. *To prepare lampblack for outlining the gold in crimson.*—Distemper it with ox-gall, then let it dry in the sun, and when you use it grind it with gum water.

67. *To make aqua fortis.*[1]—Take one pint of the strongest vinegar, oz. iiij of verdigris, oz. vj of sal ammoniac, oz. vj of common salt, oz. ij of arsenic, and boil them until one-third of the mixture has evaporated.

68. *Paste for the aqua fortis.*—Take of Greek pitch oz. j, of wax oz. 1 ss, and of gum arabic oz. ij; liquefy and melt these ingredients in water, and make a cerate, which must be rubbed gently all over the previously heated iron; it must then be blackened by the smoke of a lantern, after which the design must be drawn with the needle. You must then put wax round it like a box; and the space thus enclosed must be filled with aqua fortis, which must be left there for 4 or 6 hours.

69. *To write green letters.*—Take strong vinegar, powdered gum arabic, verdigris, and roche alum, all at discretion, mixed with the juice of rue, and made so liquid that the mixture will flow like ink.

70. *To make paper transparent as glass.*—Take of nut oil lb. ss. and of powdered white litharge oz. j ss, mix them well in a

[1] The aqua fortis and paste were for etching.

Come si purghi il cinaprio et minio per miniare.—Volendo che il cinaprio o minio venghi bello, macinalo con orina che sia subito fata, e riuscirà.

Secretto per fare un verde che non ha pari.—Si piglia i Gilij Pauonazzi, cioè i fiori, e si piglia le semplici foglie poi si pestano tanto che siano amaccati, e si lasciano principiar a putrefarsi, piglia poi alume di rocca bruciato a discretione, e con l' alume macina li gilii, et incorpora bene l' alume, e poi lasciali sul macinino per cinque o sei hore, poi prepara le conchilie, e piglia una pezza di lino usata, e metti li Gilij dentro, e con destrezza va premendo sopra le conchilie o vasi, e lascierai seccare all' ombra et haverai un bel verde, e volendolo far più chiaro vi porrai un poco di calcina viva a tua discrezione.

Per accomodar negro di fumo per profilar l' oro in cremesino.—Si distempra con fiel di bue, poi si mette a sciugar al sole e dovendolo adoperare si macina con acqua gommata.

Per far acqua forte.—Una pinta d' accetto fortiss^{mo} verderame ℥ iiij sal armoniaco ℥ vj sal comune ℥ vj arsenico ℥ ij bollito insieme e consumato il terzo.

Pasta per l' acqua forte.—R. Pece Greca ℥ j cera ℥ 1 ss., goma arabica ℥ ij, il tutto liquefatto e fuso in acqua, se ne forma cerotto, il quale scaldato prima il ferro si toccarà sottilm^{te}, e tutto si farà negro sopra il fumo della lucerna, poi con l' ago si farà il disegno, e si porà della cera attorno a foggia di scatola, e s' empirà il luogo di d^{ta} acqua forte, e si lascierà per spacio di 4 o 6 hore.

Per scrivere lettere verdi.—Si piglia accetto forte, gomma arabica in polvere, verderame, alume di rocca, tutto a discrezione, mescolati con succo di ruta, e si fa liquido in modo che possa correre a modo d' inchiostro.

Per far carta trasparente come vetro.—R. Oglio di noce lb. ss. litargirio bianco polverizzato ℥ j ss. il tutto mescolato in-

new pipkin, and heat them gently for the space of an hour, but do not boil them. Let the mixture then settle for 24 hours, and pour this purified oil into another pipkin with ℥ viij of powdered white Greek pitch, and dissolve them gently by heating them without boiling as above.

71. *To make white bone black.*—Take of litharge and quicklime each oz. 6, mix them with common water, and place them over the fire to boil; put in the white bone, stirring continually until the water boils. Then take the vessel from the fire, and do not cease stirring until the water is cold, when the bone will be black.

72. *To make bone as soft as wax.*—Take equal quantities of Roman vitriol and common salt, pound them well, put them into an alembic and distil them, and preserve the water, and when you wish to soften the bone, put it in this water, and it will become soft as wax.

73. *To make white bone green.*—Take a bocale of strong vinegar, of powdered verdigris and brass filings each oz. 3, and of rue j. handful. Pound each ingredient, put them all together into a glazed vase with the bone; close up the mouth of the vase, and put it in a cellar for a fortnight, when the bone will be green.

74. *A most beautiful green for miniature painting.*—Take equal quantities of verdigris, litharge of gold, and quicksilver, grind them all to a fine powder with urine, and put them into a bottle, which you must bury in horse dung for 20 days; then take it out, grind the verdigris again, and you will have a most noble green for miniatures, writing, and painting.

75. *To change bone to a most beautiful green colour.*—Take well pounded verdigris, steep it in goat's milk and leave it until it becomes green; then put it into a copper vase with the bone, close up the vase air tight, bury it in dung for a week, when you will find the bone of a green colour, which will be still more beautiful if the bone is afterwards boiled in nut oil.

76. *Another way of making transparent paper.*—Take warm olio di abezzo; there is nothing better.

77. *To make rosetto di verzino.*—Take verzino or red sandal

sieme in pignatino novo, si fa lentamente scaldare per lo spacio d' un hora ma però non bolli, cosi fato lasciassi posare per hore 24, poi si mete in un altra pignata il d^{to} oglio purificato con ℥ viij di pece greca pesta e bianca, e si farà fondere a puoco a puoco ma che non bolli come sopra.

Osso bianco che diventi negro.—Litargirio, calce viva, an. oz 6, mistica con l' acqua comune e meti a bollire, e ponivi l' osso bianco sempre menando per fin che comincia a bollire, e levalo dal foco, e non restar di menare sin che l' acqua si raffreddi e sarà negro.

Osso come si facci mole come cera.—Piglia vitriolo Romano sal com. an. e ben pesti mettili in lambico, e distila e serva l' acqua, e quando vorai molificare l' osso mettilo dentro la d^{ta} acqua, e verà mole come cera.

Osso bianco che diventi verde.—Accetto forte boccali uno, verderame polverizzato, limatura d' ottone, an. oz. 3 ; ruta man. j, pesta ogni cosa, e metti in vaso invitriato, e metti l' osso dentro, e tura il vaso bene, e metti il detto vaso in cantina per quindici dì, e saranno verdi.

Verde belliss^{mo} per miniare.—R. verderame, litargirio d' oro, argento vivo an : macina tutto insieme sottil^{te} con orina di puto, e poni il tutto in boccia sepelita in lettame di cavallo per venti giorni, e poi cavalo fuori, e di novo tornalo a macinare, et haverai verde nobiliss^{mo} per miniare, scrivere, e dipingere.

Per far osso verde bellissimo.—Piglia verderame ben rotto, e ponilo in latte di capra e lascialo sino che diviene verde, di poi metilo in vaso di rame e ponivi l' osso, poi copri benissimo che non sfiati, e ponilo in letame otto giorni, e lo troverai verde, e con farlo bollire nel oglio di noce, sarà più bello.

Per far carta lucida in altro modo.—Piglia oglio d' abezzo caldo per farla belliss^{ma} non v' è meglio.

A fare rossetto di verzino.—Pigla verzino overo sandali rossi,

wood, cut it into small pieces, and soften it in rain water, in which it is to be left for three days; then boil it until the water is reduced to half its original quantity, and for every pound add oz. 1. of roche alum with a scruple of gum arabic, and boil it until all the ingredients are liquefied, strain it, and it will be finished.

78. *Mode of colouring bones so that they will appear like emeralds.*—Take aqua fortis which dissolves metals and let it dissolve as much brass or copper as it will, put into it the bone which you wish to colour, having first carved it as you please, and leave it in the water for one night, when its colour will be beautiful.

79. *To make a beautiful green.*—Take the ripe berries of the buckthorn, pound them, boil them with roche alum water, and incorporate with them some of the yellow made from the buckthorn and a little saffron, and thus a most beautiful green will be made.

80. *To make brazil wood of four colours.*—Take brazil wood, and steep any quantity you please (so that it is more than a third part) in clear water until the colour is very red. Then divide this colour into 4 parts: if you wish to make a rose colour use it pure; if you wish it purple add lime water, but the water must be tepid; if you wish a violet colour add a ley to it; and if you desire that it should be of a mulberry colour add tartar.

81. *To make a green for writing and miniature painting.*—Take verdigris, litharge, and quicksilver; grind them all together with urine, and write or paint with this, which will be beautiful, and of the colour of an emerald.

82. *To make a green for miniatures and painting.*—Take verdigris, dissolve it with vinegar, and when it is well dissolved strain it through a fine cloth; then grind it up well on the porphyry slab with clear water, adding honey during the grinding. Let it dry, and again grind it up with gum water, and it will be done.

83. *To render any colour more brilliant and permanent.*—Take

e taglia sottilm^{te} e mettansi a molle in acqua piovana, e lasciali per tre giorni, e poi falli bollire al calo della metà, e per ogni lib. agiongi oz. uno alume di rocca, et un scrupolo di gomma arabica, e facciasi bollire, tanto che le d^{te} cose siano liquefate, e colalo che sarà fatto.

Modo di tingere ossa che parerano smeraldi.—Piglia acqua forte da partire, et falle mangiare, e disolvere tanto rame, o ottone quanto ne può disolvere, et in essa metti le ossa che voi tingere, havendole prima fate lavorare a tuo modo e lasciali in d^{ta} acqua una note, e saranno belliss^{mi}.

A fare un bel verde.—Piglia bacche di spincervino ben mature, e pestali, e falli ben bollire con aqua d' alume di rocca, e incorpora giallo di spincervino e un poco di zaffarano, e sarà fato un verde belliss^{mo}.

A fare il verzino in quattro colori.—Piglia verzino e concialo in acqua chiara quella quantità che voi tanto che sia più del terzo, e tanto che il color sia ben rosso. Poi parti questo colore in quattro parti; e volendo fare color rosato adopralo come si trova, e volendo pavonazzo, aggiongi acqua di calcina, averti che il verzino vol tepido, se violato poni liscia, e se lo voi morello poni alume di feccia.

A far verde per scrivere e miniare.—R. verderame, litargirio, et argento vivo, e trita tutto insieme con orina di putto e scrivi o minia che sarà belliss^{mo} e sarà colore di smeraldo.

A far verde per miniare e dipingere.—R. verderame e con accetto il farai disfare, e quando sarà ben disfatto il colerai con pano sottile, e poi lo macinarai sul porfido bene con acqua chiara e vi porai del miele nel macinarlo, e lascialo poi sciugare, poi ritorna a macinarlo con acqua gommata e sarà fato.

Ut vividior, et maxime constans quilibet reddatur color.—R.

the rectified spirit of urine in a glass phial, and mix your colour with this. Leave it, mixed, in the gentle heat of ashes, or of hot water, for half an hour, the mouth of the phial being stopped. Then separate the colour from the spirit, and you will find it more florid, and much more permanent. But if the spirit is not to be obtained, a ley prepared from calcined tartar, nitro fixo,[1] and the salt of urine may be used.

If in this ley are boiled crimson woollen cloths, a most wonderful cochineal colour is obtained, which is commonly called "scarlato col secreto." The same may be said of the other colours.

If copper is dissolved in the spirit of nitre [nitric acid] and then precipitated by a solution of salt of tartar, there will be a green colour much less corrosive than the other colours.

If by the same spirit ceruse is dissolved, and then precipitated by a solution of gold, there will be a very white and delicate colour.

84. *To make green letters.*—Take the juice of rue, verdigris, and saffron, grind them together, and write with gum water.

85. *To make blue ink.*—Take "endico bagatello," grind it to a fine powder, liquefy it with the above-mentioned gum water, and if you wish the colour to be very fine add to it roche alum (without gum water it would not flow well), and it is then finished.

86. *To make the lily green.*—Take the purple lilies, pick off the most highly coloured petals, and leave them to ferment for a day; then pound them in a mortar, put the juice in a cup, then tie up some quicklime and alum in a piece of linen rag, put it into the juice, stirring it about until the green colour is developed; then keep it dry in paper, and let it be made in fine weather.

87. *Mode of extracting the colour of brazil wood.*—Take of rasped or filed brazil wood, say, oz. 2, and white of egg at discretion, but in sufficient quantity to soak the brazil wood; then take two-eighths of burnt roche alum, and put the whole together in a pipkin, and stir it with a wooden spatula until you see that

[1] Nitre deflagrated in a crucible along with charcoal. See Nuovo Plico, p. 123.

spiritum defecatum urinæ in vitrea phiala, cum eo misce colorem. Relinque mixtum in leni cinerum vel aquæ calidæ calore, per semihoram clauso phiale ore. Separa deinde colorem a spiritu et invenies floridiorem, maximeque constantem, loco spiritu urinæ si desit adhiberi potest lixivium ex tartaro calcinato nitro fixo, et urinæ sale confectum.

Si in hoc lisivio coquantur vellera panni carmesini extrahetur inde color mirificus coccineus qui vulgo dicitur scarlato col secreto idem dic de cæteris coloribus.

Si nitri spiritum solvatur cuprum, ac deinde lixivio salis tartari præcipitetur habebitur color viridis alios colores minime rodens.

Si eodem spiritu solvatur cerusa, ac deinde solis aqua præcipitetur, habebitur candidissimus delicatissimusque color.

A far lettere verdi.—R. ruta e cavane il succo, verderame, e zafferano e macina insieme, e scrivi con acqua gommata.

A far inchiostro turchino.—R. endico bagatello macinalo sottile, e liquefalo con acqua di gomma della soprad^{ta}. e chi lo vol fare belliss^{mo} li meta alume di rocca, e senza acqua di gomma non correrebbe ed è fatto.

Per fare il verde gilio.—Si piglia i gilij pavonazzi, e se li levano le parte più colorite poi si pone per un giorno a putrefarsi, poi si pestano in mortaro, e si cava il suco, si pone in tazza, poi si mete calce viva et alume, e messo in pezza di lino si pone nel detto suco facendolo girare sin che si vede ricavato il colore verde e conserva poi asciuto in carta, e si fa in tempo bono.

Modo di cavar il colore dal brasile.—Piglia il brasile raspato o limato u. g. *(sic)* oz. 2. piglia bianchi d' ova a discretione che tutto resti inzuppato, poi piglia due ottavi alume di rocca abrucciato, e il tutto metti insieme dentro una scudella poi con spatola di legno rimena il tutto sintanto che vedrai il tutto ben colorito,

the whole is well coloured, strain it through a linen rag, and immediately expose it to the sun that it may dry; and if you wish to make a beautiful purple, take Campeachy wood (?), and do the same with that.

88. *To make the Indian varnish. First notice.*—You must first heat an earthen vase, and while it is very hot put into it the gum lac pounded and sifted through a silk sieve; then add to it about $\frac{1}{4}$ of an ounce of colophony, and at the same time, that it may have a body, collect it on the end of a stick in order to present all parts of it to the fire, that it may all be of the same colour, and as soon as it is liquefied you will add to it, a little at a time, the powdered colours, observing that they must be quite dry when they are put in.

89. *For green.*—Take 15 drachms of orpiment, a drachm of indico, more or less dark in colour, for the sky-blue, sulphur well pounded with indico at discretion, and so with the other colours. After the colours are well mixed on their sticks with the gum lac they must be frequently beaten on the marble, or in a hot mortar, in order to mix them well; they are afterwards worked in the hands, and little tablets are made of them for use when they are wanted. For dark blue, indico alone; for yellow, orpiment; for red, cinnabar or minium; for olive, burnt orpiment; for flesh colour, sulphur and minium; and so for all the other colours.

90. *To extract the colour of the gum lac, so that it will serve for bright colours.*—Pulverize coarsely the gum, and put it into a ley of rosewood or vinewood, which will extract its colour; you must then separate the water from the gum, and evaporate it carefully until it begins to thicken. You must then take it from the fire, and stir it with a silver spoon, and let it settle till the next morning, and when it is sufficiently thick, you must place it on a slab of marble, dry it and use it for giving a lustre to the gum and to all colours. Observe that this colour mixed with white lead makes a most beautiful flesh colour.

The remainder of the gum lac must be washed in the ley until it has entirely lost its red colour; it will then do for melt-

colla per pezza, e poni al sole subito a seccare; se voi fare un bel pavonazzo, piglia il campuccio e fa l' istesso.

Per fare la vernice indiana, p° avertimento.—Bisogna far scaldare un vaso di terra, essendo ben caldo metti della gomma lacca pesta e crivelata al setazzio di seta, ponivi insieme circa ¼ d' oz. collofonia e nell' istesso tempo ch' haverà fatto corpo, la coglierete alla cima d' un bastone per presentarla al foco voltandola da tutte le parti a fin che prendi ugualm^te^ il colore, e subito liquefatta che sarà, li metterai a poco a poco li collori ben pesti osservando che siano ben secchi nel ponerli.

Per il verde.—Vi bisognano 15 dramme d' orpimento, e una dramma d' indico più o meno oscuro, per il turchino solfaró ben pesto con indico a discretione, e cosi dell' altri colori. Doppo che li colori saranno ben mescolati sopra li bastoni con la gomma lacca, bisogna batterli sopra il marmo, o dentro un mortaro caldo molte volte per renderlo ben mescolato, e dopo voltarlo nelle mani e farne tavolette, per servirsene ne bisogni, il turchino scuro, l' indico solo, il gialo l' orpimento, il rosso il cinaprio, o minio, color d' oliva orpimento abbruciato, color di carne, solfaro e minio, e cosi di tutti li altri colori.

Per tirare il colore della gomma lacca che serve per li colori vivi.—Polveriza grossam^te^ la detta gomma, e ponila in liscia di legno di rosa o di vite, e la detta liscia tirerà il colore, bisogna separare le acque dalla gomma, e farle svaporare sotil^te^ sin tanto ch' essa cominci a divenir spessa. All' hora bisogna levarla dal fuoco, e moverla con un chuchiaro d' argento, poi lasciarla riposare insino alla mattina, e quando haverà fatto corpo, metterla sopra una pietra di marmo e farla seccare, e ve ne servirete per dare il lustro alla gomma, e a tutti li colori. Nota che questo colore con biacca fa color di carne bellissimo.

La residenza della gomma lacca bisogna lavarla nella liscia, sin tanto ch' habbi lasciato il color rosso, e vi servirà per fon-

ing with the other colours, as cinnabar, orpiment, and others, because the gum being passed through the ley, is clarified [or bleached], and all the impurities of the inside will pass off with the colour.

The wood should be covered with a coat of yellow made with orpiment, and the colours placed on it, ad libitum. But this must be after having spread the yellow with a willow wand or some other stick.

91. *To purify the gum lac, so that it will give a lustre like crystal.*—Take the clearest gum, break it in a strong and clear cloth bag, 2 fingers in breadth, and at the two extremities of the bag tie two sticks, so that they may keep the bag closed, which you will present to the fire, and continue turning it round until the gum passes through the cloth, which you must scrape with a wet knife, on the marble, and continue to do so until the whole has passed through, taking care that you do not burn yourself, and this gum, thus purified, serves for giving a lustre to all works.

92. *An amber varnish.*—Take common turpentine, make it to boil for a quarter of an hour, add to it some amber well powdered on the marble, boil it for half an hour until the amber is liquefied, and take it from the fire. As soon as it is cold it will become hard; when you wish to use it, dilute it with oil of turpentine in order that it may liquefy, and it will be better to heat it slightly that it may be more manageable, taking notice that while it is hot, it should be passed through a cloth, and the part which passes through will be the best part. Apply it with the pencil or with the warm hand. It is necessary to acquaint you that this composition should be washed in hot water, after it has been well strained, that it may be clean and pure.

93. *Another secret to make the true Indian varnish.*—Take gum lac and oil of spike, both of them clean and pure. The oil must be cleansed from its impurities with an equal quantity of litharge of gold; it must then be redistilled and again left to settle until it becomes clear after being passed twice

dere con li colori, come cinaprio, orpimento, et altri, perchè la gomma essendo passata per la liscia si renderà chiara, e tutte le sporchezze di dentro se ne anderanno alla tintura.

Bisogna coprire il legno di gialdo fatto con l' orpimento e di poi mettergli li altri colori ad libitum sopra, ma questo dopo haver bene disteso il detto colore gialo con un bastone di salice o altro.

Per purificare la gomma lacca che darà il lustro come cristallo.—Prendi la gomma più chiara conquassala dentro un sachetto di tella forte e chiara, che sii stretto due dita, et alle due estremità del sacco, lega due bastoni che tengano serato il sacco, qual presenterai al fuoco, voltandolo sempre sino che la gomma passi fuori della tella, qual raschierai con cortello bagnato sopra il marmo, e seguiterai sino che è passata, ma averti di non abbrucciarla, e questa gomma cosi purificata serve per lustrare tutti li lavori.

Vernice d'ambra.—Piglia grassa terbentina, fala bollire per $\frac{1}{4}$ d' hora, e ponili del ambra sul marmo ben in polvere fata, e falla bollire per mez' hora sin che l' ambra sia liquefata, levala dal fuoco, e subito fredda, diverà dura, volendola adoperare bisogna aiutarla con l' oglio di terbentina, acciò si liquefaccia, e fala un poco scaldare per maneggiarla bene, avvertendo che quando e calda di farla passare per un panno et quello che passerà sarà il buono, applicandolo con pennello overo con la mano ben calda. Bisogna avertire che tutta questa compositione, si deve lavare nel acqua calda dopo d' haverla ben colata acciò sii ben netta e purgata.

Altro secreto per fare la vernice vera d' India.—R. Gomma lacca, et oglio di spiga tutti neti e puri, l' oglio bisogna che sia netatto dalla sua grossezza con tanto di letargirio d' oro, quanto di oglio, e questo bisogna far passare per un vetro per distillatione, e si torna a riposare, sino che sia ridotto chiaro, e pas-

through the still. Another vessel shaped like this must be procured, and for every 4 ounces of spike must be taken one ounce of gum lac (if it is very yellow and clear there is no doubt of its goodness); the whole is then to be placed over a charcoal fire and to be boiled until the colour is changed, and the varnish becomes like honey. To know whether it is good, put a drop on a knife, and if it remains united it is good; it must afterwards be poured through a linen cloth into a vase of majolica and preserved.

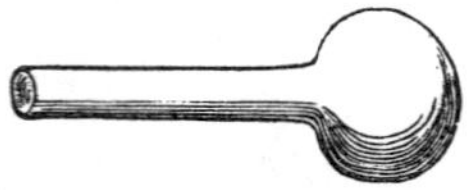

Cinnabar is ground up with pure water, and dried on the stone; then ground for a quarter of an hour with seven times its quantity of varnish. The varnish is then applied with a pencil, and the work is to be exposed to the air for 2 hours in order that the odour may pass away; for the same reason the work is to be kept in a warm place; any colour may then be laid on 5 or 6 times.

After this it must be made perfectly clean and again varnished, continually dipping the pencil in oil of spike. Whenever you varnish you must dry the whole perfectly.

In using the yellow colour you must wait some time for the dissolution of the gum, or you must dissolve it over a slow fire if you do not wish to wait long.

94. *A very clear varnish for pictures and paper alla Fiaminga.*—Take 7 ounces of highly rectified spirit of wine, 2 oz. of sandarac, and 2 ounces of olio d'abezzo. The sandarac, which should be very clear, must be pulverized and put in a bottle with the olio d'abezzo, which also must be very clear. The spirit of wine must then be added, and the whole boiled gently over the fire, until the whole is dissolved, keeping the mouth of the vessel well closed, that the spirit of wine may not evaporate. The varnish must then be strained into a glass vase, leaving the impurities at the bottom. When it is used it must be put into a majolica cup, the picture also must be heated, and the varnish applied with the pencil.

sato due volte si piglia un altra bozza come qui e per ogni quattr' oncie di spiga, si piglia un' oncia di gomma lacca, e come sarà ben giallo, e chiaro, non si dubiti della sua bontà, questa tutt' insieme si mette sopra foco di carboni, e si

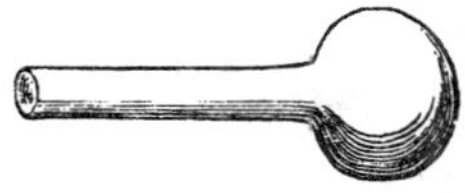

fa tanto bollire sin che si muta il colore, e diventi come mele, per conoscer questo s' è buono, si mette una goccia sopra un cortello, e restando tutto unito, e buono, e poi s'infonde per panno lino in vaso di Majolica e si conserva.

Il cinabrio si macina con acqua pura, e si fa seccare nella pietra, poi si piglia sette volte più di vernice che di colore, si macina ben bene insieme per un quarto d'hora, poi si piglia un pennello, e si mette alla robba, poi si fa stare all' aria due hore acciò passi l' odore, e si tiene la robba a loco caldo acciò più presto passi l' odore, e porre il color che piace 5. o 6 volte.

Poi si netta polito, poi si piglia la vernice, e si dá sopra il lavoro un' altra volta, con bagnare il pennello nel oglio di spiga sempre. Ogni volta che darai la vernice lascierai ben asciugare il tutto.

Il color gialo l' hai d' attendere per disolutione della gomma, overo la farai a fuoco lento, se non voi aspettar tanto.

Vernice lucidissima per pitture e carte alla fiamenga.—R. oz. 7. acquevita sflemattma oz. due Sandaraca, oz. due abiezzo. La sandaracca sia ben chiara si polverizzi, e si meti in bozza insieme con l' abbiezzo, che deve essere chiarissimo, et poi ponivi l' acquevite, e falla bollire dolcemte al foco sino che tutto diventi acqua tenendo stopata la bozza acciò l' acqua vite non svapori, e poi si coli in vaso di vetro facendo restar a dietro il fondo, e quando si vol adoperare si mette in tazzine di Majolica, e si fà scaldare anco il quadro, e con pennello si và seguentemente dandola vernice.

95. *Mode of engraving and painting on glass.*[1]—The engraving you wish to transfer must be soaked in water for the space of 24 hours or more, according to the size of the paper.

Then take a glass cup containing an ounce of turpentine, and place it to boil over a slow fire for half a quarter of an hour; add to it a drachm of powdered mastic, and let it again boil for half a quarter of an hour. Take the glass [to which the print is to be transferred], heat it well on one side only, then lay the print on a cloth in order to absorb the superfluous moisture, and lay the glass on it, which should not be very hot; then turn it over and remove the air-bubbles with the fingers and also the paper, so that it may come off without force. When it is dry, take a wet rag, and rub until the design begins to clear; then, when it is dry, heat it a little by the fire on the side opposite the print, let it cool, and again rub off the paper with the wet rag, and, when it is dry, heat it by the fire more strongly than before, in order that the varnish may soak into the print and make one body, and the work will be clear and beautiful.

96. *Mode of gilding and painting on glass.*—First grind the colours with boiled oil, that is, oil prepared in this manner. Take half a pound of litharge of gold and one pound of nut oil; grind the litharge and put the whole into a varnished pipkin, and boil the oil until it is reduced to two-thirds of its previous quantity. Preserve it for painting on glass.

To make the mordant for gilding on glass, take equal quantities of white lead, terra gialla, and minium; grind the whole together with nut oil, and mix what is ground in a shell or vase with oil boiled as above, boil the whole together a little, and then use it.

97. *To make most perfect water of "grana."*—Take good white wine, put it into a glazed pipkin, and add to it an ounce of verzino, and a drachm of grana; boil it down to half of its original quantity, then add to it three quarters of an ounce of

---

[1] This should rather be entitled, "Mode of transferring an engraving on to glass."

Modo di stampare e dipingere in vetro.—L'imagine che vorai fare la porai in acqua comune per spacio di 24 hore o più secondo la grossezza della carta.

Poi piglia tazza di vetro con un oncia di termentina e ponila a bollire a foco lento per mezo quarto d' hora, poi vi ponerai una dramma di mastice pistato e lascia bollire un altro mezo quarto d'hora, piglia poi il vetro, e scaldalo bene da una parte sola, habbi poi l' imagine preparata sopra una pezza, ma che non v' abbondi acqua per di sopra, e applica d^{to} vetro non troppo caldo sopra, e poi rivolterai, e anderai con le dita levando le vesighe, e parimente la carta che senza forza se ne viene, quando sarà secca piglia pezza bagnata e và fregando per insino comincia a schiarire il disegno, poi quando sia secca scaldala un poco al foco da quella parte dove non v' è materia, e poi lasciala rafreddare, e torna di nuovo con la d^{ta} pezza bagnata a levar la carta, poi secca che sia, scaldala al foco più forte che prima acciò l' arteria insupi nella materia e facci un corpo, e venirà chiara e bella.

Modo d' indorare e dipingere sopra vetro.—Prima macina i colori con oglio coto, cioè fato in questo modo. Piglia meza lib. di litargirio d' oro, et una lib. d' oglio di noce, e pesta bene il litargirio, e meta il tutto dentro un pignatino verniciato, e falo bollire sino che cali il terzo. Serve per dipingere in vetro.

Per indorare in vetro, piglia per fare il mordente, Biacca, terra giala, minio, tanto dell' uno come del altro, macina il tutto insieme con oglio di noce, e poi metti il macinato in conchiglia o vaso con oglio cotto come sopra, e fallo bollire un poco e poi adopralo.

A far acqua di grana perfett^{ma}.—R. Vino bianco bono e metilo in pignata invitriata et poneli oz. una di verzino, et una drama di grana, et falla bollire tanto che calli per metà, et quanto sarà calata metili tre quarti d' oncia d' alume

roche alum, and a quarter of an ounce of "alume di piuma," that is, "flower of stone." Put these ingredients over the fire, mix well till they are all dissolved and until all the gums [i. e. the two kinds of alum] are well incorporated (they should be previously well pulverized), then strain through a fine linen cloth which should be previously wetted with white wine in order that the cloth may not absorb too much of the water, but take care to press out the wine before you strain it.

98. *To make fine lake.*—Take lime water in which brazil wood has been infused, and add to it flour, so that it may become thick, and when the whole is well mixed, let the flour sink to the bottom, make it into a small loaf, dry it in an oven not too hot, then grind it up, and with lime water make it into pellets, and let them dry in the shade.

99. *Varnish for gold.*—Fine sugar lb. 1, gum lac oz. 1, and socotrine aloes dr. 2; pulverize each separately, then take of oil of turpentine oz. 8, and distemper the whole, strain through a coarse sieve; it is to be used cold.

100. *To make crimson from the "solatro Indiana."*—The ripe "solatro" being bruised, must be boiled with any quantity of water, gum arabic, and roche alum, over a slow fire, until the water is reduced to two-thirds; it must then be left to clear, and the sediment must be dried in the shade, and then ground.

101. *Yellow.*—Socotrine aloes distempered with clear water. Dry buckthorn berries, pounded finely with pulverized saffron, are boiled with alum water until the water is reduced to two-thirds; it is then strained and dried in the sun. The quantities may be varied at pleasure.

102. *To make the finest Indian varnish.* — Take oz. 8 of gum lac, oz. 4 of the white resin of Arabia,[1] oz. 3 of mastic, and oz. ½ of borax; liquefy the whole in a glazed basin. When dissolved, strain them through a silk cloth; then take an ounce and a half of the composition, reduce it to powder, put the powder into a receiver, and throw on to it half a pound of spirit of

---

[1] Is not this white resin of Arabia, Oriental Copal?

di rocca, et un quarto d' alume di piuma, cioè fior di piera e questa cosa fa che sia posta al fuoco, e mescola bene tanto che si disolva, e fa che siano ben incorporati insieme tutte le d^{te} gomme, e fa che siano perfettamente polverizate, e poi cola per pezza di lino sottile e bagnala prima con vino bianco, acciò la pezza non ricevi troppo di quell' acqua, con struccarla però prima bene dal vino.

Per far lacca fina.—R. acqua di calcina nella quale vi sii stato infuso del brasile, et in essa poni fior di farina, tanto che s' inspessisca, e meschiata bene ogni cosa si lascia poi andar la farina al fondo, della quale fatto un pastoncello si ponga à seccare nel forno non molto caldo, tritalo poi e con acqua di calcina formane ballottine, e lasciale seccare all' ombra.

Vernice da oro.—Zuccaro fino lib. j., goma lacca oz. j., aloe sucottrino dramme 2. si polverizi il tutto separatamente, poi piglia oglio di trementina oz. 8. si stemperi il tutto insieme poi si coli per sedaccio si pone in opera fredda.

Far cremesi di solatro Indiano.—Ammaccato il solatro maturo senza groppo, si fa bollire con acqua e gomma arabica, et allume di rocca, il tutto a discretione a fuoco lento sino al calo di due terzi, dipoi si lasci schiarire, e la feccia si lasci seccare all' ombra e poi si macina.

Giallo.—Aloe sucottrino si stempera con acqua chiara. Spincervino secco pesto minutamente con zafferanno polverizzato si fa bollire con acqua alumata tanto che cali due terzi poi si cola e si secca al sole il tutto a discrettione.

Modo di far la vernice all' Indiana finiss^{ma}.—R. oz. 8. di gomma lacca, oz. 4 di raggia bianca d' Arabia, oz. 3 mastice, oz. $\frac{1}{2}$ borace, il tutto fa liquefare in catino invitriato, distrutto si cola per tella di seta poi piglierai un oz. e mezza di d^{ta} compositione, la ridurai in polvere, la qual polvere metterai in recipiente, e le porai sopra meza lib. d' acqua vite rafinata quattro volte, e

wine rectified 4 times, and put the receiver into hot ashes or a sand bath until the powder is entirely dissolved. The varnish will then be finished. It is then used in the following manner: —Add to it a 6th part, by weight, of Spanish red,[1] and with this give 7 or 8 coats to the wood which you wish to varnish, leaving each coat 5 or 6 hours before the next is laid on. After it is quite dry, it must be polished with a small brush and olive oil; then two coats of varnish must be applied, and when it is dry it must be rubbed very softly with goatskin and with Tripoli powder and oil, when it will be done; but I warn you that you must follow the recipe exactly.

103. *Another Chinese varnish.*—Take of white carabe [amber] oz. 2, of gum lac oz. ¼, of sandarac oz. ¼, and of rectified spirit of wine lib. 1. The gums must all be pounded, and put into a long-necked bottle, and left in infusion for 2 days, in order that they may be perfectly dissolved, keeping the bottle well closed. The bottle must then be put in a very gentle sand-bath for 7 or 8 hours, and left to cool, when it will be done.

104. *Clear varnish.*—Take lib. 1 of spirit of wine, oz. 4 of fine turpentine, a quarter of an ounce of white mastic, and the same quantity of sandarac. Put the whole into a bottle, as in the preceding recipe, and in the same manner place it for 6 hours in a sand-bath of such a heat that the varnish will boil. It will then be finished.

105. *Lustro di rasa.*—Lustro di rasa, for grinding bright colours [for painting] on glass, is made with equal parts of spirit of turpentine and Greek pitch, placed over a moderate fire until the pitch is melted.

106. *Varnish is made as follows.*—Take one ounce of juniper gum [sandarac], oz. ¼ of pure and clear oglio d'abezzo, which is called oglio d'abiezzo for making varnish, oz. ½ of the best 7 times rectified spirit of wine. The sandarac must be ground up, and made into a paste with the abezzo. It must then be put into a bottle, the spirit of wine must be added, and

[1] The Almagre of the Spanish writers. A pigment is still sold at Venice

porrai il recipiente a fuoco d' arena o cenere sin tanto che la detta polvere sia tutta distrutta, e cosi la vernice sarà fatta. Si adopera poi come sotto, mettendovi dentro la sesta parte del peso, di rosso di spagna quanto sarà il peso della vernice, e doppo con un pennello dare sette o otto mani sopra il legno che si vorà accomodare, faccendo distanza de una mano all' altra cinque o sei hore, e doppo che serà ben secca bisogna pulire le dete opere con del settolino con oglio d' oliva, e poi applicarvi due mani di vernice, e secco che sarà, lo stropiciarai pian piano con la camozza, e del tripoli in polvere con oglio, e sarà fata. Ma averti che bisogna stare a quello è scritto.

Altra vernice alla China.—Carabe bianco oz. 2. gomma lacca oz. $\frac{1}{4}$, sandaracca oz. $\frac{1}{4}$, spirito di vino disflemato lib. j. si pestano tutte le gomme, e poi si mette in bocia dal colo longo, e vi si lasci in infusione per due giorni acciò si disolvi le sod^te^ gomme tenendo benissimo turato la boccia, e poi si mete a fuoco di sabia gradatiss^mo^ per sette o otto hore, e poi si lascia rafreddare e così sarà fatta.

Vernice chiara.—Lib. una spirito di vino, oz. 4 trementina fina, un quarto d' oncia di mastice bianco, et un quarto di sandracca, il tutto messo in boccia come l' altra vernice, e le si da fuoco per sei hore però di sabia tantochè si vede a bollire, e poi è fatta.

Lustro di rasa.—Il lustro di rasa si fa per macinar colori vivi in vetro con parti uguali d' acqua di raggia, e pecce greca sopra foco moderato sino si liquefacci la pecce greca.

La vernice si fa come sotto.—Oz. una gomma di ginepro, oz. $\frac{1}{4}$ oglio d' abezzo puro e chiaro, quale si addimanda oglio d' abbiezzo per far vernice oz $\frac{1}{2}$ acqua vite boniss^ma^ di sette cotte. Si macina la sandaracca e si fa pasta con l' abiezzo e si mette in bozza, e se li mette sopra la d^ta^ acquavite e si mette sopra fuoco dolce, tanto che il tutto s' incorpori, fatto questo

by the name of Terra Rossa di Spagna, but it is believed to be identical with the Terra Rossa d'Inghilterra, and to be actually brought from England.

it must be placed over a slow fire until it is well incorporated. When this is done, the wood or glass which is to be varnished is painted with a tuft of feathers.

107. *A varnish for miniatures and picture frames.*—Take of spirit of turpentine lib. 1, of benzoin oz. 4, and of mastic oz. 2. Reduce the mastic to a very fine powder, and mix it with the benzoin in a varnished pipkin. Then put the spirit of turpentine into a bottle, which you must heat by means of a water-bath, and then mix it with the benzoin and mastic in the pipkin; afterwards incorporating it with the other things over a slow fire, &c.

When this varnish is used on picture frames, you must add to it two ounces of sandarac also well pounded, and you must mix with the varnish the colour which you wish to apply on the frames.

108. *To make very pure white lead.*—Take the calcined lead of the potters, or litharge of gold or silver in proper quantity; pound it finely, pass it through a coarse sieve of silk, and having placed it in an earthen vessel with very strong white vinegar (if distilled it will be better), leave it for 3 or 4 days, frequently stirring it, and letting the impurities of the lead go to the bottom. Then decant the vinegar, and pour over the lees fresh vinegar in such quantity that no odour may proceed from it and that the precipitate may be almost black. Then take rain or well water with the proper quantity of salt, and with this salt water precipitate the lead which is in solution, and wash it with common water until it has no more odour or savour; then dry it, by placing it on leaves of blotting paper until it is dry.

109. *To make a colour like carmine.*—Take powdered cochineal, put it into a ley, and add to it some finely pulverized crystallized arsenic, which is proper for precipitating the colour; it will then turn out well.

110. *Colours for miniature painting.*

White lead,	Burnt yellow [earth],
Paris carmine,	Burnt lake,

con pennello di piuma si pinge il legno, o vetro se vole invernigare.

Vernice per miniature e cornici.—Acqua rasa lib. una, bigione oz. 4, mastice oz. 2, pestasi il mastice in sotill^{ma} polvere, e si mescola col bigione dentro una pignata vernicata, l' acqua rasa si mette in una boccia di vetro, qual si farà scaldare al bagno maria e dappoi la mescolerai col bigione, e mastice nella pignata, facendola poi incorporare con le altre cose a fuoco lento, etc.

Per mettere sopra le cornici vi metterai due oncie di sandaracca anche ben pista, et il colore che vi vorai mettere, lo macinerai con la vernice.

Per far biacca purgatiss^{ma}.—Si piglia piombo calcinato da boccallari o litargirio d'oro o d' argento, la quantità che si vuole, si pesti sottil^{te}, poi si passi per settaccio di seta, e posto questo con acetto fortissimo bianco, e se fosse distillato sarebbe migliore, si lasci in un vaso di terra tre o quattro giorni mescolandolo spesso, lasciando andare al fondo la terestreita del piombo, di poi si decanti, e sopra le residenze si ponga novo accetto sin tanto che non dia più sapore facendosi la terra quasi nera. Si prende poi acqua pluviale, o di pozzo con del sale alla quantità che si vole et poi con d^{ta} acqua salata si precipiti il piombo soluto, poi si lavi con acqua commune sin a tanto che non habbi più odore ne sapore, e poi s' asciughi, e si ponghi sopra foglii di carta strazza sin tanto sij secca.

Per fare un colore com' è il carmino.—Piglia cosoniglia pista, e si mete in liscia, e se li mette arsenico cristallino ben polverizzato, che questo è atto a precipitare il colore, e si cava beniss^{mo}.

Colori per miniare.

Bianco di piombo,	Gialo bruggiato,
Carmino di Parigi,	Lacca bruggiata,

Dutch vermilion,
Rosso delle aguze,
Red from Roman vitriol,
Red from rust of iron,
Terra d' Inghilterra,
Stone yellow,[1]
Flanders yellow,
Brown from burnt terre verte,
Burnt umber,
Indian black [ink ?],
Black from burnt acorns,
Ultramarine,
Lily green,
Indico.

111. *Secret preparation of the scammony.*—Take out what you consider a proper quantity of clean scammony, liquefy it by means of a gentle heat with strong spirit of wine, with which a little salt of tartar has previously been distempered, and afterwards filter the solution; then evaporate one-half of it in a water bath, and when it becomes tolerably cool, add to it as much rose water as is sufficient to make the very pure resin of the scammony fall to the bottom of the vase, which should be of glass, free from all ungrateful savour, odour, and malignity. Then pour off the water, dry the powder, and keep it for use. The dose is half or even a scruple in some convenient vehicles, &c.

112. *Lily green.*—Take the juice of the flowers of purple lilies, but the juice of the buds will be better, and having purified two glasses full of it, add a piece of lime of the size of a small pea, and the same quantity of unburnt roche alum with a little pulverized candied sugar; and when they are well dissolved and incorporated, the colour must be dried by exposure to the air.

113. *To make very fine lake.*[2]—Take oz. ½ of lac, half a drachm of crystals of tartar pulverized, and a scudella of hot water. First dissolve the tartar, then take the lac which has been ground, put it on a clean linen rag, and tie it into the form of a ball, and then cut off the superfluous part of the rag, and put the ball into the above-mentioned hot water, placing the scudella over some hot cinders, and leaving it there until the

[1] Probably native yellow ochre. The best kinds are sold in the lump, and not in powder.

[2] In the original MS., this recipe is broken into two parts by a repetition

Minio d' olanda,
Rosso delle aguze,
Rosso di vitriolo Romano,
Rosso di rugine di ferro,
Terra d' Inghilterra,
Gialo di pietra,
Gialo di Fiandra,
Biondo di terra verde bruggiata,
Terra d'ombra bruggiata,
Nero d' India,
Nero de' giande brugiato,
Oltramarino,
Verde gilio,
Indico.

Preparazione segreta della scammonea.—Piglia quella quantità che voi di scamonea netta, liquefatta à dolce caldo con acqua vite gagliarda, dove prima sia stato distemperato un poco di sal tartaro a discretione, poi stemperata feltra la solutione, poi in bagno maria fa sfumare la metà, poi rafredato alquanto il d[to] liquore metivi dentro tanto d' acqua rosa quanto basti per far cadere nel fondo del vaso, che vol essere di vetro, la resina puriss[ma] della scamonea libera à fatto da qual si voglia ingrato sapore, odore e malignità. Poi leva l' acqua, secca la polvere e conservela per i bisogni. La dose e mezo, o pure un scrupolo in vehicoli convenienti, etc.

Per fare verde gilio.—Si cavi il succo da fiori di gilij pavonazzi, da bottoni sarà migliore, e purgato nella quantità di due bichieri, si mette quanto un cece di fior di calcina, e un altro d' alume di rocca non abruggiato con un poco di zuccaro candido spolverizato, il che disfatto che sia, e ben incorporato, si sciuga all' aria.

Per far lacca finiss[ma].—Si piglia lacca mez' oncia, cristallo di tartaro in polvere meza dramma, et una scudella d' acqua calda, si pone prima il cristallo, e si fa disolvere, poi si piglia la lacca macinata e si pone in un pezzetto di lino pulito, e si trenge in forma di balla poi si.

Per far lacca finiss[ma].—Osserva li due segni neri.|| Si piglia lacca, mez' oncia; di cristallo Tartaro in polvere meza; ||

---

of the title and the first line; as this was evidently a mistake, I have avoided it in the translation.

water becomes well coloured. When this is the case, take the ball from the water, and evaporate the water gently over the hot cinders until the colour is condensed at the bottom; it will then be done.

115. *To make a most beautiful purple lake.*—Take an ounce of fine grana or cochineal, a quarter of an ounce of roche alum, and about a bocale full of common water. Boil the water with a quarter of an ounce of fennel seed until it is diminished one-third; then add the grana or cochineal finely pulverized, and boil the whole over a slow fire for a quarter of an hour; then add the pulverized roche alum, and let it boil for another quarter of an hour. After this take it from the fire, strain it through a linen cloth into a new and unglazed earthen porringer, and leave it there for 8 days. You must then decant the water, or take it up gently with a sponge, evaporating the little which remains until the colour is condensed, which you must afterwards keep in shells, adding to it a little lemon-juice.

116. *Another sort of fine lake.*—Take 12 grains of powdered cochineal or fine grana, add to it 2 ounces of ley; leave the infusion for about 2 hours; strain it through a linen cloth, and put it over hot cinders. When it boils, add to it pulverized roche alum of the size of 2 peas, when the ley will make a thick red scum; as soon as this happens throw it all on to a stretched linen cloth, when the clear ley will pass through, leaving the coagulum on the cloth, which coagulum must afterwards be dried and made into tablets.

117. *To make a red Parisino* [Parisian] *colour.*—Take oz. $\frac{1}{4}$ of Brazil wood, and half a bocale of clear ley; put the ley into a new glazed pipkin, and when it is hot, add to it the Brazil wood, keeping it over a slow fire for a quarter of an hour. It must then be strained through cloth into a new pipkin, and some pulverized roche alum of the size of a grain of rice must be added to it, and the mixture must be stirred without heat for 7 or 8 minutes. The whole must then be put

taglia il superfluo di d^{ta} pezzetta, si mette la detta balla nella soprascritta acqua calda, applicando la scudella ad un poco di cenere calda, et ivi si lascia sino che l' acqua sij ben colorita, all' hora si leva la balla dall' acqua, e si fa svaporare l' acqua pian piano sopra la cenere calda sin à tanto che il colore si condensa nel fondo, e sarà fatta.

Per fare una lacca pavonazza belliss^{ma}.—Si piglia un' oncia di grana fina, o cocciniglia, allume di Rocca un quarto d' oncia, acqua commune circa un bocale, si fa bollire la detta acqua con un quarto d' oncia di seme di finocchio, sino alla diminutione d' un terzo, poi nella d^{ta} acqua si aggiunge la d^{ta} grana, o cocciniglia macinata bene, e si fa bollire a fuoco lento per un quarto d' ora, poi vi si aggiunge l' allume di rocca fatto in polvere, e si lascia bollire per un altro quarto d' hora, ciò fatto si leva dal fuoco, si cola per pano lino in scudella nova di terra non vitriata, e si lascia per otto giorni, qual poi si decanta o si leva $gentil^{te}$ con spugna facendo evaporare quel poco che resterà sin tanto che il colore si condensa, quale si conserva nelle conchiglie applicandovi un poco di succo di limone.

Un altra sorte di lacca fina.—R. Piglia 12 grani di cocciniglia, o grana fina fatta in polvere, si pone in due oncie di lissivio lasciandola in infusione due hore incirca poi si cola per pano lino, e si mette sopra cenere calda, quando vorrà bollire vi si aggiunge quanto due piselli d' allume di rocca in polvere, quando il liscivo farà schiuma grossa incarnata all' hora si getta tutto in un panno lino steso, e passarà il lissivo chiaro restando la schiuma nel panno, quale si fa seccare, e si fa tavolette.

Per far color rosso Parisino.—La quarta parte d' un' oncia di legno di Brasile, mezo boccale di lissivio chiaro, si pone il liscivo in pignata nova invitriata, scaldato che sij, vi si aggionge il d^{to} legno tenendolo a foco lento per un quarto d' hora, dopo si cola per pezza in pignata nova, e vi si agionge quanto una rizzolla d' allume di rocca in polvere, e si mena senza foco per mezo quarto d' ora poi si pone il tutto in un sacco accuminato, e si

into a pointed bag and passed through twice, as in straining wine. It may be kept in shells, &c.

118. *To make rose colour.*—Take the above-mentioned colour, heat it over the fire, and when quite hot add to it a little fish-bone (that is, sepia) in powder, but in very small quantity, that the colour may not be too dry; then stir the whole well in the sun until it is cool. It may be kept without adding gum, but must be distempered with parchment glue.

119. *To prepare minium.*—Take the minium, steep it in water, beat it up well; then decant the finest part, and let it dry. It is to be incorporated with parchment size and a little purified honey.

120. *To make violet colour.*—Take bastard madder,[1] grind very finely a small quantity of it, and put it in hot [liquid] "color di verzino," but take care there is no roche alum in it, which precaution you ought also to observe with the rose colour.

121. *Straw colour.*—Take lead yellow [massicot], wash it with a very strong and clean ley, then decant the ley, and distemper the colour with parchment glue.

122. *A most beautiful white.*—Take some powdered Venice crystal [glass], add to it a third part of powdered sulphur, place it in a well-luted pipkin over lighted charcoal, and leave it there until the pipkin becomes well heated and red hot; then take it off; and when it is cold break it, and collect the pigment which is in it, grind it and preserve it.

123. *Another violet colour.*—Incorporate 2 parts of the above-mentioned rose colour with 1 part of turchino or turnsole, and it is done.

124. *A most beautiful black.*—Burn the books of gold-leaf, leaf by leaf separately; let the ashes fall into clean water, then take them and incorporate with parchment glue. The colour will be most beautiful.

125. *A most beautiful blue.*—Take "smaltino," pass it

---

[1] Galium Mollugo, Galium Album. The great ladies' bed straw, or wild Bastard Madder.

passa due volte come il vino colato, e si conserva in conchiglie &c.

Per far color di rosa.—Si piglia il color soprad^{to}, si pone al foco acciò si scaldi bene scaldato vi si giunge un poco d' osso di pesce in polvere cioè di seppa, ma pochiss^{ma} quantità acciò il colore non riesca troppo secco, si move il tutto bene al sole sin tanto che sij raffredato, e si conserva senza porvi gomma, ma si stempera con cola di pergamena.

Per preparare il minio.—Si piglia il minio posto nel acqua, si sbatte beniss^{mo}; poi si decanta la parte più suttile, e si lascia asciugare; s' incorpora con acqua pergamena liquida con poco miele purificato.

Per far color di viole.—Pietra [piglia?] Galica bianca, si macina ben sottile in poca quantità, e si pone in color di verzino caldo, ma che non vi sii alume di rocca, il che si deve avvertire nel color di rose ancora.

Gialdo di Paglia.—Piglia gialdo di piombo, si lava con liscivo ben forte e netto, poi si decanta il liscivo, e si stempera il colore con cola pergamena.

Un bianco belliss^{mo}.—Si piglia cristallo di Venetia fatto in polvere, vi si agionge la 3^{a} parte di solfo in polvere, si pone in pignata tutto ben lutata sopra li carboni accesi, e si lascia sin a tanto che la pignata sij ben infocata, et accesa, poi si rimove e fredda che sij si spezza, e la matteria che vi sarà dentro si macina e serve.

Altro color di viole.—Doi terzi di color di rose soprad^{to} s' incorpora con un terzo di color turchino, o tornasole ed è fatto.

Un belliss^{mo} nero.—Li libbri del oro in foglio abbrucciati a foglio per foglio al lume, e far cascare l' abbrucciato nel acqua netta, piglia poi quella robba incorporala con colla pergamena ed è belliss^{mo} &c.

Un Turchino belliss^{mo}.—Si piglia smaltino passa per settaccio sottile, incorpora con biacca e gomma macinata.

through a fine sieve, incorporate it with white lead, and grind it with gum.

126. *Mountain green.* — Grind the mountain green with parchment size and "succo verde."

127. *Sap green.*—Take the berries which grow on the hedges in bunches like grapes, collecting them 24 days before the feast of St. Michael. When they are ripe, place them in a pipkin, and dry them well with pounded alum for 2 days in the sun. Then add to them clear ley, and boil them over a slow fire until reduced two fingers' breadth; then strain the liquor, and pour it into a bladder and expose it to the air that it may dry.

128. *To prepare saffron for painting.*—Take the saffron, tie it up in a rag, and steep it in white vinegar, with a little gum or white of egg beaten and strained; but if you make use of the white of egg, use no gum.

129. *To make gold colour.*—Take orpiment which has been well ground with ox gall, put it into a pipkin with saffron and white wine, and let it boil over a slow fire until it has a body. When you wish to use it distemper it with white wine mixed with the above-mentioned gall.

130. *To make verdigris.*—Take pieces of copper anointed with purified honey, and fasten them to the cover of a well-glazed pipkin, which must be full of hot vinegar made with strong wine; then cover it and place it in a warm situation for 4 or 5 weeks, and when you uncover it, remove the colour which you will find on the pieces of copper, and it will be most beautiful.

131. *To make a colour of dragon's blood.*—Dragon's blood is ground up with sal ammoniac and pounded gum; it will be much better for the addition of white lead and minium.

132. *Distempering of cinnabar.*—When the cinnabar is well ground, it is to be incorporated with a strong white; it is then dried on the stone, and reground with well-beaten white of egg and a small portion of Hepatic aloes. It may then be preserved, and when used it should be distem-

Verde di montagna.—Si macina il verde di montagna con cola pergamena liquida e succo verde.

Succo verde.—Si pigliano bacche che vengano per le sieppi in forma d'uve, si raccogliono 24 giorni avanti S. Michele quando sono matture, si pongono in pignata, e s' abbruciono bene con alume pestato due giorni al sole in infusione, poi si aggionge liscivo chiaro, e si pone al foco lento acciò bolli sino al calo di due detta poi si cola e si pone in vescica all' aria acciò secchi.

Accomodar il zafarano.—Si piglia il zaffarano, si pone in pezzetta legata, si pone in acetto bianco con un poco di gomma, overo bianco d' ova ben sbattute e passate, ma senza gomma se adopri il bianco dell' ovo.

Per far color d'oro.—Orpimento ben macinato con fiele di bue si pone in pignata con zaffarano, e vino bianco, e si lascia bollire a foco lento sin tanto che piglij corpo, poi si distempera con vino bianco, quando lo voi adoperare misturato con fiele soprad^{ta}.

A far verde rame.—Piglia pezzette di Rame onte con miele purificato, attaccali al coperchio d' una pignata ben vitriata che sij piena d' acetto caldo di vin forte fata, poi coprila e ponila in loco caldo per quattro o cinque settimane e scoprendola leverai il colore che troverai sopra li detti pecci di rame che sara belliss^{mo}.

Per far color di sangue di Drago.—Sangue di drago si macina con salmiaco, e gomma pista riuscirà più bello con agiongervi un poco di biacca e minio.

Tempra del Cinaprio.—S' incorpora il cinaprio con un bianco forte quando sarà ben macinato, poi si lascia seccare sopra la pietra, e si macina di nuovo con chiara d' ovo ben sbatutto, et una picciola parte d' aloe epatico, si conserva, et quando si

pered with spring water and a little white of egg, and it will flow more freely if a little myrrh be added.

133. *To make giallo santo.*[1]—Take the berries of the buckthorn towards the end of the month of August, boil them with pure water, until the water is loaded and thick with colour; add a little burnt roche alum and then strain it. You may boil the strained liquor to make the colour deeper, mixing with it some very pure gilder's gesso; then make the colour into pellets, and dry them in the shade.

134. *Secret for making lake.*—To 2 pints of common water add 2 ounces of pulverized soda, and leave the mixture in this state for 24 hours; then strain it, and put into the ley 6 ounces of "pastella;" then leave it again for 24 hours, strain it through [a bag shaped like] a capuchin's hood, add alum water, stir it with a stick, and add water to it in order to remove the salt. When the colour has fallen to the bottom, pour off the water, collect the lake which will be at the bottom, dry it, and it will be finished.

135. *To make a carmine colour.*—Take powdered cochineal, add ley to it, and instead of alum water, add well pulverized crystallized arsenic, for this will precipitate the colour, which will be brighter if treated as above.

136. *To extract the colour from Chinese grapes for painting and miniatures.*—Take the grapes when quite ripe, pound them, pass them through a press, filter through linen rag, and evaporate the juice over hot cinders; when all the moisture is evaporated, take spirits of urine, which you must pour on to the juice, and let it remain until you see that it is well coloured. Then take some spirits of wine, and add them, so that the colour may be precipitated, or evaporate it, and preserve the colour in small bags of parchment or skin.

137. *To make most beautiful sap green.*—Take the berries of the buckthorn when they are quite ripe, which will be about the

---

[1] In the Nuovo Plico, Giallo Santo is said to be made of the flowers of the Erba Lizza, Barba di Becco (yellow goat's beard). We may, there-

vorà adoperare si piglia acqua di fonte con un poco di chiara d' ovo, e perchè corri meglio aggiongi un poco di mira.

Per far gialo santo.—Piglia grana di spincervino nel fine d' agosto, fallo bollire con acqua pura sin tanto che sij ben carico, e spesso di colore con poco d' alume di rocca non bruggiato, poi si coli quale per farlo per farlo (*sic*) più colorito si può farlo bollire, e con detta colatura s'impasti gesso purgato di quello d' indoratori, e se ne faccino ballotte quali si seccano all' ombra.

Secretto per la lacca.—Piglia due pinte d' acqua comune, e meti dentro due oz. di soda polverizata e lascialo per 24 hore poi si cola, e poi metti nella d[a] liscia oz. 6 pastella, e si lascia per 24 hore, poi passala per capuccio, poi metti acqua alumata, poi mescola con bastone et aggiongi acqua per levare la salsedine, quando il colore sarà andato al fondo decanta l' acqua poi piglia la lacca che sarà al fondo, falla seccare e sarà fata.

Per far colore di carmino.—Piglia consoniglia pesta, meti in liscia, e in cambio d' acqua alumata meti arsenico cristalino ben polverizato che questo precipita il colore e si fa più vivo a fare come sopra.

Per cavare il colore dall' uva della China per dipingere e miniare.—Si piglia la d[ta] uva ben matura, poi si pesta, e si passa per torchio, poi si feltra per pezza di lino, poi si fa evaporare sopra le ceneri calde, passata tutta l' humidità piglia spirito di vino, si pone nel succo sin che si vede ben colorito, piglia poi spirito d' orina, e si mette acciò precipiti il colore, overo fallo svaporare, e conservalo in sacchetti di carta capretta o pelle.

A far pasta verde belliss[ma].—Si piglia la grana di spinselvino ben mattura, che sarà quando l' uva è matura, si pista, e

---

fore, safely infer that it was a yellow lake made sometimes with the juice of one plant, and sometimes with that of another.

time when grapes are ripe; pound and boil them as soon as they are gathered, and add to them a little roche alum ad libitum, and when the liquor becomes of a beautiful green, which will happen in about an hour, take them from the fire, and when cold filter, and keep what passes through in a bladder in the chimney that it may dry well.

138. *To make excellent boiled hair.*—Take the manes, forelocks, and tails of oxen, horses, cows, and calves (but remember that the tails of horses are not good), place them in fresh water, and wash them so that there may not remain any grease or dirt; then string them on a cord, afterwards put them into a vessel with ley and let them boil for 6 hours.

139. *To make super-excellent carmine.*—Take an egg, make a hole in it so that the white will run out, then take mercury and fill the egg with it, stop up the hole and lute it according to the best of your ability; then bury it two feet deep in horse-dung which is very much exposed to the sun, and do this in the dog days. Leave it in this situation for 40 days, then take it out, with great care, lest it should break; then break it, and you will find in it a living animal; let the animal die, and preserve it, it will fall to powder; use this powder, which will be a most splendid carmine, for painting and miniatures, but you must beware of the smell at the beginning.

140. *To colour canes and to imitate those of India.*—Polish well the cane, then take gum water, and mix with it white lead and smaltino according to your fancy; this is the composition which you must sprinkle on the cane with a pencil; then shaking the cane hold it over the fire with sulphur until the cane becomes black. Then polish it with a wet rag, afterwards rub it well with a little olive oil, taking care to do this from knot to knot.

141. *To blacken the wood of the apple, pear, olive, box, service, cherry trees, and elm (?).*—When the wood has been polished with burnt pumice stone it must be well rubbed with a coarse cloth and with the said powder, bathing the work with German size that it may be more polished; it must then be cleaned with another rag.

si fa bolire come si trova, e si aggiunge un poco d'alumme di Rocca ad libitum, quando vedrai un verde belliss^{mo}, che verà in spacio d' un hora, si leva dal foco, e fatta fredda falla passare per feltro, e conservala in vesica sotto il camino acciò si secchi bene.

Per fare crino bollito belliss^{mo}.—Si piglia le cume e zuffe, cove di bovi, cavalli, vache, vitelli, ma averti che le cove de' cavalli non sono bone. Si pongono in acqua fresca, e si lava acciò non le resti untume ne sozzure alcune, di poi falle fillare in corda poi si pone in parollo (sic) di liscia, e si fa bollire per 6 hore.

Per fare Chermino sopraeccellentissimo.—Piglia un ovo, fali un buco tanto che n' eschi la chiara, poi piglia mercurio, et empi l' ovo, e di poi tura bene il bucco, e lutalo secundum artem, e ponilo in Ruto di cavalo sepolto un braccio fondo in loco chevi giocchi il sole più sii possibile in tempo di Canicola fallo, e fallo stare quaranta giorni; poi levalo con avertenza che non si rompi, poi più avertito rompilo che vi troverai un animale vivo, lascialo poi morire, e serbalo che anderà in polvere, e di quella serviti, che sarà un chermino non più visto da dipingere et miniare, ma guardati dal tuto alla prima.

Per far Canne tinte e finte d' India.—Polisci bene la canna, poi piglia acqua di gomma, biacca, e smaltino, à tuo modo unissi con d^{ta} gomma, farai la composizione da spruzza su la canna con pennello, e dibattendo la canna la porrai sopra il fuoco con zolfaro sinche la canna venghi nera poi la pollirai con straccio bagnandola con acqua, e poi con un poco d' oglio d' olivo, e la sfregherai bene, avertendo di far questa fattura a nodo per nodo.

Per far negro Pomo, pero, olivo, Busso, zorbolo, cerasa, verna [*e orno?*].—Pulito che sarà il legno con pomice bruggiata, si freghi bene il lavoro con canovazzo, e detta polvere bagnando il lavoro con acqua di cola tedesca acciò venga più pulito poi si neti bene con altra pezza.

142. *A water for blackening the above-mentioned works.*—Boil the rind of the pomegranate in water until a third part is consumed, and lay it all over the work, which must be quite hot, with a pencil of hog's bristles; then let it dry in the shade, and in the same manner give 3 coats, having the water always quite hot, and always leaving it to dry in the shade.

Item, take Campeachy wood (?) which has been boiled in water with a little roche alum until a third part has evaporated, and while it is still hot, give 3 coats of it as above, leaving it to dry in the shade. Item, for putting on the black. The strongest white or red wine, in which you must put a quantity of iron filings at discretion, bearing in mind that the more iron filings you add the blacker will the composition be, and it should be left in infusion for 24 hours; it will thus make a most beautiful black. When the 24 hours are past you may add to it ox gall at discretion, afterwards boiling it until it is reduced one third. You must apply 3 coats of it while hot on the work, allowing each coat to dry in the shade, and the more coats you lay on, the blacker will the work be.

143. *To polish the work.*—Rub it well with new cloth; then take fine Tripoli powder which has been well rasped and pounded finely with goatskin, and rub the work well, so that it will have a lustre; then take white wax, if you wish it to be still brighter, and rub it over the work, which will thus become most beautiful.

144. *To grind lake.*—Spirits of wine or candied sugar, at discretion, with gum water and a few drops of oil of tartar.

145. *Beautiful smaltino.*—Grind it up with spirits of wine; then regrind it with dragon's blood in tears before the spirits have evaporated, and it will be beautiful. It should also be incorporated with burnt Roman vitriol or burnt "pietra focaia,"[1] &c.

146. *To make the Turkish paper waved with divers colours.*—The colours which succeed best on this paper are fine orpi-

[1] See ante, p. 537, n.

Acqua per dare il nero a sopradti lavori.—Scorze di pomo granato si faccino bollire in acqua che consumi un terzo, poi con pennello di setola si dij sopra il lavoro, che sij ben calda. Doppo coperto tutto il lavoro di detta acqua si lasci sciugare all' ombra, e di quest' acqua sempre calda se ne dij tre mani, e si lasciano sciugare all' ombra sempre.

Item si piglij compuccio a discrezione bollito in acqua comune alla consumatione del terzo con un poco d' alume di rocca, e cosi calda si dij sopra tre mani come sopra, e si lasci sciugare all' ombra. Item per dare il negro. Vin fortissmo bianco o negro nel quale porrai dentro quella quantità di limatura di ferro a discretione, avertendo che quanta più ne sarà verrà sempre più nero, e si deve lasciare in infusione hore ventiquattro, e farà nero bellissmo passate poi le 24 hore, o che il ferro sij consumato vi si pone dentro fiele di bue a discrettione, poi falla bollire all' callo (*sic*) d' un terzo. E la darai sopra il lavoro calda tre mani, e lascia sciugare mano per mano all' ombra e con più mani più nero verrà.

Per lustrare il lavoro.—Sfrega bene il lavoro con canevazzo novo, e poi piglia tripolo fino e ben pesto raspato sottilte con pelle di camozza si freghi il lavoro ben bene, che si lustrerà, e piglia cera bianca per darli più lustro, e frega sopra il lavoro che verrà bellissmo.

Per macinar lacca.—Spirito di vino o zucchero candito a discrettione con acqua gommata con qualche goccia d' oglio di tartaro.

Smaltino bello.—Si macini con spirito di vino, e poi rimacinarlo con sangue di drago in lacrima, cosi bagnato e sarà bello, et con rosso di vitriolo romano abbrugiato o pietra focaia brugiata incorporati &c.

Per fare la carta turchesca ondata di diversi colori.—Li colori quali riescono meglio in questa carta sono, orpimento, lacca

ment or common lake, cinnabar, that is dark morello, indico, that is purple, and white lead; but the eye must be the judge of the mixture and making of the colours.

The colours are to be kept separate, but because the orpiment is rather light coloured, it should be mixed with cinnabar during the grinding, and thus it will be of the colour of gold. The lake should be ground up with cinnabar, which will sink to the bottom, so that it requires to be mixed with lake; purple, not being found in nature, is made with indico and lake; green is made with orpiment and indico; sky-blue with indico and white lead; and black with ivory calcined in an uncovered crucible, but not too much calcined, as in that case it will become white, and indico is the colour which gives it body. These then alone are the colours which succeed; they must be well ground up with simple water and moderately liquid, so that they may be collected on the stone and placed in their respective vases. They are to be distempered with spirit made from good and not spoiled wine, afterwards adding to them 5 or 6 drops of the gall of an ox or calf, which makes them spread over the gum water of which we shall speak; and if you do not think that the colour spreads sufficiently, add a drop or two more, and every time that the colours dry add spirit of wine. When they are ground you must add no more water, but spirit, which has the property of fastening the colours to the papers. We have now spoken of all that pertains to the disposition of the colours, and it remains for us to speak of the method of employing them.

You will take, therefore, a tray of the size of the paper which you wish to paint, with the sides 3 fingers high, and entirely covered with pitch; you will fill it with water, but you must first put the water into a vase, and for one measure of the water you will add an ounce and a half of gum, or one ounce if it is pure and good, adding a little more water, because the gum will absorb part. Leave it in infusion for 2 days and 2 nights, and then mix and squeeze it with the hand into the vase 2 or 3 times a day in order to perfect the water; and while

fina, o commune, cinabrio, cioè morello scuro, indico cioè pavonazzo, biaca overo bianco di piombo, sij giudice l' occhio nel mischiare i colori e nel farli.

Questi servono separati, ma perchè l' oropimento sia troppo chiaro si mischia col cinabrio nel macinarlo, e cosi piglia il color d' oro, la lacca si macina col cinabrio, il cinabrio va à fondo da lui si che richiede compagna la lacca, per fare il pavonazzo, non trovandosi naturale si fa con l' indico et lacca, il verde si fa con orpimento et indico, per il celeste si fa con indico et biacca, il nero si fa con l' avoglio in crociolo scoperto calcinato, ma averti che non stia troppo perchè diviene bianchiss^{me} e l' indico è quello che li da corpo. Questi dunque solamente sono li colori che riescono, quali vanno macinati benissimo, e si macinano con acqua semplice e mezanamente liquidi si che si possano raccogliere sopra la pietra, e posti nelli vasi si stemprano con acqua vite fatta di vin bono e non guasto, di poi vi si pone 5, o 6 goccie di fiel di bue o vitello maschio, che questo fa stendere sopra l' acqua di gomma che si dirà, e se parerà che si stenda poco vi porrai una o due goccie di più, et ogni volta che li colori sciugheranno, aggiongi acqua vite, ne da che sono macinati vi porrai più acqua semplice, ma acqua vita, che ha virtù di far attaccare li colori alla carta, e questo e quanto appartiene alla disposicione dè colori, resta ora che disponiamo il corpo di quelli.

Piglierai adonque una cassetta fatta granda come la carta che voi dipingere, con le sponde alte tre dit atutta impegolata, empirai la cassetta d' acqua, ma prima porrai l' acqua in un vaso e per la misura di detta acqua vi porrai un oz. e meza di gomma, e se la gomma sarà pura e bella basterà un oz. averti porvi un poco più d' acqua, perchè la gomma sorbisce la sua parte, e lasciala in infusione due giorni, e due noti, e poi la mescolarai e premerai con la mano nel vaso due o tre volte al giorno per perfetionar l' acqua, e nel porla nella cassa falla

pouring it into the tray, make it pass through a strong rag. To know whether the gum is too thick, take a feather and lead it backwards from one side to the other frequently in this manner 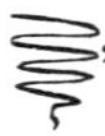, first pouring in one or two colours; and if these colours flow after the feather, it will be perfect; and if, on the contrary, they do not follow the feather, the mixture is too thick, and will require to be mixed with some spring water, which must be stirred by the hand, moving it all over the tray. But this imperfection may also arise from a defect in the colours, for instance, when there are not sufficient ingredients, that is, too little gall or not sufficient spirit of wine; the remedy for this can only be learned by experience. We may also warn you that if there is too much spirit the colour will be too light. For each vase of colour you must have a pencil, and must place one colour after the other, a drop for each colour; but you must not touch the water with the pencil, and by its motion you must make the paint fall at equal distances. The colours being placed according to your fancy, you must conduct the pencil from one side to the other as previously directed, merely touching, however, the surface of the water. You must afterwards make a comb of thin wood as long as the breadth of the tray, in which you will insert hog's bristles in this manner, 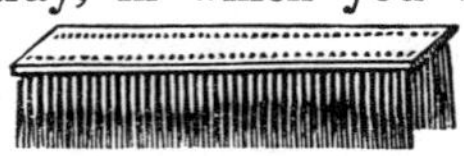 and the thicker they are the more delicate will be the waves of colour. With this comb you will pass over the whole tray, taking care to touch only the surface of the water, and you will thus succeed well. If you choose, you may make with the feather, circles, snakes, labyrinths, and similar things.

147. *To cause a rose or carnation to become white.*—Burn sulphur in such a manner that the flower may be exposed to the fumes, and it will become quite white; but take care that the companion, which is on the same branch, may not feel it.

148. *To make fruits grow without kernels.*—Cleave the young plant to the root, take out the pith on both sides; then unite the parts, plaster them with ox-dung, and tie them together. This will succeed admirably.

passare per pezza forte. Per conoscere poi se la gomma è troppo spessa piglia una penna alla rovescia, e guidala da una parte e dall' altra spesso in questo modo 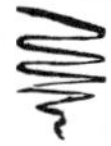 ma prima vi porrai un colore o due, se quelli colori corrono dietro la penna sarà perfetta, altrimenti sarà troppo spessa e converrà porvi acqua di pozzo e mischiarla con la mano per la cassa, ma averti che ciò può anche avenire per difetto de colori, quando non vi sono ingredienti a sufficienza cioè poco fiele, o poc' acqua vite et in ciò l' esperienza vi farà pratico, averti di più che quando vi sarà tropp' acqua vite, il colore sarà troppo chiaro. Per ciascun vaso di colore haverai un pennello, e vi porrai un color doppo l' altro una goccia per ciascun colore, ma non toccar l' acqua col pennello, ma con il moto di quello farai cader la pittura in egual distanza; posti li colori a tuo modo, li condurrai con la penna da una parte e dall' altra come ho detto di sopra, toccando però solo la superficie del acqua. Di poi farai un pettine longo come il traverso di detta cassa, e lo farai d' asse sottile, nella quale v' inserirai delli pelli di porco in questo modo 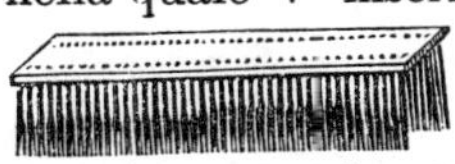 et quanto saranno più spessi, le onde saranno più delicate, e con il pettine scorrerai tutta la cassetta, ma averti di toccar solo la superficie dell' acqua, che cosi riuscirà bello, e se vorai con la penna vi farai de' circoli, biscie, laberinti, e simili.

Per far una rosa o garofalo che divenghi bianco.—Piglia foco di zolfo e con delicatezza fallo sentire al fiore che riuscirà bianchiss^{mo}; ma averti non lo senta il compagno ch' è sopra la rama medema.

Fare che li frutti naschino senza armella.—Schioppa la pianta giovine sino alla radice, e levali l' anima da una parte e dal altra, poi unisse le parti, e con sterco di bue impiastra, e legale insieme, che riuscirà mirabile.

MODO DA TENER NEL DIPINGER.

BY

GIAN BATISTA VOLPATO.

VOLPATO MANUSCRIPT.

PRELIMINARY OBSERVATIONS.

GIOVANNI BATISTA VOLPATO, the author of the following MS., was a painter, born at Bassano in 1633. He was a pupil of Novelli, who had studied under Tintoretto. He settled at his native place, where, after the ancient school of the Bassani had become extinct, he practised the art, and had several pupils. He left some writings on painting, which were preserved in the select and valuable library of Conte Giuseppe Remondini. From the Remondini family the MSS. passed into the public library at Bassano, where they are now preserved. One of these works, entitled 'La Verità Pittoresca,' is believed to be still unpublished, although it was announced for publication at Vicenza in 1685.

In the preface to this work, says Lanzi, Volpato protests that he had no master, but in a MS. at Castelfranco it is stated that he was a pupil of Novelli. He adds that the work is full of good observations, whence it may be supposed he was well acquainted with the theory of the art. Mr. Eastlake remarks[1] that this MS.

---

[1] Notes to Goethe on Colours, p. 406.

afterwards formed the groundwork of Verci's 'Notizie intorno alla Vita e alle Opere de' Pittori di Bassano.'

Volpato left also another MS. in his own handwriting, entitled 'Modo da tener nel Depingere,' which is now published for the first time in the following pages, and the original of which was kindly lent to me by Sig. Baseggio, the librarian and president of the Athenæum of Bassano, with a permission to copy it if we could, for the hand-writing was so bad as to render this extremely problematical. With some trouble, however, we deciphered the MS., with the exception of six or eight words, of which I took fac-similes.

The MS. appears to have been composed in the latter part of the seventeenth or beginning of the eighteenth century. That it was not written previous to 1670 is certain, because Volpato quotes the work of Padre Lana, which was published in that year, and it was probably later, because he alludes to the practice of Canziani, the Veronese painter, who survived Volpato five or six years, being still living in 1712.[1] The terms also in which Volpato speaks of his recollection of the face of S. Pietro Martire in Titian's celebrated picture, suggest the idea of its having been written by an old man. On these grounds, therefore, I am of opinion that the notices in this MS. respecting painting in oil, are to be considered as applying to paintings of the Venetian school at the conclusion of the seventeenth century.

The MS. purports to be a dialogue between two apprentices of painters, in which the elder explains to

---

[1] See Orlandi's Abecedario.

the younger, who appears to have just entered the profession, the various technical details in which he is to be employed, such as preparing the grounds of the pictures, grinding the colours, setting the palette, tracing the outline, and other mechanical processes, on which the apprentices[1] were usually employed.

Volpato commences by describing the kind of canvas proper for painting, and observes that smooth canvas requires a thin ground only. He then teaches how to prepare grounds, of which he describes several, and states the advantages and disadvantages of each kind, and particularly the effects of gesso on grounds, which he illustrates by referring to the practice of Bassano. He also shows the advantages arising from making the surfaces of pictures smooth. After speaking of the preparation of grounds for pictures, Volpato treats of the preparation of walls for painting with oil colours.

The next subject discussed is the different methods of transferring the design to the canvas, which is said to be the work of the boy and not of the artist; and then he takes occasion to speak of tracing paper and the method of using it, and of other mechanical contrivances for copying pictures.

Volpato then treats of grinding and preserving the colours, and of cleaning the palette and brushes, of the preparation of boiled oil, by boiling it with litharge, of the different kinds of varnish, of which he mentions three, namely, the "vernice grossa," amber varnish, and mastic varnish. He says that he purchases the two former ready made; the latter he makes himself,

---

[1] See also the Brussels MS., pp. 771, 772, 782.

and in this part of the dialogue he refers to the works of Armenini da Faenza and Raffaello Borghini, "who," he adds, "teach all things pertaining to our trade, and how to make all kinds of varnish, as well as the proper mode of using them."

Again, in speaking of the method of distempering the colours, of setting the palette, and preparing the sketch for the finishing, he speaks of these works, and says the directions given to him for this purpose by his master, "correspond exactly with those of Armenini, and you may write them out also, for besides this he teaches the whole process." These passages certainly afford a fair presumption, that the method of painting in the Venetian school was on the whole like that described by Armenini and Borghini, modified probably by the peculiar habits and style of every artist.

He then speaks of the choice, preparation, and tests of the goodness of the colours, and of the means of rendering certain colours more drying.

Volpato also alludes to the mode of preparing the sketches. He says, "I wash the sketches, I oil them, I varnish them, and on some of them I lay the white of egg, according to his (the master's) orders;" and it is on this occasion that he refers to the work of Armenini.[1] After describing some other mechanical operations, he mentions the injuries done to pictures by cleaning them, and in particular by copyists, whose bad practices he describes and reprehends in the strongest terms, and he adduces one instance (the S. Pietro Martire of Titian) of the ill effects of applying oil (which he says

---

[1] See Armenini, Dei veri Precetti della Pittura, cap. ix.

is not good on pictures) on the surface of a painting, in order that the copyist might see it more distinctly. "This picture," observes Volpato, "has been oiled so many times by the sacrilegious blockheads who have copied it, that he [the figure of the martyr] is so blackened and spoiled, that there is no telling what sort of face he has, and yet," he adds, "I recollect when he was beautiful, and you may observe the children [the angels in the upper left-hand corner of the picture] which, being above the reach of similar influences, are in excellent condition." This difference, however, is not so perceptible as it was in the time of Volpato, for the Pietro Martire was sent to Paris, where it underwent the operation of cleaning, and of a partial repainting. It is now in the church of S. S. Giovanni e Paulo at Venice.

In the fly-leaf, but in different hand-writing, are the following words:—

Licinio.
Silvio.

ꝑ. netar quadri lume di feccia.
Il libro delle stampe del Ricci, d. L. ii
mi conto' . . . lire 4.
4.
Conto di . . . 3.
Spesi . . . . 6.
5 .. 18.

COPY OF AN AUTOGRAPH MANUSCRIPT

OF

GIAN BATISTA VOLPATO,

ENTITLED

"THE MODE TO BE OBSERVED IN PAINTING."

PRESERVED IN THE PUBLIC LIBRARY AT BASSANO.

F. My Silvius, on what subject shall we converse?

S. I have been but a few days with Sig. Floriani, therefore I should like you to teach me the mode of preparing canvas, colours, and those things which pertain to the business in which I am engaged, as I have had but little practice in such things.

F. Come, you fool, eat, eat, this is not the time for study; when you have appeased your appetite I will tell you all.

S. You are right, give me a glass of that wine which you praise as being so exquisite.

F. Here, take it, you will find it most delicate.

S. To the health of our masters.

F. I know you are not a servant, but a friend of your master, because servants, being enemies of their masters, desire that they may have all kinds of misfortunes, and not success; therefore you do not deserve the name of a servant, but that of a friend.

S. My master's kindness obliges me to act thus.

F. My master is not at all inferior to yours, and I would shed my blood for him; I will therefore join you in drinking their healths.

S. Truly, the wine is not inferior to the capon, and they both deserve to be consumed in a proper manner.

F. There is no one waiting for us, therefore we can take our time, and when we have finished, I will willingly instruct you,

MODO DA TENER NEL DIPINGER.

COPIA TRATTA DALL' AUTOGRAFO

DI

GIAN BATISTA VOLPATO,

CHE SI CONSERVA NELLA PUBLICA BIBLIOTECA DI BASSANO.

F. Silvio mio, e che volevi discorrer?

S. Pochi giorni sono che stò con il S. Floriani, e per ciò vorrei che m' insegnasti il modo di preparar telle, colori, e tutto ciò, che fa bisogno per servirlo, perchè ho poco pratica di simil cose.

F. Hò, pazzo, mangia, mangia, che non è tempo questo d' applicatione, che fornito ti farò veder il tutto.

S. Hai raggione. Da mi un bichiere di quel vino che mi celebri così squisito.

F. Eccolo, e sentirai una cosa delicatissima.

S. Alla salute de' nostri patroni.

F. Conosco bene che non sei servo, ma amico del padrone, perchè li servi essendo nemici de' padroni, le desiderano bensi tutte le disgratie, ma non la salute, e perciò non meriti nome di servo ma d' amico.

S. La sua bontà m' obliga a questo.

F. Veramente, ne anco il mio non è punto inferiore che spanderei il sangue per lui, et io istessamente ti rendo in loro salute ragione.

S. Veramente, il vino non è punto inferiore al capone, e meritono l' uno e l' altro esser devorati come si deve.

F. Non vi è alcuno che ci aspetti. Se la potremo prender comoda, che poi volentieri t' insegnerò principiando dal pre-

beginning with the preparation of the canvas, and gradually going through all those things which belong to the art, because such pertain not to painters, but to those who serve them.

S. We have now finished, therefore you may have the table cleared, but leave the wine, which will season our discourse.

F. Drink away, for I have more of it.

S. I will not disobey you.

F. Now I will tell you what you desire to know. First, you must be told that the canvas must be good, strong, smooth, and well made; that it must bė prepared with a thin ground, and must be so durable as to last as long as the picture, and it is the duty of him who buys the canvas to ascertain this, for if the canvas is bad it decays in a short time. Smooth canvas requires but little ground for priming, for if the priming be too thick, the colours become black from the abundance of oil which is used, and the repetition of so many primings; wherefore you must take good canvas, stretch it on the frame, and give it a coat of glue made of the parings of very young pigs' skins, that it may be softer, for such glues as parchment glue, being strong and harsh, cause a certain shrinking of the canvas, which has a bad effect, therefore do as I teach you. When this coat is dry, polish it with pumice stone, give it another coat of glue, as before, and let it neither be too weak nor too strong; for if too weak it will not defend the canvas from the oil, and if too strong it will cause the colour to crack; that which is of the proper consistence will be soft like jelly when it is cooled.

S. If the priming were to be laid on with pure oil, without glue, what would be the result?

F. When the canvas has no glue to defend it from the oil, it loses its strength, for the oil dries, so that it becomes like the bark of a tree, and when the canvas is taken off the stretching frame it cracks and splits.

S. In some shops where they prime canvas, I have seen flour paste used: is this improper?

F. Flour paste is very bad, because if it is too stiff it causes

parar tele, e poi di mano in mano di tutte quelle cose che ci appartengono, perchè queste cose non sono da pittori, ma ben da chi li serve.

S. Siamo al fine, puoi sbratar, lasciendo il vino, qual servirà per stemprar li nostri discorsi.

F. Bevi pur alegramente, che ne ho dell' altro.

S. Non dubitar che non le mancherò.

F. Hora ti dirò ciò che brami, e prima sarai havertito che le telle sijono buone, forte, liscie, ben lavorate, che con poca materia restino impresse, la bontà serve che tanta dura il quadro, quanta dura la tela, ed è dovere di chi le compra, che come sono cative in breve si consumano; le telle liscie poca materia l' imprime, che come vi è troppa materia anerisse li colori per l' abondanza de l' olio che vi si pone ed il replicar molte primiture; e però piglia buona tela, e tirata in telaro, gli darai una mano di colla di retagli di nonnate o maschiette per che riesce più dolce, che le colle come di bergamina, essendo forte e crude, fa certe ritiramente nelle tele che fa cativo effetto, e perciò fà come t' insegno: asciuta la lisciarai con la pomice, e li darai un altra mano di cola come prima et osserverai, che non si troppo dolce ne troppo forte, la troppo dolce non difende la tela dall' olio, e la troppo forte fà crepar il colore, e la buona serà tenera come gelo quando è rafredata.

S. Chi dasse la primitura con olio puro senza cola, che sarebbe?

F. Quando la tela non hà la cola, che la difende dall' olio, non può conservar la sua fortezza, che l' olio si disecca in modo che viene come una cortecia d' arbore, che volendosi maneggiare giù del telaro si taglia e si rompe.

S. Ho veduto in certe botteghe ove si imprimisce tele usar colla di farina, che forse non è buona?

F. La cola di farina è pessima, perchè come è un poco gag-

the colour to crack and scale off, and if it is too weak the damp causes the canvas to decay, and the rats eat it. These persons use it because they prime very bad canvas, which perishes in eight or ten years, and because the flour paste fills up the holes of the canvas.

S. And those who use gesso?

F. To use gesso, is to tempt fortune, for many old paintings are to be seen spoiled by the gesso, yet many are in good preservation, but this arises from the quality of the glue, which may be either too strong or too weak, but weak glue is best, because the strong absolutely spoils the canvas, whereas with the former very little gesso is required, for I have observed in the works of Bassano, that those pictures which have been primed with but little gesso are in good preservation, while those on which too much gesso has been used scale off; and you may distinguish these from the others by the texture of the canvas, the threads of which are visible, although being painted they are covered with gesso, priming, and colours; while others which have smooth surfaces, from having too much gesso, scale off. Besides the pictures on canvas, we have examples of this in old paintings on wood, which are well preserved in consequence of this practice of using glue. But dust also is very injurious to old pictures, as you will observe in those belonging to the nuns "Riformati," and Capuchins, whose pictures being kept free from the dust, the colours are preserved admirably. In order to avoid this difficulty, I use simple glue, as I have told you, which I lay on twice, using the pumice stone after each coat when dry, that the canvas may become smooth. I afterwards give them the priming ground up with linseed oil. All earths are good for this purpose according to the taste of him who uses them. I use "terra da bocali,"[1] terra rossa, and a little umber

[1] Terra da boccali, called by Baldinucci (Voc. Dis.) Terra di Cava or Terretta. "The earth or clay used in making earthenware for table services, which, being mixed with powdered charcoal, was employed for making grounds, and for painting chiariscuri, and even in the tints, and which was also used, tempered with glue, upon canvases on which triumphal arches, perspectives, and other scenes, were to be painted. It is better adapted for

liarda crepa il colore e si scorza, e se pur è poca, al umido marcisce le tele, e li topi le mangiano, e queli l' adoperano perchè imprimono tele tristissime, che in otto o dieci anni restano consumate, e perchè la cola di farina ottura li buchi della tela, si servono di questa.

S. Quelli poi che adoperano il gesso?

F. Con il gesso si gioca di fortuna, perchè si vede assai pitture antiche sconcerti per il gesso, e molte ancora si conservono, il che proviene dalla qualità della cola, o troppo forte, o troppo dolce, ma la meglio è la dolce, che la forte sciupa assolutamente, et in questo modo ci vol pochissimo gesso, che ho osservato nell' opere del Bassano, che quelle che hano poco gesso si conservano, e quelle che ne ha troppo si scorzano, e ciò si conosce dala tessitura dela tela che si scopre li relevi di detta, ben chè habia gesso, primitura, e colori, essendo dipinte, e quelle liscie che hano assai gesso si scorzano, et oltre le telle si vede l'esempio nelle tavole antiche, che assai si conservono, e ciò proviene da questa pratica della cola; ma anco la polvere rovina assai, che osserverai dalle monache, da Riformati, e Capucini, che tengono le sue pitture nete da la polvere si conservano benissimo, et in fatti il gesso si vede che conserva molto bene il colorito. Ma per levar queste difficoltà, io adopro cola semplice come ti ho detto, che data doi volte apomicando ogni volta dopo asciuta aciò la tela venga liscia, li do poi la primitura macinata ad olio di lino, e tutte le terre sono buone per questa faccenda, secondo il gusto di chi comanda, io piglio terra da bocali, terra rossa, et un poca di terra d' ombra distemperate dopo fate in polvere sotile e passate in foco con olio di lino senza macinarle, le do con il cortelo supra dela tela, e dopo asciuta e pomicata, le do un altra mano macinata, e così resta impressa benissimo, e questo è un modo il più sicuro e migliore per la riuscita. Ho veduto anco metter

---

modelling than any other clay, because its particles are so minutely divided, that works made of it can not only receive the highest degree of polish, but the most minute works can be executed in it. It is dug at Rome, near St. Peter's, and at Monte Spertoli, 13 miles from Florence." It appears to be like what is called in England "China Clay."

finely powdered and mixed with linseed oil and stirred together for a short time, but not ground, over the fire. I then spread this preparation over the canvas with a knife, and when dry and pumiced, I give the canvas another coat of the same colours, but these must be previously ground, and thus the canvas will be well primed; this is the best mode and the most certain in its results. I have also seen some persons steep the "terra da bocali" in water to soften, when it liquefies immediately; then, removing as much water as possible, the same quantity of linseed oil as of the water which remains behind is to be added; then the different ingredients are stirred together with a spatula until well incorporated. The priming is then applied to the canvas for the first time, but for the second coat the ingredients must be previously ground as I have before said. This method succeeds well and is quickly done, as little colour is required in the second coat, the canvas being already made smooth with the first. To the first coat made with earth distempered with water is added the oil which is pressed from the pencils when cleaning them, and which, being boiled with the sediment of the colours, dries like a mordant in the winter time; but umber is sufficient to make the second coat (which is ground) drying, and it does not require the boiled oil. This is the mode which I sometimes follow in preparing the canvas for my master, but the first mode which I mentioned to you is the best.

S. How shall I know whether the glue is too strong or too weak, when it is made, since it is used hot?

F. I touch it with two fingers, and feel whether it is tacky, and thus I ascertain the fact; if it is too strong, I add water, and do not let it boil any longer; and if too weak, I let it boil until I consider it is of the proper consistence; but take care you do not add to the glue either terretta or gesso, or anything, because these scale off in time; but use the pure glue, in order to spread the priming, and that the canvas may retain its strength, as I have told you.

S. When painters wish to paint on walls, how do they prepare them?

a mole nell' acqua la terra da bocale la quale si liquefa subito, e gitata poi fuori tutta l' acqua che può uscire, li getono tanto olio di lino quanto può esser l' acqua che vi è rimasta, e poi con una spatola la meschiono fino che s' incorpora, e poi la dano sopra le tele la prima volta, ma la seconda la dano macinata come t' ho detto, e riesce benissimo et è negotio breve che la seconda mano poco colore fa bisogno, essendo già fatta liscia con la prima, nella prima fatta di terra stemprata con l' acqua vi si pone olio che si neta li peneli, che bulito con questa fece di colori, seca come mordente nel tempo del verno, et ne la seconda che si macina, basta la terra d' ombra per far secante, ne ci vol olio coto. Questo è il modo che tengo alle volte preparar le tele al mio patrone, ma la meglio è nel primo modo che ti ho discorso.

S. Per conoscer la cola quando si fà, se è troppo forte, o dolce, perchè si da calda ?

F. Io toco con due dita e sento se ha picico nel asciugarsi, e da quelo m' accorgo, se è troppo forte v' agiungo dell' acqua e lascio levar il bolo, e se è dolce la lascio bolir fino che mi pare fatta giusto al bisogno, ma haverti di non por cosa alcuna, ne terreta, ne gesso, nella cola, perchè con il tempo si scorzano, ma solo si dà la cola pura, aciò si possa distender la primitura, e che la tela conservi la sua forza come t' ho detto.

S. Quando li Pitori vogliono dipinger sopra muri in qual modo si preparano ?

F. On walls, neither glue nor gesso is used, because they would scale off in a short time, but the wall should merely be anointed with linseed oil, and after several days, when it is quite dry, a tint should be applied of earths ground up as a priming, and, when this is dry, the wall is ready for painting on. And in the same manner, to make coloured sketches on paper, a tint should first be laid with the brush, but let the paper be strong and well sized, such as the blue or the white.

S. And how is paper made transparent?

F. Some sheets of huckster's paper, I do not exactly know what it is called, are glued together, according to the size of the picture or figure which is intended to be traced; these sheets are then anointed with common oil, or, still better, with nut oil. There is also a good mode of oiling paper for the use of children when drawing, and also for laying over writing; it is prepared thus:—Take, &c.[1]

Spread the oiled paper over the picture, and with a pencil or charcoal outline the figures, which are visible through the paper very clearly; and if they are too black, they may be touched slightly with gesso on the darkest parts, not doing as some clumsy and imprudent persons do who outline the paintings with lake ground with oil, and afterwards oil the paper above it, and then press it with the hand until the above-mentioned outlines are impressed on the oiled paper. Such people ought to have their hands cut off as a punishment for the crime of spoiling such gems, especially when they are able to accomplish their object otherwise in a better manner; but this is only practised by tracers, who rule their lines, and can do nothing but daub canvas, for virtuosi do not make marks on pictures. These proceed with proper respect, and those who have valuable pictures in their custody should be aware of this practice, and if they catch any of those clumsy fellows, they should kick them out, and send them to the gallows as

1 A blank in the original, in which it was doubtless intended to copy a recipe.

F. Sopra muri non ci vol cola ne geso perchè assolutamente in breve si scorzano, ma solo si unge con olio di lino il muro, e passati diversi giorni che sij benissimo asciuto se la da una tinta macinata di tere come primitura qual benissimo seca, può il Pittore dipingervi sopra. E cosi le carte per far modeli coloriti, si le da una tinta con il penelo, ma che la carta si forte, e che habi buona cola, come l' azzurra o bianca ma di quella reale.

S. Et lucidi come si farà ?

F. S' incola della carta da fatorela, non so il nome, quanta è la grandezza del quadro overo la figura che ci vuol lucidare, e poi si ungi ad olio comune overo di noce, che è meglio ; ma vi è anco un modo belo per unger carta qual serve a fanciuli per dissegnar et anco per imponar a scrivere et è si, Piglia &c.—(*sic*)

(*sic*)

e detta carta unta si distendi sopra il quadro e si contorna con lapis o carboni le figure che gia spicono benissimo e se fossero troppo nere si può legermente tocar con gesso nella parte più perse, e non far come certi sgratiati e temerarj che contornano le pitture con lacca a olio, e poi l' ogliono la carta di sopra, e con la mano le vano ritocando fino che resta impressi li sudetti contorni, che a questi bisognerebbe troncar le mani in pena di tal delitto, volendo guastar gioje cosi rare potendo in miglior modo conseguire il loro intento, ma ciò non viene usato se non da calcanti che vano rigando, e che non sano se non impiastrar telle, che li virtuosi non mettono le noti sopra le pitture. Codesti si va con que' rispeti che si deve et a ciò dovrebbero haver l' ochio chi le hano in custodia, che capitando di que' sgratiati scatiarli, e mandarli alle forche come indegni, ne lasciarli acostar a gioje si pretiose.

unfit to live, and not suffer them to approach such precious gems.

S. I myself have seen persons do this more than once; but, having made this tracing paper, how is it used?

F. A leaf of paper is covered with dry white lead or gesso, which, being placed between the tracing paper and the canvas, where it is oiled, the outlines of these figures are pressed with a needle of bone, and the coloured paper, which is placed between the two, leaves impressed all those marks which you have indented with the needle, and thus you will remove in regular order this coloured paper, having, however, fixed the tracing paper in two places that it may not move. I also do this, although I am not a painter, because it requires no skill in painting, but it is properly our business. And in the same manner, in order to transfer the design to white paper, the paper is coloured with charcoal, or with black or red chalk.

S. The "velo" which I have seen on a cartoon of my master's, how is it used? [1]

F. It is applied on the painting like the tracing paper, and the outline is drawn on it with gesso. It is then removed to the primed canvas, and the marks, being pressed with a piece of linen held in the hand, are thus transferred to the primed canvas, or the gesso is again passed over the outlines which are transferred to the priming.

S. How is the Graticola [2] used?

F. The Graticola is used in two ways: the picture which is to be copied is either crossed with white threads, or the Graticola, being made on a frame, is applied over the picture, and the same number of squares are to be struck on the primed canvas, which, whether it is larger or smaller than the painting, is to be divided in the same proportion.

---

1 The "Velo" was used in a different manner by L. B. Alberti, who describes it in his Treatise on Painting, Lib. II. It consisted of a piece of transparent gauze stretched on a frame, and divided into equal parts by

S. Ho veduto più d' una volta ancor io a far di queste, ma fato questo lucido, come s' adopra ?

F. Si tinge un foglio di carta con biaca suta ovvero giesso, qual posta tra il lucido e la tella ove sarà ogliato e con un ago di osso si calca li contorni di quelle figure, e quella carta tinta che fra posti, lascia impressi tutti quei segni, che haverai calcato con l' ago, e cosi trasporterai per ordine quella carta tinta havendo però saldata da due parti il lucido aciò non si mova ; e questa la facio ancor io, benchè non son pittore, che in ciò non vi entra artificio di pittura, ma è una pura operatione nostra, e cosi per calcar sopra carta bianca, si tinge con carbone, lapis nero, ovvero rosso.

S. Il velo che ho veduto in un cartone del mio padrone come s' adopra ?

F. Quelo si aplica sopra la pittura come il lucido, e si contorna con il gesso, e poi si trasporta sopra la tella imprimita, e con una peza di lino si va con la mano calcando sopra quei segni e cosi restono impressi sopra la tella primita, overo che di nuovo si replica con il giesso sopra li contorni, quali trapasseno sopra la primitura.

S. La Graticola come s' adopera ?

F. La Graticola si fa in due modi, cio è o sopra il quadro che si vuol copiare con fili bianchi, overo fata in un telaro, si aplica sopra il medesimo quadro, e con l' istesso comparto si bate sopra la tella primita, che essendo magiore o minore de la pittura si divide con la stessa proportione.

---

threads drawn across it. It was placed perpendicularly between the painter and his subject, so that the rays of the visual cone might pass through it. The points of intersection were marked with a pencil, and thus a correct outline was obtained, which was afterwards transferred to a panel or wall.

2 Graticola. A square divided by white crossed threads.

S. How are the lines struck?

F. A thread is rubbed with dry gesso or white lead, and is beaten over the compartments exactly as the joiners do with terra rossa over their wood; and the painters strike the lines of the architecture in their paintings in the same manner, drawing the lines to the point of sight.

S. Why do the painters use these tracing papers or graticola?

F. In the first place, to avoid the tediousness of drawing their works, which, in fact, is not their business, but ours; and, in the second place, to profit by it, as it enables their scholars to copy their works with greater perfection; and this plan was employed by Bassano, and my master has a chest half full of the tracings by the sons of Bassano from the works of their father, which, being touched up by the master, pass as his works.

S. How are colours ground?

F. The white lead is ground with nut oil; "verde eterno,"[1] Indigo, and all other blues, charcoal and the other colours, with linseed oil.

S. How are the stones cleaned after the colours are ground?

F. With bran, and then with a piece of rag, and the palettes are cleaned in the same manner; but take care that, when you leave off using the bran, you do not leave any flour behind, which may have an injurious effect on the colours; for when you grind up fine lake, or "verde eterno," it will whiten and spoil, therefore the bran is better after it has been used several times.

S. And suppose it should happen that you forget to clean the palette, so that the colour dries on it, how should it be cleaned?

F. With a little water and a pumice-stone.

S. How are the colours which have been ground preserved?

---

[1] Purified or, as it is sometimes called, distilled verdigris.

S. Come si bate?

F. Si tinge un filo con giesso overo biaca suta, e si bate sopra li comparti come fano li marangoni con la terra rossa sopra li legnami, e li pittori cosi batono l' architettura che fano sopra li quadri volendoli tirar al punto.

S. Perchè li Pittori usano questi lucidi o graticola?

F. Prima per levarti il fastidio di queste faccende non essendo sue ma di noi altri, e per valersi aciò li scolari copiino le loro opere con maggior perfetione, il che usò il Bassano, che apunto il mio Padrone ne ha meza una cassa di lucidi de figli del Bassano trati dalle opere del padre, che in tal guisa ritocate da maestri corrono come sue.

S. Li colori come si macinano?

F. La Biaca con olio di noce, il verde eterno, e l' Endico e cosi tutti gl' azzurri, et anco il carbone et gl' altri con olio di lino.

S. Come si neta le petre quando si è macinato li colori?

F. Con la semola di formento e poi con un pezo di stratio, e cosi istessamente le tavolozze; ma averti che quando la semola non è più stata adoperata, lascia qualche poco di farina si che habi l' actio, che se macinarai laca fina o verde eterno bianchegiono e si guastono, e perciò la semola è meglio come si è adoperata diverse volte.

S. E se per caso si scordasse di netar che il color si secasse, come si neta?

F. Con un poca d' acqua et una pietra pomica.

S. Li colori macinati come si tengono?

F. In divers ways, viz.—in folded papers, in small saucers, and in bladders; and this last is the best mode, for the colours keep better; but white lead is kept in a vase with water; the palettes also are placed in water, just as they are set in order, that the colours may not dry when the painter wishes to use them the following day; but remember that lake, giallo santo, and verderame are spoiled by the water, and they must be taken off the palettes before they are put under water.

S. How are the pencils preserved?

F. They are kept in linseed oil, and with that they are cleaned, pressing out the colour with a knife on a palette suspended over a vessel of oil, which oil you may afterwards keep for distempering the primings, as I have before told you; but the large brushes should be cleaned with soap and water, especially if they are afterwards to be used with blues, but as soon as they are dry wipe them well with a linen rag; then wind a thread round them from the handle to the extremity of the hairs, to keep them closer together, otherwise they will spread like flattened fungi.

S. How is boiled oil prepared?

F. The linseed oil is put into a clean pipkin or saucepan with some litharge of gold,[1] which is tied up in a rag, and fixed to a small piece of wood, which being laid across the pipkin or saucepan, suspends the rag so that it does not touch the bottom, because, if it should touch, it would burn, and the oil would become black, and when the oil boiled it would rise to the brim of the pipkin and flow over, but when the litharge is suspended these effects are not so easily produced. If the oil is boiled very much it will be more drying, and so whether you use much or little litharge; you may also boil with it a little umber, this will have the same effect, except that the oil will not be so light coloured. Sometimes also the oil, soiled with the colours pressed from the brushes, is boiled with olio di abezzo, and is applied to the backs of old pictures, which are scaling off their grounds, in order to fix them.

[1] It is unnecessary to observe that litharge of gold and silver are the

F. In diversi modi cioè nelle carte piegate, ne scudelini, nelle vesiche, e questo è il meglio che si conservano più, ma la biaca si tiene in un vaso con acqua che apunto le tavolozze come sono preparate si metono nel acqua a ciò li colori non si sechino, volendoli adoperare il pittor il giorno dietro, ma averti che la lacca, il gialo santo, et il verderame patiscono, e bisogna levarli avanti che si meta nel acqua.

S. Li peneli come si tengono?

F. Si tengono nell' olio di lino, e con quelo si netano, cavandoli il colore con un cortelo sopra d' una tavoluza pendente sopra il catino dell' olio, qual olio poi ti serve per stemprar le primiture come t' ho detto, ma li grandi il meglio è netarli con sapone et acqua, massime come devono esser adoperati con azurri, ma haverti che come sono neti asciugali bene con una peza di lino, e poi legali con filo dal manico fino alla estremità delle sete aciò restino più unite che altrimenti s' alargono come le vesce sponate [spianate?].

S. L' olio coto come si fa?

F. Si pone l' olio di lino in un pignato o calderola neta e vi si pone del retargirio d' oro, legato in una pezzetta, legato con un filo e saldata ad un legneto che passi attraverso del pignato o calderola, lo sostenti che non tochi il fondo, perchè come tocha il fondo s' abbrucia, e l' olio vien nero, et anco volendo sormonta l'orlo del vaso e si spande, che cosi sospeso non fa tal effetto cosi facilmente, se bole assai si fa più disecante, e cosi dal porvi più o meno retargirio si puo anco cucinar con un pezzo di terra d' ombra e fa l' istesso, ma non resta cosi chiaro. Si cucina alle volte anco l' olio sporco con colori con olio d' abete e questo si da dal rovescio alli quadri che vechij che si scorzano per saldarli.

---

same things. They derived their names from being extracted from ores which contained gold or silver. Litharge is the semi-vitrified oxide of lead.

S. How are varnishes made?

F. Varnishes are of different kinds: some we make ourselves, others, such as the "vernice grossa" and amber varnish, we purchase, but I make the mastic varnish myself.

S. Tell me how you make it?

F. I take pulverized white mastic, and put it into a pipkin with spirit of turpentine, or naphtha, in such quantities that the spirit of turpentine may rise two-thirds above the mastic in the pipkin. I then set the pipkin over the fire, and boil it until the mastic is perfectly dissolved, and sometimes add to it a little "olio d'abezzo." This serves for varnishing finished pictures, but if you wish to see divers modes of preparing these varnishes, consult Armenino da Faenza and Rafael Borghini, who teach all things pertaining to our trade, and how to make other kinds of varnishes, as well as the proper mode of using them.

S. I have not these books, nor can I see them.

F. Borrow them, and write down what you wish to know on this subject; perhaps your master may have the works, and then you may use them, because as they wrote of other things appertaining to painters, if your master studies painting, he will most certainly have them.

S. If they treat of painting, they will not write on these things which pertain neither to the art nor the artist, for this would be unbecoming, because our operations are merely vile and mechanical, and require no skill, but merely the labour of the hands.

F. They were not prudent enough to separate these things, and it is very proper that painters should understand them and know their use, so as to give orders to those whose business it is to prepare them, and to know whether the things made are perfect, and also to know good colours, but then they are not obliged to manufacture these things themselves.

S. How are good colours known from bad, because sometimes my master sends me [to purchase colours], and I have not had much experience on this subject?

F. Many are known by the eye, others by grinding them on the stone, others on the palette, in using them, and others dur-

S. Le vernici come si fanno?

F. Le vernici sono diverse, altre le facciamo noi, altre si comprano, come la vernice grossa, quella d' ambra si compra, quella di mastice la facio io.

S. Dimi dunque come fai?

F. Si piglia mastici bianchi polverizati, si pone in una ampola con acqua di ragia overo olio di sasso, la sua proporzione si che l' acqua di rasa sormenti due terzi sopra li mastici, si pone al foco, si fa bolir sino che li mastici siino bene liquefati, se le può agiunger anco un poco d' olio d' abezzo, e questa serve per dar sopra li quadri forniti, e se voi vedere diversi modi circa queste vernici, vedi Armenino da Faenza e Rafael Borgini (*sic*) che insegnano tutte le cose appartenenti al nostro mestiere, altri diverse sorte di vernice con il modo proprio di adoperarle.

S. Io non li ho, non li posso vedere.

F. Trova l' imprestito e scrivi ciò che ti fa bisogno in questi particolari; e forse il tuo Patrone li haverà e te ne potrai servire perchè scriveva altre cose appartenenti a Pittori, e se è già studioso della pittura li haverà certamente.

S. Se tratono di pittura non scriverano di queste materie che non s' apartengono ne a l' arte ne agli artefici che saria cosa indecente; che le nostre operationi sono vili e mecaniche, ne vi entra altro artificio che un lavorar di mani.

F. Non hano havuto questa prudenza di separar le cose, è bene che il pittor le conosca e sapia, per potersi far bene servire et ordinar a chi toca tale operatione, e per conoscer le cose fate, se sono perfette, come anco il conoscer li buoni colori, ma non sono tenuti a fabricarli.

S. Come si conosce li buoni colori da cattivi, perchè alle volte il mio padrone mi manda e non ho molta pratica?

F. Molti si conoscon nel vederli, altri sopra la pietra nel macinarli, altri sopra la tavolozza nel adoperarli, et altri posti

ing the painting, but the knowledge of the last is the painter's business, and not ours, for we do not paint.

S. Give me some rule by which I may know them.

F. The first rule is, that they must be of beautiful colour, as white lead, lake, the blues, cinnabar, red lead, "gialorino," "giallo santo," &c.; those colours which are in powder must be very finely pulverized. But with respect to the others, "smaltino" should be very bright, and so should all other blues. If you wish to know whether the ultramarine is adulterated, put it over the fire in a spoon; if it resists, it is good, but if it blackens, it is bad. The lakes should not only be beautiful and of lively colour, but in the grinding they should have body and not be liquid. The giallo santo, on the contrary, should be of fine colour, and in grinding should become very liquid so as to require very little oil in distempering, and should dry very quickly, which is a sign that it is pure; but if it hardens and requires a great deal of oil in grinding, that is a proof that it contains dirt or other impurities, and in this case it dries slowly and fades on the pictures. In the same manner, the lake which dries quickly is the best, and the "verde eterno" should be crystalline, clear, and of a lively colour. And the last test for the colours is to place the pictures in the sun; if they are not injured they are good, but if the colours fade they are bad, especially the giallo santo, the lake, and the indico. The earths in the lump are best, because they are natural, and there is no other material mixed with them; but the venders are accustomed to falsify everything in order to promote their own interests, and for this reason Borghini teaches the making of all colours, so that we may learn to manufacture them and to have them perfect, i. e., those which are most important, because it is much better to buy some colours ready made.

S. Are there not many colours which require to be burnt? how is this done?

F. Umber, yellow, green, and red earths should all be burnt in the fire, placing them over a slow fire that they may not break from the excessive heat; they are gradually made hotter until

in opera, e questa cognitione e del pittor che noi non dipingemo.

S. Dami un poco di regola per conoscerli.

F. La prima cognitione e che siino di bellissimo colore, comè la biaca, la laca, gl' azurri, il cinaprio, e el minio, gialorino, e gialo santo etc. queli che sono in polvere siino sottilissimi. Ma gl' altri, il smaltino e che sii chiaro di colore, e cosi tutti gl' altri azurri, l' oltremarino per conoscerlo se è adulterato, si pone al foco sopra un guchiaro, se resiste è buono, se anerisce è cattivo. Le lache deno esser non solo belissime di color vivace ma che nel macinar abino corpo, e che non inliquidiscon. Il giallo santo il contrario sii bello di colore, ma che nel macinar venga liquido che con pochissimo olio si stempera, et asciuga prestissimo che è segno che è puro, ma come s' indurisce e che ci vole assai olio nel macinarlo, e segno che ha delle feci o di materia cativa e stenta asciugarsi, e nelle piture si perde, e così anche la laca che asciuga presto e la meglio, il verde eterno si cristalino chiaro e di color vivace. E la prova ultima che si da ai colori è il por li quadri al sole, se resistono sono buoni, ma come svaniscono sono cativi, massime il gialo santo, la laca, e l' endico; le terre le grezze sono migliori, perchè sono naturali, e non v' è altra materia mista perchè uson per interesse a falsificar tutte le cose, e perciò il Borgini insegna a far tutti li colori, si che noi potiamo aprender il modo di fabricarli per haverli perfetti, cioè li più importanti perchè di molti è meglio il trovarli fatti.

S. Non vi sono molti colori che si abruciono? dimi in qual maniera.

F. La terra d' ombra, la giala, la verde, e la rossa, tutte s' abruciono nel foco ponendole a foco lento aciò non si spezino per la troppa veemenza del calore, ma a poco a poco si riscal-

they have a most vehement heat and are roasted; they are then sufficiently burnt. The yellow, however, is pulverized, and then burnt on a fire-shovel until it blackens, and when it cools it becomes of a dark red colour.

S. Tell me, pray, do you set your master's palette?

F. Certainly; I also distemper all the powder colours, and it is sufficient for him to tell me what he is going to paint, for I know what colours I ought to put on the palette; I wash the abbozzi, I oil them, I varnish them, and on some I lay the white of egg according to his orders; and then he has given me in writing full instructions in the distempering of the colours that I may know what to do, and his directions exactly correspond with those of Armenino da Faenza, and thus you also may write them out, for besides this he teaches the whole process. Father Lana[1] also, a Jesuit, has treated of this matter in his discourse on painting. And remember to put boiled linseed oil

---

[1] The treatise is contained in a larger work, entitled, "Prodromo overo Saggio di alcune Inventione nuove premesso al opera che prepara il P. Francesco Lana, Bresciano, della Compagnia de Gesù;" Brescia, 1670, fol. The part which relates to painting begins at p. 135. Four chapters are devoted to this subject; Cap. I. treats of Invention, Cap. II. of Design, Cap. III. of Colouring, and Cap. IV. of different methods of Painting and Drawing. The chapter on Colouring contains the usual directions for painting with four colours—a recommendation to mix ultramarine with all the flesh tints—full directions for mixing various tints on the palette, but none as to the mixing of the pigments with any liquid—as to the distribution of the light—and of the light in which a painting is to be placed while in progress. The directions as to "oiling out" are precise. Lana recommends for this purpose "boiled linseed oil, that is to say, linseed oil to which have been added two ounces of litharge for each pound of oil, warmed until it begins to boil." "This application," he says, "is not injurious to the picture, as some have imagined; and the advantage is that it dries quickly, for raw oil is a long time in drying."

According to P. Lana, "The priming consists in covering the picture with some colour, which is usually umber finely ground with a little white lead and terra rossa, in linseed oil; this mixture being very stiff, and less liquid than the other colours, is spread evenly and thinly over the picture with a large knife; when it is dry, another coat is to be applied, and after this, a third coat; which I do not approve of, because, being too thick, it causes the colours which are laid on it to change, for these sink into it so much, that they

dono, e poi se li da foco vehemente fino che s' arrossiscono; et allora sono arse. La giala, però, si spolveriza e s' abrucia sopra la paleta da fuocco, fino che anerisce, che rafredata divene rossa oscura.

S. Dimi in grazia, prepari tu la tavolozza al tuo padrone?

F. Certo che si, li stempro anco tutti li colori che sono in polvere, e mi basta che mi dica ciò che vol dipinger, che so quali devo pore sopra la tavolozza, lavo gli abozzi, li ungo, li do la vernice, et altri ancora la chiara d' uova secondo mi comanda, e poi mi ha dato in scrito tutto ciò che occore nel distemperar de colori, a ciò sapia ciò che devo fare, et è apunto come insegna Armenino da Faenza, e cosi li potrai scriver ancor tu che insegna il tutto et anco il P. Lana Gesuita ha scritto di questa materia nel suo discorso di pittura. Et haverti che nè colori che difficilmente s' asciugono di porvi de l' olio coto et anco verderame, come nel nero fumo et aspalto, e così l' azuro di Spagna

---

participate of the colour of the priming itself. But in order that the colours should retain their brilliancy, the same colour should be repeated several times upon the first, and the parts should be more charged with colour than the life; for instance, in colouring the cheeks, or other parts, with cinnabar and lake, they should be made a little more rosy than the natural carnations, because, after a time, they sink, and are toned down to their natural hue; without this precaution, they would become too pale and dead."—p. 158.

In Cap. IV. Lana treats of the different methods of painting, in distemper, in oil, and fresco; also of miniature painting, painting on marble, on silk, tapestry, mosaics, and metals.

In page 165, he observes that, " when the painting is finished, some painters are accustomed to varnish it, in order that the work may be more smooth and brilliant."

He then mentions an invention of his own for painting on glass, and afterwards treats of engraving.

The remainder of the work treats of other inventions. I have been thus particular in detailing the technical processes described in this Treatise, because the work itself is rare; and, as it treats on other subjects, it is not likely to form part of the library of a painter. Indeed, it is so little known, that the scanty notice of it in the work of Volpato is the only reference I have ever found to it; and it was not without considerable research that I at last ascertained, that the Treatise of Padre Lana, on Painting, was contained in the above-mentioned work.

and verdigris with the colours which dry slowly, such as lamp black and asphaltum. And in like manner the Spanish blue[1] should be distempered as stiffly as possible with nut oil. The painters make it flow with spirit of turpentine, and ultramarine with naphtha.

S. How do you varnish with the white of egg?

F. I apply the white of egg upon those [pictures] which he finishes without having varnished the abozzo, and which he completes by merely "oiling out" and then retouching until finished, and on the others I apply mastic varnish. I beat up this white of egg well with a spoon, agitating it till it flows well through a rag, and adding to it a little garlic cut small, which has a good effect, and this was used by Canziani on his paintings. Your master will order all the rest that you may have to do.

S. I am in a great fright and do not know what course to take; the other day I let a canvas fall against a box, and injured it so much that there is a large lump on one side; and what makes the matter worse is, that my master is going to use the canvas so soon that I shall not have time to prepare another, nor can I get any canvas of that size, and I should not like my master to know it and be vexed about it; what would you advise me to do?

F. Are the threads broken?

S. There is no hole in it, but it is in such a state that it cannot be used.

F. What will you give me to tell you how to set it to rights?

S. Whatever you please, for I am very much annoyed at the accident, as it is a large canvas and of some value.

F. We will share the reward between us, for I wish you only, as it were, to change wine for water.

S. Most willingly; but how is this change to be effected?

---

1 This was probably the "azzurri di Spagna" mentioned by Malvasia, Felsina Pittrice, Vol. II., p. 349, which I consider (see Art of Fresco Painting, Int., p. xlviii.) to be the native Blue Carbonate of Copper.

stemperalo più sodo che si può con olio di noce, li pittori lo fano score con l'acqua di rasa, e l' oltremarino con l' olio di sasso.

S. Dimi come le dai la chiara d'ovo?

F. Quelli che fornisce senza dar vernice sopra l' abozzo, che solo con il lavor li fornisce e con l' unger li ritocca, a queli li do la chiara d' uovo, et a gl' altri la vernice di mastici; e questa chiara la rompo benissimo con un guchiaro, agitandola fra pezza, ponendovi dentro un poco d' alio tagliato minuto, che fa bell' effetto, e cio usava il Canziani sopra de suoi quadri e poi il tuo patrone ti ordinarà ciò che devi fare.

S. Io son molto intricato, ne so qual partito pigliare, l' altro giorno è cascata una tela sopra uno scrigno, et è sfondata con un rilevo bestiale, et il Patrone la deve pore in opera in breve, che non ho tempo di prepararne altra, ne di quella misura non ne trovo, perchè non vorrei che s' acorgesse e ricever qualche mortificazione, cosa mi consigli che facia?

F. E rota?

S. Non è forata, ma in quel modo non si può adoperare.

F. Cosa mi voi donare che t' insegno il modo di agiustarla?

S. Ciò che voi, perchè mi preme; essendo tela grande di qualche consideratione.

F. Goderemo insieme il mercato, che altro non voglio da te che in tal guisa contracambierai vino per acqua.

S. Più che volentieri, ma in che modo farò questo cambio?

---

2 Gio. Batista Canziani was a native of Verona and pupil of Antonio Calza; he flourished about 1712. Vide Crespi, Pittori di Bologna, p. 189.

F. Bathe with tepid water the back of the canvas, and it will become even.

S. I am very much obliged to you, for I did not at all know what to do, but I have another difficulty; my master has several pictures soiled by smoke, and has told me to wash them, but I do not know how.

F. It must be some trick he wishes to play a friend or patron, because good pictures either never are washed or the owners perform this operation themselves; and it is not merely a mechanical operation, because the pictures are easily spoiled, for if washed too much, those last retouchings which are the perfection of the work are effaced, and I have seen many paintings spoiled in this manner by ignorant persons who know not what mischief they do. And I have even seen them wash paintings on panel and on canvas, in such a way that after being washed they have scaled off, because the gesso underneath was affected by the moisture, and swelled; therefore it is great folly to wash good paintings.

S. I do not understand, or know anything about it.

F. Your master ought to know this himself.

S. But how should I wash them?

F. Take some ashes, which have been sifted very fine that there may not be any pieces of charcoal or any large substances which may scratch the picture; put them into a small pipkin with pure water, and with a sponge spread them all over the painting, and clean it by moving about the sponge gently, then wash it off quickly with pure water, because the ashes corrode the colour. Afterwards wash it well with clear water, dry it with a linen cloth, and then varnish it with white of egg.

S. But should it not be oiled?

F. No, for the oil is not good on pictures, except on their backs when they are scaling off, as I have told you; and in proof of this, see the Saint Peter the Martyr, at Venice, who having been oiled so many times by sacrilegious blockheads who have copied him, is so spoiled and blackened, that there is no telling what sort of face he has, and yet I recollect when he

F. Bagna con acqua tiepida dal rovescio dela tela, che il servitio sarà fato, e resterà ugualgiato.

S. Ti ringratio infinitamente, perchè era molto intricato; ma un altra cosa, il mio Patrone ha diversi quadri afumicati, m' ha detto che vol che li lavi, io non so come fare.

F. Sarà qualche stratio per agradir qualche suo amico o patrone perchè quadri buoni, o che non si lavono mai, overo che lo fano loro, e non è cosa da manuali, perchè si possono guastar facilmente, che con il lavarli troppo se le consuma què ultimi ritochi che sono la perfetione de l' opera, come ne ho veduti tanti cosi guasti, per mezo di ignoranti che non sano ciò che fano. E di più ho veduto anco lavar quadri in tavola e cosi in tela, che dopo lavati si sono scorzati, perchè il gesso di sotto risente quell' umido e si rileva; e perciò è gran pazzia lavar quadri buoni.

S. Non me ne intendo, ne so quel che sia.

F. Lo deve saper lui.

S. Come dovrò fare per lavarli?

F. Prendi un poca di cenere sedazata sotilmente aciò non vi sii carbone o materia grossa che possa raschiar il quadro, ponila in una scudela con acqua pura, e con una sponga distendila sopra il quadro, e leggermente maneggia la sponga netandolo, ma fa presto a levar con acqua chiara la sud[ta] cenere per che rode il colore. Lavato bene con acqua chiara, asciugala con un drapo di lino, et asciuto come si, dali la chiara d'ovo.

S. Che lo ungessi?

F. Non lo fare, che l' olio non fa bene a quadri, se non dal rovescio, come si scorzano come ti ho detto, e che ciò sia vero, vedi il S. Pietro Martire di Venezia, che unto tante volte da sacrilegi e sgratiati che lo copiano l' hano cosi guasto et anerito che non si vede più che facia egli abia; e pur a miei giorni era bellissimo, e puoi osservare li putini che essendo alti lontani da

was beautiful, and you may observe the children, which being above the reach of similar influences, are in excellent preservation, therefore these blackguards should be forbidden to copy such excellent works. This privilege should only be permitted to those who have a proper respect for pictures. Do you wish me to tell you anything else ?

S. One thing, about which I am curious : my master has made me grind up several colours with pure water, and tells me he wants to make crayons of them for colouring on paper. What are these crayons, and how are they made ?

F. You will see, because he will make the tints with the knife, and will make you point the crayons for use. But in order that the white lead and the powder colours may adhere together, he will tell you to add gum-water to them to make them firm so that they may be used, but the lamp black is formed into a paste with the "terra da bocali," and dried by the fire, and is sometimes used instead of charcoal for drawing.

S. How is charcoal made ?

F. An iron tube is provided, the pieces of wood are pressed tightly into this, and the ends of the tube are stopped up with ashes that the smoke may not escape, and when the tube is red hot and no more smoke is given out, the charcoal is made ; the whole is then thrown into water.

S. What sort of wood is used ?

F. The plum-tree and the willow.

S. Why is the tube fastened up air-tight ?

F. Because if the wood were to burn, it would fall to ashes without making charcoal : when the crayons are made they are anointed with common oil, so that when used the marks may not be cancelled. Is there anything else you wish to know, for I would willingly communicate everything to you ?

S. I am very much obliged to you, and I think I want no more instructions for my functions ; if I have any difficulty I will consult you. It is now time, however, for you to go to the "piazza," and take your salad for supper ; our masters will perhaps come home late this evening.

simili influsi sono conservati belissimi, e perciò si dovrebbe vietare a questa sorte di canagle il copiar opere si fatte, e solo permeterlo a soggetti che portano a quadri li dovuti rispetti. Desideri saper altro da me?

S. Una curiosità. Il mio patrone mi ha fatto macinar diversi colori con acqua pura, e mi dice che vol far delle pastele per colorir sopra le carte. Cosa sono queste pastele e come si fanno?

F. Lo vederai perchè farà le tinte con il cortelo, e poi ti farà far le punte a te per adoperarli. Ma perchè la biaca e queli che sono in polvere stijno saldi, ti farà meter un poca d' acqua di goma a ciò siino salde per poterle adoperare, ma il nero fumo s' impasta con terra da bocali, e si seca al foco e serve anco per carbone da disegnare.

S. Il carbone come si fa?

F. Si piglia una cana di fero, vi si pone dentro li stechi di legno ben serati, si atura con cenere delle parti di detta cana essendo posta nel focco aciò il fumo non esali, e come la cana è infocata, e che si vede che non esala più fumo, il carbone è fato, s' estingue il tutto nel acqua.

S. Che sorte di legno s' adopera?

F. Si piglia il susin, ed il salice.

S. Perchè s' atura e non si lascia respirare?

F. Perchè ardendo andarebbe in cenere, ne si faria carbone, qual fatto si unge con olio comune aciò che adoperato non si canceli. Vedi s' altro ti occore, che ti dirò il tutto volontieri.

S. Ti ringrazio infinitamente, che per la mia fontione altro non fa bisogno, e se haverò qualche difficoltà ti verò a trovare. Fra tanto è hora che vadi alla piazza a piglar l'insalata per la cena, li nostri patroni forse verano tardi questa sera.

F. Mine is not gone far. They will come home at the usual time; but before you go, I beg you will take a glass of wine, come.

S. This cellar is very cool.

F. Take this wine and taste it, it will taste as if it were iced.

S. To the health of our masters!

F. To theirs and to our own!

S. Truly, it is very cool.

F. Now I will taste it, in confirmation of what you say.

S. I will take another glass.

F. Two or three, if you like.

S. One will do for the present.

F. Take it.

S. And with this I will drink your good health.

F. May you long continue in good health.

F. E poco lontano. Verano all' ora solita. Avanti che ti parti, bevi un bichier di vino. Andiamo.

S. Questa cantina è molto fresca.
F. Prendi e gusterai il vino che pare che sii in giaza.

S. Alla salute de nostri patroni!
F. Alla sua et alla nostra ancora!
S. Veramente è freschissimo.
F. Hora lo gusterò anch' io alla confirmatione di quanto hai detto.
S. Ne voglo un altro bichier.
F. Anco doi e tre se ti gusta.
S. Un sol mi basta per hora.
F. Prendi.
S. E con questo ti lascio la buona salute.
F. In buon vigore conservati.

BRUSSELS MANUSCRIPT,

ENTITLED

"RECUEUIL DES ESSAIES DES MERVEILLES DE LA PEINTURE."

BY

PIERRE LEBRUN, PAINTER,

1635.

BRUSSELS MANUSCRIPT.

PRELIMINARY OBSERVATIONS.

THE following pages are copied from the commencement of a MS., preserved in the Public Library at Brussels, numbered 15,552, written in 1635 by Pierre Le Brun, a painter. The MS. is in small octavo, the writing extremely small and difficult to read, and the ink very pale. It appears to have been intended for publication, as it contains many drawings. The part of the MS. uncopied treats of Sculpture, Architecture, and Perspective.

It appears from the MS. that Pierre Le Brun was contemporary with the Carracci, with Rubens, Laurens Dubry the Fleming, and Vouet; and the scattered notices he has given relative to painting in oil must be considered as indications of the practice of this art in France, or rather at Paris, during the middle of the seventeenth century. The manner in which the author speaks of contemporary artists shows that he was living at Paris when the MS. was written.

The object of the author in writing the treatise seems to have been to give amateurs such a knowledge of the mechanical parts of the art, and of technical terms, as would enable them to speak on the subject of painting with propriety, and without incurring ridicule.

In the first chapter, therefore, he describes the implements used in the mechanical part of the art, and then recapitulates a number of technical expressions, some few of which he explains, especially those relating to the light in which a picture should be viewed. This part of the work bears much resemblance to the Treatise of Bulengerus, De Pictura, Plastice, et Statuaria, lib. ii. cap. ii., a work which must have obtained some reputation, since it has passed through three editions, and has been translated into English.[1]

The author then treats of painting in distemper and in fresco; and he cites, as authority for the rules he lays down for fresco-painting, Father L'Ange and Father Antoine the Capuchin, and M. Thierson, a painter. The latter he mentions frequently in the course of the work.

The fourth chapter treats of painting on glass; and I find, by comparing this chapter with the second part of Le Vieil's "Art de la Peinture sur Verre," that the method described in the MS. was that which was generally followed in France. The practice of the art, therefore, appears to have changed but little from the time of Le Brun (1635) to the date of the work of Le Vieil, 1774.

In the fifth and sixth chapters, Le Brun treats of the proportion of the human body and of the beauty of the

---

1 The first Latin edition was printed at Leyden in 1621, and the English translation in 1657. The work is mentioned in the letters of Rubens, who merely states that he had received the work, but had not had time to read it. It appears from the explanations of many of the technical terms being in French, that the author was a Frenchman. His name, probably, was Boulanger.

face, and in the seventh he teaches the nature and composition of colours. He describes six kinds of azure, the first of which, called Cerulée or "Turchino," is the azure of Pozzuoli, of Vitruvius, and the smaltino of the Italians. The second, formed of mercury, sulphur, and sal ammoniac, has been called Venetian azure. The third, which is called "Ultramarine," is said to consist of calcined silver, aqua fortis, and sal ammoniac. The fourth is the Carbonate of Copper, mentioned in the first chapter under the name of "La Cendrée." The fifth is Indico, composed of the scum of woad, starch, &c.; and the sixth is the true Ultramarine.

The eighth chapter, entitled Secrets in Painting, consists of detached hints relative to the technical parts of the art. From these it appears that white was to be excluded from shadows (see No. 1), which we know was in accordance with the precept of Rubens.

In No. 42, Umber and Lake are mentioned as forming a beautiful colour for shadows. The directions given in No. 7, "Il faut fort ombrer en esbauchant," and the reason given for it, "cela ayde a parachever avec plus grande facilité," appear to me to recommend the Flemish practice of getting in the subject in chiaroscuro, after which it was necessary merely to apply the lights and local colours, leaving the deep shadows free from solid or opaque colour. In No. 10 it is recommended not to use umber in the grounds, because the colours sink into it. No. 19 shows that the colour of the grounds was generally of a yellow colour, the method of preparing which appears to be described in Chapter I. In No. 32 a process is mentioned by

which a canvas can be prepared so quickly that a person may paint on it the same day. The author also advises the use of mineral colours, which were to be previously ground with oil (see Cap. I.), and recommends that paintings should be exposed to the air. Nos. 23, 24, and 25 describe the method of preparing both drying and fat oils, which were to be used for promoting the drying of certain colours, among which we find white lead, which is not usually placed among the slow dryers. Ground glass and verdigris are also said to be mixed with colours to make them dry.

The method of applying the azure in powder, described in No. 39, is curious, but not uncommon, since it is mentioned several times in the MS. of De Mayerne in the British Museum.

No. 40 shows that even so late as 1635 statues or bassi rilievi were painted with colours.

In order to preserve pictures from dust and fly marks, it is recommended (No. 22) to wash them with white of egg, and the reason for using this is stated to be that it may be easily washed off with a damp sponge. It is added, "this cannot be done with varnish." From this then it appears that it was not always usual to varnish paintings in oil, and this certainly implies that they were painted with a vehicle *which rendered varnishing unnecessary*; thus affording evidence of the truth of Vasari's statement that pictures painted in the manner of Van Eyck did not require varnishing.

The MS. contains no directions as to the vehicle; it is merely stated that the colours were to be ground with

---

[1] See Mr. Eastlake's 'Materials,' &c., vol. i. p. 455, 456.

oil, and that certain colours were to be used with drying oil, in order to make them more siccative. In No. 14, Oil of "Camamine" (Chamomile) is mentioned,[1] but on account of the difficulty of deciphering the MS., it is scarcely possible to distinguish whether Le Brun has written "bonne pour peindre," or "bonne pour prendre." The supposition, coupled with the conclusion of the sentence, "it is as clear as rock water," is certainly in favour of the first reading, whence we may suppose that oil of chamomile was used to dilute the colours in the same manner as spirit of turpentine is now used.

With regard to the varnishes described in the MS., it will be observed that they are not oleo-resinous. The first varnish for pictures consists of mastic and "huile de sapin," which appears to be synonymous, or nearly so, with the "olio di abezzo" of the Italians. The second consisted of turpentine liquefied over the fire, thinned with oil of spike. The "Vernis Gros" ("vernice grossa" of the Italians) or common varnish was made of turpentine, oil of turpentine, and resin melted together. The two former, at least, were probably light-coloured varnishes; the colour of the last seems doubtful. A passage in Chapter I. (No. 16) suggests the idea of a high-coloured varnish having been used occasionally "to lower the brilliancy of the colours." This may have been a relic of an older practice, and

[1] The distilled oil of chamomile (Oleum Anthemidis) is sometimes of a blue colour: that which is found in the shops is generally foreign, of a yellowish or brownish yellow colour, and becomes viscid by age.—Brande's Dictionary, &c.

appears more applicable to an oleo-resinous varnish than to one of those described in the MS.

Chapter IX. teaches how to speak of beautiful paintings; and Chapter X. is an account of the greatest painters in the world. The author commences this chapter with an extract from Quintilian (ch. 16, l. 12), giving a brief account of a few of the great painters of antiquity. He then speaks of the moderns, among whom he mentions Michael Angelo as a distinct person from Buonarotti. From the painters of the cinquecento he passes to the artists who were contemporary with him, among whom he enumerates the Carracci, Rubens, and Simon Vouet, and he concludes this part of the work with observing that his friend M. Thierson, to whom he was indebted for many hints for his work, "is also a very clever man."

Chapter XI. treats of the various methods of gilding, and the work concludes with the recipes for varnish before mentioned.

COLLECTION OF ESSAYS,

ETC.

COLLECTION OF ESSAYS ON THE WONDERS OF PAINTING,

By PIERRE LEBRUN, PAINTER, 1635.

PREFACE TO THE READER.

When Alexander the Great visited Apelles the Great, and began to talk of colours and paintings, the apprentices burst into a loud laugh, so that their master was frightened and ashamed of them, and whispered to Alexander, saying, "Sire, I entreat you will not speak of the profession, for the boys who are grinding the colours are bursting with laughter at the mistakes you make: you are good for conquering worlds, we for representing them on pictures; your sword and our pencils in the same hand do not agree, and, to do well, every one should speak of his own trade, otherwise he furnishes a subject of laughter to the whole company." Alexander was silent, and laughed. Reader—my dear friend, I desire to free you from this annoyance, and from the fear that your ignorance should be the subject of derision, when you speak of painting on a flat surface, one of the most noble arts of the world. The greatest deceiver in the world is the greatest painter of the universe and the most excellent workman; for, to tell the truth, eminence in this art consists in a deception, innocent, and full of enthusiasm and divine spirit. Poets have their inspirations in the head, which is the seat of the poetic nerve; painters in the tips of the fingers, and in the flowing point of the pencil. But the eye must be deceived, or the picture is worth nothing; this must appear

RECUEUIL DES ESSAIES DES MERVEILLES DE LA PEINTURE,

De PIERRE LEBRUN, PEINTRE, 1635.

PRÉFACE AU LECTEUR DE LA PEINTURE.

Quand le grand Alexandre visitant Apelles le grand voulut parler des couleurs et des peintures, les Apprentis esclattèrent si fort de rire que le maistre en eust peur et honte. Sire (dit-il tout bas) ne parlez point de le mestier car les garçons qui broient les couleurs crevent de rire vous entendant ainsi begayes : vous estes bon pour conquerir les mondes, et nous pour les coucher sur nos tableaux. Vostre espée et nos pinceaux ne s'accordent pas bien en une mesme main, et pour bien faire chacun doit parler de son mestier autrement on appreste à rire à toute la compagnie. Alexandre se teut et se print à rire. Je desire lecteur mon grand amy, vous delivrer de ceste peine, et de la peur qu'on ne se gausse de vostre niaiserie quand vous voudrez parler de la platte peinture, l'un des nobles artifices du monde, le plus grand trompeur du monde c'est le meilleur peintre de l'univers et le plus excellent ouvrier, car à vray dire l'eminence de le mestier ne consiste qu'en une tromperie innocente et toute pleine d'entousiasme et de divin esprit, les poetes ont leurs inspirations dans la teste ou est la nerve poëtique, et les peintres au fin bout des doigts et à la pointe scarante du pinceau. Mais faut tromper l'œil ou tout n'y vaut rien : il faut qu'on croie que celà est creux et enfoncé, cela enflé, et boursoufflé, cecy hors d'œuvres et qui se jette entièrement hors du

hollow and concave, that swollen and convex ; this appear to project and stand out from the picture, that must appear distant a good league ; this of a prodigious height, that perforated ; this living and full of movement. Let the horse gallop and foam at the mouth through its hard breathing ; let the dog bark loudly ; let the blood flow from the wound ; let the clouds really thunder and be torn to pieces by frequent flashes of lightning ; let this dying man appear with his soul issuing from his lips ; let this bird tire his beak by pecking at the grapes ; let the spectators call for the curtain to be raised, so as to see what is behind ; yet there is no reality in this, for the surface on which the objects are represented is flat, and truth is imitated so artfully that nature appears to have animated the picture in order to assist painting to deceive us, and to laugh at our folly ; hence it is that one painter wrote in his works "*res ipsa*"—*it is the thing itself*, not the imitation ; and another, "*fecit Apelles*," which that great artist wrote on three works in which he surpassed art, nature, and himself ; on the others he wrote "faciebat," that is to say, "*he was doing it.*" He would not finish his designs lest he should make Nature blush, for she had already acknowledged herself conquered by genius and art,—not like those simpletons who were such fools as to paint an ox or an ass for a horse, and so wretchedly was the imitation daubed, that it was necessary to write under it in large letters, "Gentlemen, this is an ass ;" or, "Gentlemen, this is an ox ;" but even in this they lied, for there were two asses ; he [the painter] was the first, and the brute he had painted the second. Therefore, to know how to discourse on this noble profession, you must have frequented the studio and disputed with the masters, have seen the magic effects of the pencil, and the unerring judgment with which the details are worked out by the

of the wonders of nature by René François, the King's preacher.

tableau, cecy esloigné d'une bonne lieue, cela d'une hautesse extrême, celà perce à jour, cecy tout vif et plein de mouvement, que le cheval court et escume à force de souffler, que ce chien jappe vivement, que le sang coule de la plaie, que les nuées tonnent en effet, et que les nuages soient tout descousus à force d'esclaires qu'on voie sortir coup sur coup ; que cest homme rende l'esprit, et qu'on voie l'ame sur ses leuvres, que les oyseaux bequettent ces raisins, et se lassent le becque, qu'on crie haut qu'il faut oster le rideau afin de voir ce qui est caché, cependant il n'y a rien de tout celà, car tout celà est plat, pris bas mort et contrefait si artistement qu'il semble que la nature se soit couchée la-dessus pour aider la peinture à nous tromper finement et se mocquer de nostre bestise, de la vient qu'un deux escrit en les ouvrages *res ipsa*, c'est la chose même non pas la peinture, et l'autre *fecit Apelles;* ce qu'il mit en trois piéces ou il surmonta l'art, la nature et soy-mesme, aux autres il mettait *faciebat*, c'est à dire il faisoit, et à dessein n'a point vouluz achever de peur de fair rougir la nature qui se fut confessée vaincue par l'esprit et par l'art, ce n'est pas comme ces badaux qui étaient si niaiz que pour peindre un cheval ils faisoient une asne ou un bœuf et encore si mal fagotté qu'il falloit escrire en gros cadeaux : Messieurs cecy est une asne, cecy est un bœuf, encore mentoient-ilz, car ilz estoient deux, luy le beau premier, et celuy qu'il avoit peint l'autre ; Pour scavoir donc parler de ce noble mestier, il faut avoir esté à la boutique disputé avec les maistres, veu le traint de pinceau, et le jugement asseuré pour esplucher toute chose par le menu .[1] . . may des . . . merveilles de nature par René François Predicat. du Roy.

---

[1] The words omitted are illegible in the MS.

CHAPTER I.

OF FLAT PAINTING.

1. The muller (that is, the stone with which the colours are ground) must be of flint or whetstone, so as to grind the colours on the porphyry and to incorporate them better with the oil. The amassette[1] is of horn, and with this the colours are collected after grinding, and spread upon the stone.

2. The scaffold or easel of the painter is used to support the paintings for working.

3. The pencils are made of a soft kind of hair, but which has sufficient resistance to keep itself straight, and to make a firm point for painting; the hairs of bears are very good, so are those of martens and similar animals. Small brushes made of hogs' or pigs' bristles are also used, and pencils of fishes' hair[2] for softening.

4. The pinceliere is a vase in which the pencils are cleaned with oil, and of the mixture of oil and dirty colours is made a grey colour, useful for certain purposes, such as to lay on the first coats, or to prime the canvas. The pincelier is a vase containing oil, in which the pencils are placed that they may not dry.

5. A palette set for painting flesh colour must contain terre verte, cendre verte et bleue, brown pink, yellow ochre, vermilion, red ochre, lake, umber, bone black, and charcoal black, with white lead in the middle.

6. The painter's palette is the mother of all colours; for, from the mixture of 3 or 4 principal colours, his pencil will create, and, as it were, cause to flourish all kinds of colours. They say *to set a palette* for the carnations (that is to say, to make the flesh colour), with green, &c.; and this is the work of the boy. The principal colours are, 1st, white lead (so called because it is found in lead mines); 2ndly, fine azure

---

[1] Amassette—instrument with which the colours are collected and scraped together on the stone.

CHAPITRE PREMIER.

DE LA PLATTE PEINTURE.

1. Il faut que la moulette soit de caillou (c'est à dire la pierre à broyer) de gré ou de queux, afin de mieux broyer les couleurs sur le porphir et les mieux incorporer avec l'huile. L'amassette est de corne, et amasse la couleur broyée, et éparse sur la pierre.

2. L'Estodi, l'eschafaux ou chevallet du peintre, c'est sur quoy on posse les tableaux pour travailler.

3. Les pinceaux sont fait d'un poil doux toutefois qu'il ait une résistance pour se tenir droit et faire une pointe assez ferme pour peindre, les poils d'ouris [ours] y sont tres bons, moustoil, foines et autres semblables; on se sert aussi de petite bruissette fait de soye de pourceau (ou cochon). L'on a aussi des pinceaux fait de poil de poisson pour adoucir.

4. La pinceliere est un vase où l'on nestoie les pinceaux avec l'huile, et de ce meslange on fait un gris et bon à certains ouvrages comme à faire les premières couches ou imprimer la thoile. Le pincelier est un vase où l'on met tramper les pinceaux dans de l'huile, de peur qu'il ne se seichent.

5. Une pallette de carnation est du verd de terre, cendre verd et bleuse, stil de grun [grain], ocre jaune, vermillon, ocre rouge, lac, terre d'ombre, noir dos et de charbon, avec blanc de plomb au milieu.

6. La pallette du peintre est la mère de toutes les couleurs, car du meslange de trois ou quatre maistresse couleurs, son pinceau fait naistre et comme fleurir toutes sortes des couleurs, on dit préparer une palette de carnation (c'est à dire, pour faire la charnure) du verd, &c. Et c'est l'ouvrage du garçon. Les meres des couleurs sont premièrement le blanc de plomb (à cause qu'il se trouve en mine de plomb). 2 le fin azur et

---

[2] Probably seal's fur.

and ultramarine; 3rdly, Venetian lake, which makes a most brilliant flesh colour and scarlet; 4thly, Spanish vermilion; 5thly, la cendrée; 6thly, charcoal black; 7thly, massicot, which serves for the fine yellow; 8thly, "verd de terre;" 9thly, dragon's blood; and, 10thly, "la rosette."[1] These are the florid colours, the others are common.

7. The canvases are covered with parchment glue or flour paste before they are primed with potter's earth, yellow earth, or ochre ground with linseed or nut oil. The priming is laid on the canvas with the knife or amassette to render it smoother, and this is the work of the boy.

8. To take the portrait of a person, or to draw from the life. Anciently, the art did not extend beyond drawing the outlines; in later times the outline was covered with a single colour. To give expression and character; to open the mouth, the eye; to give a smile; to paint the soul, the character, the passions, &c.

9. To paint the portrait after the life, to leave the work at the discretion of the pencil, and to the chance of the hand; to heighten and relieve the colours, i. e. to give the colours lustre and light; item to varnish, and cover with varnish to produce lustre.

10. Outlines, gestures, symmetry, proportions, expressions, and character, give renown to the pencil, and are the principal points to be aimed at. The inner part is easily done; but the outline, the finishing touches, and the roundings off of the different objects are difficult.

11. To shade or shadow the works, put in the darks and shadows, to give prominence to some parts, and make others recede, and to throw back the landscapes to a still greater distance, and compress them into a small space. The light and shade should be intermixed so that the diversity of colour may heighten and give roundness to both.

---

[1] La Rosette. See Chap. VII. No. 11.

l'outremarin. 3e. la lacque de Venise qui a un incarnat et une escarlatte fort vive. 4°. le vermillon d'Espagne. 5°. la cendrée, 6° le noir de charbon, 7° le massicot qui est le fin jaune, 8° le verd de terre, 9° le sang de dragon, 10° la rosette : voilà les couleurs gayes, les autres sont rudes.

7. Les toilles s'encolles avec colle de parchemin ou de farine auparavant que les imprimer ; on les imprime avec terre de potier, terre jaune ou ocre broyés avec huille de noix ou de lin. La dite imprimure se couche sur les toilles avec un cousteau ou avec l'amassette pour les rendres plus unie, et c'est l'ouvrage du garçon.

8. Pourtraire et enlever au vif une personne, du commencement on ne faisoit que porfiller, puis après on couvrit le pourfil d'une seule couleur. Donner contenance, sans images et bonnes mines, ouvrant la bouche, l'œil, le rire, &c., peindre l'esprit, les mœurs, les passions, &c.

9. Faire le pourtrait au naturel, laisse l'ouvrage à la discretion du pinceau et au hasard de la main, rehausser les couleurs et relever l'ouvrage, c'est donner le lustre et le jour aux couleurs. item vernisser et coucher du vernis pour faire esclate.

10. Les pourfils, les gestes, les simmetries et proportions, et mines et bonnes contenances sont celles qui donnent bruit au pinceaux ; et le point principal de tout c'est cela. Le dedans se fait aisément, mais le pourfil, les derniers traits, et l'arrondissement de la besogne est mal aisée.

11. Ombrer ou ombrager les ouvrages, faire des nuits, des ombrages pour faire esclatte, les autres reculer, les paysages bien loin et en petit volume. L'ombragement et le jour s'entremeslent afin que la diversité des couleurs facent rehausser et arondir l'une et l'autre.

12. Besides the light and the shade, there is the half light,[1] which is something between light and shade, and is a colour composed of a mixture of the two, and is that which separates the colours; it is called "dejettement," and in Greek "armoge."

13. To paint landscapes on a flat ground in architecture, in the air, and as if among the clouds, covering but a small surface of canvas; the ancients had two sorts, and afterwards three, the Ionic, Sicyonic, and Attic. To make figures, flowers, fancy subjects, rivers, to raise mountains, and tempests, &c.

14. To paint landscapes, grotesques, arabesques, rustic scenes, fancies, chimeras, vignettes, tufts of trees, precipices, falls of water, sea pieces, storms, with a thousand poetical inventions of the kind.

15. To paint draperies, and clothe the figures, that is to say, to dress them with drapery, always using more than one colour, but there must be a mixture of colours. There is simple drapery, and there is drapery damasked and embroidered with historical subjects; there are robes tucked up and with folds, which the painters cover with crape, and which are visible through the veil and the transparent gauze; others which are broken with shadows in order to lower the brilliancy of the colours.

16. To lower the too great brilliancy of the colours with varnish, which is like talc or crape spread over the painting; to infuse into the painting the soul, the affections, the conceptions of genius (the inimitable invention of Apelles), in fact to paint that which cannot be painted, such as thunder, lightning, the voice, the breath, &c. To lay on the colours with cleanliness, with harshness.

17. Ceruse is made of lead and vinegar; it is good in the flesh colour and similar things. Burnt ivory, which was used

---

1 Millin gives a different signification to this term. He says, that in painting a picture, it is said to be in a false light, when it is placed in an apartment in such a manner that the natural light enters on the side oppo-

12. Outre le jour et l'ombragement, il y a encore le faux-jour, qui tien du jour et de l'ombre et est un lustre composé des deux, ce qui sépare les couleurs, il s'appelle le "dejettemans" et en Grec "armoge."

13. Peindre en paysage, à fond plat, en architecture, en l'air, et comme parmy les nuees, peindre en petit volume. Les anciens estoient à deux sortes et puis à trois, à l'Ionique, à la Sycionienne, et à l'Attique. Faire les personnages, les fantages, les fleurs, les fantasies, les rivières, dresser des montagnes, soulever des tempêtes, &c.

14. Peindre des paysages, des grotesques, arabesques, la rustique, des fantasies, et des chimeres, vignettement, touffe de bois, precipices, chutes d'eaux, baricanes, la marine, et les orages et mille gentillesses et inventions poëtiques de la même taille.

15. Faire la draperie, et drapper l'image, c'est l'habiller or en drappant, jamais on ne met une seule couleur; mais il y faut du meslange. Il y a simple drapperie; il y a celle qui est damassée, historiée à brodure, les robes retroussées et les replis puisurés (*sic*), les feintres les couvertes de crespe, et qui percen le voile et la thoille desliée, les autres qui sont meurtries avec les ombrages qui rabattent le trop grand esclat.

16. Meurtrir la trop grande gayeté des couleurs avec vernix qui semble du talc ou du crespe ou de lairs espars sur le tableau; l'ame, les affections, peindre les conceptions d'esprit sur le tableau (invention d'Appellés inimitable), enfin peindre ce qui ne se peut peindre, comme les tonnerres, esclairs, la voix, la respiration, &c. asseoir les couleurs propremen, estre trop rude à charge des couleurs.

17. La ceruse se fait de plomb et de vinaigre; elle est bonne pour incarner playe et chose semblable; l'isvoire bruslée fait un

---

site the artificial light which is supposed to illuminate the objects in the painting. Millin, Dict. des Beaux Arts.

by Apelles, is a most excellent black, for if it is dissolved in vinegar and dried in the sun it cannot be effaced. There are some works of powerful colouring, others feeble ; the latter, after the first painting, must be heightened with vigorous colours.

18. A good picture should possess great invention, well observed proportions, pleasing and natural colouring, lively flesh colour, rich drapery, distant landscape, accurate perspective, and tints so natural that the eye may easily be deceived.

19. The heightenings are produced by throwing lights upon them, the hollows and retiring parts are produced with the shades, and thick darkness must be surrounded with light. Softening is that tender union of the colours by which one colour is almost lost in the other. By glazing is meant the last thin coat [of transparent colour] which softens and gives brilliancy, by glazing the white, the purple, the green, the yellow, &c.

20. The painting should be placed in its proper light or in a full light, and concerning this you must know that all painting supposes generally that the light comes from the right towards the left ; the false light[1] is when the light shines from left to right, and in this case all the shadows are on the opposite side. Therefore, to place a painting in its proper light is to expose it to the light whence the painter supposes the light to come, turning it towards the window, so that all the parts may appear as if hidden behind that part of the body which is illuminated. It sometimes happens that the light falls from above ; when this is the case the head, face, and nose are highly illuminated, and the rest of the neck, body, and person do not participate in the light except in a few places where streaks or rays of light fall on the folds and other parts which appear to swell and project out of the work. Again, it sometimes happens in the opposite manner, when the light shines from below, and in

[1] This is now called Faux jour. See Millin, Dictionnaire des Beaux Arts.

noir excellent dont se servoit Apeles, car s'il est desmelé et deffait en vinaigre, et ars au soleil, il ne se peut effacer. Il y a des ouvrages de haulte couleur, d'autre blaffarde, mais après la première couche il faut donner la charge avec quelques couleurs vigoureuse.

18. Un beau tableau doit avoir l'invention gaillarde, les proportions bien gardées, le coloris plaisant et naturel, la carnation vive, la drapperie riche, les paysages fort esloigné, la perspective bien observée, la teinte si naturelle que l'œil soit aisément contrain d'estre trompé.

19. Les rehauts se font à force de jour qu'on verse dessus, les enfondremens, les creux, les rentremens, se font avec les ombres et les nuicts espaisses ceint de jour et de lumière. L'adoucissement se fait par une si douce liaison des couleurs qu'elle se perde quasi l'une dans l'autre, glace, c'est mettre les derniers adoucissements et la couche dernière delicate qui donne l'esclat avec le blanc glacé, ou pourpre glacé, verd glacé, jaune glacé, &c.

20. La peinture se doit mettre à son jour, ou estre à contre-jour; surquoy il faut scavoir que tout peindre suppose d'ordinaire que le jour vienne du costé droite vers le gauche; le contrejour, c'est la gauche à droicte, alors tous les ombrages sont du costé opposé donc le jour vient; de façon que mettre une peinture à son jour, c'est la tourner vers le jour que le peindre suppose devoir estre le jour, à la tourner vers la fenestre en telle façon que tout les membres soient comme cachés derriere la partie du corps qui est enluminée. Il advient aussi que le jour se donne d'en hault, et a l'heure la teste, le visage, le nez, sont fort esclairez; et le reste du col, du corps, et de la personne ne participes point du jour que par certains esclairs ou filet de jour qui esclate sur les replis et autres parties qui sembles s'enfler et se jeter hors l'ouvrage. Il y en a au contraire qui prennent le jour par en bas, et se doivent mettre bien hautes, alors les pieds, genoux, et autres parties bien éminentes sont fort esclairées le

this case the figures would be raised very high, and the knees and other prominent parts would be strongly illuminated, while the face and other parts would be half eclipsed. The light must therefore always be suffered to enter on the side whence the painter supposes it to shine, that is to say, the shadows must never appear to be thrown towards the window.

21. In a painting there must be the point of sight, the vanishing point, the hollows and retirements of the members, the perspective, the receding and approaching parts, the feints and deceptions; there is even the movement of the eyes, which, by a miracle of the pencil, are made to appear to be looking everywhere, which they never do in nature; they even appear to be moved by the eyelids; nothing is wanting to the figures but speech and life.

22. To take the proper light, or the false light, that is to say, the side light which the window affords the painter; the feigned light from another source, like the light on the angel in the Nativity; the full light, when the light shines on the front of the whole portrait, and in this case there is no shadow.

23. Foreshortening, retreating, or retiring, which causes some objects to appear distant. These parts must be painted tenderly, that is, with softness, for if the colours were too strong the objects would appear too near.

24. The shadows give roundness, the colours shade and give force to the work. The false light which appears where it should not; a concealed light, such as that of a flambeau, a lamp.

25. Drapery. To cast the drapery and to drape the figures, to add the ornaments, that is to say, to imitate the embroidery, or to paint vases or flowers on the robes which are of gold or of "dorage," that is to say, like fine gold; and there are several sorts of "dorage," according to the lightness or darkness of the colour.

26. To represent the death of a stag or other animal. To paint a landscape you must begin with the air, *i. e.*, where there are no clouds, that it [the landscape] may appear nearer, and

visage et autre partie sont a demy esclipsez. Il faut donc tousjours donner le jour du costé que le peintre le suppose et jamais le contrejour, c'est à dire ne tourner jamais les ombrages du costé de la fenestre.

21. Il y a au tableau le point de jour, le tiers point, les enfondremens, rentremens de membres, la perspective, les esloignemens, les aproches, les fintes et tromperies ; il y a mesme du mouvement des yeux par un miracle du pinceau qui fait que l'œil regarde de toute part, ce que la nature ne fit onque ; mesmes avec les paupières on fait remuer les yeux, il ne s'en faut rien que les images ne parlent et ne soient animées.

22. Prendre le droit jour ou le contre jour, c'est à dire le jour du costé que la fenestre le donne au peintre ; le jour feint qui se prend d'ailleurs, comme à la nativité la clarté de l'ange, un jour de pleine face c'est à dire qui donne à tout le pourtrait un jour de front ; et la il n'y a point d'ombre.

23. A racourcissement, rentrement, renfondrement, pour faire paroistre la peinture loing il faut que la chose soit peinte flouement, c'est à dire doucement, car si elle estoit rude et non pas floue, elle paroistroit de trop près.

24. Les ombrages font dejetter les couleurs ombrer et faire rude la besongne, faux-jour qui se fait ou il ne faut pas, clarté desrobée c'est une lampe, flambeau, &c.

25. Drapper, faire la drapperie et faire le drap, faire l'enrichissement, c'est à dire feindre la broderie ou semer des corbettes, c'est à dire des vases ou fleurs sur les robbes qui se font d'or, ou de cirage [dorage?], c'est à dire comme de l'or fein ; et il y a plusieurs sortes de cirages [dorages?] selon que la couleur est plus claire ou sombre.

26. Faire un atterassement de cerf ou autre beste ; pour faire un paysage il faut commencer à peindre l'air, c'est à dire, ou il n'y a point de nuées, afin qu'il paroisse plus près et les autres

the rest behind. The foreground, that is, the ground which sustains the whole work, is to be painted with forcible colours.

27. To paint or represent a dark night pierced by a single ray of light; to round the figure, *i. e.*, to make it appear in relief, which is done by means of light and shade. "Derober un jour," that is, to represent a rising or setting sun in a corner, behind a mountain or something similar, which gives light to the whole.

28. There are different kinds of light; the "jour de droit fil" is, when the light comes from the right side; "jour caché ou derobé," as when the sun is supposed to be behind a mountain, not yet throwing its golden rays on the surface of the earth, at the rising of Aurora, or when she has opened the gates of light to the beautiful son of Latona, to restore the agreeable day-light, and to show her golden wig to the habitants of this low universe, and this is called "jour derobé." "Jour feint" is a light at midnight, as in the Nativity of Our Lord; and "faux jour" is when one cannot discern whence the light proceeds.

29. Distance of the works, when they appear distant, the colours being faint. Deception is the perfection of the art, deceiving the eye, which imagines it sees what in fact it sees not. To paint with black and white, or in distemper, or with nut oil, which is the usual way, and the best, or in fresco.

30. To work with crayons or charcoal, to sketch, to outline, to make the first design, to draw a rough sketch, to put on the first touches, to make the rough outline with crayon, chalk, charcoal, plumbago, vermilion, or to draw on the paper with ink. To sketch the first thoughts on the canvas, then at leisure to search for perfection and particularize all the parts; to draw the subject, to rub out the false touches of the rough sketch; the "maistre traict" still remains to guide the sketched work.

31. To represent a full face, that is, all the face; thus—

[This part of the work is illustrated with drawings.]

32. To paint the outline or profile, *i. e.* the half or side face.

derrière. la terrasse est fort rude, c'est à dire, la terre qui soutien toute l'ouvrage.

27. Peindre ou faire une nuict épaisse trenchée d'un petit filet de jour desrobé : arondir la figure, c'est à dire faire qu'elle semble de relief, et qui se fait par le jour et l'ombrage. Desrober un jour, c'est faire en un coin derrière une montagne ou autre chose un soleil qui porte le jour, qui se leve, ou qui se couche.

28. Il y a divers sortes de jour ; le jour de droit fil c'est quand on le faict venir du costé droict, jour caché ou desrobé comme par supposition que le soleil fut derrière une montagne, ne jetant encore ses rayons dorés sur la surface de la terre, au lever de l'Aurore ou quand elle a ouvert les portes du jour a ce beau fils de Latone pour rédonner les agréables clartés et faire voir sa perruque dorée aux habitans de ce bas univers, et s'appele jour desrobé.

Jour feint c'est un jour en plain minuit, comme a la Nativité de Nostre Seigneur, et faux-jour, c'est quand on ne peut dicerner de quel costé il vient.

29. Esloignement des ouvrages quand ils semblent loing, estant flouée ; feindre, c'est le haut point de l'art, trompant l'œil qui croit voir ce qu'il ne voit pas. Peindre de blanc et noir, ou a destrampe, ou a huijle de noix, qui est l'ordinaire et la meilleure, ou a fresque.

30. Crayonner, charbonner, griffonner, porfiler ; jetter la première ordonnance, figuer grossement, jetter les premiers traicts, faire le griffonnement avec crayon, craye, charbon, mine de plomb, vermillon ou figuer sur le papier avec l'ancre, Jetter des premières pensées sur la toile, puis à loisir en rechercher la perfection et particularisant toutes les parties, retirer la chose pourtraicte, effacer les faulx traicts du griffonnement ; le maistre traict demeure tout jours pour guider la besongne esbauchée.

31. Peindre de front ou en face ou en plain ; c'est tout le visage ainsi.

32. Peindre de profil ou pourfil, c'est la moictié.

33. To paint back views, *i. e.* backwards, when only the hinder part is painted.

34. To paint with glories, as they paint saints.

35. By "ordonnance" and design are meant the first touches, for painting refers to the colours which are applied upon the portrait. The size of the picture may be increased or reduced to a small scale; it may be pricked and laid on the ground and outlines, and pounced with pounce. The design thus executed is called "poncif," but it is the work of the apprentice.

36. The colouring is very forcible, the colours well arranged; the lights disposed in their proper places; the drapery well cast; the painter has a good touch, *i. e.* he paints the flesh well, *i. e.* the flesh colour of the face, hand, and foot, for the other part of the body is clothed.

37. Moresques are pencils or horns drawn round a painting, and they are made of gold on a ground of the colour of gold.

38. Grotesques, in addition to these, contain figures.

39. Arabesques consist of foliage and flowers.

39*a*. Estampes (engravings) are copper plates. The word comes from estamper, which signifies to print in Italian.

40. Cartouches are almost the same things, except that the "quartouche"[1] partakes of the grotesque.

41. Terms are figures which are placed under brackets or cornices, which they support by their heads, like pilasters; they have the form of human beings down to the waist, the lower part being shaped into columns or pillars.

41*a*. Busts or models are generally half-figures; such, generally, are portraits.

42. Cameos are figures composed of black and white or red, or some other colour.

43. The design of Michael Angelo, the colouring of Raf-

[1] Cartouches were ornaments of painting, sculpture, &c. They repre-

33. Peindre à dos c'est tout à rebours, quand on peint le derrière seulement.

34. Peindre en gloire, comme on fait les saints ou saintes.

35. On appelle ordonnance et dessein ces premiers traits, et pourtraire, car peindre c'est avec les couleurs qui surviennent dessus le pourtraict. Si on veut aggrandir on peut reduire le tout au petit pied, le piquant et l'appliquant sur son fonds, et le poncer avec la ponce, et ce dessein ainsi fait se nomme le poncif, mais c'est pour les apprentifs.

36. Le coloris est fort vif, les couleurs bien posées, et bien mises; les rehauts fait bien a propos, le drap bien drappé, le peintre touche bien c'est à dire fait bien la carnation du nud, c'est à dire de la face, de la main, du pied, car le reste est habillé.

37. Moresques sont des pinceaux et des cornets autour d'un tableau qui se font d'or sur l'or couleur.

38. Les Grotesques ont de plus de personnages.

39. Arabesques sont feuillages et fleurs.

39 *a*. Estampes sont tailles douces: ce mot vient d'estamper, qui signifie imprimer en Italien.

40. Cuiver (?) quarts touches sont quasi les mesmes choses, sinon que le quartouche participe de la grotesque.

41. Termes: ce sont figures que l'on mets sous trez ou poultres, ou sous corniches, les soutenans de la teste en guisse de pillastres et portent visage d'hommes et de femmes et le corps jusques à la ceinture, le bas estant fait en forme de colonne et pillier.

41 *a*. Bustes ou modeles sont figures a demy, comme on fait d'ordinaire les pourtraicts.

42. Camaieux, ce sont figures faites de blanc et noir ou de rouge ou de quelqu'autre couleur.

43. Le profil de Michel-ange, le coloris de Raphael, l'inven-

---

sented scrolls of paper, rolled or twisted. Their principal use was for inscriptions. The word "cartouches" was derived from "charta."

faello, the invention and boldness of Parmigianino, and the night scenes of Bassano united, would present to an artist the beau ideal of good painters; they constitute the four elements of a perfect painter.

CHAPTER II.

PAINTING IN DISTEMPER.

1. For painting in distemper without oil, the colours must be ground with water or glue; gum is used for illuminating and giving lustre and brilliancy to the colours which are heightened and rendered gay by the gum; just as varnish gives a beautiful lustre to oil paintings, serving as gauze and talc to defend them from the dust; and as crystal, to give lustre and light to that which seems gloomy and eclipsed.

2. Painters use several colours in finishing the pictures and in painting in gum, oil, or water, without trituration, grinding, &c. We shall only mention in this place those which are used with water, viz., black from burnt stag-horns, Flanders black, black stone, and ink, which the dark tan colours approach very nearly in colour, and from which the paler tawny colours are far removed; dark violet, Indigo, turnsol, the violet from logwood [?], distilled and boiled in vinegar; the paste which is made of a little white mixed with the preceding colour; blue, which has several degrees of price and vivacity, that which is called "blanchette" and "mourante;" light blue and sky-blue; brown-red, common pure lake, the colour of armour, which is composed of this lake and saffron mixed with urine; gamboge and lake made from [Brazil] wood, vermilion, pure vermilion, minium as common as blanchette and as that which is called "rouge-blanc;" "laque blanchette forte," with or without ceruse, of the colour of flesh; the carnations, composed of vermilion, lake, and white; or of minium, vermilion, and white; true flesh-colour; the colour of dead flesh, gamboge, brown-pink,

tion et la hardiesse de Parmesan, et les nuicts de Bassan font un peintre l'idée des bons peintres; ce sont les quatres elemens d'un parfait peintre.

CHAPITRE SECOND.

PEINDRE À DESTRAMPE.

1. Pour travailler en destrampe et sans huyle il faut broyer les couleurs avec de l'eau ou de la colle, la gomme sert pour illuminer et donner l'esclat et le rayon aux couleurs qui s'esveillent et se rendent gaies à la faveur de la gosme, comme aussi le vernix donne un beau jour aux ouvrages en huyle, leur servant de crespe et de talc, pour le garantir de poussière, et de crystal pour donner lustre et tirer au jour ce qui semble morne et esclipsé.

2. Les peintres se servent de plusieurs couleurs pour achever leurs tableaux, et pour peindre en gomme, en huile, et a l'eau, sans trituration et broyement, ou autrement. Se mete seulement icij celles dont ils usent à l'eau, à savoir, le noir de cerf bruslé, de flandre, et de pierre noir, et d'ancre, dont les tannez bruns approchent de bien pres, car le tannez mourant en est plus esloigné, et puis ils usent du violet noir, de l'inde, du tournesol : du violet de bois de perse distillé et cuit en vinaigre, du paste qui se fait d'un peu de blanc meslé avec le précedent : de l'azur qui a plusieurs degrez de prix et de vivacité, de celui que l'on appele blanchette et mourante, du bleu blanc et celeste, du rouge brun, de la laque pure commune, de la couleur d' armure qui se compose de la dite laque et du safran avec l' urine, de la gomme goutte et de la lacque couleur de bois, du vermillon, du vermillon pure, de la mine tant commune que blanchette, et de celle que l'on appelle rouge-blanc, de la lacque blanchette forte avec ou sans la céruse; de la couleur de chair; vermillonnée, composée de vermillon, de laque, et de blanc : de la mine, et vermillon, [et ?] blanc, de la vraye couleur

saffron, which is mixed with massicot, pale yellow, golden yellow, brown minium and "cendres," and the colour of dead leaves, sap-green, calcined [vitriol ?] "du mourant ;" sea-green and "du gay," saffron, green-yellow made from the berries of the buckthorn ; distilled verdigris [?], green-blue and mountain-blue, terre verte, grey-brown, grey [made of] white and black, turnsol and white, and several other compositions ; ceruse and Venice white, white lead, and chalk-white. I omit several other colours which are distilled and obtained from minerals and metals, as well as those used with oil, the different mixtures of which would fill a whole book.

3. Indigo mixed with orpiment makes a beautiful green for distemper.

4. Orpiment makes a beautiful yellow, and is good for "dorages."

5. The shadows are composed of white lead, vermilion, lake, umber mixed with flesh colour, that is to say, with divers colours,—yellow ochre, ochre de ru, that is, dark-coloured ochre, massicot, "verde doye," sea green.

6. Gold and silver of Germany, of Flanders, and of Paris, are also used with the colours, and in paintings with water colours ; but it must be remarked, that, when gold is to be applied on wood, iron, or copper, it must first have two coats of white, and the gold must be polished with the tooth of a dog or wolf ; and if it is to be laid on an oil ground, it must have one coat of white, two of red, and then one of gold colour : the gold is laid on this. As to the gold leaf, it is applied with a pencil of badger's hair, and with the cotton.

7. Illuminating is working on vellum with white of egg or gum to distemper the colours, and in painting on them, powdered gold (not leaf gold) must be used, and "azur d'Acre," that is to say, the finest which is brought with gold from the mines ; this is ultramarine, and is brought from Spain and the Indies.

de chair, de la couleur de chair morte, de la gomme goutte, de la graine d'avignon, du saffran que l'on mesle avec le massicot, du jaune pasle et du dore, du minium brun et cendre et de la feuille morte, du verd de vessie, du calciné, du mourant, du verd de mer et du gay, du safrans, du verd jaune du composé avec la graine d'avignon: du distillé, du verd bleu et de montagne, du verd de terre; du grisz brun, du gris blanc et noir, du tournesol et blanc, et de plusieurs autres composés: du blanc de ceruse et de venise, du blanc de plomb, et du blanc de craye. Je laisse plusieurs autres couleurs qui sont distillées, et que l'on tire des mineraux et des métaux, et toutes celles qui sont à huylle, dont les différentes compositions méritent un livre entier.

3. L'inde, meslée avec de l' orpin, fait un tres beau verd en destrampe.

4. L'orpin fait de très beau jaune, et est bon à faire des cirages [dorages ?].

5. Blanc de plomb, vermillon, lacque, la terre d'ombre pour faire les ombrages meslé la carnation c'est à dire de diverses couleurs, l'ocre jaune, l'ocre dru [de rue] c'est à dire plus brun, massicot, verd doye, verd de mer.

6. L'on use aussi de l'or et de l'argent d'allemagne, de flandres, et de Paris dans les couleurs et peintures à l'eau, mais il faut remarquer que l'or s'applique tellement sur le bois, sur le fer, et sur le cuivre, qu'il faut premièrement mettre deux couches de blanc sur le bois, et qu'il faut pollir l'or avec le dent de chien ou de loup: et si on le couche en huile il faut mettre une couche de blanc, deux de rouge, et puis l'or de couleur sur lequel on met l'or; quant à l'or en feuille, on l'applique avec le pinceau fait de poil de blereau et avec le coton.

7. Enluminer c'est travailler sur du velin avec du blanc d'œuf qui destrampe les couleurs ou de la gomme, puis on peint avec de l'or moulu (non pas en feuille) et azur d'Acre c'est à dire le plus fin qui vient avec l'or dans la carrière c'est l'outremarin, on l'apporte d'Espagne,[1] ou des Indes.

[1] Pacheco, whose work was published only six years after the date of

CHAPTER III.

FRESCO PAINTING.

Fresco painting is the art of painting on the wall while the first coats [of plaster] are still damp, that the colours may be absorbed and penetrate into them. It is generally executed in distemper, and lasts twice as long as any other kind of painting. If the following conditions[1] are observed, it will withstand all weathers.

First. If the wall has not been plastered, you must apply three coats or beds composed of sand and old lime, the older the better. The first coat must be of coarse river sand, passed through a coarse sieve, and old lime, as we have said before,—7 parts of sand and 1 of lime.

The second coat must be of the same material, except that the sand should be finer, and the lime in less quantity, that is to say, the sand must be passed through a finer sieve. Distemper with milk of lime, which is made by putting old lime in a vessel with water, to reduce it as it were to a milk and clear broth.

The third coat must be composed of the same material, always diminishing the quantity of lime, and using sand of fine quality.

The three first coats should be whitened with the same milk [of lime]: in working, the tool must be passed from right to left, and afterwards from top to bottom, that all the holes may be filled; it must then be left a short time before working on it.

If the wall has already been fresh plastered, it will require but two beds or coats.

The pencils are made with tolerably coarse hogs' bristles.

---

this MS., says, p. 391, that Ultramarine was not used by the Spanish painters on account of the expense. The azure sent from Spain to Flanders or France, therefore, may have been the native blue carbonate of copper. In the Bolognese MS. it is identified with Azzurro della Magna, which has been proved to be the native blue carbonate of copper.

CHAPITRE TROIS.

POUR PEINDRE A FRESQUE.

PEINDRE à fresque ou à frais, c'est travailler sur l'aparoir les couches premières encore toutes fraisches afin que les couleurs s'imbibent et penetrent au dedans, et se fait d'ordinaire en destrampe, et s'y dure deux fois autant que d'autre. Ceste peinture tien bon contre tout temps.

Premier.—Si le mur n'est crespy nij reduit, faut faire trois couches ou lict avec sable ou chaux vielle, tant plus vielle elle est et tant mieux vaut. La première couche sera de gros sable de rivière, grossièrement passé, et de chaux vielle, comme dit est, les sept pars sable et la huitiesme chaux.

Le second lict sera de la mesme matière, sinon que le sable sera plus deliés, et la chaux en moindre quantité, c'est-à-dire le sable plus menu passé destrampe dans du lait de chaux, lequel se fait en mettant dans un pot de la chaux vielle et de l'eau, pour la reduire en laict et claire bouillye.

Le troisième lict sera encore composé de la mesme matière, diminuant toutjours la quantité de la chaux et affinant le sable.

Les trois couches premières seront blanchies du mesme laict, en tirant de gauche à droicte, et puis après de hault-à-bas, afin que tous les trous se remplissent, et fait on les laisse un peu reposer pour y travailler.

Sy le mur est jà recrespy, il n'y sera besoin que deux lict et couches.

Les pinceaux sont fait de soye de pourceau, et assez grossiers.

---

1 This is the method of Father L'Ange and P. Antoine, the Capuchin. M. Thierson adopts the same method, as he himself informed me.—*Marginal note by Author.*

The colours are lime white and charcoal black (any kind of charcoal will do), and black stone, the one being blacker and the other browner, which last serves for the shadows.

This painting is done in distemper without oil, and the colours are clear and liquid as fluid ink.

The painting is executed while the above-mentioned coats are still damp, by which the colours penetrate and are absorbed.

If the beds or coats should dry before the work is finished, they may be moistened by throwing over them three or four jugs of water.

The niches in which the figures are painted are generally red.

Under the beams may be placed "terms" or figures of the natural height, sustaining the beams with their hands and heads; these figures are generally painted red.

This kind of painting lasts nine or ten times longer than any other kind, and the more it is exposed to the rain the better it lasts.

The ancients used to practise this kind of painting very much, and the Italians still do so. In the ruins of ancient Rome some beautiful examples of it are found, which testify its durability.

When it is wished to represent a person, or some other figure, previous to laying on the coats of lime and sand, the design is to be drawn with charcoal or black earth, on several large sheets of paper glued together. The design having been drawn with charcoal made of the spindle tree, or of black chalk, the coats [of lime and sand] are then to be applied, and while these are still wet the niches and borders are drawn. When this is done, the paper containing the design is applied, and the principal lines having been pricked with a pin on to the niche, the designs are rubbed with the feathers of turkeys, or of some other bird. When the design is removed, the person or figure which was on it is found impressed on the plaster.

Les couleurs sont, scavoir, le blanc de la chaux, et le noir de charbon, il n'importe de quel bois et de pierre noire, l'un estant plus noir et l'autre plus brun, ce qui sert à faire les ombrages.

Ceste peinture se fait à destrampe sans huile, et sont les couleurs assez claires et liquides comme de lancre coulante.

La peinture se fait sur les dites couches encore fraisches par le moyen de quoy les couleurs s'imbibent et penetres au dedans.

Que si les couches et licts venaient a se seicher auparavant la perfection de l'ouvrage, on les rafraichit en jettant dessus trois ou quatre potées d'eau.

Les niches dans lesquels on peint les personnages sont ordinairement rouge.

Soulz les taz et poultres on y peut mettre des termes ou personnages de haulteur naturel soutenant à deux mains et de la teste les dites poultres ; et sont ordinairement de rouge.

La dite peinture dure neuf ou dix fois plus que l'autre, et tant plus elle est bastie des eaux pluvialles tant mieux vault.

Les anciens se servoient fort de ceste peinture, et encore aujourdhuy les Italiens, il se rencontre dans les anciennes ruines de Rome des pieces de ceste peinture encore fort belles qui tesmoignent sa durée.

Lorsque l'on veult representer un personnage ou quelque autre figure, on en fait le dessein auparavant que faire les dites couches, sur plusieurs grandes feuilles de papier collée ensemble. Ce dict dessein fait de noir de charbon de fusain ou pierre noir, puis on fait les couches et icelles estant fraisches on y fait les niches et les bordures et filets, cela estant fait on applique le papier portant le dessein piquetté et percé avec une espingle de principaux traicts dans la niche, puis avec plumes de coq d'Inde oisaux ou aultre on frotte le dit dessein, lequel estant osté, le personnage ou la figure portée en icelluy se trouve imprimée sur les couches.

The back of the design is applied against the said fresh plaster; and, as only the principal lines are marked, the design is fixed upon boards near the painter, that he may imitate it in finishing, perfecting, and shading the pierced drawing.

Gypsum is of no use for making the plaster, for it swells and decays when exposed to the rain.

CHAPTER IV.

PEINTURE D'APREST—(PAINTING ON GLASS).

A "BEL APREST" is a painting executed on glass, baked and re-baked in the fire with colours that can stand the fire, such as the mineral colours.

1. To make good black for drawing the outlines on the pieces of glass, you must take equal parts of clean scales of iron and rocaille;[1] grind them on a plate of copper for five hours with a little urine.

2. You must provide some crow-quills for writing[2] and for drawing on the glass, for they are more delicate and firm than other quills.

3. You must draw the figures as delicately as possible, keeping them very clean; and whilst drawing them, be careful not to touch the surface of the glass with the fingers,[3] for that would injure it, but you must take the glass by the edges, and then leave it to dry.

4. The glass being dry, you must have a pencil with a brush at each end, which is used for washing and shading the figures.

5. The colours are to be applied smoothly on the figures which have been previously drawn; and when they are dry

---

[1] Rocaille—The white glass or flux to which different minerals were added for the composition of the various coloured glasses used for painting.

Le dos du dessein s'applique contre les dites couches fraiches ; et, d'aultant qu'il n'y a que les principaux traicts de ponces, on met le dict dessein dessus une esse [ais] pres de soy pour l'imiter en ragreant, perfectionnant, et baillant les ombrages au poncif.

Le plastre ne vaut rien à faire les couches, d'aultant qu'il renfle et se pourrit à la pluie.

CHAPITRE IV.

POUR TRAVAILLER D'APREST.

Un bel aprest c'est une peinture faite sur le verre cuite et recuite au feu avec des couleurs qui puissent souffrir le feu comme sont les mineralles.

1. Pour faire son noir pour rétirer les oualles, il faut prendre des escailles de fer des plus nettes et de la rocaille, autant de l'un que de l'autre ; et les broyer l'espace de cinq heures sur une platine de cuivre avec un peu d'hurine.

2. Il faut avoir des plumes de corbeau pour escrire et retirer les oualles, car elle sont plus délicate et ferme que d'autre.

3. Il faut retirer des figures le plus délicattement que l'on peut, et les tenir tousjours nettes ; et en les maniant, ne mettre jamais les doigts dessus, car cela y nuict, mais il les faut prendre par les costés, puis il les faut laisser seicher.

4. Les oualles estant seiches, on a un pinceau émanché par les deux boutz, duquel on se sert pour laver ses figures et leur donner les ombrages.

5. L'on couche les couleurs tout unie sur les figures qu'on a retirés auparavant, puis quand elles sont seiches on a un pin-

---

Le Vieil says the best kind of rocaille was brought from Venice. See Le Vieil, "L'Art de la Peinture sur Verre," p. 106.

2 To write on glass—the technical expression for painting on glass.

3 Le Vieil says that during the drawing, the glass should be covered with a sheet of white paper.

you must take a very hard pencil of hogs' bristles, with which the figures are scratched where lights are required, so as to remove the colour and leave the glass white.

6. Observe, that the under layer of colours must be dry before laying on more colour.

7. The secret of this kind of painting consists in making the black properly. It is said the addition of a little urine does everything when it is neither in too great nor too small quantity.

8. The figures are to be much softened (or shaded) with grey before colouring them, then the colours are glazed smoothly upon this.

9. The yellow is made with silver, copper, and a little yellow ochre, the whole ground up together on a plate of copper.

10. The furnace must be heated for 12 whole hours, first with a small charcoal fire for 4 hours, the heat being gradually increased; then for the last four hours the furnace must be strongly heated. But take care to remove the charcoal frequently for fear of burning the pieces of glass which are underneath, and heat the furnace so that the fire does not smoke, for this spoils the work; but make a clear and strong fire.

11. The pieces of glass are to be placed on a pan of iron on an iron tripod or fillet, just in the middle of the fire, so that the flame rises all round it without injuring them.

12. Beds or layers of lime are laid between the pieces of glass above and below, that they may not break.

13. You must provide some pieces of glass for experiments, which may be withdrawn from the fire in order to ascertain whether the colours are sufficiently baked.

14. These are the principal points to be observed in this art, for, as regards the outline, one cannot fail in this on account of the design which is placed under the glass, the outlines of which have been traced as delicately as possible with black as has been before observed.

ceau de soye de pourceau fort rude, avec lequel on grate ses figures a l'endroit qu'il faut les jours, pour les emporter et laisser le verre blanc.

6. Notté, qu'il faut que les couleurs de desoubz soient seiches auparavant que d'en remettre une autre dessus.

7. Le secret de ceste peinture est quand le noir est bien fait, un peu d'hurine comme dit est fait tout quand il n'y en a trop n'y trop peu.

8. L'on adoucit fort ses figures avec un gri auparavant que les colorer, puis les couleurs se glassent par dessus tout unie.

9. Le jaune se fait avec de l'argent, du cuivre, et un peu d'ocre jaune, le tout broyez ensemble sur une platine de cuivre.

10. Il faut chauffer le fourneau douze heures entières, premièrement à petit feu de charbon quatre heures, puis en augmentant tousjours, les quatres dernières heures il le faut chauffer avec des esclat, et avoir soin de retirer souvent le braise de peure de brusler les oualles de desoubs, et le chauffer si bien que le feu ne face point de fumée, car elle gaste l'ouvrage, mais un feu clair et flambant.

11. On met les oualles dans une poille de ferre sur un trepied ou bande de fer justement au milieu du feu, de sorte que la flamme tourne tout autour sans endommager les oualles.

12. On fait des lictz et couches de chaux entre les oualles dessus et dessoubs de peur qu'elle ne se cassent.

13. L'on a des essais que l'on retire pour veoir si elle sont assez cuites.

14. Voila les principaux poincts de ceste sciences, car pour ce qui est du crayon, l'on ni peut manquer par le moien du dessein qu'on a dessous ses oualles, duquel on en fait le porfil avec du noir comme dit est le plus delicattement qu'il est possible.

15. As for the colours, there are works which teach the manner of composing them, but practice and experience do a great deal.

CHAPTER V.

OF THE PROPORTIONS OF THE HUMAN BODY.

PYTHAGORAS was right when he said that man was the measure of all things—first, because he is the most perfect of all corporeal creatures, and according to the maxim of philosophers that which is the most perfect and first of its class is the measure for all the rest; second, because in reality the common measures of the foot, the inch, the cubit, the pace, have taken their names and length from the human body; third, because the symmetry and well fitting of the parts is so admirable that all well-proportioned works, and especially buildings, temples, ships, columns, and similar pieces of architecture, are in some degree composed according to the proportions of man; we know that the ark of Noah, built by the command of God, was 300 cubits in length, 50 in breadth, and 30 in height or depth, so that its length was 6 times its breadth and 10 times its depth. Now let a man lie down at full length, and he will be found to have the same proportions as to length, breadth, and depth.

Villalpandus, speaking of that inimitable chef-d'œuvre and model of good architecture, the temple of Solomon, has curiously remarked the same proportion in certain parts, and also by means of this he has observed such rare symmetry throughout the whole work, that he has dared to assure us that from a single part of this large building, such as a base or a capital of a column, one might calculate the measures of this beautiful edifice.

Other architects tell us that the foundations of houses and the bases of columns are like the feet; the capitals, the roofs, and copings are like the head, and the rest of the building

15. Pour les couleurs, l'on a des recueilles qui enseignent la manière de les composer ; la pratique et l'experience y font de beaucoup.

CHAPITRE V.

DE LA PROPORTION DU CORPS HUMAIN.

Protagoras avait raison de dire que l'homme est la mesure de toutes choses, 1° parce qu'il est le plus parfait entre touts les creatures corporelles, et selon la maxime des philosophes ce qui est le plus parfait et le premier en son rang, mesure tout le reste, 2c parcequ'en effet les mesures ordinaires de pied, de pouce, de coudées, de pas, ont pris leur noms et leur grandeur du corps humain, 3° parceque la symetrie et bien seans de ces parties est si admirable que toutes les ouvrages bien proportionnés, et nommément des bastimens, des temples, des navires, des colonnes, et semblables pieces d'architecture, sont en quelque façon composée selon ses proportions ; nous scavons que l'arche de Noé, bastie par le commandement de Dieu, estoit longue de 300 coudées, large de 50, et haulte ou profonde de 30, tellement que la longueur contenoit six fois la largeur et dix fois la profondeur. Or, qu'on couche un homme de son long, on trouvera la mesme proportion en sa longeur, largeur, et profondeur.

Villapande, traitant du temple de Salomon, ce chef-d'œuvre inimitable et modelle de toute bonne architecture, a remarqué curieusement en certaines pièces la mesme proportion, et par ce moien en tout le gros de l'ouvrage, une symmetrie si rare qu'il a bien osé asseurer que d'une seule partie de ce grand bastiment, d'une base ou d'un chapiteau de quelque colonne, on pouvoit coignoistre les mesures de ce bel édifice.

Les autres architectes nous advisent que les fondemens des maisons et les bases des colonnes sont comme le pied ; les chapiteaux, les toicts et couronnement, comme la teste, le reste comme

like the body. There is also similarity as well in form as in name, and those who have been rather more curious have remarked that, as in the human body, the single parts, such as the nose, the mouth, are in the centre; the others, which are double, are placed on the sides; so the same order is observed in architecture. Indeed, some have made researches more curious than solid, assimilating all the ornaments of a cornice to the parts of the face, to the forehead, eyes, nose, and mouth; comparing the volutes of the capitals to the flowing of the hair, and the flutings of the columns to the folds in the dresses of ladies; indeed, so many resemblances do they find, that it would really seem that as art imitates nature, so the building being the most artistical of all works, should be imitated from the chef-d'œuvre of nature, which is man, for the body of man is to other works what the statue of Polycletus was to other statues, which gave the rule to all others. It is for this reason that Vitruvius (book v.), and all the best architects, treat of the proportions of man, and among others Albert Dürer has written a whole work on the subject, measuring him from the foot to the head, whether he is taken in face or in profile, down to the smallest parts.

[*The proportions of the human figure, inserted at this place in the original, being well known, are omitted.*]

Knowing the proportions of man, it is easy for painters, statuaries, and image makers to proportion and perfect their works, and by these means is rendered credible what some have related of Grecian statuaries, viz., that some of these having one day undertaken that each should form separately a part of the face of a man, the different parts were afterwards conjoined, and formed a beautiful and well-proportioned face. It is certain that from knowing the proportions one may know Hercules by his footsteps, the lion by his claw, the giant by his thumb, and the whole of a man by a sample of his body. It was thus that Pythagoras, having measured the foot of Her-

le corps. Il y a de la convenance aussi bien en effet qu'au surnom, et ceux qui ont esté un peu plus curieux ont encore remarqué que, comme au corps humain, les parties qui sont unicques comme le nez, la bouche, le nombril, sont au milieu; les autres, qui sont doubles, sont mises de costé, et d'autre avec une parfaicte esgalité, de mesme en architecture. Voire mesme quelqueuns ont fait des recherches plus curieuses que solides, appariants tous les ornements d'une corniche aux parties de la face au front, aux yeux, au nez, à la bouche, comparant les volutes des chapiteaux aux cheveux entortillez et les cavelures des colonnes aux plis de la robe des dames, tant y a qu'il semble avec raison que comme l'art imite la nature, le bastiment estant l'œuvre le plus artiste, devoit prendre son imitation du chef-d'œuvre de nature, qui est l'homme, de façon que son corps en comparaison des ouvrages, est comme la statue de Polyclete, qui regloit toutes les autres.

C'est pourquoi Vitruve, (liv. v.) et tous les meilleurs architectes, traictent des proportions de l'homme, et entre autre Albert Durer en a fait un livre entier, le mesurant depuis le pied jusquà à la teste, soit qu'on le prenne de front ou de profil, jusques au moindre parties.

* * * * * *

Sachant les proportions de l'homme, il est facile aux peintres statuaires et imagères (?) de proportionner et perfectionner leurs ouvrages; et par le mesme moien est rendu croyable ce que quelques uns racontes des statuaires de Grece qu'ayant un jour entrepris de former chacun a part et en divers une partie de la face d'un homme toutes les parties estant puis après assemblées, la face se trouva très belle et bien proportionnée. C'est chose claire que la faveur des proportions on peut cognoistre Hercule par ses pas, le lyon par son ongle, le geant par son poulce, et tout un homme par un eschantillon de son corps. Car c'est ainsi que Pithagore ayant pris la grandeur du pied

cules, according to the impression which he had left on the earth, was enabled to calculate his height; it was thus that Phidias from the claw of a lion could represent the whole animal conformable to its prototype; and finally, it was thus that the painter Timanthes having represented some pigmies who were measuring with a fathom line the thumb of a giant, could give a good idea of his size.

CHAPTER VI.

OF THE BEAUTY OF THE FACE.

THE beauty of the face consists in a forehead large, square, open, clear, and serene; the eyebrows being well-arranged, fine, and separated; the eye well opened, gay, and brilliant; the nose , the mouth small; the lips coralline; the chin short and forked; the cheeks full and dimpled, the ear round and well turned; and the whole combined with a clear, fair, and smooth complexion.

There are several points to be considered with regard to beauty. The beauty of man properly consists in the form and size of his body: the other kinds of beauty are for women; there are two kinds of beauty—one still, which does not move, and which consists in the due proportion and colour of the limbs, the body not being puffed or swollen, the sinews not visible nor the bones piercing the skin, but the body full of blood, vigorous, and plump, the muscles raised, the skin polished, the colour vermilion. The other kind is moving and is called grace, consisting in the movement of the limbs, and especially of the eyes; one kind is as it were dead, the other living and acting; there is rude, fiery, and severe beauty, and there is soft beauty as well as insipid beauty.

Beauty described.

1. The skin of the whole body like jasper or porphyry, interrupted by small and graceful azure veins.

d'Hercule suivant les traces qu'il en avoit laissées sur la terre colligea tout sa hauteur, c'est ainsi que Phydias ayant seulement l'cngle d'un lyon figura toute la beste entierement conformes a son prototype. Ainsi le peintre Timante ayant peint des pigmées qui mesuroient avec une toise le poulce d'un géant donne suffisamment a cognoistre la grandeur du géant.

CHAPITRE VI.

DE LA BEAUTÉ DU VISAGE.

La beauté du visage[1] gist en un front large, quarré, tendu, clair et serain, sourcils bien ranges menu et deliés, l'œil bien fendu gay et brillant, nez bien , bouche petite aux levres coralines, menton court et fourchu, joues relevées et au milieu le plaisant gelasin, oreille ronde et bien troussée, le tout avec un teint vif, blanc, et vernie.

Il y a diverses considerations en la beauté ; celle des hommes est proprement la forme et la taille du corps, les autres beautés sont pour les femmes, il y a deux sortes de beauté ; l'une arestée qui ne se remue point et est en la proportion et couleur deue des membres, un corps qui ne soit enflé ny bouffy, auquel d'ailleurs les nerfs ne paroissent point, ni les os ne percent la peau, mais plain de sang, d'esprits et enbonpoint ayant les muscles releves, le cuir poli, la couleur vermeille ; l'autre mouvante, qui s'appelle grace, qui est la conduite des mouvemens des membres, surtout des yeux ; celle là seule est comme morte, celle cy est agente et vivante ; il y a de beautés rudes, fières, aigres ; d'autre douces voir encore fades.

De la beauté descripte en dix-huict articles.

1. La peau de tout le corps comme jaspe ou porphyre, entrecoupée de petites veines azurées trenchant de bonne grace, c'est y voir mouvant.

---

[1] Lecaron—L. de la sagesse.—*Marginal note by Author.*

2. The hair flaxen, golden, and curling naturally.

3. The forehead gently arched, serene like the sky, polished like alabaster.

4. Two eyes on a level with the head, large, sparkling, and beaming mildly.

5. The eyebrows black, fine, well arranged, and arched.

6. The cheeks like lilies and roses, indented by two dimples.

7. The mouth flesh-coloured, and like pinks or coral.

8. Oriental pearls or diamonds, set in the scarlet gums, even, all of the same size, close, not pressed together, and not yellowish.

9. The chin round and dimpled, not pointed or flat, or creased.

10. The whole complexion soft and smooth, without wrinkles or creases.

11. The neck like snow or coagulated milk, beautifully round and of proper size.

12. The temples well filled up, not deep and hollow.

13. The cheeks not sunken, hollow, pendent, or withered, but slightly raised, without, however, being too much swollen or puffed.

14. The profile of the nose aquiline, dividing the face into two equal parts.

15. The ears small, vermilion, close, and in no wise torn or drooping, or deeply marked.

16. The head well rounded and proportioned to the other parts of the body, neither too small and thin, nor too long and pointed.

17. The colour lively and fresh, and neither too red nor of a pale saffron colour, nor with similar defects of complexion.

18. The deportment grave, or gay without affectation or art, full of simple sweetness.

2. Cheveux blond, doréz et frisez par nature fort naïfs.

3. Le front mollement vouté, serain comme un ciel, polly comme albastre.

4. Deux yeux a fleur de teste, estincelant, d'une belle grandeur et doucement rayonnant.

5. Les sourcis de brins d'ébene fort menus, bien arrangez, et ayencez en façon d'arc.

6. Les joues comme de lys et de roses entasmées de deux fossettes.

7. La bouche incarnadine, et d'œillets ou de corail.

8. Des perles orientales ou diamans enchassez dans l'escarlatte des gencives, et tout a l'esgal, et de mesme grandeur, non entrouvertes, n'y entrebassantes, ny jaunissantes.[1]

9. Le menton rond et fosselu, non pointu, ny applaty, ny fendu.

10. Tout le teint uny et delié sans estre detranche de rides, ny fendu de sillons.

11. Le col de neige ou de laict caillé d'une belle rondeur et grandeur proportionnée.

12. Les temples bien remplies, et non enfoncées et creuses.

13. Les joues non point abbatues, effamées, deschargées, pendantes ou flestries, mais doucement enflées sans estre pourtant trop bouffies et boursoufflées.

14. Le nez aquilin a pourfil, et fendant a droicture le visage party esgallement.

15. Les oreilles petites, vermeilles, fermées et nulement arachées ou languissantes, et trop avallées.

16. La teste bien arrondie, d'une grosseur avenante au reste du corps, non trop menue ni mince, ny trop longue et pointue.

17. La couleur vive et animée sans excez de rougeur, de pasle couleur de safran ou pareille ternissure de visage.

18. Le maintien grave, gay sans feintes et artifices, plein de naïfve douceur.

---

[1] P. Binet, 'Essay de Nature.'

CHAPTER VII.

OF COLOURS.

1. Colours [pigments] are formed in the earth and in mines, or are composed by mixtures and combination, or are extracted from herbs or otherwise.

2. Black is made either with the soot and smoke of resin or with vine twigs and shavings of pine, reduced to charcoal, pounded, and mixed with glue, or finally, with the burnt lees of good wine, dried and mixed with glue. This is very black, and imitates the Indian colour which is called "morée."[1]

3.[2] "Cerulée," which is called blue or "turquin," is made by grinding sand with flower of nitre until it becomes as fine as flour. Some brass filings are then sprinkled over it and incorporated with the other ingredients; the whole is then made into pellets and ground between the hands, then placed in a furnace; the brass and sand then mix, from the heat of the fire, change their nature, and are reduced to a blue colour.

4. "Buslé" is made of "mottée de sil"[3] heated, and extinguished in vinegar, thus forming a purple colour.

5. Ceruse or white lead is made by putting vine branches in butts, pouring vinegar on to them, fixing sheets of lead on the top, and fastening them up air-tight; then, after some time the ceruse will be found attached. If it be heated in a furnace, its colour will be changed, and it will be converted into "sandaracque" or massicot. When plates of copper or brass are attached in the same manner verdigris is made.

6. Ochre-coloured earth being taken from the veins of marble, when burnt and extinguished in vinegar, assumes the appear-

---

[1] Probably Indian ink.

[2] A marginal note states that this recipe was extracted from the "Essay de Nature." This pigment is the Vestorian Azure of Vitruvius, the Azzurro di Pozzuoli and Smaltino of the Italian writers; the term *turquin*—turchino, evidently shows its Italian origin.

CHAPITRE VII.

DES COULEURS.

1. Les couleurs se concréent en la terre et en miniers, ou bien se composent par mixtions et temperatures, ou naissent en herbe ou autrement.

2. Le noir se fait ou de suye et fumée de poix raisine, ou de sarmens de vigne et coipeau de pin, redigez en charbon pilez et meslez avec la colle, ou enfin de lie de bon vin bruslée, sechée et meslée avec la colle, celà devient fort noire, et imite la coulour d'Inde, qu'on nomme morée.

3. La cerulée qu'on nomme bleu ou turquin, se fait broyant du sable avec la fleure de nitre, si delie qu'il devient comme farine, on prend de la limaille d'airain de Cypre et en saupoudre en cela afin de s'incorporer, on moule des pélottes entre ses mains, on les mets dans un vaisseau et dans une fournaise, lairain et le sable par la force du feu s'entredonnant leurs sueurs, changent de nature, et se reduisent en couleur cerulée.

4. Le bruslé se fait de mottée de sil, embrassées et desteintes en vinaigre, d'ou se fait la couleur de pourpre.

5. La ceruse ou blanc de plomb se fait mettant des branches des sarmens dans des tonneaux, les surfondant avec du vinaigre, et par dessus asseans des lames de plomb estoupant les queulles afin qu'il ne sort ny vent ny halene, au bout de quelque temps on trouve la ceruse atachée. Si on la cuit en une fournaise, elle change de couleur et se convertit en sandaracque ou massicot, et quand on assied les lames de cuyvre ou dayrain ils en font du verdegris.

6. Le sil qui s'approche de l'ocre estant tiré des veines de marbres si on le brusle et esteind en vinaigre il prend semblance

---

3 The " mottée di sil " here mentioned is stone ochre. Motte or Mote signifies a stone, *gleba*. The term " sil " denotes a mineral earth of which colours are made ; it appears to be always applied to iron ores.

ance of purple or crimson inclining to violet; some think it is ultramarine azure.

7. "Rubricks," or "bloodstones,"[1] are also taken out of the earth; orpiment, cinnabar, green chalk, or "verd de terre,"—that brought from Smyrna is the best. "Sandaraque," which some think is massicot, comes from Pontus, and in some places it is found ready prepared by nature, without the necessity of grinding, sifting, or pounding.[2]

8. Minium is made of lead melted in an earthen vessel over the fire, and stirred with a stick until the whole is changed into minium, which is found attached to the sides of the vessel.

9. *Indigo*[3] is made with the flowers of woad; that is to say, the flower and starch mixed with urine and vinegar; then made into pellets, and dried in the sun.

10. "Verdet"[4] is made of brass or copper filings, sprinkled with urine and sal ammoniac, then dried in the sun on a board, and sprinkled [with the same] until they become green.

11. The "rosette" is made with brazil wood boiled over the fire with "grain" [grana, or kermes] and gum; and, if a light red is desired, pulverized alum is added.

12. Rose-colour is made with very small chips of brazil wood mixed with ceruse and roche alum, the whole distempered together, then covered with urine, and left in this state for some time; it is then strained through a cloth, put into a glazed vessel, and placed in a dark situation to dry.

13. Purpurino is made with fine molten brass mixed with mercury, and made into a paste; sulphur and sal ammoniac, which have been well ground in a wooden mortar, is then taken,

---

[1] Hæmatites, or red ores of Iron. The Lapis Amatito of Cennino and other old writers.

[2] Native red orpiment is plainly alluded to in this last sentence.

[3] A marginal note shows that this definition was extracted from the work of D. Alessio Piemontese.

[4] Verdetto. Baldinucci says this is a mineral colour produced in the mines

de pourpre ou cramoisi violet ; aucuns pensent que c'est l'azur d'outremer.

7. Les rubriches ou pierres sanguines se tirent aussi de la terre ; l'orpiment, le cinnabre, la craye verte ou verd de terre vient de la terre de Smyrne et est la plus excellente. La sandaracque qu'aucuns croyent estre le massicot, vient du pont et croit en certains lieux toute préparée par nature sans qu'il la faille moudre, cribler, sasser, ny piler.

8. La mine se fait avec du plomb que l'on met fondre dans une vaisselle de terre sur le feu, en le remuant avec un baston jusque à ce qu'il soit tout converti en mine, laquelle on trouve attachée autour du pot.

9. L'Inde se fait avec fleurs de pastel ou gueste, c'est a scavoir, florée et farine d'amidon meslée avec urine et vinaigre ; puis on en fait des pelottes que l'on met seicher au soleil.

10. Le verdet se fait avec airain et cuijvre limé, arousé d'urine vielle et sel armoniac, puis seiché au soleil sur un ais et s'arrouse jusque a ce qu'il vienne verd.

11. On fait la rosette avec bresil que l'on met bouillir sur le feu avec graind et gomme ; si on veut avoir un rouge leger, on y adjouste de l'alun pulverisé.

12. La rose se fait avec bresil derompu bien menu, meslé avec ceruse et alun de roche, le tout destrempé ensemble, puis on verse dessus de l'urine tant que tout soit couvert, et ainsi on la laisse une espace de temps après, il la faut couler par un linge et la mettre en un pot plombé en un lieu ou il n'y entre ny soleil ny clarté, et la laisser ainsi seicher.

13. La couleur purpurine se fait avec fin estain fondu, et argent vif meslé ensemble, et en fait on une paste, puis on prend soulfre et sel armoniac très bien broyez en un mortier de bois,

---

of Germany. It cannot then have been synonymous with the colour mentioned in the text, which corresponds in some measure with the *Verdete* of the Spanish writers, which is verdigris. Neither does it correspond with the Verdetto of Lomazzo and the Paduan MS., which is a kind of Brown Pink.

and the whole is incorporated together and put into a luted phial in the furnace over a slow fire; a gold-coloured yellow is thus obtained.

14. Common lake is made by putting some cuttings of fine scarlet [cloth][1] into a strong ley, which is boiled until the whole is dissolved; some roche alum is then added, and it is passed through a bag, adding to it some raspings of brazil wood and gum arabic, mixing all these ingredients together, and then making them into small pellets, which must be suffered to dry.

15. Fine lake is made like common lake, except that no brazil wood is added.[2]

16. Cinnabar or vermilion is made of sulphur and mercury ground together on the porphyry, then burnt in the furnace until they are sublimed.

17. Azure is made by pulverizing mercury, sal ammoniac, and sulphur, and then burning them in an alembic.

18. Ultramarine is made with calcined silver, aquafortis, and sal ammoniac; these are placed for some time in a well-closed leaden vessel.

19. The modern mode of making verdigris is to take some clean scales of copper, common salt, tartar of red wine, sal ammoniac, and leaven of wheat, distempered with vinegar; the whole is then to be put into a glass vessel, and covered with dung for a certain time.

20. "Rouget" is made with bruised brazil wood, lime water, and roche alum, all boiled together.

21. Sap-green is made with the bruised fruit of the buckthorn, which is boiled in a new pipkin with pounded roche alum, then left to stand in a warm place for 6 or 8 days; it is afterwards put in a bladder, so that no air may have access to it. Sometimes a little Spanish blue is used.

22. "Stil de grain" is made with [white] earth mixed with the juice of the flowers.[3]

---

[1] The cuttings of fine scarlet cloth were dyed with grana (kermes).

[2] This is Lacca di Cimatura of the Italians.

[3] The words "fleur de geneste" are written in the margin of the MS.,

on incorpore le tout ensemble, puis se met en une fiolle lutée sur le fourneau a petit feu, ainsi l'on a un jaune qui imite la couleur d'or.

14. La grosse lacque se fait mettant de la tondure de fine escarlate dans de la forte lessive, que l'on fait bouillir tant qu'elle soit dissoulde en eau, on y met de l'alun de roche, puis on la passe dans un sachet, en y ajoustant bresil racle et gomme arabiques, le tout meslé ensemble, puis on en fait des petites pommes qu'on laisse seicher.

15. La fine lacque se fait ainsi que la grosse, sinon qu'on n'y met pas de brésil.

16. Le Sinabre ou vermillon est composé de soulfre et mercure broyé sur le porphir, puis bruslé au fourneau à sublimer.

17. L'azur se fait avec sel armoniac, soulfre, et mercure, le tout pulverisé [et] bruslé en l'alembic.

18. L'outremarin se fait avec argent calciné, eaue forte et sel armoniac qu'on met en un pot plombé tres-bien bouché quelque temps.

19. Le verdegris à la moderne se fait avec escaille de cuivre bien nettoyée, de pouldre, sel comun, tartre de vin rouge, sel armoniac, levain de froment, le tout destrempé en vin aigre, ainsi se met dans un pot verre soub le fumier un certain temps.

20. Le rouget se fait avec bresil brisé, eau de chaux, allun de roche, le tout bouillé ensemble.

21. Le ver de vessie se fait avec fruict de burguespine froissez, qu'on met en un pot neufve bouillir avec un peu d'alun de roche pilé, ainsi se laisse reposer en lieu chaud par l'espace de six ou huict jours, puis se met en une vessie, de peur qu'il ne scorente ; on y adjouste si l'on veut, un peu de bleu d'espagne.

22. Le stil de grun se fait avec terre et le suc de certaines fleurs meslé dedans.

---

opposite the word "certaines," which shows that the stil de grain was sometimes made from the flowers of the Genista Tinctoria, Common Dyer's Genista or broom, Dyer's green, Le Genêt des teinturiers.

23. English red, otherwise called brown red,[1] red ochre, yellow ochre, umber, and yellow earth, are formed in the earth.

NAMES OF THE COLOURS.[2]

1. Snow-white, lime-white, milk-colour, black, vine-colour, silver-colour, lead-colour, water-colour, grey or mouse colour, livid-colour, straw-colour, flaxen-colour, gold-colour, Isabel-colour, violet-colour, saffron-colour, aurora-colour, flame-colour, scarlet red, rose-colour, green, colour of pastel ou verd naissant, citron-colour, flesh-colour, amaranth-colour, leek-colour, colour of verdigris, chesnut-colour, sad-colour, brunette.

2. There are 4 principal colours,—white, red, green, and black, or obscure.

3. Colours which have great brightness,—snow-white, silver-colour, pale gold, green, scarlet, water-colour, blue, and purple; all these colours are in the rainbow.

4. A purple colour is formed when an opaque whiteness is intermixed with the rays of the sun, as at daybreak.

CHAPTER VIII.

SEVERAL SECRETS IN PAINTING.

1. Light colours should be intermixed with dark colours, as they give grace and adorn the picture; red ought to be intermixed with blue and green, white with grey and yellow; but

---

[1] Terra Rossa d'Inghilterra, the red Hæmatite.

23. Le rouge d'Angleterre autrement dit rouge brun, l'ocre rouge et jaune, terre d'ombre et terre jaune, se concreent en la terre.

NOMS DES COULEURS.

1. La couleur blanche comme neige, couleur blanche comme chaux, couleur de laict, couleur noir, couleur provine, couleur d'argent, couleur de plomb, couleur d'eau, couleur grise ou de souris, couleur livide, couleur paille, couleur blonde, couleur jaune comme l'or, couleur Isabel, couleur qui est entre violette, couleur de safran, couleur d'aurore, couleur de flame, escarlatte rouge, couleur vermeille comme le rose, couleur verde, couleur de pastel ou verd naissant, couleur citrine, couleur incarnadine, couleur amaranthe, couleur de poireau, couleur de verdegris, couleur ternée dit de chastaigne, couleur de deuil, couleur brunette.

2. Elles sont quatre principalles, la blanche, la rouge, la verde, et obscure.

3. Couleurs qui ont grand clarté, la blanche comme neige, couleur d'argent, d'or candide, verde, escarlatte, couleur d'eau, cendree, et de pourpre, lesquelles couleurs sont toutes en l'arc celeste.

4. La couleur de pourpre se fait quand une blancheur obscure est entremeslée aux rayons du soleil, comme en l'aube du jour.

CHAPITRE VIII.

PLUSIEURS SECRETS DE PEINTURE.

1. Les couleurs clairs doivent avoir lieu entre les obscures, elles donnent grace et ornement en la peinture ; la rouge couleur doibt estre entremeslée entre la bleue et la verde, la

---

[2] It appears from a marginal note that the names of the colours are taken from Cardan, Lib. IV., de Subtilitate.

you must take care not to use too much white, for it is like poison, inasmuch as its splendour diminishes the grace and beauty of the painting; it also weakens other colours, and spoils their shadows.

2. Terre verte is used in the shades of flesh colour, but it must be employed sparingly, for, as the colours become old, they appear raw, and would thus produce a bad effect.

3. Some use red ochre in their flesh colours, and with this make a beautiful colouring.

4. To imitate a laughing face, the corners of the mouth must be turned up; if they are turned down, the figure will appear sorrowful and weeping.[1]

5. The Italians use coal[2] black for painting external works, because it is a black which resists the injuries of time longer than any other colour.

6. The Italians burnish their mouldings, and then apply the gold with strong glue.

7. You must shade very much in sketching, as that will enable you to finish with greater facility.

8. Umber is of no use in the primings, for it absorbs the colours which are laid on it, and this produces a bad effect.[3]

9. To make very beautiful green for glazing, verdigris must be used with varnish which should be very brilliant and beautiful, and thus it will not fade soon.[4]

10. Fat oil is added to orpiment to make it dry, otherwise it would never dry; it is also added to indigo.

11. This orpiment is very beautiful in "dorage" and ornament.

---

[1] A marginal note ascribes this well-known fact to "M. Thierson, peintre."

[2] Common coal was also used by the Flemings in painting in oil. See the authorities cited by Mr. Eastlake, 'Materials, &c.,' p. 467.

blanche entre la grise et la jaune. Mais il faut prendre garde de auser trop de la blanche aux peintures, car elle est comme le venin et pour sa splendeur elle oste de la peinture la grace et la beauté, elle diminue les autres couleurs et corrompt l'ombre des autres choses.

2. On met de la terre verd aux ombrages de la carnation, mais il faut prendre garde d'en trop mettre, car les couleurs venant a vieillir, elles demeurent crues, et cela feroit un mauvais effet.

3. Aucuns usent d'ocre rouge dans les carnations, et avec icelluy font un très beau coloris.

4. Pour faire un visage riant, il faut que les extremités de la bouche montent en haut, si l'on les abaisse il sera triste et pleurant.

5. Les Italiens se servent de noir de charbon de terre pour travailler hors d'œuvres, comme estant un noir qui resiste plus longtemps à l'injure du temps que pas ung autre.

6. Les Italiens brunissent leurs moulures, puis appliquent l'or dessus avec de la colle forte.

7. Il faut fort ombrer en esbauchant, cela ayde a parachever avec plus grande facilité.

8. La terre d'ombre dans l'imprimure n'y vaut rien, car elle fait imbiber les autres couleurs qu'on mets dessus, et cela fait un mauvais effets.

9. Pour faire de très beau verd glassé, faut emploier le verdegris avec du verny ; cela sera fort beau et luisant, et si ne mouvera pas si tost.

10. L'on met dans l'orpin de l'huile grasse pour le faire seicher, car autrement il ne seicheroit jamais, pareillement dans l'inde.

11. Le dit orpin est très beau en cirage [dorage ?] et ornement.

---

3 The reader will not fail to notice this condemnation of dark grounds.

4 Palomino and Lionardo da Vinci give similar instructions respecting the use of verdigris.

12. Verdigris also is very good if employed with fat oil.

13. Perspective and geometry are the foundations of painting, and serve to give proportions and measures to all things, and to give an appearance of reality.

14. Oil of chamomile is very good for painting,[1] and is as clear as rock water.

15. Enamel is cleaned with a ley made of ashes, and then washed with clean water. Soap is very efficient for cleaning brushes.

16. Vermilion is adulterated with lime; to detect this, it must be put on the blade of a knife [and heated]; if good, it will, when cold, be of the same colour as before, but if one side of the knife remain black, and then become brown and blackish, it will be evident that the vermilion has been adulterated.

17. Vermilion may be kept under cover for a long time, but when it is exposed to the air, the sun and moon spoil its beauty and diminish its brilliancy and vivacity.

18. Fat colours preserve their beauty longer than any others; hence it arises that gold lasts longer than any colour; on account of the "or de couleur," which is fat. To render the colours more durable, they must be used very thick, and must not be spared when they are used.[2]

19. The colour of the primed canvas is called "couleur mate," that is to say, "dead," on account of the fat oil; and gold is applied only on a "couleur mate," called "or couleur," which is made of divers colours, and is good for receiving the gold of gildings and cornices.[3]

---

[1] It is uncertain whether this word is written in the text "peindre" or "prendre." The former is most probable. I am not aware that oil of chamomile is used in painting; but from the manner in which it is mentioned in the text, I should think it possible that it may have been used to dilute the colours or varnish in the same way as distilled linseed oil, oil of

12. Le verdegris est aussi fort beau emploié avec huille grasse.

13. La perspective et la géometrie sont les fondemens de la peinture, et servent à donner les proportions et mesures à toutes choses, et faire les reconnoissances.

14. L'huile de camamine est très bonne pour prendre [peindre ?] et est claire comme eau de roche.

15. On degraisse lesmaille avec laissive que l'on fait avec cendre, puis on la lave avec eaue nette. Le savon est très bon pour degraisser et nettoier les brosses.

16. On sophistique le vermillon avec de la chaux, pour l'esprouver il le faut mettre sur une lame, si il est loyal et marchant, estant refroidy, il aura sa mesme couleur, mais s'il garde une costé noire, et devient brun et noirastre, c'est signe qu'il a de la mechanceté.

17. Le vermillon se conserve longtemps s'il est à couvert, mais à l'air le soleil et la lune massacrent sa beauté, et meurtrissent l'esclat de sa vivacité.

18. Les couleurs grasses demeurent plus longtemps belles, d'ou vient que l'or dure plus qu'aucunes couleurs, cela provient de l'or de couleur qui est gras, aussi pour faire demeurer ses couleurs plus longtemps belles, il les faut emploier grasse, et ne point espargner les couleurs en travaillant.

19. La couleur de la thoille imprimée se dit couleur mate, c'est-à-dire, qui est comme mort, à cause de l'huile grasse, et l'or ne se met sinon sur une couleur mate, ce qu'on dit or couleur qui se fait de diverses couleurs, et est bonne pour recevoir l'or des dorures des corniches.

---

spike, naphtha, &c. Oil of chamomile is mentioned in the Bolognese MS., p. 518.

[2] Lebrun quotes the authority of M. Thiesson for these observations.

[3] Couleur mate. See this subject, *supra*.

From this, as well as No. 7, Cap. I., it appears that yellow grounds were used at this period.

20. In pictures exposed to the air, artificial colours should not be employed, but mineral colours and earths only, such as red and yellow ochre, yellow earth, umber, green earth, English red, "cendrées," smalt, and similar pigments. Smalt becomes more beautiful by being exposed to the sun than by being left in a close situation; also paintings are much better when exposed to the air than when kept in a moist and dark place.

20 *a*. The design must be bold, that is to say, the attitude of the person represented, making him look over the shoulder, for that gives grace and elegance to a picture.

21. Indigo entirely fades if exposed to the sun, and so does minium; indigo also fades if exposed to water.

22. To preserve pictures from dust and fly-marks you must take some white of egg and beat it until it becomes like rock-water, and varnish the pictures with this: when necessary, the white of egg may be cleaned by passing a wet cloth over the picture, which easily removes the white of egg, together with the dust attached to it. This cannot be done with varnish.

22 *a*. One of the principal points in painting is to balance the figures well in the picture, so that the head should not be beyond the foot on which the figure is placed, for this would give rise to great faults.

23. Drying-oil is made by putting some nut-oil into a pipkin, into which is put a rag containing umber and minium, which is suspended to the handle of the pipkin, and then boiled.

24. Fat oil is made by putting a bag of litharge into a pipkin with oil, and boiling it.

25. Or the litharge may be ground on the porphyry with oil made into a little ball and dried. When it is wanted for use it is boiled until the litharge is dissolved, and when cold the oil becomes as clear as rock-water.

20. Un tableau pour mettre à l'air, on n'y doibt point emploier couleurs qui sont composées, mais seulement les minerales et qui proviennent de terre comme ocre rouge et jaune, terre jaune, terre d'ombre, terre verd, rouge d'Angleterre, cendrées, esmailles et autres semblables. L'esmail devient plus belle au soleil qu'en lieu fermé, aussi un tableau se porte toujours mieux à l'air que en un lieu humide et obscure.

20 *a*. Il faut que le crayon soit hardi, c'est-a-dire, le posture du personnage qu'on represente, en la faisant regarder par dessus l'espaule, et cela donne de la grace et orne mieu un tableau.

21. L'inde devient toute blafarde si elle est mise au soleil, la mine toute de mesme si elle est à l' eau ; de mesme pour l'inde.

22. Pour conserver les tableaux de poussière et chiure de mouches, il faut prendre de la glaire d'œuf et la battre tant qu'elle soit devenue comme eaue de roche, puis les vernir avec, lesquels on nettoie quant on veut, car prenant un linge mouillé et en passant par dessus, on emportera facillement ladite glaire avec la poussière attachée dessus, ce qui ne se peut faire avec verny.

22 *a*. C'est un des principaux points de peinture que de bien planter les figures dans le tableau, en sorte que la teste n'excede la pied sur lequel la figure se pose ; car autrement il y auroit de lourdes fautes.

23. L'huile siccative se fait mettant en une chopine de l'huile de noix dans laquelle on y met un linge plain de terre d'ombre et mine, que l'on pend à lance du pot, puis la fait on bouillir.

24. Huille grasse se fait avec de la litarge que l'on met dans un sachet en une chopine avec de l'huile, puis on la fait bouillir.

25. Autrement on broie la litarge avec huille sur le porphyre, et en fait on petite balle que l'on fait seicher, puis quand on s'en veult servir, on les fait bouillir jusques a ce que la litarge soit fondue ; puis estant froide, elle devient clair comme eaue de roche.

26. This oil is very good for drying the colours which do not dry, such as common lake, fine lake, white lead, black, ochre, [?] and other similar colours, which dry slowly.

27. To counterfeit ebony, take lamp-black, with which ink and a little glue are mixed; some persons add vinegar instead of the glue; the mouldings are then passed over 3 or 4 times with this composition, and afterwards rubbed with a piece of rag or a reed to polish them. After this they are rubbed with a waxed cloth or with a piece of wax, to make them shine like ebony. If there are any spots, they are to be removed by rubbing with reeds.

28. To make all kinds of polished woods take the colour of ebony, so as to deceive by them.

The wood which is to be made the colour of ebony must be rubbed with a coat of "eau forte d'esteinte," (?) and when dry, 3 or 4 coats of good ink which does not contain any gum, must be applied. The wood must then be rubbed with a rag or cloth, or a brush made with Spanish reeds, and afterwards for a long time with wax; and lastly, wiped with a clean cloth, when it will be like ebony.

Note that the wood of the pear tree is more proper than any other wood.

29. Ground glass mixed with the colours is good to make them dry.

30. To make wood of the colour of Brazil wood, rub it with distempered quicklime. The lime penetrates and thus makes it of a red colour. If the wood be afterwards rubbed with oil it will be more beautiful. Remember that pear-tree wood is more proper for this than any other wood, because it is naturally much inclined to redden.

31. To fix the tin on coats of arms, take some parchment glue with a little honey, and boil them together. Some per-

26. La dite huille est très bonne pour faire seicher les couleurs qui ne seichent point, comme lacque fine et commune, blanc de plomb, noir, ocree, [?] et autres semblables couleurs qui sont long temps à seicher.

27. Pour contrefaire le bois d'ebene, on prend de noir de fumée avec de l'ancre, et un peu de colle meslée dedans, aucuns y mettent du vinaigre au lieu de la dite colle, puis on passe par dessus les moulures trois ou 4 fois avec la dite composition; après on les frottes avec un chiffre ou jonq pour les polir, cela estant fait on les frottes avec un linge ciré ou avec un morceau de cire, pour les rendre luisantes comme ebene, s'il y a quelques taches, on les fait en aller avec des joncs à force de frotter.

28. Faire prendre couleur d'ebene a toute sorte de bois, pourveu qu'il soit polli, en sorte qu'on si pourra tromper.

It faut frotter le bois qu'on desire teindre en couleur d'ebene, d'une couche d'eau forte d'esteinte, puis estant seiche, faire trois ou quatre couches de bonne ancre qui ne soit point gommée, faut frotter le dit bois avec un chiffre, ou linge, ou brosse faite avec joncqs d'Espagne, puis le refrotter longuement de cire, après l'essuier d'un morceau de drap net, et sera, comme ebene.

Notté, que le poirier y est plus propre qu'autre bois.

29. Le cristal broyé mis dans les couleurs est très bon pour les faire seicher.

30. Pour faire bois de couleur de bresil, il faut prendre de la chaux vive destrempée, et en frotter très-bien le bois qu'on desir avoir de couleur de bresil. La chaux pénétrant au dedans le fait devenir ainsi rouge, si on le frotte puis après avec de l'huile il en sera plus luisant; notté que le poirier y est plus propre qu'autre bois, à cause que de soy il ne demande qu'à rougir.

31. Pour asseoir l'estain sur des armoiries, on prend de la colle de parchemin avec un peu de miel que l'on fait bouillir

sons use flour-paste. If the tin is to be fixed with oil, "or de couleur"[1] is to be used.

32. To prime a canvas quickly, so that a person may paint on it the same day that it has been primed, you must grind together some parchment glue and oil priming,[2] and immediately prime the canvas with this; it will harden directly, but this priming is very apt to scale off when the canvas is rolled up.[3]

33. Minium in the flesh colour makes a beautiful colouring without ochre, because it naturally contains ochre, provided that it is not exposed to the air; for the sun causes it to fade and lose its beauty.

34. The longer the canvas has been primed the more valuable is it, for the colours which are afterwards laid on it become brighter.[4]

35. If one desire to paint in oil on wax, the wax must first receive a coat of well beaten white of egg to cause the colours to adhere, and also to enable one to paint on it more easily; the white of egg must also be applied on glass and lead.

36. A similar coat of white of egg is also applied on marble and alabaster before laying on the colours, whether they are used with gum or with oil.

37. Ivory must be washed with the water which is found under horse-dung, for the colours cannot be applied without this secret and invention.

38. The stones of peaches and plums burnt and extinguished in vinegar make a most excellent black.

39. To make blue draperies which are very beautiful, and which are made with azure in powder, first paint them with black and white, the lights being very strong (i. e. very white)

---

1 Or de couleur. See p. 836.

2 Oil priming. See ante, p. 772.

ensemble, aucuns se servent de colle de farine. Sy l'on le veult asseoir en huile, on prend or de couleur.

32. Pour imprimer une thoille promptement en sorte qu'on y puis peindre le meme jour qu'elle aura esté imprimée, il faut prendre colle de parchemin et imprimure en huille, puis broyer le tout ensemble et aussitôt en imprimer sa toille, et durcit incontinent, mais le dit imprimure est suject a s'escailler sitôt que l'on enrolle la toille.

33. La mine dans la carnation fait un beau coloris sans ocre, à cause que de soy elle porte son ocre, pourveu qu'elle ne soit point mise à l'air, car le soleil la fait devenir toute blaffarde et massacre sa beauté.

34. Plus les thoilles sont vieilles imprimées tant mieux vallent, les couleurs qu'on met pas après dessus en deviennent plus belles.

35. Sy l'on desire peindre sur la cire avec des couleurs en huyle, il faut luy donner auparavant que d'y appliquer les couleurs, une couche de blanc d'œuf battu pour les faire tenir, et afin aussi d'y peindre plus facilement, il faut faire le semblable sur le verre et sur le plomb.

36. On donne à l'albastre et au marbre semblable couche de glaire d'œuf auparavant que d'y mestre les couleurs, soit en gomme ou en huile.

37. Sur l'yvoire il faut que se soit avec l'eau qui se trouve sous le fumier de cheval, car on n'y peut peindre autrement; les couleurs n'y pouvant estre appliquées que par ce secret et invention.

38. Les noieaux des pesches et des prunes bruslées, et d'estains en vinaigre font un noir très excellent.

39. On fait des habits bleu qui sont fort beau et se font avec azur à poudrer, il les faut faire de blanc et noir, lesquelz il faut que le rehaut soit fort clair (c'est à dire fort blanc), et les

---

3 It must be previously glued with flour paste.—*Note by Author.*

4 Because the surface is quite hard, and the colours do not sink into it.

and the shades very dark, so as to appear very beautiful; they must then be powdered with "azur."[1]

40. To illuminate figures or medals, either of plaster, alabaster, wood, earth, or similar things. First apply a coat of clear fish-glue, and then the colours may be laid on with gum. Nothing is so beautiful and brilliant as these figures. This secret is considered rare, and is of the first importance to the illuminator. The glue does not in any manner fill up the folds and hollows of the figures as other glues do; for even when painted one may perceive their finest lines and most delicate hairs.[2]

40 *a*. Lamp-black is poison among the other colours, as well as verdigris. This black lasts a long time, and is very easy to use.

41. If some minium be mixed with white lead and a little fine lake a most beautiful carnation will be formed, as I know from experience.

42. If a little umber be mixed with bone-black and common lake, or if "stil de grain" be mixed with common lake and a little minium, a most beautiful colour for shadows will be produced.

43. The purple colour made with fine lake and white lead harmonizes very well with green, white, and yellow draperies.

44. Verdigris is added to charcoal black, or lamp black, to make these colours dry, but it is used only with the shadows, for it is a poison in painting, and kills all the colours with which it is mixed.

---

1 Azure in powder. This appears to be a good method of painting blue draperies, because no oil is necessary but that which cements the black and white. This method of employing azure in powder was common in France, as appears from a passage in the Traité de Mignature de Cristophe Ballard (Lyon, 1693—the first Edition was published in 1682), p. 217. In the

ombrages fort noirs pour paroistre fort beaux, puis les poudrer avec azur.

40. Si l'on veult enluminer quelques images ou medale soit de plastre, albastre, bois, terre, et autres choses semblables, il faut passer par dessus une couche de colle de poisson fort claire, puis appliquer dessus ses couleurs avec de la gomme; on ne voit rien de si beau et luisant comme sont les images (ce secret est tenu rare et est des premier pour l'enlumineur) la dite colle ne remplit aucunement les plis et creux des images comme font les autres, car encore bien qu'elle soient peintes, on y peut remarquer jusques au moindres traictz et cheveux les plus délicats qui se voient.

40 *a.* Le noir de fumée est venin parmy les autres couleurs, ainsi que le verdegris. Ce noir dur fort long temps, et s'y est fort facille à employer.

41. Si l'on mesle parmy le blanc de plomb de la mine avec un peu de fine lacque, cela fera une très belle carnation, ainsy que je l'ay esprouvé.

42. Si l'on y mesle un peu de terre d'ombre avec noir d'os et grosse lacque, il fera un fort belle ombrage, ou bien stil de grun et grosse lacque avec un peu de mine.

43. La couleur de pourpre faite avec fine lacque et blanc de plomb revient fort bien avec les habitz verds, et les blancs, ensemble avec les jaulnes.

44. On met dans le noir, soit de charbon, ou fumée, du ver de gris pour le faire seicher, il ne s'en faut servir que dans les ombrages, car il est venin dans la peinture, et fait mourir tous les couleurs parmy lesquelz il est meslez.

---

latter work the azure is called "email," and was probably smalt or the Italian Smaltino, which all persons agree was extremely difficult to use on account of its gritty texture. And see Mr. Eastlake's 'Materials, &c.,' p. 455.

[2] P. Anselme.—*Marginal note by Author.*

CHAPTER IX.

HOW TO SPEAK OF BEAUTIFUL PAINTINGS.

1. THAT is not painting, it is nature; and those figures look at the spectators, but with so natural a look that you would swear they are alive.

2. Do you see those fish? Why they would swim if you were to pour water on them! Then look at those birds, which would fly away and pierce the sky unless they were secured, they are so well done.

3. Is it possible that the pencil can have given such softness by such rough touches, and that such apparent carelessness should be so attractive?

4. When painting was in its infancy, and a suckling, painters handled the pencil so clumsily, and their works were so badly executed, that they were obliged to write under an object "this is an ox," otherwise you might have taken it for a quarter of veal, but at the present time painters are obliged to write under the figures "these are painted," lest the spectator should fancy that they are dead figures glued to the canvas, and they appear like living beings without motion, from being so well executed.

5. Rich pictures must be spoken of as if they were real objects, not imitation. See how those dolphins play in the water which they have so agitated, and look at the birds, some of them warbling on the branches, others flying away and disappearing in the clouds!

6. Apelles painted what could not be painted: one might hear the roar of the thunder, and the crackling of the clouds, flashing with lightning.

7. See how well the folds of that drapery are arranged! Look at those snow white hands, where the veins seem to swell at each beat of the pulse! See how those muscles grow and swell! One may count the ribs, and the body is as well done as if Nature herself had formed it! Is it natural and real, or is it produced by art?

8. Why did you give this horse a bridle, this horse which is

CHAPITRE IX.

LA FAÇON DE PARLER DES BEAUX TABLEAUX.

1. Cela n'est pas peinture, mais nature et ces personnages là regardent tous ceux qui les regardent, mais d'une œillade si naïfve que vous jureriez qu'ils sont en vie.

2. Voyez-vous ces poissons là, si vous versez dessus de l'eau ils nageront, car rien ne leur manque et les oyseauz s'ils n'estoient attachez ils prendroient l'air, et fendroient le ciel, tant sont ils bien faitz.

3. Comme est il possible que le pinceau ait couché tant de douceurs sous ces traitz si rudes, sous des couleurs si rudes, et que parmy tant de nonchalance, on ait couché tant d'attraits.

4. Quand la peinture estoit encore au berceau et à son premier laict, le pinceau estoit si niais, les ouvrages si lourds, qu'il falloit escrire dessus : c'est un bœuf, autrement vous eussiez pris cela pour un quartier de veau, maintenant il faut mettre dessous, qu'un tel peignoit de peur qu'on ne crut que ce sont des morts qu'on a collé sur la toile, et des personnages vivants sans vie tant le tout est bien fait.

5. Pour parler des riches peintures, il en faut parler comme si les choses estoient vrayes, non pas peintes. Voyez, je vous prie, comme ces dauphins follastrent dans ces bouillons d'eau qu'ils soulevent. Comme ces oyseaux, perchez sur ces ramées gazouilles, voi les qu'ils s'envolent et se cachent dans les nuées.

6. Apelles peignoit ce qui ne se pouvoit peindre : on oyoit craquer les tonnerres et les tintamares des nuées esclattantes et toutes trenchées d'esclaires.

7. Voyez comme ce drap est bien plissé, voyez ces mains de neige ou les veines s'enflent et semblent battre à la cadance du poux ; voyez ces muscles comme ils se poussent et s'enflent ; on peut conter les costes de ce corps, tout le corps est aussi bien fait que si la nature l'avoit faconné de ses mains, mais encore est ce peinture ou nature, verité ou artifice ?

8. Mon amy, pourquoy avez vous donné une bride à ce che-

running at full gallop, foaming at the mouth, and looking as if it were out of breath? I did it on purpose, for with two more bounds he would have been out of the road and out of the canvas, so you see I was obliged to hold him back by a bit; see how it makes him rear and caper!

9. How finely and gracefully this ground is broken and trellised!—you would swear that it was hollow and very deep.

10. See how these springs rise on the tops of the mountains, and how the pencil of the painter makes these brooks to flow as well as Nature could do! They pursue their course full of small ripples, so agreeable to those lively little fish that swim between the waves. Look at the ducks gliding among the herbs, and see how they dive, raising heaps of little threads or hair-like lines of water! but you had better move back a little, lest they should sprinkle or splash you by shaking and beating the water with their feet.

11. The pictures of Philostratus are excellent in this respect, and will make you very rich in these matters.

CHAPTER X.

A TREATISE CONCERNING THE GREATEST PAINTERS OF THE WORLD.

The first painters of reputation whose works are seen with admiration, and that not only on account of their antiquity, are Polygnotus and Ataglarphon,[1] whose simple method of using one colour only is even now practised by some, and is so esteemed, that these first elements of the new-born art are preferred to the works of the great masters who followed them, from a certain ambition, as I presume, of attributing to themselves a more particular knowledge of things out of the common way. After-

---

[1] Probably Aglaopho.

val qui court de tout sa puissance et jette son escume à gros bouillons et est hors d'haleine? Je l'ay fait a dessein, car en deux bonds il se fut jetté hors de la carrière et hors la thoile; il la fallu retenir par forche, voyez comme par despit il s'en cabre.

9. Mon Dieu, que ce fonds est haché bien menu et trellissée de bonne grace, vous jureriez que c'est une chose creuse et bien profonde.

10. Voyez comme ces fontaines sordent des croupes de ces montagnes, comme la main du peintre meine les ruisseaux aussi bien que scauroit faire la nature, ils poussent hors par endroits tout plein de petits surjons bouillonnans commode à ces petits follastres de poissons qui nagent entre flot et flot. Voyez comme ces canards se coulent parmy ces herbes et couvillent. Voyez la comme ils se plongent boursoufflant contre mont de petits brins et filet d'eau, retirez vous un peu à l'escart, de peur qu'il ne vous aspergent et mouillent en fretillant ainsi des pattes et battant l'eau.

11. Philostrate en ses tableaux est excellent en cecy, et vous fera riche en ceste matière.

CHAPITRE X.

TRAICTÉ TOUCHANT LES PLUS EXCELLENS PEINTRES DE L'UNIVERS.

Les premiers peintres de réputation dont les ouvrages se voient avec admiration, et non seulement en recommendation et faveur de leur antiquité, furent Polygnotus et Ataglarphon,[1] desquels le traict tout simple et d'une seule couleur, se fait encore aujourd'huy par aucuns tellement estimer, qu'ils préferent ces premiers elementz de l'art qui ne faisoit encore que de naistre, aux ouvrages de ces grands maistres qui ont esté depuis, par certaine ambition, comme je présume, de s'attribuer

---

[1] Quintilian, ch. xvi., liv. 12.—*Marginal note by Author.*

wards Zeuxis and Parrhasius, almost contemporaries, contributed greatly to the advancement of this art. Zeuxis is said to have discovered the art of painting in relief by means of light and shade, while Parrhasius proceeded to study delicacy and neatness of touch, for Zeuxis was the first who gave substance and living flesh to the limbs of his figures, as he found this manner more magnificent and august. In this he is said to have imitated Homer, who represents the most robust figures as the most beautiful, even when speaking of women. Parrhasius limited and determined all that concerns painting, so that he has acquired the name of the Legislator, inasmuch as all succeeding painters, as if compelled by necessity, have followed him in his manner of representing the gods and heroes. The art of painting flourished principally in the time of Philip and Alexander, but in different degrees of perfection. Protogenes was studiously elaborate; Pamphilus and Melanthius possessed a fine style; Antiphilus worked with great facility; Theo of Samos was wonderfully inventive and full of great imagination in design; Apelles excelled in the beautiful and ingenious disposition of his subjects, and in his unequalled grace in painting amorous subjects, of which he made his boast; and Euphranor was admired because, being among those most skilled in literature, he occasionally proved himself an excellent painter and sculptor. Among the modern painters we may mention Michael Angelo, Raffaello d'Urbino, Chivoly (Cigoli?) Buonarotti [!] Parmigiano, Salviati, Polidor of Parma, and Titian. But Michael Angelo was greater in sculpture than in painting. Bassano was one of the most esteemed of his time, although there was a certain roughness in his style.[1] Antonio Tempesta, an Italian, designed very cleverly, and for hunting scenes is unequalled. The Carracci are three Italian brothers,[2] who are unequalled by any of their contemporaries, and paint with such grace that they are

[1] Leonardo da Vinci, one of the most remarkable of painters, was never satisfied with his works, few of which he completed, because, it is said, that he could never realise with his hand the conceptions of his mind.

[2] This is a mistake. Annibale and Agostino Carracci were brothers; Ludovico was their elder cousin.

une propre et plus particulière intelligence de telles choses au dela du commun. En suite Zeuxis et Parrhasius, presque contemporains, adjoustèrent grandement à cest art de peinture. On tient que Zeuxis trouva la manière de peindre de relief par le moien des jours et des ombres, et que Parrhasius s'etudia d'avantage à la délicatesse et netteté du traict, car Zeuxis fut le premier qui donna du corps et de la chair vive aux membres de ses figures, trouvant ceste manière plus magnifique et plus auguste ; et comme ils tiennent imitant en cela le poëte Homere, qui nous represente les figures les plus robustes pour les plus belles, mesmes en femmes ; quant à Parrhasius, il a tellement compris et determiné tout ce qui concerne la peinture, qu'il en a remporté le nom de legislateur, d'autant que tous les auteurs comme par necessité forcée, le suyvent en sa manière de representer les dieux et les héros. Or la peinture fleurit principalement environ le temps de Philippe, et jusques aux successeurs d'Alexandre, mais en diverses parties de perfection, a part Protogenes estoit grandement studieux de bien élaborer ses ouvrages, Pamplius et Melanthius tenoient une belle manière, Antiphilius travailloit avec grande facilité, Theon de Samos estoit merveilleusement inventif et plain d'imaginations pour le dessein, Apelles excelloit en belle et ingenieuse disposition et grace nompareille de peindre amoureusement dont luy-mesme se vantoit. Euphranor se fait admirer en se questant des mieux pourveu de bonnes lettres, il estoit quant et quant un merveilleux ouvrier de peinture et sculpture, ensuit de ceux cy sont ensuivi plusieurs excellents maistres comme Michel-Ange, Raphael, Urbain, Chivoly, Bonnarot, Parmesan, Salviat, Polidore de Parme et du Titian, mais Michel-Ange estoit tenu pour plus grand ouvrier en fait de sculpture que de platte peinture. Basan estoit des mieux estimé de son temps, toutefois avoit une manière rude en ses ouvrages. Anthonio Tempeste Italien

[1] Leonard de Vinci, peintre singulier entre les autres, ne se contentoit jamais d'ouvrage qu'il peut faire, et n'en menoit que peu au point jusqu'a totale perfection, et disoit que cestoit a cause que sa main ne pouvoit atteindre à la conception de son entendement.—*Note by Author.*

admired by every one. Peter Paul Rubens is a very clever man and a Fleming; it was he who worked at the Luxembourg. Laurence Dubry,[1] a Fleming, is considered one of the best landscape painters. M. Bunel[2] is the best painter in France; he worked at the Tuileries and in the galleries of the Louvre; his two best paintings are an Assumption and a "Pentecost;" one is at the "Feuillans" and the other at the Augustines at Paris; they are his latest works, and were executed a short time before he died. Freminet,[3] who left the unfinished paintings at Fontainebleau, has been highly esteemed. Vouet[4] is considered one of the best of the present day. Vaulezar is reputed to be very clever in painting and perspective. Lallemand [5] also is highly esteemed. M. Thiesson is also a very clever man.

CHAPTER XI.

OF "ESTOFFERIE,"[6] OR HOW TO GILD.

PAINTERS use three kinds; viz. ground gold, *aurum contusum*, which serves for illuminating images, or writing with the pencil; burnished gold, *aurum politum;* this word "bruni" has two meanings; sometimes it means to shade and make brown, sometimes to polish and lighten; and "or mat," *aurum impolitum.* "Mat" comes from the Greek *ματαιος*, stultus, de-

---

1 Perhaps one of those painters brought from the Netherlands by Ambrose du Bois and Jean de Hoïy, and who assisted in painting in the Luxembourg. (Felibien, Vol. II. p. 114.)

2 Jacob Bunel, painter to the King of France. He was born at Blois in 1558. His father, François Bunel, was also a painter. Jacob painted with Breuïl in the small gallery of the Louvre. Felibien, &c. Vol. I. p. 712.

3 Martin Freminet, a native of Paris. He succeeded Du Breuïl in the works of the Louvre and Fontainebleau, and was chosen painter in ordinary to the King. He was in great favour with Henry IV. and Louis XIII.,

très habil homme pour le dessein, mais pour des chasses il est sans pareille. Les Caraches sont trois frères italiens des meilleurs qui soit pour les present, et peignent de si belle grace qu'il se font admirer de tout le monde. Pierre Paul Rubens tres habil homme flaman de nation, c'est celuy qui a travaillé a Luxembourc. Laurens Dubry flaman est tenu des meilleurs pour le paysage. Monsieur Bunel estoit le meilleur peintre de la France, il a travaillé aux Thuilleries et aux galleries du Louvre, les deux meilleurs pièces qu'il ait jamais fait sont une assomption et une pentecost; l'une est aux feuillan et l'autre aux Augustins à Paris; ce sont les deux dernières pieces qu'il fist quelque peu de temps auparavant que de mourir. Freminet a esté aussi grandement estimé, c'est celuy qui a laissé les peintures de fontaine blau imparfaite. Vouet est estimé des meilleurs d'aujourd'huy. Vaulezar est estimé très habile homme pour la peinture mesme pour la perspective. Lallemand est aussi fort estimé. Monsieur Thiesson est aussi très habil homme.

CHAPITRE XI.

DE L'ESTOFFERIE, OU MANIERE DE DORER.

Les peintres se servent de trois sortes, d'or moulu, *aurum contusum* qui est propre pour enluminer les images ou escrire avec le pinceau; d'or bruni, *aurum politum*, ce mot brunir a deux significations, quelquefois il signifie rendre brun et obscure et quelquefois pollir et esclaircir; et d'or mat, *aurum impolitum*, mat vient du grecq mataios, stultus, demens, inneptus; et en

but did not live long to enjoy his honours, dying in 1619, before he had completed the chapel at Fontainebleau. See Felibien, p. 114.

[4] Vouet, Simon, born at Paris in 1582, died 1641. Félibien says that France is indebted to him for having revived the good manner of painting, and for having educated a number of pupils, many of whom afterwards rose to eminence.

[5] Lallemand, Georges, a native of Nancy. He executed a number of designs for tapestry, and many pictures in churches.

[6] Estofferie—the Estofado of the Spanish. See Pacheco, p. 352.

mens, ineptus; and in Italian *mat* signifies *silly*, so that "or mat" is *silly gold*, without brilliancy and splendour. Matois, i. e. a do-nothing, a fool, and a good-for-nothing fellow; it is generally taken for a sharp and cunning man, *per antiphrasim quasi minime stultus.* It would also seem that this word, check-mate, and give check, and "mate," are derived from this root, meaning to stun a person, and exhaust all his resources; the Italians are great chess-players, the expression check-mate being derived from them.

It may also be said that this word *mat* or *mate* is derived from the game of chess, so common among the Indians and Persians, for both nations call this by the same name. They call this game *Scha*, i. e. king; and *Schatrah*, i. e. the game of king; as also *schamate*, which means "the king is dead," just as we say check-mate; so that "or mat" is a dead or dull gold, as opposed to a lively and brilliant gold. These words are taken from the author of the 'States and Empires,' in the abridgment of his history of the kings of Persia, article 'Nexere anauxion, 31 Roy.' "Mat" signifies also a moist or flat colour.

First, ground Gold.[1]—To grind fine gold, so that one may paint or write with it with the pencil, you must take gold leaf with 4 drops of honey, mix the whole together, and put it in a small glass vessel; when wanted for use, it must be distempered with gum-water.

Another mode of grinding Gold.—A proper quantity of beaten gold or silver is to be spread inside a smooth glass cup, and moistened with clear water. The leaves are then rubbed with the finger, wetting them occasionally, and not spreading them too much while rubbing; this process is continued until all the leaves of gold are well ground, continually adding water. When they are properly ground, the cup

---

[1] Ground gold. *Note by Author*, "Le Sieur Alexis." It is a transla-

langue italique, mat, signifie sot, de façon que or mat est un or qui est sot et sans esclat et splendeur. Matois, id est homme vain qui ne fait rien qui vaille un plaisant et vaurain [vaurien]. On le prend ordinairement pour un homme fin et rusé *per antiphrasim quasi minime stultus,* il semble aussi que ce mot des eschets mat, comme donner eschets, et mat vient delà, voulant dire rendre une personne toute estourdie et au bout de son roulait; les Italiens sont fort grands joueurs d'eschets, leur ayant donné ce mot de mat.

On peut aussi dire que ce mot de mat ou mate est derivé du jeu des Eschets fort familier aux peuples Indiens et Persans qui tous deux usent en icelluy de mesme noms, car ils appellent ce jeu *scha,* c'est à dire roy et *schatrah* jeu de roy, comme aussi *schamate* qui signifie le roy est mort, c'est ce que nous disons eschets et mat; de sorte que or mat c'est un or mort ou morte qui n'est point vif ny esclattant; ces mots icy sont tirés de l'autheur des Estats et Empires en l'abregé de l'histoire des roys de Perse, article de Nexere anauxion 31 roy.

Mat, signifie aussi une couleur moite et grasse.

Premier, Or moulu.—Pour broyer l'or fin duquel on puis peindre ou escripre avec le pinceau. Il faut prendre feuilles d'or battu et quatre gouttes de miel, meslez le toute ensemble et les mettres en un cornet de verre, et quand on s'en veult servir, il le faut detremper avec de l'eau de gomme.

Autre manière de broyer l'Or.—On prend autant d'or et d'argent battu que l'on veut et les estend on en une tasse de verre bien unie mouillée d'eau clair, puis les broyer avec le doigt en les mouillant aucune fois, mais il ne les faut pas trop estendre en les broyant et ainsi continuer jusque a ce que toutes les feuilles d'or soient bien moulues en y adjoustant tousjours de l'eau et quand ils semblent assez broyée il faut

---

tion of a recipe in the first part of the Secreti of D. Alessio Piemontese, Lib. V.

must be filled with fresh water and stirred well. The gold is then left for ½ an hour to settle, after which the water is poured off, and the gold remains at the bottom of the cup. This is dried, and when used is distempered with gum-water. This is the best way of grinding gold.

Burnished Gold.—To make the ground for burnished gold, you must take Armenian bole of the size of a nut, according to the quantity which is to be made; bloodstone, of the size of a bean; roche alum, of the size of a pea; and a little vermilion, to colour the mordant, with a burnt crust of bread to make it dry; the whole ground on the porphyry with a little water and glue.

Another mode:—Take Armenian bole of the size of a bean, a little more or less according to the quantity which is to be made; half as much of bloodstone, with a clove of garlic, and a little tallow, the whole ground up together with soap-suds and a little glue.

Another way:—You must take gypsum of the size of a nut, Armenian bole of the size of a bean, the same quantity of hepatic aloes, and one-third as much of sugar candy; powder each ingredient separately, then, putting them all together, you must finally add a little "civette" or a little honey.

Another way:—Take equal quantities of fine gypsum, hepatic aloes, and Armenian bole, distempered with some white of egg which has been strained through a linen cloth. If this composition is too stiff, it is to be distempered with fresh water.

Another way:—Lay on the gold with well-gummed water alone; and this method is very good for gilding parchment or skin. You may also use fresh white of egg or fig juice alone in the same manner.

emplir la tasse d'eau fraiche, et l'esmouvoir très bien ; cela fait il les faut laisser reposer une demye heure, puis on coule l'eau hors, l'or demeurant au fond de la tasse qu'on laisse seicher, et l'or que l'on s'en veut aider et servir, on le destrempe avec de l'eau gommée, cecy est la plus belle manière qui soit pour faire l'or moulu.

Or bruni.—Pour faire l'assiette à dorer d'or bruny, il faut prendre bol armenique environ la grosseur d'une noix selon la quantité que l'on en veult faire, la grosseur d'une febvre de sanguine, allun de roche la grosseur d'un poix, et un peu de vermillon pour donner couleur à la dite assiette, avec une crouste de pain bruslée qui sert pour faire seicher, le tout broyez avec un peu d'eau et colle sur le porphyre.

Autrement :—On prend la grosseur d'une febvre de bol armenie peu plus peu moins, selon la quantité que l'on desire en faire, et la moitié d'autant de sanguine, avec l'œil d'un ail, et un peu de suif de chandelle, le tout broyé avec de l'eau savonnée en y ajoustant un peu de colle.

Autrement :—Il faut prendre gipsum de la grosseur d'une noix, bol armenique la grosseur d'une febvre, aloe épatique la grosseur d'une febvre, et un tiers de succre candy ; étampé chacun à part soy et mettant l'un sur l'autre on y applique à la fin un peu de civette ou de miel.

Autrement :—On prend gipsum fin, aloe épatique, bole armenique, autant de l'un que de l'autre, destrempé avec de la glair d'œuf frais, laquelle on aura coulé par un linge ; et si la dite assiette est trop forte, on la destrempe avec de l'eau fraiche.

Autrement :—On prend de l'eau bien gommée, et avec icelle seule on met l'or ; et est (la dite assiette) bonne sur parchemin ou sur peaux. Le mesme peut on faire avec de la glaire d'œuf fraiz, et aussi avec laict de figue seulle.

Remember, that, previous to laying on the gold, the subject to be gilded must have seven coats of Spanish white distempered with tolerably strong parchment glue,[1] which must be smoothed with a linen cloth dipped in clear water, and then rasped or polished to make it smoother. When this is done, two coats of the above-mentioned mordant are laid on it, and when these are dry, it is cleaned with a piece of frieze. When the gold is to be applied, the preparation is moistened with a pencil dipped in clear water, and the gold laid on. It is then allowed to dry, after which it is polished with the tooth of a dog or wolf, and a beautiful burnished gold is the result.

If there are any defects in the gold after it is polished, a piece of gold is to be laid on the defective part, and attached with the breath, and then polished.

To gild on copper with burnished gold, the copper must first be polished and made red hot, in order to apply the gold with the agate burnisher, and it must then be heated again. Two or three coats must be laid on in this manner, after each of which coats it must be replaced over a slow charcoal fire, in order to polish it. When gold is applied on or paper, the front tooth of an ox may be used.

"*Or mat,*" *to make* "*or de couleur.*"—You must take all the dirty colours, and put them to boil on a chafing dish in an earthen vessel, with fat oil out of the pinceliere.[2] After this has been thus boiled, it is passed through a loose cloth and again boiled; and if the said "or de couleur" is not sufficiently yellow, you must add some yellow ochre, a little coarse massicot and minium, which must be well ground; and this will make it dry well.

Another mode. Take Armenian bole, ground up with lin-

---

1 *Note by Author.* "Before boiling the glue, it must be purified by washing it with ashes and hot water, until it is cleansed from the impurities and becomes white; it is then boiled, and afterwards passed through a sieve or strainer."

2 See *ante*, p. 771, No. 4.

Nottez qu'il faut que au préalable, la pièce que l'on veult dorer soit blanchie sept fois avec blanc d'Espagne et colle de parchemin assez forte,[1] laquelle piece on adoucit avec un linge mouillé dans de l'eau clair, puis on la racle ou oppresse pour la rendre unie. Ainsi faite, on passe par dessus deux fois de la ditte assiette cy dessus, laquelle estant seiche, on la torche d'un morceau de frise, et lors que l'on y veult appliquer l'or, on la mouille d'un pinceau avec de l'eau claire a mesure qu'on applique l'or, puis on laisse seicher le dit or, lequel estant seicq, on le pollit avec une dent de chien ou de loup, cela fait on a un très belle or bruny.

Si d'avanture il y a quelque faute à l'or après qu'il est poly, on y remette un morceau d'or, qu'on fait tenir avec le hasle puis se pollit.

Pour employer l'or poly et bruny sur le cuivre, il faut premièrement polir le dit cuivre et le faire rougir, afin d'appliquer l'or avec le caillou, et puis il le faut recuire, ce que l'on fait en mettant 2 ou 3 couches, l'une sur l'autre, et en le remestant tousjours a feu de charbon leger pour le polir, et lorsque l'on l'applique sur de la   ou sur du papier, le dent de bœuf du devant y doit servir.

Or mat pour faire or de couleur.—Il faut prendre toutes les salles couleurs, et les mettre bouillir sur le rechault dans une vaisselle de terre avec de l'huile grasse que l'on prend dans le pinceliere, ainsi bouillie on le passe par dedans un linge deliez, et puis on le fait derechef un peu bouillir, et sy le dit or de couleur n'est pas assé jaune, on y adjoustera de l'ocre jaune, un peu de gros massicot et mine, le tout bien broyez ; et cela sert à le faire seicher.

Autrement : on prend boli-armenique broyez avec l'huile de

[1] *Note marginale.*—On degresse la colle auparavant que de la mettre bouillir avec des cendres et de l'eau chaude, en la lavant très-bien tant qu'elle soit toute nestoiée de son ordure, et devenue blanche ; puis on la fait bouillir, et la passe par après dans un balot ou dedans une couloire.

seed or nut oil, and when gold is to be laid on the mordant, it must be neither too moist nor too dry.[1]

Another way.[2] " Or de couleur " is made with yellow earth or ochre, with a little white lead (to make it more similar to gold in colour), which is left to thicken on the porphyry, stirring it morning and evening lest it should skin over in drying. This mode is the best, because fire tarnishes and obscures the gold.

The " or de couleur " may be exposed to the sun in order to make it dry more quickly.

1. To make beautiful " or mat," a half dry brush must be passed over the " or de couleur," so as to freshen and render it fat and shining (that is, supposing the " or de couleur " is laid over the subject to be gilded).

2. Fat oil is very good if added to the " or de couleur," as it makes it brilliant and shining. Also, if a coat of this oil be passed over the " or de couleur," when it is half dry, it will produce a gold as brilliant as burnished gold.

3. Observe, that the " or couleur " must be nearly dry before the gold is laid on it, otherwise the gold would become dull without any brilliancy or splendour.

4. To make beautiful " or mat," such as is seen on mirrors. The subject to be gilt must be whitened in distemper, in the same manner as for burnished gold ; you must prime it with oil, using some very drying colours, and when dry you must pass over it some new and fat nut oil, and then apply the gold at the proper time.

To make very good varnish for varnishing gold and all other things.—Take benzoin, and grind it as finely as possible between two pieces of paper, then put it into a phial and pour on it some very good spirit of wine, which must cover the benzoin to the depth of 3 or 4 fingers, and leave it in this state for a day or two ; then to half a phial of this spirit of wine you must add 5 or 6 blades[3] of saffron, slightly bruised, but not broken in pieces.

---

[1] *Note by the Author.* " This size [assiette] is very good on marble."

[2] *Note by the Author.* " M. Thiesson the painter."

lin ou de noix, et quand on veut mettre l'or dessus le dit assiette, il faut qu'elle ne soit ny trop seiche ny trop humide.

Autrement : or de couleur se fait avec de la terre jaune, ou ocre avec un peu de blanc de plomb (pour le rendre plus aprochant de l'or) qu'on laisse engraisser sur le porphyre en le remuant du matin au soire, de peure qu'il ne s'y face des peaux. C'est [cette] manière est la meilleure, parceque le feu fait ternir l'or et le rend obscure. Aussi on peut mettre ledit or de couleur au soleil pour le faire plustot engraisser.

1. Pour faire de bel or mat, il faut passer par dessus l'or de couleur avec une brosse estant a demy seicq pour le rafraichir et le tenir gras et luisant (cela s'entend quand il est couché sur la pièce qu'on desire dorer.)

2. L'huile grasse est aussi très bonne dans l'or de couleur, pour le rendre beau et luisant ; aussi, passant une couche de cest huile par dessus l'or de couleur estant a demy seicq, cela fera un or fort esclatant comme or bruny.

3. Nottez, qu'il faut que le dit or couleur soit quasi seicq auparavant que d'y appliquer l'or dessus, car autrement l'or deviendroit tout morne et sans esclat et splendeur.

4. Pour faire de bel or mat comme l'on void de les miroirs, il faut blanchir en destrampe la piece que l'on veut dorer tout ainsi que l'on fait pour l'or bruny ; puis il faut prendre des couleurs fort seccative pour l'imprimer en huille ; estant seicher il faut repasser par dessus avec de l'huille de noix qui soit nouvelle et grasse, puis appliquer son or en temps et heure.

Pour faire de très beau verny pour vernir l'or et toute autres ouvrages.—Il faut prendre benioin, et le broyer le mieux qu'il sera possible entre deux papiers, puis le mettre en quelque phiolle, et y verser dessus de l'eau-de-vie très bonne tant qu'elle passe le benioin de trois ou quatre doigts, et le laisser ainsi un jour ou deux, puis on y adjoust pour demye fiole de telle eaue de vie cinq ou six brin de safran legerement estampé et tout

[3] Brins de Saffron. The hair-like filaments of the saffron is the part in which the colouring matter resides.

When you have done this, strain it, and varnish with it something that has been gilt, which will then become very beautiful and shining; this varnish will dry quickly, and will last several years. Now, if it is wished to apply silver in the way in which gold is laid on, common white salt must be used instead of saffron. This varnish is very good for varnishing all things, as well painted as unpainted, such as tables and boxes of nut tree, ebony, &c., gilt or not gilt, or copper, for it causes to shine, preserves, and brings out colours, dries quickly without contracting dust or dirt, and may be cleaned with a cloth or fox-tail.

To make a varnish with mastic for oil paintings.[1]—Take 2 ounces of hard mastic and 1 ounce of huile de sapin, put the last into a small new pot, melt the mastic over a slow fire, then add the oil, which must boil when mixed with it, and must be kept boiling very slowly; for if it were to boil too fiercely, the varnish would become too viscous. To know when it is done you must dip a hen's feather in it; if this is burnt, the varnish will have been sufficiently boiled; then pour it into a phial or bottle to preserve it from the dust. When required for use it must be warmed in the rays of the sun.

Fine varnish[2] is made with turpentine melted over the fire; when melted, remove it from the fire, and add oil of spike with mastic, and, if required, sandarac.

Gros[3] [vernis] is made with turpentine, oil of turpentine, and resin, melted up together.

---

[1] Varnish of Benzoin. *Note by Author.* "Le Sieur Alexis Piemontois."

entiers ; ce fait on le coule, et d'un pinceau on en verni quelque chose dorée, laquelle devient très belle et luisante et seiche incontinent durant plusieurs années. Or si l'on veut accomoder l'argent comme l'or, au lieu de safran on y met du sel commun blanc, le dit verny est très bon pour vernir toutes choses tant peintes que non peintes, et aussi pour faire reluire les tables et coffres de bois de noier, d'ebene, et de toutes autres choses, pareillement aussi ouvrage de cuivre dorée et non dorée, car il fait reluire, preserve, ayde aux couleurs, et se seiche incontinent sans recevoir pouldre, n'ordure ; et se peut nettoier d'un linge ou d'une queue de renard.

Pour faire verni de mastic pour mettre sur les peintures faites en huile.—On prend deux once de mastic ferme, et une once d'huile de sapin ; que l'on met dans un petit pot neufve, on fait fondre le mastic a petit feu, puis on y adjouste l'huile qu'on laisse quelque peu bouillir en le meslant tousjours afin qu'il ne bouille presque pas, car s'il bouilloit fort le verny deviendroit trop visqueux, et pour scavoir s'il est cuit, on met une plume de poulle dedans le pot, et si elle se brusle incontinent c'est signe qu'il est fait, puis on le met en quelque fiolle ou bouteil pour le garder de la pouldre, et quand on s'en veult servir, on le met au soleil pour l'eschauffer.

Le fin verny se fait avec de la terebantine que l'on fait fondre sur le feu, puis on la retire, et on y met de l'huile d'aspic avec du mastic, ou si l'on veult on y met du sandarac.

Le gros se fait avec de la terrebantine, huile de terrebantine et poix resine, le tout fondu ensemble.

---

[2] *Note by Author.* "M. Thiesson."

[3] The *Vernice grossa* of the Italians. See also Pierre Pomet, Histoire Générale des Drogues, Vol. II. p. 64.

EXTRACTS

FROM

AN ORIGINAL MANUSCRIPT,

ENTITLED

STORIA DELLA ORGANIZZAZIONE CIVILE DELLE BELLE ARTI
IN VENEZIA PER SERVIRE AL PIANO DI SISTEMA
STABILE DI QUESTA IMPERIALE E REALE
VENETA ACCADEMIA. AN. 1833.

BY

SIG. GIOVANNI O'KELLY EDWARDS,

OF

VENICE.

SIG. EDWARDS'S MANUSCRIPT.

PRELIMINARY OBSERVATIONS.

THE consideration which induces me to publish these extracts is, that they treat of the restoration of the paintings of Venice from injuries arising from damp, moisture, and other causes, which probably have a similar operation in England.

This restoration by Sig. Pietro Edwards has been noticed in the Art Union. I endeavoured to learn the method adopted, but the extracts I was able to procure relative to this subject are extremely meagre.

The author of this MS. is the only son of Sig. Pietro Edwards, to whom the restoration of the public pictures of Venice was entrusted.

Sig. Pietro Edwards practised the art at Venice, and was employed by that jealous Republic, and subsequently by the Austrian Government, in restoring the public pictures. He died in 1821, at the age of 76, and is still remembered with esteem for his knowledge, skill, and integrity. The family were originally English, and lay claim to more than noble descent, but both father and son were born in Venice, and the circumstance of the father having been employed by the Government in the restoration of the national

pictures, shows the estimation in which he was held by those whom it may be presumed were competent judges. Sig. O'Kelly Edwards was also employed in their restoration under the superintendence of his father.

It appears from the statement I have made in the general Introduction, that the art of restoring pictures is now practised in the north of Italy by professors of skill and eminence. I have noticed Sig. Fidanza as having practised this art all his lifetime; and when I saw him he had been engaged in this employment at Milan for thirty-six years. These professors are not only employed by private individuals, but by the Austrian Government, in cleaning, repairing, and restoring the national pictures. The art has in some cases descended in families; and I have scarcely a doubt but that many of those who now practise it, either from tradition, or from the accidental discovery of MS. recipes, or from both, and from some of them having analyzed the materials used in these old paintings, possess the knowledge, which they claim, of having ascertained the pigments and vehicles used by the great Italian masters, and the mode of their use and application.

The MS. from which the following extracts were made was written by Sig. O'Kelly Edwards with a view to publication; but in the Venetian territories works on the fine arts are not permitted to be published without especial permission from the Academy of Venice. This permission was refused; but the authorities at Vienna, to whom the MS. had been submitted, directed that a copy of it should be made and preserved in the Academy at Venice. I saw this copy among

the Edwards' papers in the office of the secretary of the Academy.

The first part of the book contains the history of the several academies of painting, &c., in Venice.

The beginning of the second part gives an interesting account of some of the public pictures; of the search that was made for some that were missing; and of the collecting of the best pictures from all parts of the Venetian territories, in order to form a public gallery at Venice, which should show the rise, progress, and decline of the art. The extracts contained in the following pages which treat of the general restoration of the public pictures under the direction of Sig. Pietro Edwards, and of the causes of their decay, are from this part of the work.

Sig. Edwards relates that his father, in 1776, restored the only picture painted in distemper on a wall by Paolo Veronese. This painting is on the ceiling of the Collegio in the Palazzo Ducale; it is still in existence, but is in bad condition.

In 1777 Sig. Pietro Edwards painted the head of the principal figure in Titian's beautiful picture of "Faith" (now in the Sala delle quattro Porte), which had been cut out and carried away; and so well has this been done, that it is impossible to detect the part newly painted, and as his son observes, neither the French Commissioners, who removed the picture to Paris, nor the painters of that country ever detected the modern work. Sig. P. Edwards also painted the head of one of the Magi in the "Adoration" of Bonifazio, which had likewise been cut out and stolen.

The number of public pictures restored by Sig.

Edwards, and those who worked under him, between the years 1770 and 1817, amounted to upwards of 759.

The third part of the work is uninteresting to the English reader, and therefore has not been transcribed.

In consequence of a report from England, which reached me when I was in Venice, that Sig. Pietro Edwards had discovered the old method of painting in oil, and had sold his secret to the Government, I endeavoured to ascertain whether this was the fact. By the kindness of the Count and Countess Spiridion Papadopoli I obtained permission from the President of the Academy to inspect the papers left by Sig. P. Edwards, which are preserved in the Academy, and, from what I saw there, I am enabled to state my firm belief that no secret was either bought or sold; but I saw among these papers much interesting matter relative to the restoration of pictures, which would be extremely useful, and of which Sig. O'Kelly Edwards promised to send me copies. I have reason to expect the Venetian jealousy has interfered, and that Sig. Edwards has been prevented from performing his promise. Fortunately, however, while I was looking over the papers at the Academy, I employed my son in making extracts from some of the most useful parts, translations of which will be found in the notes.

As this MS. is rather historical than technical, I have thought it unnecessary to publish the original text.

ON THE RESTORATION OF THE ROYAL PAINTINGS

UNDER THE

Venetian Government.

From the year 1725 to the year 1775 no less than 751 Reports of the College of Painters, concerning the necessity of the restoration of the public paintings, are enumerated. All these mentioned the gradual decay of the pictures, and in each the attention of the public was earnestly called to this subject, and to the urgent necessity of repairing the greater part of them, and of restoring them to their ancient lustre and splendour.

A fact authenticated by so great a number of depositions, and attested not on the credit of a few intelligent persons only, but by the common consent of the professors of the art, determined the Venetian Senate to consider the subject of a general restoration.

And although the individuals, the Government, and the members of the above-mentioned College were changed, this feeling still remained constant in the minds of the good citizens of Venice, and the Government was more and more inclined every day to attend to the public remonstrances.

For if, in forming their judgment on other important subjects, the Senate relied on the opinion of one or two persons skilled in the various questions upon which they were sometimes required to decide, it could have had no difficulty in deciding on this subject, which was supported by the opinions of a long succes-

sion of men, all agreeing on the same point, and incapable of entertaining views of promoting private interests.

Nor could there be any doubt of the integrity of these men, because the business of restoring paintings was not, at that time, an employment to which masters of any reputation applied themselves, but, on the contrary, the society of which these were members, experienced continual difficulties and embarrassments on that account.

It may be said that the names alone of Sebastian Ricci,[1] Lazzarini,[2] Balestra,[3] Tiepolo, Trevisano, and many others, were

---

[1] Sebastiano Ricci, or, as he was called by the Venetians, Rizzi, was a native of Belluno; he was born in 1659 or 1660, and died in 1734. He painted in Venice, Milan, Bologna, Florence, and Rome; and traversed every part of Italy, where he accepted every commission and any terms he was offered. He afterwards visited Germany, England, and Flanders, where he perfected himself in colouring. "In such a variety of schools," says Lanzi (Vol. III. p. 225), "he filled his mind with beautiful images, and copying many, he familiarized his hand with different styles. Like Giordano he possessed the power of imitating every manner, and several of his pictures, after Bassano or Paolo, have deceived many, as was the case with one of his pictures at Dresden, which was attributed to Correggio." In addition to this power of imitating other painters, a most admirable and essential qualification for a restorer of pictures, he possessed excellences which were peculiarly his own, and which entitled him to rank highly among the original painters of that period. Zanetti, della Pittura Veneziana, p. 437, observes, "if his pictures have in some degree darkened, the fault must be attributed to the bad preparations of the canvas and colours which were in use at that period."

[2] Gregorio Lazzarini, the scholar of Rosa, whose dark style he repudiated and banished from the Venetian school, of which, for the correctness of his design, he may almost be considered the Raffaelle. At first sight it might be supposed he had been educated at Bologna, or rather at Rome. Lanzi says he was never out of Venice, but Moschini[a] proves that he was a scholar of Girolamo Forabosco at Padua. His genius secured him the esteem of the most learned professors of the art, and especially of Carlo Maratti, who had but little respect for his contemporaries.

It is related "that the Venetian ambassador at Rome, having proposed to Maratti to paint a picture for the Sala del Scrutinio, he refused the employment, expressing astonishment that they should seek him at Rome, when they had a Lazzarini at Venice; and well did Lazzarini answer the

---

[a] Moschini, della Origine e delle Vicende della Pittura in Padova, p. 120.

sufficient to authorize this decision, but to these were also added the evidence of the eyes, and the voice of all the citizens of taste.

For if the public could be persuaded of the necessity of a general restoration of their paintings fifty years previously, how much more should they be of this opinion in 1770, when the damaged pictures showed visible signs of decay, and it was feared that they would be entirely lost; and when people spoke no more of the impending destruction, but of the ruin which was already visible!

The disadvantages of this otherwise excellent climate, and their destructive influence on manufactures and natural productions, are well known; for even marbles, metals, and the hardest articles are injured, and the action of the moist and saline particles of our atmosphere is particularly visible on the colours, and on the soft and porous grounds of canvas and panels on which these colours are used, and which are well adapted for the reception and retention of the minute particles which are introduced with the air.

From this action of the atmosphere in diminishing the resistance of the glutinous parts, which consequently crack and cease to hold the colours in strong cohesion, it would follow

---

expectations formed of him by Maratti in two pictures he painted in this apartment, in memory of the triumph of Morosini, surnamed 'Il Peloponnesiaco.' But he particularly signalized himself in the picture of S. Lorenzo Giustiniani in S. Pietro di Castello, which is, perhaps, the best picture in oil that the Venetian school has produced in this century for the taste of the composition, the elegance of the contours, and the originality and variety of the faces and attitudes. It is also distinguished for the force of the colouring, in which he was not always equally successful." This picture is still in excellent preservation. The date of his death is uncertain: some authors say it took place in 1730; others not until 1740.

3 Antonio Balestra, born at Verona in 1666, died there in 1740. He painted in Venice, where he was much esteemed. His Nativity, in the Convent of La Carità (now the Academy), and the Deposition from the Cross, may compete with the best paintings of the age. His S. Vincenzio is one of the best preserved of his pictures; for his method of painting with boiled oil has spoiled not a few. Those painted with oil less boiled have changed less. Lanzi, iii., p. 230.

that after the lapse of a certain time, pictures would be more deteriorated in a few years, than during a period three times as long as that which preceded it.

This natural reasoning, proved by experience, removed all perplexity from the Venetian Government, and perhaps from this they concluded that the restoration required by the greater part of the works of the Venetian masters not having been properly effected since the year 1725, the pictures should naturally have suffered more injury during the last fifty-two years (from 1725 to 1777) than in the previous century and a half, and that therefore their condition required immediate reparation.

It was, however, very fortunate that the Government should have acted with great circumspection until the year 1777, in consenting to the general and universal restoration of all the royal paintings, because the art of repairing paintings damaged by time had not then obtained perfection, and the greatest painters considered the employment as beneath their dignity, and projected it merely with a view to obtain some office which might confer honour on themselves. The reparations, therefore, fell to the lot of the unemployed artists, who are generally the worst, and who, when there was no part of the picture to be entirely removed, thought that any indifferent painter was equal to washing, strengthening, and introducing the proper juices for restoring the picture to its ancient beauty.

In fine, a catalogue of the pictures, which were in a state requiring immediate restoration, being ordered in 1727 to be prepared, the number was found to amount to twenty, and the Society of Painters selected Sebastiano Ricci to restore three of hose which required renovation, while, for repairing the others, they nominated five other painters, who worked very badly, and whose existence would, perhaps, never have been known, had not these works been spoiled by their hands.

It is not, however, wonderful, that even among professional persons such miserable blindness and wrong notions should have prevailed. The art of repairing paintings damaged by the injuries of time was new to the world, and, until this period,

nothing was known of it beyond the occasional necessity of repairing rents and superficial blemishes and the corrosions which, at that date, the pictures had only begun to suffer from the hidden ravages of time.

Necessity introduced the arts, and the art of restoring the works of the pencil from the decay to which they were liable from age could not arise unless pictures grew old and lost their beauty: therefore different modes of restoring them to their former state were tried.

The learning and skill necessary for such a profession, following the common order of things, were acquired by gradual steps only; meanwhile public faith and the innocent error of the painters themselves kept occupied a few devastating hands, who left behind them much cause for grief.

At last the eyes of men were opened, and by long and continual experience it was discovered, that the restoration of ancient paintings was not a work of such small importance as to be entrusted to the hands of any person; for it was sometimes found that the most gentle washes would determine the fate of a painting, and some operations, after the ephemeral splendour of a few years, accelerated the destruction of the pictures, and it was discovered that it did not require less knowledge to restore the paintings to their pristine state, than skill to paint them.

This last observation, which, on the authority of the beforementioned Ricci, passed into a proverb among those who followed this profession, elevated the study of the art of restoring paintings among the Venetians. One after another, all professors of merit aspired to it; and although the first trials showed that the art was not yet well understood, yet the second errors were far less dangerous than the first.

It was here, however, that party enmity broke forth in the Society of Painters. The manifest necessity of restoring the Venetian paintings, and the already declared desire of the Government to repair them, gave rise to the belief that the period of some decisive resolution was not far distant; meanwhile the

watchful crowd of artists, who saw themselves in danger of being ungraciously dismissed from their high stations, was anxiously expecting this moment, and with all the cunning which can be found in the idleness of the unemployed, and which human sagacity, sharpened by poverty, can suggest, they endeavoured to determine the event in their favour.

On the first announcement that there had been some deliberations on this subject, it is impossible to describe the ferment which was excited in that agitated circle, in order to carry into effect their preconcerted wiles. Hence it arose that men intruded themselves into the works of restoration, who had no right but that of their own temerity, and who endeavoured to evade the prudence of the person who presided, and to obtain by trickery a consent which it was easy to procure in the confusion of such intricate and violent practices.

Thus were united, to the injury of the ancient Venetian paintings, first the errors and afterwards the monopolies of those same artists, who themselves would be most injured by so deplorable a ruin, and this was certainly the principal reason why the public mind vacillated for seven years (from 1770 to 1777), uncertain which course to pursue.

Nevertheless, as to abandon entirely the restoration of the public paintings would have been the same as to lose them entirely, three decrees were promulgated which contained orders to provide for this event, and the direction was entrusted to Commissioners of high rank. These were afterwards five in number.

It is difficult to understand (but the fact is nevertheless well proved) why all the authority and vigilance of the Venetian Commissioners up to the above-mentioned epoch were insufficient to form a regular system of public restoration, since the authority of the Commissioners themselves, and the intervention of the Society of Painters, armed both parties.

This Society, called in the year 1770 to give its vote confirmed by an oath on this affair, did justice to Bertani, a most useful man at that time, and the first who instituted a good

mode of restoration, whom the Senate had praised for having restored the ceiling of Paolo [Veronese] in the room called the "Sala della Bussola," for which work he was paid 220 ducats; yet, with all this, such were the underhand dealings, that at last even this honoured artist protested against his commission if it were to be obtained by such means, and if he were to be dependent on the whole band of his competitors.

It was evident, therefore, that the assistance of this great painter was only to be obtained through the interposition of the Society of Painters, and that everything would end badly if they could not be induced to agree together, and if, to promote their own private views, the contending parties continued obstinate in not proposing useful means for proceeding. This was the motive which at once put an end to the designs of the Senate and the activity of the plans set in operation for effecting the general restoration; nor did it produce any matured arrangements for rescuing the pictures from the long threatened injury to which they were subjected first by the ignorance, and afterwards by the artifices and poverty of the artists.

If, however, the great necessity for restoring the celebrated paintings of the Venetians from the damage which had arisen from natural causes and from the injuries which they had suffered from the inexperienced hands of those who had operated on them, and the intrigues by which the best provisions were frustrated, had not been motives strong enough to determine the formation of a well-arranged system relative to the beforementioned general restoration, there ought not to have been any hesitation on the subject, considering the quantity of money which had been thrown away, the dishonour with which the native glory and credit of Venetian genius was tarnished, and the disadvantages to which it subjected the liberal arts.

It is true that the pecuniary value of these precious paintings has no regular standard, and that their real value consists principally in the combination of social circumstances; the Venetians should, therefore, for this reason hold their national and classical pictures in the highest esteem.

If the half of a painting by Titian, which was at one time in a church of this city, and which was reputed to be almost ruined, was sold by a dealer for 8000 ducats; if a single picture by Paolo [Veronese], the greatest ornament of a noble house, was desired by a rich stranger at the price of 20,000 ducats;[1] and if more than 70,000 ducats were paid at that time to the Duke of Modena[2] for his collection, which consisted chiefly of small paintings; most certainly a very great sum was worthy of being spent on the wonderful pictures possessed only by the then Government of Venice.

What must have been their value, for such property could not be valued according to the rules by which the treasures of private individuals and the wealth of merchants are determined, but as gems destined to enhance the splendour of the royal crown of a sovereign?

Small indeed is the sum, in this view of the question, of a few thousands disbursed in the course of many years, with the object of recovering riches to the amount of some millions, and maintaining the public dignity, which could not certainly be adorned by more beautiful ornaments than those created by the genius of her sons.

---

1 The Family of Darius at the feet of Alexander, in the Cà Pisani. This exquisite picture is in a perfect state of preservation: the colours appear to have undergone but little change; the flesh tints are beautiful, and the whites quite fresh. Sig. Edwards informed me it had been restored by Bertani in 1778, under the superintendence of Sig. Pietro Edwards, his father; that it then required but very little reparation. It was lined and cleaned, and some small touches of colour were replaced where necessary; the blue sky, which had been painted in oil, was restored to its original colour, and the picture was re-varnished, and since that time the varnish has never changed, but the blue sky has again acquired a slight greenish tinge. Sig. Edwards told me the colour used for the sky was "Turchino," not ultramarine. The high degree of preservation in which this picture now is, may, perhaps, be partly attributable to the fortunate circumstance of its having always remained in the same family, to its being hung on an internal wall of a room apparently always inhabited, and, above all, to the prudent resolution of the owner not to allow either whole or partial copies to be made of it, on account of the destruction of so many first-class pictures by copyists.

2 This collection is now in the Dresden Gallery.

For these reasons it may be remarked, that as one cannot judge of the greatness of the genius with which a nation is endowed from the secret resources of that nation, but from those objects which it most esteems and which are visible; so the rivals of the Venetians, from the general abandonment of so many sublime works, which had been the objects of their studies, would have had a very good argument for deductions rather unfavourable to that people.

Well and wisely, then, would the Venetians have acted if they had bestowed all their care in forming a certain system of public restoration of their splendid paintings, which, besides being the object of an almost superstitious veneration, had been frequently sought for with so lavish an expenditure of gold, by those to whom nature had denied a Titian and a Paolo, and which had so gloriously contributed to the national renown, and which deserved to be respected, not only from gratitude, but also from the precious deposit of fame which their authors had confided to the fidelity of their country.

Nor could the Venetians allege in excuse the sanguinary incursions of barbarians and the perversion of political systems, which have been cited by some nations as apologies for the state of decay to which the famous pictures of the ancient masters were reduced; nor can they exculpate themselves by pleading that the decline of taste was occasioned by the great number of excellent works left them by their native authors of the golden time. The humiliation of the Venetian genius would have been further increased by neglecting to restore them to their ancient beauty, and the indifference they showed concerning their absolute destruction.

On the contrary, we will say something more, namely, that the custody of the pictures being at that time entrusted to persons who had little love towards the fine arts, specimens of them are very rare which are not either blackened, torn, badly situated, badly repainted, or in some way or other entirely spoiled; and for this reason the public testimonies of such neglect would have authorized the universal contempt, the increasing perver-

sion of taste in painting; and would also have put an end to the wonder of those who could not perhaps understand how, with the flattering applause of strangers, nearly all the rich galleries of the state should have been emptied in less than seventy years; and that only a very few private collections[1] should still

[1] The principal private collections now existing in Venice are those in the Manfrini and Barberigo palaces. Among the latter are the Magdalen of Titian, and his St. Sebastian, left unfinished by this great artist, who was working on it when he was attacked, at the age of 99, with the plague. For those who are desirous of studying the method of Titian, there cannot be a better opportunity than that afforded by this picture. It should be studied with the work of Boschini in the hand. In the sky, on the left of the Saint, may be seen, distinct and unsoftened, those vigorous touches of terra-rossa, ocrea, biacca, and nero, of which he speaks. The distant landscape, bounded by mountains, and a group of trees in the background, are merely indicated. The face and head are finished, the colours on the upper part of the body have been repeated, but the rest of the body is merely an "abbozzo." It is easy to see, from the length and boldness of the strokes, that the artist used a large brush when painting, and stood at a distance from the picture.

Most of the pictures in this collection are injured by cleaning, having apparently been washed with some solvent, such as spirits of wine or an alkali, which has removed all the glazings, which have never been replaced. From this cause all the pictures in this collection by the Bassani resemble pictures in distemper. The removal of the glazings also gave me an opportunity of remarking that the dark leaves of the trees, and other extreme darks, as well as lake drapery, &c., in a picture by Tintoretto, were painted with colours mixed with varnish, while the rest of the picture looked dull; and I cannot help thinking that as these colours mixed with varnish resisted the action of the corrosive liquid which had been applied to the picture, an oleo-resinous varnish must have been used.

The Magdalen by Titian has suffered much from copyists, who have applied oil and other substances to it in order to see to copy it. The celebrity of this picture may be estimated by the fact, that one artist employed himself solely for eight years in making copies of it. In return for the liberality of the nobleman who had granted him this indulgence, the artist injured the sky by the tricks he employed to develop the colours, to such an extent, that he thought it necessary to repaint it, in order to conceal the mischief he had done. This part of the picture does not now harmonize with the rest.

The Venus also has been much injured, and part of it appears to have been repainted. Part of the drapery has changed to a dull flat black, all the lights and shades being lost, apparently by the action of some chemical application.

remain embellished with the dusty remnants of this art, banished from the dwellings of the nobles.

It has been already observed, in the first part of this work, concerning the organization and state of the arts, that at the epoch of which we are speaking, the spirit of frivolity having put an end to the cultivation of high art, works of puerile taste were substituted, which stamped with dishonour the character of the eighteenth century; that the few good artists were driven to starvation, or to follow the common plan; that the growing and youthful nobility, who should have been able to promote the arts, continued to form the first notions of artificial beauty, both simple and sublime, from the study of the productions of the puerile, the ridiculous, and the hyperbolical style which, by a strange fascination of the mind, was then admired: and that thus artists and their patrons joined hand and heart in ruining the genius of the nation while they cultivated the arts.

As little or nothing, therefore, could be hoped for in these bad times, or in those which were preparing, no hopes remained of the renaissance of the Venetian School, which, in the short space of a few years, had entirely lost not only the original art itself, but those persons who could direct the taste of the artists; the characters of its lost style could no longer be distinctly traced, and that number of examples which pointed out the various paths of excellence to native genius, were rapidly decaying.

But the loss of the Venetian paintings which would have ensued through not organizing a system for restoring them, would not have produced the above-mentioned injuries only. In the rise and decline of painting is also included the history of the progress and decline of nearly all the inferior arts which are derived from it, such as the laws of well-adjusted design, the judicious choice of forms, and the various imitations of natural and artificial beauty.

The art of painting has always influenced the productions of the chisel, and all kinds of work in which enthusiasm and

the inventive faculties take part, and the pictorial discipline influences more than all the rest the general taste of the people, presenting to it lasting lessons, which are understood even by idiots; encouraging that delicacy of finish and neatness in the manufactures of industry, which, when they are brought to the highest degree of perfection, are said to be *executed by the pencil*, and, to use the words of Buonarotti, fixing the compasses of elegance and proportion in the eyes of artists.

The destruction, therefore, of the pictures of this State, which might by some be considered the object of idle and superfluous cares, would have occasioned the universal ruin of those social arts which are based on design, a misfortune so much the greater because it would have happened at the period of the general decay of these arts themselves, and at a time when voices were heard from other regions inviting them to leave this their ancient dwelling.

These considerations were of greater weight than all others, because the nearer the danger, the greater was the force of envy, and the value of the monuments of native genius which might still be saved, and so much the more was it the duty of the Venetians to put in operation the most active and efficacious measures for promoting the arts.

It ought, however, to be observed, that without the appointment of a Director well skilled in the Arts, especially in the theory and practice of the different styles of Venetian Painting, the regulation concerning the restoration of the public paintings would always have been essentially defective. This was ultimately determined in 1778.

If the system of a general restoration had been confided to any other person, even though he were a man reputed very learned in the art, it might be believed that such a knowledge would extend to the proposing of a method of external custody only; and thus the different examination of various buildings in which the pictures were contained, the best defences from accidental injuries, and other similar provisions, would have

formed the sum of what was to be changed and what to be established.

But when the contrary to this had become well known, and the fact of many unfortunate experiments, before the time of Bertani and Diziani,[1] had proved that the art of restoration had not yet attained any certain method and science, the Venetian Government entrusted to the most learned person conversant with the art the whole undertaking (more important than any previous system partially effected), the object of which was to retard the decay of the Royal paintings as much as possible beyond the natural course of things; and this may truly be called preservation.

But although these researches reflected so much honour on the Government, they were equally calculated to perplex every man of honour, how well soever he might be informed on these matters. On the one hand, there were no authorized instructions of classic artists, no example of successful experiments conducted on good methods; and on the other, it was useless to say that the paintings were perishing because no one knew how to restore them. Hence, while the biting irony of empirics in painting, who mysteriously pretended that they alone knew what was unknown to all others, grew louder, great difficulty

---

1 Gaspero Diziani, of Belluno. He was a pupil of Sebastiano Ricci, and a scene painter, in which branch of the art he had great facility. He also painted cabinet pictures which were much esteemed.

The following extract from the Decree of the Venetian Senate of the 3rd Sept., 1778, for restoring the pictures in the Ducal Palace, will show the estimation in which Bertani was then held :—

" The Senate having maturely considered that it was not prudent to entrust so decisive and important, but necessary, an operation to the plan proposed by J. ——, and being aware of the difficulty and risk of selecting a person of reputation and experience skilled in the most difficult art of restoring the injured paintings, hereby declare it convenient and in accordance with the express sentiments of the same conference, and with a perfect knowledge of the ability and probity of Prof. Giuseppe Bertani, proved on several occasions, to appoint him, in conjunction with his two usual associates Baldassini and Diziani, to be assisted by them only, to execute this important task," &c.

was found in making every one understand the theoretical reasonings and practical observations which could undeceive the minds of people, confine their hopes to more just measures, and justify the moderation of those who only promised what could be expected from the limited strength of human ingenuity.

However, at this period the Venetian Government began to place much confidence in the President[1] of the College of Painting. This person, who had opposed the decision of ten artists who had condemned as irrecoverable, and who had proposed to remove, the only work in tempera painted on a wall by Paolo Veronese on the ceiling of the college of the ducal palace,[2] undertook, in the year 1776, to save this splendid work from impending destruction, and to restore it to its pristine splendour. The improvement he effected may be estimated by comparing with the present appearance of the picture an apposite description of it by the pen of the President of the College of Painting, which is still preserved; for without his ingenious operations and certainty of result, this painting most certainly would not now be in existence.

About the year 1777 occurred the robbery of the head of the celebrated Faith, painted by Titian, and now existing in the "Sala delle Quattro Porte," and the Senate had recourse to the

[1] Sig. Pietro Edwards, the father of the author of this work. Sig. Pietro Edwards is mentioned in the decree of the 3rd of Sept., 1778, in the following terms:—"The already suggested appointment of an inspector of intelligence and of tried probity, who, with attention and care, should assist this work and decide on the quality and merit of the works, being of equal importance, the Council has therefore determined to intrust this important charge to Sig. Edwards, the other Professor, who alone is considered worthy to fulfil so delicate a task, having already shown his ability in various operations, and especially in the public work of restoring the ceiling by Paolo Veronese in the Sala dell' Anti Collegio, then in danger of perishing, and who was by the Senate, in preceding decrees, acknowledged honest and skilful, and who has obligingly consented to accept the employment for certain considerations."

[2] The picture is still in existence and in its original situation, but it is much injured.

It appears from the description by Sig. Edwards of the state of this picture in 1776, that it was in danger of falling in pieces from the ceiling, and that Sig. Edwards secured it in its situation by a multitude of iron cramps.

same (not mercenary) pencil to supply this loss; nor could the French Commissioners who transported it to their country, or the painters of that country, ever discover the modern substitution.[1] In the same manner the pencil of this person had, with exact imitation of style, filled up the empty space remaining in the Adoration[2] of Bonifazio, by inserting the head of one of the Magi which, at about the same epoch, had been cut out, perhaps by the same hand that had had the opportunity and audacity to cut out that other most beautiful head of Faith.

These and other experiments, as well public as private, which had satisfied the minds of learned observers, added to the notoriety of his profound theoretical knowledge and superior probity, determined the Venetian Senate to trust the undertaking of the general restoration to the President of the College of Painters.

It was required to preserve 92 paintings of Paolo, 57 of Bonifazio, 41 of Giacomo Tintoretto, 11 of the best of the Bassani, and a few by the great Titian, with many others by various classical masters, in all 405 pictures, which were restored between the years 1779 and 1785. These pictures were contained in thirty-two public buildings in the districts of St. Mark and the Rialto; after which 270 more were restored, between the last-mentioned period and the year 1788, under the direction of the same person, making a total of 675 public paintings restored out of 1187.[3]

---

[1] Sig. O'Kelly Edwards, the author of the MS., told me that the piece cut out of the picture was nearly square, and about 4 or 5 inches larger than the head, and had evidently been stolen for the purpose of framing. He also told me that he and another person who was then restoring pictures in the Ducal Palace, procured a ladder and examined the picture; that the seams where it was joined can be felt on the back of the picture, by pressing it against the wall. I went purposely to see this picture twice, but from the distance at which I stood, it was impossible to detect any difference in the tone of the colours, or to distinguish the seams. This fine picture is injured in many places, and appears to be decaying fast. The paint is scaling from the canvas in many of the dark parts.

[2] The Adoration, by Bonifazio. This picture is now in the Academy at Venice.

[3] The expenses incurred in the restoration of these 405 pictures are

In order to guide us in determining with certainty the merit of any pictorial restoration, with reference to the difficulties overcome, the propriety of the means used, and the probable success of the result, it is most essential to be fully acquainted with the three following points, namely, the previous state of the restored works, the particular nature of the paintings, and the characteristic style of the authors.

The partial or total want of these three requisites for judging reasonably of the skill, diligent practice, patient investigation, and sure discoveries, which might direct and accompany the above-mentioned undertaking, was perhaps the principal cause of the silence of the learned Venetians concerning the benefits to be derived from this public provision.

But as all agree in praising the worth and immense value of these royal pictures, and as the fact of the 751 Reports representing their perishing state is notorious, as well as their general restoration, and as there are in the public acts more than fifty written testimonials approving of this operation, so much public and private applause redounds to the honour of the art of restoring at that period firmly established.

It may be thought useful to indicate briefly some of the results of this restoration from its commencement and during its progress; these may with propriety be compared with those restorations which in later times were practised with less successful methods, and under the influence of a different management.

Almost all the pictures, therefore, which adorn the Royal ex-Ducal Palace, were preserved by the general restoration, and to this we owe the existence of the paintings illustrative of some of the most splendid events in Venetian history. The painting by Andrea Vicentino, representing the arrival of

---

stated by Sig. Edwards in his MS. to have been 48,595 florins, in which sum were included the expense of repairing and regilding the frames, and the sub-director's salary of one florin a day. The pictures of the first class which were restored, computed by Italian square feet, comprised an area of 6458 feet 26 inches; of the second class, 6407 square feet and 5 inches —total in square feet, 12,865 and 31 inches.

Henry III., now in the "Sala delle Quattro Porte," in the Ducal Palace, was restored to its ancient beauty, as well as that by Leandro Bassano, representing the Victorious Return of the Doge Ziani and the Meeting with Alexander III., which adorns the Council Chamber of the X.; and that other picture by Marco Vecellio, the nephew of Titian, in which is represented the Confirmation of the Peace of Italy; and, together with these, after many misfortunes, were at length repaired the paintings existing there by Bazzacco, by Paolo, by Zelotti, and by Aliense, so that they were again enabled to resist the climate and seasons.

By this general restoration were restored the greater part of the public paintings which now adorn the new public library, and which were previously injured by various causes and menaced with ruin. Among these we may cite the painting by Domenico Tintoretto, representing the Taking of Zara, and as a testimony of the well-directed restorations effected about the year 1779, the Universal Judgment by Jacopo Palma. As examples of the execution and duration of works which have remained unaltered more than half a century, we may cite the paintings of Jacopo Tintoretto, of Palma, of Dolabella in the "Sala del Pregadi," with many others which are omitted, and which form rich ornaments, and afford most excellent instruction to the learned subjects of this most peaceable kingdom.

In spite, however, of the great practice and knowledge acquired by about twenty-six artists retained in the public service during the general restoration, it was very doubtful whether the skill they had acquired would become hereditary.

It would undoubtedly have done so if they had not been very jealous of their superior information, of their almost inspired knowledge, and discoveries of secrets, especially when an opposition school was formed by some of this profession, in which most excellent future restorers, to whom the public works might be trusted, were instructed.

The best informed persons being dead, there was still less

hope that the art would be transmitted as the patrimony of posterity; nor could other expectations be entertained from those who succeeded them, who, notwithstanding the estimation to which they had been raised by the instructions of others and on account of the scarceness of other workmen, were, in fact, but idiots and mechanical artists only.

These, nevertheless, were the men who, watched over and assisted by the assiduous lessons of the Royal Inspector of pictorial restorations, continued to work well in Venice even until the year 1798-9, in restoring about eighty-two of the public pictures, and under the safeguard of the primitive Imperial and Royal Government of

AUSTRIA.

This remembrance is always a proof of the gratitude of the Venetian nation, who experienced the effects of the royal and paternal solicitude of his Majesty.

It is also satisfactory to consider, that even without the example of the Venetians, the august genius of the monarch should have not only continued, but commenced this undertaking, it being well known that the royal munificence had expended, between the years 1777 and 1781, 75,000 florins in the restoration of the Imperial Gallery.

Now all that was provided or proposed, from 1798-9 to 1805, on this subject, at Venice, through the care of the Prince Reitz, of the Commissioner and President Pellegrini, and of his Excellency Count Bissingen, was much praised, both for the prudence with which it was executed and the judgment with which it was planned, and ever afterwards for the value of the paintings, the restoration of which was the object of the attention of the Government.

Under its superintendence fifty-four paintings were restored (on the 15th of January), 1797-8, to their places in the ex-ducal palace. Some of these which, under the previous Government of Venice, had been removed for the necessary restorations were restored, and if the painting by the school of Marco Vecellio,

representing the consecration of San Lorenzo Giustiniani, is still to be seen in the Sala del Pregadi, it is owing to this superintendence. The other picture by Pietro Bellotti, representing the demolition of Margaritino, was restored to its pristine beauty, as well as the taking of Cattaro by Andrea Vicentino, in the "Sala dello Scrutinio."

These were proofs, which satisfied the Royal Government of his Majesty, that the art of restoring injured pictures was proceeding in the right way in which it had been directed since the year 1779. Additional proofs were also afforded by the two immense paintings of Jacopo Tintoretto, which were again placed in the church of the "Madonna dell' Orto" in this city; and one of which, representing the Last Judgment, had lost its colour in many places, and especially in some of the principal figures, which had been twice re-painted.

In the year 1803, the Government, after particular inspection, deliberated on the propriety of restoring twenty-eight other pictures, which had not been repaired at the time of the general restoration, and which had been much injured by the Commission for the necessary external defence.

It appears, from the notes of the Government of the 3rd of September, 1803 (No. 16,475), that—

In the Sala del Maggiore Consiglio :—

The large painting by Domenico Tintoretto, of the taking of Zara (a subject similar to that in the "Sala dello Scrutinio"), "had in many ways suffered from the weather and the previous bad restorations," which had been executed by the painter Cardinali, who had the execrable habit of re-painting old pictures with oil.

In the same apartment :—

The Apotheosis of Venice, a very large work, by Paolo Veronese, on the ceiling, "required the removal of many spots occasioned by the intrinsic change of colour and the irregular sinking in of the colours." The other two octagons painted by him, representing the Taking of Smyrna and the Liberation of

Scutari,[1] were previously "almost destroyed by the decay of the colour," and in 1803 the former "was much injured by rain water, and other causes, which had occasioned great alteration of colour," and to the same causes was attributed the decay of the picture representing the Fortification of the Isthmus of Corinth, by Leonardo Corona.

Again, with regard to the Rout of the Dukes of Ferrara and of the Germans, painted by Francesco Bassano, and the Rout of the Arragonese, by Jacopo Tintoretto; the first is represented as "entirely decayed," the second as "obscured and injured by the rains to which it had been exposed," and there was reason to "fear that it would become worse," and it was "also torn" in several places, and "had greatly suffered by the action of water, with which it had been saturated," and, consequently, that the "necessary operations for preserving it could not be omitted." The picture of Otho, presented to Alexander III., was "dis-

---

1 I had an opportunity of closely examining one of these works which had been removed from the ceiling for the purpose of being repaired. The picture had been lined, but much of it had absolutely decayed, and there were large blanks on the new canvas. The ground of the picture was extremely thin, and was not visible; the painting was much worn in places, and some of it had scaled off. The varnish also was removed except in one part, which did not appear to have been retouched. I saw that neither the blue pigment nor the lake had changed. The former was of a beautiful colour. The last colour was laid on transparently, and was deeper in the crevices than on the surface of the marks left by the brush. Vermilion also had been laid on the lights of one drapery, but it had been much rubbed, and I could see the solid painting and white lights beneath. There was a figure in the foreground with a sabre wound on the head. The blood was painted with vermilion, glazed with deep lake, which appeared *varnishy* in the darkest parts, and was of a very fine colour. There were also some lights on a yellow drapery, painted solidly and glazed with a transparent yellow resembling Indian yellow. Part of an embroidered drapery was painted with an orange colour, resembling red orpiment, or that pigment now almost unknown in Italy, called "Rauschel Minerale" (if, indeed, they are not synonymous). It was contrasted with a rich warm green, and a lake-coloured drapery of the usual bluish tint was near it. The lights of this drapery were white; the lake was glazed on the shadows, and softened off exactly as it is used in painting in water colours.

figured by the running of damp (colatura) from the top to the bottom."

Finally, we read the following remarks on the Paradise, by Jacopo Tintoretto :—" It suffered much damage from the last disaster of the penetration of the rain through the large roof. Independently of this misfortune its injuries are indescribable, and would require the hand of its author to repair them, because they are not restricted to particular parts of the picture, but extend to the general harmony, to the distinction of the masses, and to the entire effect of a composition of excessive richness, and almost entirely dependent for effect on the separation of tint and chiaroscuro, which are now so much altered, that they leave great doubt concerning the true and primitive conception of the master. To these great difficulties relative to the essential part of the painting, are added other serious and hazardous operations belonging to the mechanism of the work, to the necessity of cutting the picture, to the mode of reuniting it, to the uncertainty of working on the parts in a divided state, and to the difficulty of comparing the whole together previous to replacing it in the proper situation," &c.

In the " Sala dello Scrutinio :"—

Although the Taking of Padua by Night, painted by Francesco Bassano, " did not appear to be injured by the water which lay on it ;" yet, for the sake of prudence, " it was secured with appropriate precautions from injury." The Rout of the Pisans by Giovanni Michele at the Port of Rhodes, painted by Andrea Vicentino, " was lined, and the surface of the paint fixed to the ground." The Morea in Chains, and the Fame, painted by Lazzarini, had " suffered great injuries, and will still suffer more from the corrosive droppings of the moisture which collects on the marbles of the architecture," such as that of which the monument of the Doge Peloponnesiaco (Morosini) is constructed. Of the Victory gained over Ruggiero King of Sicily, and painted by Marco di Tiziano, it is remarked, " great is the damage which it has received from the calcareous drop-

pings by which it is disfigured; it appears also to be otherwise damaged."

In the "Sala delle Quattro Porte:"—

The work of Carletto Caliari, representing the Ambassadors of Persia introduced at the Collegio dei Savii, was restored to its present state, and to show its former condition we quote the following passage, in which it was thus described:—"This beautiful work has contracted a general obscurity from being exposed to the sun; and it is besides much spotted by the rain and snow which penetrated by the side of the window, so as to cover half the picture."

In the "Sala del Pregadi:"—

The painting by Jacopo Tintoretto, representing the Doge Leonardo Loredano imploring the protection of the Virgin Mary, was restored; and the three paintings of Palma Giovane, in which are represented the League of Cambray, the Union of Candia to the Venetian Dominion, and the Tributes of Various Cities, "were so much damaged that they ought to be repaired." To these was added, the Dead Christ supported by Angels, of which we read, "its greatest injury resulted from being washed in an improper manner, by which it was injured, and from a very great blackness which seems to be incorporated with the colour; hence success cannot be promised." And lower down we read, relative to the oval painting on the ceiling, painted by the same author, and to the other two by Marco Vecellio and Dolabella, that they had suffered "from the same misfortunes."

It would also have been desirable to restore to their former splendour six frescoes,[1] of whose existence few are now aware,

---

[1] Frescoes of Titian. Since this was written the whitewash has been removed from one of these frescoes, the S. Cristoforo over the door leading down to the Church of S. Nicolò. Kugler says the head is fine, the rest of the figure very mediocre. The surface of the picture is broken in a few places as if from accident, and the surface is dirty. The figures are perfect, and have never been retouched. The colours are dark like those of a

which were painted by Titian in the small church of St. Nicholas, in the same ex-ducal palace, and which, unknown to the Government, were whitewashed by the troops[2] who were quartered there. The Commissioners, who still remember them, believe that they have perished from the effects of time. These paintings had been overlooked during the researches of the members of the College of Painters, who visited the public places. If no operation has yet been put in practice to recover them, some laudable efforts might now, at all events, be easily made, to remove from the walls the calcareous crust which encloses them, as was done to the celebrated Last Supper of Leonardo da Vinci, engraved by Morghen, and which, after being covered for two centuries with whitewash, was again brought to light by a traveller.

---

painting in oil, the red (terra rossa) drapery is of a good colour, but it was impossible to say whether the inner drapery had been blue or green. The sky was also a heavy dirty grey. It is rather singular that Boschini (Ricche Minere, p. 54, Ed. 1674) mentions the five other frescoes, painted in the Church of S. Nicolò,[a] but he does not mention this S. Cristoforo. Sig. P. Edwards frequently suggested to the Government by memorials (one of which I have seen among his papers in the Academy) the propriety of removing the whitewash from these pictures, but no notice was taken of his communications. His son, the author of the MS., told me he should himself offer to remove the whitewash. Boschini notices that these pictures were injured, he says, from the effects of time, but probably the injury arose from other causes, since the frescoes painted by Titian in the Scuola of S. Antonio at Padua are still in good preservation.

[2] In 1798. See the Report of Edwards for the years 1805, 1810, in the Academy. I have copied this date from a marginal note by Sig. Edwards, written in a copy of Boschini's Ricche Minere which he lent me at Venice.

---

[a] Boschini says, "Passing onwards a few steps, and on the left of the Scala de' Giganti, and the open stairs, we shall find the small Church of S. Nicolò, where Titian painted in fresco by the altar the four Evangelists, two on each side; and in the Lunette the Virgin and Child with S. Nicolò kneeling on her right hand, and the Doge Gritti on the left.

"Opposite the altar in the Lunette over the door is S. Mark sitting on the Lion, and all these pictures are, as I have said, by Titian."

The public restoration of paintings being directed by the same inspector, produced good results also under the

ITALIAN GOVERNMENT.

Few pictures were restored during this period, except those which were effected for the ornament of the vice-regal palaces of Venice and of Strà: and it will readily be supposed that these are sufficient to demonstrate the necessity of publicly teaching this art, thus diligently promoted by the above-mentioned inspector, who, besides being the guardian of the royal pictures, had been elected conservator of the Picture Gallery of the Academy.

This was also proved by the restored paintings destined for the Vice-regal Gallery of Milan, among which were many portraits of Venetian senators, some of the best of Tintoretto's, and some even by the great Titian, which, on account of their extreme blackness,[1] required to undergo a process of cleaning, at once so difficult and dangerous, that the pictures would probably have been destroyed had the task been conducted under the direction of another man.

If an opportunity be desired of studying some of the effects of the first restoration, as well as that executed in 1814, on works painted in various styles and all by classical masters, it will be found in the rooms of the Old Library and of the Procuratie Nuove. There is the Virgin by Cima [da Conegliano], another by Bellino, and the Christ of Albert Dürer, in restoring which, in the year 1779, 128 days of work were spent. Then there is the Noah's Ark, by Bassano, which, being recovered about the above-mentioned period from a foreign country, was restored to Venice in a most ruinous condition, folded in several places, and in several parts detached from the ground. Then,

---

[1] The cause of this darkening of the pictures of Titian and Tintoretto is ascribed in Venice to the excessive use of Asphaltum, not only on the shadows, but in glazing and harmonizing the picture. The tendency of this pigment to grow darker in time is well known.

as examples of the more recent restorations, there is the San Marco saving the Saracen from Shipwreck, the Adoration of the Magi, and the St. Joachim driven out of the Temple, with many others, the daily and private ocular inspection of which, united with assiduous lessons of art, were always entrusted to the above-mentioned Conservator of the Academy.

It must not be attributed to partiality in the writer, if he wander from his subject, in order to draw attention to the great knowledge and artistic skill which constitutes the merits of these restorations, in which it is well known that the characteristic style of the authors was not departed from, or the original beauties diminished or obscured.

But the great excellence of the most eminent works of this kind can never include an idea more perfect than that corresponding to the original condition of this or that work just as it came from the hands of its author, and for this reason, if, after this date, a picture began to show symptoms of decay, it would be unjust to pretend that when restored to its pristine youth, it should also acquire an incorruptibility, which it did not possess in its first state.

Hence, if after a long course of years some of the restored paintings should have again begun to decay, this is only a continuation and consequence of their inseparable tendencies, and not a defect of the art, the scope of which can never be to change nature, but only to give it help and succour. Then the reciprocal affinity between the most active elements of this Venetian atmosphere, and the material substance of the paintings, and more especially of oil paintings, and the various mechanical methods employed by their authors, being accurately known, more physical causes of insensible destruction are to be found than are sufficient to produce, in spite of the most skilful restorations, greater alteration in the before-mentioned pictures than we find to have occurred between the year 1779 and the present time. But excepting all these innumerable and accidental causes, the results of the public restoration of the royal pictures between 1779 and 1814, although sixty years ago,

prove, even in their present state, that they were directed with uncommon learning and great skill.

From this it is manifest, that if a superintendent be provided with sufficient knowledge, prudence, true zeal, and superior probity, the Government may at all events rest quietly in the certainty of its confidence being well placed. It is now time to see from the facts which follow, whether, from 1814 to the present day, the restorations of the royal paintings have proceeded with equal success, and whether the pictures themselves have been safely preserved.

In the year 1816, the Venetian Academy, having become possessed of 250 paintings, presented to them by the royal munificence for the decoration of the public picture gallery, raised a doubt, notwithstanding the successful experiments of sixty years since the commencement of the public restoration, whether it would be of greater utility and security to leave the above-mentioned paintings in the state in which they then were, or to repair them in the usual manner.

The votes being taken, there was not found to be a sufficient majority in favour of the definitive determination of the Government to promote an undertaking, the execution of which would have decided the fate of so valuable a portion of the public property, of the honour of the art of restoration among the Venetians, of the reputation of the Royal Academy, in the bosom of which it ought to be exercised, of the fame of the celebrated "Capi-Scuola," recommended in their works to the fidelity of their country, and, finally, of the utility which would arise to the public in the education of the rising artists.

Objects of such importance obliged them to entrust to the experience of the above-mentioned aged director of the public restorations and conservator of the picture galleries of the Academy, the commission of writing an official Report[1] on the necessity

[1] The Report here alluded to is preserved in the Academy at Venice. It is a most interesting document, but owing to circumstances which I could not control, I was prevented from taking a copy of it. I, however, procured an extract to be made from it, a translation of which will be found

and utility of the restoration of the pictures, in which might also be demonstrated the advantages that would arise from the establishment of a public school for this purpose. The practicability of the subject first suggested being abundantly proved, it was adopted in the year 1817, and the restoration was permitted, but, as will be easily believed, in the full confidence that the execution of such operations should be directed by that same conservator to whom it exclusively belonged by reason of his office.

A decree so well considered, through the care of his Excellency the Governor (Count Göess), did not limit to a certain period of time so delicate an enterprise, for accomplishing which many years and many restorers were necessary; the Government well knowing that had they acted differently, they could not have expected a result corresponding with the views which, in their provisions, they had contemplated.

The President of the Academy,[1] having given to this judicious decree an interpretation which could not possibly have been contemplated, waiving the above-mentioned considerations, and reflecting that the slow re-establishment of the health of the Conservator, who was then indisposed, was incompatible with the rapidity with which he desired to complete the splendid decorations of the room destined for the annual distribution of the prizes in August, 1817, resolved to commence immediately the restoration of those pictures which were to be used for this purpose. The exclusion of so important a surveillance was the first error of the then President; we think proper to make this remark on account of the importance of his influence.

In addition to this, the whole work was confided to two artists only, on whom the Inspector of restorations thought he could not depend unless he kept them under his daily ocular inspection, and directed their labours with assiduous artistical lessons, and the best of whom he did not consider sufficiently careful to

in p. 885, which will show Mr. Edwards's opinion as to the best method of rendering paintings in oil durable.

[1] The Conte Cicognara, author of the works on Sculpture and on Nielli.

be proposed as master of the school of pictorial restoration projected in 1816. This second oversight was not inferior to the first; indeed it was worse, inasmuch as these artists were generally reputed for various reasons to require the most rigorous and careful superintendence.

But when it is considered that the labour of the two artists above-mentioned was limited to the short space of four months, when five or six years were really necessary, and that within this time they were required to repair thirty paintings of great size,[1] both on panel and on canvas, one may easily be con-

[1] Among the pictures restored in this hasty manner was the Assumption of the Virgin by Titian, formerly in the Church of the Frari, but now in the Gallery of the Academy. I saw the contract for the restoration of this picture among the papers of Sig. Pietro Edwards. It was made between Sig. Edwards, as Director of the Restorations, and Sig. Floriani, by whom the picture was restored. It contained the following stipulations:—

"The above-mentioned restorations shall be made upon a ground of gesso, tempered with weak 'colla di ritaglj;' and the parts to be repainted, as well as the indispensable reparation of portions of the old colour, shall be executed with varnish, the use of oil being absolutely excluded; and for this purpose Sig. Edwards shall supply eight pounds of varnish, which shall be delivered into the charge of Sig. Floriani."

The date of this document was the 21st of February, 1816. From the bills of expenses which accompanied it, I ascertained that the varnish supplied by Edwards consisted of "acqua di ragia" and mastic;[a] that the paste used for lining the picture was composed of flour paste, Flanders glue, and ox-gall. The use of the latter ingredient was to preserve the paste from the attacks of insects.

The method of pressing freshly lined pictures pursued by Sig. Edwards differed from that practised in this country. The process was described to me by his son; it was as follows:—

The face of the picture being secured by pasting paper over it, it was laid on the polished Venetian floor, or, as it is called, "Terrazzo," and the lining was fixed to it. Hot sand was then laid all over it, beginning always in the middle of the picture, whence the sand gradually spread to the edge, and the picture was covered to a certain height. By this means the air was pressed out from between the canvas and the picture, and an equal

[a] According to Sig. Edwards, the best proportions for making this varnish are 1½ oz. of spirit of turpentine to 1 oz. of mastic.

vinced, even by merely considering the probabilities of the case, that the result would be anything but satisfactory. This was the third blunder committed while the Academy was under the guidance of this President; nor is it easy to understand how, when the effects were so evident on these precious monuments of art, and on the other objects which relate to them, even independently of their belonging to royalty, it should have been decided to employ such dangerous measures.

The result of his zeal corresponded with the anticipations of the Conservator of the Academy, and justified his respectful disapprobation. We cannot do otherwise than believe that the former President was ignorant both of his anticipations and of his disapprobation, for in the annual discourse for 1817 his activity in bringing to new life those splendid monuments of

---

degree of warmth and pressure was communicated at the same time to the whole surface, much more safely and effectually than with a hot iron.

The information I had obtained relative to technical processes used by Sig. Edwards in restoring the Venetian pictures, naturally induced me to examine carefully some of the paintings that had been repaired under his superintendence, and especially the "Assumption of the Virgin" above-mentioned. The general effect of this picture is fresh and beautiful in the extreme, but on looking into it, many parts are perceived which appear to have been retouched with meguilp, for they exhibit the cracks to which paintings executed with this vehicle are liable. In other parts the colour is lowered, as if oil had been used, evidently showing that the painting had been repaired with more than one vehicle. The darks of the picture look as if they had been injured by the application of something corrosive. From these remarks I think it very probable that the picture has been repaired more than once since its restoration under Sig. Edwards in 1816, now 30 years ago. At the same time, I must acknowledge that Sig. O'Kelly Edwards frequently lamented the extreme haste with which the painting had been repaired, and which perhaps will account sufficiently for the numerous cracks in the new parts.

Titian's picture of the "Presentation in the Temple" is also much cracked in several parts, apparently from the effects of restorations. The same may be observed of the Miracle of St. Mark by Tintoretto.

I have been informed that Sig. Edwards used no varnish but that of mastic in restoring the decayed pictures, but this is objected to by many modern Venetian restorers of the Government pictures, some of whom use raw linseed oil only, others linseed oil boiled on litharge. It is unnecessary to comment on the effects of such restorations.

which, according to his cautious expression, he was the "passive keeper," is highly praised.

Some of the injuries effected by the restoration of 1817 are visible to all intelligent persons, but there are others which work secretly and which are only known to a few—time will show the result of these. He who does not know the previous state of the pictures, or who is unacquainted with the nature of the painting, and the mode in which the picture was executed by its author, who cannot distinguish the intrinsic and inherent defects incident to the works themselves, from those which are the consequence of bad restorations, who possesses or trades with paintings restored in the same manner as those of which we are speaking, and lastly, who is contented with an apparent illusion, cannot be a judge in these affairs.

A written report was wanting, from which might be known the state of the paintings of the Royal Academy at the time of the above-mentioned restoration, and fifteen years previous, as well as the methods then established, which were to be observed in the practical execution, in order to form just conclusions as to the former, and to recognize, by evidence, the latter, and hence to judge of the consequent injuries suffered by the pictures. But this deficiency is supplied by the catalogues[1] of the defunct Conservator, in which is described the state of the royal paintings from 1808, at which time they were collected in the public depository of St. Antonio, where they were carefully preserved.

But even without this, how well soever the nature of the paintings may be known as we have just observed, and the various executive methods of the different styles, it is easy to distinguish, by comparing the parts of the pictures which are intact with those which are nearest to them, the defects originally inherent in the paintings, from those which were caused in them by the influence of the climate or seasons, and from the injuries arising from the want of skill or negligence of others.

[1] These catalogues are now preserved in the Academy.

It is certain that in the peculiar nature of this or that picture is to be found the intrinsic cause of its greater or less resistance depending on the nature of the material, and on the method of the work.

The use of ill-prepared and fleeting colours, the mixture of substances which act upon each other reciprocally, the want of skill in employing alone and in large masses colours which do not well receive the cementation of the oils unless they are united with other bodies, such as vitreous and sandy colours;[1] the introduction of various liquids calculated to produce changes in various degrees in the body of a painting, and to cause it to separate in laminæ[2] of various consistence, instead of forming one single homogeneous and uniform body, and the excessive liquidity of the too-dilute colours;[3] all these are defects inherent in the solid part of the paintings, proceeding from the mechanical execution, and which cannot be remedied.

To this may be added the rigidity of the friable glues, the bad choice of the preparations and grounds used by the different painters, the thinness of the coats of colour, the glazings and the *sfregazzi*,[4] so much loved by the Venetian school, and indeed perhaps indispensable, the retouches applied by the painter to

1 The difficulty of employing vitreous colours, such as smalt, is acknowledged by all writers on art.

2 I may mention as a fact that Sig. Schiavone assured me, that in restoring pictures by Titian, he had removed eight or nine layers of colour.

3 The ill effects of employing the colours too liquid are frequently mentioned by Malvasia and Lanzi.

4 *Sfregazzi* or *sfregature*. By this term is meant a peculiar thin kind of glazing, which is executed by dipping the finger into the colour and drawing it once lightly and evenly along the part of the picture on which it was to be applied, such as the shade on the cheek, the limbs, &c., or wherever it is wished to lay a soft thin shadow. It is easy to understand that the layer of colour must be very thin. These sfregazzi are distinguished from the glazings by the manner in which they are executed, as well as their effects. The glazings which are commonly mixed with varnish may be applied either with a brush or with the hand, but instead of drawing the finger once along the part to be painted, it may be rubbed in with the whole hand. Glazings are used for laying a flat transparent tint, but sfregazzi for soft shadows only.

the picture when in a state too dry and hard, with a hundred other things, are all defects inherent in the pictures and which spoil them, making them appear as if injured by the climate, and preventing the perfect union of the surface and of the interior.

Hence, besides the decay of the finer parts exposed to the contact of the external air, the whole substance of the picture becomes porous, which increases the facility of ingress to the dissolving acids, and these give rise to a secret disunion of parts, and form various combinations which are afterwards manifested by change of colour, blackness, and other marks of destruction.

In addition to these, there are the intrinsic defects peculiar to painting in oil, notwithstanding the misapplied praises of many writers. The nature of the vegetable oils obtained by expression causes them to blacken in the paintings; the peculiar loss or sinking in of the half-tints, which takes place more frequently in this kind of painting than in distemper or fresco; the drying and want of cohesion in the small particles of the colours;[1] the

[1] The effects produced on pictures by their hanging for a period of 100 or 200 years on a south wall were described to me by Sig. Schiavone. He says such pictures invariably appear as if painted in distemper, from the evaporation of the thin and fluid parts of the oil. Such pictures preserve the purity of their colours, which Sig. Schiavone assured me would wash off with water. He denies that the Venetians painted any part of their pictures with water colours, and says the appearance of it is to be attributed to this cause only. He also told me that paintings which had hung on north walls never had this appearance, but always perished from damp.

Mr. Edwards also concurred in this, and in order to show the effects produced on an old picture which had always hung on a north wall, by exposure to the sun, he related to me the following account of a Capo d'Opera painted by Cima da Conegliano, for an altar-piece in a church at Venice, which was intended to be hung on a north wall :—

The picture was on wood, and in order to preserve it from damp, the wall against which it was to be placed was lined with wood, and the space between this wood and the picture was filled with charcoal. The contrivance succeeded, and the picture was preserved until recently in a perfect state; but the late Abbate required new garments for the priests, and not having ready money available, the picture was sold. The purchaser mortgaged the picture, which was deposited for safety with a restorer of pic-

rigidity of the painting, which acquires almost the transparency of talc; the coagulation of some colours, which contract into distinct, dark-coloured, and very hard globular particles, a great and invincible defect, which is known among artists by the name of *sobbollimento.*

Although these liquids are very capable of being volatilized, the proportion of their elements is restored to equilibrium by the regularity of the evaporation, after which no part of them remains but the dregs (feccie), which are incapable of being sublimed,[1] and which are called by the chemists "inflammable earth,"[2] which, in the slow operation of years and in the state of commixtion in which it is found, acquires greater friability and perhaps also greater blackness than is remarked in the artificial separation by distillation,[3] and instead of considering it as the

---

tures, who, without considering that the picture had hung ever since it was finished on a north wall, left it on the floor of a room exposed to the mid-day sun. In the mean time the old Abbate died and a new one was appointed, who, thinking the picture had been unlawfully disposed of, instituted law proceedings against the purchaser and recovered the picture. But the picture was no longer of the same value, for it was found dried up, cracked, and almost destroyed by the exposure to the sun.

[1] The oil is converted into resin by the evaporation of the watery particles.

[2] It is almost unnecessary to remark that this theory, founded upon Stahl's "Theoria Chemicæ Dogmaticæ," the doctrines of which were inculcated as the infallible code of professors of chemistry for almost a century, is now found to be incorrect.

Stahl supposed that light and heat were occasioned by the emission of a common inflammable principle, which he called Phlogiston.

[3] These remarks of Mr. Gio. Edwards are evidently founded on the opinion of his father, expressed in the Report from which I have given an extract at page 885.

Mr. Edwards appears to have been well acquainted with the distillation of oils, the residue of which is a kind of resin, liquid when heated, but solid when cold; black in colour when viewed in the mass, but a transparent brown yellow when spread on a light ground. It is without any smell, and may be diluted to any extent by the volatile oil which has been distilled from it. The smell of this volatile oil is extremely pungent and unpleasant, and as oil paintings cease to smell when perfectly dry, it may fairly be presumed that all the volatile parts of the oil have evaporated (especially if the

usual residuum of all oils, it may be considered as a result similar to that mentioned in the observations of Kunckel, who, by uniting a vegetable essential oil to a highly concentrated acid, obtained from the residue after distillation a dry and shining earth (terra) which was infusible.

For if the substance of this oily cement is supposed to change so materially, in the same manner we may readily suppose the change which it induces in the various bodies to which it is united. The strong smell of oil colours is sufficient to show the effervescence of the parts of the fresh composition, and the formation of the last combinations among the different principles which disengage themselves and unite together.

Hence, the scrutinizing and experienced eye, investigating the changes of an old painting of this kind, will find, among many other things, impure concretions of sulphur,[1] which was never used, and indeed could not have been used on that part of the picture, a phenomenon obtained artificially, as Boyle and Stahl obtained it, by simple digestion of the vegetable oils with sulphuric acid.

---

picture has been placed in the sun and air), and that the resin alone is left. The change therefore produced in oils by drying is a *chemical* change, for different salts come over with the volatile parts in the process of distillation. These become visible when the distilled oil is cooled to a temperature of 40° Fahrenheit, when it becomes a mass of white needle-shaped crystals which again disappear on warming the distilled oil. If this distilled oil be rectified by distilling it a second time upon water, the salts are removed and the volatile oil remains limpid and clear in the coldest weather. The good effects therefore of exposing newly painted pictures to the sun and dew, by which the volatile particles and salts or rather acids are evaporated, become apparent.

In addition to the partial decomposition of the oil, and the evaporation of the volatile acids from paintings in oil which have been exposed to the sun and dew, another important chemical change is effected, and the resinous part of the oil is bleached by the action of the chemical rays of light, and by the absorption of oxygen from the air, and especially from the dew which contains much air and free oxygen.

[1] Mr. Edwards told me his father had sometimes found particles of sulphur on old paintings, and that he had more than once called his attention to the subject, and had pointed out to him the grains of sulphur, which he had picked out of the paintings.

Besides these defects naturally inherent in the painting, there is the following, namely, that in an oil painting 200 or 300 years old, no efforts of art can remove the fixed and blackened part which cannot be evaporated. Lead, copper, and mercury are also subject to almost the same alterations when they are used on the same agents.

From these facts we conclude that the changes of these bodies in some parts of the painting can frequently be revived, but this should be understood, with very great restrictions, for some tints, especially those composed of metallic green, blackened by an excess of acid, which enters into a sulphurous combination with the oil, although once restored by the use of an alkali properly diluted, do not permanently better their condition.

There are also the injuries arising from the climate, which is the most active enemy of paintings, and only in a few cases, perhaps, can they be defended from its universal and incessant action, and although climate is most important everywhere, it is especially so at Venice, for if a writer were to make a long description of the phenomena peculiar to all the different climates of the world, he would characterize that of Venice by merely indicating its singular property of corroding all paintings in a very short space of time.

Having related the different effects of the immovable causes which we have indicated, with their modifications, I would observe that they can, by a very easy comparison, be distinguished from those which are produced by bad restorations. For example, the impossibility of increasing the thickness of the coats of colour in painting, is not a fault of the art of restoration, but the continual attenuation of them with corrosive substances is so; it is not the fault of the art if that which causes them to divide into thin laminæ cannot be removed, but it is a fault to introduce a menstruum which disjoins the parts still more; it is not a fault if the unequal porosity of the mass of colour in a painting cannot be reduced to the consistence of a body fused all at one time, but the want of skill consists in rendering its surface even by rasping and by stippling it. So it is not to be

imputed to ignorance if the volatile and light nature of the mezze tinte are not changed into solid and resisting substances, but it shows great ignorance to increase and make them heavy with that kind of re-painting called "di corpo," nor is it an artistical error if the heterogeneous and improper ingredients which enter into the composition of the different mixtures cannot be separated from the other substances, but it is very wrong to use those things which decompose them.

In order to verify the accuracy of these observations on the visible injuries of which we are speaking, we think it sufficient to refer to the concordant testimony of the academic body to whom the anterior state of the chosen pictures, and the mode followed in their restoration, is well known.

EXTRACTS

FROM

A DISSERTATION READ BY SIG. PIETRO EDWARDS IN THE ACADEMY OF FINE ARTS AT VENICE ON THE PROPRIETY OF RESTORING THE PUBLIC PICTURES.

DATED MARCH, 1812.

Of gesso and oil grounds.—The practice of painting in distemper having almost entirely ceased towards the end of the fifteenth century, another century, at least, elapsed before there was any necessity for the frequent reparation of paintings in oil. After this period the use of gesso grounds being abandoned, with great injury to the Venetian colouring, the practice of employing grounds prepared with oil was introduced, which led to the adoption of different methods of painting.

Of the art of restoring pictures.—At this time the experience derived from previous trials must necessarily have been wanting, and no experiment could be said to have been properly tried until it had stood the test of a long course of years. Meanwhile each artist adopted the method which to him seemed best, or followed, without examination, the custom which then prevailed, until the year 1730 or 1740, when, warned by the many past errors and few fortunate results, some artists adopted a better method. This reform gradually progressed, so that we can maintain on the base of indisputable facts, proved by the testimony of more than sixty years, that the art is now carried to a point of the highest utility, and has become so much the more valuable and important inasmuch as the necessity of our having recourse to its aid is daily augmenting.

Nor is any discredit thrown on the art by general accusations

founded on the unsuccessful result of its undertakings, when they are considered collectively without distinction of times, and when all the dates of so dubious a career are put together from its first beginning. The commencement of all the arts was feeble and insignificant, and even at the height of their renown they always numbered among their professors some obtuse or bad workmen. Hence, if it is wished to insinuate that the restoration of paintings should be absolutely forbidden, on the pretence that it is generally productive of the worst effects, it is necessary to show, previously to such a conclusion, that all the testimony that has been, or that can be, adduced in favour of good restorations, by means of which many valuable works of art, now admired, and formerly considered useless or entirely lost, were recovered, is evidently false or dictated by a foolish anticipation; it is also necessary to prove that the opinions of the most expert professors on pictures valued at 20 or 30 before their restoration, and actually sold for 100 or 1000 after it, were absurd, or that they were all purchased by bribery; and, finally, it must be proved that, in this general condemnation, the whole course or state of the art must be comprehended, so that from its commencement until the present time, neither work nor workman can be pointed out deserving of praise.

But if all this cannot be demonstrated, the lamentable belief of this universal falling off should be partially removed, because, while it does not correspond with historical truth, it drives to despair all those amateurs and artists who wish that by systematic laws the chefs-d'œuvre of ancient pencils may in a few years afford us no occupation but that of weeping over their legally consummated misfortunes. I well know that all this is not sufficient to change the firm opinions of my opponents who, though they cannot contradict my statements, still believe that they derive a strong argument against the restoration from some essential defects inseparable from it, and on which I ought not even to touch, lest I should increase the tedium of this long discourse; yet, that my silence may not be attributed to

an endeavour to avoid answering this objection which is reputed to be the Achilles of its party, and so give rise to suspicion against my cause, let me entreat you to suffer me to allude briefly to the alteration of tints by retouchings "di corpo" in ancient pictures, of which so much has been said.

My adversaries being persuaded that so gigantic an objection must be insuperable, inquire, almost smilingly, *What colour now used will be the same hereafter?* To this I have a most decided and short answer. That colour whose liquid cement shall be quickly absorbed by the ground on which it is placed, and which shall be afterwards covered with an appropriate varnish, by which it is preserved from immediate contact with the air, *that* will be the colour which, being used to-day, will remain permanently the same for more than a century. The assertion that all colours in all cases must change is gratuitously put forward without the slightest evidence. I might therefore dispense with adducing proofs of the correctness of my answer, were it not that the respect due to the honourable assembly which hears me obliges me to say something on the subject, with a proper regard to the greatness of your knowledge before which alone I am permitted to justify my expressions, merely observing, that from the chemical doctrines of the fermentation of the mixtures into which fluid components enter, results the cause of the intrinsic or internal alteration of the colours; that from the same doctrines of the action of the inflammable gases and carbon which float about in the atmospheric air as well as from the aqueous vapours of the same atmosphere, are derived what may be called the extrinsic change in the same colours when thoroughly consolidated; that from the knowledge, also derived from chemical science, of the attractions or affinities of aggregation alone, is demonstrated the power possessed by certain absorbent earths, such as our gesso after calcination, of attracting to themselves the oils as well expressed as essential, not miscible with water; that the most subtle and fluid portion of these substances being absorbed, and the cause of fermentation being thus removed, the most viscous and resinous parts

which remain, withdraw into themselves and condense the particles of the mixture into more strict cohesion, which thus acquires a uniform consistence most proper for preventing the penetration of the dissolving principles contained in the external air; that the interposition of a varnish between the painting and this external air, as it prevents their immediate contact, so it preserves the surface of the colours derived from metallic oxides, which by their affinity for the before-mentioned inflammable gases might be deprived of their oxygen and be revivified; that the foundation of these theories may be seen expressed in the old chemical terms in the works of the celebrated Bergman, of Boumé, and of Macquer; and in the formulæ of modern chemistry, which we have used, in the works of Fourcroy and other moderns, not omitting, with respect to the article of varnishes, the useful practical treatise of Watin, praised by the before-mentioned Macquer, besides all those passages in the works of various respectable authors which in a purely physical sense may be compared with them; that, finally, the truth of my proposition is proved by the incontrovertible, though rarely occurring, fact of ancient pictures painted in oil with very few repaintings on grounds of gesso not hardened, (mark well,) not hardened by strong glue, or on canvas having a thin coating of gesso, whose colours have been preserved with as much freshness as if just painted. Such are the three paintings representing the legend of Sta. Cristina, and another, the subject of which is the Annunciation, all of which are the works of Paolo [Veronese], now existing in our Royal Academy, and already prepared in the "Gran Sala" for any observations you may wish to make on them, which being considered solely with reference to the colours not being obscured by any intrinsic change, would be judged to have been painted but two days instead of upwards of two centuries, yet not having been defended by varnish they have suffered great injuries in the parts most deficient in solid colour, being consumed by repeated rubbings or indiscreet applications on pictures remarkably rigid and dry, as well as by the continual, though imperceptible action of the

surrounding atmosphere; so also in those small portions which present a surface of metallic colour to the contact of the air, such as the copper greens and a certain mineral blue which is no longer used, they have manifestly suffered in a small degree from the activity of the inflammable principles, according as the substance adapted to feel their action was combined in a greater or less degree with other ingredients, agreeable to the practice of Paolo, who, differing from other Venetian masters, scarcely ever used the above-mentioned colours unless mixed with others.

You will perceive, learned academicians, that I omit adding a hundred other things on this special proposition, as I ought to do in every other division of my discourse, because each by itself would have required a particular treatise; but your penetration will certainly understand, even from what I have hitherto stated concerning the apprehended alteration of colours in the retouchings "di corpo," that it was not the impossibility of making the colours of the restored parts remain always the same, that occasioned their change, which in part originated in the then unknown bad effect of stuccoes and grounds incapable of absorbing the more fluid part of the recent painting, and, consequently, of permitting it to dry; it was the want of an universal knowledge of the theories necessary for the secure practice of the art, and these effects were sometimes produced by the desire of increasing the prospect of gain by hastening the work, aided by the stuccoes being either naturally unabsorbent or being saturated with oil previous to the retouching, or being formed of the colour itself, distempered with what ought afterwards to serve for the retouches themselves, all these being common errors on such a subject.

ADDITIONAL NOTES AND CORRECTIONS.

Note, p. clxxv.

The Bolognese MS. (p. 454) contains a recipe, which I had overlooked, in the later handwriting, for making lake from "lac overo grana." Lake made from kermes was known, therefore, in the fifteenth century, and previous to the time of Neri.

P. clxxxviii.

I am informed by a friend that the Germans consider the terms Morellen Salz, Eisen Oxyd, and Caput Mortuum as synonymous.

P. cclxi.

By the earliest varnish used in Italy, I mean to say, that which was in general use after the revival of the arts.

Note, p. ccxcv.

Since this Introduction was written, it has been pointed out to me by a friend, on whose judgment I have perfect reliance, that Paolo Pino was alluding, in the passage I have quoted, to the *drawing*, which the old masters were accustomed to finish with great accuracy, and not to the commencement of the *picture* in chiaroscuro. On a closer examination of the passage in Paolo Pino's Dialogue, I am satisfied my friend is right. I must, however, observe, that although there may be no documentary evidence that Gian Bellino began his pictures in chiaroscuro, we have still the testimony of an eminent Venetian artist that this was his usual practice. See p. cxxxiii.

Page 50, No. 11.

Several kinds of ley are mentioned in these MSS. Common ley was made by an infusion or decoction of the ashes of burnt wood in water. This was called *Ranno* in Tuscany, *Liscia* in other parts of Italy. It was also called *Colato* [1] and *Bucato*, which is the ley used by laundresses. Strong ley was called *Liscia fortissima*, weak ley *Liscia dolce*. *Capitello* was by some persons considered the same as *Liscia;* but D. Alessio says that Capitello was made of strong ashes and of soda with quicklime, like that of which soap is made. It was then *caustic ley*. *Ranno da Mezzo* is the same as Capitello,[2] and *Ranno da Capo* [3] is probably the same. The strength of the ley was determined during the middle ages in the same manner as it is now—namely, by laying a fresh egg upon it: if the egg sank, the ley was

[1] D. Alessio. [2] Alberto's Dict. [3] Bol. MS., p. 354.

too weak; if it swam, it was of the proper strength. See Bol. MS., p. 498.

Page 70, No. 48.

Tutia, Tuzia, or Tuchia, is an impure oxide of zinc found in the chimneys of the furnaces in which zinc ores are roasted, or in which zinciferous lead-ores are smelted. (Note by the Translators of Beckmann's Inventions, Art. Zinc.) Alexandrine Tuzia was prepared artificially by placing in the furnaces where the ore was smelted rods of iron, to which the zinc, being sublimed by the heat, adhered. (See Ricettario Fiorentino.) Oxide of zinc was called by the Romans Pompholyx and Bulla, Pompholige by the Italians, Tuzia by the Arabs; at a later period it has been known by the names of Lana philosophica, nil album, flowers of zinc, &c. Matthioli (Diosc., lib. v., cc. 43, 44, 45) distinguishes between the real Tutia, which he calls Cadmia Minerale, and Alexandrine Tutia. Depping (Hist. du Commerce, &c., vol. i. p. 144) says—"La tuthie, poudre de l'arbre *Goan*, que les Egyptiens tiraient d'Alexandrie; Pegoletti la nomme *ispodio*, d'après le mot *spodos*, que donnaient à cette drogue les Grecs et les Arabes." In this he is not correct. Tutia and Spodio are not to be confounded. The difference between them is pointed out by Matthioli, who, quoting Galen, says—"By *pompholige* was understood the more subtle part which rose to the top of the furnace; and by *spodio* the grosser particles which fell to the bottom." The same author mentions an artificial kind of spodio which was stated by Avicenna to be prepared from different vegetables, chiefly from canes, and it is this artificial kind of spodio which Depping has confounded with Tutia. See Matthioli's Diosc., lib. v. cap. 45.

P. 86, note 5.

The "lot" is not a liquid measure, but a weight. See the 'Note on the Weights and Measures,' p. 898.

Note, p. 112.

The proof that S. Audemar was a Frenchman and an ecclesiastic is to be found in No. 165 (p. 131), where he says, "in hac nostra patria Galliæ ut in tota Francia crescit," and "quedam herba......cujus flores nos crocum laici vero safran vocant."

P. 178.

Since writing the passage in the text I have had reason to think that the glass described in the page referred to may have been black, and not blue, but as yet I have no proof of this fact.

P. 205, No. 232.

Cuprum ustum or *Æs ustum*, called also Ferretta di Spagna, was, according to Cesalpino (De Metallicis, lib. iii. c. 5), nothing but calcined copper. In modern chemistry it is denominated the protoxide of copper. The terms Ferret and Ferretta di Spagna were also applied to the native red ore of iron, called Hæmatite. See Art of Fresco-painting, p. xxxii.

P. 209.

Copper was at first called *æs cyprium:* but in course of time *cyprium* only; from which was at length formed *cuprum.* See Beckmann's Inventions, tit. Zinc.

Page 211, No. V.

Admovitrius.—This should be *ammonitrum* or *hammonitrum*, the ancient term for the "frit" or first mixture obtained by the fusion of the sand and alkali. See Pliny, lib. xxxvi. cap. 26. Cesalpino speaks positively on this point: he says that "of sand and nitre is made a mass which Pliny calls *hammonitrum*, and which is now called 'fritte.'" See Merret's Notes to Neri's Arte Vetraria, cap. viii.

Page 227, No. XXII.

Paramentum.—The saline efflorescence which is found on old walls. It is more acrid than common salt. Merret says that he had a specimen in his cabinet which was transparent, and very similar to alum. It is more acrid to the taste than sea-salt. See Merret's Notes to Neri's Arte Vetraria, cap. vii.

Page 244, No. L.

ALUMEN.—The name formerly given to all salts which had sulphuric acid for a base. In medieval MSS. these salts are also called "Glassa," or "Glace." It appears that the Romans gave this name to sulphate of iron. "The difference, that the vitriols are combinations of sulphuric acid with a metallic oxide, either that of iron, copper, or zinc, and alum on the other hand with a peculiar white earth, called on this account alumina, has been established only in modern times."[1]

Many kinds of alumen are mentioned in medieval MSS. A pigment of this name, which appears to have been Allume Scagliuolo, is twice alluded to in the third book of Eraclius. See pp. 245 and 232.

Alumen glacie, Alumen glarum, Alun de glace, Alumen jameni.—There is little doubt that these were merely different names for Roche Alum.[2] *Allume di feccia*—Tartar of wine dried in the sun during the dog-days.[3] Carbonate of potash. *Allume catino*—Carbonate of soda. *Allume di piume, Alun de plume*—called also *Allume Scissile.* It is a natural alum, composed of many threads, which are white, straight, fine, and shining like crystal, which form here and there certain fringes or beards like feathers. It is frequently confounded with the stone called Amyanthus, or Fiore di pietra.[4] *Allume di Rocca, Roche Alum, Alun de Roche*—The best kinds of alum are known by this name. The genuine is of a pale red colour; but this is frequently imitated by colouring the common kinds of alum. The origin of the term

---

1 Beckmann, Inventions, tit. *Alum.*

2 See MS. of Le Begue, Nos. 42, 93, 299, and Table of Synonymes; and the Bol. MS., No. 3.

3 Ricettario Fiorentino.

4 Alb., Diz. Enc.; and see Ricett. Fior.

Roche alum is doubtful. Beckmann thinks, with Leibnitz, that the name was derived from Rocca, in Syria. *Allume Scagliuolo*—A kind of stone resembling talc, of which, when calcined, is made the "gesso da oro," or gesso of the gilders, and which is also used for the grounds of pictures. The heat renders it opaque like gesso, and causes it to split into layers.[1] It has been observed (p. cliii.) that this was probably the pigment called *Alumen* by Eraclius. *Allume Zuccarino*—Roche alum pounded with sugar, white of egg, and rose water.[2]

Page 258, note.

In a dissertation, published at Vicenza in 1845, entitled 'La Carta,' Sig. Giuseppe Riva, author of several archæological works, endeavours to prove that the manufacture of paper was known to the Romans, and described by Pliny; and in the Appendix to the Second Edition of this Treatise, published in the following year, Sig. Riva mentions two medieval documents which are among the earliest known to be written on paper. They are preserved in glass cases in the Archivio Capitolare at Verona. The first, which is of the ninth century and of the reign of Charlemagne, was signed by Bishop Ratoldo in the year 814, as appears in the Italia Sacra of Ughelli (2nd edit., tom. v. pp. 707, 708). The other is about a century earlier, and was subscribed by Diodato, son of the Doge Orso. (See Maffei, Verona Illustrata, iii. p. 1, p. 298, and Apol. Rifl., p. 25 and 27.) Both documents, which were examined by Sig. Riva and other antiquaries, were found to be on paper similar to what is now in use, and in excellent preservation; but it could not be ascertained whether the paper was made of linen or cotton.

P. 303, No. 322.

Since this work was printed, I have been favoured with another copy of this recipe which appears to be more correct than my version; I therefore subjoin the variations:—

Pour or mouler recipe. R. tres fin or lime bien menu, &c. . . . . . Mais avant ce doit estre bien limanze d'or bien lave en un bachin ou une conche de limee en [a] un pincel et a ce mortier dessus dit molez tant or que l'eaue qui y sera mise soit au departir clere. Et en telle maniere pourrez molir cuivre, argent estaing ou tout autre metal mais gardez que lor ne se paerde car il faudroit remoudre de rechief, &c.

A recipe for grinding gold. Take some very fine gold filings, &c. . . . . . but your filings should be previously well washed in a basin or shell with a pencil. Then grind all your gold in the above-mentioned mortar, until the water passes off clear. And in this way you may grind copper, silver, tin, and all other metals, but take care that the gold is not lost, for it would then be necessary to regrind it, &c.

Page 313, No. 341.

The word "glas" occurs frequently in medieval MSS. It is sometimes

---

[1] Alb., Diz. Enc.; Ricett. Fior.; Matthioli, p. 1430. [2] Ricett. Fior.

written "glasse" or "glasse aromatique," and sometimes it is joined with alum; for instance, "alun de glace," "alumen glacie," "alumen jameni vel glasso." The term has many significations. It was applied during the middle ages to alum; the name being probably given from the resemblance of the crystallised salts to glass, in the same manner as the sulphates of iron, copper, and zinc were called "Vitriols" from their glassy appearance. (See Agricola, De Metallicis.) In Welsh, Armoric, and Irish, the herb woad, which was used as an alkali in glass-blowing, was denominated "glas" (glastum or vitrum): the same term was also applied by these people to the colours blue and green. (See Edinburgh Review for July, 1847, p. 201, n.) The Romans gave the name of glessum to amber, which was called by the Germans "glas." The latter term was also applied to Sandarac, the principal ingredient in the Italian "Vernice liquida," and this has occasioned much confusion.

The following passage from Mr. Eastlake's 'Materials' (p. 246) will serve as a guide in determining the meaning of "glas" when used with reference to varnishes:—"Where both terms [vernix and glas] appear together, they mean distinct things, and the text can alone show which of the two meanings each conveys; but in general *glas* means amber, and *vernix* sandarac." With this view of the subject, therefore, the word "vernix" in No. 207 of the MS. of S. Audemar (p. 163) means sandarac, and "glasse" in the following recipe amber: the same may be observed of the passage in No. 274 of the Paris copy of Eraclius, "si autem *vernix* non habueris, accipies *glassam*." But with respect to the term "glasse aromatique" in the Le Begue MS., p. 341, there is no positive evidence which ingredient is meant.

As late as the year 1617 the word "glasse" was synonymous with the English word varnish. See Minshew's 'Guide unto Tongues,' London, 1617.

There is yet another signification of the word "glace" which has become obsolete, namely, "glace d'étain," the old name for bismuth.

P. 327.

"La Cornoaille fournissait au commerce du moyen-âge son étain. On l'envoyaient brut dans l'île de Majorque, en Provence, et à Venise, pour le foudre. Celui qu'on avait apprêté à Venise était le plus estimé dans le Levant."—Balducci Pegoletti, Prattica della Mercatura, cap. xxix., quoted by Depping, Histoire du Commerce.

P. 334.

This observation refers to the second kind of Giallolino, which is described in p. clviii.

P. 606, last line but 4.

This passage has been inserted by mistake—powdered glass is not, I believe, mentioned in the Marciana MS.

P. 636, line 16.

Instead of the present translation, read thus—

When making the varnish, you must boil and skim it well, if necessary, that it may be clear and thick.

P. 649, note 5.

It may be necessary to remark that the name "Biadetto" was given both to the native and the artificial blue carbonate of copper. See p. ccii.

P. 822, note.

The reference to the 'Traité de Mignature de Cristophe Ballard' is incorrect. The method described in this work of applying the blue pigment differs from that in the text. See p. ccviii.

NOTE

ON THE WEIGHTS AND MEASURES WHICH OCCUR IN THIS WORK.

The weights and measures mentioned in the different MSS. vary so much that it may be necessary to give a short account of them.

Those which occur in the French MSS. are the following—namely, the pound, the quarteron, the ounce, the denier, the blanc, and the esterlin: the last was, properly speaking, an English weight.

The pound varied in different parts of France. At Paris it contained 16 oz.; at Lyons 14; at Toulouse and in Provence 13½ oz.; and at Rouen 16½ oz. and ⅚ths of the Paris weight. The weights mentioned by Le Begue were those used at Paris; and those in the recipes brought from England, which have French names, were probably the same as were then used in the Anglo-French provinces.

The Paris pound, used to weigh gold, silver, and the richer commodities, was thus sub-divided—

24 grains = 1 pennyweight or denier.
3 deniers = 1 gros.
8 gros = 1 ounce.
8 ounces = 1 marc = 2 quarterons.
2 marcs = 1 pound = 7560 grains Troy.

The grain was sub-divided by the moneyers in the following manner—

1 grain = 20 mites.
1 mite = 24 droits.
1 droit = 20 periots.
1 periot = 24 blancs.[1]

The Esterlin was a goldsmith's weight, equal to 18½ grains.[2] It was introduced into England by the Anglo-Saxons, who were called Easterlings or

---

[1] See p. 86, No. 94.

[2] See p. 88.

Esterlings, whence the name of the coin. From this it is easy to perceive the derivation of the term "sterling" now applied to English money generally.

The English weights have their first composition from the silver penny, which ought to weigh 32 wheat corns taken from the middle of the ear (some authors add, which should be well dried). The silver denarius was, in its diminished state, the pattern of the English and Gothic penny; and as the denarius gave name to the weight used on the Continent, the penny gave its name to our pennyweight. The weight of the penny, from the Conquest to the 28th Edward I., was originally 24 grs.,[1] but in the reign of Edward III.[2] it fell to 18.[3] This, it will be observed, was only half a grain less than the goldsmith's weight called Esterlin, and it is extremely probable that this Esterlin was of the same weight as those Anglo-Gallic pence coined in the reign of Edward III., by himself and his son the Black Prince, which were actually denominated "Sterlings" and "Aquitaine Sterlings."[4] Twenty pence (of the weight of 32 wheat corns) made an ounce, and 12 ounces 1 pound. This was Troy weight, called by Fleta "Trone weight."[5] It was used to weigh gold, silver, precious stones, medicinal preparations, and bread. The quantities then, in the recipes given by Theodore of Flanders to Le Begue, must be calculated by Troy weight, and not by the Paris weight.

Italian weights and measures are mentioned in those parts of the Le Begue MS. which were translated from the Italian.

The Italian pound was divided as follows—

G	24 grains	= 1 Scropolo (scruple) or danaro, the French denier and English pennyweight.
℈	3 scruples	= 1 dragma (drachm).
ʒ	8 drachms	= 1 ounce.
℥	12 ounces	= 1 pound, equal to 12 oz. of the Imperial pound avoirdupois, or to $\frac{3}{4}$ths of that standard.

The Venetian ounce contained 9 drachms. The modern Roman pound was equal to 1 marc $\frac{1}{2}$ gros 14 grs. French.

At Genoa and Venice goods were weighed either by the *peso grosso* or the *peso sottile*. The latter was used for weighing gold, silver, and valuable articles; the former for other things.

100 pounds of the *peso sottile* of Venice were equal to 61$\frac{2}{7}$ths commercial pounds of Amsterdam.

100 pounds of the *peso grosso* = 94$\frac{4}{5}$ths of the same pounds.

The following table will show the relative proportion of the several weights used in the countries mentioned in the MSS.—

[1] Redding, Annals, vol. i. p. 388.

[2] Enc. Brit., tit. *Medals*.

[3] Edward III. died in 1377, only five years before the earliest date mentioned by Alcherius.

[4] See Akerman's Numismatic Manual, p. 377, 379, and 383.

[5] Some authors derive the name of Troy weight from *Troy Novant*, the monkish name for London, the former capital of the Trinobantes, as the inhabitants of Middlesex and Essex are called by Cæsar (B. G. 5, 20).

	lbs.	oz.	
100 pounds of England are equal to	91	8	of Amsterdam, Paris, &c.
	137	4	of Genoa.
	132	11	of Leghorn.
	153	11	of Milan.
	152		of Venice.[1]

A Rotolo is a Venetian weight of 32 oz.: also a Sicilian weight of 2½ lbs.

The "loth" mentioned in Nos. 96 and 97 (p. 86), and still used in Germany, Denmark, and other parts of the north of Europe, was probably introduced into England by the Anglo-Saxons. It is equivalent to half an ounce. The German pound is divided in the following manner:—

4 drachms = 1 loth.
2 loths = 1 ounce.
8 ounces = 1 marc.
2 marcs = 1 livre or pound.

In No. 97 "creeres de Inde" are mentioned. The term "creeres" may have been a corruption of "seer," the common Indian pound, which is equal to 12 Paris ounces.

MEASURES.

In the MS. of Le Begue the pint, the quart, and the chopine are mentioned. Their relative value was as follows:—

The old Paris quart was equal to 2 pints.
1 pint ,, 2 chopines.
1 chopine ,, 2 demi setiers.

The Paris pint was nearly equivalent to the English wine quart. These measures are mentioned in the recipes given by Theodore of Flanders to Alcherius.

ROMAN LIQUID MEASURES.

			Eng. wine gallon.
4 cartocci	=	1 *Foglietta*, equal to	0·0868
4 fogliette	=	1 *Boccale* ,,	0·3471
32 boccali	=	1 Barrile ,,	11·1072

TURIN LIQUID MEASURES.

2 *Boccali*	=	1 *pinta*, equal to	0·$\frac{1}{12}$ths
6 *pinte*	=	1 Rubbo ,,	2·½

FLORENTINE LIQUID MEASURES.

2 *quattrini*	=	1 Mezzetta or metadella	0·13125
2 *mezzette*	=	1 boccale	0·2625
2 *boccali*	=	1 fiascho	0·525
20 *fiaschi*	=	1 barrile	10·5
10 barrili	=	1 congo	105

The words in Italics occur in the Italian MSS.; and in those parts of the Le Begue MS. which were translated from the Italian.

---

[1] From the Enc. Brit., art. *Weights*.

INDEX.

C.

D.

H.

M.

N.

O.

T.

W.

THE END.

A CATALOG OF SELECTED

DOVER BOOKS

IN ALL FIELDS OF INTEREST

A CATALOG OF SELECTED DOVER BOOKS IN ALL FIELDS OF INTEREST

STICKLEY CRAFTSMAN FURNITURE CATALOGS, Gustav Stickley and L. & J. G. Stickley. Beautiful, functional furniture in two authentic catalogs from 1910. 594 illustrations, including 277 photos, show settles, rockers, armchairs, reclining chairs, bookcases, desks, tables. 183pp. 6½ x 9¼. 23838-5 Pa. $11.95

AMERICAN LOCOMOTIVES IN HISTORIC PHOTOGRAPHS: 1858 to 1949, Ron Ziel (ed.). A rare collection of 126 meticulously detailed official photographs, called "builder portraits," of American locomotives that majestically chronicle the rise of steam locomotive power in America. Introduction. Detailed captions. xi + 129pp. 9 x 12. 27393-8 Pa. $12.95

AMERICA'S LIGHTHOUSES: An Illustrated History, Francis Ross Holland, Jr. Delightfully written, profusely illustrated fact-filled survey of over 200 American lighthouses since 1716. History, anecdotes, technological advances, more. 240pp. 8 x 10¾. 25576-X Pa. $12.95

TOWARDS A NEW ARCHITECTURE, Le Corbusier. Pioneering manifesto by founder of "International School." Technical and aesthetic theories, views of industry, economics, relation of form to function, "mass-production split" and much more. Profusely illustrated. 320pp. 6⅛ x 9¼. (USO) 25023-7 Pa. $9.95

HOW THE OTHER HALF LIVES, Jacob Riis. Famous journalistic record, exposing poverty and degradation of New York slums around 1900, by major social reformer. 100 striking and influential photographs. 233pp. 10 x 7⅞. 22012-5 Pa. $11.95

FRUIT KEY AND TWIG KEY TO TREES AND SHRUBS, William M. Harlow. One of the handiest and most widely used identification aids. Fruit key covers 120 deciduous and evergreen species; twig key 160 deciduous species. Easily used. Over 300 photographs. 126pp. 5⅜ x 8½. 20511-8 Pa. $3.95

COMMON BIRD SONGS, Dr. Donald J. Borror. Songs of 60 most common U.S. birds: robins, sparrows, cardinals, bluejays, finches, more–arranged in order of increasing complexity. Up to 9 variations of songs of each species. Cassette and manual 99911-4 $8.95

ORCHIDS AS HOUSE PLANTS, Rebecca Tyson Northen. Grow cattleyas and many other kinds of orchids–in a window, in a case, or under artificial light. 63 illustrations. 148pp. 5⅜ x 8½. 23261-1 Pa. $4.95

MONSTER MAZES, Dave Phillips. Masterful mazes at four levels of difficulty. Avoid deadly perils and evil creatures to find magical treasures. Solutions for all 32 exciting illustrated puzzles. 48pp. 8¼ x 11. 26005-4 Pa. $2.95

MOZART'S DON GIOVANNI (DOVER OPERA LIBRETTO SERIES), Wolfgang Amadeus Mozart. Introduced and translated by Ellen H. Bleiler. Standard Italian libretto, with complete English translation. Convenient and thoroughly portable–an ideal companion for reading along with a recording or the performance itself. Introduction. List of characters. Plot summary. 121pp. 5¼ x 8½. 24944-1 Pa. $3.95

TECHNICAL MANUAL AND DICTIONARY OF CLASSICAL BALLET, Gail Grant. Defines, explains, comments on steps, movements, poses and concepts. 15-page pictorial section. Basic book for student, viewer. 127pp. 5⅜ x 8½. 21843-0 Pa. $4.95